THE JERUSALEM TALMUD

FIRST ORDER: ZERAÏM

TRACTATES *MA'ASER ŠENI, ḤALLAH, 'ORLAH,*

AND *BIKKURIM*

STUDIA JUDAICA

FORSCHUNGEN ZUR WISSENSCHAFT
DES JUDENTUMS

HERAUSGEGEBEN VON
E. L. EHRLICH

BAND XXIII

WALTER DE GRUYTER · BERLIN · NEW YORK
2003

THE JERUSALEM TALMUD
תלמוד ירושלמי

FIRST ORDER: ZERAÏM
סדר זרעים
TRACTATES *MA'ASER ŠENI, ḤALLAH, 'ORLAH,* AND *BIKKURIM*
מסכות מעשר שני, חלה, ערלה, ובכורים

EDITION, TRANSLATION, AND COMMENTARY

BY

HEINRICH W. GUGGENHEIMER

WALTER DE GRUYTER · BERLIN · NEW YORK
2003

ISBN 978-3-11-068130-7
e-ISBN (PDF) 978-3-11-090675-2

This volume is text- and page-identical with the hardback published in 2003.

Library of Congress Control Number: 2020942761

Bibliographic information published by the Deutsche Nationalbibliothek
The Deutsche Nationalbibliothek lists this publication in the
Deutsche Nationalbibliografie;
detailed bibliographic data are available on the Internet at http://dnb.dnb.de.

Printing and binding: CPI books GmbH, Leck

www.degruyter.com

Preface

The present volume is the fifth and last in a series covering the first order of the Jerusalem Talmud. The principles of the edition regarding text, vocalization, and commentary have been spelled out in detail in the Introduction to the first volume. The text in this volume is based on the recently published manuscript text of the Yerushalmi by the Academy of the Hebrew Language, Jerusalem 2001. The only systematic difference between this text and the *editio princeps* is that the manuscript shows less influence of Babylonian spelling. Most noticeable, של is a separate word in the print but a prefix in the manuscript, .

The extensive commentary is not based on emendations; therefore the preliminary translations of Roger Brooks (1993) and Jacob Neusner (1991) of the Tractates included have not been consulted. The main commentaries used are the same as in the prior volumes. Biographical notes have been attached to the names of those personalities not already mentioned in the previous volumes.

Again I wish to thank my wife, Dr. Eva Guggenheimer, who acted as critic, style editor, proof reader, and expert on the Latin and Greek vocabulary. Her own notes on some possible Latin and Greek etymologies are identified by (E. G.).

Contents

Introduction to Tractate Ma'aśer Šeni 1

Ma'aśer Šeni Chapter 1, מעשר שני
Halakhah 1 3
Halakhah 2 13
Halakhah 3 26
Halakhah 4 37

Ma'aśer Šeni Chapter 2 , מעשר שני ניתן
Halakhah 1 44
Halakhah 2 60
Halakhah 3 60
Halakhah 4 62
Halakhah 5 64
Halakhah 6 65
Halakhah 7 67
Halakhah 8 72
Halakhah 9 74
Halakhah 10 75

Ma'aśer Šeni Chapter 3, לא יאמר אדם
Halakhah 1 79

Halakhah 2 83
Halakhah 3 88
Halakhah 4 92
Halakhah 5 93
Halakhah 6 96
Halakhah 7 100
Halakhah 8 105
Halakhah 9 111
Halakhah 10 115
Halakhah 11 117

Ma‘aśer Šeni Chapter 4, המוליך פירות
Halakhah 1 120
Halakhah 2 126
Halakhah 3 129
Halakhah 4 135
Halakhah 5 143
Halakhah 6 144
Halakhah 7 146
Halakhah 8 151
Halakhah 9 154

Ma‘aśer Šeni Chapter 5, כרם רבעי
Halakhah 1 168
Halakhah 2 177
Halakhah 3 182
Halakhah 4 189
Halakhah 5 191
Halakhah 6 201
Halakhah 7 208
Halakhah 8 213
Halakhah 9 218

Introduction to Tractate Ḥallah 225

Ḥallah Chapter 1, חמשה דברים
Halakhah 1 227
Halakhah 2 252
Halakhah 3 253
Halakhah 4 254
Halakhah 5 263
Halakhah 6 269
Halakhah 7 272
Halakhah 8 275
Halakhah 9 277
Halakhah 10 282

Ḥallah Chapter 2, פירות חוצה לארץ
Halakhah 1 285
Halakhah 2 290
Halakhah 3 295
Halakhah 4 299
Halakhah 5 303
Halakhah 6 305

Ḥallah Chapter 3, אוכלין עראי
Halakhah 1 315
Halakhah 2 323
Halakhah 3 326
Halakhah 4 328
Halakhah 5 330
Halakhah 6 336
Halakhah 7 339

Ḥallah Chapter 4, שתי נשים

Halakhah 1 354
Halakhah 2 357
Halakhah 3 359
Halakhah 4 361
Halakhah 5 363
Halakhah 6 366
Halakhah 7 369
Halakhah 8 375
Halakhah 9 378
Halakhah 10 379
Halakhah 11 382
Halakhah 12 388

Introduction to Tractate ‘Orlah 397

‘Orlah Chapter 1, הנוטע לסייג
Halakhah 1 398
Halakhah 2 413
Halakhah 3 422
Halakhah 4 425
Halakhah 5 437
Halakhah 6 442
Halakhah 7 446
Halakhah 8 447

‘Orlah Chapter 2, התרומה ותרומת מעשר
Halakhah 1 451
Halakhah 2 466
Halakhah 3 472
Halakhah 4 475

Halakhah 5 478
Halakhah 6 482
Halakhah 7 488
Halakhah 8 494
Halakhah 9 496
Halakhah 10 498
Halakhah 11 502

'Orlah Chapter 3, בגד
Halakhah 1 504
Halakhah 2 521
Halakhah 3 526
Halakhah 4 528
Halakhah 5 529
Halakhah 6 531
Halakhah 7 533
Halakhah 8 531

Introduction to Tractate Bikkurim 543

Bikkurim Chapter 1, יש מביאין
Halakhah 1 544
Halakhah 2 549
Halakhah 3 553
Halakhah 4 559
Halakhah 5 564
Halakhah 6 569
Halakhah 7 572
Halakhah 8 575
Halakhah 9 580
Halakhah 10 581
Halakhah 11 583
Halakhah 12 584

Halakhah 13 586

Bikkurim Chapter 2, התרומה

Halakhah 1 589
Halakhah 2 604
Halakhah 3 614
Halakhah 4 618
Halakhah 5 619
Halakhah 6 622
Halakhah 7 624
Halakhah 8 626
Halakhah 9 629

Bikkurim Chapter 3, כיצד מפרישין

Halakhah 1 631
Halakhah 2 633
Halakhah 3 634
Halakhah 4 648
Halakhah 5 651
Halakhah 6 654
Halakhah 7 657

Epilogue

On the Tosephta 661
On the Editors of the Yerushalmi 663

Indices

Index of Biographical Notes 667
Index of Biblical Quotations 667
Index of Greek and Latin Words 669
Index of Hebrew and Arabic words 669
General Index 670

Introduction to Tractate Ma'aser Šeni

The main theme of the Tractate is the "Second Tithe" introduced in *Deut.* 14:22-27. This tithe is the property of the farmer who is supposed to take it, or money representing its value, and eat or spend it in purity at the Temple precinct on the occasion of his pilgrimage. Similar rules apply to the yield of the fourth year of a newly planted vineyard or orchard, *Lev.* 19:24; this is a second subject of the Tractate. The common themes, taking up most of the text, are the rules of redemption of sanctified food in all its forms and the rules to handle sanctified food which became impure. These rules have become irrelevant today in the absence of a Temple since the tithe can be redeemed for a token sum; cf. Chapter 4, Notes 35-36. The fourth Chapter contains a long section on the interpretation of dreams, one of three such texts in Talmudic literature. The final Chapter is dedicated mostly to the farmer's declaration in the Temple that he fulfilled all his obligations for heave and tithes, *Deut.* 26:12-15.

For the interpretation, as always the main guides are Maimonides and R. Simson of Sens. Of the Eighteenth Century commentators, the most useful is R. Eliahu Fulda; the least useful are R. Moses Margalit (פני משה), R. Eliahu Wilna and, from the Twentieth Century, R. H. Kanievski, all of whom tend to emend away the difficult portions and the disagreements with Babylonian tradition. Similarly, the preliminary translation and explanation by Roger Brooks (Chicago, 1993) heavily depends on the emended Wilna text and a presumed but untenable identification of the Tosephta underlying the Yerushalmi with the Tosephta in our hands. In some places, the text is in bad shape and invites emendation. However, since there are many possibilities of emendation and very few of them would represent the original text, discussions of possible emendations are left to the commentary. Of modern commentaries, R. Saul Lieberman's *Tosefta ki-fshutah,* New York, 1955 and R. Y. Qafeḥ's commented edition and translation of Maimonides's Commentary are most useful. Other sources are quoted by name when used.

מעשר שני פרק ראשון

(fol. 52b) **משנה א:** מַעֲשֵׂר שֵׁינִי אֵין מוֹכְרִין אוֹתוֹ וְאֵין מְמַשְׁכְּנִין אוֹתוֹ וְאֵין מַחֲלִיפִין אוֹתוֹ וְלֹא שׁוֹקְלִין כְּנֶגְדּוֹ וְלֹא יֹאמַר אָדָם לַחֲבֵירוֹ בִּירוּשָׁלֵם הֵילָךְ יַיִן וְתֵן לִי שֶׁמֶן וְכֵן כָּל־שְׁאָר הַפֵּירוֹת אֲבָל נוֹתְנִין זֶה לָזֶה מַתְּנַת חִנָּם.

Mishnah 1: One does not sell Second Tithe[1], one does not take it as a pledge, one does not barter it, and one does not weigh corresponding to it[2]. One should not say to his neighbor in Jerusalem, here you have wine, give me its value in oil, but they may give free gifts to one another.

1 One may not sell Second Tithe as such, that it should be Second Tithe in the hand of the buyer. One may exchange Second Tithe for money (*Deut.* 14:25), transfer its holiness to the money, and render the produce profane which then may be sold; cf. Mishnah 4:1. The money has to be spent for pure food in Jerusalem to be consumed by the rules of holiness.

2 As long as it retains its status as Second Tithe.

הלכה א: מַעֲשֵׂר שֵׁינִי אֵין מוֹכְרִין אוֹתוֹ. אֵין מוֹכְרִין אוֹתוֹ מִפְּנֵי שֶׁכָּתוּב בּוֹ קְדוּשָּׁה. אֵין מְמַשְׁכְּנִין אוֹתוֹ מִפְּנֵי שֶׁכָּתוּב בּוֹ בְּרָכָה. כֵּיצַד אֵין מוֹכְרִין אוֹתוֹ. לֹא יֹאמַר אָדָם לַחֲבֵירוֹ הָא לָךְ אֶת הַמָּנֶה הַזֶּה שֶׁלְּמַעֲשֵׂר שֵׁנִי וְתֵן לִי בוֹ חֲמִשִּׁים זוּז שֶׁלְּחוּלִין.

Halakhah 1: "One does not sell Second Tithe." One does not sell it because holiness is written for it[3]. One does not use it as a pledge because blessing is written about it[4]. "[5]How may one not sell it? A person should not say to his neighbor, here you have this mina's worth of Second Tithe, give me 50 *zuz* profane for it."

3 *Lev.* 27:30.

4 *Deut.* 14:24. Taking a loan and giving a pledge is not a sign of blessing.

5 A similar text in Tosephta 1:1: "How may one not sell it? One should not say, here is 200 [*zuz*] worth, give me 100 in exchange." If Second Tithe were sold, it would not be redeemed and the buyer would have to eat the produce in purity and sanctity in Jerusalem (assuming the existence of the Temple.)

מָאן תַּנָּא אֵין מוֹכְרִין אוֹתוֹ רִבִּי מֵאִיר. בְּרַם כְּרִבִּי יוּדָה בְּדִין הוּא שֶׁיְּהֵא מוּתָּר לְמוֹכְרוֹ מִקַּל וָחוֹמֶר. מַה אִם תְּרוּמָה שֶׁהִיא אֲסוּרָה לְזָרִים מוּתָּר לְמוֹכְרָהּ. מַעֲשֵׂר שֵׁינִי שֶׁהוּא מוּתָּר לְזָרִים אֵינוֹ דִין שֶׁיְּהֵא מוּתָּר לְמוֹכְרוֹ. לֹא. אִם אָמַרְתָּ בִתְרוּמָה שֶׁאֵינָהּ טְעוּנָה מְחִיצָה תֹּאמַר בְּמַעֲשֵׂר שֵׁינִי שֶׁהוּא טָעוּן מְחִיצָה. בִּיכּוּרִים יוֹכִיחוּ שֶׁהֵן טְעוּנִין מְחִיצָה וּמוּתָּר לְמוֹכְרָן. לֹא. אִם אָמַרְתָּ בְּבִיכּוּרִין שֶׁאֵינָן תּוֹפְסִין אֶת דְּמֵיהֶן. תֹּאמַר בְּמַעֲשֵׂר שֵׁינִי שֶׁהוּא תוֹפֵשׂ אֶת דָּמָיו. שְׁבִיעִית תּוֹכִיחַ שֶׁהִיא תוֹפֶסֶת אֶת דָּמֶיהָ וּמוּתָּר לְמוֹכְרָהּ. אָמַר רִבִּי יוּדָן מִזּוֹ מְכִירָתָהּ שֶׁל שְׁבִיעִית הִיא חִילּוּלָהּ.

Who is the Tanna of "one does not sell it"? Rebbi Meïr[6]! But for Rebbi Jehudah it should be logical that it be permitted to be sold, by an argument *a minore ad majus*: If it is permitted to sell heave[7] which is forbidden to lay people, since Second Tithe is permitted to lay people, one should certainly be permitted to sell it. No, if you assert this for heave which does not need an enclosure, what can you imply for Second Tithe which needs an enclosure[8]? First Fruits shall prove it which need an enclosure[9] and one may sell them! No, if you assert this for First Fruits which do not implicate their monetary substitute[10], what can you imply for Second Heave which implicates its monetary substitute[11]! The Sabbatical shall prove it which implicates its monetary substitute[12] and it is permitted to sell it! Rebbi Yudan said, from this? The sale of Sabbatical produce is its redemption[13].

6 R. Meïr considers Second Tithe as property of Heaven given to the farmer for consumption in holiness. For R. Jehudah, Second Tithe is private property. Their disagreement is in Mishnah *Qiddušin* 2:8, cf. *Demay* Chapter 1, Notes 185-186.

7 As mentioned many times in Mishnah *Terumot*; e. g. Mishnah 4:1.

8 *Deut.* 14:24 requires that Second Tithe be consumed "at the place chosen by the Eternal, your God." This place must be designated somehow. We have no record that the sanctuary at Shilo was within walls, but some enclosure must have defined the sacred space. It is accepted that the ancient walls of Jerusalem defined the sacred space for Second Tithe. In contrast, heave may be consumed by the priests anywhere in the Land.

9 Since they have to be brought to the Temple. The operative enclosure here is the courtyard of the Tabernacle or the outer wall of the Temple. The receiving priest is permitted to sell to another priest.

10 The money is profane.

11 The money must be taken to Jerusalem as Second Tithe, *Deut.* 14:24. The argument could have been formulated: The sale of First Fruits is a sale, the sale of Second Tithe is a redemption.

12 Mishnah *Ševi'it* 8:8.

13 The sale of Sabbatical produce, as authorized in Mishnah *Ševi'it* Chapter 8, cannot be characterized as a sale but is a redemption which does not impinge on the holiness of the produce which remains Sabbatical. But exchanged Second Tithe is totally profane. Therefore, there is no proof that R. Jehudah would permit the sale of unexchanged Second Tithe.

אָמַר רִבִּי יִרְמְיָה מָאן תַּנָּא אֵין מוֹכְרִין אוֹתוֹ רִבִּי מֵאִיר. בְּרַם כְּרִבִּי יוּדָן בְּדִין הוּא שֶׁיְּהֵא מוּתָּר לְמוֹכְרוֹ מִקַּל וָחוֹמֶר מַה אִם שְׁבִיעִית שֶׁאֵין פּוֹרְעִין חוֹב

מִדָּמֶיהָ מוּתָּר לְמוֹכְרָהּ. מַעֲשֵׂר שֵׁינִי שֶׁפּוֹרְעִין חוֹב מִדָּמָיו אֵינוֹ דִין שֶׁיְּהֵא מוּתָּר לְמוֹכְרוֹ. הָא אַשְׁכַּחְנָן שֶׁפּוֹרְעִין חוֹב מִדָּמָיו כַּיי דְתַנִּינָן תַּמָּן מָשַׁךְ הֵימֶנּוּ מַעֲשֵׂר בְּסֶלַע וְלֹא הִסְפִּיק לִפְדּוֹתוֹ עַד שֶׁעָמַד בִּשְׁתַּיִם. אָמַר רִבִּי יוֹסֵי שַׁנְיָיא הִיא. שֶׁמִּשָּׁעָה הָרִאשׁוֹנָה מַעֲשֵׂר שֵׁינִי חַייָב. אִילּוּ חַייָב הָיָה לוֹ וְנוֹתֵן לוֹ מֵעֲשֵׂר יְאוּת. אָמַר רִבִּי יוּדָן מַתְנִיתָא אָמְרָה כֵן שֶׁהוּא אָסוּר לְמוֹכְרוֹ. דְּתַנִּינָן תַּמָּן מֵזִיד קִידֵּשׁ שׁוֹגֵג לֹא קִידֵּשׁ. אִם אַתְּ אוֹמֵר יְהֵא מוּתָּר לְמוֹכְרוֹ יְהֵא מוּתָּר לְקַדֵּשׁ בּוֹ. וְכָל־שֶׁהוּא אָסוּר לְמוֹכְרוֹ אָסוּר לְקַדֵּשׁ בּוֹ. וְהָתַנִּינָן אֵין לוֹקְחִין עֲבָדִים וְקַרְקָעוֹת וּבְהֵמָה טְמֵיאָה מִדְּמֵי שְׁבִיעִית. וְאִם לָקַח יֹאכַל כְּנֶגְדָּהּ. אָמַר רִבִּי יוֹסֵי זֹאת אוֹמֶרֶת שֶׁאָסוּר לִיקַּח לוֹ אִשָּׁה מִדְּמֵי שְׁבִיעִית. דִּלֹכֵן מַה בֵּין קוֹנֶה אִשָּׁה מַה בֵּין קוֹנֶה שִׁפְחָה. רִבִּי יוֹסֵי בְשֵׁם רִבִּי זְעִירָא רִבִּי יוּדָן בְּשֵׁם רִבִּי יִילָא דִּבְרֵי הַכֹּל הִיא מִפְּנֵי פִּילְפּוּלוֹ. רִבִּי יוֹסֵי בְשֵׁם רִבִּי אָחָא דִּבְרֵי הַכֹּל הִיא כְּדֵי שֶׁיְּהוּ הַכֹּל זְקוּקִין לְמְחִיצָתָן.

Rebbi Jeremiah said, who is the Tanna of "one does not sell it"? Rebbi Meïr[6]! But for Rebbi Jehudah it should be logical that it be permitted to be sold, by an argument *a minore ad majus*: If it is permitted to sell Sabbatical produce with which one may not liquidate one's debts[14], it is logical that it should be permitted to sell Second Tithe since with it one may liquidate one's debts. We find that one may liquidate one's debts with Second Tithe, following what we stated[15]: "If he took from him tithe worth one tetradrachma and did not come to exchange it until it was worth two." Rebbi Yose said, there is a difference since from the start the value of Second Tithe was due. If he had owed before, it would be an argument[16]. Rebbi Yudan said, a Mishnah said that it is forbidden to sell it, as we stated there[17]: "If intentional, he married, if in error, he did not marry." If you say that he may sell it, he should be able to use it for marriage but anything he may not sell he may not use for marriage. But did we not state[18]: "One does not buy slaves, real estate, and unclean animals from Sabbatical money. If he bought them, he has to eat their worth." Rebbi Yose said, this means that it is forbidden to acquire a wife with Sabbatical money. Otherwise, what is the difference between one who acquires a wife and one who acquires a slave girl?

Rebbi Yose in the name of Rebbi Zeïra, Rebbi Yudan in the name of Rebbi Ila, everybody agrees because of these arguments. Rebbi Yose in the name of Rebbi Aḥa, everybody agrees that all should need the enclosures[19].

14 *Demay* 3:1, Notes 13-14.

15 Mishnah *Ma'aser Šeni* 4:6. The text quotes only the beginning of the Mishnah but the argument is from the second part: If the buyer took possession of the Second Tithe when it was worth 2 tetradrachmas but did not exchange it until its value decreased to 1 tetradrachma, he gives the seller one tetradrachma of profane money (for redemption); the second tetradrachma he may take out of his own Second Tithe money. This means that he may use his Second Tithe money to liquidate the debt he incurred when he took possession of the Second Tithe.

16 There is no proof that Second Tithe money may be used for anything but Second Tithe or profane food to be turned into Second Tithe.

17 Mishnah *Qiddušin* 2:8. The Mishnah states that no tithe may be used for the money due the bride at the preliminary marriage ceremony (cf. *Demay* 1:3, Notes 185-187; *Peah* 6:2 Note 46, 7:6 Note 135). R. Jehudah holds that if the groom criminally alienated Second Tithe from its intended use and used it as bridal money, the former Second Tithe now is his private property (for which restitution is due) which may be used as bridal money. But this implies that Second Tithe cannot be used in the absence of criminal intent since if it was used inadvertently, without criminal intent, Second Tithe is Heaven's property and the preliminary marriage is invalid.

18 *Ševi'it* Mishnah and Halakhah 8:8, Notes 114, 115, 118.

19 The first opinion of R. Yose

states that the previous arguments showed that R. Jehudah agrees that Second Tithe may not be sold but only exchanged. The second opinion states that this is not a biblical law but a rabbinic institution so that, if the Temple is rebuilt, everybody has an interest in seeing to it that the walls of Jerusalem will be in good shape.

כֵּיצַד אֵין מְמַשְׁכְּנִין אוֹתוֹ הַנִּכְנָס לְתוֹךְ בֵּיתוֹ שֶׁל חֲבֵירוֹ לְמַשְׁכְּנוֹ (fol. 52c) אַל יְמַשְׁכֵּן מַעֲשֵׂר שֵׁינִי שֶׁלּוֹ. תַּנֵּי וְלֹא מַרְהִינִין אוֹתוֹ וְלֹא יִתְּנֶנּוּ לְחֶנְוָנִי שֶׁיֹּאכַל עָלָיו. עָבַר וּמִישְׁכֵּן עָבַר וְהִירְהֵן. יָבֹא כְּהָדָא הָאוֹכֵל מַעֲשֵׂר שֵׁינִי שֶׁלּוֹ בֵּין שׁוֹגֵג בֵּין מֵזִיד יִצְעַק לַשָּׁמַיִם דִּבְרֵי רַבָּן שִׁמְעוֹן בֶּן גַּמְלִיאֵל. רִבִּי אוֹמֵר שׁוֹגֵג יִצְעַק לַשָּׁמַיִם מֵזִיד יַחְזְרוּ דָּמָיו לִמְקוֹמָן. וְאִם הָיוּ מָעוֹת. שׁוֹגֵג יִצְעַק לַשָּׁמַיִם מֵזִיד יַחְזְרוּ דָּמָיו לִמְקוֹמָן דִּבְרֵי רַבָּן שִׁמְעוֹן בֶּן גַּמְלִיאֵל. רִבִּי אוֹמֵר בֵּין שׁוֹגֵג בֵּין מֵזִיד יַחְזְרוּ דָּמָיו לִמְקוֹמָן. רִבִּי זְרִיקָה בְּשֵׁם חִזְקִיָּה הֲלָכָה כְּרִבִּי בְּמָעוֹת וּכְרַבָּן שִׁמְעוֹן בֶּן גַּמְלִיאֵל בְּפֵירוֹת. אָמַר רִבִּי יֵילָא מַעֲשֶׂה הָיָה וְהוֹרוּ כְּרִבִּי בְּמָעוֹת.

"[20]How does one not take it as a pledge? He who enters another's house to take a pledge should not take his debtor's Second Tithe as pledge." It was stated: "One does not give it as a deposit and he should not give it to a grocer to receive food in its value.[21]" If one transgressed and took as pledge, trangressed and gave as deposit? It shall be as the following[22]: "If somebody eats his Second Tithe, whether in error or intentionally, he shall cry out to Heaven[23], the words of Rabban Simeon ben Gamliel. Rebbi says, in error he shall cry out to Heaven, intentionally the money's worth shall be restituted. If it was money, in error he shall cry out to Heaven, intentionally the money's worth shall be restituted, the words of Rabban Simeon ben Gamliel. Rebbi says, whether in error or intentionally, the money's worth shall be restituted." Rebbi Zeriqa in the name of Ḥizqiah: Practice follows Rebbi for money and Rabban Simeon ben Gamliel for produce. Rebbi Ila said, there was a case about money and they instructed following Rebbi.

20 Tosephta 1:1.

21 In Tosephta 1:2: One does not give it as a deposit; he should not say, keep this tithe in your hands and give me profane [produce] for its value.

22 Tosephta 3:9-10; the Yerushalmi text is parallel to the Erfurt ms.

23 There is no replacement; his sin can be forgiven only by divine mercy.

אוֹ יִיָבֹא כְּהָדָא אֵין נוֹטְעִין וְאֵין מַבְרִיכִין וְאֵין מַרְכִּיבִין עֶרֶב שְׁבִיעִית פָּחוֹת מִשְּׁלֹשִׁים יוֹם לִפְנֵי רֹאשׁ הַשָּׁנָה וְאִם נָטַע אוֹ הִרְכִּיב אוֹ הִבְרִיךְ יַעֲקוֹר. לֹא עָקַר פֵּירוֹתָיו מַה הֵן. רִבִּי בָּא רִבִּי אִמִּי הֲווֹן יְתִיבִין בְּצוֹר אָתָא עוּבְדָּא קוֹמֵיהוֹן הוֹרֵי רִבִּי אִילָא יִשָּׁפְכוּ פֵּירוֹתָיו. אָמַר רִבִּי בָּא אֲנִי לֹא נִמְנֵיתִי עִמָּהֶן בַּעֲלִיָּיה. נֶפְקִין וְשָׁמְעוּן רִבִּי יוֹנָה וְרִבִּי יִצְחָק בַּר טֶבֶלַיי בְּשֵׁם רִבִּי לָעְזָר אֵין מְחַדְּשִׁין עַל הַגְּזֵירָה. אָמַר רִבִּי יוֹסֵי רִבִּי יִצְחָק בַּר טֶבֶלַיי בְּשֵׁם רִבִּי לָעְזָר אֵין מוֹסִיפִין עַל הַהֲלָכָה.

Or it may follow this: [24]"One does not plant, sink, or graft in the year preceding a Sabbatical year later than thirty days before the New Year; if he planted, grafted, or sank he has to uproot it." If one did not uproot, what is with its yield? Rebbi Abba [and] Rebbi Immi[25] were sitting in Tyre when a case came before them. Rebbi La taught that the fruits should be thrown away. Rebbi Abba said, I was not counted with them on the upper floor. They said, let us go out and study. They went out and heard Rebbi Jonah and Rebbi Isaac bar Tevele in the name of Rebbi Eleazar: One does not make a new restriction. Rebbi Yose, Rebbi Isaac bar Tevele in the name of Rebbi Eleazar: One does not add to an established practice.

24 The entire paragraph is in *Ševi'it* 32:6, Notes 42-47.

25 In *Ševi'it*: Rebbi La. The next sentence shows that this is the correct text.

רִבִּי יַעֲקֹב בַּר אָחָא בְּשֵׁם רִבִּי זְעִירָא מִן מַה דְּתַנֵּי אֵין מְמַשְׁכְּנִין אוֹתוֹ וְלֹא מַרְהִינִין אוֹתוֹ הָדָא אֲמָרָה עָבַר וּמִישְׁכֵּן עָבַר וְהִרְהִין קוֹנְסִין בּוֹ.

Rebbi Jacob bar Aḥa in the name of Rebbi Zeïra: Since it was stated, "one does not take it as a pledge nor give it as a deposit", this means that if one transgressed and took it as a pledge, trangressed and gave as a deposit, one fines him for it[26].

26   The court will remove pledge or deposit (Maimonides, *Ma'aser Šeni* 3:18).

וְלֹא שׁוֹקְלִין כְּנֶגְדּוֹ מָעוֹת אֲפִילוּ סֶלַע שֶׁלְּחוּלִין לַעֲשׂוֹת סֶלַע שֶׁלְּמַעֲשֵׂר שֵׁנִי. הָיָה לוֹ סֶלַע שֶׁלְּמַעֲשֵׂר וְהִיא מְסוּיֶּימֶת לוֹ מַהוּ שֶׁיִּשְׁקוֹל כְּנֶגֶד הַסֶּלַע שֶׁלְּמַעֲשֵׂר שֵׁנִי אַחֶרֶת וּתְהֵא מְסוּיֶּימֶת לוֹ. הָאַחִין שֶׁחָלְקוּ מַהוּ שֶׁיִּשְׁקְלוּ זֶה כְּנֶגֶד זֶה.

"[27]One does not use it[28] to weigh coins[29], not even a profane tetradrachma to turn it into a tetradrachma of Second Tithe." If he had a tetradrachma of Second Tithe whose weight was known to him, may he use it to weigh another tetradrachma of Second Tithe so that its weight should be known to him? May brothers who split [an inheritance] weigh one against the other[30]?

27   Tosephta 1:1, in slightly different wording.

28   Coins of Second Tithe whose weight is known may not be used on scales to determine the weight of other things.

29   To see whether they have the legal weight.

30   To split the Second Tithe money evenly. The questions are not answered but if the answer to the first question were in the negative, the second question could not have been asked. Therefore, the answer to the first question must be affirmative and by the parallelism of the questions one may infer that the second question also must be answered in the affirmative: Second Tithe money may be weighed for purposes of Second Tithe. (In the

Babli, the questions would be put into a lengthy rhetorical frame centered on the expression אם תמצי לומר.}

תְּנָן לֹא יֹאמַר אָדָם לַחֲבֵירוֹ בִּירוּשָׁלֵם הָא לָךְ יַיִן וְתֵן לִי שֶׁמֶן. הָא לָךְ שֶׁמֶן וְתֵן לִי יַיִן. אֲבָל אוֹמֵר לוֹ הָא לָךְ יַיִן שֶׁאֵין לָךְ יַיִן הָא לָךְ שֶׁמֶן שֶׁאֵין לָךְ שֶׁמֶן. הָא לָךְ יַיִן שֶׁאֵין לִי שֶׁמֶן הֲוֹון בָּעְיֵי מֵימַר אָסוּר. אַשְׁכַּח תַּנֵּי מוּתָּר. וְאֵינוֹ אָסוּר מִשּׁוּם חֲלִיפִין. מִכֵּיוָן שֶׁאֵינוֹ יָכוֹל לְהוֹצִיאוֹ מִמֶּנּוּ בְּדִין אֵין אֵילּוּ חֲלִיפִין. וְלֵיידָא מִילָּא אָמַר הָא לָךְ יַיִן שֶׁאֵין לִי שֶׁמֶן. דְּאִילּוּ הֲוָה לִי מְשַׁח הֲוֵינָא מִיתַּן לָךְ.

We have stated[31]: "One should not say to his neighbor in Jerusalem, here you have wine, give me its value in oil, here you have oil, give me its value in wine. But he may say to him, here you have wine since you have no wine, here you have oil since you have no oil[32]." Here you have wine since I have no oil, they wanted to say that this is forbidden. They found stated: "It is permitted." Is it not forbidden because of barter? Since he cannot enforce it in a court, this is not barter. Why could he have said: Here you have wine since I have no oil? If I had oil, I would give you that also.

31 It should read תני; תנן is Babylonian Aramaic for a quote from the Mishnah.

32 Tosephta 1:2: "How does one not barter? A person should not say, here you have wine, give me its value in oil, here you have oil, give me its value in wine. But he may say to him, here you have wine since *I* have no *oil*, *and the other one says*, here you have oil since *I* have no *wine*. It turns out that they exchange but do not barter; they do favors for one another." With this text, the discussion in the paragraph becomes unnecessary.

אֲבָל נוֹתְנִין זֶה לָזֶה מַתְּנַת חִנָּם. מַתְנִיתִין דְּרִבִּי מֵאִיר דּוּ רִבִּי מֵאִיר אָמַר אֵין מַתָּנָה כְּמֶכֶר. אָמַר רִבִּי יוֹסֵי דִּבְרֵי הַכֹּל הִיא הָכָא כְּהָדָא דְתַנֵּי. הָיָה אוֹמֵר אָדָם לַחֲבֵירוֹ[33] מַה אָכַלְתָּ הַיּוֹם וְהוּא אוֹמֵר לוֹ קַיִץ וְהָיָה יוֹדֵעַ שֶׁהוּא בְּכוֹר. מַה הַקַּיִיץ נִמְכַּר בְּזוֹל. אַף הַבְּכוֹר נִמְכַּר בְּזוֹל. הָיָה אוֹמֵר לוֹ מָן וְהָיָה יוֹדֵעַ שֶׁהוּא מַעֲשֵׂר שֵׁינִי. מַה הַמָּן נִיתַּן בְּמַתָּנָה אַף מַעֲשֵׂר שֵׁינִי נִיתַּן בְּמַתָּנָה. הָתִיבוּן הֲרֵי מַעֲשֵׂר בְּהֵמָה דִּבְרֵי הַכֹּל אֵינוֹ נִמְכַּר וְאַתְּ אָמְרַת נִיתַּן בְּמַתָּנָה. אַף זֶה נִיתַּן בְּמַתָּנָה. רִבִּי מָנָא לֹא אָמַר כֵּן אֶלָּא כְּרִבִּי יוּדָה דְּרִבִּי יוּדָה אָמַר עָשָׂה אוֹתוֹ כִּנְכָסָיו. הָתִיבוּן הֲרֵי מַעֲשֵׂר בְּהֵמָה דִּבְרֵי הַכֹּל אֵינוֹ כִּנְכָסָיו וְאַתְּ אָמַר נִיתַּן בְּמַתָּנָה. אַף זֶה נִיתַּן בְּמַתָּנָה.

"But they may give free gifts to one another." Our Mishnah is Rebbi Meïr's since Rebbi Meïr says a gift is not like a sale[34]. Rebbi Yose said, here it is everybody's opinion, following what was stated: A person says to his neighbor [in Jerusalem]: What did you eat today? If that one says summer figs[35], he knows that it was firstling. Just as summer figs are sold cheaply, so firstlings are sold cheaply[36]. If that one said manna, he knows that it was Second Tithe. Just as manna was given as a gift, so Second Tithe may be given as a gift. They objected: Everybody agrees that animal tithe cannot be sold[37]; do you say it can be given as a gift? This also can be given as a gift. Rebbi Mana did not say so but was following Rebbi Jehudah since Rebbi Jehudah said He made it one's property[38]. They objected: Everybody agrees that animal tithe is not one's property[39]; do you say it can be given as a gift? This also can be given as a gift[40].

33 The Rome ms. adds: בירושלם This is required by the context.

34 *Ma'serot* 2:1, Note 5.

35 As explained in *Ekhah Rabbati* 1, in Jerusalem one always talked in hints.

36 A first-born animal becomes property of a Cohen. It may not be sold by weight or in a store and the buyers can only be Cohanim unless it is

a blemished animal which may not be used as a sacrifice. Therefore, it can only be sold cheaply.

37 Animal tithe (*Lev.* 27:32) must be eaten as a sacrifice; if without blemish its blood and fat are burned on the altar and the meat may be eaten by any pure person in the holy precinct (i. e., inside the walls of Jerusalem.) The rancher who brings the sacrifice may invite anybody to partake of the meat. Since it is holy it may not be sold; it follows that the meat may be given as a gift. It is impossible to distinguish between Second Tithe and animal tithe in this respect.

38 Mishnah *Qiddušin* 2:8, quoted in the next Halakhah, notes that for R. Meïr, Second Tithe is Heaven's property but for R. Jehudah it is the farmer's property. Cf. also *Demay* 1:3, Note 185.

39 By being counted as tenth animal, it becomes automatically dedicated as a sacrifice.

40 As noted in Note 37. The animal tithe is the only sacrifice which is totally given to the rancher who brings it. The parts which go onto the altar, blood and fat, are those which may not be eaten even from a profane animal. The Cohanim do not receive any part, neither is any edible part burned on the altar.

(fol. 52b) **משנה ב:** מַעֲשֵׂר בְּהֵמָה אֵין מוֹכְרִין אוֹתוֹ תָּמִים חַי. וְלֹא בַּעַל מוּם חַי וְשָׁחוּט וְאֵין מְקַדְּשִׁין בּוֹ אֶת הָאִשָּׁה. הַבְּכוֹר מוֹכְרִין אוֹתוֹ תָּמִים חַי. וּבַעַל מוּם חַי וְשָׁחוּט וּמְקַדְּשִׁין בּוֹ אֶת הָאִשָּׁה. וְאֵין מְחַלְּלִין מַעֲשֵׂר שֵׁנִי עַל אַסֵּימוֹן וְלֹא עַל הַמַּטְבֵּעַ שֶׁאֵינוֹ יוֹצֵא וְלֹא עַל הַמָּעוֹת שֶׁאֵינָן בִּרְשׁוּתוֹ.

Mishnah 2: One may not sell animal tithe unblemished alive, or blemished[41] alive or slaughtered, and one may not use it for preliminarily marrying a woman[42]. One[43] may sell a firstling unblemished alive, blemished alive or slaughtered[44], and one may use it for preliminarily marrying a woman. One does not exchange Second Tithe by a blank[45], or by a coin not in circulation[46], or on money not in his possession[47].

41 A blemished tenth animal (or firstling) is holy but must be eaten as profane food away from the Temple.

42 *Peah* 6:2, Note 46. The husband has to give his bride something of his possessions. For R. Meïr, Second Tithe is not the farmer's property but given to him by Heaven.

43 Not the rancher whose animal produced a firstling but the Cohen who receives it. The firstling becomes the property of the Cohen. Since his bride becomes a member of the tribe upon consummation of the marriage, she then will have full use of the firstling for food even if it is unblemished.

44 A slaughtered blemished firstling may be sold by the Cohen as food even to a Gentile (*Bekhorot* 28a).

45 Greek ἄσημος, -ον "without mark; uncoined", a blank for coining. Cf. D. Sperber, *Roman Palestine 200-400, Money and Prices* (Ramat Gan, 1974), Note 12 on p. 208.

46 Any coin which is not legal tender at the place of redemption is merchandise, not money.

47 Second Tithe cannot be exchanged pledging future income, or outstanding loans, or by one's own but inacessible money.

(fol. 52c) **הלכה ב:** הַשָּׁחוּט מוּתָּר. תַּנֵּי דְבֵי רִבִּי יַנַּאי לֹא שַׁנְיָיא בֵּין חַי בֵּין שָׁחוּט בֵּין תָּמִים בֵּין בַּעַל מוּם. וְלֵיי דָא מִילָּה תְּנָן חַי וְלֹא שָׁחוּט. כְּגוֹן נִיתְנֵי דְבַתְרָהּ הַבְּכוֹר מוֹכְרִין אוֹתוֹ תָּמִים חַי וּבַעַל מוּם חַי וְשָׁחוּט.

Halakhah 2: Therefore, once it was slaughtered, is it permitted[48]? It was stated by the House of Rebbi Yannai: There is no difference between alive and slaughtered, unblemished and blemished[49]. For what did we state then "live but not slaughtered?" For example, what was stated after this: "One may sell a firstling unblemished alive[50], blemished alive or slaughtered[51]."

48 Why does the Mishnah make a difference between unblemished and blemished animal tithe?

49 This is also a *baraita* in Babli *Bekhorot* 31b.

50 To a Cohen, and certainly when it was slaughtered and its blood and fat brought to the altar.

51 To a Jew, not necessarily a Cohen. The animal may be sold to a Gentile only slaughtered since it has to be slaughtered ritually.

רִבִּי אַבָּא בַּר יַעֲקֹב בְּשֵׁם רִבִּי יוֹחָנָן נֶאֱמַר כָּאן לֹא יִגָּאֵל. וְנֶאֱמַר בְּחֶרְמֵי כֹהֲנִים לֹא יִמָּכֵר וְלֹא יִגָּאֵל. מַה לֹא יִגָּאֵל הָאָמוּר בְּחֶרְמֵי כֹהֲנִים אֵינוֹ לֹא נִמְכַּר וְלֹא נִגְאַל. אַף לֹא יִגָּאֵל הָאָמוּר כָּאן אֵינוֹ לֹא נִמְכַּר וְלֹא נִגְאַל. רִבִּי יַעֲקֹב דְּרוֹמִייָה בָּעָא קוֹמֵי רִבִּי יוֹסֵי כְּלוּם כְּתִיב בִּבְכוֹר לֹא תִפָּדֶה בְּבַעַל מוּם. מַעֲשַׂר בְּהֵמָה לֹא חִלְּקָה הַתּוֹרָה בֵּין חַי בֵּין שָׁחוּט בֵּין תָּמִים בֵּין בַּעַל מוּם.

Rebbi Abba bar Jacob in the name of Rebbi Joḥanan[52]: It is said here (*Lev.* 27:33): "It may not be redeemed." It has been said about Cohanim's bans (*Lev.* 27:28) "It may not be sold or redeemed." Since "it may not be redeemed" for Cohanim's bans includes sale, so "it may not be redeemed" here includes sale. Rebbi Jacob the Southerner asked before Rebbi Yose: Is it not written about a firstling (*Num.* 18:17) "it should not be redeemed?" About a blemished animal[53]. For animal tithe, the Torah made no difference between living and slaughtered, unblemished and blemished.

52 In the Babli (*Bekhorot* 32a) this is quoted in the names of R. Joḥanan and Rav and rejected. For Tannaïtic sources, cf. *Sifra Beḥuqotay Pereq* 13(4), quoted Babli *Bekhorot* 31b, *Temurah* 5b, 40a.

53 *Num.* 18:17 refers only to unblemished animals. No restrictions are put on blemished firstlings other than that they have to be given to a Cohen.

אֵין מְקַדְּשִׁין בּוֹ אֶת הָאִשָּׁה. אֲבָל מְקַדְּשִׁין בְּגִידָיו וּבַעֲצָמָיו וּבְקַרְנָיו[54] וּבִטְלָפָיו. אָמַר רִבִּי לָעְזָר מִפְּנֵי שֶׁכָּתוּב בּוֹ בְּרָכָה. וִיקַדֵּשׁ בִּבְשָׂרוֹ. אָמַר רִבִּי יוֹסֵי כְּלוּם לָמְדוּ מַעֲשֵׂר אֶלָּא מֵחֶרְמֵי כֹהֲנִים מַה חֶרְמֵי כֹהֲנִים אֵין מְקַדְּשִׁין בּוֹ אֶת הָאִשָּׁה. אַף כָּל־הַקֳּדָשִׁים אֵין מְקַדְּשִׁין בּוֹ אֶת הָאִשָּׁה. מֵעַתָּה לֹא יְקַדְּשׁוּ לֹא בְגִידָיו וְלֹא

בַּעֲצָמָיו וְלֹא בְקַרְנָיו וְלֹא בִטְלָפָיו. הֲוֵי צוֹרְכָא לְהַהִיא דְּאָמַר רִבִּי לֶעְזָר מִפְּנֵי שֶׁכָּתוּב בָּהֶן בְּרָכָה.

"One may not use it for preliminarily marrying a woman." But one may use its sinews, bones, horns, and hooves for preliminary marriage[54]. Rebbi Eleazar said, because a blessing is mentioned for it[55]. Why can one not use its meat for preliminary marriage? Rebbi Yose said, they learned tithe only from Cohanim's bans. Since one may not use Cohanim's bans for preliminary marriage, one may not use any sacrifices for preliminary marriage. Then one should not be able to use its sinews, bones, horns, and hooves for preliminary marriage. One needs what Rebbi Eleazar said, because a blessing is mentioned for it.

54 This is not mentioned in the Babli or in Maimonides's Code. The inedible parts of a sacrifice, totally stripped of their meat, are profane after the meal.

55 *Deut.* 12:15: "But for all your desire you may slaughter and eat meat, by the blessing the Eternal, your God, gave you in all your gates; the impure and the pure should eat it, like deer and gazelle." This deals with dedicated animals which developed a blemish or the blemished animal which became tithe (*Sifry Deut.* 71). On this, the Babli (*Bekhorot* 32a) elaborates: "What is the sacrifice in which there is blessing only after slaughter? This is the animal tithe." As Rashi explains, dedicated sacrifices which developed a blemish may be exchanged and returned to profane status. The blemished firstling may be sold when alive. Only animal tithe remains holy even if blemished until it is ritually slaughtered and used as human food.

רִבִּי יוּדָן בָּעֵי אָמַר לְאִשָּׁה מִשְׁכִּי לִי מַעֲשֵׂר בְּהֵמָה זֶה שֶׁתִּתְקַדְּשִׁי לִי בוֹ לְאַחַר שְׁחִיטָה. מֵאַחַר שֶׁיֵּשׁ בְּיָדוֹ לִשְׁחוֹט מְקוּדֶּשֶׁת מִכְּבָר. אוֹ לְאַחַר שְׁחִיטָה.

Rebbi Yudan asked: If somebody said to a woman, draw this animal tithe to you from me[56] and be preliminarily married to me by it after slaughtering[57]. Since it is in his hand to slaughter, is she immediately preliminarily married or only after slaughtering?

56 This is an act of acquisition. But since animal tithe cannot be alienated while alive, the acquisition will be completed only upon ritual slaughter of the animal.

57 It is clear from Mishnah *Qiddušin* 2 that conditional betrothals are valid under certain conditions. In this case, one has to assume that either the animal is unblemished and the discussion takes place in the outer courtyard of the Temple or the animal is blemished. In both cases, the animal could be slaughtered immediately and all questions avoided. Therefore, no answer is needed.

רִבִּי זְעִירָא בְשֵׁם רִבִּי בָּא בַּר מָמָל הַגּוֹנֵב מַעֲשַׂר בְּהֵמָה שֶׁלְּחֲבֵירוֹ אִם הָיָה קַייָם מַחֲזִירוֹ לוֹ בְעֵינוֹ. אֲכָלוֹ מַה שֶׁאָכַל אָכַל. רִבִּי לָעְזָר בְּשֵׁם רִבִּי מָנָא אֵין אוֹמֵר לוֹ שֶׁיִּתֵּן מִילְּתָא אוֹ פָּחוֹת מִשָּׁוֶה פְרוּטָה אֵין אוֹמֵר לוֹ שֶׁיִּתֵּן. אָמַר רִבִּי חִינְנָא הָדָא דְאָתָא בְּשֶׁאֵינוֹ שָׁוֶה פְרוּטָה מֵעִיקָּרוֹ. אֲבָל אִם הָיָה יָפֶה שָׁוֶה פְרוּטָה מֵעִיקָּרוֹ אוֹמֵר לוֹ שֶׁיִּתֵּן.

Rebbi Zeïra in the name of Rebbi Abba bar Mamal: If someone steals someone else's animal tithe, if it still exists he returns it as is, if he ate it, he ate what he ate[58]. Rebbi Eleazar in the name of Rebbi Mana[59]: He cannot ask him to give anything; if it is worth less than a *perutah*[60] one cannot say that he should give[61]. Rebbi Ḥinena said, that is, if it was worth less than a *perutah* from the start. But if it was worth a *perutah* from the start, one tells him to pay[62].

58 Since the living animal tithe is property of Heaven, he does not have to pay the fines imposed on the thief of private property (cf. *Terumot* 6, end of

Halakhah 4). His atonement is between him and Heaven.

59 R. Mana I.

60 Cf. *Ma'serot* Chapter 3, Note 13.

61 This is another version of R. Zeïra's argument: Since a live animal tithe is not marketable it has no value, and the theft is not prosecutable in court since the court will not take cognizance of a case worth less than a *perutah*.

62 This is a remark pertaining to tort law, not to our case here. In torts, the value of a claim is computed for the time the damage was done, which may be different from the value of the object today. A similar statement is in Babli *Baba Mezi'a* 55a.

רִבִּי יוּדָה בַּר פָּזִי בְּשֵׁם רִבִּי יְהוֹשֻׁעַ בֶּן לֵוִי חַי לֹא שָׁחוּט. תַּמָּן תַּנִּינָן הַמְקַדֵּשׁ בְּחֶלְקוֹ מִקָּדְשֵׁי קָדָשִׁים וּבְקָדָשִׁים קַלִּין אֵינָהּ מְקוּדֶּשֶׁת. אָמַר רִבִּי יוּדָה בֶּן פָּזִי רִבִּי יוּדָה יְלִיף כָּל־הֶקְדֵּשׁ מִבְּכוֹר. מַה בְּכוֹר מְקַדְּשִׁין בּוֹ אֶת הָאִשָּׁה. אַף הַקֳּדָשִׁים מְקַדְּשִׁין בָּהֶן אֶת הָאִשָּׁה. רִבִּי מֵאִיר יְלִיף כָּל־הַקֳּדָשִׁים מִמַּעֲשֵׂר בְּהֵמָה. מַה מַּעֲשֵׂר בְּהֵמָה אֵין מְקַדְּשִׁין בָּהֶן אֶת הָאִשָּׁה אַף כָּל־הַקֳּדָשִׁין אֵין מְקַדְּשִׁין בָּהֶן אֶת הָאִשָּׁה. מִחְלְפָה שִׁיטָּתֵיהּ דְּרִבִּי יוּדָה בַּר פָּזִי תַּמָּן הוּא אָמַר בֵּין חַי בֵּין שָׁחוּט. וְהָכָא הוּא אוֹמֵר חַי וְלֹא שָׁחוּט. תַּמָּן בְּשֵׁם גַּרְמֵיהּ. וְהָכָא בְּשֵׁם רִבִּי יְהוֹשֻׁעַ בֶּן לֵוִי. אֲפִילוּ תֵימַר כָּאן וְכָאן בְּשֵׁם גַּרְמֵיהּ. בִּמְקַדֵּשׁ בְּחַי וּבְרָאוּי לִיפּוֹל לוֹ וּלְאַחַר שְׁחִיטָה. מַאי טַעֲמָא דְּרִבִּי יְהוֹשֻׁעַ בֶּן לֵוִי. וּבְשָׂרָם יִהְיֶה לָךְ כַּחֲזֵה הַתְּנוּפָה. וּמַאי טַעֲמָא דְּרִבִּי יוּדָן בֶּן פָּזִי. יִהְיֶה לָךְ אֲפִילוּ לְאַחַר שְׁחִיטָה. מַה מְקַיֵּם רִבִּי יְהוֹשֻׁעַ בֶּן לֵוִי יִהְיֶה לָךְ. רִיבָּה לוֹ הֲוָייָה אַחֶרֶת שֶׁיְּהֵא נֶאֱכָל לִשְׁנֵי יָמִים וְלַיְלָה אֶחָד.

[63]Rebbi Jehudah bar Pazi in the name of Rebbi Joshua ben Levi: Alive, but not slaughtered[64]. There[65], we have stated: "If somebody betrothes a woman with his share in most holy or simple holy sacrifices, she is not betrothed." Rebbi Jehudah bar Pazi said, Rebbi Jehudah learns all dedicated things from the firstling. Just as one may betrothe a woman with a firstling, so all sacrifices may be used to betrothe a woman. Rebbi

Meïr learns all sacrifices from animal tithe. Just as one may not betrothe a woman with animal tithe, so no sacrifices may be used to betrothe a woman. The opinion of Rebbi Jehudah bar Pazi is inverted. There[66], he says, alive or slaughtered. But here, he says alive, but not slaughtered. There in his own name, here in the name of Rebbi Joshua ben Levi. Even if you say there and here in his own name; if he betrothes while it is still alive and with what is scheduled to fall to him[67]. After slaughter, what is the reason of Rebbi Joshua ben Levi? (*Num.* 18:18): "Their meat shall be for you, like the breast of weaving[68]." And what is the reason of Rebbi Jehudah ben Pazi? "*Shall be for you*", even after slaughtering. How does Rebbi Joshua ben Levi uphold "*shall be for you*"? He added another *being*[69] that it should be eaten during two days and one night.

63 This paragraph also is in *Qiddušin* 2:8 (fol. 62d-63a).

64 The Mishnah, which states that a live firstling may be given as a marriage gift, is interpreted to mean that after slaughter it will be permitted to the bride.

65 Mishnah *Qiddušin* 2:8; also quoted *Demay* 1:3, Notes 185-187: "If somebody uses his share in the holiest sacrifices or simple holy sacrifices as marriage gifts, the marriage is not valid. With Second Tithes, be it intentional or in error, the marriage is not valid, the words of R. Meïr. Rebbi Jehudah said, if in error, the marriage is not valid, if intentional, the marriage is valid." Rebbi Meïr declares that holiest sacrifices, the Cohen's share of simple sacrifices, and the Second Tithe are all Heaven's property offered, as the case may be, to the Cohen, his family, or the layman and his family for consumption in Jerusalem. Hence, for R. Meïr, the basic conditions for a valid marriage are not satisfied.

R. Jehudah agrees that under normal circumstances, Second Tithe in Jerusalem cannot be exchanged. However, since it must be redeemed if it became ritually impure, it can also be exchanged unlawfully. His position is explained in *Peah*, Chapter 7, Note 135. He also holds that the Cohen's share of the sacrifices is his personal property. Hence, at least as far as simple sacrifices are concerned, the woman becomes his wife through the marriage and can legally consume the meat given to her. R. Jehudah also asserts that Second Tithe is always the owner's property, even before exchange. However, it cannot be used as a marriage gift directly since there is a lien on it that it should be used only for consumption, and that lien must first be removed by conscient redemption or exchange.

The Babli (*Qiddušin* 52b) goes to great lengths to find a case in which a woman might receive a Cohen's part of the holiest sacrifices which must be eaten by male Cohanim in those parts of the Temple yard into which others may enter only when required by the necessities of sacrificial rites. It also holds (*Baba Qama* 12b) that the statement about the firstling is valid only in the absence of a Temple; a position difficult to reconcile with the first part of the Mishnah.

66 In *Qiddušin* 2:8.

67 This is a very hypothetical answer which, as seen in the following text, is immediately discarded. It is possible to marry a woman by a future benefit as, e. g., the offer of future services (*Qiddušin* 3:6). However, since the Cohen's part of sacrificial meat is defined only at the moment of distribution, one runs into the problem of retroactivity (*Demay* 6:10, Note 160).

68 The part of the Cohen from a family sacrifice, to be eaten by the Cohen's family but not the Cohen's property. The verse identifies the holiness of the firstling with that of the Cohen's share in a Temple sacrifice.

69 "Their meat *shall be for you*; like the breast of weaving and the right thigh it *shall be for you*." It is implied that the Cohen has maximal use of the firstling. This is taken to mean that the period after slaughter in which the firstling may be eaten is the maximal period found in the Torah for any sacrifice.

In the Babli, *Zebaḥim* 57a, the discussion is quoted in the name of Tannaïm of the first and second generations.

מַתְנִיתִין דְּלָא כְּרִבִּי יוֹסֵי. דְּתַנֵּי מְחַלְּלִין מַעֲשֵׂר שֵׁינִי עַל אֲסִימוֹן דִּבְרֵי רִבִּי דוֹסָא וַחֲכָמִים אוֹסְרִין. מַה טַעֲמָא דְּרִבִּי דוֹסָא. וְצַרְתָּ הַכֶּסֶף דָּבָר שֶׁהוּא נִצְרָר

מְחַבֵּירוֹ וְיֵשׁ לוֹ צוּרָה וְיוֹצֵא עַל גַּב צוּרָתוֹ. רִבִּי יוֹסֵי בְּשֵׁם רִבִּי יוֹחָנָן דִּבְרֵי רִבִּי יוֹסֵי מְחַלְּלִין מַעֲשֵׂר עַל לִיטְרָא שֶׁלְּכֶסֶף. אִילּוּ אָמַר כֶּסֶף הֲוִינָן (fol. 52d) אָמְרִין כְּשֵׁם שֶׁאָמַר כֶּסֶף כָּךְ אָמַר זָהָב. אִילּוּ אָמַר כֶּסֶף הֲוִינָן מָרִין לְהוֹצִיא שִׁבְרֵי קְעָרוֹת וּמְתַּמְחוּיִין הֲוֵי מֵהֶן לִיטְרָא שֶׁלְּכֶסֶף.

[70]Our Mishnah does not follow Rebbi Yose[71], as it was stated[72]: "One may exchange Second Tithe for a blank, the words of Rebbi Dosa, but the Sages forbid it." What is Rebbi Dosa's reason? (*Deut.* 14:25) "You should bundle the money;" something which is bundled together, or which has a form and is current because of its form[73]. Rebbi Yose in the name of Rebbi Johanan: The word of Rebbi Yose that one exchanges [Second] Tithe for a pound of silver[74]. If he had [only] said "silver", we would have said just as he said silver, so he said gold. If he had [only] said "silver", we would have taught to exclude broken pots and baskets from which one could get a pound of silver.

70 Here starts the discussion of the redemption of Second Tithe.

71 The name tradition in this paragraph is confusing. The Tosephta quoted is in the name of R. Dosa (probably R. Dosa ben Hyrcanus, of the first generation of Tannaïm) in all sources except the Rome ms. of the Yerushalmi (ר' יוסה); but the statement of R. Yose (the Amora) shows that R. Yose (the Tanna) accepts the position of R. Dosa. Therefore, no emendation of the text is necessary.

72 Mishnah *Idiut* 3:2, quoted Babli *Baba Mezi'a* 47b; in different formulation Tosephta 1:4.

73 A quote from *Sifry Deut.* 107 (reproduced in Babli *Baba Mezi'a* 47b), shortened to unintelligibility. The verses *Deut.* 14:24-26 form the basis of the rules of redemption of Second Tithe; see the Introduction. V. 14:25 states: "Give silver [for it]; וצרת הכסף בידך . . ." R. Ismael reads "take the silver in your hand", i. e. "something which is bundled (√צור I, صرّ, to bind) together;" whereas R. Aqiba reads "something which has a form" (√צור III, صوّر, to form). The only explanation which fits the language of the verse is

that of R. Ismael (R. Dosa, R. Yose); it is accepted by both the Babylonian and the Palestinian Aramaic Targumim. It is difficult to see how R. Aqiba could give a straightforward translation of the verse. He also separates בידך from the preceding text. This shows that in the text before us, "or" denotes a switch from R. Ismael (R. Dosa, R. Yose) to R. Aqiba (the Sages).

74 Since coinage was invented long after the time of Moses, he takes כסף to mean just that, silver bullion, not gold, or silver which is not bullion and whose value could only be determined by a lengthy assay.

עַל אַסֵּימוֹן. הַכֹּל מוֹדִין שֶׁאֵין מְחַלְּלִין אוֹתוֹ עַל הַמָּעוֹת הַנְּתוּנוֹת לָאוֹלִייָר. הָדָא דְתֵימַר כְּדֶרֶךְ שֶׁהֵן יָפִין אֵצֶל הָאוֹלִייָר. אֲבָל כְּדֶרֶךְ שֶׁהֵן יָפִין אֵצֶל[75] הַתֵּירְמַסָּר מְחַלֵּל.

"For a blank". Everybody agrees that one does not exchange for the coins given to the *olearius*[76]. That is, the way they are used for the *olearius*. But the way they are used by the *tremissarius*[77] one may exchange.

75 Reading of the Rome ms. Leyden and Venice: על.

76 The dispensor of rubbing oil in the bathhouse, cf. *Berakhot* 2:3, Note 94.

77 Perhaps a *tremissarius* is the person who changes coins into *tremisses*, thirds of an *as*, to be given to the bath attendants (E. G.); cf. J. N. Epstein, *Tarbiẓ* 1, p. 49. The word *tremissarius* is not recorded in Latin literature but *tremes, -issis* is. If the *tremissarius* changes legal coins into *tremisses*, he will also purchase *tremisses* (at a lower rate) and pay legal coin. Also cf. *assarius*, old form of *as*.

The Babylonian tradition (Tosephta 1:4, *Baba Meẓi'a* 47b) always refers to "(small) coins given as tokens in the bathhouse."

מַטְבֵּעַ שֶׁנִּפְסַל וְהַמַּלְכוּת מְקַבְּלָתוֹ רִבִּי יוֹסֵי בְּשֵׁם רִבִּי יוֹחָנָן כְּאַסֵּימוֹן. רִבִּי חִייָה בְּשֵׁם רִבִּי יוֹנָתָן בְּמַטְבֵּעַ שֶׁלְּמְלָכִים הָרִאשׁוֹנִים (נֵימַר)[78] אִם הָיָה יוֹצֵא עַל

גַּב צוּרָתוֹ מְחַלֵּל. וְאִם לָאו אֵינוֹ מְחַלֵּל. מַטְבֵּעַ שֶׁמָּרַד כְּגוֹן בַּר כּוֹזִיבָא אֵינוֹ מְחַלֵּל. הָיוּ לוֹ מָעוֹת שֶׁלְּסַכָּנָה אָתָא עוֹבְדָא קוֹמֵי רִבִּי אִימִּי אָמַר יוֹלִיךְ הֲנָייָה לְיַם הַמֶּלַח. וְהָיוּ לוֹ מָעוֹת שֶׁל דיסגנים.[79] רִבִּי יַעֲקֹב בַּר זַבְדִּי בְּשֵׁם רִבִּי אַבָּהוּ מְחַלְּלָן כְּדֶרֶךְ שֶׁהֵן יָפִן[80] אֵצֶל הַתֵּירְמִסָּר. בִּיקֵּשׁ לְהוֹצִיאָן מְחַלְּלָן כְּדֶרֶךְ שֶׁהוּא מְחַלֵּל עֲלֵיהֶן.

A coin out of circulation which the government will accept, Rebbi Yose in the name of Rebbi Joḥanan: It is like a blank. Rebbi Ḥiyya in the name of Rebbi Joḥanan: A coin of the earlier kings, if it is currently accepted because of its coinage one exchanges, otherwise one does not exchange[81]. A revolutionary coin like that of Bar Koziba one does not exchange[82]. If he had dangerous coins[83]: such a case came before Rebbi Immi. He said, one should carry its yield to the Dead Sea[84]. If one had coins difficult to determine: Rebbi Jacob bar Zavdi: One exchanges at the value given by the *tremissarius*[85]. If he wants to spend the coins, he exchanges in his usual way.

78 Superfluous word, missing in Rome ms.

79 In Rome ms: לסגנים. Zuckermann, *Talmudische Münzen und Gewichte*, Breslau 1862, explains as **dusignum*, supposed to mean "doubly coined, overstruck", accepted by Levy, Krauss, and Sperber. However, H. L. Fleischer already has pointed out that no composites of *duo* with the singular are known. While the exact nature of these coins is unknown, from the text it is reasonable to derive the word from δυσγνωσία, ἡ, "difficulty of knowing", δύσγνωστος, ον (adj.) "hard to recognize" (E. G.).

80 Reading of Rome ms. שמחללן; an intrusion from the next sentence.

81 The statements of R. Yose and R. Ḥiyya deal with the same subject. If somebody had an old Roman coin from the time the coinage was honest, if it is recognized by its coinage and/or acceptable for payment of taxes, it is money and may be used for exchange/redemption of Second Tithe.

Otherwise it is merchandise and may not be used.

S. Lieberman, *Tosefta ki-Fshutah* p. 717, wants to restrict the meaning of "otherwise" to coins of emperors whose memory was cursed by the Senate. In the Babli, *Baba Qama* 97b, coins of earlier kings (maybe Partian coins in the Persian empire?) are declared unacceptable; the Tosephta (1:6) declares them all acceptable.

82 In Tosephta and Babli (*loc. cit.*): Bar Koziba or Jerusalem coins (from the first war against the Romans.)

83 This probably is a restatement of the previous sentence.

84 The usual description of: destroy completely.

85 If the money changer offers payment for that coin, this is its monetary value.

תַּנֵּי אֵין מְחַלְּלִין אוֹתוֹ לֹא עַל הַמָּעוֹת שֶׁהֵן[86] בְּבָבֶל וְלֹא עַל הַמָּעוֹת שֶׁבְּבָבֶל כָּן. לֹא עַל הַמָּעוֹת שֶׁכָּן בְּבָבֶל בְּעוֹמֵד בְּבָבֶל. וְלֹא עַל הַמָּעוֹת שֶׁבְּבָבֶל כָּן בְּעוֹמֵד כָּן. הָיוּ לוֹ מָעוֹת מִבָּבֶל לְבָבֶל וְהוּא עוֹמֵד כָּאן נֵימַר אִם הָיְתָה דֶרֶךְ פְּתוּחָה מְחַלֵּל וְאִם לָאו אֵינוֹ מְחַלֵּל וְטָבְבוֹ כָן.

"[87]One does not exchange it for money in Babylonia nor for Babylonian money here." Not for money from here in Babylonia if he is in Babylonia; nor for Babylonian money here when he is here. If he had Babylonian money in Babylonia but he is here, let us say that he may exchange if the road was open; but otherwise he cannot exchange and put in order here.

86 Rome ms.: שכן. This reading is assumed in the next sentence.

87 Tosephta 1:6. The Tosephta and possibly the Babli *Baba Qama* 97b allow a Babylonian in the Land of Israel to exchange his tithe for his Babylonian money in Babylonia irrespective of the political situation.

אָמַר רִבִּי אָבִין כָּל־הַמַּטְבֵּיעוֹת הָיוּ יוֹצְאוֹת בִּירוּשָׁלֵם מִפְּנֵי כֵן עַל שֵׁם יְפֵה נוֹף מְשׂוֹשׂ כָּל־הָאָרֶץ.

Rebbi Abin said, all coins were current in Jerusalem in old times, following (*Ps.* 48:3) "beautiful region, enjoyment of all the earth."[88]

88 In the Babli *Baba Qama* 97b, the fact that all coins from all countries were accepted in Jerusalem in Temple times is quoted as tannaïtic.

יָכוֹל אִם הָיוּ לוֹ מָעוֹת בְּהַר הַמֶּלֶךְ וּבְקַצְרָה מְחַלְּלָן עֲלֵיהֶן. תַּלְמוּד לוֹמַר וְצַרְתָּ הַכֶּסֶף בְּיָדְךָ. מַהוּ בְּיָדְךָ בִּרְשׁוּתְךָ. רִבִּי יוֹנָה בָּעֵי נָפַל כִּיסוֹ לְבוֹר וּבוֹ מֵאָה רִיבּוֹ וְהָיָה יָכוֹל לְהוֹצִיא חֲמִשִּׁים רִיבּוֹא לְהַעֲלוֹתָן אוֹתָן חֲמִשִּׁים רִיבּוֹא כְּמוֹ שֶׁהֵן בִּרְשׁוּתוֹ.

I could think that if someone had money on King's Mountain or in a castle[89] he might exchange based on it. The verse says (*Deut.* 14:25): "take the silver in your hand;" what means "in your hand"? In your possession! Rebbi Jonah asked, if his wallet with 1'000'000 [denars][90] fell into a cistern and he could spend 500'000 to get them out, is that as if 500'000 were in his possession[91]?

89 The Tosephta, 1:6, reads: "How [does one not exchange] if it is not in his possession? If he had monies buried on King's Mountain or a Roman army camp (קצטרא *castra*) or his wallet had fallen into a cistern, even though he knows that they are there, they cannot be used for redemption and if he used them, he did not acquire the tithe." There are no longer any Jews living on King's Mountain, only Gentiles (cf. *Demay* 5:9, Note 115), and he certainly cannot start digging in a camp of the Roman army.

90 Just before Diocletian's currency reform, that would be about $16\frac{2}{3}$ *aurei*.

91 Since the Tosephta gives a clear, negative, answer to this question, the Tosephta does not represent Yerushalmi tradition.

(fol. 52b) **משנה ג:** הַלּוֹקֵחַ בְּהֵמָה לְזִבְחֵי שְׁלָמִים וְחַיָּה לִבְשַׂר הַתַּאֲוָה יָצָא הָעוֹר לְחוּלִין אַף עַל פִּי שֶׁהָעוֹר מְרוּבֶּה עַל הַבָּשָׂר. כַּדֵּי יַיִן סְתוּמוֹת מָקוֹם שֶׁדַּרְכָּן לִימָּכֵר סְתוּמוֹת יָצָא קַנְקַן לְחוּלִין. הָאֱגוֹזִים וְהַשְּׁקֵדִים יָצְאוּ קְלִיפֵּיהֶן לְחוּלִין. הַתֶּמֶד עַד שֶׁלֹּא הֶחֱמִיץ אֵינוֹ נִלְקָח בְּכֶסֶף מַעֲשֵׂר וּמִשֶּׁהֶחֱמִיץ נִלְקָח בְּכֶסֶף מַעֲשֵׂר.

Mishnah 3: If somebody buys a domestic animal for a well-being offering[92] or a wild animal[93] for meat of desire[94], the hide becomes profane even though it may be worth more than the meat[95]. [If he buys] sealed wine jugs at a place where jugs usually are sold sealed[96], the pitcher becomes profane. The shells of walnuts and almonds become profane[97]. Afterwine before it fermented cannot be bought with tithe money[98]; after it fermented it may be bought with tithe money.

92 This is the main purpose of bringing Second Tithe money to Jerusalem, to buy there animals to eat "before the Eternal, your God" (*Deut.* 14:26). Most of the well-being offering is consumed by the family of the donor.

93 Wild animals, from the list *Deut.* 14:5, can never become sacrifices and are intrinsically profane. They are mentioned here only because of Mishnah 4.

94 The biblical expression (*Deut.* 11:15) for profane meat slaughtered outside the holy precinct.

95 The hide, as part of the live animal, has been paid for by tithe money. After the meat has been consumed according to the rules of tithe money, the hide may be used or sold as fully profane. The Halakhah will restrict this to non-professional transactions.

96 Wine is not usually sold from the barrel so that the jug would be an intrinsic part of the deal.

97 And may be used as fuel or for tanning.

98 It is water which may not be bought with tithe money, Mishnah 5.

משנה ד: הַלּוֹקֵחַ חַיָּה לְזִבְחֵי שְׁלָמִים וּבְהֵמָה לִבְשַׂר הַתַּאֲוָה לֹא יָצָא הָעוֹר לְחוּלִין. כַּדֵּי יַיִן פְּתוּחוֹת אוֹ סְתוּמוֹת מָקוֹם שֶׁדַּרְכָּן לִימָּכֵר פְּתוּחוֹת לֹא יָצָא קַנְקַן לְחוּלִין. סַלֵּי תְאֵינִים וְסַלֵּי עֲנָבִים עִם הַכֶּלִי לֹא יָצְאוּ דְמֵי הַכֶּלִי לְחוּלִין.

Mishnah 4: If somebody buys a wild animal for a well-being offering[99] or a domestic animal for meat of desire[100], the hide does not become profane. [If he buys] open wine jugs or sealed ones at a place where wine usually is sold from the barrel, the pitcher does not become profane. [If he buys] baskets of figs and baskets of grapes sold with the vessel, the price money of the vessel does not become profane[101].

99 A wild animal can never be a sacrifice. Since the animal cannot be eaten in the way it was intended, the hide cannot lose its status of tithe money. If the hide is sold, the proceeds are still tithe money and must be spent on food in Jerusalem.

100 The Halakhah will explain that domestic animals bought with tithe money must be used as sacrifices.

101 In the last two cases, the buyer will be charged separately for pitcher or basket. Since these are not edible, they should be paid for with non-tithe money.

משנה ה: הַלּוֹקֵחַ מַיִם וּמֶלַח וּפֵירוֹת הַמְחוּבָּרִים לְקַרְקַע אוֹ פֵּירוֹת שֶׁאֵינָן יְכוֹלִין לְהַגִּיעַ לִירוּשָׁלֵם לֹא קָנָה מַעֲשֵׂר. הַלּוֹקֵחַ פֵּירוֹת שׁוֹגֵג יַחְזְרוּ דָמִים לִמְקוֹמָן. מֵזִיד יַעֲלֶה וְיֵאָכְלוּ בַמָּקוֹם וְאִם אֵין מִקְדָּשׁ יֵרָקְבוּ.

Mishnah 5: If somebody buys water, or salt[102], or produce still connected to the ground, or produce that cannot reach Jerusalem, the tithe [money] does not acquire[103]. If somebody bought produce[104] in error, the money should return to its place[105]. If intentionally, he should bring them up and they should be eaten at the Place[106]; if there is no Temple they should be left to rot.

102 It will be shown in Halakhah 4 that tithe money can be spent only in Jerusalem and only on something generated by sexual reproduction (vegetal or animal).

103 The transaction is invalid: the buyer returns what he bought and the seller returns the money.

104 Outside of Jerusalem, an act forbidden by *Deut*. 14:24-25.

105 The transaction is valid but the buyer has to set aside new money for the tithe money which in error became profane.

106 The place of the central sanctuary (Siloh or Jerusalem); the language is borrowed from *Deut*. 14:24.

משנה ו: הַלּוֹקֵחַ בְּהֵמָה שׁוֹגֵג יַחְזְרוּ דָמֶיהָ לִמְקוֹמָהּ. מֵזִיד תַּעֲלֶה וְתֵאָכֵל בַּמָּקוֹם וְאִם אֵין מִקְדָּשׁ תִּיקָּבֵר עַל יְדֵי עוֹרָהּ.

Mishnah 6: If somebody buys[104] a domestic animal in error, the money should return to its place. If intentionally, he should bring it up and it should be eaten at the Place[106]; if there is no Temple it should be buried in its hide[107].

107 No use can be had from any part of this animal.

(fol. 52b) **משנה ז**: אֵין לוֹקְחִין עֲבָדִים וְקַרְקָעוֹת וּבְהֵמָה טְמֵיאָה מִדְּמֵי מַעֲשֵׂר שֵׁנִי וְאִם לָקַח יֹאכַל כְּנֶגְדָּן. אֵין מְבִיאִין קִינֵּי זָבִין וְקִינֵּי זָבוֹת וְקִינֵּי יוֹלְדוֹת מִדְּמֵי מַעֲשֵׂר שֵׁנִי וְאִם מֵבִיא יֹאכַל כְּנֶגְדָּן. זֶה הַכְּלָל כָּל־שֶׁהוּא חוּץ לַאֲכִילָה וְלִשְׁתִייָה וּלְסִיכָה מִדְּמֵי מַעֲשֵׂר שֵׁנִי יֹאכַל כְּנֶגְדּוֹ.

Mishnah 7: One does not buy slaves, real estate, and unclean animals from Second Tithe money. If he bought them, he has to eat their worth. One does not bring nests for men with gonorrhea, women with discharges, or women who have given birth from Second Tithe money. If he bought them, he has to eat their worth[108]. This is the principle: If one bought anything except for eating, drinking, and rubbing[109] from Second Tithe money, he has to eat its worth.

108 This Mishnah appears word by word, except for "Sabbatical" instead of "Second Tithe", in *Ševi'it* 8:8 and is explained there in Notes 114-116.

109 Drinking and massaging with olive oil are everywhere taken as equivalents of eating.

(fol. 52d) **הלכה ג:** תַּנֵּי בֶּן בַּגְבַּג אוֹמֵר וְנָתַתָּ הַכֶּסֶף בְּכָל־אֲשֶׁר תְּאַוֶּה נַפְשְׁךָ. תַּנֵּי לוֹקֵחַ הוּא אָדָם פָּרָה מִפְּנֵי עוֹרָהּ וְצֹאן מִפְּנֵי גִיזָּתָהּ וְיַיִן מִפְּנֵי קַנְקַנּוֹ. אָמַר רִבִּי זְעִירָה הָדָא דְתֵימָא כְּשֶׁהָיָה הַמּוֹכֵר הֶדְיוֹט. אֲבָל אִם הָיָה הַמּוֹכֵר אוּמָּן נַעֲשָׂה כְּמוֹכֵר זֶה בִּפְנֵי עַצְמוֹ וְזֶה בִּפְנֵי עַצְמוֹ. אָמַר רִבִּי זְעִירָה מַתְנִיתָא אָֽמְרָה כֵן כַּדֵּי יַיִן סְתוּמוֹת מָקוֹם שֶׁדַּרְכָּן לִימָּכֵר סְתוּמוֹת יָצָא קַנְקַן לְחוּלִין. אָמַר רִבִּי מָנָא וּמִנָּהּ כְּמַה דְתֵימַר תַּמָּן אִם הָיָה הַמּוֹכֵר אוּמָּן נַעֲשָׂה כְּמוֹכֵר זֶה בִּפְנֵי עַצְמוֹ וְזֶה בִּפְנֵי עַצְמוֹ. וְדִכְווָתָהּ אִם הָיָה הַלּוֹקֵחַ אוּמָּן נַעֲשָׂה כְּלוֹקֵחַ זֶה בִּפְנֵי עַצְמוֹ וְזֶה בִּפְנֵי עַצְמוֹ.

Halakhah 3: It was stated[110]: "Ben Bag Bag[111] says (*Deut*. 14:26): 'You shall spend the money for anything you desire.' It was stated[112]: A person may buy a cow because of its hide[113], a sheep because of its fleece, and wine because of its pitcher." Rebbi Zeïra said, that is, if the seller was a private person. But if the seller was a professional it is as if he sold this separately and that separately[114]. Rebbi Zeïra said, the Mishnah said this: "In a place where wine jugs usually are sold sealed, the pitcher becomes profane.[115]" Rebbi Mana said, from this [you conclude that] just as you say there, if the seller was a professional it is as if he sold this separately and that separately, so if the buyer was a professional it is as if he bought this separately and that separately.

110 *Sifry Deut*. 107, a longer text explaining the entire verse; reproduced Babli *Eruvin* 27b.

111 A very early Tanna, contemporary of Hillel and R. Jehudah ben Bathyra of Nisibis. His name

probably was Joḥanan.

112 This word is superfluous and does not appear in the parallel sources.

113 Since this might be his desire.

114 Since he usually sells meat and hides separately.

115 Quote and argument are incomplete. The next Mishnah says that at a place where wine usually is sold from the barrel, buying the wine in a pitcher results in two separate transactions. We infer that established trade patterns have to be followed in all but private transactions.

חוֹתֶל שֶׁלִּתְמָרִים פַּטוֹלַיְיָא שֶׁלִּתְמָרִים יָצְאוּ לְחוּלִין. קוּפּוֹת שֶׁלִּתְמָרִים אִית תַּנָּיֵי תַנֵּי יָצְאוּ וְאִית תַּנָּיֵי תַנֵּי לֹא יָצְאוּ. אָמַר רַב חִסְדָּא מָאן דְּאָמַר יָצְאוּ דְּרוּסוֹת. וּמָאן דְּאָמַר לֹא יָצְאוּ בְּשֶׁאֵינָן דְּרוּסוֹת.

Palm-leaf baskets[116] of dates, plates[117] of dates became profane. Some Tannaïm state that boxes of dates did become, some Tannaïm state that they did not become. Rav Ḥisda said, he who said they did become, when they were pressed[118]. He who said they did not become, [meant] when not pressed.

116 Definition of Rashi, *Šabbat* 20a.

117 Latin *patella*. According to the Gaonim and Maimonides (Mishnah *Kelim* 16:5), a willow-weave basket with a narrow opening used for storing or transporting dried figs.

118 This is stated explicitly in Tosephta 1:10 which notes that all containers which become unusable, such as containers for fish sauce, vinegar, oil, honey, or in which dates or figs were pressed, by necessity are paid for with the food they contain and are profane when emptied.

הַתֶּמֶד עַד שֶׁלֹּא הֶחֱמִיץ אֵינוֹ נִקַּח בְּכֶסֶף מַעֲשֵׂר וּפוֹסֵל אֶת הַמִּקְוֶה מִשֶּׁהֶחֱמִיץ נִקַּח בְּכֶסֶף מַעֲשֵׂר וְאֵינוֹ פּוֹסֵל אֶת הַמִּקְוֶה. מַתְנִיתִין דְּרִבִּי יוּדָה דְּתַנִּינָן תַּמָּן הַמְתַמֵּד וְנָתַן מַיִם בְּמִידָּה וּמָצָא כְדֵי מִידָּתוֹ פָּטוּר. רִבִּי יְהוּדָה מְחַיֵּיב. אָמַר רִבִּי אַבָּהוּ זִימְנִין אָמַר לָהּ בְּשֵׁם רִבִּי לָעְזָר וְזִימְנִין אָמַר לָהּ בְּשֵׁם רִבִּי יוֹסֵי בֵּי רִבִּי חֲנִינָא. וְהוּא שֶׁהֶחֱמִיץ. אָמַר רִבִּי יוֹסֵי דִּבְרֵי הַכֹּל הִיא שֶׁכֵּן אֲפִילוּ מֵי מֶלַח נִיקָּחִין בְּכֶסֶף מַעֲשֵׂר.

[119]"Afterwine before it fermented cannot be bought with tithe money and invalidates a *miqweh*[120]; after it fermented it may be bought with tithe money and does not invalidate a *miqweh*." Our Mishnah follows Rebbi Jehudah as we have stated there[121]: "If someone makes after-wine and pours in a measured amount of water, if he found the same amount he is free. Rebbi Jehudah declares him obligated." Rebbi Abbahu said, sometimes in the name of Rebbi Eleazar, sometimes in the name of Rebbi Yose ben Ḥanina: Only if it fermented. Rebbi Yose said, it is the opinion of everybody since even salt water may be bought with tithe money.

119 Mishnah *Ḥulin* 1:7; cf. *Ma'serot* 5:6, Notes 89-93.

120 It is water; cf. *Terumot* Chapter 10, Note 139.

121 This and the remainder of the paragraph are in *Ma'serot* 5:5, Notes 87-93.

אָמַר רִבִּי לָעְזָר לֹא קָנָה מַעֲשֵׂר. אָמַר רִבִּי יוֹסֵי בְּקַדְמִיתָא הֲוִינָן מָרִין הַלּוֹקֵחַ בְּהֵמָה לִבְשַׂר תַּאֲוָה עַל כָּרְחוֹ נִתְפַּס הַשֵּׁם לִשְׁלָמִים וְלָא הֲוִינָן אָמְרִין כְּלוּם מִן הָדָא דְאָמַר רִבִּי לָעְזָר לֹא קָנָה מַעֲשֵׂר.

Rebbi Eleazar said, the tithe [money] did not acquire[103]. Rebbi Yose said, first we said that if somebody bought a domestic animal for meat of desire, against his will it gets the name of well-being offering but we said nothing since Rebbi Eleazar said, the tithe [money] did not acquire[122].

122 *Sifry Deut.* 107 explains that from *Deut.* 14:26 "you have to eat there *before the Eternal*, your God, and *enjoy it* you and your family" one concludes that all meat bought with tithe money has to be meat of well-being offerings. Since there is no sacrifice which does not have to be dedicated first, it is logical that the transaction should be void and there is no automatic sacrifice.

The argument assumes that any

animal bought with tithe money is without blemish; otherwise, it could not become a sacrifice. The paragraph seems to imply that buying a blemished animal with tithe money is automatically an invalid transaction. Therefore, it seems that the discussion deals with rabbinical, not biblical rules.

רִבִּי יוֹסֵי בְשֵׁם רִבִּי יוֹחָנָן בְּהֵמָה מַעֲשֵׂר שֵׁינִי בִּירוּשָׁלֵם כְּרִבִּי מֵאִיר פְּטוּרָה מִן הַבְּכוֹרָה כְּרִבִּי יְהוּדָה חַייֶבֶת בִּבְכוֹרָה. רִבִּי יִרְמְיָה בָּעֵא קוֹמֵי רִבִּי זְעִירָא יָֽלְדָה בְּכוֹר אֵימוֹרָיו מַהוּ שֶׁיִּקְרְבוּ לְגַבֵּי מִזְבֵּחַ. וְלֹא חָל מַעֲשֵׂר שֵׁינִי עַל אֵימוֹרָיו וְלֹא נִמְצָא מַבְרִיחוֹ מִן הָאֲכִילָה. אָמַר לֵיהּ וְכִי הַלּוֹקֵחַ בְּשַׂר בְּהֵמָה לִבְשַׂר תַּאֲוָה לֹא חָל מַעֲשֵׂר שֵׁינִי עַל אֵימוֹרֶיהָ וְלֹא נִמְצָא מַבְרִיחָהּ מִן הָאֲכִילָה. אָמַר לוֹ בִּלְקִיחָתָהּ פָּֽקְעָה מִמֶּנָּהּ קְדוּשַּׁת מַעֲשֵׂר. אָמַר רִבִּי יוֹסֵי וַאֲנָן לֹא הֲוִינָן אָֽמְרִין כֵּן. אֶלָּא לֹא הִתִּירָה הַתּוֹרָה לִיקַּח בְּכֶסֶף מַעֲשֵׂר אֶלָּא שְׁלָמִים בִּלְבַד. מַה נַפְקָא מִבֵּינֵיהוֹן וְולָדָהּ בְּכוֹר וְהִקְדִּישָׁהּ שְׁלָמִים. מָאן דְּאָמַר לֹא הִתִּירָה הַתּוֹרָה לִיקַּח בְּכֶסֶף מַעֲשֵׂר אֶלָּא שְׁלָמִים בִּלְבַד קְרֵיבָה. מָאן דְּאָמַר בִּלְקִיחָתָהּ פָּֽקְעָה מִמֶּנָּהּ קְדוּשַּׁת מַעֲשֵׂר אֵינָהּ קְרֵיבָה.

Rebbi Yose in the name of Rebbi Joḥanan: An animal of Second Tithe in Jerusalem following Rebbi Meïr[123] is free from the rules of firstlings[124]; following Rebbi Jehudah it is under the rules of firstlings. Rebbi Jeremiah asked before Rebbi Zeïra: If it gave birth to a firstling, must its sacred parts be brought onto the altar[125]? Did not its sacred parts fall under the rules of Second Tithe and you would hide it from being eaten[126]? He said to him, if somebody bought meat as meat of desire, would not [the holiness of] Second Tithe have fallen on its sacred parts, would you not hide it from being eaten[127]? He said to him, when it was bought, the holiness of tithe left it[128]. Rebbi Yose said, we were not saying so but the Torah did permit to buy from tithe money only well-being sacrifices exclusively[122]. What is the difference between them? If it gave birth to a firstling and he dedicated it as well-being sacrifice. For him who says, the Torah did permit to buy from tithe money only well-being sacrifices exclusively, it is offered[129]. For him who says, when it was bought, the holiness of tithe left it, and it is not offered[130].

123 He holds that tithe money is Heaven's money and any animal bought with it is not the property of the farmer; cf. Note 6; *Demay* 1, Notes 185-186. R. Jehudah holds that tithe money and what is bought from it is private property. One must assume that the animal bought either was blemished and could not be a sacrifice or was unblemished but not yet dedicated as sacrifice at the time it had its young. Maimonides (*Bekhorot* 5:9) follows R. Jehudah here whereas in the rules of Mishnah 1 he follows R. Meïr (*Ma'aser Šeni* 3:17).

124 These rules apply only to "any male firstling born to *your* cattle and flock" (*Deut.* 15:19).

125 The parts detailed in *Lev.* 3 which have to be burned on the altar. The question may be asked only according to R. Jehudah.

126 If the mother is unblemished, her sacred parts already go onto the altar; the calf or lamb should be eaten by the family. How can R. Jehudah cause the family to be slack in their fulfillment of the commandment to eat all food bought with tithe money?

127 This sentence is somewhat elliptic. R. Zeïra disagrees with R. Eleazar and holds that meat may be bought with tithe money. The sentence duly expanded should read: "He said to him, if somebody bought meat as meat of desire, would not the holiness of Second Tithe have fallen on its sacred parts [if one had fulfilled the commandment to eat well-being sacrifice]? [By buying an animal as well-being sacrifice] would you not hide its sacred parts from being eaten?" He shows that R. Jeremiah's argument is inconsistent. If it is preferable to eat sacrificial meat then not all meat should be eaten but part given to the altar.

128 Since holiness cannot join holiness, the animal must be profane at the moment it is dedicated as well-being sacrifice. Therefore, acquisition must eliminate the holiness of tithe.

129 As a firstling if it was born between the act of buying and the

dedication as sacrifice, according to R. Jehudah.

130 If the holiness of tithe disappears at the consummation of the sale, it is possible to buy an animal with tithe money only if one states that the dedication should be an immediate consequence of the acquisition. But then the calf falls under the rules of young of sacrifices and not of firstlings.

אָמַר רִבִּי יוֹסֵי הָא כָּל־אִילֵּין מִילַּייָא אֲנָן מָרִין וּמַתְנִיתָא מְסַייְעָא לְרִבִּי זְעִירָא. לֹא יָבִיא מֵחִיטֵּי מַעֲשֵׂר שֵׁינִי אֶלָּא מִמָּעוֹת מַעֲשֵׂר שֵׁינִי. מַה בֵּין חִטִּים וּמַה בֵּין מָעוֹת. אֶלָּא בִּלְקִיחָתָהּ פָּֽקְעָה מִמֶּנָּהּ קְדוּשַּׁת מַעֲשֵׂר. אָמַר רִבִּי חִינְנָא קוֹמֵי רִבִּי מָנָא וְיָבִיא מִן הַחִיטִּים הַתְּרוּמָה לַכֹּהֵן וְהַשְּׁאָר לַבְּעָלִין מִפְּנֵי מָה אֵינוֹ מֵבִיא. אָמַר לוֹ הַגַּע עַצְמָךְ שֶׁנִּשְׁפַּךְ הַדָּם לֹא נִפְסַל הַלֶּחֶם.

Rebbi Yose said, we teach all these words but a Mishnah supports Rebbi Zeïra: "He should not bring from wheat of Second Tithe but from money of Second Tithe.[131]" What is the difference between wheat and money? It must be that when it was bought, the holiness of tithe left it. Rebbi Ḥinena asked before Rebbi Mana: Why should he not bring wheat, the heave[132] to the Cohen and the rest for the owners, why does he not bring[133]? He said to him, think of it, if the blood is spilled[134] does the bread not become unusable[135]?

131 Mishnah *Menaḥot* 7:5: If somebody made a vow to bring a thanksgiving sacrifice and its breads (*Lev.* 7:12) from tithe money, he may do so but the bread should be made from wheat bought with tithe money, not wheat that is Second Tithe. Since a thanksgiving sacrifice is a special kind of well-being sacrifice, he may use tithe money for it. However, since a thanksgiving sacrifice only can be eaten for one day and one night, but a regular well-being sacrifice for two days and the night in between, this practice is frowned upon.

The Babli (*Menaḥot* 81b-82a) gives as a reason for the breads that the verse requires the sacrifice to be brought *with* its breads, i. e., from the same source. Since Second Tithe itself consists of produce, it is clear that the animal itself must be bought with tithe money. Therefore, the bread also should come from tithe money. (R. Jeremiah disagrees with the Mishnah.)

The Yerushalmi disagrees and holds that tithe money is holy and the holiness of a dedicated sacrifice can fall on the wheat only if the latter is profane. This proves R. Zeïra's point.

132 This is not the usual heave but one bread from each kind brought with the thanksgiving sacrifice; it is called heave in *Lev*. 7:14.

133 He disagrees with R. Yose whose argument is tenable only if he holds with R. Meïr that tithe money is Heaven's property. But since the previous paragraph presupposes that we hold with R. Jehudah that Second Tithe and tithe money are property of the farmer, there is no reason why Second Tithe wheat should not be used since all the breads will be eaten in holiness, either by the farmer's family or by the Cohen.

134 On the way to the altar. The entire sacrifice is invalidated if its blood is not sprinkled on the altar.

135 If anything happens to the sacrifice, the bread is wasted and has to be burned. But if the breads are bought, they will be replaced by other bought breads.

אָמַר רִבִּי יוֹחָנָן גָּֽזְרוּ עַל נְקֵיבָה בַּעֲלַת מוּם מִפְּנֵי וְולָדָהּ. גָּֽזְרוּ עַל זָכָר בַּעַל מוּם מִפְּנֵי נְקֵיבָה בַּעֲלַת מוּם. וְאָֽמְרִין בְּשֵׁם רִבִּי יוֹחָנָן אֲפִילוּ תְמִימָה גְּזֵירָה. בָּרִאשׁוֹנָה הָיוּ אוֹמְרִים לוֹקְחִין בְּהֵמָה לִבְשַׂר תַּאֲוָה וְהָיוּ מַבְרִיחִין אוֹתוֹ מֵעַל גַּבֵּי הַמִּזְבֵּחַ. חָֽזְרוּ לוֹמַר לֹא יִקְחוּ אֲפִילוּ חַיָּה אֲפִילוּ עוֹפוֹת כְּהָדָא דְתַנֵּי אֶחָד שְׁבִיעִית וְאֶחָד מַעֲשֵׂר שֵׁינִי מַחֲלִיפִין אוֹתוֹ עַל נְקֵיבָה בַּעֲלַת מוּם וְעַל שְׁאָר בְּהֵמָה חַיָּה וְעוֹף בֵּין חַיִּין בֵּין שְׁחוּטִין דִּבְרֵי רִבִּי מֵאִיר. וַחֲכָמִים אוֹמְרִים אֵין מְחַלְּלִין אֶלָּא עַל הַשְּׁחוּטִין בִּלְבַד. רִבִּי יִרְמְיָה בְּשֵׁם רִבִּי שְׁמוּאֵל בַּר רַב יִצְחָק גָּֽזְרוּ אוֹתָן שֶׁלֹּא יִרְעוּ אוֹתָן עֲדָרִים עֲדָרִים. קָם רִבִּי יִרְמְיָה עִם רִבִּי זְעִירָא אָמַר לֵיהּ עַד כְּדוֹן רִבִּי שְׁמוּאֵל בַּר רַב יִצְחָק קַיָּים וְאַתּוּן תַּלְיָין בֵּיהּ מַרְטוּטֵיכִין. וְהָאָמַר בְּשֵׁם רִבִּי יוֹחָנָן אֲפִילוּ תְמִימָה גְּזֵירָה. דִּילְמָא דְלָא אִיתְאֲמָרַת אֶלָּא עַל הַשְּׁבִיעִית. אַשְׁכַּח תַּנֵּי עַל הַשְּׁבִיעִית.

Rebbi Joḥanan said, they decreed on a blemished female because of her young. They decreed on a blemished male because of the blemished female. They said in the name of Rebbi Joḥanan, even an unblemished one is a decree[136]. Earlier they said one may buy an animal for meat of desire and hide it from the altar. They turned to say, not even a wild animal, not even birds as it was stated: "Sabbatical [money] and Second Tithe [money] can be exchanged for a blemished female animal or other domestic and wild animals and birds whether alive or slaughtered, the words of Rebbi Meïr. But the Sages say, one exchanges only on slaughtered ones.[137]" Rebbi Jeremiah in the name of Rebbi Samuel ben Rav Isaac: They decreed this that one should not raise them in herds. Rebbi Jeremiah stood next to Rebbi Zeïra who said to him, Rebbi Samuel ben Rav Isaac is still alive and you hang your rags on him! Did not Rebbi Joḥanan say even an unblemished one is a decree[138]! Maybe this was said only for Sabbatical [money]? They found it stated for Sabbatical [money][139].

136 It is agreed that while it is a positive commandment to buy well-being sacrifices in Jerusalem for the meat, the verse does not forbid to buy any kosher animal or any meat. As stated later, first they forbade to buy blemished females which could not be sacrificed but might be kept to raise young. That action would clearly be forbidden since tithe money must be used for food to be consumed. In the end, they permitted only animals for well-being sacrifices to be bought with tithe money.

137 A similar *baraita* is in Babli *Sukkah* 40b, where the statement of R. Samuel ben Isaac is part of the *baraita*. The Tosephta (1:9) has a statement contradicting both Talmudim, declaring all non-sacrificial meat (in Jerusalem) as impure. This is either a remnant of teachings of the House of Shammai or Sadducee teaching of the Qumran type (MMT 2, lines 29-30).

138 Therefore, it should be forbidden to buy meat at the butcher store. This means that by rabbinical decree, with tithe money one may only buy meat in the form of live unblemished animals.

139 *Ševi'it* 8:7, Babli *Sukkah* 40b.

(fol. 52d) **הלכה ד:** תַּמָּן תַּנִּינָן אֵין לוֹקְחִין עֲבָדִים וְקַרְקָעוֹת וּבְהֵמָה טְמֵיאָה מִדְּמֵי שְׁבִיעִית וְאִם לָקַח יֹאכַל כְּנֶגְדּוֹ. וְכָא אַתְּ אָמַר הָכֵין. רִבִּי יוֹנָה אָמַר אִיתְפַּלְּגוּן רִבִּי חִיָּיה בַּר יוֹסֵף וּשְׁמוּאֵל. חַד אָמַר כָּאן דֶּרֶךְ מְכִירָה כָּאן דֶּרֶךְ חִילּוּל. וְחָרָנָא אָמַר כָּאן בְּשֶׁהַמּוֹכֵר קַיָּים. וְכָאן שֶׁהָלַךְ לוֹ הַמּוֹכֵר. וְלֹא יָדַעְנָא מָאן אָמַר דָּא וּמָאן אָמַר דָּא. מִן מַה דְּאָמַר רִבִּי יוֹסֵי בְּשֵׁם שְׁמוּאֵל נִקְנֶה הַמִּקַּח. הֲרֵי הוּא דְאָמַר כָּאן דֶּרֶךְ מְכִירָה כָּאן דֶּרֶךְ חִילּוּל.

Halakhah 4: There[140], we have stated: "One does not buy slaves, real estate, or unclean animals from Sabbatical money. If he did buy them, he has to eat their worth." And here, you say so? Rebbi Jonah said, Rebbi Ḥiyya bar Josef and Samuel disagreed. One said here as a sale[141], there as redemption. The other one said here if the seller is present[142], there if the seller went away. We did not know who said what. Since Rebbi Yose said in the name of Samuel, the buy is acquired[143], that means he is the one who said here as a sale, there as redemption.

140 Mishnah *Ševi'it* 8:8. One might as well have quoted the Mishnah here since the question is, why in Mishnah 7 the transaction is valid but the tithe money has to be restituted and used for food and in Mishnah 6 a similar transaction is declared invalid.

141 What is invalid as a sale is valid as redemption.

142 The money has to be returned.

143 If he bought slaves with tithe money. He must hold that "bought" is an inexact expression since the farmer exchanged tithe money for slaves.

מַתְנִיתִין דְּרִבִּי עֲקִיבָה דְּלֹא כְרִבִּי יִשְׁמָעֵאל. רִבִּי יִשְׁמָעֵאל דָּרַשׁ וְנָתַתָּ הַכֶּסֶף בְּכָל־אֲשֶׁר תְּאַוֶּה נַפְשְׁךָ כְּלָל. (fol. 53a) בַּבָּקָר וּבַצֹּאן בַּיַּיִן וּבַשֵּׁכָר פְּרָט. וּבְכֹל אֲשֶׁר תְּאַוֶּה נַפְשְׁךָ הֲרֵי כְּלָל אַחֵר. כְּלָל וּפְרָט וּכְלָל אֵי אַתָּה דָן אֶלָּא כְּעֵין הַפְּרָט. לוֹמַר לָךְ מַה הַפְּרָט מְפוֹרָשׁ דָּבָר שֶׁהוּא וְלַד וְלָדוֹת הָאָרֶץ. אַף אֵין לִי אֶלָּא דָּבָר שֶׁהוּא וְלַד וְלָדוֹת הָאָרֶץ. רִבִּי עֲקִיבָה מְפָרֵשׁ מַה הַפְּרָט מְפוֹרָשׁ דָּבָר שֶׁהוּא פְּרִי וְלַד פְּרִי וּמַכְשִׁירֵי פְּרִי. אַף אֵין לִי אֶלָּא דָּבָר שֶׁהוּא פְּרִי וְלַד פְּרִי וּמַכְשִׁירֵי פְּרִי. מַה נְפִיק מִבֵּינֵיהוֹן דָּגִין וַחֲגָבִין כְּמֵהִין וּפִטְרִיּוֹת. כְּרִבִּי עֲקִיבָה נִיקָּחִין בְּכֶסֶף מַעֲשֵׂר.

Our Mishnah follows Rebbi Aqiba but not Rebbi Ismael. [144]Rebbi Ismael explained (*Deut.* 14:26): "Spend the money on anything you want," a general clause. "For cattle and sheep, wine and intoxicating drink[145]", detail. "And anything you want[146]," another general clause. General, detail, and general, you may judge only in the light of the detail[147]. Just as the detail is explained as born from what is born from the earth, so only what is born from what is born from the earth[148]. Rebbi Aqiba explains[149]: Just as the detail is explained as fruit, born from a fruit, or what prepares fruit, so only what is fruit, born from a fruit, or what prepares fruit[150]. What is the difference between them? Fish, locusts, truffles, and mushrooms[151] which may be bought with tithe money following Rebbi Aqiba.

144 Parallels in *Sifra* Introduction (8); the full statement of R. Ismael. Yerushalmi *Eruvin* 3:1, fol. 20c/d; Babli *Eruvin* 27b, *Baba Qama* 54b, 63a; in slightly different version *Nazir* 35b.

145 Cattle and sheep, wine and liquor.

146 In the verse: ובכל אשר תשאלך נפשך "and anything you may wish."

147 One of the hermeneutical principles of R. Ismael. *Sifra*, Introduction (1), (8).

148 Anything grown by sexual reproduction from plant or animal

living on the land.

149 In detail explained *Sifry Deut.* 107, naturally without reference to R. Ismael's rule.

150 In *Sifry* called משביחי אכילה "food enhancers", such as costus, amomum, other spices, benjamin, asa foetida, peppers, and saffron.

151 In *Sifra*, R. Ismael explicitly excludes truffles and mushrooms.

אָמַר רִבִּי חַגַּיי מַתְנִיתָא אָמְרָה כֵן שֶׁאֵין מְחַלְלִין מָעוֹת עַל הַפֵּירוֹת בְּרִיחוּק מָקוֹם. אָמְרָהּ קוֹמֵי רִבִּי אֲבִינָא וְקַלְּסֵיהּ. אָמְרָהּ קוֹמֵי רִבִּי יִרְמְיָה וְקַנְתְּרֵיהּ. וְהָתַנִּינָן מָעוֹת בִּירוּשָׁלֵם וּפֵירוֹת בִּמְדִינָה. שַׁנְיָיא הִיא שֶׁהָיָה בְּמָקוֹם אֶחָד.[152] כַּד נְפַק רִבִּי חַגַּיי אַשְׁכַּח תַּנֵּי מָעוֹת וּפֵירוֹת בִּירוּשָׁלֵם מָעוֹת וּפֵירוֹת בִּמְדִינָה. אָמַר אִין הֲוָה שְׁמִיעַ רִבִּי יִרְמְיָה הָדָא מִילְּתָא יְאוּת קַנְטְרִי. בָּעֵא מַחֲזִיר בֵּיהּ. אָמַר לוֹ רִבִּי זְעִירָא לֹא תַחְזוֹר בָּךְ. דְּאָמַר רִבִּי לָעְזָר דְּרִבִּי מֵאִיר וְרַבָּנָן בִּדְמַאי הָא בְוַדַּאי לֹא. מִן דְּאָמַר רִבִּי לָעְזָר דְּרִבִּי מֵאִיר הִיא הָדָא אָמְרָה הוּא דְמַאי הוּא וַדַּאי.

Rebbi Ḥaggai said, a Mishnah[153] said that one does not exchange coins for fruits far from the Place. He said that before Rebbi Abinna who praised him, before Rebbi Jeremiah who needled[154] him: Did we not state, "coins in Jerusalem and produce in the countryside[155]"? There is a difference because it was in one place[156]. When Rebbi Ḥaggai left, he found it stated[157]: coins and produce in Jerusalem, coins and produce in the countryside. He said, if Rebbi Jeremiah had heard this, he would have needled me justly. He wanted to change his mind. Rebbi Zeïra said to him, do not change your mind since Rebbi Eleazar said, Rebbi Meïr and the rabbis [disagree] about *demay*; therefore not for certain [produce][158]. Since Rebbi Eleazar said, this is Rebbi Meïr's, it follows that *demay* and certain are equal.

152 Reading of the Rome ms. Leyden and Venice: אחר מקום "after place".

153 Mishnah 3:3: "If somebody has [tithe] coins in Jerusalem and needs them, and a friend has produce, he says to his friend: those coins are exchanged on your produce. The friend has to eat his produce in purity but he may use the coins. One should not do this with a vulgar [friend] except for *demay*." Since the transaction is restricted to Jerusalem, it follows that it would be illegal elsewhere.

154 Cf. *Berakhot* 2:3, Note 96.

155 Mishnah 3:4 states that money in Jerusalem may be exchanged for outside produce (which then has to be brought into the city) or Jerusalem produce may be bought with tithe money which at the moment of the transaction was outside.

156 Mishnah 3:3 which admits the transaction only in Jerusalem deals with the case that both parties are at the same place. R. Ḥaggai is still justified in not admitting redemption if both parties are outside the city.

157 A *baraita* differing with the Mishnah in his interpretation.

158 According to most commentators, this seems to refer to the *baraita* quoted at the end of Halakhah 3, that the rabbis permit redemption only for meat, not live animals, comparing with Mishnah 6 which is held to be R. Meïr's opinion. But the *baraita* was shown to refer only to Sabbatical money and is not applicable here.

According to R. H. Kanievski, the diagreement of the Sages and R. Meïr is in Mishnah *Demay* 1:2, and the statement of R. Eleazar, that the Mishnah is only R. Meïr's, to Mishnaiot 1:5-6 since in *Demay* he also holds that *demay* money can be exchanged and traded at will outside of Jerusalem. Then it follows that the opinon of the opposing Sages, that produce, illegally bought with tithe money outside of Jerusalem, should be brought up and eaten in Jerusalem, is true not only for *demay* but for all tithe money, supporting R. Ḥaggai.

רִבִּי זְבִידָא הֲוָה יְתִיב מַתְנֵי לִבְרֵיהּ. הָרוֹצֶה לְחַלֵּל מָעוֹת עַל הַפֵּירוֹת בִּזְמָן הַזֶּה בֵּין אֵילּוּ בֵּין אֵילּוּ קָדְשׁוּ כְּדִבְרֵי בֵית שַׁמַּאי. בֵּית הִילֵּל אוֹמְרִים מָעוֹת כְּמוֹת שֶׁהֵן וּפֵירוֹת כְּמוֹת שֶׁהֵן. עָבַר רִבִּי קְרִיסְפָּא אָמַר לֵיהּ לָא תַנְיָיתָהּ כֵּן אֶלָּא

פֵּירוֹת עַל הַמָּעוֹת. הָא מָעוֹת עַל הַפֵּירוֹת דִּבְרֵי הַכֹּל לֹא קָדְשׁוּ. וְהָתַנִּינָן אֵין מִקְדָּשׁ יֵרָקְבוּ. תִּיפְתָּר שֶׁהִקְדִּישָׁן בִּשְׁעַת הַמִּקְדָּשׁ וְחָרֵב הַמִּקְדָּשׁ.

Rebbi Zevida was sitting and teaching his son: [159]"If somebody wants to exchange [tithe] money for produce today, both these and those are consecrated[160], the words of the House of Shammai. The House of Hillel say, the money is as it was and the produce is as it was." Rebbi Crispus passed by and told him, do not state it so but say "produce for money.[161]" Therefore, everybody agrees that money for produce was not consecrated. But did we not state[162]: "if there is no Temple they should be left to rot"? Explain it if he dedicated it when there was a Temple and the Temple was destroyed[163].

159 A similar text in Tosephta 3:14.

160 Since there is no Temple, the produce cannot be consumed. The House of Shammai are not sure whether tithe money can be exchanged without a Temple; therefore they declare everything Second Tithe by default. The House of Hillel are certain that, since the biblical injunction to eat the produce bought for tithe money "before the Eternal, your God," cannot be followed today, tithe money cannot be exchanged (but either has to be destroyed or thrown into the Dead Sea.)

161 There is a dispute on exchanging Second Tithe produce for money (outside of Jerusalem) but there is no dispute that tithe money today cannot be used to buy anything. There is a Gaonic decree (Maimonides *Ma'aser Šeni* 2:2) that any amount of Second Tithe produce can be exchanged for the smallest coin in circulation.

162 Mishnah 5. If the produce were not consecrated it would not be forbidden. Therefore, the Mishnah seems to imply that tithe money can be exchanged in the absence of a Temple.

163 While this answer seems to be very contrived, it can be read into the Mishnah which notes the absence of the Temple only in connection with the use of the produce, not the act of redemption.

תַּנֵּי בֶּן בֵּיבַי וְנָתַתָּ אֶת הַכֶּסֶף בְּרִיחוּק מָקוֹם אַתָּה פוֹדֵהוּ. בְּקִירוּב מָקוֹם אֵין אַתְּ פוֹדֵהוּ. וְנָתַתָּ הַכֶּסֶף בְּקִירוּב מָקוֹם אַתָּה מְחַלְלוֹ וְאֵי אַתְּ מְחַלְלוֹ בְּרִיחוּק מָקוֹם.

Ben Vivian stated: (*Deut.* 14:25) "Turn it into money[164]", far from the Place[106] you redeem it[165], near the Place you cannot redeem it. (*Deut.* 14:26) "Spend the money", near the Place you exchange[166] it, far from the Place you do not exchange it.

164 The verse reads: ונתת בכסף.

165 Exchange produce for money and transfer the sanctity to the money.

166 Exchange money for produce and transfer the sanctity to the produce.

רִבִּי יוֹסֵי[167] בְּשֵׁם שְׁמוּאֵל נִקְנֶה הַמִּקָּח. רִבִּי יוֹסֵי בֶּן חֲנִינָה כִּיפּוּרָה.[168] אָמַר רִבִּי הִילָא מִן מַה דְתַנִּינָן יֹאכַל כְּנֶגְדָּן הָדָא אָמְרָה קָדְשׁוּ. אָמַר רִבִּי יוֹסֵי מִכֵּיוָן שֶׁמָּשַׁךְ נִקְנָה הַמִּקָּח מִכָּן וְאֵילַךְ מִקַּח אֶחָד הוּא. אָמַר רִבִּי יוּדָן צָרִיךְ לַחֲזוֹר וּלְהַקְדִּישׁוֹ. שֶׁהוּא סָבוּר לוֹמַר שֶׁמָּא קִידְּשׁוּ וְלֹא קִידְּשׁוּ.

Rebbi Yose in the name of Samuel: The buy is acquired[169]. Rebbi Yose ben Ḥanina: Expiation. Rebbi Hila said, since we stated "he has to eat their worth", that means it was sanctified. Rebbi Yose said, since he took it up, the buy was acquired; from there on it is one[170] buy. Rebbi Yudan said, he has to dedicate it again; he means that maybe it was sanctified when it was not sanctified.

167 The Rome ms. has here and in the third sentence: R. Jonah. However, R. Yose mentioned here is not the late Amora but the teacher from the intermediary generation between Tannaïm and Amoraïm who appears in the Babli as Rav Assi, older than R. Yose ben Ḥanina. The reading of the Rome ms. has to be rejected.

168 Reading of the Rome ms. Leyden and Venice: בי פירא "ditch house".

169 This paragraph refers to Mishnah 7: If one buys slaves, or birds, or animals for obligatory expiation sacrifices with tithe money, the transactions are valid since otherwise the money would have to be restituted and no new money taken as tithe money. This then implies that the expiatory sacrifice is valid. R. Yudan is not sure about this implication of the Mishnah, and it is possible that the authors of Mishnah 7 themselves were not sure whether the transactions are valid or not. Therefore, he requires that after the tithe money has been set aside, the birds used for the expiatory sacrifices be dedicated again since the dedication at the time of acquisition may be invalid.

170 Most commentators prefer to read אחר "another" instead of אחד "one". The change, against the testimony of the two mss., is unnecessary since R. Yose holds that the acquisition is valid in all respects.

מעשר שני ניתן פרק שני

(fol. 53a) **משנה א:** מַעֲשֵׂר שֵׁינִי נִיתָּן לַאֲכִילָה וְלִשְׁתִייָה לְסִיכָה לֶאֱכוֹל דָּבָר שֶׁדַּרְכּוֹ לוֹכַל וְלָסוּךְ דָּבָר שֶׁדַּרְכּוֹ לָסוּךְ. לֹא יָסוּךְ יַיִן וְחוֹמֶץ אֲבָל סָךְ הוּא אֶת הַשֶּׁמֶן. אֵין מְפַטְּמִין שֶׁמֶן שֶׁל מַעֲשֵׂר שֵׁינִי וְאֵין לוֹקְחִין בִּדְמֵי מַעֲשֵׂר שֵׁינִי שֶׁמֶן מְפוּטָּם אֲבָל מְפַטֵּם הוּא אֶת הַיַּיִן. נָתַן בְּתוֹכוֹ דְּבָשׁ וְתַבְלִין וְהִשְׁבִּיחוּ הַשְּׁבָח לְפִי חֶשְׁבּוֹן. דָּגִים שֶׁנִּתְבַּשְּׁלוּ עִם הַקֶּפַלּוֹטוֹת שֶׁל מַעֲשֵׂר שֵׁינִי וְהִשְׁבִּיחוּ הַשְּׁבָח לְפִי חֶשְׁבּוֹן. עִיסָּה שֶׁל מַעֲשֵׂר שֵׁינִי שֶׁאֲפָייָהּ וְהִשְׁבִּיחָה הַשְּׁבָח לַשֵּׁינִי. זֶה הַכְּלָל כָּל־שֶׁשְּׁבָחוֹ נִיכָּר הַשְּׁבָח לְפִי חֶשְׁבּוֹן. וְכָל־שֶׁאֵין שְׁבָחוֹ נִיכָּר הַשְּׁבָח לַשֵּׁינִי.

Mishnah 1: Second Tithe is to be used for eating, drinking, and anointing; to eat everything commonly eaten, to anoint with what commonly is used for anointing. One should not anoint with wine or vinegar, but with olive oil[1]. One does not use Second Tithe oil as base for perfume[2], one does not buy perfumed oil with Second Tithe money[3], but one may make spice wine. If one adds it to honey and spices and it increases in value, the increase is proportional[4]. If fish is cooked with Second Tithe leeks which increases its value, the increase is proportional. If a dough of Second Tithe when baked increased in value, the increase belongs to the Second[5]. This is the principle: In all cases in which the increase is visible[6], the increase is proportional. In all cases in which the increase is not visible, the increase belongs to the Second.

1 These two sentences are stated, for Sabbatical produce and money, in Mishnah *Ševi'it* 8:2.

2 Since then the oil is no longer

food.

3 Even though anointing with Second Tithe oil is permitted, one may buy only what is used by the majority of people, not what is reserved for a minority of the rich and pampered.

4 If some dish offered for sale in Jerusalem was prepared with Second Tithe material worth a, and profane material worth b, and now the dish is worth $c > a + b$, then $cb/(a+b)$ is profane and may be paid with Second Tithe money; the rest must be paid with profane money.

5 Since the profane fuel did not change the body of the bread, the entire bread made from Second Tithe flour has the status of Second Tithe.

6 The meaning of this expression will be discussed in the Halakhah.

(fol. 53b) **הלכה א**: מַעֲשֵׂר שֵׁינִי נִיתָּן לַאֲכִילָה כול׳. נִיתָּן לַאֲכִילָה שֶׁכָּתוּב בּוֹ אֲכִילָה. לִשְׁתִיָּה שֶׁהַשְּׁתִיָּה בִּכְלָל אֲכִילָה. מְנַיִין שֶׁהַשְּׁתִיָּה בִּכְלָל אֲכִילָה. רִבִּי יוֹנָה שָׁמַע לָהּ מִן הָדָא. עַל כֵּן אָמַרְתִּי לִבְנֵי יִשְׂרָאֵל כָּל־נֶפֶשׁ מִכֶּם לֹא יֹאכַל דָּם. מָה נָן קַייָמִין אִם בְּדָם שֶׁקָּרַשׁ. וְהָתַנֵּי דָּם שֶׁקָּרַשׁ אֵינוֹ לֹא אוֹכֶל וְלֹא מַשְׁקֶה. אֶלָּא כִּי נָן קַייָמִין כְּמוֹת שֶׁהוּא וְהַתּוֹרָה קָרָאת אוֹתוֹ אֲכִילָה. וְהָא תַנֵּי הִמְחָה אֶת הַחֵלֶב וּגְמָעוֹ הִקְפָּה אֶת הַדָּם וַאֲכָלוֹ הֲרֵי זֶה חַייָב. מַה עֲבַד לָהּ רִבִּי יוֹנָה. אֵינוֹ לֹא אוֹכֶל לְטַמֵּא טוּמְאַת אוֹכְלִין וְלֹא מַשְׁקֶה לְטַמֵּא טוּמְאַת מַשְׁקִין.

Halakhah 1: [7]"Second Tithe is to be used for eating," etc. It is to be used for eating, since eating is written regarding it[8]. For drinking, since drinking is included in eating. From where that drinking is included in eating? Rebbi Jonah understood if from the following (*Lev*. 17:12): "Therefore, I said to the Children of Israel, no person among you may eat blood." Where do we hold? If about congealed blood, did we not state[9]: "Congealed blood is neither food nor drink"? So we must hold as is[10], and the Torah called it "eating." But did we not state[11]: "If he mashed the fat[12] and sipped it, congealed the blood and ate it, he is guilty!" How does Rebbi Jonah explain? It is neither food, to accept the impurity of food, nor drink, to accept the impurity of drinks[13].

7 This and the following paragraphs (up to Note 35) are also in *Yoma* 8:3 (fol. 45a), *Ševu'ot* 3:2 (fol. 34b). The parallel discussion in the Babli is *Ševu'ot* 22b-23a.

8 *Deut.* 14:23.

9 Tosephta *Tahorot* 2:5.

10 Fluid blood.

11 Babli *Ḥulin* 120a, *Menaḥot* 21a.

12 The fat of domestic animals which from sacrifices is burned on the altar and from profane meat is forbidden as food.

13 The Tosephta *Tahorot* adds explicitly: "If he thought of [the congealed blood] as food, it accepts the impurities of food." The argument of R. Jonah is not acceptable.

חָזַר רִבִּי יוֹנָה וּשְׁמָעָהּ מִן הָכָא. וְנָתַתָּ הַכֶּסֶף בְּכָל־אֲשֶׁר תְּאַוֶּה נַפְשְׁךָ. מַה נָן קַייָמִין אִם בְּנוֹתֵן טַעַם יַיִן בְּתַבְשִׁיל. וַהֲלֹא הַטַּעַם בִּפְגָם הוּא. רַבָּנִין דְּקַיְסָרִין אָמְרִין תִּיפְתָּר בְּאִילֵּין אורזנייה וגמזוזינייה. כָּל־הַטָּפֵל לַאֲכִילָה כַּאֲכִילָה.

Rebbi Jonah changed his mind and understood it from the following (*Deut.* 14:26): "Spend the money for anything you desire[14]." Where do we hold? If one adds the taste of wine to a dish, is that not tasting badly[15]? The rabbis of Caesarea say, explain it with *'rznyyh* and *gmzvzynyyh*[16]. Anything auxiliary to food is considered food.

14 The argument is from the later part of the verse: "cattle and sheep, wine and liquor, anything you might want, and eat it there before the Eternal, your God, . . ." How does one eat wine and liquor?

15 In *Ševu'ot* and *Yoma*, the argument closes with: So we must hold as is, and the Torah called it "eating," as for the first argument.

16 In *Yoma* אורזנייא וגוממני, in *Ševu'ot* גמרייה ואורזרייה. Every commentator and author of a dictionary has his own identification. {Perhaps cf. Greek spiced liquor *Retsina*, classical Greek ῥητίνα "*pine resin*", and various kinds of gum (*gummi*, κόμμι) used in manufacture of fine liquors. (E. G.) } The variants make a reliable identification impossible. The additions involved must be such that wine (or liquor) is an essential ingredient of the recipe. In that case, one cannot say that a dish made with

wine tastes worse than wine itself. R. Yose has not proved that from Second Tithe money one may buy wine other than cooking wine.

רִבִּי יוֹסֵי שָׁמַע לָהּ מִן הָכָא שְׁבוּעָה שֶׁלֹּא אוֹכַל וְאָכַל וְשָׁתָה חַייָב שְׁתַּיִם. חֲבֶרַייָא אָמְרִין אֵינוֹ חַייָב אֶלָּא אַחַת. אָמַר לוֹן רִבִּי יוֹסֵי אָמְרִין דְּבַתְרָא שְׁבוּעָה שֶׁלֹּא אוֹכַל וְאֶשְׁתֶּה וְאָכַל וְשָׁתָה חַייָב שְׁתַּיִם. אִילּוּ מִי שֶׁהָיוּ לְפָנָיו שְׁנֵי כִּכָּרִים וְאָמַר שְׁבוּעָה שֶׁלֹּא אוֹכַל כִּכָּר זוֹ וְחָזַר וְאָמַר שְׁבוּעָה שֶׁלֹּא אוֹכַל כִּכָּר זוֹ שֶׁמָּא אֵינוֹ חַייָב שְׁתַּיִם.

[17]Rebbi Yose understood it from the following[18]: "[I swear] an oath that I shall not eat, when he ate and drank he is guilty on two counts." The colleagues said, he is guilty only on one count. Rebbi Yose said to them, we say after this, "an oath that I shall neither eat nor drink, when he ate and drank he is guilty on two counts." It is as if somebody had two loaves before him when he said: [I swear] an oath that I shall not eat this one, and then he said: [I swear] an oath that I shall not eat that one, would he not be guilty on two counts?

17 The text is difficult. The parallel in *Ševu'ot* is almost unintelligible. The best text seems to be the one in *Yoma* {commentary in braces}:

Rebbi Yose understood it from the following (Mishnah *Ševu'ot* 3:2): "An oath {meaning: I swear} that I shall not eat, when he ate or drank he is guilty on one count only." {This proves the point.} The colleagues said before Rebbi Yose, one continues after this {in the same Mishnah}, "an oath that I shall neither eat nor drink, when he ate and drank he is guilty on two counts." {This seems to disprove that drinking is subsumed under eating.} Rebbi Yose said to them, is that not as if somebody had two loaves before him when he said: an oath that I shall not eat this one, and then he said: an oath that I shall not eat that one, would he not be guilty on two counts? {Therefore, drinking in general is subsumed under eating but if somebody spells them out separately, he takes upon himself two parallel but separate obligations.)

18 This is a misquote from Mishnah *Ševu'ot* 3:2; the correct text is given by the colleagues. The second quote by R. Yose is correct.

רִבִּי חֲנַנְיָה בְּשֵׁם רִבִּי פִּינְחָס שָׁמַע לָהּ מִן הָכָא. שְׁבוּעָה שֶׁלֹּא אוֹכַל וְאָכַל אוֹכְלִין שֶׁאֵינָן רְאוּיִין לַאֲכִילָה וְשָׁתָה מַשְׁקִין שֶׁאֵינָן רְאוּיִין לִשְׁתִייָה פָּטוּר. הָא אִם שָׁתָה מַשְׁקִין שֶׁרְאוּיִין לִשְׁתִייָה חַייָב. לֹא בִשְׁבוּעָה שֶׁלֹּא אוֹכַל נִיחָא. בְּמַתְנִיתָא דְּנָן מָרִין שְׁבוּעָה שֶׁלֹּא אוֹכַל בְּרַם כְּרַבָּנִין דְּאִינּוּן מָרִין שְׁבוּעָה שֶׁלֹּא אוֹכַל וְשֶׁלֹּא אֶשְׁתֶּה.

Rebbi Ḥanania in the name of Rebbi Phineas understood it from the following[19]: "[I swear] an oath that I shall not eat, when he ate inedible food and drank undrinkable fluids he is free from punishment." Therefore, if he drank drinkable fluids he is guilty. That is correct following "an oath that I shall not eat," and in our Mishnah they teach "an oath that I shall not eat." But for those rabbis[20] who teach "an oath that I shall not eat and I shall not drink"?

19 Mishnah *Ševu'ot* 3:2.

20 The anonymous editors of the Babli, *Ševu'ot* 23a, to show that from the Mishnah one cannot infer that drinking is a subcategory of eating.

רִבִּי חִינְנָא שָׁמַע לָהּ מִן הָדָא. אָכַל וְשָׁתָה בְּהֶעְלֵם אֶחָד אֵינוֹ חַייָב אֶלָּא אַחַת. רִבִּי אַבָּא מָרִי שָׁמַע לָהּ מִן הָכָא לֹא אָכַלְתִּי בְּאוֹנִי מִמֶּנּוּ אֶלָּא שָׁתִיתִי.

Rebbi Ḥinena understood it from the following[21]: "If he ate and drank in one forgetting he is guilty only once." Rebbi Abba Mari understood it from here (*Deut.* 26:14): "I did not eat from it in my mourning", but I drank[22]?

21 Mishnah *Yoma* 8:3. A person who forgot that it was the Day of Atonement and he ate or drank must bring a sin sacrifice. But if he ate and drank in one forgetting episode he brings only one sacrifice. The argument is weak since the commandment of the Day of Atonement is "to deprive oneself", and not eating and not drinking are aspects of deprivation.

22 From the declaration the farmer makes in the Temple when he brings his Second Tithe to Jerusalem after he gave First Tithe and, if applicable, the tithe of the poor. It seems obvious that the declaration cannot be made if the farmer drank from tithe wine while in deep mourning, which is a desecration as if he had eaten. Therefore, the verse subsumes drinking under eating.

נִיחָא כְּמָאן דְּאָמַר שְׁבוּעָה שֶׁלֹּא אוֹכַל וְשָׁתָה. בְּרַם כְּמָאן דָּמַר שְׁבוּעָה שֶׁלֹּא אֶשְׁתֶּה וְאָכַל שְׁתִייָה בִּכְלָל אֲכִילָה וְאֵין אֲכִילָה בִּכְלָל שְׁתִייָה.

It is understandable[23] for him who said, "[I swear] an oath that I shall not eat", and he drank[24]. But for him who said, "an oath that I shall not drink", and he ate? Drinking is subsumed under eating, but eating is not subsumed under drinking.

23 The text in *Ševu'ot* which reads עד כדון "so far", probably is better. The entire paragraph belongs to the Mishnah in *Ševu'ot*; here ends the parallel in *Ševu'ot*.

24 The preceding argument shows that drinking is subsumed under eating. But everybody agrees that a mention of drink does not include solid food. The same conclusion is in Babli *Ševu'ot* 23a.

אִית דְּבָעֵי מַשְׁמַע מִן הָדָא לֹא תוּכַל לֶאֱכוֹל בִּשְׁעָרֶיךָ מַעֲשַׂר דְּגָנְךָ תִּירוֹשְׁךָ וְיִצְהָרֶיךָ. תִּירוֹשְׁךָ זֶה הַיַּיִן. וְיִצְהָרֶיךָ זוֹ סִיכָה וְהַתּוֹרָה קָרְאָה אוֹתָהּ אֲכִילָה. וְאֵינוֹ מְחוּוָר. אִין תֵּימַר בִּמְחוּוָר הוּא יִלְקוּ עָלָיו חוּץ לַחוֹמָה. אָמַר רִבִּי יוֹסֵי בֶּן חֲנִינָה אֵין לוֹקִין חוּץ לַחוֹמָה אֶלָּא עַל מַעֲשֵׂר שֵׁינִי טָהוֹר שֶׁנִּכְנַס לִירוּשָׁלֵם וְיָצָא. מְנַיִין שֶׁאֵינוֹ מְחוּוָר. כְּהָדָא דְתַנֵּי בְּשַׁבָּת בֵּין סִיכָה שֶׁהִיא שֶׁלְּתַעֲנוּג בֵּין

סִיכָה שֶׁאֵינָהּ שֶׁלְּתַעֲנוּג מוּתָּר. בְּיוֹם הַכִּיפּוּרִים בֵּין סִיכָה שֶׁהִיא שֶׁלְּתַעֲנוּג בֵּין סִיכָה שֶׁאֵינָהּ שֶׁלְּתַעֲנוּג אָסוּר. בְּתִשְׁעָה בְּאַב וּבְתַעֲנִית צִיבּוּר בְּסִיכָה שֶׁהִיא שֶׁלְּתַעֲנוּג אָסוּר וְשֶׁאֵינָהּ שֶׁלְּתַעֲנוּג מוּתָּר. וְהָתַנֵּי שָׁווֹת סִיכָה לִשְׁתִיָּה לְאִיסּוּר וּלְתַשְׁלוּמִין אֲבָל לֹא לְעוֹנֶשׁ. בְּיוֹם הַכִּיפּוּרִים לְאִיסּוּר אֲבָל לֹא לְעוֹנֶשׁ. וְהָתַנֵּי לֹא יְחַלְּלוּ לְהָבִיא אֶת הַסָּךְ וְאֶת הַשּׁוֹתֶה. אָמַר רִבִּי יוֹחָנָן לֵית כָּאן סָךְ. אָמַר רִבִּי אָבָּא מָרִי וְאִין לֵית כָּאן סָךְ לֵית כָּאן שׁוֹתֶה דִּלֹכֵן דָּבָר שֶׁהוּא בָּא מִשְּׁנֵי לָוִין מִצְטָרֵף.

Some want to understand it from this (*Deut*. 12:17): "You may not eat in your gates the tithe of your grain, your cider, and your shining oil."[25] 'Your cider', that is the wine. 'And your shining oil' refers to anointing and the Torah called it 'eating'. But this is not clear. If it were clear one should be whipped because of it outside the walls[26]! Rebbi Yose ben Ḥanina said, one is whipped outside the walls only for pure Second Tithe which entered Jerusalem and left[27]. From where that it is not clear? From what was stated[28]: "On the Sabbath, both anointing for pleasure and anointing not for pleasure are permitted. On the Day of Atonement, both anointing for pleasure and anointing not for pleasure are forbidden. On the Ninth of Ab and public fasts[29] anointing for pleasure is forbidden but anointing not for pleasure is permitted." Did we not state: "Anointing is equal to drinking for prohibition and replacement[30] but not for punishment, on the Day of Atonement for prohibition but not for punishment[31]"? Did we not state (*Lev*. 22:15): "They should not desecrate," to include him who anoints and him who drinks[32]. Rebbi Johanan said, there is no 'anoints' here. Rebbi Abba Mari said, if there is no 'anoints' here then there is no 'drinks' for otherwise something that comes from two different prohibitions would be added together[33]!

25 Both drinking and anointing are subsumed under "eating".

26 If the verse were a formal identification of anointing and eating as far as Second Tithe is concerned, the use of impure heave oil for anointing should be a criminal offense.

27 This amoraïc statement is part of the objection.

28 The text from here to the end of the next paragraph is only hinted at in *Yoma*; it is in *Šabbat* 9:4, fol. 12a-b, the fullest text in *Ta'aniot* 1:6, fol. 64c.

29 Fasts in a winter of draught, whose rules are modeled on those for the Ninth of Ab.

30 Referring to illegal use of heave and dedicated food by non-Cohanim and its replacement by $^5/_4$ of the value taken.

31 The only biblical prohibitions on the Day of Atonement are eating, drinking, and working. The other two, anointing and sexual relations, are rabbinic and not subject to biblical punishment.

32 The verse refers to the non-Cohen who "eats" holy food in error.

33 If the verse in *Lev*. is needed to include drinking in eating then it is incomprehensible that for inadvertently eating and drinking together on the Day of Atonement one should be responsible only for one sacrifice since in that case, one infringes on two separate biblical prohibitions and should be responsible for two separate sacrifices. Similarly, if one illegimately ate and drank heave one should be responsible for two separate fifths. Since in both cases the Mishnah treats eating and drinking together, the verse cannot express a separate status for drinking; the addition of anointing and drinking is rabbinic interpretation but not biblical law and there is no reason to exclude anointing.

מְנַיִין שֶׁהוּא מְחוּוָר בַּעֲשֵׂה. רִבִּי לִיעֶזֶר בְּשֵׁם רִבִּי סִימַיי לֹא נָתַתִּי מִמֶּנּוּ לְמֵת. מַה נָן קַייָמִין אִם לְהָבִיא לוֹ אָרוֹן וְתַכְרִיכִין דָּבָר שֶׁהוּא אָסוּר לַחַי לַחַי הוּא אָסוּר לֹא כָּל־שֶׁכֵּן לָמֵת. אֵי זֶהוּ דָבָר שֶׁהוּא מוּתָּר לַחַי וְאָסוּר לָמֵת הֱוֵי אוֹמֵר זוֹ סִיכָה.

From where that it is clear as a positive commandment[34]? Rebbi Eleazar in the name of Rebbi Simai (*Deut*. 26:14): "Nor did I give from it to the dead." Where do we hold? If it were to bring a casket and shrouds for him, that were also forbidden for a living person[35]! If something is forbidden for the living, not so much more for the dead? What is something which is permitted for the living but prohibited for the dead? That is anointing!

34 While illegitimate use of heave oil for anointing is a prohibition, it is mentioned in the framework of the farmer's declaration in the Temple which is a positive commandment. Overstepping the prohibition of anointing when it is forbidden is legally overstepping a positive commandment not under the scope of biblical penal law.

35 Only consuming Second Tithe is permitted.

כֵּיצַד לוֹכַל דָּבָר שֶׁדַּרְכּוֹ לוֹכַל. אֵין מְחַייְבִין אוֹתוֹ לֹא פַּת שֶׁעִיפֵּישָׁה וְלֹא קְנוּבַת יָרָק וְלֹא תַבְשִׁיל שֶׁעִיבְּרָה צוּרָתוֹ. וְכֵן הוּא אִם בִּיקֵּשׁ לוֹכַל תַּרְדִּין חַיִּין אוֹ לָכוּס חִיטִּין חַיּוֹת אֵין שׁוֹמְעִין לוֹ. כֵּיצַד לִשְׁתּוֹת דָּבָר שֶׁדַּרְכּוֹ לִשְׁתּוֹת. אֵין מְחַייְבִין אוֹתוֹ לִשְׁתּוֹת לֹא אֱנֵיגָרוֹן וְלֹא אֵיכְסֵיגָרוֹן וְלֹא יַיִן בִּשְׁמָרִין. הַחוֹשֵׁשׁ בְּשִׁינָּיו לֹא יְהֵא מְגַמֵּא חוֹמֶץ וּפוֹלֵט אֲבָל מְגַמֵּא בָהֶן וּבוֹלֵעַ וּמְטַבֵּל כָּל־צָרְכּוֹ וְאֵינוֹ נִמְנַע. הַחוֹשֵׁשׁ בִּגְרוֹנוֹ לֹא יְעַרְעֶנּוּ בְשֶׁמֶן אֲבָל נוֹתֵן הוּא שֶׁמֶן הַרְבֵּה לְתוֹךְ אֱנֵיגָרוֹן וְגוֹמֵעַ. לֹא יָסוּךְ יַיִן וְחוֹמֶץ אֲבָל סָךְ הוּא אֶת הַשֶּׁמֶן. הַחוֹשֵׁשׁ אֶת רֹאשׁוֹ אוֹ שֶׁעָלוּ בוֹ חֲטָטִין סָךְ שֶׁמֶן אֲבָל לֹא יָסוּךְ יַיִן וְחוֹמֶץ.

[36]What means "to eat everything commonly eaten"? "One does not oblige anybody to eat mouldy bread, or discarded leaves of vegetables, or spoiled food." On the other hand, if somebody wants to eat raw beets or chew raw wheat kernels one does not listen to him. What means "to drink everything one commonly drinks"? "One does not oblige anybody to drink oily fish sauce, or sour fish sauce, or wine with yeast. He who has a toothache should not sip vinegar and spit out but he may sip and

swallow. He may dip his food in as much [vinegar] as he wants without second thoughts. He who has a throat ache should not gargle with oil but he may load fish sauce with oil and sip it." "One should not anoint with wine or vinegar, but with olive oil." "If somebody has a headache or he has a scab, he may rub with oil but not with wine or vinegar."

36 The text, with minor orthographic changes, is identical with the text in *Ševi'it* 8:2, Notes 22-28. Since the Mishnah here does not have the sentence "to drink everything one commonly drinks" in practically all mss., the text in *Ševi'it* is original.

יַיִן שֶׁלְּמַעֲשֵׂר שֵׁינִי שֶׁפִּיטְּמוֹ אָסוּר לָסוּךְ בּוֹ. שֶׁמֶן שֶׁלְּמַעֲשֵׂר שֵׁינִי שֶׁפִּיטְּמוֹ מוּתָּר לָסוּךְ בּוֹ. מַה בֵּין זֶה לָזֶה. זֶה דַּרְכּוֹ לָכֵן וְזֶה אֵין דַּרְכּוֹ לָכֵן.

Perfumed wine of Second Tithe may not be used for anointing. Perfumed oil of Second Tithe may be used for anointing. What is the difference? For the latter it is customary, for the former it is not customary.

רִבִּי יוּדָן בָּעֵי שֶׁמֶן שֶׁלְּמַעֲשֵׂר שֵׁינִי שֶׁנִּסְרַח. אָמַר רִבִּי מָנָא מִכֵּיוָן שֶׁנִּסְרַח פָּקְעָה מִמֶּנּוּ קְדוּשָּׁתוֹ. מַה צְרִיכָה לֵיהּ. שְׁבִיעִית אַף עַל פִּי שֶׁנִּסְרַח בִּקְדוּשָּׁתוֹ הוּא.

Rebbi Yudan asked: Second tithe oil that became rancid? Rebbi Mana said, when it became rancid, its holiness burst from it. Why did he have to ask? Sabbatical [oil] even if rancid remains in its holiness[37].

37 At least as long as it still is animal feed. Second Tithe may not be used for animal feed.

שִׁמְעוֹן בַּר בָּא בְשֵׁם רִבִּי חֲנִינָא זֶה שֶׁהוּא לוֹחֵשׁ נוֹתֵן שֶׁמֶן עַל גַּבֵּי רֹאשׁוֹ וְלוֹחֵשׁ וּבִלְבָד שֶׁלֹּא יִתֵּן לֹא בְיַד וְלֹא בִכְלִי. רִבִּי יַעֲקֹב בַּר אִידִי רִבִּי יוֹחָנָן בְּשֵׁם רִבִּי

יַנַּאי נוֹתֵן בֵּין בְּיַד בֵּין בִּכְלִי. מַה בֵּינֵיהוֹן מְאִיסָה. מָאן דְּאָמַר נוֹתֵן בֵּין בְּיַד בֵּין בִּכְלִי מָאוּס הוּא. מָאן דְּאָמַר נוֹתֵן שֶׁמֶן עַל גַּבֵּי רֹאשׁוֹ וְלוֹחֵשׁ אֵינוֹ מָאוּס. אָמַר רִבִּי יוֹנָה מַעֲשֵׂר שֵׁינִי בֵּינֵיהוֹן. מָאן דְּאָמַר נוֹתֵן בֵּין בְּיַד בֵּין בִּכְלִי מַעֲשֵׂר שֵׁינִי אָסוּר. מָאן דְּאָמַר נוֹתֵן שֶׁמֶן עַל גַּבֵּי רֹאשׁוֹ וְלוֹחֵשׁ מַעֲשֵׂר שֵׁינִי מוּתָּר. אָמַר רִבִּי יוֹסֵי וְכִי כָּל־שֶׁהוּא מוּתָּר בַּשַּׁבָּת מוּתָּר בְּמַעֲשֵׂר שֵׁינִי וְכָל־שֶׁאָסוּר בַּשַּׁבָּת אָסוּר בְּמַעֲשֵׂר שֵׁנִי. וְהָתַנֵּי מַדִּיחָה הִיא אִשָּׁה בְנָהּ בְּיַיִן מִפְּנֵי הַזִּיעָה. בִּתְרוּמָה אָסוּר. הִיא תְרוּמָה הִיא מַעֲשֵׂר שֵׁינִי. מַהוּ כְדוֹן. וּבִלְבַד שֶׁלֹּא יַעֲשֶׂה בַשַּׁבָּת כְּדֶרֶךְ שֶׁעוֹשֶׂה בַחוֹל.

[38]Simeon bar Abba in the name of Rebbi Ḥanina: He who whispers[39] puts oil on his head and whispers on condition that he use neither hand nor vessel[40]. Rebbi Jacob bar Idi, Rebbi Joḥanan in the name of Rebbi Yannai: with hand or vessel[41]. In what do they differ? Whether it is repulsive. For him who says with hand or vessel, it is repulsive. For him who says neither hand nor vessel, it is not repulsive. Rebbi Jonah said, they differ about Second Tithe. For him who says with hand or vessel, Second Tithe is forbidden[42]. For him who says neither hand nor vessel, Second Tithe is permitted. Rebbi Yose said, is all that is permitted on the Sabbath permitted with Second Tithe and all that is forbidden on the Sabbath forbidden with Second Tithe? Did we not state: A woman may douse her son with wine[43] because of sweat, but this is forbidden with heave? Heave and Second Tithe are the same! How is that[44]? Only that he not do it in the way he is used to do it on weekdays.

38 The paragraph is also in *Šabbat* 14:3, fol. 14c.

39 A medical procedure where rubbing with oil is accompanied by whispered recitation of charms. The Talmud in *Šabbat* (Note 39) accepts this procedure for illnesses of the eye, intestines, and snake and scorpion bites. The Babli (*Sanhedrin* 101a) approves whispered charms only for snake and

scorpion bites; for eye and intestinal problems they approve only anointing and wrappings.

40 These rules are only given for the Sabbath when medical procedures are forbidden if there is no danger to the life of the patient.

41 "Hand" means to pour an amont of oil into one's palm and taking it from there by a finger of the other hand. "Vessel" is not the large container of the oil but a small vessel containing just enough oil for the procedure. Its use is permitted on the Sabbath for people who would be repelled by the idea of dipping the finger into the jar of cooking oil.

42 It is forbidden to use Second Tithe oil for medical purposes; it is permitted to use it for anointing. It is suggested that just smearing oil on one's head with a finger is a form of anointing; this is rejected immediately.

43 On the Sabbath. In *Šabbat* 14:3, the text reads: "Herself and her son."

44 What is the real reason for the rule of whispering? Anybody who does it with a vessel on weekdays has to do it without one on the Sabbath and vice-versa.

דָּגִים שֶׁנִּתְבַּשְּׁלוּ בְּקֶפְלוֹטוֹת שֶׁלְּמַעֲשֵׂר שֵׁינִי וְהִשְׁבִּיחוּ הַשְׁבָח לְפִי חֶשְׁבּוֹן. אָמַר רִבִּי הוֹשַׁעְיָה דְּרִבִּי יוּדָה הִיא. דְּתַנִּינָן רִבִּי יוּדָה מַתִּיר בְּצַחֲנָה שֶׁאֵינוֹ אֶלָּא לִיטּוֹל אֶת הַזּוֹהֲמָה. רַבָּנִין דְּקַיְסָרִין בָּעֵיין. וְהִיא דְאָמַר רִבִּי אַבָּהוּ בְּשֵׁם רִבִּי יוֹחָנָן כָּל־הָאִיסוּרִין מְשַׁעֲרִין כִּילּוּ בָּצָל כִּילּוּ קֶפְלוֹט דְּלֹא כְרִבִּי יוּדָה. מוֹדֵי רִבִּי יוּדָה בְּבָצָל שֶׁלְּהֶקְדֵּשׁ וּמוֹדֵי רִבִּי יוּדָה בְּבָצָל שֶׁלַּעֲבוֹדָה זָרָה.

45"If fish is cooked with Second Tithe leeks which increases its value, the increase is proportional." Rebbi Hoshaia said, it follows Rebbi Jehudah, since we have stated: "Rebbi Jehudah permits in anchovies where it only serves to remove pollutants." The rabbis of Caesarea asked: The saying of Rebbi Abbahu in the name of Rebbi Joḥanan, that all forbidden [food] is estimated as if it were onion, as if it were leeks, does this contradict Rebbi Jehudah? Rebbi Jehudah will agree regarding an onion of the Temple or an onion of idol worship.

45 This paragraph is from *Terumot* 10:1; explained there in Notes 8-12.

אָמַר רִבִּי יוֹחָנָן כָּל־שֶׁיֵּשׁ בּוֹ הוֹתִיר מִדָּה הַשְּׁבָח לְפִי חֶשְׁבּוֹן. וְכָל־שֶׁאֵין בּוֹ הוֹתִיר מִדָּה הַשְּׁבָח לַשֵּׁינִי. רִבִּי שִׁמְעוֹן בֶּן לָקִישׁ אָמַר כָּל־שֶׁטַּעְמוֹ שְׁבָחוֹ נִיכָּר הַשְּׁבָח לְפִי חֶשְׁבּוֹן. וְכָל־שֶׁאֵין טַעַם שְׁבָחוֹ נִיכָּר הַשְּׁבָח לַשֵּׁינִי. מַתְנִיתָא פְלִיגָא עַל רִבִּי יוֹנָתָן[46] עִיסָּה שֶׁלְּמַעֲשֵׂר שֵׁינִי שֶׁאֲפָייָהּ וְהִשְׁבִּיחָה הַשְּׁבָח (fol. 53c) לַשֵּׁינִי. פָּתַר לָהּ בְּשֶׁאֵין טַעַם שְׁבָחוֹ נִיכָּר. מַתְנִיתָא פְלִיגָא עַל רִבִּי יוֹחָנָן דָּגִים שֶׁנִּתְבַּשְּׁלוּ עִם הַקֶּפַלּוֹטוֹת שֶׁל מַעֲשֵׂר שֵׁינִי וְהִשְׁבִּיחוּ הַשְּׁבָח לְפִי חֶשְׁבּוֹן. רִבִּי יוֹסֵי בְּשֵׁם רִבִּי הוֹשַׁעְיָה תִּפְתָּר שֶׁבִּישֵּׁל שְׁנֵיהֶן כְּאַחַת. רִבִּי יוֹנָה בְּשֵׁם רִבִּי הוֹשַׁעְיָה בָּעֵי הַגַּע עַצְמָךְ שֶׁבִּישֵּׁל זֶה בִּפְנֵי עַצְמוֹ וְזֶה בִּפְנֵי עַצְמוֹ וְעִירְבָן. כְּלוּם יֵשׁ בְּדָגִין אֶלָּא טַעַם הַקֶּפַלּוֹטוֹת וּבַקֶּפַלּוֹטוֹת אֶלָּא טַעַם דָּגִין.

[47]Rebbi Johanan said, for everything that augments the measure, the increase [in value] is proportional, but for everything that does not augment the measure, the increase belongs to the Second [Tithe]. Rebbi Simeon ben Laqish said, for everything where the taste of the improvement is recognizable, the increase [in value] is proportional, but for everything where the taste of the improvement is not recognizable, the increase belongs to the Second [Tithe]. The Mishnah disagrees with Rebbi Jonathan[48]: "If a dough of Second Tithe when baked increased in value, the increase belongs to the Second." Explain it if the improvement cannot be tasted. The Mishnah disagrees with Rebbi Johanan: "If fish cooked with Second Tithe leeks increased in value, the increase is proportional." Rebbi Yose in the name of Rebbi Hoshaia: Explain it if he cooked them together[49]. Rebbi Jonah in the name of Rebbi Hoshaia: Think of it, if he cooked them separately and mixed them[50]! Have fish only the taste of leeks and leeks only the taste of fish[51]?

46 Reading of the Rome ms. Leyden and Venice: Joḥanan.

47 Here starts the discussion of the last part of the Mishnah.

48 It seems that the opinion of R. Simeon ben Laqish, which reaffirms the statement of the Mishnah, is that of R. Jonathan.

49 He cooked them together until they became soft and could no longer be separated. Since the profane part clinging to the heave part must be eaten in the holiness of heave, the volume of the holy part has increased.

50 In this case, there would only be a question according to R. Simeon ben Laqish but none according to R. Joḥanan.

51 Since in the latter case only little taste is absorbed, both R. Joḥanan and R. Simeon ben Laqish agree that the increase of the value of the tithe part does not have to be split.

מַתְנִיתִין פְּלִיגָא עַל רִבִּי יוֹחָנָן הָאִשָּׁה שֶׁשָּׁאֲלָה מֵחֲבֵירָתָהּ תַּבְלִין וּמַיִם וּמֶלַח לְעִיסָּתָהּ הֲרֵי אֵילּוּ כְּרַגְלֵי שְׁתֵּיהֶן. אָמַר רִבִּי בָּא תְּחוּמִין עָשׂוּ לְמִדַּת הַדִּין. תֵּדַע לָךְ שֶׁהוּא כֵן דְּתַמָּן אָמְרִין בְּשֵׁם רַב חִסְדָּא וְלָא יָדְעִינָן אִם מִשְּׁמוּעָה אִם מִן מַתְנִיתָא אֲפִילוּ עֵצִים. סָבְרִינָן מֵימַר עֵצִים אֵין בָּהֶן מַמָּשׁ. מַתְנִיתָא פְּלִיגָא עַל רִבִּי שִׁמְעוֹן בֶּן לָקִישׁ תַּבְשִׁיל שֶׁלְּמַעֲשֵׂר שֵׁינִי שֶׁתִּיבְּלוֹ בְּתַבְלִין שֶׁל חוּלִין הַשֶּׁבַח לַשֵּׁנִי. פָּתַר לָהּ בְּשֶׁאֵין טַעַם שִׁבְחוֹ נִיכָּר. וְהָתַנֵּי תַּבְשִׁיל שֶׁל חוּלִין שֶׁתִּיבְּלוֹ בְּתַבְלִין שֶׁלְּמַעֲשֵׂר שֵׁינִי לֹא יָצָא מַעֲשֵׂר שֵׁינִי מִידֵי פִּדְיוֹנוֹ. עַל דַּעְתֵּיהּ דְּרִבִּי יוֹחָנָן וְהוּא שֶׁיְּהֵא שָׁם הוֹתִיר מִדָּה. עַל דַּעְתֵּיהּ דְּרִבִּי שִׁמְעוֹן בֶּן לָקִישׁ וְהוּא שֶׁיְּהֵא שָׁם טַעַם שִׁבְחוֹ נִיכָּר.

A Mishnah disagrees with Rebbi Joḥanan: "Spices, water, or salt a woman borrowed from a friend for her dough, goes after both their feet[52]." Rebbi Abba said, for *eruv* they went according to the logical rule[53]. You should know that this is so since they say there[54] in the name of Rav Ḥisda, but we know not whether from a tradition or a Mishnah, "even logs!" Did we want to say that logs have no credible importance?

A *baraita*[55] disagrees with Rebbi Simeon ben Laqish: "If a tithe dish is prepared with profane spices, the increase belongs to Second Tithe." Explain it if the improvement cannot be tasted. But was it not stated: "If a profane dish is prepared with Second Tithe spices, the tithe cannot escape redemption[56]"? According to Rebbi Joḥanan, if the volume was increased. According to Rebbi Simeon ber Laqish if the improvement was clearly recognizable.

52 Mishnah *Bezah* 5:4. If one or both of the women had moved their domain for the holiday by an *eruv* (cf. *Peah* 8, Note 56), during the holiday the dough cannot be brought to any place not reachable by both of them. This part of Mishnah 5:4 is not discussed in Yerushalmi *Bezah* 5:4.

The Yerushalmi is difficult to understand. The Babli (*Bezah* 38b-39a) comes up with three possible explanations for the Mishnah. Abbai holds that all is only a rabbinical prohibition to be ready with a rule for the case the two women baked a cake together. Rava holds with R. Simeon ben Laqish that taste cannot be disregarded and, therefore, the spices are essential even if present only in a minute amount. As Tosaphot point out, water certainly cannot be disregarded even if most of it evaporates since without water there would be no dough. But water used to make unleavened dough does not necessarily increase the volume. This seems to be the objection of the Yerushalmi. Rav Ashi holds that one does not invoke special rules if by waiting (ubtil the end of the holiday) all problems disappear automatically.

53 Since the dish contains contributions from both of them, one does not have to try to allocate parts.

54 In Babylonia. In this version, the dish can be moved only in the common domain even if only the firewood came from a person with a different domain. Firewood cannot be bought with tithe money.

55 Tosephta 1:16.

56 Or the entire dish must be eaten under the rules of tithe. This part of the Tosephta requires explanation according to both opinions.

(fol. 53a) **משנה ב:** רִבִּי שִׁמְעוֹן אוֹמֵר אֵין סָכִין שֶׁמֶן שֶׁל מַעֲשֵׂר שֵׁינִי בִּירוּשָׁלֵם וַחֲכָמִים מַתִּירִין. אָמְרוּ לוֹ לְרִבִּי שִׁמְעוֹן הֵיקֵל בִּתְרוּמָה חֲמוּרָה לֹא נָקֵל בְּמַעֲשֵׂר שֵׁינִי הַקַּל. אָמַר לָהֶן מַה לֹא הֵקֵל בִּתְרוּמָה חֲמוּרָה מָקוֹם שֶׁהֵיקֵל בְּכַרְשִׁינִין וּבִתְלְתָּן נָקֵל בְּמַעֲשֵׂר שֵׁינִי הַקַּל מָקוֹם שֶׁלֹּא הֵיקֵל בְּכַרְשִׁינִין וּבִתְלְתָּן.

Mishnah 2: Rebbi Simeon says, one does not rub himself with oil of Second Tithe in Jerusalem[57] but the Sages permit it. They said to Rebbi Simeon, if He made it easy for the important heave[58], should we not be lenient for the lightweight Second Tithe? He said to them, this is no good[59]. He was lenient for the important heave as He was lenient for vetch and fenugreek[60]; how can we be lenient for Second Tithe where He was not lenient for vetch and fenugreek?

57 In the opinion of R. Simson and R. Isaac Simponti, R. Simeon disagrees with the previous Mishnah and Halakhah and holds that anointing is not subsumed under the notion of eating. This is contradicted by the Halakhah. In the opinion of Maimonides, R. Simeon agrees that in principle rubbing oneself is legitimate use of Second Tithe oil. However, he holds the owner of Second Tithe oil may not ask another person to massage him because the latter's hand also will be rubbed with oil and this is akin to paying for the massage with Second Tithe oil, a rabbinic transgression. The last assertion is difficult to accept; the more likely explanation is that of H. Albeck (ששה סדרי משנה[2], Jerusalem 1958), that according to R. Simeon if a person rubbed with such oil leaves Jerusalem while some of the oil still clings to his body, he will have sinned. In order to prevent inadvertent sin he forbids rubbing as a "fence of the law."

58 As explained in the next Mishnah.

59 This is the reading of the Yerushalmi mss., the Parma ms. of the Mishnah, and one ms. of a translation of the Commentary of Maimonides. All other Mishnah mss. read מה לא אם היקל "On the contrary, if He was lenient . . ."

60 As explained in Mishnah 4. If the argument is accepted, the relation of heave to Second Tithe is not that of *majus* to *minor*.

(fol. 53c) **הלכה ב**: מַה הֵיקִילוּ בִתְרוּמָה. כְּהָדָא דְתַנֵּי סָךְ הוּא כֹהֵן שֶׁלִּתְרוּמָה וּמֵבִיא בֶן בִּתּוֹ שֶׁל יִשְׂרָאֵל וּמְעַגְלוֹ עַל גַּבֵּי מֵיעָיו וְאֵינוֹ חוֹשֵׁשׁ. אָמַר רִבִּי יוֹחָנָן כָּאן הֵשִׁיבוּ דִבְרֵי סוֹפְרִים לְדִבְרֵי תוֹרָה.

Halakhah 2: How were they lenient for heave? As we have stated[61]: "A Cohen may rub himself with heave oil and bring his daughter's son by an Israel and roll him on his belly without qualms." Rebbi Joḥanan said, here they retorted with rabbinic words against the word of the Torah[62].

61 Tosephta *Terumot* 10:10. The Babli, based on biblical verses, explains in *Keritut* 7a that rubbing oil on one's body, while a permitted activity, removes the sanctity from the oil just as eating removes the sanctity from the food in the Cohen's body. Therefore, even if an unrelated adult Israel touches the oil on the Cohen's body, he does not sin.

62 Rebbi Simeon's prohibition is rabbinical, the argument of the Sages is biblical!

The Rome ms. reads דברי סופרים לדברי סופרים. This seems to be a scribal error.

(fol. 53a) **משנה ג**: תִּלְתָּן שֶׁל מַעֲשֵׂר שֵׁנִי תֵיאָכֵל צִימְחוֹנִין וְשֶׁל תְּרוּמָה בֵּית שַׁמַּאי אוֹמְרִים כָּל־מַעֲשֶׂיהָ בְטָהֳרָה חוּץ מֵחֲפִיפָתָהּ. וּבֵית הִלֵּל אוֹמְרִים כָּל־מַעֲשֶׂיהָ בְטוּמְאָה חוּץ מִשְּׁרִייָתָהּ.

Mishnah 3: Fenugreek of Second Tithe should be eaten as sprouts[63]. Of Heave[64], the House of Shammai say it must always be handled in purity except for shampooing. But the House of Hillel say, it may be handled in impurity except in soaking[65].

63 Since Second Tithe must be eaten; ripe fenugreek plants are hard as straw and its seeds also are hard; the only time fenugreek really is edible is in young sprouts.

64 As mentioned several times in *Terumot* and *Ma'serot*, heave of fenugreek is traded in bundles, the hard stem (which gives some taste) and the seeds (usable as spice). The House of Shammai hold that since it may be used as spice, it must always be treated as food and handled in purity since otherwise it must be burned as impure heave food, except that it can be used to perfume water to shampoo hair. In that case, the Cohen's action shows that the fenugreek is not food for him and if impure does not have to be burned.

65 For the House of Hillel, fenugreek is not food except if shown by an action of the Cohen to be prepared as food, e. g., soaking the seeds to use as spice. Otherwise, fenugreek is wood and cannot become impure; if it is handled in impurity it does not have to be burned.

(fol. 53c) **הלכה ג:** כֵּינִי מַתְנִיתָא מוּתֶּרֶת לְהֵיאָכֵל צִמְחוֹנִין.

So is the Mishnah: It is permitted to eat it as sprouts[66].

66 It is not a requirement. J. N. Epstein (מבוא לנוסח המשנה ע' 487) considers this to be a commentary, not a change of the Mishnah text.

מַה בֵּינֵיהוֹן. אָמַר רִבִּי יוֹנָה שׁוֹלֶה בֵּינֵיהוֹן. בֵּית שַׁמַּי אוֹמְרִים שׁוֹלֶה בְּיָדַיִם טְהוֹרוֹת וּבֵית הִלֵּל אוֹמְרִים שׁוֹלֶה בְּיָדַיִם טְמֵאוֹת. תַּנֵּי זוֹ דִּבְרֵי רִבִּי מֵאִיר. אֲבָל דִּבְרֵי רִבִּי יְהוּדָה אוֹמֵר בֵּית שַׁמַּי אוֹמְרִים כָּל־מַעֲשֶׂיהָ בְּטָהֳרָה חוּץ מֵחֲפִיפָתָהּ. וּבֵית הִלֵּל אוֹמְרִים כָּל־מַעֲשֶׂיהָ בְטוּמְאָה חוּץ מִשְּׁלִיָּתָהּ. מַה בֵּינֵיהוֹן. אָמַר רִבִּי מַתַּנְיָה מְגִיגָה בֵּינֵיהוֹן. בֵּית שַׁמַּי אוֹמֵר מוֹגֵג בְּיָדַיִם טְהוֹרוֹת. וּבֵית הִלֵּל אוֹמְרִים מוֹגֵג בְּיָדַיִם טְמֵאוֹת.

What is between them? Rebbi Jonah said, pulling out of water is between them. The House of Shammai say, one pulls out of the water with pure hands but the House of Hillel say, one pulls out of the water with impure hands[67]. It is stated[68]: "These are the words of Rebbi Meïr. But the words of Rebbi Jehudah, he says that the House of Shammai say, it must always be handled in purity except for shampooing. But the House of Hillel say, it may be handled in impurity except in pulling it out of water[69]." What is between them? Rebbi Mattaniah said, softening[70] is between them. The House of Shammai say, one softens with pure hands but the House of Hillel say, one softens with impure hands.

67 In this version, the House of Hillel require pure (i. e., washed) hands only for putting fenugreek into the water for soaking, not to make heave impure by one's own action. But they will permit taking the soaked seeds out of the water with unwashed hands since the seeds are also soaked as animal feed.

68 Tosephta 2:1.

69 The text is uncertain. The Tosephta has שרייתה "it soaking" instead of שליתה. It is possible that שליה here does not mean "to scoop out of the water", as in Yerushalmi Targumim but by a change of liquids *l* and *r* is the same as שריה, "soaking", and refers to all stages of soaking. This is not the position of Maimonides in his Code (*Ma'aser Šeni* 2:14).

70 Softening the kernels by rubbing them between one's fingers. The House of Hillel do not consider this an action transforming the seeds into food.

(fol. 53a) **משנה ד:** כַּרְשִׁינֵי מַעֲשֵׂר שֵׁנִי יֵאָכְלוּ צִמְחוֹנִים וְנִכְנָסִין לִירוּשָׁלֵם וְיוֹצְאִין. נִטְמְאוּ רִבִּי טַרְפוֹן אוֹמֵר יִתְפָּרְדוּ לְעִיסִּיּוֹת וַחֲכָמִים אוֹמְרִים יִפָּדוּ. וְשֶׁל תְּרוּמָה בֵּית שַׁמַּאי אוֹמְרִים שׁוֹרִין וְשָׁפִין בְּטָהֳרָה וּמַאֲכִילִין בְּטוּמְאָה. וּבֵית הִלֵּל אוֹמְרִים שׁוֹרִין בְּטָהֳרָה וְשָׁפִין וּמַאֲכִילִין בְּטוּמְאָה. שַׁמַּי אוֹמֵר יֵאָכְלוּ צָרִיד. רִבִּי עֲקִיבָה אוֹמֵר כָּל־מַעֲשֵׂיהֶן בְּטוּמְאָה.

Mishnah 4: Vetch[71] of Second Tithe should be eaten as sprouts; it may enter Jerusalem and leave[72]. If it became impure, Rebbi Ṭarphon says it should be divided into pieces of dough[73], but the Sages say it should be redeemed[74]. If it is heave[75], the House of Shammai say, one soaks and cleans[76] in purity and feeds in impurity, but the House of Hillel say, one soaks in purity[77] and cleans and feeds in impurity. Shammai says, it should be eaten dry[78]. Rebbi Aqiba says, all its processing is done in impurity[79].

71 It was stated (*Terumot* 11:9) that only in years of famine is vetch human food. But as sprouts it can be eaten and is not animal feed. This Mishnah also appears in *Idiut* 1:8.

72 Since sprouts cannot qualify as produce.

73 He does not permit to redeem any Second Tithe to be used as animal feed; therefore he requires the vetch, which is a legume, to be ground to flour and mixed with flour in little cakes whose volume is less than that of a chicken egg so that it may be eaten as pure human food (cf. *Terumot* 5:3).

74 And fed to animals after redemption.

75 Heave vetch is animal feed, *Terumot* 11:9.

76 Even though the intention was from the start to use it as animal feed, as long as it is not given to the animals it must strictly be treated according to the rules of heave.

77 In order not to make heave impure with one's hands.

78 It should be given dry and unwashed to the animals to avoid any question of impurity.

79 He holds that vetch is not human food unless there is a famine.

(fol. 53c) **הלכה ד:** כְּדֵי לַעֲשׂוֹת עִיסָּה וְלַחֲזוֹר כְּדֵי לַעֲשׂוֹת וְלַחֲזוֹר.

Halakhah 4: To make a dough and return it, to make it and return[80].

80 This seems to refer to the statement that Second Tithe vetch may leave Jerusalem. An identical statement is Halakhah 3:4, referring to

the opinion of Rabban Simeon ben Gamliel (Mishnah 3:5) that Second Tithe produce which entered Jerusalem may leave again. It is stated here and there that it may leave only to be processed, returned, and consumed in Jerusalem.

The duplication in the text is difficult to understand; instead of כדי לעשות ולחזור the Rome ms. reads כדי בגיסה ולחזור. The meaning of the *hapax legomenon* בגיסה (assuming it is not a corruption) is unknown. The text in 3:4 has a simple duplication כדי לעשות עיסה ולחזור. כדי לעשות עיסה ולחזור.

הלכה ה: מַתְנִיתָא דְרַבָּן שִׁמְעוֹן בֶּן גַּמְלִיאֵל אַף הַפֵּירוֹת נִכְנָסִין וְיוֹצְאִין. דִּבְרֵי הַכֹּל הִיא. הָכָא קַל הוּא שֶׁהֶקִילוּ בְּכַרְשִׁינִין וּבִלְבָד בְּעִיסָּה שֶׁלְּכַּרְשִׁינִין. וּבִלְבַד עִיסָּה שֶׁלְּמַעֲשֵׂר שֵׁינִי.

Halakhah 5: Is our Mishnah Rabban Simeon ben Gamliel's[80]? "Also produce enters and leaves"! It is the opinion of everybody. Here they were very lenient for vetch, but only dough of vetch[81], only dough of Second Tithe.

81 For the Halakhah here, dough of Second Tithe produce for Halakhah 3:4.

רִבִּי גּוֹרְיוֹן בְּשֵׁם רִבִּי יוֹסֵי בֶּן חֲנִינָא דִּבְרֵי רִבִּי טַרְפוֹן אֵין פּוֹדִין אֶת הַקֳּדָשִׁים לְהַאֲכִילָן לִכְלָבִים. אָמַר רִבִּי יוֹנָה נִרְאוּ דְּבָרִים הָרָאוּי לְאוֹכֶל אָדָם אֵין פּוֹדִין אוֹתוֹ לוֹכֶל בְּהֵמָה. וְשֶׁאֵינוֹ רָאוּי לוֹכֶל אָדָם פּוֹדִין אוֹתוֹ לוֹכֶל בְּהֵמָה.

Rebbi Gorion in the name of Rebbi Yose ben Ḥanina: Rebbi Ṭarphon implies that one may not redeem sanctified food to feed it to the dogs. Rebbi Yose said[82], it seems reasonable that anything which can be human food cannot be redeemed to be fed to animals, but anything which is not human food can be redeemed to be fed to animals.

82 He gives the rationale of the Sages opposing R. Tarphon.

רבִּי יִצְחָק בֶּן אֶלְיָשִׁיב בָּעֵי נִטְמְאוּ בִגְבוּלִין לֹא יִיפָּדוּ שֶׁאֵין פּוֹדִין אֶת הַקֳּדָשִׁים לְהַאֲכִילָן לִכְלָבִים. אָמַר רִבִּי יוֹנָה וְהֵן נוּ טִי נוּ טוּמִי.

Rebbi Isaac ben Eliashiv asked: [Is it true that] if it became impure in the countryside it should not be redeemed since one may not redeem sanctified food to feed it to the dogs? Rebbi Jonah said, that is בוטי נוטומי[83].

83 The Rome ms. reads ניטומטומי. All commentators read the expression as one of concurrence with the rule tentatively expressed by R. Isaac ben Eliashiv. The expression has not been convincingly explained. {The Latin and Greek etymologies offered by Levy, Löw (in Krauss's Dictionary), Kohout, and Lieberman (*Tarbiẓ* 3, p. 337) presuppose rewriting the consonantal text. Jastrow declares the text corrupt.}

(fol. 53a) **משנה ה:** מָעוֹת חוּלִין וּמָעוֹת מַעֲשֵׂר שֵׁנִי שֶׁנִּתְפַּזְּרוּ מַה שֶּׁלִּיקֵּט לִיקֵּט לְמַעֲשֵׂר שֵׁינִי עַד שֶׁיַּשְׁלִים וְהַשְּׁאָר חוּלִין. אִם בָּלַל וְחָפַן לְפִי חֶשְׁבּוֹן. זֶה הַכְּלָל הַמִּתְלַקְּטִין לְמַעֲשֵׂר שֵׁינִי וְהַנִּבְלָלִין לְפִי חֶשְׁבּוֹן.

Mishnah 5: Of profane and Second Tithe coins that were strewn around, what one collected goes to Second Tithe until complete, the remainder is profane[84]. If he mixed them together and took out fists full, it is in proportion[85]. That is the principle: What is picked out is for Second Tithe and what is mixed together by proportion[86].

84 One assumes that the profane and the tithe coins are indistinguishable. What is collected first has to be sanctified as Second Tithe money by a declaration, and what had been Second Tithe coins and now ends up in the profane part is then automatically redeemed by the profane coins which ended up in the tithe part.

85 If the coins are not picked up as

they fell but first are swept together with a broom to form a heap in which all coins are mixed, the coins taken out are separated into heave and profane according to the proportion heave and profane had before the accident. According to Maimonides (in his Commentary and his Code, *Ma'aśer Šeni* 6:1) the proportional split in this case holds even if some coins were lost. In this case also, a declaration of substitution has to be made.

86 For all Second Tithe, not only coins. This is spelled out more clearly in the Tosephta, 2:4.

הלכה ו: (fol. 53c) אָמַר רִבִּי זְעִירָה כְּדֵי לְשָׂכָר שֵׁינִי שֶׁמָּא יֹאבְדוּ הַשְּׁאָר וְיִהְיוּ אֵילּוּ שֶׁבְּיָדוֹ תְּפוּסִין עַל הַשֵּׁנִי. אָמַר רִבִּי זְעִירָא וְצָרִיךְ לְהַתְנוֹת וְלוֹמַר אִם אֵילּוּ שֶׁלְּמַטָּן שֵׁנִי יִהְיוּ אֵילּוּ שֶׁבְּיָדִי תְּפוּסִין עֲלֵיהֶן. אָמַר רִבִּי יוֹנָה וְהוּא שֶׁלִּיקֵּט מִכָּן וּמִכָּן אֲבָל אִם לִיקֵּט עַל אוֹמָן כְּבוֹלֵל וְחוֹפֵן הוּא.

Rebbi Zeïra said, for the profit of the Second; maybe the rest will be lost and then at least those held in his hand will be kept for Second [Tithe][87]. Rebbi Zeïra said, and one has to spell out and say, if those at the bottom are from the Second, those in my hand are taken in their stead. Rebbi Jonah said, only if he collected from all around but if he collected in a straight line it is as if he had swept and taken out fists full.

87 He explains why the person who does not first sweep all coins together must first collect for Second Tithe. The person who sweeps (and in the opinion of R. Jonah, the person who collects in systematic sweeps) does something first to avoid further losses and, therefore, can profit from more lenient rules.

רִבִּי יוֹסֵי בְּשֵׁם רִבִּי פְּדָיָה רִבִּי יוֹנָה בְּשֵׁם חִזְקִיָּה אֵין בְּלִילָה אֶלָּא בְּיַיִן וְשֶׁמֶן בִּלְבַד. רִבִּי יוֹחָנָן אָמַר עַד כְּזֵיתִים הַנִּבְלָלִים. מַתְנִיתָא פְּלִיגָא עַל רִבִּי יוֹחָנָן. אִם בָּלַל וְחָפַן לְפִי חֶשְׁבּוֹן. פָּתַר לָהּ עַד כְּזֵיתִים. הַמִּתְלַקְּטִים לְמַעֲשֵׂר שֵׁינִי

וְהַנִּבְלָלִין לְפִי הַחֶשְׁבּוֹן. רִבִּי יוֹסֵי בֵּי רִבִּי בּוּן בְּשֵׁם רִבִּי הוּנָה סָלְקַת מַתְנִיתָא הַנִּבְלָלִין וְהַנֶּחֱפָנִין לְפִי חֶשְׁבּוֹן.

[88]Rebbi Yose in the name of Rebbi Pedaiah, Rebbi Jonah in the name of Ḥizqiah, there is no mixing except for wine and oil. Rebbi Joḥanan says, it can be mixed up to the size of olives[89]. Our Mishnah disagrees with Rebbi Joḥanan: "If he mixed them together and took out fists full, it is by proportion." He explains it, up to the size of olives. "What is picked out is for Second Tithe and what is mixed together in proportion." Rebbi Yose ben Rebbi Abun in the name of Rebbi Huna: The Mishnah comes up so: What is mixed and[90] what is taken out in fists full in proprtion.

88 The first three sentences are also in *Demay* 5:5. Notes 82-83. The discussion is about the principle, applied to produce, stated at the end of the Mishnah.

89 Solid produce smaller than the size of an olive, e. g., grains, can be thoroughly mixed.

90 One should not read "mixed *or* taken out in fistfuls" but "mixed *and* taken out in fistfuls".

(fol. 53a) **משנה ו:** סֶלַע שֶׁלְמַעֲשֵׂר שֵׁנִי וְשֶׁלַחוּלִין שֶׁנִּתְעָרְבוּ מֵבִיא סֶלַע מָעוֹת וְאוֹמֵר סֶלַע שֶׁלְמַעֲשֵׂר שֵׁינִי בְּכָל־מָקוֹם שֶׁהִיא מְחוּלֶּלֶת עַל הַמָּעוֹת הָאֵלּוּ וּבוֹרֵר אֶת הַיָּפָה שֶׁבָּהֶן וּמְחַלְּלָן עָלֶיהָ מִפְּנֵי שֶׁאָמְרוּ מְחַלְּלִין כֶּסֶף עַל נְחוֹשֶׁת מִדּוֹחַק לֹא שֶׁיְּקַיֵּים כֵּן אֶלָּא חוֹזֵר וּמְחַלְּלָן עַל הַכֶּסֶף.

Mishnah 6: If a tetradrachma of Second Tithe was mixed up with a profane one[91], one brings coins in the value of a tetradrachma and says: The tetradrachma of Second Tithe, wherever it may be, is exchanged for these coins. Then he chooses the better of the two and exchanges it for them since they said, one exchanges bronze for silver in an emergency[92], not that it should stay so but that he should exchange them for silver.

91 And it is not known which of the two coins is dedicated as Second Tithe. The farmer does not want to take both coins to Jerusalem.

92 But not silver for silver. When the silver coin, the standard legal tender in the entire Roman empire, is spent in Jerusalem it is usually first converted into local bronze coin. Therefore, this exchange is legal under certain circumstances. But silver coins under normal circumstances are never exchanged into other silver coins and, therefore, such an exchange is never permitted. The bronze coins should not be kept as such because non-local bronze coins may not be accepted at full value in Jerusalem.

(fol. 53c) **הלכה ז:** תַּנֵּי בֶּן עֲזַּאי אוֹמֵר שְׁתַּיִם. רִבִּי זְעִירָא אָמַר מַה בְּחֶלְמָה מֵיכַל[93] לְעוּלָּא בַּר יִשְׁמָעֵאל קוּפְדָּה שְׁמֵינָה. לְמָחָר אָתָא שָׁאַל לֵיהּ. אָמַר לֵיהּ לָמָּה שְׁתַּיִם. אָמַר לֵיהּ מִתּוֹךְ שֶׁאַתְּ אוֹמֵר לוֹ כֵּן הוּא דוֹחֵק עַצְמוֹ וּפוֹדֶה אוֹתָהּ.

Halakhah 7: It was stated[94]: Ben Azai says, two. Rebbi Zeïra said, in a dream I had Ulla bar Ismael ate fat meat[95]. The next day he came and asked him, he said to him, why two? He said to him, since you tell him so, he will push himself to exchange it[96].

93 Reading of the Rome ms. Leyden and Venice: בר ייכל.

94 Tosephta 2:5. Ben Azai requires small change in double the value of the tithe coin.

95 R. Zeïra, the dreamer, took that to mean that Ulla was fed celestial fare which contains the secrets of the Torah.

96 If one exchanges for the exact value, the farmer will not see why he could not simply take one of the coins and declare it tithe money. But then the original tithe coin might be spent in a sinful way as profane.

חִזְקִיָּה אָמַר כְּשֶׁהוּא מְחַלְּלָהּ עוֹשֶׂה אוֹתָהּ כְּרָעָה. וּכְשֶׁהוּא מְחַלֵּל עָלֶיהָ עוֹשֶׂה אוֹתָהּ כְּיָפָה. וְהָא תַנִּינָן בּוֹרֵר אֶת הַיָּפָה שֶׁבָּהֶן וּמְחַלְּלָן עָלֶיהָ. וְיָבוֹר אֶת הָרָעָה וְיַעֲשֶׂה אוֹתָהּ כְּיָפָה. אָמַר רִבִּי יוֹנָה אֲנִי אוֹמֵר הִיא הָיְתָה מַעֲשֵׂר שֵׁינִי.

Ḥizqiah said, when he exchanges it, he treats it as bad. But if he exchanges for it, he treats it as a good one[96]. But did we not state: "He chooses the better of the two and exchanges it for them[97]"? Why can he not take the worse [coin] and treat it as a good one? Rebbi Jonah said, I say that this one was Second Tithe[98].

96 The statement of Ḥizqiah belongs to *Baba Meẓi'a* 4:5 (fol. 9d), Babli 52b-53a. The Mishnah establishes tolerances for coins; on how much they may differ from the standard weight to be acceptable in honest trade. On this Ḥizqiah remarks that if somebody has an underweight coin of tithe money, if he spends it in Jerusalem he clearly has to spend it as underweight coin, worth less than a full-weight silver coin. But if he exchanges his own Second Tithe produce for the coin, a transaction between him and himself, he may exchange it as if it were a full-weight coin.

97 The Mishnah seems to establish higher, not lower, standards for transactions involving his own Second Tithe.

98 The trick of Ḥizqiah is acceptable if a profane coin is turned into tithe money. But the moment it is dedicated as tithe, it has to be treated with the respect due the holy.

מִכָּל־מָקוֹם לֹא יָצָאת לְחוּלִין. אָמַר רִבִּי יוֹנָה לֹא יִתְכַּוֵּין לַעֲשׂוֹתָהּ חוּלִין בְּרוּרִין. תֵּדַע לָךְ שֶׁהוּא כֵן דְּתַנִּינָן לֹא שֶׁיְּקַיֵּים כֵּן אֶלָּא חוֹזֵר וּמְחַלְּלוֹ עַל הַכֶּסֶף.

Did it not become profane anyhow[99]? Rebbi Jonah said, he should not intend to make it totally profane. You should understand that this is so since we have stated: "not that it should stay so but that he should exchange it for silver".

99 Why does one have to insist that the bronze coins be changed into the present silver coin in the end? Why can the two silver coins not become totally profane?

רִבִּי חַגַּי אָמַר קוֹמֵי רִבִּי זְעִירָא מְנַחֵם בְּשֵׁם רִבִּי יוֹחָנָן כָּל־שֶׁאָֽמְרוּ בִדְמַאי מְחַלְּלִין בְּוַדַּאי מְחַלְּלִין אוֹתוֹ מְדוּחָק. וְהָתַנִּינָן מְחַלְּלִין כֶּסֶף עַל נְחוֹשֶׁת מְדוּחָק. הָא כֶסֶף עַל כֶּסֶף לֹא. רִבִּי בָּא בַּר כֹּהֵן אָמַר קוֹמֵי רִבִּי יוֹנָה רִבִּי אָחָא בְּשֵׁם רִבִּי יוֹחָנָן כָּל־שֶׁאָֽמְרוּ בִדְמַאי מְחַלְּלִין בְּוַדַּאי עָבַר וְחִילְּלוֹ מְחוּלָּל. רִבִּי יוּדָן בֶּן פָּזִי רִבִּי שִׁמְעוֹן בַּר בָּא בְּשֵׁם רִבִּי יוֹחָנָן כָּל־שֶׁאָֽמְרוּ בִדְמַאי מְחַלְּלִין בְּוַדַּאי עָבַר וְחִילְּלָן מְחוּלָּלִין.

Rebbi Ḥaggai said before Rebbi Zeïra, Menaḥem in the name of Rebbi Joḥanan: In all cases where they said about *demay* that it can be exchanged[100], for certain produce one may exchange it in an emergency[101]. But did we not state: "One exchanges bronze for silver in an emergency", therefore not silver for silver! Rebbi Abba bar Cohen said before Rebbi Jonah, Rebbi Aḥa in the name of Rebbi Joḥanan: In all cases where they said about *demay* that it should be exchanged, if he transgressed and exchanged for certain produce it is exchanged[102]. Rebbi Jehudah ben Pazi, Rebbi Simeon bar Abba in the name of Rebbi Joḥanan: In all cases where they said about *demay* that it should be exchanged, if he transgressed and exchanged for certain produce they are exchanged.

100 As explained in Mishnah *Demay* 1:2 that for tithe money of *demay* one may exchange silver for silver, silver for bronze, bronze for bronze, etc.

101 Not only the one case stated in the Mishnah here.

102 While it is illegal, the exchange is valid. Only the case stated by the Mishnah is legal. This corrects the tradition reported by R. Ḥaggai. The difference between R. Abba bar Cohen and R. Jehudah ben Pazi is a minor point of grammar.

תַּנֵּי רִבִּי לָֽעְזָר בֵּי רִבִּי שִׁמְעוֹן אוֹמֵר כְּשֵׁם שֶׁמְּחַלְּלִין כֶּסֶף עַל נְחוֹשֶׁת כָּךְ מְחַלְּלִין זָהָב עַל הַכֶּסֶף. אָמַר לוֹ רִבִּי מִפְּנֵי מַה מְחַלְּלִין כֶּסֶף עַל נְחוֹשֶׁת שֶׁכֵּן מְחַלְּלִין כֶּסֶף עַל הַזָּהָב. ויְחַלְּלוּ זָהָב עַל הַכֶּסֶף. אֵין מְחַלְּלִין זָהָב עַל נְחוֹשֶׁת. אָמַר לוֹ רִבִּי לָֽעְזָר בֵּירִבִּי שִׁמְעוֹן שֶׁכֵּן מַעֲשֵׂר שֵׁינִי שֶׁלְּזָהָב מְחַלְּלִין אוֹתוֹ עַל הַמָּעוֹת שֶׁבִּירוּשָׁלֵם. מִדִּבְרֵי שְׁנֵיהֶן מְחַלְּלִין כֶּסֶף עַל כֶּסֶף וְאֵין מְחַלְּלִין כֶּסֶף עַל נְחוֹשֶׁת.

It was stated[103]: "Rebbi Eleazar ben Rebbi Simeon says one exchanges gold for silver just as one exchanges silver for bronze[104]. Rebbi said to him: Why does one exchange silver for bronze? Because one exchanges silver for gold[105]! Should one exchange gold for silver[106]? One does not exchange gold for bronze! Rebbi Eleazar ben Rebbi Simeon answered him: Certainly one exchanges Second Tithe gold for small coins in Jerusalem!" From the arguments of both of them one exchanges silver for silver and one does not exchange silver for bronze[107].

103 Tosephta 2:7: "Rebbi Eleazar ben Rebbi Simeon says one *should be able to exchange* gold for silver just as one exchanges silver for bronze. Rebbi said to him: Why does one exchange silver for bronze? Because one exchanges silver for gold! *Then one should not be able to* exchange gold for silver *since* one does not exchange gold for bronze! Rebbi Eleazar ben Rebbi Simeon answered him: Certainly Second Tithe gold one exchanges for small coins in Jerusalem! *When has this been said? For* demay *but not for certain tithe*!" Since the Yerushalmi does not consider *demay* in this connection, the Tosephta cannot be the basis of the Yerushalmi.

104 Since this exchange (outside of Jerusalem) is authorized only in emergencies, the exchange of gold for silver also should be authorized only in emergencies.

105 The opinion of the House of Hillel in the next Mishnah.

106 The standard means of payment was the silver tetradrachma. Gold coins have to be exchanged by a competent money changer and bronze/copper coins are only local currency. In both cases one reduces the immediate availability of the money in

Jerusalem and this should be avoided.

107 While this is the text in both mss. and the *editio princeps*, it is clear that one should read: "one exchanges silver for bronze and one does not exchange silver for silver." An exchange of silver for silver would not accomplish anything.

(fol. 53a) **משנה ז:** בֵּית שַׁמַּאי אוֹמְרִים לֹא יַעֲשֶׂה אָדָם אֶת סְלָעָיו דֵּינָרֵי זָהָב. וּבֵית הִלֵּל מַתִּירִין. אָמַר רִבִּי עֲקִיבָה אֲנִי עָשִׂיתִי לְרַבָּן גַּמְלִיאֵל וְרִבִּי יְהוֹשֻׁעַ אֶת כַּסְפָּם דֵּינָרֵי זָהָב.

Mishnah 7: The House of Shammai say, a person should not turn his tetradrachmas into gold denars but the House of Hillel permit it. Rebbi Aqiba said, for Rabban Gamliel and Rebbi Joshua I turned their silver coins into gold denars.

(fol. 53c) **הלכה ח:** אָמַר רִבִּי יוֹחָנָן לֹא אָמְרוּ בֵּית שַׁמַּי אֶלָּא בְסוֹף. אֲבָל בַּתְּחִילָּה אוּף בֵּית שַׁמַּי מוֹדֵיי. מַה טַעֲמָא דְבֵית שַׁמַּי כֶּסֶף וְלֹא זָהָב. וְאֵימָא כֶּסֶף וְלֹא נְחוֹשֶׁת. וְהָתַנִּינָן הַפּוֹרֵט סֶלַע מִמָּעוֹת מַעֲשֵׂר שֵׁינִי. וְסָבְרִינָן מֵימַר כֵּינִי מַתְנִיתָא הַמְצָרֵף סֶלַע מִמָּעוֹת מַעֲשֵׂר שֵׁינִי. מַאי כְדוֹן טַעֲמָא דְבֵית שַׁמַּאי. הִיא כֶסֶף הִיא נְחוֹשֶׁת. רִבִּי שִׁמְעוֹן בֶּן לָקִישׁ אָמַר בֵּין בַּתְּחִילָּה בֵּין בְּסוֹף בֵּית שַׁמַּי פְּלִיגִין. מַה טַעֲמָא דְבֵית שַׁמַּי. כֶּסֶף רִאשׁוֹן וְלֹא כֶסֶף שֵׁינִי. וְהָתַנִּינָן הַפּוֹרֵט סֶלַע מִמָּעוֹת מַעֲשֵׂר שֵׁינִי וְסָבְרִינָן מֵימַר כֵּינִי מַתְנִיתָא הַמְצָרֵף סֶלַע מִמָּעוֹת מַעֲשֵׂר שֵׁינִי. מַאי כְּדוֹן טַעֲמָא דְבֵית שַׁמַּי. כֶּסֶף עַד כְּדֵי כֶסֶף.

Halakhah 8: Rebbi Joḥanan said, the House of Shammai said this only at the end, but at the beginning also the House of Shammai agree[108]. What is the reason of the House of Shammai? (*Deut*. 14:25) "Silver", not gold. Say "silver" but not bronze! But did we not state[109]: "If somebody gets change for coins of Second Tithe"? We wanted to say that the Mishnah means: If somebody takes[110] a tetradrachma for coins of Second Tithe. How is that? The reason of the House of Shammai is that silver and bronze have the same rule[111].

Rebbi Simeon ben Laqish said, both at the beginning and at the end does the House of Shammai disagree. What is the reason of the House of Shammai? (*Deut.* 14:25) "Silver" first and not second[112]. But did we not state: "If somebody gets change for coins of Second Tithe"? We wanted to say that the Mishnah means: If somebody takes a tetradrachma for coins of Second Tithe. How is that? The reason of the House of Shammai (*Deut.* 14:25): "Silver", it should add up to silver[113].

108 In this interpretation, the House of Shammai require that any coin of tithe money taken to Jerusalem should be a silver coin since it is written (Deut. 14:24-25): "If the way is too much for you that you cannot carry it all the way .... then *turn it into silver, take the silver in your hand* and go to the place which the Eternal, your God, will choose."

An echo of the discussion here is in Babli *Baba Meẓi'a* 45a. In the final interpretation there, the reason of the House of Shammai is rabbinical, not biblical.

109 Mishnah 2:8, seemingly about exchanging large coins for small change outside of Jerusalem. The interpretation turns the language of the Mishnah on its head and reads: "He who takes small coins of Second Tithe money and turns them into large coins," which is permitted. This interpretation is accepted by Rashi (*Bekhorot* 50b, *Qiddušin* 11b) since nobody starts out exchanging produce for silver coins.

110 מצרף is the same as the corresponding Arabic صرف "to exchange money" in the sense of giving large coins for small, in contrast to פורט, giving change for large coins. (J. N. Epstein, מבוא לנוסח המשנה ^{2}, p. 487.)

111 It is unreasonable to expect the Second Tithe of one year to amount to a tetradrachma's worth. Therefore, they must permit the original

redemption in copper coins to be turned into silver but exclude gold coins.

112 We think that he takes the verse "then *turn it into silver*" to mean that redemption of Second Tithe is possible only with silver coin.

113 He really only insists on the second part of the verse, *take the silver in your hand*, that one should not go to Jerusalem unless he has at least a silver coin of Second Tithe money to spend there. But even if one has 25 silver coins to carry there, the House of Shammai will not permit them to be changed into a gold denar. The House of Hillel interpret כסף as "money" in all these verses.

(fol. 53a) **משנה ח:** הַפּוֹרֵט סֶלַע מִמָּעוֹת מַעֲשֵׂר שֵׁינִי בֵּית שַׁמַּאי אוֹמְרִים בְּכָל־הַסֶּלַע מָעוֹת וּבֵית הִלֵּל אוֹמְרִים בְּשֶׁקֶל כֶּסֶף וּבְשֶׁקֶל מָעוֹת. רִבִּי מֵאִיר אוֹמֵר אֵין מְחַלְּלִין כֶּסֶף וּפֵירוֹת עַל כֶּסֶף. וַחֲכָמִים מַתִּירִין.

Mishnah 8: He who gives a tetradrachma for change of Second Tithe money[114], the House of Shammai say small change for the entire tetradrachma but the House of Hillel say one *šeqel*[115] silver coin and one *šeqel* small coin. Rebbi Meïr says, one does not exchange silver coin and produce for silver coin[116], but the Sages permit it.

114 Cf. Note 109. In this interpretation, the House of Hillel require bronze coins to be exchanged into silver coins at the earliest possible moment since bronze coins are more likely to deteriorate.

115 Two drachmas (silver denars), half a tetradrachma. This change is outside of Jerusalem. As R. Abraham ben David explains in his commentary to the Mishnah (*Idiut* 1:9), the House of Hillel think that if everybody brings only silver coin to Jerusalem, the money changers there will raise the price of bronze coins relative to silver.

116 If somebody has three silver

denars and produce in the value of one denar of Second Tithe, he should not exchange them together for a tetradrachma.

(fol. 53c) **הלכה ט**: רִבִּי שִׁמְעוֹן בֶּן לָקִישׁ אָמַר מַה פְּלִיגִין רִבִּי מֵאִיר וְרַבָּנִין בְּפֵירוֹת שֶׁאֵין בָּהֶן כְּדֵי כֶסֶף. אֲבָל בְּפֵירוֹת שֶׁיֵּשׁ בָּהֶן כְּדֵי כֶסֶף אוֹף רַבָּנִין מוֹדֵיי. חֲצִי דֵינָר כֶּסֶף וַחֲצִי דֵינָר פֵּירוֹת מוּתָּר. דֵּינָר כֶּסֶף וְדֵינָר פֵּירוֹת אָסוּר. כָּל־שֶׁכֵּן שְׁנֵי דֵינָרִין כֶּסֶף וּשְׁנֵי דֵינָרֵי פֵּירוֹת שֶׁאָסוּר.

Halakhah 9: Rebbi Simeon ben Laqish said, where do Rebbi Meïr and the rabbis disagree? If the produce is not worth a silver coin. But for produce worth a silver coin also the rabbis agree. Half a denar in money and half a denar's worth of produce is permitted. A denar in money and a denar's worth of produce is forbidden[117], and so much more two denars in money and two denar's worth of produce is forbidden.

117 Since silver coin should not be exchanged for silver coin; cf. Note 107.

(fol. 53a) **משנה ח**: הַפּוֹרֵט סֶלַע שֶׁלְּמַעֲשֵׂר שֵׁנִי בִירוּשָׁלֵם בֵּית שַׁמַּי אוֹמְרִים בְּכָל־הַסֶּלַע מָעוֹת וּבֵית הִלֵּל אוֹמְרִים בְּשֶׁקֶל כֶּסֶף וּבְשֶׁקֶל מָעוֹת. הַדָּנִים לִפְנֵי חֲכָמִים אוֹמְרִים בִּשְׁלֹשָׁה דֵינָרֵי כֶסֶף וּבְדֵינָר מָעוֹת. רִבִּי עֲקִיבָה אוֹמֵר בִּשְׁלֹשָׁה דֵינָרִין כֶּסֶף וּבָרְבִיעִית מָעוֹת/כֶּסֶף.[118] רִבִּי טַרְפוֹן אוֹמֵר אַרְבַּע אַסְפָּרוֹ כֶּסֶף. שַׁמַּי אוֹמֵר יַנִּחֶנָּה בֶּחָנוּת וְיֹאכַל כְּנֶגְדָּהּ.

Mishnah 8: [119]If somebody gives a tetradrachma in Jerusalem for change, the House of Shammai say for the entire tetradrachma small change but the House of Hillel say one *šeqel*[115] in silver coin and one *šeqel* in small coin. Those who argue before the Sages say three denars in silver and one denar in small change. Rebbi Aqiba says, three denars in silver and one denar in small change and silver[120]. Rebbi Ṭarphon says, four *asparo*[121] silver. Shammai says, he shall deposit it with a grocer and eat accordingly[122].

118 In the Leyden ms., the first hand has ברביעית מעות, the corrector writes ברביעית כסף. The Venice print has simply ברביעית . The Rome ms. has ורביעית מעות "and a quarter (denar) in coin." This might be the best reading in the Mishnah.

119 The same Mishnah in *Idiut* 1:10.

120 By Maimonides and the other commentators taken to mean that R. Aqiba requires $3^1/_2$ denars in silver and $^1/_2$ denar in small coin.

121 A small Persian coin, in Pahlevi *asparn*, in Persia the equivalent of a drachma. Its value in popular interpretation in the second century C. E. in Galilee is unknown. According to Maimonides it is a (12th. cent.) Greek coin, ἄσπρον, whose value is unknown to him. {As ἄσπρε, it became the smallest silver coin in early Ottoman money.} According to Arukh, "it is a fifth of a denar and Rav Hai Gaon called it אצברי meaning pieces of metal", perhaps صبارة "pebbles, small pieces of metal". Cf. also ἀσπράτουρα, ἡ, for Latin *asper* "rough, unworn, coin" (Latin gloss *aspratura*), translation of κόλλυβος, ὁ, "small coin; rate of exchange" corresponding to Hebrew חלף "change, exchange" (Liddell & Scott). .

122 And not exchange it at all but establish an account with a dealer of victuals. In this Mishnah, Shammai's rule is the most restrictive and his House's the most lenient.

משנה י: מִי שֶׁהָיוּ מִקְצָת בָּנָיו טְמֵאִין וּמִקְצָת בָּנָיו טְהוֹרִין מַנִּיחַ אֶת הַסֶּלַע וְאוֹמֵר מַה שֶׁהַטְּהוֹרִין שׁוֹתִין סֶלַע זוֹ מְחוּלֶּלֶת עָלָיו. נִמְצְאוּ טְמֵאִים וּטְהוֹרִין שׁוֹתִין מִכַּד אֶחָד.

Mishnah 10: If part of one's children were pure and part impure[123], he puts down the tetradrachma[124] and says, this tetradrachma shall be exchanged for what the pure are drinking. It turns out that the pure and the impure may drink from the same pitcher[125].

123 All are forbidden Second Tithe.

124 Of tithe money.

125 The wine must be pure so that it can become Second Tithe the moment it is poured into the cups of the pure children.

(fol. 53d) **הלכה י:** אֵלּוּ הֵן הַדָּנִין בֶּן עֲזַאי וּבֶן זוֹמָא. אֵלּוּ הֵן הַתַּלְמִידִים חֲנִינָה בֶּן חֲכִינַיי וְרִבִּי אֶלְעָזָר בֶּן מַתְיָה. עֵדָה קְדוֹשָׁה רִבִּי יוֹסֵי בֶּן הַמְשׁוּלָּם וְרִבִּי שִׁמְעוֹן בֶּן מְנַסְיָא.

Halakhah 10: These are the ones who argue: Ben Azai and Ben Zoma. These are the students: Ḥanina ben Hakiniah and Rebbi Eleazar ben Mathia[126]. The holy group, Rebbi Yose ben Hameshullam and Rebbi Simeon ben Menasiah[127].

126 In the Babli, *Sanhedrin* 17b, those who argue before the Sages are Simeon ben Azai, Simeon ben Zoma, Ḥanan the Egyptian, Ḥanina ben Hakinai, and possibly Simeon the Yemenite. According to Rashi, they argue before the Sages, or are called students, because they all died young before they could establish their own schools.

127 They are called holy because they studied all the time they could but worked to sustain their families, *Qohelet rabba* on 9:9.

הלכה יא: מַה טַעֲמָא דְשַׁמַּי שֶׁמָּה יִשְׁכַּח וְיַעֲשֶׂה אוֹתָהּ חוּלִין.

Halakhah 11: What is the reason of Shammai? Maybe he will forget and treat it as profane[128]!

128 If he has both profane and tithe moneys, he will not be able to keep them separate and might spend tithe money on unauthorized expenditures.

The Rome ms. reads וישתה for ויעשׂה, which seems to be a scribal error.

מַה נָן קַייָמִין. אִם בְּאוֹמֵר מִכְּבָר מַשְׁקֶה מְעוּרָב הוּא. וְאִם בְּאוֹמֵר לִכְשֶׁיִּשָּׁתֶה לְמַפְרֵיעַ חוּלֵי שָׁתֵי. אֶלָּא כִּי נָן קַייָמִין בְּאוֹמֵר מִכְּבָר לִכְשֶׁיִּשָּׁתֶה.

Where do we hold? If he[129] said it before, the drink is mixed. If he said it when it will be drunk, before they drank profane. But we hold that he said it before to apply at the time of drinking.

129 The father mentioned in Mishnah 10. He cannot declare part of the wine as Second Tithe before it is poured since then the impure children will also drink from Second Tithe. He cannot declare anything after the wine was consumed. He must declare beforehand that his declaration is conditional and applies only when the wine is poured and drunk.

בִּטְמֵאִין טָמֵא מֵת שֶׁאֵין כְּלִי חֶרֶשׂ מִיטַּמֵּא מֵאֲחוֹרָיו. אֲבָל בִּטְמֵאִין טוּמְאַת זִיבָה שֶׁהַזָּב מִיטַּמֵּא בְּהֶסֵּט לֹא בְדָא. בְּשֶׁאֵין אֶחָד מְעָרֶה אֲבָל אִם יֵשׁ אֶחָד מְעָרֶה אֲפִילוּ טְמֵאִין טוּמְאַת זִיבָה.

If they are impure by the impurity of the dead, for no clay vessel becomes impure from its back[130]. But if they are impure by the impurity of flux[131], since the impure from flux makes impure by carrying, this cannot be the case unless one [other person] pours. But if one [other] pours, even if they are impure by the impurity of flux.

130 What kind of impurity do the impure children have? A clay vessel can make its contents impure only if it became impure inside its cavity, *Lev.* 11:33. In this case, even an impure child may handle the pitcher and pour pure wine for his pure siblings.

131 Somebody impure because of a genital discharge causes impurity to anything he carries, *Lev.* 15:10. In this case, the impure person may not move the pitcher.

לא יאמר אדם פרק שלישי

(fol. 53d) **משנה א:** לֹא יֹאמַר אָדָם לַחֲבֵירוֹ הַעַל אֶת הַפֵּירוֹת הָאֵלּוּ לִירוּשָׁלֵם לְחַלֵּק אֶלָּא אוֹמֵר לוֹ הַעֲלֵם שֶׁנֹּאכְלֵם וְשֶׁנִּשְׁתֵּם בִּירוּשָׁלֵם אֲבָל נוֹתְנִין זֶה לָזֶה מַתְּנַת חִנָּם.

Mishnah 1: A person should not say to another: bring this produce to Jerusalem to distribute[1], but he may say bring it that we shall eat and drink it together, or they may give free gifts to one another.

1 He cannot promise the other person a piece of the Second Tithe as reward for his transporting the tithe since that would be a commercial transaction forbidden by Mishnah 1:1. He can either invite the other to join in the consumption of the tithe or he can give it all to the other as an unconditional gift; the other person will take it up to Jerusalem, and then may give it to the original owner as an unconditional gift.

(fol. 54a) **הלכה א:** לֹא יֹאמַר אָדָם לַחֲבֵירוֹ כול׳. מַה בֵּין הָאוֹמֵר שֶׁנֹּאכְלֵם וּשֶׁנִּשְׁתֵּם לָאוֹמֵר לְחַלֵּק. רִבִּי זְעִירָא בְּשֵׁם רִבִּי יוֹנָתָן מֵהִלְכוֹת שֶׁלָּעִימְעוּם הִיא. תַּמָּן תַּנִּינָן הָאוֹמֵר לַפּוֹעֵל הֵא לָךְ אִיסָּר זֶה וְלַקֵּט לִי יָרָק הַיּוֹם שְׂכָרוֹ מוּתָּר. לַקֵּט לִי בּוֹ יָרָק הַיּוֹם שְׂכָרוֹ אָסוּר. לָקַח מִן הַנַּחְתּוֹם מִכִּכָּר בְּפוּנְדְיוֹן לִכְשֶׁיִּלְקוֹט יַרְקוֹת שָׂדֶה אָבִיא לָךְ מוּתָּר. לָקַח מִמֶּנּוּ סְתָם לֹא יְשַׁלֵּם לוֹ דְמֵי שְׁבִיעִית שֶׁאֵין פּוֹרְעִין חוֹב מִדְּמֵי שְׁבִיעִית. מַה בֵּין הָאוֹמֵר לַקֵּט לִי מַה בֵּין הָאוֹמֵר לַקֵּט לִי בּוֹ. רִבִּי אָבִין בְּשֵׁם רִבִּי יוֹסֵי בֶּן חֲנִינָה מֵהִלְכוֹת שֶׁלָּעִימְעוּם הִיא. תַּמָּן תַּנִּינָן שׁוֹאֵל אָדָם מֵחֲבֵירוֹ כַּדֵּי יַיִן וְכַדֵּי שֶׁמֶן וּבִלְבַד שֶׁלֹּא יֹאמַר לוֹ

הַלְוֵנִי. מַה בֵּין הָאוֹמֵר הַלְוֵנִי מַה בֵּין הָאוֹמֵר הַשְׁאִילֵינִי. רִבִּי זְעִירָא בְּשֵׁם רִבִּי יוֹנָתָן מֵהִלְכוֹת שֶׁלָּעִימְעוּם הִיא.

Halakhah 1: [2]"One should not say to another person," etc. What is the difference between him who says "to distribute" and him who says "that we should eat and drink them?" Rebbi Zeïra in the name of Rebbi Jonathan, this is one of the practices of obfuscation. There, we have stated: If somebody says to a day-laborer: "Here you have an *as* and collect vegetables for me today", these wages are permitted. "For its value collect vegetables for me today", these wages are forbidden. If somebody bought from the baker a loaf in the value of a *dupondius* [and says], when I collect vegetables from the field I shall bring to you, that is permitted. If he took from him silently he should not pay with the proceeds of Sabbatical [produce] since one may not pay a debt with proceeds of the Sabbatical. What is the difference between him who says "collect for me" and him who says "for its value collect for me"? Rebbi Yose in the name of Rebbi Yose ben Ḥanina, this is one of the practices of obfuscation. There, we have stated: "A person may borrow from another pitchers of wine or oil but he should not say: lend me." What is the difference between him who says "let me borrow" and him who says "lend me"? Rebbi Zeïra in the name of Rebbi Jonathan, this is one of the practices of obfuscation.

פִּיתָּן רִבִּי יַעֲקֹב בַּר אָחָא בְּשֵׁם רִבִּי יוֹנָתָן עוֹד הִיא מֵהִלְכוֹת שֶׁלָּעִימְעוּם הִיא. אָמַר רִבִּי יוֹסֵי קַשְׁיָיתָהּ קוֹמֵי רִבִּי יַעֲקֹב בַּר אָחָא מַהוּ מֵהִלְכוֹת שֶׁלָּעִימְעוּם הִיא. כָּךְ אֲנִי אוֹמֵר בְּמָקוֹם שֶׁפַּת יִשְׂרָאֵל מְצוּיָה בְּדִין הוּא שֶׁתְּהֵא פַּת גּוֹיִם אֲסוּרָה וְעִימְעוּם עָלֶיהָ וְהִתִּירוּהָ. אוֹ בְּמָקוֹם שֶׁאֵין פַּת יִשְׂרָאֵל מְצוּיָה בְּדִין הוּא שֶׁתְּהֵא פַּת גּוֹי מוּתֶּרֶת וְעִימְעֲמוּ עָלֶיהָ וַאֲסָרוּהָ. אָמַר רִבִּי מָנָא וְיֵשׁ עִימְעוּם

לְאִיסוּר. וּפַת לֹא כְתַבְשִׁילֵי גוֹיִם הִיא. כָּךְ אֲנִי אוֹמֵר בְּמָקוֹם שֶׁאֵין תַּבְשִׁילֵי יִשְׂרָאֵל מְצוּיִין בְּדִין הוּא שֶׁיְּהֵא תַבְשִׁילֵי גוֹיִם מוּתָּרִין וְעִימְעֲמוּ עֲלֵיהֶן וַאֲסָרוּם. אֶלָּא כֵן הוּא בְּמָקוֹם שֶׁאֵין פַּת יִשְׂרָאֵל מְצוּיָה בְּדִין הוּא שֶׁתְּהֵא פַּת גוֹיִם אֲסוּרָה וְעִימְעֲמוּ עָלֶיהָ וְהִתִּירוּהָ מִפְּנֵי חַיֵּי נֶפֶשׁ. רַבָּנִין דְּקֵיסָרִין בְּשֵׁם רִבִּי יַעֲקֹב בַּר אָחָא כְּדִבְרֵי מִי שֶׁהוּא מַתִּיר וּבִלְבַד מִן הַפַּלְטוֹר. וְלָא עָבְדִינָן[3] כֵּן.

Their bread. Rebbi Jacob bar Aḥa in the name of Rebbi Jonathan: This also belongs to the practices of obfuscation. Rebbi Yose said, I objected before Rebbi Jacob bar Aḥa: Why should it belong to the practices of obfuscation? Do I say that at a place where Jewish bread is available, Gentile bread should be forbidden but they obfuscated about it and permitted it or that at a place where no Jewish bread is available it is logical that Gentile bread should be permitted, but they obfuscated the matter and forbade it. Rebbi Mana said: Does there exist obfuscation for prohibition? Is bread not like Gentile cooking? So we say: At a place where no Jewish cooking is to be found it is logical that Gentile cooking should be permitted, but they obfuscated the matter and forbade it. But so it was: At a place where no Jewish bread is available it is logical that Gentile bread should be forbidden, but they obfuscated the matter and permitted it as a necessity of life. The rabbis of Caesarea in the name of Rebbi Jacob bar Aḥa [hold] with the one who permits, but only from a store. But we do not follow this.

2 This paragraph and the next appear (with a natural change in the order of the first two subjects) in *Ševi'it* 8:4, and are explained there, Notes 51-62.

3 In the Rome ms. עבדין "one does", as in the text in *Ševi'it*.

תַּנֵּי לֹא יֹאמַר אָדָם לַחֲבֵרוֹ בִּירוּשָׁלֵם הַעַל חָבִית זוֹ שֶׁלְּיַיִן מִמָּקוֹם לְמָקוֹם לְחַלֵּק. אָמַר רִבִּי לָעְזָר דְּרִבִּי יוּדָה וּדְרִבִּי נְחֶמְיָה הִיא. מַה נָן קַייָמִין אִם בְּהוּא דְאָמַר לֵיהּ הֵא לָךְ הַב לִי. דִּבְרֵי הַכֹּל אָסוּר. הַב לִי וַאֲנָא יְהַב לָךְ דִּבְרֵי הַכֹּל מוּתָּר. אֶלָּא כִי נָן קַייָמִין בְּהוּא דְאָמַר לֵיהּ הַב לִי בָּרִיא לִי אֲנָא יְהַב לָךְ. רִבִּי יוּדָה וְרִבִּי נְחֶמְיָה אוֹסְרִין שֶׁאֵין יַרְקוֹת שָׂדֶה מְצוּיִין. וַחֲכָמִים מַתִּירִין שֶׁיַּרְקוֹת שָׂדֶה מְצוּיִין.

[4]It was stated: "Rebbi Jehudah and Rebbi Neḥemiah forbid it.[5]" What are we talking about? If about him[6] who says, here you have it, give me [payment], everybody agrees that it is forbidden. If he[7] says, give me and I shall give you, everybody agrees that it is permitted. But it is about one who says, give it to me and it is clear to me [where to find it], I shall bring it to you; Rebbi Jehudah and Rebbi Neḥemiah forbid it because vegetables on the field are rare; but the Sages permit it because vegetables on the field are abundant.

4 This also belongs to *Ševi'it* 8:4; it is there in rudimentary form, cf. *Ševi'it* 8, Note 69.

5 Tosephta *Ševi'it* 6:21: "If somebody buys from the baker a loaf for a *dupondius* [and says] I shall collect vegetables from the field this is permitted [in the Sabbatical]. Rebbis Jehudah and Neḥemiah forbid it."

6 The baker. In this formulation, Sabbatical vegetables would be used for the payment of a debt; this is forbidden.

7 The buyer.

מִשֶּׁהֶעֱלָה אוֹתָן מַהוּ שֶׁיֹּאמַר לוֹ טוֹל חֶלְקָךְ וַאֲנִי חֶלְקִי. מַהוּ שֶׁיֹּאמַר לוֹ טוֹל חָבִית שֶׁלְּיַיִן זוֹ וְאָנוּ אוֹכְלִין חָבִית שֶׁמֶן שֶׁיֵּשׁ לִי שָׁם. אַף בְּמַעֲשֵׂר בְּהֵמָה כֵן. מַעֲשֵׂר שֵׁינִי עַל יְדֵי שֶׁמְּכִירָתוֹ מְיוּחֶדֶת אַתְּ אָמַר מוּתָּר. מַעֲשֵׂר בְּהֵמָה עַל יְדֵי שֶׁאֵין מְכִירָתוֹ מְיוּחֶדֶת הֲרֵי אַתְּ אָמַר אָסוּר. לֵית פְּשִׁיטָא לָךְ דְּהִיא מוּתָּר. מַהוּ שֶׁיֹּאמַר לוֹ הַעַל בְּהֵמָה וְחַיָּה זוֹ וְאָנוּ אוֹכְלִים בְּשַׂר שְׁחוּטָה שֶׁיֵּשׁ לִי שָׁם.

After he transported it, may he say take your part and I shall take mine[8]? May he say to him, take this barrel of wine[9] and we shall eat the barrel of oil that is there. Is it similar with animal tithe[10]? Second Tithe, since it has special conditions for a sale[11] you say is forbidden but animal tithe since it has no conditions for a sale[12] you say is permitted. It should not be clear to you that it is permitted. May he ask him, take and transport this domesticated or wild animal, and we shall eat meat from a ritually slaughtered animal there[13]?

8 If the tithe is already in Jerusalem, is the language which was barred in the Mishnah acceptable?

9 And transport it to Jerusalem.

10 This question refers both to the situation described in the Mishnah and the two questions raised here.

11 While it is forbidden to sell Second Tithe, it may be exchanged for money and then sold.

12 Redemption and any use of animal tithe other than as sacrifice or food of the family of the original rancher is strictly forbidden; *Lev*. 27:32-33, Mishnah 1:2.

13 It is difficult to make sense of the question in the framework of tithes. The best explanation seems to be that of the author of *Sepher Nir* who emends בהמה וחיה into בהמה חיה and reads: "May he ask another person, take and transport this live animal [of tithe], and we shall eat [its] meat [once it is] ritually slaughtered [in the Temple] there?" It is possible to call meat from the sacrifice of animal tithe "slaughtered meat", an expression usually reserved for profane meat, since only the blood of the animal is sprinkled on the altar but no part of it is burned or given to a Cohen.

(fol. 53d) **משנה ב:** אֵין לוֹקְחִין תְּרוּמָה בְּכֶסֶף מַעֲשֵׂר מִפְּנֵי שֶׁהוּא מְמָעֵט בַּאֲכִילָתוֹ. וְרִבִּי שִׁמְעוֹן מַתִּיר. אָמַר לָהֶן רִבִּי שִׁמְעוֹן אִם הֵיקֵל בְּזִבְחֵי שְׁלָמִים

שֶׁהוּא מְבִיאָן לִידֵי פִּיגּוּל וְנוֹתָר וְטָמֵא לֹא יָקֵל בִּתְרוּמָה. אָמְרוּ לוֹ מַה לֹא הֵיקֵל בְּזִבְחֵי שְׁלָמִים שֶׁכֵּן מוּתָּרִין לְזָרִים נָקֵל בִּתְרוּמָה שֶׁהִיא אֲסוּרָה לְזָרִים.

Mishnah 2: One may not buy heave with tithe money because he would restrict its edibility[14], but Rebbi Simeon permits. Rebbi Simeon said to them: If He was lenient with well-being sacrifices[15] when that could bring them to be *piggul*[16], leftover[17], or impure[18], would He not be lenient with heave? They answered him but no, if He was lenient with well-being sacrifices that are permitted to outsiders[19], can we be lenient with heave which is forbidden to outsiders?

14 To Cohanim as explained in the Halakhah.

15 As established in Chapter 1, that meat bought with tithe money should be meat from well-being sacrifices.

16 A sacrifice brought with the intent of eating it at an inappropriate time or inappropriate place, a deadly sin (*Lev.* 7:18, 19:7).

17 Leftovers from sacrificial meat remaining after the allotted time, whose consumption is sinful.

18 The rules of impurity for sacrifices are much more restrictive than those for heave; in turn, the rules of impurity for heave are much more restrictive than those for Second Tithe. However, in the opinion of most tannaïtic authorities, these rules are purely rabbinical. Therefore, it is possible that "or impure" is an intrusion from the standard list of disqualifications of a sacrifice, פיגול נותר וטמא.

19 Non-Cohanim.

(fol. 54a) **הלכה ב**: תַּנֵּי שֶׁלֹּא יָבוֹא לִידֵי פְסוּל. מַהוּ לִידֵי פְסוּל. אָמַר רִבִּי יוֹנָה שֶׁנִּפְסַל בִּטְבוּל יוֹם. לְאוֹכְלוֹ אֵין אַתְּ יָכוֹל שֶׁהוּא טָמֵא דְּבַר תּוֹרָה. אֵין אַתְּ יָכוֹל שֶׁהוּא טָהוֹר דְּבַר תּוֹרָה. הֲוֵי שֶׁלֹּא יָבוֹא לִידֵי פְסוּל.

Halakhah 2: It was stated: "That it should not become unusable[20]." What is "become unusable"? Rebbi Jonah said, it becomes unusable through a *ṭevul-yom*[21]. You cannot eat it, for he is impure by the word of the Torah[22]; you cannot for he is pure by the word of the Torah[23]. That means, that it should not become unusable[24].

20 Heave from Second Tithe can become unusable in a way Second Tithe could not.

21 A previously impure person in the time between his immersion in a ritual bath and sundown; if he touches heave or sacrifices they become unusable, cf. *Terumot* Chapter 5, Note 68.

22 He really is not impure, as stated in the next clause. But since the verse says (*Lev.* 22:7): "at sundown he will be pure", in regard to heave and sacrifices he has a biblical status of not being pure.

23 The requirement of waiting till sundown is spelled out only in connection with heave and sacrifices. In all other circumstances of impurity mentioned in *Lev.*, there is only a requirement of immersion in water.

24 It will be stated in Mishnah 10 that impure Second Tithe in Jerusalem can be redeemed and eaten as impure food. But heave, suspended between purity and impurity, does not qualify for redemption or any other use.

מַהוּ מְמָעֵט בַּאֲכִילָתוֹ תְּרוּמָה אֲסוּרָה לְזָרִים. מַעֲשֵׂר שֵׁינִי מוּתָּר לְזָרִים. תְּרוּמָה אֲסוּרָה בִּטְבוּל יוֹם. מַעֲשֵׂר שֵׁינִי מוּתָּר בִּטְבוּל יוֹם. וּכְשֵׁם שֶׁהוּא מְמָעֵט בַּאֲכִילָתוֹ כָּךְ הוּא מְמָעֵט בַּאֲכִילָתָהּ. תְּרוּמָה מוּתֶּרֶת לְאוֹנֵן מַעֲשֵׂר שֵׁינִי אָסוּר לְאוֹנֵן. תְּרוּמָה אֵינָהּ טְעוּנָה מְחִיצָה. מַעֲשֵׂר שֵׁינִי טָעוּן מְחִיצָה. אַשְׁכָּח תַּנֵּי מִפְּנֵי שֶׁהוּא מְמָעֵט בַּאֲכִילָתוֹ וּבַאֲכִילָתָהּ.

What means "he would restrict its edibility"? Heave is forbidden to outsiders, Second Tithe is permitted to outsiders. Heave is forbidden to a *ṭevul-yom*, Second Tithe is permitted to a *ṭevul-yom*. And just as he would restrict its edibility, so he would restrict her[25] edibility. Heave is permitted to the deep mourner, Second Tithe is forbidden to the deep mourner[26]. Heave does not need an enclosure, Second Tithe needs an enclosure[27]. It was found stated: "Because he would restrict its edibility and her edibility".

25 "She" is heave; to make the point understandable the feminine has to be used also in the English translation.

26 The "deep mourner" is the close relative of a deceased person in the period between death and burial. While the prohibition is not spelled out, it is implied by the text of the declaration to be made at the presentation of Second Tithe in the Temple (*Deut.* 26:14): "I did not eat from it in my deep mourning."

27 Second Tithe must be eaten in the holy precinct; the expression "enclosure" is broad enough to cover the holy precinct of Shiloh and the walls of Jerusalem. {It is questionable whether the extant Turkish walls of Jerusalem would quality, cf. Mishnah *Ševu'ot* 2:2.}

תַּנֵּי אֵין לוֹקְחִין שְׁבִיעִית בְּכֶסֶף מַעֲשֵׂר. אָמַר רִבִּי יוֹסֵי בְּמַחֲלוֹקֶת. אָמַר רִבִּי יוֹנָה דִּבְרֵי הַכֹּל הִיא. אוֹכְלֵי תְרוּמָה זְרִיזִין הֵן. הָתִיב רִבִּי חֲנַנְיָה קוֹמֵי רִבִּי מָנָא וְהָא תַנֵּינָן נִתְעָרְבוּ בִבְכוֹרוֹת רִבִּי שִׁמְעוֹן אוֹמֵר אִם חֲבוּרַת כֹּהֲנִים יֵאָכֵלוּ. וְתַנֵּי עֲלָהּ יֵאָכֵלוּ כְּחָמוּר שֶׁבָּהֶן. אָמַר לוֹ אוֹכְלֵי פְסָחִים בִּשְׁעָתָן זְרִיזִין הֵן כְּאוֹכְלֵי תְרוּמָה. תֵּדַע לָךְ שֶׁהוּא כֵן דְּתַנֵּינָן אֵין צוֹלִין בָּשָׂר בָּצָל וּבֵיצָה אֶלָּא כְדֵי שֶׁיִּצּוֹלוּ. וְתַנֵּינָן מְשַׁלְשְׁלִין אֶת הַפֶּסַח לְתַנּוּר עִם חֲשֵׁיכָה.

[28]It was stated[29]: "One does not buy Sabbatical [produce] with tithe money." Rebbi Yose said, that is a disagreement[30]. Rebbi Jonah said, that is the opinion of everybody. The eaters of heave are careful[31]. Rebbi Ḥananiah objected before Rebbi Mana: Did we not state[32]: "If they[33] were mingled with firstlings, Rebbi Simeon says, if it is a company of Cohanim they should be eaten." And we have stated on that, they should be eaten following the more stringent rules. He said to him, eaters of the Pesaḥ sacrifice in its time are as careful as the eaters of heave[34]. You should know that this is so since we have stated[35]: "One roasts meat, onion, or

egg only that they should be roasted", but we have stated[36]: "One lowers the Pesaḥ sacrifice into the oven at nightfall."

28 The paragraph is also Halakhah 9:7 in *Pesaḥim*, fol. 37a.

29 A similar statement in Tosephta *Ševi'it* 7:1: "One does not exchange Second Tithe [money] on Sabbatical produce, but if it was done it should be eaten following the more stringent rules;" i. e., the rules of tithe and of Sabbatical, whichever happens to be more restrictive in a given situation. In this formulation, the discussion here is superfluous.

30 Between Rebbi Simeon and the rabbis.

31 Rebbi Simeon permits heave from tithe only because Cohanim will be careful to finish all their heave in one sitting; then the problems discussed in the previous paragraph will not arise. But between Second Tithe and the Sabbatical, he will agree with the majority.

32 Mishnah *Pesaḥim* 9:7.

33 Pesaḥ sacrifices. The Sages require that the animals be put out to graze until they develop a defect which makes them unfit for the altar. Then they can be sold and the money used for sacrifices. Rebbi Simeon notes that the ways in which Pesaḥ and firstlings are sacrificed are identical. Therefore, he permits a company of Cohanim, who are entitled to eat firstlings, to make a declaration that they intend to eat the one that should be Pesaḥ as such and the firstling as such, and eat both of them without knowing which is which. This means, he permits the firstling, usually eaten for two days and one night, to be eaten during one night only. He permits reducing the time allowed for consumption.

34 Nothing will be left beyond midnight.

35 Mishnah *Šabbat* 1:14. Since increasing or decreasing the fire on the Sabbath is a capital crime, all food has to be fully cooked by the beginning of the Sabbath.

36 Mishnah *Šabbat* 1:15. If the first day of Passover is a Sabbath, the sacrifice, which must be roasted in the night, is put over the fire just at the start of the Sabbath and we are not afraid that somebody will increase or decrease the fire. This means that prohibitions of "fence" are unnecessary for the Pesaḥ sacrifice.

(fol. 53d) **משנה ג:** מִי שֶׁהָיוּ לוֹ מָעוֹת בִּירוּשָׁלֵם וְצָרִיךְ לָהֶם וְלַחֲבֵירוֹ פֵּירוֹת אוֹמֵר לַחֲבֵירוֹ הֲרֵי הַמָּעוֹת הַלָּלוּ מְחוּלָּלִים עַל פֵּירוֹתֶיךָ נִמְצָא זֶה אוֹכֵל פֵּירוֹתָיו בְּטָהֳרָה. וְהַלָּהּ עוֹשֶׂה צוֹרְכוֹ בְּמָעוֹתָיו. וְלֹא יֹאמַר כֵּן לְעַם הָאָרֶץ אֶלָּא בִדְמַאי.

Mishnah 3: If somebody had coins in Jerusalem and his friend had produce[37], he says to his friend, these coins are exchanged for your produce. That one has to eat his produce in purity but he can use his coins for his needs. But one should not say this to a vulgar unless they were from *demay*[38].

משנה ד: פֵּירוֹת בִּירוּשָׁלֵם וּמָעוֹת בִּמְדִינָה אוֹמֵר הֲרֵי הַמָּעוֹת הָהֵם מְחוּלָּלִין עַל פֵּירוֹת הָאֵלוּ. מָעוֹת בִּירוּשָׁלֵם וּפֵירוֹת בִּמְדִינָה אוֹמֵר הֲרֵי הַמָּעוֹת הָאֵלוּ מְחוּלָּלִין עַל פֵּירוֹת הָהֵם וּבִלְבַד שֶׁיֵּעָלוּ הַפֵּירוֹת וְיֵאָכְלוּ בִירוּשָׁלֵם.

Mishnah 4: Produce in Jerusalem and coins in the countryside, he says these coins are exchanged for that produce. Coins in Jerusalem and produce in the countryside, he says that produce is exchanged for these coins; then the produce must be brought to and eaten in Jerusalem[39].

37 The coins are tithe money, the produce is profane. By the declaration, the produce becomes Second Tithe and has to be eaten in purity but the coins are profane and may be used for business.

38 The vulgar cannot be trusted to eat anything in purity; see the Introduction to *Demay*. Second Tithe from *demay* is only conditional tithe; it is not sure whether it really has to be eaten in purity. Therefore, it may be exchanged for produce of the vulgar.

39 The only exchange prohibited is that of Second Tithe produce in Jerusalem.

(fol. 54a) **הלכה ג:** רִבִּי יְהוֹשֻׁעַ בֶּן לֵוִי אוֹמֵר אֵין מוֹסִיפִין חוֹמֶשׁ אֶלָּא עַל תְּחִילַּת הַהֶקְדֵּישׁוֹת. אָמַר רִבִּי לָעְזָר וְתַנֵּי כֵן אִם בַּבְּהֵמָה טְמֵאָה וּפָדָה בְעֶרְכֶּךָ מַה בְּהֵמָה טְמֵיאָה מְיוּחֶדֶת שֶׁהִיא תְּחִילַּת הֶקְדֵּשׁ מוֹסִיף חוֹמֶשׁ. אַף כָּל־שֶׁהוּא

תְּחִילַּת הֶקְדֵּשׁ מוֹסִיף חוֹמֶשׁ. רִבִּי שְׁמוּאֵל בַּר חִייָה בַּר יְהוּדָה בְּשֵׁם רִבִּי חֲנִינָה שְׁלָמִים שֶׁלְּקָחָן בְּכֶסֶף מַעֲשֵׂר הוּמְמוּ וּפְדָייָן מוֹסִיף חוֹמֶשׁ. רִבִּי שְׁמוּאֵל בַּר חִייָה בַּר יְהוּדָה בְּשֵׁם רִבִּי חֲנִינָה שְׁלָמִים שֶׁלְּקָחָן מִדְּמֵי פֶּסַח הוּמְמוּ וּפְדָייָן מוֹסִיף חוֹמֶשׁ. אָמַר רִבִּי יוּדָן הָדָא צוֹרְכָה וְהָדָא לֹא צוֹרְכָה. אָמַר רִבִּי מָנָא פֶּסַח צוֹרְכָה שְׁלָמִים לֹא צוֹרְכָה. שֶׁלֹּא תֹאמַר הוֹאִיל וּפֶסַח מִשְׁתַּנֶּה לְשֵׁם שְׁלָמִים כְּהֶקְדֵּשׁ אֶחָד הוּא אֵינוֹ מוֹסִיף חוֹמֶשׁ.

Halakhah 3: Rebbi Joshua ben Levi says: One does add a fifth only for the first dedication[40]. Rebbi Eleazar said, this is what has been stated (*Lev.* 27:27): "If it is an impure animal, he shall redeem it for its value[41];" just as an impure animal is special in that it is a first dedication[42] so for anything which is a first dedication he has to add a fifth. Rebbi Samuel bar Ḥiyya bar Jehudah[43] in the name of Rebbi Ḥanina: If well-being sacrificial animals bought with tithe money developed a blemish and one redeemed them, he adds a fifth. Rebbi Samuel bar Ḥiyya bar Jehudah in the name of Rebbi Ḥanina: If well-being sacrificial animals bought with Passover money[44] developed a blemish and one redeemed them, he adds a fifth. Rebbi Yudan said, one is needed and one is not needed. Rebbi Mana said, Passover is needed, well-being sacrifices are not needed[45]. You should not say that since the *Pesaḥ* sacrifice is changed into well-being sacrifices it is like one dedication, he would not add a fifth[46].

40 As a rule, any money paid to the Temple in liquidation of a personal debt is paid at the rate of 125% of the debt, the value plus one fifth from above; cf. *Terumot* Chapter 6, Note 1.

41 The verse continues: "its fifth he shall add to it".

42 An impure animal, i. e., a domesticated animal whose kind is not acceptable as a sacrifice, given to the Temple can only be an original gift, never a substitution.

43 An Amora of the early second generation, student of R. Ḥanina. In the

Babli, he appears as R. Samuel ben Ḥiyya.

44 Since the *pesaḥ* sacrifice must be eaten by subscription, if more animals were bought before the holiday than were actually used, the remainder are automatically used for well-being sacrifices (Babli *Zebaḥim* 7b).

45 Since tithe money is used mainly for well-being sacrifices, this is the original dedication.

46 If the *pesaḥ* was automatically changed into a well-being sacrifice which then developed a blemish, one certainly would have to add a fifth. But in the case here the well-being sacrifice was bought with money from the redemption of a blemished *pesaḥ* sacrifice, one should not say that this is a second dedication exempt from the fifth.

אָמַר רִבִּי הוּנָא טַעֲמָא דְרִבִּי שִׁמְעוֹן דּוּ אָמַר אֵין הַפֶּסַח עוֹשֶׂה תְּמוּרָה וְשׁוֹנֶה. הֵימַר בּוֹ עוֹדֵהוּ פֶּסַח. מֵימַר בּוֹ עוֹדֵהוּ שְׁלָמִים. אָמַר לוֹ רִבִּי מָנָא וְלֹא דְמוּיֵי הֲוָה רִבִּי מְדַמֶּה לָהּ. רִבִּי בָּא רִבִּי חִיָּה בְשֵׁם רִבִּי יוֹחָנָן שְׁלָמִים שֶׁלְּקָחָן בְּכֶסֶף מַעֲשֵׂר הוּמְמוּ וּפְדָיָן עוֹד אֵינָן חוֹזְרִין לִכְמוֹת שֶׁהָיוּ לְהֵיעָשׂוֹת שֵׁנִי. רִבִּי זְעִירָא רִבִּי הִילָא תְּרֵיהוֹן בְּשֵׁם רִבִּי יוֹסֵי בֶּן חֲנִינָה. חַד אָמַר שְׁלָמִים שֶׁלְּקָחָן בְּכֶסֶף מַעֲשֵׂר פָּקְעָה מֵהֶן קְדוּשַּׁת מַעֲשֵׂר. תְּרוּמָה שֶׁלְּקָחָהּ בְּכֶסֶף מַעֲשֵׂר לֹא פָקְעָה מִמֶּנָּה קְדוּשַּׁת מַעֲשֵׂר. מִשְׁנָה שׁוֹבֶרֶת. מֵשִׁיבִין דָּבָר שֶׁפָּקְעָה מִמֶּנּוּ קְדוּשַּׁת מַעֲשֵׂר עַל דָּבָר שֶׁלֹּא פָקְעָה מִמֶּנּוּ קְדוּשַּׁת מַעֲשֵׂר. וְחָרָנָה אָמַר לֵית הָדָא אָמְרָה מֵשִׁיבִין דָּבָר שֶׁפָּקְעָה מִמֶּנּוּ קְדוּשָּׁתוֹ עַל דָּבָר שֶׁלֹּא פָקְעָה מִמֶּנּוּ קְדוּשָּׁתוֹ שֶׁהוּא אָמַר לוֹ (אָבַד עָלַי)[47] טְבִילָה אַחַת.

Rebbi Huna said, the reason of Rebbi Simeon[48] is that he says the *pesaḥ* sacrifice cannot be substituted; if he substituted a second time it still is a *pesaḥ*. If he substituted, it is a well-being sacrifice[49]! Rebbi Mana said to him, did my teacher[50] not compare the following? Rebbi Abba, Rebbi Ḥiyya in the name of Rebbi Joḥanan, if well-being sacrifices bought with tithe money developed a blemish and he redeemed them, it[51] does not return to its original status to make it a second. Rebbi Zeïra, Rebbi Hila, both in the name of Rebbi Yose ben Ḥanina, one said if well-being sacrifices were bought with tithe money, the holiness of tithe broke away from them[52]. If heave was bought with tithe money, the holiness of tithe did not break away from it[53]. The Mishnah breaks[54]: Can you object from a case in which the holiness of tithe broke away to a case in which the holiness of tithe did not break away? The other one said, this does not mean one objects from a case in which its holiness broke away to a case in which its holiness did not break away; he says to him, it is one immersion[55].

47 Words missing in the Rome ms. Since the commentators all feel obliged to emend the words to something else, they are not translated.

48 In Mishnah 2. This paragraph, for which the preceding one was the introduction, still should belong to Halakhah 2,

49 Substitution of sacrifices is forbidden (*Lev.* 27:10); if an animal was substituted, the verse prescribes that "the original and the substitute shall be holy." It is not specified how to proceed if there are degrees of holiness. On this, Mishnah *Pesaḥim* 9:6 states that if the substitution was before noon of the 14th of Nisan, when the *pesaḥ* could not have been slaughtered, the substituted animal cannot be slaughtered since nobody subscribed to it and it cannot become a well-being sacrifice since it is not a leftover *pesaḥ*. Therefore, it remains *pesaḥ* and must be left grazing until it develops a blemish when it must be sold and the money used for a well-being sacrifice. But if the substitution was after noontime of the 14th of Nisan, when the *pesaḥ* is slaughtered, the substitution is a leftover *pesaḥ* and automatically becomes a well-being sacrifice.

50 This word is missing in the Rome ms.

51 The tithe money. As explained after this, the money now is profane and well-being offerings bought with this money are first dedications rather than second.

52 Since in all respects, the rules of well-being sacrifices are more strict than those of tithe.

53 As explained in Mishnah 2.

54 The argument of R. Simeon in the Mishnah is faulty.

55 The original argument of the Sages about the *ṭevul yom* is irrelevant since the important act was the immersion of the person; waiting a short time is not really a restriction.

אֲבָל לֹא יֹאמַר כֵּן לְעַם הָאָרֶץ אֶלָּא בִדְמַיי. הָא בְוַדַּאי לֹא שֶׁאֵין מוֹסְרִין וַדַּאי לְעַם הָאָרֶץ.

"But one should not say this to a vulgar unless they were from *demay*"; therefore, not if it is certain since one does not deliver certain [tithe] to a vulgar[38].

(fol. 53d) **משנה ה:** מָעוֹת נִכְנָסוֹת לִירוּשָׁלֵם וְיוֹצְאוֹת. פֵּירוֹת נִכְנָסִין וְאֵינָן יוֹצְאִין. רַבָּן שִׁמְעוֹן בֶּן גַּמְלִיאֵל אוֹמֵר אַף הַפֵּירוֹת נִכְנָסִין וְיוֹצְאִין.

Mishnah 5: [Tithe] money enters Jerusalem and leaves; [tithe] produce enters but does not leave. Rabban Simeon ben Gamliel says, even produce enters and leaves.

(fol. 54a) **הלכה ד:** כְּדֵי לַעֲשׂוֹת עִיסָּה וְלַחֲזוֹר כְּדֵי לַעֲשׂוֹת עִיסָּה וְלַחֲזוֹר.

Halakhah 4: To make a dough and return it, to make a dough and return it[56].

56 Cf. Chapter 2, Halakhah 4, Note 80.

(fol. 53d) **משנה ו**: פֵּירוֹת שֶׁנִּגְמְרָה מְלַאכְתָּן וְעָבְרוּ בְּתוֹךְ יְרוּשָׁלַיִם. יַחֲזוֹר מַעֲשֵׂר שֵׁינִי שֶׁלָּהֶן וְיֵאָכֵל בִּירוּשָׁלֵם. וּשֶׁלֹּא נִגְמְרָה מְלַאכְתָּן סַלֵּי עֲנָבִים לְגַת. וְסַלֵּי תְאֵינִים לְמוּקְצֶה.

Mishnah 6: If fully processed produce was transported through Jerusalem, its Second Tithe should be brought back and eaten in Jerusalem[57]. If the produce was not fully processed, the baskets of grapes are for the wine-press, and baskets of figs for the *muqẓeh*.

משנה ז: בֵּית שַׁמַּי אוֹמְרִים מַעֲשֵׂר שֵׁינִי יַעֲלֶה וְיֵאָכֵל בִּירוּשָׁלֵם. וּבֵית הִלֵּל אוֹמְרִים יִפָּדֶה וְיֵאָכֵל בְּכָל־מָקוֹם. רַבִּי שִׁמְעוֹן בֶּן יְהוּדָה אוֹמֵר מִשּׁוּם רַבִּי יוֹסֵי לֹא נֶחְלְקוּ בֵית שַׁמַּי וּבֵית הִלֵּל עַל פֵּירוֹת שֶׁלֹּא נִגְמְרָה מְלַאכְתָּן שֶׁיִּיפָּדֶה מַעֲשֵׂר שֵׁינִי שֶׁלָּהֶן וְיֵאָכֵל בְּכָל־מָקוֹם. וְעַל מַה נֶחְלְקוּ עַל פֵּירוֹת שֶׁנִּגְמְרָה מְלַאכְתָּן שֶׁבֵּית שַׁמַּי אוֹמְרִים יַחֲזוֹר מַעֲשֵׂר שֵׁינִי שֶׁלָּהֶן וְיֵאָכֵל בִּירוּשָׁלֵם. וּבֵית הִלֵּל אוֹמְרִים יִיפָּדֶה וְיֵאָכֵל בְּכָל־מָקוֹם. וְהַדְּמַאי נִכְנָס וְיוֹצֵא וְנִפְדֶּה.

Mishnah 7: The House of Shammai say, the Second Tithe should be brought up and eaten in Jerusalem[58]. But the House of Hillel say, it may be redeemed and eaten anywhere. Rebbi Simeon ben Jehudah[59] said in the name of Rebbi Yose, the House of Shammai and the House of Hillel did not disagree about produce which was not fully processed, that its Second Tithe may be redeemed and eaten anywhere. Where did they disagree? About fully processed produce, where the House of Shammay said, its Second Tithe should be brought back and eaten in Jerusalem, but the House of Hillel said, it may be redeemed and eaten anywhere. *Demay* enters, leaves, and may be redeemed[60].

57 Even outside of Jerusalem it cannot be redeemed since tithes should have been separated before it was transported to Jerusalem.

58 In most Mishnah mss. this Mishnah is part of the preceding one

and continues the preceding text. Even though no tithes were due at the time the produce was in Jerusalem, the influence of Jerusalem is so great that even potential tithe cannot be redeemed.

59 A Tanna of the fifth generation, the most important student of R. Simeon bar Iohay. Sometimes, he is called R. Simeon ben Jehudah from Kefar Akko.

60 This statement is part of the statement of R. Simeon ben Jehudah. According to R. Simson and Maimonides in his Code (*Ma'aser Šeni* 2:9), it is agreed that tithe from *demay* produce which passed through Jerusalem may be redeemed anywhere but Second Tithe from *demay* may not be redeemed in Jerusalem. In his Commentary, Maimonides refers to Mishnah *Demay* 1:2 and frees Second Tithe of *demay* from the rules of Mishnaiot 4-7; this contradicts Halakhah 6.

(fol. 54a) **הלכה ה:** רִבִּי שִׁמְעוֹן בֶּן לָקִישׁ אָמַר זֹאת אוֹמֶרֶת יְרוּשָׁלֵם עָשׂוּ אוֹתָהּ כַּחֲצַר בֵּית שְׁמִירָה. מַה חֲצַר בֵּית שְׁמִירָה טוֹבֶלֶת אַף זוֹ טוֹבֶלֶת. אָמַר רִבִּי יוֹנָה בְּדִין הוּא הָיָה אֲפִילוּ בָּתִּים שֶׁשָּׁם לֹא יַטְבִּילוּ שֶׁהֵן שֶׁלְּכָל־יִשְׂרָאֵל. אֶלָּא זֹאת אוֹמֶרֶת יְרוּשָׁלֵם עָשׂוּ אוֹתָהּ כַּחֲצַר בֵּית שְׁמִירָה מַה חֲצַר בֵּית שְׁמִירָה טוֹפֶסֶת אַף זוֹ טוֹפֶסֶת. אָמַר רִבִּי הָדָא אָמְרָה כְּרִי שֶׁהוּא טָבוּל לָרִאשׁוֹן וּלְשֵׁינִי אִם הִתְרוּ בוֹ מִשּׁוּם שֵׁינִי לוֹקֶה. הָתִיב רִבִּי (fol. 54b) מָנָא. וְהָתַנִּינָן בֵּית שַׁמַּי אוֹמְרִים יַחֲזוֹר מַעֲשֵׂר שֵׁינִי שֶׁלָּהֶן וְיֵאָכֵל בִּירוּשָׁלֵם. אִית לָךְ מֵימַר עַל דְּבֵית שַׁמַּי לוֹקֶה. אֶלָּא חוֹמֶר הוּא בְמְחִיצוֹת. אוּף הָכָא חוֹמֶר הוּא בִמְחִיצוֹת.

Halakhah 5: Rebbi Simeon ben Laqish said, this means they made Jerusalem like a secure courtyard[61]. Just as a secure courtyard induces *ṭevel*, this also induces *ṭevel*. Rebbi Jonah said, it would have been logical that even its houses would not induce *ṭevel* since they are property of all of Israel[62]. But it means they made Jerusalem like a secure courtyard. Just as a secure courtyard grabs, so this grabs[63]. Rebbi [Jonah][64] said, this means if a heap was *ṭevel* for First and Second [Tithes] and he was warned

[only] about the Second[65] he is whipped. Rebbi Mana objected: Did we not state, the House of Shammai say, the Second Tithe should return and be eaten in Jerusalem? Can you say that he is whipped according to the House of Shammai[66]? But enclosures are more important; here also, enclosures are more important[67].

61 Cf. *Ma'serot* 2, Notes 100-102.

62 In the Second Commonwealth, every house in Jerusalem was built with a servitude that its owner would host some pilgrims for the holidays. The owners were indemnified by their guests with the skins of their thanksgiving, well-being, and *pesaḥ* sacrifices. Therefore, there always were unrelated people who had the right to enter courtyard or house and, by Mishnah *Ma'serot* 3:5, courtyard and house do not induce *ṭevel.*

63 Just as a secure courtyard "grabs" produce to require heave and tithes only if completely processed, so Jerusalem induces *ṭevel* for all produce only if completely processed. (Explanation of *Sefer Nir.*)

64 Missing in the mss. but required by the context, as noted by R. S. Cirillo.

65 At a moment where there was no obligation of Second Tithe since the First was not yet separated.

66 Since only the House of Shammai recognize an action of Jerusalem on produce which is *ṭevel* for First Tithe, whipping somebody for not giving Second Tithe when he was warned about it before Second Tithe was due is ruling with the House of Shammai against the House of Hillel. This is unacceptable.

67 Cf. Note 27. The rules have nothing to do with Jerusalem being like a secure courtyard and those rules are irrelevant here. It is that for simple sacrifices and tithes the walls of Jerusalem happen to be the enclosure of the holy precinct; since biblical law requires the produce to be brought into the enclosure, its rules must be applied.

רִבִּי זְעִירָא בָּעֵי הִפְרִישׁ עָלָיו שֵׁינִי מִמָּקוֹם אַחֵר נִפְטָר אוֹ כְבָר תְּפָשָׁתוֹ מְחִיצָה. רִבִּי יוֹנָה בָּעֵי עָשָׂה כוּלוֹ שֵׁינִי לְמָקוֹם אֶחָד כּוּלוֹ נִתְפָּשׂ אוֹ לֹא נִתְפָּשׂ אֶלָּא אֶחָד מֵעֲשָׂרָה שֶׁיֵּשׁ בּוֹ.

Rebbi Zeïra asked: If he separated Second Tithe for it from another place, is it freed or was it already grabbed by the enclosure[68]? Rebbi Jonah asked: If he made all of it Second Tithe for some place, is all of it taken or only one tenth of what is in it[69]?

68 If fully processed produce not yet *ṭevel* was transported through Jerusalem, is it possible to give Second Tithe for it from other produce, which then could be redeemed, or, according to the anonymous Tanna of Mishnah 5, must the Second Tithe be given from this batch only?

69 There are two possible interpretations of this question. It is possible that he is of the opinion that, after First Tithe was given, the Second Tithe is already implicitly holy and therefore does not accept any other dedication since its place is not known, or that he holds that one tenth is reserved but the rest may be used for Second tithe at another place.

הָא סַלֵּי תְאֵינִים לַאֲכִילָה וְסַלֵּי עֲנָבִים לַאֲכִילָה גְּמַר מְלָאכָה הֵן.

Therefore, baskets of table figs and baskets of table grapes are end of processing[70].

70 This refers to the Mishnah, that baskets of fruits for further processing are free from the duties of tithes.

הלכה ו: אָמְרוּ בֵּית הִלֵּל לְבֵית שַׁמַּי אֵין אַתֶּם מוֹדִין לָנוּ בְּפֵירוֹת שֶׁלֹּא נִגְמְרָה מְלַאכְתָּן שֶׁיִּפָּדֶה מַעֲשֵׂר שֵׁינִי שֶׁלָּהֶן וְיֵיאָכֵל בְּכָל־מָקוֹם. אַף פֵּירוֹת שֶׁנִּגְמְרָה מְלַאכְתָּן כֵּן. אָמְרוּ לָהֶן בֵּית שַׁמַּי לֹא. אִם אֲמַרְתֶּם בְּפֵירוֹת שֶׁלֹּא נִגְמְרָה מְלַאכְתָּן שֶׁהוּא יָכוֹל לְהַבְקִירָן וּלְפוֹטְרָן מִן הַמַּעְשְׂרוֹת. תֹּאמְרוּ בְּפֵירוֹת שֶׁנִּגְמְרָה מְלַאכְתָּן שֶׁאֵינוֹ יָכוֹל לְהַבְקִירָן וּלְפוֹטְרָן מִן הַמַּעְשְׂרוֹת. אָמְרוּ לָהֶן בֵּית הִלֵּל אַף פֵּירוֹת שֶׁנִּגְמְרָה מְלַאכְתָּן יָכוֹל הוּא לְהַבְקִירָן וּלְפוֹטְרָן מִן הַמַּעְשְׂרוֹת. וְכִי סַלֵּי תְאֵינִים וַעֲנָבִים לַאֲכִילָה שֶׁמָּא אֵין יָכוֹל לְהַבְקִירָן וּלְפוֹטְרָן מִן הַמַּעֲשֵׂר. הָדָא אָמַר סַלֵּי תְאֵינִים לַאֲכִילָה וְסַלֵּי עֲנָבִים לַאֲכִילָה

גְּמַר מְלָאכָה הֵן. אָמְרוּ לָהֶן בֵּית שַׁמַּי לֹא. אִם אֲמַרְתֶּם בְּפֵירוֹת שֶׁלֹּא נִגְמְרָה מְלַאכְתָּן שֶׁהוּא יָכוֹל לְהוֹצִיא עֲלֵיהֶן שֵׁינִי מִמָּקוֹם אַחֵר. תֹּאמְרוּ בְּפֵירוֹת שֶׁנִּגְמְרָה מְלַאכְתָּן שֶׁאֵינוֹ יָכוֹל לְהוֹצִיא עֲלֵיהֶן שֵׁינִי מִמָּקוֹם אַחֵר. הָדָא פְּשִׁטָא שְׁאֵילָה.

Halakhah 6: [71]"The House of Hillel said to the House of Shammai: Do you not agree with us that Second Tithe of not fully processed produce may be redeemed and eaten anywhere? Also with fully processed produce it is the same. The House of Shammai answered them: No. If you say this about not fully processed produce which one may abandon and thereby free from tithes, what can you say about fully processed produce which one cannot abandon and thereby free from tithes[72]. The House of Hillel replied to them: Even fully processed produce one may abandon and thereby free from tithes; are not baskets of eating figs or grapes fully processed?" This proves that baskets of table figs and baskets of table grapes are end of processing[73]. "The House of Shammai answered them: No. If you say this about not fully processed produce for which one may take Second Tithe from another place, what can you say about fully processed produce[74] for which one cannot take Second Tithe from another place!" This answers the question simply[75].

71 The first part of the argument is in Tosephta 2:11, in the name of R. Simeon ben Jehudah in the name of R. Yose. A second argument there (by the House of Hillel) is not in the text here.

72 Mishnah *Peah* 1:6 states that a person can give away any produce free of heave and tithes "until he smoothes the heap." While the Yerushalmi there holds that this statement is from the House of Shammai, R. Simson points out that the House of Hillel will agree if "smoothing the heap" is interpreted as "completing processing in one's courtyard or house." But the situation envisaged in Mishnah 6/7 is that of

produce fully processed but still not under the obligation of heave and tithes because it was processed in the field and, therefore, has to be transported to the house (via Jerusalem). Therefore, the House of Hillel will hold that produce fully processed but still not under the obligation of heave can be given away and then is not under any potential obligation of heave and tithes.

73 An amoraic note in the tannaïtic text to support the statement at the end of the preceding Halakhah.

74 Which passed through Jerusalem. Since heave of the tithe can be taken from another place for other fully processed produce, certainly Second Tithe may be taken for it from another place.

75 R. Zeïra's question in the preceding Halakhah which was not answered there.

אָמַר רִבִּי זְעִירָא רִבִּי חֲנִינָה וְרִבִּי יוֹנָתָן וְרִבִּי יְהוֹשֻׁעַ בֶּן לֵוִי עָלוּ לִירוּשָׁלֵם נִתְמַנֵּי לָהֶן פֵּירוֹת וּבִקְשׁוּ לִפְדּוֹתָן בִּגְבוּלִין. אָמַר לוֹן חַד סַבָּא אֲבוּכוֹן לָא הֲווֹן עָבְדִין כֵּן אֶלָּא מַפְקָ(ר)ן[76] חוּץ לַחוֹמָה וּפוֹדִין אוֹתָן שָׁם. סַבְתָּא הֲוָת סָבְרָה מֵימַר רוֹאִין אֶת הַמְּחִיצוֹת כְּאִילּוּ עוֹלוֹת. וְאִילֵּין רַבָּנִין הֲווֹן סָבְרִין מֵימַר אֵין רוֹאִין אֶת הַמְּחִיצוֹת כְּאִילּוּ עוֹלוֹת. סַבְתָּא הֲוָת סָבְרָה מֵימוֹר כְּרִבִּי לִיעֶזֶר וְאִילֵּין רַבָּנִין הֲווֹן סָבְרִין מֵימוֹר כְּרִבִּי יְהוֹשֻׁעַ. רִבִּי פִּינְחָס מְסָאֵב לָהּ וּפָדֵי לָהּ דּוּ חָשַׁשׁ לְדֵין וּלְדֵין.

Rebbi Zeïra said: Rebbi Ḥanina, Rebbi Jonathan, and Rebbi Joshua ben Levi ascended to Jerusalem. There happened to be produce[77] for them; they wanted to redeem it in the countryside[78]. An old woman[79] told them, your forefathers did not do that but took it outside of the wall and redeemed it there. The old woman thought one considers the enclosures as if they were risen; those rabbis thought one does not consider the enclosures as if they were risen[80]. The old woman held with Rebbi Eliezer; those rabbis held with Rebbi Joshua[81]. Rebbi Phineas made it impure and redeemed it; he took both into consideration.

76 Reading of the Rome ms. מפרן, generally considered a corruption. The Leyden text, Babylonian מפקרן "declared it abandoned", is an obvious scribal error.

77 They obtained *ṭevel* produce and had to dispose of it according to the rules in the absence of a Temple.

78 Take it outside the city as *ṭevel* and redeem the Second Tithe there, which they counld not do in the city.

79 The mss. read here סבא "an old man" but since the discussion is about the opinions of the old woman, one has to read סבתא here also. The Yerushalmi in general approves of women students of Jewish laws and tradition; cf. *Berakhot* 3:4, Note 182.

80 The old woman follows R. Joshua who declares (Mishnah *Idiut* 8:6) that one may eat Second Tithe inside the holy precinct even if the enclosures (the walls of Jerusalem) are destroyed. Therefore, it is enough to take the produce out of the part of the city that in Temple times was walled.

The rabbis hold that ritual Jerusalem is defined only by its walls; therefore, in the absence of walls there is no duty to keep the Second Tithe in Jerusalem but the city is defined by its actual extension, not that of Temple times. The Babli (*Makkot* 20a, in the name of Rabba or Rebbi Abba) chooses a third way, that holy food may be eaten only within actual walls but that the rules regarding "grabbing" are purely rabbinical and, therefore, abolished with the destruction of the sanctified walls.

81 The Yerushalmi holds that if R. Joshua thinks that the holiness of Solomon's Temple is eternal, R. Eliezer must think that it terminated with the destruction of the Temple. The Babli (*Sebaḥim* 107b) tentatively disagrees, but then must hold that the enclosure of the Temple domain is merely cosmetic, a position not accepted in other parts of the Babli. The relationship of the positions of RR. Joshua and Eliezer to the problem at hand is tenuous since permanent sanctity is asserted only for the Temple domain on the Temple Mount, not for the rest of Jerusalem. See also the discussion of this problem in the author's *Seder Olam* (Northvale NJ, 1998), pp. 257-259.

The text here is difficult; as R. M. Margalit points out it would seem that the old woman follows R. Joshua and the rabbis R. Eliezer. But that would put the rabbis on the wrong side of the law, a most unlikely situation. One has to conclude that the reference to a disagreement between RR. Joshua and Eliezer is to some *baraita* unknown to us.

רִבִּי יַעֲקֹב בַּר אִידִי וְרִבִּי יְהוֹשֻׁעַ בֶּן לֵוִי הֲלָכָה כְדִבְרֵי הַתַּלְמִיד. אָמַר רִבִּי זְעִירָא וּבִלְבַד בְּפֵירוֹת שֶׁהֵן טְבוּלִין לִדְמַיי. הָא דְּמַי עַצְמוֹ כְּבָר תְּפָשָׂתוֹ מְחִיצָה.

Rebbi Jacob bar Idi and Rebbi Joshua ben Levi[82], practice follows the student[83]. Rebbi Zeïra said, only for produce which is *ṭevel* as *demai*. But [tithe of] *demai* itself is already grabbed by the enclosure.

82 Probably one should read רבי יהושע instead of ורבי יהושע since the student, R. Jaacob bar Idi, can be a tradent of the teachings but not the equal of his teacher.

83 R. Simeon ben Jehudah in his statement about *demay*, Note 60.

(fol. 53d) **משנה ח**: אִילָן שֶׁהוּא עוֹמֵד בִּפְנִים וְנוֹטֶה לַחוּץ אוֹ עוֹמֵד לַחוּץ וְנוֹטֶה לִפְנִים מִכְּנֶגֶד הַחוֹמָה וְלִפְנִים כְּלִפְנִים. מִכְּנֶגֶד הַחוֹמָה וְלַחוּץ כְּלַחוּץ. בָּתֵּי הַבַּדִּים שֶׁפִּתְחֵיהֶן לִפְנִים וַחֲלָלָן לַחוּץ אוֹ שֶׁפִּתְחֵיהֶן לַחוּץ וַחֲלָלָן לִפְנִים בֵּית שַׁמַּאי אוֹמְרִים הַכֹּל כְּלִפְנִים וּבֵית הִלֵּל אוֹמְרִים כְּנֶגֶד הַחוֹמָה וְלִפְנִים כְּלִפְנִים מִכְּנֶגֶד הַחוֹמָה וְלַחוּץ לַחוּץ.

Mishnah 8: A tree which stands inside[83] and [its crown] extends outside, or stands outside and extends inside, what is above the wall and inside is like inside, above the wall and outside is like outside. Oil presses whose entrances are inside but their space extends to the outside or whose entrances are outside but their space extends to the inside, the House of Shammai say it is all counted as inside, but the House of Hillel say what is under the wall and inside is like inside, under the wall and outside is like outside[84].

משנה ט: הַלְּשָׁכוֹת בְּנוּיוֹת בַּקּוֹדֶשׁ וּפְתוּחוֹת לַחוֹל תּוֹכָן חוֹל וְגַגּוֹתֵיהֶן קוֹדֶשׁ בְּנוּיוֹת בַּחוֹל וּפְתוּחוֹת לַקּוֹדֶשׁ תּוֹכָן קוֹדֶשׁ וְגַגּוֹתֵיהֶן חוֹל. בְּנוּיוֹת בַּקּוֹדֶשׁ וּבַחוֹל וּפְתוּחוֹת לַקּוֹדֶשׁ וְלַחוֹל תּוֹכָן וְגַגּוֹתֵיהֶן כְּנֶגֶד הַקּוֹדֶשׁ וְלַקּוֹדֶשׁ קוֹדֶשׁ. כְּנֶגֶד הַחוֹל וְלַחוֹל חוֹל.

Mishnah 9: If chambers are built in the holy precinct and open to the profane domain, their insides are profane but their roofs holy[85]. If they are built in the profane domain but open to the holy precinct, their insides are holy but their roofs profane. If they are built in the holy and the profane and open both to the holy and the profane[86], their insides and their roofs, over the holy and in direction of the holy they are holy[87], over the profane and in direction of the profane they are profane.

83 In Jerusalem. Inside, one may not redeem Second Tithe but may eat it; outside, one may redeem Second Tithe but may not eat it. Cf. *Ma'serot* Chapter 3, Notes 171-174.

84 In all these rules, the wall appears both outside and inside. In Mishnah *Pesaḥim* 7:10 it is stated that the wall is counted as inside. Therefore, the interpretation here should be: From the wall to the outside it is outside. However, in the Tosephta (*Ma'aser Šeni* 2:15) the status of the wall is a matter of controversy.

85 In the profane domain, Second Tithe and simple sacrifices (family sacrifices) may be consumed. In the holy part, most-holy sacrifices may be consumed and simple sacrifices be slaughtered. (Most-holy sacrifices must be slaughtered inside the precinct, North of the altar.)

86 The chamber of the fireplace, where the Cohanim kept watch during the night and from which a Cohen who became impure could first descend to a subterranean *miqweh* and then leave directly into the profane domain as a *ṭevul yom*.

87 The border between holy and

profane domain was indicated by a mosaic strip. This strip takes the function of the wall which belongs to both domains.

(fol. 54b) **הלכה ז:** אָמַר רִבִּי לָעְזָר לַחוּמְרִין. רִבִּי יוֹסֵי בָּעֵי מַהוּ לַחוּמְרִין. אָמַר רִבִּי יוֹנָה הָדָא דְתַנִּינָן תַּמָּן בָּתֵּי הַבַּדִּין שֶׁפִּתְחֵיהֶן לִפְנִים וַחֲלָלָן לַחוּץ מִכְּנֶגֶד הַחוֹמָה וְלִפְנִים כִּלְפְנִים. מִכְּנֶגֶד הַחוֹמָה וְלַחוּץ כִּלְחוּץ. אֵין שׁוֹחֲטִין שָׁם קֳדָשִׁים קַלִּין כִּלְפְנִים וְאֵין פּוֹדִין שָׁם מַעֲשֵׂר שֵׁינִי כִּלְחוּץ. אֵין פִּתְחֵיהֶן לַחוּץ וַחֲלָלָן לִפְנִים מִכְּנֶגֶד הַחוֹמָה וְלַחוּץ כִּלְחוּץ. מִכְּנֶגֶד הַחוֹמָה וְלִפְנִים אֵין שׁוֹחֲטִין שָׁם קֳדָשִׁים קַלִּין כִּלְפְנִים וְלֹא פוֹדִין שָׁם מַעֲשֵׂר שֵׁינִי כִּלְחוּץ.

Halakhah 7: Rebbi Eleazar said, for restriction. Rebbi Yose asked, what means "for restriction"? Rebbi Jonah said, that is what we have stated there[88]: "Oil presses whose doors are open inside but which extend to the outside, under the wall and inside is like inside, under the wall and outside is like outside. One does not slaughter there simple sacrifices as one would inside and one does not redeem Second Tithe as outside. If their doors are open outside but extend to the inside, under the wall and outside is like outside, under the wall and inside, one does not slaughter there simple sacrifices as one would inside and one does not redeem Second Tithe as outside."

88 The text here is hopelessly garbled since oil presses (Mishnah 8) are in the city, not on the Temple Mount but sacrifices are slaughtered in the Temple precinct (Mishnah 9). As a minimum one would have to replace "slaughter" by "eat" to adapt the text to the circumstances of the city of Jerusalem.

A consistent text is in Tosephta 2:12: "Oil presses whose entrances are inside [the city] but their space extends to the outside or whose entrances are outside but their space extends to the inside, the House of Shammai say one does not redeem there Second Tithe as if it were inside and not does not eat simple sacrifices as if it were outside. But the

House of Hillel say what is under the wall and inside is like inside, under the wall and outside is like outside. Rebbi Yose said, this is the teaching of Rebbi Aqiba. The earlier teaching: The House of Shammai say one does not redeem there Second Tithe as if it were inside nor does one eat simple sacrifices as if it were outside. But the House of Hillel say, they are similar to chambers; those open to the inside are like inside, those open to the outside like outside."

It is impossible to correct the text by the Tosephta (except for "eat" instead of "slaughter") since the statement of R. Yose is quoted in a different context at the end of the Halakhah. Also, to extend the prohibition both of eating sacrifices and of redeeming tithe to the entire space would do violence to the text; in that case there would be no difference between being open to the inside or the outside. One must conclude that the place where one restricts to exclude the activities both outside and inside the walls is the place under the wall itself.

Maimonides (*Ma'aser Šeni* 2:16) formulates as follows: "Houses by the wall which open inside the wall but extend outside, under the wall and inside it is like inside the city in all respects, but under the wall and outside one does neither eat nor redeem as a restriction. If they were built inside but open to the outside, from the wall to the outside one redeems, to the inside one neither redeems nor eats as a restriction. The thickness of the wall and the loopholes are like the inside." The last sentence is Mishnah *Pesaḥim* 7:10.

אָמַר רִבִּי יַעֲקֹב בַּר אָחָא כֵּינִי מַתְנִיתָא תּוֹכָן קוֹדֶשׁ וְגַגּוֹתֵיהֶן (חוֹל)[89] מִכְּנֶגֶד הַקּוֹדֶשׁ וְלַקּוֹדֶשׁ כְּלְקוֹדֶשׁ מִכְּנֶגֶד הַחוֹל וְלַחוֹל חוֹל. בְּנוּיוֹת בַּקּוֹדֶשׁ וּפְתוּחוֹת לַקּוֹדֶשׁ וְלַחוֹל תּוֹכָן קוֹדֶשׁ. בְּנוּיוֹת בַּחוֹל וּפְתוּחוֹת לַקּוֹדֶשׁ וְלַחוֹל תּוֹכָן חוֹל. הֵן דְּאַתְּ אָמַר תּוֹכָן קוֹדֶשׁ אוֹכְלִין שָׁם קָדְשֵׁי קֳדָשִׁים וְשׁוֹחֲטִין שָׁם קֳדָשִׁים קַלִּין וְטָמֵא שֶׁנִּכְנַס שָׁם חַיָּיב.

Rebbi Jacob bar Aḥa said, so is the Mishnah[90]: "Their insides are holy and their roofs (are profane)[89], over the holy and in the direction of the holy they are holy, over the profane and in direction of the profane they are profane." "Built in the holy but open to the holy and the profane, the inside is holy. Built in the profane but open to the holy and the profane, the inside is profane. There, where you say the inside is holy one eats most holy sacrifices, slaughters simple holy sacrifices and the impure who enters is guilty."

89 The word is missing in the Rome ms.; in the Leyden ms. it is added by a second hand. Most probably it should be disregarded; as it was by R. S. Cirillo.

90 He adds one word, "is holy", to the last clause in the Mishnah. This is all that is quoted from the Mishnah.

91 Tosephta 2:15 a similar text. The last sentence looks like an amoraic gloss but a similar sentence, without the Aramaic introduction, is in Tosephta 2:14. J. N. Epstein (מבוא לנוסח המשנה[2] pp. 449-450) speculates that R. Jacob bar Aḥa quotes here a Babylonian *baraita.*

רַב יְהוּדָה בְּשֵׁם רַב אֵין לוֹקִין אֶלָּא עַל אוֹרֶךְ מֵאָה וּשְׁמוֹנִים וְשֶׁבַע עַל רוֹחַב מֵאָה וּשְׁלֹשִׁים וְחָמֵשׁ. וְהָתַנֵּי לִשְׁכָּה שֶׁהִיא בְנוּיָה בְּשִׁיווּי חוֹמַת הָעֲזָרָה אוֹכְלִין שָׁם קָדְשֵׁי קֳדָשִׁים וְשׁוֹחֲטִין שָׁם קֳדָשִׁים קַלִּין וְטָמֵא שֶׁנִּכְנַס לְשָׁם פָּטוּר. תִּיפְתָּר כְּהָדָא תַנַּיָּא דְתַנֵּי אָמַר רִבִּי יוֹסֵי זוֹ מִשְׁנַת רִבִּי עֲקִיבָה. אֲבָל דִּבְרֵי חֲכָמִים הִבְדִּילוּ הַכָּל־הַלְּשָׁכוֹת וְכָל־הַלְּשָׁכוֹת הוֹלְכִין אַחַר פִּתְחֵיהֶן.

Rav Jehudah in the name of Rav: One whips only for 187 length by 135 width[92]. But did we not state: In a chamber built flush with the wall of the Temple courtyard one eats most holy sacrifices, slaughters simple holy sacrifices, but an impure person who enters there cannot be punished[93]. Explain it following the Tanna who stated[94]: "Rebbi Yose said, these are the words of Rebbi Aqiba. But the Sages say, they classified the chambers and all chambers follow their openings."

92 The inner measurements in cubits of the enclosure of the Temple as stated in Mishnah *Middot*. In the Babli, *Zebahim* 55b, the statement of Rav Jehudah is in the name of his teacher Samuel.

93 This supports Rav but contradicts the *baraita* quoted in the preceding paragraph.

94 Cf. Tosephta 2:12, Note 88. The preceding *baraita* follows the Sages, the one quoted here R. Aqiba.

(fol. 53d) **משנה י**: מַעֲשֵׂר שֵׁנִי שֶׁנִּכְנַס לִירוּשָׁלֵם וְנִיטְמָא בֵּין שֶׁנִּיטְמָא בְּאַב הַטּוּמְאָה בֵּין שֶׁנִּיטְמָא בְּוְלַד הַטּוּמְאָה בֵּין בִּפְנִים בֵּין בַּחוּץ בֵּית שַׁמַּי אוֹמְרִים הַכֹּל יִפָּדֶה וְיֵאָכֵל בִּפְנִים. חוּץ מִשֶּׁנִּיטְמָא בְּאַב הַטּוּמְאָה בַּחוּץ. וּבֵית הִלֵּל אוֹמְרִים הַכֹּל יִפָּדֶה וְיֵיאָכֵל בַּחוּץ חוּץ מִשֶּׁנִּיטְמָא בְּוְלַד הַטּוּמְאָה בִּפְנִים.

Mishnah 10: Second Tithe which entered Jerusalem and became impure, whether from original impurity[95] or from derivative impurity[96], inside [the city] or outside, the House of Shammai say, all should be redeemed and eaten inside except what became impure from original impurity outside[97]. But the House of Hillel say, all should be redeemed and may be eaten outside except what became impure from derivative impurity inside[98].

95 One of the biblical sources of impurity such as a dead person, a person suffering from a genital discharge, a cadaver, etc.

96 By touching something impure in original impurity. Most, but not all, derivative impurities are rabbinic; cf. *Demay* 2, Notes 136-137.

97 Since by biblical law it could not be eaten when brought into Jerusalem, the enclosure never "grabbed" it (Note 63).

98 If its impurity is rabbinic in character, the biblical law will not allow it to be taken out of Jerusalem.

(fol. 54b) **הלכה ח:** כְּתִיב כִּי לֹא תוּכַל שְׂאֵיתוֹ מָה נָן קַייָמִין אִם בְּרִיחוּק מָקוֹם כְּבָר כְּתִיב כִּי יִרְבֶּה מִמְּךָ. אִם בְּקֵירוּב מָקוֹם כְּבָר כְּתִיב וְנָתַתָּ הַכֶּסֶף. אֶלָּא מַהוּ לֹא תוּכַל שְׂאֵתוֹ לֹא תוּכַל לְפָדוּתוֹ וּכְתִיב וְנָתַתָּ הַכֶּסֶף.

Halakhah 8: It is written (*Deut*. 14:24): "For you will be unable to take it." Where do we hold? If far from the Place[99], it already is written: "If [the distance] will be too much for you.[100]" If near the Place, it already is written (*Deut*. 14:26): "You shall spend the money[101]." What does it mean "for you will be unable to take it"? You cannot redeem it[102], and it is written: "You shall spend the money."

99 Shiloh or Jerusalem.

100 "(24) But if the distance is too much for you, for you will be unable to take it, for the Place, chosen by the Eternal, your God, to put His Name there, is too far from you, because the Eternal blessed you - (25) then turn it *into money*, bundle that money in your hand and go to the Place which will be chosen by the Eternal, your God. (26) Then *spend the money* for all you desire . . ."

The *Sifry Deut*. (107) explains that while *the distance* is spatial distance, *too far* is temporal distance. In any case, the clause *unable to carry* is redundant.

101 At the Place one is restricted to spending the money; the exchange of tithe for money is restricted to places far away by v. 25.

102 Since the verse cannot deal with a situation far from the Place it must be at the Place. The only case in which one cannot take tithe brought to the Place is if the tithe became impure and, therefore, inedible as tithe. Then one has to spend the [redemption] money.

The Babli (*Pesaḥim* 36b, *Baba Meẓi'a* 53a, *Makkot* 19b, *Sanhedrin* 112b) has a weird derivation of the same result from the same verse. The Babylonian identification of שׂאת as "food" contrasts with the Yerushalmi's identification (*Ḥagigah* 1:3, fol. 76b) as "gift".

תַּנֵּי בַּר קַפָּרָא אָמַר אַב הַטּוּמְאָה דְּבַר תּוֹרָה וְוֹלַד הַטּוּמְאָה מִדִּבְרֵיהֶן. רִבִּי יוֹחָנָן אָמַר בֵּין זֶה בֵּין זֶה דְּבַר תּוֹרָה. וְקַשְׁיָא דְּבֵית שַׁמַּי עַל דְּרִבִּי יוֹחָנָן דְּבֵית שַׁמַּי אוֹמְרִים הַכֹּל יִיפָּדֶה וְיֵאָכֵל בִּפְנִים חוּץ מִשֶּׁנִּטְמָא בְּאַב הַטּוּמְאָה בַּחוּץ. מַה בֵּין וְוֹלַד הַטּוּמְאָה בַּחוּץ וּבֵין אַב הַטּוּמְאָה בַּחוּץ זֶה וָזֶה דְּבַר תּוֹרָה הוּא. וַאֲפִילוּ עַל דִּבְרֵי בֵית הִלֵּל לֹא מַקְשִׁיָא. דְּבֵית הִלֵּל אָמְרִין הַכֹּל יִיפָּדֶה וְיֵאָכֵל בַּחוּץ חוּץ מִשֶּׁנִּיטְמָא בְּוֹלַד הַטּוּמְאָה בִּפְנִים. מָה בֵּין וְוֹלַד הַטּוּמְאָה בִּפְנִים מָה בֵּין אַב הַטּוּמְאָה בִּפְנִים זֶה וָזֶה לֹא דְּבַר תּוֹרָה הוּא. לֹא הֲוֵי בָהּ רַבָּנִין אֶלָּא עַל דְּבַר קַפָּרָא.

It was stated: Bar Qappara said, "original impurity" is biblical, "derivative impurity" rabbinic[103]. Rebbi Joḥanan said, in both cases it is biblical. The House of Shammai are difficult for Rebbi Joḥanan: "The House of Shammai say, all should be redeemed and eaten inside except what became impure from original impurity outside;" what is the difference between original impurity outside and derivative impurity outside; are not both biblical? Are the words of the House of Hillel not also difficult? "The House of Hillel say, all should be redeemed and may be eaten outside except what became impure from derivative impurity inside"; what is the difference between original impurity inside and derivative impurity inside; are not both biblical? The rabbis discuss only that from Bar Qappara.

103 In the interpretation of this Mishnah.

וְקַשְׁיָא דְּבַר קַפָּרָא עַל דְּבֵית שַׁמַּי דְּבֵית שַׁמַּי אוֹמְרִים הַכֹּל יִיפָּדֶה וְיֵאָכֵל בִּפְנִים חוּץ מִשֶּׁנִּיטְמָא בְּאַב הַטּוּמְאָה בַּחוּץ. מָה בֵּין אַב הַטּוּמְאָה לְוְוֹלַד הַטּוּמְאָה בֵּין בַּחוּץ בֵּין בִּפְנִים. זֶה וָזֶה לֹא דְּבַר תּוֹרָה הוּא. שֶׁלֹּא אוֹמְרִים אֵינוֹ מַעֲשֵׂר שֵׁינִי שֶׁנִּכְנַס וְיוֹצֵא. מֵעַתָּה לֹא יִיפָּדֶה שֶׁלֹּא יְהוּ אוֹמְרִים אֵינוֹ מַעֲשֵׂר שֵׁינִי נִכְנַס

לִירוּשָׁלֵם וְנִפְדָּה. בְּשָׁעָה שֶׁנִּיטְמְאוּ בִּפְנִים מְחִיצָה תוֹפַסְתּוֹ. בְּשָׁעָה שֶׁנִּיטְמָא בַּחוּץ אֵין מְחִיצָה תוֹפַסְתּוֹ. וַאֲפִילוּ עַל דְּבֵית הִלֵּל לֵית הוּא מַקְשִׁייָא. דְּבֵית הִלֵּל אוֹמְרִים הַכֹּל יִיפָּדֶה וְיֵאָכֵל בַּחוּץ חוּץ מִשֶּׁנִּיטְמָא בִּוְלַד הַטּוּמְאָה בִּפְנִים. מַה בֵּין וְלַד הַטּוּמְאָה בֵּין בַּחוּץ בֵּין בִּפְנִים זֶה וְזֶה לֹא מִדִּבְרֵיהֶן הוּא. כְּשֶׁהִכְנִיסָן עַל מְנָת דְּלֹא תִתְפָּשֶׂנּוּ מְחִיצָה.

It is difficult, according to Bar Qappara for the House of Shammai, since "the House of Shammai say, all should be redeemed and eaten inside except what became impure from original impurity outside;" what is the difference between derivative impurity and original impurity[104]; what is the difference between outside and inside, are not both biblical? That one should not say, is that not Second Tithe which enters and leaves? If it is so, it should not be redeemed, so that one should not say, is that not Second Tithe which enters Jerusalem and is redeemed[105]? If it became impure inside, the enclosure had grabbed it; if it became impure outside, the enclosure never grabbed it[106]. And is it not difficult even for the House of Hillel? For "the House of Hillel say, all should be redeemed and may be eaten outside except what became impure from derivative impurity inside"; what is the difference for derivative impurity between outside and inside; are not both rabbinic? When he brought it inside it was on condition it should not be "grabbed" by the enclosure[107].

104 This clause should be deleted, it is copied from the previous text and makes no sense here. The Rome text, הַכֹּל יִפָּדֶה וְיֵאָכֵל בִּפְנִים בֵּין מִשֶּׁנִּיטְמָא בְּאַב הַטּוּמְאָה בַּחוּץ בֵּין בְּאַב הַטּוּמְאָה is not better.

105 Which also is forbidden for pure tithe.

106 Since it never could be eaten inside the sanctified area.

107 Since *actually* it never could be eaten inside the sanctified area.

אָמַר רִבִּי זְעִירָה הָדָא אֶמְרָה מַעֲשֵׂר שֵׁינִי טָהוֹר שֶׁהִכְנִיסוֹ עַל מְנָת שֶׁלֹּא תִתְפְּשֶׂנּוּ מְחִיצָה אֵין מְחִיצָה תוֹפַסְתּוֹ. רִבִּי יוֹנָה בָּעֵי טָהוֹר דְּבַר תּוֹרָה וְאַתְּ אָמַר הָכֵין. אֶלָּא כֵּנִי עָבַר וּפָדָה פָּדוּי.

Rebbi Zeïra said, this means[108] pure Second Tithe which he brought inside on condition that the enclosure not "grab" it, the enclosure does not "grab" it. Rebbi Jonah asked, it is pure and you say so? But it must be: If he transgressed and redeemed it, it is redeemed[109].

108 Since rabbinically impure tithe is pure by biblical standards, it seems that a mental reservation of the farmer can override the biblical decree that tithe brought into the holy enclosure has to be consumed as such.

109 If he made a mental reservation and then redeemed the tithe in Jerusalem, the transaction is valid since the prohibition of redemption is a rabbinic interpretation of the biblical verse. This supports the position of Maimonides in his *Sefer Hammizwot* that rules derived from biblical verses by rabbinic interpretation are rabbinic in character.

רִבִּי יַעֲקֹב דְּרוֹמַיָּא בָּעָא קוֹמֵי רִבִּי יוֹסֵי נִטְמָא חוּץ לִירוּשָׁלֵם וְנִכְנַס לֹא יֵצֵא שֶׁלֹּא יְהוּ אוֹמְרִין רָאִינוּ מַעֲשֵׂר שֵׁינִי נִכְנַס לִירוּשָׁלֵם וְיוֹצֵא. קוֹל יוֹצֵא לְיוֹצֵא. וְאֵין קוֹל יוֹצֵא לְפָדוּי.

Rebbi Jacob the Southerner asked before Rebbi Yose: If it became impure outside of Jerusalem and was brought inside, it should not leave lest one say, we saw Second Tithe entering Jerusalem and leaving[110]? Leaving is publicized, redemption is not publicized.

110 This is a question about the House of Shammai's position which in this case requires the tithe to be removed from Jerusalem. The answer is that this case is so rare that it would be dealt with in a rabbinic court in public whereas redemption of tithe which became impure is frequent, done in private, and unremarkable.

רִבִּי חִייָה בַּר אָדָא בָּעָא קוֹמֵי רִבִּי מָנָא נִטְמָא בִּוְלַד הַטּוּמְאָה וּפְדָיוֹ וְחָזַר וְנִיטְמָא בְּאַב הַטּוּמְאָה. נֹאמַר אִם הָיוּ הַמָּעוֹת הָרִאשׁוֹנוֹת קַייָמוֹת מְחַלֵּל עֲלֵיהֶן וְאִם לָאו אֵינוֹ מְחַלֵּל עֲלֵיהֶן. וְאֵין לוֹקִין לֹא עַל הַמָּעוֹת הָרִאשׁוֹנוֹת וְלֹא עַל הַמָּעוֹת הַשְּׁנִיּוֹת. רִבִּי יוֹנָה בָּעֵי אַף לְלוֹקֵחַ כֵּן. אָמַר רִבִּי מָנָא מְחִיצָה טוֹפֶסֶת וְהַלּוֹקֵחַ טוֹפֵס. כְּשֵׁם שֶׁנֶּאֱמַר בִּמְחִיצָתָהּ כָּךְ נֶאֱמַר בְּלוֹקֵחַ.

Rebbi Ḥiyya bar Ada inquired before Rebbi Mana: If it became impure by derivative impurity and he redeemed it[111], then it became impure in original impurity[112]; do we say that if the original money is still there he redeems with it, otherwise he cannot redeem with it, and one is whipped neither for the first nor the second monies[113]? Rebbi Jonah asked, is it the same for him who buys[114]? Rebbi Mana said, the enclosure "grabs" and the buyer "grabs". What was said for the enclosure was said for the buyer.

111 As required. However, since the tithe is still pure by biblical standards, the redemption is *de facto*, not *de jure*.

112 Now it has to be redeemed by biblical decree. If the original money is still completely in the farmer's hands, he now turns the rabbinic redemption into a biblical one.

113 If he misappropriates the monies and spends them outside of Jerusalem, as described in Mishnah 1:5, he cannot be prosecuted if the produce remains rabbinically impure since the redemption is not biblical; nor can he be prosecuted if the produce becomes biblically impure and is redeemed by new money because the second redemption is a formality only since the produce was unusable as tithe.

114 Cf. Mishnaiot 1:5,6. There, it is spelled out that produce bought with tithe money outside of Jerusalem cannot be redeemed. Its status is at least as restricted as that of original tithe brought into the enclosure of Jerusalem.

משנה יא: הַלּוֹקֵחַ בְּכֶסֶף מַעֲשֵׂר שֶׁנִּיטְמָא יִיפָּדֶה. רִבִּי יְהוּדָה אוֹמֵר (fol. 53d) יִיקָּבֵר. אָמְרוּ לוֹ לְרִבִּי יְהוּדָה מָה אִם מַעֲשֵׂר שֵׁנִי עַצְמוֹ שֶׁנִּטְמָא הֲרֵי זֶה נִפְדֶּה. הַלּוֹקֵחַ בְּכֶסֶף מַעֲשֵׂר שֶׁנִּיטְמָא אֵינוֹ דִין שֶׁיִּיפָּדֶה. אָמַר לָהֶן לֹא אִם אֲמַרְתֶּם בְּמַעֲשֵׂר שֵׁינִי עַצְמוֹ שֶׁכֵּן הוּא נִפְדֶּה בְּטָהוֹר וּבְרִחוּק מָקוֹם תֹּאמְרוּ בְּלָקוּחַ בְּכֶסֶף מַעֲשֵׂר שֶׁאֵינוֹ נִפְדֶּה בְּטָהוֹר וּבְרִיחוּק מָקוֹם.

Mishnah 11: If what was bought with tithe money became impure, it should be redeemed. Rebbi Jehudah says, it should be buried[115]. They said to Rebbi Jehudah, if original Second Tithe which became impure is redeemed, what was bought with tithe money and became impure certainly should be redeemed. He said to them, no! If you said about original Second Tithe, which can be redeemed when it is pure and far from the Place, can you say the same about what was bought with tithe money which cannot be redeemed when it is pure and far from the Place?

משנה יב: צְבִי שֶׁלְּקָחוֹ בְּכֶסֶף מַעֲשֵׂר וּמֵת יִיקָּבֵר עַל יְדֵי עוֹרוֹ. רִבִּי שִׁמְעוֹן אוֹמֵר יִיפָּדֶה. לְקָחוֹ חַי וּשְׁחָטוֹ וְנִטְמָא יִיפָּדֶה. רִבִּי יוֹסֵי אוֹמֵר יִיקָּבֵר. לְקָחוֹ שָׁחוּט וְנִטְמָא הֲרֵי הוּא לוֹ כְּפֵירוֹת.

Mishnah 12: If a deer bought with tithe money died, it should be buried in its hide. Rebbi Simeon says, it should be redeemed[116]. If he bought it alive and slaughtered it, if it became impure it should be redeemed[117]. Rebbi Yose said, it should be buried. If he bought it slaughtered[118] and it became impure, he treats it following the rules of produce.

115 It is holy but cannot be eaten. It cannot be left to rot since one might eat from it inadvertently. This Mishnah is quoted in Babli *Pesaḥim* 38a, *Sanhedrin* 113a, *Baba Meẓi'a* 53b, *Zebaḥim* 49b.

116 This is explained in the Halakhah.

117 For the anonymous Tanna and R. Jehudah, it is like any other food that became impure. R. Yose extends the rules of the preceding case to this one, since a deer never can be a sacrifice.

118 This use is fully approved by the biblical verse.

(fol. 54c) **הלכה ט:** מַה טַעְמָא דְּרִבִּי יוּדָה. כֶּסֶף רִאשׁוֹן וְלֹא כֶסֶף שֵׁינִי. אֶלָּא מִן מָה דְּאִינּוּן מֵתִיבִין לֵיהּ מִקַּל וָחוֹמֶר הוּא מוֹתִיב לוֹן מִקַּל וָחוֹמֶר.

Halakhah 9: What is the reason of Rebbi Jehudah? The first money, not second money[119]. Only because they objected to him by an argument *de minore ad majus*, he answered in terms of an argument *de minore ad majus*.

119 *Deut*. 14:25: "then turn it *into the money*." The definite article is taken to restrict the money to the coins originally given. This argument is described in the Babli, *Baba Meẓi'a* 45a, as that of the House of Shammai. This is possible since R. Jehudah was a student of his father R. Ilaï, a student of R. Eliezer who started out as a disciple of the House of Shammai. The House of Hillel (the anonymous majority in Mishnah 11) hold that the repetition in the verse, "then turn it into *money*, bundle the *money* in your hand" means that monies can be exchanged; otherwise it would have said "bundle it".

רִבִּי יוֹסֵי בְּשֵׁם רִבִּי יוֹחָנָן צְבִי עָשׂוּ כְקָדְשֵׁי בֶדֶק הַבַּיִת לִטְעוֹן הַעֲמָדָה וְהַעֲרָכָה. רִבִּי יִרְמְיָה בָּעֵא קוֹמֵי רִבִּי זְעִירָא בְּהֵמָה טְמֵיאָה מַהוּ שֶׁתִּיטְעַן עֲמָדָה וְהַעֲרָכָה. אָמַר לֵיהּ אִילוּלֵי דְּאָמַר רִבִּי יוֹסֵי בְּשֵׁם רִבִּי יוֹחָנָן חַיָּה טְהוֹרָה אֵינָהּ טְעוּנָה עֲמָדָה וְהַעֲרָכָה בְּהֵמָה טְמֵיאָה לֹא. אָמַר רִבִּי הִילָא וְתַנֵּי כֵן וְאִם בַּבְּהֵמָה הַטְּמֵאָה וּפָדָה בְעֶרְכֶּךָ. מַה בְּהֵמָה טְמֵיאָה מְיוּחֶדֶת שֶׁשָּׁוָה שְׁעַת פִּדְיוֹנָהּ לִשְׁעַת הֶקְדֵּישָׁהּ. אַף אֲנִי אַרְבֶּה אֶת הַמֵּיתָה שֶׁשָּׁוָה שְׁעַת פִּדְיוֹנָהּ לִשְׁעַת הֶקְדֵּישָׁהּ. וּמוֹצִיא אֶת שֶׁאָמַר הֲרֵי זֶה הֶקְדֵּשׁ וּמֵיתָה שֶׁלֹּא שָׁוַת שְׁעַת פִּדְיוֹנָהּ לִשְׁעַת הֶקְדֵּישָׁהּ. אָמַר רִבִּי יוֹסֵי מַתְנִיתָא אָמְרָה כֵן חָמוּר מוֹעֲלִין בָּהּ וּבַחֲלָבָהּ. וְחָלָב

לָאו כְּמֵיתָה הִיא. וְכָל־שֶׁהוּא טָעוּן פִּדְיוֹן מוֹעֲלִין בּוֹ. אִין תִּפְתְּרִינֵיהּ לְשֵׁם הִילְכוֹת מֵיתָה לֹא יָכִיל דְּתַנִינָן חֲמוֹר. אָמַר רִבִּי חֲנִינָא קוֹמֵי רִבִּי מָנָא תִּיפְתָּר כְּרִבִּי שִׁמְעוֹן דְּרִבִּי שִׁמְעוֹן אָמַר קָדְשֵׁי בֶדֶק הַבַּיִת אֵין טְעוּנִין עֲמָדָה וְהַעֲרָכָה. אָמַר לֵיהּ אִין כְּרִבִּי שִׁמְעוֹן לָמָּה לִי חֲמוֹר אֲפִילוּ שְׁאָר כָּל־בְּהֵמָה.

Rebbi Yose in the name of Rebbi Joḥanan: They treated deer like dedications for the upkeep of the Temple to require standing and appraisal[120].

Rebbi Jeremiah asked before Rebbi Zeïra: Does an unclean animal need standing and appraisal? He said to him, if Rebbi Yose had said in the name of Rebbi Joḥanan that a pure wild animal does not need standing and appraisal, an unclean animal would not need it. Rebbi Hila said, we have stated thus (*Lev*. 27:27)[121]: "If an unclean animal, he should redeem it as appraised[122]." Just as an unclean animal is particular in that it is the same at the time of its redemption as at the time of its dedication[123], so I am adding the dead animal which is the same at the time of its redemption as at the time of its dedication, and I exclude the one for which he said, this is dedicated, and then it died, which is not the same at the time of its redemption as at the time of its dedication[124]. Rebbi Yose said, a Mishnah said so[125]: "One commits larceny with a donkey and its milk[126]." Is not milk comparable to its being dead[127]? With all that needs redemption one can commit larceny[128]. You cannot explain it as giving the rules of dead [animals] since we stated "a donkey"[129]. Rebbi Ḥanina said before Rebbi Mana, explain it following Rebbi Simeon since Rebbi Simeon said, dedications for the upkeep of the Temple do not need standing and appraisal. He said to him, if it is following Rebbi Simeon, why a donkey and not any animal[130]?

120 The rules of dedications of animals whose monetary equivalent should be used for the upkeep of the Temple are spelled out in *Lev*. 27. The relevant verses are 11-12 and 27. (11) "If it is any unclean animal which cannot be a sacrifice to the Eternal, one should make the animal stand before a Cohen. (12) The Cohen should appraise it, whether it is good or bad; the Cohen's appraisal shall stand." (27) "If it is an unclean animal, he should redeem it for its appraisal .." Since an unclean (nonkosher) animal *never* can be a sacrifice, the "unclean" animal of v. 11 must be a kosher animal with a blemish, which *now* cannot be a sacrifice. V. 27 therefore details the rules of nonkosher animals dedicated to the Temple. The rabbis hold that the parallel expressions "unclean animal" indicate that the rules of vv. 11-12 can be transferred to v. 27 but R. Simeon holds that in v. 27 no "standing" is mentioned, therefore it is not needed. (Details in Babli *Temurah* 32b).

The rabbis hold that any dedicated animal which cannot stand before a Cohen cannot be appraised and, therefore, cannot be redeemed. R. Simeon holds that animals which never can be sacrifices, nonkosher animals and kosher wild animals, do not need standing; they can be redeeemed even if dead.

121 *Sifra Beḥuqotay Parašah* 4(3), a similar text; quoted in Babli *Baba Meẓi'a* 54b.

122 The verse adds: "He has to add its fifth".

123 It could not be a sacrifice in either case; it was alive in both cases.

124 Even according to the Sages, it can be redeemed without standing and appraisal.

125 This is the operative rule.

126 *Meïlah* 3:5. Larceny committed on anything dedicated to the upkeep of the Temple incurs a fine of 25% and requires a sacrifice for atonement.

127 The use of masculine חמור for a female donkey is in all Mishnah mss.; it has wrongly been corrected in the editions of Babli (*Meïlah* 12b).

128 It was not there at the moment of dedication and, being a fluid, it cannot stand.

129 A live one.

130 It could even have been a blemished kosher animal.

משנה יג: הַמַּשְׁאִיל קַנְקַן לְמַעֲשֵׂר שֵׁינִי אַף עַל פִּי שֶׁגָּפָן לֹא קָנָה (fol. 53d) מַעֲשֵׂר. זָלַף לְתוֹכָן סְתָם עַד שֶׁלֹּא גָּפָן לֹא קָנָה מַעֲשֵׂר מִשֶּׁגָּפָן קָנָה מַעֲשֵׂר. עַד שֶׁלֹּא גָּפָן עוֹלוֹת בְּאֶחָד וּמֵאָה. מִשֶּׁגָּפָן מְקַדְּשׁוֹת כָּל־שֶׁהֵן. עַד שֶׁלֹּא גָּפָן תּוֹרֵם מֵאַחַת עַל הַכֹּל מִשֶּׁגָּפָן תּוֹרֵם מִכָּל־אַחַת וְאַחַת.

Mishnah 13: If somebody lends flasks[131] for Second Tithe, even if he closed the top with clay[132], tithe did not acquire it. If he filled them without saying anything[133], before he closed the top with clay[134], tithe did not acquire it; after he closed the top with clay[134], tithe acquired it. Before he closed the top with clay, one may lift by 101[135], after he closed the top with clay any one sanctifies[136]. Before he closed the top with clay, he gives heave from one for all, after he closed the top with clay he has to give heave from each single one.

131 The mss. of the Maimonides tradition have more accurately קנקניו "his own flasks"; the vintner gives one of his flasks to put in tithe wine since the wine has to be in some vessel. Before filling the wine into the flasks, he specified that the flasks were a loan to the tithe. Therefore, he does not have to redeem them, i. e., to buy food in the value of the flasks to eat in the holiness of tithe.

132 A semi-permanent seal; in this case it is needed to transport the wine to Jerusalem. Flasks were usually sealed in this way only for sale and transport.

133 He did not specify that the flask would be filled with tithe wine.

134 He declared the wine to be Second Tithe. But since the flask was sealed, if he makes no special declaration, he sanctifies the flask with its contents.

135 If heave accidentally fell into one of the flasks and it is not known where it fell, if the profane is more that 101 times the heave, the latter can be lifted following the rules of heave.

136 Since sealed flasks usually are prepared for sale, they fall under the rules of items sold singly which never can become insignificant and even one sanctified among 1000 profane makes all sanctified; cf. Mishnah *Orlah* 3:7.

(fol. 54c) **הלכה י:** אָמַר רִבִּי זְעִירָא אָמְרָה תוֹרָה פּוֹרְטֵיהוּ בַּמִּקְדָּשׁ וְכוֹנְסֵהוּ בִּגְבוּלִין מַה בְּמִקְדָּשׁ יָצָא קַנְקַן לְחוּלִין. אַף בִּגְבוּלִין נִתְפָּשׂ קַנְקַן מַעֲשֵׂר.

Halakhah 10: Rebbi Zeïra said, the Torah said, spend it in the Holy Place and assemble it in the countryside. Just as in the holy place the flask is profane[137], in the contryside can the flask be grasped by tithe?

137 As stated in Mishnah 1:4, if wine is bought in Jerusalem with tithe money, the value of the flask does not have to be estimated and an equivalent value eaten in the holiness of tithe. The argument gives the rationale for the first clause of the Mishnah.

רִבִּי חִייָה בְשֵׁם רִבִּי יוֹחָנָן כֵּינִי מַתְנִיתָא. אִם עַד שֶׁלֹּא גָּפָן קָרָא שֵׁם לֹא קָנָה מַעֲשֵׂר קַנְקַן. מִשֶּׁגָּפָן קָרָא שֵׁם קָנָה מַעֲשֵׂר קַנְקַן. עַד שֶׁלֹּא גָּפָן קָרָא שֵׁם עוֹלוֹת בְּאֶחָד וּמֵאָה. מִשֶּׁגָּפָן קָרָא שֵׁם מְקַדְּשׁוֹת כָּל־שֶׁהֵן. אִם עַד שֶׁלֹּא גָּפָן קָרָא שֵׁם תּוֹרֵם מֵאֶחָד עַל הַכֹּל מִשֶּׁגָּפָן קָרָא שֵׁם תּוֹרֵם מִכָּל־אֶחָד וְאֶחָד.

Rebbi Ḥiyya in the name of Rebbi Joḥanan, so is the Mishnah: "If before he sealed the top with clay he gave it its name[138], tithe did not acquire it; if after he sealed the top with clay he gave it its name, tithe acquired it. If before he sealed the top with clay he gave it its name, one may lift by 101, if after he sealed the top with clay any one sanctifies. If before he sealed the top with clay he gave it its name, he gives heave from one for all, if after he sealed the top with clay he gave it its name, he has to give heave from each single one."

138 He declared the contents of the flask to be Second Tithe.

בַּמֶּה דְבָרִים אֲמוּרִים בְּשֶׁל יַיִן אֲבָל בְּשֶׁלְּשֶׁמֶן בֵּין עַד שֶׁלֹּא גָּפָן בֵּין שֶׁגָּפָן לֹא קָנָה מַעֲשֵׂר קַנְקַן. בֵּין עַד שֶׁלֹּא גָּפָן בֵּין מִשֶּׁגָּפָן עוֹלוֹת בְּאֶחָד וּמֵאָה. בֵּין עַד שֶׁלֹּא גָּפָן בֵּין מִשֶּׁגָּפָן תּוֹרֵם מֵאֶחָד עַל הַכֹּל.

[139]When has this been said? For wine; but for oil, whether he closed the top with clay or did not close the top with clay, tithe did not acquire it. Whether he closed the top with clay or did not close the top with clay, he may lift by 101. Whether he closed the top with clay or did not close the top with clay, he gives heave from one for all.

139 A similar text in Tosephta 2:18 enumerates fish sauce, vinegar, *muries*, oil, and (date) honey. Fish sauce and *muries* cannot be subject to tithe. Maimonides in his Code (*Ma'aser Šeni* 8:5) copies the entire list. In both mss. and the *editio princeps* of the Tosephta, "tithe acquired it"; but Maimonides (*loc. cit.*) copies "tithe did not acquire it." It is impossible to determine whether or not the Tosephta is corrupt in this passage.

(fol. 53d) **משנה יד**: בֵּית שַׁמַּי אוֹמְרִים מְפַתֵּחַ וּמְעָרֶה לְגַת וּבֵית הִלֵּל אוֹמְרִים מְפַתֵּחַ וְאֵינוֹ צָרִיךְ לְעָרוֹת. בַּמֶּה דְבָרִים אֲמוּרִים בְּמָקוֹם שֶׁדַּרְכָּן לִימָּכֵר סְתוּמוֹת אֲבָל בְּמָקוֹם שֶׁדַּרְכָּן לִמָּכֵר פְּתוּחוֹת לֹא יָצָא הַקַּנְקַן לְחוּלִין. וְאִם רָצָה לְהַחֲמִיר עַל עַצְמוֹ לִמְכּוֹר בְּמִידָּה יָצָא הַקַּנְקַן לְחוּלִין. רִבִּי שִׁמְעוֹן אוֹמֵר אַף הָאוֹמֵר לַחֲבֵירוֹ חָבִית זוֹ אֲנִי מוֹכֵר לָךְ חוּץ מִקַּנְקַנֶּיהָ יָצָא הַקַּנְקַן לְחוּלִין.

Mishnah 14: [140]The House of Shammai say, he opens and pours into a vat, but the House of Hillel say, he opens and does not have to pour. Where has this been said? At a place where usually one sells sealed, but at a place where usually one sells open, the flask did not become profane[141]. However, if he is meticulous to sell by volume[142], the flask did become profane. Rebbi Simeon said[143], also if somebody says to another person, I am selling to you this amphora except its flask, the flask became profane.

140 This Mishnah is a continuation of the previous one. If somebody sealed the mouths of his pitchers with clay, how can he undo what he did?

141 In this case, he opened the flask for redemption because everybody does it for sale; this has no influence on the status of holiness of either the flask or its contents.

142 Even if he sells whole barrels he will measure exactly the amount it contains and does not use an approximate formula. In that case, no vessel is ever part of a sale unless paid for separately; also for his redemption of tithes the vessel will never be counted.

143 The statement of R. Simeon refers to Mishnah 1:3, that if wine usually is sold in sealed amphoras, the amphora is profane even though paid for with tithe money. R. Simeon adds that even if wine is sold in open amphoras, a stipulation may make the amphora profane. The Tosephta (2:18) shows that R. Simeon reduces the disagreement between the Houses of Hillel and Shammai to the case when all flasks are still in the wine cellar near the vat from which they were filled.

(fol. 54c) **הלכה יא:** אָמַר רִבִּי חֲנַנְיָה וְקַשְׁיָא עַל דְּבֵית שַׁמַּי מָה בֵּינָהּ לַחֲמִשָּׁה שַׂקִּין בְּגוֹרֶן. אִלּוּ חֲמִשָּׁה שַׂקִּין בְּגוֹרֶן שֶׁמָּא אֵין תּוֹרְמִין וּמְעַשְּׂרִין מִזֶּה עַל זֶה.

Halakhah 11: Rebbi Ḥananiah said, it is difficult about the House of Shammai! What is the difference between this and five sacks on a threshing floor? For five [separate] sacks on one threshing floor, can one not give heave and tithe from one for the other?

רִבִּי יְהוֹשֻׁעַ בֶּן לֵוִי אָמַר עַל הָרִאשׁוֹנָה הוּשְׁבָה. רִבִּי בָּא אָמַר עַל הַשְּׁנִיָּה.

Rebbi Joshua ben Levi said, it refers back to the first [part]. Rebbi Ba said, to the second[144].

144 Everybody agrees that Mishnah 14 refers to Mishnah 13. The question is only, does it refer to the first part, do the House of Shammai oppose the statement that a prior declaration leaves the flask as tithe money unless

the wine was entirely put in order in the vat, or does it refer to the second part, that the wine was poured without any specification.

אָמַר[145] רְבִיעִית חוּלִין יֵשׁ לִי בְּחָבִית זוֹ יָצָא קַנְקַן לְחוּלִין. רִבִּי חִייָה בְּשֵׁם רִבִּי יוֹחָנָן מַתְנִיתָה אָמְרָה כֵן רִבִּי שִׁמְעוֹן אוֹמֵר הָאוֹמֵר לַחֲבֵירוֹ חָבִית זוֹ אֲנִי מוֹכֵר לָךְ חוּץ מִקַּנְקַנָּהּ יָצָא קַנְקַן לְחוּלִין.

"If he said, a *quartarius* of profane is in this barrel, the barrel is profane[146]." Rebbi Ḥiyya in the name of Rebbi Joḥanan: The Mishnah says so, "Rebbi Simeon said, also if somebody says to another person, I am selling to you this amphora except its flask, the flask became profane.[147]"

145 Reading of the Rome ms. Leyden and Venice: אם רוב "if most of". It is unlikely that less than a *quartarius* have legal consequences.

146 A similar statement is in Tosephta 2:18: "When was it said that [the flask] became tithe money? If all was tithe. But if he added a *quartarius* (cf. *Berakhot* 3, Note 227) of profane [wine], the tithe did not acquire it whether sealed with clay or not."

147 Any reservation in this situation is valid. R. Joḥanan accepts the statement of R. Simeon as practice even though it is presented as the opinion of only one person because no opposition is noted.

המוליך פירות פרק רביעי

(fol. 54c) **משנה א:** הַמּוֹלִיךְ פֵּירוֹת מַעֲשֵׂר שֵׁנִי מִמְּקוֹם הַיּוֹקֶר לִמְקוֹם הַזּוֹל אוֹ מִמְּקוֹם הַזּוֹל לִמְקוֹם הַיּוֹקֶר פּוֹדֵיהוּ כְּשַׁעַר מְקוֹמוֹ. הַמֵּבִיא פֵּירוֹת מִן הַגּוֹרֶן לָעִיר כַּדֵּי יַיִן מִן הַגַּת לָעִיר הַשֶּׁבַח לַשֵּׁנִי וִיצִיאָה מִבֵּיתוֹ.

Mishnah 1: If somebody transports Second Tithe produce from a place of high prices to one of low prices[1] or vice versa, he redeems at the level of his place[2]. If he brings produce from the threshing floor to town or from the wine-press to town, the excess value[3] belongs to the Second but the expense is on him.

1 For some reason, Maimonides translates "from a clean to a dirty place", implying that dirty places have cheap prices, clean places high prices.

2 At the place where the redemption is actually taking place, outside Jerusalem.

3 The difference between produce, etc., in town and out in the fields is added to Second Tithe money but the cost of transportation from the field to town is on him and cannot be deducted from tithe money.

(fol. 54d) **הלכה א:** הַמּוֹלִיךְ פֵּירוֹת מַעֲשֵׂר שֵׁינִי כו'. אָמַר רִבִּי יוֹנָה לֹא אָמְרוּ הַמּוֹלִיךְ הָא כַּתְּחִילָּה אָסוּר. וּבְפֵירוֹת מַעֲשֵׂר שֵׁינִי אֲבָל בְּפֵירוֹת שֶׁהֵן טְבוּלִין לְמַעֲשֵׂר שֵׁינִי אֲפִילוּ לְכַתְּחִילָּה מוּתָּר. כְּהָדָא רִבִּי חָנָה לֵיהּ פֵּירִין הָכָא וּפֵירִין בְּבוֹתְנַיִין וַהֲוָה קְבַע מַעְשְׂרָא דְהָכָא תַּמָּן וּמְפָרֵק לוֹן בְּשַׁעֲרָא דְתַמָּן.

Halakhah 1: "If somebody transports Second Tithe produce," etc. Rebbi Mana said, they said only "if somebody transports"; therefore originally it is forbidden[4]. This is about Second Tithe produce, but for produce which is *ṭevel* for Second Tithe[5] it is originally permitted, following this: Rebbi had produce here and in Batanaia[6]; he fixed the tithes of here there and redeemed them according to the going price there.

4 If people were encouraged to transport heave from place to place (except on the way to Jerusalem), the Mishnah would have been formulated: מוליכין פירות "One transports produce". The formulation: If somebody does it, then . . . is only used for actions which are disapproved of but which are not actually forbidden.

5 Produce for which heave and First Tithe had already been given.

6 Cf. *Ma'serot* 4, Note 82.

תַּנֵּי בֵּין בְּיוֹקֶר וְהוּזְלוּ בֵּין בְּזוֹל וְהוּקְרוּ. נִיחָא בְּיוֹקֶר וְהוּזְלוּ. בְּזוֹל וְהוּקִירוּ. שַׁנְייָא הִיא שֶׁהוּא יָכוֹל לְהַעֲרִים עָלָיו וּלְפוֹטְרוֹ מִן הַחוֹמֶשׁ.

It was stated: Whether it was expensive and became cheap or cheap and became more expensive[7]. We understand "expensive and became cheap[8]". "Cheap and became more expensive"? There is a difference because he could use a trick and free it from the fifth[9].

7 It seems that the *baraita* permits redeeming at the lowest rate between the time Second Tithe was given and the time it was redeemed.

8 Since in this case, the price of redemption is the actual price at the time of redemption.

9 As explained in Mishnah 4, if a third party redeems the tithe, he does not have to add a fifth.

תַּנֵּי אַבָּא (בַּר)[10] חִילְפַיי בַּר קִרְיָיא אָמַר בַּמֶּה דְבָרִים אֲמוּרִים בְּוַדַּאי אֲבָל בִּדְמַאי בֵּין בְּיוֹקֶר וְהוּזְלוּ בֵּין בְּזוֹל וְהוּקְרוּ מוֹכְרוֹ בְזוֹל. לָמָּה מִשּׁוּם שֶׁנִּרְאֶה לְהִימָּכֵר בְּזוֹל אוֹ מִשּׁוּם שֶׁאֵינוֹ יָכוֹל לְהַחֲזִירוֹ לִמְקוֹמוֹ. מַה נְפַק מִבֵּינֵיהוֹן. הֲרֵי הוֹקִירוּ מְקוֹמוֹ. אִין תֵּימַר מִשּׁוּם שֶׁאֵינוֹ יָכוֹל לְהַחֲזִירוֹ לִמְקוֹמוֹ הֲרֵי הוֹקִירוּ. אִין תֵּימַר מִשּׁוּם שֶׁנִּרְאֶה לְהִימָּכֵר בְּזוֹל אֲפִילוּ כֵן נִרְאֶה לְמִימָּכֵר בְּזוֹל. כְּהָדָא

רִבִּי חִייָה בַּר וָוא הֲוָה בְּרוֹמֵי וַחֲמְתִין מְפָרְקִין אִילֵין נִקְלָוְסִיָּא דְהָכָא תַּמָּן בְּשַׁעֲרָא דְהָכָא. אֲמַר מָאן דְּהוֹרֵי לוֹן חִילְפַּיי בַּר קִרְוָיָא הוֹרֵי לוֹן.

It was stated[11]: "Abba Ḥilfai the small-town man[12] said, when has this been said? For certain [produce], but for *demay* whether it was expensive and became cheap or was cheap and became expensive, he may sell it cheaply." Why? Is it because it always may be sold cheaply or because it may not be returned to its place[13]? What is the difference? If later it rose in price again at its place[14]. If you say, because it may not be returned to its place, did it not increase in value? If you say, because it always may be sold cheaply also in this case it can be sold cheaply. Like this: Rebbi Ḥiyya bar Abba was in Rome and he saw them redeem there Nicolaos dates[15] from here at the price here[16]. He said, who taught them? Ḥilfai the small-town man taught them.

10 Word missing in the Rome ms. The end of the paragraph shows that "Abba" here is a title, not a name.

11 In the Tosephta, 3:1, R. Joshua ben Qorḥa states the opposite rule: *Demay* follows the rules of the Mishnah, but certain produce always is redeemed by the higher tariff.

12 In the Babli, *Baba Batra* 123a, there appears a אבא חליפא קרויא, Abba Ḥalifa Small-Towner, who, however, was a student of R. Ḥiyya bar Abba and cannot be identical with the person mentioned here.

13 So that it always could be redeemed at the cheaper place.

14 At the moment of redemption there is no cheap place.

15 Cf. *Berakhot* 6, Note 162; *Demay* 2, Notes 15,16.

16 At the much lower rate of the Land of Israel.

תַּנֵּי מִשְׁתַּכֵּר הוּא אָדָם עַד שֶׁקֶל. מִשְׁתַּכֵּר הוּא אָדָם עַד רְבִיעִית. הֵיךְ עֲבְדָא דֵּינָרָא הָכָא בִתְרֵין אֲלָפִין וּבְאַרְבְּאֵל בִּתְרֵין אֲלָפִין וְלֶקֶן וְהוּא בָּעֵי מֵיתֵן חֲמְשִׁים רִיבּוֹא וּמֵיסוּק. דִּיהַב לֵיהּ הָכָא בִתְרֵין אֲלָפִין וּבְאַרְבֵּלִין בִּתְרֵין וְלַקֶן.[17]

It was stated: A person[18] may earn up to a *šeqel*[19], a person may earn up to a quarter[20]. How is this done[21]? A denar here is worth 2000, but in Arbel 2000 and a *laqan*[22]. He wants to give 50 myriads[23] and brings it up, here by 2000 and in Arbel by 2[000] and *laqan*[24].

17 Reading of the Rome ms. Leyden and Venice: בתרין אלפין וחמשין ריבוא "with 2000 and 500'000."

18 A money changer or money dealer. This paragraph should belong to *Baba Meẓi'a.*

19 2 (silver) denars per gold denar? or aureus? The rate of 2000 denars to one aureus points to the early fourth Century.

20 A quarter of a tetradrachma, one denar. Probably the larger amount is for retail transactions, the smaller for wholesale.

21 Without transgressing the interest prohibitions.

22 A word of uncertain origin and meaning. Following M. Zuckermann, *Talmudische Münzen und Gewichte,* Breslau 1862, most Talmudic Dictionaries derive this word from Greek λευκόν "a white [thing]", supposed to mean "a small silver coin". (Jastrow, deriving the word from the root לקי "to hit, smite", takes it as translation of Greek λεπτόν, "a small copper coin.")

However, there never was a Greek coin λευκόν (whose transliteration moreover would have to be לבקן or לוקן). The efforts of H. J. Sheftel (ערך מלין לשעורי תורה Berdičev 1907, p. 39b/c) and D. Sperber (cf. Note 24) to determine the monetary value of the supposed coin are inconclusive.

The apparent meaning of לקן here and in *Baba Meẓi'a* 4:1, fol. 9c, "a small indeterminate amount of money" rather suggests a connection with Arabic لَقَن "small dish, cup" which is used in the composite عِوَض لقن "small thing given in exchange", or "trifle given as agio".

{Perhaps cf. Greek λεκάνη, ἡ and λέκος, -εως, τό, "dish, pot, pan" from which a late diminutive λεκίσκιον, τό, "small measure or weight" (E. G.)}.

23 500'000 denar = 250 aurei.

24 Cf. also D. Sperber, *Roman Palestine 200 - 400, Money and Prices,* Ramat-Gan 1974, Chap. 14.

תַּנֵּי אֵין פּוֹדִין מַעֲשֵׂר שֵׁינִי לְשֵׁם שֵׁינִי אֶלָּא לְשֵׁם חוּלִין. רִבִּי שָׁאוּל בָּעֵי הַגַּע עַצְמָךְ שֶׁהָיוּ הַכֹּל יוֹדְעִין בּוֹ שֶׁהוּא שֵׁינִי. אֲפִילוּ כֵן. תַּנֵּי אֵין פּוֹדִין מַעֲשֵׂר שֵׁינִי אֶלָּא בְּמִין עַל מִינוֹ. דְּלֹא כֵן מַה נָן אָמְרִין פּוֹדִין מִן הַחִטִּין עַל הַשְּׂעוֹרִין וּמִן הַשְּׂעוֹרִין עַל הַחִטִּין לָכֵן צְרִיכָה. אֲפִילוּ מִן הָאַגְּרוּ עַל הַשַּׁמְתִּית. וּמִן הַשַּׁמְתִּית עַל הָאַגְּרוּ.

It was stated: One does not redeem Second Tithe as Second Tithe but as profane[25]. Rebbi Saul asked: Think of it, if everybody knew that it was Second[26]? Even so. It was stated: One redeems Second Tithe only from its own kind[27]. Otherwise, what would we say? One might redeem wheat for barley, barley for wheat; even fine wheat for coarse wheat[28], coarse wheat for fine wheat.

25 Unless the person who redeems states that the produce shall be profane and the holiness of tithe transferred to the coins, there is no transfer.

26 What else could he do with it? Even so, there is no transfer without declaration.

27 Tithes do not have to be given from earmarked produce; the farmer may give tithe from one part of his harvest for all other produce of the same harvest but at other places.

28 Cf. *Peah* 2, Notes 85,86.

אָמַר רִבִּי חֲנַנְיָה רִבִּי הָיָה לוֹקֵחַ קִשּׁוּאִין בְּכוּרוֹת לַמַּלְכוּת וְקוֹבֵעַ מַעֲשֵׂר שֵׁינִי שֶׁלָּהֶן עַל כָּל־עוּקָץ וְעוּקָץ. רָאָה אוֹתָן כִּילוּ הֵן חֲתוּכוֹת. רִבִּי יוֹחָנָן בָּעֵי שְׁלֵימוֹת וְאַתְּ אָמַרְתָּ חֲתִיכוֹת. אָמַר רִבִּי יוֹנָה וְיֵאוּת אִילּוּ שְׁנַיִם שֶׁהָיוּ שׁוּתָּפִין בְּקִישּׁוּת אַחַת לְזֶה חֵלֶק אֶחָד וְלָזֶה שְׁנֵי[29] חֲלָקִים. שֶׁמָּא הוּא אוֹמֵר לוֹ טוֹל חֶלְקָךְ וַאֲנִי חֶלְקִי. אֶלָּא עַל יְדֵי זֶה וְעַל יְדֵי זֶה נִמְכַּר בְּיוֹקֶר. וְהָכָא עַל יְדֵי זֶה וְעַל יְדֵי זֶה נִמְכַּר בְּיוֹקֶר. כְּהָדָא רִבִּי שִׁמְעוֹן בַּר רִבִּי הֲוָה מַפְקִיד עַל אִילֵּין דְּרוֹמַיָּא דַּהֲווֹן מְזַלְזְלִין בָּהּ. נַסְתּוֹן בַּר קַפָּר וְקִרְטְטָא קוֹמוֹי אָמַר לֵיהּ טָב הוּא כְּלוּם. עַד כְּדוֹן מִילָּה מְקַרְטְטָה וְלָא טָבָא מִילָּה מְקַרְטְטָה וְטָבָה.

Rebbi Ḥanania said: Rebbi took early ripe green melons[30] for the government[31] and fixed their Second Tithe in each peduncle[32]. He considered them as if cut[33]. Rebbi Joḥanan asked, they were whole and you say cut? Rebbi Jonah said, that is correct! If two people were partners in a green melon, one having one part and the other two, can he say, take your part and I shall take mine? But for the two together it is sold more dearly; here also together it is sold[34] more dearly. Like this: Rebbi Simeon ben Rebbi commanded those Southerners who were disregarding it[35]. Bar Qappara lifted them and before him cut them into little pieces. He said to him, is that worth anything[36]? So far, some things are cut into little pieces and they are no good, other things are cut into little pieces and are good[37].

29 Reading of the Rome ms. Leyden: תשעה "nine".

30 Cf. *Kilaim* 1:2, Note 38.

31 To invite (Augustus or Caesar) Antoninus, cf. *Kilaim* 9:4, Note 79.

32 He then redeemed them together.

33 The peduncle with some fruit flesh cut off from the melon.

34 I. e., redeemed.

35 They disregarded Second Tithe (which without a Temple cannot be used for anything) and which, at least for produce other than grain, wine, and olive oil, was rabbinic even in the Times of the Temple.

36 If it has no monetary value, it is not subject to tithes.

37 The argument of Rebbi against Bar Qappara.

רִבִּי יְהוֹשֻׁעַ בֶּן לֵוִי אָמַר אֵין פּוֹדִין מַעֲשֵׂר שֵׁינִי אֶלָּא עַד שְׁלֹשִׁים וְשִׁשָּׁה בְּשָׁווֹי. וְאָמַר רִבִּי חִזְקִיָּה זֶה שֶׁהוּא מְחַלֵּל לֹא יְהֵא מְחַלֵּל עַל חֲצִי פְּרוּטָה שֶׁלֹּא יְהֵא כִמְחַלֵּל עַל אֲסִימוֹן. אֶלָּא עַד שָׁוֶה פְּרוּטָה.

Rebbi Joshua ben Levi said, one redeems Second Tithe only up to thirty six times [the coin's] worth. And Rebbi Ḥizqiah said, one who exchanges should not exchange for half a *peruṭah* so he should not be like one who exchanges for a blank[38]; it must be worth a *peruṭah*.

38 The *peruṭa* was an Hasmonean copper coin; in Talmudic times it was purely a unit of computation. According to Yerushalmi *Qiddušin* 1:1 (fol. 58d), one *as* (*obolus*) was counted as 6 *peruṭot*. The statement then means that for redemption purposes, a *denar* can be represented by a *peruṭah*.

Half a *peruṭah* never was an official coin; for blanks cf. Chapter 1, Note 45.

(fol. 54c) **משנה ב:** פּוֹדִין מַעֲשֵׂר שֵׁינִי כְּשַׁעַר הַזּוֹל כְּמוֹ שֶׁהַחֶנְוָנִי לוֹקֵחַ לֹא כְמוֹת שֶׁהוּא מוֹכֵר כְּמוֹת שֶׁהַשּׁוּלְחָנִי פּוֹרֵט לֹא כְמוֹת שֶׁהוּא מְצָרֵף. אֵין פּוֹדִין מַעֲשֵׂר שֵׁינִי אַכְסְרָה אֶת שֶׁדָּמָיו יְדוּעִין נִפְדֶּה עַל פִּי אֶחָד וְאֵת שֶׁאֵין דָּמָיו יְדוּעִין נִפְדֶּה עַל פִּי שְׁלֹשָׁה. כְּגוֹן הַיַּיִן שֶׁקִּיסֵּס וּפֵירוֹת שֶׁהִרְקִיבוּ וּמָעוֹת שֶׁהֶחֱלִיאוּ.

Mishnah 2: One redeems Second Tithe following the low rate at which the grocer buys[39], not at which he sells; the one at which the banker gives small coins, not at which he assembles large coins[40]. One does not redeem Second Tithe *en bloc*[41]; if the price is known it is redeemed by the information of one person, if the price is not known by the information of three, as e. g., wine getting sour, fruit rotting, or coins rusting.

39 At wholesale.

40 The banker engaged in exchange operations makes money on the spread between buying and selling rates. For redeeming tithe one values bronze coins as if one were a banker selling copper coins against silver.

41 Cf. *Demay* Chapter 2, Note 198.

(fol. 54d) **הלכה ב:** אָמַר רִבִּי אִימִּי כָּמָּה עֲלַל קוֹמֵי רִבִּי יוֹחָנָן וְרִבִּי שִׁמְעוֹן בֶּן לָקִישׁ וְאִינּוּן אָמְרֵי פּוּק וְאִישְׁלַם כְּהָדֵין תַּנָּייָה פּוֹדִין מַעֲשֵׂר שֵׁינִי כְּשַׁעַר[42] הַזּוֹל

וְלֹא כְשַׁעַר[42] הַיּוֹקֶר כְּמוֹת שֶׁהַחֶנְוָנִי[42] לוֹקֵחַ לֹא כְמוֹת שֶׁהוּא מוֹכֵר. כְּמוֹת שֶׁהַשּׁוּלְחָנִי פּוֹרֵט לֹא כְמוֹת שֶׁהוּא מְצָרֵף. עַד כְּדוֹן דָּבָר מְרוּבָּה הָיָה דָבָר מְמוּעָט. אֲפִילוּ כֵן כְּמוֹת שֶׁהַחֶנְוָנִי לוֹקֵחַ לֹא כְמוֹת שֶׁהוּא מוֹכֵר. כְּמוֹת שֶׁהַשּׁוּלְחָנִי פּוֹרֵט לֹא כְמוֹת שֶׁהוּא מְצָרֵף.

Halakhah 2: Rebbi Immi said, Kama came before Rebbi Joḥanan and Rebbi Simeon ben Laqish. They said to him, go and pay according to those Tannaïm: "One redeems Second Tithe when it is cheap, not when it is expensive; at the rate at which the grocer buys, not at which he sells; the one at which the banker gives small coins, not at which he assembles large coins." So far for large quantities, what about small ones? Even so, at the rate at which the grocer buys, not at which he sells; the one at which the banker gives small coins, not at which he assembles large coins.

רִבִּי נַחְמָן בַּר יַעֲקֹב מְחַוֵּי חוּתֶל לְנַגָּרָא וּמְפָרֵק עַל פּוּמֵיהּ. רִבִּי יַנַּאי מְחַוֵּי רוֹבַע חִטִּין לְחִטוֹנַיָּא וּמְפָרֵק עַל פּוּמֵיהּ. רִבִּי סִימוֹן חֲוֵי פֵּירִין לְרִבִּי חִלְקִיָּה. אָמַר לוֹ בְּשָׁוֵיהֶן אָמַר לוֹ כֵן. אָמַר רִבִּי חִלְקִיָּה בְּשֵׁם רִבִּי סִימוֹן אֵין פּוֹדִין מַעֲשֵׂר שֵׁינִי עַל פִּי הַשּׁוֹטִין. רִבִּי פִּינְחָס חֲוֵי פֵּירִין לִגְרוֹסָה אָמַר לֵיהּ בְּשָׁוֵייהֶן. אָמַר לֵיהּ הָכֵין אָמַר רִבִּי חִלְקִיָּה בְּשֵׁם רִבִּי סִימוֹן אֵין פּוֹדִין עַל פִּי הַשּׁוֹטִין. אָמַר רִבִּי שַׁמַּי כַּמָּה בַּר נַשׁ בָּעֵי בְטָהֳרָה טְהוֹרָה בִּתְקוּפַת תַּמּוּז בָּתַר בַּלָּנֵי מַסִּיק לְזוֹרְיֵיהּ וּמֵיתֵייהּ פְּרִיטִין וּמִיפְרְקִינֵיהּ. אָמַר רִבִּי יִרְמְיָה כַּמָּה בַּר נַשׁ בָּעֵי בָּעֲרוּבְתָא בְּפַתֵּי רַמְשָׁה מִנְשַׁיָּא קַלְעָן וּמַעֲבִיר עֲלֵיהֶן וּמֵיתֵי פְּרִיטִין וּמִפְרְקִינֵיהּ. אָמַר רִבִּי יוּדָן בַּר גַּדְיָא רִבִּי יַעֲקֹב בַּר בּוּן מַנִּיחָן עָלָיו עַד שֶׁיִּכְמוֹשׁוּ וּפוֹדֶה אוֹתָן מוֹצָאֵי שַׁבָּת מִיָּד.

Rebbi Naḥman bar Jacob[43] showed a basket of palm leaves to a carpenter and redeemed following his opinion. Rebbi Yannai showed a quarter [*qab*] wheat to a wheat dealer[44] and redeemed following his opinion. Rebbi Simon showed produce to Rebbi Ḥilqiah who asked him, by their true value? He answered, yes. Rebbi Ḥilqiah said in the name of Rebbi Simon, one does not redeem Second Tithe following the opinion of imbeciles. Rebbi Phineas showed produce to a grits-maker who asked him, by their true value? He said to him, so said Rebbi Ḥilqiah in the name of Rebbi Simon, one does not redeem following the opinion of imbeciles. Rebbi Shammai said, how much a person wants [to pay] on a clear noontime at the summer solstice when the bath master[45] takes up his bunches, he brings coins and redeems. Rebbi Jeremiah said, as much as a person wants Friday afternoon from women braiders[46] when he passes by, he brings coins and redeems. Rebbi Yudan bar Gadya[47] said, Rebbi Jacob bar Abun left it lying until it got moldy and redeemed it immediately after the Sabbath.

42 Reading of the Rome ms. and the Venice print. The Leyden text is: פּוֹדִין מַעֲשֵׂר שֵׁינִי כִּשְׁעַת הַזּוֹל וְלֹא כִּשְׁעַת הַיּוֹקֶר כְּמוֹת שֶׁהַשּׁוּלְחָנִי לוֹקֵחַ לֹא כְּמוֹת שֶׁהוּא מוֹכֵר.

43 The only known Naḥman bar Jacob is Rav Naḥman bar Jacob, Chief Judge in Babylonia and son-in-law of the Resh Galuta. Since carpenters do not make baskets from leaves, they were certainly incompetent to testify to their volume or value. The story therefore notes that in Babylonia, where tithes are rabbinic practice only, any estimate is good.

44 In the Rome ms. סיטונאי "grain wholesaler". While the Mishnah takes as standard the selling price of the wholesaler, he asked his buying price.

45 He runs a thermal bath which will not have many customers in the summer heat; he will sell his supplies cheaply.

46 They are fully occupied and will react only if they get an extraordinarily cheap buy. R. Jeremiah seems to have no compunctions to go to a women's hairdresser shop!

47 He seems to be R. Yudan bar Guria.

רִבִּי מָנָא הֲוָה לֵיהּ מְשַׁח וְאַחְתֵּיהּ לְעַכּוֹ. אָמַר לֵיהּ רִבִּי חִייָה בַּר אָדָא אִין הַהוּא מִישְׁחָךְ דְּבֵית מַעֲקֶה קַייָם הָא עוֹנָתָךְ דִּיפְרְקִינֵיהּ דְּלָא טָב שִׁיתָּא מָנֵי.

Rebbi Mana had oil which he brought down to Acco[48]. Rebbi Ḥiyya bar Ada said to him, if your oil there at the parapet[49] is still there, it is your time that you should redeem it for [there] it is not worth six minas[50].

48 Where olive oil is more expensive than at the place of production in Galilee.

49 Second Tithe money oil at your house in Galilee.

50 Instead of שיתא מני the Rome ms. has מינך "from you"; a corruption.

אָמַר רִבִּי יוֹחָנָן פּוֹדִין מַעֲשֵׂר שֵׁינִי עַל פִּי שְׁלֹשָׁה לְקוּחוֹת וַאֲפִילוּ אֶחָד מֵהֶן גּוֹי. אֲפִילוּ אֶחָד מֵהֶן בַּעַל. רִבִּי יוֹנָה בָּעֵי שְׁנֵיהֶם גּוֹיִם לֹא שְׁנֵיהֶן בְּעָלִים לֹא אֶחָד גּוֹי וְאֶחָד בַּעַל לֹא. אֶלָּא לִצְדָדִין אִיתְאֲמָרַת.

Rebbi Joḥanan said, one redeems Second Tithe by the offers of three buyers, even if one of them is a Gentile, even if one of them is an owner. Rebbi Jonah asked: Not two Gentiles, not two owners; also not one Gentile and one owner? No, it was said separately[51].

51 Only one Gentile, only one owner, but one Gentile and one owner is acceptable. This is also accepted in the Babli, *Sanhedrin* 12b, where the owner and his wife are accepted, in Rashi's interpretation on condition that the wife have her own business and not be dependent on her husband for her upkeep.

(fol. 54c) **משנה ג:** בַּעַל הַבַּיִת אוֹמֵר בְּסֶלַע וְאֶחָד אוֹמֵר בְּסֶלַע בַּעַל הַבַּיִת קוֹדֵם מִפְּנֵי שֶׁהוּא מוֹסִיף חוֹמֶשׁ. בַּעַל הַבַּיִת אוֹמֵר בְּסֶלַע וְאֶחָד אוֹמֵר בְּסֶלַע וְאִיסָּר

אֶת שֶׁל סֶלַע וְאִיסָּר קוֹדֵם מִפְּנֵי שֶׁהוּא מוֹסִיף עַל הַקֶּרֶן. הַפּוֹדֶה מַעֲשֵׂר שֵׁנִי שֶׁלּוֹ מוֹסִיף עָלָיו חֲמִישִׁיתוֹ בֵּין שֶׁהוּא שֶׁלּוֹ בֵּין שֶׁנִּיתַּן לוֹ בְּמַתָּנָה.

Mishnah 3: If the owner says[52] a tetradrachma and another says a tetradrachma, the owner is preferred since he adds a fifth. The owner says a tetradrachma and someone else says a tetradrachma and an as, the one who offers a tetradrachma and an as is preferred since he adds to the capital[53]. He who redeems his own Second Tithe adds a fifth, whether it is his own or was given to him as a gift[54].

52 He offers for redemption of his Second Tithe. He has to add a fifth of the amount, *Lev*. 27:31.

53 By contrast, for redemption of property dedicated to the Temple, the other person would have to offer more than 125% of the owner's offer before his offer would be considered. The difference between the Second Tithe and Temple dedication is (a) that redemption money of tithe remains in the hand of the owner (Babli *Arakhin* 27b) and (b) for Second Tithe, the owner can get out of the obligation to pay the additional fifth (Mishnah 4).

54 The meaning of the last clause depends on whether one holds that Second Tithe is the owner's money, then Second Tithe may be a gift, or whether it is Heaven's money in the hand of the farmer, when it can be given only as *ṭevel* but not as tithe.

(fol. 54d) **הלכה ג**: וְאֵין חוֹמְשׁוֹ שֶׁל זֶה מְרוּבֶּה עַל תּוֹסֶפְתּוֹ שֶׁל זֶה. אָמַר רִבִּי אָבִין שֶׁנְיָיא הִיא שֶׁהוּא יָכוֹל לְהַעֲרִים עָלָיו וּלְפוֹטְרוֹ מִן הַחוֹמֶשׁ.

Halakhah 3: Is not the fifth of this more than the addition of that one[55]? Rebbi Abin said, there is a difference that he can circumvent and free it from the fifth[56].

55 The "fifth" is a full drachma, an as is only $^{1}/_{96}$ of a tetradrachma.

56 As explained in the next Mishnah.

שֶׁל סֶלַע וְאִיסָּר קוֹדֵם מִפְּנֵי שֶׁהוּא מוֹסִיף עַל הַקֶּרֶן. רִבִּי יַעֲקֹב בַּר אִידִי בְשֵׁם רִבִּי סִימַיי כָּל־מַעֲשֵׂר שֵׁינִי שֶׁאֵין בְּקַרְנוֹ שָׁוֶה פְרוּטָה אֵינוֹ מוֹסִיף חוֹמֶשׁ. רִבִּי יוֹסֵי בֵּירִבִּי סִימוֹן בְּשֵׁם רִבִּי יוֹחָנָן כָּל־מַעֲשֵׂר שֵׁינִי שֶׁאֵין בְּחוּמְשׁוֹ שָׁוֶה פְרוּטָה אֵינוֹ מוֹסִיף חוֹמֶשׁ. הָתִיב רִבִּי בָּא בַּר מָמָל וְהָתַנִּינָן חָמֵשׁ פְּרוּטוֹת הֵן. וְנִתְנֵי שֵׁשׁ עַל דַּעְתֵּיהּ דְּרִבִּי סִימַאי וְקַרְנוֹ שֶׁל מַעֲשֵׂר שֵׁינִי בְּשָׁוֶה פְרוּטָה. וְשֶׁבַע עַל דַּעְתֵּיהּ דְּרִבִּי יוֹחָנָן וְחוּמְשׁוֹ שֶׁל מַעֲשֵׂר שֵׁינִי שָׁוֶה פְרוּטָה. וְעוֹד מִן הָדָא דְּאָמַר רִבִּי יוֹסֵי בְּשֵׁם רִבִּי מָנָא בַּר תַּנְחוּם רִבִּי אַבָּהוּ בְּשֵׁם רִבִּי יוֹחָנָן אֵין קַרְקַע נִקְנֶה בְּפָחוֹת מִשָּׁוֶה פְרוּטָה. וְעוֹד מִן הָדָא מַעֲשֵׂר שֵׁינִי שֶׁאֵין דָּמָיו יְדוּעִין דַּיּוֹ שֶׁיֹּאמַר הוּא וְחוּמְשׁוֹ מְחוּלָּל עַל הַסֶּלַע הַזֶּה. רִבִּי יוֹסֵי בְּשֵׁם רִבִּי קְרִיסְפָּא רִבִּי יוֹנָה בְּשֵׁם רִבִּי זְעִירָא בְּסֶלַע שֶׁלְּמַעֲשֵׂר שֵׁינִי הִיא מַתְנִיתָא. אֵי אֶיפְשַׁר שֶׁלֹּא יְהֵא שָׁם חוּלִין כָּל־שֶׁהֵן.

"A tetradrachma and an as is preferred since he adds to the capital". Rebbi Jacob bar Idi in the name of Rebbi Simai: One does not add a fifth for any Second Tithe which itself is not worth a *peruṭa*. Rebbi Yose ben Rebbi Simon in the name of Rebbi Joḥanan: One does not add a fifth for any Second Tithe for which the fifth is not worth a *peruṭa*[57]. Rebbi Abba bar Mamal objected: Did we not state[58] "there are five *peruṭot*", should one not state "six" according to Rebbi Simai, "Second Tithe which is worth a *peruṭa*!" And "seven" according to Rebbi Joḥanan, "the fifth of Second Tithe worth a *peruṭa*."[59] In addition, from what Rebbi Yose said in the name of Rebbi Mana bar Tanḥum, Abbahu in the name of Rebbi Joḥanan: Real estate cannot be acquired for less than a *peruṭa*[60]. In addition, from the following: If the value of Second Tithe is not known[61], it is enough that one say: it and its fifth shall be exchanged for this tetradrachma. Rebbi Yose in the name of Rebbi Crispus, Rebbi Jonah in the name of Rebbi Zeïra: this *baraita* deals with a tetradrachma of tithe money where it is impossible that it not contain some profane[62].

57 The Yerushalmi *Baba Meẓi'a* 4:5, fol. 9d, finds a basis for both rules in *Lev*. 27:31.

58 Mishnah *Baba Meẓi'a*, Mishnah 4.6: One cannot force an oath if the defending party has not admitted owing at least a *peruṭa*; a woman can be preliminarily married only for a gift worth a *peruṭa*; a person deriving a *peruṭa*'s worth of benefit from anything dedicated to the Temple has committed larceny; if a find is worth a *peruṭa* it must be publicized; if somebody robs another of at least a *peruṭa* and swears falsely, he cannot atone for it unless he makes restitution even if that means a very long trip.

59 The Yerushalmi *Baba Meẓi'a* 4:5, fol. 9d, considers this a contradiction to the Mishnah. The Babli, *Baba Meẓi'a* 55a, notes that the Mishnah is restricted to original obligations.

60 This is a principle accepted everywhere in the Yerushalmi, *Eruvin* 6, fol. 23c; *Qiddušin* 1:3, fol. 59d; 1:5, fol 60c. In the Babli, *Qiddušin* 13a, it is noted that the statement holds only for acquisition by money but not for barter.

61 It is unknowable because it is less than a *peruṭa* and cannot be measured by money's worth.

62 This presupposes the statement of R. Joḥanan in the next paragraph that coins given for tithe money are holy only up to the actual value of the tithe exchanged for that coin. The argument is logical since nobody would offer a tetradrachma for anything valued less than a *peruṭa*, less than 0.2% of the value of the coin.

אָמַר רִבִּי יוֹחָנָן הֶקְדֵּשׁ שֶׁפְּדָיִיוֹ יוֹתֵר עַל דָּמָיו תָּפַס אֶת הַכֹּל. מַעֲשֵׂר שֵׁינִי שֶׁפְּדָיִיוֹ יוֹתֵר עַל דָּמָיו לֹא תָפַס אֶת הַכֹּל. מַה בֵּין הֶקְדֵּשׁ מַה בֵּין מַעֲשֵׂר שֵׁינִי. אָמַר רִבִּי אִימִּי שֶׁכֵּן אָדָם מָצוּי לִהְיוֹת מַרְבֶּה בְּהֶקְדֵּישׁוֹ. רִבִּי זְעִירָא בָּעָא קוֹמֵי רִבִּי אִימִּי נִבְדַּק אוֹתוֹ הָאִישׁ וְאָמַר לֹא לְכָךְ נִתְכַּוַּנְתִּי. אָמַר לֵיהּ לִכְשֶׁיִּבְדּוֹק. רִבִּי יוֹנָה בָּעֵי כְּמָאן דְּאָמַר אֵינוֹ כִּנְכָסָיו. בְּרַם כְּמָאן דְּאָמַר כִּנְכָסָיו הוּא. מַה (fol. 55a) בֵּין הֶקְדֵּשׁ מַה בֵּין מַעֲשֵׂר שֵׁינִי. אָמַר רִבִּי יוֹסֵי לֹא כְּבָר אִתְמַר טַעֲמָא שֶׁכֵּן אָדָם מָצוּי לִהְיוֹת מַרְבֶּה בְּהֶקְדֵּישׁוֹ.

Rebbi Joḥanan said, if somebody redeemed dedications[63] for more than their worth, [the Temple] grabs everything[64]. If somebody redeemed

Second Tithe for more than its worth, it does not grab everything. What is the difference between dedications and Second Tithe? Rebbi Immi said, because a person usually adds to his dedications[65]. Rebbi Zeïra asked before Rebbi Immi: If the person[66] was checked and he said, that was not what I intended? He said to him, when he will be checked. Rebbi Jonah asked, that is following him[67] who said that it is not his property. But for him who says that it is his property, what is the difference between dedications and Second Tithe? Rebbi Yose said, the reason has already been explained, because a person usually adds to his dedications.

63 Gifts for the upkeep of the Temple, to be redeemed by the giver or to be sold by the Temple treasurer.

64 The entire sum becomes Temple property.

65 Since dedications are voluntary gifts, in contrast to tithe which is an obligation.

66 Redeeming tithe. If he is asked and declares the entire amount as holy, his word stands. But nobody has to ask.

67 R. Meïr. One can understand the reluctance to give more if the money is Heaven's money in an obligation imposed. But for R. Jehudah, who holds that tithe money is property of the farmer, why should he care which label is attached to his money since all will be spent for his own benefit?

אָמַר רִבִּי יוֹחָנָן הֶקְדֵּשׁ פְּדָייו וְלֹא הוֹסִיף חוֹמֶשׁ הֲרֵי זֶה פָּדוּי. מַעֲשֵׂר שֵׁינִי שֶׁפְּדָייו וְלֹא הוֹסִיף חוֹמֶשׁ הֲרֵי זֶה אֵינוֹ פָּדוּי. מַה בֵּין הֶקְדֵּשׁ וּמַה בֵּין מַעֲשֵׂר שֵׁינִי. אָמַר רִבִּי הִילָא הֶקְדֵּשׁ יֵשׁ לוֹ תוֹבְעִין. מַעֲשֵׂר שֵׁינִי אֵין לוֹ תוֹבְעִין. רִבִּי יוֹנָה בָּעֵי כְּמָאן דְּאָמַר אֵינוֹ כִּנְכָסָיו. בְּרַם כְּמָאן דְּאָמַר כִּנְכָסָיו הוּא. מַה בֵּין הֶקְדֵּשׁ וּמַה בֵּין מַעֲשֵׂר שֵׁינִי. אָמַר רִבִּי יוֹסֵי לֹא כְּבָר אִתְמַר טַעֲמָא הֶקְדֵּשׁ יֵשׁ לוֹ תוֹבְעִין. מַעֲשֵׂר שֵׁינִי אֵין לוֹ תוֹבְעִין.

Rebbi Joḥanan said, if somebody redeemed his dedication without adding a fifth, it is redeemed. If somebody redeemed his Second Tithe without adding a fifth, it is not redeemed. What is the difference between dedications and Second Tithe? Rebbi Hila said, dedications have claimants, Second Tithe has no claimants[68]. Rebbi Jonah asked, that is following him[67] who said, it is not his property. But for him, who says it is his property, what is the difference between dedications and Second Tithe? Rebbi Yose said, the reason has already been explained, dedications have claimants, Second Tithe has no claimants.

68 The Temple treasurer has an organization dedicated to collect monies due the Temple; Second Tithe is a matter purely between the farmer and Heaven. In the Babli, *Baba Meẓi'a* 54a, R. Eliezer holds that the fifth never precludes redemption but the Sages hold that the fifth always precludes redemption and R. Joḥanan decides with R. Eliezer for dedications because of the reason given here by R. Hila. In the Tosephta (4:5), Rebbi holds with R. Eliezer for Second Tithe on the Sabbath but not on weekdays. The argument shows that according to everybody, the position of the Sages only represents a rabbinic institution.

הַפּוֹדֶה מַעֲשֵׂר שֵׁינִי שֶׁלּוֹ מוֹסִיף עָלָיו חֲמִישִׁיתוֹ בֵּין שֶׁהוּא שֶׁלּוֹ בֵּין שֶׁנִּיתַּן לוֹ בְּמַתָּנָה. מַתְנִיתָא דְּרִבִּי מֵאִיר דְּרִבִּי מֵאִיר אוֹמֵר אֵין מַתָּנָה כְּמֶכֶר. אָמַר רִבִּי יוֹנָה דִּבְרֵי הַכֹּל הִיא תִּפְתָּר בְּפֵירוֹת שֶׁהֵן טְבוּלִין לְמַעֲשֵׂר. וְהָתַנִּינָן הַפּוֹדֶה נֶטַע רְבָעִי שֶׁלּוֹ מוֹסִיף עָלָיו חֲמִישִׁיתוֹ. אִית לָךְ מֵימַר בְּפֵירוֹת שֶׁהֵן טְבוּלִין (לְמַעֲשֵׂר שֵׁינִי. וְהָתַנִּינָן)[69] לְנֶטַע רְבָעִי. לֹא לְנֶטַע רְבָעִי עַצְמוֹ. בְּרַם הָכָא מַעֲשֵׂר הֲוֵי סוֹפָךְ מֵימוֹר.

"He who redeems his own Second Tithe adds a fifth, whether it was his own or was given to him as a gift." Our Mishnah is Rebbi Meïr's since Rebbi Meïr says, a gift is not like a sale[70]. Rebbi Jonah said, it is the opinion of everybody, explain it with produce still *ṭevel* for tithes[71]. But did we not state[72]: "He who redeems his own fourth-year tree adds a fifth, whether it is his own or was given to him as a gift"? Can you say that this speaks about produce still *ṭevel* for (Second Tithe? We have stated)[69] "fourth-year tree!" That means the fourth-year tree itself! So here, you will end up saying "tithe"[73].

69 Missing in Rome ms., probably correctly.

70 *Ma'serot* 5:1, Note 5. If a gift were a moneyless sale, the produce would not be his and be free from the fifth.

71 Since it was his property at the moment the Second Tithe became due, even without the Mishnah we would have known that he has to add the fifth.

72 Mishnah 5:5. *Lev.* 19:23-24 requires that the fruit of a newly planted tree not be eaten for the first three years. In the fourth year, "all its fruit shall be holy as a praise to the Eternal." The rules of this holiness are given in the next Chapter. Fruits far from Jerusalem have to be redeemed but, being intrinsically the Eternal's, they are not subject to heave and tithes and can never be *ṭevel*.

73 Since the wording in Mishnah 5:5 speaks about produce to be redeemed, the parallel language in the Mishnah here must also speak about tithe, not *ṭevel*, and the Mishnah must be R. Meïr's.

(fol. 54c) **משנה ד:** מַעֲרִימִין עַל מַעֲשֵׂר שֵׁינִי כֵּיצַד אוֹמֵר אָדָם לַחֲבֵירוֹ לִבְנוֹ וְלִבִתּוֹ הַגְּדוֹלִים לְעַבְדּוֹ וּלְשִׁפְחָתוֹ הָעִבְרִים הֵילָךְ מָעוֹת הָאֵילוּ וּפְדֵה לָךְ אֶת מַעֲשֵׂר זֶה. אֲבָל לֹא יֹאמַר לוֹ כֵן לִבְנוֹ וּלְבִתּוֹ הַקְּטַנִּים לְעַבְדּוֹ וּלְשִׁפְחָתוֹ הַכְּנַעֲנִים מִפְּנֵי שֶׁיָּדָן כְּיָדוֹ.

Mishnah 4: One may circumvent about Second Tithe[74]. How is this? A person may say to his neighbor, his adult son or daughter, his Hebrew male or female slave[75]: Take these coins and redeem this tithe for yourself. But he should not say so to his minor son or daughter or his Canaanite male or female slave[76] because their hand is like his hand.

74 Circumvent the payment of the fifth.

75 This rule is purely theoretical since the institution of Hebrew slavery was intrinsically bound to the land distribution by Joshua and automatically disappeared with the destruction of the first Temple, never to be re-instituted. The male Hebrew "slave" is not a slave but a servant indentured for six years (*Deut.* 15:18) and remains a legal person. The female Hebrew slave is necessarily a minor and supposed to be married by a member of the master's family.

76 They are not Canaanites but originally Gentile slaves or their offspring who became semi-Jewish by circumcision and/or immersion in water. If manumitted, they will automatically become full Jews but as slaves they have no independent legal standing.

(fol. 55a) **הלכה ד:** רִבִּי אָבוּן אָמַר אִיתְפַּלְּגוּן רִבִּי לָעְזָר וְרִבִּי יוֹסֵי בַּר חֲנִינָה. חַד אָמַר לָמָּה מַעֲרִימִין עָלָיו מִפְּנֵי שֶׁכָּתוּב בּוֹ בְּרָכָה. וְחָרָנָה אָמַר לָמָּה פּוֹדִין אוֹתוֹ בְּשַׁעַר הַזּוֹל מִפְּנֵי שֶׁכָּתוּב בּוֹ בְּרָכָה.

Halakhah 4: Rebbi Abun said, Rebbi Eleazar and Rebbi Yose bar Ḥanina disagree. One said, why may one circumvent it? For "blessing" is written about it[77]. The other said, why is it redeemed at a cheap rate? For "blessing" is written about it.

77 *Deut.* 14:24, "because the Eternal, your God, will bless you." This is taken as authorization to be lenient in several respects.

מַה נָן קַייָמִין אִם כְּשֶׁאָמַר לוֹ צֵא וּפְדֵה לִי שְׁלוּחוֹ הוּא. צֵא וּפְדֵה לָךְ שֶׁלּוֹ הֵן. אֶלָּא כִּי נָן קַייָמִין כְּשֶׁאָמַר לוֹ פְּדֵה לִי מִשֶּׁלָּךְ פְּדֵה לָךְ מִשֶּׁלִּי. וְתַנֵּי כֵן פְּדֵה לִי מִשֶּׁלָּךְ פְּדֵה לָךְ מִשֶּׁלִּי אֵינוֹ מוֹסִיף חוֹמֶשׁ. אָמַר רִבִּי יוֹחָנָן כָּל־מַעֲשֵׂר שֶׁאֵינוֹ הוּא וּפִדְיוֹנוֹ מִשֶּׁלּוֹ אֵינוֹ מוֹסִיף חוֹמֶשׁ. רִבִּי יוֹסֵי בֵּי רִבִּי בּוּן בְּשֵׁם רִבִּי חֲנִינָא טַעֲמָא דְּרִבִּי יוֹחָנָן וְאִם גָּאֹל יִגְאַל אִישׁ מִמַּעַשְׂרוֹ חֲמִישִׁיתוֹ יוֹסֵיף עָלָיו. כְּדֵי שֶׁיְּהוּ הוּא וּפִדְיוֹנוֹ מִשֶּׁלּוֹ.

How do we hold? If he said to him, go and redeem for me, he is his agent[78]; go and redeem for yourself, they are the other's property[79]. But we have to hold that he said to him, redeem for me of your property, or redeem for yourself of my property. We have stated thus: "Redeem for me of your property, or redeem for yourself of my property, he does not add a fifth." Rebbi Joḥanan said, for any tithe, where neither it nor its redemption money is his, he does not have to add a fifth. Rebbi Yose ben Rebbi Abun in the name of Rebbi Ḥanina, the reason of Rebbi Joḥanan (*Lev.* 27:31): "If a person goes to redeem of his own tithes, his own fifth he shall add to it;" both it and its redemption money must be his.

78 The status of the agent is the status of his employer; a fifth is due.

79 A fifth is due for the gift as stated in Mishnah 3.

מַה נָן קַייָמִין אִם בִּגְדוֹלָה זָכַת בְּסִימָנִין. אִם בִּקְטַנָּה קָטָן זָכָה. אָמַר רִבִּי יוּדָן בַּר שָׁלוֹם קוֹמֵי רִבִּי יוֹסֵי תִּיפְתָּר כְּמָאן דְּאָמַר הַקָּטָן תּוֹרֵם. אָמַר לֵיהּ וַאֲפִילוּ כְמָאן דְּאָמַר הַקָּטָן תּוֹרֵם קָטָן זָכָה. עַל דַּעְתִּין דְּרַבָּנִין דְּתַמָּן נִיחָא דְּתַמָּן אָמְרִין בְּשֵׁם רַב נַחְמָן בַּר יַעֲקֹב כָּל־שֶׁנּוֹתְנִין לוֹ אֱגוֹז וּמַשְׁלִיכוֹ צְרוֹר וְהוּא נוֹטְלוֹ. הַמּוֹצִיא בְּיָדוֹ כְמוֹצִיא בְּאַשְׁפָּה. אֱגוֹז וְהוּא נוֹטְלוֹ צְרוֹר וְהוּא מַשְׁלִיכוֹ גְּזֵילוֹ גֶּזֶל מִפְּנֵי דַרְכֵי שָׁלוֹם. אֱגוֹז וּצְרוֹר וְהוּא נוֹטְלָן וּמַצְנִיעָן וּמְבִיאָן לְאַחַר זְמָן גְּזֵילוֹ גֶּזֶל גָּמוּר. זָכָה לְעַצְמוֹ אֲבָל לֹא לַאֲחֵרִים. רַב הוּנָא אָמַר כְּשֵׁם שֶׁהוּא זוֹכֶה לְעַצְמוֹ כָּךְ הוּא זוֹכֶה לָאֲחֵרִים. הַכֹּל מוֹדִין שֶׁאֵין מַתָּנָתוֹ מַתָּנָה. דִּכְתִיב כִּי

יִתֵּן אִישׁ. מַתְּנַת אִישׁ מַתָּנָה וְאֵין מַתְּנַת קָטָן מַתָּנָה דִּבְרֵי חֲכָמִים. רִבִּי יוּדָה בַּר פָּזִי בְּשֵׁם רִבִּי יוֹחָנָן רִבִּי יַעֲקֹב בַּר אָחָא בְּשֵׁם רִבִּי יוֹחָנָן לְעוֹלָם אֵין גְּזֵילוֹ גֶּזֶל גָּמוּר עַד שֶׁיָּבִיא שְׁתֵּי שְׂעָרוֹת. רִבִּי אַבָּהוּ בְּשֵׁם רִבִּי יוֹחָנָן הָדָא דְתֵימָה לְהוֹצִיא מִמֶּנּוּ בְּדִין אֲבָל לְהָבִיא קָרְבַּן שְׁבוּעָה כָּל־עַמָּא מוֹדֵיי עַד שֶׁיָּבִיא שְׁתֵּי שְׂעָרוֹת. בְּרַם כְּרַבָּנִין דְּהָכָא (בְּשֵׁם)[80] רִבִּי יוֹסֵי בָּעֵי מֵעַתָּה אֲפִילוּ לְעַצְמוֹ לֹא יִזְכֶּה דִּכְתִיב אֶל רֵעֵהוּ עַד שֶׁיְּהֵא כְרֵעֵהוּ. רִבִּי יוֹסֵי בֵּי רִבִּי בוּן בְּשֵׁם שְׁמוּאֵל בַּר רַב יִצְחָק פָּתַר לָהּ בְּשִׁיטַּת אַפִּיוֹטוֹת. דְּתַנִּינָן תַּמָּן אַפִּיוֹטוֹת מִקְחָן מִקָּח וּמִמְכָּרָן מִמְכָּר בְּמִטַּלְטְלִין. וְהָתַנִּינָן אֲבָל אֵינוֹ מְזַכֶּה לֹא עַל יְדֵי בְּנוֹ וּבִתּוֹ הַקְּטַנִּים וְלֹא עַל יְדֵי עַבְדּוֹ וְשִׁפְחָתוֹ הַכְּנַעֲנִים מִפְּנֵי שֶׁיָּדָן כְּיָדוֹ. רַבָּנִין דְּקֵיסָרִין אָמְרִין כָּאן בְּקָטָן שֶׁיֵּשׁ בּוֹ דַעַת כָּאן בְּקָטָן שֶׁאֵין בּוֹ דַעַת.

How do we hold? If she[81] is an adult, she acquired [her freedom] by the signs [of puberty][82]; if she is a minor, may a minor acquire? Rebbi Yudan bar Shalom said before Rebbi Yose, explain it following him who said, a minor may give heave[83]. He said to him, even following him who said, a minor may give heave, may a minor acquire? Following the opinion of the rabbis there[84] it is acceptable since there, they say in the name of Rav Naḥman bar Jacob: One to whom one gives a nut and he throws it away, a pebble and he keeps it, what is found in his hand is as if found on a garbage heap; a nut and he keeps it, a pebble and he throws it away, what is robbed from him is robbed because of communal peace; a nut or a pebble he takes, hides them, and produces them later, what is robbed from him is total robbery. He can acquire for himself but not for others[85]. Rav Huna said, just as he can acquire for himself so he can acquire for others. Everybody agrees[86] that his gift is not a gift since it is written (*Ex.* 22:6): "If a man give." The gift of a man is a gift, but the gift of a minor is no gift, the words of the Sages. Rebbi Jehudah bar Pazi in the name of Rebbi Joḥanan, Rebbi Jacob bar Aḥa in the name of Rebbi Joḥanan, robbing from him is not total robbery unless he grew two pubic hairs. Rebbi Abbahu in the name of Rebbi Joḥanan, that is, to recover from him by a law suit, but to have to bring a sacrifice for [a false] oath only if he grew two pubic hairs[87]. But following the rabbis here, Rebbi Yose asked that even for himself he should not be able to acquire since it is written (*Ex.* 22:6): "To his neighbor", until he be like his neighbor. Rebbi Yose ben Rebbi Abun in the name of Samuel ben Rav Isaac explained it by the method of small children. As we have stated there[88]: "For school children, their buying is buying and their selling selling, for movables." But did we not state[89]: "He cannot make them acquire through his minor son or daughter or his Canaanite male or female slave, because their hand is like his hand." The rabbis of Caesarea say, here a minor with knowledge[90], there a minor without knowledge.

80 Missing in the Rome ms. and the parallels in *Eruvin* 7, fol. 24c, *Giṭṭin* 5:9, fol. 47b.

81 The female Hebrew slave who when she becomes an adult either is a wife or a free adult; cf. Note 75. The Babli (*Giṭṭin* 65a) restricts the female Hebrew slave to redeeming heave of produce not grown in the soil (in a flower pot without a hole). This answer is very questionable for many reasons.

82 It is argued (*Mekhilta Mišpaṭim* 3) that the verse (*Ex.* 21:7) which gave the father the right to sell his daughter also restricted her servitude to the period in which the father had this right, before she became an adult.

83 Cf. *Terumot* 1:1, Notes 56-58.

84 In Babylonia.

85 In the Babli, *Giṭṭin* 65a, the formulation (by Rava, student of Rav Naḥman) is: "There are three stages for minors. If he throws away a pebble and takes a nut, he can acquire for himself but not for others; for school children, their buying is buying and their selling selling, for movables; if they reached the time of vows (cf. *Terumot*, Mishnah 1:3, Note 105) their

vows and dedications are valid; but to sell inherited real estate (without permission of the court) one must be 20 years old."

86 The Babli, *Baba Qama* 106b, concurs.

87 The minor, or an adult representing him, can successfully prosecute the robber from a minor in court but if in the course of the proceedings the accused swears falsely that he did not take anything, he is not obliged to bring (or, if he has a guilty conscience, he is barred from bringing) a guilt sacrifice since his robbery was forbidden by police law, not biblical law.

88 Mishnah *Giṭṭin* 5:9. The quote here shows that ה and א were both silent.

89 Mishnah *Eruvin* 7:6. In order to turn a dead-end street into a private domain for the purpose of carrying on the Sabbath, one has to affix to it a symbolic gate and then all residents of the dead-end street have to contribute to the food for a common meal. It is acceptable that one person designate the food, e. g., a wine barrel, and then appoints somebody to acquire for the other dwellers their part for this Sabbath. The qualifications in that Mishnah are the same as in the Mishnah here, with the same questions about the qualifications of the female Hebrew slave. (Since the devices of participation and *eruv* are ascribed to King Solomon, the mention of the Hebrew slave can be justified in that case.)

90 It seems that a "minor with knowledge" is a minor who reached the time of vows, cf. *Tosaphot Sanhedrin* 68b, *s. v.* קטן.

תַּמָּן תַּנִּינָן הַשּׁוֹאֵל אֶת הַפָּרָה וְשִׁילְּחָהּ לוֹ בְּיַד בְּנוֹ בְּיַד עַבְדּוֹ בְּיַד שְׁלוּחוֹ. לֵית הָדָא אָמְרָה שֶׁהָעֶבֶד זָכָה מֵרַבּוֹ לְאַחֵר. אָמַר רִבִּי לָעְזָר תִּיפְתָּר בְּעֶבֶד עִבְרִי. אָמַר רִבִּי יוֹחָנָן אֲפִילוּ תִּיפְתְּרִינֵיהּ בְּעֶבֶד כְּנַעֲנִי תִּיפְתָּר בְּאוֹמֵר לוֹ פְּתַח לָהּ וְהִיא בָּאָה מֵאֵילֶיהָ. וְתַנֵּי כֵן הִנְהִיגָהּ הִמְשִׁיכָהּ קָרָא לָהּ וּבָאת אַחֲרָיו נִתְחַיֵּיב לָהּ לְשַׁלֵּם כְּשׁוֹאֵל.

[91]There, we have stated[92]: "If somebody borrows a cow and [the lender] sent her to him through his son, his slave, or his agent." Does this not say that a slave is able to transfer rights from his master to another

person? Rebbi Eleazar[93] said, explain it about a Hebrew slave. Rebbi Joḥanan said, you can even explain it for a Canaanite slave, it he told him, open the gate for her and she will go by herself, as we have stated: If he led her, drew her, called her[94] and she followed him, he is required to pay as a borrower.

91 Parallels to this paragraph and the next are in *Eruvin* 7, *Qiddušin* 1:3, fol. 60a.

92 Mishnah *Baba Meẓi'a* 8:4; Babli 98b. If the borrowed animal dies, the borrower is liable to pay. Therefore, it is important to determine the exact time at which the obligation of the borrower starts. This is the moment in which disposal of the cow is transferred from lender to borrower. The Mishnah states that if the borrower asks that the cow be brought to him by the lender's slave, he becomes liable as soon as the slave goes on his way. But this seems to contradict the Mishnah here; if the slave's hand (in the legal sense) is his owner's then the cow should not leave the lender's domain until she is handed over to the borrower since nobody doubts that if the owner himself drives the cow to the borrower, the latter's responsibility starts only at the moment of delivery, not during the trip.

93 In the Babli, *Baba Meẓi'a* 99a, the position of R. Eleazar is Samuel's, that of R. Joḥanan is Rav's.

94 In the Babli: Hit her with a stick.

רִבִּי זְעִירָא שָׁמַע לָהּ מִן הָכָא אֲבָל אֵינוֹ מְזַכֶּה לֹא עַל יְדֵי בְנוֹ וּבִתּוֹ הַקְּטַנִּים וְלֹא עַל יְדֵי עַבְדּוֹ וְשִׁפְחָתוֹ הַכְּנַעֲנִים מִפְּנֵי שֶׁאֵין יָדָן כְּיָדוֹ. לֵית הָדָא אָמְרָה שֶׁאֵין הָעֶבֶד זָכָה מֵרַבּוֹ לְאַחֵר. תִּיפְתָּר כְּרִבִּי מֵאִיר דְּרִבִּי מֵאִיר עֲבִיד יַד הָעֶבֶד כְּיַד רַבּוֹ. וְהָתַנֵּי אִשְׁתּוֹ. רִבִּי מֵאִיר עֲבַד יַד הָאִשָּׁה כְּיַד בַּעֲלָהּ. רִבִּי חֲנַנְיָה בְשֵׁם רִבִּי פִּינְחָס תִּיפְתָּר כְּהָדֵין תַּנַּייָה דְתַנֵּי אִשְׁתּוֹ אֵינָהּ פּוֹדָה לוֹ מַעֲשֵׂר שֵׁינִי. רִבִּי שִׁמְעוֹן בֶּן אֶלְעָזָר אוֹמֵר מִשּׁוּם רִבִּי מֵאִיר אִשְׁתּוֹ פּוֹדָה לוֹ מַעֲשֵׂר שֵׁינִי. וְהָדֵין תַּנַּייָה רִבִּי מֵאִיר עֲבַד יַד הָעֶבֶד כְּיַד רַבּוֹ וְלֹא יַד הָאִשָּׁה כְּיַד בַּעֲלָהּ.

Rebbi Zeïra understood it from here: "But he cannot make them acquire through his minor son or daughter or his Canaanite male or female slave, because their hand is not like his hand." Does this not imply that a slave is not able to transfer rights from his master to another person? Explain it following Rebbi Meïr since Rebbi Meïr makes the hand of the slave the hand of his master[95]. But did we not state[96] "his wife"? Rebbi Meïr holds that the hand of the wife is the hand of her husband! Rebbi Ḥananiah said in the name of Rebbi Phineas, explain it following the Tanna who stated[97]: "His wife cannot redeem Second Tithe for him. Rebbi Simeon ben Eleazar says in the name of Rebbi Meïr, his wife can redeem Second Tithe for him." For that Tanna, Rebbi Meïr makes the hand of the slave the hand of his master but not the hand of the wife the hand of her husband!

95 Everywhere in the Mishnah. The *baraita* denies legal standing to minors and slaves.

96 Mishnah *Eruvin* 7:6; cf. Note 89. In the list of people empowered, the wife is noted together with the adult children since her husband cannot make an *eruv* for her without her consent.

97 Tosephta 4:7. In the Babli, Rava restricts the statement of R. Simeon ben Eleazar to the case that the wife inherited Second Tithe. Since R. Meïr holds that Second Tithe is Heaven's money, the Second Tithe does not become part of the estate. If the wife now redeems the tithe with household money, the money is the husband's but the tithe is not; therefore, no fifth is due. The Babli rejects the conclusion of the Yerushalmi here.

(fol. 54c) **משנה ה:** הָיָה עוֹמֵד בְּגוֹרֶן וְאֵין בְּיָדוֹ מָעוֹת אוֹמֵר לַחֲבֵירוֹ הֲרֵי הַפֵּירוֹת הָאֵילוּ נְתוּנִין לָךְ מַתָּנָה וְחוֹזֵר וְאוֹמֵר לוֹ הֲרֵי הֵן מְחוּלָּלִין עַל מָעוֹת שֶׁבַּבַּיִת.

Mishnah 5: If somebody was standing on the threshing floor and no coins were in his hand[98], he says to a friend, this produce is given to you as a gift; then he goes on and says to him, it is redeemed[99] by coins in the house.

98 If the coins were in his hand, he could give them to another person and let him redeem the Second Tithe without paying a fifth.

99 Since now the produce is not his own, he does not have to pay the fifth. For what has to be formally given to the neighbor, cf. Note 54.

(fol. 55a) **הלכה ה:** בָּרִאשׁוֹנָה הָיוּ עוֹשִׂין כֵּן בְּמָעוֹת. הָיוּ נוֹטְלִין אוֹתָן וּבוֹרְחִין. הִתְקִינוּ שֶׁיְּהוּ עוֹשִׂין בְּפֵירוֹת. אַף עַל פִּי כֵן הָיוּ נוֹטְלִין אוֹתָן וְאוֹכְלִין אוֹתָן. הִתְקִינוּ שֶׁיְּהֵא מְזַכֶּה לוֹ אֶחָד מֵעֲשָׂרָה לְקַרְקַע.

Halakhah 5: In earlier times, they were doing so with coins[100]. They took them and fled[101]. They instituted that one does it with produce[102]. Nevertheless, they took and ate it. They instituted that he should give him the right to one in ten on the ground[103].

100 The farmer gave coins to a third party as a gift that the recipient should redeem his Second Tithe.

101 In the Tosephta (4:3), R. Joshua ben Qorḥa reports that the practice was discontinued since many people did not give the coins as gifts.

102 The procedure explained in the Mishnah.

103 As explained in *Peah* 3:8, a square inch of ground can be given to the recipient and the ownership of the produce transferred with it. In that case, ownership can be transferred without the produce actually coming into the hands of the second person who, therefore, cannot eat it. This sentence is not in the Tosephta.

רִבִּי אִינַיְיָא בַּר סִיסַי סְלַק גַּבֵּי רִבִּי יוֹנָה אָמַר לֵיהּ אֶפְרוֹק לָךְ בְּהָדָא סִילְעָא. אָמַר אִי בָּעֵי מֵינַס נַסָּא חָזַר וְנַסְתָּה מִינֵיה. אָמַר רִבִּי יוֹנָה כָּךְ שְׁעָרִית דַּעְתֵּיהּ דְּאִילּוּ נַסְתָּהּ לָא הֲוָה אָמַר לִי כְּלוּם לְפוּם כֵּן יְהָבֵת יָתָהּ לָהּ.

Rebbi Inaya bar Sisai[104] came to Rebbi Jonah and said to him, shall I redeem for you with that tetradrachma[105]? He said, if you want to take it, take it. Then he took it back from him. Rebbi Jonah said, I had judged his opinion that if I took it back he would not say anything; therefore I gave it to him[106].

104 He is R. Ḥanina bar Sisai; cf. *Berakhot* p. 493.

105 With R. Jonah's coin, in the style of earlier times, as given in the previous *baraita*.

106 If there was no danger that the other person would run away with the money, the earlier practice is preferable to that of the Mishnah.

(fol. 54c) **משנה ו:** מָשַׁךְ מִמֶּנּוּ מַעֲשֵׂר בְּסֶלַע וְלֹא הִסְפִּיק לִפְדּוֹתוֹ עַד שֶׁעָמַד בִּשְׁתַּיִם נוֹתֵן לוֹ בְּסֶלַע וּמִשְׂתַּכֵּר בְּסֶלַע וּמַעֲשֵׂר שֵׁנִי שֶׁלּוֹ. מָשַׁךְ מִמֶּנּוּ מַעֲשֵׂר בִּשְׁתַּיִם וְלֹא הִסְפִּיק לִפְדּוֹתוֹ עַד שֶׁעָמַד בְּסֶלַע נוֹתֵן לוֹ סֶלַע מֵחוּלָּיו וְסֶלַע שֶׁל מַעֲשֵׂר שֵׁינִי שֶׁלּוֹ. אִם הָיָה עַם הָאָרֶץ נוֹתֵן לוֹ מִדְּמָיו.

Mishnah 6: If [somebody] took from [another] tithe in the value of a tetradrachma[107] and did not pay to redeem it until it became worth two, he gives him a tetradrachma, gains a tetradrachma, and the Second Tithe is his. If [somebody] took from [another] tithe in the value of two and did not pay to redeem it until it became worth one tetradrachma, he gives him a tetradrachma of profane money and a tetradrachma of his Second Tithe [money][108]. If he is a vulgar, he gives him from his *demay*[109].

107 A takes from B Second Tithe produce with the understanding that he will pay B one tetradrachma which will become tithe money and which B will be obliged to take to Jerusalem and spend there. As far as the civil contract is concerned, the act of taking concludes the contract and the monetary obligation is fixed. But the verse *Deut.* 14:25 decrees that redemption of Second Tithe is the giving of money. Therefore, the redemption is carried out only at the moment of payment and an additional tetradrachma from the buyer should become tithe money for the buyer, not the seller. Then the Second Tithe becomes profane in the hand of the buyer but not before. (Explanation of כסף משנה to Maimonides, *Ma'aser Šeni* 8:7.)

108 The situation is essentially the same as before but, since it was stated in Halakhah 3 that Second Tithe cannot be redeemed for more than its market value, only one tetradrachma can be tithe money but naturally he has to fulfill his contract and pay two tetradrachmas. Therefore, the buyer must give at least one tetradrachma of profane coin which becomes tithe money; the other coin he may pay either in profane money and it remains profane or in tithe money which remains tithe money and has to be taken to Jerusalem.

109 This reading is the Maimonides tradition (the vocalization follows the Yemenite tradition) and the first explanation of R. Simson. Since tithe money may not be delivered to a vulgar, the second coin due has to be profane or from money reserved from *demay* tithe. The second explanation of R. Simson reads מִדָּמָיו (with the corrector of the ms.) "from his money" and requires that the vulgar be paid 100% in profane money where only one coin becomes tithe money.

(fol. 55a) **הלכה ו:** מַתְנִיתָא דְּלֹא כְרַבָּן שִׁמְעוֹן בֶּן גַּמְלִיאֵל דְּתַנִּינָן רַבָּן שִׁמְעוֹן בֶּן גַּמְלִיאֵל אוֹמֵר לְעוֹלָם מְשִׁיכָתוֹ שֶׁלְּמַעֲשֵׂר שֵׁינִי הִיא פִדְיוֹנוֹ.

Halakhah 6: The Mishnah does not follow Rabban Simeon ben Gamliel, as we have stated[110]: "Rabban Simeon ben Gamliel says, always the taking up of Second Tithe is its redemption."

110 In the Tosephta, 4:14, this is the majority opinion: "The redemption of Second Tithe is its sale. Rabban Simeon ben Gamliel and R. Ismael ben R. Joḥanan ben Beroqa say, also for a dedicated thing, its being taken up is its redemption." For these authors, the matter of payment is purely an affair of civil, not religious, law between the parties.

רִבִּי יוֹסֵי בְשֵׁם רִבִּי לָעְזָר אֵין מוֹסִיפִין חוֹמֶשׁ עַל הַסֶּלַע הַשְּׁנִייָה. וְהָיָה רִבִּי לָעְזָר מִסְתַּכֵּל בֵּיהּ. אָמַר לֵיהּ מָה אַתְּ מִסְתַּכֵּל בִּי. אַף רִבִּי הִילָא מוֹדֵי בָהּ כַּיי דְּאָמַר רִבִּי יוֹחָנָן כָּל־מַעֲשֵׂר שֵׁינִי שֶׁאֵינוֹ הוּא וּפִדְיוֹנוֹ מִשֶּׁלּוֹ אֵינוֹ מוֹסִיף חוֹמֶשׁ.

Rebbi Assi in the name of Rebbi Eleazar: One does not add a fifth to the second tetradrachma[111]. Rebbi Eleazar[112] stared at him. He said to him, why do you stare at me? Rebbi Hila also agrees with it, following what Rebbi Joḥanan said, for any tithe, where not it and its redemption money is his[113], he does not add a fifth.

111 The one which remains in the hand of the buyer in the first case.

112 This name tradition, found in both mss., is impossible since R. Eleazar, the originator of the rule in question, died before R. Yose's time. "Staring" is always a sign of disapproval.

113 While in this case the Second Tithe was acquired by being handed over by the seller to the buyer, this acquisition is not counted for the Second Tithe which may not be sold except for redemption. It follows that by biblical standards, the tithe at the moment of its redemption by A was still B's tithe, even if it was not B's property.

(fol. 54c) **משנה ז:** הַפּוֹדֶה מַעֲשֵׂר שֵׁינִי וְלֹא קָרָא שֵׁם רִבִּי יוֹסֵי אוֹמֵר דַּיּיו. רִבִּי יוּדָה אוֹמֵר צָרִיךְ לְפָרֵשׁ. הָיָה מְדַבֵּר עִם הָאִשָּׁה עַל עִיסְקֵי גִיטָּהּ קִידּוּשֶׁיהָ נָתַן לָהּ קִידּוּשֶׁיהָ וְלֹא פֵּירַשׁ רִבִּי יוֹסֵי אוֹמֵר דַּיּיו וְרִבִּי יוּדָה אוֹמֵר צָרִיךְ לְפָרֵשׁ.

Mishnah 7: If somebody redeemed Second Tithe and did not give it a name[114], Rebbi Yose says it is sufficient, Rebbi Jehudah says he has to be explicit. If a man was talking with a woman about her bill of divorce or her preliminary marriage and gave her [the valuable for] preliminary marriage and did not spell it out[115], Rebbi Yose says it is sufficient, Rebbi Jehudah says he has to be explicit.

114 He thought to redeem the tithe but did not voice his intention.

115 The usual interpretation is that he gave the valuable and said, take this to be married, but not: take this to be married *to me*. While in general it is required that the person should be named, if it is clear from the context, one may dispense with it following R. Yose.

(fol. 55a) **הלכה ז**: מַהוּ צָרִיךְ לְפָרֵשׁ זֶה גִיטֵּיךְ וְזֶה קִידּוּשַׁיִךְ וְהָכָא זֶה פִּדְיוֹן מַעֲשֵׂר שֵׁינִי.

Halakhah 7: How must he be explicit? "This is your bill of divorce, or this is for your preliminary marriage," and here: "This is for redemption of Second Tithe."

רִבִּי זְעִירָא חִיָיה בַּר בּוּן אָדָא[116] בַּר תַּחְלִיפָא בְּשֵׁם רַב הוֹשַׁעְיָה מַה פְּלִיגִין כְּשֶׁהִפְלִיגוּ דַעְתָּן לְעִנְיָינוֹת אֲחֵרִים אֲבָל אִם הָיוּ עֲסוּקִין בְּאוֹתוֹ עִנְיָין גֵּט הוּא.

Rebbi Zeïra, Ḥiyya bar Abun, Abba bar Taḥlifa, in the name of Rebbi Hoshaia, when do they differ? If they thought about other things but if they still were on the same subject, it is a bill of divorce[117].

116 Reading of the Rome ms., confirmed by the Leyden ms. in the quote of this statement in the next paragraph. Leyden and Venice here: אבא.

117 In the Babli, *Qiddušin* 6a, the statement is in the names of Samuel and R. Hoshaia.

רִבִּי חַגַּי בָּעָא קוֹמֵי רִבִּי יוֹסֵי רִבִּי כְּרִבִּי יוֹסֵי וְרִבִּי נָתָן כְּרִבִּי יוּדָה דְּתַנִּינָן תַּמָּן אִיפְשִׁי שֶׁתְּקַבֵּל לָהּ. אֶלָּא הָא לָךְ וְתֵן לָהּ אִם רָצָה לְהַחֲזִיר יַחֲזִיר. מַתְנִיתָא דְּרִבִּי דְּתַנֵּי אָמְרָה הָבֵא לִי גִיטִּי וְהָלַךְ וְאָמַר לוֹ אִשְׁתְּךָ אָמְרָה הִתְקַבֵּל לִי גִיטִּי הוֹלִיכוֹ לָהּ וּנְתָנוֹ לָהּ זַכֵּה לָהּ הִתְקַבֵּל לָהּ. אִם רָצָה לְהַחֲזִיר לֹא יַחֲזִיר דִּבְרֵי רִבִּי. רִבִּי נָתָן אוֹמֵר הוֹלִיכוֹ לָהּ וּנְתָנוֹ לָהּ אִם רָצָה לְהַחֲזִיר יַחֲזִיר. זַכֵּה לָהּ וְהִתְקַבֵּל לָהּ אִם רָצָה לְהַחֲזִיר לֹא יַחֲזִיר. רִבִּי אוֹמֵר (fol. 55b) בְּכוּלָּן לֹא יַחֲזִיר עַד שֶׁיֹּאמַר לוֹ אֵי אֶיפְשִׁי שֶׁתְּקַבְּלִי אֶלָּא שֶׁתּוֹלִיכִי לָהּ. וְקַשְׁיָא עַל דְּרִבִּי. הָא לָךְ מִדִּיבּוּרִי אִם רָצָה לְהַחֲזִיר לֹא יַחֲזִיר. וְקַשְׁיָיא עַל דְּרִבִּי נָתָן. הָא לָךְ מִדִּיבּוּרָא אִם רָצָה לְהַחֲזִיר לֹא יַחֲזִיר. רִבִּי חוּנָא אָמַר נַעֲשֶׂה שְׁלוּחוֹ וּשְׁלוּחָהּ. אִיסָּא אָמַר כּוּלְּהוֹן דְּתַנִּינָן שְׁלוּחוֹ וּשְׁלוּחָהּ מְגוֹרֶשֶׁת וְאֵינָהּ מְגוֹרֶשֶׁת. אָמַר לֵיהּ וּמָה בְיָדָךְ. וְאָמַר רִבִּי זְעִירָא חִיָּה בַּר בּוּן אָדָא בַּר תַּחְלִיפָא בְּשֵׁם רַב הוֹשַׁעְיָה מַה פְּלִיגִין כְּשֶׁהִפְלִיגוּ דַעְתָּן לְעִנְיָינִים אֲחֵרִים אֲבָל אִם הָיוּ עֲסוּקִין בְּאוֹתוֹ עִנְיָין גֵּט הוּא. וְהָכָא אֲפִילוּ הֵן עֲסוּקִין בְּאוֹתוֹ עִנְיָין הִיא הַמַּחְלוֹקֶת.

[118]Rebbi Ḥaggai asked before Rebbi Yose: Rebbi follows Rebbi Yose and Rebbi Nathan Rebbi Jehudah, as we have stated there[119]: "I cannot accept that you accept it for her, but here you have it and give it to her, if he wants to take it back, he may take it back." The Mishnah is Rebbi's, as it was stated[120]: "If she said, bring me my bill of divorce, but he said to him, your wife said, accept my bill of divorce for me. 'Bring it to her, give it to her, acquire it for her, receive it for her', if he wants to take it back, he may not take it back, the words of Rebbi. Rebbi Nathan says, 'bring it to her, give it to her,' if he wants to take it back, he may take it back; 'acquire it for her, receive it for her', if he wants to take it back, he may not take it back." Rebbi says, in any of these cases he may not take it back except if he says, "I cannot accept that you accept it for her, but give it to her." It is difficult for Rebbi, "here you have it from my word",

if he wants to take it back, he may not take it back. It is difficult for Rebbi Nathan, "here you have it from her word", if he wants to take it back, he may not take it back[121].

Rebbi Ḥuna[122] said, he becomes his and her agent[123]. Assi[124] said, everywhere we have stated "his and her agent", she is divorced and not divorced[125].

He[126] said to him, what do you have in your hand, did not Rebbi Zeïra, Ḥiyya bar Abun, Abba bar Taḥlifa, say in the name of Rebbi Hoshaia, when do they differ? If they thought about other things but if they still were at the same theme, it is a bill of divorce.

118 The parallel to this and the next paragraph is in *Giṭṭin* 6:1, fol. 47d.

119 Mishnah *Giṭṭin* 6:1, referring to the delivery of a bill of divorce if husband and wife are at different places. Since the verse decrees (*Deut.* 24:1): "He shall write her a bill of divorce and give it into her hand," a divorce is not valid unless the bill of divorce is written on the order of the husband and delivered into the hand of the wife. If she appoints an agent, all depends on the instruction of the agent. If he is appointed to receive the bill in her stead, she is divorced the moment the agent receives it. If he is appointed to bring her the bill, she is divorced only when the bill is delivered into her hand. In the second case, it is the majority opinion that the husband may change his mind and annul the divorce anytime the bill has not yet been delivered. Cf. *Peah* 4. Note 119; *Demay* 4, Note 83.

In the case mentioned here, the husband refuses to recognize the commission of the agent to receive the bill but appoints him his own agent to deliver the bill. Since the wife's commission was explicitly refused, the agent is now exclusively the husband's agent; there are no legal complications. The complications arise if either the agent does not exactly repeat his instructions to the husband or if the husband appoints him his agent without explicitly repudiating the wife's commission.

120 Tosephta *Giṭṭin* 6:1. The opinion ascribed in the Yerushalmi to

R. Nathan is reported in the Tosephta as that of Rabban Simeon ben Gamliel. But the *baraita* quoted in the Babli, *Giṭṭin* 63a, is the same as the text in the Yerushalmi. The Babli also notes that Mishnah *Giṭṭin* 6:1 states Rebbi's opinion.

121 The last two sentences are R. Ḥaggai's argument: If he says, "here you have it from my word," is that not invalidating the wife's commission? In that case, "give it to her" is also invalidating the wife's commission and he should be able to change his mind. For R. Nathan, the argument is the opposite: "bring it to her, give it to her," can be read as accepting the wife's commission; he should not be able to change his mind.

122 In the Babli, *Giṭṭin* 63b, this is the opinion of Rebbi Abba in the name of Rav Huna in the name of Rav.

123 The Babli explains that in this case, it is doubtful which commission the agent executes and, therefore, whether his action is legal.

124 Reading of the parallel in *Giṭṭin*.

125 She cannot remarry without a second bill of divorce and, if she is childless and the husband dies before executing the second bill, she cannot marry her brother-in-law.

126 This is now R. Yose's (the Amora) response to R. Ḥaggai, that the situation described in the Mishnah here is not comparable to that in *Giṭṭin* 6:1.

רִבִּי עֶזְרָה בָּעָא קוֹמֵי רִבִּי מָנָא אַף לְעִנְייָן מַתָּנָה כֵן. אָדָם עוֹשֶׂה שָׁלִיחַ לְקַבֵּל דָּבָר שֶׁאֵינוֹ שֶׁלּוֹ. אָמַר לֵיהּ תַּמָּן הַתּוֹרָה זִיכָּת אוֹתָהּ בְּגִיטָּהּ וְהִיא עוֹשָׂה שָׁלִיחַ לְקַבֵּל דָּבָר שֶׁהוּא שֶׁלָּהּ. אִית לָךְ מֵימַר בְּמַתָּנָה אָדָם עוֹשֶׂה שָׁלִיחַ לְקַבֵּל דָּבָר שֶׁאֵינוֹ שֶׁלּוֹ. וְעוֹד מִן הָדָא דְּאָמַר רִבִּי יוֹסֵי רִבִּי יַעֲקֹב בַּר זַבְדִּי רִבִּי אַבָּהוּ בְשֵׁם רִבִּי יוֹחָנָן אָמַר לִיתֵּן מַתָּנָה לַחֲבֵירוֹ וּבִיקֵּשׁ לַחֲזוֹר בּוֹ חוֹזֵר בּוֹ. קָם רִבִּי יוֹסֵי עִם רִבִּי יַעֲקֹב בַּר זַבְדִּי אָמַר לֵיהּ וְהֵינוֹ הִין צֶדֶק. אָמְרִין בְּשָׁעָה שֶׁאָמַר הִין צֶדֶק הֲוָה.

Rebbi Ezra asked before Rebbi Mana: Is it the same for a gift[127]? Can a person appoint an agent for something that is not his? He said to him, there the Torah gave her the right to a bill of divorce and she appoints an agent to receive what rightfully is hers[128]. Can you say in regard to a gift that a person can appoint an agent for something that is not his? [129]In addition, from what Rebbi Yose, Rebbi Jacob bar Zavdi, Rebbi Abbahu in the name of Rebbi Joḥanan said, if somebody said to give a gift to another and he wants to take it back, he may take it back. Rebbi Yose stood near to Rebbi Jacob bar Zavdi and said to him, is that a just "yes"? They said, at the moment he said it, it was a just yes.

127 Are the rules of agency for receiving a gift the same as for receiving a bill of divorce.

128 The husband cannot divorce her without handing her a bill of divorce.

129 From here to the end of the Halakhah, the text is also in *Ševi'it* 10:9, Notes 133-134.

(fol. 54c) **משנה ח:** הַמֵּנִיחַ אִיסָּר וְאָכַל עָלָיו חֶצְיוֹ וְהָלַךְ לְמָקוֹם אַחֵר וַהֲרֵי הוּא יוֹצֵא בְּפוּנְדְּיוֹן אוֹכֵל עָלָיו עוֹד אִיסָּר. הַמֵּנִיחַ פוּנְדְּיוֹן וְאָכַל עָלָיו חֶצְיוֹ וְהָלַךְ לְמָקוֹם אַחֵר וַהֲרֵי הוּא יוֹצֵא בְּאִיסָּר אוֹכֵל עָלָיו עוֹד פְּלַג. הַמֵּנִיחַ אִיסָּר שֶׁל מַעֲשֵׂר שֵׁינִי אוֹכֵל עָלָיו אַחַד עָשָׂר אִיסָּר וְאֶחָד מִמֵּאָה בְּאִיסָּר. בֵּית שַׁמַּאי אוֹמְרִים הַכֹּל עֲשָׂרָה וּבֵית הִלֵּל אוֹמְרִים בְּוַדַּאי אַחַד עָשָׂר וּבִדְמָאי עֲשָׂרָה.

Mishnah 8: He who put aside an *as* and ate for half of its worth, then went to another place where it is worth a *dupondius*, has to eat another *as* for it[130]. He who put aside a *dupondius* and ate for half of its worth, then went to another place where it would be worth an *as*, has to eat another half[131]. He who put aside an *as* of Second Tithe eats for it 11 *as* and $^{1}/_{100}$ of an *as*[132]; the House of Shammai say, 10 in total[133], but the House of Hillel say, if it is certain 11[134] and for *demay* 10.

130 He put aside a profane *as* to redeem Second Tithe and ate from his redeemed Second Tithe but it was worth only half an *as*, then half of the *as* is still profane. If now he goes to a place where his copper coin is worth a local *dupondius*, or 2 *as*, then half the coin there is worth a full *as* and he has to eat another *as*'s worth of Second Tithe since it was stated in Halakhah 4:3 that Second Tithe cannot be redeemed for more than its wholesale value. (Explanation of Maimonides's first version, R. Simson, and R. Isaac Simponti.)

131 By the same argument as before, he has to redeem Second Tithe in the worth of half the coin, which now is half an *as*.

132 Maimonides reads אוֹכֵל עָלָיו אַחַד עָשָׂר בְּאִיסָּר "he eats $^{11}/_{10}$ of an *as*." This is not the reading of the Leyden ms. of the Yerushalmi, the Mishnah in the Babli ms. Munich, and the Cambridge and Kaufmann mss. of the Mishnah. Therefore, it seems that one has to explain the Mishnah following R. Simson and R. Isaac Simponti, that this part of the Mishnah speaks about tithe money which is spent in Jerusalem. The produce is bought from a vulgar who was seen to have separated (unprepared, therefore pure) Second Tithe but who then put the Second Tithe back into his profane produce since he is in Jerusalem. If the fellow then buys from him, nine parts are presumed to be profane and one Second Tithe. Since $^{1}/_{9} = .\bar{1}$, an infinite decimal, in order to turn the *as* into profane coin, he has to buy for $^{10}/_{9}$ *as*. This means that "11 *as* and $^{1}/_{100}$ of an *as*" has to be read as "11 *as* and 11 times $^{1}/_{100}$ of an *as*".

133 The House of Shammai always, and the House of Hillel in the case of *demay*, do not believe that the vulgar separated First Tithe. Therefore, he has separately to give $^{1}/_{10}$ as First Tithe.

134 They mean, $11.\bar{1}$.

(fol. 55b) **הלכה ח:** תַּנֵּי רִבִּי חִייָה שְׁנֵי אִיסָּרִין פּוֹנְדִּיוֹן. אָמַר רִבִּי יוֹסֵי מַתְנִיתָא אָֽמְרָה כֵן הַמֵּנִיחַ אִיסָּר וְאָכַל עָלָיו חֶצְיוֹ וְהָלַךְ לוֹ לְמָקוֹם אַחֵר וַהֲרֵי הוּא יוֹצֵא בְּפוֹנְדִּיוֹן אוֹכֵל עָלָיו עוֹד אִיסָּר.

Halakhah 8: Rebbi Ḥiyya stated, two *as* equal a *dupondius*[135]. Rebbi Yose[136] said, the Mishnah says so: "He who put aside an *as* and ate for half its worth, went to another place where the coin is worth a *dupondius*, has to eat another *as* for it."

135 In the military anarchy and later, *as* and *dupondius* had long vanished from circulation and their relationship was no longer generally known.

136 Who lived after Diocletian's currency reform.

שְׁמוּאֵל אָמַר לָא מָצֵייָא תַנִּייָה. אִין יְסַב חַד לַעֲשָׂרָה צָרִיךְ לְמֵיסַב חָדָא לְמָאת. אִין יְסַב חָדָא לְמָאת. צָרִיךְ לְמֵיתַב חָדָא לְאֶלֶף. אִין יְסַב חָדָא לְאֶלֶף. צָרִיךְ מֵיסַב חָדָא לַעֲשָׂרָה אֲלָפִין.

Samuel says, you cannot state that; when he takes one in ten, he has to take one in a hundred. When he takes one in a hundred he has to take one in a thousand, when he takes one in a thousand he has to take one in ten thousand[137].

137 He refers to the statement of the House of Hillel who qote only 11 instead of 11.11111 . . . The same argument and a similar text is in *Demay* 7:8, Note 104.

בֵּית שַׁמַּי אוֹמְרִים בְּוַדַּאי אַחַד עָשָׂר וּבִדְמַאי עֲשָׂרָה. תַּנֵּי בַּר קַפָּרָא בֵּין בִּדְמַאי בֵּין בְּוַדַּאי אַחַד עָשָׂר הֵן. הוֹרֵי רִבִּי יוּדָן בֵּירִבִּי שָׁלוֹם כְּהָדָא דְתַנֵּי בַּר קַפָּרָא. בֵּית שַׁמַּאי כְּרִבִּי לִיעֶזֶר דְּרִבִּי לִיעֶזֶר אָמַר הַנֶּאֱמָן עַל הַשֵּׁינִי נֶאֱמָן עַל הָרִאשׁוֹן. אָמַר רִבִּי יוֹסֵי דִּבְרֵי הַכֹּל הִיא עָשׂוּ אוֹתוֹ כְּתוֹסֶפֶת הַבִּיכּוּרִים. מַה תּוֹסֶפֶת הַבִּיכּוּרִים נֶאֱכֶלֶת בְּטָהֳרָה וּפְטוּרָה מִדְּמַייֵ אַף זֶה נֶאֱכַל מִשּׁוּם שֵׁינִי וּפָטוּר מִן הָרִאשׁוֹן. אָתָא רִבִּי חֲנַנְיָה בְשֵׁם רִבִּי יוֹסֵי דְּרִבִּי לִיעֶזֶר הִיא.

The House of Shammai[138] say, if it is certain 11[134] and for *demay* 10. Bar Qappara stated, both for *demay* and for certain 11. Rebbi Yudan ben Rebbi Shalom taught what Bar Qappara had stated. The House of

Shammai follows Rebbi Eliezer, [139]since Rebbi Eliezer said, he who is trustworthy for the Second is trustworthy for the First. Rebbi Yose said, everybody agrees, they made it like additions to First Fruits. Just as additions to First Fruits are eaten in purity and are free from *demay*, so this is eaten as Second Tithe and is free from the First. Rebbi Ḥananiah confirmed in the name of Rebbi Issi: it is Rebbi Eliezer's.

138 It is possible that this is an error for "The House of Hillel". Since both mss. have the same reading, the error must already have been in the common *Vorlage*. It is more likely that this is a *baraita* which disagrees with the Mishnah.

139 From here to the end of the paragraph, the text is from *Demay* 4:5, Notes 60-62. Since the text there reads: "The *baraita* follows R. Eliezer," one has to accept that the text discussed here is a *baraita*.

(fol. 54c) **משנה ט**: כָּל־הַמָּעוֹת הַנִּמְצָאִין הֲרֵי אֵילוֹ חוּלִין וַאֲפִילוּ דֵינָרֵי זָהָב עִם הַכֶּסֶף וְעִם הַמָּעוֹת. מָצָא בְתוֹכָן חֶרֶשׂ וְכָתוּב עָלָיו מַעֲשֵׂר הֲרֵי זֶה מַעֲשֵׂר.

Mishnah 9: All found coins[140] are profane, even gold denars with silver or change[141]. If one found with them a potsherd reading "tithe", it is tithe.

משנה י: הַמּוֹצִיא כֵּלִי וְכָתוּב עָלָיו קָרְבָּן רִבִּי יְהוּדָה אוֹמֵר אִם הָיָה שֶׁל חֶרֶשׂ הוּא חוּלִין וּמָה שֶׁבְּתוֹכוֹ קָרְבָּן וְאִם הָיָה שֶׁל מַתֶּכֶת הוּא קָרְבָּן וּמָה שֶׁבְּתוֹכוֹ חוּלִין. אָמְרוּ לוֹ אֵין דֶּרֶךְ בְּנֵי אָדָם לִהְיוֹת כּוֹנְסִין חוּלִין בְּקָרְבָּן.

Mishnah 10: If one finds a vessel inscribed "sacrifice", Rebbi Jehudah said, if it was pottery it is profane and its contents sacrifice[142], but if it was metal it is sacrifice and its contents profane[143]. They said to him, people do not put profane in sacrifice [vessels].

משנה יא: הַמּוֹצֵיא כֵּלִי וְכָתוּב עָלָיו קוֹ״ף קָרְבָּן מֵ״ם מַעֲשֵׂר דַּלֵ״ת דְּמַאי טֵי״ת טֶבֶל. תָּ״יו תְּרוּמָה שֶׁבִּשְׁעַת הַסַּכָּנָה הָיוּ כוֹתְבִין תָּי״ו תַּחַת תְּרוּמָה. רִבִּי יוֹסֵי אוֹמֵר וְכוּלָּן שְׁמוֹת אָדָם הֵן. אָמַר רִבִּי יוֹסֵי אֲפִילוּ מָצָא חָבִית וְהִיא מְלֵיאָה פֵּירוֹת וְכָתוּב עָלֶיהָ תְּרוּמָה הֲרֵי אֵלּוּ חוּלִין שֶׁאֲנִי אוֹמֵר אֵישְׁתְּקַד הָיְתָה מְלֵיאָה פֵּירוֹת תְּרוּמָה וּפִינָּהּ.

Mishnah 11: If one finds a vessel inscribed ק it means sacrifice, מ tithe, ד *demay*, ט *ṭevel*, ת heave since in times of danger one wrote ת for heave[144]. Rebbi Yose says, all these are people's names[145]. Rebbi Yose said, even if he found an amphora full of produce and inscribed "heave", these are profane since I say last year it was full of tithe produce but he emptied it.

משנה יב: הָאוֹמֵר לִבְנוֹ מַעֲשֵׂר שֵׁינִי שֶׁבְּזָוִית זוֹ (fol. 54d) וּמְצָאוֹ בְּזָוִית אַחֶרֶת הֲרֵי אֵלּוּ חוּלִין. הֲרֵי שָׁם מְנָה וּמָצָא מָאתַיִם הַשְּׁאָר חוּלִין. מָאתַיִם וּמָצָא מְנָה הַכֹּל מַעֲשֵׂר.

Mishnah 12: If somebody said to his son, "Second Tithe is in that corner" but he found it in another corner, that is profane[146]. "There is a talent" but he found 200, the remainder is profane. "200" and he found 100, all is tithe.

140 The Maimonides autograph Mishnah and the Cambridge codex of the Galilean Mishnah add: "in Jerusalem". But in Jerusalem during the holidays, all coins found are considered tithe money, and the rest of the year coins found in the animal market are presumed to be tithe money since the main use of tithe money is for well-being sacrifices; Mishnah *Šeqalim* 7:2. Therefore, the text here is preferable and the meaning is that coins found anywhere, except in Jerusalem in the few instances enumerated in *Šeqalim* 7:2, are to be considered profane.

141 Here one could argue that silver and change are the tithe exchange for the gold coin which was the original tithe money.

142 A clay pot is too cheap to have been dedicated to the Temple. Therefore, only its contents are dedicated. The Sages do not oppose this statement.

143 Everybody agrees that metal vessels are valuable enough to be dedicated. Therefore, the vessel has to be considered Temple property (it cannot be a sacrifice). R, Jehudah holds that without further evidence, the contents of the vessel have to be considered profane, but the anonymous Sages hold that nobody uses a dedicated vessel to store profane material.

144 This proves the status of anything in the vessel. Again "sacrifice" means "dedicated to the Temple".

145 Everything is profane.

146 We assume the tithe was removed and what was found in another corner is other produce. Since 100 denar (a talent) are a part of 200, one assumes that 100 was taken and 100 remains. On the other hand, 100 cannot grow to 200; 100 must be new money.

(fol. 55b) **הלכה ט:** שֶׁלֹּא תֹאמַר הוֹאִיל וְאֵין דֶּרֶךְ בְּנֵי אָדָם לַעֲשׂוֹת כֵּן יְהֵא שֵׁינִי לְפוּם כָּךְ צָרַךְ מֵימַר חוּלִין.

Halakhah 9: That you should not say, since people do not usually act like this, one has to say "profane[147]".

147 The second part of Mishnah 9; it is not usual that people use an ostracon in a money bag.

תַּנֵּי אָלֶ״ף דָּלֶ״ת חֵי״ת טֵי״ת רֵי״שׁ מֶ״ם תָּי״ו תְּרוּמָה. אָלֶ״ף קַדְמִיתָא. דָּלֶ״ת דְּמַאי. חֵי״ת חֶלְבּוֹ. טֵי״ת טוּבוֹ. רֵי״שׁ רֵאשִׁית. מֶ״ם מַעֲשֵׂר. תָּי״ו תְּרוּמָה. בֵּי שִׁין שֵׁינִי. פֵּי שִׁין שֵׁינִי. יוּ״ד מֶ״ם מַעֲשֵׂר. מַעֲשֵׂר עִיר פֻּרְקוֹן. לְשֵׁם יוֹסֵי לְשֵׁם שִׁמְעוֹן לַעֲלוֹת לְאוֹכְלָן בִּירוּשָׁלֵם חוּלִין אֲנִי אוֹמֵר סִיבּוֹלֵיה עָשׂוּ בֵּינֵיהוֹן.

It was stated[148]: *Alef dalet het tet mem tav* heave. א "first"[149]. ד "*demay*". ח "its fat"[150]. ט "its best". ר "beginning"[149]. ת "heave". ב ש

"Second Tithe"[151], פ ש "Second Tithe"[152]. מ י׳[153] "tithe". Tithe for the City[154], redemption. Those on the name of Yose, on the name of Simeon, to take it up to eat in Jerusalem, are profane; I am saying contributions[155] they arranged among themselves.

148 Cf. Tosephta 5:1: If one found a vessel inscribed *alef dalet reš tav*, it is heave. *Yod mem* is tithe. *Pe šin* is Second. But the Sages say, all of them are people's names.

149 Heave is called "beginning" in *Num.* 18:12.

150 An expression for heave in *Num.* 18:12, 29.

151 Either ב for 2nd or ש for שני.

152 פ for פדיון or פורקן "redemption". In that case, the vessel should contain coins of the redemption money (or produce in Jerusalem).

153 י, numerical value 10, stands for 10%.

154 In Talmudic texts, "City" stands for Jerusalem, not Byzantion.

155 Greek συμβολή.

עַד כְּדוֹן חֲדָשׁוֹת. יְשָׁנוֹת אֲנִי אוֹמֵר אֶתְמוֹל הָיְתָה מְלֵיאָה תְרוּמָה וּפִינָּהּ כְּהָדָא דְּרִבִּי יוֹנָה[156] וְרִבִּי יוֹסֵי הֲווֹן שׁוּתָּפִין בְּגַרְבִּיָּה. כַּד דָּמַךְ רִבִּי יוֹנָה אָמַר רִבִּי מָנָא לְרִבִּי יוֹסֵי כָּל־גְּרָב דִּכְתִיב בּוֹ רִבִּי יוֹנָה דִּידִי. אָמַר לֵיהּ אֶשְׁתְּקַד הֲוָה דִידָךְ אֵיְשְׁתְּדָא דִידִי. מָצָא בִמְגוּפָתוֹ הֲרֵי הוּא כָתוּב עָלָיו מַעֲשֵׂר הֲרֵי זֶה מַעֲשֵׂר.

So far new ones[157]. Old ones, I am saying yesterday it was full of heave but he empties it, like this: Rebbi Jonah and Rebbi Yose were partners in a cellar of (wine)-barrels. When Rebbi Jonah died, Rebbi Mana[158] said to Rebbi Yose: Any barrel on which is written "Rebbi Jonah" is mine. He said to him, yesteryear is was yours, this year it is mine. But if he found that on the lid was written "tithe", it is tithe[159].

156 Reading of the Rome ms.; required by the following. Leyden and Venice: ר׳ יודה.

157 Containers with markings on them.

158 R. Jonah's son.

159 Since the lid is easily exchanged, he would not have reused one that said "tithe".

נִתְחַלְּפוּ לוֹ. תַּמָּן תַּנִּינָן זִימֵּן שְׁחוֹרִין וּמָצָא לְבָנִים לְבָנִים וּמָצָא שְׁחוֹרִים שְׁנַיִם וּמָצָא שְׁלֹשָׁה אֲסוּרִין. שְׁלֹשָׁה וּמָצָא שְׁנַיִם מוּתָּרִין. רִבִּי יַעֲקֹב בַּר אָחָא בְשֵׁם רִבִּי יָסָא דְּרִבִּי הִיא. דְּתַנֵּי מָאתַיִם וּמָצָא מְנָה הַמְּנָה נוּטָּל דִּבְרֵי רִבִּי. וַחֲכָמִים אוֹמְרִים חוּלִין. חָזַר וְאָמַר דִּבְרֵי הַכֹּל הִיא שַׁנְיָיא הִיא בְגוֹזָלִין שֶׁדַּרְכָּן לִפְרוֹחַ. וְהָתַנֵּי רִבִּי חֲלַפְתָּא בֶּן שָׁאוּל הִיא הַדָּבָר בְּגוֹזָלִין הִיא הַדָּבָר בְּבֵיצִים. הֲוֵי דְּרִבִּי הִיא. תַּמָּן הוּא הִנִּיחַ הוּא מָצָא בְּרַם הָכָא אָבִיו הִנִּיחַ אָבִיו מָצָא. רִבִּי בּוּן בַּר כֹּהֵן אָמַר קוֹמֵי רִבִּי יֹסֵא בְּשֵׁם רִבִּי אָחָא הוֹרֵי רִבִּי בָּא בַּר זַבְדָּא בְּמַעֲשֵׂר שֵׁינִי כְּהָדָא דְּרִבִּי.

Were these exchanged[160]? We have stated there[161]: "If he prepared black ones and found white, white and found black, two and found three, they are forbidden, three and found two they are permitted." Rebbi Jacob bar Aḥa in the name of Rebbi Assi, this[162] is Rebbi's, as we have stated[163]: "Two hundred and he found a talent, a talent was taken, the word of Rebbi, but the Sages say, it is profane." He turned around and said, this is everybody's opinion since pigeon chicks usually start to fly[164]. But did not Rebbi Ḥalaphta ben Shaul state: The same rule applies to pigeon chicks and to eggs[165]. Therefore, it is Rebbi's. There[166], he put it there and he found, here, his father put it there, did his father find it? Rebbi Abun bar Cohen said before Rebbi Yose in the name of Rebbi Aḥa: Rebbi Abba bar Zavda taught according to Rebbi for Second Tithe.

160 Here starts the discussion of Mishnah 12. Why do we assume that what was found was what was deposited?

161 Mishnah *Beẓah* 1:4. From here to the end of the paragraph, the text is found in *Beẓah* 1:5, fol. 60c.
It is a rule that on holidays, only food

may be prepared that was designated as holiday food before the start of the day; cf. *Ševi'it* 9:1, Note 24. The Mishnah deals with pigeon chicks in one's dovecot which cannot yet fly. The problem is that he designated some of these chicks to be taken the next day to be slaughtered and cooked and now on the holiday he finds others.

162 The last clause, that 2 from 3 is permitted.

163 Tosephta 5:7 and Babli *Bezah* 10b, in slightly changed wording.

164 In the Babli, *Bezah* 10b, this opinion is attributed to R. Johanan and R. Eleazar and is the final statement. The next *baraita* is not in the Babli sources.

165 If he designated eggs in his chicken coop without taking them before the holiday.

166 To show that there is comparison between the cases in *Bezah* and here. The text in *Bezah* reads: "there, his father put it there, he found it."

הֲרֵי שֶׁהָיָה מִצְטָעֵר עַל מָעוֹתָיו שֶׁלְּאָבִיו. נִרְאָה לוֹ בַחֲלוֹם כָּךְ וְכָךְ הֵם וּבִמְקוֹם פְּלוֹנִי הֵם. אֲתָא עוּבְדָא קוֹמֵי רַבָּנִין אָמְרִין דִּבְרֵי חֲלוֹמוֹת לֹא מַעֲלִין וְלֹא מוֹרִידִין. רִבִּי יוֹנָה בָּעֵי מִצְטָעֵר וַחֲמִי וְאַתְּ אָמַר הָכֵין. אָמַר רִבִּי יוֹסֵי לֹא מִסְתַּבְּרָה דְלֹא בְּהוּא דְלֹא מִצְטָעֵר וַחֲמִי. בְּרַם הָכָא כְּמָה דְבַר נַשׁ הָוֵי הוּא חָלִים. אָמַר רִבִּי אָבִין מָאן דַּעֲבַד יְאוּת עֲבַד כְּרִבִּי יוֹסֵי.

[167]Somebody was worried about his father's monies; it appeared to him in a dream that they were so and so much and at place X. This case came before the rabbis who said, dreams do not improve or detract. Rebbi Jonah asked: He is worried and you say so? Rebbi Yose said, is it not reasonable that it does not apply to somebody who is not worried but sees; but here, what the person is he sees. Rebbi Avin said, whoever wants to act, should act following Rebbi Yose[168].

167 In the Rome ms.: If somebody was worried about tithe monies. In the Tosephta, 5:6, the text is: Somebody was worried about his father's Second Tithe; the dream spirit appeared to him and said, they are so and so much and

at place X. This happened in a case; they found monies there and asked the rabbis who said, they are profane for dreams do not improve or detract. In the Babli, *Sanhedrin* 30a: If somebody was worried about the monies his father left him, the dream spirit appeared to him and said, they are so and so much, at place X, and are of Second Tithe. This case came before the rabbis who said, dreams do not improve or detract.

168 Dreams are of importance if they are unconnected to the daily activities of the dreamer. A similar statement in the name of the early R. Jonathan is in Babli *Berakhot* 55b. This is the introduction to the next section, dealing with the importance of dreams and their interpretation. The fact that all interpretations are given in Aramaic seems to indicate that only for scholars are dreams unimportant.

חַד בַּר נַשׁ אָתָא לְגַבֵּי דְּרִבִּי יוֹסֵי בֶּן חֲלַפְתָּא. אֲמַר לֵיהּ חֲמִית בְּחֶילְמַי מִתְּמַר לִי אֵיזִיל לְקַפּוֹדְקִיָּא וְאַתְּ מַשְׁכַּח מִדְלָא דְאָבוּךְ. אֲמַר לֵיהּ אֲזַל אָבוֹי דְּהוּא גַבְרָא לְקַפּוֹדְקִיָּא מִן יוֹמוֹי אֲמַר לֵיהּ לָא. אֲמַר לֵיהּ אֵיזִיל מְנִי עֶשֶׂר שׁוּרִיָּן גּוֹ בֵּייתֵיךְ וְאַתְּ מַשְׁכַּח מִידְלָא דְאָבוּךְ קַפָּא דקוריא.[169]

[170]A man came before Rebbi Yose ben Ḥalaphta and said to him, I saw in my dream that it was said to me, go to Cappadocia and you will find your father's property. He asked him, did the father of this man ever go to Cappadocia? He said to him, no. He said to him, go and count 20 rows in your house and you will find your father's property, κάππα δοκία[171].

169 In the parallel source דוקייא δοκία "beams" (δοκίον, τό, "plank").

170 The main parallel of this and the following paragraphs is *Midrash Qohelet Rabbati* 1(15) ff.; the Babylonian parallels are in Babli *Berakhot* 55b-57b. This particular paragraph is in *Qohelet Rabbati* 1(18), *Berakhot* 56b.

171 "κ (*kappa*, the Alexandrian notation for 20) beams".

חַד בַּר נַשׁ אָתָא לְגַבֵּי דְּרִבִּי יוֹסֵי בַּר חֲלַפְתָּא. אֲמַר לֵיהּ חֲמִית בְּחֶילְמַאי לְבוּשׁ חַד כְּלִיל דְּזַיִת. אֲמַר לֵיהּ דְּאַתְּ מִתְרוֹמְמָא. לְבָתַר יוֹמִין אֲתָא חַד חוֹרָן אֲמַר לֵיהּ חֲמִית בְּחֶילְמַאי לְבִישׁ כְּלִילָא דְּזַיִת. אֲמַר לֵיהּ דְּאַתְּ מַלְקֵי. אֲמַר לֵיהּ לְהַהוּא גַּבְרָא אֲמְרַת דְּאַתְּ מִתְרוֹמְמָא וְלִי אֲמְרַת דְּאַתְּ מַלְקֵי. אֲמַר לֵיהּ הַהוּא הֲוָה בִּנְצִיָּא וְאַתְּ בְּחַבָּטִיָּא.

A person came to Rebbi Yose ben Ḥalaphta and said to him, I saw in my dream that I was wearing a crown of olives. He said to him, you will rise to greatness in the future. Another person came and said to him, I saw in my dream that I was wearing a crown of olives. He said to him, you will be whipped. He said to him, to the other man you said you will rise to greatness and to me you say you will be whipped? He said to him, that other was at blossoming, you at hitting [time][172].

172 The Rome text is: בוצינא ואת באבטיחיא that other was "at light, but you among water melons." This makes no sense. In *Qohelet Rabbati* 1(16), reads: דין חמא בשעת נצבא ודין בשעת חבטה "That one saw at the time of blossoming and this at the time of hitting." The time the tree is shaken and its branches hit is harvest time. This story has no Babylonian equivalent.

חַד בַּר נַשׁ אָתָא לְגַבֵּי דְּרִבִּי יִשְׁמָעֵאל בֵּרִבִּי יוֹסֵי אֲמַר לֵיהּ חֲמִית בְּחֶלְמַיי מַשְׁקֶה זֵיתָא מְשַׁח. אֲמַר לֵיהּ תִּיפַּח רוּחֵיהּ דְּהַהוּא גַּבְרָא לְאִימֵּיהּ הוּא חֲכַם. חַד בַּר נַשׁ אָתָא לְגַבֵּי דְּרִבִּי יִשְׁמָעֵאל בֵּרִבִּי יוֹסֵי אֲמַר לֵיהּ חֲמִית בְּחֶילְמַי עֵינִי נָשְׁקָה חֲבֵירְתָהּ. אֲמַר לֵיהּ תִּיפַּח רוּחֵיהּ דְּהַהוּא גַּבְרָא לְאַחְתֵּיהּ הוּא חֲכַם. חַד בַּר נַשׁ אָתָא לְגַבֵּי דְּרִבִּי יִשְׁמָעֵאל בֵּירִבִּי יוֹסֵי אֲמַר לֵיהּ חֲמִית בְּחֶילְמַאי אִית לִי תְּלָתָא עַיינִין. אֲמַר לֵיהּ תַּנּוּרִין אַתְּ עֲבִיד תַּרְתֵּין עַיינֵיךְ וְעֵינָא דְתַנּוּרָא. חַד בַּר נַשׁ אָתָא לְגַבֵּי דְּרִבִּי יִשְׁמָעֵאל בֵּירִבִּי יוֹסֵי אֲמַר לֵיהּ חֲמִית בְּחֶילְמַאי אִית לֵיהּ אַרְבָּעָה אוּדְנִין. אֲמַר לֵיהּ מַלּוֹי אַתְּ תַּרְתֵּי אֶדְנֵיךְ וְתַרְתֵּי אוּדְנוֹי דְגַרְבָא. חַד בַּר נַשׁ אָתָא לְגַבֵּי דְּרִבִּי יִשְׁמָעֵאל בֵּירִבִּי יוֹסֵי אֲמַר לֵיהּ חֲמִית בְּחֶילְמַאי

בְּרִייָתָא עֲרְקִין מִן קוֹמוֹי. אֲמַר לֵיהּ דְּאַתְּ מֵייתֵי אִיזַיְיָא וְכָל־עָמָּא עֲרְקִין מִן קֳדָמָךְ. חַד בַּר נַשׁ אָתָא לְגַבֵּי דְּרִבִּי יִשְׁמָעֵאל בֵּירִבִּי יוֹסֵי אֲמַר לֵיהּ חֲמִית בְּחֵילְמַאי לְבִישׁ חַד פִּינַקְס דִּתְרֵי עָשָׂר לְוָחִין. אֲמַר לֵיהּ אִיסְטְוָא דְּהַהוּא גַּבְרָא אִית בָּהּ תְּרֵי עָשָׂר מַרְקָעָן. חַד בַּר נַשׁ אָתָא לְגַבֵּי דְּרִבִּי יִשְׁמָעֵאל בֵּירִבִּי יוֹסֵי אֲמַר לֵיהּ חֲמִית בְּחֵילְמַאי בְּלַע חַד כּוֹכָב. אֲמַר לֵיהּ טִיפַּח רוּחֵיהּ דְּהַהוּא גַּבְרָא יְהוּדַאי קְטַל דִּכְתִיב דָּרַךְ כּוֹכָב מִיַּעֲקֹב. חַד בַּר נַשׁ אָתָא לְגַבֵּי דְּרִבִּי יִשְׁמָעֵאל בֵּירִבִּי יוֹסֵי אֲמַר (fol. 55d) לֵיהּ חֲמִית בְּחֵילְמִי כַּרְמֵיהּ דְּהַהוּא גַּבְרָא מַסִּיק חַסִּין. אֲמַר לֵיהּ חַמְרֵיהּ דְּהַהוּא גַּבְרָא מֵיפּוֹק בַּסִּים וְאַתְּ מִינְסַב חַסִּין וּצְבַע בְּכַסִּין.

A person came before Rebbi Ismael ben Rebbi Yose[173] and said to him, I saw in my dream that I was watering an olive tree with oil. He said to him, the spirit of that person should be blown away, he made love to his mother.

A person came before Rebbi Ismael ben Rebbi Yose and said to him, I saw in my dream that my eye kissed its companion. He said to him, the spirit of that person should be blown away, he made love to his sister[174].

A person came before Rebbi Ismael ben Rebbi Yose and said to him, I saw in my dream that I had three eyes. He said to him, you are an oven maker; your two eyes and the opening of the oven[175].

A person came before Rebbi Ismael ben Rebbi Yose and said to him, I saw in my dream that I had four ears. He said to him, you are filling [amphoras]; your two ears and the two ears of the amphora.

A person came before Rebbi Ismael ben Rebbi Yose and said to him, I saw in my dream that people got out of my way. He said to him, you are carrying thorns and everybody gets out of your way[176].

A person came before Rebbi Ismael ben Rebbi Yose and said to him, I saw in my dream that I was wearing a wooden notebinder with twelve tablets. He said to him, the stone bench of this person has twelve tatters[177].

A person came before Rebbi Ismael ben Rebbi Yose and said to him, I saw in my dream that I swallowed a star. He said to him, the spirit of that person should be blown away, he killed a Jew as it is written (*Num.* 24:17): "A star went out from Jacob.[178]"

A person came before Rebbi Ismael ben Rebbi Yose and said to him, I saw in my dream the vineyard of this man grow bitter lettuce. He said to him, all your wine will be sour and you will bring bitter lettuce and dip it in the cups[179].

173 In *Qohelet Rabbati* and Babli *Berakhot*, the author is always R. Ismael.

174 In *Qohelet Rabbati*, one eye swallowed the other and the interpretation was that his children slept with one another. In the Babli, this and the preceding paragraph speak of the same person.

175 In *Qohelet Rabbati*, a baker with the glowing opening of his oven.

176 In *Qohelet Rabbati*, this and the preceding paragraph are amalgamated to an unintelligible whole.

177 In *Qohelet Rabbati*, the cover of his donkey has 12 tears.

178 In *Qohelet Rabbati*, the proof is from *Gen.* 15:5. In the Babli, *Berakhot* 56b, he is accused of selling a Jew into slavery.

179 In *Qohelet Rabbati*, all people will come to buy his vinegar to pickle the bitter lettuce.

חַד בַּר נַשׁ אָתָא לְגַבֵּי דְּרִבִּי יִשְׁמָעֵאל בֵּירִבִּי יוֹסֵי אֲמַר לֵיהּ חֲמִית בְּחֶילְמַאי מִיתַּמַּר לִי הָכֵין זְרַק אֶצְבַּעְתָּךְ נְחַת. אֲמַר לֵיהּ הַב לִי אַגְרִי וַאֲנָא אֲמַר לָךְ. אֲמַר לֵיהּ חֲמִית בְּחֶילְמִי מִיתַּמַּר לִי הָכֵין תִּיהֲוֵי נְפַח בְּפוּמָךְ. אֲמַר לֵיהּ הַב לִי

אַגְרַאי וַאֲנָא אֲמַר לָךְ. אֲמַר לֵיהּ חֲמִית בְּחֵילְמִי הָכֵין זְקִיף אֶצְבְּעָךְ. אֲמַר לֵיהּ לָא אֲמְרִית לָךְ הַב לִי אַגְרִי וַאֲנָא אֲמַר לָךְ. כַּד דְּאִיתַמַּר לָךְ הָכֵין נְחַת דִּילְפָּא בְחִיטָּךְ. כַּד אִיתַמַּר לָךְ הָכֵין אִינַפְּחָן. כַּד אִיתַמַּר לָךְ הָכֵין צֳמְחִין.

A person came to Rebbi Ismael ben Rebbi Yose and said to him, I saw in my dream that it was said to me, throw your fingers, descend. He said to him, give me my fee and I shall tell you. He said to him, I saw in my dream that it was said to me, blow with your mouth. He said to him, give me my fee and I shall tell you. He said to him, I saw in my dream that it was said to me, straighten your fingers upwards. He said to him, did I not say to you, give me my fee and I shall tell you! When it was said to you [first], [the rain] dripped down on your wheat. When it was said to you next, they became swollen. When it was said to you next, they sprouted[180].

180 In *Qohelet Rabbati* 1(15), the same story is much more wordy, finding R. Ismael in competition with a Samaritan interpreter of dreams. In the Babli, *Berakhot* 56a/b, there is a story about a Babylonian interpreter who took money and came to a bad end.

חַד כּוּתַיי אֲמַר אֲנָא אֵיזִיל מַפְלֵי בְּהָדֵין סָבָא דִיהוּדָאֵי. אֲתָא לְגַבֵּיהּ אֲמַר לֵיהּ חֲמִית בְּחֵילְמַאי אַרְבַּע אֲרָזִין וְאַרְבַּע שִׁיקְמִין מַקְנִיתָא אִדְרָא תוֹרְתָא וְהַהוּא גַבְרָא יְתִיב מִדְרָךְ. אֲמַר לֵיהּ טִיפַּח רוּחֵיהּ דְּהַהוּא גַבְרָא לֵית הָדֵין חֲלָם. אֲפִילוּ כֵן לֵית אַתְּ נְפִיק רֵיקָן. אַרְבַּעְתֵּי אַרְזֵי אַרְבַּעְתֵּי שִׁיטָּתֵיהּ דְּעַרְסָא. אַרְבַּעְתֵּי שִׁקְמֵי אַרְבַּעְתֵּי כּוֹרְעָתָא דְּעַרְסָא. מַקְנִיתָא מַרְגְּלָתָא. אִדְרָא בְּרָא דְתִבְנָא. תּוֹרְתָא אֶצְבְּעָתָא. וְהַהוּא גַבְרָא יְתִיב מִדְרָךְ. וְהוּא גַבְרָא רְבִיע בְּגַוֵּיהּ לָא חַיֵּי וְלָא מָיֵית. וְכֵן הֲוָות לֵיהּ.

A Samaritan said, I shall make fun of this elder of the Jews. He went to him and said, I saw in my dream four cedars, four sycamores, a stand, the skin of a cow[181], and this man sits and steps on it. He said to him, the spirit of that person should be blown away, this is no dream! Nevertheless, you should not go away empty-handed. The four cedars are the four sides of his bed, the four sycomores the four legs of his bed, the stand with a skin, the basis for straw, and the rows the fingers. And this man sits and steps on it: this man lies on them, he cannot live and cannot die. And that happened to him[182].

181 This is then interpreted as a pun, reading תורתא either as feminine of תור "ox, cattle", Hebrew שׁוֹר, or of תורא "row", Hebrew שׁוּר.

182 The text in *Qohelet Rabbati* 1(16) is quite different.

חָדָא אִיתָא דַּאֲתִיָא לְגַבֵּי דְּרִבִּי לִיעֶזֶר. אֲמְרָה לֵיהּ חֲמִית בְּחֶילְמַאי תִּינְיָיתָא דְבַיְתָא מִיתְבְּרָא. אֲמַר לָהּ דְּאַתְּ מוֹלַד בַּר דָּכָר אֲזָלָה וְיָלְדָה דָּכָר. בָּתַר יוֹמִין אֲזָלָה בָּעֲיָא לֵיהּ. אֲמְרִין לָהּ תַּלְמִידוֹי לֵית הוּא הָכָא. אֲמְרִין לָהּ מָה אַתְּ בָּעֲיָא מִינֵיהּ. אֲמְרָה לוֹן חֲמִית הַהִיא אִיתְתָא בְּחֶילְמַאי תִּינְיָיתָא דְבַיְתָא מִיתְבְּרָא. אֲמְרִין לָהּ דְּאַתְּ מוֹלַד בַּר דָּכָר וּבַעֲלָהּ דְּהַהִיא אִיתְתָא מַיִית. כַּד אֲתָא רִבִּי לְעָזָר תַּנּוּן לֵיהּ עוּבְדָא אֲמַר לוֹן קְטַלְתּוּן נְפַשׁ לָמָּה שֶׁאֵין הַחֲלוֹם הוֹלֵךְ אֶלָּא אַחַר פִּתְרוֹנוֹ שֶׁנֶּאֱמַר וַיְהִי כַּאֲשֶׁר פָּתַר לָנוּ כֵּן הָיָה.

[183]A woman came before Rebbi Eliezer. She said to him, I saw in my dream the pillar[184] of the house breaking. He said, you will give birth to a male child. She went and gave birth to a male. After some time she came and asked for him. His students said, he is not here. They asked her, what do you want from him? She said to them, this woman[185] saw in my dream that the pillar of the house was breaking. They said to her, you will give birth to a male child[186] and the husband of that woman[187] dies. When Rebbi Eliezer came, they told him what happened. He said to them, you killed a person for the dream goes only after its interpretation as it is

said (*Gen.* 41:13): "It was just as he had interpreted it for us, so it happened."

183 The original story is in *Qohelet Rabbati* 1(19); a text parallel to the Yerushalmi in *Gen. rabba* 89(10).

184 The unexplained word חיניתא is translated following the text in *Gen. rabba* which has שוריתא.

185 I. e., I.

186 The version here is telescoped from the text in *Qohelet Rabbati*. There, R. Eliezer himself told her twice that she would have a son; the students made the bad interpretation only the third time.

187 I. e., you.

אָמַר רִבִּי יוֹחָנָן כָּל־הַחֲלוֹמוֹת הוֹלְכִין אַחַר פִּתְרוֹנֵיהֶן חוּץ מִן הַיַּיִן. יֵשׁ שׁוֹתֶה יַיִן וְטוֹב לוֹ. יֵשׁ שׁוֹתֶה יַיִן וְרַע לוֹ. תַּלְמִיד חָכָם שׁוֹתֶה וְטוֹב לוֹ. עַם הָאָרֶץ שׁוֹתֶה וְרַע לוֹ.

Rebbi Joḥanan said, all dreams follow their interpretations except for wine. There is one who drinks and it is good for him and one who drinks and it is bad for him. A scholar drinks and it is good for him, a vulgar drinks and it is bad for him[188].

188 This is the end of the story of R. Eliezer in both *Qohelet Rabbati* 1(19) and *Gen. rabba* 89(10). In the latter text, R. Abbahu dissents and states that dreams do not improve or detract.

חַד בַּר נַשׁ אֲתֵי גַּבֵּי רִבִּי עֲקִיבָה אֲמַר לֵיהּ חֲמֵית בְּחֵילְמַאי רַגְלִי קְטִינָא. אֲמַר לֵיהּ דְּמוֹעֲדָא מַיְיתֵי וְלֵית מֵיכַל קוֹפָּד. אֲתָא חַד חוֹרָן לְגַבֵּיהּ אֲמַר חֲמֵית בְּחֵילְמַאי רַגְלִי מְסוּבְלָא. אֲמַר לֵיהּ מוֹעֲדָא מַיְיתֵי וְאִית לָךְ קוֹפָּד סַגִּי. חַד תַּלְמִיד מִן דְּרִבִּי עֲקִיבָה הֲוָה יְתִיב וְאַפּוֹי מְשַׁנְיָין אֲמַר לֵיהּ מַהוּ כֵן. אָמַר לֵיהּ חֲמִית בְּחֵילְמַאי תְּלַת מִילִין קַשְׁיָין בַּאֲדָר אַתְּ מַיִית וְנִיסָן לֵית אַתְּ חֲמֵי וּמַה דְּאַתְּ זְרַע לֵית אַתְּ כְּנַשׁ. אָמַר לֵיהּ תְּלַתֵּיהוֹן טָבָא אִינּוּן. בְּהַדְרָא דְאוֹרֵייתָא אַתְּ מְרוֹמְמָא וְנִיסִין לֵית אַתְּ חֲמֵי וּמַה דְּאַתְּ זְרַע לֵית אַתְּ כְּנַשׁ. וּמַה דְּאַתְּ מֵילִיד לֵית אַתְּ קְבַר.

[189]A person came to Rebbi Aqiba and said to him, I saw in my dream my foot shrinking. He said to him, holiday[190] is coming but you will not eat read meat[191]. Another person came and said, I saw in my dream my foot swelling. He said to him, holiday is coming and you will have plenty of red meat. A student of Rebbi Aqiba was sitting making a queer face. He said to him, why is that? He said to him, I saw in a dream three hard things: In Adar you will die, Nisan you will not see, and what you will sow you will not collect. He said to him, all three are good. In the glory[192] of the Torah you will be lifted, wonders you will not see[193], and what you will sow you will not collect, what you will have born to you you will not bury.

189 In *Qohelet Rabbati* 1(17), the author is R. Joḥanan. The last story, of the student, is told in the Babli, *Berakhot* 56b, of Bar Qappara and Rebbi.

190 A holiday of pilgrimage, which in biblical Hebrew is called "foot".

191 As *Sifry Deut.* 141 explains, the biblical command of rejoicing on a holiday can only be fulfilled by the consumption of meat from animals acceptable as holiday sacrifices.

192 A pun of אדר and הדר is possible only if ה has lost all sound.

193 In *Qohelet Rabbati* and Babli *Berakhot*, "you will not undergo temptations".

כרם רבעי פרק חמישי

(fol. 55c) **משנה א:** כֶּרֶם רְבָעִי מְצַיְּינִים אוֹתוֹ בְקוֹזָזוֹת אֲדָמָה וְשֶׁל עָרְלָה בְחַרְסִית וְשֶׁל קְבָרוֹת בְּסִיד וּמְמְחֶה וְשׁוֹפֵךְ. אָמַר רִבִּי שִׁמְעוֹן בֶּן גַּמְלִיאֵל בַּמֶּה דְבָרִים אֲמוּרִים בַּשְּׁבִיעִית וְהַצְּנוּעִין מַנִּיחִין אֶת הַמָּעוֹת וְאוֹמֵר כָּל־הַנִּלְקָט מִזֶּה מְחוּלָּל עַל הַמָּעוֹת הָאֵלּוּ.

Mishnah 1: One marks a fourth-year vineyard with lumps of earth, one of *'orlah* with potsherds[1]; graves with whitewash which is thinned and poured[2]. Rebbi Simeon ben Gamliel said, when has this been said? In a Sabbatical year. But discreet religious persons set aside some coins and say, what is taken from here is exchanged for these coins[3].

1 The fruits of newly planted trees, including vines, are forbidden for all use during the first three years; this is called *'orlah*. In the fourth year, the fruits are (*Lev*. 19:24) "holy exultation for the Eternal", they have to be eaten under the rules of Second Tithe in Jerusalem or be redeemed and the redemption money treated under the rules of tithe money.

The anonymous Tanna requires that such a vineyard be marked so that people would not inadvertently take from its fruits and sin. For him, one marks the fourth-year vineyard with temporary markings but *'orlah*, which extends over a few rainy seasons, with markers that remain after the rains. Rabban Gamliel holds that we are not responsible for thieves, cf. *Demay* 3:5, Note 135; therefore, it is only necessary to mark forbidden orchards or vineyards in the Sabbatical where everybody has the right to take the fruits.

2 Single graves in an agricultural area must be made easily recognizable so that Cohanim can avoid them.

3 If the fourth year of the vineyard is a Sabbatical, the obligation of redemption is not lifted. In that year, scrupulous followers of Rabban Simeon ben Gamliel nevertheless take precautions lest people sin inadvertently. In that case, the vineyard does not have to be marked.

(fol. 55d) **הלכה א:** זוּנָא שָׁאַל לְרִבִּי מַה נִיתְנֵי. כֶּרֶם רְבָעִי אוֹ נֶטַע רְבָעִי. אֲמַר לוֹן פֻּקוּן שְׁאָלוּן לְרִבִּי יִצְחָק רוֹבָא דְּבָחֲנִת לֵיהּ כָּל־מַתְנִיתָא. נַפְקוּן וְשָׁאֲלוּן לֵיהּ. אֲמַר לוֹן קַדְמִיָּא כֶּרֶם רְבָעִי וְתִנְייָנָא נֶטַע רְבָעִי. רִבִּי זְעִירָא קָבַל[4] לְסַבַּיָּא דַהֲווֹן בְּיוֹמוֹי דְּרִבִּי יִצְחָק רוֹבָא דְּלָא בָחֲנוּן כָּל־מַתְנִייָתָא מִינֵיהּ.

Halakhah 1: Zenon asked Rebbi: How should we state, fourth-year vineyard or fourth-year orchard? He said to them, go out and ask Rebbi Isaac the Elder[5] with whom I checked the entire Mishnah. He said to them, the first ones fourth-year vineyard, the second ones fourth-year orchard. Rebbi Zeïra complained about the old people from the time of Rebbi Isaac the Elder, that they did not check all Mishnaiot with him.

4 Reading of the Rome ms. Leyden and Venice: מקבל "receives".

5 A Tanna of the fourth generation, companion of R. Nathan, older than Rebbi.

תַּנֵּי כֶּרֶם רְבָעִי מְצַיְיְנִים אוֹתוֹ בְקוֹזְזוֹת אֲדָמָה שֶׁהוּא לְשָׁעָה. שֶׁל עָרְלָה בְּחַרְסִית בְּחִיוְורָא שֶׁהוּא יוֹתֵר מִכֵּן. וְשֶׁל קְבָרוֹת בְּסִיד דּוּ יוֹתֵר מִכֵּן. תַּנֵּי רִבִּי חֲלַפְתָּא בֶּן שָׁאוּל אִם הָיוּ יְחִידוֹת תּוֹלֶה בָהֶן אָזְנֵי חָבִיּוֹת.

It was stated: One marks a fourth-year vineyard with lumps of earth because it is temporary, one of *'orlah* with potsherds because it has to last longer; graves with whitewash because it has to last still longer. Rebbi Ḥalaphta ben Shaul stated: If [the *'orlah* trees] were isolated, one hangs amphora handles on them.

רִבִּי זְעִירָא בָּעֵי לָמָּה לֵי נָן אָמְרִין כָּל־אֶחָד וְאֶחָד לְפִי מָה שֶׁהוּא. כְּהָדָא דְתַנֵּי אִילָן שֶׁלְהֶקְדֵּשׁ סוֹקְרִין אוֹתוֹ בְסִיקְרָא. בָּתֵּי עֲבוֹדָה זָרָה מְפַחֲמִין אוֹתָן בְּפְחָמִין. בַּיִת מְנוּגָּע נוֹתְנִין עָלָיו אֶפֶר מַקְלֶה. מָקוֹם הָרוּג בְּדָם. מָקוֹם עֶגְלָה עֲרוּפָה בַחֲגוֹרָה שֶׁל אֲבָנִים. וְחָשׁ לוֹמַר שֶׁמָּא אִילָן שֶׁהוּא מְנַבֵּל פֵּירוֹתָיו הוּא. וְלֹא כֵן תַּנֵּי אִילָן שֶׁהוּא מְנַבֵּל פֵּירוֹתָיו סוֹקְרִין אוֹתוֹ בְסִיקְרָא וּמַטְעִינִין אוֹתוֹ אֲבָנִים וּמְבַהֲתִין לֵיהּ דִּי עֲבַד. תַּמָּן דְּלָא יַתִּיר פֵּירוֹי. בְּרַם הָכָא דְּיַעֲבִד כַּתְּחִילָּה. רִבִּי יוֹנָה בָּעֵי וְלָמָּה לֵי נָן מָרִין חוּט כְּחוּט שֶׁלְסִיקְרָא זֵכֶר לַמִּזְבֵּחַ. כְּיי דְתַנִּינָן תַּמָּן חוּט שֶׁלְסִיקְרָא חוֹגְרוֹ בְאֶמְצַע לְהַבְחִין בֵּין דָּמִים הָעֶלְיוֹנִים לַדָּמִים הַתַּחְתּוֹנִים. תַּנֵּי רִבִּי חִיָּא סוֹקְרִין עָלָיו בְּסִיקְרָא הֶקְדֵּשׁ.

Rebbi Zeïra asked, why do we not enumerate all for what they are: As we have stated[6]: "A dedicated tree one colors with vermilion, houses of idol worship one blackens with charcoal, a leprous house one indicates by burned ashes, the place of a slain person by blood, the place where the neck of a calf was broken[7] by a stone enclosure." Is one not afraid that it will be said it is a tree which sheds its fruits[8]? Did we not state[9]: "If a tree sheds its fruits, one colors it red with vermilion, loads it with stones, and frightens it into producing." They said, there that it should not loosen its fruits, here that it should start to produce[10]. Rebbi Jonah asked: Why do we not teach "a line", like the vermilion line as remembrance of the altar, as we have stated there[11]: "A vermilion line is like a belt in the middle to distinguish between upper and lower blood." Rebbi Ḥiyya stated, one writes on it with vermilion: "dedicated."

6 Tosephta 5:13.

7 To atone for an unsolved murder case, *Deut.* 21:1-9. The place is permanently forbidden for agricultural use, v. 4.

8 The tree painted vermilion; one might come to profanely use its fruits.

9 *Ševi'it* Chapter 4, Notes 65-69; cf. Babli *Šabbat* 67a, *Ḥulin* 77b.

10 This sentence is copied from

Ševi'it; it makes no sense here. The correct answer is given in the next sentence.

11 Mishnah *Middot* 3:1, describing the altar in the courtyard of the Temple. The blood of burnt offerings and animal purification offerings has to be poured on the upper wall of the altar; the blood of all other sacrifices goes on the lower part. The borderline is indicated by a red line, one cubit below the walkway around the altar. R. Jonah proposes to make the dedication mark narrow in contrast to the coloring of a misbehaving tree.

רִבִּי יוֹסֵי וְרַבָּן שִׁמְעוֹן בֶּן גַּמְלִיאֵל אָֽמְרוּ דָּבָר אֶחָד. כְּמָה דְּרִבִּי יוֹסֵי אָמַר אֵין אָנוּ אַחֲרָאִין לְרַמָּאִין. כֵּן רַבָּן שִׁמְעוֹן בֶּן גַּמְלִיאֵל אוֹמֵר אֵין אָנוּ אַחֲרָאִין לְרַמָּאִין. מִסְתַּבְּרָא רִבִּי יוֹסֵי יוֹדֵי לְרַבָּן שִׁמְעוֹן בֶּן גַּמְלִיאֵל רַבָּן שִׁמְעוֹן בֶּן גַּמְלִיאֵל לֹא יוֹדֵי לְרִבִּי יוֹסֵי. רִבִּי יוֹסֵי יוֹדֵי לְרַבָּן שִׁמְעוֹן בֶּן גַּמְלִיאֵל שֶׁאֵין אָנוּ אַחֲרָאִין לְרַמָּאִין. רַבָּן שִׁמְעוֹן בֶּן גַּמְלִיאֵל לֹא יוֹדֵי לְרִבִּי יוֹסֵי. שֶׁאֵין דֶּרֶךְ חָבֵר לְהוֹצִיא מִבֵּיתוֹ דָּבָר שֶׁאֵינוֹ מְתוּקָּן.

[12]Both Rebbi Yose and Rabban Simeon ben Gamliel said the same thing. Just as Rebbi Yose said, we are not responsible for the dishonest, so Rabban Simeon ben Gamliel says, we are not responsible for the dishonest. It is reasonable that Rebbi Yose will agree with Rabban Simeon ben Gamliel; Rabban Simeon ben Gamliel will not agree with Rebbi Yose. Rebbi Yose will agree with Rabban Simeon ben Gamliel that we are not responsible for the dishonest. Rabban Simeon ben Gamliel will not agree with Rebbi Yose, because it is not fitting for a *ḥaver* that anything not in order should leave his house[13].

12 This is from *Demay* 3:5, Notes 135-136, where R. Yose states that one does not have to give tithes to save the nonobservant from sin. The statement of Rabban Simeon ben Gamliel is in the Mishnah here.

13 This is quoted in the Babli (*Erubin* 32a, *Pesaḥim* 9a) in the name of R. Ḥanina (there called R. Ḥanina from Khusistan.)

מְנַיִין לְצִיּוּן. רִבִּי בֶּרֶכְיָה רִבִּי[14] יַעֲקֹב בַּר בַּת יַעֲקֹב בְּשֵׁם רִבִּי חוֹנְיָה דִבְרַת־חַוְורָן רִבִּי יוֹסֵי אָמַר לָהּ רִבִּי יַעֲקֹב בַּר אָחָא בְשֵׁם רִבִּי חוֹנְיָה[15] דִבְרַת־חַוְורָן. רִבִּי יוֹסֵי אָמַר לָהּ רִבִּי יַעֲקֹב בַּר אָחָא בְשֵׁם רִבִּי חֲנַנְיָה דִבְרַת־חַוְורָן. רִבִּי חִזְקִיָּה רִבִּי עוּזִּיאֵל בְּרֵיהּ דְּרִבִּי חוֹנְיָה דִבְרַת־חַוְורָן בְּשֵׁם רִבִּי חוֹנְיָה דִבְרַת־חַוְורָן וְטָמֵא טָמֵא יִקְרָא. כְּדֵי שֶׁתְּהֵא הַטּוּמְאָה קוֹרָא לָהּ בְּפִיהָ וְאוֹמֶרֶת לָךְ. פְּרוֹשׁ. רִבִּי הִילָא בְשֵׁם רִבִּי שְׁמוּאֵל בַּר נַחְמָן וְעָבְרוּ הָעוֹבְרִים בָּאָרֶץ וְרָאָה עֶצֶם אָדָם וּבָנָה אֶצְלוֹ צִיּוּן. [16]מִכָּן שֶׁמְּצַיְּינִים עַל הָעֲצָמוֹת. אָדָם מִכָּן שֶׁמְּצַיְּינִים עַל הַשִּׁיזְרָה וְעַל הַגּוּלְגּוֹלֶת. וּבָנָה. מִכָּן שֶׁמְּצַיְּינִים עַל אֶבֶן קְבוּעָה. אִם אוֹמֵר אַתְּ עַל תְּלוּשָׁה אַף הִיא הוֹלֶכֶת וּמְטַמְּא בְּמָקוֹם אַחֵר. אֶצְלוֹ. בְּמָקוֹם טָהֳרָה. צִיּוּן. מִכָּן לְצִיּוּן.

[17]From where about marks? Rebbi Berekhiah, Rebbi Jacob the son of the daughter of Jacob[18], in the name of Rebbi Onias from Hauran. Rebbi Yose said it in the name of Rebbi Jacob bar Aḥa in the name of Rebbi Onias from Hauran. Rebbi Ḥizqiah, Rebbi Uziel the son of Rebbi Onias from Hauran in the name of Rebbi Onias from Hauran (*Lev.* 13:45): "impure, impure, he shall call out;" the impurity itself has to call out and say to you: go away! Rebbi Hila in the name of Rebbi Samuel bar Naḥman (*Ez.* 39:15): "The emissaries shall crisscross the land; if one sees a bone of a human he builds a sign near it." [*A bone*,] from here that one makes signs for bones. *A human*, from here that one makes signs for spine and skull. *He builds*, from here that one makes signs on fixed stones. If you say on loose ones, it would move and make other places impure. *Near it*, on a place of purity. *A sign*, from here the marks.

14 Reading of the parallels. Here בר' "son of Rebbi".

15 Reading of the Rome ms. and the parallels. Leyden and Venice ר' חנניה.

16 Here the quote עצם is missing;

added in translation from the parallels.

17 This and the following two paragraphs are also in *Šeqalim* 1:1, fol. 46a; *Mo'ed Qaṭan* 1:1, fol. 80b/c. Similar arguments, in the name of different authorities, in Babli *Mo'ed Qaṭan* 5a. The discussion is about the note in the Mishnah that graves have to be marked.

18 A third generation Galilean Amora.

תַּנֵּי מָצָא אֶבֶן אַחַת מְצוּיֶּינֶת אַף עַל פִּי שֶׁאֵין מְקַיְּימִין כֵּן הַמַּאֲהִיל עָלֶיהָ טָהוֹר. אֲנִי אוֹמֵר מֵת קַמְצוֹץ[19] הָיָה נָתוּן תַּחְתֶּיהָ. הָיוּ שְׁתַּיִם הַמַּאֲהִיל עֲלֵיהֶן טָהוֹר וּבֵינֵיהֶן טָמֵא. הָיָה חָרוּשׁ בֶּנְתַיִים הֲרֵי הֵן כִּיחִידִיּוֹת בֵּינֵיהֶן טָהוֹר וּסְבִיבוֹתָן טָמֵא.

It was stated[20]: If one found a single marked stone, even though one should not keep it so, if somebody forms a tent over it he is pure; I say a compressed corpse[21] was under it. If there were two, he who forms a tent over any one of them is pure; between them he is impure. If between them was a ploughed strip they are single stones, between them the area is pure and around them[22] impure.

19 Reading of the parallels. Text here: קמצון "stingy", but in the ms. the reading ן is in doubt.

20 Tosephta *Šeqalim* 1:5. This Tosephta follows the Yerushalmi, against the Babli, *Moëd Qaṭan* 6a, which reads "impure" in the first sentence.

21 A corpse buried with its head between the legs, so it fitted under the stone. This is not a Jewish burial custom. If the body is not that of a Jew, a person standing over him and forming a "tent" (*Num.* 19) with his body does not become impure (Babli *Yebamot* 60b-61a). If only one stone was needed, the corpse must be under it and cannot be Jewish since the previous *baraita* explained that the mark must be on a pure place. But then at least two markers are needed to define the impure spot.

22 Any place the whitewash was splashed on the earth around the stone.

תַּנֵּי אֵין מְצַייְנִין עַל הַבָּשָׂר שֶׁמָּא יִתְאַכֵּל הַבָּשָׂר. רִבִּי יוּסְטֵי בַּר שׁוּנֵם בָּעֵא קוֹמֵי רִבִּי מָנָא וְלֹא נִמְצָא מְטַמֵּא אֶת הַטַּהֲרוֹת לְמַפְרֵעַ. אָמַר לוֹ מוּטָּב שֶׁיִּתְקַלְקְלוּ בוֹ לְשָׁעָה וְלֹא יִתְקַלְקְלוּ בוֹ לְעוֹלָם.

It was stated[23]: One does not mark flesh, for perhaps it will decompose[24]. Rebbi Justus bar Shunem asked before Rebbi Mana: Will that not cause pure food to be retroactively made impure[25]? He said to him, it is better that these should become unusable for a limited time than that [the earth] become unusable forever.

23 In Tosephta *Šeqalim* 1:5, the reading is: One does not mark flesh or bones which do not induce tent-impurity.

24 Then it is no longer impure.

25 If the carrier of pure food learns that he has crossed a place where human flesh (without a bone) was buried.

חֲבֵרַייָא אָמְרֵי יְאוּת אָמַר רַבָּן שִׁמְעוֹן בֶּן גַּמְלִיאֵל וְקַשְׁיָא עַל דְּרַבָּנִין. לֹא בַיּוֹם הוּא מְצַיֵּין. לֹא בַלַּיְלָה הוּא גוֹנֵב. אָמַר לוֹן רִבִּי מָנָא מִבְּיוֹם כַּיי דְּאָמַר רִבִּי חֲנִינָה חָתַר בַּחוֹשֶׁךְ בָּתִּים יוֹמָם חִתְּמוּ לָמוֹ לֹא יָדְעוּ אוֹר. מִיּוֹמָם חִתְּמוּ לָמוֹ. כָּךְ הָיוּ אַנְשֵׁי דוֹר הַמַּבּוּל עוֹשִׂין הָיוּ רוֹשְׁמִין בָּאֲפּוֹבַלְסָמוֹן וּבָאִין וְגוֹנְבִין בַּלַּיְלָה. כָּךְ דָּרְשָׁהּ רִבִּי חֲנִינָא בְצִיפּוֹרִין. אִיתְעֲבִיד תְּלַת מְאָה חַתִּירָן בָּתִּים.

The colleagues said, Rabban Simeon ben Gamliel says it correctly, it is difficult for the rabbis! Does one not mark for the day, does he not steal in the night[26]? Rebbi Mana said to them, following what Rebbi Ḥanina[27] said (*Job* 24:16): "He dug in the darkness under houses, by day they designated for them, they did not see light[28]." That is what the generation of the flood did, they were making signs with balsamum[29] resin and came to steal in the night. So did Rebbi Ḥanina preach in Sepphoris; there were 300 houses undermined.

26 What use is marking forbidden fruit if they are stolen in the dark of night.

27 In the Babli, *Sanhedrin* 109a, the explanation is by the Babylonian Rava and the sermon by R. Yose the Tanna. In *Gen. Rabba* 27, the explanation is anonymous, the sermon by R. Ḥanina.

28 In the masoretic text, לֹא יָדְעוּ אוֹר. The version לא ראו אור is in both Talmudim.

29 Greek ὀποβάλσαμον, τό, "juice of the balsam-tree".

וִיצַיֵּין. אִם מְצוּיָּין הוּא הֵיאַךְ נִקְרָא הוּא צָנוּעַ.

Why can't he mark[30]? If it [his vineyard] is marked, how can he be called discreet?

30 This refers to the last statement of the Mishnah, that discreet people in the Sabbatical put coins aside so that everybody may take the fourth-year fruits.

אָמַר רִבִּי יוֹחָנָן אַתְיָא דְּרַבָּן שִׁמְעוֹן בֶּן גַּמְלִיאֵל כְּמָאן דְּאָמַר לְעִיתּוֹתֵי עֶרֶב. דְּתַנֵּי רִבִּי דוֹסָא אוֹמֵר כָּל־מַה שֶׁיְּלַקְטוּ עֲנִיִּים בֵּין הָעֳמָרִים הֶבְקֵר הֲרֵי הוּא הֶבְקֵר. רִבִּי יוּדָה אוֹמֵר לְעִיתּוֹתֵי עֶרֶב וַחֲכָמִים אוֹמְרִים אֵין הֶבְקֵר אֲנָסִין הֶבְקֵר שֶׁאֵין אָנוּ אֲחֵרָאִין לְרַמָּאִין. (fol. 56a) בְּרַם כְּמָאן דְּאָמַר בְּשַׁחֲרִית לֹא אַתְיָא. וְיֵשׁ אָדָם מַבְקִיר בִּמְחוּבָּר לַקַּרְקַע. אָמַר רִבִּי יִרְמְיָה אֲפִילוּ כְּמָאן דְּאָמַר בְּשַׁחֲרִית אַתְיָא הוּא. וְלָאו רַבָּן שִׁמְעוֹן בֶּן גַּמְלִיאֵל הִיא. וְעוֹד הוּא אִית לֵיהּ מְשִׁיכָתוֹ שֶׁלְּמַעֲשֵׂר שֵׁינִי הִיא פְּדִייָתוֹ. אָמַר רִבִּי יוֹסֵי הַיְינוּ וְקָם לוֹ. אִילּוּ רָאָה כִּכָּר מִתְגַּלְגֵּל בַּנָּהָר וְאָמַר כִּכָּר זֶה הֶקְדֵּשׁ שֶׁמָּא כְלוּם אָמַר. אָמַר רִבִּי יִרְמְיָה עַד דְּאַתְּ מַקְשֵׁי לֵיהּ בְּשַׁחֲרִית קַשְׁיָיתָהּ לְעִיתּוֹתֵי עֶרֶב. אָמַר לֵיהּ מָאן דְּאִיתֵיהּ לֵיהּ לְעִיתּוֹתֵי עֶרֶב. לֵית לֵיהּ לְאִילֵּין קַשְׁיָיתָא.

Rebbi Joḥanan said, Rabban Simeon ben Gamliel parallels him who says "in the evening", as we have stated[31]: "Rebbi Dosa says, 'everything the poor will collect between the sheaves shall be abandoned', it is abandoned.

Rebbi Jehudah says, in the evening. But the Sages say, a declaration of abandonment under duress is not an abandonment, for we are not responsible for tricksters." But he is not parallel to him who says "in the morning". Can one abandon anything if it is standing on the ground[32]? Rebbi Jeremiah said, it is even parallel to him who says "in the morning". Is it not Rabban Simeon ben Gamliel's[33]? In addition, he holds that taking Second Tithe is its redemption[34]. Rebbi Yose said, is that (*Lev.* 27:19): "It shall be his[35]"? If somebody saw a loaf floating in a river and said, that loaf shall be dedicated, did he say anything[36]? Rebbi Jeremiah said, before you ask all these questions regarding "in the morning", ask them regarding "in the evening!" He answered him, he who holds "in the evening" does not have all these questions[37].

31 Tosephta *Peah* 2:5: "R. Jehudah says, in the morning the farmer has to say: Everything the poor did collect (ms. Erfurt: will collect) from the sheaves shall be abandoned; R. Dosa says, in the evening. But the Sages say, a declaration of abandonment under duress is not an abandonment, for we are not responsible for tricksters." Since the rules for collecting single stalks are rather restrictive, RR. Jehudah and Dosa hold that the farmer should declare that anything the poor take in excess of what is legal shall be abandoned to them to protect the poor from sin. The Sages hold that we can only force all the poor to strictly follow the rules if they have to fear sinning when they overstep the legal bounds.

The parallel discussion to this paragraph is in Babli *Baba Qama* 69 a/b. There are major differences between Yerushalmi and Babli. The name tradition of the Tosephta is that of the Babli, the opposite of the Yerushalmi. In the text, the main (Vienna ms.) text, "will collect", is the original reading of the Babli, the Erfurt text is the (conditionally) corrected reading of the Babli and the original reading of the Yerushalmi. The Babli (in the name of R. Joḥanan) rejects the notion that the "discreet religious ones" follow Rabban Simeon, the position implied by R. Johanan's statement in the Yerushalmi.

32 "In the morning" means before the day's harvest. Then the grain is still standing and no stalks lie on the ground that it should be possible to define what can be abandoned. Since the farmer does not want to abandon the field, his declaration is void.

33 Chapter 4:6. Even if the declaration by the farmer in the morning is legally invalid, it becomes activated once the stalks are taken up if we hold that the rules of Second Tithe and abandoned stalks are identical.

34 He thinks that the entire declaration is unnecessary; but if somebody wants to do it out of religious scruples, he may put aside something of value for people to take.

35 (*Lev*. 27:19): "If the person dedicating his field will redeem it, he shall add a fifth of its value and it shall be his." This verse clearly ties the transfer of title to the property to the payment of money. If we hold that the rules of redemption are the same for dedicated property and Second Tithe, then taking up the tithe cannot be its redemption.

36 Since he cannot dispose of the loaf, he cannot dedicate it. Similarly, he cannot dedicate stalks to the poor if it is totally unknown which ones they will be.

37 Since in the evening all grain has been cut for the day and bound in sheaves, it is now well-defined what is there for the poor and the owner can make any declaration he wishes. The same holds for the discreet religious ones who can redeem the well-defined fruits of their fourth-year vineyard or orchard.

(fol. 55c) **משנה ב:** כֶּרֶם רְבָעִי עוֹלֶה לִירוּשָׁלֵם מַהֲלָךְ יוֹם אֶחָד לְכָל־צַד וְאֵי זוֹ הִיא תְחוּמָהּ אֵילַת מִן הַדָּרוֹם וְאַקְרַבָּה מִן הַצָּפוֹן וְלוֹד מִן הַמַּעֲרָב וְהַיַּרְדֵּן מִן הַמִּזְרָח. וּמִשֶּׁרָבוּ הַפֵּירוֹת הִתְקִינוּ שֶׁיְּהֵא נִפְדֶּה סָמוּךְ לַחוֹמָה. וּתְנַיי הָיָה הַדָּבָר אֵימָתַי שֶׁיִּרְצוּ יַחֲזוֹר הַדָּבָר לִכְמוֹת שֶׁהָיָה. רִבִּי יוֹסֵי אוֹמֵר מִשֶּׁחָרַב בֵּית הַמִּקְדָּשׁ

הָיָה הַתְּנַיי הַזֶּה וּתְנַיי אֵימָתַי שֶׁיִּיבָּנֶה בֵית הַמִּקְדָּשׁ בִּמְהֵרָה בְיָמֵינוּ יַחֲזוֹר הַדָּבָר לִכְמוֹת שֶׁהָיָה.

Mishnah 2: [Grapes from] a fourth-year vineyard have to be brought to Jerusalem from a distance up to a day's march. What is this? Eilat from the South[38], Aqrabeh from the North, Lydda from the West, the Jordan from the East. When the fruits increased[39] they decreed that they might be redeemed [even] close to the city wall. There was a condition made that anytime they decided, they could return to the previous situation[40]. Rebbi Yose says, this condition was introduced when the Temple was destroyed, *viz.*, that one would return to the previous situation if the Temple would be rebuilt soon, in our days[41].

38 An unknown place somewhere South of Hebron. One has to assume that the distance between Jerusalem and Eilat was approximately the same as the distance between Jerusalem and Aqrabeh, SE of Nablus.

39 And ruined the trade in fruits on the markets in Jerusalem.

40 Usually a rule imposed by a rabbinic assembly could be nullified or amended only by an assembly more prestigious than the first. This rule is explicitly waved in the present case.

41 For R. Yose, no exemption for a future rabbinical assembly is created; the original assembly already fixed the terms for the disestablishment of the rule.

(fol. 56a) **הלכה ב**: אָמַר רִבִּי הִילָא בָּרִאשׁוֹנָה הָיוּ עוֹשִׂין יַיִן בְּטָהֳרָה לִנְסָכִים וְלֹא הָיוּ עֲנָבִים מְצוּיוֹת. הִתְקִינוּ שֶׁיְּהֵא עוֹלֶה לִירוּשָׁלֵם מַהֲלָךְ יוֹם לְכָל־צַד. אַף הֵן מְחַלְּקִין אוֹתוֹ לִקְרוֹבִין וְלִשְׁכֵנִין וְלִמְיוּדָעִין. אֲפִילוּ דָּבָר קַל הָיָה מְעַטֵּר אֶת הַשּׁוּק.

Halakhah 2: Rebbi Hila said, at the start they made wine in purity for Temple libations and grapes[42] were rare. They decreed that it[43] had to be brought to Jerusalem from a distance up to a day's march. They used to distribute it to relatives, neighbors, and acquaintances[44], and a small quantity adorned the market[45].

42 Eating grapes.

43 The yield of fourth-year vineyards.

44 Since the buyer knew that they were fourth-year grapes, the price would be depressed and the grapes could as well be distributed. (Explanation of S. Lieberman.) In the Tosephta, 5:14, R. Simeon restricts the rule to vineyards in the sense of the formal definition (Mishnah *Kilaim* 4:6); the yield of single vines should always be redeemed and the redemption money used under the rules of tithe money.

45 This implies that in contrast to Second Tithe, the grapes from a fourth-year vineyard may be redeemed in Jerusalem proper, which makes the grapes profane and marketable. The reason given by R. Hila is attributed in the Babli (*Beẓah* 5a, *Roš Haššanah* 31b) to R. Joḥanan or R. Joshua ben Levi.

הָדָא פְלִיגָא עַל נֻקַיי. נֻקַיי הֲוָה שַׁמָּשׁ בְּמִגְדָּל צְבָעַיָּה.[46] בְּכָל־עֲרוּבָא שׁוּבָא מִן דַּהֲוָה עֲבִיד קַנְדֵּילוֹי הֲוָה סְלִיק שָׁבַת בְּבֵית מִקְדָּשָׁא וְנָחִית וּמַדְלִיק לוֹן. וְאִית דְּאָמְרִין סַפָּר הֲוָה. בְּכָל־עֲרוּבָא שׁוּבְתָא הֲוָה סְלַק פָּשַׁט סִדרוֹי לְבֵית הַמִּקְדָּשׁ וְנָחִית שָׁבַת בְּבֵיתֵיהּ.

This disagrees with Nukai[47]. Nukai was community servant in Magdala of the dyers[48]. Every Sabbath eve, after preparing his candles[49], he went up, rested in the Temple, and went down to light them. Some say, he was the Torah reader. Every Sabbath eve he went up, prepared his reading in the Temple, and went down for the Sabbath in his home.

46 Reading of the Rome ms. Leyden and Venice: וצבעייא.

47 Since נקיי, together with מתיי, "Matthew", appears as name of one of the disciples of Jesus, one might identify נקיי with Lucas by a change in liquids. The story is also in *Ekhâ Rabbati* on *Thr.* 3:9; there, the person is only identified by his occupation, not by name. The following stories, except

that of Mahalul, are also in that source.

48 Probably a quarter of Magdala, N. of Tiberias. In *Ekhâ Rabbati*, the place is simply called Magdala.

49 For the Friday night service in the synagoge. Latin *candela* "wax light, tallow candle, taper".

טַרְטִירוֹי דְּמַהֲלוּל הֲוָה סְלִיק שָׁבַת לְגַו בֵּית מִקְדְּשָׁא וְלָא הֲוָה בַּר נַשׁ קָרֵץ לְתְאֵינַיָּא קֳדָמוֹי מִינֵּיהּ.

The cap maker[50] of Malul[51] went up to observe the Sabbath in the Temple but nobody got up[52] for his fig trees before him.

50 Arabic طرطور "pointed cap". [Perhaps also cf. late Latin *triturator* "thresher", *tritor* "grinder" (E. G.).

51 In lower Galilee.

52 Sunday morning.

בְּנוֹת צִפּוֹרִי הֲווֹ סַלְקוֹן שַׁבְּתוֹן בְּגַו בֵּית מִקְדְּשָׁא וְלָא הֲוָה בַּר נַשׁ קָרֵץ לְתְאֵינַיָּא קֳדָמוֹי מִינְהוֹן. בְּנוֹת לוֹד הָיוּ לָשׁוֹת עִיסָּתָן וְעוֹלוֹת וּמִתְפַּלְּלוֹת וְיוֹרְדוֹת עַד שֶׁלֹּא יַחְמִיצוּ.

The daughters[53] of Sepphoris went up, kept the Sabbath in the Temple, but nobody got up[52] for their fig trees before them. The daughters of Lod were kneading their bread dough, went up, prayed, and descended before it became sour[54].

53 The unmarried women.

54 It seems that in Lod one never spoke Aramaic. The parallel to the sentence in *Ekhâ Rabbati* also is in Hebrew.

חַד בַּר נַשׁ הֲוָה קָאִים רְדִי. פָּֽסְקַת תּוֹרְתֵיהּ קוֹמוֹי. הֲוַת פָּֽרְיָא וַהֲוָה פָּרֵי פָּֽרְיָא וְהוּא פָּרֵי עַד דְּאִשְׁתְּכָח יְהִיב בְּבָבֶל. אָֽמְרוּ לֵיהּ אֵימַת נָֽפְקַת. אָמַר לוֹן יוֹמָא דֵין. אָֽמְרִין בְּהֵיידָא[55] אָתִיתָא. אָמַר לוֹן בְּדָא. אָמַר לוֹן אִיתָא חָמֵי לוֹן. נְפַק בְּעֵי מֵיחְמַייָא וְלָא חַכִּים בְּהֵיידָא.

[56]A person was ploughing. His cow broke away before him and started running. He ran and ran after her until he found himself in Babylonia. They asked him, when did you leave? He answered, today. They asked him, by which [road] did you come? He answered them, by this one, come and see it. He went out, wanted to see it, and did no longer recognize it.

55 In the Rome ms: בהיידא איסרטא "on which road".

56 In *Ekhâ Rabbati*, the story is quite different and not connected with instant travelling of long distances.

מִכְּלָל דִּפְלִיגָא. וַאֲפִילוּ תֵימַר לֵית הוּא פְלִיגָא מְחִילוֹת הֲווֹ וְנִגְנְזוּ. הָדָא הוּא דִכְתִיב גָּדַר דְּרָכַיי בְּגָזִית נְתִיבוֹתַיי עִוָּה.

From here, that they disagree. Even if you say it does not disagree, there were tunnels and they were hidden. That is what is written (*Thr.* 3:9): "He fenced my way with ashlar, my paths he destroyed."

רִבִּי יוֹנָה בְּשֵׁם רִבִּי זְעִירָה אֲפִילוּ כֶרֶם שֶׁהָיָה סָמוּךְ לַחוֹמָה הָיָה נִפְדֶּה.

Rebbi Jonah in the name of Rebbi Zeïra: Even a vineyard reaching to the wall was redeemed[57].

אָמַר רִבִּי אָחָא זֹאת אוֹמֶרֶת שֶׁבֵּית הַמִּקְדָּשׁ עָתִיד לְהִיבָּנוֹת קוֹדֶם לְמַלְכוּת בֵּית דָּוִיד דִּכְתִיב וְדַם עֵינָב תִּשְׁתֶּה חָמֶר. וְאַתְּ אָמַר הָכֵין.

Rebbi Aḥa said, this implies that the Temple will be rebuilt before the kingdom of David's dynasty[58] as it is written (*Deut.* 32:14): "From the blood of a grape you will drink as wine"[59]. And you say so!

57 This explains what "outside the walls" means in the Mishnah.

58 Since the decree, according to R. Yose, mentions only the rebuilding of the Temple and not the coming of the Messiah, it implies that the two events

are independent of one another.

59 This is an allusion to the explanation of this verse, describing the plenty induced by the Temple, either in *Sifry Deut.* 317: You will not have to work to press and make wine, but bring it in on a wagon, put it in a corner, and drink from it as from a barrel; or in Babli *Ketubot* 111b: It teaches you that each grape will produce 30 barrels of wine; read (following a pronunciation which has the same sound for ָ and ֹ) חָמֶר as חֹמֶר (30 *seah*); cf. *Peah* 7:4.

(fol. 55c) **משנה ג:** כֶּרֶם רְבָעִי בֵּית שַׁמַּי אוֹמְרִים אֵין לוֹ חוֹמֶשׁ וְאֵין לוֹ בִּיעוּר. וּבֵית הִלֵּל אוֹמֵר יֵשׁ לוֹ. בֵּית שַׁמַּי אוֹמְרִים יֵשׁ לוֹ פֶּרֶט וְיֵשׁ לוֹ עוֹלֵלוֹת וַעֲנִיִּים פּוֹדִין לְעַצְמָן. וּבֵית הִלֵּל אוֹמְרִים כּוּלּוֹ לְגַת.

[61]**Mishnah 3**: A fourth-year vineyard, the House of Shammai say, is not subject to a fifth and is not subject to removal; but the House of Hillel say, it is. The House of Shammai say, it is subject to single berries and gleanings and the poor redeem for themselves, but the House of Hillel say, all goes to the winepress.

61 The entire Halakhah is from *Peah* 7:6; explained there in Notes 99–145.

(fol. 26a) **הלכה ג:** תַּנֵּי רִבִּי אוֹמֵר בַּמֶּה דְּבָרִים אֲמוּרִים בִּשְׁבִיעִית אֲבָל בִּשְׁאָר שְׁנֵי שָׁבוּעַ בֵּית שַׁמַּי אוֹמְרִים יֵשׁ לוֹ חוֹמֶשׁ וְיֵשׁ לוֹ בִּיעוּר. עַל דַּעְתֵּיהּ דְּהָהֵן תַּנָּיָיה לֹא לָמְדוּ נֶטַע רְבָעִי אֶלָּא לְמַעֲשֵׂר שֵׁינִי כְּמָה דְתֵימַר אֵין מַעֲשֵׂר שֵׁינִי בִּשְׁבִיעִית. וְדִכְוָותֵיהּ אֵין נֶטַע רְבָעִי בִּשְׁבִיעִית. מֵעַתָּה אַל יְהִי לוֹ קְדוּשָּׁה. וּקְדוּשָּׁתוֹ מֵאֵילָיו לָמְדוּ. קוֹדֶשׁ הִילּוּלִים. כְּקוֹדֶשׁ שֶׁקּוֹרִין עָלָיו אֶת הַהַלֵּל. וִיהֵא מוּתָּר לְאוֹנֵן. תַּנֵּי מַגִּיד שֶׁהוּא אָסוּר לְאוֹנֵן. וִיהֵא חַיָּיב בְּבִיעוּר. בְּגִין רִבִּי שִׁמְעוֹן. דְּרִבִּי שִׁמְעוֹן פּוֹטֵר מִן הַבִּיעוּר. וְיִיפָּדֶה בִּמְחוּבָּר לְקַרְקַע.

Halakhah 3: It was stated: Rebbi says, the House of Shammai said this only for the Sabbatical year, but in all other years of the Sabbatical cycle, the House of Shammai say that it is subject to a fifth and subject to removal. According to that Tanna, they learned the rules of the fourth-year orchard only from Second Tithe; since you say that there is no Second Tithe in the Sabbatical year, so there is no fourth-year orchard in the Sabbatical year. But then should there be no holiness in it? Its holiness comes from the verse (*Lev.* 19:24): "Holy for praises," it has the status of those holy fruits over which praises are said. And should it be permitted to the fresh mourner? It is stated: This implies that it is forbidden to the fresh mourner. And should it be subject to removal? Following Rebbi Simeon, since Rebbi Simeon frees it from removal. And should it be redeemed while still connected to the ground?

תַּנֵּי רַבָּן שִׁמְעוֹן בֶּן גַּמְלִיאֵל אוֹמֵר אֶחָד שְׁבִיעִית וְאֶחָד שְׁאָר שְׁנֵי שָׁבוּעַ בֵּית שַׁמַּי אוֹמְרִים אֵין לוֹ חוֹמֶשׁ וְאֵין לוֹ בִּיעוּר. עַל דַּעְתֵּיהּ דְּהָדֵין תַּנָּייָא לֹא לָמְדוּ נֶטַע רְבָעִי מִמַּעֲשֵׂר שֵׁינִי כָּל־עִיקָּר. מֵעַתָּה אַל יְהֵא לוֹ קְדוּשָּׁה. וּקְדוּשָּׁתוֹ מֵאֵילָיו לָמְדוּ. קוֹדֶשׁ הִילּוּלִים. הֲרֵי כְקוֹדֶשׁ שֶׁקּוֹרִין עָלָיו אֶת הַהַלֵּל. וִיהֵא מוּתָּר לְאוֹנֵן. מַגִּיד שֶׁהוּא אָסוּר לְאוֹנֵן. וִיהֵא חַיָּיב בְּבִיעוּר. בְּגִין דְּרִבִּי שִׁמְעוֹן. דְּרִבִּי שִׁמְעוֹן פּוֹטֵר מִן הַבִּיעוּר. וְיִפָּדֶה בִּמְחוּבָּר לְקַרְקַע.

Rabban Simeon ben Gamliel stated: Both in the Sabbatical year and in the rest of the years of the Sabbatical cycle, the House of Shammai say, there is no fifth and no removal. According to that Tanna, they did not at all learn the rules of the fourth-year orchard from Second Tithe. But then should there be no holiness in it? Its holiness comes from the verse (*Lev.* 19:24): "Holy for praises;" it has the status of those holy fruits over which praises are said. And should it be permitted to the fresh mourner? It is stated: This implies that it is forbidden to the fresh mourner. And should it be subject to removal? Following Rebbi Simeon, since Rebbi Simeon frees it from removal. And should it be redeemed while still connected to the ground?

רִבִּי זְעִירָא בָּעָא קוֹמֵי רִבִּי אַבָּהוּ מְנַיִין שֶׁהוּא טָעוּן פִּדְיוֹן קוֹדֶשׁ הִילּוּלִים קוֹדֶשׁ חִילּוּלִים לָא מִתְמַנְעִין רַבָּנִין דָּרַשׁ בֵּין הֵ״א לְחֵי״ת.

Rebbi Zeïra asked before Rebbi Abbahu: From where that it needs redemption? (*Lev.* 19:24) "Holy for praises," holy for redemption. The rabbis never refrain from explaining ה by ח.

תַּנֵּי רִבִּי אַיְיבוּ בַּר נַגָּרִי קוֹמֵי רִבִּי לָא דְּרִבִּי יִשְׁמָעֵאל אִם גָּאֹל יִגְאַל אִישׁ מִמַּעַשְׂרוֹ חֲמִישִׁיתוֹ יוֹסֵף עָלָיו. פְּרָט לְנֶטַע רְבָעִי שֶׁאֵין חַייָבִין עָלָיו חוֹמֶשׁ. חָזַר וְתַנָּא קוֹמוֹי שְׁתֵּי גְאוּלוֹת הֵן אַחַת לְמַעֲשֵׂר שֵׁינִי וְאַחַת לְנֶטַע רְבָעִי.

Rebbi Ayvu bar Naggari stated before Rebbi La following Rebbi Ismael (*Lev.* 27:31): "If a man redeems part of his tithes, he should add their fifth to it." That excludes the fourth-year orchard; one is not obligated by it for a fifth. Then he turned around and stated: There are two terms of redemption, one for the Second Tithe and one for the fourth-year orchard.

תַּמָּן תַּנִּינָן רִבִּי יוּדָה אוֹמֵר אֵין לְנָכְרִי כֶּרֶם רְבָעִי. וַחֲכָמִים אוֹמְרִים יֵשׁ לוֹ. אָמַר רִבִּי לָעְזָר כֵּינִי מַתְנִיתָא אֵין לְנָכְרִי כֶּרֶם רְבָעִי כָּל־עִיקָּר. רִבִּי בִּיבִי אָמַר קוֹמֵי רִבִּי זְעִירָא בְּשֵׁם רִבִּי לָעְזָר אַתְיָא דְּרִבִּי יוּדָה כְּבֵית שַׁמַּי. עַל דַּעְתֵּיהּ דְּרִבִּי כְּמָה דְּבֵית שַׁמַּי אוֹמֵר לֹא לָמְדוּ נֶטַע רְבָעִי אֶלָּא מִמַּעֲשֵׂר שֵׁינִי כְּמַה דְּתֵימַר אֵין מַעֲשֵׂר שֵׁינִי בִּשְׁבִיעִית. וְדִכְוָותָהּ אֵין נֶטַע רְבָעִי בִּשְׁבִיעִית. כֵּן רִבִּי יוּדָה אוֹמֵר לֹא לָמְדוּ נֶטַע רְבָעִי אֶלָּא מִמַּעֲשֵׂר שֵׁינִי כְּמַה דְּאַתְּ אָמַר אֵין מַעֲשֵׂר שֵׁינִי בְּסוּרְיָא וְדִכְוָותָהּ אֵין נֶטַע רְבָעִי בְּסוּרְיָא. אָמַר לֵיהּ חֲמִי מַה אָמַר. לֹא אָמַר

אֶלָּא אֵין לוֹ חוֹמֶשׁ וְאֵין לוֹ בִּיעוּר הָא שְׁאָר כָּל־הַדְּבָרִים יֵשׁ לוֹ. רִבִּי יְהוּדָה אוֹמֵר אֵין לְנָכְרִי כֶּרֶם רְבָעִי בְּסוּרְיָא.

There we have stated: Rebbi Jehudah says, there is no vineyard in the fourth year for the Gentile, but the Sages say there is. Rebbi Eleazar said, so says the Mishnah: There is never a vineyard in the fourth year for the Gentile. Rebbi Bibi said before Rebbi Zeïra in the name of Rebbi Eleazar: According to the opinion of Rebbi, the statement of Rebbi Jehudah turns out to be like the statement of the House of Shammai. Since the House of Shammai said that they learned the rules of the vineyard of the fourth year only from Second Tithe; since you say that there is no Second Tithe in the Sabbatical year, so there is no fourth-year orchard in the Sabbatical year. Similarly, Rebbi Jehudah said that they learned the rules of the vineyard of the fourth year only from Second Tithe; since you say that there is no Second Tithe in Syria, so there is no fourth-year orchard in Syria. He said to him, look what he said! He said only, it is not subject to a fifth and is not subject to removal, hence, it is subject to all other rules; Rebbi Jehudah says, there is no vineyard in the fourth year for the Gentile in Syria.

שְׁמוּאֵל בַּר אַבָּא בָּעֵי הָא בֵית שַׁמַּי אוֹמְרִים לֹא לָמְדוּ נֶטַע רְבָעִי אֶלָּא מִמַּעֲשֵׂר שֵׁינִי כְּמָה דְתֵימַר אֵין מַעֲשֵׂר שֵׁינִי בִשְׁבִיעִית. וְדִכְוָותָהּ אֵין נֶטַע רְבָעִי בִשְׁבִיעִית. וְדִכְוָותָהּ שְׁלִישִׁית וְשִׁישִּׁית הוֹאִיל וְאֵין בָּהֶן מַעֲשֵׂר שֵׁינִי לֹא יְהֵא בָהֶן נֶטַע רְבָעִי. אָמַר רִבִּי יוֹסֵי שְׁלִישִׁית וְשִׁישִּׁית אַף עַל פִּי שֶׁאֵין בָּהֶן מַעֲשֵׂר שֵׁינִי יֵשׁ בָּהֶן מַעְשָׂרוֹת. שְׁבִיעִית אֵין לוֹ מַעְשָׂרוֹת כָּל־עִיקָּר.

Samuel bar Abba asked: Since the House of Shammai said that they learned the rules of the vineyard of the fourth year only from Second Tithe; since you say that there is no Second Tithe in the Sabbatical year, there is no fourth-year orchard in the Sabbatical year. Similarly, in the third and sixth years of the Sabbatical cycle, since there is no Second Tithe, there should not be any fourth-year orchard. Rebbi Yose said, even though there is no Second Tithe in the third and sixth years, there are the tithes. In the Sabbatical year, there are no tithes at all.

חֵיפָא שְׁאַל הָא רִבִּי יוּדָה אָמַר לֹא לָֽמְדוּ נֶטַע רְבָעִי אֶלָּא מִמַּעֲשֵׂר כְּמָה דְתֵימַר אֵין מַעֲשֵׂר שֵׁינִי בְּסוּרְיָא. וְדִכְוָותָהּ אֵין נֶטַע רְבָעִי בְסוּרְיָא. וְדִכְוָותָהּ לֹא לָֽמְדוּ תְרוּמַת תּוֹדָה אֶלָּא מִתְּרוּמַת מַעֲשֵׂר. כְּמָה דְתֵימַר אֵין תְּרוּמַת מַעֲשֵׂר בַּמִּדְבָּר וְדִכְוָותָהּ לֹא תְהֵא תְרוּמַת תּוֹדָה בַּמִּדְבָּר. אָמַר רִבִּי יוֹסֵי לֹא לָֽמְדוּ מִמֶּנָּה אֶלָּא לְשִׁיעוּרִין.

Ḥeipha asked: Since Rebbi Jehudah said that they learned the rules of the vineyard of the fourth year only from Second Tithe; since you say that there is no Second Tithe in Syria, there is no fourth-year orchard in Syria. Similarly, they learned the rules of the heave of the thanksgiving sacrifice only from the heave of the tithe; since you say that there was no heave of the tithe in the desert, will it follow that there was no heave of the thanksgiving sacrifice in the desert? Rebbi Yose said, they learned from it only in regard to quantities.

תַּנֵּי רִבִּי יוֹסֵי בֵּי רִבִּי יוּדָה אוֹמֵר רִבִּי לָֽעְזָר בֵּי רִבִּי שִׁמְעוֹן אוֹמֵר לֹא נִתְחַייְבוּ יִשְׂרָאֵל בְּנֶטַע רְבָעִי אֶלָּא לְאַחַר אַרְבַּע עֶשְׂרֵה שָׁנָה שֶׁבַע שֶׁכִּיבְּשׁוּ וְשֶׁבַע שֶׁחִילְּקוּ. אָמַר רַב חִסְדָּא אַתְיָא דְרִבִּי יוֹסֵי בֵּי רִבִּי יוּדָה בְּשִׁיטַּת רִבִּי יוּדָה אָבִיו. כְּמָה דְרִבִּי יוּדָה אָמַר לֹא לָֽמְדוּ נֶטַע רְבָעִי אֶלָּא מִמַּעֲשֵׂר שֵׁינִי כְּמָה דְתֵימַר אֵין מַעֲשֵׂר שֵׁינִי בְּסוּרְיָא וְדִכְוָותָהּ אֵין נֶטַע רְבָעִי בְּסוּרְיָא. כֵּן רִבִּי יוֹסֵי בֵּי רִבִּי יוּדָה אוֹמֵר לֹא לָֽמְדוּ נֶטַע רְבָעִי אֶלָּא מִמַּעֲשֵׂר. כְּמָה דְתֵימַר אֵין מַעֲשֵׂר שֵׁינִי אֶלָּא לְאַחַר אַרְבַּע עֶשְׂרֵה שָׁנָה. וְדִכְוָותָהּ אֵין נֶטַע רְבָעִי אֶלָּא לְאַחַר אַרְבַּע

עֶשְׂרֵה שָׁנָה. אָמַר רִבִּי יוֹסֵי וְהִיא בְשִׁיטַּת בְּנוֹ סוּרְיָא לְמֵידָה מֵאַרְבַּע עֶשְׂרֵה שָׁנָה אֵין אַרְבַּע עֶשְׂרֵה שָׁנָה לְמֵידָה מִסּוּרְיָא.

It was stated: Rebbi Yose ben Rebbi Jehudah said, Rebbi Eleazar ben Rebbi Simeon said, Israel did become obligated for the fourth-year orchard only after 14 years, seven during which they conquered and seven during which they divided up the land. Rav Ḥisda said, it turns out that the argument of Rebbi Yose ben Rebbi Jehudah is identical with that of his father Rebbi Jehudah. Just as Rebbi Jehudah said that they learned the rules of the fourth-year orchard only from Second Tithe, since you say that there is no Second Tithe in Syria, so there is no fourth-year orchard in Syria. Similarly, Rebbi Yose ben Rebbi Jehudah said that they learned the rules of the fourth-year orchard only from Second Tithe, since you say that they did become obligated for the fourth-year orchard only after 14 years,, similarly there was no fourth-year orchard until after 14 years. Rebbi Yose said, he follows his son's argument; Syria was inferred from "after 14 years;" "after 14 years" was not inferred from Syria.

כְּתִיב וּבַשָּׁנָה הַחֲמִישִׁית תֹּאכְלוּ אֶת פִּרְיוֹ לְהוֹסִיף לָכֶם וגו׳. רִבִּי יוֹסֵי הַגְּלִילִי אוֹמֵר הֲרֵי אַתְּ כְּמוֹסִיף פֵּירוֹת חֲמִישִׁית עַל פֵּירוֹת רְבִיעִית מַה פֵּירוֹת חֲמִישִׁית לִבְעָלִים. אַף פֵּירוֹת רְבִיעִית (fol. 56b) לִבְעָלִים. רִבִּי זְעִירָא רִבִּי יָסָא בְשֵׁם רִבִּי יוֹחָנָן אַתְיָא דְּרִבִּי יוֹסֵי הַגְּלִילִי כְּרִבִּי יְהוּדָה. כְּמָה דְּרִבִּי יְהוּדָה עוֹשֶׂה אוֹתוֹ כִּנְכָסָיו כֵּן רִבִּי יוֹסֵי הַגְּלִילִי עוֹשֶׂה אוֹתוֹ כִּנְכָסָיו.

It is written (*Lev.* 19:25): "In the fifth year, you shall eat its yield to add for you, etc." Rebbi Yose the Galilean says, here one adds the fruits of the fifth to the fruits of the fourth year. Just as the fruits of the fifth year are for the proprietors, so the fruits of the fourth year are for the proprietors. Rebbi Zeïra, Rebbi Yasa, in the name of Rebbi Joḥanan: It turns out that

Rebbi Yose the Galilean argues like Rebbi Jehudah. Just as Rebbi Jehudah makes it his property, so Rebbi Yose the Galilean makes it his property.

רִבִּי יִרְמְיָה בָּעָא קוֹמֵי רִבִּי זְעִירָא כְּדִבְרֵי מִי שֶׁהוּא עוֹשֶׂה אוֹתוֹ כִּנְכָסָיו מַהוּ שֶׁיְּהֵא חַייָב בְּמַעְשְׂרוֹת. אֲמַר לֵיהּ כַּיי דְּאָמַר רִבִּי יְהוֹשֻׁעַ בֶּן לֵוִי דְּאָמַר רִבִּי אָבִין בְּשֵׁם רִבִּי יְהוֹשֻׁעַ בֶּן לֵוִי לֹא סוֹף דָּבָר הֲלָכָה זוּ אֶלָּא כָּל־הֲלָכָה שֶׁהִיא רוֹפֶפֶת בְּבֵית דִּין וְאֵין אַתְּ יוֹדֵעַ מַה טִיבָהּ צֵא וּרְאֵה הֵיאַךְ הַצִּיבּוּר נוֹהֵג וּנְהוֹג. וַאֲנָן חָמִיּין צִיבּוּרָא דְּלָא מַפְרְשִׁין. אֲמַר רִבִּי מָנָא אִילּוּ אָמַר כְּבֵית שַׁמַּי וְיֵשׁ צִיבּוּר כְּבֵית שַׁמַּי. אֲמַר רִבִּי אָבִין כְּלוּם לָמַדְנוּ נֶטַע רְבָעִי אֶלָּא מִמַּעֲשֵׂר שֵׁינִי כְּמָה דְּתֵימַר אֵין מַעֲשֵׂר שֵׁינִי חַייָב בְּמַעְשְׂרוֹת. וְדִכְוָותָהּ אֵין נֶטַע רְבָעִי חַייָב בְּמַעְשְׂרוֹת.

Rebbi Jeremiah asked before Rebbi Zeïra: According to those who declare it his property, should it not be subject to tithes? He said to him, according to what Rebbi Joshua ben Levi said, as Rebbi Abin said in the name of Rebbi Joshua ben Levi, not only this practice, but in any practical question which is weak in court and you do not know how to decide, go out and see how the public acts, and act accordingly. And we see that they do not give. Rebbi Mana said, that is, if the practice would follow the House of Shammai. But is there any public that acts according to the House of Shammai? Rebbi Abin said, they learned the rules of the vineyard of the fourth year only from Second Tithe; just as you say that Second Tithe is not subject to tithes, so the yield of the fourth year is not subject to tithes.

רִבִּי בָּא רִבִּי חִייָה בְּשֵׁם רִבִּי יוֹחָנָן עִיסַּת מַעֲשֵׂר שֵׁינִי בִּירוּשָׁלֵם כְּרִבִּי מֵאִיר פְּטוּרָה מִן הַחַלָּה כְּרִבִּי יוּדָה חַייֶבֶת בְּחַלָּה. אֲמַר רִבִּי יוֹנָה[62] לֹא אָמְרוּ אֶלָּא בִּירוּשָׁלֵם אֲבָל בִּגְבוּלִין לֹא.

Rebbi Abba, Rebbi Ḥiyya, in the name of Rebbi Joḥanan: A dough of Second Tithe in Jerusalem, following Rebbi Meïr, is free from *ḥallah*, following Rebbi Jehudah it is subject to *ḥallah*. Rebbi Jonah said, they said this only for Jerusalem, but not for the countryside.

62 Reading of the Rome ms. and the text in *Peah*. Leyden and Venice: ר' יודה

רִבִּי בָּא בַּר כֹּהֵן בָּעָא קוֹמֵי רִבִּי יוֹסֵי כְּדִבְרֵי מִי שֶׁהוּא מְחַייֵב בְּפֶרֶט מַהוּ שֶׁתְּהֵא חַייֶבֶת בְּחַלָּה. אָמַר לֵיהּ וְלֹא רִבִּי יוּדָה הִיא וְסָבְרִינָן מֵימַר כָּל־הָדָא הִלְכְתָא רִבִּי יוּדָה כְּבֵית שַׁמַּי.

Rebbi Abba bar Cohen asked before Rebbi Yose: Does he who declares it obligated for single berries also declare it obligated for *ḥallah*? He said to him, is that not Rebbi Jehudah? And it is our opinion that in all this practice, Rebbi Jehudah follows the House of Shammai.

(fol. 55c) **משנה ד:** כֵּיצַד פּוֹדִין נֶטַע רְבָעִי מַנִּיחַ אֶת הַסֶּלַע עַל פִּי שְׁלֹשָׁה וְאוֹמֵר כַּמָּה אָדָם רוֹצֶה לִפְדּוֹת לוֹ בְּסֶלַע עַל מְנָת לְהוֹצִיא יְצִיאוֹת מִבֵּיתוֹ וּמַנִּיחַ אֶת הַמָּעוֹת וְאוֹמֵר כָּל־הַנִּקְלָט מִזֶּה מְחוּלָּל עַל הַמָּעוֹת הָאֵילּוּ. מִכָּךְ וְכָךְ סַלִּים בְּסֶלַע.

Mishnah 4: How does one redeem a fourth-year orchard? He puts a tetradrachma[63] before three [experts] and asks, how much does a person redeem for himself for a tetradrachma when all expense[64] is on him? Then he puts down the money and says, all that is collected under this is exchanged for this money; so and so many baskets per tetradrachma.

משנה ה: וּבַשְּׁבִיעִית פּוֹדֵיהוּ בְּשָׁוְיוֹ אִם הָיָה הַכֹּל מוּבְקָר אֵין לוֹ אֶלָּא שְׂכַר לְקִיטָה. הַפּוֹדֶה נֶטַע רְבָעִי שֶׁלּוֹ מוֹסִיף עָלָיו חֲמִישִׁיתוֹ בֵּין שֶׁהוּא שֶׁלּוֹ בֵּין שֶׁנִּיתַּן לוֹ בְּמַתָּנָה.

Mishnah 5: In a Sabbatical, he redeems its full value[65]. If all of it was abandoned[66], he has only the cost of harvesting. He who redeems a fourth-year orchard adds its fifth whether it was his or was given to him as a gift[67].

63 Most Mishnah mss. read הסל "the basket" but in addition to the Leyden ms. the reading here is in a ms. of the Babli and in a Mishnah ms. from the Geniza. Therefore, it does not seem permissible to treat the reading here as a scribal error.

64 The entire expense for growing this year's yield.

65 Since there is no agricultural work, no costs accrue that could be deducted.

66 In a non-Sabbatical year, the amount invested before it was abandoned is not deductible by the person who acquires the ownerless property; he may only deduct his own expenses of harvesting.

67 Following the House of Hillel, Mishnah 3. If it was given as a gift it becomes the recipient's property only if delivered before the time of heave and tithes since later the yield is Heaven's property.

(fol. 56b) **הלכה ד:** לִפְדּוֹת לוֹ בְּסֶלַע לוֹקֵחַ לוֹ בְּסֶלַע. אֵין לוֹ אֶלָּא שְׂכַר לְקִיטָה אֵין לוֹ אֶלָּא שְׂכַר עֲקִיצָה. רִבִּי הוֹשַׁעְיָה מְפַק תְּלָתָה אִיסְתּוֹנְנְסִין וּמְפָרֵק עַל פִּימוֹן.

Halakhah 4: To redeem for a tetradrachma [means] he buys for himself for a tetradrachma. "He has only the cost of harvesting" including the cost of removing the pedicles[68]. Rebbi Hoshaia took three wholesalers[69] [?] and redeemed on their word.

68 And any post-harvest processing needed.

69 Jastrow reads סיטונין for איסתוננסין. Buxtorf and Mussaphia read ἀστυνόμοι "street police"; R. M. Margalit reads "asthenics" who in his view are vegetarians and know the price of fruits.

(fol. 55c) **משנה ו:** עֶרֶב יוֹם טוֹב הָרִאשׁוֹן שֶׁלְּפֶסַח שֶׁלְּרְבִיעִית וְשֶׁלְּשְׁבִיעִית הָיָה בִּיעוּר. כֵּיצַד הָיָה בִּיעוּר נוֹתְנִין תְּרוּמָה וּתְרוּמַת מַעֲשֵׂר לִבְעָלֶיהָ וּמַעֲשֵׂר רִאשׁוֹן לִבְעָלָיו וּמַעֲשֵׂר עָנִי לִבְעָלָיו. מַעֲשֵׂר שֵׁינִי וּבִיכּוּרִים מִתְבָּעֲרִים בְּכָל־מָקוֹם. רִבִּי שִׁמְעוֹן אוֹמֵר הַבִּיכּוּרִין נוֹתְנִין לַכֹּהֲנִים כִּתְרוּמָה. הַתַּבְשִׁיל בֵּית שַׁמַּי אוֹמֵר צָרִיךְ לְבָעֵר. וּבֵית הִלֵּל אוֹמְרִים הֲרֵי הוּא כִמְבוֹעָר.

Mishnah 6: The removal[70] was on the day before the first[71] day of Passover in the fourth and the seventh year [of the Sabbatical cycle.] What is the removal? One gives heave and heave of the tithe to its recipients[72], First Tithe to its recipients[73], tithe of the poor to its recipients. Second Tithe and First Fruits are removed on the spot[74]. Rebbi Simeon says, first fruits one gives to the Cohanim like heave. A cooked dish the House of Shammai say one has to remove, but the House of Hillel say it is as if removed[75].

70 The removal is the same as for Sabbatical produce (*Ševi'it* 9:8); no produce may remain in the hands of the owner. {Maimonides holds that the leftovers have to be burned.}

71 This is the reading of both Yerushalmi mss. and a majority of the Mishnah mss. However, the Cambridge ms. of the Galilean Mishnah as well as the Maimonides autograph read "last" day; and this reading is necessary in Halakhah 7. In *Sifry Deut.* 302, the mss. are divided about evenly between "first" and "last". One might speculate that the reading "first" is derived from some mss. in which יום טוב אחרון was

abbreviated to 'י״ט א' which was read as י״ט אחד (ראשון).

72 The Cohanim.

73 The Levites.

74 Outside of Jerusalem, they cannot be eaten. If anything is left, it must be destroyed. This rule shows that in Jerusalem one needs the entire holiday of Passover to dispose of Second Tithe.

75 This sentence seems to have been part of the next Mishnah since it is discussed at the beginning of Halakhah 6.

(fol. 56b) **הלכה ה:** כְּתִיב מִקְצֵה שָׁלֹשׁ שָׁנִים תּוֹצִיא אֶת כָּל־מַעְשַׂר תְּבוּאָתְךָ בַּשָּׁנָה הַהִוא וְהִנַּחְתָּ בִּשְׁעָרֶיךָ יָכוֹל פַּעַם אַחַת בְּשָׁבוּעַ אַתְּ חַייָב לְהוֹצִיא אֶת הַמַּעְשְׂרוֹת וּלְהוֹצִיא מַעֲשֵׂר עָנִי. תַּלְמוּד לוֹמַר מִקְצֵה שָׁלֹשׁ שָׁנִים אַחַת לְשָׁלֹשׁ שָׁנִים. וְלֹא אַחַת לְשֶׁבַע. אֶלָּא בִשְׁלִישִׁית וּבִשְׁבִיעִית שְׁנֵי פְעָמִים בַּשָּׁבוּעַ. אוֹ קוֹרֵא אֲנִי רֹאשׁ הַשָּׁנָה יָכוֹל כֵּיוָן בְּרֹאשׁ הַשָּׁנָה אַתְּ חַייָב לְבָעֵר אֶת הַמַּעְשְׂרוֹת וּלְהוֹצִיא מַעֲשֵׂר עָנִי תַּלְמוּד לוֹמַר מִקְצֵה שָׁלֹשׁ. אֵין מִקְצֵה אֶלָּא בְסוֹף שָׁנָה אַתְּ מְבָעֵר. וְאֵין אַתְּ מְבָעֵר בְּרֹאשׁ הַשָּׁנָה. אִי בְסוֹף שָׁנָה יָכוֹל כֵּיוָן בְּרֹאשָׁהּ שֶׁל רְבִיעִית אַתְּ וְחַייָב לְבָעֵר אֶת הַמַּעְשְׂרוֹת וּלְהוֹצִיא מַעֲשֵׂר עָנִי תַּלְמוּד לוֹמַר כִּי תְכַלֶּה לַעְשֵׂר אֶת כָּל־תְּבוּאָתְךָ כְּשֶׁתְּכַלֶּה לַעְשֵׂר אֶת כָּל־הַפֵּירוֹת. אִי כְּשֶׁתְּכַלֶּה לַעְשֵׂר כָּל־הַפֵּירוֹת יָכוֹל אֲפִילוּ בַּחֲנוּכָּה. נֶאֱמַר כָּאן מִקְצֵה. וְנֶאֱמַר לְהַלָּן מִקְצֵה שֶׁבַע שָׁנִים בְּמוֹעֵד שְׁנַת הַשְּׁמִיטָּה בְּחַג הַסּוּכּוֹת. מַה מִקֵּץ שֶׁנֶּאֱמַר לְהַלָּן בְּמוֹעֵד אַף כָּאן בְּמוֹעֵד. אִי מַה מִקֵּץ שֶׁנֶּאֱמַר לְהַלָּן בְּחַג הַסּוּכּוֹת אַף כָּאן בְּחַג הַסּוּכּוֹת. תַּלְמוּד לוֹמַר כִּי תְכַלֶּה לַעְשֵׂר אֶת כָּל־מַעְשַׂר תְּבוּאָתְךָ. אֵימָתַי הוּא מְכַלֶּה לַעְשֵׂר אֶת כָּל הַפֵּירוֹת בְּפֶסַח שֶׁלָּרְבִיעִית.

Halakhah 5: It is written (*Deut*. 14:28): "At the end of three years you shall take out all tithe of your produce, in that year, and deposit it in your gates." I could think that once in a Sabbatical cycle you have to distribute the tithes including the tithe of the poor[76]. The verse says "at the end of three years," once in three years and not once in seven; i. e., in the third and the seventh[77], twice in a Sabbatical cycle. Do I understand at New

Year's Day, that on New Year's Day you have to distribute the tithes including the tithe of the poor? The verse says "at the end of three years." "At the end" means at its conclusion you remove, you do not remove on New Year's Day. If it is at the end of the year, I could understand that at the beginning of the fourth you have to remove the tithes including the tithe of the poor; the verse says (*Deut.* 26:12): "If you have finished tithing [all tithe of][78] your produce," when you have tithed all your fruits. [79]If it is when you have tithed all your fruits, could I understand even on Ḥanukkah[80]? It says here, "at the end of;" it says further (*Deut.* 26:12): "At the end[81] of seven years, on the fixed time of the Sabbatical year, on the festival of booths." Since "at the end" there means at a fixed time, so here also at a fixed time. Since there "at the end" means the holiday of booths, does it here also mean the holiday of booths? The verse says "if you have finished tithing all tithe of your produce," when you have finished tithing all of your fruits? On Passover of the fourth year[82].

76 The tithe of the poor is mentioned separately since the paragraph in question introduces the tithe of the poor.

77 This formulation is inconsistent. It must either be the 3rd and the 6th year for the obligation of tithes, or the 4th and the 7th which are finally determined to be the times of delivery.

78 In the masoretic text, missing in the quote.

79 From here on, including the tannaitic parts of the next two paragraphs, a similar text is in *Sifry Deut.* §109; in very shortened form also §302.

80 Since Ḥanukkah is not connected with the agricultural year and is not a biblical holiday, its mention does not make much sense, in particular because the tithing year for trees and their fruits ends only on the 14th of Ševaṭ, more than a month and a half after the start of Ḥanukkah. The 15th of Ševaṭ is mentioned as "New Year of trees" in Mishnah *Roš Haššanah* 1:2; in the opinion of the House of Shammai it

is the first of Ševaṭ. This indetermination in itself disqualifies the New Year of trees as a biblical date. The discussion of the date is in *Roš Haššanah* 1:2 (fol. 57a), Babli 14a.

81 In the biblical text, מקץ not מקצה.

82 Since this is the first biblical holiday after the end of tithing fruits of the preceding year.

בַּשָּׁנָה הַהִיא אַתְּ זָקוּק לְבַעֲרוֹ וְאֵין אַתְּ זָקוּק לְבַעֲרוֹ בִּשְׁאָר כָּל־הַשָּׁנִים. בַּשָּׁנָה הַהִיא אַתְּ זָקוּק לְבָעֵר. אֵין אַתְּ זָקוּק לְבָעֵר יָרָק שֶׁיָּצָא מֵרֹאשׁ הַשָּׁנָה עַד הַפֶּסַח. חֲבֵרַייָא אָמְרֵי שֶׁאֵינוֹ מִתְוַדֶּה בָּרְבִיעִית אֶלָּא בַחֲמִישִׁית. אָמַר רִבִּי הִילָא שֶׁאֵינוֹ מְעַכֵּב וִדּוּי בָּרְבִיעִית אֶלָּא בַחֲמִישִׁית. מַה נְפַק מִן בֵּינֵיהוֹן עָבַר וְנִתְוַדָּה. עַל דַּעְתֵּיהוֹן דַּחֲבֵרַיָּא פָּסוּל. עַל דַּעְתֵּיהּ דְּרִבִּי הִילָא כָּשֵׁר.

(*Deut.* 14:28) "In that year" your are obliged to remove it but you are not obliged to remove it in any other year[83]. "In that year" you are obliged to remove; you are not required to remove vegetables which grew between New Year's Day and Passover[84]. The colleagues say, because he can make a declaration[85] [for the latter] only in the fifth year[86]. Rebbi Hila said, because it does not hinder the declaration in the fourth, only in the fifth. Where do they differ? If he transgressed and included it in his declaration. According to the colleagues it is invalid, according to Rebbi Hila is it valid[86].

83 In the *Sifry*, this sentence refers to a later discussion which in the Yerushalmi is purely amoraic.

84 Since the vegetable belongs to the following, not to *this* year.

85 The declaration in the Temple that he fulfilled all his duties for tithes, *Deut.* 26:13-15.

86 Since the declaration is for *all* tithes, a declaration for part of the vegetables of a year is unacceptable.

87 For the colleagues the declaration is a lie since not all tithes of the fourth year are included; for R. Hila it is incorrect but the inclusion may be disregarded. The problem does not arise for the tithes of the sixth year since the Sabbatical is exempt from tithes.

בַּשָּׁנָה הַהִיא אַתְּ מוֹצִיאוֹ מִן הַטָּמֵא עַל הַטָּהוֹר וְאֵין אַתְּ מוֹצִיאוֹ בִּשְׁאָר כָּל־הַשָּׁנִים מִן הַטָּמֵא עַל הַטָּהוֹר. אָמַר רִבִּי לָעְזָר כֵּינִי מַתְנִיתָא בַּשָּׁנָה הַהִיא אַתְּ מוֹצִיאוֹ מִמְּקוֹם טוּמְאָה לִמְקוֹם טָהֳרָה. וְאֵין אַתְּ מוֹצִיאוֹ בִּשְׁאָר כָּל־הַשָּׁנִים מִמְּקוֹם טוּמְאָה לִמְקוֹם טָהֳרָה. אַתְיָא דְּרִבִּי לָעְזָר כְּמָאן דְּאָמַר אֵין מוֹצִיאִין מַעֲשֵׂר לִכְהוּנָּה. בְּיוֹמוֹי דְּרִבִּי יְהוֹשֻׁעַ בֶּן לֵוִי בִּיקְשׁוּ לְהִימָּנוֹת שֶׁלֹּא לִיתֵּן מַעֲשֵׂר לִכְהוּנָּה. אָמְרִין מָאן יֵיעוֹל רִבִּי יְהוֹשֻׁעַ בֶּן לֵוִי דְּהוּא מְסַייֵּעַ לְלִיוָאֵי. עָאַל וְסִייֵּעַ לְכָהֲנֵי אָמַר בְּעֶשְׂרִים וְאַרְבַּע מְקוֹמוֹת נִקְרְאוּ הַכֹּהֲנִים לְוִיִּים וְזֶה אֶחָד מֵהֶן וְהַכֹּהֲנִים הַלְוִיִּם בְּנֵי צָדוֹק.

"In that year" you take it out from impure for pure but in other years you do not take it out from impure for pure. Rebbi Eleazar said, so is that *baraita*: "'In that year' you have to take it from an impure place to a pure but in other years you do not have to take it from an impure place to a pure.[88]" This statement of Rebbi Eleazar follows the opinion that one does not give tithe to Cohanim. In the days of Rebbi Joshua ben Levi they wanted to vote not to give tithe to Cohanim. They said, why should we come to Rebbi Joshua ben Levi[89] since he will help the Levites. He came and helped the Cohanim and said: In 24 places are Cohanim called Levites and this is one of them (*Ez.* 44:15): "The Cohanim Levites, the descendants of Ẓadoq.[90]"

88 The version of R. Eleazar is the version of *Sifry Deut.* 109; the first version is unintelligible. The extra "in this this year" mentioned in *Deut.* 14:28 is interpreted to mean that in that year, the third (or sixth) of the Sabbatical cycles, *all* tithes have to be treated equally. Since Second Tithe, as long as it is not redeemed, has to be kept in purity (for consumption in Jerusalem), it follows that First Tithe also, which is to be given to the Levites, has to be kept in purity in these years. But this implies that in other years it may be left to become impure (after heave was taken). This is taken to mean that in

other years it should not be given to the Cohen together with the heave.

89 Who was a Levite.

90 This is also his argument in Babli *Yebamot* 86b, *Ḥulin* 24b.

רִבִּי בִּנְיָמִין בַּר גִּידוּל וְרִבִּי אָחָא הֲוֹון יְתִיבִין אָמְרוּן וְהָא כְתִיב וְהָיָה הַכֹּהֵן בֶּן אַהֲרוֹן עִם הַלְוִיִּם בַּעְשֹׂר הַלְוִיִּם לִיתֵּן לוֹ תְרוּמַת מַעֲשֵׂר. וְהָכְתִיב וְהַלְוִיִּם יַעֲלוּ אֶת הַמַּעֲשֵׂר. רִבִּי חוּנָא וַחֲבֵרַיָּא חַד מִינְהוֹן אָמַר לִבְנֵי לֵוִי מַה תַּלְמוּד לוֹמַר וְלִבְנֵי אֶלָּא מִכָּן שֶׁנּוֹתְנִין מַעֲשֵׂר לִכְהוּנָּה. וְחָרָנָא אָמַר אֲפִילוּ לֵית כְּתִיב אֶלָּא לִבְנֵי נוֹתְנִין מַעֲשֵׂר לִכְהוּנָּה. אִילּוּ מָאן דְּאָמַר פְּלָן בְּרִי יְסַב מִקָּמַת פְּלָן וּשְׁאָר נְכָסַיי יִרְשׁוּ בָנַיי דִּילְמָא לָא נְסַב עִמְּהוֹן.

Rebbi Binjamin bar Gidul and Rebbi Aḥa were sitting together and saying, is it not written (*Neh.* 10:39): "The Cohen, descendant of Aaron, will share with the Levites in the Levite's tithe"? To give him heave of the tithe. But is it not written (*Neh.* 10:39): "The Levites shall bring [the tithe of][91] the tithe"? Rebbi Ḥuna and the colleagues, one of them said "to the descendants of Levi". Why does the verse say (*Num.* 18:21): "And to the descendants of Levi[92]"? From here that one gives tithes to Cohanim. The other said, even if it were only written "to the descendants" one would give tithes to Cohanim. If somebody would say, my son X shall take property Y [before distribution] and the rest of my properties my sons shall inherit, does he not participate with them?

91 From the masoretic text, missing in the quote, but carrying the essence of the proof. The first argument was that the verse associates Cohanim with Levites in receiving tithe. This was countered by the argument that Cohanim always receive the heave of the tithe and, therefore, are always getting part of the Levite's tithe. That argument is disproved since the heave of the tithe is explicitly mentioned in the second part of the verse, "the Levites shall bring the tithe of the tithe to the Temple."

This establishes that the right of Cohanim to take tithe was part of the constitution of Nehemiah. This is the accepted doctrine of the Babli (*Yebamot* 86b) which only discusses the reason behind the decree but does not deny that the right of Cohanim to tithe is purely rabbinical. The Yerushalmi denies this since it continues to find the pentateuchal basis for the rights of Cohanim.

92 "And to the descendants of Levi I gave all tithes in Israel as inheritance." The first argument is that the beginning "and" also includes the Cohanim. The second argument notes that the verse declares tithes to follow the laws of inheritance. If somebody in his will gives some special part to a son before the general distribution, that son is not excluded from taking part in the division of the inheritance. Therefore, the fact that the Cohanim got heave and the heave of the tithe does not exclude them from the ranks of "descendants of Levi". If the verse had been addressed instead to "the Levites", the Cohanim would have been excluded.

רִבִּי יוֹנָה יְהַב מַעְשְׂרוֹי לְרִבִּי אָחָא בַּר עוּלָּא לֹא מִשּׁוּם דַּהֲוָה כֹהֵן אֶלָּא מִשּׁוּם דַּהֲוָה לָעֵי בְּאוֹרַיתָא. מַה טָעֲמָא וַיֹּאמֶר לָעָם לְיוֹשְׁבֵי יְרוּשָׁלַ͏ִם לָתֵת מְנָת הַכֹּהֲנִים וְהַלְוִיִּם לְמַעַן יֶחֶזְקוּ בְּתוֹרַת יי. רִבִּי הוּנָא לָא נְסַב מַעֲשֵׂר רִבִּי אָחָא לָא נְסַב מַעֲשֵׂר. רִבִּי חִיָּה בַּר בָּא הוֹרֵי עַל גַּרְמֵיהּ לָצֵאת לְחוּץ לָאָרֶץ בְּגִין דְּלָא מֵיסַב מַעֲשֵׂר. שָׁאַל בַּר נַשׁ רִבִּי שְׁמוּאֵל בַּר נַחְמָן שָׁאַל לְרִבִּי יוֹנָתָן מַהוּ דִּנְסַב. אָמַר לוֹ סַב וּמַה דְּנָפַל לְשִׁבְטָךְ נָפַל לָךְ.

Rebbi Jonah gave his tithes to Rebbi Aḥa bar Ulla, not because he was a Cohen but because he studied Torah. What is the reason? (*2Chr.* 31:4) "He said to the people, the inhabitants of Jerusalem, to give the part of the Cohanim and the Levites, so they should be strong in the Torah of the Eternal." Rebbi Huna did not take tithe, Rebbi Aḥa did not take tithe. Rebbi Ḥiyya bar Abba instructed himself to go outside the Land, not to take tithe[93]. A person[94] asked Rebbi Samuel bar Naḥman who asked

Rebbi Jonathan, may one take? He said to him, take, what fell to your tribe fell to you.

93 The circumstances are narrated in *Ševi'it* 3:1, Notes 5-6.

94 Who was a Cohen.

רִבִּי יַנַּאי מְפַקֵּד לְקָרִיבוֹי כַּד תְּהֵוֹיְיָן חַכְרָן אֲרָע לָא תַחְכְּרוּן אֶלָּא מִן דְּחֵילוֹנַיָּא. וְאַף עַל גַּב דְּאַתְּ אָמַר אֵין נוֹתְנִין מַעֲשֵׂר לִכְהוּנָּה מוֹדֶה שֶׁאֵין מוֹצִיאִין שֶׁלּוֹ מִיָּדוֹ. מַה טַעֲמָא כִּי תִקְחוּ מֵאֵת בְּנֵי יִשְׂרָאֵל אֶת הַמַּעֲשֵׂר אֲשֶׁר נָתַתִּי לָכֶם מֵאִתָּם בְּנַחֲלַתְכֶם וַהֲרֵמוֹתֶם מִמֶּנּוּ אֶת תְּרוּמַת יי מַעֲשֵׂר מִן הַמַּעֲשֵׂר. מֵאֵת בְּנֵי יִשְׂרָאֵל אַתְּ מוֹצִיא וְאֵין אַתְּ מוֹצִיא מִמַּכָּרֵי כְהוּנָּה וּלְוִיָּה. וְאַתְיָא כַּיי דְּאָמַר רִבִּי לָעְזָר כִּי תִקְחוּ מֵאֵת בְּנֵי יִשְׂרָאֵל אֶת הַמַּעֲשֵׂר. מֵאֵת בְּנֵי יִשְׂרָאֵל אַתְּ מוֹצִיא וְאֵין אַתְּ מוֹצִיא מִן הַגּוֹי.

Rebbi Yannai ordered his relatives, when you lease[95] a field, lease only from lay people since even if you say one does not give tithes to Cohanim you have to agree that one does not take his own[96] out of his hand. What is the reason? (*Num.* 18:26) "If you take from the Children of Israel the tithe which I gave you from them as your inheritance, you should lift from it the heave of the Eternal, a tithe of the tithe." From the Children of Israel you take out[97] but not from those contracting with Cohanim or Levites. It parallels what Rebbi Eleazar said, "if you take the tithe from the Children of Israel," from the Children of Israel you take out but not from the Gentile[98].

95 The Leyden ms. has חכר "to lease", the Rome ms. and the Venice print חבר "to connect". In view of H. L. Fleischer's discussion (in Levy's Dictionary, Vol. 2, p. 204b) of the original meaning of the Aramaic / Arabic root חכר as "keep tight, hold together, hold back" (in modern Arabic only "to hoard") there is no difference of meaning involved.

96 The tithe but not heave, cf. *Peah* Chapter 1, Note 291.

97 If needed, by a court order.

98 He holds that the produce of the Gentile farmer in the Land is exempt from heave and tithes. Since this is a matter of dispute between Tannaïm, cf. *Peah* Chapter 4, Notes 131-134, one might read the statement here to say that tithe voluntarily given by a Gentile cannot be obtained from him by a court order; he may give to you but you cannot take from him.

רִבִּי אַבָּהוּ אָמַר אִיתְפַּלְּגוּן רִבִּי יְהוֹשֻׁעַ בֶּן חֲנַנְיָה וְרִבִּי לֶעְזָר בֶּן עֲזַרְיָה . רִבִּי יְהוֹשֻׁעַ בֶּן חֲנַנְיָה אָמַר אֵין נוֹתְנִין מַעֲשֵׂר לִכְהוּנָּה. וְרִבִּי לֶעְזָר בֶּן עֲזַרְיָה אָמַר נוֹתְנִין מַעֲשֵׂר לִכְהוּנָּה. מָתִיב רִבִּי יְהוֹשֻׁעַ בֶּן חֲנַנְיָה לְרִבִּי לֶעְזָר בֶּן עֲזַרְיָה וְהָא כְתִיב וַאֲכַלְתֶּ[ם] אוֹתוֹ בְּכָל־מָקוֹם בּוֹא וְאוֹכְלוֹ עִמּוֹ בַּקֶּבֶר. אָמַר לוֹ מַהוּ בְּכָל־מָקוֹם בַּעֲזָרָה. אָמַר לוֹ וְהָכְתִיב אַתֶּם וּבֵיתְכֶם וְאִשָּׁה נִכְנֶסֶת לָעֲזָרָה. רִבִּי בָּא הֲוָה מִשְׁתָּעֵי הַהֵן עוֹבְדָא . רִבִּי לֶעְזָר בֶּן עֲזַרְיָה הֲוָה יְלִיף מֵיסַב מַעְשְׂרָא דְחָדָא גִינָּה. וְהָיָה לְאוֹתָהּ גִינָּה שְׁנֵי פְתָחִים אֶחָד לִמְקוֹם טוּמְאָה וְאֶחָד פָּתוּחַ לִמְקוֹם טָהֳרָה. נְפַק רִבִּי עֲקִיבָה לְגַבֵּיהּ אָמַר לֵיהּ פְּתַח הָהֵן וּסְתוֹם הָהֵן. אִין אֲתָא אֱמַר לֵיהּ בֹּא בְּדֶרֶךְ הַזּוֹ. אָמַר לֵיהּ אִין שְׁלַח תַּלְמִידֵיהּ אֱמוֹר לֵיהּ אַתֶּם כְּתִיב. שָׁמַע רִבִּי לֶעְזָר בֶּן עֲזַרְיָה וְאָמַר מִרְצֵעָה (fol. 56c) דַּעֲקִיבָה בֶּן יוֹסֵף בָּא לְכָאן. בְּאוֹתָהּ שָׁעָה הֶחֱזִיר רִבִּי לֶעְזָר בֶּן עֲזַרְיָה כָּל־הַמַּעְשְׂרוֹת שֶׁנָּטַל. אָמַר רִבִּי יִצְחָק בַּר לֶעְזָר בְּשֵׁרוּתָא בָּעֲיָא מוֹלֵיי סִבָא דְקִיסָּא מִינֵיהּ וּבֵיהּ כָּל־גּוּמְרָא דְלָא כְוִיָּה בְשַׁעְתָּהּ לָא כְוִיָּה.

Rebbi Abbahu said, Rebbi Joshua ben Ḥananiah[99] and Rebbi Eleazar ben Azariah[100] disagreed. Rebbi Joshua ben Ḥananiah said, one does not give tithe to Cohanim but Rebbi Eleazar ben Azariah said, one gives tithe to Cohanim. Rebbi Joshua ben Ḥananiah objected to Rebbi Eleazar ben Azariah: Is it not written (*Num.* 18:31): "You shall eat it everywhere", come and eat it by a grave[101]! He said to him, what means "everywhere"? In the courtyard[102] of the Temple. He retorted, but is it not written (*Num.

18:31): "You and your house[103]"? Does a woman enter the courtyard of the Temple? Rebbi Abba understood it from the following occasion: Rebbi Eleazar ben Azariah was used to take tithes from a certain garden. That garden had two exits, one to a place of impurity[104] and one open to a place of purity. Rebbi Aqiba went to him[105] and said, open this one and lock the other one. If he will come, tell him to come by that way. He also said, if he sends a student, tell him "you" is written[106]. Rebbi Eleazar ben Azariah heard this and said, that is Aqiba ben Joseph's whip. At that moment, Rebbi Eleazar ben Azariah returned all tithes he had taken[107]. Rebbi Isaac bar Eleazar said, for dinner one has to fill up completely with wood fibers[108]; any coal which does not cause a burn at the beginning will not cause one.

99 A Levite. In the Babli, *Yebamot* 86a/b, the opponent of R. Eleazar ben Azariah is R. Aqiba at all stages.

100 A Cohen, direct descendant of Ezra.

101 A place forbidden to Cohanim.

102 He must mean the courtyard of the priests since women are invited to enter the women's courtyard and may enter the men's courtyard for ceremonies required for sacrifices.

103 The expression "house" often is used to represent someone's wife.

104 A cemetery.

105 The owner of the vegetable garden. He persuaded him to leave only the cemetery door open and to lock the other.

106 Cf. *Demay* 6:1, Note 8, that an emphasis on "you" means one personally unless an expression of inclusion is added; *Terumot* 1:1 Note 76, Babli *Qiddušin* 41b.

107 This remark, establishing the practice that tithes are not for Cohanim, is missing in the Babli which holds strongly that tithes should be given to Cohanim in preference to Levites.

108 To make a point one has to take strong action immediately; later it is useless. The text is doubtful; the proverb appears three times; for סבא here one reads סמא in *Bezah* 2:3 and כסא in *Ḥagigah* 2:3.

משנה ז: מִי שֶׁהָיוּ לוֹ פֵּירוֹת בִּזְמַן הַזֶּה וְהִגִּיעָה שְׁנַת הַבִּיעוּר בֵּית שַׁמַּי(fol. 55c) אוֹמְרִים צָרִיךְ לְחַלְּלָן עַל הַכֶּסֶף. בֵּית הִלֵּל אוֹמְרִים אֶחָד שֶׁהֵן כֶּסֶף וְאֶחָד שֶׁהֵן פֵּירוֹת.

Mishnah 7: He who had produce[109] in this time and the year of removal came, the House of Shammai say he has to exchange it for money; the House of Hillel say, either money or produce.

משנה ח: אָמַר רִבִּי יְהוּדָה בָּרִאשׁוֹנָה הָיוּ שׁוֹלְחִין אֵצֶל בַּעֲלֵי בָתִּים שֶׁבַּמְּדִינוֹת מַהֲרוּ פֵּירוֹתֵיהֶם עַד שֶׁלֹּא תַגִּיעַ שְׁעַת הַבִּיעוּר עַד שֶׁבָּא רִבִּי עֲקִיבָה וְלִימֵּד שֶׁכָּל־הַפֵּירוֹת שֶׁלֹּא בָאוּ לְעוֹנַת הַמַּעְשְׂרוֹת פְּטוּרִין מִן הַבִּיעוּר.

Mishnah 8: Rebbi Jehudah said, in earlier times they sent to the rural farmers, speed up your produce before the time of removal, until Rebbi Aqiba came and taught that any produce which did not reach the time of tithing is exempt from removal[110].

משנה ט: מִי שֶׁהָיוּ פֵּירוֹתָיו רְחוֹקִים מִמֶּנּוּ צָרִיךְ לִקְרוֹת לָהֶן שֵׁם. מַעֲשֶׂה בְּרַבָּן גַּמְלִיאֵל וְהַזְּקֵנִים שֶׁהָיוּ בָאִין בִּסְפִינָה אָמַר רַבָּן גַּמְלִיאֵל עִישּׂוּר שֶׁאֲנִי עָתִיד לָמוֹד נָתוּן לִיהוֹשֻׁעַ וּמְקוֹמוֹ מוּשְׂכָּר לוֹ. עִישּׂוּר אַחֵר שֶׁאֲנִי עָתִיד לָמוֹד נָתוּן לַעֲקִיבָה שֶׁיִּזְכֶּה בוֹ לָעֲנִיִּים וּמְקוֹמוֹ מוּשְׂכָּר לוֹ. אָמַר רִבִּי יְהוֹשֻׁעַ עִישּׂוּר שֶׁאֲנִי עָתִיד לָמוֹד נָתוּן לְאֶלְעָזָר בֶּן עֲזַרְיָה וּמְקוֹמוֹ מוּשְׂכָּר לוֹ. וְנִתְקַבְּלוּ זֶה מִזֶּה שָׂכָר.

Mishnah 9: If somebody's produce was far from him[111], he has to give it a name. It happened that Rabban Gamliel was on a ship with the elders when Rabban Gamliel said, a tenth which I shall measure in the future is given to Joshua and its place is rented to him[112]; another tenth which I shall measure in the future is given to Aqiba[113]; he should distribute it to the poor, and its place is rented to him. Rebbi Joshua said, a tenth[114] which I shall measure in the future is given to Eleazar ben Azariah and its place is rented to him. They paid the rent to each other[115].

109 Of Second Tithe. Since there is no Temple, the tithe cannot be eaten in Jerusalem. The House of Shammai hold that *Deut.* 14:25 requires that any tithe produce which cannot be eaten in purity in the holy precinct has to be exchanged for money. Since that money cannot be used it must be destroyed or safely buried. The House of Hillel, the authors of Mishnah 1:5, hold that either the coins must be destroyed or the produce left to rot.

110 If it is exempt from removal, the fact that the farmer has untithed produce does not prevent him from reading the declaration of tithes (*Deut.* 26:13-15). The fact that R. Aqiba had to rule on the matter supports Maimonides (*Ma'aser Šeni* 7:4) that the declaration should be made even if there is no Temple.

111 At the time of removal he has to tithe and transfer ownership of his tithes in order to be able to make the declaration.

112 Real estate can be rented in the way it is acquired, by contract, payment, or taking actual possession. If real estate is acquired, movables on it can be acquired with it. Therefore, the future tithe is acquired by payment of the rent. Cf. Babli *Qiddušin* 26b/27a, *Baba Meẓi'ai* 11a, and Rashi's commentary there.

113 He was overseer of charities and as such could receive the tithe of the poor due at the time of removal.

114 The heave of the tithe given by the Levite to the Cohen.

115 R. Eleazar ben Azariah to R. Joshua, RR. Joshua and Aqiba to Rabban Gamliel.

(fol. 56c) **הלכה ו**: הַכֹּל מוֹדִין בְּפַת וְשֶׁמֶן שֶׁהוּא צָרִיךְ לְבָעֵר. בְּיַיִן וּבְתַבְלִין שֶׁהוּא כִמְבוּעָר. מַה פְלִיגִין בְּתַבְשִׁיל בֵּית שַׁמַּי אוֹמְרִים צָרִיךְ לְבָעֵר. וּבֵית הִלֵּל אוֹמְרִים אֵין צָרִיךְ לְבָעֵר.

Halakhah 6: Everybody agrees that bread and oil have to be removed, wine and spices are as if removed. Where do they disagree: A cooked dish the House of Shammai says one has to remove, but the House of Hillel say one does not have to remove[116].

116 This is the discussion of the last sentence of Mishnah 6. A profane dish containing tithe oil is subject to removal, one containing tithe wine or spices is not since these are not recognizable. A dish made from tithe vegetables is not subject to removal since cooked vegetables are not the same as raw ones, according to the House of Hillel.

מַה טַעֲמָא דְבֵית שַׁמַּי. וְצַרְתָּ הַכֶּסֶף בְּלְבַד בְּיָדְךָ. מַה טַעֲמָא דְבֵית הִלֵּל. אֲפִילוּ מְחַלְּלוֹ מַה הוּא מוֹעִיל.

[117]What is the reason of the House of Shammai? (*Deut*. 14:25): "Bundle" only "the money in your hand.[109]" What is the reason of the House of Hillel? Even if he exchanges, what good does it do[118]?

117 This is the discussion of Mishnah 7.

118 Since the following injunction of the verse, to bring the money to the Holy Precinct, cannot be fulfilled, the entire verse becomes inapplicable.

וְלֹא טֶבֶל הוּא. רִבִּי הִילָא בְּשֵׁם שְׁמוּאֵל זֹאת אוֹמֶרֶת שֶׁהַטֶּבֶל קָרוּי קוֹדֶשׁ.

[119]Is it not *ṭevel*? Rebbi Hila in the name of Samuel: This implies that *ṭevel* is called holy[120].

119 This is the discussion of Mishnah 8. Since the declaration reads: "I removed the holy produce from the house", meaning heave and tithes as well as fourth-year growth, why should untithed produce be subject to removal and hinder the declaration?

120 R. Aqiba agrees that *ṭevel* must be brought in order but he counsels not to bring new produce to the state of *ṭevel*.

אָמַר רִבִּי יוּדָה מַעֲשֶׂה בְּרַבָּן גַּמְלִיאֵל וְהַזְּקֵנִים שֶׁהָיוּ יוֹשְׁבִין עַל מַעֲלוֹת הָאוּלָם בְּהַר הַבָּיִת. וְהָיָה יוֹחָנָן הַכֹּהֵן הַסּוֹפֵר הַלָּז יוֹשֵׁב לִפְנֵיהֶן. אָמְרוּ לוֹ צֵא וּכְתוֹב אַחֵינוּ בְּנֵי גָלִילָא עִילָּאָה בְּנֵי גָלִילָא אַרְעִיתָא שְׁלָמְכוֹן יִסְגֵּא. מוֹדַעְנָא לְכוֹן דְּמָטָא זְמַן בִּיעוּרָא תַּפְקוּן מַעְשְׂרַיָּא מִן מַעֲטָנֵי זֵיתָאֵי. לְאַחָנָא בְּנֵי דְרוֹמָא עִילָּאָה וּבְנֵי דְרוֹמָא אַרְעִיתָא מוֹדַעְנָא לְכוֹן דְּמָטָא זְמַן בִּיעוּרָא תַּפְקוּן מַעְשְׂרַיָּא מֵעֳמְרֵי שִׁיבֳּלַיָּא. לְאַחָנָא בְּנֵי גָלוּתָא דְבָבֶל וּבְנֵי גָלוּתָא דְמָדַי וּבְנֵי גָלוּתָא דְיָוָן וּשְׁאָר כָּל־גַּלְוָותְהוֹן דְּיִשְׂרָאֵל שְׁלָמְכוֹן יִסְגֵּא. מוֹדַע אֲנָא לְכוֹן דְּאִימְרַיָּא רְכִיכִין וְגוֹזָלַיָּא דְקִיקִין וּשְׁפַר בְּאַנְפַּיי וּבְאַנְפֵּי חֲבֵרַיי מוֹסְפָא עַל שַׁתָּא זֶה תַּלְתִּין יוֹמִין.

[121]Rebbi Jehudah said, it happened that Rabban Gamliel[122] and the elders were sitting on the steps of the Hall on the Temple Mount and Johanan, the Cohen, their scribe, was sitting before them. They said to him, go and write:

To our brothers of Upper and Lower Galilee, may you have much peace. We inform you that the time of removal is approaching; take out tithes from the ripening vats[123] of olives.

To our brothers of Upper and Lower South country, we inform you that the time of removal is approaching; take out tithes from the sheaves of grain[124].

To our brothers of the diasporas of Babylonia, Media, Greece, and all other diasporas of Israel, may you have much peace. I am informing you that the lambs are young and the young pigeons small[125], so it is good in my eyes and the eyes of my colleagues to add thirty days to this year.

121 The text of the letters is also in *Sanhedrin* 1:2 (fol. 18d), Tosephta *Sanhedrin* 2:6, Babli *Sanhedrin* 11b. The best text is preserved (although in Hebrew) from *Midrash Tannaïm* in *Midrash Haggadol Deut.* (2 ed. S. Fisch, Jerusalem 1975), pp. 597-598. There is an Introduction, a discussion between R. Neḥonia bar Haqanah and R. Joshua, whether the expression "I removed the

holy produce from the house" implies that potentially titheable produce outside the house does not preclude the recitation of the declaration. R. Joshua replies that he never heard anything about it but he remembered Rabban Simeon ben Gamliel (I, later the president of the revolutionary government in the first war against the Romans) and Rabban Joḥanan ben Zakkai writing the letters in which they required tithing of unfinished produce, in accordance with R. Jehudah's description of the earlier practice.

122 While this is the text in both Talmudim and the Tosephta, and the Babli explicitly identifies this Rabban Gamliel with the head of the Synhedrion at Jabneh, for historical reasons the only acceptable reading is that of *Midrash Tannaïm*: Rabban Simeon ben Gamliel I (ben Simeon ben Hillel).

123 A vat in which olives were stored before pressing and where they softened. On the basis of Arabic عطن one might translate "soaking vat".

124 Neither unthreshed grain nor unpressed oil olives are subject to heave and tithes in normal years. In *Midrash Tannaïm*, Rabban Simeon writes as excuse that he has to write because it is an old established practice.

125 In the parallel sources, "it does not look like spring". This letter is not in *Midrash Haggadol* since its subject is not tithes.

הָדָא אָֽמְרָה שֶׁאֵין נוֹתְנִין מַֽעֲשֵׂר לִכְהוּנָּה. שַׁנְייָא הִיא שֶׁהָיָה רִבִּי יְהוֹשֻׁעַ בֶּן חֲנַנְיָה תַּמָּן. אָמַר רִבִּי חֲנַנְיָה הָדָא אָֽמְרָה שֶׁהָיָה רַבָּן גַּמְלִיאֵל צָרִיךְ לְזַכּוֹת. אָמַר רִבִּי יְהוֹשֻׁעַ בְּפֵירוֹת מְחוּבָּרִין לְקַרְקַע. אִילּוּ קוּפָּתוֹ שֶׁל רַבָּן גַּמְלִיאֵל נְתוּנָה לְתוֹךְ בֵּיתוֹ שֶׁל רִבִּי יְהוֹשֻׁעַ וְאוֹמֵר יִזְכֶּה לְמַֽעֲשֵׂר שֶׁבָּהּ כְּלוּם עָשָׂה עַד שֶׁיְּסַייֵם.

[126]That means that one does not give tithe to Cohanim. There is a difference, since Rebbi Joshua ben Ḥananiah was there[127]. Rebbi Ḥananiah said, it means that Rabban Gamliel had to transfer[128]. Rebbi Joshua[129] said, for produce standing on the ground[130]. Even if Rabban

Gamliel's box were standing in Rebbi Joshua's house and he would say, he should acquire its tithe, would he have done anything if he did not label it[131]?

126 Here starts the discussion of Mishnah 9. Why did Rabban Gamliel choose the complicated way of giving to the Levite, could he not have given everything to the Cohen who would not have had to rent space for his heave of the tithe?

127 A poor Levite is preferable to a very rich Cohen under any circumstances.

128 The Mishnah requires only "to give a name". But Rabban Gamliel actually transferred property rights.

129 An Amora whose identity cannot be determined. The editors of the Leyden ms. suggest to read צריך לזכות את רבי יהושע בפירות "he has to transfer the produce to R. Joshua (ben Ḥanania)."

130 It was not yet in orderly heaps.

131 Goods in a vessel of the giver (or seller) in the house of the recipient (or buyer) cannot be acquired by proxy unless their place is exactly described. If Rabban Gamliel's grain had been in orderly heaps, he could have said the Northernmost 10% are First Tithe, the Southernmost 10% tithe of the poor. But in the situation he was in, he could only rent out ground for future use. This remark leads to the consideration of right of acquisition.

רִבִּי רְדִיפָה אָמַר אִיתְפַּלְּגוּן רִבִּי יִרְמְיָה וְרִבִּי יוֹסֵי. חַד אָמַר הָרָאוּי לִיטּוֹל זָכָה. וְחַד אָמַר הָרָאוּי לִיתֵּן זָכָה. מָאן דָּמַר הָרָאוּי לִיטּוֹל זָכָה כָּל־שֶׁכֵּן רָאוּי לִיתֵּן. וּמָן דְּאָמַר הָרָאוּי לִיתֵּן הָא לִיטּוֹל לֹא.

[132]Rebbi Redifa said, Rebbi Jeremiah and Rebbi Yose disagree. One says, he who may take may acquire; the other says, he who may give may acquire. He who says "he who may take" certainly includes him who may give. He who says "he who may give," excludes him who may take.

132 The text from here to the end of the Halakhah is also in *Peah* 4:6 and explained there, Notes 113-125. The question is about the power of a person to acquire property for a third party..

הָא מַתְנִיתָא פְלִיגָא עַל מָאן דְּאָמַר הָרָאוּי לִיטּוֹל זָכָה. וְתַמָּן תַּנִּינָן תֵּן גֵּט זֶה לְאִשְׁתִּי שֶׁכֵּן רָאוּי הוּא לְקַבֵּל גֵּט בִּתּוֹ. וּשְׁטָר שִׁחְרוּר זֶה לְעַבְדִּי שֶׁכֵּן הוּא רָאוּי לְקַבֵּל שְׁטָר שִׁחְרוּרוֹ. וְתַנִּינָן הִתְקַבֵּל גֵּט זֶה לְאִשְׁתִּי אוֹ הוֹלֵךְ גֵּט זֶה לְאִשְׁתִּי אִם רָצָא לְהַחֲזִיר יַחֲזִיר. וְהָעֶבֶד רָאוּי לְהוֹלִיךְ אֶת הַגֵּט. פָּתַר לִצְדָדִין הִיא מַתְנִיתָא.

The following Mishnah disagrees with him who says that he who may take may acquire, since we have stated: "Give this divorce document to my wife," because he may receive the divorce document of his minor daughter. "And the document of manumission to my slave," since he may receive his own document of manumission. But did we not state: "Receive this divorce document for my wife or bring this divorce document to my wife; if he wants to change his mind . . . he may do so." Is a slave empowered to bring a divorce document? Explain it by different cases contained in the Mishnah.

מַתְנִיתָא פְלִיגָא עַל מָאן דְּאָמַר הָרָאוּי לִיתֵּן זָכָה. דְּתַנִּינָן תַּמָּן עִישּׂוּר אֶחָד שֶׁאֲנִי עָתִיד לִימוֹד נָתוּן לַעֲקִיבָה בֶּן יוֹסֵף שֶׁיִּזְכֶּה בוֹ לָעֲנִיִּים וּמוּשְׂכָּר לוֹ מְקוֹמוֹ. וְרִבִּי עֲקִיבָה רָאוּי הוּא לִיטּוֹל. פָּתַר לָהּ עַד שֶׁלֹּא הֶעֱשִׁיר. וַאֲפִילוּ תֵּימַר מִשֶּׁהֶעֱשִׁיר תִּיפְתָּר כְּשֶׁהָיָה פַּרְנָס וְיַד הַפַּרְנָס כְּיַד הֶעָנִי.

A Mishnah disagrees with him who says that he who may take may acquire, since we have stated there: "One tithe that I will measure in the future is given to Aqiba ben Joseph that he should let the poor acquire it, and its place is rented to him." But is Rebbi Aqiba entitled to take? Explain it, before he got rich. And even if you say, after he became rich, when he was an administrator, and the hand of the administrator is equal to the hand of the poor.

מִילְתֵיהּ דְּרִבִּי יְהוֹשֻׁעַ בֶּן לֵוִי אָמְרָה הָרָאוּי לִיטּוֹל זָכָה. דְּרִבִּי יְהוֹשֻׁעַ בֶּן לֵוִי אָמַר בְּבַעַל הַבַּיִת עָשִׁיר נֶחְלְקוּ. אֲבָל בְּבַעַל הַבַּיִת עָנִי מִתּוֹךְ שֶׁרָאוּי לִיטּוֹל זָכָה.

The word of Rebbi Joshua ben Levi is that he who may take may acquire, since Rebbi Joshua ben Levi said: They disagree about a rich owner. But in the case of a poor owner, since he has the right to take it, the other person acquired it.

(fol. 55c) **משנה י:** בְּמִנְחָה בְּיוֹם טוֹב הָיוּ מִתְוַדִּין כֵּיצַד הָיָה הַוִּידּוּי בִּיעַרְתִּי הַקּוֹדֶשׁ מִן הַבַּיִת זֶה מַעֲשֵׂר שֵׁינִי וְנֶטַע רְבָעִי. וּנְתַתִּיו לַלֵּוִי זֶה מַעְשַׂר לֵוִי. וְגַם נְתַתִּיו זֶה תְרוּמָה וּתְרוּמַת מַעֲשֵׂר. לַגֵּר לַיָּתוֹם וְלָאַלְמָנָה זֶה מַעְשַׂר עָנִי. הַלֶּקֶט הַשִּׁכְחָה וְהַפֵּיאָה אַף עַל פִּי שֶׁאֵינָן מְעַכְּבִין אֶת (fol. 55d) הַוִּידּוּי. מִן הַבַּיִת זֶה הַחַלָּה. כְּכָל מִצְוָתְךָ אֲשֶׁר צִוִּיתָנִי. הָא אִם הִקְדִּים מַעֲשֵׂר שֵׁנִי לָרִאשׁוֹן אֵינוֹ יָכוֹל לְהִתְוַדּוֹת. לֹא עָבַרְתִּי מִמִּצְוֹתֶיךָ. לֹא הִפְרַשְׁתִּי מִמִּין עַל שֶׁאֵינוֹ מִינוֹ לֹא מִן הַתָּלוּשׁ עַל הַמְּחוּבָּר וְלֹא מִן הַמְּחוּבָּר עַל הַתָּלוּשׁ לֹא מִן הֶחָדָשׁ עַל הַיָּשָׁן וְלֹא מִן הַיָּשָׁן עַל הֶחָדָשׁ. וְלֹא שָׁכַחְתִּי מִלְּבָרֶכְךָ וּמִלְּהַזְכִּיר שִׁמְךָ עָלָיו.

Mishnah 10: In the afternoon of the holiday[133] they made the declaration. How was the declaration? (*Deut.* 26:13) "I removed the holy produce from the house," is Second Tithe and fourth-year growth. "I gave it to the Levite," is the Levite's tithe. "Also I gave it," includes heave and heave of the tithe. "To the sojourner, the orphan, and the widow," is the tithe of the poor. "From the house," is *ḥallah*. "Following Your entire Commandment which You commanded me;" therefore, if he gave Second

Tithe before the First he cannot make the declaration. "I did not transgress Your Commandments," I did not give from one kind for another, not from the harvested on the standing or from the standing on the harvested, not from new for old or from old for new. "And I did not forget," to praise and mention Your Name over it.

משנה יא: לֹא אָכַלְתִּי בְאוֹנִי מִמֶּנּוּ הָא אִם אֲכָלוֹ בָאֲנִינָה אֵינוֹ יָכוֹל לְהִתְוַדּוֹת. וְלֹא בִיעַרְתִּי מִמֶּנּוּ בְּטָמֵא הָא אִם הִפְרִישׁוֹ בְטוּמְאָה אֵינוֹ יָכוֹל לְהִתְוַדּוֹת. וְלֹא נָתַתִּי מִמֶּנּוּ לְמֵת. לֹא לָקַחְתִּי מִמֶּנּוּ אָרוֹן וְתַכְרִיכִין לְמֵת. וְלֹא נְתַתִּים לְאוֹנְנִים אֲחֵרִים. שָׁמַעְתִּי בְּקוֹל יי אֱלֹהָי הֱבֵאתִיו לְבֵית הַבְּחִירָה. עָשִׂיתִי כְּכֹל אֲשֶׁר צִוִּיתָנִי. שָׂמַחְתִּי וְשִׂימַּחְתִּי בוֹ.

Mishnah 11: (*Deut.* 26:14) "I did not eat from it in my deep mourning;" therefore if he ate from it in deep mourning[134] he cannot make the declaration. "I did not remove any of it in impurity;" therefore if he separtated it in impurity he cannot make the declaration. "I did not give from it to the dead," I did not buy from it a casket or shrouds for a dead person nor did I give it to other deep mourners. "I listened to the voice of the Eternal, my God," I brought it to the Selected House[135]. "I did all You commanded me," I enjoyed and gave joy to others with it[136].

133 This is the text in the Mishnah mss. of the Yerushalmi and Maimonides traditions, unspecified between first and last days of Passover. However, the Halakhah seems to presume a reading of "last day".

134 Cf. *Demay* Chapter 1, Note 70.

135 A standard name for the Temple.

136 Fulfilling part of the commandment (*Deut.* 16:14) "enjoy your holiday" with festive meals.

(fol. 56c) **הלכה ז:** וְיִתְוַדֶּה בְּיוֹם טוֹב הָרִאשׁוֹן שֶׁלְּפֶסַח. כְּדֵי שֶׁיְּהֵא לוֹ מַה לוֹכַל בְּרֶגֶל. וְיִתְוַדֶּה בְּשַׁחֲרִית. עַד כָּאן מְצֻוֶּה הוּא לוֹכַל.

Halakhah 7: Could he not make the declaration on the first day of Passover? So he should have something to eat for the holiday[137]. Could he not make the declaration in the morning? While he is commanded to eat.

137 Since the declaration can only be recited if no Second Tithe, tithe money, and fourth-year growth are left, if he would make the declaration early he could not eat of his fruits or buy well-being sacrifices during the holiday.

תַּנֵּי וְהַבִּיכּוּרִים. מָאן תַּנָּא בִּיכּוּרִין רַבָּנִין. מָאן לֹא תַנָּא בִּיכּוּרִין רִבִּי שִׁמְעוֹן. דְּתַנִּינָן וְחַיָּבִין בְּבִיעוּר וְרִבִּי שִׁמְעוֹן פּוֹטֵר.

It was stated[138]: "And First Fruits." Who stated "First Fruits"? The rabbis. Who did not state "First Fruits"? Rebbi Simeon. As we have stated[139]: "They are subject to removal but Rebbi Simeon frees them."

138 In the list of holy offerings that were removed before the declaration (Mishnah 10).

139 Mishnah *Bikkurim* 2:2.

נְתַתִּיו לַלֵּוִי מִכָּן שֶׁאֵין נוֹתְנִין מַעֲשֵׂר לִכְהוּנָּה.

"I gave it to the Levite," from here that one does not give tithe to Cohanim[140].

140 This is the final word of the Yerushalmi in this matter.

אָמַר רִבִּי יוֹנָה זֹאת אוֹמֶרֶת נִשְׂרַף טִיבְלוֹ אֵינוֹ יָכוֹל לְהִתְוַדּוֹת. אִית תַּנָּיֵי תַנֵּי כָּל־הַמִּצְוֹת שֶׁבַּתּוֹרָה מְעַכְּבוֹת. אִית תַּנָּיֵי תַנֵּי כָּל־הַמִּצְוֹת שֶׁבַּפָּרָשָׁה מְעַכְּבוֹת. רִבִּי אָחָא בַּר פַּפָּא בָּעֵי קוֹמֵי רִבִּי זְעִירָא אֲפִילוּ הִקְדִּים לִתְפִילָּה שֶׁלָּרֹאשׁ לִתְפִילָּה שֶׁלְּיָד אָמַר לֵיהּ אוּף אֲנָא סָבַר כֵּן.

Rebbi Jonah said, this means that if his *ṭevel* was burned he cannot make the declaration[141]. Some Tannaïm say, all commandments in the Torah prevent him[142]; some Tannaïm say, all commandments in the paragraph prevent him. Rebbi Aḥa bar Pappos[143] asked before Rebbi Zeïra, even if he put on head phylacteries before phylacteries on his arm[144]? He said to him, that is also what I am thinking.

141 If he had *ṭevel*, he is required to give heave and tithes. If the produce was burned before he gave, he cannot fulfill the condition "I gave it to the Levite" and is disqualified. If his produce was burned before it became obligated, he never was under an obligation and may make the declaration for his other produce.

142 A literal interpretation of the text "I did not transgress Your Commandments."

143 A Babylonian, student of Rav Huna, known in Babylonia as "the long Rav Aḥa", who immigrated into Galilee in the times of R. Immi and R. Abbahu.

144 This is the proverbial description of a minor infraction, disregarding a positive commandment which is inferred from the structure of the text. The commandment to carry the words of the Torah on one's hands and head is spelled out four times (*Ex.* 13:9, 16; *Deut.* 6:8, 11:18). In each of these verses, hand is mentioned before head. It is inferred that putting them on the hand must precede putting them on the head.

אָמַר רִבִּי יוֹסֵי בֵּי רִבִּי בּוּן צָרִיךְ לוֹמַר חַלָּה עַל כֹּל תְּרוּמָה עַל הַכֹּל. לַיי זֶה שֵׁם הַמְּיוּחָד. מְנַיִין לֹא עָשָׂה כְּלוּם עַד שֶׁיְּשַׁיֵּיר מִקְצָת. תַּלְמוּד לוֹמַר מֵרֵאשִׁית וְלֹא כָּל־רֵאשִׁית.

Rebbi Yose ben Rebbi Abun said, he must say "*ḥallah* for all," "heave for all."[145] "To YHWH," that is the particular Name[146]. From where that he did not do anything until he left some [as profane]? The verse says (*Num.* 15:21): "Of the beginning" and not all the beginning[147].

145 The main place of this paragraph is at the end of the first Chapter of *Ḥallah*. It is inserted here as another example of rules to be followed to be able to make the declaration. It was established in the first Chapter of *Terumot* that heave may be given only from produce whose location is exactly pinpointed. Therefore, in taking heave one must declare all produce that should be freed by this heave. *Ḥallah* is called "heave" in *Num*. 15:19-20; it has to follow the rules of heave.

146 It is written about *ḥallah* (*Num*. 15:19): "Lift a heave to YHWH." About heave, it is written (*Num*. 18:12): "Their first gifts which they will give to YHWH". It is inferred that in separating heave of *ḥallah*, God may not be addressed as Elohim (which in absence of a definite article or other identifyer only means "extraordinary power"), but only as YHWH (in its substitute pronunciation) which is His particular Name.

147 This refers to Mishnah *Ḥallah* 1:9: He who says, everything on my threshing floor shall be heave, all my dough shall be *ḥallah*, did not say anything unless he leaves a [profane] remainder."

מְנַיִין שֶׁהוּא עוֹבֵר בַּעֲשֵׂה. רִבִּי לָעְזָר בְּשֵׁם רִבִּי סִימַיי לֹא נָתַתִּי מִמֶּנּוּ לְמֵת. מַה נָן קַיָּמִין אִם לְהָבִיא לוֹ אָרוֹן וְתַכְרִיכִין דָּבָר שֶׁהוּא אָסוּר לַחַי לַחַי הוּא אָסוּר לֹא כָּל־שֶׁכֵּן לַמֵּת. אֶלָּא אֵי זֶהוּ דָבָר שֶׁהוּא מוּתָּר לַחַי וְאָסוּר לַמֵּת הֱוֵי אוֹמֵר זוֹ סִיכָה.

148From where that he would transgress a positive commandment? Rebbi Eleazar in the name of Rebbi Simai (*Deut*. 26:14): "Nor did I give from it to the dead." Where do we hold? If it were to bring a casket and shrouds for him, that were also forbidden for a living person! If something is forbidden for the living, not so much more for the dead? What is something which is permitted for the living but prohibited for the dead? That is anointing!

148 This is from Chapter 2, Notes 34-35 and refers to the prohibition to use any tithe or tithe money for funeral rites.

(fol. 55d) **משנה יב:** הַשְׁקִיפָה מִמְּעוֹן קָדְשְׁךָ מִן הַשָּׁמַיִם. עָשִׂינוּ מָה שֶׁגָּזַרְתָּ עָלֵינוּ אַף אַתְּ עֲשֵׂה מָה שֶׁהִבְטַחְתָּנוּ. הַשְׁקִיפָה מִמְּעוֹן קָדְשְׁךָ מִן הַשָּׁמַיִם וּבָרֵךְ אֶת עַמְּךָ אֶת יִשְׂרָאֵל בְּבָנִים וּבְבָנוֹת. וְאֵת הָאֲדָמָה אֲשֶׁר נָתַתָּ לָנוּ בְּטַל וּבְרוּחוֹת וּבְמָטָר וּבְוַלְדוֹת בְּהֵמָה. אֲשֶׁר נִשְׁבַּעְתָּ לַאֲבוֹתֵינוּ אֶרֶץ זָבַת חָלָב וּדְבָשׁ כְּדֵי שֶׁיִּתֵּן טַעַם בַּפֵּירוֹת.

Mishnah 12: (*Deut.* 26:15) "Look down from Your Holy Abode, from Heaven," we did what You decided[149] for us, You also do what You promised us: "Look down from Your Holy Abode, from Heaven, and bless Your people Israel" with sons and daughters, "and the land You gave us," with dew, winds, rain and young of the domestic animals, "that You had sworn to our forefathers, a Land flowing with milk and honey" to give taste to the fruits[150].

149 This use of גזר is in the sense of Biblical Hebrew "to cut" in the meaning of גזר דין = פסק דין "(judicial) decision"; not the rabbinical גזר = גדר; cf. *Demay* 1:2, Note 89.

150 The verse is the continuation of the declaration. The commentary is a paraphrase of *Deut.* 28:4.

(fol. 56c) **הלכה ח:** רִבִּי הוּנָא בַּר אָחָא בְּשֵׁם רִבִּי אֲלֶכְסַנְדְּרָא בּוֹא וּרְאֵה כַּמָּה גָדוֹל כּוֹחָן שֶׁל עוֹשֵׂי מִצְוֹת שֶׁכָּל־הַשְׁקָפָה שֶׁבַּתּוֹרָה אֲרוּרָה וְזֶה בִלְשׁוֹן בְּרָכָה. אָמַר רִבִּי יוֹסֵי בֶּן חֲנִינָא וְלֹא עוֹד אֶלָּא שֶׁכָּתוּב בָּהּ הַיּוֹם הַזֶּה. תְּנָיֵי יוֹמָא.

Halakhah 8: Rebbi Huna bar Aḥa[151] in the name of Rebbi Alexandros: Come and see the power of those who keep the Commandments because all "lookings down" in the Torah[152] are curses but this one is in the language of blessing. Rebbi Yose ben Ḥanina said, not only that but it is written[153] (*Deut.* 26:16) "this day," the condition of every day.

151 He is not otherwise known.

152 *Gen.* 18:16, 19:28 (Sodom), 26:8 (Abimelekh and Rebekka), *Ex.* 14:24 (Egyptians on the Sea). This refers only to *hiph'il* of שקף.

153 Starting words of the next paragraph guaranteeing instant response.

רִבִּי יוּדָה בַּר פָּזִי פָּתַח בָּהּ אָבוֹא בִּגְבוּרוֹת יי אֱלֹהִים. כְּתִיב אֵלֶּה שְׁנֵי בְּנֵי הַיִּצְהָר הָעוֹמְדִים עַל אֲדוֹן כָּל־הָאָרֶץ. רִבִּי אַבָּהוּ אָמַר אִיתְפַּלְּגוּן רִבִּי יוֹחָנָן וְרִבִּי (fol. 56d) שִׁמְעוֹן בֶּן לָקִישׁ. חַד אָמַר אֵילּוּ שֶׁהֵן בָּאִין בְּטִרוֹנְיָא לִפְנֵי הַקָּדוֹשׁ בָּרוּךְ הוּא. וְחָרָנָה אָמַר אֵילּוּ שֶׁהֵן בָּאִין מִכּוֹחַ הַמִּצְוֹת וּמַעֲשִׂים טוֹבִים לִפְנֵי הַקָּדוֹשׁ בָּרוּךְ הוּא.

Rebbi Judah bar Pazi started[154] with this: (*Ps.* 71:16): "I shall come in strength, Eternal, God.[155]" It is written (*Zach.* 4:14): "These are the two oil-sons who stand over the Lord of all the earth." Rebbi Abbahu said, Rebbi Joḥanan and Rebbi Simeon ben Laqish disagree. One says, these are the ones who come in novitiate[156] before the Holy One, praised be He. The other one says, these are the ones who come by the power of [kept] commandments and good deeds before the Holy One.

154 Started a sermon.

155 While the verse is quite clear: "When I reach old age, o Master, Eternal, I shall remember only Your justice!", it is taken here out of context to note that it seems to be possible to come in strength before the Eternal.

156 From Latin *tiro, -onis* "novice, recruit" to mean "come without accumulated merit before the Eternal. (The commentaries and dictionaries all derive the word from Greek τυραννίς, because of a similar homily in the next paragraph using באין בזרוע "being

strong-armed". But then it should read טורוניא and a clear meaning of the sentence can only be obtained by distorting the meaning of the word.}

רַב הֲוָה לֵיהּ כִּיתָּן וְלָקַת. שָׁאַל לְרִבִּי חִייָה רוֹבָא מַהוּ מִיכּוֹס צִפַּר וּמִגְבְּלָה אַדְמֵיהּ בִּזְרַע כִּיתָּן. אָמַר לֵיהּ נְבֵילָה. וְלָמָּה לֹא אָמַר לֵיהּ טְרֵיפָה. בְּגִין דְּרִבִּי מֵאִיר. דְּרִבִּי מֵאִיר אָמַר טְרֵיפָה חַייֶבֶת בְּכִיסּוּי. לֹא כֵן אָמַר רִבִּי אִמִּי מִשֵּׁם רִבִּי שִׁמְעוֹן בֶּן לָקִישׁ מִשֶּׁעָלוּ מִן הַגּוֹלָה לֹא לָקַת פִּשְׁתָּן וְלֹא הֶחֱמִיץ יַיִן וְנָתְנוּ עֵינֵיהֶן בִּזְכוּת רִבִּי חִייָה הַגָּדוֹל וּבָנָיו. וְרַב כְּהָדָא שִׁמְעוּ אֵלַי אַבִּירֵי לֵב הָרְחוֹקִים מִצְּדָקָה. רִבִּי אַבָּהוּ אָמַר אִיתפַּלְגוֹן רִבִּי יוֹחָנָן וְרִבִּי שִׁמְעוֹן בֶּן לָקִישׁ. חַד אָמַר שֶׁכָּל־בָּאֵי עוֹלָם בָּאִין בִּצְדָקָה וְאֵילּוּ בָּאִין בִּזְרוֹעַ. וְחָרְנָה אָמַר שֶׁכָּל־טוֹבוֹת וְנֶחָמוֹת הַבָּאוֹת לְעוֹלָם בִּזְכוּתָן וְהֵן אֵין נֶהֱנִין מֵהֶן כְּלוּם. כְּגוֹן מָר זוּטְרָא דְּמַצְלֵי עַל חוֹרָנִין וּמִתְעַנֵּי וְעַל נַפְשֵׁיהּ לֹא מִתְעַנֵּי.

Rav had flax which was blighted[157]. He asked the elder Rebbi Ḥiyya, may one slaughter a bird and mix its blood with flax seed? He said, a cadaver[158]. Why did he not say to him, a torn one[159]? Because of Rebbi Meïr, for Rebbi Meïr said [the blood of] a torn [bird] must be covered. But did not Rebbi Immi say in the name of Rebbi Simeon ben Laqish: From the time when they came from the diaspora, flax was never blighted and wine never became vinegar; they considered this to be due to the merit of the Great Rebbi Ḥiyya and his sons[160]. But Rav is like (*Is.* 46:12): "Listen to me, mighty of heart, who are far from charity!"[161] Rebbi Abbahu said, Rebbi Joḥanan and Rebbi Simeon ben Laqish disagree. One says, all the world depend on charity but these on strong arms[162]. But the other one said that all good things and consolations come to the world in their merit but they themselves do not profit at all[163]. For example Mar Zuṭra[164] who prayed and fasted for others but for himself he never fasted.

157 In the Babli, *Ḥulin* 85b-86a, the story is told of R. Ḥiyya and Rebbi. There, the decision goes against R. Meïr.

158 He could not use the blood of a regularly slaughtered kosher bird since that has to be covered with earth (*Lev.* 17:13). It seems that his agricultural practice did not allow using the blood of a non-kosher bird.

159 A kosher bird regularly slaughtered but which was found to have a bodily defect which made it forbidden. In Mishnah *Ḥulin* 6:2, the anonymous majority (which in the Babli is identified as R. Simeon and his followers) free the blood from the obligation of covering since the bird is not to be eaten but R. Meïr requires covering.

160 How could Rav's flax be blighted when his uncle's merit should have shielded it.

161 In the Babli, *Berakhot* 17b, the explanation is by either Rav and Samuel or R. Joḥanan and R. Eleazar.

162 Since Rav only trusted his own merit, he was not shielded by another's merit.

163 According to the Babli, no flax in all the Land of Israel was blighted in the times of R. Ḥiyya except his own.

164 He seems to be identical with Mar Zuṭra Ḥasida mentioned in the Babli, whose time cannot be ascertained. What is told here of the Babylonian Mar Zuṭra is told in the Babli (*loc. cit.*) of the Palestinian R. Ḥanina ben Dosa.

תַּנֵּי לְמַחְלוֹקֶת נִתְּנוּ דִּבְרֵי רִבִּי יוּדָה. רִבִּי יוֹסֵי אָמַר לְבֵית דִּירָה נִיתְּנוּ. אַתְיָא דְּרִבִּי יוּדָה כְּרִבִּי יוֹסֵי וּדְרִבִּי מֵאִיר כְּדַעְתֵּיהּ דְּתַנִּינָן מַעֲלוֹת הָיוּ שָׂכָר לַלְוִיִּם דִּבְרֵי רִבִּי יוּדָה. רִבִּי יוֹסֵי אוֹמֵר לֹא הָיוּ מַעֲלוֹת לָהֶן שָׂכָר.

[165]It was stated: They were given to be distributed, the words of Rebbi Jehudah. Rebbi Yose said, they were given as dwellings. It turns out that Rebbi Jehudah holds with Rebbi Yose[166] and Rebbi Meïr follows his own opinion as we have stated: "They[167] were paying rent to the Levites, the words of Rebbi Jehudah; Rebbi Yose says they were not paying rent."

165 The origin of this paragraph is in *Makkot* 2:7 (fol. 32a); the statement is alluded to in *Soṭa* 9:2 (fol. 23c). Here, it refers to the disagreement between R. Yose and R. Meïr on the status of Levites and Cohanim, whether they may read the declaration which refers to "the land You gave us." If the Levitical cities and the cities of refuge were parcelled out to their inhabitants, then they own land given by God. But if the cities were tribal property and the houses given to the inhabitants as living quarters by the tribal council, not as property, then individual Levites and Cohanim never obtained land and cannot read the declaration.

166 The name tradition is garbled. In *Makkot* 2:7, the text reads: It turns out that Rebbi Yose holds with Rebbi Jehudah. The reference is to the statement of R. Yose in the next Mishnah, which parallels R. Yehudah's opinion in *Makkot* 2:7. Mishnah *Makkot* 2:15 (Babli 2:8) reads: "They were paying rent to the Levites, the words of Rebbi Jehudah; Rebbi Meïr says they were not paying rent." Therefore, the text of the preceding sentence must be: R. Meïr says, they were given as dwellings.

167 In all old sources, the verb is in the feminine 3rd person plural. The object of the Mishnah are homicides which by the court in whose jurisdiction the crime was committed were sentenced to exile in a city of refuge. Rashi explains that the question was whether the homicide's home town has to pay rent in the city of refuge (presumably to be charged to the criminal's family). R. Jacob Ettlinger (*Arukh leNer Makkot* 13a) notes that Rashi is forced to explain this because "city" עיר is feminine. It is assumed here that the explanation is that lodging a criminal in a private home clearly requires payment but if the cities of refuge were given as tribal property subject to a lien that they had to accept all homicides, then no extra rent is due. Rava in the Babli, *Makkot* 13a, holds that in a city of refuge no rent can be due; the only question was about the other 42 Levitic cities which might give temporary refuge to the homicide between crime and trial. This cannot be the position of the Yerushalmi.

(fol. 55d) **משנה יג:** מִיכָּן אָמְרוּ שֶׁיִּשְׂרָאֵל וּמַמְזֵרִים מִתְוַדִּים אֲבָל לֹא גֵרִים וְלֹא עֲבָדִים מְשׁוּחְרָרִים שֶׁאֵין לָהֶן חֵלֶק בָּאָרֶץ. רִבִּי מֵאִיר אוֹמֵר אַף לֹא כֹהֲנִים וּלְוִיִּם שֶׁלֹּא נָטְלוּ חֵלֶק בָּאָרֶץ. רִבִּי יוֹסֵי אוֹמֵר יֵשׁ לָהֶן עָרֵי מִגְרָשׁ. יוֹחָנָן כֹּהֵן גָּדוֹל הֶעֱבִיר הוֹדָיַית מַעֲשֵׂר. אַף הוּא בִּיטֵּל אֶת הַמְעוֹרְרִים וְאֶת הַנּוֹקְפִים עַד יָמָיו הָיָה פַּטִּישׁ מַכֶּה בִירוּשָׁלֵם וּבְיָמָיו אֵין אָדָם צָרִיךְ לִשְׁאוֹל עַל הַדְּמַאי.

Mishnah 13: Because of this[168], they said that Israel persons and *Mamzerim*[169] may make the declaration but not proselytes and freed slaves who have no part in the Land. Rebbi Meïr says, also excluding Cohanim or Levites who did not receive any part of the Land. Rebbi Yose says, they have their cities with surroundings[170]. [171]The High Priest Joḥanan disestablished the declaration of tithes. He also eliminated the arousers and the hitters[172]. Up to his days the hammer was hitting in Jerusalem[173] and in his days nobody had to ask about *demay*.

168 The statement "the land You gave us" in the declaration.

169 Children born from adultery or incest who are forbidden to marry regular Israelites (*Deut*. 23:3). Since the disability is hereditary, R. Ṭarphon in Mishnah *Qiddušin* 3:14 counsels male bastards to live with a non-manumitted slave girl and at the birth of a child (which is his biologically but not legally) manumit the child which by this act automatically becomes a full Jew free of his father's disability. Today he would have to marry a non-Jewish woman and convert the child at birth.

170 This was discussed in the preceding paragraph.

171 From here it is also Mishnah *Soṭah* 9:10. The historical identity of this High Priest cannot be determined. {Cf. Eliahu Katz, "Who was Joḥanan the High Priest?" *Šanah bešanah* 1979, pp. 368-373 (Hebrew).} In the Babli (*Yoma* 9a) it is reported that he acted as High Priest for 80 years; an assertion of doubtful accuracy like most historical stories in the Babli. According to a possible interpretation of Tosephta *Soṭah* 13:6, he was the Hasmonean Joḥanan Hyrkanos; cf. Notes 188,189.

172 This will be discussed in the

Halakhah.

173 This is explained only in the Babli, *Makkot* 11b and *Soṭah* 48a and Tosephta *Soṭah* 13:10. On the intermediate days of the holiday week urgent work may be done. But since metal work is very noisy, and Jerusalem was full of holiday pilgrims at these times, he decreed that, in Jerusalem only, noisy work should not be performed.

(fol. 56d) **הלכה ט**: רִבִּי יִרְמְיָה רִבִּי חִייָה בְּשֵׁם רִבִּי שִׁמְעוֹן בֶּן לָקִישׁ מַתְנִיתָא מִשֶּׁנֶּחְשְׁדוּ לִהְיוֹת נוֹתְנִין מַעֲשֵׂר לִכְהוּנָּה. הָדָא מְסַייְעָא לְרִבִּי יוֹחָנָן בְּחָדָא וּפְלִיגָא עָלוֹי בְּחָדָא. פְּלִיגָא עָלוֹי דְּתַנִּינָן וְכֵן בַּת כֹּהֵן לְלֵוִי לֹא יֹאכְלוּ בִתְרוּמָה וְלֹא בְמַעֲשֵׂר. נִיחָא בִתְרוּמָה לֹא תֹאכֵל. בְּמַעֲשֵׂר מַה נַפְשָׁךְ כֹּהֶנֶת הִיא תֹאכֵל לְוִייָה הִיא תֹאכֵל. רִבִּי אִילָא בְשֵׁם רִבִּי יוֹחָנָן כְּמָאן דְּאָמַר אֵין נוֹתְנִין מַעֲשֵׂר לִכְהוּנָּה. הֲוָה הוּא אָמַר נוֹתְנִין מַעֲשֵׂר לִכְהוּנָּה.

Halakhah 9: Rebbi Jeremiah, Rebbi Ḥiyya in the name of Rebbi Simeon ben Laqish: Our Mishnah[174] after the people were suspected of giving tithe to Cohanim. There is support for Rebbi Joḥanan in one and disagreement with him in one. Disagreement with him as we have stated[175]: "Similarly, the daughter of a Cohen [married] to a Levite should eat neither heave nor tithe." We understand that she should not eat heave[176]. But tithe any way you take it, if she is a Cohen's daughter she should eat, if she is a Levite's wife she should eat. Rebbi Hila in the name of Rebbi Joḥanan: [It follows] him who says one does not give tithe to Cohanim. That means, he himself[177] says one gives heave to Cohanim.

174 Which states that Joḥanan the High Priest abolished the recitation of the declaration. He held that people who do not follow the rules cannot make the declaration and giving tithe to Cohanim breaks the rules. In order not to be inquisitive he let nobody recite.

175 Mishnah *Yebamot* 9:6. In the interpretation of the Yerushalmi, one

speaks about the daughter of a Cohen preliminarily married to a Levite, who has lost her Cohen status and not yet acquired Levitic status. In the interpretation of the Babli (*Yebamot* 86a) which holds that tithes should regularly be given to Cohanim, the Mishnah is explained away: The daughter of a Cohen married to a Levite may eat tithes but she cannot receive tithes from an Israel as a precaution since an Israel woman married to a Cohen should not accept heave or tithe from an Israel since we are afraid her husband might die without issue and then she would be barred from heave and tithes.

176 Since legally she is married; cf. *Peah* 6, Note 46.

177 If R. Joḥanan considers the Mishnah contrary to his position, he must hold that Cohanim may receive tithe according to biblical law.

מְסַייְעָא לֵיהּ דּוּ אָמַר כּוּלָּן לְשֶׁבַח. דְּאָמַר רִבִּי יוֹחָנָן יוֹחָנָן כֹּהֵן גָּדוֹל שָׁלַח וּבָדַק בְּכָל־עָרֵי יִשְׂרָאֵל וּמְצָאָן שֶׁלֹּא הָיוּ מַפְרִישִׁין אֶלָּה תְרוּמָה גְדוֹלָה בִּלְבַד. אֲבָל מַעֲשֵׂר רִאשׁוֹן וּמַעֲשֵׂר שֵׁינִי מֵהֶן הָיוּ מַפְרִישִׁין וּמֵהֶן לֹא הָיוּ מַפְרִישִׁין. אָמַר הוֹאִיל וּמַעֲשֵׂר רִאשׁוֹן בְּמִיתָה. וּמַעֲשֵׂר שֵׁינִי בַּעֲוֹן טֵבֶל יְהֵא אָדָם קוֹרֵא שֵׁם לִתְרוּמָה וְלִתְרוּמַת מַעֲשֵׂר וְנוֹתְנוֹ לְכֹהֵן וּמַעֲשֵׂר שֵׁינִי מְחַלְּלוֹ עַל הַמָּעוֹת וְהַשְּׁאָר מַעֲשֵׂר עָנִי הַמּוֹצִיא מֵחֲבֵירוֹ עָלָיו הָרְאַייָה.

It supports him because he says it is all praise, as Rebbi Joḥanan said[178], Joḥanan the High Priest sent and checked in all localities of Israel and found that they separated only Great Heave. But First and Second Tithes some were separating and some did not. He said, since [omitting] First Tithe is a deadly sin and [omitting] Second Tithe [implies] the sin of *ṭevel*, a person should give a name to heave[179] and heave of the tithe and give them to the Cohen; Second Tithe he exchanges for coins. About the remaining tithe of the poor, he who has a claim on another person must bring proof.

178 Tosephta *Soṭah* 13:10; a slightly different text Babli *Soṭa* 48a. The passage is explained in the Introduction to Tractate *Demay*.

179 This must be the instruction to the farmer, not the buyer who can be sure that heave was taken. The ms. evidence of the Tosephta does not permit deleting the reference to heave.

וְיִתְוַדֶּה. אָמַר רִבִּי הִילָא כַּעַס הוּא לִפְנֵי הַמָּקוֹם מִי שֶׁהוּא אוֹמֵר עָשִׂיתִי וְהוּא לֹא עָשָׂה. מֵעַתָּה מִי שֶׁהוּא מַפְרִישׁ מִתְוַדֶּה. מִי שֶׁאֵינוֹ מַפְרִישׁ לֹא יִתְוַדֶּה. כְּהָדָא דְתַנֵּי עַד הַשְׁקִיפָה הָיוּ אוֹמְרִים קוֹל נָמוּךְ. מִיכָּן וְהֵילָךְ הָיוּ אוֹמְרִים קוֹל גָּבוֹהַּ.

Why should he not make the declaration[180]? Rebbi Hila said, he causes anger before the Omnipresent by saying "I did" when he did not. If it is so, he who separated should make the declaration, he who did not separate should not make the declaration, as we have stated: "Up to 'Look down' they were saying it in an undertone, from 'Look down' onwards in a high voice."

180 Why should the necessity of introducing *demay* lead to the disestablishment of the declaration? The remedy indicates that the not too religiously scrupulous could omit the incriminating passages without anybody noticing, which shows that Joḥanan's order was not followed in subsequent generations.

אֶת הַמְעוֹרְרִין. אוֹתָן שֶׁהָיוּ אוֹמְרִים עוּרָה לָמָּה תִישַׁן יי הָקִיצָה אַל תִּזְנַח לָנֶצַח. וְכִי יֵשׁ שֵׁינָה לִפְנֵי הַמָּקוֹם. וַהֲלֹא כְּבָר נֶאֱמַר הִנֵּה לֹא יָנוּם וְלֹא יִישָׁן שׁוֹמֵר יִשְׂרָאֵל. וּמָה תַלְמוּד לוֹמַר וַיִּקַץ כְּיָשֵׁן יי אֶלָּא כִבְיָכוֹל כְּאִלּוּ לְפָנָיו שֵׁינָה בְּשָׁעָה שֶׁיִּשְׂרָאֵל בְּצָרָה וְאוּמּוֹת הָעוֹלָם בִּרְוָוחָה. וְכֵן הוּא אוֹמֵר וּבְהַמְּרוֹתָם תָּלַן עֵינִי.

"The arousers." Those who were saying (*Ps.* 44:24): "Be roused, why do You sleep, o Eternal, please awake, do not abandon forever.[181]" Does there exist sleep before the Omnipresent? Has it not already been said (*Ps.* 121:4): "Lo, He will not slumber nor sleep, the Guardian of Israel!" Why does the verse say (*Ps.* 78:65): "Like a sleeper awoke the Eternal, like a hero exhilarated by wine." But in a symbolic way it is as if sleep were before Him when Israel is in trouble and the other peoples are at ease. So it says (*Job* 17:2): "When they apostasize, My eye will rest."

181 According to Babli *Sota* (*loc. cit.*) and Tosephta *Soṭah* 13:9, this was a daily song of the Levites in the Temple.

אֶת הַנּוֹקְפִים. אוֹתָן שֶׁהָיוּ מַכִּין עַל גַּבֵּי הָעֶגֶל בֵּין קַרְנָיו. אָמַר לָהֶם יוֹחָנָן כֹּהֵן גָּדוֹל עַד מָתַי אַתֶּם מַאֲכִילִין אֶת הַמִּזְבֵּחַ טְרֵיפוֹת. וְעָמַד וְעָשָׂה לָהֶן טַבָּעוֹת. רִבִּי בָּא בְשֵׁם רִבִּי יְהוּדָה טַבָּעוֹת עָשָׂה לָהֶן טַבָּעוֹת רְחָבוֹת מִלְּמַטָּן וְצָרוֹת מִלְּמַעְלָן.

"The hitters." Those who were hitting the calf between its horns[182]. Johanan the High Priest said to them, how long will you feed torn animals to the altar[183]? He went and made them rings[184]. Rebbi Abba in the name of Rebbi Jehudah: He made rings for them, rings wide below and narrow at the top.

182 In the Rome ms.: בין חרצו "in its depression." To stun the animal before slaughter. According to Tosephta *Soṭah* 13:10, this was usually done with animals brought to pagan slaughter.

183 If the membrane covering the brain is torn, the animal is forbidden food.

184 To immobilize the neck of the animal to be slaughtered. The word in parentheses is not in the Rome ms.

עַד יָמָיו הָיָה פַּטִּישׁ מַכֶּה בִירוּשָׁלֵם עַד תְּחִילַּת יָמָיו. וּבְיָמָיו אֵין אָדָם צָרִיךְ לִשְׁאוֹל עַל הַדְּמַאי שֶׁהֶעֱמִיד זוּגוֹת.

"Up to his days the hammer was hitting in Jerusalem,"[173] up to his early days. "And in his days nobody had to ask about *demay*" because he sent out teams[185].

185 Who made the rounds through all agricultural areas and saw to it that every farmer tithed.

מִילְתֵיהּ דְּרִבִּי יְהוֹשֻׁעַ בֶּן לֵוִי אֲמְרָה מֵהֶן לִגְנַאי וּמֵהֶן לְשֶׁבַח. דְּאָמַר רִבִּי יוֹסֵי בְּשֵׁם רִבִּי תַנְחוּם בַּר חִייָה. רִבִּי חִזְקִיָּה רִבִּי אֶלְעָזָר בֵּי רִבִּי יוֹסֵי רִבִּי תַנְחוּם בַּר חִייָה בְּשֵׁם רִבִּי יְהוֹשֻׁעַ בֶּן לֵוִי בָּרִאשׁוֹנָה הָיָה מַעֲשֵׂר נַעֲשֶׂה לִשְׁלֹשָׁה חֲלָקִים. שְׁלִישׁ לְמַכָּרֵי כְהוּנָּה וּלְוִיָּה וּשְׁלִישׁ לָאוֹצָר וּשְׁלִישׁ לָעֲנִיִּים וְלַחֲבֵירִים שֶׁהָיוּ בִירוּשָׁלֵם. אָמַר רִבִּי יוֹסֵי בֵּירִבִּי בּוּן מָן דַּהֲוָה סְלִיק לְמֵידִין בִּירוּשָׁלֵם עַד דִּתְלָת אִיגְּרָן הֲוָה יְהַב מִדִּידֵיהּ מִכָּן וְאֵילָךְ מִשֶּׁלָּאוֹצָר. מִשֶּׁבָּא אֶלְעָזָר בֶּן פְּחוֹרָה וִיהוּדָה בֶּן פְּטִירָה הָיוּ נוֹטְלִין אוֹתוֹ בִּזְרוֹעַ וְהָיָה סִפֵּיקָן בְּיָדָן לִמְחוֹת וְלֹא מִיחָה. וְהֶעֱבִיר הוֹדָיַית הַמַּעֲשֵׂר. וְזוֹ לִגְנַאי. וְאֶת הַמְּעוֹרְרִין לְשֶׁבַח. וְאֶת הַנּוֹקְפִין לְשֶׁבַח.

The word of Rebbi Joshua ben Levi implies some[186] are censure and some praise. Since Rebbi Yose said in the name of Rebbi Tanḥum bar Ḥiyya, Rebbi Ḥizqiah, Rebbi Eleazar ben Rebbi Yose, Rebbi Tanḥum bar Ḥiyya in the name of Rebbi Joshua ben Levi, originally tithe was split into three parts. One third to his acquaintances among Cohanim and Levites, one third to the public treasury, one third to the poor and the fellows in Jerusalem. Rebbi Yose ben Rebbi Abun said, a person who went to court in Jerusalem, up to three letters[187] he paid for himself, from there on from the public treasury. When Eleazar ben Paḥora[188] and Judah ben Patora[189] came, they took it by force and it would have been in his hand to stop this but he did not but disestablished the declaration of tithes[190], and this is for censure. But the arousers for praise and the hitters for praise.

186 Of the recorded actions of the High Priest Joḥanan.

187 Summons to the opposing party to appear before the court.

188 In the Babli (*Qiddušin* 66a) he is called Eleazar ben Po'era, described as a Sadducee, and placed in Alexander Yannai's time.

189 In the parallel in *Soṭah* 9:10 he is called בן פכורה. They might have been Cohanim and taking the tithe by force for themselves but more likely were royal officials who took all for the public treasury.

190 Since the tithe was taken by force, the biblical rules could not be kept. If the identification of this High Priest with Joḥanan Hyrkanos is true, he himself would have been a beneficiary of the corrupt system.

עַד יָמָיו הָיָה פַּטִּישׁ מַכֶּה בִירוּשָׁלֵם עַד תְּחִילַּת יָמָיו. רִבִּי חֲסִידָא שָׁאַל לְרִבִּי חִזְקִיָּה לֹא מִסְתַּבְּרָא עַד סוֹף יָמָיו. אֲמַר לֵיהּ אוּף אֲנָא סָבַר כֵּן.

"Up to his days the hammer was hitting in Jerusalem," up to his early days[191]. Rebbi Ḥasida[192] asked Rebbi Ḥizqiah, is it not reasonable to the end of his days. He said, I also am of that opinion.

191 In that case, he would be praised for stopping the practice. If he tolerated it and only his successors abolished it, he would be mentioned for censure.

192 A fourth generation Amora, asking not only R. Ḥizqiah but also R. Yose.

דְּמַאי רִבִּי יוֹסֵי בְשֵׁם רִבִּי אַבָּהוּ רִבִּי חִזְקִיָּה בְשֵׁם רִבִּי יוּדָה בֶּן פָּזִי דְּמַאי דָּמִי תִיקֵּן. דָּמִי לֹא תִיקֵּן.

{What means] *demay*? Rebbi Yose in the name of Rebbi Abbahu, Rebbi Ḥizqiah in the name of Rebbi Jehudah ben Pazi: Maybe he put in order, maybe he did not put in order[193].

193 Cf. Introduction to Tractate Demay, p. 348.

Introduction to Tractate Ḥallah

The Tractate explains the verses *Num.* 15:17-22: "The Eternal spoke to Moses, saying: Speak to the Children of Israel and say to them: At your coming to the Land to which I am bringing you, it shall be that for your eating from the bread of the Land you shall lift a heave for the Eternal. The first of your kneading-troughs you shall lift *ḥallah* as a heave. Just like the heave from the threshing floor so you shall lift it. From the first of your kneading-troughs you shall give heave to the Eternal, for your generations." The verses make it quite clear that the duty of *ḥallah* is restricted to bread dough (defined in Chapter One), to the Land (whose definition from *Ševi'it* is repeated in Chapter Four), and has to follow the rules of heave as developed in Tractates *Terumot* and *Ma'serot*. The detailed application of these rules to bread dough is not without complications, as explained in Chapters Two and Three. The Tractate ends with a discussion of the obligation of heave and *ḥallah* in the regions surrounding the Land and a general rejection of public displays of religious behavior unsupported by general rules.

For the interpretation, as always the main guides are Maimonides and R. Simson of Sens. In addition, for this Tractate, the extended commentary on the Mishnah by Menaḥem Meïri (edited by A. Sofer, Jerusalem 1960) is very valuable. Of the Eighteenth Century commentators, the most useful is R. Eliahu Fulda; the least useful are R. Moses Margalit (פני משה), R. Eliahu Kramer of Wilna and, from the Twentieth Century, R. H. Kanievski, all of whom tend to emend away the difficult portions and the disagreements with Babylonian tradition. Similarly, the preliminary translation and explanation by Jacob Neusner (Chicago, 1991) heavily depends on the emended Wilna text and a presumed but untenable identification of the Tosephta underlying the Yerushalmi with the Tosephta in our hands. Of modern commentaries, R. Saul Lieberman's *Tosefta ki-fshutah* (New York, 1955), R. Y. Qafeḥ's commented edition and translation of Maimonides's Commentary, and *Ozar Mefarshe Hattalmud* (Jerusalem 1993) are most useful.

חמשה דברים פרק ראשון

(fol. 57a) **משנה א:** חֲמִשָּׁה דְּבָרִים חַייָבִין בַּחַלָּה הַחִיטִּים וְהַשְּׂעוֹרִין וְהַכּוּסְמִין וְשִׁיבּוֹלֶת שׁוּעָל וְהַשִּׁיפוֹן הֲרֵי אֵלּוּ חַייָבִין בַּחַלָּה. וּמִצְטָרְפִין זֶה עִם זֶה וַאֲסוּרִין בֶּחָדָשׁ לִפְנֵי הַפֶּסַח וּמִלִּקְצוֹר לִפְנֵי הָעוֹמֶר. וְאִם הִשְׁרִישׁוּ קוֹדֶם לָעוֹמֶר הָעוֹמֶר מַתִּירָן וְאִם לָאו אֲסוּרִין עַד שֶׁיָּבוֹא הָעוֹמֶר הַבָּא.

Mishnah 1: Five kinds are subject to *ḥallah*: wheat, barley, spelt, foxtail, and oats[1]. These are subject to *ḥallah* and combine with one another[2]. They are forbidden as new grain before Passover[3] and may not be cut before the *'omer*[4]. If they formed roots before the *'omer*, the *'omer* permits them[5]; otherwise, they are forbidden until the next *'omer*.

1 For the determination of these grains, see *Kilaim* 1, Notes 2-3. In current practice, שיפון is interpreted as rye, following Rashi. Flour made from these and only these grains qualifies as bread flour. All other flours are cake flours; bread made from them is legally cake.

2 Mixed dough is subject to *ḥallah* if the volume of flour used is at least that specified in Mishnah 2:6.

3 *Lev*. 23:14.

4 The *'omer* is the sheaf of barley cut first in the spring harvest and brought to the Temple (*Lev*. 23:10), in rabbinic interpretation on the second day of Passover, the 16th of Nisan.

5 While the first harvest is that of barley, all other grains, including wheat, are immediately permitted for profane use. Only for the Temple is new wheat forbidden until the Festival of First Fruits, *Lev*. 23:16.

הלכה א: חֲמִשָּׁה דְבָרִים חַייָבִין בַּחַלָּה כו'. כְּתִיב וְהָיָה בַּאֲכָלְכֶם מִלֶּחֶם הָאָרֶץ תָּרִימוּ תְרוּמָה לַיי. יָכוֹל יְהוּ כָל־הַדְּבָרִים חַייָבִין בַּחַלָּה. תַּלְמוּד לוֹמַר מִלֶּחֶם וְלֹא כָל־לֶחֶם. אִם מִלֶּחֶם וְלֹא כָל־לֶחֶם אֵין לִי אֶלָּא חִיטִּין וּשְׂעוֹרִין בִּלְבַד. כּוּסְמִין שִׁיבּוֹלֶת שׁוּעָל וְשִׁיפוֹן מְנַיִין. תַּלְמוּד לוֹמַר רֵאשִׁית עֲרִיסוֹתֵיכֶם רִיבָּה. וְרִיבָּה הַכֹּל. רִבִּי יוֹסֵי בְּשֵׁם רִבִּי שִׁמְעוֹן תַּנֵּי רִבִּי יִשְׁמָעֵאל כֵּן.

Halakhah 1: [6]"Five kinds are subject to *ḥallah*", etc. It is written (*Num*. 15:19): "It shall be when you eat of the bread of the Land you shall lift a heave[7] for the Eternal." I could think that everything[8] is subject to *ḥallah*; the verse says "of the bread" and not all bread. If "of the bread" and not all bread, that might be only wheat and barley[9]. From where spelt, foxtail, and oats? The verse says (*Num*. 15:20,21) "the first of your dough,[10]" this includes. Does it include everything[11]? Rebbi Yose in the name of Rebbi Simeon[12]: Rebbi Ismael stated this.

6 This and the next paragraphs are also in *Pesaḥim* 2:4 (fol. 29b).

7 This is *ḥallah* which follows the rules of heave.

8 Since לחם can also mean "food", cf. *Gen*. 47:12.

9 Since bread is usually made from these.

10 The expression is emphasized by repetition. One has to include every grain usable for making dough.

11 According to this argument, rice and millet for example should also be included.

12 This must be R. Simeon ben Laqish. R. Yose asserts that R. Ismael accepted the inference as valid; "dough" includes every bread-dough made from grains similar to the bread grains wheat and barley.

רִבִּי יוֹנָה רִבִּי זְעִירָא רִבִּי שִׁמְעוֹן בֶּן לָקִישׁ בְּשֵׁם רִבִּי יִשְׁמָעֵאל. אָמַר רִבִּי מָנָא אָזְלִית לְקֵיסָרִין וְשָׁמְעִית רִבִּי אַחַוָה בֶּן[13] רִבִּי זְעִירָא וְאַבָּא הֲוָה אָמַר לֵיהּ בְּשֵׁם רִבִּי יִשְׁמָעֵאל. נֶאֱמַר לֶחֶם בְּפֶסַח וְנֶאֱמַר לֶחֶם בַּחַלָּה. מַה לֶחֶם שֶׁנֶּאֱמַר בְּפֶסַח דָּבָר שֶׁהוּא בָא לִידֵי מַצָּה וְחָמֵץ אַף לֶחֶם שֶׁנֶּאֱמַר בַּחַלָּה דָּבָר שֶׁהוּא בָא

לִידֵי מַצָּה וְחָמֵץ. וּבָדְקוּ וּמָצְאוּ שֶׁאֵין לָךְ בָּא לִידֵי מַצָּה וְחָמֵץ אֶלָּא חֲמֵשֶׁת הַמִּינִין בִּלְבַד. וּשְׁאָר כָּל־הַדְּבָרִים אֵינָן בָּאִין לִידֵי מַצָּה וְחָמֵץ אֶלָּא לִידֵי סִירְחוֹן.

Rebbi Jonah, Rebbi Zeïra, Rebbi Simeon ben Laqish in the name of Rebbi Ismael. Rebbi Mana said, I went to Caesarea and heard Rebbi Aḥava ben Rebbi Zeïra[14], but my father said it in the name of Rebbi Ismael[15]: "Bread" is mentioned for Passover[16] and "bread" is mentioned for *ḥallah*[17]. Since bread mentioned in a discussion of Passover is something that can be either *mazzah* or leavened, bread mentioned for *ḥallah* must be something that can be either *mazzah* or leavened. They checked and found that only the five kinds can be either *mazzah* or leavened; all others cannot be *mazzah*[18] or leavened but would spoil.

13 Reading of the parallel in *Pesaḥim*. Here: ר' אחווה ור' זעירא.

14 The son of R. Zeïra who had been a *baraita* teacher in his father's academy. The father of R. Mana was R. Jonah.

15 A similar text *Sifry Num.* 110. As regards Passover only, Babli *Pesaḥim* 35a, *Mekhilta deR. Ismael Bo* Chap. 8, 17; *Sifry Num.* 146.

16 *Deut.* 16:2.

17 *Num.* 15:19.

18 Rice cakes, while unleavened, cannot be called *mazzah* since rice bread (not containing gluten) does not qualify as leavened bread. If left standing with leavening it will not rise but spoil.

תַּנֵּי אָמַר רִבִּי יוֹחָנָן בֶּן נוּרִי קָרְמִית חַיֶּיבֶת בַּחַלָּה. רִבִּי יוֹחָנָן בֶּן נוּרִי אָמַר בָּאָה הִיא לִידֵי מַצָּה וְחָמֵץ וְרַבָּנִין אָמְרִין אֵינָהּ בָּאָה לִידֵ מַצָּה וְחָמֵץ. וְיִבְדְּקוּהָ. עַל עִיקַּר בְּדִיקוּתָהּ הֵם חוֹלְקִין. רִבִּי יוֹחָנָן בֶּן נוּרִי אָמַר בְּדָקוּהָ וּמְצָאוּהָ שֶׁהִיא בָּאָה לִידֵ מַצָּה וְחָמֵץ. וְרַבָּנִין אָמְרִין בְּדָקוּהָ וְלֹא מְצָאוּ אוֹתוֹ שֶׁהִיא בָּאָה לִידֵי מַצָּה וְחָמֵץ.

It was stated[19]: "Rebbi Joḥanan ben Nuri said, *qeramit*[20] is obligated for *ḥallah*." Rebbi Joḥanan ben Nuri said, it can be either *mazzah* or leavened, but the rabbis say, it cannot be either *mazzah* or leavened. Let them check! They disagree about the outcome of the checking. Rebbi Joḥanan ben Nuri said, they checked and found it can be either *mazzah* or leavened, but the rabbis say, they checked and did not find that it can be either *mazzah* or leavened.

19 Tosephta 1:1; cf. Tosephta *Pesaḥim* 2:17; Babli *Pesaḥim* 35a.

20 According to the Geonim (*Ozar Hageonim Pesaḥim* p. 33) a grain growing wild among reeds in swamps, used as human food in times of famine. In the opinion of I. Löw (*Flora der Juden* 1, p. 703) *Glyceria fluitans*, a grain preferring swampy ground, frequently used for animal feed, also for soups and flour. {Also cf. Latin *gramen, -inis*, n. "grass, dog's grass" (*Plin. Hist. Nat.* 24,19,118, #178) (E. G.)}.

תַּמָּן תַּנִּינָן תַּפּוּחַ שֶׁרִיסְקוֹ וּנְתָנוֹ לְתוֹךְ עִיסָּה וְחִימִּיצָהּ הֲרֵי זוֹ אֲסוּרָה. תַּנֵּי רִבִּי יוֹסֵי אוֹמֵר מוּתָּר. רִבִּי אָחָא רִבִּי אַבָּהוּ בְּשֵׁם רִבִּי יוֹסֵי בֶּן חֲנִינָה מַפְלִיגִין בְּמְחַמֵּץ בְּמֵימָיו אֲבָל בִּמְחַמֵּץ בְּגוּפוֹ דִּבְרֵי הַכֹּל מוּתָּר. רִבִּי יוֹסֵי כְּדַעְתֵּיהּ דּוּ אָמַר תַּמָּן אֵין תַּבְשִׁילוֹ תַּבְשִׁיל בָּרוּר. כֵּן הוּא אָמַר הָכָא אֵין חִימּוּצוֹ חִימּוּץ בָּרוּר.

There[21], we have stated: "If a mashed apple is added to dough which soured, [the dough] is forbidden" It was stated: Rebbi Yose says, it is permitted. Rebbi Aḥa, Rebbi Abbahu in the name of Rebbi Yose ben Ḥanina: They disagree when it becomes sour from the juice [of the apple]. But if it becomes sour from its solid substance it is permitted according to everybody. Rebbi Yose stays with his opinion; just as he says there, its cooking is not clearly cooking, so he says here, its souring is not clearly souring.

21 *Terumot* 10:2. The paragraph is explained there, Notes 15-19.

וּכְמָא דְאַתְּ אָמַר אֵין לָךְ בָּא לִידֵי מַצָּה וְחָמֵץ אֶלָּא חֲמֵשֶׁת הַמִּינִין בִּלְבַד. וְדִכְוָותָהּ אֵין לָךְ מְגָרֵר עִם כּוּלָּן אֶלָּא חִטִּים וּשְׂעוֹרִים בִּלְבַד. רִבִּי הִילָא בְשֵׁם רִבִּי שִׁמְעוֹן בֶּן לָקִישׁ לֹא שָׁנִינוּ אֶלָּא הָעוֹשֶׂה עִיסָּה מִן הַחִיטִּים וּמִן הָאוֹרֶז וְאֵינוֹ נִגְרָר אֶלָּא עִם (fol. 57b) הַחִיטִּין בִּלְבַד.

And just as you say only the five kinds can become *mazzah* and leavened, so only wheat and barley can be dragged with anything[22]. Rebbi Hila said in the name of Rebbi Simeon ben Laqish, we have only stated: "He who makes dough from wheat and rice;" only wheat can be dragged in.

22 They can be dragged to be subject to *ḥallah* even if only a small part of the dough is grain and the rest is filler. The reference is either to Mishnah 3:6 or Tosephta 2:1, a cake made from rice and wheat is subject to *ḥallah* if it tastes like bread. The question is whether "wheat" stands for any grain or only for wheat itself and the grains closely related to it.

מַהוּ שֶׁיְּהוּ חַייָבִין עַל קָלִי שֶׁלּוֹ מִשּׁוּם חָדָשׁ. אָמַר רִבִּי זְעִירָה כְּתִיב וְלֶחֶם וְקָלִי וְכַרְמֶל לֹא תֹאכְלוּ. אֶת שֶׁחַייָבִין עַל לֶחֶם שֶׁלּוֹ מִשּׁוּם חָדָשׁ חַייָבִין עַל קָלִי שֶׁלּוֹ מִשּׁוּם חָדָשׁ. אֶת שֶׁאֵין חַייָבִין עַל לֶחֶם שֶׁלּוֹ מִשּׁוּם חָדָשׁ אֵין חַייָבִין עַל קָלִי שֶׁלּוֹ מִשּׁוּם חָדָשׁ.

Is one guilty because of new grain[23] when it is roasted? Rebbi Zeïra said, it is written (*Lev.* 23:14): "Bread, parched or fresh grain you should not eat." Anything for whose bread you would be guilty because of new grain you are guilty for parched grain because of new grain; but anything for whose bread you would not be guilty because of new grain you are not guilty for parched grain because of new grain.

23 New grain is forbidden until the sheaf of barley is brought to the Temple on Passover; *Lev*. 23:9-14. It is stated here that the definition of "bread" established for Passover and *ḥallah* is valid for the prohibition of new grain also.

רִבִּי יִרְמְיָה בָּעָא קוֹמֵי רִבִּי זְעִירָא עִירֵב אַרְבַּעַת קַבִּין בִּפְנֵי עַצְמָן וְחִימְּצָן. וְאַרְבַּעַת קַבִּין בִּפְנֵי עַצְמָן וְעִירְבָן הֲרֵי בִשְׁעַת חִיּוּבָן לָבֹא לִדֵי מַצָּה וְחָמֵץ. [אָמַר לֵיהּ מִינוֹ בָא לִידֵי מַצָּה וְחָמֵץ.][24] אַתְיָיא דְּרִבִּי יוֹנָה כְרִבִּי יִרְמְיָה. וּדְרִבִּי יוֹסֵי כְרִבִּי זְעִירָא. אַתְיָיא דְּרִבִּי יוֹנָה כְרִבִּי יִרְמְיָה. כְּמָה דְרִבִּי יִרְמְיָה אָמַר עַד שֶׁיְּהֵא קָרוּי לֶחֶם. כָּךְ רִבִּי יוֹנָה אָמַר עַד שֶׁיְּהֵא קָרוּי לֶחֶם. דְּרִבִּי יוֹסֵי כְרִבִּי זְעִירָה כְּמָה דְרִבִּי זְעִירָה אָמַר מִינוֹ קָרוּי לֶחֶם כֵּן רִבִּי יוֹסֵי אָמַר מִינוֹ קָרוּי לֶחֶם. אַתְיָא דְּרִבִּי יוֹסֵי כְּרִבִּי הִילָא אַף עַל גַּב דּוּ פָּלִיג עָלוֹי.

Rebbi Jeremiah asked before Rebbi Zeïra: One mixed four *qab*[25] separately and made them leavened, and another four *qab*[26] separately and mixed them. Then at the moment of their obligation[27] for *ḥallah* can they become *mazzah* or leavened? [He said to him, its kind becomes *mazzah* or leavened.[28]] Rebbi Jonah parallels Rebbi Jeremiah, Rebbi Yose parallels Rebbi Zeïra. Rebbi Jonah parallels Rebbi Jeremiah, just as Rebbi Jeremiah says, only if it is called bread, so Rebbi Jonah says, only if it is called bread[15,16]. Rebbi Yose parallels Rebbi Zeïra, just as Rebbi Zeïra said only if its kind is called bread, so Rebbi Yose said only if its kind is called bread[12]. Rebbi Yose parallels Rebbi Hila[29] even though he disagrees with him.

24 Reading of the Rome ms., sentence missing in Leyden ms. and Venice print.

25 Since Mishnah 2:6 states that dough made from $^{5}/_{4}$ *qab* of flour is subject to *ḥallah*, it is clear that one has to read here "quarter *qab*" instead of *qab*. The leavened flour by itself is not enough to induce an obligation of

ḥallah.

26 Another $^5/_4$ *qab* of rice, millet, or pea flour which cannot be leavened and which by themselves never induce an obligation of *ḥallah.*

27 After he mixed the leavened dough with the non-grain flour, he now has 2 *qab* which potentially are obligated for *ḥallah.*

28 If the leavened flour were more than the unleavened, the unleavened could be disregarded and all would be subject to *ḥallah* but when is it evenly split it does not satisfy our crtiteria.

29 He says in Halakhah 3:6 that there can be no obligation of *ḥallah* unless more then 50% is bread flour and the finished product tastes like bread. R. Zeïra in that Halakhah is quoted as stating that R. Hila got the names of the Tannaïm wrong in his *baraita.*

רִבִּי שְׁמוּאֵל בַּר נַחְמָן שָׁמַע כּוּלְּהוֹן מִן אָהֵן קְרָייָא וְשָׂם חִיטָּה שׂוֹרָה וּשְׂעוֹרָה נִסְמָן וְכֻסֶּמֶת גְּבוּלָתוֹ. וְשָׂם חִיטָּה אֵלּוּ הַחִיטִּים. שׂוֹרָה זֶה שִׁיבּוֹלֶת שׁוּעָל וְלָמָּה נִקְרָא שְׁמָהּ שׂוֹרָה שֶׁהִיא עֲשׂוּיָה כְּשׁוּרָה. שְׂעוֹרָה אֵלּוּ הַשְּׂעוֹרִים. נִסְמָן זֶה הַשִּׁיפוֹן. וְכֻסֶּמֶת זֶה הַכּוּסְמִין. גְּבוּלָתוֹ לֶחֶם. עַד כָּאן גְּבוּלוֹ שֶׁלְּלֶחֶם. וּלְמֵידִין מִן הַקַּבָּלָה. אָמַר רִבִּי סִימוֹן מִן מָה דִכְתִיב וְיִסְּרוֹ לַמִּשְׁפָּט אֱלֹהָיו יוֹרֶנּוּ. כְּמוֹ שֶׁהוּא דְּבַר תּוֹרָה.

Rebbi Samuel ben Naḥman understood it from the following verse (*Is.* 28:28): "He puts wheat, *śorāh*, barley; *nismān* and spelt are its limit." "He puts wheat", that is wheat[30]. "*Śorāh*" is foxtail and why is it called *śorāh*? Because it is made in a line[31]. "Barley", that is barley. "*Nismān*" is oats. "Spelt" is spelt. "Its limit", bread: So far the definitions of bread. Does one infer anything from tradition[32]? Rebbi Simon said, since it is written (*Is.* 28:29): "He instructs in the law, his God will teach him,[33]" it is as if it were a word of the Torah[34].

30 The rabbinic equivalents to the biblical Hebrew names are given for all five kinds.

31 The expression חטה שׂורה probably means "ripe wheat", cf. Accadic *šer'u* "ripe grain". All expressions are

explained here as names of grains. The interpretation of שׂורה as שורה shows that in Talmudic times in Galilee, *š* was heard as *s*, under the influence of Greek. Cassuto in his biblical commentary accepts the interpretation as genuine.

32 The common name for Prophets and Hagiographs. These are sources of moral teachings but have no standing as books of law.

33 This interpretation, in contrast to that of the next paragraph, follows the masoretic division of the text.

34 But the next paragraph immediately contradicts this statement; there is no source of biblical law other than the Torah. {Prophets and Hagiographs are used as basis for rabbinic decrees.}

אָמַר רִבִּי סִימוֹן אִילֵּין נְשַׁיָּא דְאָמְרָן לָא נֵיעוֹל בְּנֵינָן לִכְנִישְׁתָּא אִין חֲמֵי לֵיהּ מֵילַף מֵילַף הוּא. לָא עָבְדִין טַבָּאוּת אֶלָּא וְיִסְּרוֹ לַמִּשְׁפָּט אֱלֹהָיו יוֹרֶנּוּ.

Rebbi Simon said, those women who say: we shall not send our sons to the communal school; if he is good at learning he will learn [by himself]; they do not act well, but (*Is*. 28:29): "He shall be instructed in his God's law, it will teach him."

רִבִּי יוּדָה בַּר פָּזִי בְשֵׁם רִבִּי יוֹנָתָן דְּרִבִּי יִשְׁמָעֵאל בְּנוֹ שֶׁל רִבִּי יוֹחָנָן בֶּן בְּרוֹקָא הִיא. דְּתַנֵּי רִבִּי יוֹחָנָן רִבִּי יִשְׁמָעֵאל בְּנוֹ שֶׁל רִבִּי יוֹחָנָן בֶּן בְּרוֹקָא אוֹמֵר יָכוֹל תָּבִיא מִן הַכּוּסְמִין וְשִׁיבּוֹלֶת שׁוּעָל וְהַשִּׁיפוֹן. וְדִין הוּא וּמָה אִם הַחִיטִּים שֶׁכָּשְׁרוּ לִשְׁאָר כָּל־הַמְּנָחוֹת לֹא כָשְׁרוּ לְמִנְחַת הָעוֹמֶר. כּוּסְמִין וְשִׁיבּוֹלֶת שׁוּעָל וְהַשִּׁיפוֹן שֶׁלֹּא כָשְׁרוּ לִשְׁאָר כָּל־הַמְּנָחוֹת אֵינוֹ דִין שֶׁלֹּא יִכָּשְׁרוּ לְמִנְחַת הָעוֹמֶר. הַשְּׂעוֹרִין יוֹכִיחוּ שֶׁלֹּא כָשְׁרוּ לִשְׁאָר כָּל־הַמְּנָחוֹת וְכָשְׁרוּ לְמִנְחַת הָעוֹמֶר. לֹא אִם אָמַרְתָּ בִּשְׂעוֹרִין שֶׁמִּנְחַת סוֹטָה בָאָה מֵהֶן. תֹּאמַר בְּכוּסְמִין וְשִׁיבּוֹלֶת שׁוּעָל וְשִׁיפוֹן שֶׁאֵין מִנְחַת סוֹטָה בָאָה מֵהֶן. יָצְאוּ הַחִיטִּים מִן הַכָּתוּב וְכוּסְמִין וְשִׁיבּוֹלֶת שׁוּעָל וְהַשִּׁיפוֹן מִקַּל וְחוֹמֶר.

Rebbi Jehudah bar Pazi in the name of Rebbi Jonathan: This[35] is from Rebbi Ismael the son of Rebbi Joḥanan ben Beroqa, as Rebbi Joḥanan stated; "Rebbi Ismael the son of Rebbi Joḥanan ben Beroqa said, I could think you could bring spelt, foxtail and oats. But is it not logical: If wheat which is usable for all other cereal offerings is not acceptable for the *'omer* offering, spelt, foxtail and oats which are not usable for any other cereal offerings certainly are not acceptable for the *'omer* offering. No; you might say about barley from which the offering of the straying wife[36] is brought; what can you say about spelt, foxtail and oats which are not usable for the offering of the straying wife? Wheat is excluded by the verse[37]; spelt, foxtail and oats are excluded by a reasoning *a minore ad majus*."

35 The Mishnah which forbids harvesting any of the five kinds of grain before the *'omer*. The statement of R. Ismael ben R. Joḥanan ben Beroqa is in *Sifra Wayiqra Paršata* 13(5). The problem is *Lev*. 2:14-16, speaking of the cereal offering of first fruits. The verse cannot speak of individual first fruits (*Deut*. 26:1-11) since no cereal offering is connected with these. For any other cereal offering, the flour is specified. It is always wheat except for the *'omer* sheaf (*Lev*. 23:9-14) and the offering for the wife suspected of infidelity (*Num*. 5:15). *Lev*. 2:14 does not specify the kind of cereal for the offering. The cereal offering of first fruits is identified as the *'omer* offering; this determines the flour as barley flour.

36 In *Sifra*, the second argument also refers to the *'omer*.

37 The nature of the grain cut for the *'omer* is not specified in *Lev*. 23:9-14. But since the "new grain" for the cereal offering of the 50th day is specified as fine wheat flour, the earlier offering cannot possibly be wheat.

אָמַר רִבִּי יוֹסֵי מִיסְבּוֹר סָבוּר רִבִּי יוּדָה בֶּן פָּזִי שֶׁמִּנְחַת הָעוֹמֶר בָּאָה מִן הַכּוּסְמִין וְשִׁיבּוֹלֶת שׁוּעַל וְשִׁיפוֹן. אִלּוּ מָן דְאָמַר תְּאֵינִים שְׁחוֹרוֹת עָלַי שֶׁמָּא

אֵינוֹ מוּתָּר בִּלְבָנוֹת. אֶלָּא שְׁחוֹרוֹת אָמַר לְבָנוֹת לֹא אָמַר. וְהָכָא שְׂעוֹרָה אָבִיב אָמַר שִׁבּוֹלֶת שׁוּעָל אָבִיב לֹא אָמַר.

Rebbi Yose said, who would think that Rebbi Jehudah ben Pazi could think that the cereal offering of the *'omer* could come from spelt, foxtail, or oats? If somebody said, black figs are [forbidden] to me, is he not permitted white ones? But "black ones" he said, "white ones" he did not say. And here, "milky white barley" was said[38], "milky white foxtail" was not said.

38 *Ex.* 9:31. The first-grain cereal offering is described in *Lev.* 2:14 as "milky white, parched in fire." The argument shows that the Mishnah can be the opinion of everybody. A similar argument is attributed in the Babli, *Menaḥot* 68b, to R. Eliezer.

בְּרַם כְּרַבָּנִין שְׁלֹשָׁה מִינִין הֵן. הַשִּׁיפוֹן מִין כּוּסְמִין. שִׁבּוֹלֶת שׁוּעָל מִין שְׂעוֹרִים. רַבָּנִין דְּקֵיסָרִין בָּעֵייָן מָה תַנִּינָן חֲמִשָּׁה מִינִין לֹא חֲמִשָּׁה דְּבָרִים. שְׁנֵי דְבָרִים מִין אֶחָד וּשְׁנֵי דְבָרִים מִין אֶחָד.

But for the rabbis they are three kinds! Oats are a kind of spelt, foxtail are a kind of barley[39]. The rabbis of Caesarea asked: Did we ever state: Five species? No, five kinds. Two times two kinds are one species.

39 In Mishnah *Kilaim* 1:1, oats and spelt, barley and foxtail, are described as "not *kilaim* one with the other." Therefore, they must be counted as one botanical species.

תַּמָּן תַּנִּינָן אֵיזֶהוּ מִין בְּמִינוֹ הַחִיטִּים אֵין מִצְטָרְפִין עִם הַכֹּל אֶלָּא עִם הַכּוּסְמִין. הַשְּׂעוֹרִין מִצְטָרְפִין עִם הַכֹּל חוּץ מִן הַחִיטִּים. רִבִּי יוֹסֵי אָמַר לָהּ סְתָם. רִבִּי יוֹנָה בְשֵׁם רִבִּי יוֹחָנָן תַּמָּן בְּנָשׁוּךְ וְכָאן בְּבָלוּל. תַּנֵּי רִבִּי חִיָּיה כֵן וְכוּלָּן שֶׁבָּלְלָן

תְּבוּאָה קְמָחִין וּבָצֵיקוֹת מִצְטָרְפוֹת. עִירֵס רָאשֵׁי עִיסִּיּוֹת. אָמַר רִבִּי יוֹסֵי וְהָהֵן נָשׁוּךְ לָאו כִּמְעִירֵס הוּא. אַתְּ אָמַר אֵינוֹ מִצְטָרֵף וְהָכָא אֵינוֹ מִצְטָרֵף.

There[40], we have stated: "What means one species with itself? Wheat does not go together with anything but spelt. Barley goes together with everything except wheat." Rebbi Yose said it without attribution, Rebbi Jonah in the name of Rebbi Joḥanan: "There if it bites[41], here if it was mixed[42]. Rebbi Ḥiyya stated: All those which he mixed as grains, flour, or dough, go together." If he mixed the ends of doughs together? Rebbi Yose said, is biting not like mixing together? You say they do not go together, so here they do not go together[43].

40 Mishnah 4:2, which seems to contradict the statement of the Mishnah here that the five kinds of grains can be added together for the minimal amount needed for the obligation of *ḥallah*.

41 If different doughs are placed together so they touch one another and, if separated again, small parts of one dough will cling to the other. Then all pieces together form one dough for *ḥallah* if made from compatible flours.

42 If there is only one dough made from mixed flour, it is subject to *ḥallah* as if it were of homogeneous flour.

43 Since biting is a weak form of mixing, the rule of the Mishnah here applies only if the entire doughs are mixed, following R. Ḥiyya (the elder).

מַהוּ שֶׁיִּלְקוּ עַל חַלָּתָן דְּבַר תּוֹרָה. רִבִּי יוֹנָה בְשֵׁם שְׁמוּאֵל רִבִּי יוֹסֵי רִבִּי אַבָּהוּ בְשֵׁם רִבִּי שִׁמְעוֹן בֶּן לָקִישׁ אֵין לוֹקִין עַל חַלָּתָן דְּבַר תּוֹרָה. אָמַר רִבִּי יַעֲקֹב בַּר אָחָא רִבִּי שִׁמְעוֹן בֶּן לָקִישׁ כְּדַעְתֵּיהּ דְּאִיתְפַּלְּגוֹן הַפִּיגּוּל וְהַנּוֹתָר שֶׁשְּׁחָקָן רִבִּי יוֹחָנָן אָמַר לֹא בִיטְּלוּ זֶה אֶת זֶה. וְרִבִּי שִׁמְעוֹן בֶּן לָקִישׁ אָמַר בִּיטְּלוּ זֶה אֶת זֶה. אָמַר רִבִּי יוֹסֵי וְלֹא דָמְיָין. תַּמָּן אָמַר זֶה אָסוּר וְזֶה אָסוּר. בְּרַם הָכָא שְׁנֵי דְבָרִים רָבִים עַל אֶחָד וּמְבַטְּלִין אוֹתוֹ. וּכְבָר בִּיטְּלוּ עַד שֶׁלֹּא נַעֲשֶׂה אִיסּוּר.

אִילּוּ אָמַר עָשָׂה חָמֵשׁ עִיסִּיּוֹת מֵחֲמִשָּׁה מִינִין וְעִירְבוֹ. וְאָמַר רִבִּי שִׁמְעוֹן בֶּן לָקִישׁ אֵין לוֹקִין עַל חַלָּתָן דְּבַר תּוֹרָה יָאוּת.

Can they whip because of their *ḥallah* as a biblical law[44]? Rebbi Jonah in the name of Samuel, Rebbi Yose, Rebbi Abbahu in the name of Rebbi Simeon ben Laqish: one cannot whip because of their *ḥallah* as a biblical law[45]. Rebbi Jacob bar Aḥa said, Rebbi Simeon ben Laqish stays with his opinion, as they differed[46]: If somebody ground and mixed *piggul*[47] and leftover [sacrificial meat], Rebbi Joḥanan said they do not cancel one another, but Rebbi Simeon ben Laqish said they do cancel one another[48]. Rebbi Yose said, the cases are not similar[49]. There, one says this is forbidden and that is forbidden. But here, two kinds are more than the third and cancel it; they cancelled it before it became forbidden[50]. If one made five doughs[51] from five different kinds and then mixed them, if Rebbi Simeon ben Laqish would say that one cannot whip because of their *ḥallah* as a biblical law, then the argument would be correct.

44 If somebody made a dough from different kinds of flour that cannot be combined according to Mishnah 4:2 and ate from the bread without taking *ḥallah* following Mishnah 1:1, he ate *ṭevel*. Can he be convicted and sentenced to be whipped on the testimony of two eye witnesses?

45 Mishnah 4:2 is the biblical, Mishnah 1:1 the rabbinic standard.

46 Also quoted Babli *Zebaḥim* 75a. The Babli states that R. Simeon ben Laqish must hold (a) that different prohibitions are not cumulative but competing and (b) that criminal intent can only be proved by a warning that specifies the exact paragraph of the penal code the perpetrator was warned about; cf. *Kilaim* Chapter 8, Note 9. Here, R. Yose argues only about point (a), not (b).

47 From the verse *Lev*. 19:6-7 it would seem that פגול (Arabic فجل "soft, mushy") refers to sacrificial meat left after the time allotted for its consumption. However, since leftover

meat already is forbidden in *Lev.* 7:17-18, פגול is defined as meat from sacrifices which were slaughtered with the intention of eating them outside the holy precinct. Similarly, "leftover" does not really denote leftover meat but meat from sacrifices slaughtered with the intention of eating them after the allotted time. Eating פיגול is a deadly sin, eating leftover meat a sin, and both invalidate the sacrifice. If the sacrifice was slaughtered correctly, then an accidental leftover or piece outside the precinct is still forbidden but does not invalidate the sacrifice.

48 If somebody makes chopped meat out of *piggul* and leftover in approximately equal amounts and then eats the volume of an olive of the mixture, for R. Joḥanan he ate a punishable amount of forbidden meat and committed a crime. For R. Simeon ben Laqish, he ate less than an olive-sized piece of either *piggul* or leftover and cannot be punished for either one.

49 It is possible that R. Joḥanan agrees with R. Simeon ben Laqish about *ḥallah*.

50 Eating from dry flour is not forbidden. The prohibition comes only with the obligation of *ḥallah*, with the production of dough ready to be baked. Therefore, the case here involves no competition of laws. However, if the dough is large enough that one single kind already would induce the obligation of *ḥallah*, then everybody agrees that eating the bread without taking *ḥallah* is a criminal act.

51 Each one large enough to induce the obligation of *ḥallah*.

הִלֵּל הַזָּקֵן הָיָה כוֹרֵךְ שְׁלָשְׁתָּן כְּאַחַת. אָמַר רִבִּי יוֹחָנָן חֲלוּקִין עַל הִלֵּל הַזָּקֵן וְהָא רִבִּי יוֹחָנָן כָּרַךְ מַצָּה וּמָרוֹר. כָּאן בִּשְׁעַת הַמִּקְדָּשׁ כָּאן שֶׁלֹּא בִשְׁעַת הַמִּקְדָּשׁ. וַאֲפִילוּ תֵּימַר כָּאן וְכָאן בִּשְׁעַת הַמִּקְדָּשׁ שְׁנֵי דְבָרִים רָבִים עַל אֶחָד וּמְבַטְּלִין אוֹתוֹ. רִבִּי יוֹסֵי בְשֵׁם רִבִּי לָעְזָר כְּשֵׁם שֶׁאֵין הָאִיסּוּרִים מְבַטְּלִין זֶה אֶת זֶה כָּךְ אֵין הַמִּצְוֹת מְבַטְּלוֹת זוֹ אֶת זוֹ.

"Hillel the elder used to make a sandwich of all three together[52]." Rebbi Joḥanan said, they disagreed with Hillel the elder[53]. But did not Rebbi Joḥanan make a sandwich of *mazzah* and bitter herbs[54]? There in Temple times, here not in Temple times[55]. Even if you say here and there in Temple times, two kinds are more than the third and cancel it.[56] Rebbi Yose in the name of Rebbi Eleazar[57]: Just as forbidden things do not cancel one another, so commanded things do not cancel one another.

52 Also quoted in the Babli, *Pesaḥim* 115a, *Zebaḥim* 79a. It is written about the Passover sacrifice (*Ex.* 12:8): "They shall eat the meat in that night, roasted on the fire, and *mazzot*, on bitter herbs they shall eat it." Similarly, it says about the second Passover (*Num.* 9:11): "They shall eat it on *mazzot* and bitter herbs." Hillel held that this means one has to eat of meat, *mazzah*, and bitter herbs together in one bite.

53 The Babli, *Pesaḥim* 115a, explains R. Joḥanan to say that in Temple times, when all three commandments are biblical, one has the choice to follow Hillel or eat the three ingredients separately. This cannot be the position of the Yerushalmi since then the discussion would not even start.

54 In the Babli, Rav Ashi (who lived after the compilation of the Yerushalmi) rules that one eats twice, once each item singly and once as a sandwich. Naturally, there cannot be any meat mentioned here; cf. the author's *The Scholar's Haggadah* (Northvale NJ, 1995) pp. 332-338. Since R. Joḥanan here is accused of inconsistency, he cannot have followed the custom established by Rav Ashi.

55 In the absence of a Temple, only *mazzah* is a biblical commandment since it is prescribed separately from any Temple service, *Ex.* 13:6-7. Bitter herbs are mentioned only as accessory to the sacrifice; therefore, today one eats bitter herbs purely as a remembrance of the Temple as rabbinical ordinance. R. Joḥanan must hold that a rabbinic ordinance cannot interfere with a biblical commandment. Therefore, it is possible to eat *mazzah* and bitter herbs together. But he holds that in Temple times, each of the three ingredients must be recognized by its taste. This position is the opposite of that of the Babli.

56 This explains the rejection of Hillel's position in Temple times. Since there are three biblical obligations, they cancel one another and none of them is fulfilled.

57 Babli *Zebaḥim* 79a. R. Eleazar supports R. Joḥanan's position against

R. Simeon ben Laqish and his making a sandwich in the manner of Hillel. He must hold that R. Johanan reports that most authorities of Hillel's time disagreed but he himself agrees.

רִבִּי יְהוֹשֻׁעַ דְּרוֹמִיָּא בָּעֵי עָשָׂה עִיסָּה מֵחֲמֵשֶׁת הַמִּינִין וְחָזַר וְעָשָׂה חָמֵשׁ עִיסִּיּוֹת מִמִּין אֶחָד וְעִירְבוֹ. חִיטִּין שֶׁבּוֹ מַהוּ שֶׁיְּבַטְּלוּ חִיטִּין שֶׁבּוֹ וּשְׂעוֹרִין שֶׁבּוֹ מַהוּ שֶׁיְּבַטְּלוּ שְׂעוֹרִין שֶׁבּוֹ. אָמַר רִבִּי חִיָּיא בַּר אָדָא לֹא כֵן אָמַר רִבִּי יוֹסֵי שְׁנֵי דְּבָרִים רַבִּים עַל אֶחָד וּמְבַטְּלִין אוֹתוֹ. לֹא צוּרְכָא דְּלֹא עָשָׂה חָמֵשׁ עִיסִּיּוֹת מֵחֲמִשָּׁה מִינִין וְעִירְבָן וְחָזַר וְעָשָׂה חָמֵשׁ עִיסִּיּוֹת מֵחֲמִשָּׁה וְלֹא עִירְבָן. חִיטִּים שֶׁכָּן מַהוּ שֶׁיְּבַטְּלוּ חִיטִּים שֶׁכָּן וּשְׂעוֹרִין שֶׁכָּן מַהוּ שֶׁיְּבַטְּלוּ שְׂעוֹרִין שֶׁכָּן.

Rebbi Joshua the Southerner asked: If somebody made dough from five kinds and then made five doughs from one kind each and put them together[58]. Does wheat in one cancel the wheat in the other and barley in one cancel barley in the other? Rebbi Ḥiyya bar Ada said, did not Rebbi Yose say that two kinds are more than the third and cancel it[59]? It is only needed for the following: If somebody made five doughs from one kind each and put them together[60] and again made five doughs from one kind each and did not put them together[61]. Does wheat in one cancel the wheat in the other and barley in one cancel barley in the other[62]?

58 This paragraph is rather cryptic and each commentator has his own scenario to make sense of the text; *Sefer Nir* even has two radically different interpretations. Therefore, the interpretation given here must be considered as tentative.

The first dough is made from five kinds of flour. But Mishnah 4:2 states that if dough is made from wheat and barley then all other kinds of grain add to the dough and cannot be treated separately (spelt adds to wheat and all except wheat add to barley). Therefore, the questions can be asked only about wheat and barley but not about the other three kinds. "Wheat" has to be interpreted as "wheat and spelt" and similarly for barley.

The first dough is subject only to rabbinic *ḥallah* as explained above, Notes 44-45. The other doughs are too small to be subject to *ḥallah* by themselves. If they are taken together, does the wheat in the "rabbinic" dough prevent the pure wheat dough to be counted as biblically obligated?

59 The answer to the preceding question is obviously "no".

60 The five doughs are all subject to *ḥallah*. Since they were obligated before being mixed, that obligation cannot go away, cf. Note 50.

61 These doughs are not subject to *ḥallah* before being put in contact with the large one.

62 The question is not answered but since the preceding question was answered in the negative, it is implied that this one also is answered in the negative.

וַאֲסוּרִין בֶּחָדָשׁ מִלִּפְנֵי הַפֶּסַח. אִית תַּנָּיֵי תַנֵּי מִלִּפְנֵי הַפֶּסַח אִית תַּנָּיֵי תַנֵּי מִלִּפְנֵי הָעוֹמֶר. מַאן דְּאָמַר מִלִּפְנֵי הַפֶּסַח מְסַייֵעַ לְרַבִּי יוֹחָנָן. מַאן דְּאָמַר מִלִּפְנֵי הָעוֹמֶר מְסַייֵעַ לְחִזְקִיָּה. דְּאָמַר רַבִּי יוֹנָה בְשֵׁם חִזְקִיָּה בִּשְׁעַת הַקָּרְבָּן הַקָּרְבָּן מַתִּיר שֶׁלֹּא בִשְׁעַת הַקָּרְבָּן הַיּוֹם מַתִּיר. רַבִּי יוֹסֵי בְשֵׁם חִזְקִיָּה בִּשְׁעַת הַקָּרְבָּן הַקָּרְבָּן מַתִּיר. מוֹדֵי חִזְקִיָּה שֶׁלֹּא בִשְׁעַת הַקָּרְבָּן הַיּוֹם מַתִּיר. רַבִּי יוֹחָנָן אָמַר בֵּין בִּשְׁעַת הַקָּרְבָּן בֵּין שֶׁלֹּא בִשְׁעַת הַקָּרְבָּן הַיּוֹם מַתִּיר.

"They are forbidden as new grain before Passover[3]." Some Tannaïm state: before Passover; some Tannaïm state: before the *'omer*[63]. He who said "before Passover" supports Rebbi Joḥanan; he who said "before the *'omer*" supports Ḥizqiah. As Rebbi Jonah said in the name of Ḥizqiah: If there is sacrifice[64], the sacrifice permits; if there is no sacrifice, the day permits. Rebbi Yose in the name of Ḥizqiah: If there is sacrifice, the sacrifice permits. Ḥizqiah agrees that if there is no sacrifice, the day permits[65]. Rebbi Joḥanan said: Whether there is sacrifice or there is no sacrifice, the day permits[66].

63 *Lev*. 23:14 reads: "Bread, parched and green grains you shall not eat until that day proper, until your bringing of your God's sacrifice, a permanent rule for your generations in all your dwelling places." *Sifra Emor, Parašah* 10(10) points out that the sacrifice must be the *'omer*, the sheaf of barley brought to the Temple. If it would refer to the accompanying sacrifice (v. 13), then "doing" would be used instead of "bringing (in from the outside)". Since the two conditions, the day proper (the morning light) and the *'omer*, are formulated in parallel, rather than sequential, it is not clear which one is determining when there is a Temple. If there is no Temple, the day is determining by default. The position of Ḥizqiah seems to follow the simple meaning of the verse. Contrary arguments are detailed in the next paragraphs.

64 When there is a Temple.

65 The difference between R. Jonah and R. Yose is purely in the formulation. According to R. Yose, if there is no sacrifice the meaning of the verse is clear and does not need rabbinic interpretation. In the Babli (*Menaḥot* 68a), the position of Ḥizqiah is that of his cousin Rav and of Samuel.

66 In the Babli, *Menaḥot* 5a/b, 68a, R. Joḥanan and R. Simeon ben Laqish.

אָמַר רִבִּי הִילָא טַעֲמָא דְרִבִּי יוֹחָנָן עַד עֶצֶם הַיּוֹם הַזֶּה מְלַמֵּד שֶׁהַיּוֹם מַתִּיר. יָכוֹל אֲפִילוּ בִשְׁעַת הַקָּרְבָּן תַּלְמוּד לוֹמַר עַד הֲבִיאֲכֶם אֶת קָרְבַּן אֱלֹהֵיכֶם. יָכוֹל הֲבָאָה מַמָּשׁ. תַּלְמוּד לוֹמַר עַד עֶצֶם הַיּוֹם הַזֶּה. הָא כֵיצַד טוֹל מִבֵּינְתַיִים זְמַן הֲבָאָה.

Rebbi Hila said: The reason of Rebbi Joḥanan is (*Lev*. 23:14): "until that day proper," teaches that the day permits. I could think, even if there is sacrifice? The verse says, "until your bringing of your God's sacrifice." I could think, until it is actually brought? The verse says, "until that day proper." How is that? Allow for the time needed for bringing[67].

67 Even R. Joḥanan will agree that new grain is not permitted early in the morning of the day after Passover. The Babli, *Menaḥot* 5a/b, holds that R,

Joḥanan and R. Simeon ben Laqish hold that dawn is "the day proper" and new grain is permitted immediately.

מוֹדֵי רִבִּי יוֹחָנָן בְּאִיסּוּר שֶׁהוּא אָסוּר. אִיסּוּרוֹ מַהוּ. רִבִּי יִרְמְיָה אָמַר אִיסּוּרוֹ דְּבַר תּוֹרָה. רִבִּי יוֹנָה וְרִבִּי יוֹסֵי תְּרֵיהוֹן אָמְרִין אִיסּוּרוֹ מִדִּבְרֵיהֶן. אָמַר רִבִּי יוֹסֵי מִילֵּיהוֹן דְּרַבָּנִין מְסַייְעִין לָן. דְּתַנִּינָן תַּמָּן אֵין מְבִיאִין מְנָחוֹת וּבִיכּוּרִים וּמִנְחַת בְּהֵמָה קוֹדֶם לָעוֹמֶר וְאִם הֵבִיא פָּסוּל. וְאָמַר (fol. 57c) רִבִּי יְהוֹשֻׁעַ דְּרוֹמִיָּא רִבִּי יוֹנָה רִבִּי אִימִּי בְּשֵׁם רִבִּי יוֹחָנָן לֹא שָׁנוּ אֶלָּא שְׁלֹשָׁה עָשָׂר וְאַרְבָּעָה עָשָׂר וַחֲמִשָּׁה עָשָׂר. הָא שִׁשָּׁה עָשָׂר עָבַר וְהֵבִיא כָּשֵׁר. אִין תֵּימַר אִיסּוּרוֹ דְּבַר תּוֹרָה הִיא לֹא שַׁנְייָא הִיא שְׁלֹשָׁה עָשָׂר הִיא אַרְבָּעָה עָשָׂר הִיא חֲמִשָּׁה עָשָׂר הִיא שִׁשָּׁה עָשָׂר עָבַר וְהֵבִיא פָּסוּל. וְעוֹד מִן הָדָא דְּאָמַר רִבִּי זְעִירָא עַל יְדֵי דְּרַב בַּר בֵּי דַּעְתּוֹן דִּבְנוֹי דְּרִבִּי חִייָה רֹבָה הוּא סָבַר דִּכְוָותְהוֹן אִין תֵּימַר אִיסּוּרוֹ דְּבַר תּוֹרָה רַב בַּר דַּעְתֵּיהּ דְּרִבִּי יוֹחָנָן.

Rebbi Joḥanan agrees that it is forbidden[68]. How is it forbidden? Rebbi Jeremiah said, it is forbidden from the Torah. Rebbi Jonah and Rebbi Yose both say, it is forbidden from their words[69]. Rebbi Yose said, the words of the rabbis support us, we have stated there[70]: "One may not bring cereal offerings[71], first fruits, and cereal offerings accompanying animal sacrifices[72] before the *'omer* and if he brought they are invalid." And Rebbi Joshua the Southerner, Rebbi Jonah, Rebbi Immi said in the name of Rebbi Joḥanan, they taught that only for the thirteenth, fourteenth, and fifteenth[73]. Therefore, on the sixteenth if he transgressed and brought, it is acceptable. If you would say it is forbidden from the Torah there should be no difference; whether he brought on the thirteenth, fourteenth, fifteenth, or sixteenth, if he transgressed and brought, it should be invalid. In addition from the following, as Rebbi Zeïra said: Since Rav grew up with the opinions of the sons of the elder

Rebbi Ḥiyya[74], he holds with them. If you say that it is forbidden from the Torah, he would follow[75] Rebbi Joḥanan!

68 Since the verse stated two conditions for permission to use new grain and in Temple times at dawn of the 16th of Nisan only one condition is satisfied, he holds that new grain still is forbidden, but not as a criminal act, until after the *'omer* was brought.

69 As rabbinic decree.

70 Mishnah *Menaḥot* 6:10, Babli *Menaḥot* 68b.

71 This can only be the cereal offering of the suspected wife (*Num.* 5:15), which is barley flour. All other cereal offerings are of wheat flour and these cannot be from new harvest until Pentecost (Rashi).

72 These are always from wheat flour and cannot be from new grain even after the *'omer*. They are mentioned here only because of the next sentence in the Mishnah, not quoted here, that they may not be brought from new wheat before Pentecost but if brought are not invalid.

73 Jehudah and Ḥizqiah, his cousins and fellow students of their father.

74 Of Nisan.

75 Also follow. There would be no disagreement left.

וְהָתַנִּינָן מִשֶּׁחָרַב בֵּית הַמִּקְדָּשׁ הִתְקִין רַבָּן יוֹחָנָן בֶּן זַכַּיי שֶׁיְּהֵא יוֹם הֶנֶף כּוּלּוֹ אָסוּר. אִין תֵּימַר אִיסּוּרוֹ אִיסּוּר תּוֹרָה נִיחָא אִין תֵּימַר אִיסּוּרוֹ מִדִּבְרֵיהֶן יֵשׁ תַּקָּנָה אַחַר תַּקָּנָה. אָמַר רִבִּי יוֹסֵי בֵּי רִבִּי בּוּן מִפְּנֵי הָרְחוֹקִין.

Did we not state[76]: "When the Temple was destroyed, Rabban Joḥanan ben Zakkai instituted that the entire day of elevation[77] should be forbidden." If you say it is forbidden from the Torah, it is fine[78]. If you say it is forbidden from their words, is there an institution after an institution[79]? Rebbi Yose bar Abun said, because of those far away[80].

76 Mishnah *Menaḥot* 6(10):5; *Sifra Emor Parašah* 10(10); cf. Mishnah *Sukkah* 3:13, *Roš Haššanah* 4:3.

77 The day of bringing the *'omer*. The language is from *Lev.* 23:11: "He shall *elevate* the sheaf before the

Eternal for acceptance in your behalf; on the day after the Sabbath the Cohen shall *elevate* it."

78 As the Babli, *Menaḥot* 68b, puts it: Maybe the Temple will be rebuilt instantaneously by a miracle on the second day of Passover and then new grain will be forbidden by biblical law until the *'omer* can be brought.

79 As a matter of principle, there should be no "fence" to guard against infringements of rabbinical decrees.

80 They will not know when the *'omer* was presented and, since in classical times longitudes could not be determined with any degree of confidence, were not able to convert Jerusalem local time into their own local time.

רִבִּי יִרְמְיָה בְשֵׁם רִבִּי חִייָא בֵּין בִּשְׁעַת הַקָּרְבָּן בֵּין שֶׁלֹּא בִשְׁעַת הַקָּרְבָּן הַיּוֹם מַתִּיר. אָמַר רִבִּי הוּנָא מַתְנִיתָא דְחִזְקִיָּה פְלִיגָא עָלוֹי. עַד עֶצֶם הַיּוֹם הַזֶּה מְלַמֵּד שֶׁהַיּוֹם מַתִּיר. יָכוֹל אֲפִילוּ בִשְׁעַת הַקָּרְבָּן תַּלְמוּד לוֹמַר עַד הֲבִיאֲכֶם אֶת קָרְבַּן אֱלֹהֵיכֶם. וְתַנִּינָן מִשֶּׁחָרַב בֵּית הַמִּקְדָּשׁ הִתְקִין רַבָּן יוֹחָנָן שֶׁיְּהֵא יוֹם הֶנֶף כּוּלּוֹ אָסוּר. אָמַר רִבִּי יוֹנָה אִיתְּתָבַת קוֹמֵי רִבִּי יִרְמְיָה וְאָמַר אֵין יִסְבּוֹר חִזְקִיָּה כְּרִבִּי יוּדָה. דְּרִבִּי יוּדָה אָמַר אָמַר וַהֲלֹא מִן הַתּוֹרָה אָסוּר.

Rebbi Jeremiah in the name of Rebbi Ḥiyya: Whether there is sacrifice or there is no sacrifice, the day permits. Rebbi Huna said, a *baraita* of Ḥizqiah disagrees with him (*Lev.* 23:14): "Until that day proper," which teaches that the day permits. I could think, even if there is sacrifice? The verse says, "until your bringing of your God's sacrifice." And we have stated: "When the Temple was destroyed, Rabban Joḥanan [ben Zakkai] instituted that the entire day of elevation should be forbidden." Rebbi Jonah said, this objection came before Rebbi Jeremiah[81] and he said, possibly Ḥizqiah thinks like Rebbi Jehudah[82], since Rebbi Jehudah said it is forbidden by the Torah.

81 The objection from the previous paragraph that the institution of Rabban Joḥanan makes sense only if the prohibition of new grain on the day of the *'omer* is biblical.

82 Mishnah *Menaḥot* 6(10):5; *Sifra Emor Parašah* 10(10). R. Jehudah interprets **בעצם היום הזה** as: "including the essence of the day", meaning the entire day in the absence of the Temple (Rashi). The Babli, *Menaḥot* 68b, holds that Rabban Joḥanan agrees with R. Jehudah and, therefore, he did not institute a rabbinic decree but decreed the correct interpretation of the biblical law.

תַּמָּן חָשִׁין לְצוֹמָא רַבָּא תְּרֵין יוֹמִין. אָמַר לוֹן רַב חִסְדָּא לָמָּה אַתֶּם מַכְנִיסִין עַצְמֵיכֶם לְמִסְפָּק הַזֶּה הַמְּרוּבֶּה חֲזָקָה שֶׁאֵין בֵּית דִּין מִתְעַצְּלִין. אָבוּהּ דְּרִבִּי[83] שְׁמוּאֵל בַּר רַב יִצְחָק חָשׁ עַל גַּרְמֵיהּ וְצָם תְּרֵין יוֹמִין אִפְסַק כְּרוּכָה וּדְמָךְ.

There, they were apprehensive to have the great fast for two days[84]. Rav Ḥisda said to them, why do you bring yourselves into that great uncertainty[85]. One may trust that the Court is never lazy[86]. The father of Rebbi Samuel bar Rav Isaac was apprehensive for himself and fasted two days; his intestines split and he died.

83 Reading of the parallel text in *Roš Haššanah* 1:4 (fol. 57b). Text here: **בר אבוי** "son of his father". The paragraph might have been inserted here to indicate that the "16th of Nisan" to be counted in the diaspora is the 17th.

84 Since all holidays in the diaspora are two days, originally because the exact calendar dates could not quickly be transmitted from the Synhedrion to the diaspora. The Babli, *Roš Haššanah* 21a, reports that some rabbis in Babylonia fasted two consecutive days; the same is reported from early Medieval German rabbis.

85 The "great uncertainty" is what in the Babli is called "possible danger to one's life".

86 Since up to now it never happened that the first of Tishre was not the 30th of Elul (cf. *Ševiït* 10:2, p. 639), if it should happen the Synhedrion would immediately have sent signals to that effect.

אִם הִשְׁרִישׁוּ קוֹדֶם לָעוֹמֶר הָעוֹמֶר מַתִּיר. רִבִּי יוֹנָה אָמַר קוֹדֶם לַהֲבָאָה. רִבִּי יוֹסֵי אָמַר קוֹדֶם לִקְצִירָה. אָמַר רִבִּי יוֹנָה הֲבָאָה מַתֶּרֶת לַהֲבָאָה הַקְּצִירָה מַתֶּרֶת לִקְצִירָה. אָמַר רִבִּי יוֹסֵי קְצִירָה מַתֶּרֶת הֲבָאָה וּקְצִירָה. לְפוּם כֵּן רִבִּי יוֹסֵי חַוֵי בָהּ קָצַר לָרַבִּים וְנִטְמָא חָזַר הַיָּחִיד לְאִיסּוּרוֹ.

"If they formed roots before the *'omer*, the *'omer* permits them." Rebbi Jonah said, before presentation[87]. Rebbi Yose said, before cutting. Rebbi Jonah said, presentation permits bringing[88], cutting permits to cut. Rebbi Yose said, cutting permits bringing and cutting. Therefore, Rebbi Yose gave his opinion: If he cut for the public and it became impure, private persons are again forbidden.

87 The summer grain must have formed roots before the presentation of the *'omer* in the Temple. Rebbi Yose requires that the roots already be formed at the time of the harvesting of the barley sheaf, usually on the preceding evening.

The Babli, *Menahot* 70b, quotes this tradition and the switched one in the inverse order of the Yerushalmi.

88 He agrees that a private person may start harvesting the moment the sheaf has been cut for the Temple. Though usually one may not perform agricultural work on the intermediate days of a holiday, cutting new grain for the enjoyment of the holiday is permitted since it was impossible to do so before the holiday. But the Temple will not accept a barley cereal offering from new grain before the presentation of the *'omer*. If the barley cut for the Temple became impure before presentation, it cannot be used and its cutting retroactively is invalid. {While the barley and its flour never became wetted, putting the flour in a Temple vessel prepares it for impurity.}

רִבִּי יוֹנָה אָמַר קוֹדֶם לִקְצִירָה. רִבִּי יוֹסֵי אָמַר קוֹדֶם לַהֲבָאָה. אָמַר רִבִּי יוֹנָה מִילְתֵיהּ דְּכַהֲנָא מְסַייְעָא לִי דְּכַהֲנָא אָמַר וְאִם תַּקְרִיב מִנְחַת בִּיכּוּרִים לַיי. זוֹ בִיכִּירָה הָאַחֶרֶת לֹא בִיכִּירָה. הַגַּע עַצְמָךְ אֲפִילוּ עֲשָׂבִים אֲפִילוּ הִשְׁרָשָׁה הָעוֹמֶר בָּא וּמַתִּיר. וְלֹא קוֹדֶם לִקְצִירָה אֲנָן קַייָמִין. וְעוֹד מִן הָדָא דְתַנֵּי הַמְנַכֵּשׁ

בִּשְׁלֹשָׁה עָשָׂר וְנִתְלַשׁ הַקֶּלַח בְּיָדוֹ הֲרֵי זֶה שׁוֹתְלוֹ בְּמָקוֹם הַטִּינָא אֲבָל לֹא בְּמָקוֹם הַגְּרִיד. הֲרֵי יֵשׁ כָּאן שְׁלֹשָׁה עָשָׂר וְאַרְבָּעָה עָשָׂר וַחֲמִשָּׁה עָשָׂר וּמִקְצַת הַיּוֹם כְּכוּלּוֹ.

Rebbi Jonah said, before presentation. Rebbi Yose said, before cutting. Rebbi Jonah said, Cahana's word supports me, as Cahana said (*Lev.* 214): "If you bring a cereal gift of first fruits[89] to the Eternal." This one is first fruit, the others are not first fruit. Think of it, even if it were only grasses or only roots the *'omer* comes and permits it. Do we not hold before cutting[90]? In addition, from the following which was stated[91]: "If somebody weeds on the thirteenth and a stalk remains in his hand, he should replant it in a moist spot but not a dry one." Here you have the 13th, the 14th, the 15th, and part of a day is counted as whole[92].

89 This is the sheaf of barley, cf. Notes 35, 63.

90 As usual, the argument is from a part of the verse which is not quoted explicitly: "If you bring a cereal gift of first fruits to the Eternal; milky white roasted in fire, farina from soft kernels you should bring as cereal offering to your God." The verse prescribes that the barley after cutting must be threshed, roasted, and milled before presentation. But the expression "milky white" specifies which plants are sufficiently ripened to be candidates for cutting. Therefore, the verse must speak of the time of cutting.

91 In the Babli (*Pesaḥim* 55a), the *baraita* is in the name of R. Jehudah who states in Mishnah *Ševiït* 2:6 that any transplant which does not form roots in three days will not survive.

92 If the action of the *'omer* would be counted from presentation, then replanting on the 14th would still leave three days, part of 14th, 15th, part of 16th, to form a root. Since the *baraita* specifies the 13th as last day for replanting, it follows that the operative time of the *'omer* is early in the night of the 16th, the time of cutting the barley.

אָמַר רִבִּי יוֹסֵי מִילְתֵיהּ דְּרִבִּי אֲבִינָּא מְסַייְעָא לִי דְּאָמַר רִבִּי אֲבִינָּא תִּיפְתָּר כְּהָדָא מַתְנִיתָא בְּמָקוֹם שֶׁנָּהֲגוּ שֶׁלֹּא לַעֲשׂוֹת מְלָאכָה בְּאַרְבָּעָה עָשָׂר אֲבָל בְּמָקוֹם שֶׁנָּהֲגוּ לַעֲשׂוֹת מְלָאכָה בְּאַרְבָּעָה עָשָׂר לֹא בְּתָלוּשׁ שֶׁמָּא בִּמְחוּבָּר. אַשְׁכַּח תַּנֵּי מָקוֹם שֶׁנָּהֲגוּ לַעֲשׂוֹת מְלָאכָה בְּתָלוּשׁ עוֹשִׂין אֲפִילוּ בִּמְחוּבָּר.

Rebbi Yose said, the word of Rebbi Abinna supports me, since Rebbi Abinna said, explain it[93] following this *baraita*: "In a place where one does not usually work on the 14th, but not in a place where one is used to work on the 14th." If it is cut; maybe also when it is standing[94]? It was found stated[95]: "In a place where people are used to work on cut produce, one may work even on standing grain."

93 Mishnah *Pesaḥim* 4:1 states: "In a place where one is used to work in the morning of the 14th [of Nisan], one may work; in a place where one is not used to work in the morning of the 14th [of Nisan], one may not work." If work on the 14th is forbidden, it is obvious that the 13th is the last day for weeding and the *baraita* quoted in the preceding paragraph does not prove anything about the *'omer*. Since it is stated that one may replant on the 14th, it follows that only the presentation of the *'omer* is relevant.

94 An objection by R. Jonah. Maybe agricultural work, while permitted on the morning of the 14th, is restricted.

95 Tosephta *Pesaḥim* 3:18: "In a place where one is used to work on standing grain on the 14th until noon, one may do so."

וְאִם לֹא אֲסוּרִין עַד שֶׁיָּבוֹא הָעוֹמֶר הַבָּא. רִבִּי לָעְזָר שָׁאַל מַהוּ שֶׁיָּבִיא הָעוֹמֶר מֵהֶן. אֵיפְשָׁר לוֹמַר חָדָשׁ וְיָשָׁן אֵין תּוֹרְמִין וּמְעַשְּׂרִין מִזֶּה עַל זֶה. וְאַתְּ אָמַר הָכֵין. הָתִיבוּן הֲרֵי שְׁאָר הַמִּינִין הֲרֵי הֵן תְּלוּיִין בָּעוֹמֶר וְאֵין הָעוֹמֶר בָּא מֵהֶן. לֹא אִם אָמַרְתָּ בִּשְׁאָר הַמִּינִין שֶׁלֹּא כָשְׁרוּ לְמִנְחַת הָעוֹמֶר תֹּאמַר בִּשְׂעוֹרִין שֶׁכָּשְׁרוּ לְמִנְחַת הָעוֹמֶר. חֲבֵרַייָא בְשֵׁם רִבִּי לָעְזָר רֵאשִׁית קְצִירְךָ וְלֹא סוֹף קְצִירְךָ. רִבִּי זְעִירָא בְשֵׁם רִבִּי לָעְזָר בִּיכּוּרִין אֵין אֵלֶּה בִּיכּוּרִין. מַה נְפַק

מִבֵּינֵיהוֹן. עָבַר וְהֵבִיא. עַל דַּעְתְּהוֹן דַּחֲבֵרַיָּא פָּסוּל. עַל דַּעְתֵּיהּ דְּרִבִּי זְעִירָא כָּשֵׁר. דִּבְרֵי חֲכָמִים רִבִּי יוֹסֵי בֵּירִבִּי בּוּן רִבִּי חִייָה בְּשֵׁם רָבִין בַּר חִייָה וְהֵן שֶׁהֵבִיאוּ שְׁלִישׁ לִפְנֵי רֹאשׁ הַשָּׁנָה. אֲבָל הֵבִיאוּ שְׁלִישׁ לְאַחַר רֹאשׁ הַשָּׁנָה הָעוֹמֶר בָּא מֵהֶן.

"Otherwise, they are forbidden until the next *'omer*." Rebbi Eleazar asked, may they[96] be used to bring [next year's] *'omer*? It is impossible to say so: Old and new produce, one does not give heave and tithe from one for the other, and you say so[97]? They objected, are there not the other kinds[98] which are dependent on the *'omer* but cannot be used for the *'omer*? No, what you said is for the other kinds which are never usable for the *'omer*; what can you say about barley which can be used for the *'omer*? The colleagues in the name of Rebbi Eleazar: (*Lev.* 23:10) "The first of your harvest," not the last of your harvest. Rebbi Zeïra in the name of Rebbi Eleazar: (*Lev.* 2:14) "First fruits," these are not first fruits. What is the difference between them? If somebody transgressed and brought. In the opinion of the colleagues it is disqualified. In the opinion of Rebbi Zeïra it is acceptable[99]. The words of the Sages, Rebbi Yose ben Rebbi Abun in the name of Rabin bar Ḥiyya[100] That is only if it was one third ripe before New Year's Day. But if it only was one third ripe after New Year's Day, the *'omer* comes from it.

96 If it is barley.

97 In this version, nothing sown before the New Year can be used for the *'omer*.

98 All grains which are not barley.

99 It is explained in *Sifra Wayyiqra Pereq* 15(1) that "first fruits" is a requirement that is waived if no ripe barley is found in the fields by Passover. Since it can be disregarded under certain circumstances this cannot be an absolute requirement.

100 He is R. Abin bar Ḥiyya, student of R. Zeïra.

(fol. 57a) **משנה ב**: הָאוֹכֵל מֵהֶן כְּזַיִת מַצָּה בַּפֶּסַח יָצָא יְדֵי חוֹבָתוֹ. כְּזַיִת חָמֵץ חַיָּב בְּהִיכָּרֵת. נִתְעָרֵב אֶחָד מֵהֶן בְּכָל־הַמִּינִין הֲרֵי זֶה עוֹבֵר בַּפֶּסַח. הַנּוֹדֵר מִן הַפַּת וּמִן הַתְּבוּאָה אָסוּר בָּהֶן דִּבְרֵי רַבִּי מֵאִיר. וַחֲכָמִים אוֹמְרִים הַנּוֹדֵר מִן הַדָּגָן אֵינוֹ אָסוּר אֶלָּא מֵהֶן. וְחַיָּבִין בַּחַלָּה וּבְמַעְשְׂרוֹת.

Mishnah 2: If somebody eats the volume of an olive of *mazzah* from them[101] on Passover[102], he did his duty, the volume of an olive of leavened [bread], he is subject to being cut off[103]. If one of them is mixed with other kinds[104] one transgresses on Passover. He who takes a vow not to use bread or produce[105] is forbidden them, the words of Rebbi Meïr; but the Sages say, he who takes a vow not to use flour is only forbidden these[106]. They are subject to *hallah* and tithes[107].

101 The five kinds mentioned in Mishnah 1.

102 More exactly, the first night of the holiday as spelled out in *Ex.* 12:18: "In the evening you have to eat *mazzah*." The remaining days of Passover, leavened bread is forbidden but *mazzah* is not required; one might live without bread.

103 *Ex.* 12:19. The punishment of "being cut off" is divine punishment, not of the earthly court.

104 It is sinful to keep on Passover any leavened mixture made from flour of one of the five kinds mixed with other edible material.

105 In the talmudic vocabulary, תבואה only means "grain." But as shown in Halakhah 3, in biblical language the word means "any agricultural yield."

106 This is a shortened version of Mishnah *Nedarim* 7:2: "He who takes a vow not to use flour is forbidden even dry Egyptian bean, the words of R. Meïr; but the Sages say, he is only forbidden the five kinds. R. Meïr says, he who takes a vow not to use grain is forbidden only the five kinds."

107 As a matter of biblical law.

(fol. 57c) **הלכה ב**: אָמַר רִבִּי יַעֲקֹב בַּר זַבְדִּי זֹאת אוֹמֶרֶת שֶׁלּוֹקִין עַל חַלָּתָן דְּבַר תּוֹרָה. רִבִּי יִרְמְיָה בְּשֵׁם רִבִּי חִיָּיה בַּר וָוא תִּיפְתָּר שֶׁאָכַל כְּזַיִת מִזֶּה וּכְזַיִת מִזֶּה.

אָמַר רִבִּי יוֹסֵי אֲפִילוּ תֵּימַר כְּזַיִת מִכּוּלְּהוֹן. שַׁנְייָא הִיא שֶׁכּוּלְּהֹן לְשֵׁם חָמֵץ. מִחְלְפָה שִׁיטָּתֵיהּ דְּרִבִּי יוֹסֵי. תַּמָּן הוּא אָמַר שְׁנֵי דְבָרִים רָבִים עַל אֶחָד וּמְבַטְּלִין אוֹתוֹ וְהָכָא הוּא אָמַר הָכֵין. אָמַר רִבִּי יוֹסֵי בֵּירִבִּי בוּן כֵּינִי מַתְנִיתָא אִי כְּזַיִת מִזֶּה וּכְזַיִת מִזֶּה.

Halakhah 2: Rebbi Jacob bar Zavdi said, this means that one whips because of their *ḥallah* as a word of the Torah[108]. Rebbi Jeremiah in the name of Rebbi Ḥiyya bar Abba, explain it if it contains the volume of an olive of any one of them. Rebbi Yose said, you might even say one volume of an olive of all of them. It is different since the category of "leavened" applies to all of them. The argument of Rebbi Yose seems inverted. There[51], he says two kinds are more than the third and cancel it; here, he says so! Rebbi Yose ben Rebbi Abun said, so is the Mishnah: "Either the volume of an olive from this one or from another.[109]"

108 The language of the Mishnah, "the volume of an olive of *mazzah* from them", seems to mean that a *mazzah* made of mixed dough is acceptable on Passover and subject to *ḥallah* by biblical decree. This contradicts R. Simeon ben Laqish (Note 51) who held that different kinds, each of which measures less than the necessary volume, cannot be taken together to be subject to biblical *ḥallah*.

109 The argument is accepted; the Mishnah permits mixed *mazzah* on Passover only if at least one kind of grain is present in a sufficient amount for an acceptable *mazzah* by itself.

חלכה ג: הָא הַנּוֹדֵר מִן הַפַּת וּמִן הַתְּבוּאָה אָסוּר בַּכֹּל כְּרַבָּנָן. רִבִּי חִיָּיה בְשֵׁם רִבִּי יוֹחָנָן כֵּינִי מַתְנִיתָא הַנּוֹדֵר מִן הַדָּגָן אֵינוֹ אָסוּר אֶלָּא מֵהֶם. מַה נָן קַייְמִין אִם בְּאוֹמֵר פַּת תּוֹרָה מֵעַתָּה אַף הָאוֹמֵר תְּבוּאָה תוֹרָה יְהֵא אָסוּר בַּכֹּל דִּכְתִיב וּתְבוּאַת הַכָּרֶם. אִי בְּאוֹמֵר פַּת סְתָם אֵין לָךְ קָרוּי פַּת סְתָם אֶלָּא חִיטִּין וְשְׂעוֹרִין בִּלְבַד. אָמַר רִבִּי יוֹסֶה קִייַמְתִּיהָ בְּמָקוֹם שֶׁאוֹכְלִין פַּת כֹּל. אֵין לָךְ קָרוּי פַּת סְתָם אֶלָּא חֲמֶשֶׁת הַמִּינִין בִּלְבַד.

Halakhah 3: [110]Therefore, is he who makes a vow not to use bread or produce forbidden everything[111] according to the rabbis? Rebbi Ḥiyya in the name of Rebbi Joḥanan, so is the Mishnah: "He who makes a vow not to use flour is only forbidden these." How do we hold? If he uses "bread" in the biblical sense then also if he says "produce" it is meant in the biblical sense. He should be forbidden everything since it is written (*Deut.* 22:9): "The produce of the vineyard." If he simply says "bread"; only from wheat or barley is it simply called "bread"[112]. Rebbi Yose said, I confirmed it, at a place where one eats bread from all [kinds], only from the five kinds it is simply called "bread".

110 Here begins the discussion of the statement about vows.

111 Everything vegetal.

112 Spelt or oatmeal bread would have to be called spelt-bread or oatmeal-bread buit never "bread" without a qualifier.

(fol. 57a) **משנה ג**: אֵילוּ חַיָּבִין בַּחַלָּה וּפְטוּרִין מִן הַמַּעְשְׂרוֹת. הַלֶּקֶט הַשִּׁכְחָה וְהַפֵּיאָה וְהַהֶבְקֵר וּמַעֲשֵׂר רִאשׁוֹן שֶׁנִּיטְּלָה תְרוּמָתוֹ וּמַעֲשֵׂר שֵׁנִי וְהֶקְדֵּשׁ שֶׁנִּפְדּוּ וּמוֹתַר הָעוֹמֶר וּתְבוּאָה שֶׁלֹּא הֵבִיאָה שְׁלִישׁ. רִבִּי לְעָזָר אוֹמֵר תְּבוּאָה שֶׁלֹּא הֵבִיאָה שְׁלִישׁ פְּטוּרָה מִן הַחַלָּה.

Mishnah 3: The following are subject to *ḥallah* but exempt from tithes: Gleanings, forgotten sheaves, and *peah*[113], as well as abandoned property[114], First tithe of which its heave had been taken[115], second tithe and dedicated [grain] that were redeemed[116], the excess of the *'omer*[117], and grain not yet one-third ripe[118]. Rebbi Eleazar said, grain not yet one-third ripe is exempt from *ḥallah*.

113 Cf. *Peah* 4, Note 97. Since the poor may sell the grain collected as gleanings, etc., the flour from these grains is subject to all rules of regularly harvested grain. The detailed arguments for exemption are in *Ma'serot* 1, Notes 18-23.

114 Cf. *Peah* 6, Note 1, for the exemption from heave and tithes.

115 This is purely profane; there is no reason why it should not be subject to *ḥallah*. The statement which is needed is that flour made from first tithe taken before the great heave becomes profane upon separation of the heave of the tithe (*its* heave, in the language of the Mishnah) without any great heave.

116 But unredeemed second tithe in Jerusalem is free from *ḥallah* for R. Meïr who holds that it is Heaven's property; cf. *Ma'aser Šeni* 4, Note 67.

117 The flour from the barley cut for the *'omer* presentation which was not needed in the Temple. This was redeemed and sold by the Temple as profane.

118 According to the majority opinion, dough made from flour of green kernels, not yet one-third ripe, can become leavened and therefore is subject to *ḥallah*.; cf. Notes 15-20.

(fol. 57c) **הלכה ד**: רִבִּי הוֹשַׁעְיָה שָׁאַל לְכַהֲנָא מְנַיִין שֶׁהֵן חַייָבִין בַּחַלָּה וּפְטוּרִין מִן הַמַּעְשְׂרוֹת. אָמַר לֵיהּ לֹא תֵימַר לִי תָּרִימוּ וְכֵן תָּרִימוּ. חָזַר וְאָמַר מֵאַרְבַּע עֶשְׂרֵה. מַה אַרְבַּע עֶשְׂרֵה חַייָבִין בַּחַלָּה וּפְטוּרִין מִן הַמַּעְשְׂרוֹת אַף אֵילּוּ חַייָבִין בַּחַלָּה וּפְטוּרִין מִן הַמַּעְשְׂרוֹת.

Halakhah 4: Rebbi Hoshaiah asked Cahana: From where that these are subject to *ḥallah* but exempt from tithes? He said to him, do not tell me (*Num.* 15:19): "you shall lift"; (*v.* 20) "so you shall lift."[119] He came back and said, from 14 [years][120]. Just as in the 14 years they were subject to *ḥallah* but exempt from tithes, so these are subject to *ḥallah* but exempt from tithes.

119 "It shall be when you eat from the bread of the Land, *you shall lift* a heave for the Eternal. The first of your doughs, *ḥallah* you shall lift as heave, as the heave of the threshing floor so *you shall lift it*." At first

glance, the second verse seems to imply that anything exempt from great heave should be exempt from *ḥallah*. Cahana assumes that R. Hoshaiah's question was, why should the items enumerated in the Mishnah ever be subject to *ḥallah*?

120 The years of conquest and distribution under Joshua, when they ate *from the bread of the Land* but did not harvest themselves. Cf. *Seder Olam* 11 [in the author's edition (Northvale NJ 1998), pp. 116-117, Note 2]; *'Orlah* 1:2, Note 55.

רִבִּי יוֹחָנָן בְּשֵׁם רִבִּי יַנַּאי זֶה אֶחָד מִשְּׁלֹשָׁה מִקְרִיּוֹת שֶׁהֵן מְחוּוָרִין בַּתּוֹרָה. וּבָא הַלֵּוִי כִּי אֵין לוֹ חֵלֶק וְנַחֲלָה עִמָּךְ מָה שֶׁיֵּשׁ לָךְ וְאֵין לוֹ אַתְּ חַייָב לִיתֵּן לוֹ. יָצָא הֶבְקֵר שֶׁיָּדָךְ וְיָדוֹ שָׁוִין בּוֹ. הִיא לֶקֶט הִיא שִׁכְחָה הִיא פֵּאָה הִיא הֶבְקֵר.

[121]Rebbi Johanan in the name of Rebbi Yannai: This is one of three well-explained verses in the Torah (*Deut.* 14:27): "The Levite shall come, for he has neither part nor inheritance with you." You must give him from what you have but he has not. This excludes ownerless property where your and his hands are equal. There is no difference between gleanings, forgotten sheaves, *peah*[122], and abandoned property.

121 *Terumot* 1, Note 159.

122 All poor are entitled to these, irrespective of their tribal affiliation.

מַעֲשֵׂר רִאשׁוֹן שֶׁנִּטְּלָה תְרוּמָתוֹ וּמִכֵּיוָן שֶׁנִּטְּלָה תְרוּמָתוֹ לֹא כְחוּלִין הוּא. תִּיפְתָּר שֶׁהִקְדִּימוֹ בַשִּׁיבֳּלִין. דְּאָמַר רִבִּי אַבָּהוּ בְשֵׁם רִבִּי שִׁמְעוֹן בֶּן לָקִישׁ מַעֲשֵׂר רִאשׁוֹן שֶׁהִקְדִּימוֹ בַשִּׁיבֳּלִין פָּטוּר מִתְּרוּמָה גְדוֹלָה. אָמַר רִבִּי יוֹסֵי כְּתִיב אֶת כָּל־חֶלְבּוֹ אֶת מִקְדְּשׁוֹ מִמֶּנּוּ לֹא חֶלְבּוֹ וְחֵלֶב חֲבֵירוֹ. אָמַר רִבִּי יוֹסֵי כְּתִיב וַהֲרֵמוֹתֶם מִמֶּנּוּ אֶת תְּרוּמַת יי מַעֲשֵׂר מִן הַמַּעֲשֵׂר וְלֹא תְרוּמָה וּמַעֲשֵׂר מִן הַמַּעֲשֵׂר. בְּשֶׁמֵּירַח וְאַחַר כָּךְ הִפְרִישׁ תְּרוּמַת מַעֲשֵׂר שֶׁבּוֹ. אֲבָל אִם הִפְרִישׁ תְּרוּמַת מַעֲשֵׂר וְאַחַר כָּךְ מֵירְחוֹ לֹא בְדָא. כְּשֶׁהִפְרִישׁ מִמֶּנּוּ עָלָיו אֲבָל אִם הִפְרִישׁ מִמָּקוֹם אַחֵר לֹא בְדָא.

"First tithe of which its heave had been taken;" since its heave was taken, is it not like profane? Explain it if he gave it early, from ears, as Rebbi Abbahu said in the name of Rebbi Simeon ben Laqish: First tithe given early, from ears, is free from [the obligation of] great heave[123]. Rebbi Yose said, it is written[124] (*Num.* 18:29): "From all its best, the holy part from it;" not its best and the best of another person. Rebbi Yose said, it is written (*Num.* 18:26): "You shall lift from it the heave of the Eternal, tithe of the tithe," but not heave and tithe from the tithe. When he[125] made a heap and then gave its heave of the tithe. But if he gave heave of the tithe and then made a heap[126] this does not apply. When he gave from itself for it, but if he gave from another place[127] this does not apply.

123 Babli *Berakhot* 47a, *Šabbat* 127b, *Eruvin* 31b, *Pesaḥim* 35b, *Beẓah* 13b, in the name of R. Simeon ben Laqish; Yerushalmi *Bikkurim* 2:3, 2:4 (fol. 65a).

124 The two verses quoted are written about heave of the tithe. The MT of 18:28 reads מִכָּל־חֶלְבּוֹ.

125 The Levite who threshed the ears given to him as tithe.

126 This starts the obligation of heave which then must be given. In the Babli, this is an observation ascribed to Abbaye.

127 This is permitted but then it is not "from it"; the verses do not apply.

מַעֲשֵׂר שֵׁנִי וְהֶקְדֵּשׁ שֶׁנִּפְדּוּ. רִבִּי זְעִירָא רִבִּי יוֹסֵי רִבִּי חָמָא בַּר עוּקְבָּא רִבִּי הִלֵּל בֶּן הֶלֵיס מָטֵי בָהּ בְּשֵׁם רִבִּי יוּדָה דְּמִן הָדָא. מַעֲשֵׂר רִאשׁוֹן שֶׁהִקְדִּימוֹ בַשִּׁיבּוֹלִין (fol. 57d) פָּטוּר מִתְּרוּמָה גְדוֹלָה.

"Second Tithe and dedicated [grain] that were redeemed[116]". Rebbi Zeïra, Rebbi Assi, Rebbi Ḥama bar Uqba, Rebbi Hillel ben Vales[128] argued in the name of Rebbi Jehudah from the following: "First tithe given early, from ears, is free from [the obligation of] great heave"[129].

128 The name appears as הליס, אליס, ולס.

129 The Mishnah states that redeemed second tithe is obligated for *ḥallah* but free from tithe. How can tithe be free from tithe? It must be that it is not free from tithe but from heave which is subsumed under the name of tithes.

רִבִּי יוֹנָה בָּעֵי כְּמָאן דְּאָמַר אֵינוֹ כִנְכָסָיו בְּרַם כְּמָאן דְּאָמַר כִּנְכָסָיו הוּא חַיָּב. אָמַר לֵיהּ אוֹף אֲנָא סָבַר כֵּן הֲוֵי מַעֲשֵׂר שֵׁינִי הוֹאִיל וְכָל־עַמָּא מוֹדֵיי שֶׁהוּא כִנְכָסָיו חַיָּב. הֲוֵי פְלִיגָא הוּא. מָאן דְּאָמַר חַיָּב אֲפִילוּ תְרוּמָה שֶׁבּוֹ חַיֶּיבֶת. מָאן דְּאָמַר פָּטוּר אֲפִילוּ חוּלִין שֶׁבּוֹ פְטוּרִין.

Rebbi Jonah asked: Following him who holds that it is not like his property[116]; but following him who holds it is like his property he must be obligated[130]. He[131] said to him, I also am of this opinion. For second tithe, since everybody agrees that it is like his property, he is obligated, there is a disagreement. For him who holds it is obligated[132], even its heave is obligated. For him who holds it is free[133], even its profane part is free.

130 If second tithe is the farmer's property even before redemption, then redemption should make no difference in the obligation of *ḥallah*. This means that the Mishnah is R. Meïr's; it cannot follow R. Jehudah.

131 An unidentified person; probably it is R. Jonah's usual partner R. Yose.

132 While everybody agrees that early first tithe preempts heave, nothing has been said about second tithe given early. If early second tithe is subject to heave, any dough made from it is subject to *ḥallah*, including what still has to be given as heave.

133 The only second tithe that possibly is free is unredeemed second tithe consumed in Jerusalem. For him who holds it is Heaven's property, any second tithe dough in Jerusalem is exempt from *ḥallah*.

מָאן דְּאָמַר חַייָב עֲשָׂאוֹ תְרוּמַת מַעֲשֵׂר עַל מָקוֹם אַחֵר מַה אַתְּ עֲבַד לָהּ כְּגָדִישׁ שֶׁנִּדְמַע כְּעִיסָּה שֶׁנִּדְמְעָה. רִבִּי יוֹחָנָן אָמַר אֲנָא בָעִיתָהּ. רִבִּי יֹאשִׁיָּה אָמַר אֲנָא בָעִיתָהּ. מַה בֵּין גָּדִישׁ שֶׁנִּדְמַע לְעִיסָּה שֶׁנִּדְמְעָה. גָּדִישׁ שֶׁנִּדְמַע אַתְּ אָמַר חַייָב. עִיסָּה שֶׁנִּדְמְעָה אַתְּ אָמַר פְּטוּרָה. רִבִּי תַנְחוּמָה בְּשֵׁם רִבִּי חוּנָה. גָּדִישׁ שֶׁנִּדְמַע עַד שֶׁלֹּא נִדְמַע עָבַר וְהִפְרִישׁ מִמֶּנּוּ תְרוּמָה אֵינָהּ תְּרוּמָה. עִיסָּה שֶׁנִּדְמְעָה עַד שֶׁלֹּא נִדְמְעָה עָבַר וְהִפְרִישׁ מִמֶּנּוּ חַלָּה אֵינָהּ חַלָּה דְּתַנִּינָן תַּמָּן הַמַּפְרִישׁ חַלָּתוֹ קֶמַח אֵינָהּ חַלָּה וְגֶזֶל בְּיַד כֹּהֵן.

For him who holds it is obligated[134], if he used it as heave of the tithe for some other produce, how do you treat it? Like a heap of sheaves which became *dema'*[135] or like a dough which became *dema'*[136]? A heap of sheaves which became *dema'* you say is obligated, a dough which became *dema'* you say is free! Rebbi Tanḥuma in the name of Rebbi Ḥuna: Concerning a heap of sheaves which became *dema'* if he transgressed and gave heave before it became obligated, is it not heave[137]? A dough which became *dema'* if he transgressed and gave *ḥallah* from it before it became obligated[138] is not *ḥallah* as we have stated there[139]: "If somebody gives *ḥallah* from flour it is not *ḥallah* and will be robbery in the hand if the Cohen.[140]"

134 Early Second Tithe obligated for heave. It was established in *Terumot* 2:1 that heave of the tithe may be given from one batch for an unrelated batch.

135 Profane mixed with heave; cf. *Terumot* 3:2.

136 Which is exempt from *ḥallah*, cf. Mishnah 4.

137 The Constantinople print (Benvenist) has this as a declarative sentence: "It is heave." The heap of sheaves is not processed but if heave is given, automatically all tithes are also due.

138 A (sufficiently large) bread dough is potentially obligated for *ḥallah* the moment it is no longer dry flour.

139 Mishnah 2:5.

140 The two cases have been explained but the original question was not answered.

וּמוֹתַר הָעוֹמֶר. מַתְנִיתָא דְּלֹא כְרִבִּי עֲקִיבָה דְּרִבִּי עֲקִיבָה מְחַייֵב בִּתְרוּמָה וּבְמַעְשְׂרוֹת.

"The excess of the *'omer.*" The Mishnah is not Rebbi Aqiba's since Rebbi Aqiba makes it liable for heave and tithes[141].

141 Mishnah *Menaḥot* 10(6):4; Babli *Menaḥot* 66b-67a.

וּתְבוּאָה שֶׁלֹּא הֵבִיאָה שְׁלִישׁ. מַה טַעֲמָה דְּרַבָּנִין נֶאֱמַר לֶחֶם בְּפֶסַח וְנֶאֱמַר לֶחֶם בְּחַלָּה מַה לֶחֶם שֶׁנֶּאֱמַר בְּפֶסַח דָּבָר שֶׁהוּא בָא לִידֵי מַצָּה וְחָמֵץ אַף לֶחֶם שֶׁנֶּאֱמַר בְּחַלָּה דָּבָר שֶׁהוּא בָא לִידֵי מַצָּה וְחָמֵץ. מַה טַעֲמָא דְּרִבִּי לְעָזָר כִּתְרוּמַת גּוֹרֶן כֵּן תָּרִימוּ אוֹתָהּ. מַה תְּרוּמַת גּוֹרֶן מִפֵּירוֹת שֶׁהֵבִיאוּ שְׁלִישׁ. אַף זוֹ מִפֵּירוֹת שֶׁהֵבִיאוּ שְׁלִישׁ. וְלֵית לְרִבִּי לְעָזָר לֶחֶם לֶחֶם. אַשְׁכַּח תַּנֵּי בְשֵׁם רִבִּי לְעָזָר אֵינָהּ חַייֶבֶת בְּחַלָּה וְאֵין אָדָם יוֹצֵא בָהּ יְדֵי חוֹבָתוֹ בְּפֶסַח.

"And grain not yet one-third ripe ". What is the rabbis' reason? "Bread" is mentioned in connection with Passover and "bread" is mentioned in connection with *ḥallah.* "Bread" mentioned in connection with Passover includes all that may be *mazzah* or leavened, [therefore] also "bread" mentioned in connection with *ḥallah* includes all that may be *mazzah* or leavened[15-18,118]. What is Rebbi Eleazar's reasoning? (*Num.* 15:20) "You shall lift it like heave from the threshing floor." Since heave from the threshing floor is only from produce at least one-third ripe[142], that also is only from produce at least one-third ripe. Does Rebbi Eleazar not have "bread, bread[143]"? It was found stated in the name of Rebbi Eleazar: It[144] is not subject to *ḥallah* and nobody can use it to fulfill his duty on Passover.

142 Cf. *Ma'serot* 1:3, Note 78.

143 If there is an established tradition that the word "bread" means the same in both cases, R. Eleazar also must agree that the same standard applies in both cases.

144 Bread or dough made from flour milled from grain not yet one-third ripe.

מַהוּ שֶׁחַייָבִין עַל לֶחֶם שֶׁלּוֹ מִשּׁוּם חָדָשׁ. אָמַר רִבִּי יוּדָן כְּתִיב וְלֶחֶם וְקָלִי וְכַרְמֶל לֹא תֹאכְלוּ. אֶת שֶׁחַייָבִין עַל קָלִי שֶׁלּוֹ מִשּׁוּם חָדָשׁ חַייָבִין עַל לֶחֶם שֶׁלּוֹ מִשּׁוּם חָדָשׁ. אֶת שֶׁאֵין חַייָבִין עַל קָלִי שֶׁלּוֹ מִשּׁוּם חָדָשׁ אֵין חַייָבִין עַל לֶחֶם שֶׁלּוֹ מִשּׁוּם חָדָשׁ.

[145]Is one guilty for bread from it because of new grain? Rebbi Yudan said, it is written (*Lev.* 23:14): "Bread, parched or fresh grain you should not eat." Anything for whose parched grain you would be guilty because of new grain you are guilty for bread because of new grain; but anything for whose parched grain you would not be guilty because of new grain you are not guilty for bread because of new grain.

145 This formulation is exactly the inverse of the same argument in Halakhah 1, Note 23.

אָמַר רִבִּי זְעִירָא כְּתִיב עַשֵּׂר תְּעַשֵּׂר אֵת כָּל־תְּבוּאַת זַרְעֶךָ. דָּבָר שֶׁהוּא נִזְרַע וּמַצְמִיחַ יָצָא פָּחוּת מִשְּׁלִישׁ שֶׁאִם נִזְרַע אֵינוֹ מַצְמִיחַ.

[146]Rebbi Zeïra said: It is written (*Deut* 14:22): "You shall certainly tithe all your seed-yield." Anything which will grow when sown; this excludes seeds less than one-third ripe which when sown will not grow.

146 *Ma'serot* 1:3, Note 78.

פְּשִׁיטָא עַל דְּרַבָּנִין בְּהָהֵן פָּחוּת מִשְּׁלִישׁ שֶׁאֵינוֹ נִגְרָר לְעִנְייַן הַמַּעְשְׂרוֹת. רִבִּי חִיָּיה בַּר יוֹסֵף שָׁאַל עַל דַּעְתֵּיהּ דְּרִבִּי לָעְזָר מַהוּ שֶׁיְּהֵא נִגְרָר לְעִנְייַן חַלָּה כְּעִיסַּת

הָאוֹרֶז. שְׁמוּאֵל בַּר אַבָּא בָּעֵי אֵי זֶהוּ חָדָשׁ וְיָשָׁן שֶׁבַּחַלָּה. שְׁתֵּי שָׂדוֹת אַחַת הֵבִיאָה שְׁלִישׁ וְאַחַת פָּחוֹת מִשְּׁלִישׁ לַחַלָּה אַחַת לְמַעְשְׂרוֹת שְׁתַּיִם. אַחַת פָּחוֹת מִשְּׁלִישׁ וְאַחַת עֲשָׂבִים לַחַלָּה שְׁתַּיִם לְמַעְשְׂרוֹת אַחַת. אַחַת הֵבִיאָה שְׁלִישׁ וְאַחַת עֲשָׂבִים בֵּין לַחַלָּה בֵּין לְמַעְשְׂרוֹת שְׁתַּיִם.

It is obvious: For the rabbis, that "less than a third" is not dragged in concerning the matter of tithes. Rebbi Ḥiyya bar Josef asked: According to Rebbi Eleazar, is it dragged in in the matter of *ḥallah* like a rice dough[147]? Samuel bar Abba asked: How does one treat old and new for *ḥallah*[148]? Two fields, one one-third ripe, one less than one-third ripe, are one for *ḥallah*[149] and two for tithes. One less than one-third ripe and one of grasses[150] are two for *ḥallah* and one for tithes. One one-third ripe and one of grasses are two both for *ḥallah* and tithes.

147 Since grain less than one-third ripe is not subject to tithes, if such grain is mixed with ripe grain, only the ripe grain is subject to heave and tithes. The green kernels cannot become subject to tithes. Cf. Note 22. On the other hand, it is stated in Mishnah 3:6 that if a dough made from rice and grain tastes of grain, the entire dough is obligated for *ḥallah* and the bread baked from it is acceptable for Passover.

149 It is forbidden to give heave from the new harvest for last year's. Since *ḥallah* is called heave, how does one treat dough made from flour which is a mixture of last year's and this year's grain? No answer is given; it seems obvious that one does not have to investigate the origin of the flour one buys on the market.

150 According to the rabbis, flour from both fields is subject to *ḥallah* when made into a dough but only the riper one is subject to heave and tithes.

151 The grain seeds are somehow used to make flour. That flour cannot be measured in the minimal amount needed for *ḥallah* (Mishnah 2:6). But as human food it is subject to (rabbinic) tithes.

(fol. 57a) **משנה ד**: אֵילּוּ חַייָבִין בְּמַעְשְׂרוֹת וּפְטוּרִין מִן הַחַלָּה. הָאוֹרֶז וְהַדּוֹחַן וְהַפְּרָגִים וְהַשּׁוּמְשְׁמִין וְהַקִּטְנִיּוֹת וּפָחוֹת מֵחֲמֵשֶׁת רְבָעִים בִּתְבוּאָה. הַסּוּפְגָּנִים וְהַדּוּבְשָׁנִים וְהָאִיסְקָרִיטִין וְחַלַּת הַמַּשְׂרֵת וְהַמְּדוּמָּע פְּטוּרִין מִן הַחַלָּה.

Mishnah 4: The following are obligated for tithes but free from *ḥallah*: Rice, millet, poppies, sesame, legumes[151], and less than five quarter [*qab*] of grain[152]. Bismarcks[153], honey cakes[154], roasted cakes[155], pancakes[156], and *dema'*[157] are free from *ḥallah*.

151 Anything from which a kind of flour can be extracted, other than grasses. The main examples are peas and beans.

152 A dough made with more than this volume of flour is subject to *ḥallah*; Mishnah and Halakhah 2:6.

153 The traditional spelling pronunciation is הַסּוּפְגָּנִים but better Mishnah sources write the word without ו , derived from Greek σπόγγος, Armenian and Syriac *spung* "sponge". According to *Arukh*, they are what in Arabic is called إِسْفَنْج *isfunj*, spherical spongy cakes fried in oil. In modern Hebrew, the word is used in the feminine: סופגניות.

154 Defined in the Halakhah as "milk and honey". The readings of the Kaufmann ms. of the Mishnah, הדיבשנים, or of the Munich ms. of the Babli, הדבשנים, are preferable.

155 Greek, [ἄρτος] ἐσχαρίτης, ὁ, "[bread] baked over the fire".

156 Cf. *2S*. 13:9.

157 Profane and heave mixed together, forbidden to all but Cohanim.

(fol. 57d) **הלכה ה**: בֵּינְתַּיִים מַהוּ. רִבִּי יוֹנָה בְשֵׁם רִבִּי שִׁמְעוֹן בֶּן לָקִישׁ בֵּינְתַיִם כְּבָרִאשׁוֹנָה. רִבִּי יוֹסֵי בְשֵׁם רִבִּי שִׁמְעוֹן בֶּן לָקִישׁ בֵּינְתַיִים כְּבָאַחֲרוֹנָה. אֵי זֶהוּ בֵּינְתַיִים. הָעוֹשֶׂה עִיסָּה מִן הַטֵּבֶל חַלָּה חַייֶבֶת בִּתְרוּמָה וּתְרוּמָה חַייֶבֶת בַּחַלָּה. מְנַיִין שֶׁחַלָּה חַייֶבֶת בִּתְרוּמָה. רִבִּי יִצְחָק בְּשֵׁם רִבִּי שְׁמוּאֵל בַּר מַרְתָּא בְשֵׁם רַב חַלָּה תָרִימוּ תְרוּמָה. מֵחַלָּה תָרִימוּ תְרוּמָה. מְנַיִין שֶׁהַתְּרוּמָה חַייֶבֶת בַּחַלָּה מִן קוֹשׁוֹי פֳּתְרִין הָהֵן קְרָיְיָא מֵאוֹתָהּ שֶׁכָּתוּב בָּהּ רֵאשִׁית תָּרִימוּ חַלָּה.

Halakhah 4: What are the rules "in between"[158]? Rebbi Jonah in the name of Rebbi Simeon ben Laqish: "In between" follows the rules of the first state[159]. Rebbi Yose in the name of Rebbi Simeon ben Laqish: "In between" follows the rules of the final state. What means "in between"? [160]If somebody makes dough from *ṭevel*, its *ḥallah* is obligated for heave and its heave for *ḥallah*. From where that *ḥallah* is obligated for heave? Rebbi Isaac in the name of Rebbi Samuel ben Martha in the name of Rav: (*Num*. 15:20) "*Ḥallah* you shall lift heave," from *ḥallah* you shall lift heave. From where that heave is subject to *ḥallah*? From our difficulty to explain that verse, the one where it is written: "Beginning . . . you shall lift *ḥallah*"[161].

158 In between obligations, if dough is made from flour that is not totally profane.

159 All prior obligations also fall on the *ḥallah* taken from the dough.

160 Cf. *Demay* 5:1, Notes 23 ff.; Tosephta *Terumot* 4:10.

161 The full verses read: "The beginning of your doughs, *ḥallah* you shall lift heave; like heave of the barn, so you shall lift it. From the beginning of your doughs you shall give a heave to the Eternal, for your generations." The second verse states that *ḥallah* is due as a heave from the moment the kneading of the dough starts. But then the first "beginning" is redundant; it is taken to refer to actual heave which is called "beginning" in *Num*. 18:12. Then the second clause of the first verse is read not "*ḥallah* you shall lift [as] heave" but "[from] *ḥallah* you shall lift heave."

הַסּוּפְגָּנִים טְרִיקְטָא. הַדּוּבְשָׁנִים מְלִי גָּאלָא. וְהָאִיסְקְרִיטִין חֲלִיטִין דְּשׁוּק. וְחַלַּת מַסְרֶת חֲלִיטִין דְּמַיִי.

Bismarcks are *tracta*[162]. Honey cakes μελίγαλα[163]. `Εσχαρίτης are bake-meats[164] of the market, pancakes dumplings in water.

162 Latin *tractum, tracta*, Greek τρακτόν, τό, "long piece of dough drawn out in making pastry" (Liddell & Scott). Mentioned in Apicius (*De re coquinaria*, Ed. M. E. Milham, Leipzig 1969) Bk. IV iii as used in serving fish, Bk. Vi1 using "three small *tracta* balls" for *pultes tractogalatae.*

163 "Honey-milk" baked goods.

164 The root of חליטה seems to be Arabic خلط "to mix", from which Arabic مخلوطا "baked from a mixture of lentils, peas, and farina." The Babli, *Pesaḥim* 37a, defines חַלַּת מַסְרֶת as "non-commercial חָלוּט"; a better opposite to "commercial חלוט" of the Yerushalmi.

The Babli, *Pesaḥim* 37b, also defines חלוט as "dough cooked by pouring boiling water over it" in contrast to מעיסה "dumpling" made by dropping lumps of dough into boiling water but the Yerushalmi (Halakhah 7) switches the meanings of both terms.

רִבִּי יוֹחָנָן אָמַר טְרִיקְטָא חַייֶבֶת בְּחַלָּה וְאוֹמֵר עָלָיו הַמּוֹצִיא לֶחֶם מִן הָאָרֶץ. וְאָדָם יוֹצֵא בָהּ יְדֵי חוֹבָתוֹ בַּפֶּסַח. רִבִּי שִׁמְעוֹן בֶּן לָקִישׁ אָמַר טְרִיקְטָא אֵינָהּ חַייֶבֶת בְּחַלָּה וְאֵין אוֹמֵר עָלָיו הַמּוֹצִיא לֶחֶם מִן הָאָרֶץ. וְאֵין אָדָם יוֹצֵא בָהּ יְדֵי חוֹבָתוֹ בַּפֶּסַח. רִבִּי יוֹסֵי אָמַר תַּרְתֵּיי רִבִּי יוֹחָנָן אָמַר טְרִיקְטָא חַייֶבֶת בְּחַלָּה וְאוֹמֵר עָלֶיהָ הַמּוֹצִיא לֶחֶם מִן הָאָרֶץ. וְאָדָם יוֹצֵא בָהּ יְדֵי חוֹבָתוֹ בַּפֶּסַח. רִבִּי שִׁמְעוֹן בֶּן לָקִישׁ אָמַר טְרִיקְטָא אֵינָהּ חַייֶבֶת בְּחַלָּה וְאֵין אוֹמֵר עָלֶיהָ הַמּוֹצִיא לֶחֶם מִן הָאָרֶץ. וְאֵין אָדָם יוֹצֵא בָהּ יְדֵי חוֹבָתוֹ בַּפֶּסַח. רִבִּי יוֹסֵי אָמַר חוֹרֵי. רִבִּי יוֹסֵי אָמַר רִבִּי יוֹחָנָן כָּל־שֶׁהָאוּר מְהַלֵּךְ תַּחְתָּיו חַייָב בְּחַלָּה וְאוֹמֵר עָלָיו הַמּוֹצִיא לֶחֶם מִן [הָאָרֶץ] וְיוֹצֵא בָהּ יְדֵי חוֹבָתוֹ בַּפֶּסַח. רִבִּי שִׁמְעוֹן בֶּן לָקִישׁ אוֹמֵר כָּל־שֶׁהָאוּר מְהַלֵּךְ תַּחְתָּיו אֵינוֹ חַייָב בְּחַלָּה וְאֵין אוֹמֵר עָלָיו הַמּוֹצִיא לֶחֶם מִן הָאָרֶץ וְאֵין אָדָם יוֹצֵא בָהּ יְדֵי חוֹבָתוֹ בַּפֶּסַח. אָמַר לוֹ רִבִּי יוֹחָנָן וּבִלְבַד עַל יְדֵי מַשְׁקֶה.

Rebbi Johanan said, *tracta* is subject to *ḥallah*[165], one recites for it "He Who produces bread from the earth,[166]" and one may satisfy one's Passover obligation with it[167]. Rebbi Simeon ben Laqish said, *tracta* is not subject to *ḥallah*, one may not recite for it "He Who produces bread from the earth," and one may not satisfy one's Passover obligation with it. Rebbi Yose said both together: Rebbi Joḥanan said, *tracta* is subject to *ḥallah*, one recites for it "He Who produces bread from the earth," and one may satisfy one's Passover obligation with it; Rebbi Simeon ben Laqish said, *tracta* is not subject to *ḥallah*, one may not recite for it "He Who produces bread from the earth," and one may not satisfy one's Passover obligation with it. Rebbi Yose said another [statement] (Rebbi Yose): Rebbi Joḥanan said, everything[168] under which the fire burns is subject to *ḥallah*, one recites for it "He Who produces bread from the earth," and one may satisfy one's Passover obligation with it. Rebbi Simeon ben Laqish said, anything under which the fire burns is not subject to *ḥallah*, one may not recite for it "He Who produces bread from the earth," and one may not satisfy one's Passover obligation with it. Rebbi Joḥanan said, only in a fluid[169].

165 The obvious contradiction to the Mishnah is resolved in the next paragraph.

166 The benediction required for bread and bread alone; *Berakhot* 6:1.

167 To eat *maẓẓah* defined as unleavened *bread*; cf. Note 15.

168 Every dough baked in an oven. Their ovens were shaped as conical frustums, where the dough was clinging to the inclined wall directly over the fire.

169 Dough baked in a pan whose bottom is filled with liquid (including oil) cannot become bread.

מַתְנִיתָא פְלִיגָא עַל דְּרִבִּי יוֹחָנָן. הַסּוּפְגָּנִים וְהַדּוּבְשָׁנִים וְהָאִיסְקָרִיטִין וְחַלַּת הַמַּשְׁרֵת וְהַמְּדוּמָּע פְּטוּרִין מִן הַחַלָּה. פָּתַר לָהּ בְּסוּפְגָּנִין שֶׁנַּעֲשׂוּ בָאוּר. וְאֵין יוֹצְאִין בְּסוּפְגָּנִין שֶׁנַּעֲשׂוּ בַחַמָּה. יוֹצְאִין בְּסוּפְגָּנִין שֶׁנַּעֲשׂוּ בָאוּר. וְלֵית הָדָא פְלִיגָא עַל רִבִּי שִׁמְעוֹן בֶּן לָקִישׁ. פָּתַר לָהּ בְּשֶׁהָיָה הָאוּר מְהַלֵּךְ מִן הַצָּד.

The Mishnah disagrees with Rebbi Johanan: "Bismarcks, honey cakes, roasted cakes, pancakes, and *dema'* are free from *ḥallah*!" He explains it for Bismarcks made on the fire: One does not fulfill one's obligation with Bismarcks baked by the sun[170]; one may fulfill one's obligation with Bismarcks baked on the fire. Does this not disagree with Rebbi Simeon ben Laqish? He explains it if the fire extends to the sides[171].

170 He restricts the Mishnah to that unlikely case; this is accepted in the Babli, *Pesaḥim* 37a.

A Genizah text has a more complete version: פתר לה בסופגנים שנעשו בחמה. ותני כן יוצאים בסופגנים שנעשו באור ואין וצאים בסופגנים שנעשו בחמה "He explains it for Bismarcks baked by the sun. It was stated thus (Tosephta *Pisḥa* 2:19): One may fulfill one's obligation with Bismarcks baked on fire but one may not fulfill one's obligation by Bismarcks baked in the sun."

171 Since the oven is much larger at the botton than in the upper part where the bread is baked, the heat comes from all sides. R. Simeon considers baking with heat coming just from one direction as cooking, not baking. In the Babli, *Pesaḥim* 37b, R. Simeon defines as cooking anything prepared in a vessel in the oven; he accepts as baking only what is in the oven without any vessel. This may be the same as his opinion explained here.

מִילֵּיהוֹן דְּרַבָּנִין פְּלִיגִין. כַּהֲנָא שָׁאַל לִשְׁמוּאֵל לֹא מִסְתַּבְּרָא בְּהָהֵן מְדוּמָּע. דְּתַנִּינָן הָכָא שֶׁרוּבָּהּ תְּרוּמָה תְרוּמָה. אָמַר לֵיהּ אוּף אֲנָא סָבַר כֵּן אֶלָּא כַּד תֵּיסוֹק לְאַרְעָא דְיִשְׂרָאֵל אַתְּ שְׁאַל לָהּ. כַּד סְלַק לְהָכָא שָׁמַע רִבִּי יָסָה בְשֵׁם רִבִּי יוֹחָנָן אֲפִילוּ סְאָה אַחַת שֶׁנָּפְלָה עַל תִּשְׁעִים וְתֵשַׁע חוּלִין. אָמַר רִבִּי אַבָּהוּ כָּךְ מֵשִׁיב רִבִּי שִׁמְעוֹן בֶּן לָקִישׁ לְרִבִּי יוֹחָנָן הַסְּאָה פוֹטֶרֶת אֶת הַכֹּל. אָמַר לֵיהּ וְכִי עִיגּוּל בְּעִיגּוּלִין דָּבָר בָּרִי שֶׁהַתְּרוּמָה עוֹלָה בְיָדוֹ וְאַתְּ אָמְרַת דָּבָר קַל הוּא אַף הָכָא קַל הוּא. וִיתִיבִינֵיהּ שַׁנְיָיא הָא בְעִיגּוּלִין שֶׁכְּבָר בָּטְלוּ. רִבִּי יוֹנָה וְרִבִּי יוֹסֵי תְּרֵיהוֹן בְּשֵׁם רִבִּי זְעִירָא אֲפִילוּ חִטִּין בְּחִטִּין טוֹחֵן וּמַתִּיר.

[172]The words of the rabbis disagree. Cahana asked Samuel: Is it not reasonable that the *dema'* which we stated here contains mostly heave? He said to him, that is also my opinion, but when you go to the Land of Israel do ask about this. When he went, he heard what Rebbi Assi said in the name of Rebbi Joḥanan, even one *seah* that fell into 99 [which were] profane. Rebbi Abbahu said, thus did Rebbi Simeon ben Laqish answer Rebbi Joḥanan: That one *seah* frees everything? Is a fig cake among fig cakes such a sure thing that heave came up in his hand? But you must say it is [to be taken] lightly; here also it is [to be taken] lightly. Could he not have objected: Is it different with fig cakes which already are disregarded? Rebbi Jonah and Rebbi Yose, both in the name of Rebbi Zeïra: Even wheat and wheat he may grind and lift.

172 This paragraph appears, with minor spelling differences, in *Terumot* 4 and was explained there, Notes 76-81.

פָּחוֹת מֵחֲמֵשֶׁת רְבָעִים כִּתְבוּאָה. אָמַר רִבִּי אָבִינָא הָדָא אֶמְרָה כְּשֶׁהָיוּ פָּחוֹת מֵחֲמֵשֶׁת רְבָעִים. אֲבָל אִם הָיוּ חֲמֵשֶׁת רְבָעִים מְצוּמְצָמִין לֹא בְדָא. רִבִּי יוֹסֵי בֵּירִבִּי בּוּן בְּשֵׁם רִבִּי אֲבוּנָא לֹא עַל הָדָא אִתְאֲמָרַת. אֶלָּא עַל הָדָא דְּאָמַר רִבִּי יוֹחָנָן מְדוּמָּע פָּטוּר מִן הַחַלָּה. סָפֵק מְדוּמָּע וְהַנֶּאֱכַל מִשּׁוּם דִּימּוּעַ חַייָב בַּחַלָּה עָלֶיהָ. רִבִּי יוֹסֵי בֵּירִבִּי בּוּן בְּשֵׁם רִבִּי אֲבוּנָא הָדָא דְאִיתְמַר כְּשֶׁהָיוּ יוֹתֵר מֵחֲמֵשֶׁת רְבָעִים אֲבָל אִם הָיוּ חֲמֵשֶׁת רְבָעִים מְצוּמְצָמִין פְּטוּרָה מִן הַחַלָּה.

"Less than five quarter [*qab*] of grain." Rebbi Abina said, this you said if it was less than five quarter [*qab*] of grain. But if it were exactly five quarters, this does not apply[173]. Rebbi Yose ben Rebbi Abun in the name of Rebbi Abuna, it was not said on that but on the following: Rebbi Joḥanan said, *dema'* is free from *ḥallah* but *ḥallah* is obligated for what is possible *dema'*[174] and is eaten because of *dema'*[175]. Rebbi Yose ben Rebbi Abun in the name of Rebbi Abuna, when has this been said? For more than five quarter [*qab*], but for exactly five quarters it is exempt from *ḥallah*.

173 This is implied by the Mishnah which exempts only volumes strictly less that $^5/_4$ *qab*, against the opinion of R. Yose (Mishnah *Idiut* 1:2) who requires strictly more than $^5/_4$ *qab*.

174 If there were two boxes and heave fell into one of them but it is not known into which, the contents of both must be eaten by Cohanim but are not exempt from *ḥallah*.

175 It seems that in the text one should read סָפֵק מְדוּמָּע נֶאֱכַל מִשּׁוּם דִּימּוּעַ חַייָב בַּחַלָּה as in Tosephta *Ḥallah* 1:5, *Terumot* 7:8.

(fol. 57a) **משנה ה**: עִיסָּה שֶׁתְּחִילָּתָהּ סוּפְגָּנִים וְסוֹפָהּ סוּפְגָּנִים פְּטוּרָה מִן הַחַלָּה. תְּחִילָּתָהּ עִיסָּה וְסוֹפָהּ סוּפְגָּנִים תְּחִילָּתָהּ סוּפְגָּנִים וְסוֹפָהּ עִיסָּה חַייֶבֶת בַּחַלָּה. וְכֵן הַקְּנוּבְקָאוֹת חַייָבוֹת.

Mishnah 5: Dough intended for Bismarcks and made into Bismarcks is free from *ḥallah*.[176] If it was started as bread dough but made into Bismarcks, or started as Bismarck dough and used as bread dough, is obligated for *ḥallah*. Similarly, *qenubqa'ot*[177] are obligated.

176 According to Maimonides, only if baked in the sun.

177 A word of unknown etymology, cf. Note 182. {Perhaps cf. Latin *clibanicius* (*viz.*, *panis*) "bread baked in a *clibanus*, an earthen or iron vessel for baking bread; oven, furnace" (Lewis & Short) (E. G.).}

(fol. 57d) **הלכה ו**: הָדָא אִיתָא שָׁאֲלַת לְרִבִּי מָנָא בְּגִין דַּאֲנָא בָּעְיָיא לְמֵיעְבַּד אִצְוָותִי אִטְרֵי מָהוּ דְיִנְסְבֶּנָּה וּתְהֵא פְטוּרָה מִן הַחַלָּה. אָמַר לָהּ לָמָּה לֹא. אָתָא שְׁאִיל לְאָבוֹי. אָמַר לֵיהּ אָסוּר שֶׁמָּא תִימָּלֵךְ לַעֲשׂוֹתָהּ עִיסָּה.

Halakhah 6: A woman asked Rebbi Mana: Since I want to make *iṭry*[178] in my kneading-trough, may I take from it so that it should be free from *ḥallah*[179]? He said to her, why not? He went to ask his father[180]. He said to him, it is forbidden; maybe she would change her mind to use it[181] as bread dough.

178 Cf. Greek ἴτριον "a kind of cake;" in later usage, any cake (L.&S.). In Modern Hebrew, איטריות are "noodles"; cf. Arabic اطرية "vermicelli".

179 While the total dough in the trough is more than the minimum for *ḥallah*, the dough taken to make bread will be less than the minimum. This should be exempt from *ḥallah*.

180 R. Jonah.

181 More than the minimum for *ḥallah*.

וְכֵן הַקְּנוּקָעוֹת חַיָּבוֹת. רִבִּי יְהוֹשֻׁעַ בֶּן לֵוִי אָמַר קְרַמְבִּיטֵס. רִבִּי חֲנַנְיָה בֶּן עָגוּל בְּשֵׁם חִזְקִיָּה אָמַר בוקרלטא שֶׁלֹּא (fol. 58a) תֹאמַר הוֹאִיל וְהוּא עָתִיד לְהַחֲזִירָהּ לְסוֹלְתָהּ תְּהֵא פְטוּרָה מִן הַחַלָּה. אָמַר רִבִּי בָּא בַּר זַבְדָּא עִיסַּת מַבְרִין חַייֶבֶת בַּחַלָּה. שֶׁלֹּא תֹאמַר הוֹאִיל וְהוּא עָתִיד לְהַחֲזִירָהּ לְסוֹלְתָהּ תְּהֵא פְטוּרָה מִן הַחַלָּה.

"Similarly, *qenubqa'ot* are obligated". Rebbi Joshua ben Levi said, *Zwieback*. Rebbi Ḥananiah ben Agul in the name of Ḥizqiah said *boqrlṭa*. That you should not[182] say that because in the end it will be turned into a kind of farina it should be free from *ḥallah*. Rebbi Abba bar Zavda said, dough for the sick is obligated for *ḥallah*, that you should not say that because in the end it will be turned into a kind of farina it should be free from *ḥallah*.

182 J. N. Epstein [*Tarbiz* 1(1929) p. 124-125] identifies קרמביטס as Greek κράμβιτας "*Zwieback*" {cf. Greek κραμβαλέος "dried, parched, roasted" (E. G.)} and בוקרלטא (in the Peterburg fragment בוקולתא) as Greek βούκκελλα {really from the Latin *bucella* (E. G.)} "small loaf"). The following is the text of *Or Zaru'a* (R. Isaac from Vienna, 13th Cent.; §219): הַקְנוּבְקָאוֹת חַיָּבוֹת בחלה. פירש רבנו יצחק מסימפונט אין ידוע לנו ומסתבר עוֹשִׂין אוֹתוֹ מן [הקמח] ואוֹפין אוֹתוֹ בשמש אוֹ בתנוּר וּכשרוֹצה סולת כוֹתשין אוֹתוֹ אפילוּ הכי חייבת בחלה. ירוּשלמי: וכן הַקְנוּבְקָאוֹת חַיָּבוֹת בחלה ר' חנינא בר עיגול בשם חזקיה שקילטא שֶׁלֹּא תֹאמַר הוֹאִיל וְהוּא עָתִיד לְהַחֲזִירָהּ לְסוֹלְתָהּ תְּהֵא פְּטוּרָה מִן הַחַלָּה. "*qenubqa'ot* are obligated for *ḥallah.* R. Isaac Simponti explains that we do not know what it is but it seems that one makes it from [flour], bakes it in the sun or the oven, and if one needs farina one pounds it; nevertheless it is obligated for *ḥallah.* Yerushalmi: 'Similarly, *qenubqa'ot* are obligated for *ḥallah.* R. Ḥanina bar 'Agil in the name of Ḥizqiah, *šqylṭ'*; that you should not say that because in the end it will be turned into a kind of farina it should be free from *ḥallah.*'" In the Wilna Talmud edition of R. Isaac Simponti בן קלטא instead of שקלטא. There, he adds: "In our language (Italian) one calls loaves made in ring form בנקלטא". There is no reasonable conjecture about the meaning of שקילטא, but בנקלטא probably should be read בוקלטא parallel to the reading of the Geniza fragment.

The *Arukh* defines *qenubqa'ot* by Italian *mostaccioli* (from *mostaccio* "snout"), a kind of ginger-bread cookie.

R. Ḥanina bar 'Agil was a third generation Galilean Amora who is quoted elsewhere in the Yerushalmi as transmitting statements of Ḥizqiah (*Yebamot* 6:6) and in the Babli as asking R. Ḥiyya bar Abba.

רַב אָמַר עִיסַּת כּוּתָח חַיֶּיבֶת בַּחַלָּה. אָמַר רִבִּי בּוּן שֶׁמָּא תִּימָּלֵךְ לַעֲשׂוֹתָהּ חֲרָרָה לְבָנָה. אָמַר רִבִּי מָנָא צְרִיכִין אָנוּ מַכְרִיזִין בְּאִינֵין דְּעָבְדִין עָבִיצִין דְּיֵיאוּן עָבְדִין לוֹן פָּחוֹת מִכְּשִׁיעוּר דְּאִינּוּן סָבְרִין שֶׁהִיא פְטוּרָה וְהִיא חַייֶבֶת.

Rav said, dough for *kutaḥ*[183] is subject to *ḥallah.* Rebbi Abun said, perhaps she will change her mind to make it white *Zwieback.* Rebbi

Mana said, we have to announce publicly that those who make *'abiṣin*[184] should make less than the measure since they think it is exempt but it is obligated.

183 A Babylonian specialty cheese for which the active bacteria come from mold growing on bread. If the bread is never intended to be eaten, it should be exempt from *ḥallah*. In the Babli (*Berakhot* 37b/38a), R. Ḥiyya is quoted that such dough is exempt. The statement is then explained away because if one makes bread to grow mold, it is subject to *ḥallah* but if the mold is grown on a kind of porridge it is exempt.

184 In the Babli, חביצין, Arabic خبيص, baked starch with milk and dates.

(fol. 57a) **משנה ו**: הַמְּעִיסָּה בֵּית שַׁמַּי פּוֹטְרִין וּבֵית הִלֵּל מְחַייְבִין. הַחֲלִיטָּה בֵּית שַׁמַּי מְחַייְבִין וּבֵית הִלֵּל פּוֹטְרִין. חַלּוֹת תּוֹדָה וּרְקִיקֵי נָזִיר עֲשָׂאָן לְעַצְמוֹ פָּטוּר לִמְכּוֹר בַּשּׁוּק חַייָב.

Mishnah 6: The House of Shammai free parboiled dough but the House of Hillel obligate it. The House of Shammai obligate dumplings but the House of Hillel free it[185]. The loaves for a thanksgiving sacrifice[186] and those needed by the *nazir*[187], if he made them for himself they are exempt[188], to sell on the market obligated.

185 In both cases, the dough will be baked in the end. In the Babli, *Pesaḥim* 37b, the definition of מעיסה and חליטה are switched; the Babli essentially follows the Yerushalmi here. The disagreement of the Houses of Hillel and Shammai is also quoted in Mishnah *Idiut* 5:2.

186 *Lev.* 7:12.

187 *Num.* 6:15.

188 Since they are dedicated when baking they are exempt as sacrifice.

הלכה ה: תַּנֵּי רִבִּי יִשְׁמָעֵאל בֵּירִבִּי יוֹסֵי אָמַר מִשּׁוּם אָבִיו אֵי זוֹ הִיא הַמְּעִיסָּה הַנּוֹתֵן חַמִּין לְתוֹךְ קֶמַח. חֲלִיטָה קֶמַח לְתוֹךְ חַמִּין. (fol. 58a)

It was stated[189]: "Rebbi Ismael ben Rebbi Yose said in his father's name: What is parboiled? If one adds hot water to flour. Dumpling, flour into hot water."

189 Tosephta 1:1. The Babli quotes this in the opposite way (cf. Note 164) and insists that the water be not just hot but boiling.

אִתָה חֲמִי נֶחְלְטָה כָּל־צוֹרְכָהּ בֵּית שַׁמַּי מְחַיְיבִין. לֹא נֶחְלְטָה כָּל־צוֹרְכָהּ בֵּית שַׁמַּי פּוֹטְרִין. רִבִּי יָסָא בְשֵׁם חִזְקִיָּה רִבִּי חִייָה בְשֵׁם רִבִּי הוֹשַׁעְיָא שְׁנֵי תַלְמִידִים שָׁנוּ אוֹתָהּ. רִבִּי אִימִּי בְּשֵׁם רִבִּי יוֹחָנָן עַל הַדָּבָר הַזֶּה הָלַכְתִּי אֶצֶל רִבִּי הוֹשַׁעְיָא רוֹבָא לְקַיְסָרִין וְאָמַר לִי שְׁנֵי תַלְמִידִים שָׁנוּ אוֹתָהּ.

Come and look: If it is completely parboiled, the House of Shammai obligate, not completely parboiled, the House of Shammai exempt[190]? Rebbi Assi in the name of Ḥizqiah, Rebbi Ḥiyya in the name of Rebbi Hoshaia: Two students stated this[191]. Rebbi Ammi in the name of Rebbi Johanan: For this matter I went to the elder Rebbi Hoshaia to Caesarea[192] and he said to me, two students stated this.

190 Flour dumped into boiling water can become cooked and edible; if boiling water is poured over flour, the dough needs baking. It would be reasonable to require *ḥallah* in the second case; why do they require it only in the first?

191 The Mishnah is composed of two incongruous pieces. There is no difference in the rules between parboiled flour and dumplings, but one student holds that the House of Shammai forbids and that of Hillel permits (both for חליטה and מעיסה) while the other holds that the House of Hillel forbids and the House of Shammai permits.

192 Caesarea Philippi.

וַחֲכָמִים אוֹמְרִים לֹא כְדִבְרֵי זֶה וְלֹא כְדִבְרֵי זֶה אֶלָּא הַנֶּאֱפָה בַתַּנּוּר חַיָּב. בְּאִילְפָּס וּבִקְדֵירָה פָּטוּר.

"[193]But the Sages say, not following either one of them[194], but what was baked in the oven is obligated, in a pan or a pot is free."

193 Continuation of Tosephta 1:1.

194 Of the Houses of Hillel and Shammai.

אֵי זֶהוּ חָלוּט בָּרוּר. אָמַר רִבִּי זְעִירָה כָּל־שֶׁהָאוּר מְהַלֵּךְ תַּחְתָּיו. אָמַר רִבִּי יוֹסֵי אֲפִילוּ הָאוּר מְהַלֵּךְ תַּחְתָּיו מִכֵּיוָן שֶׁהוּא עָתִיד לַעֲשׂוֹתוֹ בָצֵק חַיָּב בַּחַלָּה. קֶמַח קָלִי שֶׁעֲשָׂאוֹ בָצֵק חַיָּב בַּחַלָּה. רִבִּי יוֹסֵי בְשֵׁם רִבִּי יוֹחָנָן וְהוּא שֶׁאֲפִייָן.

What is certainly parboiled[195]? Rebbi Zeïra said, everything the fire burns under. Rebbi Yose said, even if the fire burns under it, since he will use it as dough in the future it is obligated for *ḥallah*[196]. Roasted flour which he used as flour is obligated for *ḥallah*. Rebbi Yose in the name of Rebbi Joḥanan: Only if he baked it.

195 If it was cooked in boiling water, it is exempt from *ḥallah*.

196 Anything that may be used in a bread dough, even if baked completely as, e. g., *matzah* meal, *is subject to* ḥallah *when first made.*

חַלּוֹת תּוֹדָה וּרְקִיקֵי נָזִיר עֲשָׂאָן לְעַצְמוֹ פָּטוּר דִּכְתִיב רֵאשִׁית עֲרִיסוֹתֵיכֶם וְלֹא שֶׁלָּהֶקְדֵּשׁ. לִמְכּוֹר בַּשּׁוּק חַיָּב. לֹא בְדַעְתּוֹ הַדָּבָר תָּלוּי. בְּדַעַת הַלְּקוּחוֹת הַדָּבָר תָּלוּי. שֶׁמָּא יִמְצָא הַלְּקוּחוֹת וְנִטְבְּלוּ מִיַּד.

"The loaves for a thanksgiving sacrifice and those needed by the *nazir*, if he made them for himself they are exempt," for it is written[197] "the first of your baking troughs;" "to sell on the market he is obligated", it does not depend on his intention but on that of his customers. Maybe he will find a customer; therefore, it becomes *ṭevel* immediately[198].

197 *Num.* 15:20. The sentence as addressed to the people, not to the priests of he Temple all whose food is dedicated.

198 The same argument is found in *Ma'serot* 1:5, cf. there, Note 115, 125.

(fol. 57a) **משנה ז**: נַחְתּוֹם שֶׁעָשָׂה שְׂאוֹר לְחַלֵּק חַייָב בַּחַלָּה וְנָשִׁים שֶׁנָּתְנוּ לְנַחְתּוֹם לַעֲשׂוֹת לָהֶם שְׂאוֹר אִם אֵין בְּשֶׁל אַחַת מֵהֶן כְּשִׁיעוּר פְּטוּרָה מִן הַחַלָּה.

Mishnah 7: A baker who made sour dough for distribution is obligated for *ḥallah*. But women who gave to a baker that he should make sour dough for them are free from *ḥallah* if no individual gave a full measure.[199]

199 This Mishnah was explained in *Ma'serot* 5:6. The following Halakhah 8 is identical with Halakhah *Ma'serot* 5:6 and was explained there, Notes 95-109. It is presupposed that the baker made sour dough for retail sale from more than $^{5}/_{4}$ *qab* of flour.

(fol. 58a) **הלכה ח**: הַמְמָרֵיחַ כְּרָיו שֶׁל חֲבֵירוֹ שֶׁלֹּא מִדַּעְתּוֹ. רִבִּי יוֹחָנָן וְרִבִּי שִׁמְעוֹן בֶּן לָקִישׁ. רִבִּי יוֹחָנָן אָמַר נִטְבַּל. וְרִבִּי שִׁמְעוֹן בֶּן לָקִישׁ אָמַר לֹא נִטְבַּל. מָתִיב רִבִּי יוֹחָנָן לְרִבִּי שִׁמְעוֹן בֶּן לָקִישׁ וְהָתַנִּינָן וְכֵן נָשִׁים שֶׁנָּתְנוּ לְנַחְתּוֹם לַעֲשׂוֹת לָהֶן שְׂאוֹר אִם אֵין בְּשֶׁלְּאַחַת מֵהֶן כְּשִׁיעוּר פְּטוּרָה מִן הַחַלָּה. וְאֵין בְּשֶׁלְּכוּלְּהֶן כְּשִׁיעוּר. אָמַר לֵיהּ שַׁנְיָיא הִיא שֶׁכֵּן הָעוֹשֶׂה עִיסָּה עַל מְנָת לְחַלְּקָהּ בָּצֵק פְּטוּרָה מִן הַחַלָּה. אָמַר לֵיהּ וְהָתַנִּינָן נַחְתּוֹם שֶׁעָשָׂה שְׂאוֹר לְחַלֵּק חַייָב בַּחַלָּה. אָמַר לֵיהּ לֹא תְתִיבֵינִי נַחְתּוֹם. נַחְתּוֹם לֹא בְדַעְתּוֹ הַדָּבָר תָּלוּי בְּדַעַת הַלְּקוּחוֹת הַדָּבָר תָּלוּי. שֶׁמָּא יִמְצָא לְקוּחוֹת וְהוּא חוֹזֵר וְעוֹשֶׂה אוֹתָהּ עִיסָּה. אָמַר לֵיהּ וְהָתַנִּינָן חוֹרֵי הַנְּמָלִים שֶׁלָּנוּ בְּצַד הָעֲרֵימָה חַייֶבֶת הֲרֵי אֵילּוּ חַייָבִין.

הָא בְצַד עֲרֵימָה פְטוּרָה פְּטוּרִין. אָמַר רִבִּי יוֹנָה אָמַר (לוֹ) רִבִּי יוֹסֵי רִבִּי אַבָּהוּ בְּשֵׁם רִבִּי יוֹחָנָן מִשּׁוּם יֵיאוּשׁ. שְׁמוּאֵל בַּר אַבָּא אָמַר וְהֵן [שֶׁגֵּרְרוּ רָאשֵׁי][200] שִׁיבֳּלִין.

Halakhah 8: If somebody made a heap [of somebody's grain] without the latter's knowledge: Rebbi Johanan and Rebbi Simeon ben Laqish. Rebbi Johanan said, it is *ṭevel*, Rebbi Simeon ben Laqish said, it is not *ṭevel*. Rebbi Johanan objected to Rebbi Simeon ben Laqish, did we not state: "And similarly women who gave to a baker to make sour dough for them, if none of them had the required amount it is free from *ḥallah*." (But what if all of them had the required amount?) He said to him, because if somebody makes dough in order to distribute it, the dough is exempt from *ḥallah*. But we have stated: "A baker who made sour dough for distribution is obligated for *ḥallah*." He said to him, do not answer back about a baker. For a baker, it does not depend on his opinion but on the opinions of his customers; maybe he will find a customer and will make bread dough for him[140]. He said to him, but was it not stated: "The holes of ants which were overnight near an obligated heap are obligated," therefore, near an exempt heap they are exempt. Rebbi Jonah said, Rebbi Yose, Rebbi Abbahu in the name of Rebbi Johanan: Because of resignation. Samuel ben Abba said, only [if they dragged tips of] ears.

מָתִיב רִבִּי שִׁמְעוֹן בֶּן לָקִישׁ לְרִבִּי יוֹחָנָן וְהָתַנִּינָן הִקְדִּישָׁן עַד שֶׁלֹּא נִגְמְרוּ וּגְמָרָן הַגִּיזְבָּר וְאַחַר כָּךְ פְּדָיָין פְּטוּרִין. הֲרֵי גִּיזְבָּר כְּאַחֵר הוּא וְאַתְּ אָמַרְתְּ מַה שֶׁעָשָׂה עָשׂוּי. אָמַר לוֹ תִּיפְתָּר כְּמָאן דְּאָמַר גִּיזְבָּר כִּבְעָלִים וּדְלֹא כְרִבִּי יוֹסֵי דְּרִבִּי יוֹסֵי אָמַר הוּא גִּיזְבָּר הוּא אַחֵר.

Rebbi Simeon ben Laqish objected to Rebbi Joḥanan: Did we not state: "But if he dedicated it before it was finished, the treasurer finished it, and then the owner redeemed it, it is free." Is not the treasurer a different person and you say what he did is valid? He said to him, this follows him who says the treasurer has the status of owner and goes against Rebbi Yose since Rebbi Yose said, the treasurer is a different person.

רִבִּי חֲנַנְיָה חֲבֵרוֹן דְּרַבָּנִין בָּעֵי וַאֲפִילוּ יֵשׁ בְּשֶׁלְאַחַת מֵהֶן כְּשִׁיעוּר יֵעָשֶׂה כְּדָבָר שֶׁלֹּא נִגְמְרָה מְלַאכְתָּן וִיהֵא פָּטוּר מִן הַחַלָּה. דְּאָמַר רִבִּי יוֹסֵי בְּשֵׁם רִבִּי זְעִירָא רִבִּי יוֹנָה רִבִּי זְעִירָא בְּשֵׁם רִבִּי לָעְזָר אַף בְּמַה שֶׁבְּלָגִין לֹא נִטְבַּל מִפְּנֵי שֶׁהוּא עָתִיד לְהַחֲזִיר לְדָבָר שֶׁלֹּא נִגְמְרָה מְלַאכְתּוֹ.

Rebbi Ḥananiah the colleague of the rabbis asked: And even if one of them was[201] of full measure it should be like something not completely processed, since Rebbi Yose said in the name of Rebbi Zeïra, Rebbi Jonah, Rebbi Zeïra in the name of Rebbi Eleazar, even what is in a flask did not become *ṭevel,* in case it was not fully processed, since he would in the end return it not fully processed.

200 From the text in *Ma'serot* and a Genizah fragment; not in the Leyden ms. and the Venice print.

201 This is slightly different from the text in *Ma'serot* but does not change the meaning.

(fol. 57a) **משנה ח**: עִיסַּת הַכְּלָבִים בִּזְמַן שֶׁהָרוֹעִים אוֹכְלִין מִמֶּנָּה חַיֶּיבֶת בַּחַלָּה וּמְעָרְבִין בָּהּ וּמִשְׁתַּתְּפִין בָּהּ וּמְבָרְכִין עָלֶיהָ וּמְזַמְּנִין עָלֶיהָ וְנַעֲשֵׂית בְּיוֹם טוֹב

וְיוֹצֵא בָהּ אָדָם חוֹבָתוֹ בְּפֶסַח. וְאִים אֵין הָרוֹעִים אוֹכְלִין מִמֶּנָּה אֵינָהּ חַיֶּיבֶת בְּחַלָּה וְאֵין מְעָרְבִין בָּהּ וְאֵין מִשְׁתַּתְּפִין בָּהּ וְאֵין מְבָרְכִין עָלֶיהָ וְאֵין מְזַמְּנִין עָלֶיהָ וְאֵינָהּ נַעֲשֵׂית בְּיוֹם טוֹב וְאֵין אָדָם יוֹצֵא בָהּ חוֹבָתוֹ בְּפֶסַח. בֵּין כָּךְ וּבֵין כָּךְ מִטַּמֵּא טוּמְאַת אוֹכְלִין.

Mishnah 8: A dog biscuit, if the shepherds eat from it, is obligated for *ḥallah*[202], one may use it for *eruv* and participation[203], one may recite the blessing over it[204] and one invites[205] for it, it may be made on a holiday[206], and a person may fulfill his duty with it on Passover[207]. If the shepherds do not eat from it, it is not obligated for *ḥallah*, one may not use it for *eruv* and participation, it may not be made on a holiday, and no person may fulfill his duty with it on Passover. In any case it can become impure in the impurity of food[208].

202 Since it is written (*Num.* 15:19): "When *you* eat from the bread of the Land", to exclude bread as animal feed from the obligation of *ḥallah* (*Sifry Suṭa Šelaḥ* 21).

203 To allow carrying on the Sabbath in a common courtyard or dead-end street, cf. *Demay* 1, Notes 192-193.

204 The blessing "Who produced bread from the earth" appropriate for bread; Mishnah *Berakhot* 6:1.

205 To recite grace in a group, which is done only for a meal with bread; Mishnah *Berakhot* 7:1.

206 Since only human food may be cooked or baked on a holiday, *Ex.* 12:16. This rule is not unchallenged; R. Aqiba holds that animal feed also may be cooked on a holiday, *Yom Tob* 1:11 (fol. 61a), Babli *Beẓah* 21b.

207 If it is unleavened and from the approved five kinds of flour, it is counted as bread.

208 Animal feed may be human food in an emergency; it is susceptible to impurity even if there is no intent to use it as human food.

(fol. 58a) **הלכה ט**: אֵיזֶהוּ עִיסַּת כְּלָבִים רִבִּי שִׁמְעוֹן בֶּן לָקִישׁ אָמַר כָּל־שֶׁעֵירֵב בָּהּ מוּרְסָן.

Halakhah 9: What is dog biscuit? Rebbi Simeon ben Laqish said, any with coarse bran mixed in.

מַתְנִיתָא אָמְרָה בִּזְמַן שֶׁהָרוֹעִין אוֹכְלִין מִמֶּנָּה. פְּעָמִים שֶׁאֵין הָרוֹעִים אוֹכְלִין מִמֶּנָּה. רִבִּי יוֹחָנָן אָמַר כָּל־שֶׁעָשָׂה כָּעְכִּין וְתַנֵּי כֵן עֲשָׂאָן כָּעְכִּין חַיֶּיבֶת עֲשָׂאָהּ לִימּוּדִין פְּטוּרָה. רִבִּי בָּא בְּשֵׁם שְׁמוּאֵל רִבִּי אִמִּי בְּשֵׁם רִבִּי חִיָּיה רוֹבָא אֲפִילוּ עֲשָׂאָהּ קָלוֹסְקִין. וְהָתַנִּינָן אִם אֵין הָרוֹעִין אוֹכְלִין מִמֶּנָּה. תִּיפְתָּר שֶׁעֲשָׂאָהּ מִשָּׁעָה רִאשׁוֹנָה שֶׁלֹּא יֹאכְלוּ הָרוֹעִים מִמֶּנָּה.

The Mishnah said: "if the shepherds eat from it." Maybe sometimes the shepherds will not eat from it. Rebbi Joḥanan said, any he made into cracknels[209]. We also have stated so[210]: "Any he made into cracknels is obligated; if he made it connected[211] it is free." Rebbi Abba in the name of Samuel, Rebbi Ammi in the name of the elder Rebbi Ḥiyya, even if he formed it as rolls[212]. But did we not state, "if the shepherds do not eat from it?[213]" Explain it if he made it from the start [thinking] that the shepherds should not eat from it[214].

209 Arabic كعك "ring-shaped pastry; pretzel"; definition of *Arukh* based on Gaonic sources. R. Joḥanan disagrees with R. Simeon ben Laqish and holds that the composition of the bread does not define its legal status, only the intent of the baker as expressed in the shape he is baking..

210 Tosephta 1:6, in the name of R. Jehudah, reading of the Erfurt ms.

211 Several loaves connected together; from a Hebrew root למד "to connect", cf. S. Krauss's Note to *Arukh* *s. v.* למד[3].

212 Greek κόλλιξ; cf. *Berakhot* 6, Note 103.

213 It is obvious that a shepherd will eat a small cake which he does not have to share with his dog but even from a large loaf he may cut a piece for himself before giving the remainder to the dog. It is difficult to see why the shape of the loaves should have any influence on their legal status.

214 One disagrees with R. Simeon ben Laqish but also with R. Johanan. The status of the bread is determined by the intent of the baker.

וְנַעֲשֵׂית בְּיוֹם טוֹב. מַתְנִיתָא דְּרִבִּי שִׁמְעוֹן בֶּן אֶלְעָזָר דְּתַנֵּי אֵין עוֹשִׂין מִיּוֹם טוֹב לְמוֹצָאֵי יוֹם טוֹב. וְהָתַנֵּי מְמַלְאָה אִשָּׁה קְדֵירָה בָּשָׂר אַף עַל פִּי שֶׁאֵינוֹ אוֹכֵל מִמֶּנָּהּ אֶלָּא חֲתִיכָה אַחַת. קוּמְקוּם חַמִּין אַף עַל פִּי שֶׁאֵינוֹ שׁוֹתֶה מִמֶּנּוּ אֶלָּא כּוֹס אֶחָד. אֲבָל לְאוֹפוֹת אוֹתָהּ אֵינָהּ אוֹפָה אֶלָּא צוֹרְכָהּ. דְּתַנֵּי רִבִּי שִׁמְעוֹן בֶּן אֶלְעָזָר אוֹמֵר מְמַלְאָה הִיא אִשָּׁה אֶת הַתַּנּוּר פַּת מִפְּנֵי שֶׁהַפַּת יָפֶה בְּשָׁעָה שֶׁהַתַּנּוּר מָלֵא.

"It may be made on a holiday." The Mishnah is Rebbi Simeon ben Eleazar's, as it was stated[215]: "One does not make [food] on a holiday for use after the holiday." Also, it was stated: "A woman may fill a pot with meat even if one eats only one piece from it, a water pot[216] with hot water even if one drinks only one cup from it. But baking, she should bake only what she needs." For it is stated: "Rebbi Simeon ben Eleazar says, a woman may fill the entire oven with bread because the bread turns out well if the oven is filled.[217]"

215 Tosefta *Yom Ṭob* 2:3, reading of the Erfurt ms. and the Yerushalmi *Yom Ṭob* 2:1 (fol. 61b). The Babli (*Beẓah* 17a) and the Vienna ms. read אין אופין "one does not bake". In all Tosephta sources, the second quote is formulated in the masculine but even the Babli quotes it as speaking of a woman cook.

216 Latin *cucuma, ae, f.*, "kettle".

217 Since the Mishnah here is anonymous and permits the preparation of dog biscuits unconditionally, it determines practice following R. Simeon ben Eleazar [*Yom Ṭob* 2:1 (fol. 61b), Babli *Beẓah* 17a.]

תַּנֵּי מַצָּה גְזוּלָה אָסוּר לְבָרֵךְ עָלֶיהָ. אָמַר רִבִּי הוֹשַׁעְיָה עַל שֵׁם וּבוֹצֵעַ בֵּרֵךְ נִאֵץ יי. אָמַר רִבִּי יוֹנָה הָדָא דְתֵימָא בַּתְּחִילָּה אֲבָל בַּסּוֹף לֹא דָמִים הוּא חַייָב לוֹ. רִבִּי יוֹנָה אָמַר אֵין עֲבֵירָה מִצְוָה. רִבִּי יוֹסֵי אָמַר אֵין מִצְוָה עֲבֵירָה. אָמַר רִבִּי הִילָא אֵלֶּה הַמִּצְוֹת אִם עֲשִׂיתָן כְּמִצְוָתָן הֵן מִצְוֹת וְאִם לָאו אֵינָן מִצְוֹת.

It was stated: It is forbidden to recite a benediction over a robbed *mazzah*[218]. Rebbi Hoshaia said, because of (*Ps.* 10:3): "He who recites the blessing over a piece of bread blasphemes.[219]" Rebbi Jonah said, that is, originally. But in the end, does he not incur a monetary obligation[220]? Rebbi Jonah said, no sin can be a good deed[221]. Rebbi Yose said, no good deed can be a sin[222]. Rebbi Hila said, (*Lev.* 27:34): "These are the commandments." If you did them they way they were commanded they are a good deeds; otherwise they are not good deeds[223].

218 The parallel is in *Šabbat* 13:3 (fol. 14a); in the Babli (*Sanhedrin* 6b, *Baba Qama* 94a) and in Yerushalmi *Sanhedrin* 1:1 (fol. 18b) this is a tannaïtic statement. Here, the argument is that a religious obligation, like eating *mazzah* on Passover, cannot be fulfilled in a sinful way. The Babli insists that not even the regular benedictions before and after eating can be recited if the food is stolen or robbed.

219 Usually, the verse is read to mean: "Certainly, the wicked one praises his own desires; *he who blesses unlawful gain slanders the Eternal*!" The Tosephta (*Sanhedrin* 1:2) explains the verse as referring to judges who do not follow the rules.

220 The robber certainly cannot recite a benediction for robbed food, but after he ate it he acquired the food (or if he robbed flour he acquired it by baking) and is no longer required to return the robbed piece but has to pay. In that stage, the robber seems to be in the same position as a buyer who is slow in paying and one does not understand why he should not recite grace.

221 A good deed done by immoral means is no good deed at all and no religious obligation can be satisfied in this way. He declares his first argument faulty.

222 He accepts R. Jonah's logic, cf. Note 159.

223 He sides with R. Jonah against R. Yose.

(fol. 57a) **משנה ט**: הַחַלָּה וְהַתְּרוּמָה חַייָבִין עֲלֵיהֶן מִיתָה וְחוֹמֶשׁ וְאֲסוּרָה לְזָרִים וְהֵן נִכְסֵי כֹהֵן וְעוֹלִין בְּאֶחָד וּמֵאָה וּטְעוּנִין רְחִיצַת יָדַיִם וְרַגְלַיִים וְהַעֲרֵב שֶׁמֶשׁ וְאֵינָן נִיטָּלִין מִן הַטָּהוֹר עַל הַטָּמֵא אֶלָּא מִן הַמּוּקָף וּמִן הַדָּבָר הַגָּמוּר. הָאוֹמֵר כָּל־גּוֹרְנִי תְרוּמָה וְכָל־עִיסָּתִי חַלָּה לֹא אָמַר כְּלוּם עַד שֶׁיְּשַׁייֵר מִקְצָת.

Mishnah 9: *Ḥallah* and heave. [234]About them one is liable to death[235] and a fifth[236], they are forbidden to laymen[237], are Cohen's property, can be lifted in 101[238], need washing of the hands[239] (and feet)[240] and sundown[241], are not taken from pure for impure[242] but only from what is earmarked[243] and completed[244]. He who says, all my threshing floor is heave or all my dough is *ḥallah* did not say anything unless he left out a small amount.

234 Most of these rules have been spelled out for heave in Tractate *Terumot*; the sentence spells out that *ḥallah* is not only called "heave" (*Num.* 15:20-21) but actually follows all rules of heave.

235 *Lev.* 22:3.

236 *Terumot* 6:1.

237 *Lev.* 22:10. Since this rule is mentioned after the penalties, it must mean that consumption by laymen of quantities too small to merit judicial attention is still forbidden.

238 *Terumot* Chapter 5.

239 An extension of the injunction *Ex.* 30:17-21.

240 A scribal error in the ms. and some sources dependent on it; cf. *The Mishnah with variant readings, Zera'im* II (Jerusalem 1975), p. 325, Note 74.

241 *Lev.* 22:7.

242 *Terumot* 2:1.

243 *Terumot* 1:1, Note 6.

244 Completely processed; *Ma'serot* 1.

(fol. 58a) **הלכה י**: רִבִּי יוּדָה בַּר פָּזִי רִבִּי חָנִין בְּשֵׁם רִבִּי שְׁמוּאֵל בַּר רַב יִצְחָק חַלָּה חוּלִין הוּא הָיִיתִי אוֹמֵר מוּתָּר לְגַלְגֵּל בָּהֶן. לְפוּם כֵּן צָרִיךְ מֵימַר הַחַלָּה וְהַתְּרוּמָה חַייָבִין עֲלֵיהֶן מִיתָה וְחוֹמֶשׁ.

Halakhah 10: Rebbi Judah bar Pazi, Rebbi Ḥanin in the name of Rebbi Samuel bar Rav Isaac, *ḥallah* might be profane[245], I would say it is permitted to wait[246] with it. Therefore, it was necessary to say: "*Ḥallah* and heave. About them one is liable to death and a fifth".

245 One might think that the root of the word חלה is (rabbinic) חול (Arabic حلّ) "to be permitted, to be profane".

246 "To roll around", used to characterize long drawn-out processes. Since *ḥallah* is invalidated by impurity, it should be delivered to a Cohen at the first opportunity.

עֶשֶׂר מִצְוֹת אָדָם עוֹשֶׂה עַד שֶׁלֹּא יֹאכַל פְּרוּסָה מִשּׁוּם לֹא תַחֲרוֹשׁ. בַּל תִּזְרַע בַּל תַּחְסוֹם. לֶקֶט שִׁכְחָה וּפֵיאָה. תְּרוּמָה וּמַעֲשֵׂר רִאשׁוֹן וּמַעֲשֵׂר שֵׁינִי וְחַלָּה. רִבִּי יִצְחָק כַּידוֹ אָתֵי מֵיסַב לְיָדוֹי הוּא פָּשַׁט עֲשַׂרְתֵּי אֶצְבְּעָתֵיהּ וְאָמַר הֲרֵי קִייַּמְתִּי עֶשֶׂר מִצְווֹת.

Ten commandments does a person fulfill before he eats a piece of bread: Do not plough[247], do now sow[248], do not muzzle[249], gleanings[250], forgotten sheaves[251], and *peah*[252], heave, first tithe, second tithe, and *ḥallah*. Before Rebbi Isaac went to dinner, he spread out his ten fingers and said, I kept ten commandments.

247 "With ox and donkey together", *Deut*. 22:10.

248 "Your field do not sow as *kilaim*", *Lev*. 25:4.

249 "Your ox while threshing", *Deut.* 25:4.

250 *Lev.* 19:9.

251 *Deut.* 24:14.

חַלָּה עַל הַכֹּל תְּרוּמָה עַל הַכֹּל. תְּרוּמָה לַיי זֶה שֵׁם הַמְּיוּחָד. מְנַיִין שֶׁלֹּא עָשָׂה כְלוּם עַד שֶׁיְּשַׁיֵּיר מִקְצָת תַּלְמוּד לוֹמַר מֵרֵאשִׁית וְלֹא כָל־רֵאשִׁית.

[252]"*Ḥallah* for all, heave for all." "To YHWH," that is the particular Name. From where that he did not do anything until he left some [as profane]? The verse says (*Num.* 15:21): "Of the beginning" and not all the beginning.

252 This paragraph is a truncated quote from *Ma'aser Šeni* Chapter 5 and is explained there, Notes 145-147. The paragraph should start: Rebbi Yose ben Rebbi Abun said, he must say "*ḥallah* for all," . . .

פירות חוצה לארץ פרק שני

(fol. 58a) **משנה א:** פֵּירוֹת חוּצָה לָאָרֶץ שֶׁנִּכְנְסוּ לָאָרֶץ חַייָבִין בְּחַלָּה. יָֽצְאוּ מִכָּאן לְשָׁם רִבִּי לִיעֶזֶר מְחַייֵב וְרִבִּי עֲקִיבָה פּוֹטֵר.

Mishnah 1: Foreign produce imported into the Land is obligated for *hallah*. If it was exported, Rebbi Eliezer declares it obligated but Rebbi Aqiba declares it free.

(fol. 58b) **הלכה א:** פֵּירוֹת חוּצָה לָאָרֶץ כול׳. כְּתִיב אֶל הָאָרֶץ אֲשֶׁר אֲנִי מֵבִיא אֶתְכֶם שָׁמָּה. שָׁמָּה אַתֶּם חַייָבִין. אֵין אַתֶּם חַייָבִין חוּץ לָאָרֶץ. תַּנֵּי זוֹ דִבְרֵי רִבִּי מֵאִיר. אֲבָל דִּבְרֵי רִבִּי יְהוּדָה פֵּירוֹת חוּצָה לָאָרֶץ שֶׁנִּכְנְסוּ לָאָרֶץ רִבִּי לִיעֶזֶר פּוֹטֵר וְרִבִּי עֲקִיבָה מְחַייֵב. מַה טַעֲמָא דְּרִבִּי אֱלִיעֶזֶר לֶחֶם הָאָרֶץ. לֹא לֶחֶם חוּץ לָאָרֶץ. מָה טַעֲמָא דְּרִבִּי עֲקִיבָה אֶל הָאָרֶץ אֲשֶׁר אֲנִי מֵבִיא אֶתְכֶם שָׁמָּה. שָׁמָּה אַתֶּם חַייָבִין בֵּין בְּפֵירוֹת הָאָרֶץ בֵּין בְּפֵירוֹת חוּץ לָאָרֶץ.

Halakhah 1: "Foreign produce," etc. It is written (*Num.* 15:17) "To the Land into which I am bringing you.[1]" There you are obligated, you are not obligated outside the Land. It was stated: These are the words of Rebbi Meïr. But the words of Rebbi Jehudah[2] are: Foreign produce imported into the Land, Rebbi Eliezer declares it free but Rebbi Aqiba declares it obligated. What is the reason of Rebbi Eliezer? (*Num.* 15:18) "From the Land's bread," not foreign bread. What is the reason of Rebbi Aqiba? (*Num.* 15:17) "To the Land into which I am bringing you." There you are obligated, both for produce of the Land and foreign produce."

1 "When you come into the Land into which I am bringing you, (v. 18) it shall be that on the occasion of your eating from the bread of the Land you shall lift a heave for the Eternal."

2 Who is a better authority than R. Meïr. The same statement in *Sifry Num.* 110. In *Ma'serot* 5:4 (Note 83), R. Jehudah's interpretation of the position of R. Aqiba is presented as genuine.

מָה מְקַיֵּים רִבִּי אֱלִיעֶזֶר טַעֲמָא דְּרִבִּי עֲקִיבָה אֶל הָאָרֶץ אֲשֶׁר אֲנִי מֵבִיא אֶתְכֶם שָׁמָּה. חֲבֵרַייָא בְשֵׁם רִבִּי לָעְזָר רִבִּי בָּא בְשֵׁם רִבִּי לָעְזָר. רִבִּי הִילָא בְשֵׁם רִבִּי שִׁמְעוֹן בֶּן לָקִישׁ. כָּךְ מֵשִׁיב רִבִּי עֲקִיבָה אֶת רִבִּי לִיעֶזֶר אֵין אַתְּ מוֹדֵי לִי בְשָׁעָה שֶׁנִּכְנְסוּ יִשְׂרָאֵל לָאָרֶץ וּמָצְאוּ קְמָחִין וּסְלָתוֹת שֶׁהֵן חַייָבִין בְּחַלָּה. וְלָאו גִּידּוּלֵי פְטוֹר הֵן וְהוּא מְקַבֵּל מִינֵיהּ. אָמַר רִבִּי יוֹסֵי תְּמִיהָנִי אֵיךְ רִבִּי עֲקִיבָה מוֹתִיב אֶת רִבִּי לִיעֶזֶר וְהוּא מְקַבֵּל מִינֵּיהּ. תַּמָּן עַד שֶׁלֹּא נִכְנְסוּ לָהּ לְמַפְרֵיעָה יָרְשׁוּ דְּאָמַר רִבִּי הוּנָא בְשֵׁם רִבִּי שְׁמוּאֵל בַּר נַחְמָן לְזַרְעֲךָ אֶתֵּן אֵין כְּתִיב כָּאן אֶלָּא לְזַרְעֲךָ נָתַתִּי כְּבָר נָתַתִּי.

How does Rebbi Eliezer explain the reason of Rebbi Aqiba, (*Num.* 15:17) "To the Land into which I am bringing you?" The colleagues in the name of Rebbi Eleazar, Rebbi Abba in the name of Rebbi Eleazar, Rebbi Hila in the name of Rebbi Simeon ben Laqish: So did Rebbi Aqiba object to Rebbi Eliezer: Do you not agree that when Israel entered the Land and found there coarse and fine flour[3] that this was subject to *hallah*? Did it not grow while exempt? He accepted that[4]. Rebbi Yose said, I am wondering how could Rebbi Aqiba object to Rebbi Eliezer and how could the latter accept it? There, before they entered they had inherited it retroactively, as Rebbi Huna said in the name of Rebbi Samuel ben Naḥman: It is not written "to your posterity I shall give" but (*Gen.* 15:18): "to your posterity I gave", I already gave it.

3 R. Simson and R. Solomon ben Adrat read: "(coarse) flour and doughs". This is from a textual tradition different from our mss.; it is very likely a late change since (a) in talmudic Hebrew, קמח means only "coarse flour"; the re-emergence of the biblical meaning "flour" (irrespective of quality) is definitely Medieval rabbinic; (b) only R. Aqiba (later in this Halakhah and in Mishnah 3:5) moves the obligation of ḥallah from kneading the dough to baking it. It is unreasonable to expect R. Eliezer to accept this position.

4 As seen later, without giving up his interpretation of the verses for current practice.

מָה מְקַיֵּים רִבִּי עֲקִיבָה טַעֲמָא דְּרִבִּי אֱלִיעֶזֶר לֶחֶם הָאָרֶץ. בִּסְפִינָה שֶׁנִּכְנְסָה לָאָרֶץ. אִם קִירְמוּ פָּנֶיהָ מִן הַחוּט וְלִפְנִים חַייֶבֶת. מִן הַחוּט וְלַחוּץ פְּטוּרָה. עַל דַּעְתֵּיהּ דְּרִבִּי עֲקִיבָה הִיא סְפִינְתָא הִיא עִיסַּת הַגּוֹי הִיא הַכְנָסָתָן שֶׁהַכֹּל הוֹלֵךְ אַחַר קְרִימָה בַּתַּנּוּר. מוֹדִין חֲכָמִים לְרִבִּי עֲקִיבָה בְּהַכְנָסָתָן לָאָרֶץ שֶׁהַכֹּל הוֹלֵךְ אַחַר קְרִימָה בַּתַּנּוּר. מִן מָה דְּרִבִּי עֲקִיבָה מָתִיב לְרִבִּי לִיעֶזֶר וְהוּא מְקַבֵּל מִינֵּיהּ.

How does Rebbi Aqiba explain the reason of Rebbi Eliezer, (*Num.* 15:18) "From the Land's bread?" About a ship which entered the Land. If it made a crust in the oven inside the line[5] it is obligated, outside the line it is exempt. In the opinion of Rebbi Aqiba, the same rule applies to a ship, Gentile's dough[6], and their entry; everything depends on forming the crust in the oven. The Sages agree with Rebbi Aqiba when it enters the Land that everything depends on forming the crust in the oven. This is implied by what Rebbi Aqiba objected to Rebbi Eliezer and the latter accepted it.

5 The imaginary line drawn from the Northernmost point on the coast of the Biblical Land of Israel to the Southernmost, which defines the territorial waters of the Land according to the majority opinion; cf.

Ševi'it 6:2, Notes 92-94; *Ḥallah* 4:8. For the role of baking in determining the obligation cf. Halakhah 3:5.

6 Which is exempt if baked by a Gentile, obligated if baked by a Jew.

רִבִּי יוֹנָה בָּעָא קוֹמֵי רִבִּי יִרְמְיָה בְּשָׁעָה שֶׁנִּכְנְסוּ יִשְׂרָאֵל לָאָרֶץ וּמָצָא קָמָה לֵחָה מַהוּ שֶׁתְּהֵא אֲסוּרָה מִשּׁוּם חָדָשׁ. אָמַר לוֹ לָמָּה לֹא. עַד כְּדוֹן לֵחָה אֲפִילוּ יְבֵישָׁה. אָמַר לֵיהּ אֲפִילוּ יְבֵישָׁה אֲפִילוּ קְצוּרָה. מֵעַתָּה אֲפִילוּ חִיטִּין בָּעֲלִייָה. כָּךְ אֲנִי אוֹמֵר לֹא יֹאכְלוּ יִשְׂרָאֵל מַצָּה בְּלֵילֵי הַפֶּסַח. אָמַר רִבִּי יוֹנָה מִן דְּנַפְקוֹת תָּהִית דְּלֹא אָמְרָת לֵיהּ שַׁנְיָיא הִיא שֶׁמִּצְוַות עֲשֵׂה דוֹחָה לְמִצְוַות לֹא תַעֲשֶׂה. עַל דַּעְתֵּיהּ דְּרִבִּי יוֹנָה דּוּ אָמַר מִצְוַת עֲשֵׂה דוֹחָה בְּלֹא תַעֲשֶׂה אַף עַל פִּי שֶׁאֵינָהּ כְּתוּבָה בְּצִידָּהּ נִיחָא. עַל דַּעְתֵּיהּ דְּרִבִּי יוֹסֵי דּוּ אָמַר אֵין מִצְוַת עֲשֵׂה דוֹחָה לְמִצְוֹת בְּלֹא תַעֲשֶׂה אֶלָּא אִם כֵּן הָיְתָה כְתוּבָה בְּצִידָּהּ מַה שֶׁיִּהְיוּ תַגָּרֵי גוֹיִם מוֹכְרִין לָהֶם וּכְרִבִּי יִשְׁמָעֵאל. דְּרִבִּי יִשְׁמָעֵאל אָמַר כָּל־בִּיאוֹת שֶׁנֶּאֶמְרוּ בַתּוֹרָה לְאַחַר אַרְבַּע עֶשְׂרֵה שָׁנָה נֶאֶמְרוּ שֶׁבַע שֶׁכִּיבְּשׁוּ וְשֶׁבַע שֶׁחִילְּקוּ. הָתִיב רִבִּי בּוּן בַּר כַּהֲנָא וְהָכְתִיב וַיֹּאכְלוּ מֵעֲבוּר הָאָרֶץ מִמָּחֳרַת הַפֶּסַח. לֹא בְשִׁשָּׁה עָשָׂר. הָתִיב רִבִּי לָעְזָר בֵּירִבִּי יוֹסֵי קוֹמֵי רִבִּי יוֹסֵי וְהָכְתִיב מִמָּחֳרַת הַפֶּסַח יָצְאוּ בְנֵי יִשְׂרָאֵל בְּיַד רָמָה בְּעֵינֵי כָּל־מִצְרָיִם. לֹא בַחֲמִשָּׁה עָשָׂר.

Rebbi Jonah asked before Rebbi Jeremiah: When Israel entered the Land and found there green grain standing, would that have been forbidden as new[7]? He said to him, why not? So far green, even dry? He said to him, even dry, even cut. Then even grain in storage! So I am saying, Israel should not have eaten *mazzot* in the Passover nights[8]! Rebbi Jonah said, after I left there, I wondered that I did not say to him, it is different because a positive commandment overrides a prohibition[9]. In the opinion of Rebbi Jonah who said, a positive commandment overrides a prohibition even if it is not written next to it, it is understood. But according to Rebbi Yose who said, a positive commandment overrides a prohibition only if it is written next to it[10]? What Gentile traders sold them, or following Rebbi Ismael, since Rebbi Ismael said, any "coming"[11] mentioned in the Torah means after 14 years, seven of their conquest, seven of the distribution[12]. Rebbi Abun bar Cahana objected: Is it not written (*Jos.* 5:11): "They ate from the produce of the Land the day after the *Pesah*," on the sixteenth! Rebbi Eleazar ben Rebbi Yose objected before Rebbi Yose: Is it not written (*Num.* 33:3): "The day after the *Pesah*, the Children of Israel left with raised hand before the eyes of all of Egypt." Not on the fifteenth[13]?

7 Before the *'omer*, cf. Chapter 1, Notes 3-5.

8 But they observed *Pesaḥ* on the 14th (*Jos.* 5:10); how could they have fulfilled the commandment to eat the meat "with *mazzot* and bitter herbs" when all grain was forbidden as new since the preceding year there could not have been any *'omer* and, according to the argument of the preceding paragraph, the laws were applicable retroactively?

9 This is the position accepted everywhere in the Babli where, however, the principle is severely restricted (*Yebamot* 3b/4a).

10 The disagreement between Rebbis Jonah and Yose is also discussed *Yom Ṭov* 1:3 (fol. 60b, bottom) and commented upon by *Or Zarua'* vol. 2, #234. The position of R. Yose is not mentioned in the Babli. As *Tosaphot* note in *Qiddušin* 38a (an opinion attributed by *Or Zarua'* to R. Jacob ben Meïr of Provins), the argument of R. Jonah is weak since even according to him, only the first bite of *mazzah* would be permitted as a positive commandment; all further consumption of new bread would have been sinful.

11 Any commandment introduced with the remark: "When you *come* to the Land."

12 Cf. *Ševi'it* 6, Note 10. The statement of R. Ismael is discussed at length in Babli *Qiddušin* 37a-38a; it is quoted in Yerushalmi *'Orlah* 1:2 (fol. 60d), *Soṭah* 7:4 (fol. 21c), 9:1 (fol. 23c).

13 *Pesaḥ* in Biblical texts is only the sacrifice of the afternoon of the

14th of Nisan. Only in rabbinic texts does *Pesah* stand for the holiday of unleavened bread, usually called Passover, starting on the 15th. The objection of R. Abun bar Cahana is anachronistic.

יָצְאוּ מִכָּאן לְשָׁם רִבִּי לִיעֶזֶר מְחַייֵב וְרִבִּי עֲקִיבָה פוֹטֵר. אָמְרוּ רִבִּי לִיעֶזֶר מִן אַתְרֵיהּ וְרִבִּי עֲקִיבָה מִן אַתְרֵיהּ. רִבִּי לִיעֶזֶר מִן אַתְרֵיהּ מָה טַעֲמָא דְּרִבִּי לִיעֶזֶר לֶחֶם הָאָרֶץ בְּכָל־מָקוֹם שֶׁהוּא. מָה טַעֲמָא דְּרִבִּי עֲקִיבָה אֶל הָאָרֶץ אֲשֶׁר אֲנִי מֵבִיא אֶתְכֶם שָׁמָּה אַתֶּם חַייָבִין. וְאֵין אַתֶּם חַייָבִין חוּץ לָאָרֶץ.

"If it was exported[14], Rebbi Eliezer declares it obligated but Rebbi Aqiba declares it free." They said, Rebbi Eliezer [is explained] from his quote, Rebbi Aqiba from his quote. Rebbi Eliezer from his quote; what is the reason of Rebbi Eliezer? (*Num.* 15:18) "From the Land's bread," wherever it may be. What is the reason of Rebbi Aqiba? (*Num.* 15:17) "To the Land into which I am bringing you;" there you are obligated; you are not obligated outside the Land.

14 Outside the Land of Israel.

(fol. 58a) **משנה ב:** עָפָר חוּצָה לָאָרֶץ הַבָּא בִסְפִינָה לָאָרֶץ חַייָב בְּמַעְשְׂרוֹת וּבִשְׁבִיעִית. אָמַר רִבִּי יְהוּדָה (fol. 58b) אֵימָתַי בִּזְמַן שֶׁהַסְּפִינָה גוֹשֶׁשֶׁת. עִיסָּה שֶׁנִּילוֹשָׁה בְמֵי פֵירוֹת חַייֶבֶת בְּחַלָּה וְנֶאֱכֶלֶת בְּיָדַיִם מְסוֹאָבוֹת.

Mishnah 2: [Growth of] earth from outside the Land which came to the Land in a ship is under the obligation of tithes and Sabbatical. Rebbi Jehudah said, when is this? When the ship touches the ground. Dough kneaded with fruit juice is subject to *ḥallah* which can be eaten with unclean hands[15].

15 Pure fruit juice, without addition of water, does not make food susceptible to impurity (cf. *Demay* 2, Notes 136-137.) Therefore, *ḥallah* from such a dough cannot become impure and may be eaten by a pure Cohen without washing of his hands (cf. *Berakhot* 8, Note 46).

הלכה ב: רַבָּנִין דְּקַיְסָרִין בְּשֵׁם רִבִּי חֲנִינָה בְּמַחְלוֹקֶת. כָּל־מָקוֹם אֲשֶׁר תִּדְרוֹךְ כַּף רַגְלֵיכֶם בּוֹ לָכֶם יִהְיֶה. אֵין בִּכְלָל אֶלָּא מַה שֶׁבִּפְרָט וּכְרִבִּי יוּדָה. מֵתִיבִין לְרִבִּי יוּדָה אִם בִּסְפָרֵי אֶרֶץ יִשְׂרָאֵל וְהָכְתִיב מֵהַמִּדְבָּר וְהַלְּבָנוֹן הַזֶּה וְעַד הַנָּהָר הַגָּדוֹל נְהַר פְּרָת כָּל־אֶרֶץ הַחִתִּים וְעַד הַיָּם הַגָּדוֹל מְבוֹא הַשֶּׁמֶשׁ יִהְיֶה גְּבוּלְכֶם. אֶלָּא אִם אֵינוֹ עִנְיָין לִסְפָרֵי יִשְׂרָאֵל תְּנֵיהוּ עִנְיָין לִסְפָרֵי חוּץ לָאָרֶץ. מֵעַתָּה מַה שֶׁהָיָה דָוִד הוֹלֵךְ וּמְכַבֵּשׁ בַּאֲרָם נַהֲרַיִם וּבַאֲרָם צוֹבָה יְהוּ חַייָבִין בְּחַלָּה. שַׁנְייָא הִיא שֶׁהָיָה דָּוִד מַנִּיחַ סְפָרֵי אֶרֶץ יִשְׂרָאֵל (fol. 58c) וּמְכַבֵּשׁ סְפָרֵי חוּץ לָאָרֶץ.

Halakhah 2: The rabbis of Caesarea in the name of Rebbi Ḥanina: The disagreement: (*Deut*. 11:24) "Any place[16] your foot will tread on shall be yours," the general statement contains only the detail[17], and following Rebbi Jehudah[18]. They object to Rebbi Jehudah: If this is about the boundaries of the Land of Israel, is there not written: (*Jos*. 1:4) "From the prairie and this Lebanon up to the great river, the Euphrates, all the land of the Hittites[19] and to the great ocean at sunset shall be your borders." If it[20] cannot deal with the border regions of the Land of Israel, consider it for the border regions outside the Land[21]. Then, what David was conquering in Aram of the rivers and Aram Ẓova should be subject to *ḥallah*! There is a difference, because David was neglecting the border regions of the Land of Israel and conquering the border regions outside the Land[22].

16 In the masoretic text: בל המקום. כל מקום is in the parallel *Jos.* 1:3 which cannot be the verse quoted here.

17 The full verse reads: Any place your foot will tread on shall be yours, from the prairie and the Lebanon, from the river Euphrates to the Western Sea shall be your border region. It is a hermeneutic principle (*Sifra*, Introduction, 7) that a general statement followed immediately by a clarification means only what is intended in the clarification. Therefore, "Any place" means only the region described here in general terms and in detail in *Num.* 34:1-12; "river Euphrates" here can only mean the region of Dura Europos, nearest to the Mediterranean.

18 Who defines the Western Sea as the Atlantic Ocean (at the Straits of Gibraltar) rather than the Mediterranean; cf. *Ševi'it* 6, Note 93.

19 The Hittite settlement in the region after the disappearance of the Hittite empire in central Anatolia.

20 The general statement "any place".

21 That, if conquered, would become part of the Land of Israel.

22 The Northern part of the Land, the region of Phoenicia, as described in *Num.* 34:1-12 never was part of David's empire. Therefore, he was not authorized to conquer the regions East of the promised Land. The argument appears in greater detail in *Sifry Deut.* 51.

הֲווֹ בָּעֵיי מֵימַר מָה דְאָמַר תַּמָּן חַייָב אוּף הָכָא חַייָב. מָה דְאָמַר תַּמָּן פָּטוּר אוּף הָכָא פָּטוּר. אֲפִילוּ כְּמָאן דְּאָמַר תַּמָּן פָּטוּר הָכָא חַייָב. כֵּיוָן שֶׁנִּכְנְסוּ יִשְׂרָאֵל נִתְחַייְבוּ. כְּתִיב הוּא הֵשִׁיב אֶת גְּבוּל יִשְׂרָאֵל מִלְּבוֹא חֲמָת עַד יָם הָעֲרָבָה כִּדְבַר יי אֱלֹהֵי יִשְׂרָאֵל אֲשֶׁר דִּבֶּר בְּיַד עַבְדּוֹ יוֹנָה בֶן אֲמִתַּי הַנָּבִיא אֲשֶׁר מִגַּת הַחֵפֶר. רִבִּי חֲנַנְיָה וְרִבִּי מָנָא חַד אָמַר כָּל־מָה שֶׁכִּיבֵּשׁ יְהוֹשֻׁעַ כִּיבֵּשׁ זֶה. וְחָרָנָה אָמַר יוֹתֵר מִמָּה שֶׁכִּיבֵּשׁ יְהוֹשֻׁעַ כִּיבֵּשׁ זֶה. תַּנָּא רִבִּי סִידוֹר מְסַייֵעַ לְרִבִּי מָנָא יָמִים קַלִּים עָשׂוּ יִשְׂרָאֵל בְּאוֹתָהּ הָאָרֶץ,

They wanted to say, according to him[23] who said, there it is obligated, also here it is obligated; according to him[24] who said, there it is exempt, also here it is exempt. Even according to him who says, there it is exempt, here it is obligated for when Israel entered they became obligated[25]. It is written (*2K*. 14:25): "He reëstablished the borders of Israel from Lebo-Ḥamat[26] to the sea of the Arabah, following the word of the Eternal, the God of Israel, which He had said through Jonah ben Amittai, the prophet from Gat-Ḥepher." Rebbi Ḥananiah and Rebbi Mana, one said that all that Joshua had conquered this one conquered. The other said, more than Joshua had conquered this one conquered. Rebbi Sidor[27] stated, in support of Rebbi Mana: Few days only did Israel hold on to this land[28].

23 Rebbi Ḥananiah (?, probably Ḥaninah), who later in the paragraph holds that all the land conquered by Jeroboam II has the status of land conquered by Joshua.

24 Rebbi Mana I, later in this paragraph.

25 Even R. Mana will agree that under Joshua, the Land became obligated immediately upon being taken.

26 Lebweh in the Beqaa valley in Lebanon, the Northernmost city in Solomon's kingdom.

27 An early Galilean Amora, perhaps called Isidor, possibly a student of Jehudah, the son of the elder R. Ḥiyya.

28 Which, therefore, did not acquire the status of "Land of Israel." Since R. Mana is identified as "the other", R. Ḥananiah (Ḥaninah) must be the author of the first opinion.

עָפָר חוּץ לָאָרֶץ שֶׁבָּא לְסוּרְיָא נַעֲשָׂה כְסוּרְיָא. יָצָא מִשָּׁם לְכָאן נִתְחַייֵב.

Earth from outside the Land which came into Syria[29] becomes like Syria. Coming from there to here it becomes obligated.

29 The land temporarily conquered by David outside the biblical borders; cf. *Peah* 7, Note 119. Since most agricultural rules of the Land held in Syria by rabbinic decree, Syria is not "outside the Land." But it is not part of the Land either.

אָמַר רִבִּי יוּדָה אֵימָתַי בִּזְמַן שֶׁהַסְּפִינָה גוֹשֶׁשֶׁת. אָמַר רִבִּי חַגַּיי רִבִּי יוּדָה כְּדַעְתֵּיהּ דְּרִבִּי יוּדָה פּוֹטֵר בְּמַיִם שֶׁאֵין בָּהֶן מַמָּשׁ. אָמַר רִבִּי אָבִין לֹא מִסְתַּבְּרָא דְלֹא מִחְלְפָה שִׁיטָּתֵיהּ. לֹא הָיְתָה אֶת הַסְּפִינָה גוֹשֶׁשֶׁת כְּמוֹ שֶׁהַסְּפִינָה גוֹשֶׁשֶׁת. לֹא הָיְתָה הַסְּפִינָה גוֹשֶׁשֶׁת מַעְשְׂרוֹתֶיהָ מֵהֲלָכָה תּוֹרְמִין מִמֶּנָּה עַל עָצִיץ שֶׁאֵין נָקוּב וּמֵעָצִיץ שֶׁאֵין נָקוּב עָלֶיהָ. כְּהָדָא דְתַנֵּי עָצִיץ שֶׁאֵינוֹ נָקוּב מַעְשְׂרוֹתָיו מֵהֲלָכָה וּתְרוּמָתוֹ אֵינָהּ מְדַמַּעַת וְאֵין חַייָבִין עָלָיו חוֹמֶשׁ. רִבִּי הִילָא בְשֵׁם רִבִּי לְעָזָר הַקּוֹנֶה עָצִיץ נָקוּב בְּסוּרְיָא אַף עַל פִּי שֶׁלֹּא קָנָה עָפָר שֶׁתַּחְתָּיו וְקַרְקַע שֶׁעַל גַּבָּיו קָנָה לְחַייְבוֹ לְמַעְשְׂרוֹת וְלַשְּׁבִיעִית אֲפִילוּ נָתוּן עַל גַּבֵּי שְׁתֵּי יְתֵידוֹת. אַף רִבִּי יוּדָה מוֹדֵי בָהּ. מָה בֵינוֹ לְבֵין הַסְּפִינָה. סְפִינָה עוֹלָה וְיוֹרֶדֶת וְזֶה בִמְקוֹמוֹ הוּא.

"Rebbi Jehudah said, when is this? When the ship touches ground." Rebbi Ḥaggai said, Rebbi Jehudah follows his opinion[30] since Rebbi Jehudah exempts water[31], as it has no consistency[32]. Rebbi Abin said, it is more reasonable to assume his opinion changed; if the ship does not touch ground, would it not be as if the ship touched ground[33]? If the ship does not touch ground, its tithes are of practice; one tithes from it for a flower pot without hole and from a flower pot without hole for it, as it was stated[34]: "The tithes from a flower pot without hole are of practice[35], its heave does not create *dema'* and one does not owe a fifth for it." Rebbi Hila in the name of Rebbi Eleazar: If somebody acquires a flower pot with a hole in Syria, even if he did not acquire the earth under it or the ground on which it stands, he acquired it to be obligated for tithes and the Sabbatical, even if it sits on two pegs. Even Rebbi Jehudah will agree with this. What is the difference between this case[36] and that of a ship? A ship rises and falls, this [flower pot] rests in its place.

30 In the Babli it is held that if R. Jehudah asks in the Mishnah, when is this?, he does not disagree with the anonymous Tanna but explains the latter's position (*Eruvin* 81a-82b, *Sanhedrin* 24b). This is not the position of the Yerushalmi; cf. *Ševi'it* 7, Note 90.

31 Mishnah *Bezah* 5:4: "If somebody borrows vessels before the holiday, they follow the feet of the borrower, on the holiday, the feet of the lender. Similarly, if a woman borrowed from another spices, water, or salt, they follow the feet of both of them. Rebbi Jehudah exempts water, for water has no consistency." If both the borrower and the lender made an *eruv* (cf. *Peah* 8, Note 56), the borrowed things can only be moved inside the territory accessible to both of them. R. Jehudah exempts water since it is permitted on a holiday to drink water from a brook; that water was outside the permitted domain when the holiday started.

32 In this interpretation, the water is disregarded and the wooden ship is considered as lying on the gound.

33 According to R. Ḥaggai, the condition that the boat touch ground seems unintelligible.

34 *Kilaim* 7:6, Note 84.

35 Without any biblical basis. The flower pot is of clay which may be impermeable. Plants growing in a flower pot are considered growing on the ground only if the flower pot has a hole letting the earth in the pot absorb moisture from the ground. A wooden ship touching ground can always be said to be connected to the earth under it; it might only be compared to a flower pot with a hole.

36 The flower pot with a hole permanently fixed on pegs above ground is obligated, the ship anchored but not touching ground is exempt.

הלכה ג: רִבִּי יוֹסֵי בֵּירִבִּי חֲנִינָה אָמַר דְּרִבִּי אֶלְעָזָר בֶּן יְהוּדָה אִישׁ בִּירְתוֹתָא הִיא דְּתַנִּינָן תַּמָּן רִבִּי לְעָזָר בֶּן יְהוּדָה אִישׁ בִּירְתוֹתָא אוֹמֵר מִשֵּׁם רִבִּי יְהוֹשֻׁעַ פָּסַל אֶת כּוּלָּהּ. וְרִבִּי עֲקִיבָה אוֹמֵר מִשְּׁמוֹ לֹא פָּסַל אֶלָּא מְקוֹם מַגָּעוֹ. רִבִּי שִׁמְעוֹן בֶּן לָקִישׁ אָמַר מָה פְלִיגִין. בְּשֶׁהוּכְשְׁרָה וְאַחַר כָּךְ נִילוֹשָׁה שֶׁמֵּי פֵירוֹת מְחוּוָרִין לְהַכְשִׁיר. אֲבָל אִם נִילוֹשָׁה וְאַחַר כָּךְ הוּכְשְׁרָה אֵין מֵי פֵירוֹת מְחוּוָרִין

לְהַכְשִׁיר. רִבִּי חִייָה בְשֵׁם רִבִּי יוֹחָנָן דִּבְרֵי הַכֹּל הִיא. אַף עַל גַּב דְּרִבִּי עֲקִיבָה אָמַר תַּמָּן אֵין מֵי פֵירוֹת מְחוּוָרִין לְטוּמְאָה מוֹדֵי הוּא הָכָא שֶׁמֵּי פֵירוֹת מְחוּוָרִין לַחַלָּה.

Halakhah 3[37]: Rebbi Yose ben Rebbi Ḥanina said, this is the opinion of Rebbi Eleazar ben Jehudah from Birtota, as we have stated there[38]: "Rebbi Eleazar ben Jehudah from Birtota says in the name of Rebbi Joshua, he made everything unusable. But Rebbi Aqiba says in the latter's name, he made unusable only the place where he touched." Rebbi Simeon ben Laqish said, when do they disagree? When it was prepared for impurity and after that was kneaded, when fruit juices clearly do prepare. But if it was kneaded and after that only prepared, fruit juices are not clear to prepare[39]. Rebbi Ḥiyya in the name of Rebbi Joḥanan: It is everybody's opinion. Even though Rebbi Aqiba says there that fruit juices have no clear connection with impurity, he agrees here that fruit juices are clearly for *ḥallah*[40].

37 The Halakhah discusses the statement of the Mishnah: "Dough kneaded with fruit juice is subject to ḥallah which can be eaten with unclean hands".

38 *Ṭevul Yom* 3:6: "Dough which was prepared by fluids and kneaded with fruit juice, if a *ṭevul yom* touches it, Rebbi Eleazar ben Jehudah from Birtota . . ." The Mishnah deals with heave in case the grain or the flour was prepared for impurity by contact with one of the fluids that activate impurity (cf. *Demay* 2, Notes 136-137). The *ṭevul yom* (cf. *Terumot* 5, Note 68) makes heave unusable by his touch; he has no influence on the purity status of profane food.

39 Fruit juice clearly does not prepare for impurity according to everybody. According to R. Simeon ben Laqish, R. Eleazar ben Jehudah holds that fruit juice keeps the dough together and it becomes unusable if part of it is unusable. R. Aqiba holds that fruit juices cannot have any

influence on the status of purity; one disregards the fact that the dough now forms a solid mass.

40 For *ḥallah*, R. Aqiba holds that anything used as bread falls under the rules of bread.

רִבִּי בָּא רִבִּי חִייָה בְּשֵׁם רִבִּי יְהוֹשֻׁעַ בֶּן לֵוִי אֵין לָךְ מְחוּוָר אֶלָּא שִׁבְעַת הַמַּשְׁקִין בִּלְבַד. רִבִּי יוֹסֵי בָּעֵי מָה אִיתְאֲמָרַת לַחַלָּה לְטוּמְאָה. אִין תֵּימַר לַחַלָּה כָּל־שֶׁכֵּן לְטוּמְאָה. אִין תֵּימַר לְטוּמְאָה הָא לַחַלָּה לֹא. רִבִּי יוֹנָה פְּשִׁיטָא לֵיהּ לַחַלָּה כָּל־שֶׁכֵּן לְטוּמְאָה. רִבִּי יוֹנָה כְּדַעְתֵּיהּ דְּרִבִּי יוֹנָה תַּנֵּי דְּרִבִּי שִׁמְעוֹן בֶּן יוֹחַי. רִבִּי יְהוֹשֻׁעַ בֶּן לֵוִי תַּנֵּי דְּרִבִּי שִׁמְעוֹן בֶּן יוֹחַי דְּתַנֵּי רִבִּי שִׁמְעוֹן בֶּן יוֹחַי רִבִּי טַרְפוֹן אוֹמֵר נֶאֱמַר כָּאן חַלָּה. וְנֶאֱמַר לְהַלָּן חַלַּת לֶחֶם שֶׁמֶן. מָה חַלָּה שֶׁנֶּאֶמְרָה לְהַלָּן עֲשׂוּיָה בְּשֶׁמֶן. אַף חַלָּה שֶׁנֶּאֱמַר כָּאן עֲשׂוּיָה בְּשֶׁמֶן. וְשֶׁמֶן אֶחָד מִשִּׁבְעַת הַמַּשְׁקִין הוּא.

Rebbi Abba, Rebbi Ḥiyya in the name of Rebbi Joshua ben Levi: Nothing is clear except the seven fluids[41]. Rebbi Yose asked: Was this said for *ḥallah*[42] or for impurity? If you say for *ḥallah*, so much more for impurity. If you say for impurity, then not for *ḥallah*. It is obvious for Rebbi Jonah that it had been said for *ḥallah*, so much more for impurity. Rebbi Jonah sticks to his opinion, for Rebbi Jonah stated from Rebbi Simeon ben Ioḥai; Rebbi Joshua ben Levi stated in Rebbi Simeon ben Ioḥai's name, as Rebbi Simeon ben Ioḥai stated: Rebbi Ṭarphon said, it is stated here[43] *ḥallah,* and it is stated there[44], a *ḥallah* of oil cake. Since the *ḥallah* mentioned there is prepared with oil, so the *ḥallah* prepared here must be prepared with oil. And oil is one of the seven fluids.

41 The 7 fluids enumerated in Mishnah *Makhširin* 6:4: Dew, water, wine, oil, blood, milk, bee's honey.

42 Does R. Joshua ben Levi disagree with the Mishnah and hold that only dough kneaded with one of the 7 fluids is subject to *ḥallah*?

43 *Num.* 15:20.

44 *Lev.* 8:26. About the theory of invariable meaning of words, cf. *Kilaim* 8, Note 4.

רִבִּי יוֹסֵי בְּשֵׁם רִבִּי שַׁבְּתַי רִבִּי חִייָה בְּשֵׁם רִבִּי שִׁמְעוֹן בֶּן לָקִישׁ לַחַלָּה וְלִנְטִילַת יָדַיִם אָדָם מְהַלֵּךְ אַרְבַּעַת מִילִין. רִבִּי אַבָּהוּ בְּשֵׁם רִבִּי יוֹסֵי בֶּן חֲנִינָה הָדָא דָתֵימַר לְפָנָיו אֲבָל לַאֲחָרָיו אֵין מַטְרִיחִין עָלָיו.

[45]Rebbi Yose in the name of Rebbi Sabbatai and Rebbi Ḥiyya in the name of Rebbi Simeon ben Laqish: For *ḥallah* and for washing one's hands, he has to walk up to four *mil*. Rebbi Abbahu in the name of Rebbi Yose ben Rebbi Ḥanina: That is, going forward; but one does not bother him to return on his way.

45 From here to the end of the Halakhah, the text is from *Berakhot* 8:2; explained there in Notes 52-71.

שׁוֹמְרֵי גַּנּוֹת וּפַרְדֵּיסִין מַה אַתְּ עֲבַד לוֹן כִּלְפְנֵיהֶן כִּלְאַחֲרֵיהֶן. נִשְׁמְעִינָהּ מִן הָדָא הָאִשָּׁה יוֹשֶׁבֶת וְקוֹצָה חַלָּתָהּ עֲרוּמָה. וַהֲדָא אִשָּׁה לֹא בְתוֹךְ בֵּיתָהּ יוֹשֶׁבֶת וְתֵימַר אֵין מַטְרִיחִין עָלָיו. וְהָכָא אֵין מַטְרִיחִין עָלָיו.

How does one treat watchmen in gardens and orchards, as before them, as after them? Let us hear it from this (Mishnah *Ḥallah* 2:3): "A woman may sit down naked and separate her *ḥallah*" Is that woman not sitting inside her house and you say that one does not bother her? Also here, one does not bother him.

תַּנֵּי הַמַּיִם שֶׁלִּפְנֵי הַמָּזוֹן רְשׁוּת וְשֶׁל אַחַר הַמָּזוֹן חוֹבָה. אֶלָּא שֶׁבָּרִאשׁוֹנִים נוֹטֵל וּמַפְסִיק. וּבַשְּׁנִייִם נוֹטֵל וְאֵינוֹ מַפְסִיק. מַהוּ מַפְסִיק. רִבִּי יַעֲקֹב בַּר אָחָא אָמַר נוֹטֵל וְשׁוֹנֶה. רִבִּי שְׁמוּאֵל[46] בַּר רַב יִצְחָק בָּעֵי נוֹטֵל וְשׁוֹנֶה וְאַתְּ אָמַרְתְּ רְשׁוּת. אִין דְּבָעֵי מֵימַר אַרְבַּעַת מִילִין וְאַתְּ אָמַרְתְּ רְשׁוּת.

It has been stated: "Water before the meal is conditional, after the meal it is obligatory. Only that for the first one he takes and interrupts; for the second he takes and may not interrupt." What does he interrupt? Rebbi Jacob bar Aḥa said, he takes and repeats. Rebbi Samuel bar Isaac asked: "He takes and interrupts" and you say it is conditional? One requires four *mil* and you say it is conditional?

46 Reading of the Rome ms. and the text in *Berakhot*. Venice text: יעקב.

אָמַר רִבִּי יַעֲקֹב בַּר אִידִי עַל הָרִאשׁוֹנִים נֶאֱכַל בְּשַׂר חֲזִיר. עַל הַשְּׁנִיִּים יָצְאָה אִשָּׁה מִבֵּיתָהּ. וְיֵשׁ אוֹמְרִים שֶׁנֶּהֶרְגוּ עָלֶיהָ שָׁלֹשׁ נְפָשׁוֹת.

Rebbi Jacob bar Idi said: Because of the first, pork was eaten. Because of the second, a woman had to leave her house; some say, three persons were killed because of it.

(fol. 58b) **משנה ג:** הָאִשָּׁה יוֹשֶׁבֶת וְקוֹצָה חַלָּתָהּ עֲרוּמָּה מִפְּנֵי שֶׁהִיא יְכוֹלָה לְכַסּוֹת עַצְמָהּ אֲבָל לֹא הָאִישׁ. מִי שֶׁאֵינוֹ יָכוֹל לַעֲשׂוֹת עִיסָּתוֹ בְטָהֳרָה יַעֲשֶׂנָּה קַבִּין וְאַל יַעֲשֶׂנָּה בְטוּמְאָה. רִבִּי עֲקִיבָה אוֹמֵר יַעֲשֶׂנָּה בְטוּמְאָה וְאַל יַעֲשֶׂנָּה קַבִּין שֶׁכְּשֵׁם שֶׁהוּא קוֹרֵא לַטְּהוֹרָה כָּךְ הוּא קוֹרֵא לַטְּמֵיאָה. לְזוֹ קוֹרֵא חַלָּה בְּשֵׁם וּלְזוֹ קוֹרֵא חַלָּה בְּשֵׁם. אֲבָל קַבִּים אֵין לָהֶן חַלָּה בְּשֵׁם.

Mishnah 3: A woman may sit down naked and separate her *ḥallah*[47] because she can cover herself, but a man may not. If somebody cannot make his dough in purity he should make single *qabim*[48] and not make it in impurity. Rebbi Aqiba says, he should make it in impurity and not make it single *qabim*, since just as he names the pure one, he names the impure. But single *qabim* have no named *ḥallah*[49].

47 And pronounce the benediction needed; cf. *Berakhot* 8:2, Note 60.

48 Each separate dough being made from less than the minimum amount subject to *ḥallah*. (The mss. of the Maimonides tradition, including the autograph ms., read קביים "two *qab*". This forces Maimonides to declare that the measures of *qab* mentioned in this Tractate are non-standard.)

49 The first Tanna would abolish any mention of *ḥallah* in impurity since he holds that it is sinful to cause food to be burned just for the formal observance of a commandment (Tosephta 1:9). In Halakhah 3:1, the Yerushalmi decides practice following R. Aqiba.

(fol. 58c) **הלכה ד**: הָדָא אָֽמְרָה עֲגָבוֹת אֵין בָּהֶן מִשּׁוּם עֶרְוָה. הָדָא דְאַתְּ אָמַר לִבְרָכָה אֲבָל לְהַבִּיט אֲפִילוּ כָּל־שֶׁהוּא אָסוּר. כְּהָדָא דְתַנֵּי הַמִּסְתַּכֵּל בַּעֲקֵיבָהּ שֶׁל אִשָּׁה כְּמִסְתַּכֵּל בְּבֵית הָרֶחֶם. וְהַמִּסְתַּכֵּל בְּבֵית הָרֶחֶם כִּילּוּ בָּא עָלֶיהָ. שְׁמוּאֵל אָמַר קוֹל בְּאִשָּׁה עֶרְוָה מַה טַעַם וְהָיָה מִקּוֹל זְנוּתָהּ וַתֶּחֱנַף הָאָרֶץ וְגוֹ'.

Halakhah 4: [50]This means that buttocks are no sex organs. That is, for benedictions[51], but to look at them[52] in any way is forbidden. As it was stated: He who looks at a woman's heel is as if he looked at her genitals and he who looks at her genitals is as if he had intercourse with her. Samuel said, a woman's voice is a sex organ. What is the reason[53]? (*Jer.* 3:9) "From the sound of her whoring the land became polluted, etc."

50 Similar statements in Babli *Berakhot* 24a.

51 Benedictions and prayers may not be said in an indecent state. But since a woman may sit down flat on the ground with her legs tightly together, she may recite the benediction for *ḥallah* while naked. There is nowhere a prohibition for a woman to nurse her baby while others are present.

52 Except one's own wife.

53 The Babli quotes here *Cant.*

2:14: "For your voice is sweet and your looks refreshing." Neither of the verses prove what is required.

רַב הוּנָא אָמַר עוֹמֵד הוּא אָדָם עַל הַצּוֹאָה וּמִתְפַּלֵּל וּבִלְבַד שֶׁלֹּא יְהֵא בְשָׂרוֹ נוֹגֵעַ בַּצּוֹאָה. יָשַׁב וְלֹא קִינֵּחַ אָסוּר. אָמַר רִבִּי מָנָא אַף עַל גַּב דְּלֹא אָמַר רִבִּי יוֹסֵי הָדָא מִילְתָא אָמַר דִּכְוָותָהּ דְּרַב הוּנָא אָמַר עוֹמֵד הוּא אָדָם עַל גַּבֵּי צוֹאָה וּמִתְפַּלֵּל וּבִלְבַד שֶׁלֹּא יְהֵא בְשָׂרוֹ נוֹגֵעַ בַּצּוֹאָה. יָשַׁב וְלֹא קִינֵּחַ הֲרֵי בְשָׂרוֹ נוֹגֵעַ בַּצּוֹאָה.

Rav Huna said: A person may stand near excrement and pray[54], on condition that his flesh not touch the excrement. If he sat down[55] and did not cleanse himself, it is forbidden. Rebbi Mana said, even though Rebbi Yose did not say this, he said something equivalent. As Rav Huna said: A person may stand near excrement and pray, on condition that his flesh not touch the excrement. If he sat down and did not cleanse himself, his flesh touches the excrement.

54 In *Berakhot* (Babli 25a/b, Yerushalmi 3:5) it is stated that the *Šema'* may not be recited within 4 cubits of any excrement. There are no separate rules there for prayer.

55 To defecate.

מָה פָּחוּת מֵאַרְבַּעַת מִיל יַעֲשֶׂנָּה בְטָהֳרָה. אַרְבַּעַת מִיל יַעֲשֶׂנָּה קַבִּין. אִי אַרְבַּעַת מִיל יַעֲשֶׂנָּה בְטָהֳרָה יוֹתֵר מֵאַרְבַּעַת מִיל יַעֲשֶׂנָּה קַבִּין. נִשְׁמְעִינָהּ מִן הָדָא דְּאָמַר רִבִּי חִיָּיא בַּר וָוא כְּגוֹן קַיְסָרִין. וְקַיְסָרִין לָאו אַרְבַּעַת מִילִין הִיא. הָדָא אָמְרָה אַרְבַּעַת מִיל יַעֲשֶׂנָּה בְטָהֳרָה יוֹתֵר מֵאַרְבַּעַת מִיל יַעֲשֶׂנָּה קַבִּין. רִבִּי אִמִּי הוֹרֵי בִּכְפַר שַׁמַּי לַעֲשׂוֹת עִיסָּה גְדוֹלָה בְטוּמְאָה. וַהֲלֹא אֵין שָׁם אַרְבַּעַת מִיל. מִכֵּיוָן דְּנַהֲרָא מַפְסִיק כְּמִי שֶׁיֵּשׁ שָׁם אַרְבַּעַת מִיל. מַתְנִיתָא דְּרִבִּי עֲקִיבָה דְּרִבִּי עֲקִיבָה אָמַר יַעֲשֶׂנָּה בְטוּמְאָה וְאַל יַעֲשֶׂנָּה קַבִּין. עִיסָּה גְדוֹלָה הָיְתָה נוֹחַ הָיָה לוֹ לְהַלֵּךְ כַּמָּה וְלֹא לַעֲשׂוֹתָהּ קַבִּין.

How is this[56]? Less that four *mil* he should make it in purity, four *mil* he sould make single *qabim*, or four *mil* he should make it in purity, more than four *mil* he sould make single *qabim*? Let us hear from the following, since Rebbi Ḥiyya bar Abba said, for example Caesarea[57]. Is Caesarea not four *mil*? That means, four *mil* he should make it in purity, more than four *mil* he sould make single *qabim*. Rebbi Ammi instructed in Kefar Sammai[58] to make a large dough in impurity. Is that not less than four *mil*? Since a brook interrupts it is as if there were four *mil*. This teaching follows Rebbi Aqiba since Rebbi Aqiba says, he should make it in impurity and not make it single *qabim*. It was a large dough and it would have been easier for him to walk a distance than to make it single *qabim*[59].

56 This refers to the statement in Halakhah 3 (Note 44) that for *ḥallah* one does not have to go more than four *mil* (about one hour) to immerse himself in a *miqweh* to remove one's impurity.

57 This is difficult to understand since Caesarea (Philippi) is on the Jordan. Probably it means that from the farthest outskirts of the city to the *miqweh* it might be four *mil*.

58 Also called *Kefar Simai*, on the road from Sepphoris to Acco. Since this is reported as an actual instruction given in the third generation of Amoraïm, in the middle of the third Century, it follows that people were careful to remove any impurity on their bodies before making dough even if they could not remove the impurity caused by contact or closeness to the dead, in the absence of ashes of the red heifer.

59 The instruction of R. Ammi does not prove that practice follows R. Aqiba.

מִחְלְפָה שִׁיטָתֵיהּ דְּרִבִּי עֲקִיבָה. תַּמָּן הוּא אָמַר נוֹטֵל מִקַּב חַלָּה וְכָא הוּא אָמַר
הָכֵין. תַּמָּן לְשֶׁעָבַר בְּרַם הָכָא לְכַתְּחִילָּה.

The arguments of Rebbi Aqiba are switched. There[60], he says one takes *ḥallah* from a *qab*, and here he says so? There after the fact, here before the fact.

60 Mishnah 4:4: "If somebody took *ḥallah* from [a dough being only] one *qab*, R. Aqiba says it is *ḥallah*, but the Sages say it is not." Here, he declares that a dough of one *qab* is exempt.

(fol. 58b) **משנה ד:** הָעוֹשֶׂה עִיסָּתוֹ קַבִּין וְנָֽגְעוּ זֶה בָזֶה פְּטוּרִין מִן הַחַלָּה עַד שֶׁיִּשּׁוֹכוּ. רִבִּי אֱלִיעֶזֶר אוֹמֵר אַף הָרוֹדֶה וְנוֹתֵן לַסַּל הַסַּל מְצָֽרְפָן.

Mishnah 4: If somebody makes his dough single *qabim* and they are touching one another[61], they are free from *ḥallah* unless they are biting[62]. Rebbi Eliezer says, also if one takes them out of the oven and puts them in a basket, the basket combines them together[63].

משנה ה: הַמַּפְרִישׁ חַלָּתוֹ קֶמַח אֵינָהּ חַלָּה וְגֶזֶל בְּיַד כֹּהֵן. הָעִיסָּה עַצְמָהּ חַייֶבֶת בְּחַלָּה. וְהַקֶּמַח אִם יֵשׁ בּוֹ כְּשִׁיעוּר חַייֶבֶת בְּחַלָּה וַאֲסוּרָה לַזָּרִים דִּבְרֵי רִבִּי יְהוֹשֻׁעַ. אָֽמְרוּ לוֹ מַעֲשֶׂה וּקְפָשָׂהּ זָקֵן זָר אָמַר לָהֶן אַף הוּא קִלְקֵל לְעַצְמוֹ וְתִיקֵּן לְאַחֵר.

Mishnah 5: If somebody gives *ḥallah* from flour it is not *ḥallah* and will be robbery in the hand if the Cohen. The dough itself is subject to *ḥallah*; the flour, if it is a full measure[64], is obligated for *ḥallah* and forbidden to laymen, the words of Rebbi Joshua. They said to him, it happened that a layman rabbi grabbed[65] it. He said to them, he destroyed himself[66] and put others in order[67].

61 The different loaves touch one another in the oven.

62 The baked loaves cling to one another and cannot be cleanly separated.

63 If the basket contains more than $^5/_4$ *qab* of bread from one bake run, it is obligated for *ḥallah.*

64 The flour given as *ḥallah* measures more than $^5/_4$ *qab.*

65 קבש stands for כבש, showing that the ק had lost its guttural sound. He took and ate it without it being given to him to show that it had no holiness.

66 He sinned.

67 Others who follow his teaching will not sin since they would follow rabbinical instructions; their sins in this matter will all be charged to the rabbi who gave the wrong instructions.

(fol. 58c) **הלכה ה**: רִבִּי יוֹנָה רִבִּי חִייָה בְשֵׁם רִבִּי יוֹחָנָן רִבִּי יוֹסֵי רִבִּי אִימִּי בְשֵׁם רִבִּי יוֹחָנָן וְהֵן שֶׁנֶּשְׁכוּ. אִית תַּנָּיֵי תַנֵּי הַסָּל מְצָרֵף וְאֵין הַתַּנּוּר מְצָרֵף. וְאִית תַּנָּיֵי תַנֵּי הַתַּנּוּר מְצָרֵף וְאֵין הַסָּל מְצָרֵף. אָמַר רִבִּי יוֹחָנָן אִיתִיתֵיהּ מִדְּחִילְפַיי נֶשְׁכוּ כָאן וְכָאן מְצָרֵף. לֹא נֶשְׁכוּ כָאן וְכָאן אֵינוֹ מְצָרֵף. מַתְנִיתָא כְּגוֹן אִילֵּין רִיפְתָּא דְּבָבֶל.

Halakhah 5: Rebbi Jonah, Rebbi Ḥiyya in the name of Rebbi Joḥanan; Rebbi Ammi in the name of Rebbi Joḥanan[68]: Only if they were biting[62]. There are Tannaïm stating: The bag combines them together but not the oven[69], and there are Tannaïm stating: The oven combines them together but not the bag. Rebbi Joḥanan said, one follows Ḥilfai: If they bite in both places they are combined together, if they do not bite in both places they are not combined together. The Mishnah applies, e. g., to Babylonian bread[70].

68 In the Babli, *Pesaḥim* 48b, this is the position of R. Joshua ben Levi explaining Mishnah 4.

69 In the Babli, *loc. cit.*, this may be the position of R. Eliezer and the other position that of R. Joshua.

70 Rashi explains in *Pesaḥim* 48b that they are large and circular; they will always bite in the oven and have to be broken apart to be put into a bag.

אָמַר לָהֶן אַף הוּא קִלְקֵל לְעַצְמוֹ וְתִקֵּן לָאֲחֵרִים. קִלְקֵל לְעַצְמוֹ דַּאֲכָלָהּ וְאִיתְעֲנָשׁ וְתִקֵּן לָאֲחֵרִים דְּאִינּוּן אָכְלִין וְתָלְיִי בֵּיהּ. אִית תַּנֵּי תַּנָּיֵי תִּקֵּן לְעַצְמוֹ וְקִלְקֵל לָאֲחֵרִים. תִּקֵּן לְעַצְמוֹ מִכָּל־מָקוֹם אֲכָלָהּ. וְקִלְקֵל לָאֲחֵרִים דְּאִינּוּן סָבְרִין מֵימַר שֶׁהוּא פָּטוּר וְהִיא חַיֶּיבֶת.

"He said to them, he destroyed himself and put others in order." He destroyed himself by eating and exposed himself to punishment; he put others in order since they eat and unload [their sin] on him. Some Tannaïm state: He put himself in order and destroyed others. He put himself in order since anyhow he ate. But he destroyed others since they tend to say it is free when it is obligated.

(fol. 58b) **משנה ו:** חֲמֵשֶׁת רְבָעִים קֶמַח חַייָבִין בְּחַלָּה הֵן וְסוּבָּן וּמוּרְסָנָן חֲמֵשֶׁת רְבָעִים חַייָבִין. נִיטַּל מוּרְסָנָן מִתּוֹכָן וְחָזַר לְתוֹכָן הֲרֵי אֵלּוּ פְּטוּרִין.

Mishnah 6: Five quarters[71] of coarse flour[72] are obligated for *ḥallah*; including hulls and bran it is obligated by five quarters. If the bran was sifted out and later returned[73], it is free.

71 The measure involved is discussed in the Halakhah.

72 The same holds for fine flour which never contains bran. It is stated here that milled grain is called "coarse flour" before being sifted.

73 Usually the bran is sifted out before the flour is used for bread dough. Since normally bran is not returned, the rules for flour mixed with bran are like those for flour mixed with rice flour.

(fol. 58c) **הלכה ו:** רִבִּי אִימִּי בְּשֵׁם רִבִּי יַנַּאי קַב טִיבֵּרְנִי חַייָב בְּחַלָּה. חַד חֲלִיטָר שָׁאַל לְרִבִּי יוֹחָנָן אָמַר אֵיזִיל עֲבִיד אַרְבַּע וּפְלִיג. וְיֹאמַר לֵיהּ תְּלָתָא (fol.

(58d וּפְלִיג. אָמַר רִבִּי זְעִירָא קַבַּיָּא בְּאַתְרֵיהוֹן רוֹבְעַיָּא אִיזְדָּרְעוֹן וְיֹאמַר לֵיהּ
חֲמִשָּׁה פָּרָא צִיבְחָר. שֶׁלֹּא יָבוֹא לִידֵי סָפֵק חִיּוּב חַלָּה.

Halakhah 6: Rebbi Immi in the name of Rebbi Yannai: A Tiberian *qab* is obligated for *ḥallah*[74]. A maker of fried food asked Rebbi Joḥanan: He said, go, make four, and separate[75]. Could he say to him, three and separate[76]? Rebbi Zeïra said, in their places, *qabim* in their places are measured by quarters[77]. Could he have said to him five minus a little bit? That there should not be any doubt of obligation of *ḥallah*.

74 Which is larger than the standard *qab* of the Mishnah. Mishnah *Idiut* 1:2 states that originally the amount was fixed at 1.5 *qab*. Tosephta *Idiut* 1:2 reads: "The Sages estimated 7 + something *qabim* which are 5 quarters in Sepphoris or 1.5 *qab* in Jerusalem." According to Rashi (*Pesaḥim* 48b), Maimonides and R. Abraham ben David (*Idiut* 1:2) the argument is the following: Since *Num.* 15:21-21 speaks about "the beginning of your doughs," the reference is to the size of the doughs made in the desert, which was 1 *'omer* of manna. The *'omer* is defined in *Ex.* 16:36 as a tenth of an *ephah* which is 3 *seah* or 18 *qab*, 72 quarter *qabim*. This makes the *'omer* 7.2 biblical quarter *qabim*. The Jerusalem small measure is defined as $^1/_6$ larger than the biblical, the Sepphoris $^1/_6$ larger than the Jerusalem. This makes the *ephah* 60 Jerusalem quarters and 50 Sepphoris ones and the amount subject to *ḥallah* is 7.2 biblical quarters = 6 Jerusalem quarters = 5 Sepphoris quarters.

Maimonides defines the *qab* (Sepphoris) as 4×4×10.8 digits. The digit is $^1/_{24}$ of a cubit normally taken to be 55 cm; this makes the *qab* 2101 cm^3 = 2.1 liter and the amount of dry flour so that a dough made from it should be subject to *ḥallah* equal to 2.65 liter. A Jerusalem *qab* would then be 2.52 liter and it is possible that the Tiberian measure was equal to the Jerusalem one and R. Yannai's statement errs on the side of caution, in the spirit of the last sentence of this paragraph.

75 Make batches of 4 quarters of dough and separate the batches so they will never touch. Since fried dough is

not subject to *ḥallah* by biblical law, it is preferable to prepare the dough so the question of *ḥallah* should never arise.

76 Why did he say "make four" without saying what he meant? Could it be four *qabim* or three *qabim* or maybe three quarters of a *qab*?

77 In his place, the *qab* was never used as a commercial measure; the standard was the quarter of about 0.5 liter.

אָמַר רִבִּי יוֹחָנָן דֶּרֶךְ עִיסָּה שָׁנוּ. אָמַר רִבִּי שִׁמְעוֹן בֶּן לָקִישׁ דְּרַבָּן שִׁמְעוֹן בֶּן גַּמְלִיאֵל הִיא. דְּרַבָּן שִׁמְעוֹן בֶּן גַּמְלִיאֵל אוֹמֵר לְעוֹלָם אֵינָהּ חַייֶבֶת בְּחַלָּה עַד שֶׁיְּהֵא בָהּ דָּגָן כְּשִׁיעוּר. תַּלְמִידוֹי דְּרִבִּי חִייָה רוֹבָא בַּר לוֹלִיתָא בְּשֵׁם רִבִּי יְהוֹשֻׁעַ בֶּן לֵוִי דִּבְרֵי הַכֹּל הִיא. אָמַר רִבִּי מָנָא אַף עַל גַּב דְּלֹא אָמַר רִבִּי יוֹסֵי רִבִּי הָדָא מִילְתָא אָמַר דִּכְווָתָהּ דְּאָמַר רִבִּי יוֹחָנָן דֶּרֶךְ עִיסָּה שָׁנוּ. וְכָאן מִכֵּיוָן שֶׁנִּיטַּל מוּרְסָנָן וְחָזַר לְתוֹכָן אֵין זֶה דֶּרֶךְ עִיסָּה.

[78]Rebbi Joḥanan said, they taught the way dough is made[79]. Rebbi Simeon ben Laqish said, it follows Rabban Simeon ben Gamliel, since Rabban Simeon ben Gamliel said[80] it is never subject to *ḥallah* unless it contain the full measure of grain. The students of the elder Rebbi Ḥiyya, Bar Lolita[81] in the name of Rebbi Joshua ben Levi, it is the opinion of everybody. Rebbi Mana said, even though my teacher Rebbi Yose did not say this, he said something equivalent: that Rebbi Joḥanan said, they taught the way dough is made. In this case, since the bran was removed and then put in again, it is not the way dough is made.

78 This refers to the last sentence of the Mishnah.

79 As noted at the end, mixing the bran in again was not usually done in talmudic times.

80 Tosephta 2:1: If somebody makes dough from grain and rice, it is never subject to *ḥallah* unless it contain the full measure of grain. For R. Simeon ben Laqish, bran has the status of non-cereal.

81 He is not otherwise mentioned.

(fol. 58b) **משנה ז:** שִׁיעוּר הַחַלָּה אֶחָד מֵעֶשְׂרִים וְאַרְבָּעָה. הָעוֹשֶׂה עִיסָּה לְעַצְמוֹ וְהָעוֹשֶׂה לְמִשְׁתֶּה בְנוֹ אֶחָד מֵעֶשְׂרִים וְאַרְבָּעָה. נַחְתּוֹם שֶׁהוּא עוֹשֶׂה לִמְכּוֹר לַשּׁוּק וְכֵן הָאִשָּׁה שֶׁהִיא עוֹשָׂה לִמְכּוֹר בַּשּׁוּק אֶחָד מֵאַרְבָּעִים וּשְׁמוֹנָה. נִיטְמֵאת עִיסָּה שׁוֹגֶגֶת אוֹ אֲנוּסָה אֶחָד מֵאַרְבָּעִים וּשְׁמוֹנָה נִטְמֵאת מֵזִידָה אֶחָד מֵעֶשְׂרִים וְאַרְבָּעָה כְּדֵי שֶׁלֹּא יְהֵא חוֹטֵא נִשְׂכָּר.

Mishnah 7: The rate[82] of *ḥallah* is one in 24. If somebody makes dough for himself or his son's wedding feast, one in 24. A baker who makes to sell on the market, and also a woman[83] who makes to sell on the market, one in 48. If the dough became impure[84] by error or accident, one in 48. If it became impure intentionally, one in 24 so the sinner should not be rewarded.

82 If a dough is subject to *ḥallah*, the amount to be taken is $^1/_{24}$ by rabbinic decree. Since *ḥallah* is a heave, it has no lower limit in biblical law. The rabbinic amount is more than twice the rabbinic rate of heave which is one in 50.

83 In contrast to the baker she has no store but bakes at home to sell out of her basket on the market.

84 In this case, the *ḥallah* must be burned and there is no reason to give the Cohen a larger portion. Today, when all dough is impure, these rabbinic rules have been disestablished and biblical law reinstated.

(fol. 58d) **הלכה ז:** תַּנֵּי אָמַר רִבִּי יוּדָה מִפְּנֵי מָה אָמְרוּ בַּעַל הַבַּיִת אֶחָד מֵעֶשְׂרִים וְאַרְבָּעָה. וְנַחְתּוֹם אֶחָד מֵאַרְבָּעִים וּשְׁמוֹנָה. אֶלָּא שֶׁהַנַּחְתּוֹם עֵינוֹ יָפָה בְעִיסָּתוֹ וּבַעַל הַבַּיִת רָעָה בְעִיסָּתוֹ. וַחֲכָמִים אוֹמְרִים לֹא מִשֶּׁם (הוּא זֶה[85]) וְלֹא מִטַּעַם זֶה. אֶלָּא וּנְתַתֶּם מִמֶּנּוּ אֶת תְּרוּמַת יי לְאַהֲרוֹן הַכֹּהֵן עֲשֵׂה שֶׁיִּינָּתְנוּ לַכֹּהֵן בִּכְהוּנָּתוֹ. אֶלָּא שֶׁהַנַּחְתּוֹם עִיסָּתוֹ מְרוּבָּה וְיֵשׁ בָּהּ כְּדֵי מַתָּנָה לַכֹּהֵן וּבַעַל הַבַּיִת עִיסָּתוֹ מְעוּטָּה וְאֵין בָּהּ כְּדֵי מַתָּנָה לַכֹּהֵן.

It was stated[86]: "Rebbi Jehudah said, why did they say the private person one in 24 but the baker one in 48? Because the baker is generous[87] with his dough but the private person is stingy[86] with his dough. But the Sages say, not because of this category or reason, but (*Num.* 18:28): "You shall give from it the Eternal's heave to Aharon the priest;" they should be given to the priest in his status as priest[88]. The baker makes a large dough with enough to make a gift to the Cohen but the private person makes a small dough that would not be enough to make a gift to the Cohen[89].

85 Missing in the Rome ms., resulting in a smoother text.

86 A different text in Tosephta 1:7. In *Sifry Num.* 110 there is another version, based on *Num.* 15:21, not mentioning R. Jehudah but incorporating his argument in the version: A man is generous but a woman stingy. This is the version which Maimonides follows in his Commentary. In *Sifry*, R. Simeon ben Iohai allows *ḥallah* to be treated as heave, with a minimum gift of $^1/_{60}$.

87 This is the text of both mss.; both Tosephta mss. and R. Simson switch the places of "stingy" and "generous". The text of the Tosephta makes better sense but the principle of *lectio difficilior* speaks for the Yerushalmi. It is possible that Maimonides bases himself on *Sifry* to avoid choosing between Talmud and Tosephta.

In the interpretation of Maimonides of the Yerushalmi text, one prescribes $^1/_{24}$ for home-baked bread in the hope that at least $^1/_{48}$ will be taken whereas the baker calculates his selling price including the full cost of the *ḥallah* which he has to give to the Cohen to keep his standing of kosher baker in the community.

88 Compare *Terumot* 5, Note 22.

89 The percentages given to the Cohen must be larger than the percentages fixed for heave since dough is perishable and *ḥallah* must be delivered immediately whereas heave of agricultural produce can be accumulated until it reaches the required amounts.

וְהָתַנִּינָן הָעוֹשֶׂה עִיסָּה לְעַצְמוֹ וְהָעוֹשֶׂה לְמִשְׁתֶּה בְנוֹ אֶחָד מֵעֶשְׂרִים וְאַרְבָּעָה. שֶׁלֹּא תַחְלוֹק לְעִיסַּת בַּעַל הַבַּיִת .וְהָתַנִּינָן וְכֵן הָאִשָּׁה שֶׁהִיא עוֹשָׂה לִמְכּוֹר בַּשּׁוּק אֶחָד מֵאַרְבָּעִים וּשְׁמוֹנָה בְּשָׁעָה שֶׁהִיא עוֹשָׂה לְבֵיתָהּ עֵינָהּ רָעָה בְעִיסָּתָהּ. בְּשָׁעָה שֶׁהִיא עוֹשָׂה לִמְכּוֹר בַּשּׁוּק עֵינָהּ יָפָה בְעִיסָּתָהּ. אָמַר רִבִּי מַתְנִיתָא בִּלִימוּדֶת לִהְיוֹת מַפְרֶשֶׁת אֶחָד מֵאַרְבָּעִים וּשְׁמוֹנָה אֲבָל בִּלִימוּדֶת לִהְיוֹת מַפְרֶשֶׁת אֶחָד מֵעֶשְׂרִים וְאַרְבָּעָה נִיתְנֵי כְּדֵי שֶׁלֹּא יְהֵא הַחוֹטֵא נִשְׂכָּר.

But did we not state: "If somebody makes dough for himself or his son's wedding feast[90], one in 24?" Not to make a distinction in doughs of a private person. But did we not state: "And also a woman[91] who makes to sell on the market, one in 48?" When she makes it for herself, she is stingy[87] with her dough; when she makes to sell on the market she is generous[87] with her dough. Rebbi[92] said, the Mishnah speaks about one[93] used to give one in 48, but about one who is used to give one in 24, we should state that "the sinner should not be rewarded[94]".

90 Then he bakes a large quantity and the argument of the Sages does not apply.

91 She bakes at home and by the preceding argument should not change her rate of 1 in 24.

92 Probably a name is missing.

93 The woman selling bread on the market gets the baker's rate only if she regularly bakes for the market. If she does it only occasionally, she is held to the rate of 1 in 24 in accordance with the explanation given for the infrequent wedding feast.

94 If she works only occasionally for sale, she should not be invited to give less for her domestic bread.

(fol. 58b) **משנה ח:** רִבִּי לִיעֶזֶר אוֹמֵר נִיטֶּלֶת מִן הַטָּהוֹר עַל הַטָּמֵא כֵּיצַד עִיסָּה טְהוֹרָה וְעִיסָּה טְמֵיאָה נוֹטֵל כְּדֵי חַלָּה מֵעִיסָּה שֶׁלֹּא הוּרְמָה חַלָּתָהּ וְנוֹתֵן פָּחוֹת מִכְּבֵיצָה בְּאֶמְצַע כְּדֵי שֶׁיִּטּוֹל מִן הַמּוּקָף. וַחֲכָמִים אוֹסְרִין.

Mishnah 8: Rebbi Eliezer says, it may be taken from pure for impure[95]. How is this? With pure and impure dough, he takes the amount needed for *ḥallah* from dough from which *ḥallah* was not yet taken and gives less than the volume of an egg in the middle[96] so he should take from the earmarked. But the Sages forbid it.

95 This is forbidden for heave, *Terumot* 2:2.

96 Since food less in volume than an egg cannot transmit impurity (*Terumot* 5:1), the two doughs can be put in the same vessel to be earmarked for heave together (*Terumot* 2, Note 6). The Mishnah is quoted in Babli *Soṭah* 30a/b; there a version is quoted which has "gives the volume of an egg". The explanation is that the impure dough is impure in the first degree (cf. *Berakhot* Chapter 8, Note 46). It makes the dough in between impure in the second degree. The pure dough, while *ṭevel*, is under the rules of profane food for which no third degree exists. Therefore, the dough in the middle cannot transmit impurity to the pure dough irrespective of size. This is the position taken by Maimonides in his Code (*Bikkurim* 7:12).

(fol. 58d) **הלכה ח:** וְאֵין הַבַּיִת מְצָרֵף. דָּבָר שֶׁהוּא מַקְפִּיד עַל תַּעֲרוּבָתוֹ אֵין הַבַּיִת מְצָרֵף וּשֶׁאֵין מַקְפִּיד עַל תַּעֲרוּבָתוֹ הַבַּיִת מְצָרֵף. עִיסָּה טְמֵאָה עִיסָּה טְהוֹרָה עָשׂוּ כְּדָבָר שֶׁהוּא מַקְפִּיד עַל תַּעֲרוּבָתוֹ.

Halakhah 8: Does the house not combine them together[97]? Things which one objects to being mixed the house will not combine together; if one would not object to their being mixed the house will combine them. The status of impure and pure dough is that one is assumed to object to their being mixed.

97 Why does R. Eliezer need the expedient with food less than the volume of an egg? Could one not say that the house is a container which earmarks the two doughs together?

וְעִיסָּתָהּ חַלָּה. אֲבָל בְּעִיסָּה שְׁנִייָה אֵין לַשֵּׁינִי מַגַּע אֶצֶל הַטֵּבֶל.

If the dough is *ḥallah*[98]. But a dough of secondary [impurity] has no [invalidating] touch for *ṭevel*[99].

99 R. Simson and R. Isaac Simponti read: ועיסתה תחילה "if the dough is [impure in the] first degree."

100 A dough impure in the second degree which touches profane pure dough does not transmit impurity. This proves that *ṭevel* goes under the rules of profane food; cf. Note 96.

תַּנֵּי רִבִּי לַעְאִיי אוֹמֵר מִשּׁוּם רִבִּי לִיעֶזֶר תּוֹרְמִין מִן הַטָּהוֹר עַל הַטָּמֵא בְּלַח. כֵּיצַד כָּבַשׁ זֵיתִין בְּטוּמְאָה וְהוּא מְבַקֵּשׁ לְתוֹרְמָן בְּטָהֳרָה מֵבִיא מַשְׁפֵּךְ שֶׁאֵין בְּפִיו כְּבֵיצָה וּמְמַלֵּא אוֹתוֹ זֵתִים וְנוֹתְנוֹ עַל פִּי חָבִית. וְנִמְצָא תוֹרֵם מִן הַמּוּקָּף. לָמָּה לִי פָּחוּת מִכְּבֵיצָה. אֲפִילוּ כְבֵיצָה וְלֹא פֵּירוּרִין אִינּוּן. שֶׁלֹּא לְטַמְּאוֹת זֵיתִים הַרְבֵּה. אָמְרוּ לוֹ אֵין לָךְ קָרוּי לַח אֶלָּא יַיִן וְשֶׁמֶן בִּלְבַד. הֵיךְ עֲבִידָא קוֹרָה אַחַת לִשְׁתֵּי בוֹרוֹת. שְׁתֵּי קוֹרוֹת לְבוֹר אֶחָד. [נִיחָא קוֹרָה אַחַת לִשְׁנֵי בוֹרוֹת. אֶלָּא שְׁנֵי קוֹרוֹת לְבוֹר אֶחָד] מִכֵּיוָן שֶׁנִּיטְמָא מִקְצָתוֹ אֵין כּוּלּוֹ טָמֵא. רִבִּי הִילָא בְשֵׁם רִבִּי יָסָא תִּפְתַּר שֶׁהָיָה בְדַעְתּוֹ לַעֲשׂוֹת תְּפִיסָה אַחַת וְנִמְלַךְ לַעֲשׂוֹתָן שְׁתֵּי תְפִיסוֹת. אָמַר רִבִּי יוֹסֵי בֵּירִבִּי בּוּן הָדָא דְתֵימַר בְּשֶׁנִּיטְמָא בְּשֶׁשִּׁילֶּה וּמִשֶּׁקִּיפֶּהּ שֶׁכְּבָר נִרְאֶה לְתוֹרְמָן בְּטָהֳרָה. אֲבָל אִם נִיטְמָא עַד שֶׁלֹּא קִיפֶּה וְעַד שֶׁלֹּא שִׁילֶּה לֹא בְדָא. רִבִּי טָבִי רִבִּי יֹאשִׁיָּה בְּשֵׁם יַנַּאי הֲלָכָה כְּרִבִּי לִעֶזֶר. רִבִּי יִצְחָק בַּר נַחְמָן בְּשֵׁם רִבִּי הוֹשַׁעְיָה כְּרִבִּי לִיעֶזֶר. רִבִּי הוּנָא בְשֵׁם רִבִּי חֲנִינָה אֵין הֲלָכָה כְּרִבִּי לִיעֶזֶר. רִבִּי יוֹסֵי בֵּירִבִּי בּוּן רַב יְהוּדָה בְשֵׁם שְׁמוּאֵל אֵין הֲלָכָה כְּרִבִּי לִיעֶזֶר. אָתָא עוּבְדָא קוֹמֵיהּ וְלֹא הוֹרֵי אָמַר תַּרְתֵּיי כָּל־קֳבֵיל תְּרֵי אִינּוּן. אָמְרִין לֵיהּ וְהָא רִבִּי יִצְחָק בַּר נַחְמָן מוֹדֵי. אֲפִילוּ כֵן לֹא הוֹרֵי.

[100]It was stated: "Rebbi Illaï says in the name of Rebbi Eliezer: For food in fluids, one gives heave from pure for impure. How is this? If somebody pickled olives in impurity and wants to give heave in purity, he brings a funnel whose opening is less than [the width of] an egg, fills it with olives and puts it on top of the amphora; it turns out that he gives heave from what is earmarked." Why does it have to be less than [the width of] an egg? Are these not single pieces? It is only that not many olives should become impure. "They said to him, the only food fluids called *fluid* are wine and olive oil." How is that? One beam for two pits or two beams for one pit. [One understands one beam for two pits, but two beams for one pit?][101] Is it not that if it is partially impure it is totally impure? Rebbi La in the name of Rebbi Assi: Explain it, if he had intended to process it in one batch, and he changed his mind to make it in two batches. Rebbi Yose ben Rebbi Abun said, this applies if it became impure after he siphoned off [the froth] and [the seeds] formed lumps. But if it became impure before lumps were formed and he siphoned off, it does not apply. Rebbi Tabi, Rebbi Joshia in the name of Rebbi Yannai: Practice follows Rebbi Eliezer. Rebbi Isaac bar Naḥman in the name of Rebbi Hoshaia followed Rebbi Eliezer[102]. Rebbi Ḥuna in the name of Rebbi Ḥanina: Practice does not follow Rebbi Eliezer. Rebbi Yose ben Rebbi Abun, Rav Jehudah in the name of Samuel: Practice does not follow Rebbi Eliezer. There came a case before [Rebbi Immi][103] and he did not decide; he said there are two against two. They said to him, but Rebbi Isaac bar Naḥman agreed! Nevertheless, he gave no opinion.

100 This paragraph is from *Terumot* 2:1 and explained there, Note 35-44.

101 This sentence is in *Terumot* and here in the Rome ms., missing in the

Leyden ms.

102 In *Terumot*: "Rebbi Isaac bar Naḥman in the name of Rebbi Hoshaia: Practice follows Rebbi Eliezer." In view of the penultimate sentence, the formulation here is preferable.

103 From the *Terumot* text; name missing here in both mss.

אוכלין עראי פרק שלישי

(fol. 58d) **משנה א:** אוֹכְלִין עֲרַאי מִן הָעִיסָּה עַד שֶׁתְּגַלְגֵּל בְּחִיטִּים וּתְטַמְטֵם בַּשְּׂעוֹרִים. גִּילְגְּלָהּ בְּחִיטִּים וְטִימְטְמָהּ בַּשְּׂעוֹרִין הָאוֹכֵל מִמֶּנָּה חַייָב מִיתָה. כֵּיוָן שֶׁהִיא נוֹתֶנֶת אֶת הַמַּיִם מַגְבַּהַת חַלָּתָהּ וּבִלְבַד שֶׁיְּהֵא שָׁם חֲמֵשֶׁת רְבָעִים קֶמַח.

Mishnah 1: One may eat a snack[1] from the dough until it was rolled[2] if wheat dough or compacted[3] if barley dough. After it was rolled if wheat dough or compacted if barley dough, one who eats from it commits a deadly sin. After she added water she may lift its *ḥallah*[4] on condition that there be five quarters of flour[5].

1 Without taking *ḥallah*.

2 After kneading it was shaped ready to be baked. This is the end of preparation of dough and, as for all heave, the completion of processing induces the obligation of heave.

3 Barley dough does not hold together well and after shaping it has to be squeezed together to close the holes.

4 While the obligation of *ḥallah* starts only with completion of the dough, the possibility of giving *ḥallah* legally exists from the moment the preparation of the dough has begun. In *Pesaḥim* 3:3 (fol. 30a), R. Yose ben R. Abun notes that it became customary to give *ḥallah* from pure dough at the earliest possible moment, to protect it from possible impurity during processing.

5 This is the reading of the Yerushalmi mss., the Munich ms. of the Babli, and a number of good Mishnah mss. In this version, at least 5 quarters of flour have to be wetted before the possibility of giving *ḥallah* starts. The Maimonides autograph, a number of important Mishnah mss., and an Amora in the Halakhah read: on condition that there *not* be five quarters of flour, meaning that the flour which is still

dry cannot be of the minimal volume which triggers an independent duty of *ḥallah* since in that case, the *ḥallah* taken would not free the dough made later from the dry flour. The early Medieval authors all report that there are two conflicting readings, both of which seem to be genuine.

(fol. 59a) **הלכה א**: אוֹכְלִין עֲרַאי מִן הָעִיסָּה כול'. אָמַר רִבִּי חַגַּיי לֹא שָׁנוּ אֶלָּא עֲרַאי אֲבָל קֶבַע אָסוּר. מִפְּנֵי שֶׁהוּא מַעֲרִים לְפוֹתְרָהּ מִן הַחַלָּה. אָמַר רִבִּי יוֹסֵי אִי מִן הָדָא לֵית שְׁמַע מִינָהּ כְּלוּם שֶׁאֲפִילוּ שֶׁהוּא נוֹטֵל מִמֶּנָּה שְׁתַּיִם שָׁלֹשׁ מִקְרָצוֹת מִכֵּיוָן שֶׁהוּא עָתִיד לְהַחֲזִירוֹ לְדָבָר שֶׁלֹּא נִגְמְרָה מְלַאכְתּוֹ מוּתָּר. דְּאָמַר רִבִּי יוֹסֵי בְּשֵׁם רִבִּי זְעִירָא [רִבִּי יוֹנָה וְרִבִּי זְעִירָה] בְּשֵׁם רִבִּי לְעָזָר אַף מַה שֶׁבְּבָלְגִין לֹא נִטְבָּל מִפְּנֵי שֶׁהוּא עָתִיד לְהַחֲזִירוֹ לְדָבָר שֶׁלֹּא נִגְמְרָה מְלַאכְתּוֹ.

Halakhah 1: "One may eat a snack from the dough", etc. Rebbi Ḥaggai said, they taught only as a snack, but as a meal[6] it is forbidden since he would use a subterfuge to free it from *ḥallah*. Rebbi Yose said, if that were the reason, one could not infer anything since even if he takes from it two or three pieces of dough, since he will return the remainder to something not fully processed; it is permitted following[7] what Rebbi Yose said in the name of Rebbi Zeïra, [Rebbi Jonah, Rebbi Zeïra][8] in the name of Rebbi Eleazar, even what is in a flask did not become *ṭevel,* in case it was not fully processed, since he would put it back in the end.

6 Using the mixture of flour and water as a cereal for a sit-down meal.

7 The reference is to *Ma'serot* 4:3, Notes 61 ff. where in a similar case it is stated that taking food not fully processed will never create an obligation of heave if the remainders can be returned to be processed further.

8 Reading of the Rome ms. and the text in *Ma'serot*. Missing in the Leyden ms.

וְהָדָא אָֽמְרָה מִי שֶׁאֵינוֹ יָכוֹל לַעֲשׂוֹת עִיסָּתוֹ בְטָהֳרָה מִפְּנֵי שֶׁאֵינוֹ יָכוֹל. הָא אִם הָיָה יָכוֹל לֹא בְדָא. הָדָא אָֽמְרָה שֶׁאָסוּר לְאָדָם לַעֲשׂוֹת עִיסָּתוֹ קַבִּין.

But that[9] means, he who cannot process in purity, because he is unable. Therefore, if he is able this does not apply. This means that it is forbidden for a person to make his dough *qab* sized[10].

9 This does not refer to the Mishnah here but to Mishnah 2:3 which is formulated: If somebody *cannot* make his dough in purity. This implies that if he is able to make the dough in purity he may not make it in small loaves.

10 Unless the total volume of the flour used for all loaves is less than the minimum 5 quarters.

וּשְׁאָר כָּל־הַדְּבָרִים אַתְּ מְהַלֵּךְ בָּהֶן אַחַר הַטִּימְטוּם. עָשָׂה עִיסָּה מִן הַחִטִּים וּמִן הָאוֹרֶז אַחַר מִי אַתְּ מְהַלֵּךְ אַחַר הַגִּילְגּוּל אוֹ אַחַר הַטִּימְטוּם. תַּנֵּי רִבִּי הוֹשַׁעְיָה חַלָּה כְּמִין גַּבְלוּל. מִשֶּׁתִּתְגַּלְגֵּל בַּחִיטִּים וּתְטַמְטֵם בַּשְּׂעוֹרִים. רִבִּי לָֽעְזָר בְּשֵׁם רִבִּי הוֹשַׁעְיָה מִשֶּׁתֵּעָשֶׂה גַּבְלוּלִין גַּבְלוּלִין. מָה וּפְלִיג. כָּאן לַהֲלָכָה. כָּאן לִדְבַר תּוֹרָה.

For all other things[11] one goes after compacting. If one made a dough from wheat and rice, after what do you go, after rolling or after compacting? Rebbi Hoshaiah stated: *ḥallah* in a form[12], after it was rolled for wheat flour or compacted for barley flour. Rebbi Eleazar in the name of Rebbi Hoshaiah, after if was well formed. Do they differ? One is for practice, the other for study matters[13].

11 All flour other than wheat and barley.

12 This translation is tentative since גבלול appears only here. The meaning is guessed from rabbinic Hebrew גבל "to form into dough," Arabic جبل "to form".

13 Since none of the authors of religious codes quotes this paragraph, it is difficult to ascertain which opinion is the one that should guide practice.

תַּנֵּי רִבִּי יְהוּדָה בֶּן בְּתֵירָה אוֹמֵר מִשֶּׁתֵּעָשֶׂה מִקְרָצוֹת מִקְרָצוֹת. מָה טַעֲמָא דְּרִבִּי יוּדָה בֶּן בְּתֵירָה כִּתְרוּמַת גּוֹרֶן כֵּן תָּרִימוּ אוֹתָהּ. מָה תְרוּמַת גּוֹרֶן נִיטֶּלֶת מִן הַגָּמוּר אַף זוֹ נִיטֶּלֶת מִן הַגָּמוּר. מֵעַתָּה לִכְשֶׁתֵּאָפֶה. רִבִּי מַתַּנְיָה לֹא הוּקְשָׁה לִתְרוּמַת גּוֹרֶן אֶלָּא לִמְלֶאכֶת הָעִירוּס בִּלְבַד.

It was stated: Rebbi Jehudah ben Bathyra says after it was made into separate cuttings[14]. What is Rebbi Jehudah ben Bathyra's reason? (*Num.* 15:20) "You shall lift it like the heave of the threshing floor." Since heave of the threshing floor is taken after the end of processing, so this also is taken after the end of processing. Then after it was baked? Rebbi Mattaniah: It is compared to heave only for doughmaking[15].

14 Tosephta 1:12, speaking of a convert who accepts Judaism while making a dough.

15 Since *Num.* 15:20 defines *ḥallah* as "start of your doughs" and not "start of your breads".

רִבִּי יוֹסֵי בְּשֵׁם רִבִּי שִׁמְעוֹן בֶּן לָקִישׁ דְּרִבִּי עֲקִיבָה הִיא. דְּתַנִּינָן תַּמָּן הַנּוֹטֵל חַלָּה מִן הַקַּב רִבִּי עֲקִיבָה אוֹמֵר חַלָּה. וַחֲכָמִים אוֹמְרִים אֵינָהּ חַלָּה. כְּלוּם אָמַר רִבִּי עֲקִיבָה אֶלָּא לְשֶׁעָבַר שֶׁמָּה בַּתְּחִילָּה. וְהָכָא כַּתְּחִילָּה נָן קַיָּימִין. רִבִּי יוֹנָה רִבִּי חִייָה בְּשֵׁם רִבִּי שִׁמְעוֹן בֶּן לָקִישׁ יָרְדוּ לָהּ בְּשִׁיטַּת רִבִּי עֲקִיבָה.

Rebbi Yose in the name of Rebbi Simeon ben Laqish: This[16] is Rebbi Aqiba's, as we have stated there[17]: "If somebody took *ḥallah* from a single *qab*, Rebbi Aqiba says it is *ḥallah*, but the Sages say it is no *ḥallah*." Rebbi Aqiba said that only for the past, maybe for the start[18]? Here we deal with the start. Rebbi Jonah, Rebbi Ḥiyya in the name of Rebbi Simeon ben Laqish, they followed the manner of Rebbi Aqiba[19].

16 This refers to the last statement of the Mishnah, that legal *ḥallah* can be taken as soon as the flour is moistened. R. Simeon ben Laqish must read with Maimonides that *not* 5 quarters are still dry. The Mishnah then does not imply

that 5 quarters of flour are already moistened; one might object that then there is no obligation of *ḥallah*.

17 Mishnah 4:4.

18 If R. Aqiba validates *ḥallah* which was taken against the rules, it does not mean he will accept that one may start with the intention of giving *ḥallah* as long as the dough does not contain five quarters.

19 Mishnah 3:1 cannot be derived from 4:4 but the Sages who declare *ḥallah* from less than 5 quarters invalid cannot accept Mishnah 3:1 (in the Maimonides version.)

אָמַר רִבִּי יוֹחָנָן דִּבְרֵי הַכֹּל הִיא כֵּיוָן שֶׁהִיא נוֹתֶנֶת אֶת הַמַּיִם זוֹ הִיא רֵאשִׁית עֲרִיסוֹתֵיכֶם. דְּתַנֵּי מַעֲשֵׂר טֵבֶל שֶׁנִּתְעָרֵב בְּחוּלִין אוֹסֵר כָּל־שֶׁהוּא אִם יֵשׁ לוֹ פַּרְנָסָה מִמָּקוֹם אַחֵר מוֹצִיא לְפִי חֶשְׁבּוֹן. וְאִם לָאו רִבִּי לָעְזָר בֶּן עֲרָךְ אוֹמֵר יִקְרָא שֵׁם לִתְרוּמַת מַעֲשֵׂר שֶׁבּוֹ וְיַעֲלֶה בְּאַחַת וּמֵאָה. רִבִּי יַעֲקֹב גְּבוּלַיָּא בְּשֵׁם רִבִּי חֲנִינָה הֲלָכָה כְּרִבִּי אֶלְעָזָר בֶּן עֲרָךְ. אָמַר רִבִּי יוֹחָנָן מִמָּה שֶׁלִּימְּדוּ אֶת הַכֹּהֲנוֹת הָדָא אָמְרָה אֵין הֲלָכָה כְּרִבִּי לָעְזָר בֶּן עֲרָךְ. מָה לִימְּדוּ אֶת הַכֹּהֲנוֹת הֲרֵי זֶה חַלָּה עַל הָעִיסָּה הַזֹּאת וְעַל שְׂאוֹר הַמִּתְעָרֵב בָּהּ וְעַל הַקֶּמַח שֶׁנִּשְׁתַּיֵּיר בָּהּ וְעַל הַקֶּרֶץ שֶׁנִּיתָּן תַּחְתֶּיהָ לִכְשֶׁתַּעֲלֶה כוּלָּהּ גּוּשׁ אֶחָד הוּקְדַּשׁ זֶה שֶׁבְּיָדִי לְשֵׁם חַלָּה חוּץ מִן הַטָּמֵא שֶׁבָּהּ. וְאָמַר הוּא וְהַטָּמֵא שֶׁבָּהּ. וְיַעֲלֶה בְּאֶחָד וּמֵאָה. רִבִּי יוֹנָה אָמַר רִבִּי שְׁמוּאֵל קַפּוֹדָקִיָּא וְחַד מִן רַבָּנִין חַד אָמַר כָּאן בְּשֶׁיֵּשׁ בּוֹ כְּדֵי לְהַעֲלוֹת. וְכָאן שֶׁאֵין בָּהּ כְּדֵי לְהַעֲלוֹת מִכֵּיוָן שֶׁהוּא זָקוּק לְהַעֲלוֹת כְּמִי שֶׁיֵּשׁ לוֹ פַּרְנָסָה מִמָּקוֹם אַחֵר.

Rebbi Joḥanan said, it is everybody's opinion since when she starts pouring the water it is (*Num.* 15:20) "the beginnining of your doughs," as it was stated[20]: [21]*Ṭevel* tithe that was mixed with profane food makes it forbidden[22] in the minutest amount. If it can be taken care of from another place, one gives in proportion[23]. Otherwise, Rebbi Eleazar ben Arakh says he should give a name to the heave of the tithe and lift it by 101[24]." Rebbi Jacob from Jabul[25] in the name of Rebbi Ḥanina: Practice follows Rebbi Eleazar ben Arakh. Rebbi Joḥanan said, what they taught the Cohanot[26] implies that practice does not follow Rebbi Eleazar ben Arakh. What did they teach the Cohanot? "This is *ḥallah* for this dough, and the sour dough in it, for the flour contained in it, and for the flat bread under it[27]. If all these are counted together the amount in my hand shall be dedicated as *ḥallah* except what might be impure in it[28]." She says, except what might be impure! Could it not be lifted by 101? Rebbi Jonah said, Rebbi Samuel from Cappadocia and one of the rabbis[29], one said in one case there is enough to lift[30], in the other case there is not enough to lift[31]; since it would have been expected to be lifted it is as if care might be taken of it from another place[32].

20 The Rome ms. reads תני instead of דתני. In that case, the Tosephta is not quoted by R. Joḥanan to bolster his case but by the editors in order to question his argument. Then one should read ". . . your doughs." It was stated . . .

21 Tosephta *Terumot* 5:15, quoted in *Demay* 7:9, Note 137.

22 To laymen.

23 Since heave of the tithe does not have to be earmarked, if the Levite has other tithe from which heave of the tithe was not yet taken, he can include the heave for the mixed tithe in the heave he gives from his other tithe and make the mixture profane.

24 Heave cannot be removed unless declared as such, even if only implicitly by saying, for example: Heave shall be in the Northern part of the grain heap. "Lifting" a replacement of the impure heave was explained in *Terumot* 4, Note 62.

25 An Amora of the second generation, living near Bet Shean.

26 Wives or unmarried daughters of Cohanim. Since they had to watch over purity in their homes, they were called to take *ḥallah* in purity for lay wives.

27 From the text of the declaration it is clear that *ḥallah* is taken at the very first moment, when there still is some flour not moistened, the sour dough not thoroughly worked in, and

some pieces being separated. Flatbread in Arabic is قُرص.

28 If practice would follow R. Eleazar ben Arakh, the Cohenet should lift an amount corresponding to the impurity and then take pure *ḥallah.*

29 He said the same as R. Samuel from Cappadocia but did not mention the latter's name.

30 Then one follows R. Eleazar ben Arakh.

31 Then one formulates the declaration following the Cohanot.

32 One has to follow the Cohanot since in this case even R. Eleazar ben Arakh would not permit taking from the dough without their special declaration.

אָמַר רִבִּי יוֹסֵי נִרְאִין דְּבָרִים בְּעַרְבֵי שַׁבָּתוֹת שֶׁזֶּה מֵבִיאָה וְזֶה מֵבִיאָה כְּמַפְרִישׁ מִן חִיּוּב עַל חִיּוּב. אֲבָל בְּחוֹל תִּיקְנוּ בְּחַלָּה שֶׁתְּהֵא נִיטֶּלֶת מִן הַטָּהוֹר עַל הַטָּמֵא וְשֶׁלֹּא מִן הַמּוּקָּף. שֶׁמָּא מִפְּטוֹר עַל הַחִיּוּב. אָמַר רִבִּי יוֹנָה לֹא מִסְתַּבְּרָה דְּלֹא בְחוֹל. אֲבָל בְּעֶרֶב שַׁבָּת צְרִיכָה לוֹמַר הִיא וְהַטָּמֵא שֶׁבָּהּ. לָמָּה. עַד שֶׁלֹּא תֵּעָשֶׂה גוּשׁ אֶחָד הִיא נִיטֶּלֶת לְשׁוּם חַלָּה. מִשֶּׁתֵּעָשֶׂה גוּשׁ אֶחָד הִיא קְדֵישָׁה לְשֵׁם חַלָּה. אִם אוֹמֵר אַתְּ חוּץ מִן הַטָּמֵא שֶׁבָּהּ נִמְצָא טֵבֶל טָמֵא מְעוּרָב בַּחַלָּה. מִתּוֹךְ שֶׁאַתְּ אוֹמֵר הִיא וְהַטָּמֵא שֶׁבָּהּ חוּלִין טְמֵאִין הֵן. לֹא מוּטָּב לְהַפְרִישׁ מִן הַפְּטוֹר עַל הַחִיּוּב וְלֹא יְהֵא טֵבֶל טָמֵא מְעוּרָב בַּחַלָּה. אָמַר רִבִּי שְׁמוּאֵל בַּר אֶבְדּוּמָא וְלֹא לְמַפְרֵיעוֹ הִיא קְדֵישָׁה. מִכֵּיוָן שֶׁהִיא קְדֵישָׁה לְמַפְרֵיעָהּ כְּמַפְרִישׁ מֵחִיּוּב עַל חִיּוּב.

Rebbi Yose said, the statement is reasonable on Sabbath eves; since everybody is bringing, it is as if she separated from what is obligated for what is obligated. But on weekdays, while they instituted that *ḥallah* may be taken from pure for impure and not earmarked, but from what is exempt for what is obligated[33]? Rebbi Jonah said, it is only reasonable on weekdays, but on Sabbath eve she would have to say "all, including the impure." Why? Since [some dough] is taken before all is one mass, when all is made into one mass the former is sanctified as *ḥallah.* If one would say "except the impure contained in it", it would turn out that impure *ṭevel* is mixed with *ḥallah*[34]. If you say "all, including the impure," it is impure profane; therefore, it is better to give from what is exempt[35] for what is obligated to avoid impure *ṭevel* mixed with *ḥallah*. Rebbi Samuel ben Eudaimon said, does it not become dedicated retroactively? Since it is dedicated retroactively, it is as if one gave from what is obligated for the obligated[36].

33 Fridays every woman will bake more than the minimal amount. Therefore, at the moment the Cohenet takes the dough for *ḥallah*, it becomes *ḥallah*. But during the week, if the amount barely is obligated, the piece taken by the Cohenet is exempt because it is less than 5 quarters. Therefore, if all flour is kneaded and the obligation of *ḥallah* established, designating now that extra piece as *ḥallah* would be satisfying one's obligation with exempt food and this is forbidden for all types of heave.

34 Since the declaration by the Cohenet excludes any impurity in the dough taken for *ḥallah*, that part remains *ṭevel*. Since it is impure and a small quantity, it makes the *ḥallah* dough forbidden for everybody, including the Cohen.

35 A part carefully made in purity by the Cohenet. R. Jonah must hold that the prohibition to give heave from exempt food is purely rabbinical and can be voided if there is no other way out.

36 R. Samuel ben Eudaimon disagrees with the entire discussion, both by R. Yose and R. Jonah. Since at the moment of declaration nothing happens, all remains *ṭevel* at this moment. If the kneaded dough reaches critical mass, the *ḥallah* becomes dedicated retroactively; there is no *ṭevel* and no exempt dough remaining. Therefore, the declaration of the Cohenet is valid both on a regular weekday and on a Friday.

לָמָּה לִי וּבִלְבַד שֶׁלֹּא יְהֵא שָׁם חֲמֵשֶׁת רְבָעִים קֶמַח. אָמַר רִבִּי מַתְנִיתָא קוֹדֶם שֶׁלֹּא לִמְּדוּ אֶת הַכֹּהֲנוֹת.

Why "on condition that there not be five quarters of flour?[37]" Rebbi[38] said, the Mishnah was formulated before they instructed the Cohanot.

37 This is Maimonides's reading in the Mishnah. Since we have decided that *ḥallah* can be given conditionally, the unmixed flour mentioned by the Cohanot should not be limited.

38 Either a name has disappeared from both mss. or this is Rebbi's reason to change the prior formulation of the Mishnah to the text transmitted in both Talmudim.

(fol. 58d) **משנה ב**: נִידְמְעָה עִיסָּתָהּ עַד שֶׁלֹּא גִילְגְּלָה פְּטוּרָה שֶׁהַמְּדוּמָּע פָּטוּר וּמִשֶּׁגִּלְגְּלָה חַיֶּיבֶת. נוֹלַד לָהּ סָפֵק טוּמְאָה עַד שֶׁלֹּא גִילְגְּלָה תֵּיעָשֶׂה בְטוּמְאָה וּמִשֶּׁגִּילְגְּלָה תֵּיעָשֶׂה בְטָהֳרָה.

Mishnah 2: If the dough became *dema'*[39] before it was rolled[2] it is exempt since *dema'* is exempt from *ḥallah*.[40] If a doubt of impurity arose before it was rolled it may be processed in impurity[41] but after it was rolled it must be processed in purity[42].

39 Heave fell in the dough and there is not enough profane dough to lift the heave. Then the entire dough may be eaten only by Cohanim (cf. *Demay* 4, Note 27).

40 Mishnah 1:4.

41 If the dough later becomes obligated for *ḥallah*, the possible impurity already exists while the entire dough is profane. There is no prohibition to cause impurity to profane food (Babli *Niddah* 6b). The *ḥallah* will be forbidden and has to be burned, as if it were certainly impure.

42 At the moment the obligation of *ḥallah* was created, the dough and its *ḥallah* were pure. If later *ḥallah* is taken, it is *ḥallah* which may be

impure. It is forbidden to the Cohanim but it is also forbidden to directly make it impure (cf. *Pesahim* 1:7).

(fol. 59a) **הלכה ב**: אָמַר רִבִּי יוֹנָה תַּרְתֵּין מִילִּין תַּנֵּי רִבִּי חִייָא רוֹבָא וְאִינּוּן פְּלִיגִין חָדָא עַל חָדָא. טֶבֶל מִנְיָנוֹ בְחוּלִּין וְכָל־הַסָּפֵק פּוֹסֵל אֶת הַתְּרוּמָה וּפוֹסֵל אֶת הַחוּלִּין מִלֵּעָשׂוֹת תְּרוּמָה. וְקַשְׁיָא אִם טֶבֶל ממנו בְחוּלִּין לָמָּה לִי פּוֹסֵל אֶת הַחוּלִּין מִלֵּעָשׂוֹתָן תְּרוּמָה. וְהָא מִנְיָנוֹ בִתְרוּמָה. אָמַר רִבִּי יוֹנָה אוּף אֲנָן תַּנִּינָן תַּרְתֵּיהוֹן טֶבֶל מִנְיָנוֹ בְחוּלִּין. דְּתַנִּינָן תַּמָּן אוֹכֶל מַעֲשֵׂר שֶׁהוּכְשַׁר בְּמַשְׁקֶה וְנָגַע בּוֹ טְבוּל יוֹם אוֹ יָדַיִם מְסוֹאָבִין מַפְרִישִׁין מִמֶּנּוּ תְּרוּמַת מַעֲשֵׂר בְּטָהֳרָה מִפְּנֵי שֶׁהוּא שְׁלִישִׁי. הָדָא אָמְרָה שֶׁהַטֶּבֶל מִנְיָנוֹ בְחוּלִּין. וְכָל־הַסָּפֵק פּוֹסֵל אֶת הַתְּרוּמָה וּפוֹסֵל אֶת הַחוּלִּין מִלֵּעָשׂוֹתָן תְּרוּמָה. דְּתַנִּינָן תַּמָּן נוֹלַד לָהּ סָפֵק עַד שֶׁלֹּא גִילְגְּלָה תֵּיעָשֶׂה בְטוּמְאָה מִשֶּׁגִּילְגְּלָה תֵּיעָשֶׂה בְטָהֳרָה. אָמַר רַב שֵׁשֶׁת דְּרִבִּי עֲקִיבָה הִיא דְּרִבִּי עֲקִיבָה אָמַר יֵעָשֶׂנָּה בְטוּמְאָה וְאַל יֵעָשֶׂנָּה קַבִּין. אָמַר רִבִּי זְעִירָא דִּבְרֵי הַכֹּל הִיא יֵעָשֶׂנָּה קַבִּין בִּסְפֵיקָן. הָתִיב רִבִּי חִייָה בֵּירִבִּי בּוּן קוֹמֵי רִבִּי זְעִירָא וְהָתַנֵּי אַף בִּשְׁאָר הַמִּינִין כֵּן. אִית לָךְ מֵימַר יֵעָשֶׂנָּה קַבִּין בִּסְפֵיקָן. רִבִּי זְבִידָא אָמַר אֲנָא בְעִיתָהּ. רִבִּי יוֹסֵי בְשֵׁם רִבִּי הִילָא בְּדִין הָיָה שֶׁיְּטַמֵּא אָדָם טִבְלוֹ דְּבַר תּוֹרָה דִּכְתִיב וַאֲנִי הִנֵּה נָתַתִּי לְךָ אֶת מִשְׁמֶרֶת תְּרוּמוֹתָי. תְּרוּמָה צְרִיכָה שִׁימּוּר. אֵין הַטֶּבֶל צָרִיךְ שִׁימּוּר. מַה אֲנִי מְקַייֵם וּנְתַתֶּם מִמֶּנּוּ אֶת תְּרוּמַת יי לְאַהֲרֹן הַכֹּהֵן. עֲשֵׂה שֶׁיִּינָּתֵן לְאַהֲרֹן הַכֹּהֵן בִּכְהוּנָּתוֹ. וְכָאן הוֹאִיל וְאֵין אַתְּ יָכוֹל לִתְּנוֹ לַכֹּהֵן בִּכְהוּנָּתוֹ רַשַּׁאי אַתְּ לְטַמְּאוֹתוֹ.

Halakhah 2: Rebbi Jonah said: The elder Rebbi Ḥiyya stated two contradictory things, that *ṭevel* is counted with profane food[43] and that every doubt invalidates heave and disables profane food from becoming heave[44]. This is difficult; if *ṭevel* is counted with[45] profane food why should it disable profane food from becoming heave? That means, it is counted with heave! Rebbi Jonah said, we also have stated both statements! We have stated there[46]: "If tithe food was prepared with a fluid and a *ṭevul yom*[47] or unwashed hands touched it, one still may in purity take heave of the tithe from it because it is of the third degree." This implies that *ṭevel* is counted with profane food. But every doubt invalidates heave and disables profane food from becoming heave, as we have stated there[48]: "If a doubt of impurity arose before it was rolled it may be processed in impurity but after it was rolled it must be processed in purity." Rav Sheshet said, this follows Rebbi Aqiba, since Rebbi Aqiba said[49], he should make it in impurity and not make it single *qab*. Rebbi Zeïra said, it is the opinion of everybody that in a case of doubt he should make single *qabim*. Rebbi Ḥiyya bar Abun objected before Rebbi Zeïra, did we not state[50]: "This applies also to other kinds"? Can you say she should make single *qabim* in cases of doubt[51]? Rebbi Zabida said, I asked that[52]. Rebbi Yose in the name of Rebbi Hila: It is the law that a person may make his *ṭevel* impure by biblical standards as it is written (*Num.* 18:8): "I put on you the watch over my heaves." Heave has to be watched, *ṭevel* does not have to be watched. How do I confirm (*Num.* 18:28): "You should give from it the Eternal's heave to Aaron the priest?" You have to give it to Aaron in his quality of priest, but here, since you cannot give it to a Cohen in his quality of priest[53], you may make it impure.

43 The difference between profane food and heave in matters of ritual impurity is that profane food can be impure in the first and second degrees but heave also in the third (cf. *Berakhot* 5, Note 19). It is stated that *ṭevel*, produce under the obligation of heave, cannot become impure in the third degree.

44 If there is a doubt that *ṭevel* may contain impurity in the second degree, it can no longer be a source of heave. Then the remainder of the profane food should be of third degree, i. e.,

pure and acceptable for heave.

45 Reading מנינו instead of ממנו; originally the left stroke of מ was very short. The Rome ms. has a shorter and better version: אִם פּוֹסֵל אֶת הַחוּלִין מִלַּעֲשׂוֹתָן תְּרוּמָה יְהֵא מִנְיָנוֹ בִתְרוּמָה. "If it invalidates profane food so that it cannot be made into heave, it should be counted as heave."

46 Mishnah *Ṭevul Yom* 4:1.

47 Cf. *Terumot* 5, Note 68. A *Ṭevul Yom*, a formerly severely impure person after immersion in a *miqweh* but before sundown, is impure in the second degree by biblical standards. Unwashed hands of an otherwise pure person are impure in the second degree by post-biblical, rabbinic and Sadducee, standards.

48 Here, in Mishnah 2.

49 Mishnah 2:3. Rav Sheshet holds that the Mishnah here is R. Aqiba's but not the Mishnah *Ṭevul Yom* 4:1.

50 Tosephta 1:11: "If a doubt of impurity arose before it was rolled it may be processed in impurity but after it was rolled it must be processed in purity; its *ḥallah* is suspended {it cannot be eaten since it may be impure, and it cannot be burned since it may be pure.} What kind of doubt are we talking about? Doubt for *ḥallah* {involving third degree impurity which is inactive for profane food.} Similarly, produce for which a doubt of impurity arose before it was fully processed {before any obligation of heave} should be processed in impurity but after it was fully processed it must be processed in purity; its heave is suspended. What kind of doubt are we talking about? Doubt for heave."

51 The amount is irrelevant for heave. Therefore, R. Zeïra's argument is irrelevant.

52 He claims priority over R. Ḥiyya bar Abun.

53 The priest is obligated to consume heave in purity. Since the heave in question may not be consumed, it is not destined for the priest.

(fol. 58d) **משנה ג:** הִקְדִּישָׁה עִיסָּתָהּ עַד שֶׁלֹּא גִילְגְּלָה וּפְדָיָתָהּ חַיֶּיבֶת. הִקְדִּישָׁתָהּ עַד שֶׁלֹּא גִילְגְּלָה וְגִילְגְּלָהּ הַגִּיזְבָּר וְאַחַר כָּךְ פְּדִייָתָהּ פְּטוּרָה שֶׁבִּשְׁעַת

חוֹבָתָהּ הָיְתָה פְטוּרָה. כְּיוֹצֵא בוֹ הַמַּקְדִּישׁ פֵּירוֹתָיו עַד שֶׁלֹּא בָאוּ לְעוֹנַת הַמַּעְשְׂרוֹת וּפְדָיָין חַיָּבִין מִשֶּׁבָּאוּ לְעוֹנַת הַמַּעְשְׂרוֹת וּפְדָאָן חַיָּבִין. הִקְדִּישָׁן עַד שֶׁלֹּא נִגְמְרוּ וּגְמָרָן הַגִּזְבָּר וְאַחַר כָּךְ פְּדָיָין פְּטוּרִין שֶׁבִּשְׁעַת חוֹבָתָן הָיוּ פְטוּרִין.

Mishnah 3: If she dedicated her dough and redeemed it before she rolled [the dough], it is obligated. If she dedicated before she rolled, the Temple treasurer had it rolled, and then she redeemed it, it is exempt since at the moment of obligation it was exempt. [54]Parallel to this, if somebody dedicated his produce before the time of tithes and redeemed it, it is obligated; after the time of tithes, it is obligated. But if he dedicated it before it was fully processed, the treasurer finished it, and then the owner redeemed it, it is free since at the time of obligation it was free.

54 This second part of the Mishnah is also in Mishnah *Peah* 4:5; the principle is explained there, Notes 76-81. Since Temple property is common and not individual property, the duties of *ḥallah* and heave, addressed to individuals, are not existing for the Temple.

(fol. 59a) **הלכה ג**: וְלָמָּה תַּנִּינָתָהּ תְּרֵין זִימְנִין. רִבִּי חוּנָה רִבִּי חִיָּיה רִבִּי יְהוֹשֻׁעַ בֶּן לֵוִי בְּשֵׁם רִבִּי פְּדָיָה אַחַת לְמֵרוּחַ וְאַחַת לִשְׁלִישׁ. רִבִּי יוֹסֵי אָמַר רִבִּי בָּא וַחֲבֵרַיָּא. חֲבֵרַיָּא אָמְרִין אַחַת לְמֵרוּחַ וְאַחַת לִשְׁלִישׁ. רִבִּי בָּא מְפָרֵשׁ לַחַלָּה לְמֵירוּחַ. וּפֵיאָה לִשְׁלִישׁ.

Halakhah 3: [55]And why is it stated twice? Rebbi Huna, Rebbi Ḥiyya, Rebbi Joshua ben Levi in the name of Rebbi[56] Pedaiah: One for smoothing, one for one third. Rebbi Yose said, Rebbi Abba and the colleagues. The colleagues say, one for smoothing, one for one third. Rebbi Abba explains: At *Ḥallah* for smoothing, at *Peah* for one third.

וּמַתְנִיתָא דְּרִבִּי עֲקִיבָה. דְּרִבִּי עֲקִיבָה אָמַר אַחַר שְׁלִישׁ הָרִאשׁוֹן אַתְּ מְהַלֵּךְ. וְאִיתְפַּלְּגוּן שָׂדֶה שֶׁהֵבִיאָה שְׁלִישׁ לִפְנֵי גּוֹי וּלְקָחָהּ יִשְׂרָאֵל רִבִּי עֲקִיבָה אוֹמֵר הַתּוֹסֶפֶת פְּטוֹר וַחֲכָמִים אוֹמְרִין הַתּוֹסֶפֶת חִייוּב. מַיי כְדוֹן. תִּיפְתָּר אוֹ כְּרִבִּי עֲקִיבָה בְּמַחְלוֹקֶת אוֹ כְדִיבְרֵי הַכֹּל בְּקוֹצֵר מִיַּד.

Our Mishnah is from Rebbi Aqiba since Rebbi Aqiba said that you go after the first third. And they differed: A field that was one-third ripened in the possession of a Gentile, and a Jew bought it after that time, Rebbi Aqiba said the additional growth is free, but the Sages say he is obligated for the additional growth. How is that? Explain it either for Rebbi Aqiba in a disagreement, or according to everybody if he harvested immediately.

55 The entire Halakhah appears also in *Peah* 4:5, Notes 82-96.

56 In *Peah* correctly: Bar Pedaiah.

(fol. 58d) **משנה ד**: נָכְרִי שֶׁנָּתַן לְיִשְׂרָאֵל עִיסָּה לַעֲשׂוֹת לוֹ פְּטוּרָה מִן הַחַלָּה. נְתָנָהּ לוֹ מַתָּנָה עַד שֶׁלֹּא גִילְגֵּל חַייֶבֶת. וּמִשֶּׁגִּילְגֵּל פְּטוּרָה. הָעוֹשֶׂה עִיסָּה עִם הַנָּכְרִי אִם אֵין בְּשֶׁל יִשְׂרָאֵל כְּשִׁיעוּר חַלָּה פְּטוּרָה מִן הַחַלָּה.

Mishnah 4: A dough[57] which a Non-Jew gave to a Jew to make is exempt from *ḥallah*. If he gave it as a gift before it was rolled it is obligated, after it was rolled it is free. If somebody makes dough in partnership with a Non-Jew, it is exempt from *ḥallah* if the Jew's part is less than the measure[58].

57 Flour or dough not fully mixed. Property of the Non-Jew is not subject to Jewish ritual law.

58 If the Jew contributed less than 5 quarters of flour.

(fol. 59a) **הלכה ד**: מָה בֵינָהּ לְעִיסַּת אַרְנוֹנָא. שֶׁמָּה אֵינָהּ חַייֶבֶת בְּחַלָּה. תַּמָּן בִּרְשׁוּת יִשְׂרָאֵל הוּא שֶׁמָּא יִמְלוֹךְ הַגּוֹי לִיטְלָהּ. בְּרַם הָכָא לְדַעְתּוֹ הִיא תְלוּיָה.

Halakhah 4: What is the difference between this and a dough of *annona*? Is the latter not obligated for *ḥallah*[59]? There it is in the possession of the Jew until the Gentile decides to take it[60]. But here it depends on the latter's opinion.

59 Tosephta 1:4: "An *annona* dough (which has to be delivered to the army; cf. *Peah* 1, Note 85) is obligated since one is responsible until it is delivered." The Babli (*Pesaḥim* 6a) considers the possibility that delivery of *annona* may be replaced by a cash payment. In that case, the *annona* dough is clearly the Jew's and is not necessarily made exclusively for the Gentile government. This seems not to be the position of the Yerushalmi; it might indicate a difference between Roman and Persian administrative practices.

60 Medieval authors (e. g., R. Simson, R. Asher ben Ieḥiel, R. Nissim Gerondi) read: "Maybe the Gentile decides not to take it." It is also the reading of the ms. of R. S. Cirillo; this leads one to suspect that the reading is an attempt at harmonization with the Babli (Note 59).

In a second opinion, the Babli holds that *ḥallah* of the *annona* is purely rabbinical since people might think that the person baking does not give *ḥallah* for his own bread. This is not the Yerushalmi's general attitude; cf. *Kilaim* 2, Notes 34-40.

(fol. 59b) תַּנֵּי רִבִּי יוּדָה מְלַאי שֶׁלְיִשְׂרָאֵל וּפוֹעֲלִין גּוֹיִם עוֹשִׂין לְתוֹכוֹ חַייָב בְּחַלָּה. מְלַאי שֶׁלְגּוֹי וּפוֹעֲלֵי יִשְׂרָאֵל עוֹשִׂין בְּתוֹכוֹ פָּטוּר מִן הַחַלָּה. אָמַר רִבִּי יוֹסֵי אוּף אֲנָן תַּנִּינָן נָכְרִי שֶׁנָּתַן לְיִשְׂרָאֵל לַעֲשׂוֹת לוֹ עִיסָּה פְּטוּרָה מִן הַחַלָּה.

Rebbi Jehudah stated[61]: "If the inventory belongs to a Jew but Gentile workers make it, it is subject to *ḥallah*. If the inventory belongs to a Gentile and Jewish workers make it, it is not subject to *ḥallah*." Rebbi

Yose said, we also have stated this: "A dough which a Non-Jew gave to a Jew to make is exempt from *ḥallah*."

61 Tosephta 1:3, an anonymous statement.

רִבִּי בּוּן בַּר חִייָה בָּעָא קוֹמֵי רִבִּי זְעִירָא וַאֲפִילוּ יֵשׁ בְּשֶׁל יִשְׂרָאֵל כְּשִׁיעוּר. יֵיעָשֶׂה כְּקַב מִכָּן וְקַב מִכָּן וְקַב הַגּוֹי בְּאֶמְצַע. אָמַר לֵיהּ רִבִּי זְעִירָה וְאֵינוֹ מְעוּרָב עַל יְדֵי גוֹיִם.

Rebbi Abun bar Ḥiyya asked before Rebbi Zeïra: Even if the Jew's was a full measure, can it not be considered like a *qab* here, a *qab* there, and a Gentile's *qab* in the middle[62]? Rebbi Zeïra told him, is it not mixed by Gentiles?

62 Why should the dough of a Jew made in partnership with a Gentile ever be subject to *ḥallah*? In Mishnah 4:3 it is stated that if a dough is made in three parts of one *qab* each, two of wheat and one of rice, and the rice dough separates the two pieces of wheat dough, there is no obligation of *ḥallah* since the exempt rice prevents the two wheat doughs from being counted together. Similarly, the exempt flour belonging to the Gentile should prevent the Jew's flour from being counted as an entity.

63 The analogy is invalid; well-mixed dough made of two parts wheat flour and one part rice is subject to *ḥallah*. Even if the Gentile mixes, the Jewish parts will be connected and are subject to *ḥallah*.

(fol. 58d) **משנה ה:** גֵּר שֶׁנִּתְגַּייֵר וְהָיְתָה לוֹ עִיסָּה אִם נַעֲשֵׂית עַד שֶׁלֹּא נִתְגַּייֵר פָּטוּר. וּמִשֶּׁנִּתְגַּייֵר חַיָּיב. וְאִם סָפֵק חַייָב וְאֵין חַייָבִין עָלֶיהָ חוֹמֶשׁ. רִבִּי עֲקִיבָה אוֹמֵר הַכֹּל הוֹלֵךְ אַחַר הַקְּרִימָה בַּתַּנּוּר.

Mishnah 5: If a proselyte became Jewish while he had dough, if it was made[64] before he became Jewish it is exempt, after he became Jewish it is obligated. In case of doubt it is obligated but one does not owe a fifth[65] because of it. Rebbi Aqiba says, all goes after forming a crust in the oven[66].

64 While he was undergoing the conversion ceremony, his servants made dough in his house.

65 As penalty if the *hallah* was misappropriated; cf. Mishnah *Terumot* 6:1.

66 The question is whether R. Aqiba disagrees with all preceding statements that designate rolling (of wheat dough, or compacting of barley dough) as final processing or he holds that only baking is final processing for the proselyte.

(fol. 59b) **הלכה ה**: תַּמָּן תַּנִּינָן גֵּר שֶׁנִּתְגַּייֵר וְהָיְתָה לוֹ פָּרָה נִשְׁחֶטֶת עַד שֶׁלֹּא נִתְגַּייֵר פָּטוּר מִשֶּׁנִּתְגַּייֵר חַייָב. וְאִם סָפֵק פָּטוּר שֶׁהַמּוֹצִיא מֵחֲבֵירוֹ עָלָיו הָרְאָייָה. תַּמָּן אַתְּ אָמַר סָפֵק פָּטוּר. וְהָכָא אַתְּ אָמַר סָפֵק חַייָב. אָמַר רִבִּי אָחָא אִיתְתָּבַת קוֹמֵי רִבִּי אִמִּי וְאָמַר מִי יֹאמַר לִי שֶׁהוּא נוֹטֵל דָּמָיו מִן הַשֵּׁבֶט. רִבִּי יַעֲקֹב בַּר זַבְדִּי רִבִּי חִייָה בְּשֵׁם רִבִּי לָעְזָר נוֹטֵל הוּא דָמָיו מִן הַשֵּׁבֶט. וְיַפְרִשׁ תַּמָּן וְיִטּוֹל דָּמָיו מִן הַשֵּׁבֶט. אָמַר רִבִּי יוֹסֵי חַלָּה שֶׁהִיא טֶבֶל וּבַעֲוֹן מִיתָה מַפְרִישׁ וְלֹא יִטּוֹל דָּמָיו מִן הַשֵּׁבֶט עַל שֵׁם הַמּוֹצִיא מֵחֲבֵירוֹ עָלָיו הָרְאָיָה.

Halakhah 5: There, we have stated[67]: "If a proselyte became Jewish while he had a cow, if she was slaughtered before he became Jewish he is free, after he had become Jewish he is obligated. In case of doubt he is free because the burden of proof is on the claimant." There you say in doubt he is free, here you say in doubt he is obligated. Rebbi Abba said, this was challenged before Rebbi Ammi and he said, who would tell me that he takes its value from the tribe[68]! Rebbi Jacob bar Zavdi, Rebbi

Ḥiyya in the name of Rebbi Eleazar, he takes its value from the tribe. Why can he not put aside there[69] and take its value from the tribe? Rebbi Yose said, *ḥallah* which is *ṭevel* and a deadly sin he puts aside and does not take its value from the tribe since the burden of proof is on the claimant[70].

67 Mishnah *Ḥulin* 10:4. The chapter deals with the obligatory gifts to the Cohen from profane slaughter: forearm, jawbone and first stomach (*Deut.* 18:3). These gifts are totally profane; no holiness is attached to them at any moment. Therefore, a Cohen who claims these gifts would have to prove by legal standards that the gifts are due. Because of the nature of the doubt, this proof is precluded.

68 Since the duty of *ḥallah* is questionable, he suggests that the proselyte sell his *ḥallah* to a Cohen.

69 In the case of profane slaughter, why can we not require that the Cohen's gifts be sold exclusively to Cohanim?

70 There is no problem whatsoever; the same rules apply in both cases. The Cohen's share in a profanely slaughtered animal is profane; therefore, all rules of civil claims apply. *Ḥallah* is separated because of religious scruples; no money can be collected since the proselyte cannot prove that he is not obligated.

אָמַר רִבִּי בּוּן בַּר חִייָה שְׁנֵי גוֹיִם שֶׁעָשׂוּ שְׁנֵי קַבִּין וְחִלְּקוּ וְהוֹסִיפוּ זֶה עַל שֶׁלּוֹ וְזֶה עַל שֶׁלּוֹ חַייָבִין שֶׁלֹּא הָיְתָה לָהֶן שְׁעַת חוֹבָה וְנִפְטְרוּ. שְׁנֵי יִשְׂרָאֵל שֶׁעָשׂוּ שְׁנֵי קַבִּין וְחִלְּקוּ וְהוֹסִיפוּ זֶה עַל שֶׁלּוֹ וְזֶה עַל שֶׁלּוֹ פְּטוּרִין שֶׁכְּבָר הָיָה לָהֶן שְׁעַת חוֹבָה וְנִפְטְרוּ. יִשְׂרָאֵל וְגוֹי שֶׁעָשׂוּ שְׁנֵי קַבִּין וְחִלְּקוּ וְהוֹסִיפוּ זֶה עַל שֶׁלּוֹ וְזֶה עַל שֶׁלּוֹ. נִיחָא חֶלְקוֹ שֶׁלְּיִשְׂרָאֵל חַייָב. חֶלְקוֹ שֶׁלְּגוֹי מַהוּ. כְּלוּם חֶלְקוֹ שֶׁלְּגוֹי חַייָב לֹא מֵחֲמַת חֶלְקוֹ שֶׁלְּיִשְׂרָאֵל. חֶלְקוֹ שֶׁלְּיִשְׂרָאֵל חַייָב וְחֶלְקוֹ שֶׁלְּגוֹי פָּטוּר.

Rebbi Abun bar Ḥiyya said: Two Gentiles who made a dough of two *qabim*, split, and then each of them added to it, are obligated[71] because they never were potentially obligated but exempted. Two Jews who made a dough of two *qabim*, split[72], and then each of them added to it, are exempted because they were potentially obligated but exempted. A Jew and a Gentile made a dough of two *qabim*, split, and then each of them added to it, it is clear that the Jew's part is obligated[73]. What is the status of the Gentile's part? Would the Gentile's part not be obligated only because of the Jew[74]? The Jew's part is obligated, the Gentile's is exempt[75].

71 The Gentiles made a dough which, if made by a Jew, would have been subject to *ḥallah*. They split the dough in two and converted to Judaism. Then each of them took his part, made from less than 5 quarters of dough, and added to reach the threshhold of *ḥallah*. This then are new doughs and obligated.

The entire paragraph is based on the anonymous opinion that forming the dough for baking causes the obligation of *ḥallah*. For Rebbi Aqiba, the questions are irrelevant.

72 One has to explain with R. Joseph Caro that they made the dough with the explicit understanding that they would split before the final shaping. Then the obligated dough would become exempt at the time of splitting. If they make the dough in common and only later decide to split, it is not different from smaller breads taken together in a basket where the basket combines them, cf. Mishnah 2:4. R. Abraham ben David (Note to Maimonides, *Bikkurim* 7:9) declares the sentence to be meaningless.

73 This is more or less the case treated in the Mishnah.

74 R. Abraham ben David reads: Would the Jew's part not be obligated only because of the Gentile? This reading is accepted by R. Joseph Caro who explains that without the Gentile's flour the Jew's dough certainly would be exempt. But if the Gentile becomes Jewish and is now obligated for *ḥallah*, the question makes sense the way our text is written.

75 Maimonides (*Bikkurim* 7:10) takes this as a declarative sentence. R. Joseph Caro points out that Maimonides goes out of his way to spell out that the Jew and the Gentile make the entire dough in partnership,

implying that at the start they did not intend to split. Therefore, had the Gentile already been Jewish the dough would have been obligated when kneaded.

R. Abraham ben David declares that the sentence makes sense only if read as a rhetorical question: "The Jew's part is obligated, can the Gentile's be exempt?", which implies that both doughs are obligated.

רִבִּי עֲקִיבָה אוֹמֵר הַכֹּל הוֹלֵךְ אַחַר קְרִימָה בַּתַּנּוּר. חֲבֵרַייָא בְשֵׁם רִבִּי לָעְזָר מוֹדֶה רִבִּי עֲקִיבָה לַחֲכָמִים בְּעִיסַּת הֶדְיוֹט שֶׁגִּילְגּוּלָהּ טִיבּוּלָהּ. רִבִּי הִילָא בְשֵׁם רִבִּי לָעְזָר מוֹדֶה רִבִּי עֲקִיבָה לַחֲכָמִים בְּעִיסַּת הֶקְדֵּשׁ שֶׁגִּילְגּוּלָהּ פּוֹטְרָהּ. כַּהֲנָא אָמַר דִּבְרֵי רִבִּי עֲקִיבָה אֵין מֵירוּחַ פּוֹטֵר בִּמְקוֹם הֶקְדֵּשׁ. אוֹמֵר רִבִּי יוֹנָה הָדָא דְכַהֲנָא פְלִיגָא עַל רִבִּי לָעְזָר. מָן דְּאָמַר גִּילְגּוּל פּוֹטֵר הַמֵּירוּחַ פּוֹטֵר. וּמָאן דְּאָמַר אֵין גִּילְגּוּל פּוֹטֵר אֵין הַמֵּירוּחַ פּוֹטֵר. בְּרַם כְּרַבָּנִין גִּילְגּוּל פּוֹטֵר בִּרְשׁוּת הַגּוֹי אֵין הַמֵּירוּחַ פּוֹטֵר בִּרְשׁוּת הַגּוֹי. וְקַשְׁיָא עַל דְּרַבָּנִין גִּילְגּוּל פּוֹטֵר בִּרְשׁוּת הַגּוֹי אֵין הַמֵּירוּחַ פּוֹטֵר בִּרְשׁוּת הַגּוֹי. שַׁנְייָא הִיא דִכְתִיב וְכָל־מַעְשַׂר הָאָרֶץ מִזֶּרַע הָאָרֶץ. וְהָכָא לֵית כְּתִיב מִלֶּחֶם הָאָרֶץ. מִלֶּחֶם וְלֹא כָל־לֶחֶם. אָמַר רִבִּי חֲנִינָה בְּרֵיהּ דְּרִבִּי הִלֵּל מִן הָדָא דְרַבָּנִין אֲנָן יָלְפִין דְּלֵית הָדָא דְכַהֲנָא פְלִיגָא עַל רִבִּי לָעְזָר. כְּמָה דְרַבָּנִין אָמְרִין גִּילְגּוּל פּוֹטֵר בִּרְשׁוּת הַגּוֹי אֵין הַמֵּירוּחַ פּוֹטֵר בִּרְשׁוּת הַגּוֹי. כֵּן רִבִּי עֲקִיבָה אוֹמֵר אֵין גִּילְגּוּל פּוֹטֵר בִּרְשׁוּת הַגּוֹי וְאֵין הַמֵּירוּחַ פּוֹטֵר בִּרְשׁוּת הֶקְדֵּשׁ.

"Rebbi Aqiba says, all goes after forming a crust in the oven." The colleagues in the name of Rebbi Eleazar: Rebbi Aqiba agrees with the Sages that rolling the dough of a layman makes it *tevel*. Rebbi Hila in the name of Rebbi Eleazar: Rebbi Aqiba agrees with the Sages that rolling the dough by the Temple exempts[76]. Cahana said, the words of Rebbi Aqiba imply that shaping the heap by the Temple does not exempt[77]. Rebbi Jonah said, that of Rebbi Cahana disagrees with that of Rebbi Eleazar. He who says rolling exempts, [says] shaping exempts. And he who says rolling does not exempt, [says] shaping does not exempt[78]. But according to the rabbis, rolling exempts in the Gentile's power, shaping does not exempt in the Gentile's power. It is difficult for the rabbis, if rolling exempts in the Gentile's power, why does shaping not exempt in the Gentile's power[79]? There is a difference since it is written (*Lev.* 27:30): "All tithe from the Land from the seed of the Land.[80]" But is here[81] not written (*Num.* 15:19): "From the bread of the Land?" *From* the bread, not all bread[82]. Rebbi Ḥanina the son of Rebbi Hillel said, from the rabbis we infer that Cahana's statement does not disagree with Rebbi Eleazar. Just as the rabbis say, rolling exempts in the Gentile's power but shaping does not exempt in the Gentile's power, so Rebbi Aqiba says, rolling does not exempt in the Gentile's power and shaping does not exempt in the power of the Temple[83].

76 In R. Eleazar's opinion, R. Aqiba accepts Mishnah 3:3 without change. R. Eliahu Fulda notes that "layman" is mentioned only as contrast to "Temple". This seems to contradict the statements in Halakhah 2:1, Notes 5-6.

77 Shaping the heap is the end of grain processing, which triggers the obligation of heave and tithes. R. Aqiba states in Mishnah *Menaḥot* 10:4 that leftover flour made by Temple personnel from barley for the *'omer* offering is obligated for tithes. Since the cut grain has to be cleaned before milling, that cleaning process is the equivalent of shaping the heap in a regular harvest. The anonymous majority holds everywhere that all Temple grain is exempt from heave and tithes.

Everybody in that Mishnah agrees that dough made from this flour is subject to *ḥallah*.

78 This argument is brought without a dissenting voice in Babli *Menaḥot* 67a.

79 The Babli, *Menaḥot* 67a, holds that this is not biblical but purely rabbinic.

80 The ethnicity of the farmer is not mentioned. The questioner, and the rabbis quoted in the last sentence, must

hold with R. Meïr that possession by a Gentile does not remove the obligations imposed on produce of the Land; cf. *Peah* 4, Notes 129-131.

81 In the laws of *ḥallah.*

82 If this מ is partitive, there is no reason why in *Lev.* 27:30 it cannot be partitive also. The argument of R. Jonah is rejected.

83 It is implied that in the matter of grain grown by a Gentile in the Land, R. Meïr reports the position of R. Aqiba.

A Genizah text reads רִבִּי עֲקִיבָה אוֹמֵר אֵין גִּילְגּוּל פּוֹטֵר בִּרְשׁוּת הֶקְדֵּשׁ אֵין הַמֵּירוּחַ פּוֹטֵר בִּרְשׁוּת הֶקְדֵּשׁ. "Rebbi Aqiba says, rolling does not exempt in the Temple's power and shaping does not exempt in the power of the Temple". This may be the better text.

(fol. 58d) **משנה ו**: הָעוֹשֶׂה עִיסָּה מִן הַחִיטִּים וּמִן הָאוֹרֶז אִם יֵשׁ בָּהּ טַעַם דָּגָן חַיֶּיבֶת וְיוֹצֵא בָהּ אָדָם יְדֵי חוֹבָתוֹ בַפֶּסַח. וְאִם אֵין בָּהּ טַעַם דָּגָן אֵינָהּ חַיֶּיבֶת בַּחַלָּה וְאֵין אָדָם יוֹצֵא בָהּ יְדֵי חוֹבָתוֹ בַפֶּסַח.

Mishnah 6: If somebody makes dough from wheat and rice, if it has the taste of flour it is subject to *ḥallah* and a person may satisfy his Passover obligation with it. If it does not have the taste of flour it is not subject to *ḥallah* and a person may not satisfy his Passover obligation with it.

(fol. 59b) **הלכה ו**: מַתְנִיתָא כְּדְרַבָּן שִׁמְעוֹן בֶּן גַּמְלִיאֵל דְּרַבָּן שִׁמְעוֹן בֶּן גַּמְלִיאֵל אוֹמֵר לְעוֹלָם אֵינָהּ חַייֶבֶת עַד שֶׁיְּהֵא בָהּ דָּגָן כְּשִׁיעוּר. רִבִּי יַעֲקֹב בַּר אִידִי בְשֵׁם רִבִּי שִׁמְעוֹן בֶּן לָקִישׁ הֲלָכָה כְּרַבָּן שִׁמְעוֹן בֶּן גַּמְלִיאֵל. אָמַר רִבִּי הִילָא בֵּין כְּרַבָּנִין דְּהָכָא בֵּין כְּרַבָּנִין דְּתַמָּן[84] אָמְרִין עַד שֶׁיְּהֵא רוּבָּהּ דָּגָן וְטַעֲמָהּ דָּגָן. רַב הוּנָא אָמַר טַעֲמָהּ דָּגָן אַף עַל פִּי שֶׁאֵין רוּבָּהּ דָּגָן. מַתְנִיתָא פְלִיגָא עַל רַב הוּנָא עִירֵב בָּהּ שְׁאָר הַמִּינִין עַד שֶׁיְּהֵא בָהּ רוּבָּהּ דָּגָן וְטַעֲמָהּ דָּגָן. פָּתַר לָהּ בְּמִינִים

אֲחֵרִים. מַתְנִיתָא פְלִיגָא עַל רִבִּי הִילָא הַנּוֹטֵל שְׂאוֹר מֵעִיסַּת חִיטִּין וְנוֹתְנָהּ לְתוֹךְ עִיסַּת הָאוֹרֶז אִם יֵשׁ בָּהּ טַעַם דָּגָן חַייֶבֶת בַּחַלָּה וְאִם לָאו פְּטוּרָה. בְּגִין נִתְנוּ דְבַתְרָהּ הַטֶּבֶל אָסוּר כָּל־שֶׁהוּא מִין בְּמִינוֹ. שֶׁלֹּא בְמִינוֹ בְּנוֹתֵן טַעַם.

Halakhah 6: The Mishnah follows Rabban Simeon ben Gamliel since[85] "Rabban Simeon ben Gamliel says it is never obligated unless it contain the measure of grain." Rebbi Jacob bar Idi in the name of Rebbi Simeon ben Laqish: Practice follows Rabban Simeon ben Gamliel. Rebbi Hila said, both following the rabbis here or the rabbis there, they say not unless the greater part be grain and the taste that of grain. Rav Huna said, the taste of grain even if the greater part is not grain. A *baraita* disagrees with Rav Huna: If he mixed other kinds in, not unless the greater part be grain and the taste that of grain. He explains it for other kinds[86]. A Mishnah[87] disagrees with Rebbi Hila: "If somebody takes sourdough from grain dough and adds it to a rice dough, if it imparts the taste of grain[88] it is subject to *ḥallah*, otherwise it is exempt." Because it was stated after that[89]: "*Ṭevel* is forbidden in the most minute amount in its own kind. Not in its own kind if it can be tasted."

84 Reading of a Genizah fragment. The two mss. read התם, a Babylonism.

85 Tosephta 2:1. Since, in general, "imparting taste" needs only minute quantities (as discussed in *Terumot* 10), it is stated here that in the Mishnah a substantial amount is needed and "having the taste" does not mean "it tastes like rice cake but an admixture of wheat is noticeable" but "it actually tastes like wheat bread." Since Rabban Simeon ben Gamliel is the only author reported to have quantified this statement, we have to follow him.

86 Other than rice and millet which substitute for grain.

87 Mishnah 3:8.

88 Sourdough is used in small quantities.

89 The problem addressed is that of active sourdough taken from dough subject to *ḥallah* but of which *ḥallah*

was not yet taken. That sourdough is *ṭevel* for *ḥallah* and subject to more restrictive rules. In this case, "can be tasted" means the minute amounts discussed in *Terumot* 10, Halakhot 7-10; the quote is irrelevant for the discussion here.

רִבִּי יוֹסֵי הֲוָה מְסַמֵּךְ לְרִבִּי זְעִירָא שָׁמַע קָלֵיהּ דְּרִבִּי הִילָא יְתִיב מַתְנֵי רִבִּי חִיָּיה[90] בְּשֵׁם רִבִּי יוֹחָנָן אָמַר טַעֲמָהּ דָּגָן אַף עַל פִּי שֶׁאֵין רוּבָּהּ דָּגָן. רִבִּי יָסָא[90] בְּשֵׁם רִבִּי יוֹחָנָן עַד שֶׁיְּהֵא רוּבָּהּ דָּגָן וְטַעֲמָהּ דָּגָן. אָמַר מִחְלְפָה הִיא בְיָדֵיהּ סֵימָן הֲוָה לָן רִבִּי יוֹסֵי כְּרַב הוּנָא.

Rebbi Yose was supporting Rebbi Zeïra. He heard the voice of Rebbi Hila who was sitting and stating: Rebbi Ḥiyya in the name of Rebbi Joḥanan: the taste of grain even if the greater part is not grain; Rebbi Assi in the name of Rebbi Joḥanan: The greater part grain and the taste that of grain. He said, he got it wrong: we had a note that Rebbi Assi teaches like Rav Huna.

90 Reading of the Genizah fragment. In both mss., ר' חייה בשם is missing but is required by the next sentence. Similarly, only the Geniza ms. reads יסא in the next sentence but even it reads יוסי in the last. But even there, one must read יסא for יוסי the last two times. R. Zeïra must have been very old when he was walking supported by his student's student R. Yose while he himself was mainly a student of R. Assi's contemporary R. Ḥiyya bar Abba.

(fol. 58d) **משנה ז**: הַנּוֹטֵל שְׂאוֹר מֵעִיסָּה שֶׁלֹּא הוּרְמָה חַלָּתָהּ וְנוֹתֵן לְתוֹךְ עִיסָּה שֶׁהוּרְמָה חַלָּתָהּ אִם יֵשׁ לוֹ פַּרְנָסָה מִמָּקוֹם אַחֵר מוֹצִיא לְפִי חֶשְׁבּוֹן וְאִם לָאו מוֹצִיא חַלָּה אַחַת עַל הַכֹּל. כְּיוֹצֵא בוֹ זֵיתֵי מַסִּיק שֶׁנִּתְעָרְבוּ עִם זֵיתֵי נִיקוּף. עִינְּבֵי בָצִיר עִם עִינְּבֵי עוֹלֵלוֹת אִם יֵשׁ לוֹ פַּרְנָסָה מִמָּקוֹם אַחֵר מוֹצִיא לְפִי חֶשְׁבּוֹן. וְאִם לָאו מוֹצִיא תְּרוּמָה וּתְרוּמַת מַעֲשֵׂר לַכֹּל וּשְׁאָר מַעֲשֵׂר וּמַעֲשֵׂר שֵׁינִי לְפִי חֶשְׁבּוֹן.

Mishnah 7: If somebody takes sourdough from a dough from which no *ḥallah* was taken and adds it to dough from which *ḥallah* was taken[91], if he can provide for it from another place[92] he should take in proportion; otherwise he should take *ḥallah* for everything[93]. Similarly, if harvested olives were mixed with plucked olives[94], or harvested grapes with gleanings, if he can provide for it from another place he should take in proportion; otherwise he should take heave and heave of the tithe for everything[95] but the remainder of tithe and Second Tithe in proportion[96].

משנה ח: הַנּוֹטֵל שְׂאוֹר מֵעִיסַּת חִיטִּים וְנוֹתֵן לְתוֹךְ עִיסַּת הָאוֹרֶז אִם יֵשׁ בָּהּ טַעַם דָּגָן חַיֶּיבֶת בַּחַלָּה וְאִם לָאו פְּטוּרָה מִן הַחַלָּה. וְאִם כֵּן לָמָּה אָמְרוּ הַטֶּבֶל אָסוּר כָּל־שֶׁהוּא מִין בְּמִינוֹ. וְשֶׁלֹּא בְמִינוֹ בְּנוֹתֵן טַעַם.

Mishnah 8: If somebody takes sourdough from grain dough and adds it to a rice dough, if it imparts the taste of grain it is subject to *ḥallah*, otherwise it is exempt from *ḥallah*. Then why did they say[97] *ṭevel* is forbidden in the most minute amount? In its own kind; not in its own kind if it can be tasted.

91 This is now *ṭevel* for *ḥallah* but most of it is exempt from *ḥallah*.

92 From a third dough which is obligated for *ḥallah*. Since *ḥallah* as a heave must be given from what is earmarked, the Tosephta (2:2) requires that one make a *new* dough and put it in the same place as the problematic *ṭevel* dough to earmark it and take there the full *ḥallah* for the new dough

and a proportionate amount for the offending sourdough. Maimonides in his Commentary follows the Tosephta but in his Code (*Bikkurim* 7:11) he requires simply that the second dough be subject to *ḥallah*. The latter is the reasonable interpretation of the Mishnah.

93 He must take *ḥallah* from the *ṭevel* dough in the required amount, $^1/_{24}$ of the entire dough. Even though in general it is forbidden to give heave from what already is freed from the obligation, it is stated in the next Mishnah that the dough in question is only rabbinically *ṭevel*; for biblical standards the sourdough has disappeared in the dough whose obligation was already satisfied. Therefore, the *ṭevel* extended to the entire dough is rabbinic in character and the rabbinic obligation of *ḥallah* overrides the, in this case rabbinic, requirement to give from obligated dough.

94 Olives are harvested by shaking the trees and are subject to heave and tithes; plucked olives are collected by the poor after the harvest and are exempt. Similarly, harvested grapes are obligated and gleanings exempt.

95 Including the poor people's part since not giving heaves is a deadly sin and it is not clear whether what he takes is actully obligated or free.

96 Since the exempt olives or grapes were mixed with the farmer's, it is assumed that the farmer bought them from the poor. If not, he has to buy them now so he may take out the tithe. Technically, the farmer has to take full tithe in order to give heave of the tithe but then he may retain the part attributable to the exempt fruits for himself.

97 This is a rabbinic prohibition; by biblical standards *ṭevel* disappears in a majority of permitted food. If the prohibition were biblical, *ṭevel* sour dough in rice cake would have to be treated according to the previous Mishnah.

(fol. 59b) **הלכה ז**: רִבִּי בּוּן בַּר חִייָה בָּעָא קוֹמֵי רִבִּי זְעִירָא מִנְחָה שֶׁנִּתְעָֽרְבָה
בְחוּלִין קוֹמֵץ וּמַתִּיר אֶת הַשִּׁייְרִיים לָאֲכִילָה. קוֹרֵא אֲנִי עָלֶיהָ וְהַנּוֹתֶרֶת מִן
הַמִּנְחָה לְאַהֲרֹן וּלְבָנָיו. אָמַר לֵיהּ וְכִי טֵבֶל שֶׁנִּתְעָרֵב בְּחוּלִין קוֹרֵא אֲנִי עָלָיו[98]
וּנְתַתֶּם מִמֶּנּוּ אֶת תְּרוּמַת יי לְאַהֲרֹן הַכֹּהֵן. אָמַר לֵיהּ וְכֵן[99] אָמְרִית לָךְ שֶׁאֵינוֹ
מוֹצִיא מִמֶּנּוּ עָלָיו וְלֹא מִמֶּנּוּ לְמָקוֹם אַחֵר. אִין תַּפְשִׁיטָא לָךְ שֶׁאֵינוֹ מוֹצִיא

מִמֶּנּוּ עַל מָקוֹם אַחֵר אֲפִילוּ מִמֶּנּוּ עָלָיו אֵינוֹ מוֹצִיא. מַתְנִיתָא אָמְרָה שֶׁהוּא מוֹצִיא מִמֶּנּוּ עָלָיו דְּתַנִּינָן וְאִם לָאו מוֹצִיא חַלָּה אַחַת עַל הַכֹּל.

Halakhah 7: Rebbi Abun bar Ḥiyya[100] asked before Rebbi Zeïra: If a cereal offering was mixed with profane flour, may [the Cohen] take a fistful and permit the remainder to be eaten[101]? Do I read for this (*Lev.* 2:3): "The remainder of the offering is for Aaron and his sons?" He said to him: If *ṭevel* was mixed with profane, do I read (*Num.* 18:28) "you shall give *from it* the Eternal's heave to Aaron the Cohen"[102]? He answered him, did I say to you that he cannot take from itself for itself and not from it for another place? If it is clear to you that he cannot take from it for another place[103] then even from itself for itself he should not be able to take! The Mishnah said that he can take from itself for itself as we have stated: "Otherwise he should take *ḥallah* for everything".

98 Reading of the Genizah fragment. Mss.: עליה.

99 Reading of the Genizah fragment. Mss.: וכי.

100 In the Rome ms. "R. Yose ben Rebbi Abun bar Ḥiyya"; this is unlikely to be correct.

101 On the face of it, it would seem that the question does not even start since if the two kinds of flour are mixed it seems impossible to take out a fistful of the offering and burn it on the altar since it is forbidden to burn profane material on the altar. On the other hand, the remainder may be eaten only after the fistful was brought to the altar (*Lev.* 6:9). Even the explanation by R. H. Kanievski, that at some place the original offering is still recognizable, does not work since the fistful may be taken only out of the Temple vessel in which the offering was dedicated. One must conclude that the question of practical use is considered a technicality which can be left to the Sages at the time of the Messiah.

Since flour offerings before the lifting of the fistful are forbidden to everybody, Cohen and layman, it is reasonable to compare the laws of these offerings to those of *ṭevel*,

102 Mishnah 7 states clearly that in absence of other produce, the *ṭevel* mixed with profane flour can be put in order by taking the heave *from itself*.

103 Nobody accepts that *ṭevel* mixed with profane can be used to put certain *ṭevel* in order!

אָֽמְרִין לֵית הָדָא דְּרִבִּי זְעִירָה תְּתִיבָה עַל רִבִּי בּוּן בַּר חִיָּה. מַה בֵין הַמּוֹצִיא מִמֶּנּוּ עָלָיו מָה בֵין הַמּוֹצִיא מִמֶּנּוּ לְמָקוֹם אַחֵר. בְּשָׁעָה שֶׁהוּא מוֹצִיא מִמֶּנּוּ עָלָיו הוֹאִיל וְאֵין אוֹתוֹ הַטֵּבֶל רָאוּי לְהֵיעָשׂוֹת תְּרוּמָה כְּיוֹצֵא בוֹ חוּלִין שֶׁבּוֹ מְבַטְּלִין אוֹתוֹ. בְּשָׁעָה שֶׁהוּא מוֹצִיא מִמֶּנּוּ לְמָקוֹם אַחֵר הוֹאִיל וְאוֹתוֹ הַטֵּבֶל רָאוּי לְהֵיעָשׂוֹת חוּלִין כְּיוֹצֵא בוֹ לֹא בָטֵל. אָמַר רִבִּי יוֹסֵי הָדָא אָֽמְרָה טֵבֶל שֶׁנִּתְעָֽרְבָה בִתְרוּמָה הוֹאִיל וְאוֹתוֹ הַטֵּבֶל רָאוּי לְהֵיעָשׂוֹת כִּתְרוּמָה כְּיוֹצֵא בוֹ לֹא בָטֵל.

They said, Rebbi Zeïra's is no answer to Rebbi Abun bar Ḥiyya's question. What is the difference between him who takes from itself for itself and him who takes from it for another place? When he takes from itself for itself, since this *ṭevel* is not qualified to become heave for anything similar, the profane admixture makes it disappear[104]. When he takes from it for another place since this *ṭevel* is qualified to become profane for something similar, it cannot disappear[105]. Rebbi Yose said, that means that if *ṭevel* was mixed with heave, since this *ṭevel* is qualified to become heave for something similar, it cannot disappear[106].

104 As explained in the Mishnah, if the amount of *ṭevel* in the profane is small, it has disappeared by biblical standards and it is not legally *ṭevel*. In this case, *ṭevel* and profane, even if consisting of similar material, are considered two distinct kinds and the rules of annulment apply. The requirement to give heave from the entire heap is purely rabbinical; any reference to a biblical source is inappropriate.

105 In that case, the *ṭevel* is genuine; part of it is destined to become heave.

If a minute amount of it fell into heave, it would fall into its own kind and could not disappear.

In the Genizah fragment, the cases have been telescoped into one: בְּשָׁעָה שֶׁהוּא מוֹצִיא מִמֶּנּוּ עָלָיו הוֹאִיל וְאוֹתוֹ הַטֵּבֵל רָאוּי לְהֵעָשׂוֹת חוּלִין כְּיוֹצֵא בוֹ לֹא בָטֵל. The scribe left out from להעשות to להעשות.

106 This is the inverse case, in which a minute amount of heave fell into *ṭevel*. Since part of *ṭevel* is going to be heave, this also is falling into its own kind and no part of it can be disregarded.

וְלֵית הָדָא דְּרִבִּי בּוּן בַּר חִיָּיה תְּתִיבָה עַל דְּרִבִּי זְעִירָא. מָה נַפְשָׁךְ אִם שֶׁלְּמַעֲלָן בָּטֵל אַף שֶׁלְּמַטָּן בָּטֵל. אִם שֶׁלְּמַטָּן לֹא בָטֵל אַף שֶׁלְּמַעֲלָן לֹא בָטֵל שֶׁכְּבָר קִידֵּשׁ.[107]

But Rebbi Abun bar Ḥiyya's is no answer to Rebbi Zeïra[108]. As you take it, if the upper disappears then the lower has disappeared. If the lower did not disappear, neither did the upper since it was already sanctified.

107 Reading of the Rome ms. Leyden, Venice, and the Genizah fragment take this word together with the first of the next paragraph and read קדשתנו.

108 The case introduced by R. Abun bar Ḥiyya must be that profane flour fell onto a flour offering that was in a Temple vessel. Flour dedicated for an offering but not yet placed in a Temple vessel is not yet a flour offering. Since flour is not fluid, we have to assume that the offering is at the bottom and the flour on top with an unrecognizable boundary in between. If the upper flour is assimilated to the lower then there is no offering since the upper flour was not dedicated. If the lower part remains an offering then the upper becomes suspended unusable since it was sanctified by the Temple vessel but is not an offering because it is not dedicated. Therefore, the entire flour is invalid for any use.

תַּנֵּי[107] וְאִם לָאו מֵבִיא אַרְבַּע רוֹבָעִין וּמַשִּׁיךְ.[109] רִבִּי יוֹנָה בְּשֵׁם רִבִּי זְעִירָא זֹאת אוֹמֶרֶת רוֹבַע שְׂאוֹר שֶׁנִּטְבַּל בִּמְקוֹמוֹ טוֹבֵל אַרְבַּעַת רוֹבָעִין בְּמָקוֹם אַחֵר.

It was stated[110]: Otherwise, he brings four quarters and makes it bite. Rebbi Jonah in the name of Rebbi Zeïra: This means that one quarter of sour dough which became *ṭevel* at its place makes four other quarters *ṭevel*.

109 Word missing in Rome ms. but necessary for the text.

110 This refers to the first case in the Mishnah, *ṭevel* sour dough in a dough which already is fully profane. A similar statement is in Tosephta 2:2: "If somebody takes sourdough from a dough from which *ḥallah* was not taken, he brings flour from another place and adds to obtain four quarters to make it obligated in proportion." In the formulation of the Halakhah, the *ṭevel* dough is made from exactly one quarter. Therefore, if one makes a new dough of exactly one *qab* which is made to "bite" the profane dough, one has a total of 5 quarters of obligation and may take only *ḥallah* of the obligated, not from the already exempt. This means in general that if the amount of sour dough is x, the amount needed to avoid giving *ḥallah* for everything is (5 quarters - x). In this way, neither does one take *ḥallah* from another place nor does one have to take *ḥallah* for everything.

הָדָא אָמְרָה שֶׁהַנָּשׁוּךְ תּוֹרָה. אָמַר רִבִּי אִימִּי אִיתְפַּלְּגוֹן רִבִּי יוֹחָנָן וְרִבִּי שִׁמְעוֹן בֶּן לָקִישׁ. רִבִּי יוֹחָנָן אָמַר הַנָּשׁוּךְ תּוֹרָה. רִבִּי שִׁמְעוֹן בֶּן לָקִישׁ אָמַר אֵין הַנָּשׁוּךְ תּוֹרָה. רִבִּי חִייָה בַּר בָּא מַחֲלִיף שְׁמוּעָתָא. בָּעוּן קוֹמֵי רִבִּי יוֹסֵי אַתְּ מָה שְׁמָעַת מִן רִבִּי יוֹחָנָן. אָמַר לוֹן אֲנָא לֹא שְׁמָעִית כְּלוּם. אֶלָּא נְפָרֵשׁ מִילֵּיהוֹן דְּרַבָּנִין מִן מִלֵּיהוֹן. דְּתַמָּן תַּנִּינָן הַמְּכַנֵּיס חַלּוֹת עַל מְנָת לְהַפְרִישׁ וְנָשְׁכוּ בֵּית שַׁמַּי אוֹמֵר חִיבּוּר בִּטְבוּל יוֹם וּבֵית הִלֵּל אוֹמֵר אֵינוֹ חִיבּוּר. אָמַר רִבִּי שִׁמְעוֹן בֶּן לָקִישׁ מִמָּה דְתַנִּינָן אֵינוֹ חִיבּוּר. הָדָא אָמְרָה שֶׁאֵין חַייָבִין עָלָיו בְּשֵׁם[111] טָמֵא אוֹכֵל טָהוֹר. אָמַר לוֹ רִבִּי יוֹחָנָן שַׁנְייָא הִיא בִּטְבוּל יוֹם דִּכְתִיב בֵּיהּ טָהוֹר וְטָמֵא טָהוֹר לְחוּלִין מִבְּעוֹד יוֹם וְלִתְרוּמָה מִשֶּׁתֶּחְשַׁךְ. הֲוֵי רִבִּי יוֹחָנָן דּוּ אָמַר דָּבָר[112] שֶׁאֵינוֹ חִבּוּר בִּטְבוּל יוֹם תּוֹרָה הוּא. דּוּ אָמַר הַנָּשׁוּךְ תּוֹרָה. וְרִבִּי שִׁמְעוֹן בֶּן

לָקִישׁ דּוּ אָמַר אֵינָהּ תּוֹרָה דְּהוּא אָמַר אֵין הַנָּשׁוּךְ תּוֹרָה. וְהָתַנִּינָן (fol. 57c) וְאִם לָאו מֵבִיא אַרְבַּע רוֹבָעִין וּמַשִּׁיךְ. אָמַר רַב הוֹשַׁעְיָה תִּיפְתָּר שֶׁבָּא מֵעִיסַּת הַנָּשׁוּךְ.

This means that biting is biblical[113]. Rebbi Immi said, Rebbi Joḥanan and Rebbi Simeon ben Laqish differ. Rebbi Joḥanan said, biting is biblical. Rebbi Simeon ben Laqish said, biting is not biblical[114]. Rebbi Ḥiyya bar Abba switches the traditions[115]. They asked before Rebbi Yose, what did you hear about Rebbi Joḥanan? He said, I did not hear anything but let us explain the words of the rabbis from their own words, as we have stated there[116]: "If somebody collects loaves in order to separate [*ḥallah*] and they bit, the House of Shammai say it is a connection for a *ṭevul yom* but the House of Hillel say it is not a connection." Rebbi Simeon ben Laqish said, since we stated it is no connection, that means that nobody can become guilty under the heading "impure person eating pure [food]"[117]. Rebbi Joḥanan said to him, that is different for a *ṭevul yom* because for him is written both pure and impure[118]; pure for profane food during daytime hours and for heave after dark. That identifies Rebbi Joḥanan as the one who said that what is not a connection for the *ṭevul yom* is biblical[119]. Therefore, he says biting is biblical. And Rebbi Simeon ben Laqish is he who says it is not biblical since he says biting is not biblical. But did we not state: "Otherwise, he brings four quarters and makes it bite?" Rebbi Hoshaia said, explain that it was part of the dough which was bitten[120].

111 Reading of the Geniza fragment. Mss.: משום.

112 The Geniza fragment here has an additional שהוא טיבולא which seems to be a duplication.

113 The *baraita* (or Tosephta)

quoted in the previous paragraph, that a dough prepared from 4 quarters if it bites a dough with 1 quarter of *ṭevel* produces dough obligated for *ḥallah*.

114 He has to declare all of Mishnaiot 7-8 as purely rabbinical.

115 R. Joḥanan says not biblical, R. Simeon ben Laqish says biblical.

116 Mishnah *Ṭevul Yom* 1:1. The loaves cannot be baked yet; the Tanna must hold that *ṭevel* does not have the status of profane food. The *Ṭevul Yom* (Chapter 2, Note 37, *Terumot* 5, Note 68) is almost pure; his touch disables heave but has no influence on profane food. According to the House of Hillel, the touch of a *Ṭevul Yom* disables the *ḥallah*-heave in one loaf only.

117 This refers to *Lev*. 22:7. The *Ṭevul Yom* may eat of the loaves even before sundown (after *ḥallah* was taken). This is obvious for those who hold that *ṭevel* is like profane in matters of contamination with impurity.

The commentators who did not have the Genizah text before them either omitted the words אוכל טהור with R. S. Cirillo's ms. or switched טמא אוכל טהור into טהור אוכל טמא. In any case, the implication is that while the House of Hillel accept biting as a conduit for impurities other than that of the *Ṭevul Yom*, these derivative impurities can never be biblical.

118 *Lev*. 22:6-7.

119 Since the exceptional status of the *Ṭevul Yom* is based on biblical verses, for all other forms of impurity the rules of the *Ṭevul Yom* do not apply; biting for them is a conduit of impurity.

120 If the sour dough only became *ṭevel* because of another dough biting the one it was taken from, the *ṭevel* is only rabbinical and nothing can be inferred about the biblical status of biting (R. Eliahu Fulda).

רִבִּי זְעִירָה בָּעֵי אוֹ מַה פְלִיגִין רִבִּי יוֹחָנָן וְרִבִּי שִׁמְעוֹן בֶּן לָקִישׁ בְּנָשׁוּךְ מֵאֵילָיו. אֲבָל אִם הִשִּׁיכוֹ בְּיָדוֹ כָּל־עַמָּא מוֹדֵיי שֶׁהַנָּשׁוּךְ תּוֹרָה. אֲפִילוּ תֵּימַר הִשִּׁיכוֹ בְיָדוֹ הִיא מַחֲלוֹקֶת נֹאמַר רִבִּי שִׁמְעוֹן בֶּן לָקִישׁ כְּדַעְתֵּיהּ. דְּאָמַר רִבִּי שִׁמְעוֹן בֶּן לָקִישׁ בְּשֵׁם חִזְקִיָּה טֶבֶל בָּטֵל בְּרוֹב. רִבִּי יוֹסֵי בֵּירִבִּי נְהוֹרַאי אָמַר טֶבֶל בָּטֵל בְּרוֹב. אָמַר רִבִּי יוֹחָנָן אֵין הַטֶּבֶל בָּטֵל בְּרוֹב. רִבִּי בָּא בַּר מָמָל וְרִבִּי הִילָא אָעֲלוֹן עוֹבְדָא קוֹמֵי רִבִּי יָסָא סָבְרִין מֵימַר שְׁנַיִם רָבִין עַל אֶחָד. וְלָא שְׁמִיעִין דְּאָמַר

רִבִּי סִימוֹן בְּשֵׁם רִבִּי יְהוֹשֻׁעַ בֶּן לֵוִי אֵין הַטֶּבֶל בָּטֵל בְּרוֹב. וְהָתַנִּינָן וְאִם לָאו מוֹצִיא מֵאֶחָד עַל הַכֹּל. אוֹמֵר רִבִּי יוֹסֵי כָּל־עַמָּא מוֹדֵיי שֶׁהוּא מַפְרִישׁ. מָה פְלִיגִין לַחוּשׁ לְהַפְרָשָׁה שְׁנִייָה. מָאן דְּאָמַר טֶבֶל בָּטֵל בְּרוֹב אֲרִימָהּ וְנֶפְלַת לְאָתָר חוֹרָן אֵינוֹ חוֹשֵׁשׁ לְהַפְרָשָׁה שְׁנִייָה. מָאן דְּאָמַר אֵין טֶבֶל בָּטֵל בְּרוֹב אֲרִימָהּ וְנֶפְלַת לְאָתָר חוֹרָן חוֹשֵׁשׁ לְהַפְרָשָׁה שְׁנִייָה.

Rebbi Zeïra asked: Do Rebbi Joḥanan and Rebbi Simeon ben Laqish differ if it bites by itself but if he made it bite with his hand everybody agrees that biting is biblical? Even if you say that the disagreement arises if he made it bite with his hand, Rebbi Simeon ben Laqish sticks with his opinion since Rebbi Simeon ben Laqish said in the name of Ḥizqiah: *ṭevel* disappears in a plurality[121]. Rebbi Yose ben Rebbi Nahorai said, *ṭevel* disappears in a plurality. Rebbi Joḥanan said, *ṭevel* does not disappear in a plurality. Rebbi Abba bar Mamal and Rebbi Hila brought a case before Rebbi Assi; they wanted to say that two form a majority against one. They had not heard that Rebbi Simon said in the name of Rebbi Joshua ben Levi that *ṭevel* does not disappear in a plurality. But did we not state[122]: "Otherwise, he takes from one for all"? Rebbi Yose said, everybody agrees that he separates. Where do they differ? To worry about a second taking. For him who says *ṭevel* disappears in a plurality, if one lifted it out but if fell into another place, he does not worry to take it out a second time[123]. For him who says *ṭevel* does not disappear in a plurality, if one lifted it out but if fell into another place, he worries to take it out a second time.

121 Cf. *Terumot* 4:1, Note 10, *Ma'serot* 5:2, Note 25 ff.

122 This must refer to a *baraita* in the style of the Mishnah, probably dealing with several doughs in one vessel where for all of them there is a

doubt and *ḥallah* cannot be taken from another place. This can only happen if the *ṭevel* is a small part of the entire dough; in all cases of the Mishnah there is a plurality of profane matter.

123 If heave was taken from a mixture of *ṭevel* and profane food, with more profane than *ṭevel*, and that heave was then mixed again (as minority component) with profane food, according to R. Simeon ben Laqish there is no doubt that the second mixture never can be biblical *dema'* even in a time when all agricultural commandments in the Land are biblical. Since, in principle, rabbinic ordinances are valid only as "fences around the Law", there can be no reason to take heave a second time. For R. Joḥanan, if all agricultural commandments in the Land are biblical the second mixture is *dema'* and the heave has to be lifted.

אָמַר רִבִּי בָּא מַפְלִיגִין רִבִּי יוֹחָנָן וְרִבִּי שִׁמְעוֹן בֶּן לָקִישׁ בְּטֶבֶל שֶׁנִּטְבַּל דְּבַר תּוֹרָה. אֲבָל בְּטֶבֶל שֶׁנִּטְבַּל מִדִּבְרֵיהֶן כָּל־עַמָּא מוֹדֵיי שֶׁהַטֶּבֶל בָּטֵל בְּרוֹב. הָתִיב רִבִּי בָּא בַּר כַּהֲנָא קוֹמֵי רִבִּי יוֹסֵי. וְהָתַנִּינָן כְּיוֹצֵא בוֹ זֵיתֵי מַסִּיק שֶׁנִּתְעָרְבוּ עִם זֵיתֵי נִיקּוּף עִינְּבֵי בָצִיר שֶׁנִּתְעָרְבוּ עִם עִינְּבֵי עוֹלֵלוֹת. וְלֹא טֶבֶל שֶׁנִּטְבַּל מִדִּבְרֵיהֶן הוּא. אָמַר רִבִּי מָנָא קִייַמְתִּיהָ בְּשֶׁמֶן שֶׁל זֵיתֵי מַסִּיק שֶׁנִּתְעָרֵב בְּשֶׁמֶן שֶׁל זֵיתֵי נִיקּוּף.

Rebbi Abba said: Rebbi Joḥanan and Rebbi Simeon ben Laqish differ about *ṭevel* by biblical standards. But for *ṭevel* which is *ṭevel* only by rabbinic decree, everybody agrees that *ṭevel* disappears in a plurality. Rebbi Abba bar Cahana objected before Rebbi Yose: Did we not state: "Similarly, if harvested olives were mixed with plucked olives, or harvested grapes with gleanings," is that not *ṭevel* only by rabbinic standards[124]? Rebbi Mana said, I confirmed it: If oil from harvested olives was mixed with oil from plucked olives!

124 Biblical heave is due only for grain, wine, and olive oil.

מָתִיב רִבִּי יוֹחָנָן לְרִבִּי שִׁמְעוֹן בֶּן לָקִישׁ. נוֹטֵל אָדָם כְּדֵי חַלָּה מֵעִיסָּה שֶׁלֹּא הוּרְמָה חַלָּתָהּ לַעֲשׂוֹתָהּ בְּטָהֳרָה לִהְיוֹת מַפְרִישׁ עָלֶיהָ וְהוֹלֵךְ. מִכֵּיוָן שֶׁקָּדַשׁ רוּבָּהּ לְשֵׁם חַלָּה תִּבָּטֵל בְּרוֹב. אָמַר בְּרוֹשֶׁם. תֵּדַע לָךְ שֶׁהוּא כֵן. דְּתַנִּינָן תַּמָּן הָרוֹצֶה לְהַפְרִישׁ תְּרוּמָה וּתְרוּמַת מַעֲשֵׂר כְּאַחַת. לְאֵי זֶה דָבָר הוּא מְסַיֵּים לֹא כְדֵי שֶׁיִּבָּטֵל בְּרוֹב. אָמַר רִבִּי יִצְחָק בַּר לְעָזָר שֶׁלֹּא יְהֵא אוֹמֵר תְּרוּמַת הַכְּרִי הַזֶּה וְזֶה בְּזֶה. חָזַר רִבִּי יִצְחָק בַּר לְעָזָר וְאָמַר לֹא אֲמַרְנָא כְלוּם. וְלֹא רִבִּי יוֹחָנָן כִּי אָמַר תְּרוּמַת כְּרִי הַזֶּה וְזֶה בְּזֶה. רִבִּי יוֹחָנָן אָמַר מָקוֹם שֶׁנִּתְרְמָה תְּרוּמָתוֹ שֶׁל רִאשׁוֹן נִסְתַּיְּימָה תְּרוּמָתוֹ שֶׁלְשֵׁינִי.

Rebbi Joḥanan objected to Rebbi Simeon ben Laqish: "A person may take his *ḥallah* from a dough from which *ḥallah* was not taken[125] to have it available in purity to separate from it[126]." After most of it became *ḥallah*, should not the remainder[127] disappear in the plurality? He answered, when he notes it[128]. You should know that this is so since we have stated there: "He who wants to separate heave and heave of the tithe together[129]." Why does he have to define its place? Is it not that it should not disappear in a plurality? Rebbi Isaac bar Eleazar said, that he should not say the heave of this and that heap should be in this one[130]. Rebbi Isaac bar Eleazar changed his mind and said, I did not say anything! Is it not Rebbi Joḥanan who said, if somebody said the heave of this and that heap should be in this one, at the place where the heave of the first ended, there the second also ends[131].

126 To watch this piece in purity while he may make more dough, possibly in impurity. It is assumed that the grain is *demay* since from *demay* flour *ḥallah* may be taken from the pure for the impure.

127 Mishnah 4:6.

128 Which still is *ṭevel* and

according to R. Simeon ben Laqish should disappear in whatever the plurality is.

129 He makes a physical sign to mark the part which is now *ḥallah*. Then the remainder cannot disappear in the *ḥallah*.

130 Mishnah *Demay* 5:2. He is required to declare exactly the amount taken and indicate its place in the heap from which it is going to be taken.

131 This is discussed in *Terumot* 3:5, Note 60. The rabbis require that the places of heaves and tithes should be indicated in detail.

132 Since R. Joḥanan implies that the designation is automatic, there is no objection to R. Simeon ben Laqish's explanation.

לָקַט דְּלַעַת לִהְיוֹת מַפְרִישׁ עָלֶיהָ וְהוֹלֵךְ הֲרֵי זֶה לוֹקֵט וּבָא וְרוֹשֵׁם עַד כָּאן תְּרוּמָה וְעַד כָּאן תְּרוּמָה דִּבְרֵי רִבִּי. רַבָּן שִׁמְעוֹן בֶּן גַּמְלִיאֵל אוֹמֵר לוֹקֵט וּמְחַשֵּׁב כְּמוֹת שֶׁהוּא לָמוּד. הֲוֹון בָּעֵיי מֵימַר מָאן דְּאָמַר עַד כָּאן תְּרוּמָה וְעַד כָּאן תְּרוּמָה טֶבֶל בָּטֵל בְּרוֹב. מָאן דְּאָמַר לוֹקֵט וּמְחַשֵּׁב כְּמוֹת שֶׁהוּא לָמוּד אֵין הַטֶּבֶל בָּטֵל בְּרוֹב. אָמַר רִבִּי בָּא כְּדֵי שֶׁיְּהֵא זָקוּק לִיתֵּן לַשֵּׁבֶט בֵּינֵיהֶן.

[132]"If somebody harvested a pumpkin to use to give now and in the future, any time he harvests he has to come and note, up to here is heave, up to here is heave, the words of Rebbi. Rabban Simeon ben Gamliel says, he harvests and computes as is usual for him." They wanted to say, for him who says up to here is heave, up to here is heave, *ṭevel* disappears in a plurality but for him who says he harvests and computes as is usual for him, *ṭevel* does not disappear in a plurality[133]. Rebbi Abba said, between them is the duty to immediately give it to the tribe[134].

132 Tosephta *Terumot* 5:1. He puts one pumpkin aside to watch in purity for heave of the harvest of an entire field.

133 This would prove that there is disagreement also for heave which is purely rabbinical.

134 According to Rebbi, he has not only to make a physical sign on the pumpkin but he has to cut off the

heave part and deliver it to a Cohen on the day of harvest. According to Rabban Simeon, he may wait until the entire pumpkin is heave.

הָיָה צָרִיךְ לִתְרוֹם אַרְבַּע חָמֵשׁ חָבִיּוֹת מִן הַבּוֹר מַעֲלֶה אֶת הָרִאשׁוֹנָה עַל פִּי הַבּוֹר וְאוֹמֵר הֲרֵי זוֹ תְרוּמָה. וְכֵן הַשְּׁנִייָה וְכֵן הַשְּׁלִישִׁית דִּבְרֵי רַבָּן שִׁמְעוֹן בֶּן גַּמְלִיאֵל. רִבִּי אוֹמֵר מַעֲלֶה כוּלָּן עַל פִּי הַבּוֹר וְאוֹמֵר הֲרֵי אֵילּוּ תְרוּמָה. הֲווֹן בָּעֵיי מֵימַר מָאן דְּאָמַר מַעֲלֶה אֶת הָרִאשׁוֹנָה עַל פִּי הַבּוֹר טֶבֶל בָּטֵל בְּרוֹב. וּמָאן דְּאָמַר מַעֲלֶה כוּלָּן עַל פִּי הַבּוֹר אֵין הַטֶּבֶל בָּטֵל בְּרוֹב. רִבִּי אַבָּהוּ בְשֵׁם רִבִּי יוֹחָנָן הַקֵּיף בֵּינֵיהֶן. מָאן דְּאָמַר מַעֲלֶה כוּלָּן עַל פִּי הַבּוֹר תּוֹרֵם מִן הַמּוּקָּף. וּמָאן דְּאָמַר מַעֲלֶה אֶת הָרִאשׁוֹנָה עַל פִּי הַבּוֹר אֵין תּוֹרֵם מִן הַמּוּקָּף. רִבִּי שְׁמוּאֵל רִבִּי אַבָּהוּ בְשֵׁם רִבִּי יוֹחָנָן מַחֲלִיף מָאן דְּאָמַר מַעֲלֶה אֶת הָרִאשׁוֹנָה עַל פִּי הַבּוֹר תּוֹרֵם מִן הַמּוּקָּף. וּמָאן דְּאָמַר מַעֲלֶה כוּלָּן עַל פִּי הַבּוֹר אֵין תּוֹרֵם מִן הַמּוּקָּף. אָמַר לוֹ רִבִּי זְעִירָה וְאֵינוֹ מְעוּרָב עַל יְדֵי גִידִין.

"[135]If he had to give heave for four or five amphoras in a cistern, he lifts the first one to the mouth of the cistern and says, this is heave. The same for the second and third, the words of Rabban Simeon ben Gamliel. Rebbi says, he lifts all of them to the mouth of the cistern and says, this is heave." They wanted to say, for him who says he lifts the first one to the mouth of the cistern, *ṭevel* disappears in a plurality but for him who says he lifts all of them to the mouth of the cistern, *ṭevel* does not disappear in a plurality[136]. Rebbi Abbahu in the name of Rebbi Joḥanan: They differ about earmarking. For him who says he lifts all of them to the mouth of the cistern, he has to give from what is earmarked[137] but for him who says he lifts the first one to the mouth of the cistern he does not have to give from what is earmarked[138]. Rebbi Samuel, Rebbi Abbahu in the name of Rebbi Joḥanan switches: For him who says he lifts the first one to the mouth of the cistern, he has to give from what is earmarked but for him who says he lifts all of them to the mouth of the cistern he does not have to give from what is earmarked. Rebbi Zeïra said to him, is it not united by sinews[139]?

135 Continuation of Tosephta *Terumot* 5:1. The language is difficult. One would assume that amphoras full of wine are in a מרתף, a wine cellar, not in a בור, which is either a cistern or the vat into which the pressed grape juice flows and where it is turned into wine. In addition, one has to separate the prospective heave from the amphora before turning it into heave, otherwise it would diffuse in the entire amphora and turn everything into *dema*'. Since the statement is the continuation of the one about pumpkins, one has to say that an amount of *ṭevel* wine sufficient for the entire cistern was first taken out, put in a separate vessel, but not declared to be heave. Then the wine in the cistern is taken out by filling it into amphoras one by one. Rabban Simeon ben Gamliel, who in the first part did not require that the place of heave be indicated, permits here successive declarations that a certain part of the separated wine should be heave. Rebbi, who in the first part did require that the place of heave be indicated, permits only giving heave for all together since in a fluid no parts can be indicated.

137 All commentators, from R. Eliahu Fulda to R. S. Lieberman, note that one has to switch the places of "disappear" and "not disappear", against the evidence of both mss. As has been noted before, the two mss. have a common source which already must have contained the error. The problem is for Rabban Simeon who permits giving heave piecemeal, when it is unavoidable that at some point most of the contents of the vessel will be heave.

138 One puts the vessel containing the potential heave in the middle of all amphoras to be put in order.

139 That seems to be an impossible statement since heave has to be given from what is earmarked (Mishnah 1:9). The meaning is that giving piecemeal, even if the amphora to be put in order touches the vessel containing the potential heave, might not be considered earmarked since the wine which becomes heave is undefined.

140 One might put a thread around

all amphoras. But this seems to be unnecessary, cf. Note 137 and the end of Halakhah 4.

שתי נשים פרק רביעי

(fol. 59c) **משנה א**: שְׁתֵּי נָשִׁים שֶׁעָשׂוּ שְׁינֵי קַבִּין וְנָגְעוּ זֶה בָזֶה אֲפִילוּ הֵן מִמִּין אֶחָד פְּטוּרִין. וּבִזְמַן שֶׁהֵן שֶׁלְאִשָּׁה אַחַת מִין בְּמִינוֹ חַייָב וְשֶׁלֹּא בְמִינוֹ פָּטוּר.

Mishnah 1: If two women each made a *qab*[1] and they touched one another, even if they are of the same kind they are exempt. But if both belong to the same woman and are of the same kind they are obligated[2], different kinds[3] are exempt.

1 They separately made bread dough and now are baking it together in the same oven. Separately, the doughs are exempt but both together are obligated since $2 > {}^{5}/_{4}$.

2 If the doughs touch or are on the same baking sheet.

3 This is defined in Mishnah 4:2.

(fol. 59d) **הלכה א**: שְׁתֵּי נָשִׁים שֶׁעָשׂוּ שְׁינֵי כול'. אָמַר רִבִּי יוֹחָנָן סְתָם אִשָּׁה אַחַת אֵינָהּ מַקְפֶּדֶת שְׁתַּיִם מַקְפִּידוֹת הֵן. אִשָּׁה אַחַת שֶׁהִיא מַקְפֶּדֶת עָשׂוּ אוֹתָהּ כִּשְׁתֵּי נָשִׁים. שְׁתֵּי נָשִׁים שֶׁאֵינָן מַקְפִּידוֹת עָשׂוּ אוֹתָם כְּאִשָּׁה אַחַת. אִם אֵינָהּ מַקְפֶּדֶת לָמָּה הִיא עוֹשָׂה אוֹתָהּ כִּשְׁנֵי מְקוֹמוֹת. אָמַר רִבִּי יוֹנָה בְּשֶׁאֵין לָהּ מָקוֹם לָלוּשׁ. מִילְתֵיהּ דְּרִבִּי יוֹנָה אָמַר הָיָה לָהּ מָקוֹם הֵיכָן לָלוּשׁ וְהִיא עוֹשָׂה אוֹתָן כִּשְׁנֵי מְקוֹמוֹת מַקְפֶּדֶת הִיא. נָקִי וְקֵיבָר מַקְפֶּדֶת הִיא. אָמַר רִבִּי לָעְזָר שְׁתֵּי דֵיעוֹת עָשׂוּ אוֹתָן כִּשְׁתֵּי נָשִׁים. שְׁמוּאֵל בַּר אַבָּא בָּעֵי אֲפִילוּ רוֹצוֹת.

Halakhah 1: "Two women who each made," etc. Rebbi Joḥanan said, usually for women, one does not mind, two do mind[4]. They gave to one woman who minds[5] the status of two women, to two women who do not mind the status of one woman. If she does not mind, why does she make it at two different places? Rebbi Jonah said, because she has not enough space to knead. The word of Rebbi Jonah implies that if she had enough space to knead but she[6] makes it in two portions, she does mind. Clean and coarse [flour][7], she does mind. Rebbi Lazar said, they gave two different habits the status of two women[8]. Samuel bar Abba asked, even if they come to agree[9]?

4 According to Maimonides (*Bikkurim* 7:1), followed by the later law codes, there is no difference between men and women in this matter. According to R. M. Margalit, the Mishnah specifies women because women are neat and insist that their bread be separate from that of others while men usually do not care. The later statement of R. Lazar seems to support R. M. Margalit but the uncertain gender in the text of the Halakhah might support Maimonides.

5 If for some reason she insists on keeping the two loaves strictly separated.

6 This may be read as "he".

7 One loaf of white flour, the other one of whole wheat. This is counted as two different kinds.

8 According to R. M. Margalit, this now speaks of two men. As R. Meïr notes (*Sotah* 1:7, fol. 17a; Babli *Giṭṭin* 90a) men have different standards of cleanliness. Some men will not drink any more from a cup of wine in which they found a fly, others will take the fly out and drink the remainder. A man adhering to a higher standard of cleanliness will insist to keep his bread as separate as women do.

9 What is the status of the bread if the women kneaded their doughs separately but at baking time they decide to have them together? The answer depends on one's position regarding R. Aqiba's opinion in Halakhah 3:5.

יֵשׁ דְּבָרִים שֶׁהֵן חִיבּוּר בַּחַלָּה וְאֵינָן חִיבּוּר בִּטְבוּל יוֹם. חִיבּוּר בִּטְבוּל יוֹם וְאֵינָן חִיבּוּר בְּחַלָּה. חִיבּוּר בְּחַלָּה דְּתַנִּינָן בִּזְמָן שֶׁהֵן שֶׁלְּאִשָּׁה אַחַת מִין בְּמִינוֹ חַיָּיב וְשֶׁלֹּא בְמִינוֹ פָּטוּר. וְאֵין חִיבּוּר[10] בִּטְבוּל יוֹם דְּתַנִּינָן תַּמָּן הַמְּכַנִּיס חַלּוֹת עַל

מְנָת לְהַפְרִישׁ וְנָשְׁכוּ בֵּית שַׁמַּי אוֹמְרִים חִיבּוּר בִּטְבוּל יוֹם. וּבֵית הִלֵּל אוֹמְרִים אֵינָן חִיבּוּר. בִּטְבוּל יוֹם דְּתַנִּינָן תַּמָּן בְּשַׂר הַקּוֹדֶשׁ שֶׁקָּרַם[11] עָלָיו הַקּוּפָּה. הָא שְׁאָר כָּל־הַקּוּפָּה חִיבּוּר וְאֵין סוֹפוֹ לְחוֹתְכוֹ. וְאֵינָן חִיבּוּר[10] בְּחַלָּה דְּאָמַר רִבִּי יוֹחָנָן הָעוֹשֶׂה עִיסָּה עַל מְנָת לְחַלְּקָהּ בְּבָצֵק פְּטוּרָה מִן הַחַלָּה.

Certain situations are connections for *ḥallah* but not for a *ṭevul yom*[12], [others] for a *ṭevul yom* but not for *ḥallah*. A connection for *ḥallah* as we have stated: "But if they belong to the same woman the same kind are obligated, different kinds are exempt." They are not obligated for a *ṭevul yom* as we have stated there[13]: "If somebody collects pieces of *ḥallah* in order to separate them again, the House of Shammai say it is a connection for a *ṭevul yom*, but the House of Hillel say it is no connection for a *ṭevul yom*." We also stated there[14]: "Sanctified meat on which the sediment[15] congealed." Therefore, in all other cases congealed sediment is a connection[16] even if at the end one will remove it. But one is not obligated for *ḥallah*; as Rebbi Joḥanan said[17], if somebody makes dough in order to distribute it, the dough is exempt from *ḥallah*.

10 Reading of a Genizah text. Leyden and Venice: חייבין.

11 Reading of the Mishnah *Ṭevul Yom* 2:5 and a Genizah text here. Reading of the Leyden ms. and Venice print: שקדם, of the Rome ms. שקדש, showing that the misreading ד-ר, ס-ם was already in the common source of the two mss.

12 The touch of a *ṭevul yom* makes heave (including *ḥallah*) unusable and sacrifices impure (*Demay* 6:6, Notes 138,140). But since the *ṭevul yom* has been purified, only his immediate touch is damaging, not the touch by an intermediary object. Therefore, if the *ṭevul yom* touches a loaf of *ḥallah*, he makes the *ḥallah* inedible, including everything connected with it. It is now stated that the rules of connection regarding the obligation of *ḥallah* are not identical with the rules governing an eventual disqualification of the *ḥallah* taken.

13 Mishnah *Ṭevul Yom* 1:1, dealing with a Cohen who collects *ḥallah* from several households to carry home in one basket but does not intend to eat the different morsels together.

14 If the *ṭevul yom* touches one piece of *ḥallah*, that piece is unusable but all the others are unimpaired.

15 Mishnah *Ṭevul Yom* 2:5: "Sanctified meat on which the sediment congealed; if a *ṭevul yom* touched the sediment, the pieces are permitted. If he touched a piece, it and all that clings to it are connected. Rebbi Joḥanan ben Nuri says both are connected to one another." "Sediment" are the remainders of spices, single fibers from the meat, and assorted matrer which usually clings to the sides of the cooking pot. Since any such sediment will be scraped or washed off before the meat is eaten, it is considered separate.

16 Separate pieces of sediment on one piece of meat are considered as one; in the case of *ḥallah* they would not be considered one as indicated by the next statement by R. Joḥanan.

17 Chapter 1:8, first paragraph.

(fol. 59c) **משנה ב:** אֵי זֶהוּ מִין בְּמִינוֹ הַחִטִּים אֵינָן מִצְטָרְפוֹת עִם הַכֹּל אֶלָּא עִם הַכּוּסְמִין. הַשְּׂעוֹרִין מִצְטָרְפִין עִם הַכֹּל חוּץ מִן הַחִטִּין. רִבִּי יוֹחָנָן בֶּן נוּרִי אוֹמֵר שְׁאָר הַמִּינִין מִצְטָרְפִין זֶה עִם זֶה.

Mishnah 2: What is the same kind? Wheat combines[18] with nothing but spelt. Barley combines with everything except wheat. Rebbi Joḥanan ben Nuri said, the remaining kinds all combine with one another.

18 Cf. Chapter 1, Notes 40 ff.

(fol. 59d) **הלכה ב:** מַהוּ שִׁיֵּירְתָא רַב הוּנָא אָמַר אִם אָמַר אַתְּ הַשִּׁיפוֹן מִין כּוּסְמִין מִצְטָרֵף עִם הַחִיטִּים. שִׁיבּוֹלֶת שׁוּעַל מִין שְׂעוֹרִין אֵינוֹ מִצְטָרֵף עִם הַחִיטִּים. רִבִּי יוֹחָנָן בֶּן נוּרִי אוֹמֵר שְׁאָר הַמִּינִין מִצְטָרְפִין זֶה עִם זֶה. אִית תַּנָּיֵי

תַּנֵּי כָּל־הַמִּינִין מִצְטָרְפִין זֶה עִם זֶה. עַל דַּעְתֵּיהּ דְּהַךְ תַּנָּייָא בָּרְיָא מַה בֵּין נָשׁוּךְ מַה בֵּין בָּלוּל. אָמַר רִבִּי יוּדָן אָבוּהּ דְּרִבִּי מַתַּנְיָה בְּשֶׁחִלְּקָן וְהוֹסִיף עֲלֵיהֶן. נְשׁוּכִין חַייָבִין. בְּלוּלִין פְּטוּרִין.

Halakhah 2: Was is left[19]? Rav Huna said, if you say that oats are a kind of spelt, they combine with wheat; foxtail is a kind of barley which does not combine with wheat! "Rebbi Joḥanan ben Nuri said, the remaining kinds all combine with one another." There are Tannaïm who state: "All kinds combine with one another.[20]" In the opinion of that outside Tanna, what is the difference between bitten and mixed? Rebbi Yudan, the father of Rebbi Mattaniah said, when he split and then added; it is obligated when biting[21], exempt when mixed.

19 What is left in the statement of the anonymous Tanna that R. Joḥanan ben Nuri could disagree with? It was stated in Halakhah 1:1 (Note 39) that oats are a kind of spelt, foxtail a kind of barley. Since the Mishnah here, in contrast to Mishnah *Kilaim* 1:1, combines spelt and wheat, there are only two kinds as far as the rules of *ḥallah* are concerned and the statement of R. Joḥanan ben Nuri seems to be meaningless.

20 In this formulation, the difference bentween the anonymous Tanna and R. Joḥanan ben Nuri is clear but then one has to ask what is the difference between Mishnaiot 1:1 and 4:2.

21 Since by Mishnah 1 the doughs of two different owners never were obligated, if one of them increases his dough to $^5/_4$ *qab* the obligation of *ḥallah* is new and valid. The exemption of the mixed dough is explained in Chapter 3, Note 72.

(fol. 59c) **משנה ג:** שְׁנֵי קַבִּין וְקַב אוֹרֶז וְקַב תְּרוּמָה בְאֶמְצַע אֵינָן מִצְטָרְפִין. דָּבָר שֶׁנִּיטְּלָה חַלָּתוֹ בְאֶמְצַע מִצְטָרְפִין שֶׁכְּבָר נִתְחַייֵב בַּחַלָּה.

Mishnah 3: Two *qabim* and a *qab* of rice or[22] heave between them do not combine[23]. If a thing of which *ḥallah* was taken is between them, they do combine since already they are subject to *ḥallah*.

22 Reading of the Rome ms. and the Constantinople print: או תרומה; this probably is a gloss.

23 Two loaves made of bread flour each of which is too small to be subject to *ḥallah* are both touching an exempt dough (which is either from material intrinsically exempt or from flour exempt because of its status of sanctity) cannot become obligated since the exempt dough acts as a barrier as if it were of iron. But a dough which is not exempt cannot separate, even if it now is no longer subject to *ḥallah*.

(fol. 59d) **הלכה ג:** נִיתְנֵי אוֹרֶז וְלֹא נִיתְנֵי תְרוּמָה. אִלּוּ תַנִּינָן אוֹרֶז וְלֹא תַנִּינָן תְּרוּמָה הֲוִינָן אָמְרִין אוֹרֶז עַל יְדֵי שֶׁאֵינוֹ מִמִּינוֹ אֵינוֹ מִצְטָרֵף. תְּרוּמָה עַל יְדֵי שֶׁהִיא מִמִּינָהּ מִצְטָרֵף. הֲוֵי צוֹרְכָה מִתְנֵי תְרוּמָה. אוֹ אִילּוּ תַנִּינָן תְּרוּמָה וְלֹא תַנִּינָן אוֹרֶז הֲוִינָן אָמְרִין תְּרוּמָה עַל יְדֵי שֶׁהִיא אֵינָהּ נִגְרֶרֶת אֵינָה מִצְטָרֶפֶת. אוֹרֶז עַל יְדֵי שֶׁהוּא נִגְרָר מִצְטָרֵף. הֲוֵי צוֹרְכָה מִתְנֵי אוֹרֶז וְצוֹרְכָה מִתְנֵי תְרוּמָה.

Halakhah 3: Should one have stated "rice" but not "heave"? If we had stated "rice" but not "heave", we would have said that rice does not combine because it is not of that kind[24], but heave[25], which is of that kind, should combine. It is necessary to state "heave." If we had stated "heave" but not "rice", we would have said that heave does not combine because it is not dragged in[26], but rice, which is dragged in[27], should combine. It is necessary to state "rice" and "heave".

24 Rice dough is never subject to *ḥallah*.

25 Of bread dough.

26 *Dema'* dough containing heave

flour is exempt from *ḥallah* (Mishnah 3:2).

27 Dough containing rice is subject to *ḥallah* if it tastes like bread (Mishnah 3:6).

קַב אוֹרֶז אֵינוֹ מִצְטָרֵף קַב מְדוּמָּע אֵינוֹ מִצְטָרֵף. קַב תְּרוּמָה אֵינוֹ מִצְטָרֵף. קַב הַגּוֹי אֵינוֹ מְצָרֵף. קַב מִין אַחֵר מְצָרֵף. קַב אִשָּׁה אַחֶרֶת מְצָרֵף. קַב חָדָשׁ מְצָרֵף. קַב דָּבָר שֶׁנִּיטְּלָה חַלָּתוֹ מִן הָאֶמְצַע מִצְטָרֵף. וְרִבִּי בּוּן בַּר חִייָה בָּעֵי קַב חַלָּה מַהוּ שֶׁיְּצָרֵף. תַּנֵּי רִבִּי חֲלַפְתָּא בֶּן שָׁאוּל קַב הֶקְדֵּשׁ מְצָרֵף. קַב חַלָּה אֵינוֹ מְצָרֵף. מַה בֵּין הֶקְדֵּשׁ וּמַה בֵּין חַלָּה. הֶקְדֵּשׁ רָאוּי הוּא לְפְדוֹתוֹ וּלְחַייְבוֹ. חַלָּה אֵינוֹ רָאוּי לְפְדוֹתָהּ וּלְחַייְבָהּ.

"[28]A *qab* of rice does not combine; a *qab* of *dema'* does not combine, a *qab* of heave does not combine. A Gentile's *qab* does not combine. A *qab* of another kind[29] combines. A *qab* of another woman combines. A *qab* of new grain combines[30]. A *qab* of something of which *ḥallah* was taken in the middle does combine[31]." Rebbi Abun bar Ḥiyya asked: Does a *qab* of *ḥallah* combine? Rebbi Ḥalaphta ben Shaul stated: "A dedicated *qab* does combine, a *qab* of *ḥallah* does not combine." What is the difference between dedicated [dough] and *ḥallah*? Dedicated [dough] may be redeemed and made obligated, *ḥallah* cannot be redeemed and made obligated[32].

28 In different formulation, Tosephta 2:3-4.

29 In the Tosephta, for wheat dough this is restricted to spelt which can combine both with wheat and with barley. The Tosephta follows R. Joḥanan ben Nuri in the Mishnah; the Yerushalmi *baraita* in the Leyden version follows the Tanna of the reformulated statement (Note 19); the Rome ms. reads אינו מצרף "it does not combine"; possibly following the anonymous Tanna in Mishnah 2.

30 The two doughs at the two sides are made from last year's grain harvest, the one in the middle is from this

year's grain; cf. Mishnah 4.

31 This is a case of the Mishnah.

32 One could have argued that *ḥallah* is a heave; then R. Abun bar Ḥiyya's question is answered in the Mishnah.

הלכה ד: חֲצִי קַב חִטִּים וַחֲצִי קַב שְׂעוֹרִים וַחֲצִי קַב כּוּסְמִין נוֹטֵל מִן הַכּוּסְמִין לְפִי מַה שֶׁהֵן. קַב חִטִּים וְקַב שְׂעוֹרִים וְקַב כּוּסְמִין תּוֹרֵם מִכָּל־אֶחָד וְאֶחָד לְפִי מַה שֶׁהוּא. לֹא אָמַר אֶלָּא קַב חִטִּין קַב שְׂעוֹרִין קַב כּוּסְמִין הָא קַב חִטִּים וְקַב שְׂעוֹרִין וְקַב כּוּסְמִין בְּאֶמְצַע לֹא בְדָא. רִבִּי בּוּן בַּר חִייָה אָמַר רִבִּי חֲנִינָה חֲבֵרוֹן דְּרַבָּנִין בָּעוּ מַה בֵּין כּוּסְמִין בְּאֶמְצַע מַה בֵּין שְׂעוֹרִין בְּאֶמְצַע. רִבִּי כֹּהֵן בְּשֵׁם רַבָּנִין דְּקַיְסָרִין אֵין הַכּוּסְמִין מִצְטָרְפִין עִם הַחִטִּים מִפְּנֵי שֶׁהוּא בְמִינוֹ אֶלָּא שֶׁהוּא מְדַמֶּה לוֹ. מִכֵּיוָן שֶׁהוּא רָחוֹק מִמֶּנּוּ אֵינוֹ מְדַמֶּה לוֹ.

Halakhah 4: "Half a *qab* of wheat, half a *qab* of barley, half a *qab* of spelt: He takes from spelt for what is needed[33]. A *qab* of wheat, a *qab* of barley, a *qab* of spelt, he takes heave from each one for what is needed.[34]" He said only, a *qab* of wheat, a *qab* of barley, a *qab* of spelt, therefore this is not about a *qab* of wheat, a *qab* of barley, and a *qab* of spelt in the middle. Rebbi Abun bar Ḥiyya said, Rebbi Ḥanina the colleague of the rabbis asked: what is the difference whether spelt or barley is in the middle? Rebbi Cohen in the name of the rabbis of Caesarea: Spelt combines with wheat not because it is the same kind but because it looks similar. Since it is far from it, it does not look similar.

33 Tosephta 2:5. There, the reading is: "He takes from the spelt." The meaning is the same as in the *baraita* here, that the entire heave is taken from spelt since that combines with both wheat and barley.

34 A similar text in Tosephta 2:4: "A *qab* of wheat, a *qab* of barley, a *qab* of spelt do combine. If he takes heave, he takes from each one separately since one does not give heave from one species for another." In this version,

the rules for *ḥallah* and heave are different; the discussion shows that this is not the position of the Yerushalmi. It follows that the *baraita* represents a tradition different from the Tosephta. It is not necessary to assume with Maimonides that the *qab* here is a larger measure, equal to $^5/_4$ standard *qab* which causes separate obligations of *ḥallah*. As R. Eliahu Fulda explains, the barley in the middle is also subject to *ḥallah*; it is not different from dough of which *ḥallah* already was taken. Therefore, the obligation of *ḥallah* exists and has to be satisfied following the rules of heave.

רִבִּי יוֹנָה בָּעֵי אַף לְעִנְייַן מַעֲשַׂר בְּהֵמָה כֵן. כְּמָה דְתֵימַר תַּמָּן הָיוּ לוֹ חָמֵשׁ חִייוּב בִּכְפָר חֲנַנְיָה וְחָמֵשׁ חִיּוּב בִּכְפָר עוֹתְנַי.[35] וְחָמֵשׁ פָּטוּר בְּצִיפּוֹרִין. כְּמָה דְתֵימַר תַּמָּן דָּבָר שֶׁנִּיטְּלָה חַלָּתוֹ מִן הָאֶמְצַע מְצָרֵף. אוֹף הָכָא כֵן. אִין תֵּימַר שַׁנְייָא הִיא חַלָּה שֶׁהוּא בְנָשׁוּךְ וְהָהֵן שִׁשָּׁה עָשָׂר מִיל לֹא כְנָשׁוּךְ הוּא. מָצִינוּ חַלָּה מֵהֲלָכָה לֹא מָצִינוּ מַעֲשַׂר בְּהֵמָה מֵהֲלָכָה.

Rebbi Jonah asked: Is it the same for animal tithe[36]? As you say there, if he had five obligated ones in Kefar Ḥananiah, five obligated in Kefar Othnay, and five free ones in Sepphoris? As you say there, if something of which *ḥallah* was taken is between them, they do combine; is it the same in this case? If you say that *ḥallah* is different since there it bites, are these 16 *mil* not as if it did bite? We find *ḥallah* from practice, we do not find animal tithe from practice[37].

35 Reading of the Rome ms. and the parallels in Babli *Bekhorot* 55a, Tosephta *Bekhorot* 7:3. Leyden and Venice: בנותני, an unidentified place. Kefar Othnai was near the location of ancient Megiddo.

36 *Lev.* 27:32; from the verse it is clear that the minimum number of newborn animals subject to tithe is 10. The Mishnah (*Bekhorot* 9:7) states that animals are close to one another to be counted together for tithes if they are within grazing distance of one another; this is fixed at 16 *mil*. It is stated that the distance from Kefar Ḥananiah to Sepphoris is 16 *mil*, from Sepphoris to

Kefar Othnai also 16 *mil*. Tosephta (*Bekhorot* 7:3) and Babli (*Bekhorot* 55a) state that there is an obligation of animal tithe if the total number of newborn animals of a single owner in Kefar Ḥananiah, Sepphoris, and Kefar Othnai is at least ten with at least one being at Sepphoris. R. Jonah now asks whether it is sufficient that the owner had animals at Sepphoris which were in the past counted for tithe, similar to the situation described in Mishnah 3.

37 The rule of Mishnah 3 is rabbinic; for animal tithe only biblical standards apply. R. Jonah's question is answered in the negative.

(fol. 59c) **משנה ד:** קַב חָדָשׁ וְקַב יָשָׁן שֶׁנָּשְׁכוּ זֶה בְזֶה רִבִּי יִשְׁמָעֵאל אוֹמֵר יִטּוֹל מִן הָאֶמְצַע. וַחֲכָמִים אוֹסְרִין. הַנּוֹטֵל חַלָּה מִן הַקַּב רִבִּי עֲקִיבָה אוֹמֵר חַלָּה. וַחֲכָמִים אוֹמְרִים אֵינָהּ חַלָּה.

Mishnah 4: If a *qab* of new grain and one of old bit one another[38], Rebbi Ismael says one should take from the middle but the Sages prohibit this. If somebody takes *ḥallah* from a single *qab*, Rebbi Aqiba declares it to be *ḥallah* but the Sages say, it is not *ḥallah*.

משנה ה: שְׁנֵי קַבִּין שֶׁנִּיטְּלָה חַלָּתָן שֶׁל זֶה בִּפְנֵי עַצְמוֹ וְשֶׁל זֶה בִּפְנֵי עַצְמוֹ וְחָזַר וַעֲשָׂאָן עִיסָּה אַחַת רִבִּי עֲקִיבָה פּוֹטֵר וַחֲכָמִים מְחַייְבִין נִמְצָא חוּמְרוֹ קוּלּוֹ.

Mishnah 5: If *ḥallah* of two *qabim* was taken separately, when he then combinrd them together into one dough, Rebbi Aqiba exempts but the Sages obligate; it turns out that the severity[39] becomes a leniency.

38 While two doughs together are obligated for *ḥallah* as noted in the previous Halakhah, it is forbidden to give heave from one year's harvest for another year's (Mishnah *Terumot* 1:5). Everybody agrees that *ḥallah* must be given from both kinds of grain; the question is only how this has to be done.

39 Of R. Aqiba who treats *ḥallah* from less than the minimal volume as genuine *ḥallah*.

(fol. 59d) **הלכה ה**: יְאוּת אָמַר רִבִּי יִשְׁמָעֵאל כּוּסְמִין וְחִיטִּין שְׁנֵי מִינִים הֵן. עַל יְדֵי שֶׁהוּא מְדַמֶּה לוֹ אַתְּ אוֹמֵר מִצְרֵף. חָדָשׁ וְיָשָׁן לֹא כָּל־שֶׁכֵּן. אָמַר רִבִּי הִילָא טַעֲמָא דְרַבָּנָן כּוּסְמִין וְחִיטִּין שְׁנֵי מִינִין וְאֵין בְּנֵי אָדָם טוֹעִין לוֹמַר שֶׁתּוֹרְמִין וּמְעַשְּׂרִין מִזֶּה עַל זֶה. חָדָשׁ וְיָשָׁן מִין אֶחָד הוּא אִם אוֹמֵר אַתְּ כֵּן אַף הוּא סָבוּר לוֹמַר שֶׁתּוֹרְמִין וּמְעַשְּׂרִין מִזֶּה עַל זֶה.

Halakhah 5: Is Rebbi Ismael not correct? Spelt and wheat are two species. Since they are similar, you say they combine; new and old not so much more? Rebbi Hila said, the reason of the rabbis is that spelt and wheat are two species and people will not err to say that one may give heave and tithes from one for the other[40]. New and old are one species and if you say so, one will think that one may give heave and tithes from one for the other[41].

40 *Terumot* Mishnah 2:4.

41 This is forbidden, *Terumot* Mishnah 1:5. It follows that the prohibition of the rabbis is rabbinic, not biblical. R. Eliahu Fulda points out that the argument is weak since even R. Ismael requires that *ḥallah* be taken in such a way that dough from both sides is taken; the difference between him and the rabbis is only whether *ḥallah* can be taken together or must be taken separately.

רִבִּי עֲקִיבָה מְדַמֵּי לָהּ לַפֵּירוֹת שֶׁלֹּא נִגְמְרוּ מְלַאכְתָּן. עָבַר וְהִפְרִישׁ מֵהֶן תְּרוּמָה הֲרֵי זוֹ תְרוּמָה. וְרַבָּנִין מְדַמִּין לָהּ לִתְבוּאָה שֶׁלֹּא הֵבִיאָה שְׁלִישׁ. עָבַר וְהִפְרִישׁ מִמֶּנּוּ חַלָּה אֵינָהּ חַלָּה. חָזְרוּ לוֹמַר אֵינָן דּוֹמִין לֹא לַפֵּירוֹת שֶׁלֹּא נִגְמְרָה מְלַאכְתָּן וְלֹא לִתְבוּאָה שֶׁלֹּא הֵבִיאָה שְׁלִישׁ. אֶלָּא רִבִּי עֲקִיבָה מְדַמֵּי לָהּ לוֹמַר הֲרֵי זוֹ תְרוּמָה עַל הַפֵּירוֹת הָאֵילוּ לִכְשֶׁיִּתְלְשׁוּ וְנִתְלְשׁוּ. וְרַבָּנִין מְדַמִּין לָהּ לוֹמַר הֲרֵי זוֹ תְרוּמָה עַל הַפֵּירוֹת הָאֵילוּ לִכְשֶׁיִּתְלְשׁוּ.

Rebbi Aqiba compares it to not fully processed produce; if one transgressed and gave heave from it it is heave[42]. But the rabbis compare it to produce not yet one-third ripe; if one transgressed and gave heave from it it is not heave[43]. They had second thoughts and said, it is similar neither to not fully processed produce nor to produce not yet one-third ripe[44]! But Rebbi Aqiba compares it to the case of him who says, this is heave for these fruits when they will be taken, and they were taken; but the rabbis compare it to the case of him who says, this is heave for these fruits when they will be taken[45].

42 Mishnah *Terumot* 1:10.

43 Mishnah *Ḥallah* 1:3, following R. Eleazar.

44 Since it also must follow the majority opinion in Mishnah *Ḥallah* 1:3.

45 Everybody agrees that produce tentatively designated as heave cannot be heave if there is nothing it can be given for. Similarly, they will hold that *ḥallah* tentatively designated for the case the dough will reach critical size cannot be *ḥallah* if no obligated dough is available at the time of designation.

הֲוֹון בָּעֵי מֵימַר מַה דְאָמַר רִבִּי עֲקִיבָה נִיטַּל חַלָּה מִקַּב חַלָּה מֵהֲלָכָה. הָא מִדְּבַר תּוֹרָה לֹא. מִן מַה דְתַנִּינָן רִבִּי עֲקִיבָה פּוֹטֵר וַחֲכָמִים מְחַייְבִין הָדָא אָמְרָה אֲפִילוּ מִדְּבַר תּוֹרָה.

They wanted to say what Rebbi Aqiba said, *ḥallah* may be taken from a *qab* from practice, not as a biblical standard. Since we have stated: "Rebbi Aqiba exempts but the Sages obligate," this implies that it is by biblical standards[46].

46 Since the combined dough of 2 *qab* is subject to biblical *ḥallah* in everybody's opinion, R. Aqiba must declare *ḥallah* from a single *qab* as biblical *ḥallah*.

In R. Aqiba's statement, "one *qab*" must be taken litterally; it is not an expression meaning "less than $^{5}/_{4}$ *qab*" since in Mishnah *Idiut* 1:2, Shammai is reported to fix the obligation of *ḥallah* at one *qab* (and Hillel at 2 *qabim*). R. Aqiba must hold that any amount which is declared *ḥallah* in any tradition must be recognized as biblical *ḥallah* (Maimonides in his Commentary.)

נִמְצָא חוּמְרוֹ קוּלוֹ. אִית תַּנּוֹיֵי תַּנֵּי קוּלוֹ חוּמְרוֹ. מָאן דְּאָמַר חוּמְרוֹ קוּלוֹ רִבִּי עֲקִיבָה. (fol. 60a) קוּלוֹ חוּמְרוֹ רַבָּנִין.

"It turns out that the severity becomes a leniency." Some Tannaïm state: "The leniency becomes a severity". He who says the severity becomes a leniency, [refers to] Rebbi Aqiba; he who says the leniency becomes a severity, [refers to] the rabbis.

(fol. 59c) **משנה ו:** נוֹטֵל אָדָם כְּדֵי חַלָּה מֵעִיסָּה שֶׁלֹּא הוּרְמָה חַלָּתָהּ לַעֲשׂוֹתָהּ בְּטָהֳרָה לִהְיוֹת מַפְרִישׁ עָלֶיהָ וְהוֹלֵךְ חַלַּת דְּמַיי עַד שֶׁתִּסְרַח שֶׁחַלַּת דְּמַיי נִיטֶּלֶת מִן הַטָּהוֹר עַל הַטָּמֵא וְשֶׁלֹּא מִן הַמּוּקָף.

Mishnah 6: A person may take for *ḥallah* from a dough prepared in purity and from which *ḥallah* has not yet been taken, to use it continuously for *ḥallah* of *demay*[47] until it decays, since *ḥallah* of *demay* may be taken from pure for impure and from what is not earmarked[48].

47 It is not very clear what "*ḥallah* of *demay*" is since *ḥallah* has the status of Great Heave which everybody is supposed to have given. It seems, with R. Simson, that "*ḥallah* of *demay*" is *ḥallah* taken for bread bought from an untrustworthy baker, as described in Mishnah *Demay* 5:1. According to Maimonides, in his Code and the later version of his Commentary, "*ḥallah* of *demay*" refers to any *ḥallah* whose status as biblical obligation is in doubt.

48 Since dough or bread bought from an untrustworthy person always has the status of ritual impurity, the pure dough set aside for *ḥallah* cannot be combined with the impure for which it is designated. Therefore, the

procedure described here is restricted to the case where the heave (i. e., *ḥallah*) does not have to be earmarked.

(fol. 60a) **הלכה ו**: מַהוּ עַד שֶׁתִּסְרַח מֵאוֹכֶל אָדָם אוֹ עַד שֶׁתִּפְסוֹל מֵאוֹכֶל הַכֶּלֶב. נִשְׁמְעִינָהּ מִן הָדָא נִסְרְחָה מֵאוֹכֶל אָדָם מְטַמֵּא טוּמְאַת אוֹכְלִין וְשׂוֹרְפִין אוֹתָהּ בְּטוּמְאָה. מְטַמֵּא טוּמְאַת אוֹכְלִין וְאַתְּ אָמְרַת מֵאוֹכֶל הַכֶּלֶב. אֶלָּא מֵאוֹכֶל אָדָם.

Halakhah 6: What means "until it decays"? That it is no longer human food or until it is unfit as dog food[50]? Let us hear from the following[51]: "If it decayed and no longer is human food it is impure by the impurity of food and one burns it in impurity[52]." It is impure by the impurity of food and you say until unfit as dog food? It must be as human food.

50 No food prohibitions do apply to anything unfit as dog food.

51 Another version is in Tosephta *Terumot* 9:10: "Rebbi Ḥananiah the Second of the Cohanim says: Heave which is no longer human food but is dog food is impure by the impurity of food and one burns it in its place." Since there is a name attached to this statement, it is implied that the majority will deny that anything which is not human food can become impure in the impurity of food. The Babli (*Pesaḥim* 15b, 45b) quotes a similar but anonymous *baraita*. It follows that the Babli decides with R. Ḥananiah the Second of the Cohanim but the Yerushalmi against him. Maimonides (*Hilkhot Ṭum'at Okhlin* 2:14) follows the Yerushalmi, against the protests of R. Abraham ben David.

52 One burns it immediately as impure; one does not treat it as suspended as would be required if the status of impurity were in doubt.

הָדָא אָמְרָה שֶׁתּוֹרְמִין מִן הָרַע עַל הַיָּפֶה. וְאַתְיָיא כַּיי דָּמַר רַב שְׁמוּאֵל בַּר רַב נַחְמָן בְּשֵׁם רִבִּי יוֹנָתָן שֶׁתּוֹרְמִין מֵעֲלֵי אִיסְטָפְנִינֵי עַל הָאִיסְטָפְנִינֵי בְּמָקוֹם

שֶׁאוֹכְלִין אוֹתָהּ. כְּהָדָא גַּמְלִיֵּיל זוּגָא אִינְשִׁי מְתַקְנָה אִיסְטַפְנִינוֹתֵיהּ. אֲתָא שָׁאַל לְרִבִּי יוֹחָנָן אָמַר לֵיהּ אִית תַּמָּן קְנִיבָה אַפְרִישׁ מִן קְנוּבְתָּהּ.

This means[53] that one may give heave from bad for good. It parallels what Rebbi Samuel bar Rav Naḥman said in the name of Rebbi Jonathan, one gives heave from the leaves of carrots[54] for carrots at a place where [the leaves] are eaten. This happened with Gamliel the twin who had forgotten to put his carrots in order. He came and asked Rebbi Joḥanan who said to him: Is there greenery? Give heave from the greenery!

53 The Mishnah which permits using dough close to being spoiled as *ḥallah* (i. e., heave) for freshly prepared dough.

54 Cf. *Demay* 2, Note 63.

תַּנֵּי תְּרוּמַת מַעֲשֵׂר שֶׁלְּדְמַאי. אִיתָא חֲמִי תְּרוּמַת מַעֲשֵׂר שֶׁלְוַדַּאי נִיטֶּלֶת מִן הַטָּהוֹר עַל הַטָּמֵא תְּרוּמַת מַעֲשֵׂר שֶׁלְּדְמַאי לֹא כָּל־שֶׁכֵּן. אָמַר רִבִּי יוֹסֵי בִּסְפֵק תְּרוּמָה גְדוֹלָה אֲנָן קַייָמִין סָפֵק הִפְרִישׁ תְּרוּמָה סָפֵק לֹא הִפְרִישׁ כְּמַה דְתֵימַר מִן הַוַּדַּאי עַל הַדְּמַאי תְּרוּמָה לֹא תֵאָכֵל עַד שֶׁיּוֹצִיא תְרוּמָה וּמַעְשְׂרוֹת וְאָמַר מִן הַדְּמַאי עַל הַדְּמַאי כֵּן. אָמַר רִבִּי שִׁמְעוֹן בֶּן כַּרְסָנָא כָּאן בְּרוֹצֶה לְאוֹכְלָהּ כָּאן בְּרוֹצֶה לְשׂוֹרְפָהּ.

It was stated: "Heave of the tithe of *demay*[55]." Come and see, since certain heave of the tithe may be taken from pure for impure[56], heave of the tithe of *demay* not so much more? Rebbi Yose said, we deal with a doubt of Great Heave when it is not sure whether Great Heave was taken or not[57]. As you say, "from certain produce for *demay*, it is heave that should not be eaten unless heave and tithes were taken for it;"[58] he asserts that from *demay* for *demay* it is the same. Rebbi Simeon ben Karsana[59] said, there[60] he wants to eat it, here he wants to burn it.

55 Quote from an otherwise unknown *baraita*. From the text one may understand that the *baraita* stated that heave of the tithe of *demay* follows the same rules as *ḥallah* for *demay* dough as spelled out in the Mishnah.

56 Mishnah *Bikkurim* 2:5; cf. *Terumot* 2, Note 9.

57 But in general, the term *demay* implies that Great Heave was taken and only tithes and heave of the tithe are questionable. This supports the interpretation that also in the Mishnah, *demay* is used in a loose, non-technical way.

58 *Demay* 5:10, Note 144.

59 Also called R. Simeon ben Barsana.

60 The *baraita* is needed; its contents cannot be derived from the Mishnah here since the heave of the tithe is to be eaten whereas in the Mishnah the dough reserved for *ḥallah* has to be burned in the end when it becomes inedible.

(fol. 59c) **משנה ז:** יִשְׂרָאֵל שֶׁהָיוּ אֲרִיסִין לְגוֹיִם בְּסוּרְיָא רִבִּי לִיעֶזֶר מְחַייֵב בְּפֵירוֹתֵיהֶן בְּמַעְשְׂרוֹת וּבַשְּׁבִיעִית. וְרַבָּן גַּמְלִיאֵל פּוֹטֵר. רַבָּן גַּמְלִיאֵל אוֹמֵר שְׁתֵּי חַלּוֹת בְּסוּרְיָא. וְרִבִּי לִיעֶזֶר אוֹמֵר חַלָּה אַחַת אָחֲזוּ קוּלּוֹ שֶׁלְרַבָּן גַּמְלִיאֵל וְקוּלּוֹ שֶׁלְרִבִּי לִיעֶזֶר. חָזְרוּ לִנְהוֹג כְּדִבְרֵי רַבָּן גַּמְלִיאֵל בִּשְׁתֵּי דְרָכִים.

Mishnah 7: Jews were sharecroppers for Gentiles in Syria[61]; Rebbi Eliezer obligates their produce for tithes and the Sabbatical but Rabban Gamliel exempts them. Rabban Gamliel says there are two *ḥallot* in Syria[62] but Rebbi Eliezer says one *ḥallah*[63]. They took the leniency of Rabban Gamliel and the leniency of Rebbi Eliezer but then returned to follow Rabban Gamliel in both cases.

61 The parts of David's kingdom not conquered by the 12 tribes under Joshua; cf. *Peah* 7, Note 119. R. Eliezer holds that the laws of the Holy Land extend to Syria but Rabban Gamliel holds that Syria is essentially outside

the Land and only selected laws of the Land are extended to apply there.

62 As explained in Mishnah 8. Biblical law restricts the duty of *ḥallah* to the Land (*Num.* 15:18-19). Rabbinic practice extends the obligation to the rest of the world but, since the soil outside the Land is intrinsically impure, any *ḥallah* outside the Land is impure and must be burned. Nevertheless, in order to remind people that the original duty is to give *ḥallah* to a Cohen, it was established that some dough should be given to a Cohen. This dough cannot be sanctified, otherwise it would be forbidden to the recipient.

63 He denies that Syrian soil is impure.

(fol. 60a) **הלכה ז**: רִבִּי אַבָּהוּ בְּשֵׁם רִבִּי יוֹחָנָן לֹא חִייֵב רִבִּי לִיעֶזֶר אֶלָּא בַּחֲכִירֵי אָבוֹת כְּגוֹן מֵהִלֵּל דְּבֵית רִבִּי. תַּנֵּי רִבִּי חֲלַפְתָּא בֶּן שָׁאוּל קְנָס קְנָסוֹ רִבִּי לִיעֶזֶר. מָה נְפַק מִבֵּינֵיהוֹן אָרִיס לְשָׁעָה. מָאן דְּאָמַר קְנָס חַייָב. מָאן דְּאָמַר בַּחֲכִירֵי בָּתֵּי אָבוֹת פָּטוּר.

Rebbi Abbahu in the name of Rebbi Joḥanan: Rebbi Eliezer obligated only hereditary tenants[64], for example from Hillel to the House of Rebbi[65]. Rebbi Ḥalaphta ben Shaul stated: Rebbi Eliezer fined him[66]. Where do they differ? For a temporary sharecropper. For him who says a fine, he is obligated. For him who says hereditary tenants, he is exempt.

64 These have acquired the hereditary right to remain tenants; this is a kind of lien on the real estate.

65 For 200 years in one family.

66 To take away an incentive to leave the Land for more profitable farming in Syria.

הַלּוֹקֵחַ מִן הַנַּחְתּוֹם בְּסוּרְיָא צָרִיךְ לְהַפְרִישׁ חַלַּת דְּמַיי דִּבְרֵי רַבָּן גַּמְלִיאֵל וַחֲכָמִים אוֹמְרִים אֵינוֹ צָרִיךְ לְהַפְרִישׁ חַלַּת דְּמַיי. אָמַר רִבִּי חֲנַנְיָה קוֹמֵי רִבִּי מָנָא וְיֵאוּת אָמַר רַבָּן גַּמְלִיאֵל מַה טַעֲמְהוֹן דְּרַבָּנִין. אָמַר לוֹ כְּשֵׁם שֶׁלֹּא נֶחְשְׁדוּ יִשְׂרָאֵל עַל תְּרוּמָה בָּאָרֶץ כָּךְ לֹא נֶחְשְׁדוּ עַל חַלָּה בְּסוּרְיָא.

"He who buys from a baker in Syria[67] has to separate *ḥallah* as *demay*, the words of Rabban Gamliel, but the Sages say he does not have to separate *ḥallah* as *demay*.[68]" Rebbi Ḥananiah said before Rebbi Mana: Rabban Gamliel said it right, what is the reason of the Sages? He said to him, just as Israel are not suspected in matters of heave in the Land, so they are not suspected in matters of *ḥallah*[69] in Syria.

67 Since Rabban Gamliel holds that Syria is essentially a foreign country, he holds that there *ḥallah* even in Temple times is only rabbinic in character and the vulgar will not give *ḥallah*.

68 Tosephta 2:5. This is part of a longer statement by R. Eleazar ben R. Ẓadoq who explains the position of Rabban Gamliel that the sharecropper is exempt because the grain is processed in the possession of the Gentile but *ḥallah* whose obligation starts in the house of the Jew follows exactly the laws of the Land.

69 Whose rules are those of the Great Heave.

רִבִּי אָבוּן בַּר חִיָּה בָּעֵי כְּמַה דְאִתְאֲמָרַת שְׁתֵּי חַלּוֹת בְּסוּרְיָא וְדִכְוָותָהּ שְׁתֵּי תְרוּמוֹת בְּסוּרְיָא. אָמַר רִבִּי חַגַּיי חַלָּה אֵין אַחֲרֶיהָ כְּלוּם תְּרוּמָה יֵשׁ אַחֲרֶיהָ כְּלוּם. אִם אוֹמֵר אַתְּ כֵּן נִמְצֵאת אוֹתָהּ תְּרוּמָה שֶׁהוּא מַפְרִישׁ טְבוּלָה לְמַעְשְׂרוֹת.

Rebbi Abun bar Ḥiyya asked: Since you said that there are two *ḥallot* in Syria, should there not be two heaves[70] in Syria? Rebbi Ḥaggai said, there comes nothing after *ḥallah*[71] but after heave there comes something. If you would say so, it would turn out that the heave he separates[72] were *ṭevel* for tithes!

70 The first to be burned and the second to be eaten.

71 Taking *ḥallah* makes dough and bread totally profane.

72 The second one which cannot be real heave or it would have to be burned.

בִּיקֵּשׁ רַבָּן גַּמְלִיאֵל בֶּן רִבִּי לְהַנְהִיג אֶת הַדְּמַיי בְּסוּרְיָא וְלֹא הִנִּיחַ לוֹ רִבִּי הוֹשַׁעְיָה. אָמַר לֵיהּ מֵעַתָּה יְחוּשׁוּ הַכֹּהֲנִים עַל חַלָּתָן. מִחְלְפָה שִׁיטָּתֵיהּ דְּרִבִּי הוֹשַׁעְיָה. תַּמָּן אָמַר אֵימַת קֳדָשִׁים עָלָיו וְאֵינוֹ נוֹתֵן לַכֹּהֵן דָּבָר שֶׁאֵינוֹ מְתוּקָּן וְכָא הוּא אָמַר הָכֵן. אָמַר רִבִּי בּוּן בַּר חִייָה אֲנִי אוֹמֵר אוֹתָהּ שֶׁלְּאוּר נוֹתֵן לוֹ. אָמַר לֵיהּ רִבִּי מָנָא לֹא תַנֵּי רִבִּי הוֹשַׁעְיָה אֶלָּא מֵעַתָּה יְחוּשׁוּ הַכֹּהֲנִים עַל חַלָּתָן. הַלּוֹקֵחַ מִן הַנַּחְתּוֹם וּמִן הָאִשָּׁה שֶׁהִיא עוֹשָׂה לִמְכּוֹר לַשּׁוּק צָרִיךְ לְהַפְרִישׁ חַלַּת דְּמַיי. מִבַּעַל הַבַּיִת וְהַמִּתְאָרֵחַ אֶצְלוֹ אֵינוֹ צָרִיךְ לְהַפְרִישׁ חַלַּת דְּמַיי. רִבִּי יוֹנָה בְּשֵׁם רִבִּי חֲנַנְיָה חֲבֵרוֹן דְּרַבָּנָן בְּמִתְאָרֵחַ אֶצְלוֹ לְעִיסָּתוֹ. אָמַר רִבִּי יוֹנָה וְהֵן שֶׁרָאוּ אוֹתוֹ מְגַבֵּל אֶצֶל אַחֵר. חֶזְקַת בַּעֲלֵי בָּתִּים בְּסוּרְיָא אֵינוֹ צָרִיךְ לְהַפְרִישׁ חַלַּת דְּמַיי. אִם יוֹדֵעַ שֶׁרוֹב מִכְנָסוֹ מִשֶּׁלּוֹ צָרִיךְ לְהַפְרִישׁ חַלַּת דְּמַיי. רִבִּי בּוּן בַּר חִייָה בָּעֵי לֵית הָדָא פְלִיגָא עַל רִבִּי הוֹשַׁעְיָה. אָמַר רִבִּי מָנָא כָּאן בָּאָרֶץ כָּאן בְּחוּץ לָאָרֶץ.

Rabban Gamliel the son of Rebbi wanted to institute *demay* in Syria[73] but Rebbi Hoshaiah did not let him do it. He said to him, then Cohanim would have to worry about their *ḥallah*[74]! The argument of Rebbi Hoshaiah seems inverted. There[75], he says the fear of sacred things is on him and he will not give to the Cohen anything that is not in order, and here he says so? Rebbi Abun bar Ḥiyya said, I am saying that he gave him that of the fire[76]. Rebbi Mana said to him, Rebbi Hoshaiah only stated: then Cohanim would have to worry about *their ḥallah*[77]! "[78]He who buys from a baker and from a woman who bakes to sell on the market has to separate *ḥallah* of *demay*[79]; from a private person and if he is a guest[80] he does not have to separate *ḥallah* of *demay*." Rebbi Jonah in the name of Rebbi Ḥananiah the colleague of the rabbis, if he is a guest for his dough. Rebbi Jonah said, only if they saw him kneading at another's place[81]. It is a standing assumption that from a private person in Syria one does not have to separate *ḥallah* of *demay*; but if he knows that most of what is in his storage is his own produce, he has to separate *ḥallah* of *demay*[82]. Rebbi Abun bar Ḥiyya asked, does this not disagree with Rebbi Hoshaiah[83]? Rebbi Mana said, here in the Land[84], there outside the Land.

73 Against Mishnah *Demay* 1:3 which restricts *demay* to the Land of Israel. One may assume that in his time the center of Jewish population had moved from Galilee to Syria.

74 Since *ḥallah* is legitimate only if the dough was made from tithed flour.

75 *Demay* 1, Note 172, explaining the statement of the Mishnah that *ḥallah* of a vulgar is exempt from the laws of *demay*.

76 Since it is burned, the vulgar will not worry if heave of the tithe was not given.

77 The language of the statement excludes the argument of R. Abun bar Ḥiyya.

78 Tosephta 1:8. Cf. *Tosefta ki-Fshutah*, p.799.

79 I. e., give heave of the tithe and afterwards *ḥallah*.

80 In the Tosephta, "from a private person and his guests." Even if he is the baker's guest but eats from the bread the baker makes for himself and his family (R. Abraham ben David). The reading of the Rome ms., ומתארח אצלו "from a private person and he is his guest" supports Maimonides (*Bikkurim* 8:15). *Hilkhot Tašbeẓ* explains: "If one buys from a private person one has to give extra *ḥallah* except if one is his guest or saw him knead for another person."

81 That other people trust him to give their *ḥallah*.

82 Since in this case, a field in Syria is subject to tithes; Mishnah *Demay* 6:11.

83 Since he denies *demay* in Syria.

84 Mishnah *Demay* 1:3 deals only with the Land where all vulgars can be trusted to give *ḥallah* as they give Great Heave.

(fol. 59c) **משנה ח:** רַבָּן גַּמְלִיאֵל אוֹמֵר שָׁלֹשׁ אֲרָצוֹת לַחַלָּה מֵאֶרֶץ יִשְׂרָאֵל וְעַד גְּזִיב חַלָּה אַחַת. מִגְּזִיב וְעַד הַנָּהָר וְעַד אֲמָנֹס שְׁתֵּי חַלּוֹת אַחַת לָאוּר וְאַחַת לַכֹּהֵן. שֶׁלְאוּר יֵשׁ לָהּ שִׁיעוּר וְשֶׁלְכֹּהֵן אֵין לָהּ שִׁיעוּר. מֵהַנָּהָר וּמֵאֲמָנֹס וְלִפְנִים שְׁתֵּי חַלּוֹת אַחַת לָאוּר וְאַחַת לַכֹּהֵן. שֶׁלְאוּר אֵין לָהּ שִׁיעוּר וְשֶׁלְכֹּהֵן יֵשׁ לָהּ שִׁיעוּר. וּטְבוּל יוֹם אוֹכְלָהּ. רִבִּי יוֹסֵי אוֹמֵר אֵינוֹ צָרִיךְ טְבִילָה.

Mishnah 8: Rabban Gamliel says: There are three domains for *ḥallah*[85]. The Land of Israel[86] up to Akhzib, one *ḥallah.* From Akhzib to the Euphrates or Amanus[87], two *ḥallot*, one for the fire and one for the Cohen. The one for the fire has a measure[88], the one for the Cohen has no measure[89]. From Euphrates or Amanus inside[90], two *ḥallot*, one for the fire and one for the Cohen. The one for the fire has no measure[91], the one for the Cohen has a measure but a *ṭevul yom* may eat it[92]. Rebbi Yose says one does not need immersion[93].

85 In the biblical Land of Israel.

86 The actual Land of Israel of the Second Commonwealth; cf. Mishnah *Ševi'it* 6:1, Note 3, for the geographic details.

87 One has to add, with Mishnah *Ševi'it* 6:1, "any place held by the immigrants from Egypt," i. e., the regions North of Akhzib described as tribal territories in the book of Joshua.

88 The true *ḥallah* which cannot be eaten since the impurity of Gentile lands is extended rabbinically to any region not inhabited by Jews. The "measure" is that for *ḥallah* of the Land, Mishnah 2:7.

89 A purely symbolic *ḥallah* to be eaten in impurity, as a remembrance of the rules to be restored in the times of the Messiah.

90 The rest of Syria, domain of biblical promise; cf. *Ševi'it* 6:1, Note 3.

91 Both *ḥallot* are symbolical since that region was not under obligation of *ḥallah* even during the First Commonwealth.

92 He is forbidden true *ḥallah.*

93 This also shows that the symbolic *ḥallah* is no true heave, cf. *Berakhot* 1, Note 3.

(fol. 59c) **משנה ט:** וַאֲסוּרָה לְזָבִין וּלְזָבוֹת לְנִידּוֹת וּלְיוֹלְדוֹת וְנֶאֱכֶלֶת עִם הַזָּר עַל הַשּׁוּלְחָן וְנִיתֶּנֶת לְכָל־כֹּהֵן.

Mishnah 9: But it[94] is forbidden to people suffering from genital flux[95], and to women during menstruation[96] or after childbirth[97]. It may be eaten at one table with a layman and may be given to any Cohen[98].

94 The purely symbolic *ḥallah* mentioned last in Mishnah 8. By rabbinic ordinance, it is forbidden for people whose impurity originates in their own body.

95 *Lev.* 15:1-15, 25-30.

96 *Lev.* 15:19-24.

97 *Lev.* 12:1-8.

98 Even a vulgar who cannot be expected to follow all rules of purity.

(fol. 60a) **הלכה ח:** רִבִּי חוּנָא אָמַר כֵּינִי מַתְנִיתָא מִגְּזִיב וְעַד הַנָּהָר מִגְּזִיב וְעַד אֲמָנֹס. תַּנֵּי אֵי זוּ הִיא הָאָרֶץ וְאֵי זוּ חוּץ לָאָרֶץ. כָּל־שֶׁהוּא שׁוֹפֵעַ מִטַּוְורוֹס אֲמָנֹס וְלִפְנִים אֶרֶץ יִשְׂרָאֵל. מִטַּוְרוֹס אֲמָנֹס וּלְחוּץ חוּצָה לָאָרֶץ. הַנִּיסִין שֶׁבְּיָם אַתְּ רוֹאֶה אוֹתָן כְּאִילּוּ חוּט מָתוּחַ מִטַּוְורוֹס אֲמָנֹס וְעַד נַחַל מִצְרַיִם. מֵהַחוּט וְלִפְנִים אֶרֶץ יִשְׂרָאֵל. מֵהַחוּט וּלְחוּץ חוּץ לָאָרֶץ. רִבִּי יוּדָה אוֹמֵר כָּל־שֶׁהוּא כְּנֶגֶד אֶרֶץ יִשְׂרָאֵל הֲרֵי הוּא כְּאֶרֶץ יִשְׂרָאֵל שֶׁנֶּאֱמַר וּגְבוּל יָם וְהָיָה לָכֶם הַיָּם הַגָּדוֹל וּגְבוּל זֶה יִהְיֶה לָכֶם גְּבוּל יָם. שֶׁבַּצְּדָדִין מֵהֶן אַתְּ רוֹאֶה אוֹתָן כְּאִילּוּ חוּט מָתוּחַ מִקֶּפַלָּרִיָּא וְעַד אוֹקֵייָנוֹס מִנַּחַל מִצְרַיִם וְעַד אוֹקֵייָנוֹס מֵהַחוּט וְלִפְנִים אֶרֶץ יִשְׂרָאֵל. מֵהַחוּט וּלְחוּץ חוּץ לָאָרֶץ.

[99]Rebbi Huna said: So is the Mishnah: "Between Akhzib and Euphrates, between Akhzib and Amanus." It was stated: What is the Land and what is outside the Land? From the slopes of Taurus Amanus inwards is the Land of Israel[3], from Taurus Amanus to the outside is outside the Land. About the islands in the sea, one looks at them as if a string were drawn from Taurus Amanus to the brook of Egypt; from the string to the inside is the Land of Israel, from the string to the outside is

outside the Land. Rebbi Jehudah said, all that lies before the Land of Israel is like the Land of Israel since it is said (*Num.* 34:6): "The Western border shall be for you the Great Sea as border; that shall be for you the sea border." Assuming that a string were drawn from Cephalaria to the Ocean, from the brook of Egypt to the Ocean; inside the string is the Land of Israel, outside is outside the Land.

99 This and the following paragraph are from *Ševi'it* 6:1, Notes 90-95.

אָמַר רִבִּי יוּסְטָא בַּר שׁוּנֵם כְּשֶׁיַּגִּיעוּ הַגָּלִיּוֹת לְטַוְורוֹס אֲמָנֹס הֵן עֲתִידוֹת לוֹמַר שִׁירָה. מַה טַעַם תָּשׁוּרִי מֵרֹאשׁ אֲמָנָה.

Rebbi Justus bar Shunem said, when the people of the Diaspora arrive at Taurus Amanus they will sing. What is the reason? (*Cant.* 4:8) "Sing from the top of Amanah".

אִית תַּנָּיֵי תַּנֵּי הַיַּרְדֵּן מֵאֶרֶץ יִשְׂרָאֵל. אִית תַּנֵּי הַיַּרְדֵּן מֵחוּצָה לָאָרֶץ. אִית תַּנֵּי הַיַּרְדֵּן גְּבוּל בִּפְנֵי עַצְמוֹ. מָאן דְּאָמַר הַיַּרְדֵּן מֵאֶרֶץ יִשְׂרָאֵל וְהָעֲרָבָה וְהַיַּרְדֵּן וּגְבוּל. מָאן דְּאָמַר הַיַּרְדֵּן מֵחוּץ לָאָרֶץ וְהַיַּרְדֵּן יִגְבּוֹל אוֹתוֹ לִפְאַת קֵדְמָה. וּמָאן דְּאָמַר הַיַּרְדֵּן גְּבוּל בִּפְנֵי עַצְמוֹ וְהוּא שֶׁיְּהֵא בְּמָקוֹם אֶחָד. עָשָׂה יַרְדֵּן שֶׁנָּטַל מִזֶּה וְנָתַן לְזֶה מַה שֶּׁנָּטַל נָטַל וּמַה שֶּׁנָּתַן נָתַן. וּמַה נָן קַייָמִין אִם בְּמָקוֹם שֶׁהָיָה אֶרֶץ יִשְׂרָאֵל וְנַעֲשָׂה בְסוּרִיָּא חֶזְקָתוֹ לְמַעְשְׂרוֹת וְלִשְׁבִיעִית. רִבִּי יִרְמְיָה רִבִּי אִימִּי בְשֵׁם רִבִּי יוֹחָנָן רִבִּי סִימוֹן בְּשֵׁם רִבִּי יְהוֹשֻׁעַ בֶּן לֵוִי לְחַזָּקוֹת וּלְבִיעוּרִין וּלְמַעֲשַׂר בְּהֵמָה. רִבִּי הִילָּא בְּשֵׁם רִבִּי שִׁמְעוֹן בֶּן לָקִישׁ וְהוּא שֶׁמָּשַׁךְ עָפָר.

[100]Some Tannaïm state: The Jordan is part of the Land of Israel. Some state, the Jordan is outside the Land. Some state, the Jordan is a boundary by itself. He who says the Jordan is part of the Land of Israel: (*Deut.* 3:17) "The prairie, the Jordan, and the border." He who says the Jordan is

outside the Land: (*Jos*. 18:20): "The Jordan shall form its border Eastward." He who says the Jordan is a boundary by itself, if it is in one place. [101]"If the Jordan took from one place and gave to another, what it took, it took, and what it gave, it gave." What are we dealing with? If it was from the Land of Israel and became Syria[102], it already is under the presumptive obligation of tithes and Sabbatical! Rebbi Jeremiah, Rebbi Immi in the name of Rebbi Joḥanan, Rebbi Simon in the name of Rebbi Joshua ben Levi, for claims of possession[103], removals[104], and animal tithe[105]. Rebbi Hila in the name of Rebbi Simeon ben Laqish: Only if it removed earth.

100 A similar discussion in Babli *Bekhorot* 55a. There, the first opinion is declared to be that of R. Simeon ben Ioḥai, the second that of R. Jehudah ben Bathyra, and the third that of R. Meïr.

101 Tosephta *Ketubot* 8:4, *Baba Qama* 10:23, Babli *Baba Meẓi'a* 22a. The argument there is that a change in the river bed is an act of God against which the property owners are powerless; one may therefore assume that the owners have given up hope to recover their land; the part taken by the river now is ownerless.

102 This is a very unlikely scenario. The Jordan is meandering only between the Land of Israel and Transjordan.

103 It is assumed that people do not keep documents for more than three years. Therefore, a person who claims to have legal possession of real estate by sale or inheritance, in the absence of a title can prove his claim by showing undisturbed possession for three years. Such a claim cannot be brought simultaneously for property inside and outside the Land.

104 The required consumption of Sabbatical produce which varies from region to region, *Ševi'it* 9:2.

105 This is the topic of Babli *Bekhorot* 55a.

הלכה ט: שֶׁלְאוֹר יֵשׁ לָהּ שִׁיעוּר שֶׁהוּא דְּבַר תּוֹרָה. שֶׁלְכֹּהֵן אֵין לָהּ שִׁיעוּר שֶׁהִיא מִדִּבְרֵיהֶן. וְיַפְרִישׁ לָאוֹר וְלֹא יַפְרִישׁ לַכֹּהֵן. שֶׁלֹּא יְהוּ אוֹמְרִים רָאִינוּ תְרוּמָה טְהוֹרָה נִשְׂרֶפֶת. וְיַפְרִישׁ לַכֹּהֵן וְלֹא יַפְרִישׁ לָאוֹר. שֶׁלֹּא יְהוּ אוֹמְרִים רָאִינוּ תְרוּמָה טְמֵיאָה נֶאֱכֶלֶת. מִתּוֹךְ שֶׁהוּא מַפְרִישׁ שְׁתֵּיהֶן לִכְשֶׁהוּא בָא לְכָאן הוּא נִשְׁאָל.

Halakhah 9: "The one for the fire has a measure," for it is biblical[88]. "The one for the Cohen has no measure," for it is rabbinical[89]. Should he give for the fire and not for the Cohen? That they should not say, we saw pure heave being burned[106]. Should he give for the Cohen and not for the fire? That they should not say, we saw impure heave being eaten[107]. Since he gives both of them, when he comes here[108], he will ask.

106 The territory of the Land of Israel during the First Commonwealth which was not reoccupied by Jews during the Second Commonwealth is pure by biblical standards, impure only rabbinically. One might have a point considering that heave as pure. The second *ḥallah* shows that the obligation is only rabbinical and it is impure only by rabbinical standards.

107 Since it is impure by actual standards.

108 The two *ḥallot* are required mainly to make sure that immigrants to the Holy Land inquire about the rules to be followed in the Land.

וְזוֹ וְזוֹ מִדִּבְרֵיהֶן הוּא. מוּטָּב לְרַבּוֹת בְּנֶאֱכֶלֶת וְלֹא לְרַבּוֹת בְּנִשְׂרֶפֶת.

But both are rabbinical[109]! It is better to increase the one to be eaten, not the one to be burned.

109 This now refers to the *ḥallah* of Syria outside the Promised Land. Since both *ḥallot* are rabbinical, why is one subject to a minimum amount but not the other.

הלכה י: אוף רִבִּי יוֹסֵה[110] מוֹדֶה בָהּ חוֹמֶר הוּא בְּדָבָר שֶׁהַטּוּמְאָה יוֹצְאָה מִגּוּפוֹ.

Halakhah 10: Even Rebbi Yose[111] agrees; it is more severe if impurity stems from someone's body.

110 Reading of the Rome ms., confirming the conjecture of most commentators. Leyden and Venice: 'ר יודה.

111 In Mishnah 8, he states that purely rabbinic *ḥallah* does not need purification of the Cohen by immersion. He agrees with the anonymous Mishnah 9 that persons whose impurity is caused by their bodies are excluded from eating even rabbinic *ḥallah*.

הוֹרֵי רִבִּי אַבָּהוּ בְּבוֹצְרָה שֶׁהִיא צְרִיכָה רוֹב. אָמַר רִבִּי יוֹנָה מְלַמֵּד שֶׁהִיא עוֹלָה בְּפָחוֹת מִמֵּאָה וְאֵינָהּ נֶאֱסֶרֶת בְּאֶחָד וּמֵאָה. אָמַר רִבִּי זְעִירָא מַתְנִיתָא אָמְרָה אֲפִילוּ בְּאֶחָד וְאֶחָד. דְּתַנִּינָן וְנֶאֱכֶלֶת עִם הַזָּר עַל הַשּׁוּלְחָן.

Rebbi Abbahu instructed in Bostra that it needs a plurality[112]. Rebbi Jonah said, it teaches that it is lifted by less than 100 and is not forbidden up to 101[113]. Rebbi Zeïra said, the Mishnah implies even one in one, as we have stated: "It may be eaten at one table with a layman[114]".

112 The *ḥallah* from territories never possessed by the tribes of Israel or the returnees from Babylonia, if mixed with profane food, does not create *dema'* if the profane is more than the *ḥallah*. This is accepted by the Babli for all heave of the Diaspora (*Bekhorot* 21a).

Bostra is a town in Syria just outside the domain settled by the returnees from Babylonia; cf. *Demay* 2, Note 8.

113 The rabbinic *ḥallah*, subject of Mishnah 9, does not follow the rules of heave explained in *Terumot* 9. He is not specific about the amounts needed to annul the rabbinic *ḥallah*.

114 He disagrees with both R. Abbahu and R. Jonah and holds that foreign *ḥallah* never creates *dema'* since mixing the *ḥallah* with profane food cannot usually be avoided if both are on the same table.

The name tradition is confirmed by all written sources but it seems to be impossible. Either "R. Jonah" is incorrect since R. Jonah was a student of R. Zeïra's student R. Jeremiah and R. Zeïra cannot conduct a polemic against his opinion, or instead of "R. Zeïra" one has to read "R. Yose".

אָמַר רִבִּי יוֹחָנָן רַבּוֹתֵינוּ שֶׁבַּגּוֹלָה הָיוּ מַפְרִישִׁין תְּרוּמָה וּמַעְשְׂרוֹת עַד שֶׁבָּאוּ הָרוֹבִין וּבִטְּלוּ אוֹתָן. מָאן אִינּוּן הָרוֹבִין תַּרְגְּמוֹנַיָּא. רִבִּי זְעִירָא רַב יְהוּדָה בְּשֵׁם שְׁמוּאֵל חַלַּת חוּץ לָאָרֶץ וּתְרוּמַת חוּץ לָאָרֶץ אוֹכֵל וְאַחַר כָּךְ מַפְרִישׁ. רִבִּי בָּא בְּשֵׁם שְׁמוּאֵל לֹא חָשׁוּ אֶלָּא לִתְרוּמַת דָּגָן תִּירוֹשׁ וְיִצְהָר. רִבִּי הִילָא בְּשֵׁם שְׁמוּאֵל לֹא חָשׁוּ אֶלָּא לִתְרוּמָה בִּלְבָד. אֲבָל לִירָקוֹת אוֹ אֲפִילוּ לִתְרוּמָה גְדוֹלָה לֹא חָשׁוּ. כְּהָדָא (fol. 60b) דְּתַנֵּי אִיסִּי בֶּן עֲקַבְיָה אוֹמֵר מַעְשְׂרוֹת לִירָקוֹת מִדִּבְרֵיהֶן.

Rebbi Joḥanan said, our teachers in the Diaspora[115] used to separate heave and tithes until the youngsters came and dissuaded them. Who are the youngsters? The interpreters[116]. Rebbi Zeïra, Rav Jehudah in the name of Samuel: For *ḥallah* from outside the Land and heave from outside the Land one may eat before one separates[117]. Rebbi Abba in the name of Samuel: They only worried about heave of grain, cider, and oil. Rebbi Hila in the name of Samuel: They only worried about heave[118], but for vegetables they did not worry even about the Great Heave, as it was stated: Issi ben Aqabiah says that tithes for vegetables are rabbinical[119].

115 In Babylonia.

116 Those who explain difficult passages. Their identity is unknown. In *Gen. rabba* 51(12) a R. Hoshaia the Interpreter and in 65(6) a Ḥizqiahu the Interpreter are mentioned. The time of the first cannot be determined; the second must be later than R. Berekhiah of the last generation of Galilean Amoraïm. The Babli does not mention any change of practice.

117 One may eat from what in the Land would be *ṭevel* and declare the remainder as *ḥallah* or heave. This is quoted in the name of Samuel, as practice, by the Babli (*Beẓah* 9a,

Bekhorot 27a).

118 In Babylonia they only gave Great Heave for grain, wine, and olive oil, but no tithes. This is confirmed by the fact that tithes from outside the Land (including Transjordan and Syria) are never mentioned in either Talmud.

119 Even in the Land there is no biblical obligation for any produce other than grain, wine, and olive oil. Therefore, outside the Land there is no reason to observe heaves and tithes even as a remembrance of the Land.

תַּנֵּי חַלַּת הַגּוֹי בָּאָרֶץ וּתְרוּמַת הַגּוֹי בְּחוּץ לָאָרֶץ מוֹדִיעִין אוֹתוֹ שֶׁאֵינוֹ צָרִיךְ וְאוֹכֵל וְנִיתֶּנֶת לְכָל־כֹּהֵן בֵּין לְכֹהֵן חָבֵר בֵּין לְכֹהֵן עַם הָאָרֶץ.

It was stated[120]: "Concerning a Gentile's *ḥallah* in the Land and a Gentile's heave outside the Land, one informs him that it is unnecessary, he might eat it[121], and it may be given to any Cohen, be he Fellow or vulgar."

120 The Babylonian version (Tosephta 2:6, Babli *Menaḥot* 67a) reads: Concerning a Gentile's *ḥallah* in the Land and a Gentile's heave outside the Land, one informs him that he is not obligated, the *ḥallah* may be eaten by outsiders and the heave does not create *dema'*.

The Gentile is a "Friend of the Synagogue", as they are frequently mentioned as donors in Synagogue inscriptions in the Diaspora. Since R. Meïr holds that possession of real estate by a Gentile in the Land does not free his property from the duties of heave and tithes (even though this is not practice to be followed), a Gentile's heave in the Land is heave.

121 Since he dedicated it in error, the dedication is invalid and he may retract it. But if he insists on giving, it must be given to a Cohen. One must assume that in this case also, the heave is forbidden to a Cohen whose body is a source of impurity.

(fol. 59c) **משנה י:** אֵילוּ נוֹתְנִין לְכָל־כֹּהֵן הַחֲרָמִים וְהַבְּכוֹרוֹת וּפִדְיוֹן הַבֵּן וּפִדְיוֹן פֶּטֶר חֲמוֹר וְהַזְּרוֹעַ וְהַלְּחָיַיִם וְהַקֵּיבָה וְרֵאשִׁית הַגֵּז וְשֶׁמֶן שְׂרֵיפָה וְקָדְשֵׁי מִקְדָּשׁ וְהַבִּיכּוּרִים. רִבִּי יְהוּדָה אוֹסֵר בְּבִיכּוּרִים. כַּרְשִׁינֵי תְרוּמָה רִבִּי עֲקִיבָה מַתִּיר וַחֲכָמִים אוֹסְרִין.

Mishnah 10: The following may be given to any Cohen[122]: *ḥērem*-dedications[123], firstlings[124], the redemption money for a [firstborn] son[125], the redemption value of a firstling donkey[126], foreleg, jawbone, and first stomach[127], the first shearing[128], oil to burn[129], Temple sacrifices, and First Fruits[130]. Rebbi Jehudah forbids First Fruits[131]. Heave vetch[132] Rebbi Aqiba permits but the Sages forbid.

122 Irrespective of his level of observance and knowledge of the Law. Some of the prescribed gifts are given to priests serving in the Temple; there, they are under supervision and instruction. The other gifts are purely profane; they cannot be impaired by the impurity of the Cohen.

123 *Num.* 18:14. According to most sources, this special dedication is not for the upkeep of the Temple but for the Cohanim [*Sifra Behuqotay Pereq* 12(9), Babli *Sanhedrin* 88a, *Arakhin* 28a]. However, Babylonian practice follows the dissenting opinion (*Arakhin* 29a).

124 *Ex.* 13:1, *Num.* 18:15.

125 *Ex.* 13:1,13, *Num.* 3:47, 18:15.

126 *Ex.* 13:1,13.

127 *Deut.* 18:3.

128 *Deut.* 18:4.

129 Impure heave olive oil.

130 *Deut.* 26:1-11.

131 Since they have to follow rules of heave, Mishnah *Bikkurim* 2:1.

132 This is animal fodder except in times of famine.

(fol. 60b) **הלכה יא:** יֵשׁ מֵהֶן נוֹתְנִין לְאַנְשֵׁי מִשְׁמָר וְיֵשׁ מֵהֶן נוֹתְנִין לְכָל־כֹּהֵן. הַבְּכוֹרוֹת וְהַבִּיכּוּרִים לְאַנְשֵׁי מִשְׁמָר וּשְׁאָר כּוּלְּהוֹן לְכָל־כֹּהֵן. רִבִּי יִרְמְיָה בָּעָא קוֹמֵי רִבִּי זְעִירָא מְנַיִין שֶׁחוֹרָמִים[133] לְאַנְשֵׁי מִשְׁמָר. אָמַר לוֹ כִּשְׂדֵה הַחֵרֶם לַכֹּהֵן תִּהְיֶה אֲחוּזָּתוֹ. אֲחוּזָּה עַצְמָהּ מַהוּ שֶׁתְּהֵא לְאַנְשֵׁי מִשְׁמָר בְּגִין דִּכְתִיב

לַכֹּהֵן תִּהְיֶה אֲחוּזָּתוֹ. (אֲחוּזָּה עַצְמָהּ מַהוּ שֶׁתְּהֵא לְאַנְשֵׁי מִשְׁמָר.) וְהָכְתִיב וְנָתַן לַכֹּהֵן הַזְּרוֹעַ וְהַלְּחָיַיִם וְהַקֵּיבָה. מֵעַתָּה לְאַנְשֵׁי מִשְׁמָר. רִבִּי אָחָא רִבִּי אַבָּהוּ בְּשֵׁם רִבִּי יוֹחָנָן כָּל־חֵרֶם קֹדֶשׁ קָדָשִׁים הוּא לַיי. מַה קָדְשֵׁי קָדָשִׁים לְאַנְשֵׁי מִשְׁמָר אַף חֲרָמִים לְאַנְשֵׁי מִשְׁמָר.

Halakhah 11: Some of them[134] are given to the people of the watch[135]; some of them are given to any Cohen. Firstlings[136] and First Fruits[137] to the people of the watch; all others to any Cohen. Rebbi Jeremiah asked before Rebbi Zeïra, from where that *ḥērem*-dedications[123] are for the people of the watch? He said to him: (*Lev.* 27:21) "Like the *ḥērem*-dedicated field it shall become the property of the Cohen[138]." From where that the property itself should be given to the people of the watch? Because it is written "it shall become the property of the Cohen." (From where that *ḥērem*-dedications are for the people of the watch?)[139] But is it not written: (*Deut.* 18:3) "He shall give to the Cohen foreleg, jawbone, and first stomach," should it not be for the people of the watch[140]? Rebbi Aḥa, Rebbi Abbahu in the name of Rebbi Joḥanan: (*Lev.* 27:28) "Every *ḥērem*-dedication shall be most holy to the Eternal." Just as most holy sacrifices are for the people of the watch[141], so *ḥērem*-dedications are for the people of the watch!

133 Reading of the Rome ms. Leyden and Venice: הדמים "the money". The latter reading cannot be correct since redemption of special dedications would have to refer to movables which in the next paragraph are declared to be for any Cohen.

134 The items listed in the Mishnah.

135 The families of certified Cohanim, admitted to service in the Temple, were divided into 24 sections, each of which was the watch serving in the Temple for one week. Except for the High Priest, no Cohen had the right to officiate in the Temple except during holidays and the week assigned

to his watch.

136 Unblemished firstlings which are a sacrifice of which the owners receive no part. Blemished firstlings, unfit for sacrifice, may be given to any Cohen locally.

137 Have to be delivered to the Cohen in the Temple.

138 Since the chapter deals with transactions by the Temple treasurer, it follows that a specially dedicated field has to be given by the treasurer to the Cohen officiating in the Temple, i. e., to the watch of the week. The same argument in Babli *Sanhedrin* 88a, *Arakhin* 28a.

139 A dittography in both mss.; it must be an old error.

140 If "Cohen" in the first verse means "Cohen of the current watch" then in the second verse it should have the same meaning. But since *Deut*. 18:3 clearly speaks about profane slaughter, away from the Temple, the meaning of the word must include any Cohen.

The Babli (*Arakhin* 28b) disagrees and compares "Cohen" in this verse, about which it is written (v. 16) " If . . . a man declares holy for the Eternal" to the Cohen mentioned in the law about the repentant offender in case the person he injured or defrauded has died heirless, where it is written: (*Num*. 5:6) "The money must be returned to the Eternal for the Cohen". The latter money is distributed among the people of the current watch.

141 All most holy sacrifices are either totally burned or eaten by Cohanim only.

מֵעַתָּה אַף הַמִּיטַלְטְלִין. דְּתַנֵּי מַה בֵּין הַקַּרְקָעוֹת לַמִּטַלְטְלִין. אֶלָּא שֶׁהַקַּרְקָעוֹת לְאַנְשֵׁי מִשְׁמָר וְהַמִּטַלְטְלִין לְכָל־כֹּהֵן. רִבִּי יוֹסֵי בֵּי רִבִּי בּוּן רִבִּי חִיָּיה בְּשֵׁם רַב שֵׁשֶׁת אִשֵּׁי יי וְנַחֲלָתוֹ יֹאכֵלוּן. מַה אִישִּׁים לְאַנְשֵׁי מִשְׁמָר אַף נַחֲלָה לְאַנְשֵׁי מִשְׁמָר.

If this is the case, also movables[142]? As we have stated: What is the difference between real estate and movables[143]? Only that real estate is given to the people of the watch but movables to any Cohen. Rebbi Yose ben Rebbi Abun, Rebbi Ḥiyya in the name of Rav Sheshet: (*Deut*. 18:1) "The gifts[144] to the Eternal and His inheritance[145] they shall eat." Since the gifts are for the people of the watch, so is the inheritance.

142 The argument based on *Lev.* 27:28 cannot be true because *ḥerem*-dedicated movables may be given to any Cohen but are also called "most holy" in the verse.

143 Referring to *ḥerem*-dedications.

144 Sacrifices.

145 The term נחלה is used only for real estate; usually only for what was given the family under Joshua.

עֶשְׂרִים וְאַרְבָּעָה מַתָּנוֹת נִיתְּנוּ לְאַהֲרוֹן וּלְבָנָיו. עֶשֶׂר בַּמִּקְדָּשׁ. אַרְבַּע בִּירוּשָׁלֵם. עֶשֶׂר בִּגְבוּלִין. אֵילּוּ הֵן שֶׁבַּמִּקְדָּשׁ חַטָּאת וְאָשָׁם וְזִבְחֵי שַׁלְמֵי צִיבּוּר וְחַטָּאת הָעוֹף וְאָשָׁם תָּלוּי וְלוֹג שֶׁמֶן שֶׁלִּמְצוֹרָע שְׁתֵּי הַלֶּחֶם וְלֶחֶם הַפָּנִים וּשְׁיֵרֵי מְנָחוֹת וְהָעוֹמֶר. וְאֵילּוּ הֵן שֶׁבִּירוּשָׁלֵם הַבְּכוֹרוֹת וְהַבִּיכּוּרִים וְהַמּוּרָם מִן הַתּוֹדָה וּמֵאֵיל נָזִיר וְעוֹרוֹת הַמּוּקְדָּשִׁין. אֵילּוּ הֵן שֶׁבִּגְבוּלִין הַתְּרוּמָה וּתְרוּמַת מַעֲשֵׂר וְחַלָּה וְהַזְּרוֹעַ וְהַלְּחָיַיִם וְהַקֵּיבָה וְרֵאשִׁית הַגֵּז וְגֶזֶל הַגֵּר וּפִדְיוֹן הַבֵּן. וּפִדְיוֹן פֶּטֶר חֲמוֹר וַחֲרָמִים וּשְׂדֵה אֲחוּזָּה.

[146]24 gifts were given to Aaron and his sons, ten in the Temple, four in Jerusalem, and ten in the countryside. These are the ten in the Temple: Purification offering[147], reparation offering[148], public well-being offerings[149], purification offering of a bird[150], the reparation offering for suspected guilt[151], the *log* of oil of the skin-diseased[152], the two breads[153], the shew-bread[154], the remainders of cereal offerings[155], and the *'omer*[156]. These are in Jerusalem: Firstlings[157], First Fruits[158], what was lifted from thanksgiving sacrifices and from the *nazir*'s ram[159], and the skins of sacrifices[160]. These are in the countryside: Heave, Heave of the Tithe, *ḥallah*, foreleg, jawbone, and first stomach[127], the first shearing[161], robbery of the proselyte[162], redemption of the firstborn[163], redemption of the firstborn donkey[163], *ḥērem*-dedications, and fields of inheritance[164].

146 Tosephta *Ḥallah* 2:7-9, Babli *Baba Qama* 110b, *Ḥulin* 132b, *Sifry Qoraḥ* #119 ("12 in the Temple, 12 in the countryside"), *Midrash Tanḥuma Bemidbar* 24, *Num. rabba* 5(1).

147 *Lev.* 6:19.

148 *Lev.* 7:7.

149 *Lev.* 23:19. Even though this sacrifice is labelled "well-being offering", being a public offering it is treated as most holy and must be eaten by Cohanim in the Temple precinct.

150 While there is no separate verse commanding that the purification offering of a bird must be eaten, since the burnt offering of a bird is consumed on the altar it follows that the purification offering must be eaten.

151 *Lev* 5:17-18.

152 *Lev* 14:10,21. The unused part of the oil becomes property of the Cohen.

153 *Lev.* 23:17.

154 *Lev.* 24:9.

155 *Lev.* 2:3, 6:9-11.

156 *Lev.* 23:10-11.

157 While these are sacrifices, after the blood was sprinkled on the altar wall the animal was eaten by the Cohen and his family anywhere in the city.

158 Cf. Mishnah *Bikkurim* 3:10.

159 In fact, any part lifted for the Cohen from any well-being sacrifice is for the Cohen and his entire family, to be eaten outside the Temple precinct. Cf. *Lev.* 7:34, *Num.* 18:11.

160 Only of most holy sacrifices (burnt, purification, and reparation offerings); *Lev.* 7:8.

161 *Deut.* 18:4.

162 *Num.* 5:8. It is assumed that the only person without legal heirs is the proselyte who had no children after his conversion.

163 *Ex.* 13.

164 Dedicated and not redeemed; *Lev.* 27:16-21.

רִבִּי יוּדָה אוֹסֵר בְּבִיכּוּרִים. רִבִּי יוּדָה כְדַעְתֵּיהּ דּוּ רִבִּי יוּדָה אָמַר אֵין נוֹתְנִין אוֹתָן אֶלָּא לְחָבֵר בְּטוֹבָה.

"Rebbi Jehudah forbids First Fruits." Rebbi Jehudah follows his own opinion since[165] "Rebbi Jehudah says, one gives them only to a fellow for goodwill."

165 Mishnah *Bikkurim* 3:12. The anonymous majority requires them to be given to the people of the watch who have to eat them under the rules of simple sacrifices.

אָמַר רִבִּי יוֹנָה רִבִּי עֲקִיבָה כְדַעְתֵּיהּ דוּ רִבִּי עֲקִיבָה אָמַר כָּל־מַעֲשֵׂיהֶן בְּטוּמְאָה. אָמַר רִבִּי יוֹסֵי אֲפִילוּ תֵימָא מִחְלְפָא שִׁיטָּתֵיהּ שַׁנְייָה הִיא שֶׁאֵין אָדָם מָצוּי לְטַמֵּא אוֹכְלֵי בְהֶמְתּוֹ.

Rebbi Jonah said, Rebbi Aqiba[166] follows his own opinion since "Rebbi Aqiba says, all its processing is done in impurity"[167]. Rebbi Yose said, even if you say that he changed his method; there is a difference because a person usually does not make his animal's fodder impure[168].

166 In the Mishnah.

167 Mishnah *Ma'aser Šeni* 2:4.

168 Even if he agrees with the House of Hillel that Second Tithe vetch (in a famine) must be cooked in purity, he holds that vetch in a regular year is only animal fodder, is never soaked, never prepared for impurity, and may be handled by any impure person without consequences.

מִפְּנֵי מָה לֹא גָֽזְרוּ עַל הַבִּקְיָיה. בְּמִנְעֲלֵיהֶן יָצָאת עִמָּהֶן מֵאַלֶכְסַנְדְּרִיאָה. אֵימָתַי גָּֽזְרוּ עַל הַכַּרְשִׁינִין. רִבִּי יוֹסֵי אוֹמֵר בִּימֵי רְעָבוֹן. רִבִּי חֲנַנְיָה בְּשֵׁם רִבִּי בִּימֵי דָוִד. אָֽמְרִין הִיא הָדָא הִיא הָדָא.

Why did they not decree about *vicia*[169]? On their shoes it came out with them from Alexandria[170]. When did they decree about black vetch[171]? Rebbi Yose says, in a famine; Rebbi Ḥananiah in the name of Rebbi: In David's time. They said, both are the same.

169 Why was vetch not included originally in the duty to give heave and tithes from vegetables (cf. *Ma'serot* 5, Note 136)?

170 In Egypt it is simply a weed.

171 Which is a kind of *vicia*; cf. H. L. Fleischer in Levy's Dictionary, vol. 2, p. 458b.

(fol. 59d) **משנה יא:** נִתַּיי אִישׁ תְּקוֹעַ הֵבִיא חַלּוֹת מִבֵּייְתוּר וְלֹא קִיבְּלוּ מִמֶּנּוּ. אַנְשֵׁי אֲלֶכְסַנְדְּרִיאָה הֵבִיאוּ חַלּוֹתֵיהֶן מֵאֲלֶכְסַנְדְּרִיאָה וְלֹא קִיבְּלוּ מֵהֶן. אַנְשֵׁי הַר צְבוֹעִים הֵבִיאוּ בִּיכּוּרֵיהֶם קוֹדֶם לָעֲצֶרֶת וְלֹא קִיבְּלוּ מֵהֶן. מִפְּנֵי הַכָּתוּב שֶׁבַּתּוֹרָה וְחַג הַקָּצִיר בִּיכּוּרֵי מַעֲשֶׂיךָ אֲשֶׁר תִּזְרַע בַּשָּׂדֶה.

Mishnah 11: Nittai from Tekoa brought *ḥallot* from Baithur[172] but they did not accept from him[173]. The people of Alexandria brought their *ḥallot* from Alexandria but they did not accept from them[174]. The people from Hyena Mountain[175] brought their First Fruits before Pentecost but they did not accept from them because of the verse in the Torah: (Ex. 23:16) "The pilgrimage holiday of harvest[176], the First Fruits of your work from sowing the field."

172 This place has not been convincingly identified. Possibly it is the place of origin of the family Ben Bathyra, the leading rabbinical authorities in the region of Nisibis on the upper Tigris during the centuries of the Mishnaic period.

173 Since it is impure by coming from outside the Land, the rabbinic authorities of the day forbade any Cohen to accept it.

174 Probably near the place צבעים (*Neh*. 11:34, *1S*. 13:18), West of Jerusalem.

175 Pentecost.

משנה יב: בֶּן אֲטִיטַס הֶעֱלָה בְּכוֹרוֹת מִבָּבֶל וְלֹא קִבְּלוּ מִמֶּנּוּ. יוֹסֵף הַכֹּהֵן הֵבִיא בִּיכּוּרָיו יַיִן וְשֶׁמֶן וְלֹא קִבְּלוּ מִמֶּנּוּ. אַף הוּא הֶעֱלָה אֶת בָּנָיו וְאֶת בְּנֵי בֵיתוֹ לַעֲשׂוֹת פֶּסַח קָטָן בִּירוּשָׁלֵם וְהֶחֱזִירוּהוּ שֶׁלֹּא יִקְבַּע הַדָּבָר לְדוֹרוֹת. אֲרִסְטוֹן הֵבִיא בִּיכּוּרָיו מֵאַפָּמְיָא וְקִבְּלוּ מִמֶּנּוּ. מִפְּנֵי שֶׁאָמְרוּ הַקּוֹנֶה בְסוּרְיָא כְקוֹנֶה בְּפַרְוָר יְרוּשָׁלֵם.

Mishnah 12: Ben-Atitas[176] brought firstlings from Babylonia and they did not accept them[177]. Joseph the Cohen[178] brought his First Fruits as wine and oil and they did not accept them. He also brought his children and members of his household[179] to make the second Passover in Jerusalem but they turned him back so as not to create a precedent for the future. Ariston brought his First Fruits from Apamea and they accepted them for they said, he who buys in Syria is like him who buys in the suburbs of Jerusalem[180].

176 In the quote Babli *Temura* 21a Ben Antigonos (Venice print), Ben Eutitas (Responsa R. Salomon ben Adrat vol. 1, #331).

177 In the Temple, since firstlings can only be brought from places from which heave and tithes are obligatory [*Sifry* on *Deut.* 14:23 (#106); Babli *Bekhorot* 53a].

178 A Tanna of the Temple period, mentioned in Mishnah *Miqwa'ot* 10:1 and several *baraitot* in the Babli.

179 Women, slaves, and minor children who are exempt from bringing the *Pesaḥ* sacrifice on the 14th of Iyar if they were unable to bring it on the 14th of Nisan, since it is a positive obligation due at a fixed time. It seems that Joseph the Cohen was sufficiently known for the Temple authorities to be afraid that his example would be imitated and in the end create a baseless obligation.

180 Cf. Mishnah *Demay* 6:11.

(fol. 60b) **הלכה יב**: תַּנֵּי רִבִּי חִייָה גָּֽזְרוּ עֲלֵיהֶן וְהֶחֱזִירוּם לִמְקוֹמָן. אָמַר רִבִּי בָּא בַּר זַבְדָּא אֵיפְשַׁר לְאוֹכְלָהּ אֵין אַתְּ יָכוֹל שֶׁלֹּא יֹאמְרוּ רָאִינוּ תְּרוּמָה טְמֵאָה שֶׁנֶּאֱכֶלֶת. לְשׂוֹרְפָהּ אֵין אַתְּ יָכוֹל שֶׁלֹּא יְהוּ אוֹמְרִים רָאִינוּ תְּרוּמָה טְהוֹרָה נִשְׂרֶפֶת. לְהַחֲזִירָהּ לִמְקוֹמָהּ אֵין אַתְּ יָכוֹל שֶׁלֹּא יְהוּ אוֹמְרִים רָאִינוּ תְּרוּמָה יוֹצֵא מִן הָאָרֶץ לְחוּץ לָאָרֶץ. הָא כֵיצַד מַנִּיחָהּ עַד עֶרֶב פֶּסַח[181] וְשׂוֹרְפָהּ.

Halakhah 12: Rebbi Ḥiyya[182] stated: They decided about these and turned them back to their places of origin. Rebbi Abba bar Zavda said, this is impossible. One may not eat it lest people say we saw impure heave being eaten. One may not burn it lest people say we saw pure heave[183] being burned. One may not return it to its place of origin lest people say we saw heave being exported from the Land. What to do? He lets it lie until Passover eve[184] and burns it.

181 Reading of the Rome ms. Leyden and Venice: הפסח, a text correct by biblical but not rabbinical usage.

182 This is R. Ḥiyya the elder. The discussion is about the foreign *ḥallah* which was rejected by the authorities advising the Cohanim.

183 While the heave/*ḥallah* is impure as foreign produce, it did not become impure in the Land and people will not know that it was imported.

184 When all leavened matter, including heave, must be burned. Nobody will notice the special status of this *ḥallah*.

אָמַר רַבָּן שִׁמְעוֹן בֶּן גַּמְלִיאֵל אֲנִי רָאִיתִי אֶת שִׁמְעוֹן בֶּן כַּהֲנָא שׁוֹתֶה יַיִן שֶׁלִּתְרוּמָה בְּעַכּוֹ שֶׁאָמַר זֶה הוּבָא מִקִּילִיקְיָה וְגָזְרוּ עָלָיו וּשְׁתָייו בִּסְפִינָה. וְאֵין בְּנֵי אָדָם טוֹעִין לוֹמַר שֶׁמְּבִיאִין תְּרוּמָה מֵחוּצָה לָאָרֶץ לָאָרֶץ. נֹאמַר לֹא יָרַד לְעַכּוֹ אֵיכָן שְׁתָייוֹ מִן הַחוּט וּלְחוּץ מִן הַחוּט וְלִפְנִים נֹאמַר מִן הַחוּט וּלְחוּץ. אָמַר רִבִּי יוֹנָה אֲפִילוּ תֵימַר מִן הַחוּט וְלִפְנִים לֹא חָשׁוּ לְמַרְאִית הָעַיִן בִּסְפִינָה.

Rabban Simeon ben Gamliel said, I saw Simeon ben Cahana drinking heave wine in Acco[185]. When he said, this was brought from Cilicia, they decided about him and he drank it on a ship. Would not people say that one imports heave from outside into the Land? Let us say, he did not go into Acco[186]. Where did he drink it? Outside the string[187] or inside? Let us say, outside the string[188]. Rebbi Jonah said, even if you say inside the string, they did not worry about bad appearances on a ship.

185 This in itself is problematic since part of Acco belongs to the Land, part to Syria (cf. *Ševi'it* 6:1, Note 30).

186 Since "they decided", the rabbinical authorities of Acco must have been asked about the situation. It is reasonable to assume that the question was asked before the wine

was unloaded.

187 The imaginary line defining the territorial waters of the Land; cf. above, Note 99.

188 This is unlikely since the ship would have had to leave port and go far out to sea.

אֵימָתַי הָיָה שִׁמְעוֹן בֶּן כַּהֲנָא בִּימֵי רִבִּי לְעֶזֶר. רִבִּי שִׁמְעוֹן בַּר כַּהֲנָא הֲוָה מְסַמֵּךְ לְרִבִּי לִיעֶזֶר עֲבְרוּן עַל חַד סְיָיג. אֲמַר לֵיהּ אַייְתִי חַד קִיסָּם נֵיחֲצֵי שִׁינַּיי. חֲזַר וְאָמַר לֹא תֵּיתֵי לִי כְּלוּם אֲמַר דְּאִין אָתֵי כָּל־בַּר נַשׁ וּבַר נַשׁ מֵיעֲבַד כֵּן הֲוָה אָזִיל סְיָיגָא דְּגוּבְרָא. רִבִּי חַגַּיי הֲוָה מְסַמֵּךְ לְרִבִּי זְעִירָא עֲבַר חַד טָעִין חַד מוֹבָל דְּקִיסִּין. אֲמַר לֵיהּ אַייְתִי לִי חַד קִיסָּם נֵיחֲצֵי שִׁינַּיי. חֲזַר וְאָמַר לֵיהּ לֹא תֵּיתֵי לִי כְּלוּם דְּאִין אָתֵי כָּל־בַּר נַשׁ וּבַר נַשׁ מִתְעֲבֵד כֵּן הָא אָזְלָא מוֹבְלָא דְּגַבְרָא. רִבִּי זְעִירָה כָּשֵׁר כָּל־כָּךְ. אֶלָּא מִילִּין דְּיָצְרָן שָׁמַע לָן נַעַבְדִינָן.

When did Simeon ben Cahana live? In the days of Rebbi Eliezer. [189]Rebbi Simeon bar Cahana was supporting Rebbi Eliezer. They passed by a fence. He said to him, bring me a sliver as a toothpick. He changed his mind and told him, do not bring me anything; if everybody would do that, the fence of this man would be gone. Rebbi Ḥaggai was supporting Rebbi Zeïra. A person passed by who was carrying a load of chips. He said to him, bring me a chip as a toothpick. He changed his mind and told him, do not bring me anything; if everybody would do that, the load of this man would be gone. Is not Rebbi Zeïra particularly pious? No, he told us that we should observe the words of our Creator.

189 From *Demay* 3:2, Notes 52-56. Taking somebody else's property is not a crime as long as the value of the thing taken is less than the smallest coin in circulation.

אַנְשֵׁי אֲלֶכְסַנְדְּרִיאָה הֵבִיאוּ חַלּוֹתֵיהֶן מֵאֲלֶכְסַנְדְּרִיאָה וְלֹא קִיבְּלוּ מֵהֶן. אָמַר רִבִּי בָּא מָרִי וְלֹא רִבִּי חִייָה רוֹבָא הִיא עוֹד הוּא אִית לֵיהּ וְגָזְרוּ עֲלֵיהֶן וְהֶחֱזִירוּם.

"The people of Alexandria brought their *ḥallot* from Alexandria but they did not accept from them." Rebbi Abba Mari said, is that not also from Rebbi Ḥiyya the elder[190]? He holds that they decided about these and ordered them to be returned.

190 Does R. Ḥiyya (Note 182) simply state a ruling of the Sages of the day in the case of Nittai or does he express a generally valid halakhic statement?

אַנְשֵׁי הַר צְבוֹעִים הֵבִיאוּ בִּיכּוּרֵיהֶם קוֹדֶם לָעֲצֶרֶת וְלֹא קִיבְּלוּ מֵהֶן. תַּנִּינָן תַּמָּן אֵין מְבִיאִין בִּכּוּרִים מַשְׁקִין. רִבִּי הִילָא בְּשֵׁם רִבִּי לָעְזָר כֵּינִי מַתְנִיתָא אֵין עוֹשִׂין בִּכּוּרִים מַשְׁקִין אֲפִילוּ מִשֶּׁזָּכוּ בָהֶן בְּעָלִים. וְהָתַנֵּי דָּרַךְ בִּיכּוּרִים מַשְׁקֶה לַהֲבִיאָן מְנַיִין שֶׁיָּבִיא תַּלְמוּד לוֹמַר תָּבִיא. תִּיפְתָּר שֶׁלְּקָטָן מִשָּׁעָה הָרִאשׁוֹנָה עַל מְנָת כֵּן. וְכָאן לֹא לְקָטָן מִשָּׁעָה רִאשׁוֹנָה עַל מְנָת כֵּן.

"The people from Hyena Mountain brought their First Fruits before Pentecost but they did not accept from them." [191]There[192], we have stated: "One does not bring First Fruits as drinks." Rebbi Hila in the name of Rebbi Eleazar: So says the Mishnah, "one does not turn First Fruits into drinks" even after they became property of the owners. But did we not state: "If he pressed First Fruits as a drink in order to bring them, from where that he should bring them? The verse says (*Ex*. 23:19, 34:26), 'bring!'". That is, if he harvested them from the start for this purpose. But here, if he did not harvest them from the start for this purpose[193].

191 The discussion is not about the quote from the Mishnah but about Joseph the Cohen who brought his First Fruits as wine and oil.

192 *Terumot* 11:3. The text of the discussion is also from there, Notes 62-65. The Mishnah states: "One does not bring First Fruits as drinks except for grapes and olives." This text is implied in the discussion here.

193 But fruits other than grapes and olives may not be made into juice under any circumstances.

וְאַתְיָיא כְּמָאן דְּאָמַר פִּסְחָן שֶׁל נָשִׁים רְשׁוּת. תַּנֵּי הָאִשָּׁה עוֹשָׂה פֶּסַח הָרִאשׁוֹן לְעַצְמָהּ וְהַשֵּׁינִי טְפֵילָה לָאֲחֵרִים דִּבְרֵי רִבִּי מֵאִיר. רִבִּי יוֹסֵי אוֹמֵר הָאִשָּׁה עוֹשָׂה פֶּסַח שֵׁינִי לְעַצְמָהּ אֲפִילוּ בְשַׁבָּת וְאֵין צְרִיכָה לוֹמַר הָרִאשׁוֹן. רִבִּי שִׁמְעוֹן בֶּן אֶלְעָזָר אוֹמֵר הָאִשָּׁה עוֹשָׂה פֶּסַח רִאשׁוֹן טְפֵילָה לָאֲחֵרִים וְאֵינָהּ עוֹשָׂה פֶּסַח שֵׁינִי. מַה טַעֲמָה דְּרִבִּי מֵאִיר אִישׁ שֶׂה לְבֵית אָבוֹת. אִם רָצוּ שֶׂה לַבָּיִת. מַה טַעֲמָה דְּרִבִּי יוֹסֵי אִישׁ שֶׂה לְבֵית אָבוֹת כָּל־שֶׁכֵּן לַבָּיִת. מַה טַעֲמָה דְּרִבִּי שִׁמְעוֹן בֶּן אֶלְעָזָר אִישׁ וְלֹא אִשָּׁה. מַה מְקַיְּימִין רַבָּנִין אִישׁ. פְּרָט לְקָטָן. אָמַר רִבִּי יוֹנָה וַאֲפִילוּ לְמָאן דְּאָמַר חוֹבָה שַׁנְיָיא הִיא שֶׁהַדָּבָר מְסוּיָּים שֶׁמָּא יִקָּבַע הַדָּבָר חוֹבָה. לֹא כֵן סָבְרִינָן מֵימַר קוֹדֶם לִשְׁתֵּי חַלּוֹת לֹא יָבִיא אִם הֵבִיא כָּשֵׁר. שַׁנְיָיא הִיא שֶׁהַדָּבָר מְסוּיָּם שֶׁמָּא יִקָּבַע הַדָּבָר חוֹבָה. וְלֹא כֵן תַּנִּינָן אִם בָּאוּ תְמִימִין יִקְרָבוּ. שַׁנְיָיא הִיא שֶׁהַדָּבָר מְסוּיָּם שֶׁמָּא יִקָּבַע הַדָּבָר חוֹבָה.

Does it follow him who says the *Pesaḥ* of women is voluntary[194]? It was stated[195]: "A woman may make the First *Pesaḥ* by herself and the Second joining others[196], the words of Rebbi Meïr. Rebbi Yose says, a woman may make the Second *Pesaḥ* by herself, even on the Sabbath[197], and certainly the First. Rebbi Simeon ben Eleazar says, a woman may make the First *Pesaḥ* joining others but does not make the Second." What is the reason of Rebbi Meïr? (*Ex.* 12:3) "Every man a sheep for the family," if they want "a sheep for the house[198]." What is the reason of Rebbi Yose, "Every man a sheep for the family," *a fortiori* "a sheep for the house." What is the reason of Rebbi Simeon ben Eleazar? "Every man", not woman. How do the rabbis uphold "man"? A man, not a minor[199]. Rebbi Jonah said, even according to him who says it is an obligation, it is different here since the occasion was news, that it should not become an obligation[200]. Did we not hold[201]: "Before the Two Breads one should not bring but if somebody brought it is acceptable?" It is different here since the occasion was news, that it should not become an obligation. Did we not state[202]: "If they were without blemish they should be sacrificed"? It is different here since the occasion was news, that it should not become an obligation.

194 That they refused to let Joseph the Cohen bring the Second *Pesaḥ* for his entire family. The same discussion in *Pesaḥim* 8:1 (fol. 35d), *Qiddušin* 1:8 (fol. 61c); cf. Babli *Pesaḥim* 93a, *Mekhilta R. Ismael Ba* 3, *Mekhilta R. Simeon bar Iohai* p. 10.

195 Tosephta *Pesaḥim* 8:10. There, the opinion of R. Meïr is attributed to R. Jehudah.

196 Joining a group of men who are biblically obligated; cf. Note 177.

197 If the 14th of Iyar is a Sabbath, the sacrifice has precedence over the Sabbath.

198 Everywhere in rabbinic Hebrew, "house" of a family is the wife.

199 In the Tosephta (Note 195) the reason they turned back Joseph the Cohen was not that he brought his wife and children but his minor grandson. In that version, there is no place for disagreement or special situation.

200 If a renowned authority does something, everybody will rush to emulate him and in the next generation it will already be a common standard and acquire the status of "practice of the forefathers from time immemorial". Even R. Yose will agree that in such a situation one should not allow a public display of special devotion. The Babli *Pesaḥim* 93a quotes a Tosephta which includes women impure because of childbirth in the list of persons obligated to observe the Second *Pesaḥ*.

201 Mishnah *Menaḥot* 10:6, Babli *Menaḥot* 69a, speaking of First Fruits. There seems to be no reason why the people from Hyena Mountain should not be permitted to bring their first fruits early. The answer is, they would have been permitted had some of them come as individuals. But that the

people from an entire region should come publicly to do what is only tolerated is unacceptable.

202 Mishnah *Temurah* 3:5. Why should Ben-Atitas not be permitted to bring his firstlings?

אֲרִסְטוֹן הֵבִיא בִּיכּוּרָיו מֵאַפָּמֵיָא וְקִבְּלוּ מִמֶּנּוּ. תַּמָּן תַּנִּינָן אֵין מְבִיאִין תְּרוּמָה מֵחוּץ לָאָרֶץ לָאָרֶץ. וְיָבוֹאוּ בִּיכּוּרִין. אָמַר רִבִּי הוֹשַׁעְיָה בִּיכּוּרִים בְּאַחֲרָיוּת הַבְּעָלִים. תְּרוּמָה אֵינָהּ בְּאַחֲרָיוּת בְּעָלִים. אִם אָמַר אַתְּ כֵּן אַף הֵן מְרַדְּפִין לְאַחֲרֶיהָ לְשָׁם.

"Ariston brought his First Fruits from Apamea and they accepted them." There[203], we have stated: "One does not bring heave from outside the Land into the Land." Should they be brought as First Fruits? Rebbi Hoshaia said, First Fruits are the responsibility of the owners, heave is not the responsibility of the owners. If you would say so, they would run after it there[204].

203 *Ševi'it* 6:6. The discussion is there, Note 152.

204 Therefore, the rabbinic prohibition for heave from Syria is reasonable; there is no reason to prohibit First Fruits from Syria which must personally be delivered to the Temple.

Introduction to Tractate 'Orlah

The Tractate explains the verse *Lev.* 19:23: "When you come to the Land and plant any food tree, you shall treat its 'foreskin', namely its fruit, as foreskin; three years it shall be considered as foreskin by you; it shall not be eaten." Since plants have nothing that could be seen as foreskin, "foreskin" is taken here as symbol of anything that has to be removed for holiness. From this it is deduced in Halakhah 3:1 that the (budding) fruits of the first three years not only have to be discarded but that any use of of these fruits is forbidden. This makes the Tractate into a general source of the rules of forbidden usufruct.

The First Chapter deals with the definition of what is a food tree and what is counted as fruit, and also with the definitions of planting and replanting. The other Chapters detail the rules of many cases of forbidden usufruct and the circumstances under which minute amounts of substances may or may not be disregarded, in particular when such substances are chemically active or very valuable.

הנוטע לסייג פרק ראשון

(fol. 60c) **משנה א**: הַנּוֹטֵעַ לַסְּייָג וּלְקוֹרוֹת פָּטוּר מִן הָעָרְלָה. רִבִּי יוֹסֵי אָמַר אֲפִילוּ אָמַר הַפְּנִימִי לְמַאֲכָל וְהַחִיצוֹן לִסְייָג הַפְּנִימִי חַייָב וְהַחִיצוֹן פָּטוּר.

Mishnah 1: If somebody plants for fences or building logs he is exempt from *'orlah*. Rebbi Yose says, even if he says the inner part is for food, the outer part for a fence[1], the inner part is obligated but the outer is exempt.

1 A tree planted at the border between an orchard and the public domain. If he intends that the part facing the public domain should be integrated into a fence then the part facing the public is exempt from *'orlah* if he does not intend to harvest its yield in the future. But the inner part which will be harvested is obligated.

הלכה א: הַנּוֹטֵעַ לַסְּייָג וּלְקוֹרוֹת פָּטוּר כול'. כְּתִיב וּנְטַעְתֶּם כָּל־עֵץ מַאֲכָל. אֶת שֶׁהוּא לְמַאֲכָל חַייָב. לִסְייָג וּלְקוֹרוֹת וּלְעֵצִים פָּטוּר. מֵעַתָּה אוֹתוֹ שֶׁלְּמַאֲכָל אֲפִילוּ חִישֵּׁב עָלָיו לִסְייָג יְהֵא חַייָב. תַּלְמוּד לוֹמַר עֵץ מַאֲכָל.

Halakhah 1: "If somebody plants for fences or building logs he is exempt," etc. It is written (*Lev.* 19:23): "If you plant any food tree." What is for food is obligated; for fencing, logs, or wood it is exempt. Then the one for food even if he intended it as a fence should be obligated! The verse says, "a food tree[2]."

2 It says "a food tree", not "a fruit tree" as in the Creation story (*Gen.* 1:11-12); it must be intended for food; a fruit tree grown for its timber is exempt. A similar argument in *Sifra Qedošim Parsha* 3(2).

רִבִּי יוֹסֵי לָמַד[3] דָּבָר מִתְּחִילָּתוֹ. מִמַּשְׁמַע שֶׁנֶּאֱמַר שָׁלֹשׁ שָׁנִים יִהְיֶה לָכֶם עֲרֵילִים לֹא יֵאָכֵל. וְכִי אֵין יוֹדְעִין שֶׁבְּעֵץ מַאֲכָל הַכָּתוּב מְדַבֵּר מַה תַלְמוּד לוֹמַר וּנְטַעְתֶּם כָּל־עֵץ מַאֲכָל אֵת שֶׁהוּא לְמַאֲכָל חַיָּיב לְסִייָג וּלְקוֹרוֹת וּלְעֵצִים פָּטוּר. רִבִּי יוֹנָה לָמַד דָּבָר מִסּוֹפוֹ. מִמַּשְׁמַע שֶׁנֶּאֱמַר וּבַשָּׁנָה הַחֲמִישִׁית תֹּאכְלוּ אֶת פִּרְיוֹ לְהוֹסִיף לָכֶם תְּבוּאָתוֹ. וְכִי אֵין אָנוּ יוֹדְעִין שֶׁבְּעֵץ מַאֲכָל הַכָּתוּב מְדַבֵּר מַה תַּלְמוּד לוֹמַר וּנְטַעְתֶּם כָּל־עֵץ מַאֲכָל אֵת שֶׁהוּא לְמַאֲכָל חַיָּיב לְסִייָג וּלְקוֹרוֹת וּלְעֵצִים פָּטוּר.

Rebbi Yose understood the text from its beginning, from the meaning of what is said (*Lev.* 19:23): "Three years it shall be like ‘foreskin’ for you, it may not be eaten." Does this not imply that the verse speaks about a fruit tree? Why does the verse say: "If you plant any food tree"? What is for food is obligated, for fencing, logs, or wood is exempt. Rebbi Jonah understood the text from its end, from the meaning of what is said (*Lev.* 19:25): "In the fifth year you shall eat its fruit, to increase its yield for you." Does this not imply that the verse speaks about a fruit tree? Why does the verse say: "If you plant any food tree"? What is for food is obligated; for fencing, logs, or wood it is exempt.

3 Reading of the Rome ms. Leyden and Venice: ילמד. The Leyden text implies that one discusses the position of R. Yose the Tanna, "R. Yose might understand the text . . . " But the parallel with R. Jonah shows that *R. Yose* here is the late Amora, colleague of R. Jonah, and both discuss the position of R. Yose the Tanna in the Mishnah. This not only shows that the Rome version is correct but it strongly supports the position of Maimonides (in

his Code, *Ma'aser Šeni* 10:3, and the third version of his Commentary) that R. Yose in the Mishnah explains the rule and is not a lone dissenter.

תַּנֵּי רַבָּן שִׁמְעוֹן בֶּן גַּמְלִיאֵל אוֹמֵר בַּמֶּה דְבָרִים אֲמוּרִים בִּזְמַן שֶׁנָּטַע לְסִייָג וּלְקוֹרוֹת וּלְעֵצִים דָּבָר שֶׁהוּא רָאוּי לָהֶם. נָטַע דָּבָר שֶׁאֵינוֹ רָאוּי לָהֶן חַייָב. יְאוּת אָמַר רַבָּן שִׁמְעוֹן בֶּן גַּמְלִיאֵל. מַה טַעֲמוֹן דְּרַבָּנִין. אָמַר רִבִּי זְעִירָא בְּמִשְׁנֶה סֵדֶר נְטִיעָתָם לָעֵצִים בְּרוֹצֵף לְקוֹרוֹת בְּמַשְׁפֶּה לְסִייָג מְקוֹם הַסִּייָג מוֹכִיחַ עָלָיו.

It was stated[4]: "Rabban Simeon ben Gamliel says, when has this been said? If he planted for fencing, logs, or wood, kinds appropriate for that use. If he planted an inappropriate kind it is obligated." Rabban Simeon ben Gamliel said it correctly, what is the reason of the rabbis? Rebbi Zeïra said, if he changed the way it is usually planted[5]: For wood tightly together, for logs cutting off branches, for a fence the location of the fence proves it.

4 Tosephta 1, *Sifra Qedošim Parsha* 3(3).

5 For the majority, a tree bearing edible fruit is exempt only if from the start it is treated so that any passer-by will see that the tree is not intended as fruit tree. In this version, the restriction of the rabbis is rabbinic. For Rabban Simeon ben Gamliel it all depends on the planter's intention, an attitude rejected by R. Simeon ben Ioḥai in Mishnah *Ševi'it* 2:1.

The Rome ms. does not read במשנה; then R. Zeïra's is a straight declarative sentence: "The way it is usually planted: . . ." In this version, the rabbis eliminate the intention of the planter as a matter of biblical law.

תַּנֵּי בְשֵׁם רִבִּי מֵאִיר כָּל־הָאִילָנוֹת בָּאִין לְמַחֲשֶׁבֶת פְּטוֹר חוּץ מִן הַזַּיִת וּמִן הַתְּאֵינָה. רִבִּי מֵאִיר כְּדַעְתֵּיהּ דְּאָמַר כָּל־אִילָנוֹת אִילָן סְרָק חוּץ מִזַּיִת וּתְאֵינָה.

It was stated in the name of Rebbi Meïr: "All trees can be exempted by intention except olive and fig trees." Rebbi Meïr is consistent since he says[6] all trees are futile except olive and fig trees.

6 Mishnah *Kilaim* 6:6. He holds there that any "futile" fruit-bearing tree may be planted in a vineyard to support the spreading vines without infringing on the prohibition of mixing species in a vineyard.

תַּנֵּי בְשֵׁם רִבִּי שִׁמְעוֹן אֵין לָךְ בָּא לְמַחֲשֶׁבֶת פְּטוֹר אֶלָּא שְׁלֹשֶׁת הַמִּינִין בִּלְבַד רִימּוֹן וְשִׁקְמִים וּצְלָף. מַהוּ שֶׁיְּהוּ חַייָבִין בְּמַעֲשֵׂר. תַּפְלוּגְתָא דְרִבִּי בָּא בַּר מָמָל וּדְרִבִּי הִילָא. דְּאִיתפַּלְגוֹן הַמְשַׁמֵּר פֵּירוֹתָיו לָעֵצִים רִבִּי בָּא בַּר מָמָל אָמַר חַייָב. רִבִּי הִילָא בְשֵׁם רִבִּי יוֹסֵי אָמַר פָּטוּר. רִבִּי בָּא בַּר מָמָל אָמַר חַייָב. מִן הָדָא וּבָא הַלֵּוִי כִּי אֵין לוֹ חֵלֶק וְנַחֲלָה עִמָּךְ. מִמָּה שֶׁיֵּשׁ לָךְ וְאֵין לוֹ אַתְּ חַייָב לִיתֵּן לוֹ. יָצָא הֶבְקֵר שֶׁיָּדָךְ וְיָדוֹ שָׁוִין בּוֹ. הוּא לֶקֶט הִיא שִׁכְחָה הִיא פֵּיאָה הִיא הֶבְקֵר.

It was stated in the name of Rebbi Simeon: The only kinds admitting an intention of exemption are three: [buckthorn][7], sycamore, and caper bush. Are these obligated for tithes[7]? This is a dispute between Rebbi Abba bar Mamal and Rebbi Hila. They differed: If somebody kept his fruit trees for wood, Rebbi Abba bar Mamal said he is obligated, Rebbi Hila said he is exempted. Rebbi Abba bar Mamal said he is obligated, from the following[9]: (*Deut*. 14:29) "The Levite shall come, because he has neither part nor inheritance with you." You are obliged to give him from what you have but he has not[10]. This excludes abandoned property for which your and his hands are equal. Gleanings, forgotten sheaves, *peah*, and abandoned property are all equal.

7 Reading with R. S. Cirillo רימין for רימון, defined by Maimonides (*Demay* 1:1) by Arabic נַבק "buckthorn, lotus fruit." Pomegranate trees (רימון)

have valuable fruits and are not planted for their wood. Cf. *Demay* 1, Note 4.

8 Which parts of the caper bush may be subject to tithes is the object of Mishnah *Ma'serot* 4:6.

9 *Ma'serot* 1:1, Note 20.

10 Since the fruits of the tree destined to be cut down as fire wood remain private property, they are subject to tithes. The next two sentences are irrelevant here; they are just copied from the source in *Ma'serot*.

רִבִּי הִילָא בְשֵׁם רִבִּי יוֹסֵי אָמַר פָּטוּר מִן הָדָא כּוּסְבָּר שֶׁזְּרָעָהּ לְזֶרַע יַרְקָהּ פָּטוּר. שַׁנְיָיא הִיא כּוּסְבָּר שֶׁיֵּשׁ לוֹ גוֹרֶן אַחֶרֶת. וְהַיי דָא אָמַר דָּא הַמְקַיֵּים מְלֵיאָה שֶׁלְכְּרוּב לְזֶרַע בָּטְלָה דַעְתּוֹ קְלָחִין יְחִידִין לֹא בָטְלָה דַעְתּוֹ. אָמַר רִבִּי יוֹנָה וְהוּא שֶׁלִּיקֵּט יָרָק. אֲבָל לֹא לִקֵּט יָרָק כָּךְ אָנוּ אוֹמְרִים עֵצִים חַייָבִין בְּמַעְשְׂרוֹת.

Rebbi Hila in the name of Rebbi Yose said he is exempt, from the following[11]: "If coriander is sown for its seed, its greenery is free." Coriander is different since it has a different threshing floor[12]. But he says from the following[13]: "If someone keeps cabbage for seeds, his opinion is inoperative; for single stalks it is not inoperative." Rebbi Jonah said, only if he collected greens. But if he did not collect greens, do we say that wood is subject to tithes[14]?

11 Mishnah *Ma'serot* 4:5.

12 The seeds. Exempting the greenery is not exempting the entire plant.

13 *Ma'serot* 1:1, Notes 32-36. If somebody keeps an entire cabbage patch to grow seeds it does not exempt the patch from tithes even though the seeds are inedible.

14 Fruits from trees grown for their wood are subject to the laws of *'orlah* only if they are taken down. Since it is stated later that *'orlah* is forbidden for any use, declaring the fruits as wood makes them usable.

מַהוּ שֶׁיְּהוּ אֲסוּרִין מִשּׁוּם גֶּזֶל. וְכִי עֵצִים אֵינָן אֲסוּרִין מִשּׁוּם גֶּזֶל. מַה צְרִיכָה לֵיהּ כְּגוֹן אִילֵּין תּוּתַיָּא דְּלָא אִית בְּהוֹן מַמָּשׁ.

Are these forbidden because of robbery? Is wood not also forbidden because of robbery? What is his problem? For example, mulberry trees having no solidity[15].

15 If a mulberry tree visibly is grown for firewood (Note 5), is it permitted for strangers to take mulberries without paying for them since these cannot be used as firewood? The question is not answered. (Explanation of R. Eliahu Fulda.)

רִימּוֹן שֶׁנְּטָעוֹ לְשֵׁם רִימּוֹן. בְּנוֹת הֲדַס שֶׁנְּטָעָן לְשֵׁם בְּנוֹת הֲדַס. (fol. 60d) אִית תַּנָּיֵי תַנֵּי חַיָּיב. אִית תַּנָּיֵי תַנֵּי פָּטוּר. אָמַר רַב חִסְדָּא מָאן דְּאָמַר חַיָּיב בְּמָקוֹם שֶׁרוֹב מְשַׁמְּרִין. מָאן דְּאָמַר פָּטוּר בְּמָקוֹם שֶׁאֵין הָרוֹב מְשַׁמְּרִין. רִבִּי יוֹסֵי בָּעֵי אִם בְּמָקוֹם מְשַׁמְּרִין לָמָּה לִי חִישֵּׁב אֲפִילוּ לֹא חִישֵּׁב. כָּךְ אָנוּ אוֹמְרִים זַיִת וּתְאֵינָה עַד שֶׁיְּחַשּׁוֹב עֲלֵיהֶן. אֶלָּא אֲפִילוּ מֶחֱצָה מְשַׁמְּרִין וּמֶחֱצָה שֶׁאֵין מְשַׁמְּרִין. אָמַר רִבִּי מַתְיָא מִן דְּבַתְרָתָהּ מָקוֹם שֶׁאֵין רוֹב מְשַׁמְּרִין אֲפִילוּ לֹא חִישֵּׁב פָּטוּר.

A buckthorn[7] planted for buckthorn berries, a myrtle planted for myrtle berries[16], some Tannaïm stated: obligated, some Tannaïm stated: exempt. Rav Ḥisda said, he who said "obligated", at a place where most are guarded[17]; he who said "exempt", at a place where the majority do not guard. Rebbi Yose asked, if it is at a place where most do guard why does he have to think, even if he did not think! Are we saying: Olive trees and fig trees only if the thinks about them[18]? But even if one half do guard, one half do not guard[19]! Rebbi Matthew[20] understood this from the final statement: "At a place where the majority[21] do not guard" even if he did not think it is exempt.

16 These trees are not usually planted for their berries.

17 The rare places where the berries of these bushes are eaten and valuable.

18 Since these are always guarded and used for their fruit, nobody thinks that they are subject to *'orlah* only if expressly planted for their fruit. Therefore, at a place where myrtle berries customarily are used in food, the individual's intent should be irrelevant.

19 In that case, no preponderant use is established.

20 In the Rome ms.: R. Mattaniah.

21 "The majority do not" means "strictly more than one-half".

רִבִּי יוֹחָנָן בְּשֵׁם רִבִּי שִׁמְעוֹן בֶּן יוֹצָדָק גֶּפֶן שֶׁעָלַת בְּמָקוֹם חוֹרְשִׁין פְּטוּרָה מִן הֶעָרְלָה. אָמַר רִבִּי יוֹסֵי אֲפִילוּ נְטָעָהּ. וְהָתַנִּינָן הָעוֹלֶה מֵאֵילָיו חַייָב בְּעוֹרְלָה. תַּמָּן בְּשֶׁנְּטָעָן בְּמָקוֹם יִישּׁוּב. בְּרַם הָכָא שֶׁנְּטָעָהּ בְּמָקוֹם חוֹרְשִׁין. אָמַר רִבִּי לָעְזָר הָדָא דְתֵימַר בְּשֶׁאֵינָהּ עוֹשָׂה כְדֵי טְפֵילָתָהּ. אֲבָל אִם הָיְתָה עוֹשָׂה כְדֵי טְפֵילָתָהּ חַייֶבֶת.

Rebbi Johanan in the name of Rebbi Simeon ben Jozadaq: A vine growing in a copse is exempt from *'orlah*. Rebbi Yose said, even if he planted it. But did we not state: "If it grew by itself it is obligated for *'orlah*"? There, when it was planted in a cultivated place, but here if it was planted in a copse. Rebbi Eleazar said, this means if its yield is not worth its tending but if its yield is worth its tending it is obligated.

רַב חוּנָה שָׁאַל אֶתְרוֹג שֶׁנְּטָעוֹ לְמִצְוָותוֹ מַהוּ שֶׁיְּהֵא חַייָב בְּעָרְלָה. חָזַר רַב חוּנָה וְאָמַר אֶתְרוֹג שֶׁנְּטָעוֹ לְמִצְוָתוֹ חַייָב בְּעָרְלָה. וְלֹא כֵן תַּנִּינָן וּלְקַחְתֶּם לָכֶם וְלֹא מִן הַמִּצְוָה. תַּמָּן וּלְקַחְתֶּם לָכֶם בְּדָמִים לֹא מִן הַמִּצְוָה. בְּרַם הָכָא כְּמַה דְתֵימַר גַּבֵּי שׁוֹפָר יוֹם תְּרוּעָה יִהְיֶה לָכֶם מִכָּל־מָקוֹם. וְכָא שָׁלֹשׁ שָׁנִים יִהְיֶה לָכֶם עֲרֵילִים לֹא יֵאָכֵל מִכָּל־מָקוֹם. מַה בֵינוֹ לִמְשַׁמֵּר פֵּירוֹתָיו לְעֵצִים. כְּשֵׁם שֶׁהוּא רוֹצֶה בְּפִרְיוֹ כָּךְ הוּא רוֹצֶה בְּעֵצוֹ. בְּרַם הָכָא רוֹצֶה הוּא בְּפִרְיוֹ וְאֵין רוֹצֶה בְּעֵצוֹ. וְעוֹד מִן הָדָא דְּאָמַר רִבִּי חֲנִינָה פְּרִי אִם אוֹמֵר עֵצוֹ אֵין אָדָם יוֹצֵא בָהּ יְדֵי

חוֹבָתוֹ בְחָג. מַה דָמֵי לָהּ. זַיִת שֶׁנְּטָעוֹ לְהַדְלִיק בּוֹ בַחֲנוּכָּה. אָמַר רִבִּי יוֹסֵי בַּר בּוּן זֶה דְּבַר תּוֹרָה זֶה מִדִּבְרֵיהֶם וְאַתְּ אָמַר הָכֵין. מַה דָמֵי לָהּ. זַיִת שֶׁנְּטָעוֹ לְהַדְלִיק בּוֹ אֶת הַמְּנוֹרָה. זֶה דְּבַר תּוֹרָה וְזֶה דְּבַר תּוֹרָה.

Rav Ḥuna asked: If an *etrog* tree[22] was planted for its obligation, is it obligated for *'orlah*? Rav Ḥuna came back and said: An *etrog* tree planted for its obligation is obligated for *'orlah*. Did we not state there: (*Lev.* 23:40) "You shall buy for yourselves" and not from the obligation[23]? There, "you shall buy *for yourselves*" with money, not from the obligation. But here, as you say in the matter of *shofar*, (*Lev.* 23:24) "a day of blasts it shall be *for you*", from anywhere[24]. And here, (*Lev.* 19:23): "Three years it shall be like 'foreskin' *for you*, it may not be eaten," in any way. What is the difference between this[25] and him who guards his fruits to use as wood? He wants the tree itself just as he wants the fruits. But here, he wants the fruit and is not interested in the tree. In addition, as Rebbi Ḥanina said, (*Lev.* 23:40) "fruit"; if you say it is part of the tree nobody can acquit himself of his obligation on the holiday! What can be compared to it? An olive tree planted for light on Ḥanukkah. Rebbi Yose bar Abun said, one is biblical, the other rabbinic! And you say so? What can be compared to it? An olive tree planted to light the candelabrum[26]; then both are biblical.

22 The *etrog* is identified as the "fruit of the splendid tree" (*Lev.* 23:40) to be taken in procession on the holiday of Tabernacles. If *'orlah* did apply, then the fruits of the young tree would not be usable. The question presupposes that the *etrog* is edible, the fruit of *Citrus medica cedrata*, cf. *Ma'serot* 1, Note 86, but it is not intended to be eaten.

23 The "four kinds", *etrog*, palm fronds, myrtle, and willow twigs, should be acquired for the holiday, not taken from what is already obligated

for religious purposes; in the case of the *etrog* this refers to fruits of Second Tithe brought to Jerusalem for the holiday.

24 Since "religious obligations are not for usufruct", a *shofar* can be used for blowing even if it is forbidden for usufruct.

25 Using the *etrog* for Tabernacles instead as food.

26 An olive tree planted with the idea that its fruits should be used exclusively to produce oil for the candelabrum in the Temple. By the preceding argument, it is subject to the rules of *'orlah.*

רִבִּי שִׁמְעוֹן בֶּן יָקִים בָּעָא קוֹמֵי רִבִּי יוֹחָנָן נְטָעוֹ צַד הַתַּחְתּוֹן לְסִייָג וְהָעֶלְיוֹן לְמַאֲכָל. צַד הַתַּחְתּוֹן לְמַאֲכָל וְהָעֶלְיוֹן לְסִייָג. אָמַר לֵיהּ הִיא הָדָא הִיא הָדָא. הִיא צַד הַתַּחְתּוֹן לְסִייָג וְהָעֶלְיוֹן לְמַאֲכָל. הִיא צַד הָעֶלְיוֹן לְסִייָג וְהַתַּחְתּוֹן לְמַאֲכָל. כֵּיצַד הוּא יוֹדֵעַ. אָמַר רִבִּי יוֹנָה מֵבִיא זְמוֹרָה[27] וּמְסַיֵּים עַד כָּאן לְסִייָג מִכָּן וְאֵילָךְ לְמַאֲכָל.

Rebbi Simeon ben Yaqim asked before Rebbi Joḥanan: If he planted the lower part as fence but the upper part for food, or the lower part for food but the upper part as fence? He said to him, one is like the other, whether the upper part for food but the lower part as fence, or the lower part for food but the upper part as fence[27]. How does one know? He brings a string and ties it as a sign: So far as fence, the excess for food.

27 Reading of the Rome ms. Leyden (corrected) זמודה, Leyden uncorrected and Venice ומודה "and agrees".

28 The part destined as fence is exempt, the remainder obligated (Maimonides *Ma'aser Šeni* 10:4).

רִבִּי זְעִירָא בָּעֵי נִיחָא צַד הַתַּחְתּוֹן לְסִייָג וְהָעֶלְיוֹן לְמַאֲכָל. צַד הַתַּחְתּוֹן לְמַאֲכָל וְהָעֶלְיוֹן לְסִייָג גָּדֵל מִתּוֹךְ אִיסּוּר וְאַתְּ אָמַר הָכֵן. רִבִּי זְעִירָה כְּדַעְתֵּיהּ. דְּאָמַר רִבִּי זְעִירָא בְּשֵׁם רִבִּי יוֹנָתָן בְּבָצָל שֶׁלְּכִלְאֵי הַכֶּרֶם שֶׁעֲקָרוֹ וּשְׁתָלוֹ אֲפִילוּ מוֹסִיף כַּמָּה אָסוּר שֶׁאֵין גִּידּוּלֵי אִיסּוּר מַעֲלִין אֶת הָאִיסּוּר.

Rebbi Zeïra asked: One understands if the lower part is for a fence but the upper part for food, but the lower part for food but the upper part as fence? It grows out of something forbidden and you say so? Rebbi Zeïra follows his own opinion[29], as Rebbi Zeira said in the name of Rebbi Jonathan: An onion from *kilaim* in a vineyard which he removed from the soil and planted anew is forbidden even if it increases manifold, since growth of what is forbidden can never justify forbidden produce.

29 *Kilaim* 5:7, Note 76.

נְטָעוֹ לְסִייָג וְחִישֵׁב עָלָיו לְמַאֲכָל בָּא בְמַחֲשָׁבָה. לְמַאֲכָל וְחִישֵׁב עָלָיו לְסִייָג לֹא כָּל־הֵימֵינוּ. נְטָעוֹ שָׁנָה רִאשׁוֹנָה לְסִייָג מִכָּאן וְאֵילָךְ חִישֵׁב עָלָיו לְמַאֲכָל מִכֵּיוָן שֶׁחִישֵׁב בָּהּ מַחֲשֶׁבֶת חִיּוּב יְהֵא חַייָב. וְהָתַנִּינָן רִבִּי יוֹסֵי אוֹמֵר אֲפִילוּ הַפְּנִימִי לְמַאֲכָל וְהַחִיצוֹן לְסִייָג הַפְּנִימִי חַייָב וְהַחִיצוֹן פָּטוּר. תַּמָּן לְמַאֲכָל לְמַאֲכָל לְעוֹלָם. לְסִייָג לְסִייָג לְעוֹלָם. בְּרַם הָכָא מִכֵּיוָן שֶׁעִירֵב בּוֹ מַחֲשֶׁבֶת חִיּוּב יְהֵא חַייָב.

If he planted as a fence and then thought to use it for food, it goes after his thought. [If he first thought to use it] for food and then thought to use it as a fence, his [intent] cannot be accepted[30]. If he planted as a fence the first year and afterwards thought to use it for food, since he thought to obligate it is obligated. But did we not state: "Rebbi Yose says, even if the inner part is for food, the outer part as fence, the inner part is obligated but the outer is exempt"? There, what is for food is always for food, for a fence always for a fence, but here, since he proceeded with a thought of obligation, it is obligated.

30 An obligation can be created by intent; it cannot be removed by intent.

נְטָעוֹ שָׁלֹשׁ שָׁנִים לְסִייָג מִיכָּן וָאֵילָךְ חִישֵּׁב עָלָיו לְמַאֲכָל וְהוֹסִיף תּוֹסַפְתּוֹ. רִבִּי יִרְמְיָה אָמַר הַתּוֹסֶפֶת פְּטוֹר. רִבִּי בָּא אָמַר הַתּוֹסֶפֶת חִיּוּב. אָמַר רִבִּי יוֹסֵי הָדָא דְרִבִּי יִרְמְיָה מִתְחַמְיָא קַשְׁיָא וְלֵית הִיא אֶלָּא נִיחָא. כְּהָדָא דְתַנֵּי שָׂדֶה שֶׁהֵבִיאָה שְׁלִישׁ לִפְנֵי גוֹי וּלְקָחָהּ יִשְׂרָאֵל רִבִּי עֲקִיבָה אוֹמֵר הַתּוֹסֶפֶת פְּטוֹר. וַחֲכָמִים אוֹמְרִים הַתּוֹסֶפֶת חִיּוּב. וְהָכָא עִיקָּרוֹ פְּטוֹר וְתוֹסַפְתּוֹ חִיּוּב.

If he planted as a fence for three years, afterwards thought to use it for food, and it grew more? Rebbi Jeremiah said the addition is exempt, Rebbi Abba said the addition is obligated. Rebbi Yose said, the opinion of Rebbi Jeremiah seems to be difficult but it is only reasonable, as we have stated[31]: "If a field became one-third ripe in the possession of a Gentile and a Jew bought it, Rebbi Aqiba says the addition is exempt. But the Sages say, the addition is obligated." In our case the stem is exempt and its addition should be obligated[32]?

31 *Ma'serot* 5:4, Note 66. It seems that R. Jeremiah follows R. Aqiba in holding that any branches grown after the first three years are exempt from *'orlah*.

32 This is R. Yose's argument that R. Jeremiah's position is reasonable: Grain one-third grown is only potentially subject to tithes, after harvesting and processing. Since usually grain is not harvested one-third grown, any additional growth after one-third is normally subject to tithes. But after three years, the stem of a tree has totally outgrown any obligation of *'orlah*.

אָמַר רִבִּי יוֹחָנָן דִּבְרֵי רִבִּי יִשְׁמָעֵאל כָּל־שֶׁאֵין לוֹ עָרְלָה אֵין לוֹ רְבָעִי. רִבִּי יוֹחָנָן בָּעֵי עַד שֶׁיְּהֵא לוֹ שָׁלֹשׁ שָׁנִים עָרְלָה. אָמַר רִבִּי יוֹנָה עִיקַּר עָרְלָה צְרִיכָה לֵיהּ וְאֵין עִיקַּר עָרְלָה פָּחוֹת מִשָּׁלֹשׁ שָׁנִים. אָמַר רִבִּי יוֹסֵי עִיקַּר רְבָעִי צְרִיכָה לֵיהּ כָּל־שֶׁאֵין לוֹ שָׁלֹשׁ שָׁנִים אֵין לוֹ עָרְלָה אֵין לוֹ רְבָעִי[33].

Rebbi Joḥanan said, the words of Rebbi Ismael: Anything not subject to *'orlah* is not subject to the fourth year[34]. Rebbi Joḥanan asked: Until it was subject to *'orlah* for three years? Rebbi Jonah said, he asked about the principle of *'orlah* and no principle of *'orlah* is less than three years[35]. Rebbi Yose said, he asked about the principle of the fourth year; anything not having three years is not subject to *'orlah* and not subject to the fourth year[36].

33 The text given here is that of the Rome ms. The text of the first hand of the Leyden ms. is almost identical: אָמַר רִבִּי יוֹנָה עִיקַּר עָרְלָה צְרִיכָה לֵיהּ וְאֵין עִיקַּר עָרְלָה פָּחוֹת מִשָּׁלֹשׁ שָׁנִים. אָמַר רִבִּי יוֹסֵי עִיקַּר רְבָעִי צְרִיכָה לֵיהּ כָּל־שֶׁאֵין לוֹ שָׁנִים אֵין לוֹ עָרְלָה אֵין לוֹ רְבָעִי ; the text of the first corrector is אָמַר רִבִּי יוֹנָה עִיקַּר עָרְלָה צְרִיכָה לֵיהּ וְאֵין עִיקַּר עָרְלָה פָּחוֹת שָׁנִים. אָמַר רִבִּי יוֹסֵי עִיקַּר רְבָעִי צְרִיכָה לֵיהּ כָּל־שֶׁאֵין לוֹ עָרְלָה אֵין לוֹ רְבָעִי . It seems clear that the corrector could not understand the text because of the missing שלש in the last sentence; his correction can be disregarded.

34 The year following the three years of *'orlah* when (*Lev.* 19:24) "in the fourth year all its fruit shall be holy for praises of the Eternal."

35 According to R. Jonah, no period of *'orlah* less than three years can induce the holiness of the fourth year fruits.

36 According to him, any period of *'orlah* which ends at the end of the third year after planting induces the holiness of the fourth year fruits; no plant not surviving a full three years can be subject to *'orlah*.

תַּנֵּי אִילָן שֶׁמִּקְצָתוֹ נָטוּעַ בָּאָרֶץ וּמִקְצָתוֹ חוּץ לָאָרֶץ מִכֵּיוָן שֶׁמִּקְצָתוֹ נָטוּעַ בָּאָרֶץ כִּילּוּ כּוּלּוֹ בָּאָרֶץ דִּבְרֵי רִבִּי. רַבָּן שִׁמְעוֹן בֶּן גַּמְלִיאֵל אוֹמֵר צַד הַנָּטוּעַ בָּאָרֶץ חַיָּיב צַד[37] הַנָּטוּעַ חוּץ לָאָרֶץ פָּטוּר. רִבִּי אַבָּהוּ בְּשֵׁם רִבִּי יוֹחָנָן נַעֲשָׂה כְּטֶבֶל וְכִמְעוּשָּׂר מְעוּרָבִין מִזֶּה עַל זֶה.

It was stated[38]: "If a tree is partially planted in the Land and partially outside the Land, since it is partially planted in the Land it is as if completely planted in the Land, the words of Rebbi. Rabban Simeon ben Gamliel says, the part planted in the Land is obligated, the part planted outside the Land is free." Rebbi Abbahu in the name of Rebbi Joḥanan: It is as if *ṭevel* and tithed are mixed together[39].

37 Reading of the Rome ms., word missing in the Leyden ms.

38 Tosephta *Ma'serot* 2:22. A different text in the Babli (*Giṭṭin* 22a, *Baba Batra* 27b; also *Nedarim* 59b) attributes to Rebbi the statement here of R. Joḥanan. "Outside the Land" excludes Syria, cf. Mishnah 3:9.

39 This implies that, for Rebbi, fruits from this tree cannot be used as heave and tithe for other trees, neither can any fruit from this tree be freed from the obligation of heave and tithes by anything but other fruits from the same tree. The reason is that each fruit is both obligated and not obligated; taking from another tree would be potentially tithing from what is obligated for what is not obligated.

רִבִּי זְעִירָא בְּשֵׁם רִבִּי יוֹחָנָן שׁוֹרֶשׁ פָּטוּר פּוֹטֵר. מַה כְרִבִּי דְּרִבִּי אָמַר שׁוֹרָשִׁין חַיִין זֶה מִזֶּה. דִּבְרֵי הַכֹּל הִיא. הָכָא שׁוֹרֶשׁ פָּטוּר פּוֹטֵר. הֵן דְּתֵימַר שׁוֹרֶשׁ פָּטוּר פּוֹטֵר בְּשׁוֹרֶשׁ יָשָׁן שֶׁהִשְׁרִישׁ מִתּוֹךְ שֶׁלּוֹ לְתוֹךְ שֶׁל חֲבֵירוֹ אֲבָל אִם הִשְׁרִישׁ מֵחוּץ לָאָרֶץ בָּאָרֶץ לֹא בְדָא.

Rebbi Zeïra in the name of Rebbi Joḥanan: An exempt root exempts. Is that following Rebbi who said roots live off one another? It is the opinion of everybody. Here, an exempt root exempts. When you say that an exempt root exempts, [you deal with] an old root that expanded from its own ground to that of another's[40]; but if it extended from outside the Land into the Land it[41] does not apply.

40 If an older fruit tree develops a new stem from an old root, the new stem is exempt from the rules of *'orlah* since it is considered a branch of the old tree. This is important for "sinking" branches (*Kilaim* 7:1, Note 1).

41 The previous argument. An "exempt root" is not one exempt from the start but one that has outgrown its *'orlah* status.

שׁוֹרֶשׁ פָּטוּר פּוֹטֵר. וְהָתַנִּינָן רִבִּי יוֹסֵי אוֹמֵר אֲפִילוּ הַפְּנִימִי לְמַאֲכָל וְהַחִיצוֹן לְסִייָג הַפְּנִימִי חַייָב וְהַחִיצוֹן פָּטוּר. וְיִפְטוֹר צַד הַחִיצוֹן לְצַד הַפְּנִימִי. רִבִּי זְעִירָא אָמַר לָהּ סְתָם רִבִּי לָא בְשֵׁם רִבִּי לָעְזָר רָאוּי הוּא לַחֲשׁוֹב עָלָיו לְחַייְבוֹ.

An exempt root exempts. But did we not state: "Rebbi Yose says, even if the inner part is for food, the outer part as fence, the inner part is obligated but the outer is exempt"? Should not the outer part make the inner exempt? Rebbi Zeïra said it anonymously, Rebbi La in the name of Rebbi Eleazar: He might think about it to obligate it.[42]

42 The roots are not exempt; part of the tree is exempt by force of the (revocable) intention of the planter.

רִבִּי יָסֵי בְשֵׁם רִבִּי יוֹחָנָן שָׁרָשִׁים אֵין בָּהֶם מַמָּשׁ. אָמַר רִבִּי זְעִירָא לְרִבִּי יָסָא בְּפֵירוּשׁ שְׁמַעְתָּנָהּ מִן דְּרִבִּי יוֹחָנָן אוֹ בְעָרְלָה הֲוִיתוֹן קַייָמִין וְאִתְדַּכָּרַת הָדָא מִילְתָא בְּבִיכּוּרִין. וְאָמַר שָׁרָשִׁין אֵין בָּהֶם מַמָּשׁ. אָמַר רִבִּי זְעִירָא הֵן דְּתֵימַר שׁוֹרָשִׁין אֵין בָּהֶם מַמָּשׁ. בְּהִשְׁרִישׁוּ מֵחוּץ לָאָרֶץ לָאָרֶץ. אֲבָל מִשֶּׁהִשְׁרִישׁוּ מֵהָאָרֶץ לְחוּצָה לָאָרֶץ. שָׁרָשִׁים יֵשׁ בָּהֶם מַמָּשׁ.

Rebbi Assi in the name of Rebbi Joḥanan: Roots do not count. Rebbi Zeïra said to Rebbi Assi, did you hear that explicitly from Rebbi Joḥanan or did you discuss *'orlah* and this came up relating to First Fruits when he said, roots do not count[43]? Rebbi Zeïra said, what we say, roots do not count, if the roots spread from outside the Land into the Land. But when they spread from the Land to outside the Land they do count[44].

43 Since in presenting First Fruits to the Temple the farmer has to declare (*Deut.* 26:10): "Here I brought the first of the fruits of the land You gave me," one might think that a tree on the farmer's land whose roots extend under the land of another owner would be disqualified for First Fruits. Maybe the statement of R. Johanan means only that any tree on the farmer's land qualifies, without implications for the rules of *'orlah*?

44 Any tree in the Land is obligated, even if its root started growing outside the Land. Any tree growing on any root which started to grow in the Land is also obligated.

סִיפְּקָהּ לִזְקֵינָה פָּטוּר לְחוּץ לָאָרֶץ פָּטוּר. לְהֶקְדֵּשׁ חַייָב לְצַד הַתַּחְתּוֹן לְצַד הָעֶלְיוֹן חַייָב. לְהֶקְדֵּשׁ חַייָב שֶׁהוּא רָאוּי לִפְדּוֹתוֹ וּלְחַייְבוֹ. לְצַד הַתַּחְתּוֹן חַייָב שֶׁהוּא רָאוּי לַחֲשׁוֹב עָלָיו וּלְחַייְבוֹ.

If one bound it to an old tree[45] it is exempt, to [a tree] outside the Land it is exempt. To a dedicated [tree] it is obligated, to the lower or upper part it is obligated. To a dedicated [tree] it is obligated because one might redeem it and make it obligated. To the lower part it is obligated because he might think about and obligate it[46].

45 "Binding" is an inexact expression (cf. Mishnah *Kilaim* 6:9); the young tree is grafted or otherwise made to be fed by the old tree.

46 The same argument as above, Note 41.

רִבִּי יוֹסֵי כְּרַבָּן שִׁמְעוֹן בֶּן גַּמְלִיאֵל. אֲפִילוּ יִסְבּוֹר כְּרִבִּי עָרְלָה תָּלוּי לְדַעְתּוֹ וּמַעְשְׂרוֹת אֵינָן תְּלוּיִין לְדַעְתּוֹ.

Does Rebbi Yose[47] follow Rabban Simeon ben Gamliel[48]? He might even hold with Rebbi! *'Orlah* depends on one's intention, tithes do not depend on his intention.

47 In the Mishnah, Note 1.

48 In the Tosephta dealing with heave and tithes from a tree on the border line, Note 37.

(fol. 60c) **משנה ב:** עֵת שֶׁבָּאוּ אֲבוֹתֵינוּ לָאָרֶץ וּמָצְאוּ נָטוּעַ פָּטוּר. נָטְעוּ אַף עַל פִּי שֶׁלֹּא כִיבְּשׁוּ חַיָּב. הַנּוֹטֵעַ לָרַבִּים חַיָּב. רִבִּי יוּדָה פוֹטֵר. הַנּוֹטֵעַ בִּרְשׁוּת הָרַבִּים וְהַנָּכְרִי שֶׁנָּטַע וְהַגַּזְלָן שֶׁנָּטַע וְהַנּוֹטֵעַ בִּסְפִינָה וְהָעוֹלֶה מֵאֵילָיו חַיָּב בְּעָרְלָה.

Mishnah 2: When our forefathers came into the Land, what they found planted was exempt. If they planted even though they had not yet conquered, it was obligated. If somebody plants for the benefit of the public[49], it is obligated; Rebbi Jehudah exempts[50]. If somebody plants on public property, the Non-Jew who planted[51], the robber who planted, and he who plants on a ship, are obligated for *'orlah.*

49 But on his private property.

50 This is not discussed in the Yerushalmi. The Babli (*Pesaḥim* 23a) explains that R. Jehudah concludes from *Lev.* 19:21, "it shall be like 'foreskin' *for you* (plural)" that the commandment is addressed to the individual; a communal obligation would require the collective.

51 If he planted a tree in the Holy Land, its fruits are forbidden for Jews during the first three years. The other cases of the Mishnah are discussed in the Halakhah.

משנה ג: אִילָן שֶׁנֶּעֱקַר וְהַסֶּלַע עִמּוֹ אִם יָכוֹל לִחְיוֹת פָּטוּר וְאִם לָאו חַיָּב. נֶעֱקַר הַסֶּלַע מִצִּידּוֹ זִיעְזְעָתוֹ הַמַּחֲרֵישָׁה אוֹ שֶׁזִּיעְזְעָתוֹ וַעֲשָׂאוֹ כְעָפָר אִם יָכוֹל לִחְיוֹת פָּטוּר וְאִם לָאו חַיָּב.

Mishnah 3: If a tree was moved with its lump[52], if it can survive it is exempt, otherwise obligated. If the lump was partially moved, or the plough displaced it and turned it into dust[53], if the tree can survive it is exempt, otherwise obligated.

52 Literally "the rock". It means the roots with the earth compacted by them. If the roots are totally contained in the earth moved with the tree, it is

not a new planting and no *'orlah* is created. But if the roots are moved without sufficient earth then a new count of *'orlah* has to start.

53 Maimonides (autograph), R. Simson, the Cambridge, Munich, and Parma mss. of the Mishnah, as well as the first hand of the Kaufmann ms. and the *editio princeps* all read בעפר "it was repaired with dust", i. e., the hole created when the tree was pushed aside by the plough was filled with earth. If the tree could have survived without the new earth, it is not a new planting. *Or zarua'* (#215) reads כעפר with the Yerushalmi mss. and the corrector of the Kaufmann ms. but explains as if it were written בעפר.

(fol. 60d) **הלכה ב**: וּנְטַעְתֶּם פְּרָט לְשֶׁנָּטְעוּ גוֹיִם עַד שֶׁלֹּא בָאוּ יִשְׂרָאֵל לָאָרֶץ. רִבִּי הוּנָא בְשֵׁם רִבִּי אַבָּא הָדָא אָמְרָה שׁוֹרֶשׁ פָּטוּר פּוֹטֵר.

Halakhah 2: (*Lev.* 19:21) "When you plant," this excludes what Gentiles planted before Israel came to the Land[54]. Rebbi Huna in the name of Rebbi Abba, this implies that an exempt root exempts[55].

54 *Sifra Qedošim Parašah* 3(2).

55 Since a tree planted a day before Israel crossed the Jordan is permanently exempt.

נָטְעוּ אַף עַל פִּי שֶׁלֹּא כִיבְּשׁוּ חַיָּיב. וּכְרִבִּי יִשְׁמָעֵאל דְּאָמַר כָּל־בִּיאוֹת הָאֲמוּרוֹת בַּתּוֹרָה לְאַחַר אַרְבַּע עֶשְׂרֵה שָׁנָה נֶאֶמְרוּ. שֶׁבַע שֶׁכִּיבְּשׁוּ וְשֶׁבַע שֶׁחִלְּקוּ. רִבִּי הִילָא בְשֵׁם רִבִּי לָעְזָר מוֹדֵי רִבִּי יִשְׁמָעֵאל בְּחַלָּה וּבְעָרְלָה. וְתַנֵּי כֵן בְּבוֹאֲכֶם לְפִי שֶׁשִּׁינָּה הַכָּתוּב מַשְׁמָעוֹ שִׁינּוּ חֲכָמִים חִיּוּבוֹ. רִבִּי יוֹנָה בָּעֵי מִחְלְפָה שִׁיטָּתֵיהּ דְּרִבִּי יִשְׁמָעֵאל תַּמָּן הוּא אָמַר הִיא הֲוָיָה הִיא הֲקָמָה הִיא שְׁבִירָה הִיא נְפִיצָה הִיא גְּאוּלָּה הִיא פְּדִיָּה. וְהָכָא הוּא מְשַׁנֶּה בֵּין לִישָּׁן לְלִישָּׁן.

"If they planted even though they had not yet conquered, it was obligated." Following Rebbi Ismael who said all "comings"[56] said in the Torah refer to after 14 years, seven when they conquered and seven when they distributed? Rebbi Hila in the name of Rebbi Eleazar: Rebbi Ismael agrees in the cases of *ḥallah* and *'orlah.* It was also stated thus: (*Num.* 15:18)[57] "At your coming," because the verse changed its language, the Sages changed[58] the terms of obligation." Rebbi Jonah asked: Rebbi Ismael is inconsistent. There, he says "being" and "getting" is the same[59], "breaking" and "smashing" is the same[60], "redemption" and "deliverance" is the same[61], and here he takes note of a change in expression!

56 Any command introduced by the words "it shall be when you come into the Land" applies only after the distribution of the Land to the tribes which by rabbinic tradition was 14 years after the crossing of the Jordan, cf. *Seder Olam* Chap. 11 (in the author's edition, Northvale NJ 1998, Notes 3-5). Cf. *Ševi'it* 6, Note 10, *Ḥallah* 2:1, Note 12. The statement of R. Ismael is discussed at length in Babli *Qiddušin* 37a-38a; it is also quoted in Yerushalmi *Soṭah* 7:4 (fol. 21c), 9:1 (fol. 23c).

57 This argument, directly attributed to R. Ismael in *Sifry Šelaḥ #110,* applies only to *ḥallah* where the usual form כבאכם is used. The rules for *'orlah* start: וכי תבאו אל הארץ but it does not say וירשתם וישבתם בה "after you inherited and settled there." This kind of argument is applicable only to the Babylonian version which insists not on "coming" but on "settling". In *Sifra* (*loc. cit.* N. 53), the immediate obligation of *'orlah* after the crossing of the Jordan, whether planting was done by Jew or Gentile, is deduced from *Lev.* 19:23: "When you come into the Land and plant *any* food-tree."

58 This seems to imply that Sadducee interpretation was different.

59 In the chapter on dedications, *Lev.* 27:9 ff., the redemption of a house is described by והיה לו "it shall be his", whereas the redemption of a field is וקם לו "it shall be confirmed for him". The rules are identical even though the expressions are different. The corresponding *baraitot* in *Sifra Beḥuqqotai Pereq* 10 are anonymous.

60 Two parallel synonymous expressions in *Deut.* 12:3. In this case, *Sifry Deut.* #61 disagrees and notes that "smashing" is more than "breaking".

61 *Lev.* 27:28,29; two parallel verses.

נְטָעוֹ לָרַבִּים חַיָּיב. רִבִּי יוּדָה פּוֹטֵר. מִחְלְפָה שִׁיטָּתָן דְּרַבָּנִין. תַּמָּן אִינּוּן אָמְרִין יְרוּשָׁלֵם וְחוּץ לָאָרֶץ (fol. 61a) אֵין מִיטַּמְּאִין בִּנְגָעִין. וְהָכָא אִינּוּן אָמְרִין הָכֵין. תַּמָּן וּבָא אֲשֶׁר לוֹ הַבַּיִת. פְּרָט לִירוּשָׁלֵם שֶׁהִיא לְכָל־הַשְּׁבָטִים. בְּרַם הָכָא וּנְטַעְתֶּם מִכָּל־מָקוֹם.

"If he planted for the public benefit, it is obligated; Rebbi Jehudah exempts". The rabbis seem inconsistent. There[62], they say: "Jerusalem and outside the Land cannot become impure by skin disease," but here, they say so[63]! There (*Lev.* 14:35) "the owner of the house comes"[64], excluding Jerusalem which was not distributed among the tribes. But here, (*Lev.* 19:21) "when you plant," in any way.

62 Mishnah *Nega'im* 12:4; cf. Babli *Yoma* 12a.

63 As explained in the next Note, Jerusalem is public property and any tree planted there should be exempt as planted for public use.

64 The actual verse referred to is *Lev.* 14:34: "I shall put skin disease on a house on the Land of your inheritance." This excludes all houses in territory not distributed to the tribes; Jerusalem was conquered by David as capital not belonging to any particular tribe. *Sifra Meẓora' Parašah* 5 proves from the verse that (a) the rules did not apply before the distribution of the Land, (b) a house built on poles, not being a "house on the Land" is also not subject to the rules, (c) houses in Jerusalem (and certainly outside the Land) are excluded.

מִחְלְפָה שִׁיטָּתֵיהּ דְּרִבִּי יוּדָה. תַּמָּן הוּא אוֹמֵר אֲנִי לֹא שָׁמַעְתִּי אֶלָּא בֵּית הַמִּקְדָּשׁ. וְהָכָא הוּא אָמַר הָכֵין. תַּמָּן הוּא אָמַר אֲנִי לֹא שָׁמַעְתִּי אֶלָּא בֵּית הַמִּקְדָּשׁ שְׁמוּעָה אָמְרָהּ. בְּרַם הָכָא גַּרְמֵיהּ אָמַר.

Rebbi Judah seems inconsistent. There[65] he says, "I heard only the Temple,[66]" and here he says so! There, he says "I heard only the Temple" as a tradition, here in his own name.

65 *Sifra Meẓora' Parašah* 5(5), Tosephta *Nega'im* 6:1, Babli *Yoma* 12a, *Megillah* 26a, *Baba Qama* 82b; referring to the exemption from the laws of skin disease.

66 Since Jerusalem itself is clearly part of the domain of the tribe of Benjamin (*Jos.* 18:16), but the Temple Mount was bought by David with tax money (*2S.* 24:24, *1Chr.* 21:25) and therefore became the property of the entire people.

אָמַר רִבִּי יוֹסֵי בֵּירִבִּי בּוּן תִּפְתָּר כְּרִבִּי שִׁמְעוֹן בֶּן אֶלְעָזָר. דְּתַנֵּי רִבִּי שִׁמְעוֹן בֶּן אֶלְעָזָר אוֹמֵר מִשְּׁמוֹ הַנּוֹטֵעַ לָרַבִּים חַייָב בְּעָרְלָה. עָלָה מֵאֵילָיו פָּטוּר מִן הָעָרְלָה. הַנּוֹטֵעַ לָרַבִּים חַייָב בִּרְשׁוּת הָרַבִּים פָּטוּר. הַנּוֹטֵעַ לָרַבִּים חַייָב כְּנוֹטֵעַ בְּתוֹךְ שֶׁלּוֹ. לִרְשׁוּת הָרַבִּים פָּטוּר בְּשֶׁגָּזַל קַרְקַע. וְיֵשׁ קַרְקַע נִגְזָל. אָמַר רִבִּי הִילָא אַף עַל פִּי שֶׁאֵין קַרְקַע נִגְזָל יֵשׁ יֵיאוּשׁ לְקַרְקַע.

Rebbi Yose ben Rebbi Abun said, explain it following Rebbi Simeon ben Eleazar, as it was stated[67]: "Rebbi Simeon ben Eleazar says in his[68] name, if somebody plants for the public, it is obligated for *'orlah*. If it grew by itself[69] it is exempt from *'orlah*." [70]If somebody plants for the public, it is obligated, in the public domain it is exempt. If somebody plants for the public, it is obligated as if he planted on his own property. In the public domain it is exempt, if he robbed real estate[71]. Can real estate be robbed? Rebbi Hila said, even though real estate cannot be robbed, hope for recovery of real estate can be given up.

67 Tosephta 2.

68 R. Jehudah's. R. Simeon ben Eleazar holds that the Mishnah misrepresents R. Jehudah's position.

69 In the Tosephta: "If it grew by itself in the public domain."

709 This sentence, which has no parallel in the Tosephta, is probably part of R. Simeon ben Eleazar's *baraita*.

71 If somebody took possession of real estate by force and the original owners gave up hope of recovery, the real estate is no longer in the possession of the original owners. It cannot be legally in the possession of the robber since real estate "cannot be

robbed." Therefore, the legal status of the parcel is that of public property.

Movables are acquired by a robber or thief; the robber or thief is required to pay (eventually with a fine added) for what he took. But real estate is not mentioned in the biblical laws of restitution. There also is no rabbinic provision of monetary restitution for real estate illegally taken since it is assumed that times of lawlessness in which real estate can be taken by force are relatively short and that with the return of civilized society, genuine claims of title can be regained in court.

רִבִּי יֹאשִׁיָּה מַיְיתֵי נְטִיעוֹת מֵחוּץ לָאָרֶץ בְּגוּשֵׁיהֶן וּנְצִיב לוֹן בָּאָרֶץ. רִבִּי יוֹנָה לְשַׂכְּרוֹ שָׁנִים. רִבִּי יוֹסֵי לְשַׂכְּרוֹ רְבָעִי.

Rebbi Joshia brought saplings from outside the Land in their earth and planted them in the Land. Rebbi Jona, to gain the years[72]. Rebbi Yose, to gain the fourth year[73].

72 Since *'orlah* applies also outside the Land by tradition (Mishnah 3:9), by bringing the saplings in their earth he did not interrupt the years of *'orlah*.

73 The saplings were already three years old; R. Joshia brought them in their earth so they should not be subject to the requirement of redemption in the fourth year (*Lev.* 19:24, cf. *Peah* 7, Note 99) which does never, even rabbinically, apply to trees planted outside the Land except vines.

תַּנֵּי גּוֹי שֶׁהִרְכִּיב אִילַן מַאֲכָל עַל גַּבֵּי אִילַן סְרָק אַף עַל פִּי שֶׁאֵין יִשְׂרָאֵל רַשַּׁאי לַעֲשׂוֹת כֵּן חַיָּיב בְּעָרְלָה. עָרְלָה מֵאֵימָתַי הוּא מוֹנֶה לוֹ מִשְּׁעַת נְטִיעָתוֹ. רִבִּי שִׁמְעוֹן בֶּן לָקִישׁ אָמַר בִּלְבַד דְּבָרִים שֶׁהֵן בָּאִין בְּמַחֲשָׁבָה כְּגוֹן חָרוּבֵי צַלְמוֹנָה וְחָרוּבֵי גִידוֹדָה. אֲבָל עֲרָבָה כִּנְטוּעַ בָּאָרֶץ. רִבִּי יוֹחָנָן אָמַר אֲפִילוּ עֲרָבָה. וְהָתַנִּינָן אֵין נוֹטְעִין וְאֵין מַבְרִיכִין וְאֵין מַרְכִּיבִין עֶרֶב שְׁבִיעִית פָּחוֹת מִשְּׁלֹשִׁים יוֹם לִפְנֵי רֹאשׁ הַשָּׁנָה וְאִם נָטַע אוֹ הִבְרִיךְ אוֹ הִרְכִּיב יֵיעָקֵר. עַל דַּעְתֵּיהּ דְּרִבִּי שִׁמְעוֹן בֶּן לָקִישׁ דּוּ פָּתַר לָהּ בָּעֲרָבָה נִיחָא. עַל דַּעְתֵּיהּ דְּרִבִּי יוֹחָנָן דּוּ אָמַר

אֲפִילוּ עֲרָבָה לָמָּה לִי יֵיעָקֵר. שַׁנְיָיא הִיא שֶׁהֵן מִתְאַחִין בַּשְּׁבִיעִית. וְהֵיי דָא אָמַר דָּא הַנּוֹטֵעַ וְהַמַּבְרִיךְ וְהַמַּרְכִּיב שְׁלֹשִׁים יוֹם לִפְנֵי רֹאשׁ הַשָּׁנָה עָלְתָה לוֹ שָׁנָה שְׁלֵימָה וּמוּתָּר לְקַיְימָהּ בִּשְּׁבִיעִית פָּחוֹת מִשְּׁלֹשִׁים יוֹם לִפְנֵי רֹאשׁ הַשָּׁנָה לֹא עָלְתָה לוֹ שָׁנָה שְׁלֵימָה וְאָסוּר לְקַיְימוֹ בִּשְּׁבִיעִית. אֲבָל אָמְרוּ פֵּירוֹת נְטִיעָה זוֹ אֲסוּרִין עַד חֲמִשָּׁה עָשָׂר בִּשְׁבָט. תַּנֵּי רִבִּי יְהוֹשֻׁעַ אוֹנָיָא לֵית כָּאן מַרְכִּיב. אָמַר רִבִּי אַבָּא מָרִי אֲפִילוּ לְרִבִּי שִׁמְעוֹן בֶּן לָקִישׁ לֵית כָּאן מַרְכִּיב לְשֶׁעָבַר הָא בַּתְּחִילָּה לֹא.

It was stated[74]: "If a Gentile grafted a food-tree on a futile[75] tree, even though a Jew is not permitted to do this, it is obligated for *'orlah*." From when does one count *'orlah*? From the moment it[76] is planted. Rebbi Simeon ben Laqish said, only those for which intent is important[77]; for example carob trees from Ẓalmon or Gidud[78]; but on a willow[79] it is as if planted in the earth. Rebbi Joḥanan said, even on a willow. But did we not state[80]: "One does not plant, sink, or graft in the year preceding a Sabbatical year later than thirty days before the New Year; if he planted, sank, or grafted it should be uprooted." According to Rebbi Simeon ben Laqish who will explain it by grafting on a willow it is understandable[81]. According to Rebbi Joḥanan who said even on a willow, why should it be uprooted? There is a difference because they unite in the Sabbatical year[82]. And that is what has been said, [83]"If somebody planted, sank, or grafted 30 days before the New Year, it counts for him as a full year and he is permitted to keep it in the Sabbatical year. Less than 30 days before the New Year, it does not count for him as a full year and he is not permitted to keep it in the Sabbatical year. Truly, they said, the fruits from this planting are forbidden until the fifteenth of Shevaṭ." Rebbi Joshua from Ono[84] stated: There is no "grafted" here[85]. Rebbi Abba Mari said, even for Rebbi Simeon ben Laqish there is no "grafted" here; for the past, certainly not to start out with[86].

74 In Tosephta 5: "If a Gentile grafted a food tree on a futile tree, one counts from the moment it was planted." In this version, it is clear that the count starts with the *planting* of the futile tree, not the grafting of the fruit tree. The Tosephta was not known to the editors of the Yerushalmi.

75 A tree either without edible fruits or whose fruits are not generally objects of trade; cf. Mishnah *Kilaim* 6:6.

76 The futile stem.

77 Trees whose fruits are usually considered animal feed and only the intent of the grower can give them the status of human food.

78 These places and the kinds of carob referred to have not been identified.

79 "Willow" is taken as example of a tree whose fruits are neither human food nor animal feed.

80 Mishnah *Ševi'it* 2:6; Note 42. "Sinking" is bending a branch down to the soil to have it grow roots.

81 The forbidden graft is graft of a fruit tree on a willow.

82 אחה is usually used for "invisible mending". The two trees unite; this is forbidden agricultural activity in the Sabbatical. It has nothing to do with the rules of *'orlah.*

83 Tosephta *Ševi'it* 2:3, *Roš Haššanah* 1:8; *Ševi'it* 2:6 (Notes 50-52), *Roš Haššanah* 1:2 (fol. 57a); Babli *Roš Haššanah* 9b. The Tosephta adds: "If it is *'orlah* it remains *'orlah*, fourth year remains fourth year [until the 15th of *Ševaṭ*.]"

84 An early Amora acting as "Tanna", memorizing *baraitot.*

85 According to R. Joḥanan, grafting never creates a problem of *'orlah.*

86 Since grafting a fruit tree on a fruitless tree is forbidden, the Tosephta cannot speak only about somebody coming to ask whether he might graft on a fruit tree before *Roš Haššanah.* But in that case, R. Simeon ben Laqish agrees that *orlah* is counted for the root tree. R. Simeon ben Laqish has not stated how he would rule if somebody grafted on a willow and only afterwards came to ask.

רִבִּי יִצְחָק בַּר חֲקוֹלָה בְשֵׁם חִזְקִיָּה הַנּוֹטֵעַ בֶּעָצִיץ שֶׁאֵינוֹ נָקוּב חַיָּיב בְּעָרְלָה. רִבִּי יוֹסֵי אָמַר מִפְּנֵי שֶׁהַשָּׁרָשִׁין מְפַעְפְּעִין בּוֹ. רִבִּי יוֹנָה מַפִּיק לִשְׁנָה כְּלֵי חֶרֶשׂ עוֹמֵד לִפְנֵי שָׁרָשִׁין. רִבִּי יִרְמְיָה בָּעֵי נָטַע בּוֹ דְּלַעַת מֵאַחַר שֶׁהוּא כְנָקוּב אֵצֶל הָאִילָן כְּנָקוּב הוּא אֵצֶל זְרָעִין.

Rebbi Isaac bar Ḥaqola in the name of Ḥizqia: If somebody plants in a flower pot without a hole[87], it is subject to *'orlah*. Rebbi Yose said, because the roots break through it[88]. Rebbi Jonah uses the expression: Clay vessels withstand roots[89]. Rebbi Jeremiah asked: If he planted a gourd in it, since it is as if there were a hole for trees, is it like as if with a hole for vegetables?

87 In the Mishnah, "planting in a ship." Since the ship in question must be in the Land, it is a small river boat, sometimes made of clay. Cf. *Ḥallah* 2:2, that the ship is under the agricultural laws of the Land only if it touches the ground. The Tosephta (2-3) in ms. Erfurt has "exempt" for ship and pot without hole; the passage is missing in ms. Vienna.

88 Tree roots cause clay pots to burst.

89 Rebbi Jonah, a generation after R. Jeremiah, gives a negative answer to the latter's question. Clay vessels withstand all roots except tree roots.

רִבִּי יוֹחָנָן בְּשֵׁם רִבִּי יַנַּאי אִילָן שֶׁנְּטָעוֹ בְּתוֹךְ הַבַּיִת חַיָּיב בְּעָרְלָה וּפָטוּר מִן הַמַּעְשְׂרוֹת דִּכְתִיב עַשֵּׂר תְּעַשֵּׂר אֵת כָּל־תְּבוּאַת זַרְעֶךָ הַיּוֹצֵא הַשָּׂדֶה. וּבַשְּׁבִיעִית צְרִיכָה דִּכְתִיב וְשָׁבְתָה הָאָרֶץ שַׁבָּת לַיי. וּכְתִיב שָׂדְךָ לֹא תִזְרַע וְכַרְמְךָ לֹא תִזְמוֹר.

Rebbi Joḥanan in the name of Rebbi Yannai: A tree planted inside a house is obligated for *'orlah*[90] but free from tithes since it is written (*Deut*. 14:22): "You shall certainly tithe all yield of your seeds which comes from the *field*." For the Sabbatical it is problematic[91] since it is written (*Lev*. 25:5): "The Land shall celebrate a Sabbath for the Eternal."

And it is written (*Lev*. 25:6): "You shall not sow your *field* nor prune your vineyard."

90 Nowhere is "field" mentioned in the verses defining *'orlah*.

91 Whether the Sabbatical restrictions apply to fruit-bearing house plants.

כֵּינִי מַתְנִיתָא אִם הָיָה יָכוֹל לִחְיוֹת פָּטוּר וְאִם לָאו חַיָּב.

So is the Mishnah: If it could[92] survive it is exempt, otherwise obligated.

92 This is the discussion of Mishnah 3. If the transplanted tree could survive depending only on the earth transferred with it, without help from the earth surrounding it at the new site, no new *'orlah* is created. Cf. J. N. Epstein, מבוא לנוסח המשנה[2], p. 450.

(fol. 60c) **משנה ד:** אִילָן שֶׁנֶּעֱקַר וְנִשְׁתַּיֵּיר בּוֹ שׁוֹרֶשׁ פָּטוּר. וְכַמָּה יְהֵי בְשׁוֹרֶשׁ רַבָּן גַּמְלִיאֵל מִשּׁוּם רִבִּי לָעְזָר בֶּן יְהוּדָה אִישׁ בִּירְתּוֹתָא כְּמַחַט שֶׁלְמִתּוֹן.

Mishnah 4: If a tree was cut but there remained a root, it[93] is exempt. How large shall the root be? Rabban Gamliel[94] in the name of Rebbi Eleazar ben Jehudah from Birtota: Like a tenter's needle[95].

93 The new growth from the existing root.

94 It must be Rabban Simeon ben Gamliel, as read in some Mishnah mss., since Rebbi Eleazar ben Jehudah from Birtota was younger than Rabban Gamliel and a teacher of Rabban Simeon ben Gamliel; cf. J. N. Epstein, מבוא לנוסח המשנה[2], p. 1199.

95 Definition of *Arukh*, Maimonides, and R. Simson. The tenter is the frame holding the warp in clothmaking;

the needle is used to stretch the threads. In the Halakhah, the word appears as מיתוי. In *Kelim* 13:5, the Gaonim read מיתח, "to stretch", and explain that the weavers use broken needles to stretch the warp. Buxtorf derives the word from Greek μιτόω "to stretch".

(fol. 61a) **הלכה ג**: חִזְקִיָּה שָׁאַל פָּחוּת מִיכֵּן כְּתָלוּשׁ הוּא. הִשְׁתַּחֲוֶה לוֹ אֲסָרוֹ. כּוֹתְבִין עָלָיו גִּיטֵּי נָשִׁים. אָמְרִין חָזַר בֵּיהּ חִזְקִיָּה. אָמַר רִבִּי יוֹנָה מִן הָדָא חָזַר בֵּיהּ דְּאָמַר רִבִּי יוֹחָנָן בְּשֵׁם רִבִּי יַנַּאי מְכֵּיוָן שֶׁיֵּשׁ כְּמַחַט שֶׁל מִיתּוּי דָּבָר בָּרִיא שֶׁיֵּשׁ לוֹ שָׁלֹשׁ שָׁנִים.

Halakhah 3: Ḥizqiah asked: Less than that[96], is it as if torn out? If he worshipped it, is it forbidden? Does one write on it women's bills of divorce[97]? They say, Ḥizqiah retracted this. Rebbi Jonah said: Ḥizqiah retracted because Rebbi Joḥanan[98] said in the name of Rebbi Yannai, if it is [thick] like a tenter's needle it is certain that it is three years old[99].

96 If the root is not as thick as a tenter's needle. While any object of idolatrous worship is forbidden for usufruct, this excludes the earth and anything permanently affixed to it (Mishnah *Avodah Zarah* 3:5). It is talmudic theory that holy trees are forbidden only because statues are buried between their roots.

97 Since it is written: (*Deut.* 24:3) "He shall write for her a bill of divorce and hand it over to her," one concludes that a bill of divorce may not be written on anything that cannot be delivered immediately after signing, e. g., on a leaf connected to the ground which would have to be cut before delivery is possible (*Sifry Deut.* 269, *Giṭṭin* 3:2, Babli *Giṭṭin* 19b).

98 Who was Ḥizqiah's student and would not have transmitted a teaching rejected by his teacher.

99 If it is thinner, it is obligated for *'orlah*, which means it is planted in the earth.

חִזְקִיָּה שָׁאַל שְׁלִישׁ מַחַט שָׁנָה שְׁנֵי שְׁלִישֵׁי שְׁתֵּי שָׁנִים. חֲבֵרַיָּא בָּעֵיי מַחַט וּשְׁלִישׁ דָּבָר בָּרִיא שֶׁיֵּשׁ לוֹ אַרְבַּע שָׁנִים. אִין תֵּימַר לֹא חָזַר בֵּיהּ לָמָּה שָׁאַל כֵּן. אָמַר רִבִּי יוֹנָה מִן מִלְּתֵיהּ חָזַר בֵּיהּ דְּאָמַר רִבִּי יוֹחָנָן בְּשֵׁם רִבִּי יַנַּאי מִכֵּיוָן שֶׁיֵּשׁ כְּמַחַט שֶׁל מִיתּוּי דָּבָר בָּרִיא שֶׁיֵּשׁ לוֹ שָׁלֹשׁ שָׁנִים.

Ḥizqiah asked: A third of a needle [means] one year, two thirds two years[100]? The colleagues asked: A needle and a third, is it obvious that it is four years old? If you say, he did not retract, why would he have asked this[101]? Rebbi Jonah said: Ḥizqiah retracted this, because Rebbi Joḥanan said in the name of Rebbi Yannai. if it is [thick] like a tenter's needle it is certain that it is three yeards old[102].

100 Is the thickness proportional to the time passed after planting? The negative answer is in *Ševi'it* 5, Notes 20-21.

101 If a thin root is not in the earth it cannot count for *'orlah*. The second of Ḥizqiah's questions cannot be asked if the first is answered in the affirmative.

102 The condition of the Mishnah is sufficient but not necessary to characterize a three-year-old tree.

אָמַר רִבִּי יוֹסֵי אֲפִילוּ יֵשׁ בּוֹ שָׁלֹשׁ שָׁנִים אֵין בּוֹ כְּמַחַט שֶׁל מִיתּוּי. אָמַר רִבִּי יוּדָן מַתְנִיתָא מְסַייְעָא לְרִבִּי יוֹסֵי אָמַר רִבִּי אַף כְּשֶׁאָמְרוּ בְּנוֹת חָמֵשׁ בְּנוֹת שֵׁשׁ בְּנוֹת שֶׁבַע אֶלָּא בִגְפָנִים בְּנוֹת חָמֵשׁ. בִּתְאֵינִים בְּנוֹת שֵׁשׁ. בְּזֵיתִים בְּנוֹת שֶׁבַע. וַאֲנָן חָמֵיי הָדֵין מְרוּיתָא דִתְאֵינָה אַתְיָא בְּפֵירֵי. אָמַר רִבִּי יוּדָן כְּרִבִּי טְרִיפוֹן לְעוּבְיָהּ.

Rebbi Yose said, even three years old it will not have the thickness of a tenter's needle. Rebbi Yudan said, a *baraita* supports Rebbi Yose: [103]"Rebbi says, when they said five, six, or seven years old, for vines five years old, for figs six years old, for olives seven years old." [104]But do we not see the growth of the fig tree come with fruits? Rebbi Yudan said, according to Rebbi Tryphon we throw it on its width.

103 From here to the end of the Halakhah, the text is from *Ševi'it* 1:9, Notes 72-79. The *baraita* explains the Mishnah defining how long a tree is called "sapling." A tree which is a sapling for seven years cannot have very impressive roots after three years.

104 These two sentences belong to *Ševi'it* 1:9 and have no meaning here. In any case, the size of the root is no direct indication of a tree's age.

(fol. 60c) **משנה ה:** אִילָן שֶׁנֶּעֱקַר וּבוֹ בְּרִיכָה וְהוּא חָיֶה מִמֶּנּוּ חָזְרָה זְקֵינָה לִהְיוֹת כִּבְרִיכָה. הִבְרִכָהּ שָׁנָה אַחַר שָׁנָה וְנִפְסְקָה מוֹנֶה מִשָּׁעָה שֶׁנִּפְסְקָה. סִיפּוּק הַגְּפָנִים סִיפּוּק עַל גַּבֵּי סִיפּוּק אַף עַל פִּי שֶׁהִבְרִיכָן בָּאָרֶץ מוּתָּר. רַבִּי מֵאִיר אוֹמֵר מָקוֹם שֶׁכּוֹחָהּ יָפֶה מוּתָּר. וּמָקוֹם שֶׁכּוֹחָהּ רַע אָסוּר. בְּרִיכָה שֶׁנִּפְסְקָה וְהִיא מְלֵיאָה פֵּירוֹת אִם הוֹסִיף בְּמָאתַיִם אָסוּר.

Mishnah 5: If a tree was uprooted but it had a sunken branch[105] and now lives off that, the original trunk becomes like the sunken branch. If he sank year after year and it was interrupted, one counts[106] from the moment it was interrupted. Attachment of vines[107], attachment after attachment, even if he sank them into the earth, are permitted. Rebbi Meïr says, where it is in its force it is permitted, where it is weak it is forbidden[108]. A sunk branch which became separated but is full of fruits, if it increased by one twohundredth it is forbidden[109].

105 A branch of the tree had been bent down to the earth and part of it covered with earth so that it grew new roots from which a new tree started to grow. As long as everything remains connected, the new tree is considered part of the old and is exempt from *'orlah*. But if now the original tree is separated from its roots and the new tree must live off the new roots of the sunken branch, it reverts to *'orlah* for the next three years.

106 The new parts, no longer connected to the original trunk, become *'orlah*.

107 This term covers sinking of shoots of vines and grafting new shoots on branches of an old vine.

108 According to him, repeated grafting exempts the new limb from *'orlah* only if the previous graft had become one with the tree before the last graft.

109 Since it was stated at the beginning of the Mishnah that sinking does not create an obligation of *'orlah*, the fruits grown before the new roots were separate from the original trunk grew exempt from *'orlah*. It now is stated that *'orlah* fruits are permitted only if the exempt parts of any fruit are more than 200 times the forbidden; cf. also Mishnah 2:1; *Kilaim* 5:6.

(fol. 61a) **הלכה ד**: אִילָן שֶׁנֶּעֱקַר וּבוֹ בְּרֵיכָה וּבוֹ בְּרָכָה. רִבִּי חוּנָא בְּשֵׁם רִבִּי יוֹחָנָן וּבוֹ בְּרִיכָה. אָמַר רִבִּי מָנָא אִית בְּנֵי נָשׁ שְׁמוֹן בְּרִיכָה כְּמָאן דְּאָמַר בּוֹא בְּרוּךְ יי.

Halakhah 4: "If a tree was uprooted but it had a sunken branch;" blessing is in it. Rebbi Ḥuna in the name of Rebbi Joḥanan: There is *bĕrîkhâ* in it. Rebbi Mana said, some people are called *Bĕrîkhâ* as you say (*Gen.* 21:31): "Come, the Eternal's blessed."110

110 Both homiletic versions, that sinking branches brings blessing to the farmer, are identical. The Aramaic translation of the phrase from *Gen.* is עוּל בְּרִיכָא דַה׳ both in Onqelos (Eastern) and Yerushalmi (Pseudo-Jonathan, Western). The modern Ashkenazic version of the name is Brick, Bruck. Cf. E. and H. Guggenheimer, Jewish Family Names and Their Origins, Ktav, 1992.

רִבִּי זְעִירָא רִבִּי יַסִּי רִבִּי לָעְזָר בְּשֵׁם רִבִּי חֲנִינָא. רִבִּי בָּא רִבִּי חִייָה רִבִּי לָעְזָר רִבִּי חֲנִינָה בְּשֵׁם רִבִּי חֲנִינָה בֶּן גַּמְלִיאֵל יַלְדָּה שֶׁסִּפְּקָה לִזְקֵינָה טְהָרָה הַיַּלְדָּה. אָמַר רִבִּי חִייָה בַּר בָּא מַתְנִיתָא אָמְרָה כֵן סִיפּוּק גְּפָנִים סִיפּוּק עַל סִיפּוּק אַף עַל פִּי שֶׁהִבְרִיכָן לָאָרֶץ מוּתָּר. וְחָשׁ לוֹמַר שֶׁמָּא הִשְׁרִישָׁה הַיַּלְדָּה עַד שֶׁלֹּא

הִתְאָחָה מִן הַזְּקֵינָה. רִבִּי חֲנַנְיָה בְּרֵיהּ דְּרִבִּי הִלֵּל דְּרִבִּי יְהוּדָה הִיא. דְּרִבִּי יְהוּדָה אָמַר מִתְאָחָה הִיא עַד שֶׁלֹּא תַשְׁרִישׁ.

Rebbi Zeïra, Rebbi Assi in the name of Rebbi Ḥanina; Rebbi Abba, Rebbi Ḥiyya, Rebbi Eleazar, Rebbi Ḥananiah in the name of Rebbi Ḥanina ben Gamliel: If a young tree was attached to an old one, the young one was cleansed[111]. Rebbi Ḥiyya bar Abba said, the Mishnah says so: "Attachment of vines, attachment after attachment, even if he sank them into the earth, are permitted." Should we not say that maybe the young tree formed roots before it was well connected[112] to the old one[113]? Rebbi Ḥananiah the son of Rebbi Hillel: This follows Rebbi Jehudah, since Rebbi Jehudah says it connects well more quickly than it forms roots.

111 If an *'orlah* twig was grafted on an old vine, it is no longer *'orlah*. In the Babli, *Soṭah* 43b, this is a purely Amoraic statement by R. Abbahu. {The Bablylonian equivalent of ספק is סבך.}

112 The term מאחה usually means mending a tear in a garment so that it looks like new.

113 In case the newly grafted branch was at the same time sunk into the ground.

רִבִּי יוֹסֵי בְּשֵׁם רִבִּי יוֹחָנָן שָׁרָשִׁים אֵין בָּהֶם מַמָּשׁ. אָמַר רִבִּי זְעִירָא לְרִבִּי יוֹסֵי בְּפֵירוּשׁ שְׁמַעְתָּנָהּ מִן דְּרִבִּי יוֹחָנָן אוֹ מִן שִׁיטָּתֵיהּ דְּאָמַר רִבִּי יוֹחָנָן וְתַנֵּי כֵן הִקְדִּישׁ וְאַחַר כָּךְ נָטַע פָּטוּר מִן הָעָרְלָה. נָטַע וְאַחַר כָּךְ הִקְדִּישׁ חַיָּיב בְּעָרְלָה. וְאַתּוּן סָבְרִין מֵימַר הֶקְדֵּשׁ פָּטוּר וּזְקֵינָה פָּטוּר. וְלָא דָמְיָא הֶקְדֵּשׁ רָאוּי הוּא לִפְדוּתוֹ וּלְחַיְּיבוֹ הוֹאִיל וְרָאוּי לַחֲשׁוֹב וּלְחַיְּיבוֹ אִית לָךְ גַּבֵּי זְקֵינָה רָאוּי לַחֲשׁוֹב עָלֶיהָ וּלְחַיְּיבָהּ.

Rebbi Assi in the name of Rebbi Joḥanan: Roots do not count[114]. Rebbi Zeïra said to Rebbi Assi, did you hear that explicitly from Rebbi Joḥanan or from his argument? As Rebbi Joḥanan said, moreover it was stated[115]: "If someone dedicated[116] and then planted, it is exempt from *'orlah;* planted and then dedicated, it is subject to *'orlah*." You wanted to say, dedicated is exempt from *'orlah*, old is exempt from *'orlah*. But this is not comparable! Dedicated things can be redeemed and become obligated since he might think about it to obligate[117]; can you [say] about an old tree that one might think about it to obligate?

114 Cf. Note 42. R. Assi rejects R. Ḥananiah ben R. Hillel's solution and holds that, according to R. Joḥanan, nobody cares whether the healing of the graft or the development of new roots is faster.

115 Tosephta 4.

116 Both the sapling and the ground in which it will be planted are dedicated to the upkeep of the Temple.

117 The Tosephta states that redemption of dedicated plants induces *'orlah* to be counted from the moment of planting. This means that the obligation was latent even in the state of dedication.

רִבִּי אַבָּהוּ בְשֵׁם רִבִּי יוֹחָנָן אֶתְרוֹג שֶׁחָנַט בִּשְׁנַת עָרְלָה וְיָצָא בִשְׁנַת הֵיתֵר וְסִיפְּקוֹ לַחֲבֵירוֹ אֲפִילוּ מוֹסִיף כַּמָּה אָסוּר שֶׁאֵין גִּידוּלֵי אִיסּוּר מַעֲלִין אֶת הָאִיסּוּר. הָא יַלְדָּה שֶׁסִּיפְּקָהּ טְהוֹרָה הַיַּלְדָּה. אִין תֵּימַר לֹא טְהֲרָה אֲפִילוּ מוֹסִיף כַּמָּה אָסוּר. רִבִּי זְעִירָה בְשֵׁם רַבָּנִין אֶתְרוֹג שֶׁחָנַט בִּשְׁנַת עָרְלָה וְיָצָא בִשְׁנַת הֵיתֵר וְסִיפְּקוֹ לַחֲבֵירוֹ אֲפִילוּ מוֹסִיף כַּמָּה אָסוּר. לוֹקִין עָלָיו בִּכְזַיִת.

Rebbi Abbahu in the name of Rebbi Joḥanan: A *citrus medica* tree which formed flower buds subject to *'orlah* and the fruits grew when it was permitted[118]; if [the tree] was attached to another tree even if [the fruit] grows much it is forbidden because growth of something forbidden cannot lift what is forbidden[119]. Therefore, an attached young twig must be permitted because, if you say it is not permitted, even if it grows much it will be forbidden[120]! Rebbi Zeïra in the name of the rabbis: A *citrus medica* tree which formed flower buds subject to *'orlah* and the fruits grew when it was permitted; what was attached to another tree even if it grows much is forbidden; one whips for the size of an olive[121].

118 Its fruits stay on the tree longer than one season; therefore, for *'orlah* the determining factor is the formation of the flower, for tithes the time of collection (Mishnah *Bikkurim* 2:6). A flower fertilized in the third year cannot produce permitted fruit.

119 Even if the growth after the end of the third year is more than 200 times the volume in existence at the end of the third year, the *etrog* is forbidden.

120 This explains the Mishnah.

121 This is taken to be another formulation of the reasoning of R. Joḥanan: If eating the volume of an olive from this *etrog* (the edible kind, *citrus medica cedrata*) is criminal then all that grew after the third year must be forbidden by biblical law since otherwise there would not be the volume of an olive of biblically forbidden fruit.

אָמַר רִבִּי מַיְישָׁא לְרִבִּי זְעִירָא תַּרְתֵּין מִילִּין אַתּוּן אָמְרִין וְאִינּוּן פְּלִיגִין חָדָא עַל חָדָא. הָכָא אַתּוּן אָמְרִין שֶׁאֵין גִּידּוּלֵי אִיסּוּר מַעֲלִין אֶת הָאִיסּוּר. וְהָכָא אַתּוּן אָמְרִין לוֹקִין עָלָיו בִּכְזַיִת. וְיִלְקֶה לְפִי חֶשְׁבּוֹן שֶׁיֵּשׁ בּוֹ. אָמַר רִבִּי יוֹנָה כָּאן מֵחֲמַת עַצְמוֹ הוּא חַי. וְכָאן מֵחֲמַת הַסִּיפּוּק הוּא חַי. מֵעַתָּה אֶתְרוֹג שֶׁחָנַט בִּשְׁנַת עָרְלָה וְיָצָא בִשְׁנַת הֵיתֵר וְסִיפְּקוֹ לַחֲבֵירוֹ וְכֵן חֲבֵירוֹ סִיפְּקוֹ זֶה לָזֶה טִהֲרוּ זֶה אֶת זֶה.

Rebbi Maisha said to Rebbi Zeïra: You say two things which contradict each other. Here you say, because growth of anything forbidden cannot lift what is forbidden[122]; there you say one whips for the size of an olive. Should he not be whipped only in the proportion[123] it contains? Rebbi Jonah said, in the first case it lives because of itself[124], in the second because of the attachment[125]. Then if a *citrus medica,* which blossomed in an *'orlah* year and grew in an exempt year, is attached reciprocally[126] to a tree of the same kind they will cleanse one another[127].

122 One does not say "all growth is forbidden" but "[permitted] growth of something forbidden cannot lift the prohibition inherent in the fruit." Therefore, the essentially forbidden thing is only the fruit as it exists at the end of the *'orlah* period. Then the argument outlined in Note 121 is faulty.

123 If the volume of the fruit at the end of the *'orlah* period is *a* and the final volume is *b* (measured in volumes of olives) then using a piece of the fruit is criminal only if the size of the piece is at least $^b/_a > 1$.

124 No attaching or grafting; in this case the entire fruit is forbidden.

125 The rabbinic argument that "[permitted] growth of anything forbidden cannot lift the prohibition inherent in the fruit" applies only if the *'orlah* tree is attached to an older tree. While the act of attaching lifts the condition of *'orlah* from future fruits of the young tree, it is ineffective for the fruits already growing on the sapling at the moment of attachment.

126 The two trees keep their own roots but two branches, one of each tree, are grafted together.

127 If both of them are *'orlah*, both will be exempt at the moment one of them becomes exempt.

רִבִּי אַבָּהוּ בְשֵׁם רִבִּי יוֹחָנָן וְרַב חִסְדָּא תְּרֵיהוֹן אָמְרִין בִּסְתָם חֲלוּקִין. מַה נָן קַייָמִין אִם דָּבָר בָּרִיא הוּא שֶׁהוּא חַי מִכֹּחַ הַזְּקֵינָה דִּבְרֵי הַכֹּל מוּתָּר. וְאִם דָּבָר בָּרִיא הוּא שֶׁהוּא חַי מִכֹּחַ הַיַּלְדָּה דִּבְרֵי הַכֹּל אָסוּר. אֶלָּא כִּי נָן קַייָמִין בִּסְתָם. כֵּיצַד הוּא יוֹדֵעַ. רִבִּי בִּיבַי בְּשֵׁם רִבִּי (fol. 61b) חֲנִינָה אִם הָיוּ הֶעָלִים הֲפוּכִין כְּלַפֵּי הַיַּלְדָּה דָּבָר בָּרִיא שֶׁהוּא חַי מִכֹּחַ הַזְּקֵינָה וְאִם הָיוּ הֶעָלִים הֲפוּכִין כְּלַפֵּי הַזְּקֵינָה דָּבָר בָּרִיא שֶׁהוּא חַי מִכֹּחַ הַיַּלְדָּה. אָמַר רִבִּי יוּדָן בַּר חָנִין סֵימָנָא דְּאָכִיל מִן חַבְרֵיהּ בְּהִית מִסְתַּכְּלָא בֵיהּ. אָמַר רִבִּי יוּדָן אָבוֹי דְּרִבִּי מַתַּנְיָיה תִּיפְתָּר שֶׁנֶּשְׁרוּ הֶעָלִין.

Rebbi Abbahu in the name of Rebbi Joḥanan and Rav Ḥisda, both say: they[128] differ in the uninformed[129] case. What are we dealing with? If it is certain that it[130] lives off the old tree, everybody agrees it is permitted. If it is certain that it lives off the young tree, everybody agrees it is forbidden[131]. We must be dealing with the uninformed case. How could one know[132]? Rebbi Vivian in the name of Rebbi Ḥanina: If the leaves are turned towards the young tree one may be sure that it lives from the old one; if the leaves are turned towards the old tree one may be sure that it lives from the young one. Rebbi Yudan bar Ḥanin[133] said, a sign: He who eats from his neighbor's is ashamed to look at him. Rebbi Yudan, the father of Rebbi Mattaniah said, explain it if the leaves have fallen off.

128 Rebbi Meïr and the anonymous majority, whether attaching a young tree to an old one always frees the young one from *'orlah* or not.

129 The information required by R. Meïr is not available.

130 The *'orlah* tree.

131 It remains *'orlah*.

132 How could one measure the flow of sap?

133 One of the last authors mentioned in the Yerushalmi, a student of R. Berekhiah.

בְּרִיכָה שֶׁנִּפְסְקָה. אָמַר רִבִּי יוּדָן לֹא סוֹף דָּבָר בְּרִיכָה אֶלָּא אֲפִילוּ אִילָן דְּאָמַר רִבִּי יָסִי בְּשֵׁם רִבִּי יוֹחָנָן בָּצָל שֶׁעֲקָרוֹ וּשְׁתָלוֹ כֵּיוָן שֶׁהִשְׁרִישׁ מְעַשֵּׂר לְפִי כוּלּוֹ. רִבִּי חִייָה בְּשֵׁם רִבִּי יוֹחָנָן בָּצָל שֶׁעֲקָרוֹ וּשְׁתָלוֹ כֵּיוָן שֶׁהִשְׁרִישׁ מְעַשֵּׂר לְפִי כוּלּוֹ דְּלָא תִיסְבּוֹר מֵימַר אוּף הָכָא כֵן.

"A sunk branch which became separated." Rebbi Yudan said, not only a sunk branch but even a tree[134]; as Rebbi Assi said in the name of Rebbi Joḥanan, if an onion which one uprooted and replanted grows roots he has to tithe for everything[135]. Rebbi Ḥiyya in the name of Rebbi Joḥanan, if an onion which one uprooted and replanted grows roots he has to tithe for everything, but you should not say it applies to here also[136].

134 A tree older than 3 years, full of fruits, becomes *'orlah* again if uprooted (with its roots exposed) and replanted, and the fruits will become forbidden if they grow by more than one 200th.

135 Discussed in *Ševi'it* 6:3, Note 113. The parallel statement in the Babli (*Nazir* 54b, *Menaḥot* 70a), R. Isaac in the name of R. Joḥanan, makes it clear that the onion was fully tithed before being replanted.

136 The quote from R. Joḥanan is correct, the inference is faulty; trees do not have the same rules as onions.

חִילְפַיי שָׁאַל לְרִבִּי יוֹחָנָן וּלְרִבִּי שִׁמְעוֹן תֵּבֶל מַהוּ שֶׁיֶּאֱסֹר בְּיוֹתֵר מִמָּאתַיִם. אָמְרוּ לֵיהּ אֵין תֵּבֶל בְּיוֹתֵר מִמָּאתַיִם. וְהָתַנִּינָן כָּל־הַמְחַמֵּץ וְהַמְתַבֵּל וְהַמְדַמֵּעַ. אִין תֵּימַר לְמֵאָה מָאתַיִם אֲפִילוּ לֹא חִימֵּץ. אֲפִילוּ לֹא תִיבֵּל. אֶלָּא בָּעֲנָבִים אֲנָן קַייָמִין. רִבִּי יוֹסֵי בְשֵׁם רִבִּי יוֹחָנָן בְּשֶׁלֹּא צָמְקוּ אֲבָל אִם צָמְקוּ יֵשׁ תֵּבֶל בְּיוֹתֵר מִמָּאתַיִם. רִבִּי חִייָה בְשֵׁם רִבִּי יוֹחָנָן בְּשֶׁלֹּא בִישְּׁלוֹ. אֲבָל אִם בִּישְּׁלוֹ יֵשׁ תֵּבֶל בְּיוֹתֵר מִמָּאתַיִם.

[137]Ḥilfai asked Rebbi Joḥanan and Rebbi Simeon [ben Laqish][138], do condiments forbid with more than 200[139]? They said to him, condiments are not in more than 200[140]. But did we not state[141]: "Anything which sours, spices, or creates *dema'*?" If you say about 100 or 200, even if it does not sour, spice, or create *dema'*[142]! But we deal with grapes[143]. Rebbi Assi in the name of Rebbi Joḥanan, if they were not raisins, but if they were raisins they are condiments in more than 200. Rebbi Ḥiyya in the name of Rebbi Joḥanan, if they were not cooked, but if they were cooked they are condiments in more than 200.

137 From here to the last paragraph of the Halakhah the text is also in *Nazir* 6:10 (fol. 55c). It is clear from the later paragraphs that the original place of the text is in *Nazir*.

138 Missing here, supplied from the text in *Nazir*.

139 The Mishnah implies that *'orlah* does not forbid food if the forbidden part is less than $^1/_{200}$ of the total. Does this also apply to spices which might be tasted in smaller amounts?

140 The $^1/_{200}$ rule also applies to condiments.

141 Mishnah 2:4. The Mishnah states that these ingredients, if from *'orlah*, make everything forbidden. Since no quantities are mentioned one has to infer that there is no minimal quantity below which they are not active.

142 Defined *Demay* Chapter 1, Note 175.

143 Used as condiment for another dish. The 200 rule does not apply to spices proper.

רִבִּי יָסָא[144] בְּשֵׁם רִבִּי יְהוֹשֻׁעַ בֶּן לֵוִי בְּשֵׁם בַּר[145] פְּדָיָה [נוֹתְנֵי טְעָמִים אֶחָד מִמֵּאָה. {רִבִּי חִיָּיה בְּשֵׁם}[146] רִבִּי יְהוֹשֻׁעַ בֶּן לֵוִי בְּשֵׁם בַּר[54] פְּדָיָה][147] נוֹתְנֵי טְעָמִים אֶחָד מִשִּׁשִּׁים.[148] אָמַר רִבִּי שְׁמוּאֵל בַּר רַב יִצְחָק לְרִבִּי חִיָּיה בַּר בָּא הָא רִבִּי יוֹסֵי פְּלִיג וּמַתְנִיתָא פְּלִיגָא עַל תְּרֵיכוֹן כָּל־הַמְּחַמֵּץ וְהַמְּתַבֵּל וְהַמְּדַמֵּעַ. אִין תֵּימַר לְמֵאָה מָאתַיִם אֲפִילוּ לֹא חִימֵּץ. אֲפִילוּ לֹא תִיבֵּל. אֶלָּא בְּיוֹתֵר אֲנַן קַיָּימִין. אָמַר רִבִּי יִרְמְיָה תִּיפְתָּר בָּשָׂר בְּבָשָׂר. אָמַר רִבִּי יוֹסֵי הוּא בָּשָׂר בְּבָשָׂר הִיא שְׁאָר כָּל הָאִיסּוּרִין. דְּאָמַר רִבִּי אַבָּהוּ בְּשֵׁם רִבִּי יוֹחָנָן מְשַׁעֲרִין אוֹתָן כִּילּוּ כֵן.

Rebbi Assi in the name of Rebbi Joshua ben Levi in the name of Bar Pedaiah: [All sources of taste one in a hundred[149]. Rebbi Ḥiyya in the name of Rebbi Joshua ben Levi in the name of Bar Pedaiah:] All sources of taste one in sixty. Rebbi Samuel ben Rav Isaac said to Rebbi Ḥiyya bar Abba: Rebbi Assi disagrees with you and the Mishnah disagrees with both of you: "Anything which sours, spices, or creates *dema*'? If you say about 100 or 200, even if it does not sour, spice, or create *dema*'[142]! Therefore, we hold even more. Rebbi Jeremiah said, explain it for meat in meat[150]. Rebbi Yose said, meat in meat is the same as all other prohibitions since Rebbi Abbahu said in the name of Rebbi Joḥanan, one estimates as if they were so[151].

144 From the parallel in Nazir (Note 137); the text here reads רבי יוסי.

145 From the parallel in Nazir (Note 137); the text here reads רבי פדיה . It seems that Bar Pedaiah shared his uncle Bar Qappara's open disdain of the patriarchate which caused him never to be ordained. In the Babli (*Ḥulin* 98a), the statement is by R. Joshua ben Levi in the name of Bar Qappara. The opinion of R. Assi is not mentioned there.

146 From the parallel in Nazir, missing in the Rome ms.

147 From the parallel in Nazir and the Rome ms.

148 In the Rome ms., ממאה, from the missed previous sentence. This makes it likely that the missing sentence (Note 144) was in the common *Vorlage* of both mss.

149 A forbidden substance which can be tasted will make food forbidden if it represents more than 1% (for R. Ḥiyya, more than $1\frac{2}{3}\%$) of the total.

150 He applies the $1\%/1\frac{2}{3}\%$ rule only to forbidden meat cooked with permitted, cf. *Terumot* 10:9, Notes 106-109. The discussion in the next paragraph centers on this case.

151 "So" are onions and leeks since R. Abbahu said in the name of R. Joḥanan that all forbidden [food] is estimated as if it were onion, as if it were leeks (*Terumot* 10:1, Notes 10-11). Since onions and leeks are used for their taste, it follows that admixtures of spices also follow the same $1\%/1\frac{2}{3}\%$ rule.

מַיי כְדוֹן הָהֵן אָמַר נוֹתְנֵי טְעָמִים אֶחָד מִמֵּאָה. וְהֵן אָמַר נוֹתְנֵי טְעָמִים אֶחָד מִשִּׁשִּׁים. מָאן דְּאָמַר נוֹתְנֵי טְעָמִים אֶחָד מִשִּׁשִּׁים אַתְּ עוֹשֶׂה הַזְּרוֹעַ אֶחָד מִשִּׁשִּׁים בָּאַיִל. וּמָאן דְּאָמַר אֶחָד מִמֵּאָה אַתְּ עוֹשֶׂה הַזְּרוֹעַ אֶחָד מִמֵּאָה בָּאַיִל. מָאן דְּאָמַר אֶחָד מִמֵּאָה אַתְּ מוֹצִיא אֶת הָעֲצָמוֹת מֵהַזְּרוֹעַ. וּמָאן דְּאָמַר אֶחָד מִשִּׁשִּׁים אֵין אַתְּ מוֹצִיא אֶת הָעֲצָמוֹת מִן הַזְּרוֹעַ. וּכְשֵׁם שֶׁאַתְּ מוֹצִיא אֶת

הָעֲצָמוֹת מִן הַזְּרוֹעַ כָּךְ הוֹצִיאֵם מִן הָאַיִל. לֵית יְכִל דְּתַנֵּי אֵין טִנּוֹפֶת שֶׁלִּתְרוּמָה מִצְטָרֶפֶת עִם הַתְּרוּמָה לֶאֱסוֹר אֶת הַחוּלִין. אֲבָל טִנּוֹפֶת שֶׁלְּחוּלִין מִצְטָרֶפֶת עִם הַחוּלִין לְהַעֲלוֹת אֶת הַתְּרוּמָה. רִבִּי בִּיבַי בָּעֵי טִינּוֹפֶת שֶׁלִּתְרוּמָה מָהוּ שֶׁתִּצְטָרֵף עִם הַחוּלִין לְהַעֲלוֹת אֶת הַתְּרוּמָה. מִן מַה דְּאָמַר רַב חוּנָא קְלִיפֵּי אִיסּוּר מִצְטָרְפוֹת לְהֵיתֵר. הָדָא אָמְרָה טִינּוֹפֶת שֶׁלִּתְרוּמָה מִטְצָרֶפֶת לַחוּלִין לְהַעֲלוֹת אֶת הַתְּרוּמָה.

How is this? One says, all sources of taste by one in 100; the other one says, all sources of taste by one in 60. For him who says all sources of taste by one in 60, you take the forearm as one in 60 of the ram[152]. For him who says all sources of taste by one in 100, you take the forearm as one in 100 of the ram. For him who says one in 100, you remove the bones from the forearm. But if you remove the bones from the forearm, remove them from the ram! This you cannot do, as it was stated[153]: "The waste of heave does not combine with heave to forbid the profane, but the waste of profane combines with the profane to lift the heave." Rebbi Vivian asked: Does the waste of heave combine with profane to lift the heave? Since Rav Ḥuna said, the husks of what is forbidden combine to permit, that means waste of heave combines with profane to lift the heave.

152 The entire idea that biblical law permits to disregard minute amounts of forbidden food in otherwise permitted food is derived from the ceremony which releases the *nazir* from his vow (*Num.* 6:19). In general, from a well-being sacrifice a hind leg and the breast has to be given to the Cohen to be eaten by him and his family; that part then is forbidden to lay persons (*Num.* 18:18). But the ram which is the *nazir*'s well-being offering has to be cooked before the Cohen's part, a foreleg, is separated and given to him; the remainder of the sacrifice is permitted to lay persons. From this one

concludes that if in anything cooked the ratio of forbidden to permitted is no greater than that of the forarm to the entire ram, the food remains permitted.

153 This and the rest of the paragraph is from *Terumot* 5:9, Notes 103-106, and has been explained there. Since the bones of the forearm, being inedible, are not forbidden to lay persons, not only are they not counted as forbidden but they are added to the amount of permitted food.

תַּנֵּי רִבִּי חִייָה כָּל־מַה שֶׁאָסַרְתִּי לָךְ מִמָּקוֹם אַחֵר הִתַּרְתִּי לָךְ כָּאן. לְפִי שֶׁבַּכֹּל מֵאָה אִיסּוּר וּמֵאָה וְעוֹד מוּתָּר בְּרַם הָכָא אֲפִילוּ מֵאָה מוּתָּר.

Rebbi Ḥiyya stated: All I forbade to you at other places I permitted to you here. Since everywhere 100 is a prohibition, more than 100 is permitted, but here even 100 is permitted[154].

154 In *Nazir* and the Rome ms., the statement is in the name of Ḥizqiah, R. Ḥiyya's (the elder's) son. The previous argument is not quite conclusive since as a matter of practice we require that the amount of forbidden material should be strictly less than 1% (in the opinion adopted by the Babli, < 1⅔%). But nobody asserts that the edible part of the foreleg is less than 1% of the entire ram; so one has proved only the requirement ≤ 1%. Therefore, the rule remains one of traditional practice.

(ותוב) אִם הוֹסִיף בְּמָאתַיִם אָסוּר. דְּבֵי רִבִּי יַנַּאי מְשַׁעֲרִין בְּהָדֵין יַרְבּוּזָה. כֵּיצַד הוּא יוֹדֵעַ. רַב בִּיבַי בְּשֵׁם רִבִּי חֲנִינָה לוֹקֵט אֶחָד וּמֵנִיחַ אֶחָד מַה שֶׁזֶּה פוֹחֵת זֶה מוֹסִיף.

(In addition,)[155] "if it increased by one twohundredth it is forbidden." Those of the house of Rebbi Yannai estimate by purslain. How does one know? Rav Vivian in the name of Rebbi Ḥaninah: He takes one out and leaves one in [the ground]; what the first one is less, the other did increase.

155 Missing in the text in *Nazir*; the entire paragraph is from *Kilaim* 5, end of Halakhah 6.

(fol. 60c) **משנה ו:** נְטִיעָה שֶׁלְּעָרְלָה וְשֶׁלְּכִלְאֵי הַכֶּרֶם שֶׁנִּתְעָֽרְבוּ בִנְטִיעוֹת הֲרֵי זֶה לֹא יִלְקוֹט. וְאִם לִיקֵּט יַעֲלוּ בְאֶחָד וּמָאתַיִם וּבִלְבַד שֶׁלֹּא יִתְכַּוֵּן לִלְקוֹט. רַבִּי יוֹסֵי אוֹמֵר יִתְכַּוֵּן וְיִלְקוֹט וְיַעֲלוּ בְּאֶחָד וּמָאתַיִם.

Mishnah 6: If a sapling of *'orlah* or vineyard *kilaim*[156] became mixed with [other] saplings, one should not harvest. If he harvested it can be lifted[157] by one in two hundred on condition that he did not have the intention to harvest[158]. Rebbi Yose says, he may intend to harvest[159]; it will be lifted by one in two hundred.

156 Cf. Introduction to Tractate *Kilaim*, that the usufruct of anything sown in a vineyard is forbidden. *Kilaim* also follow the rule that less than $^1/_{200}$ is not counted (Mishnah *Kilaim* 5:6).

157 One takes out $^1/_{200}$; the remainder is permitted. For this meaning of "lifting" cf. *Terumot* 4:6, Note 62.

158 Since all the rules of lifting and disregarding the forbidden part are only for accidents; it is forbidden intentionally to use forbidden substances with the idea that they should e disregarded.

159 He holds that the lifting is only after the harvest; therefore this case does not fall under the forbidden category. Maimonides in his Commentary rejects the opinion of R. Yose, in his Code he accepts it. According to the Babli (*Giṭṭin* 54b), R. Yose holds that the prohibition of intentional use of forbidden substances is rabbinic and does not apply in a situation that never will happen since nobody will risk losing 45 vines because of one extraneous plant (Mishnah *Kilaim* 5:5). For the explanation of the Yerushalmi see Note 175.

(fol. 61b) **הלכה ה**: נְטִיעָה שֶׁלְעָרְלָה נְטִיעָה שֶׁלְכִּלְאֵי הַכֶּרֶם. וַהֲלֹא כָל־הַנְּטִיעוֹת אֵינָן כִּלְאַיִם בַּכֶּרֶם. כֵּינִי מַתְנִיתָא עֲרוּגָה שֶׁלְכִּלְאֵי הַכֶּרֶם. אָמַר רִבִּי יוֹסֵי בֵּירִבִּי (מַתְנִיתָא עֲרוּגָה שֶׁלְכִּלְאֵי הַכֶּרֶם. אָמַר רִבִּי יוֹסֵי בֵּירִבִּי)[160] בּוּן בְּשֶׁהֵבִיא עָצִיץ נָקוּב וְהֶעֱבִירוֹ תַּחַת הַגֶּפֶן.

Halakhah 5: "A sapling of *'orlah* or vineyard *kilaim.*" But no saplings are *kilaim* in a vineyard[161]! So is the Mishnah: "A vegetable bed of vineyard *kilaim.*"[162] Rebbi Yose ben Rebbi (the Mishnah: "A vegetable bed of vineyard *kilaim.*" Rebbi Yose ben Rebbi) Abun said, if he brought a flower pot and temporarily put it under a vine[163].

160 Dittography; the text in parentheses is not in the Rome ms.

161 Since the verse (*Deut.* 22:9) only forbids sowing in a vineyard (grain or vegetables; never trees).

162 In that case, it is difficult to see how one could not know which vegetable bed was forbidden.

163 Mishnah *Kilaim* 7:8, Halakhah 6; cf. Note 88. A tree in a flower pot rabbinically is considered a vegetable. A discussion of this text in J. N. Epstein, [2]במוא לנוסח המשנה p. 451.

רִבִּי שִׁמְעוֹן בֶּן לָקִישׁ בְּשֵׁם חִזְקִיָּה לוֹקֵט שְׁלֹשָׁה אֶשְׁכּוֹלוֹת וּמַתִּיר. מִחְלְפָה שִׁיטָּתֵיהּ דְּרִבִּי שִׁמְעוֹן בֶּן לָקִישׁ. תַּמָּן אָמַר בְּשֵׁם רִבִּי הוֹשַׁעְיָה הָיוּ לְפָנָיו מֵאָה וַחֲמִשִּׁים חָבִיּוֹת. נִתְפַּתְּחוּ מֵאָה מוּתָּרוֹת וַחֲמִשִּׁים אֲסוּרוֹת וְהַשְּׁאָר לִכְשֶׁיִּפַּתְּחוּ יְהוּ מוּתָּרוֹת. אָמַר רִבִּי זְעִירָא לֹא אָמַר אֶלָּא לִכְשֶׁיִּפַּתְּחוּ. הָא לִיפְתַּח כַּתְּחִילָּה אָסוּר. וְהָכָא הוּא אָמַר הָכֵין. תַּמָּן בְּשֵׁם רִבִּי הוֹשַׁעְיָה וְהָכָא בְּשֵׁם חִזְקִיָּה. וְאָמְרִין תַּמָּן בְּשֵׁם רִבִּי שִׁמְעוֹן בֶּן לָקִישׁ פּוֹתֵחַ שָׁלֹשׁ חָבִיּוֹת וּמַתִּיר. וְאַתְיָא כְּחִזְקִיָּה דְהָכָא.

Rebbi Simeon ben Laqish in the name of Ḥizqiah: He harvests three bunches and permits[164]. The position of Rebbi Simeon ben Laqish is inverted! There[165], he said in the name of Rebbi Hoshaia: If there were before him 150 amphoras which were opened, one hundred are permitted, fifty are forbidden, and the remainder will be permitted if they were opened. Rebbi Zeïra said, he said only "*if* they were opened;" therefore at the start it is forbidden to open them. And here, he says so? There in the name of Rebbi Hoshaia, here in the name of Ḥizqiah. They say there[166] in the name of Ḥizqiah: He opens three amphoras and permits; one follows Ḥizqiah here.

164 If he has a vineyard with one forbidden vine whose situation is unknown, he harvests three bunches and considers them to be forbidden as fruits of the forbidden vine. Then the remainder is permitted.

165 *Terumot* 4:8, Note 83. Mishnah *'Orlah* 3:7 will explain that amphoras never can be disregarded; if there are 150 amphoras of which one is of *terumah* (which may be lifted by one in 100) that according to Hoshaia one may open only 100 and lift from them 1% as heave; the other 50 will be usable only if opened by accident (as R. Zeïra explains) because opened intentionally they will be forbidden. Why does he require only three here, not at least 50?

166 In Babylonia, where no heave is biblical and in every respect one follows the more lenient opinion. While this does not imply anything for practice in the Land, it shows that Ḥizqiah is consistent and R. Simeon ben Laqish simply reports what others have said.

וְהָא תַנִּינָן הֲרֵי זֶה לֹא יִלְקוֹט. לְשֶׁעָבַר. וְהָא תַנִּינָן אִם לִקֵּט יַעֲלוּ בְאֶחָד וּמָאתַיִם. אָמַר רִבִּי יוֹסֵי בֵּירִבִּי בוּן כָּאן בְּשֶׁלִּיקֵּט שְׁלֹשָׁה כָּאן בְּשֶׁלִּיקֵּט כּוּלְּהוֹן.

But did we not state: "One should not harvest;" after the fact. And we have stated: "If he harvested it can be lifted by one in two hundred." Rebbi Yose ben Rebbi Abun said, in the first case if he harvested three[167]; in the second case if he harvested all of them[168].

167 They are forbidden for all use, being *'orlah* or *kilaim*.

168 They are lifted by one in 200.

תַּנֵּי רִימּוֹנֵי בְּדָן שֶׁסְּפֵיקוֹ[169] מַעֲלֶה וַדָּיָין אֵינוֹ מַעֲלֶה. אַף בְּקַרְקַע כֵּן. סָפֵק קַרְקַע מַעֲלֶה וְקַרְקַע אֵינוֹ מַעֲלֶה. הֵיךְ עֲבִידָה נְטִיעָה שֶׁלְעָרְלָה וְשֶׁלְכִּלְאֵי הַכֶּרֶם שֶׁנִּתְעָרְבוּ בִנְטִיעוֹת. אֲפִילוּ סָפֵק קַרְקַע מַעֲלֶה וְקַרְקַע אֵינוֹ מַעֲלֶה. רִבִּי יוּדָן בָּעֵי אַף לְעִנְיָן נְבֵילָה כֵן. חָזַר רִבִּי יוּדָן וָמַר נְבֵילָה אֵין לָהּ עֲלִיָּה קַרְקַע יֵשׁ לוֹ עֲלִייָה.

It was stated: Pomegranates of Bedan[170] in case of doubt can be lifted, if certain cannot be lifted. It is the same on the ground[171]. A doubt on the ground can be lifted, but the ground cannot lift[172]. How is this? If a sapling of *'orlah* or vineyard *kilaim* became mixed with [other] saplings, (even) a case of doubt on the ground can be lifted, but the ground cannot lift. Rebbi Yudan asked: Is it the same for a cadaver[173]? Rebbi Yudan turned around and said, a cadaver has no lifting[174], the ground has a lifting.

169 Reading of the Rome ms. Leyden and Venice have unintelligible שסיפקו.

170 They are so expensive that they never can be disregarded, Mishnah 3:7. But this is the rule only if it is certain that any of them is present. As *Sefer Nir* points out, if it is not known whether a certain pomegranate is of the Bedan kind or not, that one will be treated as a regular pomegranate because it will never fetch Bedan prices.

171 The case of the Mishnah, trees planted in the ground. {Rashi in *Giṭṭin* 54b holds that plants in the ground can never be lifted.}

172 One cannot simply choose a tree out of more than 200, cut it down, and declare that the problem of *'orlah* or vineyard *kilaim* has disappeared.

173 If a piece of cadaver meat (or any other piece of forbidden food) was not recognizable among similar pieces of kosher meat, may one take out one, declare it as cadaver meat, and declare

the remainder as kosher. Is this a legitimate deduction from the opinion of R. Simeon ben Laqish in the name of Ḥizqiah?

174 The only things that can be lifted are heave, *'orlah*, and *kilaim*. All others are either a negligible quantity, where everything is permitted, or not, where everything is forbidden.

רִבִּי יוֹסֵי אוֹמֵר אַף יִתְכַּוֵּן וְיִלְקוֹט וְיַעֲלוּ בְּאֶחָד וּמָאתַיִם. מַה טַעֲמָא דְּרִבִּי יוֹסֵי שֶׁכֵּן דֶּרֶךְ בְּנֵי אָדָם לִהְיוֹת מֵידַל בִּגְפָנִים.

"Rebbi Yose says, he even may intend to harvest, it will be lifted by one in two hundred." What is the reason of Rebbi Yose? People are always thinning vines[175].

175 Following R. Simeon ben Laqish in the name of Ḥizqiah, the unripe bunches of grapes cut out in thinning can be used to permit the remainder. {One cannot say that "thinning" refers to thinning out vines that were planted too close to one another since then the entire vineyard would still be *'orlah*; cf. *Or Zarua'* vol. 1, #320.}

תַּמָּן תַּנִּינָן סְאָה תְרוּמָה שֶׁנָּפְלָה לְמֵאָה טְחָנָן וּפָחֲתוּ. כְּשֵׁם שֶׁפָּחֲתוּ הַחוּלִין כֵּן פָּחֲתָה הַתְּרוּמָה. מוּתָּר. תַּנֵּי[176] אַף יִתְכַּוֵּין וְיִלְקוֹט. וְיַעֲלוּ בְאֶחָד וּמָאתַיִם. אָמַר רִבִּי זְעִירָא דִּבְרֵי הַכֹּל הִיא שֶׁכֵּן דֶּרֶךְ הַכֹּהֲנִים לִהְיוֹת טוֹחֲנִין מְדוּמָּע לְתוֹךְ בָּתֵּיהֶן. מַה נְפַק מִן בֵּינֵיהוֹן. כִּלְאֵי הַכֶּרֶם עַל דַּעְתֵּיהּ דְּרִבִּי יוֹסֵי טוֹחֵן וּמַתִּיר. עַל דַּעְתּוֹן דְּרַבָּנִין אֵין טוֹחֵן וּמַתִּיר.

There, we have stated: [177]"If a *seah* of heave fell into 100 and one milled it and it lost volume, in proportion to what the profane lost, the heave lost, and it is permitted." It was stated: ["One may mill from the start to permit." The *baraita* is Rebbi Yose's, since "Rebbi Yose said,] he even may intend to harvest, it will be lifted by one in two hundred". Rebbi Zeïra said, Cohanim are used to mill *dema'* in their houses. What is the difference between them? *Kilaim* in a vineyard. In the opinion of Rebbi Yose, one mills to permit; in the opinion of the rabbis, one may not mill to permit.

176 Here, a phrase is missing which appears in *Terumot* 5:9: אַף טוֹחֵן הוּא בַּתְּחִילָּה וּמַתִּיר. מַתְנִיתָא דְּרִבִּי יוֹסֵי דְּרִבִּי יוֹסֵי אָמַר.

177 From here on, the text is from *Terumot* 5:9 and has been explained there, Notes 100, 109-111.

(fol. 60c) **משנה ז:** הֶעָלִים וְהַלּוּלָבִים וּמֵי גְפָנִים וְהַסְּמָדַר מוּתָּרִין בְּעָרְלָה וּבִרְבִיעִי וּבְנָזִיר וַאֲסוּרִין בַּאֲשֵׁירָה. רִבִּי יוֹסֵי אָמַר הַסְּמָדַר אָסוּר מִפְּנֵי שֶׁהוּא פְּרִי. רִבִּי לִיעֶזֶר אוֹמֵר הַמַּעֲמִיד בִּשְׂרָף הֶעָרְלָה אָסוּר. אָמַר רִבִּי יְהוֹשֻׁעַ שָׁמַעְתִּי בְּפֵירוּשׁ שֶׁהַמַּעֲמִיד בִּשְׂרָף הֶעָלִים וּבִשְׂרָף הָעִיקָּרִים מוּתָּר. בִּשְׂרָף הַפַּגִּים אָסוּר מִפְּנֵי שֶׁהוּא פְּרִי.

Mishnah 7: Leaves, shoots, vine sap, and the flower[178] are permitted for *'orlah*, the Fourth Year, and a *nazir*[179], but forbidden from a pagan sacred grove[180]. Rebbi Yose said, the flower is forbidden because it is a fruit. Rebbi Eliezer says, it is forbidden to use *'orlah* sap as curd. Rebbi Joshua said, I heard explicitly that one is permitted to use sap of leaves and sap of roots as curd. But the sap of unripe figs is forbidden because that is a fruit.

178 Definition of Maimonides, Arabic אַלְפַּקָּאח. He emphasized that חִצְרִם "budding fruit" is forbidden. The same definition may be found in *Arukh*: "The state between budding of the flower and development of the fruit."

179 He is forbidden (Num. 6:4) "anything made from the wine-vine".

180 Anything used in pagan worship is permanently forbidden for all

usufruct except the soil and what stands on it. Therefore the grove itself cannot be forbidden but everything taken from it is.

(fol. 61b) **הלכה ו:** הֶעָלִים וְהַלּוּלָבִים. מַתְנִיתָא דְלֹא כְרִבִּי אֱלִיעֶזֶר דְּתַנֵּי בְשֵׁם רִבִּי לִיעֶזֶר מִכֹּל אֲשֶׁר יֵעָשֶׂה מִגֶּפֶן הַיַּיִן מֵחַרְצַנִּים וְעַד זָג לֹא יֹאכֵל אַף הֶעָלִים וְהַלּוּלָבִים בְּמַשְׁמַע.

"Leaves and shoots." Our Mishnah does not follow Rebbi Eliezer, as was stated[181] in the name of Rebbi Eliezer: (*Num.* 6:4) "Anything made from the wine-vine, from seeds to skin he shall not eat," that includes leaves and shoots.

181 *Nazir* 6:1 (fol. 54d), 6:2 (fol. 55a); Babli *Nazir* 34b.

תַּנֵּי רִבִּי יוֹסֵי אוֹמֵר סְמָדַר אָסוּר מִפְּנֵי שֶׁהוּא פֶּרִי. וְקַשְׁיָא אִם אָסוּר בְּנָזִיר לָמָּה לִי פֶּרִי אִם פֶּרִי הוּא יְהֵא אָסוּר בַּכֹּל. מִלְּתֵיהּ דְּרִבִּי יִצְחָק אָמְרָה שֶׁהוּא אָסוּר בַּכֹּל. רִבִּי יִצְחָק שָׁאַל מָאן תַּנָּא אֵין מַרְכִּיבִין בְּכַפְנִיּוֹת שֶׁלְּעָרְלָה רִבִּי יוֹסֵי.

It was stated[182]: "Rebbi Yose says the flower is forbidden because it is a fruit." It is difficult! If it is forbidden for the *nazir* why a fruit[183]? If it is a fruit it should be forbidden for everybody! The word of Rebbi Isaac implies that it is forbidden for everybody. Rebbi Isaac asked: Who stated [184]"one does not graft with spathe[185] of *'orlah*"? Rebbi Yose!

182 *Nazir* 6:2, fol. 55a. There, the text reads "Rebbi Yose says the flower is forbidden *for the nazir* because it is a fruit." The discussion presupposes this text; the question is whether the Mishnah has to be interpreted in the light of the *baraita* or whether R. Yose also forbids *'orlah* flower and requires redemption in the forth year.

183 Since the rules for *'orlah* and the

fourth year explicitly refer to fruits, if a flower is counted as a fruit automatically it would be subject to *'orlah* and the Fourth Year. If R. Yose restricts the prohibition of vine flowers to the *nazir* he must hold with R. Eliezer.

184 Mishnah 9.

185 Definition of Maimonides; Arabic טַלע. *Arukh* and Rashi, based on Gaonic sources, define as "dates that never ripen." I. Löw (followed by S. Lieberman) takes it as the male flower which from an *'orlah* date palm may not be taken to hang into the branches of a female tree.

תַּנֵּי פְּרִי אַתְּ פּוֹדֶה וְאֵין אַתְּ פּוֹדֶה לֹא בוֹסֶר וְלֹא פַגִּים. הוֹרֵי רִבִּי זְבִידָא בְּאִילֵּין פָּגֵּי תְמָרָה שֶׁיִּקָּבֵרוּ. רִבִּי יוֹנָה בָּעֵי עָבַר וּפְדָיוֹ שֶׁמָּא אֵינוֹ פָּדוּי. וְתֵימַר טָעוּן קְבוּרָה.

It was stated[186]: You redeem fruit; you do not redeem either unripe grapes or unripe figs. Rebbi Zavida instructed about unripe dates that they should be buried[187]. Rebbi Jonah asked: If he transgressed and redeemed them, is it not redeemed? And you want to say, it needs to be buried!

186 *Lev.* 19:24 declares all fourth-year *fruit* holy; implying that it must be redeemed. The next verse notes that the rules for the first four years were given so the tree should increase its *yield* starting from the fifth year. The word *yield* is taken in *Sifra Qedošim Paraša* 3(10) to mean that the duty of redemption in the fourth year starts at the point in the ripening of the fruit at which in the fifth year the duty of tithing starts (*Ma'serot* 1:2); in the case of grapes if there is some sap in the fruit. The two sources seem to contradict one another but Maimonides (*Ma'aser Šeni* 9:2) adopts both of them.

187 He holds that they cannot be eaten since they cannot be redeemed; they have to be treated like a firstling which died before it could be sacrificed.

רִבִּי פְּדָת רִבִּי יוֹסֵי בְּשֵׁם רִבִּי יוֹחָנָן. רִבִּי שִׁמְעוֹן וְרִבִּי יְהוֹשֻׁעַ אָמְרוּ דָבָר אֶחָד. תַּמָּן תַּנִּינָן רִבִּי שִׁמְעוֹן אוֹמֵר אֵין לְקָטָף שְׁבִיעִית מִפְּנֵי שֶׁאֵינוֹ פֶּרִי. אָמַר רִבִּי זְעִירָה לְרִבִּי פְּדָת כְּמָה דְתֵימַר תַּמָּן הֲלָכָה כְרִבִּי שִׁמְעוֹן וְהָכָא הֲלָכָה כְּרִבִּי יְהוֹשֻׁעַ. אָמַר רִבִּי יוֹנָה וְדַמְיָא הִיא לְכָל־רַבִּיָּה קָטָף בָּטֵל עַל יְדֵי שְׂרָפוֹ. [וְאִילָן אֵינוֹ בָטֵל עַל גַּבֵּי שְׂרָפוֹ.][188] אוֹכְלֵי בְהֵמָה קְדוּשַּׁת שְׁבִיעִית חָל עֲלֵיהֶן. אֵין קְדוּשַּׁת עָרְלָה חָל עֲלֵיהֶן. אָמַר רִבִּי בּוּן אִית לָךְ חוֹרִי. רִבִּי יְהוֹשֻׁעַ אֲמָרָהּ שְׁמוּעָה. וְרִבִּי שִׁמְעוֹן בְּשֵׁם גַּרְמֵיהּ אֲמָרָהּ. לָמָּה (fol. 61c) שְׂרָף פְּרִי פַּגִּין פְּרִי. אִין תֵּימַר שְׂרָף פְּרִי עָשָׂה כֵן בִּתְרוּמָה מוּתָּר. אִין תֵּימַר פַּגִּין פְּרִי עָשָׂה כֵן בִּתְרוּמָה מוּתָּר. לָמָּה שֶׁהֲנָיַית תְּרוּמָה מוּתֶּרֶת וַהֲנָיַית עָרְלָה אֲסוּרָה.

[189]Rebbi Pedat, Rebbi Assi, in the name of Rebbi Johanan: Rebbi Simeon follows that of Rebbi Joshua, as we have stated there[190]: "Rebbi Simeon says, balsamum is not subject to the Sabbatical because it is not a fruit." Rebbi Zeïra said to Rebbi Pedat, since we say there that practice follows Rebbi Joshua, would you have to say here that practice follows Rebbi Simeon? Rebbi Jonah said, are the situations similar? It is the other way: Balsamum is essentially sap, a tree is not essentially in its sap. The holiness of the Sabbatical falls on animal feed, but the holiness of *orlah* never falls on it. Rebbi Abun said, there is another [difference]: Rebbi Joshua quoted it as a tradition, Rebbi Simeon said it in his own name. Sap may be fruit, unripe fruits may be fruit. If you say that sap has the status of fruit, if he did it with heave it is permitted. If you say that unripe fruits are fruit, if he did it with heave it is permitted. Why? Because usufruct of heave is permitted but usufruct of *orlah* is forbidden.

188 Text in *Ševi'it* and Rome ms., missing in Leyden ms. and Venice print.

189 The parallel, references switched from there to here, is in *Ševi'it* 7:7, Notes 102-113.

(fol. 60c) **משנה ח:** עַנְקוֹקְלוֹת וְהַחַרְצָנִים וְהַזָּגִים וְהַתֶּמֶד שֶׁלָּהֶן קְלִיפֵּי רִימּוֹן וְהַנֵּץ שֶׁלּוֹ קְלִיפֵּי אֱגוֹזִים וְהַגַּרְעִינִים אֲסוּרִין בְּעָרְלָה וּבָאֲשֵׁירָה וּבְנָזִיר. וּמוּתָּרִין בָּרְבִיעִי וְהַנּוֹבְלוֹת כּוּלָּן אֲסוּרוֹת.

Mishnah 8: *Anqoqlot*[190], the grape skins, the grape seeds, and the afterwine made from them, pomegranate skins and their flowers[191], nut shells, and seeds[192] are forbidden from *'orlah*, sacred groves, and for a *nazir*[193]. They are permitted in the fourth year[194]. Windfall[195] is forbidden for all of these.

190 Neither the meaning nor the etymology of this word are known as will be clear from the Halakhah. In the opinion of *Arukh*, the word designates the edible young shoots of the vine; this follows the Gaonic commentary of R. Nathan Av Hayeshivah who reads קנוקלות, or the reading of *Or Zarua* קנוקנות, "hairline sinews" (Babli *Ḥulin* 92b). This explanation is incompatible with the Yerushalmi. In the opinion of S. Krauss, the word is an expansion of עקל to which compare Arabic עקל "to produce grapes". The text of *Sifra* [*Qedošim Parasha* 3(3)] את ענקוקלות והבוסר also shows that ענקוקלות are misdeveloped grapes.

191 The remainder of the flower visible at the tip of the outer skin.

192 Of any *'orlah* tree.

193 Only the first four items.

194 Only fruits are forbidden unless redeemed.

195 Of fully formed fruits.

(fol. 61c) **הלכה ז:** עַנְקוֹקְלוֹת וְהַחַרְצָנִים. רִבִּי זְעִירָא וְחַד מִן רַבָּנִין בְּשֵׁם רַב עֲנָבִים שֶׁלָּקוּ עַד שֶׁלֹּא הֵבִיאוּ שְׁלִישׁ. אָמַר רִבִּי יוֹסֵי בֵּירִבִּי בּוּן אֲפִילוּ לָקוּ מִשֶּׁהֵבִיאוּ שְׁלִישׁ. אָמַר רִבִּי חִייָא בַּר אָדָא לְשׁוֹן נוֹטָרִיקוֹן הוּא עֲנָבִין דְּלָקֵי תַלְתֵּיהוֹן.

Halakhah 7: "*Anqoqlot* and the grape skins." Rebbi Zeïra and one of the rabbis in the name of Rav: Grapes which went bad before they were one-third ripe. Rebbi Yose ben Rebbi Abun said, even after they were one-third ripe[196]. Rebbi Ḥiyya bar Ada said, it is a stenographic expression: "Grapes becoming bad at a third[197]."

196 In contrast to בוסר, "unripe grape berry", these were spoiled before ripening.

197 He must read עֲנָבִין דְּלָקֵי :ענקולות תַּלְתֵּיהוֹן but there are no Mishnah mss. to back this up.

(fol. 60c) **משנה ט**: רִבִּי יוֹסֵי אוֹמֵר נוֹטְעִין יִיחוּר שֶׁלְעָרְלָה. וְאֵין נוֹטְעִין אֱגוֹז שֶׁלְעָרְלָה מִפְּנֵי שֶׁהוּא פֶּרִי. וְאֵין מַרְכִּיבִין בְּכַפְנִיּוֹת שֶׁלְעָרְלָה.

Mishnah 9: Rebbi Yose said, one may plant an *'orlah* shoot but not an *'orlah* nut because the latter is a fruit. Also, one does not graft with spathe[185] of *'orlah*.

(fol. 61c) **הלכה ח**: רִבִּי יוֹסֵי אוֹמֵר אֵין נוֹטְעִין יִיחוּר. אָמַר רִבִּי יוֹחָנָן עָבַר וְנָטַע מוּתָּר. עָבַר וְהִרְכִּיב אָסוּר.

Halakhah 8: "Rebbi Yose said, one may not[198] plant a shoot." Rebbi Joḥanan said, if one transgressed and planted, it is permitted; if he transgressed and grafted it is forbidden[199].

198 This contradicts the Mishnah; the word is not in the Rome ms. However, the formulation of R. Joḥanan's statement presupposes this reading; following the text of the Mishnah one would expect: "If one planted, it is permitted; if he transgressed and grafted it is forbidden." The Babli (*Avodah Zarah* 48b) disagrees: "Rav Jehudah said, Rav said that R. Yose agrees that if one planted, grafted, or sank, it is permitted." According to Rashi, that statement refers to both shoot and nut,

according to Maimonides (*Ma'aser Seni* 10:20) only to planting a nut.

There is a disagreement in principle between Babli and Yerushalmi. The Babli holds that any growth caused by the common action of a forbidden (*'orlah*) and a permitted (the ground or the stem of an older tree) factor is automatically permitted (זו וזו גורם מותר). The Yerushalmi accepts this only if no one factor alone could have caused the result; cf. Chapter 2, Note 126.

199 It is not clear whether this is a biblical or a rabbinic prohibition.

אֱגוֹז שֶׁלְעָרְלָה שֶׁנְּטָעוֹ וְכֵן בֵּיצַת עֲבוֹדָה זָרָה שֶׁנַּעֲשָׂה אֶפְרוֹחַ. רִבִּי חַגַּיי בְּשֵׁם רִבִּי יֹאשִׁיָּה אִיתְפַּלְּגוּן חִזְקִיָּה וְכַהֲנָא. כַּהֲנָא אָמַר מוּתֶּרֶת חִזְקִיָּה אָמַר אָסוּר. עַל דַּעְתֵּיהּ דְּחִזְקִיָּה אֵין אֶפְשַׁר לְבֵיצַת עֲבוֹדָה זָרָה שֶׁנַּעֲשֵׂית אֶפְרוֹחַ. מַה נָן קַייָמִין. אִם בְּשֶׁפֶּחְסָהּ אֵין כָּאן אֶפְרוֹחַ אִם בְּשֶׁהִכְנִיסָהּ לִפְנִימָה מִן הַקַּנְקֵילִין אִתָא חֲמִי וְאִילּוּ הִשְׁתַּחֲוֶה לָהּ לֹא אֲסָרָהּ מִפְּנֵי שֶׁהִכְנִיסָהּ לִפְנִימָה מִן הַקַּנְקֵילִין אֲסָרָהּ. אָמַר רִבִּי יוּדָן אֲבוֹי דְּרִבִּי מַתַּנְיָה[200] תִּפְתָּר שֶׁגָּדַר בָּהּ עֲבוֹדָה זָרָה.

[201]An *'orlah* walnut which one planted, and similarly, an egg of idol worship which turned into a chick. Rebbi Ḥaggai in the name of Rebbi Josia: Ḥizqiah and Cahana differ. Cahana said it is permitted, Ḥizqiah said it is forbidden. In the opinion of Ḥizqiah it should be impossible for an egg of idol worship to become a chick. What is this about? If someone squashed it[202], there is no chick. If he brought it inside the lattice enclosure[203], come and look: If he worshipped it it is not forbidden[204]; because he brought it inside the grating should it be forbidden? Rebbi Yudan the father of Rebbi Mattaniah said, explain it if he used it to fence in the idol[205].

200 Reading of the Rome ms. and the parallel in *Avodah Zarah*. Leyden and Venice: מתניתא.

201 This paragraph (without mentioning the walnut) and the next are also in *Avodah Zarah* 3:6 (fol. 43a).

202 Used the egg as a pagan sacrifice. The use of the egg as a pagan symbol was studied by J. J. Bachofen, *Versuch über die Gräbersymbolik der Alten*, Gesammelte Werke Bd. 4, Basel 1954.

203 Latin *cancelli*; the fence outside the pagan temple.

204 It is Ḥizqiah's own opinion in *Avodah Zarah* 3:6 (fol. 43a) that nothing becomes forbidden because of idol worship unless something was done with it. R. Joḥanan disagrees; for him an egg introduced into a pagan temple becomes forbidden.

205 There was a hole in the wall which was closed by putting an egg into the hole.

בֵּיצַת הֶקְדֵּשׁ שֶׁנַּעֲשֵׂת אֶפְרוֹחַ. אָמַר רִבִּי יַיסָא פְּלִיגֵי בָהּ כַּהֲנָא וְרִבִּי יוֹחָנָן. כַּהֲנָא אָמַר אֲסוּרָה וְרִבִּי יוֹחָנָן אָמַר מוּתֶּרֶת. אָמַר רִבִּי זְעִירָא לְרִבִּי יוֹסֵי הָא רִבִּי יוֹחָנָן אָמַר מוּתֶּרֶת אוּף הוּא פוֹדֶה[206] אוֹתָהּ בִּזְמַן זַרְעָהּ. רִבִּי חֲנִינָה וְרִבִּי יוֹנָה רִבִּי לְעָזָר בְּשֵׁם כַּהֲנָא פוֹדֶה אוֹתָהּ בִּזְמַן זַרְעָהּ. וְרִבִּי חֲנַנְיָה בְשֵׁם רִבִּי פִּינְחָס מְתַקְּנָתָהּ. כַּהֲנָא אָמַר אֲסוּרָה וּפוֹדֶה אוֹתָהּ כְּמוֹ שֶׁהִיא. רִבִּי יוֹחָנָן אָמַר מוּתֶּרֶת וּפוֹדֶה אוֹתָהּ בִּזְמַן זַרְעָהּ.

If an egg dedicated to the Temple became a chick. Rebbi Assi said, Cahana and Rebbi Joḥanan disagree about this. Cahana said it is forbidden and Rebbi Joḥanan said it is permitted. Rebbi Zeïra said to Rebbi Assi, since Rebbi Joḥanan said it is permitted, does he redeem[207] it as from the time it is sown? Rebbi Hanania[208] and Rebbi Jonah, Rebbi Eleazar in the name of Cahana: He redeems it as from the time it is sown. Rebbi Ḥanania in the name of Rebbi Phineas corrects it: Cahana said it is forbidden and he redeems it as it is now; Rebbi Joḥanan said it is permitted and he redeems it as from the time it is sown.

206 In the Leyden ms. פורח "it flies"; already corrected in the Venice print.

207 The Rome ms. and the text in *Avodah Zarah* read: does he not

redeem it? Since this is a question, there is no material difference. One does not sow an egg; the reference is to Mishnah *Terumot* 9:4 which states that growth from dedicated grain is profane but nevertheless it has to be redeemed but only for the value of the seed grain used, not of the harvest. The question then is whether R. Joḥanan holds that the chick, being different from the egg, is purely profane and needs no redemption or, while being profane, needs redemption for the value of the egg.

208 Reading of the text in *Avodah Zarah*. The reading here, R. Ḥanina, is impossible for chronological reasons.

התרומה ותרומת מעשר פרק שני

(fol. 61d) **משנה א**: הַתְּרוּמָה וּתְרוּמַת מַעֲשֵׂר שֶׁל דְּמַאי הַחַלָּה וְהַבִּיכּוּרִין עוֹלִין בְּאֶחָד וּמֵאָה וּמִצְטָרְפִין זֶה עִם זֶה וְצָרִיךְ לְהָרִים. הֶעָרְלָה וְכִלְאֵי הַכֶּרֶם עוֹלִין בְּאֶחָד וּמָאתַיִם וּמִצְטָרְפִין זֶה עִם זֶה וְאֵינוֹ צָרִיךְ לְהָרִים. רִבִּי שִׁמְעוֹן אוֹמֵר אֵינָן מִצְטָרְפִין. רִבִּי לִיעֶזֶר אוֹמֵר מִצְטָרְפִין בְּנוֹתֵן טַעַם אֲבָל לֹא לֶאֱסוֹר.

Mishnah 1: Heave, heave of the tithe of *demay*[1], *ḥallah*, and First Fruits are lifted by one and 100[2], they combine with one another[3], and one has to remove[4]. *'Orlah* and vineyard *kilaim* are lifted by one and 200, they combine with one another, and one need not remove[5]. Rebbi Simeon says, they do not combine. Rebbi Eliezer[6] says they combine in matters of perceiving the taste[7] but not to forbid.

1 All mss. of the Maimonides tradition and many of the better Mishnah mss. read: Heave, heave of the tithe, and heave of the tithe of *demay*. This text is understood in the Halakhah. By definition of *demay*, there is no heave of *demay*. Since both *ḥallah* and First Fruits are called "heave", they follow the rules of heave.

2 Mishnah *Terumot* 4:7.

3 If, e. g., heave, heave of the tithe, and *ḥallah* fell into profane dough, the dough remains permitted for lay people only if the profane was at least 100 times the combined volume of the three "heave" kinds.

4 Before the mixture is permitted to lay people one has to remove a volume equal to that which fell into the profane and give it to the Cohen under the rules of heave. The first hand of the Leyden ms. has: "One need not remove".

5 Since they are forbidden for any use, they have no owners to which the removed part should be given. It is

enough that the forbidden parts are so few that they can be considered non-existent.

6 In most Mishnah mss. and the Halakhah: R. Eleazar. This reading is required since he is mentioned after R. Simeon.

7 As long as the taste of one is recognizable in the other. But if $^1/_{201}$ *'orlah* and $^1/_{201}$ vineyard *kilaim* fall into permitted food everything is permitted since each of the forbidden quantities is less than $^1/_{201}$ of the remaining material.

(fol. 61d) **הלכה א:** הַתְּרוּמָה וּתְרוּמַת מַעֲשֵׂר כו'. לְמִי נִצְרְכָה לְרִבִּי שִׁמְעוֹן. אַף עַל גַּב דְּרִבִּי שִׁמְעוֹן אָמַר אֵין שְׁנֵי שֵׁמוֹת מִצְטָרְפִין. מוֹדֵי שֶׁכּוּלְּהֹן לְשֵׁם תְּרוּמָה מִצְטָרְפִין.

Halakhah 1: "Heave and heave of the tithe", etc. For whom is this[8] needed? For Rebbi Simeon. Even though Rebbi Simeon says that two different names do not combine, he agrees that all items called "heave" do combine.

8 The statement that all the categories mentioned in the first statement combine.

מָאן תַּנָּא תְּרוּמַת מַעֲשֵׂר שֶׁל דְּמַאי רִבִּי מֵאִיר. דְּרִבִּי מֵאִיר מַחְמִיר בְּדִבְרֵיהֶן כְּדִבְרֵי תוֹרָה. וְהָא אַשְׁכְּחָן דְּרִבִּי מֵאִיר מַחְמִיר בְּדִבְרֵיהֶן כְּדִבְרֵי תוֹרָה. אָמַר רִבִּי חֲנִינָה הַהִיא דְתַנִּינָן תַּמָּן הָרוֹאָה כֶּתֶם הֲרֵי זוֹ מְקוּלְקֶלֶת וְחוֹשֶׁשֶׁת מִשּׁוּם זוֹב דִּבְרֵי רִבִּי מֵאִיר. וַחֲכָמִים אוֹמְרִים אֵין בִּכְתָמִין מִשּׁוּם זוֹב.

Who stated "heave of the tithe of *demay*"? Rebbi Meïr, since Rebbi Meïr is as strict with their word as with the words of the Torah[9]. Where do we find that Rebbi Meïr is as strict with their word as with the words of the Torah? Rebbi Ḥanina said, the following which we have stated there[10]: "A woman who sees a stain [on her clothes] is out of order and must consider the possibility of flux, the words of Rebbi Meïr. But the Sages say that stains do not imply flux[11]."

9 Since the institution of *demay* is rabbinic, the rules for heave of the tithe of *demay* are more lenient than those for biblical heave; cf. Introduction to Tractate Demay. Only R. Meïr does not recognize these differences.

10 Mishnah *Niddah* 6:13. A woman finding a blood stain on her underwear at a time when she does not expect her period does not know when to expect her next period since possibly the stain comes from menstrual blood. A woman is impure by flux if she has episodes for three successive days at a time when menstrual blood is excluded. In that case, she may not enter the Temple without bringing a sacrifice of purification (*Lev.* 15:29-30). R. Meïr requires a sacrifice because of the possibility of impurity but the sacrifice of purification may not be eaten by the Cohanim since possibly it was unnecessary.

11 Since the verse (*Lev.* 15:25) requires "blood flowing", the impurity of stains is purely rabbinical. In the Babli, *Niddah* 52b, the position of the "Sages" is also considered a minority opinion, attributable to R. Ḥanina ben Antigonos. Since the later chapters of the Yerushalmi *Niddah* are lost, we do not know the position of the Yerushalmi in this matter.

רִבִּי יוֹנָה בָּעֵי וְלָמָּה לֹא תַנִּינָן חַלַּת דְּמַיי כְּמַה דְתַנִּינָן חַלָּה. לֹא נִיתְנֵי חַלַּת דְּמַאי[12]. וְהָתַנִּינָן תְּרוּמָה וּתְרוּמַת מַעֲשֵׂר וּתְרוּמַת מַעֲשֵׂר[13] שֶׁלִּדְּמַאי. רִבִּי חֲנַנְיָה בְּשֵׁם שְׁמוּאֵל דְּמַאי צָרִיךְ חַלָּה. אָמַר לוֹ רִבִּי חִיָּיה בַּר לוּלְיאָנִי[14] נוֹטֵל הוּא דָּמָיו מִן הַשֵּׁבֶט. אָמַר לוֹ כֵּן אָמַר שְׁמוּאֵל שֶׁהוּא נוֹטֵל דָּמָיו מִן הַשֵּׁבֶט. רִבִּי מָנָא בְּשֵׁם רִבִּי יוֹסֵי אֵינוֹ נוֹטֵל דָּמָיו מִן הַשֵּׁבֶט לְמָחָר הוּא מֵבִיא וַדַּאי וְאוֹמֵר דְּמַיי הוּא כְּדֵי לִיטּוֹל מִמֶּנּוּ דָּמִים.

Rebbi Jonah asked: Why did we not also state "*ḥallah* of *demay*"[15] as we did state "*ḥallah*"? Should we not state "*ḥallah* of *demay*" as we did state: "Heave, heave of the tithe and heave of the tithe of *demay*"?

Rebbi Ḥanania in the name of Samuel: *Demay* does not need *ḥallah*. Rebbi Ḥiyya bar Julianus said to him, one takes its value from the tribe. He answered him, that is what Samuel said, one takes its value from the tribe[16]. Rebbi Mana in the name of Rebbi Yose: One does not take its value from the tribe; tomorrow he will bring certain [*ḥallah*] and say it is *demay* in order to take its value from the tribe!

12 This sentence is not in the Rome ms.

13 Reading of the first hand of the Leyden ms., crossed out by the corrector, probably in error.

14 Reading of the Rome ms.; Leyden and Venice: לוליבא. Elsewhere he is called בן לוליאני (cf. the Italian form *Lugliani*). A fifth generation Galilean Amora, student of R. Samuel. Therefore, "Samuel" mentioned here is not the first generation Babylonian Samuel but the fourth generation Galilean R. Samuel bar Abba.

15 Which one takes if he buys bread from an untrustworthy baker; *Demay* Mishnah 5:3.

16 This explains the cryptic first statement of R. Samuel. One has to take *ḥallah* if one buys bread from an untrustworthy baker but one may sell it to a Cohen. Since the Cohen has to eat even the *demay ḥallah* under the rules of purity of heave, he will not pay much for the *ḥallah*.

רִבִּי יוֹחָנָן שָׁאַל לְגַמְלִיאֵל זוּגָא נְהִגִין אַתּוּן מַפְקִין חַלָּה מִן דְּמַייא אָמַר לֵיהּ לֹא כֵן אָמַר שְׁמוּאֵל אַחֲוָה דְרַב בְּרֶכְיָה בְּשָׁעָה שֶׁגָּזְרוּ עַל דְּמַאי רוֹב הָעָם מַפְרִישִׁין אוֹתוֹ לְתוֹךְ בָּתֵּיהֶן. אָמַר רִבִּי יוֹסֵי בֵּירִבִּי בּוּן תְּנַיי בֵּית דִּין שֶׁתְּהֵא חַלָּתוֹ בִּצְפוֹן צְפוֹנוֹ.

Rebbi Joḥanan asked Gamliel the Twin: Are you used to take *ḥallah* from *demay*? He answered him, did not Samuel, the brother of Rav Berekhia[17], say that from the moment they decreed *demay*, most people separate it in their houses[18]? Rebbi Yose ben Rebbi Abun said, it is a condition of the court that *ḥallah* be in the Northernmost part[19].

17 Galilean Amora of the fourth generation; he is not identical with his contemporary R. Samuel quoted in the preceding paragraph. Elsewhere he is given the title of Rebbi. The Gamliel the Twin who quotes him cannot be the younger contemporary of R. Joḥanan; he must be the Gamliel who asks a question from the fifth generation R. Yose ben R. Abun (*Šeqalim* 3:2).

18 Since everybody takes extra *ḥallah* from bread he buys from an untrustworthy baker, we certainly do take it.

19 He disagrees with Gamliel the Twin and asserts that if heave of the tithe is taken from *demay* in the prescribed way (*Demay* 5:2, Note 44), one always should take heave of the tithe from the Northernmost part in order to make the procedure routine; then automatically the Northernmost part is *ḥallah* if obligated for it. In that way, tithing *demay* automatically takes care of *ḥallah*.

וְעוֹלִין בְּאֶחָד וּמֵאָה. מָה אַתְּ עֲבִיד לָהּ כִּתְחִילַּת הַפְּרָשָׁה אוֹ כְסוֹף הַפְּרָשָׁה. אִין תֵּימַר כִּתְחִילַּת הַפְּרָשָׁה אֵין הַקָּטָן מַעֲלֶה וְאֵין אַחֵר מַעֲלֶה וְאֵינוֹ דוֹחֶה אֶת הַשַּׁבָּת. וְאִין תַּעַבְדִּינֵיהּ כְּסוֹף הַקָּטָן מַעֲלֶה וְאַחֵר מַעֲלֶה וְדוֹחֶה אֶת הַשַּׁבָּת. תַּמָּן תַּנִּינָן רִבִּי יְהוּדָה אוֹמֵר אַף מַעֲלִין אֶת הַמְּדוּמָּע בְּאֶחָד וּמֵאָה. וְתַנֵּי עֲלָהּ רִבִּי שִׁמְעוֹן בֶּן אֶלְעָזָר אוֹמֵר אִם רָצָה נוֹתֵן עֵינָיו בְּמִקְצָתוֹ וְאוֹכֵל אֶת הַשְּׁאָר. אָמַר רִבִּי יוֹנָה רִבִּי יוּדָה עָבַד כְּסוֹף הַפְּרָשָׁה וְרִבִּי שִׁמְעוֹן בֶּן אֶלְעָזָר עָבַד לָהּ כִּתְחִילַּת הַפְּרָשָׁה. אָמַר רִבִּי יוֹסֵי אַף רִבִּי שִׁמְעוֹן בֶּן אֶלְעָזָר עָבַד לָהּ כְּסוֹף הַפְּרָשָׁה. וְלֹא מוֹדֵי רִבִּי שִׁמְעוֹן בֶּן אֶלְעָזָר שֶׁאָסוּר לַעֲשׂוֹת כֵּן בְּוַדַּאי. מַאי כְדוֹן וּבִלְבַד שֶׁלֹּא יַעֲשֶׂה בְּשַׁבָּת כְּדֶרֶךְ שֶׁהוּא עוֹשֶׂה בְּחוֹל.

"And are lifted by one and 100". How do you treat it, as beginning of separation or end of separation[20]? If you say as beginning of separation, no minor may lift[21], no unrelated person may lift[21], and it does not push away the Sabbath[22]. If you treat it as end of separation, a minor may lift, an unrelated person may lift, and it does push away the Sabbath. There we have stated[23]: "Rebbi Jehudah says, also one may lift *dema'* by one in a hundred." On that, it was stated[24]: "Rebbi Simeon ben Eleazar says, if he wishes he earmarks part of it and eats the remainder." Rebbi Jonah said, Rebbi Judah treated it as end of separation and Rebbi Simeon ben Eleazar treated it as beginning of separation[25]. Rebbi Yose said, even Rebbi Simeon ben Eleazar treated it as end of separation[26]. Does not Rebbi Simeon ben Eleazar agree that it is forbidden to do so with certain [produce][27]? How is that? He should never do it on the Sabbath the way he does it on a weekday[28].

20 Does it follow the rules of separation of heave (*Terumot* Chapter 1) or more lenient ones?

21 Mishnah *Terumot* 1:1.

22 Mishnah *Šabbat* 2:6.

23 Mishnah *Šabbat* 21:1. In Tosephta *Šabbat* 15:5, but not in the quote Babli *Šabbat* 142b, this is an anonymous statement.

24 Tosephta *Šabbat* 15:5. There, and in the quote of the Tosephta in the Babli *Šabbat* 142b, the clause "if he wishes" is missing. In that version, R. Simeon ben Eleazar forbids lifting heave from *dema'* on the Sabbath except by mentally designating the part where the heave has to be lifted and eating the remainder, leaving the actual lifting to the time after the Sabbath.

25 He holds with the Babli that R. Simeon ben Eleazar is restrictive where R. Jehudah is permissive.

26 He reads the Yerushalmi text of the Tosephta as not prescriptive.

27 Since untithed produce is not legally edible, it cannot be used on the Sabbath and cannot be made usable on the Sabbath.

28 R. Simeon ben Eleazar does not disagree with R. Jehudah. R. Jehudah does not tell how *dema'* can be lifted on the Sabbath; R. Simeon suggests a way in which it can be done legally.

תַּמָּן תַּנִּינָן רִבִּי לִיעֶזֶר אוֹמֵר תְּרוּמָה עוֹלָה בְּאֶחָד וּמֵאָה. רִבִּי יְהוֹשֻׁעַ אוֹמֵר בְּמֵאָה וְעוֹד. תַּמָּן אָמַר חִזְקִיָּה רִבִּי אַבָּהוּ בְּשֵׁם רִבִּי לָעְזָר כָּל־מָקוֹם שֶׁשָּׁנָה רִבִּי מַחֲלוֹקֶת וְאַחַר כָּךְ חָזַר וְשָׁנָה סְתָם הֲלָכָה כִסְתָם. מִן מַה דְתַנִּינָן סְאָה תְרוּמָה

שֶׁנָּפְלָה לְמֵאָה וְאָמַר רִבִּי לָעְזָר לֵית כָּאן לוֹמַר לְתוֹךְ מֵאָה אֶלָּא לְתוֹךְ תִּשְׁעִים וְתִשְׁעָה. כְּמַה דְתַנִּינָן רִבִּי לִיעֶזֶר וְרִבִּי יְהוֹשֻׁעַ.

There, we have stated[29]: "Rebbi Eliezer says, heave is lifted at the rate of one in 100. Rebbi Joshua says by 100 and more." There[30], [Rebbi] Ḥizqiah, Rebbi Abbahu said in the name of Rebbi Eleazar, everywhere where Rebbi taught a disagreement and returned to the problem later and taught it anonymously, practice follows the anonymous opinion. Since we have stated: "A *seah* of heave which fell into 100" and Rebbi Eleazar said, one cannot say "into 100" but "into 99." As we have stated, Rebbi Eliezer and Rebbi Joshua[31].

29 Mishnah *Terumot* 4:7, Note 62.

30 *Pesaḥim* 3:3 (fol. 30b); *Ta'aniot* 2:14 (fol. 66a), both in the name of *Rebbi* Ḥizqiah. In the Babli, the statement is anonymous (*Avodah Zarah* 7a, *Yebamot* 42b).

31 Usually, practice follows R. Joshua against R. Eliezer. Since R. Eleazar requires only 99+1 = 100, he follows R. Eliezer who is supported by the anonymous Mishnah here.

מְנַיִין שֶׁהֵן עוֹלִין. אָמַר רִבִּי יוֹנָה כְּתִיב מִכָּל־חֶלְבּוֹ אֶת מִקְדְּשׁוֹ מִמֶּנּוּ. דָּבָר שֶׁאַתְּ מֵרִים מִמֶּנּוּ שֶׁאִם יִפּוֹל לְתוֹכוֹ מְקַדְּשׁוֹ. וְכַמָּה הוּא אֶחָד מִמֵּאָה. רִבִּי לִיעֶזֶר אוֹמֵר מוֹסִיף סְאָה וּמַעֲלֶה. רִבִּי יְהוֹשֻׁעַ אוֹמֵר מוֹסִיף כָּל־שֶׁהוּא וּמַעֲלֶה. רִבִּי יוֹסֵי בֶּן מְשׁוּלָּם אוֹמֵר וְעוֹד קַב לְמֵאָה סְאָה שְׁתוּת לִמְדוּמָּע.

[32]From where that they may be lifted? Rebbi Jonah said, it is written (*Num.* 18:29): "From all its best its sanctifying part from it." Something from which you lift it, so that if this falls into anything it sanctifies it. How much is this? One in one hundred. Rebbi Eliezer says, one adds a *seah* and then lifts. Rebbi Joshua says one adds a small amount and lifts.

Rebbi Yose ben Meshullam says "and more" is one *qab* per one hundred *seah*, one sixth of what makes *dema'*.

32 This is in *Terumot* Chapter 4; Notes 64-66.

תַּנֵּי רִבִּי שִׁמְעוֹן אוֹמֵר תְּרוּמָה עוֹלָה בְּמֵאָה מִקַּל וָחוֹמֶר. אִם אִיסּוּר מִתּוֹךְ אִיסּוּר עוֹלֶה אִיסּוּר מִתּוֹךְ הֵיתֵר לֹא כָּל־שֶׁכֵּן. תְּרוּמָה אִית תַּנָּיֵי תַנֵּי אִיסּוּר מִתּוֹךְ הֵיתֵר. וְאִית תַּנָּיֵי תַנֵּי הֵיתֵר מִתּוֹךְ הֵיתֵר. מָאן דְּאָמַר אִיסּוּר מִתּוֹךְ הֵיתֵר שֶׁכֵּן תְּרוּמָה אֲסוּרָה לְזָרִים. מָאן דְּאָמַר הֵיתֵר מִתּוֹךְ הֵיתֵר שֶׁכֵּן תְּרוּמָה מוּתֶּרֶת לַכֹּהֲנִים. אִית דְּפָתַר לָהּ כּוּלָּהּ לַכֹּהֲנִים מָאן דְּאָמַר אִיסּוּר מִתּוֹךְ הֵיתֵר בִּמְדוּמָע בִּתְרוּמָה טְמֵאָה. מָאן דְּאָמַר הֵיתֵר מִתּוֹךְ הֵיתֵר בִּמְדוּמָע בִּתרוּמָה טְהוֹרָה.

It was stated[33]: "Rebbi Simeon says, heave can be lifted in 100 by a conclusion *a minore ad majus*: If what is forbidden can be lifted from what is forbidden[34], so much more what is forbidden from what is permitted[35]!" Heave, some Tannaïm state "what is forbidden from what is permitted;" some Tannaïm state "what is permitted from what is permitted." He who says "what is forbidden from what is permitted", because heave is forbidden to lay persons. He who says "what is permitted from what is permitted", because heave is permitted to Cohanim. Some explain it all about Cohanim: He who says "what is forbidden from what is permitted", in the case of *dema'* by impure heave[36]. He who says "permitted from what is permitted", in the case of *dema'* by pure heave.

33 A similar, anonymous, text in *Sifry Num.* 121. In a different formulation, the argument is quoted in Tosephta *Terumot* 5:8, where, however, it is immediately rejected and proven false.

34 Heave, forbidden to lay people, is lifted from *tevel*, forbidden to

everybody, to make it profane and permitted for everybody.

35 Heave taken out from profane food turned into *dema'*.

36 In this case, what is lifted as replacement heave has to be burned.

תַּנֵּי פְּרוּסָה שֶׁלְּלֶחֶם הַפָּנִים שֶׁנִּתְעָרְבָה בְּמֵאָה פְרוּסוֹת שֶׁלְּחוּלִין וְכֵן חֲתִיכָה שֶׁלְּחַטָּאת שֶׁנִּתְעָרְבָה בְּמֵאָה חֲתִיכוֹת שֶׁלְּחוּלִין לֹא יַעֲלוּ. רִבִּי יוּדָה אוֹמֵר יַעֲלוּ. מַה טַעֲמָא דְּרִבִּי יוּדָה. וְשֶׂה אֶחָד[37] מִן הַצֹּאן וּמִן הַמָּאתַיִם מִמַּשְׁקֵה יִשְׂרָאֵל. מִדָּבָר שֶׁהוּא מוּתָּר לְיִשְׂרָאֵל. וְקַשְׁיָא כְּתִיב מָאתַיִם וְרִבִּי יוּדָה אוֹמֵר מֵאָה. כְּתִיב חַיִּים וְרִבִּי יוּדָה אוֹמֵר שְׁחוּטִין. מַה בֵּין חַיִּים לִשְׁחוּטִין. רִבִּי חִינְנָה אָמַר חַיִּין עָשׂוּ אוֹתָן כְּדָבָר שֶׁדַּרְכּוֹ לְהִימָּנוֹת.

It was stated[38]: "A piece of the showbread which was mixed with a hundred pieces of profane [bread], or a piece of purification sacrifice mixed with a hundred profane pieces [of meat], should not be lifted[39]. Rebbi Jehudah says they should be lifted." What is the reason of Rebbi Jehudah? (*Ez.* 45:15) "One sheep from 200 from the drink of Israel," from what is permitted to Israel[40]. It is difficult! It is written 200 and Rebbi Jehudah says 100[41]. It is written alive[42] and Rebbi Jehudah says slaughtered. What is the difference between alive and slaughtered? Rebbi Ḥinena said, they considered live ones under the category of what usually is counted[43].

37 In the verse: אחת.

38 Tosephta *Terumot* 8:21, in inverse order and with the position of R. Jehudah and the anonymous majority switched. Tosephta 8:22 deals with the same case but assumes that the pieces are impure. This implies that 8:21 (and the text here) deals with pure pieces. Both parts, incompatible with the Yerushalmi, are quoted in Babli *Yebamot* 81b.

39 It is not clear whether they cannot be lifted because a kind cannot become negligible in its own kind or whether sacrifices follow specific, more stringent, rules.

40 The full verse reads: "One sheep, from 200 from the drink of Israel, for cereal offering, burnt offering, and well-being offerings, to atone for them - speech of the Lord, the Eternal."

Rashi explains: "One sheep," a particular one from his flock; and so Moses said, (*Deut.* 12:11) "the best for your vows," meaning *le meilleur*. "From 200 from the drink of Israel," Our teachers explained this for the wine offering accompanying sacrifices. If 200 [volume units] were left in the vat one [volume unit] of *'orlah* or vineyard *kilaim* fell into the vat, that they become insignificant by one in 200. "From the drink of Israel," that all sacrifices should be from what is permitted to Israel, where all food is subsumed under the appellation of "drink".

41 This objection is not answered. It seems that the question depends on the definition of "Israel" in the verse. If "Israel" means "some of Israel", then the verse does not deal with the case of heave because that is permitted to Cohanim, it would be "drink of Israel." If "Israel" means "all of Israel", then one would expect that heave also needs 200 for lifting.

42 "A sheep" means a living sheep.

43 These never become insignificant, Mishnah 3:6.

עַד כְּדוֹן דָּבָר שֶׁהוּא מַעֲלֶה וּמַתִּיר לְהֶדְיוֹט. דָּבָר שֶׁהוּא מַעֲלֶה וּמַתִּיר לַגָּבוֹהַּ. נִשְׁמְעִינָהּ מִן הָדָא וְאַחַר יֹאכַל מִן הַקֳּדָשִׁים כִּי לַחְמוֹ הוּא. יֵשׁ לָךְ קֳדָשִׁים שֶׁאֵינוֹ אוֹכֵל בָּהֶן פְּרָט לְעֵירוּבִין וּלְיֶתֶר מִמֵּאָה.

So far something than one lifts and thereby permits for lay persons. Something one lifts and permits for Heaven[44]? Let us hear from the following: [45](*Lev.* 22:7) "'After that he shall eat from[46] the holy foods because it is his bread.' There exists holy food which he does not eat; that excludes mixtures of more than one in 100"[47].

44 Heave is considered Heaven's property given to the Cohen.

45 *Sifra Emor Pereq* 4(10). There, the reading is לעירובים לפחות ממאה "mixtures in less than 100 parts." The paragraph deals with sanctified food

eaten outside the Temple precinct, the common example of which is heave.

46 מן is taken as partitive: some, not all, is permitted the pure Cohen.

47 If the forbidden (impure) is more than $^{1}/_{100}$ of the permitted (pure) heave.

אֵין לִי אֶלָּא בְּאוֹכְלֵי תְרוּמָה כְאוֹכְלֵי תְרוּמָה. מְנַיִין אוֹכְלֵי תְרוּמָה כְאוֹכְלֵי חוּלִין. אוֹכְלֵי חוּלִין כְּאוֹכְלֵי תְרוּמָה. אוֹכְלֵי תְרוּמָה כְאוֹכלֵי קוֹדֶשׁ אוֹכְלֵי קוֹדֶשׁ כְּאוֹכְלֵי תְרוּמָה. מַשְׁקֶה תְרוּמָה כְמַשְׁקֶה חוּלִין. מַשְׁקֶה חוּלִין כְּמַשְׁקֶה תְרוּמָה. מַשְׁקֶה תְרוּמָה כְמַשְׁקֶה קוֹדֶשׁ. מַשְׁקֶה קוֹדֶשׁ כְּמַשְׁקֶה תְרוּמָה. מַשְׁקֶה קוֹדֶשׁ כְּמַשְׁקֶה קוֹדֶשׁ. מְנַיִין תַּלְמוּד לוֹמַר מִן הַקֳּדָשִׁים רִיבָה. רִבִּי אָבִין בְּשֵׁם רִבִּי יוֹחָנָן תִּיפְתָּר בְּלוֹג שֶׁמֶן שֶׁלִּמְצוֹרָע שֶׁנִּתְעָרֵב בְּמוֹתָר רְקִיקֵי מִנְחַת נָזִיר. וְהָתַנֵּי מַשְׁקֶה. שְׁנַיִם. אָמַר רִבִּי חֲנַנְיָה הָדָא אָמְרָה עוֹלוֹת בְּעוֹלוֹת. אֲבָל חַטָּאת בְּעוֹלוֹת הֲרֵי יֵשׁ כָּאן וַדַּאי בְּלֹא תַעֲשֶׂה.

[48]"Not only heave food in heave food[49]; from where heave food in profane food[50], profane food in heave food, heave food in sacrificial food, sacrificial food in heave food, heave drink in heave drink, heave drink in profane drink, profane drink in heave drink, heave drink in sacrificial drink, sacrificial drink in heave drink, sacrificial drink in sacrificial drink? From where? The verse says (*Lev.* 22:7) 'From the holy foods[51]', it adds." Rebbi Abin in the name of Rebbi Joḥanan: Explain it if the *log* of oil of the skin-diseased was mixed with the excess of the loaves of the gift of the *nazir*[52]; so we have stated, two drinks. Rebbi Ḥanania said, that means burned offerings in burned offerings; but purification offerings in burned offerings is certainly a prohibition[53].

48 *Sifra Emor Pereq* 4(11). The explanation follows R. Abraham ben David *ad loc.*

49 Impure heave in pure heave. An impure Cohen who eats pure heave has committed a deadly sin since it is

said: (*Lev.* 22:9) "They will die from it because they desecrated it." Impure heave is already desecrated; an impure priest eating it commits a sin but not a deadly one. The impure heave cannot become insignificant in pure since the two are of the same kind.

50 One *seah* of heave in less than 100 *seot* of pure (and certainly one *seah* of pure in less than 100 *seot* of heave) must all be treated as heave.

51 The plural implies all kinds of sanctified food. The singular is used in v. 10.

52 This explains a possible complication of "sacrificial drink in sacrificial drink". The person healed from his skin disease has to bring a reparation offering together with a *log* of oil (*Lev.* 14). Part of the oil is used on the healed person's body; the remainder is for the Cohen under the rules of the reparation offering; it must be consumed by priests in the Temple precincts. The *nazir* who has completed his vow has to bring sacrifices and a cereal offering consisting of unleavened bread made from flour mixed with oil and unleavened bread anointed with oil (*Num.* 6:13-20). The officiating Cohen receives one of these as gift added to the *nazir*'s well-being sacrifice; therefore, the loaves may be eaten by the Cohen's family anywhere in the city of the sanctuary. If there is a mix-up of the oils, the anointed loaves can be eaten only by the Cohen in the Temple precinct.

53 A mixture of pieces of elevation and purification offerings cannot be brought to the altar since of purification offerings only the fat and some inner organs are burned. They cannot be eaten since elevation sacrifices are forbidden for any use. They cannot become insignificant because (a) they are of the same kind of meat and (b) they are counted as pieces. Therefore, one has to leave the meat for the next day when all will be forbidden and has to be burned.

הֵיךְ סָבַר רִבִּי יוּדָה כְּרִבִּי לִיעֶזֶר אוֹ כְרִבִּי יְהוֹשֻׁעַ. כְּרִבִּי לִיעֶזֶר מַעֲלֶה וְאוֹכֵל. כְּרִבִּי יְהוֹשֻׁעַ מַעֲלֶה וְשׂוֹרֵף.

How does Rebbi Jehudah think[54], following Rebbi Eliezer or Rebbi Joshua[55]? Following Rebbi Eliezer he lifts and eats; following Rebbi Joshua he lifts and burns.

54 This refers to the statement above, Note 38, about pieces of showbread or purification sacrifices mixed with profane substances.

55 Their disagreement is in Mishnah *Terumot* 5:2. R. Eliezer holds that the piece lifted is the piece that fell in; according to the Sages, whose opinion is labelled that of R. Joshua, the nature of the piece lifted is unknown. Therefore, in the opinion of the Sages the nature of the piece lifted is indeterminate between profane and sanctified; it cannot be eaten and must be burned.

מָאן תַּנָּא אֵין מִצְטָרְפִין זֶה עִם זֶה רִבִּי מֵאִיר דְּאָמַר רִבִּי אַבָּהוּ בְּשֵׁם רִבִּי יוֹחָנָן דִּבְרֵי רִבִּי מֵאִיר כָּל־הָאִסּוּרִין מִצְטָרְפִין לִלְקוֹת עֲלֵיהֶן בִּכְזַיִת מִשּׁוּם לֹא תֹאכַל כָּל־תּוֹעֵיבָה.

Who stated "they combine with one another"? Rebbi Meïr, since Rebbi Abbahu said in the name of Rebbi Joḥanan[56]: The word of Rebbi Meïr is that all forbidden [foods] combine with one another to whip for them in the volume of an olive since it says: (*Deut.* 14:3) "You shall not eat any abomination[57]."

56 Quoted in Babli *Avodah Zarah* 66a. In the printed version (not in the Munich ms.) "R. Jehudah in the name of R. Meïr", a most unlikely text since R. Jehudah was half a generation older than R. Meïr.

57 There is one law which covers all forbidden food. Therefore, if somebody is warned not to eat any abomination he can be convicted if he ate the volume of an olive composed of several tiny pieces forbidden for different reasons.

הָכָא אַתְּ אָמַר צָרִיךְ לְהָרִים. וְהָכָא אַתְּ אָמַר אֵינוֹ צָרִיךְ לְהָרִים. רִבִּי יַעֲקֹב בַּר זַבְדִּי רִבִּי אַבָּהוּ בְּשֵׁם רִבִּי יוֹחָנָן מִפְּנֵי גֶזֶל הַשֵּׁבֶט. וְתַנֵּי כֵן כָּל־תְּרוּמָה שֶׁאֵין הַכֹּהֲנִים מַקְפִּידִין עָלֶיהָ כְּגוֹן (fol. 62a) תְּרוּמַת הַכְּלֵיסִין וְהֶחָרוּבִין וּשְׂעוֹרִין שֶׁבֶּאֱדוֹם אֵינוֹ צָרִיךְ לְהָרִים.

Here[60], you say one has to lift, but there[61] you say, one does not have to lift! Rebbi Jacob bar Zavdi, Rebbi Abbahu in the name of Rebbi Joḥanan, because of robbing the tribe[62]. Also, it was stated thus[63]: "Any heave for which the Cohanim do not care, e. g., the heave of *kelesin*[64], carob, and red barley, one does not have to lift."

60 Regarding heave.

61 *'Orlah* and *kilaim*.

62 Lifting is a rabbinic decree, not to cause damage to the Cohanim, since things become insignificant if they are in amounts less than 1%. Since *'orlah* and *kilaim* are worthless, they do not have to be lifted.

63 A similar text Tosephta *Terumot* 5:6, in the names of R. Simeon and R. Ismael from Shezur.

64 Cf. *Terumot* 11:4, Note 60; *Ma'serot* 2, Note 134.

הֶעָרְלָה וְכִלְאֵי הַכֶּרֶם עוֹלִין בְּאֶחָד וּמָאתַיִים. מְנַיִין שֶׁהֵן עוֹלִין. כְּתִיב מְלֵיאָה מְלֵיאָה מַה מְלֵיאָה שֶׁנֶּאֱמַר לְהַלָּן עוֹלָה אַף כָּאן עוֹלָה. אִי מַה כָּאן מֵאָה אַף כָּאן מֵאָה. לְפִי שֶׁכָּפַל הַכָּתוּב אִיסּוּרוֹ שִׁינּוּ חֲכָמִים חִייּוּבוֹ. עַד כְּדוֹן כִּלְאֵי הַכֶּרֶם עָרְלָה מְנַיִין. מַה זוֹ אִיסּוּר הֲנָייָה אַף זוֹ אִיסּוּר הֲנָייָה. מַה זוֹ עוֹלָה אַף זוֹ עוֹלָה.

"'*Orlah* and vineyard *kilaim* are lifted by one and 200." It is written "the fulness, the fulness.[65]" Just as "the fulness" which has been said there is lifted, so "the fulness" here is lifted. Then, as there by 100, so here by 100. Since the verse doubled its prohibition, the Sages changed its obligation[66]. So for vineyard *kilaim*, what about *'orlah*? Just as that is forbidden for all use, so this is forbidden for all use; just as that is lifted, so this is lifted.

65 Heave is called "fulness" in *Ex.* 22:28, *Num.* 18:27. In *Deut.* 22:9, what grows in a vineyard is called "fulness".

66 The change from 100 to 200 is

rabbinic; it is only based on a biblical hint. "Double the prohibition" is prohibition for Cohanim and laymen, in contrast to heave which only is forbidden to laymen. The position of the Yerushalmi here seems to be that lifting by one in 100 would be a biblical decree if heave were biblical.

עַד כְּדוֹן כְּרִבִּי עֲקִיבָה כְּרִבִּי יִשְׁמָעֵאל. רִבִּי יוֹחָנָן בְּשֵׁם רִבִּי יִשְׁמָעֵאל קַל וָחוֹמֶר. מַה אִם תְּרוּמָה שֶׁהִיא אֲסוּרָה לְזָרִים הֲרֵי זוֹ עוֹלָה. עָרְלָה שֶׁהִיא מוּתֶּרֶת לְזָרִים לֹא כָּל־שֶׁכֵּן. לֹא אִם אָמְרַת בִּתְרוּמָה שֶׁהֲנָייָתָהּ מוּתָּר. תֹּאמַר בְּעָרְלָה שֶׁהֲנָייָתָהּ אֲסוּרָה. רִבִּי חִינְנָא פֶּרִי פֶּרִי גְּזֵירָה שָׁוָה.

So far following Rebbi Aqiba, following Rebbi Ismael[67]? Rebbi Joḥanan in the name of Rebbi Ismael, an argument *a minore ad majus*. If heave which is forbidden to outsiders can be lifted, *'orlah* which is permitted to outsiders, not so much more[68]? No, if you said that about heave whose use is permitted, what can you say about *'orlah* whose use is prohibited! Rebbi Ḥinena: "Fruit, fruit" as equal decision[69].

67 The previous informal derivation is attributed to R. Aqiba; R. Ismael allows only formal derivations based on one of the principles enumerated in the Introduction to *Sifra*.

58 This is incomprehensible since the next sentence implies that R. Ismael also admits that any use of *'orlah* is forbidden.

69 This is a formal argument: If there is a tradition that a certain word can have only one meaning ("decision"), then the rules must be the same any time that word is used. Heave and tithes are from "fruit" (*Lev.* 27:30), *'orlah* refers to "fruit" (*Lev.* 19:23-24). *Lev.* 27:30 is written for reference; in the laws of *'orlah* the reference to "fruit" is necessary in *Lev.* 19:23 to define the subject but in *Lev.* 19:24 it might refer to the rules spelled out for heave. If that is true then R. Ismael must hold that *'orlah* and vineyard *kilaim* can be lifted by one in 100 since an "equal decision" cannot be only partially valid.

מִצְטָרְפִין זֶה עִם זֶה בֵּין לֶאֱסוֹר בֵּין לְהַתִּיר כְּדֵי לִיתֵּן טַעַם דִּבְרֵי רִבִּי מֵאִיר. רִבִּי שִׁמְעוֹן אוֹמֵר אֵינָן מִצְטָרְפִין. רִבִּי לְעֶזֶר אוֹמֵר מִצְטָרְפִין בְּנוֹתֵן טַעַם לֹא לֶאֱסוֹר.

They combine with one another either to permit or to forbid if one can taste them, the words of Rebbi Meïr. Rebbi Simeon says, they do not combine. Rebbi Eliezer says they combine if one tastes them, not to forbid[70].

70 This *baraita*, not known from another source, begins the discussion of the last part of the Mishnah asserting, as was already established (Note 57), that the anonymous Tanna of the Mishnah is R. Meïr, and that R. Meïr holds that any forbidden admixture greater than 1% remains forbidden.

(fol. 61c) **משנה ב:** הַתְּרוּמָה מַעֲלָה אֶת הָעוֹרְלָה הָעוֹרְלָה אֶת הַתְּרוּמָה. כֵּיצַד סְאָה תְרוּמָה שֶׁנָּפְלָה לְמֵאָה וְאַחַר כָּךְ נָפְלוּ שְׁלֹשֶׁת קַבִּין עָרְלָה אוֹ שְׁלֹשֶׁת קַבִּין שֶׁלְּכִלְאֵי הַכֶּרֶם. זוֹ הִיא שֶׁהַתְּרוּמָה מַעֲלָה אֶת הָעָרְלָה הָעָרְלָה אֶת הַתְּרוּמָה.

Mishnah 2: Heave lifts *'orlah* and *'orlah* heave. How is that? If one *seah* of heave fell into 100[71] and after that fell three *qab* of *'orlah* or three *qab* of vineyard *kilaim*, that is the case when heave lifts *'orlah* and *'orlah* heave.

71 Of profane grain. This makes the amount of heave insignificant; an arbitrary *seah* can be lifted as replacement of the heave. If then $^1/_2$ *seah* of something fell in that became insignificant only in quantities of at most $^1/_2$%, it becomes insignificant even if the replacement heave was not yet lifted since different forbidden matters do not combine.

משנה ג: הָעָרְלָה מַעֲלָה אֶת הַכִּלְאַיִם וְהַכִּלְאַיִם אֶת הָעָרְלָה. וְהָעָרְלָה אֶת הָעָרְלָה. כֵּיצַד סְאָה עָרְלָה שֶׁנָּפְלָה לְמָאתַיִם וְאַחַר כָּךְ נָפְלָה סְאָה וְעוֹד עָרְלָה אוֹ סְאָה וְעוֹד שֶׁלְּכִלְאֵי הַכֶּרֶם. זוֹ הִיא הָעָרְלָה מַעֲלָה אֶת הַכִּלְאַיִם וְהַכִּלְאַיִם אֶת הָעָרְלָה וְהָעָרְלָה אֶת הָעָרְלָה.

Mishnah 3: *'Orlah* lifts *kilaim, kilaim 'orlah*, and *'orlah 'orlah.* How is that? If one *seah* of *'orlah* fell into 200[72] and then fell a little more[73] than a *seah* of *'orlah* or a little more than a *seah* of vineyard *kilaim*, that is when *'orlah* lifts *kilaim, kilaim 'orlah*, and *'orlah 'orlah.*

72 This becomes insignificant. Forbidden matter which becomes insignificant by 1 in 100 is "reawakened" to become forbidden if more of the same falls into the permitted food. It is now stated that matter which becomes insignificant by 1 in 200 is never "reawakened".

73 Since now the permitted volume is 201 *seah*, the "little more" cannot exceed $^{1}/_{200}$ *seah* = $^{6}/_{200}$ *qab*.

הלכה ב: (fol. 62a) מַה פְלִיגִין. שֶׁנָּפְלוּ שְׁלֹשֶׁת קַבִּין עָרְלָה וּשְׁלֹשֶׁת קַבִּין שֶׁלְּכִלְאֵי הַכֶּרֶם. אֲבָל אִם נָפְלוּ שְׁלֹשֶׁת קַבִּין וְעוֹד עָרְלָה וּשְׁלֹשֶׁת שֶׁלְּכִלְאֵי הַכֶּרֶם הוּתָּר הַכְּרִי. לָמָּה. וְעוֹד בָּטֵל בִּשְׁלֹשֶׁת קַבִּין שְׁלֹשֶׁת קַבִּין בְּטֵילִין בְּמֵאָה. נָפְלוּ שְׁלֹשֶׁת קַבִּין עָרְלָה וּשְׁלֹשֶׁת קַבִּין כְּאֶחָד שֶׁלְּכִלְאֵי הַכֶּרֶם. כְּמוֹ שֶׁנָּפְלוּ שְׁלֹשֶׁת וְעוֹד עָרְלָה וּשְׁלֹשֶׁת קַבִּין שֶׁלְּכִלְאֵי הַכֶּרֶם. אוֹ כְמוֹ שֶׁנָּפְלוּ שְׁלֹשֶׁת קַבִּין שֶׁלְּכִלְאֵי הַכֶּרֶם וְאַחַר כָּךְ נָפְלוּ שְׁלֹשֶׁת קַבִּין עָרְלָה.

Halakhah 2: Where do they disagree[74]? If three *qab* of *'orlah* and three *qab* of vineyard *kilaim* fell[75]. But if three *qab* of *'orlah* and something additional fell in[76] and three of vineyard *kilaim*, the heap is permitted. Why? The additional "little more" is insignificant in the three *qab*[77] and three *qab* are insignificant in a hundred [*seah*]. If three *qab* of *'orlah* and three *qab* of vineyard *kilaim* fell in together, is it as if three *qab* of *'orlah* and something additional, and three *qab* of vineyard *kilaim* fell in[78], or that three *qab* of vineyard *kilaim* fell in and afterwards three *qab* of *'orlah*[79]?

74 This refers to the disagreement between R. Meïr and R. Eliezer (Note 70) on how different substances which become insignificant by 1 in 200 can combine. The problem is made urgent by Mishnah 3 which postulates that these matters, once they are insignificant, do not "reawaken" anymore.

75 First, 0.5 *seah* of *'orlah* fell into 100 *seah* of permitted profane matter and later another 0.5 *seah* of vineyard *kilaim* fell into the same heap. The next paragraph implies that in the case under consideration here, the owner did not realize what happened until the second batch had fallen in. It is held here that minute amounts are not in themselves insignificant but they become insignificant if the owner, or a responsible worker, know of the accident and determine that the event was insignificant. In our case here, everybody must agree that all is permitted since the *kilaim* fell into 201 times its volume of other matter. Even for Rebbi Meïr, the total volume is then less than $^1/_{100}$ of the whole.

The Rome text here is garbled: מַה פְּלִיגִין שֶׁנָּפְלוּ שְׁלֹשֶׁת קַבִּין עָרְלָה ***וְעוֹד*** וּשְׁלֹשֶׁת קַבִּין שֶׁל כִּלְאֵי הַכֶּרֶם ***הוּתָּד***. אֲבָל אִם נָפְלוּ שְׁלֹשֶׁת קַבִּין וְעוֹד עָרְלָה וּשְׁלֹשֶׁת שֶׁל כִּלְאֵי הַכֶּרֶם הוּתָּר הַכְּרִי.

76 First three *qab*, later at most 3/100 *qab*.

77 The language is misleading. Since the three *qab* became insignificant, $^3/_{100}$ *qab* now become insignificant in 100.5 *seah*. The next three *qab* (0.5 *seah*) of *kilaim* now become insignificant in 100.53 *seah* of permitted matter.

78 In Mishnah *Terumot* 4:7, R. Eliezer and R. Joshua disagree on the amount which makes heave insignificant. R. Meïr, who does not allow more than $^1/_{100}$ of forbidden matter under any circumstance, disagrees with both of them and fixes the limit at $^1/_{100}$. For R. Simeon and R. Eliezer all is permitted.

79 How this could be true for R. Meïr is discussed in the next paragraph.

פְּשִׁיטָא שֶׁיְּדִיעָתוֹ מַתִּרְתוֹ. יְדִיעַת חֲבֵירוֹ מָהוּ שֶׁתַּתִּירוֹ. הֵיךְ עֲבִידָא הוּא לֹא יָדַע בָּהּ. חֲבֵירוֹ יָדַע בָּהּ.

It is obvious that his knowledge permits it[80]. Does the knowledge of a third person[81] permit it? How is this possible? He is not aware of it; another person is aware of it.

80 If the owner of the food realizes that not more than half of a percent of *'orlah* or *kilaim* fell into his food, he knows that the amount is insignificant and everything is permitted. This closes the incident. If another mishap occurs, the entire amount of food is considered permitted and profane. This contrasts with Mishnah *Terumot* 5:7 which states that heave remains a candidate for potential reawakening of the prohibition; cf. Note 72.

81 Who is not the owner or one of his employees or family members. It is not decided whether the awareness of a third party leads to closure.

יְדִיעַת סָפֵק מָהוּ שֶׁתַּתִּיר כִּידִיעַת וַדַּאי. הֵיךְ עֲבִידָא. הָיוּ לְפָנָיו שְׁתֵּי קוּפּוֹת אַחַת יֵשׁ בָּהּ מָאתַיִם וְאַחַת אֵין בָּהּ מָאתַיִם. נָפְלָה סְאָה תְרוּמָה לְתוֹךְ אַחַת מֵהֶן וְאֵין יָדוּעַ לְאֵי זֶה מֵהֶן נָפְלָה וְאַחַר כָּךְ נָפְלָה בִשְׁנִיָּה. מְדָדָהּ וּמָצָא בָהּ מָאתַיִם וּשְׁתַּיִם. אִין תֵּימַר יְדִיעַת סָפֵק כִּידִיעַת וַדַּאי עוֹלָה. אִין תֵּימַר אֵין יְדִיעַת סָפֵק כִּידִיעַת וַדַּאי אֵין עוֹלָה. הָיְתָה קוּפָּה אַחַת סָפֵק יֵשׁ בָּהּ מָאתַיִים סָפֵק אֵין בָּהּ. נָפְלָה סְאָה תְרוּמָה לְתוֹכָהּ וְאֵין יָדוּעַ אִם נָפְלָה אִם לֹא נָפְלָה וְאַחַר כָּךְ נָפְלָה הַשְּׁנִיָּה. אִין תֵּימַר יְדִיעַת סָפֵק כִּידִיעַת וַדַּאי עוֹלָה. אִין תֵּימַר אֵין יְדִיעַת סָפֵק כִּידִיעַת וַדַּאי אֵינָהּ עוֹלָה.

Does uncertain knowledge permit like certain knowledge? How is this? If there were two boxes before him, one containing 200[82] and one less than 200. If one *seah* of heave fell into one of them but it is not known into which one it fell and then [another *seah*] fell into the second. It was measured and found to be 202. If you say uncertain knowledge permits like certain knowledge, it can be lifted, but if you say uncertain knowledge does not permit like certain knowledge, it cannot be lifted[83]. If there was one chest and there is a doubt whether it contains 200 or not; if one *seah* of heave fell into [some box] but it is not known whether it fell into that box or not, and then a second time something [forbidden] fell into [the box in question]: If you say uncertain knowledge permits like certain knowledge, it can be lifted, but if you say uncertain knowledge does not permit like certain knowledge, it cannot be lifted[84].

82 Meaning: containing at least 200 *seah*.

83 If the box containing 202 *seah* contains 2 *seah* of heave, the heave may be lifted and everything is permitted. But if that box originally contained 202 *seah*, then the two *seah* of heave fell into the box containing less than 200 and that box now is *dema'* and forbidden to lay persons. If uncertain knowledge is enough to bring closure of an episode then even the box containing less than 200 *seah* will contain more than 100 and heave can be lifted in all cases.

84 Since the box might contain 2 *seah* of heave and less than 200 of profane food.

אָמַר רִבִּי קוּרִייָס לֹא שֶׁהַתְּרוּמָה מַעֲלָה אֶת הֶעָרְלָה אֶלָּא שֶׁהַתְּרוּמָה מִצְטָרֶפֶת עִם הַחוּלִין לְהַעֲלוֹת אֶת הַתְּרוּמָה. נִיחָא הַתְּרוּמָה מַעֲלָה אֶת הֶעָרְלָה שֶׁכֵּן טְהוֹרָה מַעֲלָה אֶת הַטְּמֵאָה. עָרְלָה מַעֲלָה אֶת הַתְּרוּמָה כְּלוּם טְמֵיאָה מַעֲלָה אֶת הַטְּהוֹרָה. לֹא אֵצֶל הַזָּרִים. שֶׁמָּא אֵצֶל הַכֹּהֲנִים. וְהַתַנִּינָן הֶעָרְלָה מַעֲלָה אֶת הַכִּלְאַיִם וְהַכִּלְאַיִם אֶת הֶעָרְלָה וְהֶעָרְלָה אֶת הֶעָרְלָה. שַׁנְייָא הִיא תַּמָּן בֵּין אֵצֶל הַזָּרִים בֵּין אֵצֶל הַכֹּהֲנִים.

Rebbi Curius[85] said, not that heave lifts *'orlah* but heave adds to the profane to lift (heave)[86] [*'orlah*]. One understands that heave lifts *'orlah* because pure [heave] lifts the impure[87]. "*'Orlah* lifts heave", does impure [heave] lift the pure, not for laymen, maybe for Cohanim[88]? But did we not state: "'*Orlah* lifts *kilaim, kilaim 'orlah*, and *'orlah 'orlah*"? There it is different, both for lay people and for Cohanim[89].

85 R. Simson quotes him as R. Birias; nothing more is known about him. [Curius is the name of a Roman *Gens*, but the expression might not be a name at all if it represents Greek κύριος, ὁ, "Lord, master" in the acception of "head, authority". In that case, *rebbi kurios* would be a composite of two synonymous words in two languages, expressing the idea of "Chief Rabbi" (E. G.).]

86 This is the reading in all mss.; it must mean "'*orlah*". That heave is added to the profane is stated in the next paragraph; it was stated in Halakhah 1 (Note 30).

87 Mishnah *Terumot* 5:3.

88 While it is true that impure heave may be lifted out of pure profane grain as explained in Mishnah *Terumot* 5:4, impure heave which fell into pure heave makes everything forbidden to Cohanim.

89 The entire argument is rejected. Since for *'orlah* and *kilaim* the status of purity is irrelevant; no comparison with heave is possible.

סְאָה תְּרוּמָה שֶׁנָּפְלָה לְתוֹךְ מֵאָה. אָמַר רִבִּי לָעְזָר לֵית כָּאן לְתוֹךְ מֵאָה אֶלָּא לְתוֹךְ תִּשְׁעִים וְתִשְׁעָה. סְאָה עָרְלָה שֶׁנָּפְלָה לְתוֹךְ מָאתַיִם. אָמַר רִבִּי לָעְזָר לֵית כָּאן לְתוֹךְ מָאתַיִם אֶלָּא לְתוֹךְ מֵאָה תִשְׁעִים וְתִשְׁעָה.

"A *seah* of heave which fell into 100." Rebbi Eleazar said, it is not "into 100" but "into 99."[90] "A *seah* of *'orlah* which fell into 200." Rebbi Eleazar said, it is not "into 200" but "into 199."

90 This refers to Mishnah 1; it is quoted from Halakhah 1, Note 30. In all cases, R. Eleazar holds that all that is required to allow a mixture is that the forbidden part not be larger than 1% or .5% of the total.

(fol. 61c) **משנה ד:** כָּל־הַמְחַמֵּץ וְהַמְּתַבֵּל וְהַמְּדַמֵּעַ בִּתְרוּמָה וּבְעָרְלָה וּבְכִלְאֵי הַכֶּרֶם אָסוּר. בֵּית שַׁמַּאי אוֹמֵר אַף מְטַמֵּא. וּבֵית הִלֵּל אוֹמְרִים לְעוֹלָם אֵינוֹ מְטַמֵּא עַד שֶׁיְּהֵא בוֹ כְּבֵיצָה.

Mishnah 4: Anything which sours, or spices, or creates *dema'* from heave, or is *'orlah*, or vineyard *kilaim*, is forbidden[91]. The House of Shammai say, also it transmits impurity, but the House of Hillel say nothing[92] transmits impurity unless it has at least the volume of a chicken egg.

91 In the most minute amount since its action shows that it is not negligible.

92 No foodstuff, whose impurity is always derivative. Original impurity is usually created by impure material the volume of an olive; for dead crawling things the volume of a lentil is enough.

משנה ה: דּוֹסְתַּי אִישׁ כְּפַר אֵיתְמָה הָיָה מִתַּלְמִידֵי שַׁמַּי וְאָמַר שָׁאַלְתִּי אֶת שַׁמַּי הַזָּקֵן וְאָמַר לְעוֹלָם אֵינוֹ מְטַמֵּא עַד שֶׁיְּהֵא בוֹ כְּבֵיצָה.

Mishnah 5: Dositheos from Kefar Etma[93] was a student of Shammai. He said, I asked Shammai the Elder and he said, nothing transmits impurity unless it has the volume of a chicken egg.

93 In most Mishnah ms., כפר יתמה, Yetma in Samaria. Nothing more is known about him. He holds that the later followers of the House of Shammai misrepresent the position of the founder.

משנה ו: וְלָמָּה אָמְרוּ כָּל־הַמְחַמֵּץ וְהַמְּתַבֵּל וְהַמְּדַמֵּעַ לְהַחֲמִיר מִין בְּמִינוֹ לְהָקֵל וּלְהַחֲמִיר מִין בְּשֶׁאֵינוֹ מִינוֹ כֵּיצַד שְׂאוֹר שֶׁלְּחִטִּים שֶׁנָּפַל לְתוֹךְ עִיסַּת חִטִּים וְיֵשׁ בּוֹ כְּדֵי לְחַמֵּץ בֵּין שֶׁיֵּשׁ בּוֹ לַעֲלוֹת בְּאֶחָד וּמֵאָה בֵּין שֶׁאֵין בּוֹ לַעֲלוֹת בְּאֶחָד וּמֵאָה אָסוּר. אֵין בּוֹ לַעֲלוֹת בְּאֶחָד וּמֵאָה בֵּין שֶׁיֵּשׁ בּוֹ כְּדֵי לְחַמֵּץ בֵּין שֶׁאֵין בּוֹ כְּדֵי לְחַמֵּץ אָסוּר.

Mishnah 6: And why did they say, anything which sours, or spices, or creates *dema'*, is restrictive if a kind is mixed with its own kind, but permissive or restrictive if a kind is mixed with another kind[94]. How is that? Sourdough from wheat which fell into wheat dough and is enough to make the latter sour, whether it would qualify to be lifted by one in 100 or not qualify to be lifted by one in 100, is forbidden. If it does not qualify to be lifted by one in 100 it is forbidden whether it is enough to make the latter sour or not enough to make sour[95].

94 This case is dealt with in the next Mishnah.

95 The criterion of whether it sours or not may be used only to forbid, not to permit.

(fol. 62a) **הלכה ג**: רִבִּי יוֹסֵי בְּשֵׁם רִבִּי חִילְפַיי רִבִּי יוֹנָה בְּשֵׁם רִבִּי שִׁמְעוֹן בֶּן לָקִישׁ כְּתָפוּחַ עוֹשִׂין אוֹתוֹ בֵּית שַׁמַּי.

Halakhah 3: Rebbi Yose in the name of Rebbi Hilfai, Rebbi Jonah in the name of Rebbi Simeon ben Laqish: The House of Shammai made it as if swollen[96].

96 Since the matter makes sour, they add the amount of CO_2 generated to arrive at the volume of a chicken egg (*Sefer Nir*). The commentaries read כְּתַפּוּחַ "like an apple", referring to *Terumot* 10:2. But that Halakhah contradicts the position of the House of Shammai.

תַּמָּן תַּנִּינָן מֵי הַצֶּבַע פּוֹסְלִין אוֹתוֹ בִּשְׁלֹשֶׁת לוֹגִין וְאֵין פּוֹסְלִין אוֹתוֹ בְּשִׁינּוּי מַרְאֶה. אַבָּא בְּרֵיהּ דְּרַב נַחְמָן דִּבְרֵי רִבִּי מֵאִיר מִשּׁוּם שְׁאוּבָה נִיכֶּרֶת. רִבִּי חוּנָה בְּשֵׁם רִבִּי אַבָּא אַתְייָא דְּרִבִּי מֵאִיר כְּבֵית שַׁמַּי. כְּמָה דְבֵית שַׁמַּי אָמְרֵי מִשּׁוּם חִימּוּץ מַחֲמִיץ כֵּן רִבִּי מֵאִיר אָמַר מִשּׁוּם שְׁאִיבָה נִיכֶּרֶת.

There[97], we have stated: "Dyers' water disables a *miqweh* by three *log* but not by a change in color." Abba, the son of Rav Naḥman, said, the words of Rebbi Meïr because it is visibly drawn[98]. Rebbi Ḥuna in the name of Rebbi Abba: Rebbi Meïr's parallels that of the House of Shammai. Just as the House of Shammai say because of souring it makes sour[99], so Rebbi Meïr says because it is visibly drawn.

97 Mishnah *Miqwa'ot* 7:3. The statement there is in the name of R. Yose. The Yerushalmi concludes from there that R. Meïr, the presumed author of anonymous statements, disagrees and holds that a *miqweh* is disabled if colored water changes its appearance, irrespective of the amount poured in. The general rule is that a *miqweh* must contain 40 *seah* of natural water and that 3 *log* (=$^1/_8$ *seah*) of poured water make it ineffective to remove impurity; cf. *Terumot* 4, Note 112; 10, Note 139.

98 If the color is visible, everybody knows that it is not rain water or water from a spring.

99 The rising dough makes it clear that a souring agent is present.

עַד כְּדוֹן דָּבָר שֶׁיֵּשׁ בּוֹ אִיסּוּר וְטוּמְאָה. יֵשׁ בּוֹ טוּמְאָה וְאֵין בּוֹ אִיסּוּר מָהוּ.

So far something to which prohibition and impurity apply. What is the rule if impurity applies but not prohibition[100]?

100 Since there is a question only following the House of Shammai and R. Meïr but practice follows the House of Hillel and R. Yose, it is not answered.

חִימֵּץ מִמֶּנּוּ לְמָקוֹם אַחֵר נַעֲשָׂה זֶה אָסוּר וְזֶה אָסוּר. רִיבָּה עַל הָרִאשׁוֹן וּבִיטְּלוֹ נַעֲשָׂה עִיקָּר טְפֵילָה וּטְפֵילָה עִיקָּר. שְׂאוֹר שֶׁלִּתְרוּמָה שֶׁנָּפַל לְתוֹךְ הָעִיסָּה וְהִגְבִּיהוֹ. וְאַחַר כָּךְ נִתְחַמְּצָה הָעִיסָּה הֲרֵי זוֹ מוּתֶּרֶת. וְדִכְוָותָהּ תְּאֵינָה שֶׁל תְּרוּמָה שֶׁנָּפְלָה לְתוֹךְ מֵאָה. הוּגְבְּהָה אַחַת מֵהֶן וְאַחַר כָּךְ הוּכְּרָה הַתְּרוּמָה תְּהֵא מוּתֶּרֶת. תַּמָּן לֹא הוּכַח הָאִיסּוּר בְּרַם הָכָא הוּכַח הָאִיסּוּר.

If he took from it[101] for another place to make it sour, both are forbidden. If he added to the first [dough] and made it insignificant[102], the main object will be derivative and the derivative the main object. "Heave sourdough which fell into a dough and was lifted, if the dough became sour afterwards, is permitted[103]. Similarly, if a heave fig fell into 100 [figs], one was lifted, and afterwards the heave was recognized, should it be permitted? There, the prohibited [dough] was not identified; here, the prohibited [fig] is identified[104].

101 From the dough containing heave or *'orlah* sourdough.

102 He added profane flour in error so that now the heave or *'orlah* component is less than the threshhold for insignificance, and in addition the sourdough is no longer active; then the original dough will be permitted, the secondary would still be forbidden.

103 Tosephta *Terumot* 8:11. The sourdough was inactive when heave was lifted; the scenario does not contradict the Mishnah here.

104 Lifting is invalidated if the true heave is recognized.

(fol. 61c) **משנה ז**: לְהָקֵל וּלְהַחֲמִיר מִין בְּשֶׁאֵינוֹ מִינוֹ כֵּיצַד גְּרִיסִין שֶׁנִּתְבַּשְּׁלוּ עִם עֲדָשִׁים וְיֵשׁ בָּהֶן בְּנוֹתֵן טַעַם בֵּין שֶׁיֵּשׁ בָּהֶן לַעֲלוֹת בְּאֶחָד וּמֵאָה בֵּין שֶׁאֵין בָּהֶן לַעֲלוֹת בְּאֶחָד וּמֵאָה אָסוּר. אֵין בָּהֶן בְּנוֹתֵן טַעַם בֵּין שֶׁיֵּשׁ בָּהֶן לַעֲלוֹת בְּאֶחָד וּמֵאָה בֵּין שֶׁאֵין בָּהֶן לַעֲלוֹת בְּאֶחָד וּמֵאָה מוּתָּר.

Mishnah 7: Permissive or restrictive if a kind is mixed with another kind, how is that? If groats[105] were cooked with lentils, if they can be tasted, whether they would qualify to be lifted by one in 100 or not qualify to be lifted by one in 100, are forbidden. If they cannot be tasted, whether they would qualify to be lifted by one in 100 or not qualify to be lifted by one in 100, are permitted.

105 Broken grain kernels or broken beans. In our case, these are presumed to be heave, the lentils profane. "Forbidden" and "permitted" refer to laymen who might eat from the cooked dish.

(fol. 62a) **הלכה ד**: רִבִּי יוֹנָה בָּעֵי וְלָמָּה תַנִּינָן גְּרִיסִין שֶׁנִּתְבַּשְּׁלוּ עִם הָאוֹרֶז. אֶלָּא מַתְנִיתָן כְּמָאן דְּאָמַר נוֹתְנֵי טַעַם לִפְגַם מוּתָּר. וַאֲפִילוּ כְּמָאן דְּאָמַר נוֹתְנֵי טַעַם לִפְגַם מוּתָּר מוֹדֶה הוּא הָכָא שֶׁהוּא אָסוּר.

Halakhah 4: Rebbi Jonah asked, why did we [not] state: If groats were cooked with rice[106]? Our Mishnah follows him who holds that what gives a bad taste is permitted[107]. But even he who holds that what gives a bad taste is permitted, here[108] he will agree that it is forbidden.

106 For some reason he thinks that groats enhance the taste of lentils but spoil the taste of rice.

107 He would restrict the Mishnah to cases where the taste of the forbidden admixture is an improvement.

108 In the cases enumerated in Mishnah 4, what makes sour, or spicy, or induces *dema'*, any taste will make forbidden, whether good or bad.

גְּרִיסִין שֶׁלִּתְרוּמָה שֶׁנָּפְלוּ עִם עֲדָשִׁים שֶׁלְּחוּלִין וְיֵשׁ בָּהֶן נוֹתֵן טַעַם. רִיבָה עֲלֵיהֶן עֲדָשִׁים שֶׁלְּחוּלִין מוּתָּר. עַד כַּמָּה יַרְבֶּה תַּפְלוּגְתָא דְּרִבִּי וּדְרִבִּי יִשְׁמָעֵאל בֵּירִבִּי יוֹסֵי. עַל דַּעְתֵּיהּ דְּרִבִּי דּוּ אָמַר עַד שֶׁיַּרְבֶּה עַל כּוּלְּהוֹן. עַל דַּעְתֵּיהּ דְּרִבִּי יִשְׁמָעֵאל בֵּירִבִּי יוֹסֵי דּוּ אָמַר עַד שֶׁיַּרְבֶּה עַל הַנּוֹפְלִין. גְּרִיסִין שֶׁנִּתְבַּשְּׁלוּ עִם עֲדָשִׁין שֶׁלְּחוּלִין וְאֵין בָּהֶן נוֹתֵן טַעַם. רִיבָה עֲלֵיהֶן גְּרִיסִין שֶׁלְּחוּלִין מִין מְעוֹרֵר אֶת מִינוֹ לֶאֱסוֹר. לֹא תְהֵא גְדוֹלָה מִיַּיִן נֶסֶךְ. כְּמָה דְתֵימַר בְּיַיִן נֶסֶךְ אַתְּ רוֹאֶה אֶת הַהֵיתֵר כְּמִי שֶׁאֵינוֹ. אוֹתוֹ הָאִיסּוּר אִם יֵשׁ בּוֹ בְנוֹתֵן טַעַם אָסוּר וְאִם לָאו מוּתָּר. וְהָכָא אַתְּ רוֹאֶה אֶת הַהֵיתֵר כְּמִי שֶׁאֵינוֹ. אוֹתוֹ הָאִיסּוּר אִם יֵשׁ בּוֹ

בְּנוֹתֵן טַעַם אָסוּר וְאִם לָאו מוּתָּר. הָדָא אָמְרָה רִיבָה עֲלֵיהֶן גְּרִיסִין שֶׁלְּתְרוּמָה מוּתָּר.

If heave groats fell into profane lentils and can be tasted, if he added[109] profane lentils they become permitted. How much does he have to add? A disagreement between Rebbi and Rebbi Ismael ben Rebbi Yose. In the opinion of Rebbi, one says until he adds for all of them[110]. In the opinion of Rebbi Ismael ben Rebbi Yose, one says until he adds corresponding to what fell in[111]. If groats[112] were cooked with profane lentils and cannot be tasted, if he added profane groats, this kind awakes its own to make it forbidden[113]. But this should not be stronger than libation wine! As you say[114] regarding libation wine, you disregard what is permitted; if what is forbidden can be tasted it is forbidden, otherwise it is permitted[115]. Here you disregard what is permitted; if what is forbidden can be tasted it is forbidden, otherwise it is permitted. That means, if he added groats, the heave is permitted[116].

109 By accident. It is assumed that the dish was cooked again and now the groats cannot be tasted.

110 Lentils and groats.

111 He must have added lentils that the groats could not be tasted had they been cooked with the added lentils alone, in contrast to Rebbi who requires that the new lentils also must obliterate the taste the old lentils had acquired from the groats.

112 Of heave.

113 Since food of one kind cannot become insignificant in its own kind unless the permitted part is 100 (or 200) times the forbidden one, it is assumed that the dish now is *dema'* if the lentils are less than 100 times the combined, heave and profane, groats.

114 This is detailed in Halakhah 7.

115 Wine used for pagan libations is forbidden for all use; a small libation poured from an container makes the entire contents of the container into libation wine. Then it is ruled that if libation wine fell into a dish which was

prepared with wine, one estimates whether the forbidden libation wine alone would have been enough to impart the taste of wine to the entire dish. If that is the case, the dish is forbidden; otherwise it is permitted even though actually the wine can still be tasted.

116 If he added profane groats, the original heave groats become insignificant being less than 1 in 100. The Rome ms. reads: That means, if he added heave groats it is forbidden. This is a trivial statement.

(fol. 61c) **משנה ח**: שְׂאוֹר שֶׁלְּחוּלִּין שֶׁנָּפַל לְתוֹךְ עִיסָּה וְיֵשׁ בּוֹ כְּדֵי לְחַמֵּץ וְאַחַר כָּךְ נָפַל שְׂאוֹר שֶׁלִּתְרוּמָה אוֹ שְׂאוֹר שֶׁלְּכִלְאֵי הַכֶּרֶם וְיֵשׁ בּוֹ כְּדֵי לְחַמֵּץ אָסוּר.

Mishnah 8: If profane sourdough fell into dough, enough to cause souring, and afterwards sourdough of heave or of vineyard *kilaim* fell into it, also enough to cause souring, the dough is forbidden[117].

משנה ט: שְׂאוֹר שֶׁלְּחוּלִּין שֶׁנָּפַל לְתוֹךְ עִיסָּה וְחִימִיצָהּ וְאַחַר כָּךְ נָפַל שְׂאוֹר שֶׁלִּתְרוּמָה אוֹ שְׂאוֹר שֶׁלְּכִלְאֵי הַכֶּרֶם וְיֵשׁ בּוֹ כְּדֵי לְחַמֵּץ אָסוּר. וְרִבִּי שִׁמְעוֹן מַתִּיר.

Mishnah 9: If profane sourdough fell into dough and caused it to become sour when afterwards sourdough of heave or of vineyard *kilaim* fell into it, enough to cause souring, the dough is forbidden but Rebbi Simeon permits it[118].

117 Even though the dough also would have risen without the forbidden sourdough, the fact that it could have been used without the profane sourdough activates the rule of Mishnah 4.

118 R. Simeon holds that the forbidden dough does not do anything and should be treated by the 1 in 100 (or

200) rule as if it were inert. The anonymous majority hold that this case is not different from that of the preceding Mishnah.

(fol. 62a) **הלכה ה:** תַּנֵּי חֲנַנְיָה בְשֵׁם רִבִּי יוֹחָנָן אַף הָרִאשׁוֹנָה בְמַחֲלוֹקֶת. אָמַר רִבִּי יוֹנָה הֲוִינָן סָבְרִין מֵימַר מַפְלִיגִין בְּשֶׁחִימֵּץ זֶה כָּל־כּוֹחוֹ וְזֶה כָּל־כּוֹחוֹ וְנָפַל שְׂאוֹר שֶׁלְחוּלִין תְּחִילָּה. אֲבָל אִם נָפַל שְׂאוֹר שֶׁלִתְּרוּמָה תְּחִילָּה כְּבָר נִתְחַמְּצָה הָאִיסָּה.

Halakhah 5: Ḥanania[119] stated in the name of Rebbi Joḥanan: The first Mishnah also is in disagreement[120]. Rebbi Jonah said, we hold to say that they disagree when each one is full strength and the profane sourdough fell in first. But if the heave sourdough fell in first, the dough already became sour.

119 He might be R. Ḥananiah, the colleague of the rabbis.

120 The two Mishnaiot are really one and the statement of R. Simeon refers to both of them.

כָּל־נוֹתְנֵי טְעָמִים בֵּין לִפְגָּם בֵּין לִשְׁבָח אָסוּר דִּבְרֵי רִבִּי מֵאִיר. רִבִּי שִׁמְעוֹן אוֹמֵר לִשְׁבָח אָסוּר לִפְגָּם מוּתָּר. רִבִּי שִׁמְעוֹן בֶּן לָקִישׁ אָמַר מַה פְּלִיגִין. בְּשֶׁהִשְׁבִּיחַ וְאַחַר כָּךְ פָּגַם. אֲבָל אִם פָּגַם וְאַחַר כָּךְ הִשְׁבִּיחַ אוֹף רִבִּי מֵאִיר מוֹדֶה. רִבִּי יוֹחָנָן אָמַר לֹא שַׁנְיָיא הִיא הִשְׁבִּיחַ הִיא פָּגַם. הִיא פָּגַם הִיא הִשְׁבִּיחַ הִיא הַמַּחֲלוֹקֶת. תַּמָּן תַּנִּינָן שְׂעוֹרִין שֶׁנָּפְלוּ לְתוֹךְ הַבּוֹר שֶׁל מַיִם אַף עַל פִּי שֶׁהִבְאִישׁוּ מֵימָיו מֵימָיו מוּתָּרִין. וְהָדָא מַתְנִיתָא מַה הִיא. רִבִּי יוֹחָנָן אָמַר בְּמַחֲלוֹקֶת. רִבִּי שִׁמְעוֹן בֶּן לָקִישׁ אָמַר דִּבְרֵי הַכֹּל. רִבִּי יוֹסֵי בֵּירִבִּי בוּן אָמַר אִילֵּין שְׁמוּעָתָא הָדָא רִבִּי יוֹחָנָן אָמַר בְּמַחֲלוֹקֶת. רִבִּי שִׁמְעוֹן בֶּן לָקִישׁ אָמַר דִּבְרֵי הַכֹּל.

"[121]Everything that can be tasted is forbidden, whether it spoils or improves, the words of Rebbi Meïr. Rebbi Simeon says, if it improves it is forbidden, if it spoils it is permitted." Rebbi Simeon ben Laqish said, in what do they disagree? If it first improved but then spoiled. But if it spoiled and later improved, even Rebbi Meïr will agree. Rebbi Joḥanan said, there is no difference whether it improved and spoiled or spoiled and improved, it is the disagreement. There, we have stated: "If barley grains fell into a cistern of water, even though they made it stink, the water is permitted." What is the status of that Mishnah? Rebbi Joḥanan said it is a disagreement; Rebbi Simeon ben Laqish said it is the opinion of everybody. Rebbi Yose ben Rebbi Abun said this tradition here: Rebbi Joḥanan said it is a disagreement; Rebbi Simeon ben Laqish said it is the opinion of everybody.

121 This is from *Terumot* 10:2, explained there in Notes 20-25.

אָמַר רִבִּי יוֹנָה צוֹרְכָה לְהָדָה דְּרִבִּי שִׁמְעוֹן בֶּן לָקִישׁ לֹא כֵן סָבְרִינָן מֵימַר מָה פְלִיגִין בְּשֶׁחִימֵּץ זֶה כָּל־כּוֹחוֹ וְזֶה כָּל־כּוֹחוֹ וְנָפַל שְׂאוֹר שֶׁל חוּלִין תְּחִילָּה. אֲבָל אִם נָפַל שְׂאוֹר שֶׁל תְּרוּמָה תְּחִילָּה כְּבָר (fol. 62b) נִתְחַמְּצָה הָאִיסָּה. וַאֲפִילוּ נָפַל שְׂאוֹר חוּלִין תְּחִילָּה נַעֲשֶׂה כְּמִי שֶׁהִשְׁבִּיחַ מֵעִיקָּרוֹ וְאַחַר כָּךְ פָּגַם. חָזַר רִבִּי יוֹנָה וָמַר הָאִשָּׁה הַזֹּאת אֵינָהּ מְחַמֶּצֶת כָּל־צוֹרְכָהּ מְשַׁיֶּירֶת הִיא כָּל־שֶׁהוּא. אוֹתוֹ כָּל־שֶׁהוּא יֵעָשֶׂה כְּמִי שֶׁהִשְׁבִּיחַ וְלִבְסוֹף פָּגַם. וְקַשְׁיָא אִילּוּ הִשְׁבִּיחַ וְלֹא פָּגַם שֶׁמָּא כְלוּם הִיא.

Rebbi Jonah said; the statement of Rebbi Simeon ben Laqish is necessary since we wanted to say that they[122] disagree when each one is full strength and the profane sourdough fell in first. But if the heave sourdough fell in first, the dough already became sour. Even if profane sourdough fell in first, it is considered that first it improved and then spoiled[123]. Rebbi Jonah came back to this and said, that woman will not make it thoroughly sour[124], she will leave a little bit. That little bit should be considered as if it first improved and then spoiled. That is difficult, if it improved and did not spoil, is that nothing[125]?

122 The anonymous Tanna and R. Simeon in Mishnah 8.

123 In the end, there is too much sourdough which cannot but reduce the quality of the bread.

124 A full portion of sourdough will be at the lower limit of what is necessary to thoroughly leaven the dough.

125 In that case, because of the doubt R. Simeon should agree with the anonymous Tanna that the heave sourdough is active and makes the entire bread *dema'*. Therefore, the opinion of R. Simeon ben Laqish is irrelevant here; the statement of R. Joḥanan, that R. Simeon also disagrees in Mishnah 8, has to be rejected.

רִבִּי יוֹנָה בָּעֵי מַה בֵין שֶׁבַח מִזֶּה וּמִזֶּה. וּמַה בֵין פְּגַם מִזֶּה וּמִזֶּה. שֶׁבַח מִזֶּה וּמִזֶּה אָסוּר. פְּגַם מִזֶּה וּמִזֶּה מוּתָּר. אָמַר רִבִּי מָנָא שֶׁבַח מִזֶּה וּמִזֶּה אַתְּ רוֹאֶה כְּמִי שֶׁאֵינוֹ אוֹתוֹ הָאִיסּוּר אִם יֵשׁ בּוֹ כְּדֵי לֶאֱסוֹר. פְּגַם מִזֶּה וּמִזֶּה אַתְּ רוֹאֶה אֶת הַהֵיתֵר כְּמוֹ שֶׁאֵינוֹ אוֹתוֹ הָאִיסּוּר אֵין בּוֹ כְּדֵי לֶאֱסוֹר.

Rebbi Jonah asked: What is the difference if it improved from both of them or spoiled from both of them? If it improved from both of them, it is forbidden[126]. If it spoiled from both of them, it is permitted. Rebbi Mana said, if it improved from both of them, you consider [the permitted][127] as non-existent; the forbidden is enough to make it forbidden[128]. If it spoiled from both of them, you consider the permitted as non-existent; the forbidden is not enough to make it forbidden.

126 In the Babli (*Pesaḥim* 27a/b, *Sanhedrin* 80a, *Avodah Zarah* 49a, *Ḥulin* 58a, *Temurah* 31a) this premiss is questioned and the final determination is that anything caused by two agents, one permitted and the other forbidden, is permitted. In the Yerushalmi, this is accepted only if no agent alone could

have caused the result; cf. Mishnah 11.

127 Missing in the texts but implied by the parallel in the next sentence.

128 By Mishnah 5, since it acts to improve.

משנה י: (fol. 61c) תַּבְלִין שְׁנַיִם וּשְׁלֹשָׁה שֵׁמוֹת מִמִּין אֶחָד אוֹ מִשְּׁלֹשָׁה אָסוּר וּמִצְטָרְפִין. רִבִּי שִׁמְעוֹן אוֹמֵר שְׁנַיִם וּשְׁלֹשָׁה שֵׁמוֹת מִמִּין אֶחָד אוֹ שְׁנֵי מִינִין מִשֵּׁם אֶחָד אֵין מִצְטָרְפִין.

Mishnah 10: Spices[129], two or three names from one kind[130], or [one name for] three are forbidden and combine. Rebbi Simeon says, two or three names from one kind, or two kinds of the same name, do not combine.

129 Of heave, *'orlah*, etc.

130 For example black, white, and long pepper (Rashi, *Šabbat* 89b, *Avodah Zarah* 66b). Maimonides brings as example different sorts of cardamum which are never sold together.

הלכה ו: (fol. 62b) נִיחָא שְׁנֵי שֵׁמוֹת מִמִּין אֶחָד שְׁנֵי מִינִים מִשֵּׁם אֶחָד. רִבִּי אַבָּהוּ בְּשֵׁם רִבִּי לָעְזָר בְּמִינֵי מְתִיקָה שָׁנוּ.

Halakhah 6: We understand two names for one kind. But two kinds of one name? Rebbi Abbahu in the name of Rebbi Eleazar: They taught this about sweeteners.

רִבִּי אַבָּהוּ בְּשֵׁם רִבִּי יוֹחָנָן שְׁלֹשָׁה נוֹתְנֵי טְעָמִים הֵן. כָּל־שֶׁהַהֶדְיוֹט טוֹעֲמוֹ וְאוֹמֵר קְדֵירָה זוֹ אֵינָהּ חֲסֵירָה וְנָפַל זוֹ הִיא נוֹתֵן טַעַם לִשְׁבָח מוּתָּר. וַאֲפִילוּ אָמַר תַּבְלִין פְּלוֹנִי יֵשׁ בִּקְדֵירָה זוֹ. זוֹ הִיא נוֹתֵן טַעַם לִפְגָם מוּתָּר. וְכָל־שֶׁהָאוּמָן טוֹעֲמוֹ וְאוֹמֵר תַּבְלִין פְּלוֹנִי יֵשׁ בִּקְדֵירָה. זֶה הוּא נוֹתֵן טַעַם לִפְגָם אָסוּר.

Rebbi Abbahu in the name of Rebbi Joḥanan, there are three kinds of imparting taste. Anything a common person tastes and says, this dish is not missing anything, if it fell in, it may improve the taste but is permitted[131]. Even if he says, this dish contains spice x, when it spoils the taste it is permitted. But if a professional tastes it and says, this dish contains spice x[132], when it spoils the taste it is forbidden.

131 Since the person who is not a professional cook or food taster finds the dish perfect, the later addition of forbidden spice either does not add anything; then it will be permitted if it is less than $^1/_{100}$ (or $^1/_{200}$) of the whole; or it will spoil the taste and be permitted outright.

132 But a non-professional would not taste it and for him the additional spice might improve the taste, the addition is not considered spoiling and is forbidden in the most minute amount.

רִבִּי אַבָּהוּ בְשֵׁם רִבִּי יוֹחָנָן כָּל־הָאִיסוּרִין מְשַׁעֲרִין אוֹתָן כִּילוּ בָּצָל כִּילוּ קֶפָּלוֹט. עַד כְּדוֹן דָּבָר שֶׁדַּרְכּוֹ לְהִשְׁתָּעֵר בְּבָצָל וּבְקֶפָּלוֹט. דָּבָר שֶׁאֵין דַּרְכּוֹ לְהִשְׁתָּעֵר בְּבָצָל וּבְקֶפָּלוֹט בְּמָה אַתָּה מְשָׁעֲרוֹ. הַכָּמוֹן בְּמָה אַתְּ מְשָׁעֲרָן.

Rebbi Abbahu in the name of Rebbi Joḥanan, all forbidden [food] is estimated as if it were onion, as if it were leeks[133]. That is, anything usually estimated as if it were onion, as if it were leeks. Anything which is not usually estimated as if it were onion, as if it were leeks, how do you estimate it? How do you estimate cumin?

אָמַר רִבִּי יוּדָן לֹא כֵן אָמַר רִבִּי אַבָּהוּ בְּשֵׁם רִבִּי לְעָזָר בְּמִינֵי מְתִיקָה שָׁנוּ. מִינֵי מְתִיקָה עַל יְדֵי שֶׁדַּרְכָּן לְהִשְׁתָּעֵר בְּבָצָל וּבְקֶפָּלוֹט מְשַׁעֲרִין אוֹתוֹ כִּילוּ בָּצָל כִּילוּ קֶפָּלוֹט. שְׁאָר כָּל־הָאִיסוּרִין עַל יְדֵי שֶׁאֵין דַּרְכָּן לְהִשְׁתָּעֵר בְּבָצָל וּבְקֶפָּלוֹט מְשַׁעֲרִין אוֹתָן בְּמִינָן. הַכָּמוֹן מְשַׁעֲרִין אוֹתוֹ בְּמִינוֹ.

Rebbi Yudan said, did not Rebbi Abbahu say in the name of Rebbi Eleazar, they taught this about sweeteners? Since sweeteners usually are estimated as if they were onion or leeks, one estimates them as if they were onion or leeks. All other forbidden [foods], since they are not usually estimated as if they were onion or leeks one estimates in their kinds. Cumin one estimates by its kind[134].

רִבִּי מָנָא לֹא אָמַר כֵּן אֶלָּא לֹא כֵן אָמַר רִבִּי אַבָּהוּ אָמַר רִבִּי לָעְזָר בְּמִינֵי מְתִיקָה שָׁנוּ. מִינֵי מְתִיקָה עַל יְדֵי שֶׁטַּעֲמוֹן שָׁוֶה מְשַׁעֲרִין אוֹתָן כִּילּוּ בָּצָל כִּילּוּ קֶפָלוֹט. שְׁאָר כָּל־הָאִיסוּרִין עַל יְדֵי שֶׁאֵין טַעֲמוֹן שָׁוֶה אֵין מְשַׁעֲרִין אוֹתָן כִּילּוּ בָּצָל כִּילּוּ קֶפָלוֹט. הַכָּמוֹן צְרִיכָה.

Rebbi Mana did not say so but: Did not Rebbi Abbahu say in the name of Rebbi Eleazar, they taught this about sweeteners? Since sweeteners all taste the same, they are estimated as if they were onion, as if they were leeks. All other forbidden [foods], since they do not taste the same one does not estimate them as if they were onion, as if they were leeks. Cumin is a problem[135].

133 Cf. *Terumot* 10:1, Notes 8-12; Babli *Ḥulin* 97b. Any foodstuffs usually estimated as if they were onion, as if they were leeks, are ingredients for cooking. Things not usually estimated as if they were onion, as if they were leeks, such as cumin, are used on top of bread or dishes. The problem is that one may not taste the dish or bread because it contains a forbidden substance and might be forbidden.

134 Since usually one does not use forbidden cumin, one will know how much to take to induce the flavor of cumin in the finished product.

135 In the absence of standards for judging, it remains forbidden.

רִבִּי אַבָּהוּ בְּשֵׁם רִבִּי יוֹחָנָן כָּל־נוֹתְנֵי טְעָמִים אֵין לוֹקִין עֲלֵיהֶן עַד שֶׁיִּטְעוֹם טַעַם מַמָּשׁוֹ שֶׁלְּאִיסּוּר. הָתִיב רִבִּי חָמָא בַּר יוֹסֵי קוֹמֵי רִבִּי יוֹחָנָן הֲרֵי בָּשָׂר בְּחָלָב הֲרֵי

לֹא טָעַם מַמָּשׁוֹ שֶׁלְאִיסּוּר וְאַתְּ אָמַר לוֹקֶה. וְקִבְּלָהּ. מַהוּ וְקִבְּלָהּ. כְּאִינָשׁ דְּשָׁמַע מִילֵּיהּ דְּבַעַל דִּינָא קִבְּלָהּ.

[136]Rebbi Abbahu in the name of Rebbi Joḥanan: One does not whip for anything imparting taste until he tasted the forbidden thing itself[137]. Rebbi Ḥama bar Yose[138] objected before Rebbi Joḥanan: There is meat in milk, where he did not taste the forbidden thing itself[139] and you say that he is whipped! He accepted that. What means, he accepted that? Like a person who listens to the argument of the opposing party he accepted it.[140]

136 From here to the end of the Halakhah, the text is also in *Nazir* 6:1 (fol. 54d).

137 A person eating forbidden food cannot be criminally prosecuted unless he ate at least the volume of an olive of the forbidden substance. Taste makes a mixture forbidden but not criminally.

138 A student of R. Hoshaia, Amora of the early second generation in Galilee.

139 If meat is cooked in milk and then the meat is removed, the person drinking the milk is criminally liable even though he did not eat from the meat.

140 He did not find it necessary to respond since he has his own argument. The question is obviously invalid since the milk is as strictly forbidden as is the meat since milk and meat are treated as parallels in the verses.

רִבִּי אַבָּהוּ בְּשֵׁם רִבִּי יוֹחָנָן כָּל־נוֹתְנֵי טְעָמִים אֵין לוֹקִין עֲלֵיהֶן חוּץ מִנּוֹתְנֵי טַעַם שֶׁל נָזִיר. אָמַר רִבִּי זְעִירָא כָּל־נוֹתֵן טַעַם אֵין לוֹקִין עֲלֵיהֶן עַד שֶׁיִּטְעוֹם טַעַם מַמָּשׁוֹ שֶׁל אִיסּוּר וּבְנָזִיר אֲפִילוּ לֹא טָעַם טַעַם מַמָּשׁוֹ שֶׁלְאִיסּוּר. אָמַר רִבִּי בָּא בַּר מָמָל כָּל־נוֹתְנֵי טְעָמִים אֵין אִיסּוּר וְהֵיתֵר מִצְטָרְפִין. וּבְנָזִיר אִיסּוּר וְהֵיתֵר מִצְטָרְפִין. מַתְנִיתָא מְסַייְעָא לְדֵין וּמַתְנִיתָא מְסַייְעָא לְדֵין. מַתְנִיתָא מְסַייְעָא לְרִבִּי זְעִירָא. כְּזַיִת יַיִן שֶׁנָּפַל לִקְדֵירָה אָכַל מִמֶּנָּה כְּזַיִת פָּטוּר עַד שֶׁיֹּאכַל אֶת

כּוּלָּהּ. עַל דַּעְתֵּיהּ דְּרִבִּי בָּא בַּר מָמָל כֵּיוָן שֶׁאָכַל מִמֶּנָּה כְּזַיִת חַיָּיב. מַתְנִיתָא מְסַייְעָא לְרִבִּי בָּא בַּר מָמָל. מְמַשְׁמַע שֶׁנֶּאֱמַר וְכָל־מִשְׁרַת עֲנָבִים לֹא יִשְׁתֶּה וְכִי מָה הִנִּיחַ הַכָּתוּב שֶׁלֹּא אֲמָרוֹ. אֶלָּא לְפִי שֶׁנֶּאֱמַר מִכֹּל אֲשֶׁר יֵעָשֶׂה מִגֶּפֶן הַיַּיִן מֵחַרְצַנִּים וְעַד זָג לֹא יֹאכֵל. מִיַּיִן וְשֵׁכָר יַזִּיר. מַה תַּלְמוּד לוֹמַר וְכָל־מִשְׁרַת עֲנָבִים לֹא יִשְׁתֶּה. אֶלָּא שֶׁאִם שָׁרָה עֲנָבִים וְשָׁרָה פִּיתּוֹ בָּהֶן וְיֵשׁ בָּהֶן כְּדֵי לְצָרֵף בָּהֶן כְּזַיִת חַיָּיב. וּמִיכָּן אַתָּה דָן לְכָל־הָאִיסּוּרִין שֶׁבַּתּוֹרָה וּמָה אִם הַיּוֹצֵא מִן הַגֶּפֶן שֶׁאֵין אִיסּוּרוֹ אִיסּוּר עוֹלָם וְאֵין אִיסּוּרוֹ אִיסּוּר הֲנָאָה. וְיֵשׁ לוֹ הֵיתֵר אַחַר אִיסּוּרוֹ עָשָׂה בוֹ טַעַם כְּעִיקָּר. שְׁאָר כָּל־הָאִיסּוּרִין שֶׁבַּתּוֹרָה שֶׁאִיסּוּרָן אִיסּוּר עוֹלָם וְאִיסּוּרָן אִיסּוּר הֲנָייָה. אֵין לָהֶן הֵיתֵר אַחַר אִיסּוּרָן אֵינוֹ דִין שֶׁנַּעֲשֶׂה בָהֶן אֶת הַטַּעַם כְּעִיקָּר. מִכָּן לָמְדוּ חֲכָמִים כָּל־נוֹתְנֵי טְעָמִים שֶׁיְּהוּ אֲסוּרִין. וְקַשְׁיָא עַל דְּרִבִּי זְעִירָא. בְּכָל־אָתַר אָמַר עַד שֶׁיִּטְעוֹם וָכָה אַתְּ אָמַר אֲפִילוּ לֹא טָעַם.

Rebbi Abbahu in the name of Rebbi Joḥanan: One does not whip for anything imparting taste except imparting taste for the *nazir*[141]. Rebbi Zeïra said, one does not whip for anything imparting taste until he tasted the forbidden thing itself except the *nazir* even if he did not taste the forbidden thing itself[142]. Rebbi Abba bar Mamal said, for food imparting taste what is forbidden and what is permitted are not combined, but for the *nazir* forbidden and permitted do combine[143]. A *baraita* supports one and a *baraita* supports the other. A *baraita* supports Rebbi Zeïra: If wine in the volume of an olive fell into a dish and he[144] ate from it, he cannot be prosecuted unless he ate the entire dish. In the opinion of Rebbi Abba bar Mamal, if he ate the volume of an olive from it he is guilty. A *baraita*[145] supports Rebbi Abba bar Mamal: "What do we understand when it is said (*Num.* 6:3): 'Anything in which grapes were soaked he should not eat'? What did the verse leave out that was not said? But since it was said (*Num.* 6:4): 'anything made from the wine-vine, from seeds to grape skins he should not eat;' (*Num.* 6:3) 'from wine and liquor he shall abstain.' Why does the verse say 'anything in which grapes were soaked he should not eat'? That means that if he soaked grapes and then soaked his bread in that, if it[146] adds up to the volume of an olive, he is guilty. From here you argue about all prohibitions of the Torah. Since for all that comes from the vine, whose prohibition is neither permanent[147], nor a prohibition of usufruct, and whose prohibition can be lifted[148], He made taste like the thing itself; is it not logical that for all prohibitions of the Torah, whose prohibition is permanent, is a prohibition of usufruct, and whose prohibition cannot be lifted[149], that we[150] treat taste like the thing itself[151]? From here, the Sages inferred that everything imparting taste is forbidden." This is difficult for Rebbi Zeïra who says everywhere "unless he tasted[152]", and here he says, "even if he did not taste."

141 *Num.* 6.

142 R. Zeïra takes the statements of R. Abbahu in this and the preceding paragraph as one. A similar interpretation in Babli *Pesaḥim* 43b, *Nazir* 35b.

143 Since nobody can be punished for eating less than the volume of an olive of a forbidden substance, this is his interpretation of the statements of R. Abbahu.

144 A *nazir*.

145 A shortened version in *Sifry Num.* 23, a short reference to the argument is in Babli *Pesaḥim* 44a/b.

146 The amount of water soaked up by the bread.

147 It is forbidden only for the *nazir* and only for a period of time specified at the beginning.

148 The vow of a *nazir* can be annulled just as any other vow can be annulled.

149 At least one of these categories applies to any food prohibition in the Torah.

150 The principle formulated is divine for the *nazir* and rabbinic for all other prohibitions.

151 Babli *Pesaḥim* 44b.

152 The forbidden food itself.

(fol. 61c) **משנה י:** שְׂאוֹר שֶׁלְחוּלִין וְשֶׁלִתְּרוּמָה שֶׁנָּפְלוּ לְתוֹךְ עִיסָּה לֹא בְזֶה כְדֵי לְחַמֵּץ וְלֹא בְזֶה כְדֵי לְחַמֵּץ הִצְטָרְפוּ וְחִימִּיצוּ רִבִּי לִיעֶזֶר אוֹמֵר אַחַר הָאַחֲרוֹן אֲנִי בָא. וַחֲכָמִים אוֹמְרִים בֵּין שֶׁנָּפַל אִיסּוּר בַּתְּחִילָּה בֵּין בַּסּוֹף לְעוֹלָם אֵין אוֹסֵר עַד שֶׁיְּהֵא בוֹ כְדֵי לְחַמֵּץ.

Mishnah 10: If profane and heave sourdoughs fell into a dough and neither one alone could have soured it but they combined and made it sour, Rebbi Eliezer said I am going after the last one[153] but the Sages say whether the forbidden fell first or last it does not make forbidden[154] unless it alone could make it sour.

153 If heave sourdough fell in last, it causes irreparable *dema'* following Mishnah 4. If profane sourdough fell in last, the heave may be lifted if it is less than 1% of the dough. In the Babli (*Pesaḥim* 26b/27a, *Avodah Zarah* 73b, *Temurah* 12a), Abbai holds that R. Eliezer permits the dough only if the heave sourdough was lifted out before the profane was put in. There is no hint of this in the Yerushalmi.

154 By the rules of Mishnah 4.

משנה יא: יוֹעֶזֶר אִישׁ הַבִּירָה הָיָה מִתַּלְמִידֵי שַׁמַּי וְאָמַר שָׁאַלְתִּי אֶת רַבָּן גַּמְלִיאֵל הַזָּקֵן עוֹמֵד בְּשַׁעַר הַמִּזְרָח וְאָמַר לְעוֹלָם אֵין אוֹסֵר עַד שֶׁיְּהֵא בוֹ כְדֵי לְחַמֵּץ.

Mishnah 11: Yoezer from Bira was one of Shammai's students[155]. He said, I asked Rabban Gamliel I[156] when he was standing at the Eastern gate[157] and he said, it does not make forbidden unless it alone could make it sour.

155 Nothing more is known about him.

156 The head of the Synhedrion during the first decades of the current era, Hillel's grandson.

157 Of the Temple enclosure.

הלכה ז: (fol. 62b) תַּמָּן תַּנִּינָן יֵין נֶסֶךְ אָסוּר וְאוֹסֵר כָּל־שֶׁהוּא. חִזְקִיָּה אָמַר כּוֹס שֶׁמְּזָגוֹ מִן הָאִיסּוּר וּמִן הַהֵיתֵר וְנָפַל אִיסּוּר בְּסוֹף אִיסּוּר הֵיתֵר בְּסוֹף הֵיתֵר. אָמַר רִבִּי שְׁמוּאֵל בַּר רַב יִצְחָק דְּרִבִּי לִיעֶזֶר הִיא. דְּרִבִּי לִיעֶזֶר אָמַר אַחַר הָאַחֲרוֹן אֲנִי בָא. אָמַר רִבִּי יִרְמְיָה חוֹמֶר הוּא בְּיֵין נֶסֶךְ. רִבִּי יוֹסֵי בָּעֵי אִם חוֹמֶר הוּא בְּיֵין נֶסֶךְ אֲפִילוּ נָפַל הֵיתֵר בְּסוֹף יְהֵא אָסוּר. רִבִּי יָסָא בְשֵׁם רִבִּי יוֹחָנָן כּוֹס שֶׁמְּזָגוֹ מֵאִיסּוּר וּמֵהֵיתֵר אַתְּ רוֹאֶה אֶת הַהֵיתֵר כְּמִי שֶׁאֵינוֹ אוֹתוֹ הָאִיסּוּר אִם יֵשׁ בּוֹ בְנוֹתֵן טַעַם אָסוּר וְאִם לָאו מוּתָּר. אָמַר רִבִּי הוֹשַׁעְיָה וְהוּא שֶׁנָּפַל הַהֵיתֵר בְּסוֹף. רִבִּי אִימִּי בְשֵׁם רִבִּי יוֹחָנָן לֹא שַׁנְייָא בֵּין שֶׁנָּפַל אִיסּוּר בַּתְּחִילָּה וְהֵיתֵר בַּסּוֹף לְהֵיתֵר בַּתְּחִילָּה וְאִיסּוּר בַּסּוֹף. אֲפִילוּ מַיִם וְיַיִן אֲפִילוּ נִמְזָג כָּל־צוֹרְכוֹ מִן הַהֵיתֵר אַתְּ רוֹאֶה אֶת הַהֵיתֵר כְּמִי שֶׁאֵינוֹ אוֹתוֹ הָאִיסּוּר אִם יֵשׁ בּוֹ בְנוֹתֵן טַעַם אָסוּר וְאִם לָאו מוּתָּר. אָמַר רִבִּי זְעִירָא הָדָא דְאַתְּ אָמַר וְכוּלָּהּ תֵּיתְנוּיִין הֵיךְ עֲבִידָא. רִבִּי יוֹסֵי בֵּירִבִּי בוּן רִבִּי אַבָּהוּ בְשֵׁם רִבִּי יוֹחָנָן צְלוֹחִית שֶׁלְּיַיִן נֶסֶךְ שֶׁנָּפְלָה לְתוֹךְ חָבִית שֶׁלְּיַיִן וְחָזְרָה וְנָפְלָה לְתוֹךְ בּוֹר שֶׁלְּמַיִם אַתְּ רוֹאֶה אֶת הַהֵיתֵר כְּמִי שֶׁאֵינוֹ אוֹתוֹ הָאִיסּוּר אִם יֵשׁ בּוֹ בְנוֹתֵן טַעַם אָסוּר וְאִם לָאו מוּתָּר.

Halakhah 7: [158]There, we have stated: "Libation wine[159] is forbidden and makes forbidden in the most minute amount." Ḥizqiah said, if somebody mixed a cup from forbidden and from permitted [wine], if the forbidden fell in last it makes it forbidden, permitted at the end makes it permitted[160]. Rebbi Samuel ben Rav Isaac said, this follows Rebbi Eliezer, as Rebbi Eliezer said, I am going after the last one. Rebbi Jeremiah said, this is a stringency about libation wine. Rebbi Yose asked, if it were a stringency about libation wine, even if the permitted fell in last it should be forbidden[161]! Rebbi Assi in the name of Rebbi Joḥanan: If somebody mixed a cup from forbidden and from permitted [wine], one considers the permitted as nonexistent[162]; if the forbidden does impart taste it is forbidden, otherwise permitted. Rebbi Hoshaia said, only if the permitted fell in last[163]. Rebbi Ammi in the name of Rebbi Joḥanan, it does not make any difference whether the forbidden fell in first and the permitted last or the permitted first and the forbidden last, even water and wine, even if it was mixed perfectly from permitted, one considers the permitted as nonexistent; if the forbidden does impart taste it is forbidden, otherwise permitted. Rebbi Zeïra said, that which you say and everybody stated, how can this be[164]? Rebbi Yose ben Rebbi Abun, Rebbi Abbahu in the name of Rebbi Joḥanan, if a flask of libation wine fell into an amphora of wine and then[165] it fell into a water cistern, one considers the permitted as nonexistent; if it can be tasted it[166] is forbidden, otherwise permitted.

158 Mishnah *Avodah Zarah* 5:11. The entire Halakhah is from *Avodah Zarah* 5:11, fol. 45a; the parallel in Babli *Avodah Zarah* 73a/b.

159 Cf. Note 115.

160 This seems to contradict the Mishnah just quoted.

161 R. Jeremiah's position is impossible.

162 Mixed wine always contains wine and water; the amount of prohibited wine must be so small as not to give taste to the mixing water.

163 In that case, the prohibited was already insignificant in the water when the permitted fell in; nothing is changed.

164 If one speaks about mixing cups, it is most unlikely that any ever would be permitted under these rules.

165 It was immediately fished out; the amphora will be forbidden as

libation wine.

166 The water. In the Babli, *Avodah Zarah* 73a/b, both in the printed version and in the Sephardic ms. published by S. Abramson, the disagreement between Ḥizqiah and R, Joḥanan is about libation wine which fell into a water cistern and then a flask of water fell into the cistern and was fished out. The Ashkenazic version of the Munich ms. speaks of libation *and permitted* wine which fell into a water cistern; a scenario compatible with the statement of R. Abbahu.

עַד כְּדוֹן כְּשֶׁנָּפְלוּ זֶה אַחַר זֶה. נָפְלוּ שְׁנֵיהֶן כְּאַחַת מָה אָמְרַת בָּהּ. רִבִּי לָעְזָר אָמַר נִשְׁמְעִינָהּ מִן הָדָא אֵימָתַי חָמֵיצָן שֶׁלְּכּוּתִים מוּתָּר לְאַחַר הַפֶּסַח. שֶׁלְּבַעֲלֵי בָתִּים אַחַר שָׁלֹשׁ שַׁבָּתוֹת שֶׁלְּאֲפִייָה. וְשֶׁלְּנַחְתּוֹמִין בַּכְּרָכִים לְאַחַר שְׁלֹשָׁה יָמִים. וְשֶׁלְּנַחְתּוֹמִין בַּכְּפָרִים לְאַחַר שְׁלֹשָׁה תַנּוּרִים. רִבִּי שִׁמְעוֹן בֶּן אֶלְעָזָר אוֹמֵר אַף כְּשֶׁאָמְרוּ שֶׁל בַּעֲלֵי בָתִּים אַחַר שָׁלֹשׁ שַׁבָּתוֹת שֶׁלְּאֲפִייָה. וְהוּא שֶׁיְּהֵא אָדָם גָּדוֹל אוֹ שֶׁהָיָה מַשִּׂיא אֶת בְּנוֹ וְאָפָה שְׁלֹשָׁה תַנּוּרִים בְּשַׁבָּת אַחַת זֶה אַחַר זֶה וְזֶה אַחַר זֶה מוּתָּר. וְאַף כְּשֶׁאָמְרוּ שֶׁלְּנַחְתּוֹמִין בַּכְּרָכִין לְאַחַר שְׁלֹשָׁה יָמִים וְהוּא שֶׁנִּדְחָק וְאָפָה שְׁלֹשָׁה תַנּוּרִים בְּיוֹם אֶחָד זֶה אַחַר זֶה וְזֶה אַחַר זֶה מוּתָּר. תַּנֵּי רִבִּי שִׁמְעוֹן אוֹמֵר וְאַף כְּשֶׁאָמְרוּ שֶׁלְּנַחְתּוֹמִין בַּכְּפָרִים לְאַחַר שְׁלֹשָׁה תַנּוּרִין. אָסוּר עַד שְׁלֹשָׁה יָמִים אֲסוּרִין שֶׁמִּשַּׁחֲרִית הוּא כוֹרֶה לוֹ שְׂאוֹר לְכָל־אוֹתוֹ הַיּוֹם. אוֹתָהּ הָעִיסָּה שְׁנִיָּא לֹא מֵאִיסּוּר וְהֵיתֵר הִיא מִתְחַמֶּצֶת. וָמַר רִבִּי יִרְמְיָה (fol. 62c) בְּשֵׁם רִבִּי שִׁמְעוֹן בֶּן לָקִישׁ מָאן תַּנָּא חָמֵיצָן שֶׁל כּוּתִים רִבִּי לִיעֶזֶר. וְאָמַר רִבִּי יוֹסֵי לְרִבִּי חֲנִינָא עֲנְתָנַיְיָא נָהוֹר אָתִית אֲמַר אַתְּ וְרִבִּי יִרְמְיָה בְּשֵׁם רִבִּי שִׁמְעוֹן בֶּן לָקִישׁ מָאן תַּנָּא חָמֵיצָן שֶׁלְּכּוּתִים רִבִּי לִיעֶזֶר. וַאֲנָן לֵי נָן אָמְרִין כֵּן. אֶלָּא רִבִּי הִילָא בְּשֵׁם רִבִּי שִׁמְעוֹן בֶּן לָקִישׁ יָרְדוּ לְחָמֵיצָן שֶׁלְּכּוּתִין כְּרִבִּי לִיעֶזֶר. וְעוֹד מִן הָדָא דְּאָמַר רִבִּי חֲנִינָא בְּרֵיהּ דְּרִבִּי אַבָּהוּ אַבָּא הֲוָה לֵיהּ עוֹבְדָא שָׁלַח שָׁאַל לְרִבִּי חִיָּיה וּלְרִבִּי יָסָא וּלְרִבִּי אִימִּי וְאוֹרִין לֵיהּ כְּרִבִּי לִיעֶזֶר. מַה כִיחִידָיָא מוֹרֵיי. לֹא מִשּׁוּם שֶׁיָּרְדוּ לְחָמֵיצָן שֶׁל כּוּתִין כְּרִבִּי לִיעֶזֶר.

So far when they fell in one after the other. What can one say if they fell together? Rebbi Eleazar said, let us hear from the following[167]:

"When is the leavened matter of Samaritans permitted after Passover[168]? Of private persons after three weekly bakings, of city bakers after three days, of rural bakers after three baking loads. Rebbi Simeon ben Eleazar says, even when they said of private persons after three weekly bakings, if he was an important personality or he married off his son, if he baked three loads one after the other it is permitted. And even when they said of city bakers after three days, if he was under pressure[169] and baked three loads one after the other it is permitted." It was stated[170]: "Rebbi Simeon says even when they said of rural bakers after three baking loads, it is forbidden at least three days since in the morning he prepares sourdough for the entire day." Does the second dough not become sour from forbidden and permitted[171]? And Rebbi Jeremiah said in the name of Rebbi Simeon ben Laqish, who is the Tanna of the leavened matter of Samaritans? Rebbi Eliezer![172] And Rebbi Yose said to Rebbi Ḥanina Eyntanaya: Do you remember that you and Rebbi Jeremiah said in the name of Rebbi Simeon ben Laqish, who is the Tanna of the leavened matter of Samaritans? Rebbi Eliezer! But we do not say so, since Rebbi Hila said in the name of Rebbi Simeon ben Laqish, they treated leavened matter of Samaritans following Rebbi Eliezer[173]. In addition from the following: Rebbi Ḥanina said, my father Rebbi Abbahu had a case; he sent to Rebbi Ḥiyya, Rebbi Assi, and Rebbi Ammi, and they instructed him according to Rebbi Eliezer. Would they instruct according to an isolated opinion? But it is that they treated leavened matter of Samaritans following Rebbi Eliezer.

167 Tosephta *Pesaḥim* 2:1.

168 In current practice, leavened matter which was in the possession of a Jew during Passover is forever for

bidden for any use. This is a matter of considerable controversy among talmudic authorities [*Pesaḥim* 2:2 (fol. 28d), Babli *Pesaḥim* 28a/b]. Since Samaritans are Sadducees, they do not follow rabbinic rules and since for them the prohibition of leavened matter after Passover is not biblical, they do not accept it. A Samaritan might use leavened matter somehow kept from before Passover (even though it is difficult to see how that could be done legally without violating the prohibition contained in *Ex.* 13:7).

169 Because everybody needs bread after Passover, he will bake several loads the day after Passover. Once he has prepared three loads, one may assume that all sourdough still in his possession from before Passover is used up. This is the principle in all cases.

170 Tosephta *Pesaḥim* 2:2. R. Simeon disagrees with R. Simeon ben Eleazar and holds that sourdough is not made more than once a day; therefore, a three day waiting priod is required under all circumstances. On the other hand, we will allow bread for any professional baker after three days.

171 Here starts the argument. Since sourdough for the second day is made from matter left over from the first day when forbidden dough had been mixed with permitted new flour, is it not as if forbidden and permitted were taken together at the same moment? (The same could be said for the third day.)

172 If R. Eliezer says we go after the last one, he must hold that even if the forbidden dough fell simultaneously with the permitted it qualifies as "last" and makes everything forbidden.

173 This is rabbinic practice which does not logically follow from general principles; it does not prove anything for heave, *'orlah*, and vineyard *kilaim*.

אָמַר רִבִּי מָנָא קוֹמֵי רִבִּי יָסֵא הֵיךְ מַה דְתֵימַר תַּמָּן הֲלָכָה כְּרִבִּי לִיעֶזֶר. וְכָא הֲלָכָה כְּרִבִּי לִיעֶזֶר. אָמַר לוֹ וּלְכָל־דָּבָר.

Rebbi Mana said before Rebbi Yose: What do you say, there practice follows Rebbi Eliezer; does practice here follow Rebbi Eliezer[174]? He said to him, for everything?

174 *There* is leavened matter of the Samaritans, *here* are heave, *'orlah*, and vineyard *kilaim*. The answer is negative.

(fol. 61c) **משנה יג:** כֵּלִים שֶׁסָּכָן בְּשֶׁמֶן טָמֵא וְחָזַר וְסָכָן בְּשֶׁמֶן טָהוֹר. אוֹ שֶׁסָּכָן בְּשֶׁמֶן טָהוֹר וְחָזַר וְסָכָן בְּשֶׁמֶן טָמֵא. רִבִּי לִיעֶזֶר אוֹמֵר אַחַר הָרִאשׁוֹן אֲנִי בָא וַחֲכָמִים אוֹמְרִים אַחַר הָאַחֲרוֹן.

Mishnah 13: If vessels[175] were oiled first with impure oil[176] and then with pure, or first with pure and then with impure, Rebbi Eliezer says I am going after the first, but the Sages say after the last[177].

175 According to Maimonides, vessels which cannot become impure, such as stone vessels or flat wood or flat clay. It is difficult to see why these should be oiled. According to R. Simson, as well as most moderns, one speaks of leather goods, such as water skins, which have to be oiled. The leather goods become impure but they can be purified by immersion; after they have been dried, the impure oil absorbed in the leather has no influence (unless the leather becomes wet and some impure oil starts to ooze out. ,Tosephta *Terumot* 8:15.)

176 Which is cheaper than pure oil.

177 If the oiled leather becomes wet, R. Eliezer holds that the substance massaged in first is excreted first, but the Sages hold that it is the substance massaged in last. If the pure oil remains pure one has to assume that the leather was perfectly dried between first and second oiling since when wet, the most minute amount of impure oil will make impure all pure oil in contact with it.

(fol. 62c) **הלכה ח:** מַה טַעֲמָא דְּרִבִּי לִיעֶזֶר הָרִאשׁוֹן מוֹצִיא אֶת הָאַחֲרוֹן.

Halakhah 8: What is the reason of Rebbi Eliezer? The first pushes the last out[178].

178 The oil rubbed in first fills the leather, the second rubbing is essentially without continuing influence; if the leather vessel is immersed in the *miqweh* the later oil is washed away.

The Gaon of Wilna, followed by S. Lieberman, wants to emend the text and read מַה טַעֲמָא דְּרִבִּי לִיעֶזֶר [הָאַחֲרוֹן מוֹצִיא אֶת הָרִאשׁוֹן מַה טַעֲמָא דְּרַבָּנָן] הָרִאשׁוֹן מוֹצִיא אֶת הָאַחֲרוֹן, meaning that oiling leather a second time pushes the first oil out at the other side. This interpretation is explicitly rejected in the Halakhah and the emendation is contradicted by the next paragraph.

אָמַר רִבִּי יוֹחָנָן רִבִּי יְהוּדָה וְרִבִּי לִיעֶזֶר שְׁנֵיהֶן אָמְרוּ דָבָר אֶחָד. דְּתַנִּינָן תַּמָּן צְלוֹחִית שֶׁפִּיהָ צָר טוֹבֵל וּמַעֲלֶה כְדַרְכּוֹ. רִבִּי יוּדָה אוֹמֵר הַזָּיָה הָרִאשׁוֹנָה. כְּמָה דְּרִבִּי יוּדָה אָמַר הָרִאשׁוֹן מוֹצִיא אֶת הָאַחֲרוֹן. כֵּן רִבִּי לִיעֶזֶר אוֹמֵר אוּף הָכָא הָרִאשׁוֹן מוֹצִיא אֶת הָאַחֲרוֹן.

Rebbi Joḥanan said, Rebbi Jehudah and Rebbi Eliezer said the same thing. As we have stated there[179]: "In a narrow-mouthed flask he dips and takes it out normally. Rebbi Jehudah says, for the first sprinkling[180]." Just as Rebbi Jehudah said the first pushes out the last, so here Rebbi Eliezer said the first pushes out the last.

179 Mishnah *Parah* 12:2. The flask contains water, with some ashes of the red cow, drawn for the express purpose of dipping into it a branch of hyssop and sprinkling the water on the hyssop leaves on a person or things impure by the impurity of the dead (*Num.* 19).

180 R. Jehudah holds that the narrow neck will squeeze the hyssop so that the second time some water drops on the narrow neck will get on the hyssop and the second sprinkling will not all be from the new immersion of the hyssop, which for him makes the sprinkling invalid. It follows that "the first pushes out the last" means: The first makes the second inoperative.

עַד כְּדוֹן בְּשֶׁסָּךְ מִיכָּן וּמָצָא מִצַּד הַשֵּׁינִי. סָךְ מִיכָּן וּמָצָא מִיכָּן מָה אָמַר בָּהּ רִבִּי לִיעֶזֶר. נִשְׁמְעִינָהּ מִן הָדָא דְּאָמַר רִבִּי אַבָּהוּ בְּשֵׁם רִבִּי יוֹחָנָן לֹא סוֹף דָּבָר צְלוֹחִית אֶלָּא אֲפִילוּ סֵפֶל. וְאָמַר רִבִּי יוֹחָנָן רִבִּי יוּדָה וְרִבִּי לִיעֶזֶר שְׁנֵיהֶן אָמְרוּ דָּבָר אֶחָד. אִית לָךְ מֵימַר תַּמָּן בְּשֶׁסָּךְ מִיכָּן וּמָצָא בְּצַד הַשֵּׁינִי. לֹא בְּשֶׁסָּךְ מִיכָּן וּמָצָא מִיכָּן. אוּף הָכָא בְּשֶׁסָּךְ מִיכָּן וּמָצָא מִיכָּן.

So far if he rubbed in on one side and found on the other side[178]. If he rubbed on this side and found on the same side[181], what does Rebbi Eliezer say? Let us hear from the following which Rebbi Abbahu said in the name of Rebbi Johanan: Not only a flask but also a bowl[182]; and Rebbi Johanan said, Rebbi Jehudah and Rebbi Eliezer said the same thing. Can you say there, if he rubbed in on one side and found on the other side? No, if he rubbed on this side and found on the same side. Here also, if he rubbed on this side and found on the same side.

181 After the second rubbing had dried and the leather was immersed in a *miqweh* and dried, oil was again found on the oiled surface. This is a more likely occurrence.

182 R. Jehudah will never permit using hyssop more than once in the sprinkling ceremony since some drops from the first dipping will remain. The narrow-necked flask was only mentioned for the anonymous majority who will permit repeated use even under these circumstances.

(fol. 61c) **משנה יד:** שְׂאוֹר שֶׁלִּתְרוּמָה וְשֶׁלְּכִלְאֵי הַכֶּרֶם שֶׁנָּפְלוּ לְתוֹךְ עִיסָּה לֹא בְזֶה כְּדֵי לְחַמֵּץ וְלֹא בְזֶה כְּדֵי לְחַמֵּץ וְנִצְטָרְפוּ וְחִימִּיצוּ אָסוּר לְזָרִים וּמוּתָּר לַכֹּהֲנִים. רִבִּי שִׁמְעוֹן אוֹמֵר מוּתָּר לְזָרִים וְלַכֹּהֲנִים.

Mishnah 14: Sourdough of heave and vineyard *kilaim* which fell into dough and neither one of them is enough to make it sour but they combined and made sour, it is forbidden for lay people but permitted for Cohanim. Rebbi Simeon says, it is permitted for lay people and Cohanim[182].

182 This is a parallel to the disagreement between the majority and R. Simeon in Mishnah 10. The majority permits the dough to Cohanim by an analogy to Mishnah 11, where they hold that heave sourdough makes a dough forbidden to lay persons only if it is enough to sour the entire dough.

משנה טו: תַּבְלִין שֶׁלִּתְרוּמָה וְשֶׁלְּכִלְאֵי הַכֶּרֶם שֶׁנָּפְלוּ לְתוֹךְ קְדֵירָה לֹא בְאֵלּוּ כְדֵי לְתַבֵּל וְלֹא בְאֵלּוּ כְדֵי לְתַבֵּל וְנִצְטָרְפוּ וְתִיבִּילוּ אָסוּר לְזָרִים וּמוּתָּר לַכֹּהֲנִים. רִבִּי שִׁמְעוֹן מַתִּיר לְזָרִים וְלַכֹּהֲנִים.

Mishnah 15: If spices of heave and vineyard *kilaim* fell into a pot and neither one of them is enough to spice it but they combine and spice it, it is forbidden for lay people but permitted for Cohanim. Rebbi Simeon permits for lay people and Cohanim.

(fol. 62c) **הלכה ט**: שְׂאוֹר שֶׁלִּתְרוּמָה וְשֶׁלִּשְׁבִיעִית שֶׁנָּפְלוּ לְתוֹךְ הָעִיסָּה לֹא בְזֶה כְדֵי לְחַמֵּץ וְלֹא בְזֶה כְדֵי לְחַמֵּץ וְנִצְטָרְפוּ וְחִימִּיצוּ אָסוּר לְזָרִים וּמוּתָּר לַכֹּהֲנִים. רִבִּי שִׁמְעוֹן מַתִּיר לְזָרִים וְלַכֹּהֲנִים. בְּזֶה כְדֵי לְחַמֵּץ וּבְזֶה כְדֵי לְחַמֵּץ וְנִצְטָרְפוּ וְחִמִּיצוּ אָסוּר לְזָרִים וְלַכֹּהֲנִים. רִבִּי לָעְזָר בְּרִבִּי שִׁמְעוֹן מַתִּיר לַזָּרִים.

Halakhah 9: [183]"If sourdough of heave and Sabbatical produce fell into dough and neither one of them is enough to make it sour but they combine and make sour, it is forbidden for lay people but permitted for Cohanim. Rebbi Simeon permits to lay people and Cohanim. If either one of them is enough to make it sour and they combined and made sour, it is forbidden for lay people and Cohanim[184]. Rebbi Eleazar ben Rebbi Simeon permits to lay people."

183 Tosephta *Terumot* 8:13. There, the authority permitting the dish to lay people is R. Eleazar ben R. Simeon. One has to assume that for the anonymous majority, but not for R. Simeon, the finished bread is Sabbatical.

184 In the Tosephta: "It is forbidden for Cohanim." It is not necessary to say that it is forbidden to lay people. "Forbidden" as applied to Sabbatical produce may mean either that when nothing is left for the wild animals on the fields, it can only be used as unprocessed food, or it is made from aftergrowth which is forbidden according to everybody except possibly Rebbi Simeon.

הלכה י: רִבִּי אַבָּהוּ אָמַר רִבִּי יוֹחָנָן בָּעֵי מַה בֵּין תְּרוּמָה אֵצֶל הַזָּרִים מַה בֵּין שְׁבִיעִית אֵצֶל הַכֹּהֲנִים. תְּרוּמָה אֵצֶל הַזָּרִים אֲסוּרָה שְׁבִיעִית אֵצֶל הַכֹּהֲנִים מוּתֶּרֶת. חָזַר וְאָמַר רִבִּי יוֹחָנָן תִּיפְתָּר שֶׁנָּפַל שְׂאוֹר שֶׁלִּתְרוּמָה תְחִלָּה. לֹא בָאֲתָה שְׁבִיעִית אֶלָּא לִפְגּוֹם.

Halakhah 10: Rebbi Abbahu said, Rebbi Joḥanan asked: What is the difference between heave with regard to lay people and Sabbatical produce with regard to Cohanim? Heave for lay people is forbidden; is Sabbatical produce for Cohanim permitted[185]? Rebbi Joḥanan came back and said, explain it that heave sourdough fell in first; the Sabbatical produce did only spoil[186].

185 In the two cases outlined in Note 184, the prohibition also applies to Cohanim.

186 Then for R. Simeon the addition of Sabbatical sourdough did not change its status; Cohanim may disregard the Sabbatical prohibitions for the bread made with oversour dough.

רִבִּי לָעְזָר בֵּירִבִּי שִׁמְעוֹן בְּשִׁיטַּת אָבִיו. מָהוּ בְּשִׁיטַּת אָבִיו. כְּמַה דְרִבִּי שִׁמְעוֹן אָמַר נוֹתְנֵי טְעָמִים לִפְגָם מוּתָּר. כֵּן רִבִּי לָעְזָר בֵּירִבִּי שִׁמְעוֹן אוֹמֵר נוֹתְנֵי טַעַם לִפְגָם מוּתָּר. אָמַר רִבִּי אַבָּא מָרִי מָהוּ בְּשִׁיטַּת אָבִיו כְּמַה דְרִבִּי שִׁמְעוֹן אָמַר כָּל־הַסְּפִיחִין מוּתָּרִין. כֵּן רִבִּי לָעְזָר בֵּירִבִּי שִׁמְעוֹן אָמַר כָּל־הַסְּפִיחִין מוּתָּרִין.

כְּלוּם אָמַר רִבִּי שִׁמְעוֹן אֶלָּא בִּסְפִיחֵי יָרָק דִּילְמָא בִסְפִיחֵי זְרָעִים. וְקָמַת הִיא סְפִיחֵי יָרָק הִיא סְפִיחֵי זְרָעִים.

Rebbi Eleazar ben Rebbi Simeon follows his father's argument. What is his father's argument? Just as Rebbi Simeon said anything which spoils the taste is permitted, so Rebbi Eleazar ben Rebbi Simeon said anything which spoils the taste is permitted. Rebbi Abba Mari said, what is his father's argument? Just as Rebbi Simeon said all aftergrowth is permitted[187], so Rebbi Eleazar ben Rebbi Simeon said all aftergrowth is permitted. But Rebbi Simeon said that only about aftergrowth of vegetables; did he say that for aftergrowth of grains? He[188] established that aftergrowth of vegetables and aftergrowth of grains are the same.

187 Mishnah *Ševi'it* 9:1, restricted to "field vegetables."

188 R. Eleazar ben Rebbi Simeon.

רִבָּנָן דְּקַיְסָרִין אָמְרִין אַחַת בְּשִׁיטַּת אָבִיו וְאַחַת בְּשִׁיטַּת חֲכָמִים. בְּשִׁיטַּת אָבִיו מִפְּנֵי נוֹתְנֵי טַעַם לִפְגָם מוּתָּר. בְּשִׁיטַּת חֲכָמִים מִשּׁוּם שֵׁמוֹת מִצְטָרְפִין.

The rabbis of Caesarea said, in one respect he follows his father's argument, in one the argument of the Sages[189]. His father's argument, that anything which spoils the taste is permitted. The argument of the Sages, that [different] names combine.

189 They reject R. Joḥanan's explanation that the heave sourdough fell in first since this is not indicated in the Tosephta. In the second Tosephta of Halakhah 9, he follows his father since a double portion of sourdough certainly has some spoiling effect. He does not follow his father in the first since he holds with the Sages that heave and Sabbatical sourdoughs will combine.

(fol. 61c) **משנה יו:** חֲתִיכָה שֶׁל קָדְשֵׁי קֳדָשִׁים וְשֶׁל פִּיגּוּל וְשֶׁל נוֹתָר שֶׁנִּתְבַּשְּׁלוּ עִם חֲתִיכוֹת אָסוּר לַזָּרִים וּמוּתָּר לַכֹּהֲנִים. רִבִּי שִׁמְעוֹן מַתִּיר לַזָּרִים (fol. 61d) וְלַכֹּהֲנִים.

Mishnah 16: If a piece of most holy meat[190], of *piggul*[191], or of leftover meat[192], was cooked with [other] pieces. they are forbidden for lay persons and permitted[193] for Cohanim. Rebbi Simeon permits for lay persons and Cohanim.

190 From those sacrifices which must be eaten by Cohanim within the Temple precinct.

191 Sacrifices slaughtered with the intent to eat from them after their allotted time.

192 Sacrificial meat left after the allotted time for consumption, when it had been intended that all should be consumed within the legal time limit.

193 They are permitted only if either the forbidden pieces were less than $^1/_{60}$ (or, according to the Yerushalmi, $^1/_{100}$) of the permitted or, if they were recognizably another type of meat, were taken out, and did not impart taste. Since *piggul* and leftovers are automatically impure, all this meat is impure and, if permitted at all, is permitted to pure and impure persons alike. According to Maimonides, it may be permitted to Cohanim since for them the prohibition is that of a simple crime whereas for lay persons it would be an offense punishable by extirpation. For R. Simeon, forbidden is forbidden; the severity of the crime should not make any difference and if the meat becomes insignificant as food it becomes insignificant for other prohibitions. He also will not add most holy meat and leftovers as one, but is satisfied if each category alone becomes insignificant in the permitted meat.

(fol. 62c) **הלכה יא:** תַּנֵּי שֶׁל פִּיגּוּל וְשֶׁל נוֹתָר וְשֶׁל קֳדָשִׁים קַלִּים.

Halakhah 11: It was stated: "Of *piggul*, leftovers, or holy sacrifices.[194]"

194 There is a version of Mishnah 16 which adds "simply holy sacrifices." The admissibility of that version is discussed next.

אָמַר רִבִּי יוֹנָה לֹא אָמַר אֶלָּא קֳדָשִׁים קַלִּים. פִּיגּוּל וְנוֹתָר לְאַחַר זְרִיקָה לֹא כְלִפְנֵי זְרִיקָה הֵן. לֹא אָמַר אֶלָּא פִּיגּוּל וְנוֹתָר דָּבָר שֶׁאֵין זְרִיקָה מַתִּרְתּוֹ בְּקָדְשֵׁי קָדָשִׁים הָא בְקֳדָשִׁים קַלִּין הוֹאִיל וְהֵן מוּתָּרִין אַחַר זְרִיקָה אֵין לוֹקִין עֲלֵיהֶן מִשּׁוּם זָרוּת. אָמַר רִבִּי יוֹסֵי לֹא אָמְרוּ אֶלָּא קֳדָשִׁים קַלִּים. פִּיגּוּל וְנוֹתָר לְאַחַר זְרִיקָה לֹא כְלִפְנֵי זְרִיקָה הֵן. לְאֵי זֶה דָבָר נֶאֱמַר פִּיגּוּל וְנוֹתָר לְהוֹצִיא קֳדָשִׁים קַלִּים לְאַחַר זְרִיקָה. הָא לִפְנֵי זְרִיקָה הוֹאִיל וְהֵן אֲסוּרִין בְּקֳדָשִׁים קַלִּין לוֹקִין עֲלֵיהֶן מִשּׁוּם זָרוּת. אָמַר רִבִּי אָבִין לִישָּׁן מַתְנִיתָה מְסַייְעָא לְרִבִּי יוֹסֵי נִדְבוֹתֶיךָ זוֹ תוֹדָה וּשְׁלָמִים שֶׁאִם אָכַל מֵהֶן לִפְנֵי זְרִיקַת דָּמִים לוֹקֶה.

Rebbi Jonah said, one did not say "simply holy sacrifices." Are *piggul* and leftovers not after sprinkling[195] as before sprinkling? It mentions only *piggul* and leftovers, things which sprinkling does not permit, together with most holy sacrifices. Therefore, for simply holy sacrifices, which are permitted after sprinkling, one never can whip because of laity[196]. Rebbi Yose said, did one not say "simply holy sacrifices?" Are *piggul* and leftovers not after sprinkling as before sprinkling? Why were *piggul* and leftovers mentioned, not to exclude simply holy sacrifices after sprinkling? Therefore, before sprinkling when simply holy sacrifices are forbidden, lay persons will be whipped for [eating] them[197]. Rebbi Avun said, a *baraita*[198] supports Rebbi Yose: "(*Deut.* 12"17) 'Your dedications', thanksgiving and well-being sacrifices, if one ate of them before sprinkling he is whipped."

195 All sacrifices are forbidden for everybody, and for the altar, before the blood of the animal was sprinkled on the walls of the altar. After sprinkling, the parts destined for the altar may be burned, and the meat eaten according to the rules applying to the different categories of sacrifices. Taking of the meat after sprinkling is no longer larceny.

The mention of "leftovers" here is because "*piggul* and leftovers" are always mentioned together; it has no place here because leftovers are created only after the fact. But *piggul* refers to an invalid sacrificing, and that defect cannot be remedied by anything.

196 Not even before sprinkling when the meat is forbidden for everybody.

197 He disagrees with R. Jonah.

198 *Sifry Deut.* 72, Babli *Makkot* 17a; in both cases after an argument why the verse as it stands is redundant and has to be interpreted. In the Babli, the statement appears in the name of R. Simeon; in *Sifry* it is anonymous but states only "he violated a prohibition."

(fol. 61d) **משנה יז:** בְּשַׂר קָדְשֵׁי קֳדָשִׁים וּבְשַׂר קֳדָשִׁים קַלִּים שֶׁנִּתְבַּשְּׁלוּ עִם בְּשַׂר הַתַּאֲוָה אָסוּר לַטְּמֵאִים וּמוּתָּר לַטְּהוֹרִים.

Mishnah 17: Most holy meat and simply holy meat that was cooked with meat of desire[199] is forbidden to impure persons and permitted to pure[200].

199 Profane meat; the expression alludes to *Deut.* 12:20.

200 According to Maimonides, there are two cases here. Either that most holy meat (to be eaten by Cohanim in the Temple precinct) and simply holy meat (to be eaten by any pure person in the city of the sanctuary) were cooked together; they may be eaten by pure Cohanim in the Temple precinct. Or if simply holy meat was cooked with meat of desire, it can be eaten by any pure person in the city of the sanctuary, and there are no theoretical questions connected with this Mishnah.

In the opinion of R. Simson and R.

Isaac Simponti, Mishnah 17 is the direct continuation of Mishnah 16 and it is still assumed that the most holy meat is less than 1/60 of the meat permitted to pure laymen. For them, the only difference from the preceding Mishnah is that R. Simeon does not disagree since for him, most holy and simply holy are both called "holy", are one name, and do combine, just as great heave and heave of the tithe are both "heave" and do combine.

(fol. 62c) **הלכה יב:** רִבִּי שִׁמְעוֹן בֶּן לָקִישׁ אָמַר כְּמַחֲלוֹקֶת. רִבִּי יוֹחָנָן אָמַר דִּבְרֵי הַכֹּל. וְקַשְׁיָא עַל דְּרִבִּי שִׁמְעוֹן בֶּן לָקִישׁ לֹא כֵן סָבְרִינָן מֵימַר כּוּלְּהוֹן לְשׁוֹן תְּרוּמָה מִצְטָרְפִין. וְכָא יִצְרְפוּ לְשׁוֹן טוּמְאָה וּלְשׁוֹן זָרוּת. סָבַר רִבִּי שִׁמְעוֹן בֶּן לָקִישׁ כְּהָדָא. דְּתַנֵּי בַּר קַפָּרָא חֲתִיכָה שֶׁלְּקוֹדֶשׁ וְשֶׁלְּפִיגּוּל וְשֶׁלְּנוֹתָר שֶׁנִּתְבַּשְּׁלוּ עִם הַחֲתִיכוֹת רִבִּי שִׁמְעוֹן מַתִּיר. וַחֲכָמִים אוֹסְרִין.

Halakhah 12: Rebbi Simeon ben Laqish said, following the disagreement; Rebbi Johanan said, the opinion of everybody. It is difficult for Rebbi Simeon ben Laqish, do we not say that for everybody the expressions of heave do combine[201]? And here, the expressions of impurity and laity should combine! Rebbi Simeon ben Laqish follows what Bar Qappara stated: "If pieces of holy [meat], of *piggul*, or of leftovers were cooked with [profane] pieces, Rebbi Simeon permits[202] but the Sages forbid."

201 Cf. Note 8.

202 He must hold that impurity is irrelevant here and the prohibition of laity does not apply to *piggul* or leftovers since these are also forbidden to Cohanim.

בגד פרק שלישי

(fol. 62c) **משנה א**: בֶּגֶד שֶׁצְּבָעוֹ בִּקְלִיפֵּי עָרְלָה יִדָּלֵק. נִתְעָרֵב בַּאֲחֵרִים כּוּלָּן יִדָּלְקוּ דִּבְרֵי רִבִּי מֵאִיר. וַחֲכָמִים אוֹמְרִים יַעֲלֶה בְּאֶחָד וּמָאתַיִם.

Mishnah 1: Cloth dyed with *'orlah* shells[1] should be burned[2]. If it became mixed up with others, all should be burned, the words of Rebbi Meïr[3]; but the Sages said, it should be lifted by one in 200.

1 For example, walnut shells and pomegranate skin; cf. Mishnah *Ševi'it* 7:3.

2 Since *'orlah* is forbidden for all usufruct, any product obtained by using *'orlah* is also forbidden.

3 R. Meïr holds that anything sold by the piece is important and cannot become insignificant (Mishnah 7); the Sages hold that anything forbidden for usufruct becomes insignificant if it is less than half a percent of the total, except for a very limited list of items. In order to avoid having monetary gain from forbidden things, an amount of cloth equal in size to the forbidden piece has to be taken out and burned. For the notion of lifting, cf. *Terumot* 4, Note 64.

הלכא א: בֶּגֶד שֶׁצְּבָעוֹ בִּקְלִיפֵּי עָרְלָה יִדָּלֵק כול׳. כְּתִיב וַעֲרַלְתֶּם עָרְלָתוֹ אֶת פִּרְיוֹ. אִית תַּנָּיֵי תַנֵּי בְּסָמוּךְ לְפִירְיוֹ. אִית תַּנָּיֵי תַנֵּי בְּעוֹרֵל אֶת פִּרְיוֹ. מָאן דְּאָמַר בְּעוֹרֵל אֶת פִּרְיוֹ קְלִיפִּין וְגַרְעִינִין בְּמַשְׁמַע. מָאן דְּאָמַר בְּסָמוּךְ לְפִרְיוֹ קְלִיפִּין בְּמַשְׁמַע וְלֹא גַּרְעִינִין. וְגַרְעִינִין מְנַיִין. הֲוֵי סוֹפָךְ מֵימַר אֶת פִּרְיוֹ בְּסָמוּךְ לְפִרְיוֹ. אִית דְּבָעֵי נִישְׁמְעִינָהּ מִן הָדָא. וַעֲרַלְתֶּם עָרְלָתוֹ אֶת פִּרְיוֹ דָּבָר שֶׁהוּא עוֹרֵל אֶת פִּרְיוֹ וּפִרְייוֹ עוֹרְלוֹ.

Halakhah 1: "Cloth dyed with *'orlah* shells should be burned," etc. It is written (*Lev.* 19:23): "You shall treat its foreskin with its fruit as foreskin.[4]" Some Tannaïm state: What is close to the fruit. Some Tannaïm state: What envelopes the fruit. He who says what envelopes the fruit, understands shells and pits[5]. He who says what is close to the fruit understands shells but not pits[6]. From where pits[7]? You must finally conclude that "its fruit" means "What touches its fruit."[8] Some want to understand it from here: "You shall treat its foreskin with its fruit as foreskin," anything which envelopes its fruit or its fruit envelopes it.[9]

4 The problem is the word ערלתו. It seems that the verse would be perfect without it, וערלתם את פריו "you shall treat its fruit as foreskin."

5 The foreskin is an envelope around the male organ which has the shape of a solid cylinder. In the opinion of this Tanna, usually a fruit has the shape of a torus, bounded at the outside by the shell or skin and at the inside by the pit. Therefore, the envelope of the fruit must have two parts, an inner and an outer one, and "envelope" designates the union of both.

"Foreskin" as applied to fruits is only a metaphor since human foreskin is permanently forbidden but fruits of trees only the first three years.

6 He will not agree that the foreskin is an envelope but rather an outer shell since the human foreskin is only an outer shell if the male organ is considered as a cylindrical shell bounded at the inside by the urinary duct.

7 Since practice includes pits, where is a hint of the inclusion found in the biblical text?

8 This is the opinion of the Babli (*Berakhot* 36b).

9 The definition of the envelope in Note 5 is natural for modern mathematics. For Euclidean mathematics, for which all geometric figures are compact and connected [cf. H. Guggenheimer, The Axioms of Betweenness in Euclid, *Dialectica* 31(1977) 187-192], the two-sheeted hyperboloid is composed of two separate surfaces. Therefore, in the spirit of the times the reformulation is appropriate.

The discussion here is hinted at in

Ma'serot 4:6, Note 88. The Amora quoted there, Samuel, is known as strict adherent of Ptolemaic astronomy but it seems that in the quote, he prefers the modern formulation (Note 5) to the classical. This fits with his acceptance of infinite decimal expansions as numbers (*Demay* 7:8, Note 104).

רִבִּי אַבָּהוּ בְשֵׁם רִבִּי לָעְזָר. כָּל־מָקוֹם שֶׁנֶּאֱמַר לֹא תֹאכַל לֹא תֹאכְלוּ לֹא יֵאָכְלוּ אַתְּ תּוֹפֵס אִיסּוּר הֲנָייָה בְּאִיסּוּר אֲכִילָה עַד שֶׁיָּבוֹא הַכָּתוּב וִיפָרֵשׁ לָךְ כְּשֵׁם שֶׁפֵּירֵשׁ לָךְ בְּאֵבֶר מִן הַחַי וּבִנְבֵילָה. מַה פֵּירֵשׁ לָךְ בְּאֵבֶר מִן הַחַי. וּבָשָׂר בַּשָּׂדֶה טְרֵיפָה לֹא תֹאכֵלוּ. וּמַה פֵּירֵשׁ בִּנְבֵילָה. לֹא תֹאכְלוּ כָּל־נְבֵילָה לַגֵּר אֲשֶׁר בִּשְׁעָרֶיךָ תִּתְּנֶנּוּ וַאֲכָלָהּ. תַּנֵּי חִזְקִיָּה וּפְלִיג. וְכִי מָה אָסְרוֹ לַכֶּלֶב.

[10]Rebbi Abbahu in the name of Rebbi Eleazar[11]: Everywhere it is written "do not eat, do not eat[12], it shall not be eaten", you understand a prohibition of usufruct included in the probition of eating unless the verse comes and explains to you as it did explain about limbs of a living animal and a carcass. What did it explain about limbs of a living animal? (*Ex.* 22:30) "Flesh torn in the field you shall not eat[13]." And what did it explain about a carcass? (*Deut.* 14:21) "Do not eat any carcass; to the sojourner in your gates you shall give it and he may eat it." Hizqiah stated a disagreement[14]. What does one forbid to the dog?

10 The text from here to Note 44 is also in *Pesaḥim* 2:1, fol. 28c; the parallel in the Babli is *Pesaḥim* 21b-23a. The discussion is about the prohibition of usufruct of *'orlah* fruits.

11 In the Babli, R. Eleazar is not mentioned.

12 Singular or plural.

13 The verse ends: You shall throw it to the dog. Why is it necessary to permit torn limbs as dog food? R. Eleazar argues that this shows that without such permission the limb would be forbidden for all usufruct.

14 In the Babli (*Pesaḥim* 21b), Ḥizqiah accepts the statement of R. Eleazar only for the passive formulation; later (Note 31) this is clarified to be the position of Ḥizqiah and R. Joḥanan in a second version. In this first version, Ḥizqiah must hold that an inference from a verse is only

valid if there is no second verse leading to the same result. The theoretical basis is the recognition that the legal texts in the Torah are incomplete and sometimes contradictory as a system. In addition, it is held that words do not change their meaning in legal contexts. Therefore, a mechanism of translation of the Torah text into a coherent and reasonably complete system must exist. The rule appealed to by Ḥizqiah is one of the translation rules; cf. H. Guggenheimer, *Logical Problems in Jewish Tradition*, in: Ph. Longworth (ed.), Confrontations with Judaism (London 1966) pp. 171-196.

Since here the torn limb and the carcass both lead to the same argument, one of them would be superfluous and, therefore, both must be needed for other inferences. The argument of R. Eleazar is refuted.

וְהָא כְתִיב כָּל־חֵלֶב שׁוֹר וְכֶשֶׂב וָעֵז לֹא תֹאכֵלוּ. מֵעַתָּה אַתָּה תוֹפֵס אִיסּוּר הֲנָיָיה לְאִיסּוּר אֲכִילָה. שַׁנְיָיא הִיא דִּכְתִיב וְחֵלֶב נְבֵילָה וְחֵלֶב טְרֵיפָה. וְהָכְתִיב רַק אֶת הַדָּם. מֵעַתָּה אַתְּ תוֹפֵס אִיסּוּר הֲנָיָיה כְאִיסּוּר אֲכִילָה. שַׁנְיָיא הִיא דִּכְתִיב עַל הָאָרֶץ תִּשְׁפְּכֶנּוּ כַּמָּיִם. מַה מַּיִם מוּתָּרִין בַּהֲנָיָיה אַף הַדָּם מוּתָּר בַּהֲנָיָיה. וְהָכְתִיב עַל כֵּן לֹא יֹאכְלוּ בְנֵי יִשְׂרָאֵל אֶת גִּיד הַנָּשֶׁה. אָמַר רִבִּי אַבָּהוּ קִייַמְתִּיהָ בְּגִיד הַנָּשֶׁה שֶׁלַּנְּבֵילָה. וְהָכְתִיב וְלֶחֶם וְקָלִי וְכַרְמֶל לֹא תֹאכְלוּ. אָמַר רִבִּי אַבָּא מָרִי אַחֲוָה דְּרִבִּי יוֹסֵי. שַׁנְיָיא הִיא שֶׁקָּבַע לוֹ הַכָּתוּב זְמָן. וְהָכְתִיב לֹא תֹאכְלוּם כִּי שֶׁקֶץ הֵם. אָמַר רִבִּי מָנָא מִיעֵט אִיסּוּר הֲנָיָיה שֶׁבּוֹ.

But is it not written (*Lev.* 7:23): "Any fat of cattle, sheep, or goats you shall not eat"? Do you not have to understand the prohibition of usufruct from the prohibition of eating? There is a difference, for it is written (*Lev.* 7:24): "But fat of a carcass and fat of a torn animal"[15]. But is it not written (*Deut.* 12:16): "Only the blood"? There is a difference, for it is written: "You shall pour it on the ground like water."[16] Since water is permitted for use, so blood is permitted for use. But is it not written (*Gen.* 32:33): "Therefore, the Children of Israel do not eat the sinew of the schiatic muscle"? Rebbi Abbahu said, I explained it by the sinew of a carcass or a torn animal[17]. But is it not written (*Lev.* 23:14): "Bread, parched or fresh grains you shall not eat"[18]? Rebbi Abba Mari the brother of Rebbi Yose said there is a difference since the verse fixed a time for it. But is it not written (*Lev.* 11:42): "Do not eat them for they are abominations"? Rebbi Mana said, that excludes their prohibition of usufruct[19].

15 "But fat of a carcass and fat of a torn animal may be used for any work, only you shall not eat it." This paragraph discusses verses which present a difficulty for R. Eleazar.

In the opinion of the Babli, *Pesaḥim* 23a, the verse is needed to permit *any* use of profane fat since otherwise one would argue that since fat is forbidden for humans but required for the altar, fat of animals unfit for the altar should be permitted for use in the Temple but forbidden for profane use. In the *Sifra* (*Ẓaw Paraša* 10), the argument of the Babli is attributed to R. Yose the Galilean; R. Aqiba concludes that fat of domesticated animals is not food and not subject to the impurity of food.

In the opinion of the Yerushalmi, since some fat is permitted for unrestricted use, no fat can be forbidden for usufruct in the absence of an explicit verse. For Ḥizqiah, this is a third verse that could be used for R. Eleazar's argument; nobody will contest that three parallel verses invalidate the argument. In the second version of Ḥizqiah's position (below, after Note 33), he needs the verse to permit use of fat for work on Temple property.

16 "Only the blood you shall not eat; pour it on the ground like water." The Babli, *Pesaḥim* 22b, deduces from here that animal blood is a fluid which prepares for impurity only if it is spilled on the ground (cf. *Demay* 2:3, Note 136). The argument of the Yerushalmi, and an argument that animal blood prepares for impurity in all cases, is in *Sifry Deut.* 73 and later here, in the second version of Ḥizqiah.

17 The argument is more explicit in the Babli, *Pesaḥim* 22a. R. Abbahu holds that when carcass and torn meat was permitted for the sojourner (a monotheistic Gentile adhering to the Seven Commandments observed by Noe) and the pagan, the entire animal was permitted, including the fat. Then the last paragraph of Note 15 establishes that the schiatic sinew

cannot be forbidden for usufruct.

18 "Bread, parched or fresh grains you shall not eat until that very day" referring to new grains before the *'omer* ceremony.

19 The argument seems to be that the verse has to be read: "For *they* are abominations", they (snakes and centipedes) are abominations but not anything manufactured from them. (Explanation of R. H. Kanievski.)

רִבִּי אַבָּהוּ בְשֵׁם רִבִּי יוֹחָנָן. הָעוֹשֶׂה אִיסְפְּלֵנִית מִשּׁוֹר הַנִּסְקָל וּמֵחָמֵץ שֶׁעָבַר עָלָיו הַפֶּסַח אֵינוֹ לוֹקֶה. שֶׁאֵין לֹא תַעֲשֶׂה שֶׁלּוֹ מְחוּוָּר. מִכִּלְאֵי הַכֶּרֶם לוֹקֶה. דְּאָמַר רִבִּי חֲנִינָא פֶּן תִּקְדַּשׁ פֶּן תּוּקָד אֵשׁ. מֵעָרְלָה צְרִיכָה. עֲשֵׂה לְרָחֲקוֹ כְּתִיב. לֹא תַעֲשֶׂה לְאוֹכְלוֹ כְּתִיב. לֹא תַעֲשֶׂה לְרָחֲקוֹ לֵית כְּתִיב.

Rebbi Abbahu in the name of Rebbi Johanan: He who makes a wound dressing[20] from a stoned ox[21] or from leftover sour matter after Passover cannot be whipped since its prohibition is not clear. For vineyard *kilaim* he is whipped since Rebbi Ḥanina said (*Deut.* 22:9): "Lest it be sanctified", lest fire should be kindled[22]. For *'orlah* it is problematic. A prescriptive commandment to remove is written[23], a prohibition to eat is written[24], a prohibition to remove it is not written[25].

20 Latin *splenium*, Greek σπληνίον, τό, "pad, wound dressing."

21 The Babli, *Pesaḥim* 24b, explains that one might use fat from the stoned ox to cover a wound.

The ox was stoned by order of the court because it killed humans (*Ex.* 21:28,29). Its meat is forbidden for usufruct; this is derived from *Ex.* 21:28, cf. *Mekhilta Mišpaṭim* 10 (p. 282).

22 Cf. *Kilaim* 8:1, Note 6.

23 Since *Lev.* 19:23 requires that the (budding) fruit is treated as "foreskin" and the foreskin has to be removed, one may take the verse as prescribing the removal of any *'orlah* fruit.

24 Last two words of *Lev.* 19:23. Since R. Johanan reads לא יאכל as prohibition of eating, not of usufruct, he follows his teacher Ḥizqiah in rejecting the argument of R. Eleazar.

25 Transgression of a prescriptive commandment is not prosecutable.

בְּמַתְנִיתָא פְלִיגָא עַל רִבִּי יוֹחָנָן. מְמַשְׁמַע שֶׁנֶּאֱמַר סָקוֹל יִסָּקֵל הַשּׁוֹר וְכִי אֵין אָנוּ יוֹדְעִין שֶׁבְּשָׂרוֹ אָסוּר בַּאֲכִילָה. וּמַה תַלְמוּד לוֹמַר לֹא יֵאָכֵל אֶת בְּשָׂרוֹ. לְהוֹדִיעֲךָ שֶׁכְּשֵׁם שֶׁאָסוּר בַּאֲכִילָה כָּךְ הוּא אָסוּר בַּהֲנָייָה. מַה עָבַד לָהּ רִבִּי יוֹחָנָן. פָּתַר לָהּ בְּשֶׁקָּדְמוּ הַבְּעָלִים וּשְׁחָטוּהוּ עַד שֶׁלֹּא נִגְמַר דִּינוֹ.

In a *baraita*[26] one disagrees with Rebbi Joḥanan: "What does one understand from what has been said (*Ex.* 21:28): 'The ox shall certainly be stoned'? Do we not know that its meat is forbidden as food[27]? Then why does the verse say, 'its meat shall not be eaten'? To tell you that just as it is forbidden as food so it is forbidden for usufruct." What does Rebbi Joḥanan do with this? He explained it if the owners slaughtered it before sentence was pronounced[28].

26 The *baraita* as stated here is not found in any other source except the Yerushalmi parallels *Pesaḥim* 28c, *Avodah Zarah* 45b. In *Mekhilta Mišpaṭim* 19; quoted in Babli *Pesaḥim* 22b, *Qiddušin* 56b, *Baba Qama* 41a the text explicitly notes that, since "its meat shall not be eaten" is included in the statement of the sentence to be passed by the court, only after judgment is rendered does slaughter become ineffective. This may also be the rule implied by the Yerushalmi *Targum* to *Ex.* 21:28: וְלָא יִתְנְכֵס לְמֵיכוּל יַת בִּשְׂרֵיהּ "it should not be slaughtered to make its flesh edible." Since the Babli follows R. Eleazar, no discussion of the prohibition of usufruct is necessary.

27 As carcass meat.

28 This statement directly contradicts the position of the Babli. R. Yoḥanan will hold that the prescriptive commandment to stone the ox after judgment has been passed automatically makes any slaughter invalid; that would not need a proof from the verse.

רִבִּי זְעִירָה בָּעָא קוֹמֵי רִבִּי אַבָּהוּ. הָכָא אַתְּ אָמַר הָכֵין וְהָכָא אַתְּ אָמַר הָכֵין. אָמַר לֵיהּ. חָדָא מִשְּׁמֵיהּ דְּרִבִּי לָעְזָר. וְחָדָא בְּשֵׁם רִבִּי יוֹחָנָן.

Rebbi Zeïra asked before Rebbi Abbahu: Here you say so, there you say so[29]? He said to him, one in the name[30] of Rebbi Eleazar, one in the name of Rebbi Joḥanan.

29 He states contradictory theses, whether or not prohibition as food implies prohibition of usufruct.

30 In the parallel in *Pesahim*, Hebrew בשם instead of משמיה. The latter is an inadvertent Babylonism characteristic of learned scribes.

רַבָּנִין דְּקַיְסָרִין רִבִּי אַבָּהוּ בְשֵׁם רִבִּי יוֹחָנָן. כָּל־מָקוֹם שֶׁנֶּאֱמַר לֹא תֹאכְלוּ אֵין אַתְּ תּוֹפֵס אִיסּוּר הֲנָייָה כְּאִיסּוּר אֲכִילָה. בִּנְייַן אָב שֶׁבְּכוּלָּן וְכָל־חַטָּאת אֲשֶׁר יוּבָא מִדָּמָהּ אֶל אֹהֶל מוֹעֵד לְכַפֵּר בַּקּוֹדֶשׁ לֹא תֵאָכֵל בָּאֵשׁ יִשָּׂרֵף. תַּנֵּי חִזְקִיָּה מְסַייֵעַ לְרִבִּי יוֹחָנָן. מִמַּשְׁמַע שֶׁנֶּאֱמַר כָּל־חֵלֶב שׁוֹר וְכֶשֶׂב וָעֵז לֹא תֹאכֵלוּ. לְאֵי זֶה דָבָר נֶאֱמַר וְחֵלֶב נְבֵילָה וְחֵלֶב טְרֵיפָה יֵעָשֶׂה לְכָל־מְלָאכָה. בָּא לְהוֹדִיעֲךָ אֲפִילוּ לִמְלֶאכֶת הַגָּבוֹהַּ. מִמַּשְׁמַע שֶׁנֶּאֱמַר רַק הַדָּם לֹא תֹאכֵלוּ. לְאֵי זֶה דָבָר נֶאֱמַר עַל הָאָרֶץ תִּשְׁפְּכֶנּוּ כַּמָּיִם. בָּא לְהוֹדִיעֲךָ. מָה הַמַּיִם מַכְשִׁירִין אַף הַדָּם מַכְשִׁיר. מִמַּשְׁמַע שֶׁנֶּאֱמַר לֹא תֹאכְלוּ כָל־נְבֵילָה. לְאֵי זֶה דָבָר נֶאֱמַר לַגֵּר אֲשֶׁר בִּשְׁעָרֶיךָ תִּתְּנֶנּוּ וַאֲכָלָהּ. בָּא לְהוֹדִיעֲךָ שֶׁגֵּר תּוֹשָׁב אוֹכֵל נְבֵילוֹת. מִמַּשְׁמַע שֶׁנֶּאֱמַר וּבָשָׂר בַּשָּׂדֶה טְרֵיפָה לֹא תֹאכֵלוּ. לְאֵי זֶה דָבָר נֶאֱמַר לַכֶּלֶב תַּשְׁלִיכוּן אוֹתוֹ. אוֹתוֹ אַתָּה מַשְׁלִיךְ לַכֶּלֶב וְאֵי אַתָּה מַשְׁלִיךְ חוּלִין שֶׁנִּשְׁחֲטוּ בָעֲזָרָה.

The rabbis of Caesarea[31], Rabbi Abbahu in the name of Rebbi Johanan: Nowhere do you understand a prohibition of usufruct included in the probition of eating if it is written "do not eat"[32]. The paradigm[33] for all cases is (*Lev*. 6:23): "Any purification offering of whose blood was brought into the Tent of Meeting to purify the sanctuary shall not be eaten, in fire it shall be burned." Hizqiah stated support for Rebbi Johanan: If one understands what has been said (*Lev*. 7:23): "Any fat of cattle, sheep, or goats you shall not eat," why has it been said (*Lev*. 7:24): "But fat of a carcass and fat of a torn animal may be used for any work"? It comes to tell you, even for the work of Heaven[15]. If one understands what has been said (*Lev*. 12:16): "But the blood you shall not eat," why has it been said "you shall pour it on the ground like water"? It comes to tell you, as water prepares, so blood prepares[16]. If one understands what has been said (*Deut.* 14:21) "Do not eat any carcass;" why has it been said "to the sojourner in your gates you shall give it and he may eat it"? To tell you that the resident sojourner may eat carcass meat[34]. If one understands what has been said (*Ex.* 22:30): "Flesh torn in the field you shall not eat," why has it been said "throw it to the dog"? *This* you throw to the dog but not profane meat slaughtered in the Temple precinct[35].

31 A second version of the position of R. Joḥanan, differing from what was stated earlier.

32 The text is incomplete; it refers to the statement of R. Eleazar (Note11). If the prohibition of food is in the active voice it does not imply prohibition of usufruct. That implies that the passive voice does imply prohibition of usufruct.

33 This proves that the passive voice implies prohibition of usufruct; since it is the only such case where the inference is valid according to everybody. The verse is understood [*Sifra Ẓaw Pereq* 8(5), quoted in Babli *Zebaḥim* 82a, Yerushalmi *Pesaḥim* 7:9, fol. 35a] following a punctuation which differs from the masoretic: "Any purification offering, some of whose blood was brought into the Tent of Meeting to purify, in the Sanctuary it shall not be eaten, in fire it shall be burned." This is a possible reading since purification offerings can be eaten only in the Sanctuary. Then "Sanctuary" is taken also to refer to the last clause, "(in the sanctuary) in fire it shall be burned." This excludes all sacred and profane usufruct after purification.

34 The resident sojourner, in order to receive the full protection of the law, has only to follow the "precepts of the descendants of Noe", to abstain from idolatry, murder, incest and adultery, eating limbs torn from living animals, blasphemy, robbery, and anarchy.

35 In the Babli, *Pesaḥim* 22a, this is quoted as the opinion of R. Meïr. It is forbidden to slaughter anything but sacrifices in the Temple precinct, *Lev.* 17:4.

מַתְנִיתָא מְסַייְעָא לְדֵין וּמַתְנִיתָא מְסַייְעָא לְדֵין. מַתְנִיתָא מְסַייְעָא לְרִבִּי אֶלְעָזָר.[36] לֹא יֵאָכֵל חָמֵץ. לַעֲשׂוֹת אֶת הַמַּאֲכִיל כְּאוֹכֵל. אַתָּה אוֹמֵר לְכָךְ. אוֹ

אֵינוֹ אֶלָּא לְאוֹסְרוֹ בַּהֲנָייָה. כְּשֶׁהוּא אוֹמֵר לֹא תֹאכַל עָלָיו חָמֵץ לָמַדְנוּ שֶׁהוּא אָסוּר בַּהֲנָייָה. הָא מָה תַלְמוּד לוֹמַר וְלֹא יֵאָכֵל חָמֵץ.[37] לַעֲשׂוֹת אֶת הַמַּאֲכִיל כְּאוֹכֵל דִּבְרֵי רִבִּי יֹאשִׁיָּה. רִבִּי יִצְחָק אוֹמֵר אֵינוֹ צָרִיךְ. מָה אִם שְׁרָצִים קַלִּין עָשָׂה בָהֶן מַאֲכִיל כְּאוֹכֵל. חָמֵץ הֶחָמוּר אֵינוֹ דִין שֶׁנַּעֲשֶׂה בוֹ מַאֲכִיל כְּאוֹכֵל. הָא מָה תַלְמוּד לוֹמַר לֹא יֵאָכֵל חָמֵץ. לֹא בָא הַכָּתוּב אֶלָּא לְאוֹסְרוֹ בַּהֲנָייָה. בְּגִין דִּכְתִיב לֹא יֵאָכֵל. הָא מִלֹּא תֹאכַל לֵית שְׁמַע מִינָּהּ כְּלוּם. וְהָדָא מְסַייְעָא לְרִבִּי יוֹחָנָן.

A *baraita*[38] supports both of them. The *baraita* supports Rebbi Eleazar[39]. "(*Ex.* 13:3) 'Sour bread shall not be eaten', to make the feeder equal to the eater[40]. You say for this, or is it only to forbid its usufruct? Since it says (*Deut.* 16:3): 'You shall not eat sour bread with it,' we learned that usufruct is forbidden[41]. Therefore, why does the verse say, sour bread shall not be eaten? To make the feeder equal to the eater, the words of Rebbi Josia. Rebbi Isaac says, this is unnecessary. Since for crawling things, a minor prohibition[42], He made the feeder equal to the eater[43]; regarding sour bread which is a major prohibition it should only be logical that he feeder be equal to the eater. Therefore, why does the verse say, sour bread shall not be eaten? The verse comes only to forbid its usufruct." Since it is written "sour bread shall not be eaten." Therefore, from "you shall not eat" one cannot infer anything. This supports Rebbi Joḥanan.[44]

36 Reading of the text in *Pesaḥim.* The reading here, "R. Joḥanan", is a scribal error.

37 Reading of the text in *Pesaḥim.* The reading here, ולא יאכל עליו חמץ, is not a biblical verse.

38 *Mekhilta dR. Ismael, Bo* 16, p. 51.

39 The disagreement between R. Eleazar and R. Joḥanan is an old tannaïtic disagreement between Rabbis Josia and Isaac of the fourth tannaïtic generation.

40 The person who serves sour

matter to a Jew on Passover is guilty as if he ate it, to be punished by extirpation. If the server acts intentionally and the eater unintentionally, the server alone is punishable.

41 This is the position of R. Eleazar.

42 Eating forbidden living things is punished by whipping by the earthly court; but eating sour matter on Passover is punished by Heaven with extirpation.

43 *Sifra Šemini Pereq* 5(1). R. Abraham ben David in his commentary notes that this is not the position of the Babli; he does not refer to the Yerushalmi.

44 Here ends the parallel with *Pesaḥim* 2:1.

פְּשִׁיטָא שֶׁאֵין קַרְקַע נֶאֱסַר. צָר צוּרָה בְקַרְקַע נֶאֱסַר. צָבַע דָּבָר שֶׁיֵּשׁ בּוֹ רוּחַ חַיִּים. אִילּוּ הִשְׁתַּחֲוֶה לוֹ לֹא אָסוּר. מִפְּנֵי שֶׁצְּבָעוֹ אֲסָרוֹ. מִיכָּן שֶׁצְּבָעוֹ צְרִיכָה.

It is obvious that the gound cannot be forbidden[45]. If one painted a figure on the ground it is forbidden[46]. If he colored a living being, if he worshipped it, it is not forbidden[47]; because he colored it[48] did he make it forbidden? Hence, if he colored it it is of questionable status.

45 Here starts the discussion of the prohibition of usufruct from *'orlah* dyes. It is the position of the Yerushalmi that natural ground cannot be forbidden. In the case of pagan worship of sacred grounds, this means that the ground itself is always permitted but that any building or offerings deposited on the ground are forbidden for all usufruct. In that case also, the Yerushalmi (*Avodah Zarah* 3:6, fol. 42d) takes the exemption of the bare ground as obvious but the Babli (*Avodah Zarah* 51b) needs a verse to exempt worshipped bare ground.

46 The bare ground cannot be used unless the painting is disfigured first.

47 Both Talmudim (*Avodah Zarah*, Yerushalmi 3:6 fol. 41d, Babli 51b) agree that living beings cannot become forbidden even by being worshipped (but they will be disqualified from becoming sacrifices.)

48 Are the rules of *'orlah* more strict than those of idolatry?

בֶּגֶד גָּדוֹל שֶׁצְּבָעוֹ עַל מְנָת לְחוֹתְכוֹ מַה אַתְּ עֲבֵד לָהּ כִּמוּסְגָּר אוֹ כְמוּחְלָט. אִין תַּעַבְדִּינֵיהּ כִּמוּסְגָּר מוּתָּר. אִין תַּעַבְדִּינֵיהּ כִּמוּחְלָט אָסוּר.

How do you treat a large piece of cloth dyed with the intention that it should be cut into pieces? As one locked up or declared absolute[49]? If you treat it as locked up it is permitted, as declared absolute it will be forbidden.

49 Cloth which shows a sudden change in color that cannot be eliminated by washing may be "leprous", *Lev.* 13:47-59. When shown to a Cohen, it first has to be locked up for seven days. If in these days the discoloration has spread, the cloth is declared absolutely leprous, it must be burned and, therefore, all usufruct is forbidden. Mishnah *Nega'im* 11:12 states that large pieces of cloth both locked up and absolute are impure. A large piece covers at least three fingers square. The difference is that if the locked-up cloth is cut into pieces none of which is "large", all are pure since no cloth covering less than 3 fingers square can become impure. But if the large cloth is absolutely "leprous", the impurity is not eliminated by cutting the cloth into small pieces.

The comparison of leprosy of cloth to the prohibition of *'orlah* does not lead to a clear result.

צְבָעוֹ וְחָזַר וּצְבָעוֹ וְהִקְדִּיהַ. נֹאמַר אִם הָיָה צְרִיכָה לִצְבִיעָה הָרִאשׁוֹנָה אָסוּר. וְאִם לָאו מוּתָּר. צְבָעוֹ בִּקְלִיפֵּי אֱגוֹז שֶׁלְּעָרְלָה וְחָזַר וּצְבָעוֹ בִּקְלִיפֵּי אֱגוֹז שֶׁלְּחוּלִין. מָאן דְּאָמַר נוֹתְנֵי טַעַם לִפְגָּם מוּתָּר. אוּף הָכָא מוּתָּר. וּמָאן דְּאָמַר נוֹתְנֵי טַעַם לִפְגָּם אָסוּר. אוּף הָכָא אָסוּר. צְבָעוֹ בִּקְלִיפֵּי אֱגוֹז שֶׁלְּעָרְלָה וְחָזַר וּצְבָעוֹ בִּקְלִיפֵּי רִימּוֹן שֶׁלְּחוּלִין. יָיבוֹא כְהָדָא. עִיגּוּלֵי דְבֵילָה הַגְּדוֹלִים מַעֲלִין אֶת הַקְּטַנִּים וְהַקְּטַנִּים מַעֲלִין אֶת הַגְּדוֹלִים. רַב הוּנָא אָמַר כֵּינִי מַתְנִיתָא הַגְּדוֹלִים מַעֲלִין אֶת הַקְּטַנִּים בְּמִשְׁקָל וּקְטַנִּים מַעֲלִין אֶת הַגְּדוֹלִים בְּמִנְייָן. תַּמָּן מִין בְּמִינוֹ. בְּרַם הָכָא מִין בְּשֶׁאֵינוֹ מִינוֹ. צְבָעוֹ בִּקְלִיפֵּי אֱגוֹז שֶׁלְּעָרְלָה וְחָזַר וּצְבָעוֹ בִּקְלִיפֵּי חוּלִין (fol. 63a) מִין אֶחָד. יָיבוֹא כְהָדָא. רִבִּי יְהוֹשֻׁעַ אוֹמֵר תְּאֵינִים שְׁחוֹרוֹת מַעֲלוֹת אֶת הַלְּבָנוֹת וְהַלְּבָנוֹת מַעֲלוֹת אֶת הַשְּׁחוֹרוֹת. תַּמָּן הוּא רָאוּי לְחַתְּכָן. בְּרַם הָכָא אֵינוֹ רָאוּי לְחַתְּכוֹ. מָה דָמֵי לָהּ. גְּזִים גְּזִיזִית. אָמַר

רִבִּי יוֹסֵי בֵּירִבִּי בּוּן. מָה דָמֵי לָהּ. בֶּגֶד גָּדוֹל שֶׁצְּבָעוֹ עַל מְנָת לְחַתְּכוֹ. מֵיעַבְדִינֵיהּ דּוֹרְדְּסִין.

If he dyed it[50] and then dyed a second time and spoiled it[51], if it needed the first dye it is forbidden, otherwise it is permitted. If he dyed with *'orlah* walnut shells and then dyed again with profane walnut shells. According to him who said, if its taste spoils it is permitted, here also it is permitted, but according to him who said, if its taste spoils it is forbidden[52], here also it is forbidden. If he dyed with *'orlah* walnut shells and then dyed again with profane pomegranate skins, can it be compared to: "Large fig cakes lift small ones and small ones lift the large[53]?" Rav Huna[54] said, so is the Mishnah: "Large fig cakes lift small ones" by weight, "and small ones lift the large" by count. There, it is the same kind; here, different kinds. If he dyed with *'orlah* walnut shells and then dyed again with profane shells of the same kind[55], can it be compared to[56]: "Rebbi Joshua says, black figs lift the white ones, and white ones the black"? There, he may cut them[57], but here he cannot cut. To what can that be compared? He cuts it into little pieces. Rebbi Yose ben Rebbi Abun said, to what can that be compared? A large piece of cloth dyed with the intention that it should be cut to make socks[58].

50 With *'orlah* dye both times.

51 The cloth could not be sold even if it were made with permitted dyes. If the cloth was well dyed before the second dipping, it is forbidden and anything done later cannot change its status. But if the cloth did need a second dying anyhow, if then it was spoiled it was spoiled by the second action, both dyings were damaging and do not prohibit its use following R. Simeon (*Terumot* 10, Note 21).

52 Rebbi Meïr (*Terumot* 10, Note 21).

53 *Terumot* 4:8, Note 68. The implication is that the cloth should be permitted if the amount of pomegranate dye is more than 200 times that of the forbidden walnut dye.

54 In *Terumot* 4 (Note 86), Rebbi

Ḥuna. The reading in *Terumot* is preferable. It is not clear what the quote should prove if not that in these cases one uses all possible ways of saving the cloth.

55 This case should be treated by the rules of insignificance; cf. *Terumot* 10, Notes 115 ff.

56 *Terumot* 4:8, Note 67.

57 If all figs are cut into small pieces, the entire mixture is simply figs. It follows that if the cloth is not dyed whole but cut into little pieces, of which a small number is dyed with *'orlah* dye but a 200 times larger number is dyed with profane dye, the mixture will be permitted.

58 He will permit use if only a small part of the cloth was dipped into the vat of forbidden dye, then the larger part was dyed with profane dye, and only after that was made into strips which could be sewn into a kind of socks (which in Medieval rabbinic Hebrew are called בתי רגלים "houses for the feet".)

אָמַר רִבִּי יוֹחָנָן סַמְמָנִין בְּסַמְמָנִין בְּטֵילִין בְּמָאתַיִם. מֵי צְבָעִים בְּמֵי צְבָעִים בְּטֵילִין בְּרוֹב.

Rebbi Joḥanan said, pigments in pigments become insignificant in 200. Fluid dyes in fluid dyes by a majority[59].

59 The permitted dyes plus the water used in both fluids are more than 200 times the forbidden dissolved pigment.

אָמַר רִבִּי בָּא בַּר מָמָל. הֲנָיַית עָרְלָה בְּטִיבֵּרְיָא בְּרוֹב. מַתְנִיתָא פְלִיגָא עַל רִבִּי בָּא בַּר מָמָל. תַּבְשִׁיל שֶׁבִּישְּׁלוֹ בִּקְלִיפֵּי עָרְלָה יִדָּלֵק. פָּתַר לָהּ קְרִיָּה בִקְדֵירוֹת. אָמַר רִבִּי יוֹסֵי מִיסְבּוֹר סָבַר רִבִּי בָּא בַּר מָמָל. שֶׁמּוּתָּר לַעֲשׂוֹת כֵּן בִּתְחִילָּה לֹא שֶׁעָבַר. מַיי כְדוֹן. אִם יֵשׁ בּוֹ כְדֵי לִצְבּוֹעַ. אַתְּ רוֹאֶה אֶת הַהֵיתֵר כְּמִי שֶׁאֵינוֹ. אוֹתוֹ הָאִיסּוּר שֶׁבּוֹ כְדֵי לֶאֱסוֹר. אִם אֵין בּוֹ כְדֵי לִצְבֹּעַ. אַתְּ רוֹאֶה הַהֵיתֵר כְּמִי שֶׁאֵינוֹ. אוֹתוֹ הָאִיסּוּר אֵין בּוֹ כְדֵי לֶאֱסוֹר.

Rebbi Abba bar Mamal said, the use of *'orlah* in Tiberias[60] [is judged] by a majority. A Mishnah[61] disagrees with Rebbi Abba bar Mamal: "A dish cooked with *'orlah* shells must be burned." He explains it by a clay vessel[62] among pots. Rebbi Yose said, does Rebbi Abba bar Mamal say that it is permitted to do so from the start? No, to correct the past[63]. How is that? If it is enough to dye, you consider the permitted [dye] as nonexistent. The prohibited is enough to prohibit. If it is not enough to dye, you consider the permitted [dye] as nonexistent. The prohibited is not enough to prohibit.

60 We are not informed about the special techniques used by Tiberian dyers. Therefore, the meaning of this statement cannot be determined. The meaning of the sentence seems to be, not that 'orlah may be used if mixed with a larger amount of permitted dye, but that dyestuff prepared by cooking profane pigment with 'orlah fuel, whose prohibition is only secondary, can be used if mixed with a larger amount of regular profane dyestuff.

61 Mishnah 3:4. If 'orlah prohibits even as fuel, the leniency of R. Abba bar Mamal is hard to understand. In this respect, there is no difference between cooking food and boiling for dyeing.

62 Explanation of Maimonides in Mishnah Šabbat 17:6. The word is explained by Rashi and R. Ḥananel to mean "gourd"; in particular a hollowed gourd used as a vessel. Only Maimonides's explanation makes sense here. One (smaller?) vessel was used with 'orlah fuel; many larger pots were used for the other dyestuffs.

63 The previous explanation is unacceptable. It is forbidden to remove a prohibition by intentionally mixing forbidden and permitted matter. It is only a problem if the mixture was done inadvertently. Then R. Abba bar Mamal permits if a majority is permitted, as explained in Note 60. The argument used to prove this legitimate is modelled on that explained in 'Orlah 2:7, Note 162; cf. also Notes 114, 118 in Chapter 2.

תַּמָּן תַּנִּינָן אֵילוּ דְּבָרִים שֶׁלְגּוֹיִם אֲסוּרִין וְאִיסּוּרָן אִיסּוּר הֲנָייָה. הַיַּיִן. וְהַחוֹמֶץ שֶׁלְגּוֹיִם שֶׁהָיָה מִתְּחִילָתוֹ יַיִן. וְחֶרֶס הַדְרִייָנִי. רִבִּי זְעִירָה בְּשֵׁם רִבִּי יִרְמְיָה. רִבִּי מֵאִיר הִיא. דְּתַנֵּי חֶרֶס הַדְרִייָנִי אָסוּר וְאִיסּוּרוֹ אִיסּוּר הֲנָייָה. מַה נָן קַייָמִין. אִם בְּשֶׁנְּתָנוֹ בְּתַבְשִׁיל דִּבְרֵי הַכֹּל אָסוּר. אִם בְּשֶׁמְּכָרוֹ חוּץ מִדְּמֵי יַיִן נֶסֶךְ שֶׁבּוֹ דִּבְרֵי הַכֹּל מוּתָּר. אֶלָּא כִּי נָן קַייָמִין בְּשֶׁנְּתָנוֹ עַל גַּבֵּי תַבְשִׁיל.

[64]There[65], we have stated: "The following things from Gentiles are forbidden even for usufruct: Wine[66], Gentiles' vinegar which originally was wine, and Hadrianic pottery[67]." Rebbi Zeïra in the name of Rebbi Jeremiah[68]: This is Rebbi Meïr's, as we have stated: Hadrianic pottery is forbidden even for usufruct[68]. Where do we hold? If one put it into a dish, everybody agrees that it is forbidden[69]. If he sells it excluding the value of libation wine contained in it, everybody agrees that it is permitted. But we deal with the case that he put it on top of a dish[70].

64 This and the following paragraph have parallels in *Avodah Zarah* 2:3, fol. 41b. Neither of the two text is without problems.

65 Mishnah *Avodah Zarah* 2:3.

66 Since wine might have been used for a Gentile libation, it is forbidden as ancillary to idolatreous practices. Once it is forbidden, it cannot become permitted even if the wine spoils and becomes vinegar.

67 The Babli (*Avodah Zarah* 32a) explains that this is very porous pottery which Roman soldiers used to soak in wine and carry with them, so it could be soaked in water and provide a taste of wine. There is no explanation of the term in the Yerushalmi.

Perhaps the word has nothing to do with Adria, Adrianoi in Mysia, or the emperor Hadrian, and should be read הַדְרִיָינֵי "wine pots", from Greek ὑδρία, ἡ, "water pot; vessel, wine pot" (Liddel & Scott) (E. G.).

68 This name tradition, also preserved in *Avodah Zarah*, is impossible since R. Jeremiah was R. Zẹïra's student. Either the two names should be switched, or the second author is Rav Jeremiah (an unlikely scenario given the difference in time), or it should be "R. Joḥanan" instead of "R. Jeremiah". The original formulation cannot be recovered.

68 In *Avodah Zarah*: "Hadrianic" pottery is forbidden even for usufruct, the words of Rebbi Eliezer, but the Sages say, "Hadrianic" pottery is permitted for usufruct. In Tosephta (Zuckermandel) *Avodah Zarah* 4:8: ". . . and 'Hadrianic' pottery is forbidden even for usufruct." It is clear that the argument is based on the text in the Yerushalmi *Avodah Zarah*, but with "R. Meïr" in place of "R. Eliezer".

69 Since the forbidden wine will leach out into the dish.

70 As a pan-cover.

מָהוּ לִסְמוֹךְ בּוֹ כַּרְעֵי הַמִּיטָּה. רִבִּי לָעְזָר אוֹמֵר אָסוּר. רִבִּי יוֹחָנָן אָמַר מוּתָּר. רִבִּי יוֹנָה בָּעֵה קוֹמֵי רִבִּי זְעִירָא. הָהֵן בֶּגֶד דְּתַנִּינָן הָכָא מָהוּ לִסְמוֹךְ בּוֹ אֶת הַמִּיטָּה. וְאִיקְפִּיד לְקוֹבְלֵיהּ. אָמַר לֵיהּ אֲפִילוּ לְמָאן דְּאָמַר תַּמָּן מוּתָּר. הָכָא אָסוּר. תַּמָּן אֵין אִיסּוּרוֹ נִיכָּר. בְּרַם הָכָא אִיסּוּרוֹ נִיכָּר.

May it[71] be used to support the legs of a couch? Rebbi Eleazar says it is forbidden[72]; Rebbi Joḥanan said it is permitted[73]. Rebbi Jonah[74] asked before Rebbi Zeïra: May one use the cloth[75], which was discussed here, to support the legs of a couch? The latter was offended by this. He said to him, even for him who permits there, here it is forbidden. There, the prohibition is not visible[76], here the prohibition is visible.

71 "Hadrianic" pottery. The feet of a couch were often standing in vessels filled with water to protect the sleeper from worms and insects.

72 It certainly is usufruct.

73 It is a use of the pottery, not of the absorbed wine, and therefore legitimate.

74 In *Avodah Zarah*: R. Jeremiah. While the reading here is not impossible, the one in *Avodah Zarah* is more probable.

75 Died in *'orlah* dyes.

76 The legs of the couch do not touch the forbidden particles of wine.

אָמַר רִבִּי חַגַּיי. כַּד נַחְתִּית מִן אִילְפָא שְׁמָעִית קָלֵיהּ דְּרִבִּי יַעֲקֹב בַּר אָחָא יְתִיב מַתְנֵי. בֶּגֶד שֶׁצְּבָעוֹ בִּקְלִיפֵּי עָרְלָה יִדָּלֵק. וְתַנִּינָן נָטַל הֵימֶנּוּ כֶּרְכִּד[77] אָסוּר בַּהֲנָייָה. אָרַג בּוֹ אֶת הַבֶּגֶד אָסוּר בַּהֲנָייָה. יַיִן נֶסֶךְ שֶׁנָּפַל לַבּוֹר כּוּלּוֹ אָסוּר בַּהֲנָייָה. וְתַנִּינָן רַבָּן שִׁמְעוֹן בֶּן גַּמְלִיאֵל אוֹמֵר. יִימָּכֵר כּוּלּוֹ לְגוֹי חוּץ מִדְּמֵי יַיִן נֶסֶךְ שֶׁבּוֹ. אָמַר רִבִּי אָחָא בַּר יַעֲקֹב. חַגַּיי קַשְׁתֵּיהּ רִבִּי חַגַּיי קִייְמָהּ. מַיי כְדוֹן. תַּמָּן אֵין דֶּרֶךְ בְּנֵי אָדָם לִיקַּח יַיִן מִן הַגּוֹי. בְּרַם הָכָא דֶּרֶךְ בְּנֵי אָדָם לִיקַּח בֶּגֶד מִן הַגּוֹי.

Rebbi Ḥaggai said, when I descended from a ship I heard the voice of Rebbi Jacob stating: "Cloth dyed with *'orlah* shells should be burned." But did we not state[78]: "If one took from it[79] {wood to make] a weaver's shuttle, it is forbidden for usufruct. If he used it to weave cloth it is forbidden for usufruct. [80]If libation wine fell into a cistern, all is forbidden for usufruct." But did we not state[80]: "Rabban Simeon ben Gamliel says, it should all be sold to a Gentile except for the value of the libation wine contained in it." Rebbi Aḥa ben Jacob said, Ḥaggai raised the question, Rebbi Ḥaggai resolved it. What is it? There people do not buy wine from Gentiles[81]; but here people do buy cloth from Gentiles.

77 Reading of the original scribe of the Leyden ms.; Greek κερκίς, -ίδος. Reading of the corrector and the prints: ברכר.

78 Mishnah *Avodah Zarah* 3:9.

79 A tree in a Gentile holy grove, whose wood is forbidden as accessory to idolatry.

80 Mishnah *Avodah Zarah* 5:10. The question is: Why are textiles produced or processed with forbidden materials totally forbidden but wine mixed with forbidden wine, while unusable for Jews, can be sold if only the Jewish owner is not paid for the forbidden part? Why could the cloth not be sold for its value minus the cost of dying?

81 Gentile wine is automatically forbidden. It might be possible to sell the cloth for the price of undyed cloth; but it is forbidden to bring into circulation anything which might cause a Jew to commit an inadvertant sin. That would be transgressing the commandment "not to put an obstacle into the path of a blind person" (*Lev.* 19:14).

(fol. 62c) **משנה ב:** הַצּוֹבֵעַ מְלֹא הַסִּיט בִּקְלִיפֵּי עָרְלָה וַאֲרָגוֹ בְּבֶגֶד וְאֵין יָדוּעַ אֵיזֶה הוּא. רִבִּי מֵאִיר אוֹמֵר יִדָּלֵק הַבֶּגֶד. וַחֲכָמִים אוֹמְרִים יַעֲלֶה בְּאֶחָד וּמָאתַיִם.

Mishnah 2: If somebody dyes [a thread] the length of a *sîṭ*[82] with *'orlah* shells, uses it to weave cloth, and it is not known where it is, Rebbi

Meïr says the cloth should be burned but the Sages say it may be lifted by one in 200.

משנה ג: הָאוֹרֵג מְלֹא הַסִּיט מִצֶּמֶר הַבְּכוֹר בְּבֶגֶד יִדָּלֵק הַבֶּגֶד. וּמִשְּׂעַר הַנָּזִיר וּמִפֶּטֶר חֲמוֹר בַּשַּׂק יִדָּלֵק הַשַּׂק. וּבְמוּקְדָּשִׁין מְקַדְּשִׁין כָּל־שֶׁהֵן.

Mishnah 3: If somebody weaves the length of a *sîṭ* of firstling's wool[83] in a cloth, the cloth must be burned; of hair of a *nazir*[84] or firstling donkey[85] in sackcloth, the sackcloth must be burned. Of sanctified[86] it sanctifies in the most minute amount.

82 Eleazar Qalir, who represents the Yerushalmi tradition, identifies *sîṭ* with hand-breadth (סילוק לשבת שקלים). R. Ḥananel (followed by *Arukh*), defines *sîṭ* as half a hand-breadth. Rashi (*Šabbat* 106a) following the Babli defines *sîṭ* as the distance spanned between thumb and index finger; this is also the definition of Maimonides..

83 A firstling may not be shorn (*Deut.* 15:19). Since a firstling is a sacrifice, nothing from it, other than its meat, may be used.

84 It must be used to cook the *nazir*'s well-being sacrifice (*Num.* 6:18).

85 Only if the donkey was not redeemed by a lamb, *Ex.* 13:13. After redemption, the firstling donkey is fully profane.

86 All sacrifices other than firstlings need a dedication, the "sanctification". After dedication any profane use is strictly forbidden (cf. Introduction to Tractate *Kilaim*, second paragraph.)

(fol. 63a) **הלכה ב**: מָאן תַּנָּא סִיט. רִבִּי מֵאִיר. בְּרַם כְּרַבָּנִין הוּא סִיט הוּא פָּחוֹת מִסִּיט.

Halakhah 2: Who stated "*sîṭ*"? Rebbi Meïr! But for the Sages, *sîṭ* or less than a *sîṭ* follow the same rules[87].

87 The permitted thread must be more than 200 times the forbidden length.

רִבִּי יוֹסֵי בֵּירִבִּי בּוּן אָמַר לֵיהּ מִשֵּׁם רִבִּי יוֹחָנָן רִבִּי יָסָא בְשֵׁם רִבִּי יוֹחָנָן. צֶמֶר בְּכוֹר שֶׁטְּרָפוֹ בָּטֵל בְּרוֹב. אַיְתֵיהּ רִבִּי חִיָּיה צִיפּוֹרָאָה קוֹמֵי רִבִּי אִימִּי. לִיטְרָא בִשְׁמוֹנָה וְלֹא הוֹרֵי[88] אִילוּלֹא דְּאָמַר רִבִּי יָסָא. וְלֹא מַתְנִיתָא הִיא. הָאוֹרֵג מְלֹא הַסִּיט מִצֶּמֶר הַבְּכוֹר בְּבֶגֶד יִדָּלֵק הַבֶּגֶד. אָמַר לֵיהּ. אִילּוּ אִיתְתָּבַת תַּמָּן אִית הֲוָות יְאוּת.

[89]Rebbi Yose ben Rebbi Abun said in the name of Rebbi Joḥanan, Rebbi Assi in the name of Rebbi Joḥanan: Mixed firstling wool becomes insignificant in a plurality[90]. Rebbi Ḥiyya the Sepphorean[91] brought before Rebbi Ammi a pound in eight[92] but the latter refused to rule since had not Rebbi Assi[93] said, is that not a Mishnah? "If somebody weaves the length of a *sîṭ* of firstling's wool in a cloth, the cloth must be burned"? He said to him, if you had objected there it would have been correct[94].

88 Reading of the first hand of the ms. here and in *Ketubot*. Corrector (only here) and print: הורו.

89 Partial parallels are in *Ketubot* 6:6 and *Avodah Zarah* 5:12.

90 The Mishnah decrees that minute quantities make forbidden only after the wool is processed.

91 He appears only here.

92 One pound of firstling wool mixed with eight pounds of profane wool.

93 While he reports the opinion of R. Joḥanan, he personally objects to it and holds that processed and unprocessed wool follow the same rules.

94 When the question was asked (*Avodah Zarah* 5:12) whether unprocessed forbidden materials could be made insignificant in permitted ones. Since in the meantime it was ruled that processing does not make any difference, you (R. Ḥiyya the Sepphorean) cannot object now.

תַּמָּן תַּנִּינָן אֵילּוּ הֵן הַנִּשְׂרָפִין. וְתַנִּינָן אֵילּוּ הֵן הַנִּקְבָּרִין. הָכָא אַתְּ אָמַר יִשָּׂרֵפוּ וְהָכָא אַתְּ אָמַר יִקָּבֵרוּ. אָמַר רִבִּי יוֹחָנָן כָּאן בְּשַׂק כַּאן בְּשִׂיעֵר. מָה בֵין שַׂק וּמָה בֵין שִׂיעֵר. אָמַר רִבִּי חֲנַנְיָה בְּרֵיהּ דְּרִבִּי הִלֵּל שַׂק מָצוּי לְחַטְּטֵט אַחֲרָיו. שִׂיעֵר אֵין מָצוּי לְחַטְּטֵט אַחֲרָיו. רִבִּי שִׁמְעוֹן בֶּן לָקִישׁ אָמַר. כָּאן בְּמִקְדָּשׁ כָּאן

בִּגְבוּלִין. רִבִּי יוֹסֵי בֵּירִבִּי חֲנִינָא אוֹמֵר. כָּאן בְּנָזִיר טָהוֹר כָּאן בְּנָזִיר טָמֵא. וְהָתַנִּינָן פֶּטֶר חֲמוֹר. אִית לָךְ מֵימַר כָּאן בְּמִקְדָּשׁ כָּאן בִּגְבוּלִין. כָּאן בְּנָזִיר טָהוֹר כָּאן בְּנָזִיר טָמֵא. אֶלָּא כָּאן בְּשַׂק כַּאן בְּשֵׂיעָר. אָמַר רִבִּי יוֹסֵי בֵּירִבִּי בּוּן. הֵן דְּתֵימַר יִשָּׂרֵף. שְׂעָרוֹ. הֵן דְּתֵימַר יִיקָּבֵר. גּוּפוֹ.

There, we have stated: "These have to be burned[95]." And we have stated: "These have to be buried.[96]" In one case, you say they have to be burned and in the other you say they have to be buried[97]. Rebbi Joḥanan said, here about sackcloth, there about hair. What is the difference between sackcloth and hair? Rebbi Ḥanaiah ben Rebbi Hillel said, a sack can be dug out[98], hair cannot be dug out. Rebbi Simeon ben Laqish said, here in the Temple[99], there in the countryside. Rebbi Yose ben Rebbi Ḥanina says, here about a pure *nazir*, there about an impure *nazir*. But did we not state: "A firstling donkey"[100]? Can you say, here in the Temple, there in the countryside, here about a pure *nazir*, there about an impure *nazir*? It must be, here about sackcloth, there about hair. Rebbi Yose ben Rabbi Abun said, when one says it has to be burned, its hair[101]; when one says it has to be buried, its body[102].

95 Mishnah *Temurah* 7:5. The list includes *'orlah* and vineyard *kilaim*.

96 Mishnah *Temurah* 7:4. The list includes the hair of a *nazir* and the (unredeemed) firstling donkey. The "hair of a *nazir*" must refer to an impure *nazir* who must shave before starting a new period (*Num.* 6:9) since the pure hair must be burned under the well-being sacrifice.

97 In Mishnah *Temurah*, the *nazir*'s hair must be buried but in the Mishnah here, sackcloth made from such hair must be burned.

98 Therefore it must be burned by rabbinic decree.

99 By necessity this refers to pure *nazir*'s hair which must be burned by biblical decree.

100 It cannot be brought to the Temple and cannot be impure as long as it lives nor can it be pure in death.

101 The firstling donkey's.

102 If the owner prefers to kill the firstling donkey rather than give a lamb to a Cohen as redemption.

וּבְמוּקְדָּשִׁין מְקַדְּשִׁין כָּל־שֶׁהֵן. רִבִּי יוֹסֵי בְּשֵׁם רִבִּי יוֹחָנָן. הָדָא דְתֵימַר בְּקֳדָשִׁים שֶׁיֵּשׁ לָהֶן מַתִּירִין. אֲבָל בְּקֳדָשִׁים שֶׁאֵין לָהֶן מַתִּירִין צְרִיכִין סִיט. הָתִיב רִבִּי יוֹסֵי וְהָא מַתְנִיתָא פְלִיגָא. הָאוֹרֵג מְלֹא הַסִּיט מִצֶּמֶר הַבְּכוֹר בְּבֶגֶד יִדָּלֵק הַבֶּגֶד. וּבְכוֹר לֹא כְקֳדָשִׁים שֶׁיֵּשׁ לָהֶן מַתִּירִין הוּא.

"Of sanctified it sanctifies in the most minute amount." Rebbi Yose[103] in the name of Rebbi Joḥanan: That means, sacrifices that will be permitted[104]. But sacrifices that never will be permitted[105] need a *sîṭ*. Rebbi Yose objected: Does not the Mishnah disagree? "If somebody weaves the length of a *sîṭ* of firstling's wool in a cloth, the cloth must be burned"! Is a firstling not a sacrifice that will be permitted[106]?

103 This probably should be ר' יסא.

104 Sacrifices which can be redeemed and the money used for substitute sacrifices. Therefore, no leniency is required there.

105 Sacrifices slaughtered in the Temple.

106 This refers to a disagreement in Mishnah *Idiut* 5:4 (discussed in Babli *Bekhorot* 26a/b), where everybody agrees that a firstling which has been declared blemished has become profane in the hand of the Cohen. Even a blemished firstling can be used only for food but after slaughter the hide (whether from an unblemished or a blemished animal) can legally be shorn. The disagreement is if it was shorn before being slaughtered, where for Aqabia ben Mehallalel the slaughter retroactively legitimates the shearing but for the Sages the wool is forbidden by rabbinic decree, so people would not raise firstlings. The question is not answered since, for the Sages, hair taken prematurely is sanctified and will never be permitted.

אִית דְּתָנֵי לָהּ בְּשֵׁם רִבִּי מֵאִיר. אִית דְּלָא תָנֵי לָהּ בְּשֵׁם רִבִּי מֵאִיר. מָאן דְּתָנֵי לָהּ בְּשֵׁם רִבִּי מֵאִיר אִית לֵיהּ עֲשָׂרָה דְּבָרִים מְקַדְּשִׁין. מָאן דְּלָא תָנֵי לָהּ בְּשֵׁם רִבִּי מֵאִיר מְנָן אִית לֵיהּ עֲשָׂרָה דְּבָרִים מְקַדְּשִׁין. רִבִּי מֵאִיר כְּרִבִּי עֲקִיבָה. דְּרִבִּי עֲקִיבָה אָמַר אַף כְּכָּרוֹת שֶׁלְּבַעַל הַבַּיִת.

Some state this[107] in the name of Rebbi Meïr. Some do not state this in the name of Rebbi Meïr. Those who state this in the name of Rebbi Meïr hold that ten things sanctify[108]. According to those who do not state this in the name of Rebbi Meïr, could we know that he holds that ten things sanctify? Rebbi Meïr follows Rebbi Aqiba, as Rebbi Aqiba said "also privately baked loaves[109]."

107 Mishnah 3.

108 They sanctify in the most minute amounts and cannot be lifted. These include the six items listed in Mishnah 7 and the items forbidden in Mishnaiot 3,4,5,6, where Mishnah 3 is counted as one item.

109 This would leave seven items in Mishnah 7 and Mishnaiot 4,5,6 for a total of 10.

(fol. 62c) **משנה ד:** תַּבְשִׁיל שֶׁבִּישְּׁלוֹ בִקְלִיפֵּי עָרְלָה יִדָּלֵק. נִתְעָרֵב בַּאֲחֵרִים יַעֲלֶה בְאֶחָד וּמָאתַיִם.

Mishnah 4: A dish cooked with *'orlah* shells[110] must be burned. If it was mixed with others it may be lifted by one in 200[111].

משנה ה: תַּנּוּר שֶׁהִסִּיקוֹ בִקְלִיפֵּי עָרְלָה וְאָפָה בוֹ אֶת הַפַּת תִּידָּלֵק הַפַּת. נִתְעָרְבָה בַּאֲחֵרוֹת תַּעֲלֶה בְאֶחָד וּמָאתַיִם.

Mishnah 5: If one heated an oven with *'orlah* shells and used it to bake bread, the bread must be burned. If it was mixed with others it may be lifted by one in 200[111].

110 As fuel.

111 Here even R. Meïr will agree since the value added is insignificant.

(fol. 63a) **הלכה ג:** אַבָּא בַר יִרְמְיָה כַּהֲנָא בַּר יִרְמְיָה בְּשֵׁם שְׁמוּאֵל רִבִּי בָּא רִבִּי חִיָּיה בְּשֵׁם רִבִּי יוֹחָנָן. גִּידּוּלֵי עָרְלָה שֶׁעִימְּמוּ הֲרֵי אֵילּוּ מוּתָּרוֹת. וְלָאו מַתְנִיתָא

הִיא. אִם חָדָשׁ יוּתָּץ. אִם יָשָׁן יוּצָּן. רִבִּי חֲנַנְיָא אָמַר לֵית כָּאן. רִבִּי מָנָא אָמַר אִית כָּאן. בְּשֶׁהֵבִיא עֵצִים לַחִים וְנִיגְּבוּ בִקְלִיפֵּי עָרְלָה.

Halakhah 3: Abba bar Jeremiah, Cahana bar Jeremiah[112] in the name of Samuel, Rebbi Abba, Rebbi Ḥiyya in the name of Rebbi Joḥanan: Dimmed *'orlah* growth[113] is permitted. Is that not a *baraita*[114]: "If it was new it must be broken down, old it should be cooled"? Rebbi Ḥanania said, there is nothing. Rebbi Mana said, there is something: When he brought green wood and dried it with *'orlah* shells.

112 He is mentioned only here.

113 *'Orlah* wood used as coals which now is in the process of being spent. This is considered as already spent and the ashes of everything forbidden for usufruct are permitted except ashes of idolatrous objects.

114 In the Yerushalmi, that *baraita* is always quoted in this abbreviated form; cf. also Babli, *Pesaḥim* 26b and Mishnah *Avodah Zarah* 3:4. The basic text is Tosephta *'Orlah* 7: "A (clay) oven heated with *'orlah* shells if it is new (never before heated) must be torn down (since by the first firing it becomes usable); if it is old it must be cooled (not to profit from the *'orlah* fire.) If he baked or cooked with charcoal (*of 'orlah*, which can be considered spent wood) it is permitted. The ashes of anything (forbidden for usufruct) are permitted except the ashes of a holy tree (since it is *ḥerem).* The ashes of clothes affected with mold disease (*Lev.* 13:47-59) and the dust from a leprous house (*Lev.* 33:53) are forbidden for usufruct." The last sentence of the Tosephta leads up to the next paragraph.

אֲבָנִים מְנוּגָּעוֹת שֶׁעֲשָׂאָן סִיד. אִית תַּנָּיֵי תַנֵּי עָלוּ מִטּוּמְאָתָן. וְאִית תַּנָּיֵי תַנֵּי לֹא עָלוּ מִידֵי טוּמְאָתָן. מָאן דְּאָמַר עָלוּ מִידֵי טוּמְאָתָן. הֲרֵי אֵילּוּ מוּתָּרוֹת. וּמָאן דְּאָמַר לֹא עָלוּ מִידֵי טוּמְאָתָן. הֲרֵי אֵילּוּ אֲסוּרוֹת. אֲפִילוּ כְּמָאן דְּאָמַר עָלוּ מִידֵי טוּמְאָתָן. הֲרֵי אֵילּוּ אֲסוּרוֹת. דִּכְתִיב צָרַעַת מַמְאֶרֶת. תֵּן בָּהּ מְאֵירָה וְאַל תֵּיהָנֶה מִמֶּנּוּ. רִבִּי אַבָּהוּ בְּשֵׁם רִבִּי יוֹחָנָן. כָּל־הַנִּשְׂרָפִין אֲפָרָן מוּתָּר חוּץ מֵאֵפֶר הַבָּא מֵחֲמַת עֲבוֹדָה זָרָה. הָתִיב רִבִּי חִייָה בַּר יוֹסֵף קוֹמֵי רִבִּי יוֹחָנָן. הֲרֵי

אֵפֶר הַבַּיִת הֲרֵי אֵינוֹ בָא מֵחֲמַת עֲבוֹדָה זָרָה. וְאַתְּ אָמַר אָסוּר. אָמַר לֵיהּ שַׁנְיָיא הִיא. דִּכְתִיב נְתִיצָה נְתִיצָה.

If leprous stones were turned into lime, some Tannaïm state they rose from their impurity[115]; some Tannaïm state they did not rise from their impurity. For him who stated they rose from their impurity, are they permitted[116], but for him who stated they did not rise from their impurity, are they forbidden? Even for him who stated they rose from their impurity, they are forbidden since it is written (*Lev.* 14:44): "A cursed plague", it should be cursed and you shall have no usufruct from it. Rebbi Abbahu in the name of Rebbi Joḥanan: The ashes of everything burned are permitted except ashes coming from idolatry. Rebbi Ḥiyya bar Joseph objected before Rebbi Joḥanan: There are the ashes[117] of the (leprous) house which do not come from idolatry and you say they are forbidden! He said to him, there is a difference since it is written "tearing down, tearing down[118]."

115 Since they are no longer stones.

116 For usufruct.

117 The lime produced by burning limestone.

118 Since for idolatry the same root implies prohibition of usufruct (*Deut.* 12:3), including the ashes of holy trees, for the leprous house the root נתץ (*Lev.* 14:45) must mean the same (cf. *Berakhot* 7, Note 41).

(fol. 62c) **משנה ו:** מִי שֶׁהָיוּ לוֹ חֲבִילֵי תִלְתָּן שֶׁלְּכִלְאֵי הַכֶּרֶם יִדָּלְקוּ. נִתְעָרְבוּ בַּאֲחֵרִים כּוּלָּם יִדָּלְקוּ דִּבְרֵי רִבִּי מֵאִיר. וַחֲכָמִים אוֹמְרִים יַעֲלוּ בְּאֶחָד וּמָאתַיִם. שֶׁהָיָה רִבִּי מֵאִיר אוֹמֵר אֶת שֶׁדַּרְכּוֹ לְהִימָּנוֹת מְקַדֵּשׁ. וַחֲכָמִים אוֹמְרִים אֵינוֹ מְקַדֵּשׁ אֶלָּא שִׁשָּׁה דְבָרִים בִּלְבַד. רִבִּי עֲקִיבָה אוֹמֵר שִׁבְעָה.

Mishnah 6: If somebody had bundles of fenugreek of vineyard *kilaim*[119], they should be burned. If they were mixed with others, Rebbi Meïr said, all should be burned, but the Sages say, they may be lifted by one in 200, since Rebbi Meïr said, anything counted[120] sanctifies[121]; but the Sages say only six things sanctify; Rebbi Aqiba says seven[122].

119 Of which all usufruct is forbidden.

120 I. e., sold by the piece.

121 Makes all usufruct forbidden in the most minute amount.

122 Enumerated in the next Mishnah.

(fol. 63a) **הלכה ד**: וְכַמָּה הִיא חֲבִילָה עֶשְׂרִים וַחֲמִשָּׁה זֵירִין. אָמַר רִבִּי יוֹנָה אַרְבַּע מִינְהֶן מִיטָּה.

How much is a bundle? 25 plants. Rebbi Jonah said, four to a bed[123].

123 This is from *Terumot* 10:5, Notes 52,53. Fenugreek is never sold by the piece ib quantities less than a bundle. In *Terumot*, R. Joḥanan is mentioned instead of R. Jonah.

(fol. 62c) **משנה ז**: וְאֵילּוּ הֵן אֱיגוֹזֵי פֶּרֶךְ וְרִימּוֹנֵי בָּדָן. וְחָבִיּוֹת סְתוּמוֹת. וְחוּלְפּוֹת תְּרָדִין. וְקוּלְסֵי כְּרוּב וּדְלַעַת יְוָנִית. רִבִּי עֲקִיבָה אוֹמֵר אַף כִּכָּרוֹת שֶׁלְּבַעַל הַבַּיִת. הָרָאוּי לְעָרְלָה עָרְלָה לְכִלְאֵי הַכֶּרֶם כִּלְאֵי הַכֶּרֶם.

Mishnah 7: They are: Breakable walnuts[124] and pomegranates from Badan[125], sealed amphoras[126], beet roots[127], heads of cabbage[128], and Greek gourd. Rebbi Aqiba says, also non-commercial loaves[129]. This refers to *'orlah* and vineyard *kilaim*, as the case may be[130].

124 According to *Pesiqta Rabbati* #11 (ed. M. Friedmann, Wien 1880, p. 42b) there are three kinds of walnuts: Those with breakable shells (which do not need a nutcracker), normal ones, and those with extra hard shells.

125 From Wadi Badya, between Nablus and Damieh.

126 Of wine.

127 The Gaonic commentary to *Uqeẓin* 1:4 according to J. N. Epstein defines as spines of beet greens; he reads the Arabic definition as a gloss אלצלעא אלסלק; the traditional reading is אצל אלסלק "beet root". Meïri (*Beẓah*, ed. Lange-Schlesinger, Jerusalem 1965, p. 22) explains as: "A kind of beet which is not smooth but somewhat hairy, which is rough to the touch and very red; the expression חלפי comes from Alfalfa."

128 According to I. Löw, this is a double Latin-Hebrew expression *caulis* ברוב.

129 Bread baked at home; not baked in large series.

130 The first three items may be *'orlah*, the last four may be forbidden as vineyard *kilaim*.

(fol. 63a) **הלכה ה**: רִבִּי יוֹחָנָן וְרִבִּי שִׁמְעוֹן בֶּן לָקִישׁ. חַד אָמַר דִּבְרֵי רִבִּי מֵאִיר עֲשָׂרָה דְבָרִים מְקַדְּשִׁין. וְחָרָנָה אָמַר דִּבְרֵי רִבִּי מֵאִיר כָּל־הַדְּבָרִים מְקַדְּשִׁין. רִבִּי יַעֲקֹב בַּר אָחָא אָמַר שְׁמוּעָתָא. מַתְנִיתָא פְלִיגָא עַל מָאן דְּאָמַר דִּבְרֵי רִבִּי מֵאִיר עֲשָׂרָה דְבָרִים מְקַדְּשִׁין. דְּתַנִּינָן תַּמָּן אָמַר רִבִּי יוּדָה לֹא הוּזְכְּרוּ רִימּוֹנֵי בָדָן וַחֲצִירֵי גֶבַע אֶלָּא שֶׁיְּהוּ מִתְעַשְּׂרִין וַדַּאי (fol. 63b) בְּכָל־מָקוֹם.

Halakhah 5: Rebbi Joḥanan and Rebbi Simeon ben Laqish, one says according to Rebbi Meïr ten things sanctify[108]; the other says according to Rebbi Meïr all things[131] sanctify. Rebbi Jacob bar Aḥa said this as a tradition[132]. A Mishnah disagrees with him who says, according to Rebbi Meïr ten things sanctify, as we have stated there[133]: "Rebbi Jehudah[134] said, Badan pomegranates and Geba[135] leeks were mentioned only because one must tithe them as certain everywhere."

131 Sold by the piece.

132 The interpretation of the statement of R. Meïr was already a tannaïtic problem.

133 *Kelim* 17:4. The Mishnah refers to the rule that a vessel which has a

hole the size of an average pomegranate is no longer considered a vessel and cannot be impure. There is a discussion whether "average pomegranate" means "Badan pomegranate."

134 In the Mishnah: R. Yose. This reading seems to be the correct one since R. Yose is the youngest of all Tannaïm mentioned there, is mentioned last, and practice follows him.

135 This Geba is an otherwise unidentified place in Samaria. Since Badan and Geba are in Samaria and Samaritans never tithe produce for sale and reject the notion of heave and tithes for produce other than grain, wine, and olive oil, one knows that pomegranates and leeks are subject to heave and tithing since Samaritans are a Jewish sect, and their produce is certainly *ṭevel* for heave and tithes.

The reading חצירי is that of the scribe of the ms. who corrected it to חריצי, the form found in the Venice text. The text in *Kelim* reads חצירי "leeks"; neither Hebrew חריץ ""incision, furrow", nor Arabic خرص "palm branch" make any sense here.

וּשְׁאָר כָּל־הָרִימּוֹנִין אֵין דַּרְכָּן לְהִימָּנוֹת. אֶלָּא רִימּוֹנֵי בָדָן עַל יְדֵי שֶׁהֵן חֲבִיבִין דַּרְכָּן לְהִימָּנוֹת. וּשְׁאָר כָּל־הָרִימּוֹנִין עַל יְדֵי שֶׁאֵין חֲבִיבִין אֵין דַּרְכָּן לְהִימָּנוֹת.

Does one not count other pomegranates? But Badan pomegranates one usually counts because they are preferred; other pomegranates one does not usually count because they are not preferred.

הלכה ו: רִבִּי יוֹנָה בָעֵי. הָא שְׁקֵידֵי פֶרֶךְ לֹא.

Halakhah 6: Rebbi Jonah asked: Therefore, not breakable almonds[136]?

136 Since almonds are not included in the Mishnah, they are assumed to be sold by weight.

מַתְנִיתָא בִסְתוּמָה בֵּין הַסְּתוּמוֹת. אֲבָל בִּסְתוּמָה בֵּין הַפְּתוּחוֹת וְנִפְתְּחָה אוֹ פְתוּחָה בֵּין הַסְּתוּמוֹת וְנִסְתְּמָה צְרִיכוֹת שִׁיעוּר אֶחָד. הֵיךְ אֶיפְשָׁר לִפְתוּחָה אֶצֶל הַסְּתוּמוֹת. אָמַר רִבִּי זְעִירָה. תִּיפְתָּר בִּפְתוּחָה אֶצֶל הַחֶנְוָנִי שֶׁהִיא כִסְתוּמָה אֶצֶל בַּעַל הַבַּיִת. וְהָתַנֵּי וְנִסְתְּמָה. תִּיפְתָּר שֶׁחָזַר בַּעַל הַבַּיִת וּנְטָלָהּ.

The Mishnah is about sealed[137] among sealed. But a sealed one among open ones which was opened, or an open one among sealed ones which was sealed again need a measure[138]. How is an open one among sealed ones possible? Rebbi Zeïra said, explain as open at the grocer's and sealed at the private person's[139]. But did we not state "it was sealed again"? Explain it if the private person came and took it back.

137 Amphoras.

138 1 in 100 for *kilaim*, 1 in 200 for *'orlah*. When the sealed one was sealed among open amphoras, it was recognizable and no problem existed. This eliminates the rule that the barrel could never become insignificant.

139 It really is sealed all the time but since the seal of a private producer is flimsy compared to that of a winery which must prepare its amphoras for transport over longer distances, the grocer considers it as open since very little time will be needed to open it when necessary.

רִבִּי קְרִיסְפָּא בְשֵׁם רִבִּי יוֹחָנָן. כָּל־אִילֵּין קִירָיָיא וְקִרְוָותָא דַאֲנָן אָֽכְלִין דְּלַעַת יְוָנִית הֵן.

Rebbi Crispus in the name of Rebbi Joḥanan: All these gourds and pumpkins we eat fall under the rules of Greek gourd.

רִבִּי יוֹנָה בָּעֵי. וְלָמָּה לֵי נָן אָֽמְרִין הָרָאוּי לִתְרוּמָה. אָמַר לֵיהּ רִבִּי יוֹסֵי תְּרוּמָה נוֹהֶגֶת בַּכֹּל. עָרְלָה אֵינָהּ נוֹהֶגֶת בַּכֹּל.

Rebbi Jonah asked: Why do we not say it refers to heave? Rebbi Yose said to him: Heave always applies, *'orlah* does not always apply[140].

140 It is true that the rules of the Mishnah also apply to *ṭevel* and untithed Badan pomegranates mixed with tithed ones always make *ṭevel* irrespective of the amounts. But their place is not in the Mishnah since "as the case may be" does not apply to heave which is a rabbinic obligation on all produce.

(fol. 62c) **משנה ח:** נִתְפַּצְּעוּ הָאֱגוֹזִים נִתְפָּרְדוּ הָרִימּוֹנִים נִתְפַּתְּחוּ הֶחָבִיּוֹת נֶחְתְּכוּ הַדְּלוּעִים נִתְפָּרְשׂוּ הַכִּכָּרוֹת יַעֲלוּ בְּאֶחָד וּמָאתַיִם.

Mishnah 8: If the walnuts were broken, the pomegranates dispersed[141], the amphoras opened, the gourds cut, the loaves broken, they may be lifted by one in 200.

141 The shell was removed and the pomegranate broken into single berries. in all these cases, the items are sold by amount (weight or volume), not by piece.

(fol. 63b) **הלכה ז:** נָפְלוּ וְאַחַר כָּךְ נִתְפַּצְּעוּ בֵּין שׁוֹגֵג בֵּין מֵזִיד לֹא יַעֲלוּ דִּבְרֵי רִבִּי מֵאִיר. רִבִּי יוּדָה אָמַר בֵּין שׁוֹגֵג בֵּין מֵזִיד יַעֲלוּ. רִבִּי יוֹסֵי אוֹמֵר שׁוֹגֵג יַעֲלוּ מֵזִיד לֹא יַעֲלוּ. מַה טַעֲמָא דְּרִבִּי מֵאִיר. קְנָסוּ בְשׁוֹגֵג מִפְּנֵי מֵזִיד. מַה טַעֲמָא דְּרִבִּי יוּדָה. כְּבָר קְנָסוֹ בְיָדוֹ. מַה טַעֲמָא דְּרִבִּי יוֹסֵי. כַּיי דְאָמַר רִבִּי אַבָּהוּ בְּשֵׁם רִבִּי יוֹחָנָן. כָּל־הָאִיסּוּרִין שֶׁרִיבָּה עֲלֵיהֶן שׁוֹגֵג מוּתָּר. מֵזִיד אָסוּר.

Halakhah 7: If they fell down[142] and broke, whether unintentionally or intentionally they should not be lifted, the words of Rebbi Meïr. Rebbi Jehudah says, whether unintentionally or intentionally they may be lifted. Rebbi Yose[143] says, unintentionally they may be lifted, intentionally they may not be lifted. What is the reason of Rebbi Meïr? They fined for the unintentional because of the intentional. What is the reason of Rebbi Jehudah? He already paid his fine[144]. What is the reason of Rebbi Yose? As Rebbi Abbahu said in the name of Rebbi Joḥanan, any prohibited item to which [something permitted] was added[145], unintentionally it is permitted, intentionally it is forbidden.

142 Breakable walnuts among which was one of *'orlah*. Whole ones all were forbidden. Broken they are not more valuable than any other broken walnuts. Can they be lifted by 1 in 200?

143 In the parallel Babli *Giṭṭin* 54b, this is reported as the common opinion

of RR. Jehudah, Yose, and Simeon.

144 Since he can sell the broken walnuts only for the price of regular nuts, he already has suffered monetary loss. (This opinion is not quoted in the Babli.)

145 And now the mixture is permitted according to the rules; cf. also *Terumot* 2:3.

רִבִּי שִׁמְעוֹן בֶּן לָקִישׁ בְּשֵׁם רִבִּי הוֹשַׁעְיָה הָיוּ לְפָנָיו מֵאָה וַחֲמִשִּׁים חָבִיּוֹת. נִתְפַּתְּחוּ מֵאָה מוּתָּרוֹת. חֲמִשִּׁים אֲסוּרוֹת. וְהַשְּׁאָר לִכְשֶׁיִּפָּתֵחוּ יִהְיוּ מוּתָּרוֹת. אָמַר רִבִּי זְעִירָא לֹא אָמְרוּ אֶלָּא לִכְשֶׁיִּפָּתֵחוּ הָא לְפַתֵּחַ לְכַתְּחִילָּה אָסוּר.

[146]Rebbi Simeon ben Laqish in the name of Rebbi Hoshaia: If there were before him 150 amphoras which were opened: One hundred are permitted, fifty are forbidden; this remainder will be permitted if they have been opened. Rebbi Zeïra said, he said only "*if* they have been opened;" therefore at the start it is forbidden.

146 This is from *Terumot* 4:8, Note 83, and *'Orlah* 1:5, Note 165.

דְּבֵי רִבִּי יַנַּאי שָׁאֲלִין. דְּלַעַת שֶׁלְּקָהּ בְּבֵית אָבִיהָ מָהוּ שֶׁתִּטְבּוֹל לְמַעְשְׂרוֹת. לֵוִי שָׁאַל מָהוּ שֶׁתְּטַמֵּא טוּמְאַת אוֹכְלִין. שְׁלָקָהּ בִּמְחוּתֶּכֶת הִיא. מִילְּתֵיהּ דִּשְׁמוּאֵל אָמַר שֶׁהִיא מְטַמֵּא טוּמְאַת אוֹכְלִין. וְאָמַר רִבִּי יוֹסֵי בֵּירִבִּי בּוּן בְּשֵׁם שְׁמוּאֵל. תְּאֵינִים וַעֲנָבִים שֶׁצָּמְקוּ בְּאָבִיהֶן מְטַמְּאִין טוּמְאַת אוֹכְלִין. וְהָרוֹדֶה מֵהֶן בַּשַּׁבָּת חַייָב מִשּׁוּם קוֹצֵר.

They asked at the House of Rebbi Yannai: Does a gourd which was cooked[147] while connected to the ground create *ṭevel* for tithes? Levi asked, can it become impure as food? If it was cooked it is as if cut into pieces[148]. The word of Samuel says that it becomes impure as food, as Rebbi Yose ben Rebbi Abun said in the name of Samuel[149]: Figs and raisins which shriveled on the tree may become impure as food and anybody who takes them down on the Sabbath is guilty of harvesting.

147 The text follows the *editio princeps*. The ms. has שלקטה "which he collected". In the version of the ms. the question is trivial. Since gourds are sold by the piece, the collection of the gourd is the end of processing and, since it may be taken directly to market, it immediately becomes subject to heave and tithes. Therefore, the version of the print is preferable. Since gourds grow on very long tendrils, it is possible in principle to cook the gourd while it is still connected to its root.

148 Being treated as food makes it subject to the impurity of food.

149 Quoted in Babli *Ḥulin* 127b where it is pointed out that in general fruits become food only when harvested. Raisins on the vine are food regarding impurity but not yet food regarding the Sabbath. The Tosephta (*Uqeẓin* 2:11) notes that any other shriveled fruit on the branch is not food.

נִתְפָּרְסוּ כִּכָּרוֹת. מַתְנִיתָא דְּרִבִּי עֲקִיבָה. דְּרִבִּי עֲקִיבָה אוֹמֵר אַף כִּכָּרוֹת שֶׁל בַּעַל הַבַּיִת.

"If the loaves were broken". The Mishnah is Rebbi Aqiba's since "Rebbi Aqiba says, also non-commercial loaves."

(fol. 62c) **משנה ט:** סְפֵק הָעָרְלָה בְּאֶרֶץ יִשְׂרָאֵל אָסוּר וּבְסוּרִיָּא מוּתָּר. וּבְחוּצָה לָאָרֶץ יוֹרֵד וְלוֹקֵחַ (fol. 62d) וּבִלְבַד שֶׁלֹּא יִרְאֶנּוּ לוֹקֵט. כֶּרֶם נָטוּעַ יָרָק וְיָרָק נִמְכָּר חוּצָה לוֹ. בְּאֶרֶץ יִשְׂרָאֵל אָסוּר וּבְסוּרִיָּא מוּתָּר וּבְחוּצָה לָאָרֶץ יוֹרֵד וְלוֹקֵט וּבִלְבַד שֶׁלֹּא יִלְקוֹט בְּיָד. הֶחָדָשׁ אָסוּר מִן הַתּוֹרָה בְּכָל־מָקוֹם. וְהָעָרְלָה הֲלָכָה. וְהַכִּלְאַיִם מִדִּבְרֵי סוֹפְרִים.

Mishnah 9: A doubtful case of *'orlah* in the Land of Israel is forbidden[150], in Syria[151] permitted, and outside the Land one goes and buys on condition he not see the harvesting being done[152]. If a vineyard is planted with vegetables and vegetables are sold on the outside[153], in the

Land of Israel it is forbidden, in Syria permitted, and outside the Land he goes and harvests on condition he not harvest with his own hands[154]. New grain is forbidden everywhere from the Torah[155], *'orlah* from practice, and *kilaim* by rabbinic decree.

150 Since in all cases of doubt about a biblical law one has to be restrictive.

151 The part of the Promised Land not conquered by Joshua, cf. *Peah* 7, Note 119.

152 On condition he (the Jewish buyer) not see him (the Gentile seller).

153 One has to assume that the vegetables sold outside the vineyard were grown in the vineyard and are vineyard *kilaim*.

154 He (the Gentile seller) harvests on condition that he (the Jewish buyer) not harvest himself, but the Jew may see the Gentile harvesting.

155 Grain from the winter harvest before the ceremony of the *'omer*, *Lev.* 23:9-14.

(fol. 63b) **הלכה ח**: אֵי זֶהוּ סְפֵק הֶעָרְלָה. כֶּרֶם שֶׁלְעָרְלָה וַעֲנָבִים נִמְכָּרוֹת חוּצָה לוֹ. בְּאֶרֶץ יִשְׂרָאֵל אָסוּר וּבְסוּרִייָא מוּתָּר. אָמַר רִבִּי יוּדָן. אַף זֶה סְפֵיקוֹ אָסוּר בְּסוּרְיָא. אֵי זֶהוּ סָפֵק הַמּוּתָּר בְּסוּרְיָא. כֶּרֶם שֶׁלְעָרְלָה וְכֶרֶם אַחֵר בְּצִידּוֹ וַעֲנָבִים נִמְכָּרוֹת חוּצָה לוֹ. בְּאֶרֶץ יִשְׂרָאֵל אָסוּר וּבְסוּרִייָא מוּתָּר. אָמַר רִבִּי יוּדָה אַף זֶה אָסוּר בְּסוּרְיָא. אֵי זֶה סָפֵק הַמּוּתָּר בְּסוּרְיָא. כֶּרֶם נָטוּעַ יָרָק וּשְׂדֵה יָרָק בְּצִידּוֹ וְיָרָק נִמְכָּר חוּצָה לוֹ. בְּאֶרֶץ יִשְׂרָאֵל אָסוּר וּבְסוּרִייָא מוּתָּר.

Halakhah 8: What is a doubtful case of *'orlah*? An *'orlah* vineyard and grapes are sold on the outside; in the Land of Israel it is forbidden, in Syria permitted. Rebbi Yudan said, in that doubtful case also it is forbidden in Syria. What is a doubtful case in Syria? A vineyard planted with vegetables, a vegetable field next to it, and vegetables are sold on the outside; in the Land of Israel it is forbidden, in Syria permitted. [156]"Rebbi Jehudah said, that also is forbidden in Syria. Which doubtful case is permitted in Syria? If a vineyard is planted with vegetables, a field of vegetables is nearby, and vegetables are sold on the outside, in the Land of Israel it is forbidden, in Syria permitted."

156 Tosephta 4. "That also" is the scenario of the Mishnah regarding vineyard *kilaim*.

וּבְחוּץ לָאָרֶץ יוֹרֵד וְלוֹקֵט וּבִלְבַד שֶׁלֹּא יִלְקוֹט בְּיָד. אָמַר רִבִּי יוּדָן עוֹד הִיא בְּקַדְמִייָתָא חוֹזֵר וְלוֹקֵחַ וּבִלְבַד שֶׁלֹּא יִרְאֶנּוּ לוֹקֵט.

"Outside the Land he goes, he harvests on condition that he not harvest with his own hands[154]." Rebbi Yudan said, that also should be equal to the first, "he turns in and buys on condition he not see him harvesting[152]."

הֶחָדָשׁ אָסוּר מִן הַתּוֹרָה בְּכָל־מָקוֹם. מַתְנִיתָא דְּרִבִּי לְעֶזֶר. דְּתַנִּינָן תַּמָּן כָּל־מִצְוָה שֶׁאֵינָהּ תְּלוּיָה בָּאָרֶץ נוֹהֶגֶת בָּאָרֶץ וּבְחוּצָה לָאָרֶץ. וְכָל־שֶׁהִיא תְלוּיָיה בָּאָרֶץ אֵינָהּ נוֹהֶגֶת אֶלָּא בָאָרֶץ חוּץ מִן הֶעָרְלָה וּמִן הַכִּלְאַיִם. רִבִּי לִיעֶזֶר אוֹמֵר אַף הֶחָדָשׁ. מָה טַעֲמָא דְּרִבִּי לִיעֶזֶר בְּכָל־מָקוֹם. בְּכָל־מוֹשְׁבוֹתֵיכֶם בֵּין בָּאָרֶץ בֵּין בְּחוּצָה לָאָרֶץ. מָה מְקַיְימִין רַבָּנִין טַעֲמָא דְּרִבִּי לִיעֶזֶר בְּכָל־מוֹשְׁבוֹתֵיכֶם. בְּחָדָשׁ שֶׁכָּן שֶׁיָּצָא בַחוּץ.

"New grain is forbidden everywhere from the Torah." The Mishnah is Rebbi Eliezer's as we have stated there[157]: "Any commandment not connected with the Land applies both inside and outside the Land. But any connected with the Land applies only inside the Land except for *'orlah* and *kilaim*. Rebbi Eliezer says, also new grain." What is the reason of Rebbi Eliezer[158]? Everywhere, (*Lev.* 23:14) "in all your dwelling places," both inside and outside the Land. How do the rabbis explain the reason of Rebbi Eliezer, "in all your dwelling places"? New grain from here which was exported.

157 Mishnah *Qiddušin* 1:9. The parallel discussion is in the Babli, *Qiddušin* 38a/b.

158 The end of this paragraph and the next one are also in *Qiddušin* 1:9, fol. 61d.

רִבִּי יוֹנָה בָּעֵי קוֹמֵי רִבִּי יוֹסֵי. וְלָמָּה לֹא תַנִּינָן אַף הַחַלָּה עִמָּהֶן. אָמַר לֵיהּ. לֹא אֲתִינָן מַתְנִיתִין אֶלָּא דָבָר שֶׁהוּא נוֹהֵג בְּיִשְׂרָאֵל וּבַגּוֹיִם. וְחַלָּה אֵינָהּ נוֹהֶגֶת אֶלָּא בְיִשְׂרָאֵל. דִּכְתִיב רֵאשִׁית עֲרִיסוֹתֵיכֶם וְלֹא שֶׁלְגּוֹיִם.

Rebbi Jonah asked before Rebbi Yose: Why did we not state *ḥallah* with these[159]? He said to him, our Mishnah only deals with something which applies to Israel and the Gentiles[160]. But *ḥallah* only applies to Israel, as it is written (*Num.* 15:20): The first of *your* dough," not of Gentiles.

159 Which applies outside the Land by rabbinic decree.

160 Which is forbidden to Jews even if grown by Gentiles. For *kilaim*, cf. *Kilaim* 1:7, Notes 122-140.

וְהֶעָרְלָה הֲלָכָה. שְׁמוּאֵל אָמַר כְּהִילְכוֹת הַמְּדִינָה. רִבִּי יוֹחָנָן אָמַר הֲלָכָה לְמֹשֶׁה מִסִּינַי. רִבִּי יָסָא בָּעָא קוֹמֵי רִבִּי יוֹחָנָן. הֲלָכָה לְמֹשֶׁה מִסִּינַי וְאַתְּ אָמַר הָכֵין. אָמַר בְּשָׁעָה שֶׁנִּיתְּנָה הֲלָכָה לְכָךְ נִיתְּנָה. אָמַר אִילוּלֵא סְלָקִית לְאֶרֶץ דְּיִשְׂרָאֵל אֶלָּא לִשְׁמוֹעַ דָּבָר זֶה דַּיִי.

"'*Orlah* from practice". Samuel said, practice of the country[161]. Rebbi Joḥanan said, practice from Moses on Sinai. Rebbi Assi asked before Rebbi Joḥanan, practice from Moses on Sinai, and you say so[162]? He said, when practice was proclaimed, it was given in this way. He said, if I had come to the Land of Israel[163] only to hear this it would have been been enough for me.

161 The Jews in Bablylonia continued to practice the prohibition of *'orlah* by consensus. The same disagreement is discussed in the Babli, *Qiddušin* 39a.

162 If *'orlah* outside the Land is of almost biblical status, why can the Mishnah permit all doubtful cases?

163 R. Assi was a Babylonian. The opinion expressed in Tosephta 8 that *'orlah* never applies outside the Land is quoted only in the Babli.

וְהַכִּלְאַיִם מִדִּבְרֵי סוֹפְרִים. שְׁמוּאֵל אָמַר בְּכִלְאֵי הַכֶּרֶם. הָא בְּכִלְאֵי זְרָעִים מוּתָּר. רִבִּי יוֹחָנָן אָמַר בְּכִלְאֵי הַכֶּרֶם. הָא בְּכִלְאֵי זְרָעִים אָסוּר. אָמַר רַב חוּנָא כַּד נַחְתּוֹן מַעֲרָבָיָא דְּתַמָּן אָמְרוּנָהּ בְּשֵׁם רִבִּי יוֹחָנָן וְקִייְמוּנָהּ. אֶת חֻקּוֹתַיי תִּשְׁמוֹרוּ בְּהֶמְתְּךָ לֹא תַרְבִּיעַ כִּלְאַיִם שָׂדְךָ לֹא תִזְרַע כִּלְאַיִם. שַׁעַטְנֵז לֹא יַעֲלֶה עָלֶיךָ. הִקִּישׁ כִּלְאֵי זְרָעִים לְכִלְאֵי בְגָדִים וְכִלְאֵי בְהֵמָה. מַה כִּלְאֵי זְרָעִים וְכִלְאֵי בְגָדִים שֶׁאֵין תְּלוּיִין בָּאָרֶץ וְנוֹהֲגִין בָּאָרֶץ וּבְחוּצָה לָאָרֶץ. אַף כִּלְאֵי זְרָעִים אַף עַל פִּי שֶׁהֵן תְּלוּיִין בָּאָרֶץ נוֹהֲגִין בָּאָרֶץ וּבְחוּצָה לָאָרֶץ.

"And *kilaim* by rabbinic decree." Samuel said, this refers[164] to vineyard *kilaim*. Therefore, *kilaim* of seeds[165] are permitted. Rebbi Joḥanan said, this refers to vineyard *kilaim*. Therefore, *kilaim* of seeds are forbidden[166]. Rav Huna said, when Westerners descended from there[167], they said this in the name of Rebbi Joḥanan and proved it. (*Lev.* 19:19) "You must keep My basic Laws[168], your animals you should not mate *kilaim*, your field you shall not sow *kilaim*, . . . , *ša'aṭnez*[169] shall not come upon you." It bracketed *kilaim* of seeds with *kilaim* of clothing and *kilaim* of animals. Since *kilaim* of clothing and *kilaim* of animals do not depend on the Land and apply inside and outside the Land[157], so also *kilaim* of seeds, while they depend on the Land, do apply inside and outside the Land.

164 The rabbinic decree.

165 Any vegetable *kilaim* except those growing in a vineyard.

166 By biblical law. In the Babli, *Qiddušin* 39a, this is the opinion of Samuel but practice follows what here is Samuel's opinion.

167 Galilee.

168 Cf. *Kilaim* 1, Notes 122,124.

169 Cloth woven from wool and linen.

חַד בַּר נַשׁ זְרַע חַקְלֵייהּ שְׂעוֹרִין וְלֶפֶת. עֲבַר חָנִין גּוֹבִיתָא וְעָקְרִין. אָתָא עוֹבְדָא קוֹמֵי שְׁמוּאֵל וּקְנָסֵיהּ. דְּתַנֵּי אֵין עוֹשִׂין עִם יִשְׂרָאֵל בְּכִלְאַיִם. אֲבָל עוֹקְרִין עִמּוֹ בְּכִלְאַיִם מִפְּנֵי שֶׁהוּא מְמַעֵט בָּעֲבֵירָה.

A person[170] sowed his field with barley and turnips. Ḥanin from Gobya[171] passed by and tore them out. The case came before Samuel who fined him[172], as we have stated[173]: "One does not work with a Jew in *kilaim*, but one does help him to tear out *kilaim*[174] because that helps to diminish sin."

170 In Babylonia.

171 A place on the Euphrates.

172 Ḥanin.

173 Tosephta *Kilaim* 2:16. The parallel in the Babli, *Avodah Zarah* 63b/64a, while in language closer to the Tosephta than the Yerushalmi text, has "Gentile" in place of "Jew".

174 The Tosephta applies to the Land. Even so, it only permits to help the owner, not to tear out without his consent (at least in the absence of a court order). Therefore, Ḥanin was liable even according to R. Joḥanan.

תַּנֵּי אֵין עוֹשִׂין עִם הַגּוֹי בְּכִלְאַיִם בֵּין בְּכִלְאֵי הַכֶּרֶם בֵּין בְּכִלְאֵי זְרָעִים. אֲבָל עֲיָירוֹת הַמּוּבְלָעוֹת בְּאֶרֶץ יִשְׂרָאֵל כְּגוֹן בָּאִינָה וּבָאִימָה וַחֲבֵרוֹתֶיהָ עוֹשִׂין עִמָּהֶן בְּכִלְאַיִם. כְּשֵׁם שֶׁכִּלְאַיִם בָּאָרֶץ כָּךְ כִּלְאַיִם בְּחוּץ לָאָרֶץ. שְׁמוּאֵל פּוֹתֵר מַתְנִיתָא. אֵין עוֹשִׂין עִם הַגּוֹי בְּכִלְאַיִם בָּאָרֶץ. בֵּין בְּכִלְאֵי הַכֶּרֶם בֵּין בְּכִלְאֵי זְרָעִים. אֲבָל עֲיָירוֹת הַמּוּבְלָעוֹת בְּאֶרֶץ יִשְׂרָאֵל כְּגוֹן בָּאִינָה וּבָאִימָה וַחֲבֵרוֹתֶיהָ עוֹשִׂין עִמָּהֶן בְּכִלְאַיִם. כְּשֵׁם שֶׁכִּלְאַיִם בָּאָרֶץ כָּךְ כִּלְאַיִם בְּחוּץ לָאָרֶץ. כִּלְאֵי הַכֶּרֶם. הָא כִלְאֵי זְרָעִים מוּתָּר. רִבִּי יוֹחָנָן פּוֹתֵר מַתְנִיתָא. אֵין עוֹשִׂין עִם הַגּוֹי בְּכִלְאַיִם בָּאָרֶץ. בֵּין בְּכִלְאֵי הַכֶּרֶם בֵּין בְּכִלְאֵי זְרָעִים. אֲבָל עֲיָירוֹת הַמּוּבְלָעוֹת בְּאֶרֶץ יִשְׂרָאֵל כְּגוֹן בָּאִינָה וּבָאִימָה וַחֲבֵרוֹתֶיהָ עוֹשִׂין עִמָּהֶן בְּכִלְאַיִם. כְּשֵׁם שֶׁכִּלְאַיִם בָּאָרֶץ כָּךְ כִּלְאַיִם בְּחוּץ לָאָרֶץ. בְּכִלְאֵי הַכֶּרֶם. הָא בְּכִלְאֵי זְרָעִים אָסוּר.

It was stated[175]: "One does not work with a Gentile in *kilaim*[176], be it vineyard *kilaim* or *kilaim* of seeds. But in towns[177] which form enclaves in the Land of Israel such as Baïna and Baïma[178] and similar ones one may work with them in *kilaim*. Just as *kilaim* are [forbidden] in the Land, so they are outside the Land." Samuel explains the *baraita*: "One does not work with a Gentile in *kilaim*, be it vineyard *kilaim* or *kilaim* of seeds. But in towns which form enclaves in the Land of Israel such as Baïna and Baïma and similar ones one may work with them in *kilaim*. Just as *kilaim* are [forbidden] in the Land, so they are outside the Land;" that refers to vineyard *kilaim*. Therefore, *kilaim* of seeds are permitted. Rebbi Joḥanan explains the *baraita*: "One does not work with a Gentile in *kilaim*, be it vineyard *kilaim* or *kilaim* of seeds. But in towns which form enclaves in the Land of Israel such as Baïna and Baïma and similar ones one may work with them in *kilaim*. Just as *kilaim* are [forbidden] in the Land, so they are outside the Land;" that refers to vineyard *kilaim*. Therefore, *kilaim* of seeds are forbidden[179].

175 Tosephta *Kilaim* 2:16.

176 In the Land of Israel, since there the prohibition of *kilaim* also falls on Gentiles; cf. Note 168.

177 Inhabited by Gentiles.

178 These places have not been convincingly identified. In the Tosephta, one reads either *Beth Ana Imma* or *Beth Ana Umma*. Tosephta *Ahilut* 18:4 has Hippos and Ascalon as examples of such pagan enclaves. If the place is not one settled by the returnees from Babylonia (or, in Galilee, was a place of Israelites never exiled), it is formally outside the Land and the Gentile can plant or sow *kilaim* without guilt; cf. *Ševi'it* 6:1.

179 Reading of the scribe of the Leyden ms. The corrector, followed by the prints, replaced "forbidden" by "permitted." For the correct choice of the text, cf. Note 166.

Introduction to Tractate Bikkurim

The Tractate explains the obligation of presenting First Fruits to the Temple, contained in *Deut.* 26:1-11. The first Chapter defines the obligation: who has to present his First Fruits and from where they can be presented. This leads to a discussion of the status of proselytes and the definition of the "Land flowing of milk and honey." Since there is a verse (*Deut.* 12:11) in which First Fruits are called "your hand's heave", the second Chapter is a general discussion of what is common to and what is different between First Fruits, heave, and second tithe The chapter also contains discussions of death as divine punishment and of criminal responsibility of juveniles. The third Chapter discusses the details of the Temple ceremony of communal presentation of First Fruits and includes a section on the signs of respect due elders.

יש מביאין פרק ראשון

(fol. 63c) **משנה א:** יֵשׁ מְבִיאִין בִּיכּוּרִין וְקוֹרִין. מְבִיאִין וְלֹא קוֹרִין. וְיֵשׁ שֶׁאֵינָן מְבִיאִין. אֵלּוּ שֶׁאֵינָן מְבִיאִין הַנּוֹטֵעַ בְּתוֹךְ שֶׁלּוֹ וְהִבְרִיךְ בְּתוֹךְ שֶׁל יָחִיד אוֹ בְּתוֹךְ שֶׁלָּרַבִּים. וְכֵן הַמַּבְרִיךְ מִתּוֹךְ שֶׁלְּיָחִיד אוֹ מִתּוֹךְ שֶׁלָּרַבִּים לְתוֹךְ שֶׁלּוֹ. הַנּוֹטֵעַ בְּתוֹךְ שֶׁלּוֹ וְהִבְרִיךְ בְּתוֹךְ שֶׁלּוֹ וְדֶרֶךְ הַיָּחִיד וְדֶרֶךְ הָרַבִּים בָּאֶמְצַע הֲרֵי זֶה אֵינוֹ מֵבִיא. רַבִּי יְהוּדָה אוֹמֵר מֵבִיא.

Mishnah 1: Some people bring First Fruits and make the declaration[1], some bring and do not make the declaration, and some do not bring. The following do not bring[2]: He who plants in his own but provines[3] into a private or a public plot; and so he who provines from a private or a public plot into his own. If someone plants in his own and provines into his own but a private or public road is in the middle he cannot bring; Rebbi Jehudah says he brings.

1 The thanksgiving declaration *Deut*. 26:5-10. It is forbidden to bring profane food into the Temple. If there is no obligation to bring First Fruits then there is a prohibition to bring. If there is an obligation, a dedication must sanctify the First Fruits as Temple offerings.

2 The reason is explained in Mishnah 2.

3 He bends a branch of a vine down into the earth and has it reappear elsewhere; cf. *Kilaim* 7:1, Note 1.

הלכה א: יֵשׁ מְבִיאִין בִּיכּוּרִין וְקוֹרִין כול׳. הַנּוֹטֵעַ בְּתוֹךְ שֶׁלּוֹ וְהִבְרִיךְ בְּתוֹךְ שֶׁלְּיָחִיד אוֹ לְתוֹךְ שֶׁלָּרַבִּים אֲפִילוּ מִן הַזְּקֵינָה אֵינוֹ מֵבִיא. הַמַּבְרִיךְ מִתּוֹךְ

שֶׁלְיָחִיד אוֹ מִתּוֹךְ שֶׁלְרַבִּים לְתוֹךְ שֶׁלּוֹ אֲפִילוּ מִן הַיַּלְדָּה אֵינוֹ מֵבִיא. הָדָא אָמְרָה כְּשֵׁם שֶׁיַּלְדָּה חָיָה מִן הַזְּקֵינָה כָּךְ הַזְּקֵינָה חָיָה מִן הַיַּלְדָּה.

Halakhah 1: "Some people bring First Fruits and make the declaration," etc. He who plants in his own but provines into a private or a public plot cannot bring even from the old tree[4]; he who provines from a private or a public plot into his own cannot bring even from the new tree. That means that just as the new lives off the old[5], so the old lives off the new.

4 The original one growing on his own property.

5 While the buried branch will grow new roots, as long as a connection exists between the original vine and its offshoot, the internal flow of sap cannot be controlled. Since First Fruits have to be brought "from your land" (*Deut*. 26:2), any roots of the tree have to be on the farmer's own property.

אָמַר רִבִּי יוֹחָנָן כּוּלְּהוֹן מִשּׁוּם תּוֹרַת הַגּוֹזְלָן יָרְדוּ לָהֶן. אָמַר רִבִּי יוֹסֵי מַתְנִיתָא אָמְרָה כֵן. מֵאֵי זֶה טַעַם אֵינוֹ מֵבִיא מִשּׁוּם שֶׁנֶּאֱמַר רֵאשִׁית בִּכּוּרֵי אַדְמָתְךָ.

Rebbi Joḥanan said, in all cases they judged by the rules of robbers. Rebbi Yose said, that is what the Mishnah[6] means: "Why can he not bring? Because it was said (*Deut*. 26:2): 'the beginning of the First Fruits of *your* land.'"

6 Mishnah 1:2.

תַּנֵּי אִם הִבְרִיךְ בִּרְשׁוּת מֵבִיא וְקוֹרֵא. רִבִּי יוֹסֵי בְּשֵׁם רִבִּי אִימִּי וְהוּא שֶׁנָּתַן לוֹ רְשׁוּת לְעוֹלָם. הָא לְשָׁעָה לֹא. רִבִּי יוֹנָה בְּשֵׁם רִבִּי אִימִּי אֲפִילוּ לְשָׁעָה. חֵיילֵיהּ דְּרִבִּי יוֹנָה מִן הָדָא. הָיָה חוֹפֵר בּוֹר וְשִׁיחַ וּמְעָרָה קוֹצֵץ וְיוֹרֵד וְהָעֵצִים שֶׁלּוֹ. וְעֵצִים לֹא לְשָׁעָה הֵן. מַה עָבַד לָהּ רִבִּי יוֹסֵי. שָׁרָשִׁים שֶׁדַּרְכָּן לְהַחֲלִיף לְעוֹלָם. מִכֵּיוָן שֶׁדַּרְכָּן לְהַחֲלִיף לְעוֹלָם הֵן. אָמַר רִבִּי מָנָה מִילְתֵיהּ דְּרִבִּי יוֹחָנָן מְסַיֵּיעַ

לְאַבָּא. דְּאָמַר רִבִּי יוֹחָנָן כּוּלְּהֹן מִשּׁוּם תּוֹרַת הַגּוֹזְלָן יָרְדוּ לָהֶן. וְכָאן מִכֵּיוָן שֶׁנָּתַן לוֹ רְשׁוּת לְהַבְרִיךְ אֲפִילוּ לְשָׁעָה אֵין זֶה גוֹזְלָן.

It was stated: If he provined with permission[7], he brings and makes the declaration. Rebbi Yose in the name of Rebbi Ammi: Only if the permission was permanent, not temporary. Rebbi Jonah in the name of Rebbi Ammi: Even temporary. The force of Rebbi Jonah comes from the following[8]: "If somebody digs a cistern, a ditch, or a cave, he may cut down as he works and the wood is his." Is the wood not as if temporary? What does Rebbi Yose do with this? Roots always regrow; since roots do regrow it is as if permanent. Rebbi Mana said, the statement of Rebbi Joḥanan supports my father[9], as Rebbi Joḥanan said in all cases they judged by the rules of robbers. In our case, if he gave permission to provine even temporarily, the proviner is not a robber[10].

7 Of the owner of the lot on which the original vine stood or into which the new vine is drawn.

8 Mishnah *Baba Batra* 2:12. If somebody digs a cistern on his own property and in digging he comes upon roots from a neighbor's tree, he may cut off these roots and keep the wood of the roots. In the Yerushalmi, *Baba Batra* 2:12, R. Assi in the name of R. Joḥanan holds that (invisible) roots do not influence the rules of First Fruits.

9 R. Jonah.

10 First fruits can always be brought if the farmer does not make illegitimate use of public or other people's private property.

רִבִּי זְרִיקָן בָּעָא קוֹמֵי רִבִּי זְעִירָה. מַתְנִיתָא דְּרִבִּי. דְּרִבִּי אָמַר שָׁרָשִׁין חָיִין זֶה מִזֶּה. אָמַר לֵיהּ דִּבְרֵי הַכֹּל הִיא. הָכָא הַתּוֹרָה אָמְרָה רֵאשִׁית (fol. 63d) בִּכּוּרֵי אַדְמָתְךָ עַד שֶׁיְּהוּ כָּל־הַגִּידּוּלִים מֵאַדְמָתְךָ.

Rebbi Zeriqan asked before Rebbi Zeïra: Is the Mishnah Rebbi's since Rebbi said, all roots live off one another[11]? He said to him, it is everybody's opinion. Here, the Torah said (*Deut.* 26:2): "the beginning of the First Fruits of *your* land," that all growth be from *your* land.

11 'Orlah 1:1, Note 39.

עַל דַּעְתֵּיהּ דְּרִבִּי יוּדָה מַה בֵּין הַנּוֹטֵעַ לְתוֹךְ שֶׁלּוֹ וְהִבְרִיךְ לְתוֹךְ שֶׁל יָחִיד. מַה בֵּין הַנּוֹטֵעַ לְתוֹךְ שֶׁלּוֹ וְהִבְרִיךְ לְתוֹךְ שֶׁלּוֹ וְדֶרֶךְ הַיָּחִיד בְּאֶמְצַע. רִבִּי אָחָא בְשֵׁם רִבִּי מִייָשָׁא. בְּשֶׁהִבְרִיכָהּ בִּדְלַעַת אוֹ בְסִילוֹן. אִי בְּשֶׁהִבְרִיכָהּ בִּדְלַעַת אוֹ בְסִילוֹן יָבִיא וְיִקְרָא. אֲפִילוּ כְרַבָּנִין יָבִיא וְיִקְרָא. אָמַר רִבִּי יוֹנָה צְרִיכָה לְרִבִּי יוּדָה. הַמּוֹכֵר שְׁבִיל לַחֲבֵירוֹ מְקוֹם דְּרִיסָה הוּא מָכַר אוֹ עַד הַתְּהוֹם מָכַר. אִין תֵּימַר מְקוֹם דְּרִיסָה מָכַר מֵבִיא וְקוֹרֵא. אִין תֵּימַר עַד הַתְּהוֹם מָכַר. לֹא יָבִיא כָל־עִיקָּר. מִסָּפֵק מֵבִיא וְאֵינוֹ קוֹרֵא. רַבָּנִין פְּשִׁיטָא לוֹן שֶׁמָּכַר עַד הַתְּהוֹם. מָה פְלִיגִין. בְּמוֹכֵר שְׁבִיל לַחֲבֵירוֹ. אֲבָל אִם מָכַר לוֹ שָׂדֶה וְשִׁייֵר לוֹ שְׁבִיל. כָּל־עַמָּא מוֹדֵיי שֶׁשִּׁייֵר לוֹ עַד הַתְּהוֹם.

In the opinion of Rebbi Jehudah, what is the difference between him who plants on his own property and provines into a private person's and him who plants on his own and provines into his own and a private road is in between[12]? Rebbi Aḥa in the name of Rebbi Miasha, when he provined through a gourd or a pipe[13]. If he provined through a gourd or a pipe he should bring and make the declaration! Even according to the rabbis he should bring and make the declaration[14]! Rebbi Jonah said, Rebbi Jehudah had a problem. If somebody sells a path to another person[15], does he sell him the place where the foot treads or does he sell him down to the abyss? If you say, he sold the place where the foot treads, he brings and makes the declaration. If you say, he sold down to the abyss, he should not bring at all. Because of the doubt he brings but does not make the declaration[16]. For the rabbis it is obvious that he sold down to the abyss.

Where do they differ? When he sells a path to another person. But if he sold him a field and reserved a path for himself, everybody agrees that he reserved for himself down to the abyss[17].

12 In the first case, R. Jehudah agrees that he cannot bring First Fruits but in the second case he permits bringing.

13 He tunnels under the ground which is not his and shields the branch there either by a clay or metal pipe or by threading it through a pumpkin serving as a pipe. Since no roots can grow there, he does not steal from the owner of the path and is not disqualified as a robber.

14 R. Aḥa's solution is rejected.

15 But he retains ownership of the fields on both sides of the path.

16 Since R. Jehudah mentions only bringing but not making the declaration.

17 If he extends branches under the path, it is still in his property.

עַל דַּעְתֵּיהּ דְּרִבִּי יוּדָה מַה בֵּין הַנּוֹטֵעַ לְתוֹךְ שֶׁלּוֹ וְהִבְרִיךְ לְתוֹךְ שֶׁלְּרַבִּים. מַה בֵּין הַנּוֹטֵעַ לְתוֹךְ שֶׁלּוֹ וְהִבְרִיךְ לְתוֹךְ שֶׁלּוֹ וְדֶרֶךְ הָרַבִּים בְּאֶמְצַע. אָמַר רִבִּי אִימִּי אַתְיָיא דְּרִבִּי יוּדָה כְּרִבִּי לִיעֶזֶר. דְּתַנִּינָן תַּמָּן אֵין עוֹשִׂין חָלָל תַּחַת רְשׁוּת הָרַבִּים בּוֹרוֹת שִׁיחִין וּמְעָרוֹת. רִבִּי לִיעֶזֶר מַתִּיר כְּדֵי שֶׁתְּהֵא עֲגָלָה מְהַלֶּכֶת וּטְעוּנָה אֲבָנִים. כְּמָה דְרִבִּי לִיעֶזֶר אָמַר תַּמָּן תַּחַת רְשׁוּת הָרַבִּים שֶׁלּוֹ. כָּךְ רִבִּי יוּדָה אָמַר הָכָא תַּחַת רְשׁוּת הָרַבִּים שֶׁלּוֹ. רִבִּי שְׁמוּאֵל בַּר רַב יִצְחָק בָּעֵי. אִין כְּרִבִּי לִיעֶזֶר יָבִיא וְיִקְרָא. אָמַר רִבִּי יוֹסֵי מִיסְבַּר סָבַר רִבִּי שְׁמוּאֵל בַּר רַב יִצְחָק שֶׁרִבִּי לִיעֶזֶר מַתִּיר לַעֲשׂוֹת כֵּן וְהֵן שֶׁלּוֹ לְעוֹלָם. אֶלָּא רִבִּי לִיעֶזֶר מַתִּיר לַעֲשׂוֹת כֵּן וְכָל־הַקּוֹדֵם בָּהֶן זָכָה.

In the opinion of Rebbi Jehudah, what is the difference between him who plants on his own property and provines into the public domain and him who plants on his own and provines into his own and a public road is in between? Rebbi Ammi said, Rebbi Jehudah holds with Rebbi Eliezer[18], as we have stated there[19]: "One may not make a cavity under the public domain, cisterns, ditches, or caverns. Rebbi Eliezer permits it if a truck loaded with stones can pass over it." As Rebbi Eliezer said there, under the public domain, it is his, so Rebbi Jehudah said here, under the public domain, it is his. Rebbi Samuel ben Rav Isaac asked, if it follows Rebbi Eliezer, he should bring and make the declaration. Rebbi Yose said, Rebbi Samuel ben Rav Isaac thought that Rebbi Eliezer permits to do that and it remains his permanent property, but Rebbi Eliezer permits to do that but anybody quick to acquire does acquire it[20].

18 The teacher of his father R. Ilaï.

19 Mishnah *Baba Batra* 3:12.

20 A cavity under the public domain cannot be appropriated for the exclusive use of a private person. Therefore, it may be legal to provine under the public domain but the provined plant is not exclusively in the vintner's domain. The statement of R. Eliezer is not discussed in Yerushalmi *Baba Batra*. The Babli (*Baba Batra* 60a) holds that the anonymous Tanna would agree with R. Eliezer if the safety of the road could be guaranteed for all times without maintenance. This cannot be the opinion of the Yerushalmi.

(fol. 63c) **משנה ב**: מֵאֵי זֶה טַעַם אֵינוֹ מֵבִיא. מִשּׁוּם שֶׁנֶּאֱמַר רֵאשִׁית בִּכּוּרֵי אַדְמָתְךָ תָּבִיא עַד שֶׁיְּהוּ כָל־הַגִּידּוּלִים מֵאַדְמָתְךָ. הָאֲרִיסִין וְהֶחָכוֹרוֹת וְהַסִּיקָרִיקוֹן וְהַגַּזְלָן אֵין מְבִיאִין מֵאוֹתוֹ הַטַּעַם מִשּׁוּם שֶׁנֶּאֱמַר רֵאשִׁית בִּיכּוּרֵי אַדְמָתְךָ.

Mishnah 2: Why can he not bring? Because it was said (*Deut*. 26:2): "You shall bring the beginning of the First Fruits of *your* land," that all the growth should be from your land. For the same reason sharecroppers, tenant farmers, *sicarii*[21], and robbers cannot bring, since it is said: "The beginning of the First Fruits of *your* land."

21 Knife-wielding robbers who take deeds of property as ransom for the lives of the property owners. The *sicarii* mentioned in this Mishnah obviously are Jews; in Mishnah *Giṭṭin* 5:6 the *sicarii* are Gentiles.

(fol. 63d) **הלכה ב:** עַד כְּדוֹן בְּשֶׁגָּזַל קַרְקַע. גָּזַל זְמוֹרָה וּנְטָעָהּ וְלֹא דָמִים הוּא חַיָּיב לוֹ. אֶלָּא צְרִיכָא לְרַבָּנִין. מִצְווֹת כִּגְבוֹהַּ הֵן אוֹ אֵינָן כִּגְבוֹהַּ. הִין תֵּימַר כִּגְבוֹהַּ הֵן אֵינוֹ מֵבִיא. וְאִין תֵּימַר אֵינוֹ כִגְבוֹהַּ מֵבִיא. הַכֹּל מוֹדִין בָּאֲשֵׁירָה שֶׁבִּיטְּלָהּ שֶׁאֵינוֹ מֵבִיא מִמֶּנָּה גֵיזִירִין לְמַעֲרָכָה. רִבִּי שִׁמְעוֹן בֶּן לָקִישׁ בָּעֵי. מָהוּ שֶׁיָּבִיא מִמֶּנָּה לוּלָב. מִצְוֹת כִּגְבוֹהַּ הֵן אוֹ אֵינָן כִּגְבוֹהַּ. אִין תֵּימַר כִּגְבוֹהַּ הֵן אֵינוֹ מֵבִיא. אִין תֵּימַר אֵינוֹ כִּגְבוֹהַּ מֵבִיא. פְּשִׁיטָה שֶׁהוּא מֵבִיא מִמֶּנָּה לוּלָב שֶׁאֵין מִצְווֹת כִּגְבוֹהַּ. מָהוּ שֶׁיָּבִיא בִּיכּוּרִים. כְּרִבִּי יוּדָה דוּ אָמַר הוּקְשׁוּ לְקָדְשֵׁי הַגְּבוּל מֵבִיא. כְּרַבָּנִין דְּאִינּוּן מָרִין הוּקְשׁוּ לְקָדְשֵׁי מִקְדָּשׁ אֵינוֹ מֵבִיא.

Halakhah 2: So far if he robbed the real estate. If he robbed a vine and planted it, does he not owe money[22]? But the rabbis have a problem: do commandments follow the rules of Temple sacrifices[23] or not? If you say they are like Temple sacrifices he may not bring[24]; if you say they are not like Temple sacrifices he may bring. Everybody agrees that from a worshipped tree which was damaged[25] one cannot bring logs for the altar fire. Rebbi Simeon ben Laqish asked, may he take a *lulav*[26] from it? Do commandments follow the rules of Temple sacrifices or not? If you say they are like Temple sacrifices he may not take; if you say they are not like Temple sacrifices he may take. It is obvious that he may take a *lulav* from it[27] and commandments are not like Temple sacrifices. May he bring First Fruits? According to Rebbi Jehudah[28] who compares them to country sacred food[29] he may bring; according to the rabbis who compare them to Temple sacrifices he may not bring.

22 If the owners gave up hope to recover the robbed object, the robber becomes the legal owner. The transfer of ownership imposes on the robber the obligation to pay for it. Before giving up hope, the owners could have sued for the return of the stolen object; after they gave up hope but the circumstances changed and made a suit possible, they can only sue for damages. The next paragraph will make clear that this is the situation here.

23 These rules are stricter than those governing other obligations.

24 *Sifra Wayiqra Paršata* 5(2), Babli *Baba Qama* 67b: *Lev.* 1:10, "If *his* sacrifice is from the flock" implies that robbed animals cannot become sacrifices.

25 If one of the prior worshippers of the tree damages it in a manner inadmissible in pagan worship, the tree loses is idolatrous status and becomes profanely usable. But if at any time it was forbidden for the Jewish altar it remains forbidden since in *Neh.* 10:35 the supply of firewood for the altar is called a "sacrifice."

26 The palm frond used on the Holiday of Tabernacles. In the Babli, *Avodah Zarah* 47a, this is R. Simeon ben Laqish's question in the interpretation of Rav Dimi. In his interpretation, the rules of sacrifices require that anything inadmissible at some time is always inadmissible; clearly this is not the case for any non-sacrificial use.

27 The Babli (*Mo'ed Qaṭan* 26b) makes a difference between things used for commandments (such as a *lulav*) and holy things (such as a Torah scroll). Things used for commandments may be discarded after use; holy things which can no longer be used must be buried just as damaged Temple stones must be buried. It is possible that the Yerushalmi agrees with this distinction.

28 The disagreement between R. Jehudah and the Sages is in Mishnah 3:10.

29 Sacred food to be consumed by the Cohen in purity anywhere in the Land, i. e., heave, heave of the tithe, and *ḥallah*.

עַד כְּדוֹן בִּגְזֵילָה שֶׁלֹּא נִתְייָאֲשׁוּ הַבְּעָלִים מִמֶּנָּה. אֲפִילוּ בִגְזֵילָה שֶׁנִּתְייָאֲשׁוּ הַבְּעָלִים מִמֶּנָּה. סָבְרִין אָמְרִין נִישְׁמְעִינָהּ מִן הָדָא הֲרֵי אֵילוּ בִתְרוּמָה וּבְמַעֲשֵׂר מָה שֶׁאֵין כֵּן בְּבִיכּוּרִים. כְּלוּם צְרִיכָה לֹא בִגְזֵילָה שֶׁלֹּא נִתְייָאֲשׁוּ הַבְּעָלִים מִמֶּנָּה. אֲבָל בִּגְזֵילָה שֶׁנִּתְייָאֲשׁוּ הַבְּעָלִים מִמֶּנָּה אֲפִילוּ בִתְרוּמָה לֹא עָשָׂה כְּלוּם. כְּהָדָא דְתַנֵּי הָאוֹנֵס וְהַגַּנָּב וְהַגַּזְלָן. בִּזְמַן שֶׁהַבְּעָלִים מְרַדְּפִין אַחֲרֵיהֶן אֵין תְּרוּמָתָן תְּרוּמָה וְלֹא מַעְשְׂרוֹתָיו מַעֲשֵׂר וְלֹא הֶקְדֵּישָׁן הֶקְדֵּשׁ. אִם אֵין הַבְּעָלִים מְרַדְּפִין אַחֲרֵיהֶן תְּרוּמָתָן תְּרוּמָה וּמַעְשְׂרוֹתָן מַעֲשֵׂר וְהֶקְדֵּישָׁן הֶקְדֵּשׁ. רִבִּי יוֹסֵי בְּשֵׁם רִבִּי יוֹחָנָן. לֹא זֶה תוֹרֵם וְלֹא זֶה תוֹרֵם. רִבִּי אִמִּי בְשֵׁם רִבִּי יוֹחָנָן. אֲפִילוּ הַבְּעָלִין שֶׁתָּֽרְמוּ אֵין תְּרוּמָתָן תְּרוּמָה. אָמַר רִבִּי יוֹסֵי עַד כְּדוֹן אֲנָן קַייָמִין בִּגְזֵילָה שֶׁלֹּא נִתְייָאֲשׁוּ הַבְּעָלִים מִמֶּנָּה. וּלְייֵדָא מִי לָא אֲנָן תַּנִּינָן הֲרֵי אֵילוּ בִתְרוּמָה וּמַעֲשֵׂר מַה שֶּׁאֵין כֵּן בְּבִיכּוּרִין. אֶיפְשָׁר לַפֵּירוֹת לָצֵאת בְּלֹא בִכּוּרִין. אֵיפְשָׁר לַפֵּירוֹת לָצֵאת בְּלֹא תְרוּמָה וּמַעְשְׂרוֹת. אֲבָל בִּגְזֵילָה שֶׁנִּתְייָאֲשׁוּ הַבְּעָלִים מִמֶּנָּה עַד כְּדוֹן צְרִיכָה.

So far about a robbery when the owners did not give up hope[30]. Even about a robbery when the owners did give up hope? They thought to say that we can hear it from the following[31]: "This applies to heave and tithe but not to First Fruits." For what is this needed? Not for a robbery when the owners did not give up hope, but for a robbery when the owners did give up hope[32]? Even for heave he did not do anything, as we stated[33]: "A strongman[34], a thief, or a robber, as long as the owners pursue them, their heave is no heave, his tithes no tithes, and their dedications no dedications. If the owners do not pursue them, their heave is heave, their tithes are tithes, and their dedications dedications." Rebbi Yose in the name of Rebbi Joḥanan: Neither of them can give heave[35]. Rebbi Ammi in the name of Rebbi Joḥanan: Even if the owners declare heave, it is no heave. Rebbi Yose said, so far we deal with a robbery when the owners did not give up hope. Then why did we state: "This applies to heave and tithe but not to First Fruits"? It is possible for fruits to be usable without First Fruits. It is impossible for fruits to be usable without heave and tithes[36]! But a robbery when the owners did give up hope remains a question[37].

30 The hope to recover the real estate taken from them.

31 Mishnah 2:2, which states among other rules that heave applies to sharecroppers, tenant farmers, buyers of expropriated property, and robbers.

32 Most commentators want to switch the two cases, against all ms. evidence, misreading the rhetorical quality of the multiple negations.

33 A similar text in Tosephta *Terumot* 1:6 and Babli *Baba Qama* 67a, 114a/b.

34 His quality is not defined; he might be anything from a kidnapper to a corrupt politician.

35 As the Babli explains, the robber cannot give because it is not his and the owners cannot give because it is not in their possession.

36 The Mishnah does not state that Jewish robbers, etc., have to give heave but that the rules of heave and tithes apply to them. Since they cannot give heave, they never can eat the produce of the land they robbed. On the other hand, produce may be eaten of a crop from which First Fruits were not given.

37 Whether First Fruits may be brought from this land.

(fol. 63c) **משנה ג**: אֵין מְבִיאִין בִּיכּוּרִים חוּץ מִשִּׁבְעַת הַמִּינִים. לֹא מִתְּמָרִים שֶׁבֶּהָרִים וְלֹא מִפֵּירוֹת שֶׁבָּעֲמָקִים וְלֹא מִזֵּיתֵי שֶׁמֶן שֶׁאֵינָן מִן הַמּוּבְחָר. אֵין מְבִיאִין בִּיכּוּרִים קוֹדֶם לָעֲצֶרֶת. אַנְשֵׁי הַר צְבוֹעִים הֵבִיאוּ בִּיכּוּרֵיהֶן קוֹדֶם לָעֲצֶרֶת וְלֹא קִיבְּלוּ מֵהֶן מִפְּנֵי הַכָּתוּב שֶׁבַּתּוֹרָה וְחַג הַקָּצִיר בִּיכּוּרֵי מַעֲשֶׂיךָ אֲשֶׁר תִּזְרַע בַּשָּׂדֶה.

Mishnah 3: One does not bring First Fruits except from the Seven Kinds[38], nor from mountain dates, nor from valley fruits[39], nor from oil olives which are not best quality. One may not bring First Fruits before Pentecost. [40]The people from Hyena Mountain brought their First Fruits before Pentecost but they did not accept from them because of the verse in the Torah: (Ex. 23:16) "The pilgrimage holiday of harvest, the First Fruits of your work from sowing the field."

38 The fruits enumerated in *Deut.* 8:8; cf. *Berakhot* 6, Notes 15, 151.

39 Grapes, figs, pomegranates and olives. These grow better in the hills; dates grow best in the Jordan valley. The requirement of "best quality" applies to all First Fruits.

40 The remainder of the Mishnah is also Mishnah *Ḥallah* 4:11; Notes 172,173.

(fol. 63d) **הלכה ג**: אֵין מְבִיאִין בִּיכּוּרִים כול'. אִלּוּ כְּתִיב וְלָקַחְתָּ רֵאשִׁית כָּל־פְּרִי אַדְמָתְךָ הָיִיתִי אוֹמֵר כָּל־הַדְּבָרִים יְהוּ חַייָבִין בְּבִיכּוּרִין. תַּלְמוּד לוֹמַר מֵרֵאשִׁית וְלֹא כָל־רֵאשִׁית. אִם מֵרֵאשִׁית וְלֹא כָל־רֵאשִׁית אֵין לָךְ אֶלָּא חִטִּים וּשְׂעוֹרִים בִּלְבַד. תַּלְמוּד לוֹמַר פְּרִי אַדְמָתְךָ רִיבָּה. וְרִיבָּה אֶת הַכֹּל. נֶאֱמַר כָּאן אַרְצְךָ וְנֶאֱמַר כָּאן אֶרֶץ חִיטָּה וּשְׂעוֹרָה. מָה אֶרֶץ שֶׁנֶּאֱמַר לְהַלָּן בְּשִׁבְעַת הַמִּינִין הַכָּתוּב מְדַבֵּר אַף אֶרֶץ שֶׁנֶּאֱמַר כָּאן בְּשִׁבְעַת הַמִּינִין הַכָּתוּב מְדַבֵּר.

[41]"One does not bring First Fruits", etc. If it were written (*Deut.* 26:2): "You shall take the First Fruits of your land", I would have said that all kinds should be obligated for First Fruits. The verse says,"*from*[42] the First Fruits", not all firsts. If "from the first" and not all first, then you have only wheat and barley. The verse says "fruits of your land"; this is inclusive. Does it include everything? Here[43] "your land" has been said; at another place[44] "the Land of wheat and barley" has been said. Since "land" mentioned there deals with the Seven Kinds, so also "land" mentioned in this verse must deal with the Seven Kinds.

41 A similar text in *Sifra Deut.* 197(2), a third version in Babli *Menaḥot* 84b.

42 As always, prefix מ is read as partitive.

43 *Deut.* 26:2.

44 *Deut.* 8:8.

זֵית שֶׁמֶן זֶה אָגוּרִי. רִבִּי אִמִּי בְשֵׁם רִבִּי יוֹחָנָן זֶה אַוְורוֹסִי. וְלָמָּה נִקְרָא שְׁמוֹ אָגוּרִי. שֶׁהוּא אוֹגֵר שַׁמְנוֹ לְתוֹכוֹ וְכָל־הַזֵּיתִים מְאַבְּדִין שַׁמְנָן. אָמַר רִבִּי חֲנִינָה כָּל־הַזֵּתִים הַגְּשָׁמִים יוֹרְדִין עֲלֵיהֶן וְהֵן פּוֹלְטִין אֶת שַׁמְנָן וְזֶה הַגְּשָׁמִים יוֹרְדִין עָלָיו וְהוּא אוֹגֵר שַׁמְנוֹ לְתוֹכוֹ.

[45]"Oil olives" that is *agory*[46]. Rebbi Ammi in the name of Rebbi Joḥanan, that is the Avaritic[47]. Why is it called *agory*? Because it stores its oil inside. Do all other olives lose their oil? Rebbi Ḥanina said, all other olives will leach their oil if rains fall on them but this one stores its oil inside.

45 This paragraph and the following explain expressions used in *Deut.* 8:8.

46 In the Gaonic commentary to *Kelim* 17:8, the reading is איגורי. The kind of olive, the main example of a mid-sized olive, is called after a place Egor as the suffix -*y* shows. The etymology, in the name of R. Abbahu, is also in Babli *Berakhot* 39a.

47 Apparently after an Egyptian city Avaris, mentioned by Manetho. In Babli *Berakhot*, the readings are אברוטי, סמדוסי, סברוסי, סמרוסי, אברוסי. Cf. I. Löw in Krauss *Lehnwörter* p. 7; S. Liebermann, *Tosefta ki-Fshutah* p. 332.

וּדְבַשׁ. אֵילוּ הַתְּמָרִים. רִבִּי תַנְחוּמָה בְשֵׁם רִבִּי יִצְחָק בְּרִבִּי לָעְזָר. כְּתִיב וְכִפְרֹץ הַדָּבָר הִרְבּוּ בְנֵי יִשְׂרָאֵל רֵאשִׁית דָּגָן תִּירוֹשׁ וְיִצְהָר וּדְבַשׁ. וּדְבַשׁ חַייָב בְּמַעְשְׂרוֹת. אֶלָּא אֵילוּ הַתְּמָרִים שֶׁהֵן חַייָבִין בְּמַעְשְׂרוֹת.

"And honey". This refers to dates. Rebbi Tanḥuma in the name of Rebbi Isaac ben Rebbi Eleazar: It is written (*2Chr.* 31:5) "When the thing expanded, the Children of Israel did increase the first gifts[48] of grain, cider, oil, and honey." Is honey subject to tithes? But this refers to dates which are subject to tithes[49].

48 Heave and tithes.

49 Date syrup. This argument would extend the biblical duty of tithes from grain, wine, and oil to all Seven Kinds.

רִבִּי בֶּרֶכְיָה בְּשֵׁם רִבִּי שְׁמוּאֵל בַּר נַחְמָן וְלָמָּה כְּתִיב אֶרֶץ אֶרֶץ שְׁנֵי פְעָמִים. לְהוֹדִיעֲךָ שֶׁאֵין הַבַּיִת עוֹמֵד אֶלָּא עַל שְׁנֵי דְבָרִים הַלָּלוּ. וְלָמָּה נִכְלְלוּ. רִבִּי יְהוּדָה בֶּרִבִּי וְרִבִּי שְׁמוּאֵל בַּר נַחְמָן. חַד אָמַר לִבְרָכָה. וְחָרָנָה אָמַר לְשִׁיעוּרִין. מָאן דָּמַר לִבְרָכָה נִיחָא. מָאן דָּמַר לְשִׁיעוּרִין וְהָתַנִּינָן בַּהֶרֶת כִּגְרִיס לֵית הִיא מֵימָן. כַּעֲדַשָּׁה מִן הַשֶּׁרֶץ. לֵית הִיא מֵימָן.

Rebbi Berekhiah in the name of Rebbi Samuel bar Naḥman: Why is "Land, Land" written twice[50]? To tell you that a house stands only on these two things[51]. Why are [the others] included? Rebbi Jehuda ben Rebbi and Rebbi Samuel ben Naḥman, one says for benedictions[52], the other says for measures[53]. He who says for benedictions is understandable. He who says for measures, did we not state: "A shiny mark the size of half a bean[54]"? That is not reliable[55]. "The size of a lentil from a crawling thing"[56]? That is not reliable[57].

50 *Deut.* 8:8: A *Land* of wheat and barley, and vine, and fig tree, and pomegranate, a *Land* of the oil-olive and honey.

51 The necessities of life are wheat and olive oil.

52 Explained *Berakhot* 6:4, Notes 150-151, where this opinion is labelled "Babylonian".

53 In the Babli, *Eruvin* 4a/b, *Sukkah* 5b, this is reported in the name of the Babylonian Rav Ḥanin. The seven measures are: 1. A person entering a leprous house is severely

impure only if he remains long enough that he could have eaten a slice of wheat bread (*Lev.* 14:47). 2. A fragment of a human bone the size of a barley corn imparts impurity. 3. A quarter *log* of wine drunk by a *nazir* makes him subject to punishment. As a derivative, a quarter *log* of wine is the minimum for legal obligations. 4. Somebody carrying food in the volume of a dried fig from private to public domain on the Sabbath is guilty of desecrating the Sabbath. 5. A vessel having a pomegranate-sized hole is unusable and freed from the impurity of vessels. 6. The volume of an olive is the standard for most rules involving solid food. 7. Eating food in the volume of a dried date on the Day of Atonement is a desecration of the day.

54 *Lev.* 13:1-8, Mishnah *Nega'im* 6:1.. A smaller lesion does not make impure.

55 The size of the lesion does not mean anything in itself. Even if the lesion is larger, if it does not grow after being seen by the Cohen it does not make impure. If it is smaller but seen by the Cohen and then spreads, there is impurity. (Explanation of *Pene Moshe*). Another interpretation would be that this and the next measure are not standardized.

56 Mishnah *Kelim* 17:6. A fragment of a dead crawling animal (*Lev.* 11:29-31) in the size of a lentil makes impure.

57 An integral limb makes impure even if it is smaller than a lentil.

פְּשִׁיטָא הָדָא מִילְתָא. הִפְרִישׁ בִּיכּוּרִין חוּץ מִשִּׁבְעַת הַמִּינִין לֹא קָדְשׁוּ. מָה פְלִיגִין. בַּתְּמָרִים שֶׁבֶּהָרִים וּבְפֵירוֹת שֶׁבָּעֲמָקִים. רִבִּי זְעִירָא רִבִּי יָסָא בְשֵׁם רִבִּי לָעְזָר לֹא קָדְשָׁה. רִבִּי אִילָא בְשֵׁם רִבִּי אִמִּי אִיתְפַּלְגוּן רִבִּי יוֹחָנָן וְרִבִּי שִׁמְעוֹן בֶּן לָקִישׁ. רִבִּי יוֹחָנָן אָמַר לֹא קָדְשׁוּ. רִבִּי שִׁמְעוֹן בֶּן לָקִישׁ אָמַר קָדְשׁוּ. אָמַר רִבִּי יוֹנָה טַעֲמָא דְּרִבִּי שִׁמְעוֹן בֶּן לָקִישׁ. שֶׁכֵּן אִם עָבַר וְתָרַם מִן הָרַע עַל הַיָּפֶה תְּרוּמָתוֹ תְרוּמָה. אָמַר רִבִּי יוֹסֵי שֶׁמַּעְנָן פֵּירוֹת הָרָעִים חַייָבִין בְּמַעְשְׂרוֹת. שְׁמַעְנָן פֵּירוֹת הָרָעִים חַייָבִין בְּבִיכּוּרִים. מַתְנִיתָא מְסַייְעָה לְרִבִּי יוֹסֵי. אֵין מְבִיאִין מִן הַצִּיפּוֹרְנִן וּמִן הַבֵּישָׁנִין וְאִם הֵבִיא לֹא קָדְשׁוּ. אָמַר רִבִּי זְעִירָא וְתַנֵּיי תַּמָּן תְּאֵנִים סוֹכוֹת מְנוּקָּבוֹת עֲנָבִים מְאוּבָּקוֹת[58] וּמְעוּשָּׁנוֹת אֵין מְבִיאִין.

אֲבָל מְבִיאִין מִן הַתְּאֵנִים בְּנוֹת שֶׁבַע וּמִן הָעֲנָבִים הַלַּבְלוֹנִיּוֹת. מִן הַמּוּבְחָר הֵן. וְתֵימַר אֲבָל אָמַר רִבִּי אַבָּמָרִי שֶׁלֹּא תֹאמַר הוֹאִיל וְהֵן בַּסּוֹף לֹא יָבִיא.

The following is obvious: If somebody dedicated First Fruits not from the Seven Kinds it was not sanctified[1]. Where is there a disagreement? About mountain dates and valley fruits. Rebbi Zeïra, Rebbi Assi in the name of Rebbi Eleazar: They were not sanctified. Rebbi Hila in the name of Rebbi Immi: Rebbi Joḥanan and Rebbi Simeon ben Laqish disagree. Rebbi Joḥanan said they were not sanctified, Rebbi Simeon ben Laqish said they were sanctified. Rebbi Jonah said, the reason of Rebbi Simeon ben Laqish is that if somebody transgressed and gave heave from bad for good produce, his heave is heave[59]. Rebbi Yose said, we have heard that bad produce is subject to tithes; did we hear that bad produce is subject to First Fruits?[60] A *baraita* supports Rebbi Yose: "One does not bring [fruits] from Sepphoris[61] and Bet Shean[62], and if he brought they are not sanctified." Rebbi Zeïra said, but there it is stated: "Figs pierced on the branch and grapes dusted and smoked[63] one does not bring. But one brings *bat šeba* figs[64] and white grapes." The latter are highest quality. What can you say? But Rebbi Abba Mari said, one should not say that one should not bring these because they are late[65].

58 This is translated as if it were מְאוּבָּקוֹת, see Note 63.

59 Mishnah *Terumot* 2:6.

60 The argument of R. Jonah is disproved.

61 On a hilltop.

62 In a deep valley. It is not specified why fruits from these two places are unacceptable as First Fruits.

63 Cf. Mishnah *Ševi'it* 2:2.

64 White figs, cf. *Demay* 1, Note 5. (L. Goldschmidt, in his notes to Levy's dictionary, explains that in Babli *Nedarim* 27a, *bat šeba* figs are a kind different from "white figs". But "white figs" are really green ones, in contrast

to "black" or purple ones.)

64 They ripen later than other figs or grapes.

תַּנֵּי רַבָּן שִׁמְעוֹן בֶּן גַּמְלִיאֵל אוֹמֵר אֵין מְבִיאִין תְּמָרִים אֶלָּא מִירִיחוֹ וְאֵין קוֹרִין אֶלָּא עַל הַכּוֹתָבוֹת. רִבִּי שִׁמְעוֹן בֶּן אֶלְעָזָר אוֹמֵר רִימּוֹנֵי עֲמָקִים מְבִיאִין וְקוֹרִין.

It was stated[65]: Rabban Simeon ben Gamliel says, one brings dates only from Jericho and one makes the declaration only for dry ones[66]. Rebbi Simeon ben Eleazar says, one may bring valley pomegranates and make the declaration[67].

65 Tosephta 1:5.

66 Arabic قتب.

67 He only excludes valley figs.

(fol. 63c) **משנה ד**: אֵלּוּ מְבִיאִין וְלֹא קוֹרִין. הַגֵּר מֵבִיא וְאֵינוֹ קוֹרֵא שֶׁאֵינוֹ יָכוֹל לוֹמַר אֲשֶׁר נִשְׁבַּע יי לַאֲבוֹתֵינוּ לָתֵת לָנוּ. וְאִם הָיְתָה אִמּוֹ מִיִּשְׂרָאֵל מֵבִיא וְקוֹרֵא. וּכְשֶׁהוּא מִתְפַּלֵּל בֵּינוֹ לְבֵין עַצְמוֹ אוֹמֵר אֱלֹהֵי אֲבוֹת יִשְׂרָאֵל. וּכְשֶׁהוּא בְּבֵית הַכְּנֶסֶת אוֹמֵר אֱלֹהֵי אֲבוֹתֵיכֶם. וְאִם הָיְתָה אִמּוֹ מִיִּשְׂרָאֵל אוֹמֵר אֱלֹהֵי אֲבוֹתֵינוּ.

Mishnah 4: [67]The following bring but do not make the declaration. The proselyte brings but does not make the declaration since he cannot say (*Deut*. 26:3): "That the Eternal had sworn to our forefathers to give us." But if his mother was Jewish[68] he brings and makes the declaration. When he prays in private[69], he says "God of the forefathers of Israel." When he is in the synagogue, he says "God of your forefathers." But if his mother was Jewish he says "God of our forefathers."

67 The entire Mishnah is not practice, as explained in the Halakhah.

68 The child of a Jewish mother is automatically Jewish. But since Mishnah *Qiddušin* 3:12 states that "in all cases where marriage is possible and not sinful, the child is classified with the male", the child is still classified as a proselyte.

69 In the first benediction of the *'Amidah* prayer.

(fol. 64a) **הלכה ד**: וְאֵילוּ מְבִיאִין וְלֹא קוֹרִין. רִבִּי יוֹנָה וְרִבִּי יוֹסֵא תְּרֵוֵיהוֹן בְּשֵׁם רִבִּי שְׁמוּאֵל בַּר רַב יִצְחָק בִּבְנֵי קֵינִי חוֹתֵן מֹשֶׁה הִיא מַתְנִיתָא. וּבְנֵי קֵנִי חוֹתֵן מֹשֶׁה מְבִיאִין וְקוֹרִין. דִּכְתִיב לְכָה אִתָּנוּ וְהֵטַבְנוּ לָךְ. רִבִּי חִזְקִיָּה בְּשֵׁם רִבִּי לֶעְזָר לֹא אָמַר כֵּן אֶלָּא מָה טַעַם אָמְרוּ הָאֶפִּיטְרוֹפִּין וְהָעֶבֶד וְהַשָּׁלִיחַ וְהָאִישָּׁה וְטוּמְטוּם וְאַנְדְּרוֹגֵינוֹס מְבִיאִין וְלֹא קוֹרִין. שֶׁהַגֵּר הֲרֵי אָמוּר בַּפָּרָשָׁה. אָמַר רִבִּי שְׁמוּאֵל בַּר רַב יִצְחָק תִּיפְתָּר בְּהָהֵן גֵּר דְּהָכָא בִּבְנֵי קֵינִי חוֹתֵן מֹשֶׁה. וּבְנֵי קֵנִי חוֹתֵן מֹשֶׁה מְבִיאִין וְקוֹרִין.

Halakhah 4[70]: "The following bring but do not make the declaration". Rebbi Jonah and Rebbi Yose, both in the name of Rebbi Samuel bar Rav Isaac: The Mishnah speaks of a proselyte of the descendants of the Qenite, the relative of Moses by marriage, since the descendants of the Qenite, the relative of Moses by marriage, bring and make the declaration, as it is written (*Num.* 10:29): "Go with us and we shall treat you well.[71]" Rebbi Ḥizqiah in the name of Rebbi Eleazar did not say so[72] but: Why did they say[73] "the guardians, the slave, the agent, the woman, the sexless and the hermaphrodite can bring but do not make the declaration," is not the proselyte mentioned here[74]? Rebbi Samuel ben Rav Isaac said, explain it by the proselyte mentioned here[75], by the descendants of the Qenite, the relative of Moses by marriage, since the descendants of the Qenite, the relative of Moses by marriage, bring and make the declaration.

70 The different interpretations of this Halakhah are discussed in *Tosefta ki-Fshutah Zeraïm* pp. 823-825.

71 In Tosephta 1:2: "Rebbi Jehudah said, all proselytes bring but do not make the declaration, except that a Qenite proselyte brings and makes the declaration." This contradicts the opinion given here that a Qenite proselyte can make the declaration only if he is the son of a Jewish mother.

The problem is, why should the proselyte, son of a Jewish mother (Note 68), be able to make the declaration? He would not be able to declare "that the Eternal had sworn to our forefathers to give us" since the Land was distributed to males only. The daughters of Ẓelofḥad could inherit only as sole heirs of their father who was of those counted at the Exodus; the Land was never promised to the females. But since the family of Jithro were invited by Moses to join the Israelites and received part of the Land (*Jud.* 1:16), a Qenite can declare "that the Eternal had sworn to give us" from his father's side and "to our forefathers' from the mother's. {The hypothesis that the Qenites were not considered as Israelites at the conquest is difficult to accept.}

72 They do not disagree with the statement of R. Samuel ben Rav Isaac but with context and meaning. In the first version, only the sentence about the proselyte, son of a Jewish mother, refers to Qenites.

73 Mishnah 5. The first three are not owners, the last three are not male.

74 Since the proselyte cannot say "that the Eternal had sworn to our forefathers to give us" but can make the declaration if his mother is Jewish, why cannot the persons mentioned in Mishnah 5 (with the exception of the slave) make the declaration since presumably they are children of a Jewish mother?

75 Mishnah 5 in its entirety only deals with Qenites. This is difficult to accept since then the Mishnah would have become meaningless with the Babylonian exile.

אָמַר רִבִּי יוֹסֵי קִייְמָהּ בִּנְיָמִין בַּר עַשְׁתּוֹר קוֹמֵי רִבִּי חִייָה בַּר בָּא. בְּגוֹי שֶׁבָּא
בָּעֲבֵירָה עַל בַּת יִשְׂרָאֵל הִיא מַתְנִיתָא. רִבִּי יוֹנָה לֹא אָמַר כֵּן אֶלָּא רִבִּי שָׁמַע

לְאִילֵין דְּבֵי בַּר עַשְׁתּוֹר דְּאִינּוּן גֵּרִים בְּנֵי גֵרִים אוֹמְרִין אֱלֹהֵי אֲבוֹתֵינוּ. וְהָא תַנֵּינָן אִם הָיְתָה אִמּוֹ מִיִּשְׂרָאֵל אוֹמֵר אֱלֹהֵי אֲבוֹתֵינוּ. הָא גֵּרִים בְּנֵי גֵרִים לֹא. אָמַר רִבִּי יוֹסֵי קִיִּימָהּ בִּנְיָמִין בַּר עַשְׁתּוֹר קוֹמֵי רִבִּי חִייָה בַּר בָּא. רִבִּי חִזְקִיָּה בְשֵׁם רִבִּי חִייָה בַּר בָּא קִיִּימָהּ בִּנְיָמִין בַּר עַשְׁתּוֹר קוֹמֵינָן. בְּגוֹי שֶׁבָּא בָעֲבֵירָה עַל בַּת יִשְׂרָאֵל הִיא מַתְנִיתָא.

Rebbi Yose said, Benjamin bar Astor explained it before Rebbi Ḥiyya bar Abba: The Mishnah deals with a Gentile who had forbidden intercourse with a Jewish woman[76]. Rebbi Jonah did not say so, but: Rebbi[77] heard those of the family bar Astor, who were proselytes, children of proselytes[68], say "God of our forefathers." But did we not state: "If his mother was Jewish he says 'God of our forefathers'"? That means, not proselytes children of proselytes! Rebbi Yose said, Benjamin bar Astor explained it before Rebbi Ḥiyya bar Abba. Rebbi Ḥizqiah in the name of Rebbi Ḥiyya bar Abba: Benjamin bar Astor explained it before us: The Mishnah deals with a Gentile who had forbidden intercourse with a Jewish woman.

76 Since the Torah in many places requires that the proselyte and the natural born Jew be equal in rights and duties, the proselyte mentioned here cannot be the child of a proselyte who by converting became a 100% Jew. The solution given is difficult since by Mishnah *Qiddušin* 3:12 the child of an unconverted Gentile and a Jewish mother follows the mother only because there can be no marriage outside the faith in Jewish law. In similar situations, the Babli explains the rules to refer to a child of proselytes whose mother was pregnant when the parents converted. In that case, the child is Jewish but not the child of Jewish parents since at conception the parents were Gentile. E. g., if born on a Sabbath, if such a child is a male he cannot be circumcized on the Sabbath. Since a solution is chosen here which seems to contradict Mishnah *Qiddušin* 3:12, one

might infer that the Yerushalmi determines the status of the baby not by the status of the parents at conception (whose time is impossible to determine exactly) but at birth.

77 It seems that a name has disappeared here.

רִבִּי זְרִיקָן אָמַר רִבִּי זְעוּרָא בָּעֵי. כְּלוּם הוּא מִתְכַּוֵּין לֹא לְאַבְרָהָם לְיִצְחָק וּלְיַעֲקֹב. וְכִי אַבְרָהָם יִצְחָק וְיַעֲקֹב אֲבוֹתֵיהֶם הָיוּ. נִשְׁבַּע הַקָּדוֹשׁ בָּרוּךְ הוּא לֹא לַזְּכָרִים שֶׁמָּא לַנְּקֵיבוֹת.

Rebbi Zeriqan said, Rebbi Zeïra asked: Do they not refer to Abraham, Isaac, and Jacob? Were Abraham, Isaac, and Jacob their forefathers? Did not the Holy One, praise to Him, swear to the males but not to the females[78]?

78 Since the females should not be important in this respect, the Mishnah is unexplainable.

תַּנֵּי בְשֵׁם רִבִּי יְהוּדָה גֵּר עַצְמוֹ מֵבִיא וְקוֹרֵא. מַה טַעֲמָא כִּי אַב הֲמוֹן גּוֹיִם נְתַתִּיךָ. לְשֶׁעָבַר הָיִיתָ אַב לַאֲרָם. וְעַכְשָׁיו מִיכָּן וְהֵילָךְ אַתָּה אַב לְכָל־הַגּוֹיִם. רִבִּי יְהוֹשֻׁעַ בֶּן לֵוִי אָמַר הֲלָכָה כְּרִבִּי יְהוּדָה. אָתָא עוֹבְדָא קוֹמֵי דְרִבִּי אַבָּהוּ וְהוֹרֵי כְּרִבִּי יְהוּדָה.

It was stated in the name of Rebbi Jehudah: The proselyte himself brings and makes the declaration[79]. What is the reason? (*Gen.* 17:5) "For I made you the father of the multitude of Gentiles." In the past you were the father of Aram, from now onwards you will be father of all Gentiles. Rebbi Joshua ben Levi said, practice follows Rebbi Jehudah. A case[80] came before Rebbi Abbahu and he instructed following Rebbi Jehudah.

79 Since this contradicts the statement of R. Jehudah in Tosephta 1:2, it is clear that the Tosephta was not known to the editors of the Yeru

shalmi.

80 About the prayers to be recited by proselytes. Since the Babli does not take up the problem, it agrees that the proselyte everywhere says "God of our forefathers."

(fol. 63c) **משנה ה**: רִבִּי לִיעֶזֶר בֶּן יַעֲקֹב אוֹמֵר אִשָּׁה בַת גֵּרִים לֹא תִינָּשֵׂא לִכְהוּנָּה עַד שֶׁתְּהֵא אִימָּהּ מִיִּשְׂרָאֵל. אֶחָד גֵּרִים וְאֶחָד עֲבָדִים מְשׁוּחְרָרִים וַאֲפִילוּ עַד עֲשָׂרָה דוֹרוֹת עַד שֶׁתְּהֵא אִימָּן מִיִּשְׂרָאֵל. הָאֶפִּיטְרוֹפִּין וְהָעֶבֶד וְהַשָּׁלִיחַ וְהָאִישָּׁה וְטוּמְטוּם וְאַנְדְּרוֹגֵינוֹס מְבִיאִין וְלֹא קוֹרִין שֶׁאֵינָן יְכוֹלִין לוֹמַר אֲשֶׁר נָתַתָּ לִי יי.

Mishnah 5: Rebbi Eliezer ben Jacob says, a woman, daughter of proselytes, should not marry a Cohen unless her mother is from Israel[81]. There is no difference between proselytes and freedmen, even up to ten generations, unless their mothers be from Israel. The guardians[82], the slave[83], the agent[84], the woman[85], the sexless, and the hermaphrodite[86] can bring but not make the declaration, since they cannot say (*Deut.* 26:10): "Which You gave me, Eternal."

80 The dissenting opinions are in Mishnah *Qiddušin* 4:8. The discussion in the Halakhah is repeated in *Qiddušin* 4:6 (fol. 66a).

82 Administrators of orphans' property; Greek ἐπίτροπος.

83 A freed slave owning property.

84 The possibility of agency for the presentation of First Fruits is discussed in Halakhah 6.

85 Who brings First Fruits from her private property.

86 They possibly are female.

(fol. 64a) **הלכה ה**: רִבִּי לִיעֶזֶר בֶּן יַעֲקֹב אוֹמֵר כו׳. תַּמָּן תַּנִּינָן רִבִּי יְהוּדָה אָמַר בַּת גֵּר זָכָר כְּבַת חָלָל זָכָר. וְכוּלְּהוֹן מִקְרָא אֶחָד הֵן דּוֹרְשִׁין. כִּי אִם בְּתוּלוֹת

מִזֶּרַע בֵּית יִשְׂרָאֵל. רִבִּי יְהוּדָה אוֹמֵר עַד שֶׁיְּהֵא אִמּוֹ מִיִּשְׂרָאֵל. רִבִּי אֱלִעֶזֶר אוֹמֵר אוֹ אָבִיהָ אוֹ אִמָּהּ. רִבִּי יוֹסֵי אוֹמֵר עַד שֶׁיִּוָּלְדוּ בִקְדוּשַּׁת יִשְׂרָאֵל. רִבִּי שִׁמְעוֹן אוֹמֵר עַד שֶׁיָּבִיאוּ בְתוּלִים בִּקְדוּשַּׁת יִשְׂרָאֵל. תַּנֵּי בְשֵׁם רִבִּי שִׁמְעוֹן גִּיוֹרֶת פְּחוּתָה מִבַּת שָׁלֹשׁ שָׁנִים וְיוֹם אֶחָד שֶׁנִּתְגַּייְרָה כְּשֵׁירָה לִכְהוּנָּה שֶׁנֶּאֱמַר וְכָל־הַטַּף בַּנָּשִׁים אֲשֶׁר לֹא יָֽדְעוּ מִשְׁכַּב זָכָר הֶחַיּוּ לָכֶם וּפִנְחָס עִמָּהֶן. וְרַבָּנִין הֶחַיּוּ לָכֶם לַעֲבָדִים וְלִשְׁפָחוֹת.

Halakhah 5: "Rebbi Eliezer ben Jacob says," etc. There, we have stated[87]: "Rebbi Jehudah said, the daughter of a male proselyte is like the daughter of a male desecrated one[88]." They all interpret the same verse (*Ez.* 44:22): "Only virgins[89] from the seed of the House of Israel." Rebbi Jehudah says, unless his father be from Israel. Rebbi Eliezer[90] says, either her father or her mother. Rebbi Yose says, unless they are born in the holiness of Israel[91]. Rebbi Simeon says, unless they grow the hymen[92] in the holiness of Israel. It was stated in the name of Rebbi Simeon[93]: "A girl which became a proselyte being less than three years and one day of age is acceptable for the priesthood since it was said (*Num.* 31:18): 'All the female children unfit for sleeping with a male[94] you shall let live for yourselves,' and Phineas was with them." But the rabbis [say], you shall let live as slaves[95] and slave girls for yourselves.

87 Mishnah *Qiddušin* 4:6.

88 The child of a Cohen and a woman forbidden by the rules *Lev.* 21:7 (a prostitute or a divorcee) cannot be married by a Cohen. Desecration is not removable and is inherited by his descendants..

89 Since a widow is forbidden only to the High Priest, the verse describes a woman who was a virgin from the seed of Israel. Since verses in sources other than the Torah cannot be prescriptive, one speaks here about rules the Cohanim accepted over and above the ones spelled out in the Torah.

90 Ben Jacob.

91 Born after the mother became Jewish.

92 It is generally accepted talmudic medical theory that a girl who was raped when she was less than three years of age will regrow her hymen.

93 *Sifry Num.* 157; Babli *Yebamot* 60b, *Qiddušin* 76b, 78a.

94 Being less than three years of age.

95 This word has slipped in as a routine expression.

רִבִּי יָסָה בְשֵׁם רִבִּי יוֹחָנָן. הֲלָכָה כְּרִבִּי יוֹסֵי. וְכוֹהֲנִים נָהֲגוּ סִלְסוּל בְּעַצְמָן כְּרִבִּי אֱלִעֶזֶר בֶּן יַעֲקֹב. חַד כֹּהֵן נְסַב בַּת גֵּרִים. אָתָא עוֹבְדָא קוֹמֵי רִבִּי אַבָּהוּ וְאַרְבְּעֵיהּ עַל סַפְסֵילָא. אָמַר לֵיהּ רַב בֵּיבַי לֹא כֵן אַלְפּוֹן רִבִּי הֲלָכָה כְּרִבִּי יוֹסֵי. אָמַר לֵיהּ וְלֹא כֹהֲנִים נָהֲגוּ סִלְסוּל בְּעַצְמָן כְּרִבִּי אֱלִעֶזֶר. אָמַר לֵיהּ וְעַל מִנְהָג לוֹקִין. אָמַר לֵיהּ אִין כָּךְ אַתְּ חֲמִי מְפַייֵס לִי וַאֲנָא מוֹקִים לֵיהּ. מָה דְקַייְמָא אָמַר לֵיהּ הוֹאִיל וְהוּתְּרָה הָרְצוּעָה אַף אֲנִי מוּתָּר בָּהּ.

Rebbi Assi in the name of Rebbi Joḥanan: Practice follows Rebbi Yose[96] but Cohanim are used to increase their dignity following Rebbi Eliezer ben Jacob. A Cohen married the daughtor of proselytes. The case came before Rebbi Abbahu who let him kneel before the low bench[97]. Rav Bevai said to him, did the Rabbi not teach us that practice follows Rebbi Yose? He answered, but are not Cohanim used to increase their dignity following Rebbi Eliezer ben Jacob? He retorted, does one whip because of what one is used to do[98]? He said to him, if you look at it in such a way, you have appeased me and I shall let him get up. After he got up, he said to him, since the lash was withdrawn I am permitted to have her[99].

96 In the Babli (*Yebamot* 60b): R. Jacob bar Idi said practice follows R. Simeon ben Ioḥai but . . . But the final decision is that practice follows R. Eliezer ben Jacob.

97 Latin *subsellium;* to have him whipped.

98 Since there is no formal pro

hibition.

99 Since the only restriction enforceable in court is R. Yose's.

רִבִּי יַעֲקֹב בַּר אִידִי בְּשֵׁם רִבִּי יְהוֹשֻׁעַ בֶּן לֵוִי[100] מַעֲשֶׂה בְּמִשְׁפָּחָה בְדָרוֹם שֶׁהָיוּ קוֹרִין עָלֶיהָ עִרְעֵר. וְשָׁלַח רִבִּי אֶת רוֹמַינוּס לִבְדָּקָן וּבָדַק וּמָצָא שֶׁנִּתְגַּייְרָה זְקֵנָתָהּ פְּחוּתָה מִבַּת שָׁלֹשׁ שָׁנִים וְיוֹם אֶחָד וְהִכְשִׁירָהּ לִכְהוּנָּה. רַב הוֹשַׁעְיָא אָמַר כְּרִבִּי שִׁמְעוֹן הִכְשִׁירָהּ. אָמַר רִבִּי זְעִירָא דִּבְרֵי הַכֹּל הִיא. הָכָא דְּאָמַר רִבִּי זְעִירָא בְּשֵׁם רַב אָדָא בַּר אַחֲוָה רִבִּי יוּדָא מַטֵּי בָהּ בְּשֵׁם רִבִּי אַבָּהוּ בְּשֵׁם רִבִּי יוֹחָנָן וְלָד בּוֹגֶרֶת כָּשֵׁר שֶׁהוּא בְלֹא תַעֲשֶׂה שֶׁבָּא מִכֹּחַ עֲשֵׂה עֲשֵׂה. וְהוּא אִשָּׁה בִבְתוּלֶיהָ יִקָּח. כָּל־לֹא תַעֲשֶׂה שֶׁבָּא מִכֹּחַ עֲשֵׂה עֲשֵׂה הוּא. וְדִכְוָותָהּ כִּי אִם בְּתוּלָה מֵעַמָּיו יִקַּח אִשָּׁה וְלֹא גִיּוֹרֶת. כָּל־לֹא תַעֲשֶׂה שֶׁבָּא מִכֹּחַ עֲשֵׂה עֲשֵׂה הוּא. הָתִיב רִבִּי הוֹשַׁעְיָא הֲרֵי דוֹר שֵׁנִי שֶׁל מִצְרִי הֲרֵי הוּא בְּלֹא תַעֲשֶׂה שֶׁבָּא מִכֹּחַ עֲשֵׂה עֲשֵׂה הוּא. חָזַר רִבִּי הוֹשַׁעְיָא וְאָמַר לֹא דָמֵי עֲשֵׂה בְּיִשְׂרָאֵל לַעֲשֵׂה שֶׁבַּכֹּהֲנִים. עֲשֵׂה שֶׁבְּיִשְׂרָאֵל אָסוּר בַּכֹּל. וַעֲשֵׂה שֶׁבַּכֹּהֲנִים אָסוּר בַּכֹּהֲנִים וּמוּתָּר בִּלְוִיִּם וּבְיִשְׂרָאֵל.

Rebbi Jacob bar Idi in the name of Rebbi Joshua ben Levi: It happened that a family in the South was in bad reputation[101]. Rebbi sent Romanus to investigate them. He investigated and found that a grandmother had been converted at less than three years and a day of age, and he declared them fit for the priesthood. Rav Hoshaia said, he declared them fit following Rebbi Simeon. Rebbi Zeïra said, here it is everybody's opinion since Rebbi Zeïra said in the name of Rav Ada bar Ahava, Rebbi Judan brings it in the name of Rebbi Abbahu in the name of Rebbi Joḥanan: The child of an adult is fit since it is a prohibition deduced from a positive commandment[102]. (*Lev.* 21:13) "But he shall take a wife in her virginity." Any prohibition deduced from a positive commandment is a positive commandment[103]. Analogously, (*Lev.* 21:14) "only a virgin from amidst his people he shall take as wife," not a proselyte[104]. Is any prohibition deduced from a positive commandment a positive commandment? Rebbi Hoshaia objected: But the second generation of an Egyptian is a prohibition deduced from a positive commandment[105]! Rebbi Hoshaia turned around and said, a positive commandment for Israel cannot be compared to a positive commandment for Cohanim. A positive commandment for Israel implies a prohibition for everybody. A positive commandment for Cohanim implies a prohibition for Cohanim but a permission for Levites and Israel[106].

100 Reading of the parallel in *Qiddušin*. Ms. and print reading here: Bar Oshaia.

101 That all their girls were forbidden to Cohanim.

102 A High Priest is directed to marry a woman "in her virginity". This is interpreted to mean that the bride must be a virgin but not yet an adult since for adults the hymen may get soft by itself and therefore the fact of virginity cannot in all cases be established. But since the prohibition to marry an adult is only a logical consequence of the positive commandment to marry a virgin, it has no standing in penal law and, therefore, the child of woman marrying as an adult cannot be subject to any disability.

103 The Babli concurs (*Yebamot* 54b,68a; *Pesaḥim* 41b, *Zebaḥim 36a, Ḥulin* 81a.)

104 The Babli (*Yebamot* 77b) and *Sifra Emor Pereq* 2(6) conclude from the partitive מ in מעמיו that the daughter of a proselyte is acceptable.

105 The prohibition of the first two generations of descendants of an Egyptian proselyte is only inferred from the permission to the third generation to marry a Jewish partner, *Deut*. 23:9. If the previous argument is correct, only male Egyptians should be disabled in the second generation, not women. But the verse makes no gender distinction. The principle enunciated seems to contradict the Torah.

106 Since it is special legislation it cannot imply anything not spelled out explicitly.

הלכה ו: שְׁלִיחַ. רִבִּי יוֹסֵי רִבִּי שִׁמְעוֹן בֶּן לָקִישׁ בְּשֵׁם רִבִּי יוֹחָנָן. בְּשֶׁלְּקָטָן לְשַׁלְּחָן בְּיַד אַחֵר. אֲבָל אִם לַהֲבִיאָם הוּא לֹא יְשַׁלְּחֵם בְּיַד אַחֵר. וְלֹא מְחַסֵּל לָהּ. רִבִּי יוֹנָה מְחַסֵּל לָהּ. רִבִּי זְעִירָה רִבִּי אִמִּי רִבִּי שִׁמְעוֹן בֶּן לָקִישׁ בְּשֵׁם רִבִּי הוֹשַׁעְיָה. בְּשֶׁלְּקָטָן לְשַׁלְּחָן בְּיַד אַחֵר. אֲבָל אִם לְקָטָן לַהֲבִיאָן הוּא לֹא יְשַׁלְּחֵם בְּיַד אַחֵר. שֶׁכָּל־הַבִּיכּוּרִים שֶׁנִּרְאוּ לִיתּוּר בִּקְרִייָה אֵינָן נִיתָּרִין אֶלָּא בִקְרִייָה. אָמַר רִבִּי מָנָא אַף עַל גַּו דְלֹא אָמַר רִבִּי יוֹסֵי הָדָא מִילְּתָא אָמַר דִּכְוָותָהּ. אָמַר רִבִּי זְעִירָא לְרִבִּי יָסָא נְהִיר אַתְּ כַּד אִיתְאֲמָרַת הָדָא דְרִבִּי הוֹשַׁעְיָה. וְאָמַר רִבִּי יוֹסֵי בֵּירִבִּי חֲנִינָה מַתְנִיתָא פְלִיגָא. הִפְרִישׁ בִּכּוּרָיו וְאַחַר כָּךְ מָכַר שָׂדֵהוּ מֵבִיא וְאֵינוֹ קוֹרֵא. קִיימוּנָהּ בְּשֶׁנָּתַן דַּעְתּוֹ לִמְסוֹר מִשָּׁעָה רִאשׁוֹנָה. וְהָתַנִּינָן יָבֵשׁ הָאִילָן נִקְצַץ הָאִילָן עוֹד הִיא כְיָבֵשׁ מִשָּׁעָה רִאשׁוֹנָה. וּקְרִייָה מְעַכֶּבֶת. אָמַר רִבִּי שְׁמוּאֵל בַּר רַב יִצְחָק הָרָאוּי לִקְרִייָה אֵין קְרִייָה מְעַכֶּבֶת. לְקָטָן לְשַׁלְּחָם בְּיַד אַחֵר לֹא יְשַׁלְּחֵם בְּיַד אַחֵר שֶׁמָּא יִימָּלֵךְ הוּא לַהֲבִיאָן.

Halakhah 6: "The agent". Rebbi Yose, Rebbi Simeon ben Laqish in the name of Rebbi Joḥanan: When he gathered in order to send by a third person; but if he gathered to bring them himself he cannot send them by a third person. He did not finish this[107]; Rebbi Jonah finished this. Rebbi Zeïra, Rebbi Ammi, Rebbi Simeon ben Laqish in the name of Rebbi Hoshaiah: When he gathered in order to send by a third person; but if he gathered to bring them himself he cannot send them by a third person since all First Fruits which could become permitted by making the declaration[108] become permitted only by making the declaration. Rebbi Mana said, even though Rebbi Yose did not say that, he said something similar: Rebbi Zeïra said to Rebbi Assi, do you remember that when the statement of Rebbi Hoshaiah was formulated, Rebbi Yose ben Rebbi Ḥanina said that a Mishnah disagrees[109]: "If he designated his First Fruits and then sold his field he brings but does not make the declaration"! We upheld this if he had prior intention to sell[110]. But did we not state[111]: "If the tree dried up or was cut down"; that also if earlier it already was almost dry[112]. Does making the declaration prevent[113]? Rebbi Samuel ben Rav Isaac said, where making the declaration is possible, making the declaration does not prevent[114]. If he gathered to deliver them through a third person, would he be forbidden to deliver them through a third person because maybe he would change his mind to deliver them himself[115]?

107 He did not explain the reason behind this ruling.

108 In cases where the Mishnah requires making the declaration, First Fruits become permitted to Cohanim in the Temple only after the full biblical ceremony.

109 Mishnah 1:7. When he designated First Fruits he could make the declaration because the land was his; when he brings he cannot make the declaration since the land is no longer his. In this case the First Fruits should be permanently forbidden to everybody.

110 He knew at the moment of designation that he would not be able to make the declaration; then the obligation to make the declaration never started.

111 Mishnah 1:6; he brings but does not make the declaration.

112 It is not necessary that at the moment of designation it was 100% clear that he could not make the declaration; it is enough if there was a likelihood that this would be the case.

113 Is the illiterate farmer precluded from ever bringing First Fruits? Cf. Halakhah 1:7 and Mishnah 3:7.

114 In the Babli (*Baba Batra* 81b, *Makkot* 18b) this rule is attributed to R. Zeïra. In general, the omission of a required action does not prevent the validity of the act if it would have been possible to perform it (unless it is a requited חוק or תורה). But if it is impossible to perform then any omission of a required action does prevent.

115 This is unreasonable; therefore, the First Fruits were gathered with the intention to deliver without making the declaration; the declaration was never required and cannot prevent.

רִבִּי אַבָּהוּ בְּשֵׁם רִבִּי יוֹחָנָן הַיּוֹרֵשׁ מֵבִיא וְאֵינוֹ קוֹרֵא. מַה נָן קַייָמִין. אִם בְּיוֹרֵשׁ בְּחַיֵּי אָבִיו שְׁלוּחוֹ. וְאִם לְאַחַר מִיתַת אָבִיו שֶׁלּוֹ הֵן. אֶלָּא כִּי נָן קַייָמִין בְּשֶׁהָיָה אָבִיו חוֹלֶה אוֹ מְסוּכָּן.

Rebbi Abbahu in the name of Rebbi Johanan: The heir brings and does not make the declaration. How do we hold? If about an heir during his father's lifetime, he is his agent[116]. But after his father's death it is his own[117]! But we deal with the case that his father was seriously ill[118].

116 The Mishnah already states that he cannot make the declaration.

117 He can make the declaration.

118 The father had designated the First Fruits but he died before they were delivered. Then the son cannot make the declaration since he did not designate.

כְּתִיב וְשָׂמַחְתָּ בְּכָל־הַטּוֹב אֲשֶׁר נָתַן לְךָ יי אֱלֹהֶיךָ וּלְבֵיתֶךָ. מְלַמֵּד שֶׁאָדָם מֵבִיא בִיכּוּרִים מִנִּכְסֵי אִשְׁתּוֹ וְקוֹרֵא. רִבִּי שִׁמְעוֹן בֶּן לָקִישׁ אָמַר לְאַחַר מִיתָה. הָא בְּחַיִּין לֹא. וְרִבִּי יוֹחָנָן אָמַר לֹא שַׁנְייָא הִיא בְחַיִּין הִיא לְאַחַר מִיתָה. רִבִּי שִׁמְעוֹן בֶּן לָקִישׁ כְּדַעְתֵּיהּ. דְּרִבִּי שִׁמְעוֹן בֶּן לָקִישׁ אָמַר אֵין אָדָם יוֹרֵשׁ אֶת אִשְׁתּוֹ דְּבַר תּוֹרָה.

[119]"It is written (*Deut.* 26:11): 'You shall enjoy all the good things that the Eternal, your God, gave you and your house.' This teaches that a person brings First Fruits from his wife's property[120] and makes the declaration." Rebbi Simeon ben Laqish said, after her death but not during her lifetime. Rebbi Johanan said, there is no difference, during her lifetime and after her death. Rebbi Simeon ben Laqish follows his own opinion since Rebbi Simeon ben Laqish said, a person does not inherit from his wife as a biblical rule[121].

119 *Sifry Deut.* #301. The verse is the last in the paragraph about First Fruits.

120 Since a person called "a person's house" is his wife. The property here is the wife's separate property, not her dowry which becomes the husband's property subject to the wife's claim in case of dissolution of the marriage.

121 For R. Simeon ben Laqish, the husband inherits from his wife by rabbinic institution, in exchange for the obligations which the husband takes upon himself in signing the *ketubah*. This opinion is not mentioned elsewhere; *Sifry Num.* 137 derives the husband's inheritance from the verses of the law of inheritance, *Num.* 27:6-11. In the Babli, *Giṭṭin* 47b, the disagreement between R. Simeon ben Laqish and R. Joḥanan is reduced to the question whether buying usufruct, without buying the underlying real estate, transfers property rights since during the marriage the husband has the usufruct also of the wife's separate property.

הלכה ז: רִבִּי יוֹחָנָן בְּשֵׁם רִבִּי הוֹשַׁעְיָה. הֲנָחָה מְעַכֶּבֶת אֵין קְרִייָה מְעַכֶּבֶת. וְהָתַנִּינָן הָאוֹכֵל בִּיכּוּרִין עַד שֶׁלֹּא קָרָא עֲלֵיהֶן. רַב הוֹשַׁעְיָה רַב יְהוּדָה בְּשֵׁם שְׁמוּאֵל. דְּרִבִּי עֲקִיבָה הִיא. רִבִּי יוֹסֵי בָּעֵי הֵיי דָן רִבִּי עֲקִיבָה. אָמַר רִבִּי מָנָא שְׁמָעִית אַבָּא תַּנֵּי. הֲנָחָה מְעַכֶּבֶת אֵין קְרִייָה מְעַכֶּבֶת רִבִּי עֲקִיבָה אוֹמֵר קְרִייָה מְעַכֶּבֶת. רִבִּי יַעֲקֹב בַּר אָחָא בְּשֵׁם רִבִּי לְעָזָר. מַה טַעַם אָמְרוּ הֲנָחָה מְעַכֶּבֶת מִפְּנֵי שֶׁהִיא נוֹהֶגֶת בַּכֹּל. רִבִּי תַּנְחוּמָא (fol. 64b) רִבִּי הוּנָא בְּשֵׁם רִבִּי לְעָזָר. מִפְּנֵי שֶׁשָּׁנָה עָלֶיהָ. אָמַר רִבִּי אַבָּא מָרִי תַּרְתֵּיי. חָדָא כְּרִבִּי יוּדָה וְחָדָא כְּרַבָּנִין. חָדָא כְּרִבִּי יוּדָה. דְּרִבִּי יוּדָה אָמַר לְצוֹרֶךְ נִשְׁנֵית מִפְּנֵי שֶׁהִיא נוֹהֶגֶת בַּכֹּל. כְּרַבָּנִין דְּהִינּוּן מָרִיין שֶׁלֹּא לְצוֹרֶךְ נִשְׁנֵית מִפְּנֵי שֶׁשָּׁנָה עָלֶיהָ.

Halakhah 7: Rebbi Joḥanan in the name of Rebbi Hoshaia: Putting down prevents, making the declaration does not prevent[122]. But did we not state[123]: "He who eats First Fruits before the declaration was made for them"? Rav Hoshaiah, Rav Jehudah in the name of Samuel: That is Rebbi Aqiba's[124]. Rebbi Yose asked, which statement of Rebbi Aqiba?

Rebbi Mana said, I heard my father[125] state: Putting down prevents, making the declaration does not prevent; Rebbi Aqiba says, making the declaration does prevent. Rebbi Jacob bar Aḥa in the name of Rebbi Eleazar: Why did they say that putting down prevents? Because it applies to everybody. Rebbi Tanḥuma, Rebbi Huna in the name of Rebbi Eleazar: Because it is repeated[126]. Rebbi Abba Mari said both[127], one following Rebbi Jehudah, the other following the rabbis[128]. For Rebbi Judah who said it had to be repeated, because it applies to everybody[129]. For the rabbis who instruct that it did not need to be repeated, because it was repeated[130].

122 In the Babli, *Makkot* 17a, this is a statement of Rabba bar bar Ḥana in the name of R. Joḥanan. The statement does not disqualify a person who cannot read the declaration; it only applies to persons required to read, cf. Note 113. An action "prevents" if the ceremony becomes invalid if it is omitted.

123 Mishnah *Makkot* 3:3; discussed in Babli *Makkot* 18b. A Cohen who eats of First Fruits before the ceremony of dedication is whipped.

124 In *Makkot* 13a, the attribution of Mishnah *Makkot* 3:3 is given in the name of R. Joḥanan.

125 R. Jonah.

126 "Putting down" is mentioned both in *Deut.* 26:4, as an action of the Cohen, and 26:10, as an action of the farmer.

127 R. Eleazar did not change his mind; he gave two different explanations for two different schools of thought.

128 The ceremony is described in Mishnah 3:4. According to the anonymous Tanna, the farmer keeps his basket on his shoulder until he has read the entire declaration (and then hands the basket over to the Cohen who deposits it near the altar.) According to R. Jehudah, only the declaration in *Deut.* 26:3 is made with the basket on the farmer's shoulder. Then the farmer holds the basket by its handles, the Cohen puts his hands under the basket and weaves it (as required by the anonymous Mishnah 2:4). Only after that, the declaration 26:5-10 is made

and the basket deposited near the altar. For R. Jehudah, the first "putting down" is into the hands of the Cohen, the second on the floor. For him, both mentions are necessary.

The other sources more or less follow R. Jehudah. *Sifry Deut.* #300 infers from 26:4, "you shall put it down before the altar of the Eternal, your God", that in the absence of an altar there cannot be any obligation of First Fruits. In #301 it is inferred from the double mention of "putting down" that there are two, one for the declaration and one for the subsequent prostration.

The late *Targum Yerushalmi* (Pseudo Jonathan) translates 26:4: "The Cohen shall take the basket from your hand, *move it forward and backward, upward and downward*, and *at the end* put it down before the altar of the Eternal, your God." The first inserted text describes the "weaving" required by R. Jehudah. Verse 10 is translated without addition: " . . . put it down before the Eternal, your God, and prostrate yourself before the Eternal, your God."

129 For R. Jehudah the two mentions of "putting down" are needed in the description of the ceremony. For him, accepting First Fruits from a person who cannot recite is a rabbinic interpretation, unsupported by the biblical text.

130 Since for them there is only one "putting down"; the double mention is for emphasis.

(fol. 63c) **משנה ו**: הַקּוֹנֶה שְׁנֵי אִילָנוֹת בְּתוֹךְ שֶׁל חֲבֵירוֹ מֵבִיא וְאֵינוֹ קוֹרֵא. רִבִּי מֵאִיר אוֹמֵר מֵבִיא וְקוֹרֵא. יָבַשׁ הַמַּעְיָן נִקְצַץ הָאִילָן מֵבִיא וְאֵינוֹ קוֹרֵא. רִבִּי יְהוּדָה אוֹמֵר מֵבִיא וְקוֹרֵא. מִן הָעֲצֶרֶת וְעַד הֶחָג מֵבִיא וְקוֹרֵא. מִן הֶחָג וְעַד הַחֲנוּכָּה מֵבִיא וְאֵינוֹ קוֹרֵא. רִבִּי יְהוּדָה בֶּן בְּתֵירָה אוֹמֵר מֵבִיא וְקוֹרֵא.

Mishnah 6: He who buys two trees on another's property brings but does not make the declaration; Rebbi Meïr says he brings and makes the declaration[131]. If the spring dried up[132] or the tree[133] was cut down, one brings but does not make the declaration; Rebbi Jehudah says he brings and makes the declaration[134]. From Pentecost to Tabernacles one brings and makes the declaration; from Tabernacles to Ḥanukkah one brings but does not make the declaration; Rebbi Jehudah ben Bathyra says he brings and makes the declaration[135].

131 The standard contract (Mishnah *Baba Batra* 5:4) about buying trees implies that the ground on which the trees stand is sold with the trees only if the transaction involves at least three trees in one orchard. R. Meïr disagrees in that Mishnah; his standard contract implies the sale of the land also for two trees. It is clear that if the sale of the ground is expressly stipulated, the buyer can recite the declaration which is formulated for the owners of the land (Mishnah 11).

132 If the field or orchard from which the First Fruits were taken cannot bear fruit the next year since there is no longer any possibility of irrigation, it is as if the owner no longer possessed the property as agricultural land.

133 From which the First Fruits were taken.

134 Since the farmer remains the owner of the property.

135 For the anonymous majority, after Tabernacles there no longer is any joy in the harvest. Everybody agrees that there is no harvest between Ḥanukkah and Pentecost; cf. Mishnah 3.

(fol. 64b) **הלכה ח**: רִבִּי יוֹסֵי בֶּן חֲנִינָה בָּעֵי. קָנָה אִילָן אֶחָד לֹא קָנָה קַרְקַע. שְׁנַיִם לֹא קָנָה קַרְקַע. אֶחָד אֵינוֹ מֵבִיא כָּל־עִיקָּר. שְׁנַיִם מֵבִיא וְאֵינוֹ קוֹרֵא. אָמַר לֵיהּ רִבִּי לָעְזָר מִילִּין דִּצְרִיכִין לְרַבָּנִין בְּבֵית וַעֲדָא אַתְּ שָׁאִיל.

Halakhah 8: Rebbi Yose ben Ḥanina asked: If one bought a single tree he did not acquire the ground, two he did not acquire the ground. From one he does not bring at all, from two he brings and does not make the declaration[136]? Rebbi Eleazar said to him, you are asking a question to which the rabbis in assembly have no answer.

136 For real estate law, it makes no difference whether one or two trees are bought. Does one have to read the Mishnah as dealing with exactly two trees or is there no difference for the rabbis whether one buys one or two trees and the number 2 is mentioned only because of R. Meïr who will agree with the rabbis in the case of a single tree but disagrees about 2? In the latter case, the person acquiring a single fruit tree could bring but not make the declaration. In the Babli, *Baba Batra* 81a the matter is decided, that R. Meïr permits the buyer of a single tree to bring but not to make the declaration.

רִבִּי יוּדָה עֲבַד אֶת הָאִילָן כְּקַשִּׁים. תַּמָּן תְּנִינָן בֵּירַךְ עַל פֵּירוֹת הָאִילָן בּוֹרֵא פְּרִי הָאֲדָמָה יָצָא. רִבִּי חִזְקִיָּה בְּשֵׁם רִבִּי יַעֲקֹב בַּר אָחָא דְּרִבִּי יוּדָה הִיא. דְּרִבִּי יוּדָה אָמַר עֲבַד אֶת הָאִילָן כְּקַשִּׁים. אָמַר רִבִּי יוֹסֵי דִּבְרֵי הַכֹּל הִיא. פֵּירוֹת הָאִילָן בִּכְלַל פֵּירוֹת הָאֲדָמָה. וְאֵין פֵּירוֹת הָאֲדָמָה בִּכְלַל פֵּירוֹת הָאִילָן.

[137]Rebbi Jehudah treats trees like straws. There, we have stated: "If he pronounced the benediction 'Creator of the fruit of the soil' on fruits of the tree, he has fulfilled his obligation." Rebbi Ḥizqiah in the name of Rebbi Jacob bar Aḥa: This is Rebbi Yehuda's since Rebbi Jehudah treats trees like straws. Rebbi Yose said, it is everybody's opinion since fruits of a tree are also fruits of the soil but fruits of the soil are not fruits of the tree.

137 This is from *Berakhot* 6:2, Notes 117-118.

רִבִּי בּוּן בַּר כַּהֲנָא בְּעָא קוֹמֵי רִבִּי אִילָא. מָכַר לוֹ שָׂדֶה בְּקָמָתָהּ. הַלּוֹקֵחַ מַהוּ שֶׁיָּבִיא מִמֶּנָּה בִּיכּוּרִים. אָמַר לֵיהּ לָמָּה לָאו. עַד כְּדוֹן לַחָה. אֲפִילוּ יְבֵישָׁה. אָמַר לֵיהּ אֲפִילוּ יְבֵישָׁה אֲפִילוּ קְצוּרָה. מֵעַתָּה אֲפִילוּ חִיטִּין. כֵּן אָנוּ אוֹמְרִים הַלּוֹקֵחַ מִן הַשּׁוּק מֵבִיא בִּיכּוּרִין.

Rebbi Abun bar Cahana asked before Rebbi Hila: If somebody sold him a field with its standing crop, may the buyer bring First Fruits? He said to him, why not? That is, when it is moist; even when it is dry[138]? He said to him, even dry, even harvested. Then even wheat grain; do we say that the buyer on the market brings First Fruits[139]?

138 If the grain is totally dry at the moment of sale and does not ripen in the possession of the buyer.

139 There is no answer since the question is too stupid to merit one; the buyer of grain on the market does not buy the field; the only buyer who may bring First Fruits is the buyer of the field. In the Babli, *Baba Batra* 81a, the opinion that R. Meïr will allow First Fruits from grain bought on the market is shown to be impossible.

פְּשִׁיטָא הָדָא מִילְתָא. מָכַר לוֹ פֵּירוֹת וְשִׁייֵר לוֹ קַרְקַע הַמּוֹכֵר אֵינוֹ יָכוֹל לְהָבִיא שֶׁאֵין לוֹ פֵּירוֹת. חָזַר וּלְקָחָן מִמֶּנּוּ. נִישְׁמְעִינָהּ מִן הָדָא. נָתַן לָהּ קֳדָשִׁים הֲרֵי אֵילּוּ מוּתָּרִין. יֵינוֹת שְׁמָנִין וּסְלָתוֹת כָּל־דָּבָר שֶׁכְּיוֹצֵא בוֹ קָרֵב לְגַבֵּי הַמִּזְבֵּחַ אָסוּר. אֵין בִּכְלָל אֶלָּא פַּרְכִּירֵי עֲנָבִים וַעֲטָרוֹת שֶׁלְשִׁיבֳּלִין. מַה נָן קַייָמִין. אִם בְּשֶׁנָּתַן לָהּ בְּאֶתְנַנָּהּ כָּךְ אָנוּ אוֹמְרִים הַלּוֹקֵחַ מִן הַשּׁוּק מֵבִיא בִיכּוּרִים. אֶלָּא כִּי נָן קַייָמִין כְּשֶׁהָיוּ הַגְּפָנִים מִשֶּׁלָּהּ וּמָכַר לוֹ פֵּירוֹתֵיהֶן וְחָזַר וּנְתָנָם לָהּ בְּאֶתְנַנָּהּ. מִפְּנֵי שֶׁהָיָה אֶתְנַן. הָא לֹא הָיָה אֶתְנַן מֵבִיא. הָדָא אָמְרָה חָזַר וּלְקָחָן מִמֶּנּוּ מֵבִיא.

The following is obvious: If somebody sold the harvest and retained the land for himself, the seller cannot bring since he has no harvest. If he bought it back? Let us hear from the following: "If he gave her dedicated things they are permitted; wines, oils, flour, or anything of a kind admissible near the altar, are prohibited[140]. The latter adds only bundles[142] of vines and rings made of grain stalks[141]." Where do we hold? If he gave her[143] as whore's wages, do we say that the buyer on the market brings First Fruits? But we must hold in case the vines were hers, she sold him the fruits, and he gave them back to her as whore's wages. Because they are whore's wages[144]. Therefore, if they were not whore's wages she might bring. That means, if he bought back he may bring.

140 Similar statements, in different order, are Mishnah *Temurah* 6:4, Tosephta *Temurah* 4:7,9. The statements refer to the prohibition (*Deut.* 23:19) to bring a whore's wages to the Temple in fulfillment of any vow. This implies that the prostitute was paid in kind; if she is paid in money then what she buys with that money is not prohibited. Since animals or produce dedicated to the Temple cannot become objects of a new vow, these are not under the prohibition of a whore's wages.

141 This sentence is a *baraita* not otherwise recorded. Since wine, olive oil, and flour are the only vegetal products used on the altar, the addition "or anything of a kind admissible near the altar" can only refer to First Fruits which are the only other vegetables admitted in the Temple.

142 The root is פכר, to bundle, as pointed out by I. Löw. The Babli form is פרכילי with a change of liquids.

143 Fruits or grains admissible as First Fruits.

144 This is the only reason they cannot be brought to the Temple.

חֲבֵרַייָא בְשֵׁם רִבִּי יְהוֹשֻׁעַ בֶּן לֵוִי. הִפְרִישָׁן קוֹדֶם לֶחָג וְעָבַר עֲלֵיהֶן הֶחָג מֵבִיא וְאֵינוֹ קוֹרֵא. הִפְרִישָׁן קוֹדֶם לַחֲנוּכָּה וְעָבְרָה עֲלֵיהֶן חֲנוּכָּה וְנִרְקָבוּ. לְאַחַר חֲנוּכָּה לֹא קָדְשֵׁי. וְלֵית לֵיהּ לְרִבִּי זְעִירָא כְּהָדָא דַחֲבֵרַייָא. סָבַר רִבִּי זְעִירָא שֶׁכָּל־הַבִּיכּוּרִים שֶׁנִּרְאוּ לִיתּוּר בָּאָרֶץ אֵינָן נִיתּוּרִין אֶלָּא בִקְרִייָה. וְלֵית לַחֲבֵרַייָא כֵן. אִית לְהוֹן בְּשֶׁהִפְרִישָׁן קוֹדֶם לֶחָג לַהֲבִיאָן אַחַר הֶחָג. וְהָתַנִּינָן אֵין מְבִיאִין בִּכּוּרִים לֹא מִן הֶחָדָשׁ עַל הַיָּשָׁן וְלֹא מִן הַיָּשָׁן עַל הֶחָדָשׁ. מָה נָן קַייָמִין. אִם בְּפֵירוֹת שֶׁהֵבִיאוּ שְׁלִישׁ לְאַחַר רֹאשׁ הַשָּׁנָה עַל הַפֵּירוֹת שֶׁהֵבִיאוּ שְׁלִישׁ לְאַחַר רֹאשׁ הַשָּׁנָה. מִכֵּיוָן שֶׁלֹּא שֶׁהֵבִיאוּ שְׁלִישׁ לִפְנֵי רֹאשׁ הַשָּׁנָה דָּבָר בָּרוּר שֶׁלֹּא הִשְׁרִישׁוּ קוֹדֶם לָעוֹמֶר וְהֵן אֲסוּרִין עַד שֶׁיָּבוֹא הָעוֹמֶר וְיַתִּירֵם. אֶלָּא כִּי נָן קַייָמִין בְּפֵירוֹת שֶׁחָנְטוּ קוֹדֶם ט״וֹ בִשְׁבָט עַל פֵּירוֹת שֶׁחָנְטוּ אַחַר ט״וֹ בִשְׁבָט.

מִכֵּיוָן שֶׁהוּא מִן חָדָשׁ עַל הַיָּשָׁן. הָוא מִן חָדָשׁ עַל חָדָשׁ מָבִיא. וְסָבְרִינָן מֵימַר לְאַחַר חֲנוּכָּה אֲנָן קַיָּימִין. אָמַר רִבִּי חִינְנָא בִּזְמַנָּן.

The colleagues in the name of Rebbi Joshua ben Levi: If he dedicated them before Tabernacles and Tabernacles passed, he brings and does not make the declaration. If he dedicated them before Ḥanukkah and Ḥanukkah passed, they will rot[145]. After Ḥanukkah they do not become holy.

Rebbi Zeïra will not accept this of the colleagues; Rebbi Zeïra is of the opinion that all First Fruits which could become permitted by making the declaration become permitted only by making the declaration[146]. Do the colleagues not accept this? They accept it; if he dedicated before Tabernacles intending to bring them after Tabernacles[147].

Did we not state[148]: One may not bring First Fruits from the new crop for the old, nor from the old for the new. Where do we hold? If about produce[149] which was one third ripe before New Year's Day for produce which was not one third ripe before New Year's Day[150], since it was not one third ripe before New Year's Day it is obvious that it did not form roots before the *'omer* and will be forbidden until the coming *'omer* permits it[151]. But we must deal with fruits [from trees] which budded before the fifteenth of *Šebaṭ*[152] for fruits which budded after the fifteenth of *Šebaṭ*; because that would be from new for old. Therefore, from new for new one may bring[153]. We thought to say that one speaks of the time after Ḥanukkah. Rebbi Ḥinena said, in its time[154].

145 Since they must be brought to the Temple but would not be accepted, they are forbidden for any use.

146 This discusses the opinion of the colleagues that First Fruits dedicated before Tabernacles may still be

brought after Tabernacles. This seems to contradict the opinion stated in Halakhah 6 (Note 108) without opposition that First Fruits under the obligation of declaration cannot become permitted to Cohanim except by the declaration by the farmer.

147 In this case, there never was an obligation to recite the declaration.

148 It seems that תנינן should be תני since the statement is not a Mishnah. This paragraph discusses the statement that First Fruits dedicated after Ḥanukkah do not acquire sanctity.

149 In rabbinic Hebrew, פירות usually means grain but it also can be used in the Biblical sense of "fruit" in general. This ambiguity is expressed here; the first sentence speaks of grain, the second of fruits of a tree.

150 Since First Fruits are called ראשית (*Deut*. 26:2) and heave is called ראשית (*Deut*. 18:4), the rules of heave apply to First Fruits; cf. Mishnah 2:1..

151 Mishnah *'Orlah* 3:9, Note 155.

152 The New Year of fruit trees for tithing periods, cf. Mishnah *Roš Haššanah* 1:1; *Ševi'it* 5, Note 6.

153 Designating First Fruits after the 15th of *Šebaṭ* (which comes after Ḥanukkah) but before Pentecost. This is also implied by Mishnah 1:3.

154 The *baraita* does not apply to the colleagues' statement; it refers to the time between Pentecost and Tabernacles which is the actual time of First Fruits. One may not bring first fruit raisins and dried figs from former years; one may not let this year's First Fruits count for former years in which one neglected the duty to bring First Fruits to the Temple.

(fol. 63c) **משנה ז**: הִפְרִישׁ בִּיכּוּרָיו וּמָכַר שָׂדֵהוּ מֵבִיא וְאֵינוֹ קוֹרֵא. וְהַשֵּׁינִי מֵאוֹתוֹ הַמִּין אֵינוֹ מֵבִיא מִמִּין אַחֵר מֵבִיא וְקוֹרֵא. רִבִּי יְהוּדָה אוֹמֵר אַף מֵאוֹתוֹ הַמִּין מֵבִיא וְקוֹרֵא.

Mishnah 7: If he dedicated his First Fruits and then sold his field he brings but does not make the declaration. The other person cannot bring from the same kind, but from another kind he brings and makes the declaration. Rebbi Jehudah says, he may bring and make the declaration from the same kind.

(fol. 64b) **הלכה ט**: מָה טַעֲמוֹן דְּרַבָּנִין הִגַּדְתִּי הַיּוֹם. פַּעַם אַחַת הוּא מַגִּיד וְאֵינוֹ מַגִּיד פַּעַם שְׁנִיָּה. וְלֵית לְרִבִּי יוּדָה כֵן. אִית לֵיהּ בְּאָדָם אֶחָד. אֲבָל בִּשְׁנֵי בְנֵי אָדָם מַגִּיד וְחוֹזֵר וּמַגִּיד.

Halakhah 9: What is the reason of the rabbis[155]? (*Deut*. 26:3) "I am declaring today". He declares once[156] but not twice. Does not Rebbi Jehudah hold so? He does, referring to one person[157]. But two persons can declare and declare again[158].

155 That the buyer cannot bring First Fruits. It is obvious that the seller cannot make the declaration since he has no land.

156 Today but not tomorrow.

157 It is accepted without dissent that a farmer can bring First Fruits of different kinds at different times but he can read the declaration only once (Mishnah 9).

158 Even for the same crop since First Fruits are an obligation of the farmer, not of the crop.

(fol. 63c) **משנה ח**: הִפְרִישׁ אֶת בִּכּוּרָיו נָמַקּוּ נִבְזָזוּ נִגְנְבוּ אָבְדוּ אוֹ שֶׁנִּיטְמוּ מֵבִיא אֲחֵרִים תַּחְתֵּיהֶם וְאֵינוֹ קוֹרֵא וְהַשְּׁנִיִּים אֵין חַיָּבִין עֲלֵיהֶן חוֹמֶשׁ. נִיטְמוּ בָעֲזָרָה נוֹפֵץ וְאֵינוֹ קוֹרֵא.

Mishnah 8: If he dedicated his First Fruits and then they rotted, were robbed, stolen, lost, or became impure, he brings others in their stead. One is not liable for a fifth for the replacements[159]. If they became impure in the Temple court, he scatters them and cannot make the declaration[160].

משנה ט: וּמְנַיִין שֶׁהוּא חַייָב בְּאַחֲרָיוּתָן עַד שֶׁיְּבִיאֵם לְהַר הַבַּיִת. שֶׁנֶּאֱמַר רֵאשִׁית בִּכּוּרֵי אַדְמָתְךָ תָּבִיא בֵּית יי אֱלֹהֶיךָ וגו' מְלַמֵּד שֶׁהוּא חַייָב בְּאַחֲרָיוּתָן עַד שֶׁיָּבִיאֵם לְהַר הַבַּיִת.

Mishnah 9: From where that he is responsible for them until he delivers them to the Temple Mount? Because it is said (*Deut*. 26:3): "The beginning of the First Fruits of your land you shall bring to the Temple of the Eternal, your God, etc." This teaches that he is responsible for them until be delivers them to the Temple Mount.

159 But the original First Fruits go under the rules of heave (Mishnah 2:1, Note 150) and the replacement has to be 125% of the original.

160 Since delivering the basket of fruits to the Cohen to be set down near the altar is necessary; cf. Note 122.

(fol. 64b) **הלכה י**: אָמַר רִבִּי יוֹחָנָן מִשּׁוּם יְחִידִי אֲנִי שׁוֹנֶה אוֹתָהּ. וְתַנֵּי כֵן רִבִּי שִׁמְעוֹן בֶּן יְהוּדָה אוֹמֵר מִשּׁוּם רִבִּי שִׁמְעוֹן. שְׁנִיִּם אֵין חַייָבִין עֲלֵיהֶן חוֹמֶשׁ. רִבִּי שְׁמוּאֵל בֶּן רַב יִצְחָק בְּשֵׁם רַב הוּנָא. שְׁנִיִּם לוֹקְחִין אֲפִילוּ מִן הַשּׁוּק. מָה אַתְּ עֲבַד לוֹן. כְּתוֹסֶפֶת הַבִּיכּוּרִים אוֹ כְעִיטּוּר הַבִּיכּוּרִים. אִין תַּעַבְדִּינוֹן כְּתוֹסֶפֶת הַבִּיכּוּרִים פְּטוּרִין מִן הַדְּמַאי. אִין תַּעַבְדִּינוֹן כְּעִיטּוּר הַבִּיכּוּרִים חַייָבִין בִּדְמַאי.

Halakhah 10: Rebbi Joḥanan said, I am stating this as the opinion of a single individuum[161]. It was stated thus: "Rebbi Simeon ben Jehudah says in the name of Rebbi Simeon: For the replacement one is not obligated for a fifth." Rebbi Samuel ben Rav Isaac in the name of Rav Huna: The replacement one even buys on the market. How do you treat these? As addition of First Fruits or adornment of First Fruits[162]? If you treat them as addition to First Fruits they are not under the rules of *demay*. If you treat them as adornment of First Fruits they are under the rules of *demay*[163].

161 Mishnah 8, formulated anonymously, is the opinion only of R. Simeon (ben Iohai) as stated in Tosephta 1:5.

162 If one may buy on the market, the replacements are not really First Fruits. It is stated in Mishnah 3:10 that with First Fruits one brought additional fruits of the same kind as additions and fruits of other kinds as adornments.

163 Mishnah 3:10.

נִטְמְאוּ בָעֲזָרָה נוֹפֵץ וְאֵינוֹ קוֹרֵא. רִבִּי חָמָא בַּר עוּקְבָּא בְּשֵׁם רִבִּי יוֹסֵי בַּר חֲנִינָה. נִטְמְאוּ הַבִּכּוּרִים הַסַּלִּין נִיתָּנִין לַכֹּהֲנִים. דִּכְתִּיב וְלָקַח הַכֹּהֵן הַטֶּנֶא מִיָּדֶךָ.

" If they became impure in the Temple court, he scatters them and cannot make the declaration." Rebbi Ḥama bar Uqba in the name of Rebbi Yose bar Ḥanina: If the First Fruits became impure[164], the baskets are given to the priests[165] since it is said (*Deut*. 26:4): "The Cohen shall take the basket from your hand."

164 But not the baskets which cannot become impure in secondary or tertiary degree.

165 Since it was the original intent to give First Fruits in their baskets.

(fol. 63c) **משנה ט**: הֲרֵי שֶׁהֵבִיא מִמִּין אֶחָד וְקָרָא וְחָזַר וְהֵבִיא מִמִּין אַחֵר אֵינוֹ קוֹרֵא.

Mishnah 9: If he brought from one kind and made the declaration, when he comes back and brings from another kind he cannot make the declaration.

(fol. 64b) **הלכה יא**: לְמִי נִצְרְכָה לְרִבִּי יוּדָה. אַף עַל גַּב דְּרִבִּי יוּדָה אָמַר מַגִּיד וְחוֹזֵר וּמַגִּיד. הֲרֵי שֶׁהֵבִיא מִמִּין אֶחָד קָרָא וְחָזַר וְהֵבִיא מִמִּין אַחֵר הֲרֵי זֶה אֵינוֹ קוֹרֵא. אָמַר רִבִּי יוֹנָתָן תַּנֵּי רִבִּי שִׁמְעוֹן בֶּן יוֹחַאי כֵן. וְאָמַרְתָּ וְשָׂמַחְתָּ. הֲוֵי אוֹמֵר עַל הַשִּׂמְחָה.

Halakhah 11: For whom is this needed? For Rebbi Jehudah. Even though Rebbi Jehudah said, he declares and he[166] declares again, but if he brought from one kind and made the declaration, when he comes back and brings from another kind he cannot make the declaration. Rebbi Jonathan said, Rebbi Simeon ben Ioḥai stated this: (*Deut*. 26:5) "You shall say", (*Deut*. 26:11) "you shall enjoy"; you have to say it while you enjoy[167].

166 Another person; cf. Mishnah 7, Halakhah 9.

167 And a repeat performance is not the same as the first. The *Sifry* (#301) concludes from *Deut* 26:11 that the (first) presentation of First Fruits requires a family sacrifice to provide a meat meal (cf. Mishnah 3:3).

(fol. 63c) **משנה י**: אֵילוּ קוֹרִין וּמְבִיאִין וְקוֹרִין מִן הָעֲצֶרֶת וְעַד הֶחָג. מִשִּׁבְעַת הַמִּינִים מִן הַפֵּירוֹת שֶׁבֶּהָרִים מִן הַתְּמָרוֹת שֶׁבָּעֲמָקִים וּמִזֵּיתֵי שֶׁמֶן וּמֵעֵבֶר לַיַּרְדֵּן. רִבִּי יוֹסֵי הַגְּלִילִי אוֹמֵר אֵין מְבִיאִין בִּכּוּרִים מֵעֵבֶר לַיַּרְדֵּן שֶׁאֵינָהּ אֶרֶץ זָבַת חָלָב וּדְבָשׁ.

Mishnah 10: For the following one makes the declaration, one brings and makes the declaration between Pentecost and Tabernacles: From the Seven Kinds[168], from produce of the hills, from dates in the valleys[169], from oil olives[170], and from Transjordan. Rebbi Yose the Galilean says, one does not bring from Transjordan since it is not a Land flowing with milk and honey.

168 *Deut.* 8:8-9; cf. *Berakhot* 6, Note 151. Only fruits mentioned in these verses qualify as First Fruits.

169 Only these produce date honey.

170 These usually are larger than eating olives.

(fol. 64b) **הלכה יב**: רִבִּי יוֹסֵי בְּשֵׁם רִבִּי שִׁמְעוֹן בֶּן לָקִישׁ. רִבִּי יוֹנָה רִבִּי זְעִירָה בְּשֵׁם רִבִּי חֲנִינָה. שִׁשָּׁה עָשָׂר מִיל חִיזוֹר לְצִיפּוֹרִין הֵן הֵן אֶרֶץ זָבַת חָלָב וּדְבָשׁ. אָמַר רִבִּי יוֹנָה מָאן דִּמְקַדֵּד אִילֵּין שְׁגְרוֹנַיָּיה דְּבֵישָׁן מִינְהוֹן. מָאן דִּמְקַדֵּד הָדָא בְקָעַת גִּינֵּיסוֹר מִינְהוֹן. מְתִיבִין לְרִבִּי יוֹנָה. וְהָא כְתִיב וָאוֹמַר אֶעֱלֶה אֶתְכֶם מֵעֳנִי מִצְרַיִם אֶל אֶרֶץ טוֹבָה וּרְחָבָה אֶרֶץ זָבַת חָלָב וּדְבָשׁ. אָמַר לוֹן אֶרֶץ אֲשֶׁר בָּהּ זָבַת חָלָב וּדְבָשׁ.

Halakhah 12: Rebbi Yose in the name of Rebbi Simeon ben Laqish; Rebbi Jonah, Rebbi Zeïra in the name of Rebbi Ḥanina: Sixteen *mil* in a circle around Sepphoris is the Land flowing with milk and honey[171]. Rebbi Jonah said, if one measures as the crow flies[172], the outskirts of Beth Shean belong to it. If one measures as the crow flies, the valley of Genezareth belongs to it. One objected to Rebbi Jonah: (*Ex.* 3:17) "I said, I shall lift you from the deprivation of Egypt" (*Ex.* 3:8) "into a good and wide land, [to] a land flowing with milk and honey"![173] He said to them, which contains [stretches of] milk and honey.

171 In the Babli (*Ketubot* 111b), a square of side 16 *mil* centered at Sepphoris (in the name of R. Simeon ben Laqish). A phantastic tale of Rabba bar bar Ḥana puts the size of the country flowing with milk and honey at 22 parasangs (88 *mil*) square. The *mil* is 2000 average cubits; cf. *Berakhot* 3, Note 235.

172 In Babylonian texts, this appears as מקדר. The root is קדר "to cut through". The idea is that one is measuring as if tunneling through a mountain by lifting the measuring rod so that it is always horizontal (Babli *Erubin* 58b).

173 This seems to imply that the entire Land of Israel is flowing with milk and honey.

תַּנֵּי אֲשֶׁר נָתַתִּי לִי. לֹא שֶׁנָּטַלְתִּי לִי מֵעַצְמִי. מַה בֵּינֵיהוֹן. אָמַר רִבִּי אָבִין חֲצִי שֵׁבֶט מְנַשֶּׁה בֵּינֵיהוֹן. מָאן דְּאָמַר אֲשֶׁר נָתַתִּי לִי וְלֹא שֶׁנָּטַלְתִּי לִי מֵעַצְמִי חֲצִי שֵׁבֶט מְנַשֶּׁה לֹא נָטְלוּ מֵעַצְמָן. מָאן דְּאָמַר אֶרֶץ זָבַת חָלָב וּדְבָשׁ אֲפִילוּ כֵן אֵינָהּ אֶרֶץ זָבַת חָלָב וּדְבָשׁ.

It was stated: (*Deut*. 26:10) "Which You gave me", not what I took by myself.[174] About what do they differ[175]? Rebbi Abun said, half of the tribe of Manasse[176]. If one says, "which You gave me, not what I took by myself," half the tribe of Manasse did not take by themselves. If one says, (*Deut*. 26:10) "a Land of milk and honey," nevertheless it is not a land of milk and honey.

174 The *Sifry* (#301) takes this as basis to exclude guardians, etc. (Mishnah 5) from the right to declaration. For the Tanna here, the verse excludes produce from "Syria", from territories conquered by David outside the boundaries of promise.

175 The anonymous majority and R. Yose the Galilean.

176 The tribes of Reuben and Gad were sheep herders, not farmers.

(fol. 63c) **משנה יא**: הַקּוֹנֶה שְׁלֹשָׁה אִילָנוֹת בְּתוֹךְ שֶׁלַּחֲבֵירוֹ מֵבִיא וְקוֹרֵא. רִבִּי מֵאִיר אוֹמֵר אֲפִילוּ שְׁנַיִם. קָנָה אִילָן וְקַרְקָעוֹ מֵבִיא וְקוֹרֵא. רִבִּי יְהוּדָה אוֹמֵר אַף בַּעֲלֵי אֲרִיסוּת וַחֲכוּרוֹת מְבִיאִין וְקוֹרִין.

Mishnah 11: He who buys three trees in another's property, brings, and makes the declaration; Rebbi Meïr says even for two[177]. He who buys a tree and its ground[178] brings and makes the declaration. Rebbi Jehudah says, even sharecroppers and tenant farmers bring and read[179].

177 Cf. Note 131.

178 By a contract which explicitly states that the ground is sold with the tree. In the Babli, *Baba Batra* 27a, this is restricted to the case that he bought the tree with a circular domain of radius 16 cubits which can be assumed to contain all roots of the tree.

179 He disagrees with the anonymous Mishnah 2.

(fol. 64b) **הלכה יג**: תַּנֵּי חָכוֹרֵי בָּתֵּי אָבוֹת אֵינָן מְבִיאִין. רִבִּי יוּדָה אוֹמֵר הֵן עַצְמָן מְבִיאִין וְקוֹרִין.

Halakhah 13: It was stated: Hereditary tenant farmers[180] do not bring; Rebbi Jehudah says, they themselves bring and make the declaration.

180 They and their descendants have the permanent right to farm the property if they pay their rent on time.

רִבִּי זְעִירָה רִבִּי חִיָּיה בְּשֵׁם רִבִּי יוֹחָנָן. בֶּחָכוֹרֵי בָּתֵּי אָבוֹת הִיא מַתְנִיתָה. רִבִּי הִילָא רִבִּי יָסֵי בְּשֵׁם רִבִּי יוֹחָנָן בְּבַעֲלֵי אֲרִיסִיּוּת וְחָכוֹרוֹת הִיא מַתְנִיתָה. הֲוון בָּעֵי מֵימַר מָאן דְּאָמַר בְּבַעֲלֵי אֲרִיסִיּוּת וְחָכוֹרוֹת הִיא מַתְנִיתָה. הָא בְּאָרִיס וְחָכוֹר לֹא. בְּאָרִיס לְשָׁעָה וְחָכוֹר לְשָׁעָה. הָא בְּאָרִיס לְעוֹלָם וְחָכוֹר לְעוֹלָם מֵבִיא. אָתָא רִבִּי בָּא רִבִּי חִיָּיה בְּשֵׁם רִבִּי יוֹחָנָן אֲפִילוּ בְּאָרִיס לְעוֹלָם וְחָכוֹר לְעוֹלָם אֵינוֹ מֵבִיא. לָמָּה. בְּבַעֲלֵי אֲרִיסִיּוּת וְחָכוֹרוֹת הִיא מַתְנִיתָה.

Rebbi Zeïra, Rebbi Ḥiyya, in the name of Rebbi Joḥanan: The Mishnah speaks of hereditary tenant farmers[181]. Rebbi Hila, Rebbi Assi, in the name of Rebbi Joḥanan: The Mishnah speaks of owners of sharecropping or tenant farming rights[182]. They wanted to say, he who says the Mishnah speaks of owners of sharecropping or tenant farming rights, therefore not about simple sharecroppers or tenants[183]. About a temporary sharecropper or tenant farmer[184]; therefore a permanent sharecropper or tenant farmer might bring[185]. Rebbi Abba, Rebbi Ḥiyya came in the name of Rebbi Joḥanan: Even a permanent sharecropper or tenant farmer cannot bring. Why? The Mishnah speaks of owners of sharecropping or tenant farming rights[186].

181 Even these may not bring First Fruits according to the rabbis.

182 It is not clear at this moment whether the farming rights are permanent, and there is no difference in meaning between the statements of R. Zeïra and R. Hila, or whether the rights are limited in time but the contract cannot be terminated by the landlord before its expiration date. In the second interpretation, the rabbis might agree that hereditary tenants may bring First Fruits.

183 Who may be terminated at will by the landlord.

184 In this interpretation, farming rights for a limited time are treated as nonexistent for the question of First Fruits.

185 Even according to the rabbis.

186 Of any kind.

התרומה פרק שני

(fol. 64c) **משנה א:** הַתְּרוּמָה וְהַבִּיכּוּרִים חַיָּבִין עֲלֵיהֶן מִיתָה וְחוֹמֶשׁ וַאֲסוּרִין לַזָּרִים וְהֵן נִיכְסֵי כֹהֵן וְעוֹלִין בְּאֶחָד וּמֵאָה וּטְעוּנִין רְחִיצַת יָדַיִים וְהֶעֱרֵב שֶׁמֶשׁ. הֲרֵי אֵילּוּ בַּתְּרוּמָה וּבַבִּיכּוּרִים מַה שֶׁאֵין כֵּן בְּמַעֲשֵׂר.

Mishnah 1: For heave and First Fruits one incurs the penalty of death[1] or a fine of a fifth[2]; they are forbidden to lay persons, are Cohen's property[3], may be lifted by one in 100, need washing of the hands[4] and sundown[5]. This applies to heave and First Fruits but not to tithe[6].

1 Eating them in impurity is a deadly sin.

2 If misappropriated, the restitution must be 125% of what was taken; cf. *Terumot* 6, Note 1.

3 They might be traded from one Cohen to another and a Cohen may use them as gifts to marry a wife since, even if she was a lay person before, she becomes a member of the Cohen's family by marriage and may eat heave and First Fruits.

4 By rabbinic practice, hands are always impure in the second degree unless washed and watched after cleansing. Since heave and First Fruits can become impure in the third degree, touching heave or First Fruits with unwashed hands makes them unusable.

5 An impure person who cleansed himself by immersion in a *miqweh* is no longer impure, but he becomes pure for hallowed food only at sundown, cf. *Terumot* 5, Note 68.

6 First tithe of which heave of the tithe was taken is totally profane.

הלכה א: הַתְּרוּמָה וְהַבִּיכּוּרִין כול׳. כְּתִיב וַאֲנִי הִנֵּה נָתַתִּי לְךָ אֶת מִשְׁמֶרֶת תְּרוּמוֹתָיי. שְׁתֵּי תְרוּמוֹת הַתְּרוּמָה וְהַבִּכּוּרִין. תְּרוּמָה דִכְתִיב וְלֹא יִשְׂאוּ עָלָיו

חֵטְא וּמֵתוּ כוֹ כִּי יְחַלְּלוּהוּ. הַבִּיכּוּרִים דִּכְתִיב וַהֲבֵאתֶם שָׁמָּה עוֹלוֹתֵיכֶם אֵילּוּ הַבִּיכּוּרִים דִּכְתִיב וְלָקַח הַכֹּהֵן הַטֶּנֶא מִיָּדֶךָ. אוֹ נֹאמַר בַּקֳּדָשִׁים הַכָּתוּב מְדַבֵּר. כְּבָר כְּתִיב כָּרֵת בַּקֳּדָשִׁים. וִיהֵא מִיתָה וְכָרֵת בַּקֳּדָשִׁים. וְכִי יֵשׁ מֵת וְחוֹזֵר וּמֵת. כְּדָא דְתַנֵּי הַמֵּת לַחֲמִשִּׁים שָׁנָה מֵת בְּהִיכָּרֵת. לַחֲמִשִּׁים וּשְׁתַּיִם מִיתַת שְׁמוּאֵל הַנָּבִיא. לְשִׁשִּׁים מִיתָה הָאֲמוּרָה בַּתּוֹרָה. לְשִׁבְעִים מִיתָה שֶׁלְּחִיבָּה. לִשְׁמוֹנִים מִיתָה שֶׁלְּזִקְנָה. מִיכָּן וְהֵילָךְ חַיֵּי צַעַר.

Halakhah 1: "For heave and First Fruits," etc. It is written (*Num*. 18.8): "Behold, I gave to you the watch over My heaves." Two heaves, heave and First Fruits[7]. About heave it is written[8] (*Lev*. 22:9): "They should not carry sin because of it and die if they desecrate it." First fruits as it is written (*Deut*. 12:6): "There you shall bring your elevation offerings," these are First Fruits, as it is written (*Deut*. 26:4): "The Cohen shall take the basket from your hand.[9]"

Maybe we should say that the verse[10] refers to sacrifices? Extirpation is already written in regard to sacrifices[11].

Should sacrifices be subject to death and extirpation? Can somebody die and die again? As we have stated[12]: "If somebody dies at age 50, he dies of extirpation. At 52, the death of the prophet Samuel. At 60, it is the death written in the Torah. At 70, a death of love. At 80, death of old age. After that, a life of suffering."

7 In the Babli (*Šabbat* 25a, 26a; *Yebamot* 74a; and in slightly different form *Bekhorot* 34a), the two heaves are pure and impure (or pure and questionable), respectively. That tradition is in the name of the Davidic Rabba bar Abuha and may represent the autochthonous Babylonian tradition. In the Yerushalmi tradition, the verse determines the rules of First Fruits as those of heave.

8 The paragraph deals with the prohibition of impure hallowed food.

9 This statement is fragmentary

and unintelligible in the form presented. The full text is in *Sifry Deut.* 63: *There you shall bring your elevation offerings,* private and public, *your well-being offerings,* private and public, *your tithes;* R. Aqiba said, the verse deals with two different tithes, grain tithes and animal tithes, *and your hand's heaves*, these are First Fruits, as it is written: *The Cohen shall take the basket from your hand.* Other heaves do not have to be brought to the Temple.

10 *Lev.* 22:9 which imposes death by the hand of Heaven for desecrators.

11 *Lev.* 22:3 imposes the penalty of extirpation on any Cohen coming close to sacrifices while impure. Traditionally, extirpation is considered more of a punishment than death by the hand of Heaven.

12 A slightly extended form in *Śemaḥot* 3:8. The main change is in the first clause: "if somebody dies *up to* age 50." In the Babli, *Mo'ed Qaṭan* 28a, the text "at 60", is corrected to read "from 50 to 60" and the note on life after 80 is missing.

The following paragraphs discuss this statement.

מַה חֲמִית מֵימַר מֵת לַחֲמִשִּׁים מֵת בְּהִיכָּרֵת. כְּתִיב אַל תַּכְרִיתוּ אֶת שֵׁבֶט מִשְׁפְּחוֹת הַלֵּוִי וגו׳ וְזֹאת עֲשׂוּ לָהֶם וְחָיוּ וְלֹא יָמוּתוּ. עֲשׂוּ לָהֶם דָּבָר שֶׁלְּתַקָּנָה שֶׁלֹּא יְזוּנוּ עֵינֵיהֶן מִבֵּית קָדְשֵׁי הַקֳּדָשִׁים. וּכְתִיב וְלֹא יָבוֹאוּ לִרְאוֹת כְּבַלַּע אֶת הַקּוֹדֶשׁ וָמֵתוּ. וּכְתִיב וּמִבֶּן חֲמִשִּׁים שָׁנָה יָשׁוּב מִצְּבָא הָעֲבוֹדָה. רִבִּי אָבִין בְּרֵיהּ דְּרִבִּי תַּנְחוּם בַּר טְרֵיפוֹן שָׁמַע לָהּ מִן הָכָא. יְמֵי שְׁנוֹתֵינוּ בָהֶם שִׁבְעִים שָׁנָה. צֵא מֵהֶן עֶשְׂרִים שָׁנָה שֶׁאֵין בֵּית דִּין שֶׁלְּמַעֲלָן עוֹנְשִׁין וְכוֹרְתִין. נִמְצֵאת אוֹמֵר הַמֵּת לַחֲמִשִּׁים שָׁנָה מֵת בְּהִיכָּרֵת.

From where do you understand that if somebody dies at age 50, he dies of extirpation? It is written (*Num.* 4:18-19): "Do not extirpate the tribe of the families of (Levi), etc. Do the following for them that they should live and not die." Organize them that they should not enjoy seeing the holiest of holies. And it is written (*Num.* 4:20): "They should not come to look, when the holies are wrapped, and die." And it is written (*Num.* 8:25):

"At age 50, he should retire from the work force." Rebbi Abin, the son of Rebbi Tanḥum ben Rebbi Tryphon, understood it from here (*Ps*. 90:10): "The days of our lives here are 70 years." Subtract from these 20 years during which the Heavenly Court does neither punish not extirpate[13], and you will find that one who dies at up to 50 years dies in extirpation.

13 This tradition is also in the Babli, *Šabbat* 89b. While a male becomes a full member of the religious community at age 13, a female at age 12, they are treated as adults before the Heavenly court only at age 20 since in the story of the spies only the men older than 20 were punished. One has to assume that until then the parents are not absolved from responsibility for their children.

Neither "proof" has any logical consistency.

לַחֲמִשִּׁים וּשְׁתַּיִם מִיתַת שָׁאוּל הַנָּבִיא. רִבִּי אַבָּא בְּרֵיהּ דְּרִבִּי פַּפִּי. רִבִּי יְהוֹשֻׁעַ דְּסִיכְנִין בְּשֵׁם רִבִּי לֵוִי. בְּכָל־עֶצֶב יִהְיֶה מוֹתָר וּדְבַר שְׂפָתַיִם אַךְ לְמַחְסוֹר. חַנָּה עַל יְדֵי שֶׁרִיבְתָה בִתְפִילָּתָהּ קִיצְרָה בְיָמָיו שֶׁלִּשְׁמוּאֵל. שֶׁאָמְרָה וְיָשַׁב שָׁם עַד עוֹלָם. וַהֲלֹא אֵין עוֹלָמוֹ שֶׁלְּלֵוִי אֶלָּא חֲמִשִּׁים שָׁנָה. דִּכְתִיב וּמִבֶּן חֲמִשִּׁים שָׁנָה יָשׁוּב מִצְּבָא הָעֲבוֹדָה. וְחַיֵּי דְלוֹן חַמְשִׁין וְתַרְתֵּיי. אָמַר רִבִּי יוֹסֵי בֵּירִבִּי בוּן וּשְׁתַּיִם שֶׁגְּמָלַתּוּ.

"At 52, the death of the prophet Saul[14]." Rebbi Abba the son of Rebbi Pappai in[15] the name of Rebbi Levi; Rebbi Joshua from Sikhnin in the name of Rebbi Joshua ben Levi (*Prov*. 14:23): "From all toil there will be gain but from talk of lips only want." Hannah, because she prayed too much, shortened Samuel's life, since she said (*1S*. 1:22): "He shall dwell there forever.[16]" But the "forever" of a Levite is only 50 years, as it is written (*Num*. 8:25): "At the age of 50 years he shall retire from the workforce.[17]" But this one lived 52 years? Rebbi Yose ben Rebbi Abun said, two years until she weaned him.

14 Error for "Samuel", found uncorrected in ms. and the *editio princeps*. The tradition is from *Seder 'Olam* 13 (cf. the author's edition, Northvale N.J. 1998, pp. 129-135) and is reported in the Babli *Ta'anit* 5b, *Mo'ed Qaṭan* 28a. The material is Tannaïtic in *Seder 'Olam* and the Babli, a further argument that *Seder 'Olam* is a compilation of the Babylonian academies. Samuel at his retirement describes himself (*1S.* 12:2) as "old and white-haired."

15 An Amora of the fifth Galilean generation, usually reporting sayings of R. Levi.

16 However, this statement is not part of Hannah's prayer but her argument to her husband. Samuel was a Levite from the family of Gersom (*1Chr.* 6:13).

17 In verse 8:26 it is stated that the retired Levite may continue as a watchman.

לְשִׁשִּׁים מִיתָה הָאֲמוּרָה בַּתּוֹרָה. רִבִּי חִזְקִיָה בְּשֵׁם רִבִּי יַעֲקֹב בַּר אָחָא. כְּתִיב אִם יִרְאֶה אִישׁ בָּאֲנָשִׁים הָאֵלֶּה הַדּוֹר הָרָע הַזֶּה וגו'. הַגַּע עַצְמָךְ שֶׁיָּצָא מִמִּצְרַיִם בֶּן עֶשְׂרִים שָׁנָה וְעוֹד עָשָׂה בַּמִּדְבָּר אַרְבָּעִים שָׁנָה וָמֵת. נִמְצֵאת אוֹמֵר הַמֵּת לְשִׁשִּׁים שָׁנָה מִיתָה הָאֲמוּרָה בַּתּוֹרָה. וּכְתִיב תָּבוֹא בְכֶלַח עֲלֵי קָבֶר.

"At 60, it is the death written in the Torah[18]." Rebbi Ḥizqiah in the name of Rebbi Jacob bar Aḥa: It is written (*Deut.* 1:35): "If any male among these people, this evil generation, should see." Think of it, if anybody left Egypt at age 20 and then was in the desert for 40 years when he died, you find that the death written in the Torah is at age 60. And it is written (*Job.* 5:26): "You shall come into your grave *bklḥ*[19]."

18 As punishment.

19 The word כלח appears twice in Job, its etymology is unknown. The corresponding Arabic كلح means "having a stern countenance" as applied to people but "being shiny, bright" for things. The Babli, *Mo'ed Qaṭan* 28a, quotes only this verse as proof and notes that the (Alexandrian) numerical value of בכלח is 60. This seems to be the interpretation here also, the Yerushalmi being the source of the Babli.

לְשִׁבְעִים מִיתָה שֶׁלְחִיבָּה. יְמֵי שְׁנוֹתֵינוּ בָהֶם שִׁבְעִים שָׁנָה. לִשְׁמוֹנִים מִיתָה שֶׁלְזִקְנָה. שֶׁנֶּאֱמַר וְאִם בִּגְבוּרוֹת שְׁמוֹנִים שָׁנָה. וְכֵן בַּרְזִילַיי אוֹמֵר לְדָוִד בֶּן שְׁמוֹנִים (fol. 64d) שָׁנָה אָנֹכִי הַיּוֹם הַאֵדַע בֵּין טוֹב לְרָע.

At 70, a death of love. (*Ps.* 90:10): "The days of our lives are then 70 years." At 80, death of old age, as it is said: "At most, 80 years." Also thus Barzilai[20] said to David (*2S.* 19:36): "I am today 80 years of age, do I still know good from bad?"

20 In verse 33, he is described as "extremely old, 80 years of age."

אָפַר חֲמִשִּׁים שָׁנָה וְעָשָׂה דָבָר שֶׁהוּא בְהִיכָּרֵת אֲבָל רַב חָדֵי. אָפַר שִׁיתִּין וְעָשָׂה דָבָר שֶׁהוּא בָעֲוֹן מִיתָה אֲבָל חָדֵי. תַּנֵּי רִבִּי חֲנִינָה בֶּן אַנְטִיגְנָס אוֹמֵר זָקֵן שֶׁאָכַל אֶת הַחֵלֶב. וְכִי מִי מוֹדִיעֵנִיו שֶׁהוּא בְהִיכָּרֵת. כְּהָדָא דְתַנֵּי אוֹ שֶׁחִילֵּל אֶת הַשַּׁבָּת מֵת בְּהִיכָּרֵת. אֶלָּא כֵינִי. הַמֵּת לְיוֹם אֶחָד מִיתָה שֶׁלְזַעַם. לִשְׁנַיִם מִיתָה שֶׁלְבֶהָלָה. לִשְׁלֹשָׁה מֵת בַּמַּגֵּפָה. תַּנֵּי רִבִּי חֲלַפְתָּא בֶּן שָׁאוּל. מֵת בְּאֶחָד בִּשְׁנַיִם בִּשְׁלֹשָׁה בְּהִיכָּרֵת. לְאַרְבָּעָה לַחֲמִשָּׁה מִיתָה הֲדוּפָה. לְשִׁשָּׁה מִיתַת דֶּרֶךְ אֶרֶץ. לְשִׁבְעָה מִיתָה שֶׁלְחִיבָּה. מִיכָּן וְאֵילַךְ מֵת בְּיִיסוּרִין.

If he had passed[22] the age of 50 and did something punishable by extirpation, is he truly very happy[23]? If he had passed the age of 60 and did something punishable by death[24], can he truly be happy? It was stated: Rebbi Ḥanina ben Antigonos said, if an old man ate fat, who will show us that he is subject to extirpation? As we have stated, or if he desecrated the Sabbath[25] he dies by extirpation. But it must be the following[26]: He who dies in one day dies by rage, in two by urgency, in three by plague. Rebbi Ḥalafta ben Shaul stated: He who dies in one, two, three [days], dies by extirpation. Four or five is a hurried death, six a usual death, seven a death of love, longer he dies in pain[27].

21 Identifying אפר and עבר with all commentators. It is generally recognized that ע had disappeared from speech long before the Amoraic period; it appears in the Talmudim only as historical spelling. But that /ב/ = /פ/ is not usually recognized, though it appears, e. g., in ספסל = *subsellium*.

23 Most commentators change אבל into אכל without gaining anything. The meaning of אבל here is standard Mishnaic: "truly". If the punishment for a crime punishable by extirpation is death before age 50, is punishment waved for persons over age 50?

24 Death by Heaven's action.

25 In case there are no witnesses that the perpetrator had been duly warned (cf. *Kilaim* 8, Note 9), the punishment is in the hand of Heaven. The basis of this statement is *Ex.* 34:14 which decrees the judicial death penalty for the person who publicly desecrates the Sabbath and extirpation for doing work on the Sabbath.

26 Also stated in *Semaḥot* 3:9. In the Babli, *Mo'ed Qaṭan* 28a, the person who dies after 5 days of illness dies a normal death.

27 His soul avoids punishment by the Heavenly Court since he was made to suffer on Earth.

מַה חֲמִית מֵימַר מֵת לִשְׁלֹשָׁה יָמִים מֵת בְּמַגֵּפָה. חִילְפַיי בַּר בְּרֵיהּ דְּרִבִּי אַבָּהוּ אָמַר שָׁמְעִית קָלֵיהּ דְּרבי דְּרָשׁ וַיְהִי כַּעֲשֶׂרֶת הַיָּמִים וַיִּגֹּף יי אֶת נָבָל וַיָּמֹת. תָּלָה לוֹ הַקָּדוֹשׁ בָּרוּךְ הוּא שִׁבְעַת יְמֵי אֶבְלוֹ שֶׁלִּשְׁמוּאֵל שֶׁלֹּא יִתְעָרֵב אֶבְלוֹ עִם הַצַּדִּיק וְעָשָׂה עוֹד שְׁלֹשָׁה יָמִים וּמֵת בַּמַּגֵּפָה. רִבִּי חַגַּיי בְּשֵׁם רִבִּי שְׁמוּאֵל בַּר נַחְמָן לַעֲשֶׂרֶת יָמִים אֵין כְּתִיב כָּאן אֶלָּא כַּעֲשֶׂרֶת הַיָּמִים. תָּלָה לוֹ הַקָּדוֹשׁ בָּרוּךְ הוּא עֲשָׂרָה יָמִים כַּעֲשֶׂרֶת יָמִים שֶׁבֵּין רֹאשׁ הַשָּׁנָה לְבֵין יוֹם הַכִּיפּוּרִים שֶׁמָּא יַעֲשֶׂה תְשׁוּבָה וְלֹא עָשָׂה.

What did you see to assert that he who dies in three days dies from the plague[28]? Hilfai the grandson of Rebbi Abbahu said, I heard the voice of my grandfather[29] who preached (*1S.* 25:38): "It was like the ten days that the Eternal smote Nabal and he died." The Holy One, praise to Him, suspended His judgment during the seven days of mourning for Samuel[30], that mourning for him and for the just person should not overlap; then he lingered another three days and died. Rebbi Ḥaggai in the name of Rebbi Samuel bar Naḥman: It is not written "after ten days" but "like *the* ten days"; The Holy One, praise to Him, suspended His judgment for ten days, like the Ten Days between New Year's Day and the Day of Atonement[31], that he should repent, but he did not.

28 In the Babli (*loc. cit.* 26), death from the plague is within one day, based on *Ez.* 24:18.

29 Reading with *Midraš Šemuel* 23[9] סבי for רבי. The passage is quoted in *Midraš Šoḥer Ṭob* in the name of R. Hoshaia, in *Yalquṭ Šim'oni 2* #705 in the name of R. Ḥalaphta in the name of R. Abbahu. (*Yalquṭ Šim'oni*, being a compilation of excerpts, without editorial comments, is almost a ms. witness.)

In the Babli, *Roš Haššanah* 18a, only the explanation of R. Ḥaggai is given but by Rav Jehudah in the name of Rav; copied in *Yalquṭ Šim'oni 2* #134.

30 Noted in *1S.* 25:1.

31 The Days of Repentance.

כַּהֲנָא שָׁאַל לְרִבִּי זְעִירָא. זָר שֶׁאָכַל תְּרוּמָה. אָמַר לֵיהּ בְּעָוֹן מִיתָה. מִן דְּצָלִי אָמַר לֵיהּ אֲנִי יי הִפְסִיק הָעִנְיָין. רִבִּי חִייָה בְּשֵׁם רִבִּי יוֹחָנָן זָר שֶׁאָכַל תְּרוּמָה בְּעָוֹן מִיתָה. מַתְנִיתָא מְסַייְעָא לְרִבִּי יוֹחָנָן. אוֹכְלֵי תְרוּמָה בְזָדוֹן. טָהוֹר שֶׁאָכַל טָהוֹר. וְטָמֵא שֶׁאָכַל טָמֵא. וְטָהוֹר שֶׁאָכַל טָמֵא. וְטָמֵא שֶׁאָכַל טָהוֹר. בְּעָוֹן מִיתָה. אוֹכְלֵי תְרוּמָה בַכֹּהֲנִים. טָהוֹר שֶׁאָכַל טָהוֹר כְּמִצְוָתוֹ. טָהוֹר שֶׁאָכַל טָמֵא בַּעֲשֵׂה. טָמֵא שֶׁאָכַל טָהוֹר וְטָמֵא שֶׁאָכַל טָמֵא בְּלֹא תַעֲשֶׂה. מַה חֲמִית מֵימַר טָהוֹר שֶׁאָכַל טָמֵא בַּעֲשֵׂה. אָמַר רִבִּי בָּא בַּר מָמָל וְאַחַר יֹאכַל מִן הַקֳּדָשִׁים. מִן הַטְּהוֹרִין וְלֹא מִן הַטְּמֵאִין. כָּל־לֹא תַעֲשֶׂה שֶׁהוּא בָא מִכֹּחַ עֲשֵׂה עֲשֵׂה הוּא.

Cahana asked Rebbi Zeïra[32]: A layman who ate heave? He said to him, it is a deadly sin. After he had prayed, he said to him (*Lev.* 22:3): "I am the Eternal" closed the statement[33]. Rebbi Ḥiyya in the name of Rebbi Joḥanan: A layman who ate heave committed a deadly sin[34]. A *baraita* supports Rebbi Johanan: "Those who eat heave intentionally[35], whether pure [person] eating pure [heave], or impure eating impure, or pure eating impure, or impure eating pure, have commited a deadly sin. Cohanim eating heave, pure [person] eating pure [heave] fulfills its commandment; pure eating impure [has violated] a positive commandment; impure eating pure or impure eating impure [has violated] a prohibition. What did you see to say that a pure [person] eating impure [heave has violated] a positive commandment? Rebbi Abba bar Mamal said, (*Lev.* 22:7) "Afterwards he shall eat of the hallowed [food]", of what is pure but not of what is impure. Any prohibition which is implied by a positive commandment has the status of a positive commandment[36].

32 Since Cahana preceded R. Zeïra by at least one generation, the text is impossible. Later (Note 42) the statement is referred to as Rav's. Since Rav was teacher and colleague of Cahana, one has to read "Rav" instead of "R. Zeïra".

33 *Lev.* 22 deals with the rules of heave. In verse 3, Cohanim are subjected to the penalty of extirpartion for neglecting the rules of impurity. This verse closes with the remark "I am the Eternal", which usually appears at the conclusion of a commandment. R. Zeïra (Rav) concludes that no penalty has been spelled out for the rules given in verses 4 ff.

34 The prohibition is spelled out *Lev.* 22:10. For R. Zeïra it is a simple violation; for R. Johanan it falls under the punishment stated in verse 3.

35 In the Constantinople print: אוכלי תרומה בזרים "lay persons eating heave".

36 This is generally accepted also in the Babli (e. g., *Yebamot* 54b,73b; *Pesaḥim 71b; Zebaḥim* 34a, *Ḥulin* 81a). The proof is in the next paragraph. The transgression of a positive commandment is not prosecutable by a human court; the violation of a prohibition is.

The distinction between pure and impure food is read into the verse since מן "of" is partitive; there must be a category which is not included.

אָמַר רִבִּי אֲבִינָא. מִמַּשְׁמַע שֶׁנֶּאֱמַר כָּל־אֲשֶׁר לוֹ סְנַפִּיר וְקַשְׂקֶשֶׂת תֹּאכֵלוּ אֵין אָנוּ יוֹדְעִין וְכָל־אֲשֶׁר אֵין לוֹ סְנַפִּיר וְקַשְׂקֶשֶׂת לֹא תֹאכֵלוּ. לִיתֵּן עֲשֵׂה וְלֹא תַעֲשֶׂה עַל הַטְּמֵאִים. בְּגִין דִּכְתִיב. הָא אִילּוּ לֹא הֲוָה כְתִיב עֲשֵׂה הוּא. הֲוֵי כָּל־לֹא תַעֲשֶׂה שֶׁהוּא בָא מִכֹּחַ עֲשֵׂה עֲשֵׂה הוּא.

Rebbi Avina[37] said: Would one not understand that, since it is said (*Lev.* 11:9): "Any [creature in the water] having fins and scales you shall eat" we know that any creature having no fins and scales you shall not eat. To give both positive commandment and prohibition on the impure. Because it[38] is written. If it were not written, it would be a positive commandment. Therefore, any prohibition which is implied by a positive commandment has the status of a positive commandment[39].

37 In the Babli, *Ḥulin* 67b, the argument, in different style, is declared to be tannaïtic; the same in *Sifra Šemini Paraša* 3(1) in a text closely parallel to the Yerushalmi.

38 The prohibition "any having no fins or scales you shall not eat" is spelled out in *Lev.* 11:10.

39 It is impossible to say that a Jew who never eats fish transgresses the positive commandment of v. 9. Therefore, the positive formulation must have a negative implication. The eater of seafood is obligated for a purification offering as atonement for the violation of the prohibition and an elevation offering for the violation of the positive commandment.

רִבִּי יָסָא שָׁמַע לָהּ מִן הָכָא הַטָּמֵא וְהַטָּהוֹר יַחְדָּו יֹאכְלֶנּוּ. כָּאן הַטָּמֵא וְהַטָּהוֹר אוֹכְלִין בִּקְעָרָה אַחַת. בִּתְרוּמָה אֵין הַטָּמֵא וְהַטָּהוֹר אוֹכְלִין בִּקְעָרָה אַחַת. בְּקֳדָשִׁים. אָמַר רִבִּי יוֹחָנָן בַּר מַרְיָא אִין בְּגִין קֳדָשִׁים כְּבָר כְּתִיב וְהַבָּשָׂר אֲשֶׁר יִגַּע בְּכָל־טָמֵא לֹא יֵאָכֵל.

Rebbi Assi understood it from the following (*Deut.* 12:22): "The impure and the pure shall eat it together." Here, the impure and the pure shall eat it[40] from the same platter, but heave the impure and the pure may not eat from the same platter. About sacrifices[41]? Rebbi Joḥanan ben Marius said, if about sacrifices it is already written (*Lev.* 7:19): "Meat touching anything impure may not be eaten.[42]"

40 Profane meat slaughtered away from the sanctuary.

41 The verse points out the difference between profane and sacrifice meat.

42 While verse 12:22 may also apply to sacrifices, its main emphasis cannot be directed towards sacrifices but towards sanctified food eaten away from the sanctuary. This can only mean heave since the prohibition of impure sacrificial meat is already in *Lev.* 7:19.

מַתְנִיתָא פְלִיגָא עַל רַב. הַתְּרוּמָה וְהַבִּיכּוּרִין חַיָּבִין עֲלֵיהֶן מִיתָה. פָּתַר לָהּ בַּכֹּהֲנִים. וְהָא תַנִּינָן חוֹמֶשׁ. וְכִי יֵשׁ חוֹמֶשׁ בַּכֹּהֲנִים. פָּתַר לָהּ. לִצְדָדִין הִיא מַתְנִיתָא. רֵישָׁא בַּכֹּהֲנִים וְסֵיפָא בְיִשְׂרָאֵל. מַתְנִיתָא מְסַייְעָא לְרִבִּי יוֹחָנָן. וַאֲסוּרִין לְזָרִים. פָּתַר לָהּ פָּחוֹת מִכְּשִׁיעוּר.

The Mishnah disagrees with Rav[43]: "For heave and First Fruits one is liable to penalty of death." He explains it, for Cohanim[44]. But did we not state: "fifth"? Is there a fifth for Cohanim[45]? He explains that the Mishnah is case by case. The first clause for Cohanim, the last for Israel. Does the Mishnah support Rebbi Joḥanan: "They are forbidden to lay persons"?[46] He explains it, less than a legal quantity[47].

43 He denies that lay persons eating heave incur a deadly guilt, cf. Note 32.

44 Since this is explicit in *Lev.* 22:3, one would not need a Mishnah.

45 The duty of restitution of 125% is restricted to lay persons by *Lev.* 22:14.

46 If the Mishnah disagrees with Rav, it should support R. Joḥanan. But for him it is not necessary to state the prohibition to lay persons separately; it is included in the cases where mishandling heave and First Fruits is a

deadly sin!

47 Mishandling a minute quantity of hallowed food is not prosecutable by a human court or atonable by a sacrifice; therefore it is assumed that the Heavenly Court will not treat this as a deadly sin.

וְהֵן נִיכְסֵי כֹהֵן. רִבִּי בָּא רִבִּי חִיָּיה בְּשֵׁם רִבִּי יוֹחָנָן. לְךָ נְתַתִּיו לְמָשְׁחָה. לְמָשְׁחָה לִגְדּוּלָּה. לְמָשְׁחָה לִיסִיכָה. לְמָשְׁחָה לְהַדְלָקָה. הָיִיתִי אוֹמֵר בֵּין טְמֵאִים בֵּין טְהוֹרִים. רִבִּי אַבָּהוּ בְשֵׁם רִבִּי יוֹחָנָן לֹא בִעַרְתִּי מִמֶּנּוּ. מַבְעִיר אַתְּ הַתְּרוּמָה בְטוּמְאָה. רִבִּי זְעִירָא בְּשֵׁם רִבִּי לָעְזָר. מְנַיִין לְמַעֲשֵׂר שֵׁינִי עַצְמוֹ שֶׁנִּיטְמָא שֶׁאֵין מַדְלִיקִין בּוֹ. תַּלְמוּד לוֹמַר לֹא בִעַרְתִּי מִמֶּנּוּ בְּטָמֵא. רָאוּי לִפְדּוֹתוֹ וְאַתְּ אָמַר הָכֵין. לֹא אַתְיָא דְלֹא אוֹ בְלָקוּחַ בְּכֶסֶף מַעֲשֵׂר שֶׁנִּיטְמָא. אָמַר רִבִּי יְהוּדָה אוּף בְּבִיכּוּרִין שֶׁנִּיטְמְאוּ דִּבְרֵי הַכֹּל.

"They are the Cohen's property." Rebbi Abba, Rebbi Ḥiyya in the name of Rebbi Joḥanan (*Num.* 18: 8): "To you I gave it[48] as *mošḥâ*." As *mošḥâ*, for importance[49]. As *mošḥâ*, for anointing. As *mošḥâ*, as fuel[50].

I would say, both for impure and pure. Rebbi Abbahu in the name of Rebbi Joḥanan, (*Deut.* 26:14) "I did not burn any of it[51]," but one liquidates heave in impurity. Rebbi Zeïra in the name of Rebbi Eleazar: From where for Second Tithe proper which became impure that one may not use it as fuel? The verse says, "I did not burn any of it in impurity". One may redeem it and you are saying this[52]? One may only interpret it as referring to what was bought with Second Tithe money[53]. Rebbi Jehudah said[54], but for First Fruits which became impure it is the opinion of everybody.

48 In the verse נתתים "I gave them."

49 The root being משח "to anoint", as symbol of elevation.

50 In Aramaic, משח is "oil".

51 The declaration at the distribution of the tithe of the poor and the

consumption of Second Tithe in Jerusalem, including a reference to First Fruits. There is a difference in rules between heave and First Fruits in this respect.

The argument as reported in Babli *Yebamot* 73b is to take ממנו as partitive: This hallowed food cannot be burned but other (heave) can.

52 Since Second Tithe may always be redeemed for money, impure Second Tithe is redeemed and becomes totally profane. It may be burned as profane fuel.

53 In this case, R. Jehudah holds in Mishnah *Ma'aser Šeni* 3:10 that produce bought with tithe money in Jerusalem which became impure cannot be redeemed but must be buried.

54 The statement is an Amoraic interpretation of what R. Jehudah might have said, that Mishnah *Bikkurim* 1:8 implies that impure First Fruits must be destroyed even for those who permit redemption of fruits bought with tithe money.

הֲרֵי אֵילּוּ בִתְּרוּמָה וּבְבִיכּוּרִין מַה שֶׁאֵין כֵּן בְּמַעֲשֵׂר. תַּמָּן תַּנִּינָן נוֹטְלִין לְיָדַיִם לְחוּלִין וּלְמַעֲשֵׂר. וְלִתְרוּמָה וּלְקוֹדֶשׁ מַטְבִּילִין. תַּמָּן אַתְּ אָמַר. אֵין הַמַּעֲשֵׂר טָעוּן רְחִיצָה וְהָכָא אַתְּ אָמַר הַמַּעֲשֵׂר טָעוּן רְחִיצָה. הֵן דְּתֵימַר הַמַּעֲשֵׂר טָעוּן רְחִיצָה. רַבָּנִין. הֵן דְּתֵימַר אֵין הַמַּעֲשֵׂר טָעוּן רְחִיצָה. רִבִּי מֵאִיר. תַּמָּן תַּנִּינָן כָּל־הַטָּעוּן בִּיאַת מַיִם מִדִּבְרֵי סוֹפְרִים מְטַמֵּא אֶת הַקּוֹדֶשׁ וּפוֹסֵל אֶת הַתְּרוּמָה וּמוּתָּר בְּחוּלִין וּבְמַעֲשֵׂר דִּבְרֵי רִבִּי מֵאִיר. וַחֲכָמִים אוֹסְרִין בְּמַעֲשֵׂר. וְלֹא שְׁמִיעַ דְּאָמַר רִבִּי שְׁמוּאֵל בְּשֵׁם רִבִּי זְעִירָה. מַהוּ וַחֲכָמִים אוֹסְרִין בְּמַעֲשֵׂר. נִפְסַל גּוּפוֹ מִלּוֹכַל בְּמַעֲשֵׂר. מַיי כְדוֹן. הֵן דְּתֵימַר הַמַּעֲשֵׂר טָעוּן רְחִיצָה בְּרוֹצֶה לוֹכַל. הֵן דְּתֵימַר אֵין הַמַּעֲשֵׂר טָעוּן רְחִיצָה בְּרוֹצֶה לִיגַּע. לֹא הוּא רוֹצֶה לוֹכַל הוּא רוֹצֶה לִיגַּע. אֶלָּא מִשּׁוּם נְטִילַת סֶרֶךְ. וְהָתַנִּינָן תְּרוּמָה. וְכִי יֵשׁ תְּרוּמָה מִשּׁוּם נְטִילַת סֶרֶךְ. אֶלָּא בְחוּלִין שֶׁנַּעֲשׂוּ עַל גַּב הַקּוֹדֶשׁ. וְחוּלִין שֶׁנַּעֲשׂוּ עַל גַּב הַקּוֹדֶשׁ לֹא כְחוּלִין הֵן. תִּיפְתָּר אִי כְרִבִּי שִׁמְעוֹן בֶּן אֶלְעָזָר אִי כְרִבִּי לָעְזָר בֵּירִבִּי צָדוֹק. אִי כְרִבִּי שִׁמְעוֹן בֶּן אֶלְעָזָר דְּתַנֵּי רִבִּי שִׁמְעוֹן בֶּן אֶלְעָזָר אוֹמֵר מִשּׁוּם רִבִּי מֵאִיר הַיָּדַיִם תְּחִילָּה לְחוּלִין וּשְׁנִיּוֹת לִתְרוּמָה. אִי כְרִבִּי אֶלְעָזָר בֵּירִבִּי צָדוֹק דְּתַנִּינָן תַּמָּן וְחוּלִין שֶׁנַּעֲשׂוּ עַל גַּב הַקּוֹדֶשׁ הֲרֵי אֵילּוּ כְחוּלִין. רִבִּי אֶלְעָזָר בֵּירִבִּי צָדוֹק אוֹמֵר הֲרֵי אֵילּוּ כִתְרוּמָה לְטַמֵּא שְׁנַיִם וּלְפְסוֹל אֶחָד.

[55]"This applies to heave and First Fruits but not to tithe." There[56], we have stated: "One washes his hands for profane, tithe, and heave; but for sacrifices one immerses[57]." There[58], you say that tithe does not need washing and here you say, tithe needs washing! Those who say, tithe needs washing, the rabbis; he who says, tithe does not need washing, Rebbi Meïr. There[59], we have stated: "Anything needing immersion in water by rabbinic decree[60] makes sacrifices impure and heave unusable[61] but is permitted for profane food and tithe. But the Sages forbid for tithe[62]." Is that not explained by what Rebbi Samuel says in the name of Rebbi Zeïra, what means the Sages forbid for tithe? His body is disqualified from eating tithe. What is that? May you say tithe needs washing, if he wants to eat; may you say tithe does not need washing, if he wants to touch? No, wanting to touch is the same as wanting to eat[63]. So it must be washing as discipline[64]. But we have stated: "heave"! Is there washing as discipline for heave[65]? But it is about profane food prepared by the rules of sacrifices[66]. Is profane food prepared by the rules of sacrifices not profane? Explain it either[67] following Rebbi Simeon ben Eleazar or following Rebbi Eleazar ben Rebbi Ẓadoq. Either following Rebbi Simeon ben Eleazar as it was stated: Rebbi Simeon ben Eleazar says in the name of Rebbi Meïr: Hands are [impure] in the first degree for profane food, in the second for heave[68]. Or following Rebbi Eleazar ben Rebbi Ẓadoq as it was stated there[69]: "Profane food prepared by the rules of sacrifices is profane. Rebbi Eleazar ben Rebbi Ẓadoq says it is like heave, it may be impure in two degrees and invalidates a third."

55 The origin of this paragraph is in *Ḥagigah* 2:5; a parallel discussion in Babli *Ḥagigah* 18b. The statement discussed is that tithe, in contrast to

heave and First Fruits, may be eaten with unwashed hands. "Tithe" here always means Second Tithe since First Tithe whose heave of the tithe was separated is totally profane.

56 Mishnah *Ḥagigah* 2:5.

57 One has to immerse his hands in 40 *seah* of water. "Washing" means that at least a quarter *log* ($^1/_{96}$ *seah*) of water flows over the hands.

58 "There" is the Mishnah *Bikkurim* 2:1, "here" is Mishnah *Ḥagigah* 2:5.

59 Mishnah *Parah* 11:5.

60 Any impurity not explicitly stated in the Pentateuch.

61 Unwashed hands are always impure in the second degree by rabbinic decree (cf. *Berakhot* 8, Note 46). Profane food can only become impure in two degrees; the second cannot induce impurity in other profane food. Heave can become impure in three degrees; the third is called "unusable" since it cannot induce impurity in other food (except sacrifices which have four degrees.)

62 Second Tithe cannot be eaten with unwashed hands.

63 Nobody can expect a food handler not to eat.

64 Washing one's hands for profane food (in the Babli restricted to eating bread) is to teach people the discipline needed to handle heave (sources cf. Note 55).

65 For heave, washing is a biblical requirement. If heave is mentioned in a Mishnah, it cannot be dealing with washing because of rabbinic discipline.

66 This was practiced, e. g., by the Qumran sect who ate all their food under the strict rules of impurities applicable to sacrifices. Usually, strict Pharisees prepared their food under the rules of heave.

67 This use of אי' is a Babylonism not usually found in the Yerushalmi.

68 They will transfer impurity to any food but that food cannot induce other impurity.

69 Mishnah *Ṭahorot* 2:8.

(fol. 64c) **משנה ב**: יֵשׁ בְּמַעֲשֵׂר וּבְבִיכּוּרִים מַה שֶׁאֵין כֵּן בִּתְרוּמָה. שֶׁהַמַּעֲשֵׂר וְהַבִּיכּוּרִים טְעוּנִין הֲבָאַת מָקוֹם וּטְעוּנִין וִידּוּי וַאֲסוּרִין לָאוֹנֵן. רִבִּי שִׁמְעוֹן מַתִּיר. וְחַיָּבִין בְּבִיעוּר וְרִבִּי שִׁמְעוֹן פּוֹטֵר. וְאוֹסְרִין כָּל־שֶׁהֵן מִלּוֹכַל בִּירוּשָׁלֵם אַף לְזָרִים וְאַף לִבְהֵמָה. רִבִּי שִׁמְעוֹן מַתִּיר. הֲרֵי אֵילוּ בְּמַעֲשֵׂר וּבְבִכּוּרִים מַה שֶׁאֵין כֵּן בִּתְרוּמָה.

Mishnah 2: Some rules apply to tithe[70] and First Fruits but not to heave since tithe and First Fruits need to be brought to the Place[71]; they need a declaration[73] and are forbidden to the current mourner[74], but Rebbi Simeon permits[75]. They are subject to removal, but Rebbi Simeon frees from the obligation[75]. They forbid in Jerusalem the most minute amount[76] to be eaten by the unauthorized and animals; Rebbi Simeon permits.[77] These rules apply to tithe and First Fruits but not to heave.

70 Second tithe only.

71 The Temple for First Fruits, Jerusalem for second tithe.

73 For second tithe, *Deut*. 26:13-15. For First Fruits, *Deut*. 26:3-10.

74 A person who has to arrange for the burial of a close relative, between the time of death and the burial.

75 Since the אונן is explicitly forbidden second tithe (*Deut*. 26:14) and the declaration is one of removal (*Deut*. 26:13), R. Simeon can disagree only regarding First Fruits. Removal means that first and poor people's tithes were given away and second tithe brought to Jerusalem.

76 While second tithe becomes insignificant in a majority of permitted food and First Fruits by 1 in 100, this applies only outside of Jerusalem.

77 The Babylonian Mishnah has here another sentence, stating that plants grown in Jerusalem from second tithe or First Fruits also forbid in the most minute amounts; but R. Simeon permits. It is the general wisdom since the time of R. Eliahu Kramer of Wilna that the sentence is missing by an oversight of the scribe. But since the Halakhah corrects the Mishnah to insert the sentence, it is clear that it was missing in the accepted Mishnah text. In general it is safe to assume that textual corrections by R. Eliahu of Wilna are unwarranted.

(fol. 64d) **הלכה ב**: טְעוּנִין הֲבָאַת מָקוֹם. דִּכְתִיב וַהֲבֵאתֶם שָׁמָּה עוֹלוֹתֵיכֶם וְזִבְחֵיכֶם וְאֵת מַעְשְׂרוֹתֵיכֶם וְאֵת תְּרוּמַת יֶדְכֶם. תְּרוּמַת יֶדְכֶם אֵילּוּ הַבִּיכּוּרִים. דִּכְתִיב וְלָקַח הַכֹּהֵן הַטֶּנֶא מִיָּדֶךָ.

Halakhah 2: "They need to be brought to the Place." Because it is written (*Deut*. 12:6): "There, you shall bring your elevation offerings, your family sacrificies, your tithes[78], and your hand's heave." "Your hand's heave" are First Fruits since it is written (*Deut*. 26:4): "The Cohen shall take the basket from your hand."[79]

78 Animal and second tithes.

79 *Sifry Deut*. 63.

עַד כְּדוֹן מַעֲשֵׂר. בִּיכּוּרִים מְנַיִין. כַּיי דְאָמַר רִבִּי יַעֲקֹב בַּר חָמָא בְּשֵׁם רִבִּי לָעְזָר. הַקּוֹדֶשׁ הַקּוֹדֶשׁ הָעֶלְיוֹן בְּמַשְׁמַע.

So far tithe, from where First Fruits[80]? As Rebbi Jacob bar Ḥama[81] said in the name of Rebbi Eleazar (*Deut*. 26:13): "The hallowed food." That hallowed food is meant which was described in the preceding paragraph[82].

80 What implies that First Fruits, while they have their own declaration, have to be delivered on time? The farmer cannot read the declaration of second tithe if he has undelivered First Fruits at home.

81 No R. Jacob bar Ḥama is otherwise known; the commentators following R. S. Cirillo read "R. Jacob bar Aḥa" since this name is quoted in the next paragraph.

82 *Deut*. 26:1-11.

This contradicts the tannaïtic tradition (Mishnah *Ma'aser Šeni* 5:10, *Sifry Deut*. 303) that the reference is to second tithe and fourth-year yield.

וּטְעוּנִין וִידּוּי. דִּכְתִיב וְעָנִיתָ וְאָמַרְתָּ לִפְנֵי יי אֱלֹהֶיךָ. עַד כְּדוֹן מַעֲשֵׂר. בִּיכּוּרִין מְנַיִין. כַּיי דְאָמַר רִבִּי יַעֲקֹב בַּר אָחָא בְּשֵׁם רִבִּי לָעְזָר. הַקּוֹדֶשׁ הַקּוֹדֶשׁ הָעֶלְיוֹן

בְּמַשְׁמַע.

"They need a declaration." Since it is written (*Deut.* 26:5): "You should formally declare[83] before the Eternal, your God[84]." So far tithe, from where First Fruits? As Rebbi Jacob bar Ḥama said in the name of Rebbi Eleazar (*Deut.* 26:13): "The hallowed food." That hallowed food is meant which was described in the preceding paragraph.

83 Or: "You shall answer and declare", repeating the text of the declaration recited by the priest. This verse deals only with First Fruits. Cf. Halakhah 3:5; *Sifry Deut.* 301. The declaration for tithes is prescribed in v. 13.

84 This introduces the declaration of First Fruits. The next two sentences are copied from the preceding paragraph, most likely in error. They are appropriate again in the next paragraph.

וַאֲסוּרִין לָאוֹנֵן. דִּכְתִיב לֹא אָכַלְתִּי בְאוֹנִי מִמֶּנּוּ. עַד כְּדוֹן מַעֲשֵׂר. בִּיכּוּרִין מְנַיִין. כַּיי דְאָמַר רִבִּי יַעֲקֹב בַּר אָחָא בְשֵׁם רִבִּי לְעָזָר. הַקּוֹדֶשׁ הַקּוֹדֶשׁ הָעֶלְיוֹן בְּמַשְׁמַע.

"They are forbidden to the current mourner." Since it is written (*Deut.* 26:14): "I did not eat from it in my deep mourning." So far tithe, from where First Fruits? As Rebbi Jacob bar Aḥa said in the name of Rebbi Eleazar (*Deut.* 26:13): "The hallowed food." That hallowed food is meant which was described in the preceding paragraph.

תַּנִּינָן כָּל־אִילֵּין מִילַּיָּא וְרִבִּי שִׁמְעוֹן פָּלִיג. גַּבֵּי וִידּוּי לֵית רִבִּי שִׁמְעוֹן פָּלִיג. וִידּוּי זוֹ קְרִייָה. וְלֵית רִבִּי שִׁמְעוֹן פָּלִיג דִּכְתִיב וְעָנִיתָ וְאָמַרְתָּ.

In all these cases we stated that Rebbi Simeon disagrees. For the declaration Rebbi Simeon does not disagree. The declaration is the reading; there, Rebbi Simeon does not disagree since it is written (*Deut.* 26:5): "You should formally declare."

כֵּינִי מַתְנִיתָא וְאוֹסְרִין כָּל־שֶׁהֵן מִלּוֹכַל בִּירוּשָׁלֵם. רִבִּי שִׁמְעוֹן מַתִּיר. וְגִידּוּלֵיהֶן אֲסוּרִין מִלּוֹכַל בִּירוּשָׁלֵם וְרִבִּי שִׁמְעוֹן מַתִּיר. וְאַף לְזָרִים (fol. 65a) וְאַף לִבְהֵמָה רִבִּי שִׁמְעוֹן מַתִּיר. וְאוּף רַבָּנִין מוֹדוֹי לֵיהּ. מִן דּוּ מָתִיב לוֹן. אֵין אַתֶּם מוֹדִין בָּהֶן מוּתָּרִין לְזָרִים שֶׁהֵן מוּתָּרִין לַאֲכִילַת בְּהֵמָה. וְיֵשׁ מְחִצָּה לַאֲכִילַת זָרִים וְיֵשׁ מְחִצָּה לַאֲכִילַת בְּהֵמָה. כְּשֵׁם שֶׁאֵין מְחִצָּה לְזָרִים כָּךְ אֵין מְחִצָּה לַאֲכִילַת בְּהֵמָה. רַבָּנִין אָמְרִין יְרוּשָׁלֵם עָשׂוּ אוֹתָהּ כְּדָבָר שֶׁאֵין לוֹ מַתִּירִין. כְּמַה דְתֵימַר דָּבָר שֶׁאֵין לוֹ מַתִּירִין אֹסֵר כָּל־שֶׁהוּא. וְדִכְוָותֵיהּ יְרוּשָׁלֵם אוֹסֵר כָּל־שֶׁהוּא.

So is the Mishnah: "They forbid in Jerusalem in the most minute amount; Rebbi Simeon permits. Their growth[85] in Jerusalem is forbidden to be eaten and Rebbi Simeon permits. Also by the unauthorized or by animals does Rebbi Simeon permit." Do not the rabbis agree with him since he asked them[86]: Do you not agree that if they are permitted for the unauthorized, they are permitted as animal feed? Does one need walls[87] for unauthorized eating or for feeding animals? Just as one does not need walls for unauthorized eating, one does not need walls for feeding animals! The rabbis say, they made Jerusalem something which has no possibility to become permitted[88]. Anything which has no possibility to become permitted prohibits in the most minute amounts; similarly, Jerusalem prohibits in the most minute amounts.

85 Plants growing from second tithe or First Fruits used as seeds. Even though it is stated in Mishnah *Terumot* 9:4 that growth from First Fruits or second tithe is profane, this holds only outside of Jerusalem. Since both First Fruits and second tithe have to be consumed in Jerusalem, if they are mixed with profane food they still can be eaten in Jerusalem by the people entitled to eat the original hallowed food, Cohanim for First Fruits and pure Jews for second tithe.

The Tosephta (1:7) has a different version: "R. Simeon says they did not forbid the growth of First Fruits to require them to be eaten in Jerusalem." This speaks of growth of First Fruits outside of Jerusalem and contradicts Mishnah *Terumot* 9:4.

86 In a *baraita* not otherwise transmitted.

87 Food that has to be consumed in the holy precinct outside the Temple domain must be consumed inside the city walls (possibly defined as the walls of the city in First Temple times.) Since growth from dedicated seeds is intrinsically profane and does not need city walls if used as animal feed, walls are not needed and the restriction to those authorized is without basis (cf. *Tosafot Pesaḥim* 34a, *s. v.* טהרו).

88 The rabbis agree that R. Simeon might have a logical point but their position is that leniencies here are uncalled for since any food in question can be eaten in Jerusalem.

The formulation used here, דָּבָר שֶׁאֵין לוֹ מַתִּירִין "something which has no possibility to become permitted", appears in the Babli (*Beẓah* 3b,39a; *Yebamot* 82a; *Baba Meẓia* 53a) and the Tosephta (*Terumot* 5:15) as דָּבָר שֶׁיֵּשׁ לוֹ מַתִּירִין "something which has a possibility to become permitted". The language of the Babli is straightforward: For something which may become permitted without invoking the rules of insignificance (1 in 60, 100, or 200), those rules were not instituted. The standard example is that of an egg freshly laid on the Sabbath which is not food prepared for the Sabbath but becomes automatically permitted at the end of the Sabbath. If such an egg disappears in a barrel containing 1'000 eggs, all are forbidden for use until the end of the Sabbath.

The language of the Yerushalmi, "something which has no possibility to become permitted", presupposes the knowledge of the rule: If the rules of insignificance were not instituted for a certain case, they are not applicable even in the case of the smallest possible admixture. Since First Fruits and second tithe can be eaten in Jerusalem, they are always permitted for authorized people and are therefore "something which has no possibility to become permitted".

מַה פְלִיגִין רִבִּי שִׁמְעוֹן וְרַבָּנִין. בְּגִידּוּלִין. אֲבָל בְּעֵירוּבִין אוּף רִבִּי שִׁמְעוֹן מוֹדֵיי. מַה בֵין עֵירוּבִין מַה בֵין גִידּוּלִין. עֵירוּבִין בְּעֵייְנָן הֵן. גִידּוּלִין כְּבָר בָּטְלוּ. כְּמַה דְרִבִּי שִׁמְעוֹן מוֹדֵי לְרַבָּנִין בְּעֵירוּבֵי מַעֲשֵׂר. אֲבָל בְּעֵירוּבֵי בִיכּוּרִין כְּגִידּוּלִין הֵן.

וְכֵן הָיָה רִבִּי שִׁמְעוֹן אוֹמֵר. אֵין הַבִּיכּוּרִין אוֹסְרִין אֶת עֵירוּבֵיהֶן וְגִידּוּלֵיהֶן מִלּוֹכַל בִּירוּשָׁלֵם. מַה בֵּין מַעֲשֵׂר מַה בֵּין בִּיכּוּרִין. מַעֲשֵׂר אֵין לוֹ עֲלִייָה. בִּכּוּרִים יֵשׁ לָהֶן עֲלִייָה. הֲוֵי מַה דְּרִבִּי שִׁמְעוֹן מוֹדֵי לְרַבָּנִין בְּדָבָר שֶׁאֵין לוֹ עֲלִייָה. מוֹדֵי רִבִּי שִׁמְעוֹן בְּאוֹתָהּ הַסְּאָה שֶׁהֶעֱלָה מִתּוֹךְ סְאָה שֶׁהִיא טְעוּנָה מְחִיצָה וּטְעוּנָה הֲנָייָה. וְרַבָּנִין אָמְרִין כּוּלְּהֶן טְעוּנוֹת מְחִיצָה וּטְעוּנוֹת הֲנָיָיה.

About what do Rebbi Simeon and the rabbis disagree? About growth. But in mixtures even Rebbi Simeon agrees. What is the difference between growth and mixtures? In mixtures all exists. In growth it already has disappeared. Where Rebbi Simeon agrees with the rabbis is in mixtures of tithe, but mixtures of First Fruits are treated like growth. And so did Rebbi Simeon say[89]: "First fruits do not forbid their mixtures or growths to be eaten in Jerusalem." What is the difference between tithe and First Fruits? Tithe cannot be lifted[90], First Fruits can be lifted[91]. Rebbi Simeon agrees that the *seah* lifted for another *seah* needs walls and needs use[92]. But the rabbis say, all[93] need walls and need use.

89 Cf. *Tosefta* 1:7 (Note 85.)

90 Second tithe is never mentioned among foods that may be lifted; cf. *'Orlah* 1, Note 174.

91 By one in 100, cf. Mishnah 2:1.

92 It must be eaten in Jerusalem (as defined by its walls) and it may not be destroyed in small quantities as second tithe of *demay* may be; cf. *Demay* 1, Notes 105 ff.

93 Both second tithe and First Fruits.

רִבִּי יוֹחָנָן אָזַל לְחַד אֲתַר אָמַר אֲנָא בֶּן עַזַּיי דְּהָכָא. אֲתָא חַד סָב שָׁאַל לֵיהּ. אָמַר גִּידּוּלֵי תְרוּמָה תְּרוּמָה וְגִידּוּלֵי גִידּוּלִין חוּלִין. אֲבָל טֶבֶל וּמַעֲשֵׂר שֵׁינִי וּמַעֲשֵׂר רִאשׁוֹן וּסְפִיחֵי שְׁבִיעִית וּתְרוּמַת חוּץ לָאָרֶץ הַמְדוּמָּע וְהַבִּיכּוּרִין גִּידּוּלֵיהֶן חוּלִין. תַּמָּן אַתְּ אָמַר גִּידּוּלֵיהֶן מוּתָּרִין. וְהָכָא אַתְּ אָמַר גִּידּוּלֵיהֶן אֲסוּרִין. אָמַר לֵיהּ. הֵן דְּתֵימַר גִּידּוּלֵיהֶן מוּתָּרִין בְּדָבָר שֶׁזַּרְעוֹ כָלֶה. וְהֵן

דְּתֵימַר גִּידּוּלֵיהֶן אֲסוּרִין בְּדָבָר שֶׁאֵין זַרְעוֹ כָלֶה. אָמַר לֵיהּ וְהָתַנִּינָן אֵי זֶהוּ דָבָר שֶׁאֵין זַרְעוֹ כָלֶה. כְּגוֹן הַלּוּף וְהַשּׁוּם וְהַבְּצָלִים. וְהַלּוּף וְהַשּׁוּם וְהַבְּצָלִים חַייָבִין בְּבִיכּוּרִים. אָמַר אָזַל בֶּן עַזַּאי דְּהָכָא אַתְּ אָמַר. שָׁאַל לְרִבִּי יַנַּאי. אָמַר לֵיהּ לְמַעֲשֵׂר הוּשְׁבָה דָּבָר שֶׁאֵין זַרְעוֹ כָלֶה.

Rebbi Johanan went to a place and said, I am Ben Azai[94] here. There came an old man to ask him. He said, [95]"the growth from heave is heave; the growth from their growth is profane. But the growths from *ṭevel*, second tithe and first tithe, aftergrowth of the Sabbatical, heave from outside the Land, *dema'*, and First Fruits are profane." There, you say their[96] growth is permitted, why do you say here, their growth is forbidden? He said to him, where do we say their growth is permitted? For things whose seeds disappear. Where do we say their growth is forbidden? For things whose seeds do not disappear. He said to him, but did we not state[97]: "What is one whose seeds do not disappear? For example arum, garlic, and onions." Are arum, garlic, and onions obligated for First Fruits[98]? He[99] said, the Ben Azai from here went away as you say. He[99] asked Rebbi Yannai who told him, for tithe everything was classified as things whose seeds do not disappear.

94 The student of R. Joshua and colleague of R. Aqiba who could immediately answer all questions of Jewish law. The Talmudim (*Peah* 6:3, Note 79; Babli *Erubin* 29a, *Qiddušin* 20a) report that any other outstanding scholar who tried to imitate Ben Azai was quickly put down.

95 Mishnah *Terumah* 9:4 (but there, second tithe is not mentioned.)

96 Second tithe and First Fruits.

97 Mishnah *Terumah* 9:6.

98 They are not acceptable as First Fruits.

99 R. Johanan.

מִחְלְפָה שִׁיטָּתֵיהּ דְּרִבִּי יוֹחָנָן. תַּמָּן אָמַר רִבִּי יְהוֹשֻׁעַ בֶּן לֵוִי. לְקַרְנָהּ שֶׁלִּנְבֵילָה הוּשְׁבָה. אָמַר לֵיהּ לֹא כֵן אִילְפָן רִבִּי. רָאִיתִי כִגְרִיס שְׁנַיִם. וְאָמַר אוּף הָכָא וְגִידּוּלֵיהֶן. וְעוֹד מִן הָדָא. לֹא תוּכַל לֶאֱכֹל בִּשְׁעָרֶיךָ מַעְשַׂר דְּגָנְךָ. בְּאֵי זֶה מַעֲשֵׂר אֲמָרוֹ. בְּמַעֲשֵׂר שֵׁינִי הַטָּהוֹר שֶׁנִּכְנַס לִירוּשָׁלַיִם וְיָצָא. וְאוּף מִן הָדָא דְתַנֵּי לָהּ רִבִּי שִׁמְעוֹן. תַּנֵּי בְשֵׁם רִבִּי שִׁמְעוֹן יֵשׁ בְּמַעֲשֵׂר שֶׁהַמַּעֲשֵׂר אוֹסֵר דָּמָיו וְעֵירוּבָיו וְקַנְקַנָּיו וְסָפֵק עֵירוּבוֹ כָּל־שֶׁהוּא וְאֵין מַדְלִיקִין בּוֹ. וְאָמַר אוּף בְּגִידּוּלִין כֵּן. אָמַר רִבִּי הִילָא הֵן דְּתֵימַר גִּידּוּלֵיהֶן אֲסוּרִין רַבָּנִין. וְהֵן דְּתֵימַר גִּידּוּלֵיהֶן מוּתָּרִין רִבִּי שִׁמְעוֹן. אָמְרוּ לֵיהּ. וְהָתַנִּינָן גִּידּוּלֵי הֶקְדֵּשׁ וּמַעֲשֵׂר שֵׁינִי חוּלִין וּפוֹדֶה אוֹתָם בִּזְמַן זַרְעוֹ. לְאֵי זֶה דָבָר הוּא פוֹדֶה אוֹתָן. לֹא מִפְּנֵי קְדוּשָּׁה שֶׁיֵּשׁ בָּהֶן. אוּף הָכָא יִטְעֲנוּ מְחִיצָה מִפְּנֵי קְדוּשָּׁה שֶׁיֵּשׁ בָּהֶן. רִבִּי יִרְמְיָה רִבִּי אִימִּי בְשֵׁם רִבִּי שִׁמְעוֹן בֶּן לָקִישׁ. הֵן דְּתֵימַר גִּידּוּלֵיהֶן אֲסוּרִין אִיסּוּר מְחִיצָה. וְהֵן דְּתֵימַר גִּידּוּלֵיהֶן מוּתָּרִין הֵיתֵר זָרוּת. הֲרֵי אֵילּוּ בְּמַעֲשֵׂר וּבְבִכּוּרִין מַה שֶׁאֵין כֵּן בִּתְרוּמָה.

Rebbi Joḥanan's argument seems inverted. There[100], Rebbi Joshua ben Levi said, it was quoted for the horns of a cadaver. He said to him, did the teacher not teach: "I saw" the size of two beans[101]? Should he have said here also, "their growths"? In addition, from the following (*Deut.* 12:17): "You may not eat your grain's tithe in your gates." About which tithe has this been said? About pure second tithe which entered Jerusalem and left[102]. Also from the following which Rebbi Simeon stated. It was stated[103] in the name of Rebbi Simeon: "Tithe is special in that tithe forbids its money, mixtures, and vessels; the doubt of an admixture forbids in the most minute amount and one may not use it for lighting." He should say, the same holds for growth! Rebbi Hila said, he who says growth is permitted, Rebbi Simeon. Those who say growth is forbidden, the rabbis. They said to him, did we not state[104]: "Growths from dedicated [seeds] and Second Tithe are profane; one redeems them corresponding to the time of sowing." Why does he have to redeem? Not because of their inherent sanctity? Here also they should require walls because of their inherent sanctity! Rebbi Jeremiah, Rebbi Ammi, in the name of Rebbi Simeon ben Laqish: When one says the growth is forbidden, the prohibition of walls[105]. When one says the growth is permitted, the permission for unauthorized persons[106]. "These rules apply to tithe and First Fruits but not to heave."

100 It is unknown what this statement refers to. Since the tentative explanation of R. Eliahu Fulda is the only one not based on emendation of the text, it is followed here. The statement of R. Joshua ben Levi is based on the explanation of *Ex.* 21:28 given in *Mekhilta deR. Simeon ben Iohai* which contains the teachings of Ḥizqia, the teacher of R. Joshua ben Levi and the young R. Johanan (ed. Epstein-Melamed, p. 178): "If an ox gores a man or a woman and they die, the ox should be stoned, its meat may not be eaten, and the owner of the ox is free." If the ox is stoned, it becomes a carcass whose meat is forbidden anyhow; why the remark "its meat may not be eaten"? This means that if the ox has been condemned in court to be stoned but the owners slaughtered it before execution, the meat is still forbidden. What does mean: "The owner of the ox is free"? Ben Azai said, he is freed from his property; the entire animal is forbidden for all usufruct. On that, R. Joshua ben Levi adds that not only the meat but (hide and) horns are forbidden even if it died before slaughter. R. Joḥanan objects and notes that if the verse deals with two cases (stoned or slaughtered), the rules have to apply to both. In the case of R. Joshua ben Levi this means that the verse is needed to forbid hide and horns also for a correctly slaughtered ox; therefore, one does not understand why he did not object to R. Yannai that both second tithe and First Fruits should have the same rules.

101 This deals with the impurity of houses by mold disease (*Lev.* 14:33-57). Mold disease is considered impure if it is the size of a Cilician bean. It is said

(*v*. 35) that the owner has to tell the Cohen, "like *a* plague it appears to me in the house." But since it is written in *v*. 37 that the Cohen has to see "the plague in the *walls* of the house", the house is impure only if two impurities appear, each of the size of a bean.

102 The origin of this statement is unknown. In the *Sifry* the verse is interpreted to mean that grain may not be consumed unless heave and all tithes have been removed.

103 In Tosephta 1:6, an anonymous statement is close to the text here.

104 Mishnah *Terumot* 9:4; Notes 61-62.

105 It is forbidden to eat Jerusalem growth from either second tithe or First Fruits outside of Jerusalem.

106 In this respect, growth is profane as stated in Mishnah *Terumot*.

תַּמָּן תַּנִּינָן וְגַם נְתַתִּיו זוֹ תְּרוּמָה וּתְרוּמַת מַעֲשֵׂר. תַּמָּן אַתְּ אָמַר תְּרוּמָה טְעוּנָה וִידּוּי. וְהָכָא אַתְּ אָמַר תְּרוּמָה אֵין טְעוּנָה וִידּוּי. אָמַר רִבִּי הִילָא תַּנֵּיי תַמָּן הַתְּרוּמָה וְהַבִּכּוּרִים. אֶחָד הַנּוֹתְנָן וְאֶחָד הַנּוֹטְלָן טְעוּנִין וִידּוּי. אָמַר רִבִּי זְעִירָה רַבָּנִין דְּתַמָּן סָבְרִין וְרַבָּנִין דְּהָכָא אָמְרִין מִי שֶׁיֵּשׁ לוֹ מַעֲשֵׂר בִּפְנֵי עַצְמָהּ מִתְוַדֶּה. מִי שֶׁיֵּשׁ לוֹ תְּרוּמָה בִּפְנֵי עַצְמוֹ אֵינוֹ מִתְוַדֶּה. אָמַר רִבִּי יוֹסֵי מַתְנִיתָא אָמְרָה כֵן. רִבִּי יוֹסֵי אוֹמֵר יֵשׁ לָהֶן עָרֵי מִקְלָט. מַה נָן קַיָּימִין. אִם בִּתְרוּמָה וּמַעֲשֵׂר שֶׁלּוֹ הֵן. אֶלָּא כִּי נָן קַיָּימִין בִּתְרוּמָה. אָמַר רִבִּי הִילָא שְׁמָעִנָן מִי שֶׁיֵּשׁ לוֹ מַעֲשֵׂר בִּפְנֵי עַצְמוֹ מִתְוַדֶּה. מִי שֶׁיֵּשׁ לוֹ בִּיכּוּרִין בִּפְנֵי עַצְמָן מִתְוַדֶּה. שְׁמָעִנָן מִי שֶׁיֵּשׁ לוֹ תְרוּמָה בִּפְנֵי עַצְמָהּ מִתְוַדֶּה.

There[107], we have stated: "'Also I gave it,' includes heave and heave of the tithe." There, you say that heave needs declaration but here[108] you say, heave does not need declaration. Rebbi Hila said, there[109] they stated: Heave and First Fruits, both the one who gives and the one who takes need to declare[110]. Rebbi Zeïra said, the rabbis there think, and the rabbis here say, if a person has only tithe, he declares; if a person has only heave, he does not declare. Rebbi Yose said, a Mishnah[111] says so: "Rebbi Yose says, they have their cities *of refuge*." Where do we hold? If about heave and tithe, they are his. But it must deal with heave[112]. Rebbi Hila said, we [did] understand that if a person has only tithe, he declares; if a person has only First Fruits, he declares. We [now] understand that if a person has only heave, he declares.

107 Mishnah *Ma'aser Šeni* 5:10.

108 Mishnah *Bikkurim* 2:2.

109 In Babylonia.

110 The farmer has to make the declaration *Deut.* 26:3-10 for first fruit and to include in his tithe declaration (*Deut.* 26:13-14) the assertion that he duly gave his heave to the Cohen. The Cohen has to mention in his tithe declaration that he treated heave and First Fruits according to the rules.

111 Mishnah *Ma'aser Šeni* 5:14. The Mishnah, referring to Levites, speaks of "cities and their (agricultural) surroundings." The quote here, referring to Cohanim, speaks of cities of refuge (for the unintentional homicide) which were given to the Cohanim.

112 Of which he is the recipient.

(fol. 64c) **משנה ג**: יֵשׁ בִּתְרוּמָה וּבְמַעֲשֵׂר מַה שֶׁאֵין כֵּן בְּבִיכּוּרִים. שֶׁהַתְּרוּמָה וְהַמַּעֲשֵׂר אוֹסְרִין אֶת הַגּוֹרֶן וְיֵשׁ לָהֶן שִׁיעוּר וְנוֹהֲגִין בְּכָל־הַפֵּירוֹת בִּפְנֵי הַבַּיִת וְשֶׁלֹּא בִפְנֵי הַבַּיִת וּבָאֲרִיסִין וּבְחָכוֹרוֹת וּבַסִּיקָרִיקוֹן וּבַגּוֹזְלָן. הֲרֵי אֵילוּ בִתְרוּמָה וּבְמַעֲשֵׂר מַה שֶׁאֵין כֵּן בְּבִיכּוּרִין.

Mishnah 3: Some rules apply to heave and tithe but not to First Fruits since heave and tithe forbid on the threshing floor[113], they have a fixed measure[114], apply to all produce[115], are due whether the Temple exists or not, and apply to sharecroppers, tenant farmers, *sicarii*, and robbers. They apply to heave and tithe but not to First Fruits[116].

113 Once grain has been threshed and cleaned, one may not eat from it unless heave and tithes were separated. For produce other than grain, the equivalents of the threshing floor are defined in *Ma'serot*, Chap. 1.

114 Tithes by biblical decree, heave by rabbinic standard.

115 By rabbinic standard for all produce except grain, wine, and olive oil.

116 Cf. Mishnah 1:2.

משנה ד: יֵשׁ בְּבִיכּוּרִין מַה שֶׁאֵין בִּתְרוּמָה וּבְמַעֲשֵׂר. שֶׁהַבִּיכּוּרִים נִקְנִין בִּמְחוּבָּר לַקַּרְקַע עוֹשֶׂה אָדָם כָּל־שָׂדֵהוּ בִּיכּוּרִים וְחַייָב בְּאַחֲרָיוּתָם וּטְעוּנִין קָרְבָּן וְשִׁיר וּתְנוּפָה וְלִינָה.

Mishnah 4: Some rules apply to First Fruits but not to heave and tithe. For First Fruits acquire [hallowed status] when connected to the ground, a person may dedicate his entire field as First Fruits, he is responsible for them, and they need a sacrifice, song, weaving, and staying overnight.

(fol. 65a) **הלכה ג**: נִיחָא הַתְּרוּמָה אוֹסֶרֶת אֶת הַגּוֹרֶן. תִּיפְתָּר שֶׁהִקְדִּימוֹ בַּשִּׁיבּוֹלִין. דְּאָמַר רִבִּי אַבָּהוּ בְּשֵׁם רִבִּי שִׁמְעוֹן בֶּן לָקִישׁ מַעֲשֵׂר רִאשׁוֹן שֶׁהִקְדִּימוֹ בַּשִּׁיבֳּלִין פָּטוּר מִתְּרוּמָה גְדוֹלָה.

It is true that heave makes the threshing floor forbidden[117]? Explain it if he gave it[118] early, from ears, as Rebbi Abbahu said in the name of Rebbi Simeon ben Laqish: First Tithe given early, from ears, is free from [the obligation of] great heave.

117 Since heave must be given first, the obligation of heave is the one which triggers the prohibition. It is true that the obligation of heaves may stop the prohibition from being lifted, but can tithes anywhere trigger the obligation as implied in the formulation "makes forbidden"?

118 First tithe, which cannot be consumed unless heave of the tithe is given. The sentence is from *Ḥallah* 1:4, Note 123.

נִקְנִין בִּמְחוּבָּר לַקַּרְקַע דִּכְתִיב בִּכּוּרֵי כָּל־אֲשֶׁר בְּאַרְצָם.

"They acquire [hallowed status] connected to the ground", as it is written (*Num.* 18:13): "The First Fruits of anything on their land."

עוֹשֶׂה אָדָם אֶת כָּל־שָׂדֵהוּ בִּכּוּרִים. דִּכְתִיב וְרֵאשִׁית כָּל־בִּכּוּרֵי כֹל.

"A person may dedicate his entire field as First Fruits." As it is written (*Ez.* 44:30): "The first of all First Fruits of everything."

וְחַיָּבִין בְּאַחֲרָיוּתָן דִּכְתִיב רֵאשִׁית בִּכּוּרֵי אַדְמָתְךָ.

"One is responsible for them," for it is written (*Ex.* 23:19): "The beginning of the First Fruits of your land.[119]"

וּטְעוּנִין קָרְבָּן. נֶאֱמַר כָּאן שִׂמְחָה וְנֶאֱמַר לְהַלָּן שִׂמְחָה. מַה שִּׂמְחָה שֶׁנֶּאֱמַר לְהַלָּן שְׁלָמִים אַף כָּאן שְׁלָמִים.

"And they need a sacrifice." Joy is mentioned here and elsewhere. Since joy there means a well-being sacrifice, so joy mentioned here means a well-being sacrifice[120].

וְשִׁיר. נֶאֱמַר כָּאן שִׁיר וְנֶאֱמַר לְהַלָּן וְהִנְּךָ לָהֶם כְּשִׁיר עֲגָבִים.

"And song." Song is mentioned here and it is said there (*Ez.* 33:32): "Behold, you are for them like an erotic song.[121]"

וּתְנוּפָה. דִּכְתִיב וְלָקַח הַכֹּהֵן הַטֶּנֶא מִיָּדֶךָ וְהִנִּיחוֹ. לְרַבּוֹת הַבִּיכּוּרִין שֶׁיִּטְעֲנוּ תְנוּפָה כְּרִבִּי לִיעֶזֶר בֶּן יַעֲקֹב.

"And weaving[122]," as it is written (*Deut.* 26:4) "The Cohen shall take the basket from your hand and deposit it[123]," to add that First Fruits require weaving, following Rebbi Eliezer ben Jacob[124].

וְלִינָה. דִּכְתִיב וּפָנִיתָ בַבּוֹקֶר וְהָלַכְתָּ לְאוֹהָלֶךָ. הָא כָּל־הַפּוֹנוֹת שֶׁאַתָּה פוֹנֶה לֹא יְהוּ אֶלָּא בַבּוֹקֶר. אָמַר רִבִּי יוֹנָה הָדָא דְתֵימַר בְּשֶׁאֵין עִמָּהֶן קָרְבָּן. אֲבָל יֵשׁ עִמָּהֶן קָרְבָּן בְּלֹא כָךְ טָעוּן לִינָה מֵחֲמַת הַקָּרְבָּן.

"And staying overnight." As it is written (*Deut.* 16:7): "In the morning, you may leave and return to your tent." That is, all your leaving should only be in the morning[125]. Rebbi Jonah said, that is only said if there is no sacrifice accompanying them. But if there is an accompanying sacrifice, without [that Mishnah] he needs to stay overnight because of the sacrifice.

119 Cf. Mishnah 1:9.

120 It is written about First Fruits (*Deut.* 26:11): "Enjoy all the good things the Eternal gave to you and your house," and it is written about holidays of pilgrimage (*Deut.* 16:15): "You should certainly enjoy." Since a pilgrimage requires both an elevation offering and a well-being offering, the enjoyment of the holiday means eating the meat of the well-being offering.

121 As it stands, the text is unintelligible. R. Isaac Simponti and after him R. Simson of Sens and *Yalqut Šim'oni Torah* §938 read: נאמר כאן טוב ונאמר להלן יפה קול ומטיב נגן "it says here (*Deut.* 26:11) *good* things, and it is said there (*Ez.* 33:32): "a beautiful voice and *good* in music." Frequently only the first words of a verse are quoted while the reference is to another part of the verse.

Yalqut Šim'oni Torah §938 adds another derivation which ostensibly is taken from Babli *Arakhin* 11a but represents a text tradition quite different from the Venice Talmud text.

122 The movements prescribed for presenting well-being offerings (*Lev.* 7:30) to the altar and for those public flour offerings (*Lev.* 23:11,17) which have to be presented.

123 "And deposit it before the altar of the Eternal, your God." This implies a presentation before the altar.

124 Quoted with the reasoning behind R. Eliezer ben Jacob's statement in Babli *Sukkah* 47b, *Makkot* 18b, *Menaḥot* 61a/b; *Yalqut Šim'oni Torah* §938.

125 A *baraita Sifry Deut.* #134 states that this refers to bird sacrifices, as well as flour, wine, incense, and wood offerings. Whether all animal sacrifices need staying overnight is in dispute, in *Sifry* between R. Jehudah and the anonymous majority, in the Babli (*Pesaḥim* 95b) between two different interpretations of what R. Jehudah meant. The argument of R. Jonah shows that he follows the anonymous majority in *Sifry*.

משנה ה: תְּרוּמַת מַעֲשֵׂר שָׁוָה לַבִּיכּוּרִים בִּשְׁתֵּי דְרָכִים וְלַתְּרוּמָה בִשְׁתֵּי דְרָכִים. נִיטֶּלֶת מִן הַטְּהוֹרָה עַל הַטְּמֵאָה וְשֶׁלֹּא מִן הַמּוּקָּף כְּבִיכּוּרִים. וְאוֹסֵר אֶת הַגּוֹרֶן וְיֵשׁ לָהּ שִׁיעוּר כִּתְרוּמָה. (fol. 64c)

Mishnah 5: Heave of the tithe is similar to First Fruits in two ways and to heave in two ways. It may be taken from pure for impure and from produce not earmarked, like First Fruits[126]. It forbids the threshing floor[118] and it has a measure like heave[127].

126 This is explained in *Terumot* 2:1, Notes 7-15.

127 The required amount for heave of the tithe is 1% by biblical decree and that of heave is between 2.5% and 1⅔% by rabbinic usage.

הלכה ד: רִבִּי יוֹנָה אָמַר רִבִּי מַיְישָׁא וְחַד מִן רַבָּנִין. חַד מִינְהוֹן אָמַר זֹאת אוֹמֶרֶת שֶׁהַפֵּירוֹת הַטְּמֵאִין חַיָּבִין בְּבִיכּוּרִים. וְחָרָנָה אָמַר מַעֲשֵׂר רִאשׁוֹן שֶׁהִקְדִּימוֹ בַּשִּׁיבֳּלִין פָּטוּר מִתְּרוּמָה גְדוֹלָה. (fol. 65a)

Rebbi Jonah said, Rebbi Maisha and one of the rabbis. One said, this means that impure fruits are subject to First Fruits[128] and the other one said, first tithe given early, from ears, is free from [the obligation of] great heave[118,129].

128 But impure fruits cannot be brought to the Temple. Therefore, first fruits for presentation must be taken from pure fruits.

129 This explains how heave of the tithe can cause the original prohibition of use of threshed produce.

(fol. 64c) **משנה ו**: אֶתְרוֹג שָׁוֶה לָאִילָן בִּשְׁלֹשָׁה דְרָכִים וְלַיָּרָק בְּדֶרֶךְ אֶחָד. שָׁוֶה לָאִילָן בָּעָרְלָה וּבָרְבָעִי וּבַשְּׁבִיעִית. וְלַיָּרָק שֶׁבִּשְׁעַת לְקִיטָתוֹ אִישּׂוּרוֹ דִּבְרֵי רַבָּן גַּמְלִיאֵל. רִבִּי לִיעֶזֶר אוֹמֵר שָׁוֶה לָאִילָן בְּכָל־דָּבָר.

Mishnah 6: A citron[130] follows the rules of trees in three aspects and those of vegetables in one. It follows the rules of trees in *'orlah*, the fourth year, and the Sabbatical, and those for vegetables in that the moment it is harvested determines its tithe, the words of Rabban Gamliel. Rebbi Eliezer says, it follows the rules of trees in all respects.

130 The fruit of the tree *Citrus medica var. cedrata*. In Mishnah *Ma'serot* 1:4 (Note 86), citron is enumerated among vegetables, showing that the position of Rabban Gamliel is accepted as practice. The problem is that the fruit may stay on the tree for several years; therefore, the time of the budding of the fruit should not determine its status as required for fruits of a tree, whether it is subject to second tithe (in years 1,2,4,5 of the Sabbatical cycle) or to tithe of the poor (in years 3,6). R. Eliezer requires the owner of the orchard to collect fruits from different years in separate batches. The Mishnah is also discussed in Babli *Qiddušin* 2b, *Sukkah* 29b, *Roš Haššanah* 14b.

(fol. 65a) **הלכה ה**: אִם לָאִילָן לָמָּה לַיָּרָק. אִם לַיָּרָק לָמָּה לָאִילָן. תַּמָּן אָמְרִין נִכְנַס מִשִּׁישִּׁית לַשְּׁבִיעִית הֲרֵי לַבְּעָלִין כְּאִילָן וּפָטוּר מִמַּעְשְׂרוֹת כְּיָרָק. אָמַר לוֹן רַב הַמְנוּנָא. אָמְרִין דְּבַתְרָהּ. נִכְנַס מִשְּׁבִיעִית לַשְּׁמִינִית הֲרֵי הוּא הֶבְקֵר כְּאִילָן. וְחַיָּיב בְּמַעְשְׂרוֹת כְּיָרָק. וְהֶבְקֵר חַיָּיב בְּמַעְשְׂרוֹת.

Halakhah 5: If a tree why a vegetable, if a vegetable, why a tree? There[131], they say that if it grows from the sixth [year] into the Sabbatical [year] it belongs to the owners as if from a tree and is free from tithes as if a vegetable. Rav Hamnuna told them, look at the following [year]! If it grows from the Sabbatical to the eighth year, it should be ownerless as if from a tree and subject to tithes as if a vegetable. Is anything ownerless subject to tithes[132]?

131 In Babylonia, they read the Mishnah as permitting two contradictory leniencies.

132 Cf. *Peah* 1:4. Since in this case one of the leniencies becomes an impossible stringency, the original statement cannot be true.

אָמַר רִבִּי יוֹחָנָן בִּשְׁאָר שְׁנֵי שָׁבוּעַ אַתְּ מְהַלֵּךְ בּוֹ כְּיָרָק. וּבַשְּׁבִיעִית אַתְּ מְהַלֵּךְ בּוֹ כְּאִילָן. הֵיךְ עֲבִידָא. מֵחֲמִשִּׁית לְשִׁשִּׁית שִׁשִּׁית. מִשִּׁשִּׁית לַשְּׁבִיעִית שִׁשִּׁית. נִכְנַס מֵחֲמִשִּׁית לַשִּׁשִּׁית לַשְּׁבִיעִית. לְקָטָן בַּשְּׁבִיעִית שִׁשִּׁית. לְקָטָן מֵשִּׁשִּׁית חֲמִשִּׁית. נִכְנַס מִשִּׁשִּׁית לַשְּׁבִיעִית לַשְּׁמִינִית. לְקָטוֹ בַּשְּׁמִינִית שְׁמִינִית. רַבּוֹתֵינוּ חָזְרוּ וְנִמְנוּ אֶתְרוֹג בִּשְׁעַת לְקִיטָתוֹ אִישׁוּרוֹ לְמַעְשְׂרוֹת וְלַשְּׁבִיעִית.

Rebbi Joḥanan said, in the remaining years of the Sabbatical cycle you treat it as a vegetable but in the Sabbatical as a tree. How is that? From the fifth to the sixth, sixth. From the sixth to the Sabbatical, sixth. If it stayed from the fifth to the sixth to the Sabbatical, if he harvested it in the Sabbatical [it is tithed for the] sixth; if he harvested it in the sixth [it is tithed for the] fifth. If it stayed from the sixth to the Sabbatical to the eighth, if he harvested it in the eighth [it is tithed for the] eighth. "Our teachers took the problem up a second time and voted that for a citron the moment it is harvested determines its tithe and Sabbatical status.[133]"

133 According to the version of the Tosephta (*Ševi'it* 4:21) quoted in the Babli (*Roš Haššanah* 10a, *Sukkah* 40a) this happened at Usha in Galilee where the Synhedrion was reconstituted after the end of the persecutions following the war of Bar Kokhba. The same sources note that this rule was propagated in Babylonia by Rav Hamnuna.

רִבִּי יִרְמְיָה רִבִּי אִימִּי בְּשֵׁם רִבִּי יוֹחָנָן. רִבִּי סִימוֹן בְּשֵׁם רִבִּי יְהוֹשֻׁעַ בֶּן לֵוִי. הַכֹּל מוֹדִין שֶׁרֹאשׁ הַשָּׁנָה שֶׁלּוֹ בְּטוֹ בִּשְׁבָט. רִבִּי יוֹחָנָן שָׁאַל לְרִבִּי יוֹנָתָן. כְּסִדְרָן שֶׁלְּשָׁנִים אוֹ כְסִדְרָן שֶׁלִּתְקוּפוֹת. אָמַר לֵיהּ כְּסִדְרָן שֶׁלְּשָׁנִים וַאֲפִילוּ שָׁנָה (fol. 65b) מְעוּבֶּרֶת.

Rebbi Jeremiah, Rebbi Ammi, in the name of Rebbi Joḥanan. Rebbi Simon in the name of Rebbi Joshua ben Levi: Everybody agrees that its New Year is the 15th of *Šebaṭ*[134]. Rebbi Joḥanan asked Rebbi Jonathan: According to years or according to seasons[135]? He said to him, according to years and even in an intercalary year[136].

134 One cannot tithe the produce of one year for that of a different year. Even though the moment of its harvest determines its status for tithes, the year does not start on the first of Tishre as for vegetables but on the 15th of Šebaṭ as for trees (according to the House of Shammai, the 1st of Šebaṭ); cf. Mishnah *Roš Haššanah* 1:1.

135 Since the lunar year may deviate from the solar seasons by close to thirty days, does "the 15th of Šebaṭ" mean just what it says or is it a stand-in for "32 days after the winter solstice" which was its average position relative to the Julianic year in talmudic times?

136 When the 15th of Šebaṭ is approximately 25 days after the winter solstice.

מַעֲשֶׂה בְּרִבִּי עֲקִיבָה שֶׁלָּקַט אֶתְרוֹג וְנָהַג עָלָיו חוּמְרֵי בֵית שַׁמַּי וְחוּמְרֵי בֵית הִלֵּל. לָמָּה לִי [אֶתְרוֹג] אֲפִילוּ שְׁאָר כָּל־הָאִילָן. תַּנֵּי כְּחוּמְרֵי רַבָּן גַּמְלִיאֵל וּכְחוּמְרֵי רִבִּי לִיעֶזֶר. וְרַבָּן גַּמְלִיאֵל וְרִבִּי לִיעֶזֶר לֹא מִן בֵּית הִלֵּל אִינּוּן הֲווֹ. אָמַר רִבִּי יוֹסֵי בֵּי רִבִּי בּוּן. תִּיפְתָּר בְּשֶׁחָנַט קוֹדֶם לְטוֹ בִּשְׁבָט שֶׁלַּשְּׁנִייָה וְנִכְנְסָה שְׁלִישִׁית. עַל דַּעְתֵּיהּ דְּרַבָּן גַּמְלִיאֵל עִישּׂוּרוֹ עָנִי. עַל דַּעְתֵּיהּ דְּרִבִּי לִיעֶזֶר עִישּׂוּרוֹ שֵׁינִי. מַה עָשָׂה לוֹ. קָרָא שֵׁם לְמַעֲשֵׂר שֵׁינִי שֶׁבּוֹ וּפְדָייוֹ וְנוֹתְנוֹ לֶעָנִי.

[137]"It happened that Rebbi Aqiba picked a citron and observed for it the stringencies of the House of Shammai and those of the House of

Hillel.[138]" Why about a citron[139] and not about any tree? It was stated[140] "the stringencies of Rabban Gamliel and those of Rebbi Eliezer." But are Rabban Gamliel and Rebbi Eliezer not from the House of Hillel[141]? Rebbi Yose ben Rebbi Abun said, explain it that it budded before the 15th of Šebaṭ of the second year and the third year came. In the opinion of Rabban Gamliel it is subject to tithe of the poor[142]; in the opinion of Rebbi Eliezer it is subject to second tithe. How did he handle this? He gave a name to the second tithe in it, redeemed it, and gave it to the poor.

137 Almost the same text is in *Roš Haššanah* 1:1, fol. 57a.

138 Tosephta *Ševi'it* 4:21; quoted in Babli *Roš Haššanah* 14a, *Erubin* 7a, *Yebamot* 15a. In these sources, the citron was taken on the 1st of *Šebaṭ*.

139 Word missing here, supplied from the text in *Roš Haššanah*.

140 In the Tosephta this is the tradition of R. Yose ben R. Jehudah. He will not read "on the first of *Šebaṭ*."

141 After the destruction of the Temple, the authorities who developed rabbinic Judaism were all students of Rabban Joḥanan ben Zakkai of the House of Hillel, irrespective of their prior affiliations. The wholehearted support both of Rabban Gamliel and of R. Eliezer for the doctrines of the former House of Hillel is doubtful. The *Roš Haššanah* text: "Do not Rabban Gamliel and Rebbi Eliezer refer to the House of Hillel?" makes better sense.

142 The tithe of the third year of the Sabbatical cycle. The statement "it budded before the 15th of Šebaṭ" seems to be irrelevant here.

(fol. 64c) **משנה ז**: דַּם מְהַלְּכֵי שְׁתַּיִם שָׁוֶה לְדַם בְּהֵמָה לְהַכְשִׁיר אֶת הַזְּרָעִים. וְדַם הַשֶּׁרֶץ אֵין חַיָּבִין עָלָיו.

Mishnah 7: The blood of two-legged beings[143] is similar to the blood of animals in that it prepares plants, but one is not guilty because of the blood of crawling beings[144].

143 Humans and possibly big apes. Vegetables cannot become impure unless "prepared" by a desired contact with fluids (cf. *Terumot* 1, No. 7; *Demay* 2, Notes 136-141). Since all human body fluids are preparing, the assertion here is rather that blood of kosher animals prepares like human blood. On the other hand, the prohibition of blood as food extends only to birds and kosher animals (*Lev.* 7:26), not to humans.

144 "Crawling beings" are the eight species enumerated in *Lev.* 11:29-30. Since they are classified as "impure" without reference to body parts, there is no distinction made between their flesh and their blood. Eating their blood is classified as eating their flesh, a simple transgression, not punishable by extirpation like eating blood of kosher animals (*Lev.* 17:10).

(fol. 65b) **הלכה ו**: רִבִּי בָּא רַב הוּנָא בְשֵׁם רַב. אִם הִתְרוּ בוֹ לוֹקֶה. וְהָא תַנִּינָן דַּם הַשֶּׁרֶץ אֵין חַייָבִין עָלָיו. אָמַר רִבִּי בָּא אֵין חַייָבִין עָלָיו כָּרֵת. וְהָתַנֵּי דַּם מְהַלְּכֵי שְׁתַּיִם שֶׁאֵין בּוֹ טוּמְאָה קַלָּה. דַּם הַשֶּׁרֶץ שֶׁאֵין בּוֹ טוּמְאָה חֲמוּרָה. אָמַר רִבִּי חִייָא בַּר אָדָא הָדָא דְתֵימַר בְּשֶׁהִתְרוּ בוֹ מִשּׁוּם דָּם. אֲבָל אִם הִתְרוּ בוֹ מִשּׁוּם שֶׁקֶץ לוֹקֶה.

Halakhah 6: Rebbi Abba, Rav Huna in the name of Rav: If he was warned, he is whipped[145]. But did we not state: "But one is not guilty because of the blood of crawling beings"? Rebbi Abba said, one is not subject to extirpation for it[146]. But was it not stated: "The blood of two-legged beings which have no minor impurity, the blood of crawling things which have no major impurity"?[147] Rebbi Ḥiyya bar Ada said, that is, if they warned him because of blood. But if they warned him because of abomination, he is whipped[148].

145 A person cannot be criminally prosecuted unless he was duly informed about the criminality of his intended action; cf. *Kilaim* 8, Note 9. In the Babli, *Keritut* 21b, the statement is by Rav Jehudah in the name of Rav.

146 But he might be whipped for committing a misdemeanor. In the Babli, this argument is without attribution.

147 This cryptic argument is somewhat expanded in the Babli, *Keritut* 20b; the full statement is in *Sifra Ẓav Parašah* 10(11): "(*Lev*. 7:26) 'Any blood you should not eat'. I could also think the blood of two-legged beings, the blood of crawling things, the blood in eggs, the blood of locusts, and the blood of fish, are all included, but the verse says 'of birds and animals'. Birds and animals are special in that they can be the source of minor impurity (which only affects foodstuffs) and of major impurity (which affects humans, their garments and vessels), some are forbidden (as carcasses) and some are permitted (if slaughtered correctly), and they are meat. This excludes the blood of two-legged beings who cannot be the source of minor impurity (according to biblical standards), the blood of crawling things who cannot be a source of major impurity, the blood of eggs which are not meat, the blood of locusts and fish who are always permitted." The implication is that there is no biblical injunction against eating blood of crawling things.

148 Since blood is a part of the animal. In the Babli, this is reported in the name of R. Zeïra.

(fol. 64c) **משנה ח**: כּוֹי יֵשׁ בּוֹ דְרָכִים שָׁוֶה לַחַיָּה וְיֵשׁ בּוֹ דְרָכִים שָׁוֶה לַבְּהֵמָה וְיֵשׁ בּוֹ דְרָכִים שָׁוֶה לַבְּהֵמָה וְלַחַיָּה וְיֵשׁ בּוֹ דְרָכִים שֶׁאֵינוֹ שָׁוֶה לֹא לַבְּהֵמָה וְלֹא לַחַיָּה.

Mishnah 8: The *koy*[154] in some ways follows the rules for wild animals and in some those for domestic animals, in some the rules for both domestic and wild animals, and in some those for neither domestic nor wild animals.

משנה ט: כֵּיצַד שָׁוֶה לַחַיָּה. דָּמוֹ טָעוּן כִּיסּוּי כְּדַם חַיָּה וְאֵין שׁוֹחֲטִים אוֹתוֹ בְּיוֹם טוֹב. וְאִם שְׁחָטוֹ אֵין מְכַסִּין אֶת דָּמוֹ. וְחֶלְבּוֹ מְטַמֵּא בְּטוּמְאַת נְבֵילָה כַּחַיָּה. וְטוּמְאָתוֹ בְּסָפֵק וְאֵין פּוֹדִין בּוֹ פֶּטֶר חֲמוֹר.

Mishnah 9: How does it follow the rules of wild animals? Its blood must be covered like the blood of a wild animal[149]; one does not slaughter it on a holiday[150] but if it was slaughtered one does not cover its blood. Its fat can become impure in the impurity of a carcass like a wild animal[151]; that impurity is one of doubt[152]. One may not use it to redeem the first-born of a donkey[153].

149 *Lev.* 17:13. The blood of domestic kosher animals (cattle, sheep, and goats) may be used for industrial purposes but not that of wild animals or birds.

150 While one may slaughter on a holiday for immediate consumption and may cover the blood of a wild animal or bird, one may not move earth on the holiday for a questionable case.

151 Since all fat of a wild animal can be eaten, it is not distinguished from its body and, unless the animal is correctly slaughtered, its entire body becomes impure as a carcass (*Lev.* 11:39); cf. Mishnah *Uqeẓin* 3:9.

152 Since the *koy* might be a domestic animal. If a person who has become impure by touching fat from a *koy* carcass visits the Temple enclosure, he cannot be prosecuted but he will induce impurity by his touch. This rule and the one about covering the blood on a holiday are really rules distinct from those valid for domestic or wild animals.

153 *Ex.* 13:13 requires that the first-born of a female donkey be redeemed by a sheep or goat given to a Cohen.

(fol. 65b) **הלכה ז**: אֵי זֶהוּ כּוֹי. אָמַר רִבִּי לָעְזָר עֵז שֶׁעָלָה עַל גַּבֵּי צְבִי וּצְבִי שֶׁעָלָה עַל גַּבֵּי עִיזָּה. וְרַבָּנִין אָמְרִין מִין הוּא עִיקָּרוֹ וְלֹא יָֽכְלוּ חֲכָמִים לַעֲמוֹד עָלָיו.

Halakhah 7: What is a *koy*? Rebbi Eleazar said, [the offspring of] a he-goat which mated with a hind or of a stag which mated with a she-goat. But the rabbis say it is a separate kind and the Sages could not determine its nature[154].

154 Since no cognate language has any animal name close to כוי, its identity cannot be determined. It might exist only for the sake of argument.

The Babli (*Ḥulin* 80b-81a) has a long discussion about the legal differences between the offspring of a he-goat which mated with a hind or a stag which mated with a she-goat. The Babli quotes a *baraita* which ascribes the opinion of R. Eleazar to anonymous authors, the opinion of the rabbis to R. Yose, and a third, anonymous, opinion that כוי is a wild goat.

פָּדוּי בְּכוֹי חוֹזֵר וּפוֹדֶה בְשֶׂה. לְפִיכָךְ אִם מֵת אֶחָד מֵהֶן הַמּוֹצִיא מֵחֲבֵירוֹ עָלָיו הָֽרְאָיָה.

If it was redeemd by a *koy*, one has to redeem again by a sheep. Therefore, if one of them died, the claimant has to bring proof[155].

155 If the *koy* died, the Cohen cannot ask for a replacement since he cannot prove that what he got was not a sheep or goat. If the *koy* lives, the Cohen has to return it to receive the sheep or goat.

(fol. 64c) **משנה י**: כֵּיצַד שָׁוֶה לַבְּהֵמָה. חֶלְבּוֹ אָסוּר כְּחֵלֶב בְּהֵמָה וְאֵין חַייָבִין עָלָיו כָּרֵת. וְאֵינוֹ נִלְקָח בְּכֶסֶף מַעֲשֵׂר לֶאֱכוֹל בִּירוּשָׁלֵם וְחַייָב בִּזְרוֹעַ וּבִלְחָיַיִם וּבַקֵּיבָה. רִבִּי לָעְזָר פּוֹטֵר שֶׁהַמּוֹצִיא מֵחֲבֵירוֹ עָלָיו הָֽרְאָיָה.

Mishnah 10: How does it follow the rules of domestic animals? Its fat is forbidden like the fat of domestic animals[156], but one is not punished for it by extirpation. It cannot be bought with tithe money to be eaten in Jerusalem[157] and it is subject to the foreleg, the lower jaw, and the first stomach [to be given to a Cohen][158]. Rebbi Eleazar frees[159] since the claimant has to bring proof.

156 *Lev.* 7:23, prohibition restricted to "cattle, sheep, and goats."

157 Since tithe money should be used to buy well-being sacrifices (*Ma'aser Šeni* 1:4) and a *koy* cannot be a sacrifice.

158 *Deut.* 18:3, the part Cohen's of profane slaughter of cattle or sheep or goats.

159 The person slaughtering does not have to give away the foreleg, jaw, and stomach. Since these gifts are profane, the Cohen can collect only if he can prove that the *koy* is subject to these rules. R. Eleazar quoted here is the Tanna R. Eleazar ben Shamua.

(fol. 65b) **הלכה ח**: מַתְנִיתָא דְלֹא כְרִבִּי לָעְזָר. דְּתַנֵּי רִבִּי לָעְזָר אוֹמֵר כּוֹי (אֵין)[160] חַייָבִין עַל חֶלְבּוֹ אָשָׁם תָּלוּי. מַתְנִיתָא דְלֹא כְרַב. דְּרַב [אָמַר][161] כָּל־שֶׁאֵיפְשַׁר לַעֲמוֹד עַל וַדָּאוֹ לֹא יְהוּ חַייָבִין עַל סְפֵיקוֹ אָשָׁם תָּלוּי. פָּתַר לָהּ חֲלוּקִין עַל דִּבְרֵי רִבִּי לָעְזָר.

Halakhah 8: The Mishnah does not follow Rebbi Eleazar, as it was stated: Rebbi Eleazar says one must bring a "hung" sacrifice for the fat of a *koy*[162]. Is the Mishnah not following Rav? Since Rav said, for anything that can never be ascertained, one shall not be obliged for a "hung" sacrifice for this doubt. Explain it, they disagree with the words of Rebbi Eleazar.

160 Word missing in the parallel *Yebamot* 4:2 (fol. 5c).

161 Word added in the parallel *Yebamot* 4:2 (fol. 5c).

162 The "hung sacrifice" is the expiation sacrifice (*Lev.* 5:17-19) to be brought by a person who suspects that he is guilty of an offense punishable by extirpation. If he knew clearly that he is guilty, he must bring a reparation sacrifice (*Lev.* 4:27-35). If he brought a "hung" sacrifice and later ascertains that he indeed broke the law, he has in addition to bring a reparation sacrifice. In *Yebamot*, Rav holds that there is no expiation sacrifice if there cannot be a reparation sacrifice. R. Eleazar (who must be the Tanna) disagrees. Since an expiation sacrifice can be brought only for an offense subject to the penalty of extirpation, the anonymous Tanna of the Mishnah must disagree with R. Eleazar. It follows that R. Eleazar disagrees with the majority in two statements of the Mishnah, about fat and gifts, but the disagreement is noted only for one.

וַאֲפִילוּ בְּשָׁעָה שֶׁהָיוּ לוֹקְחִין בְּהֵמָה לִבְשַׂר תַּאֲוָה אֵינוֹ נִלְקָח מַעֲשֵׂר לֵיאָכֵל בִּירוּשָׁלֵם.

And even in the time they were buying animals for meat of desire it could not be bought with tithe money to be eaten in Jerusalem[163].

163 This refers to the statement that a *koy* cannot be bought with tithe money. This is obvious once the rule is enforced that tithe money can only be used to buy well-being sacrifices (*Ma'aser Šeni* 1:3, *Mishnah* 1:4). The statement here means that even when it was permitted to buy "meat of desire" (an expression for profane meat from *Deut.* 12:20), only animals that are either fit for the altar or are clearly wild animals could have been bought.

וְחַיָּב בִּזְרוֹעַ וּבִלְחָיַיִם וּבַקֵּיבָה. רִבִּי לָעְזָר פּוֹטֵר. רִבִּי לָעְזָר דּוּ אָמַר עַכְשָׁיו הוּא נִסְתַּפֵּק לוֹ דּוּ אָמַר פָּטוּר. וְרַבָּנִין דִּינוּן מָרִין מִין הוּא עִיקָּרוֹ. אִינּוּן אָמְרִין חַיָּב.

"It is subject to the foreleg, the lower jaw, and the first stomach [to be given to a Cohen]. Rebbi Eleazar frees." Since Rebbi Eleazar says that now he is in doubt, he says "free". But the Sages, who teach that it is an original species, say "obligated.[154]"

(fol. 64c) **משנה יא**: כֵּיצַד אֵינוֹ שָׁוֶה לַחַיָּה וְלַבְּהֵמָה. אָסוּר מִשּׁוּם כִּלְאַיִם עִם הַחַיָּה וְעִם הַבְּהֵמָה. הַכּוֹתֵב חַיָּתוֹ וּבְהֶמְתּוֹ לִבְנוֹ לֹא כָתַב לוֹ אֶת הַכּוֹי. אִם אָמַר הֲרֵינִי נָזִיר שֶׁזֶּה חַיָּה אוֹ בְהֵמָה הֲרֵי הוּא נָזִיר. וּשְׁאָר כָּל־הַדְּרָכָיו שָׁוִים לַחַיָּה וְלַבְּהֵמָה וְטָעוּן שְׁחִיטָה כָּזֶה וְכָזֶה. וּמְטַמֵּא מִשּׁוּם נְבֵלָה וּמִשּׁוּם אֵבֶר מִן הַחַי כָּזֶה וְכָזֶה.

Mishnah 11: How does it differ from both a wild and a domestic animal? It is forbidden as *kilaim* with wild animals and domestic animals. If somebody writes his wild or domestic animals over to his son[164], he did not include the *koy*[165]. If somebody said, I am a *nazir* if that is neither a wild nor a domestic animal, he is a *nazir*[165]. In all other ways it is like wild and domestic animals; it needs slaughtering by cutting its throat[166] like both, and as carcass it is impure like both.

164 In a gift document.

165 Since it is neither a wild nor a domestic animal.

166 *Lev.* 11:39.

(fol. 65b) **הלכה ט**: מַתְנִיתָא דְּלָא כְרַבִּי. דְּתַנֵּי הִקְדִּישׁ חַיָּתוֹ וּבְהֶמְתּוֹ לֹא הִקְדִּישׁ אֶת הַכּוֹי. רַבִּי אוֹמֵר הִקְדִּישׁ אֶת הַכּוֹי.

Halakhah 9: The Mishnah does not follow Rebbi, as it was stated: If somebody dedicated his wild and domestic animals to the Temple, he did not dedicate the *koy*. Rebbi said, he dedicated the *koy*[166].

166 In the Babli, *Nedarim* 18b, the opinion of the rabbis here is attributed to R. Eliezer and the opinion of Rebbi to the anonymous rabbis. But there, the question is not whether a *koy* is a hybrid or a separate species but whether vows should be interpreted in restricted or expansive ways.

אָמַר הֲרֵינִי נָזִיר שֶׁזֶּה חַיָּה. נָזִיר. שֶׁזֶּה בְהֵמָה. נָזִיר. שֶׁאֵין זֶה חַיָּה. נָזִיר. שֶׁאֵין זֶה בְהֵמָה. נָזִיר. שֶׁזֶּה חַיָּה וּבְהֵמָה. נָזִיר. שֶׁין זֶה לֹא חַיָּה וְלֹא בְהֵמָה. נָזִיר.

"If somebody said, I shall be a *nazir* if that is a wild animal, he is a *nazir*. That this is a domestic animal, he is a *nazir*. That this is not a wild animal, he is a *nazir*. That this is not a domestic animal, he is a *nazir*. That this is a wild and a domestic animal, he is a *nazir*. That this is neither a wild nor a domestic animal, he is a *nazir*.[167]"

167 Mishnah *Nazir* 4:9. Since all these statement are partially true, the vow of the *nazir* is valid in all cases. This is the interpretation of Maimonides in *Nazir*. The interpretation of Rashi (*Nazir* 34a) cannot be squared with the Yerushalmi.

רִבִּי חַגַּיי בָּעָא קוֹמֵי רִבִּי יוֹסֵי. לָמָּה לֹא תַנִּינָן הָרוֹבֵעַ וְהַנִּרְבַּע מִמֶּנּוּ חַייָב. אָמַר לֵיהּ תַּנֵּיתָהּ בְּסוֹפָהּ וּשְׁאָר כָּל־דְּרָכָיו שָׁוִין לַחַיָּה וְלַבְּהֵמָה.

Rebbi Ḥaggai asked before Rebbi Yose: Why did we not state that the human having active or passive sex with a *koy* is guilty? He told him, it was stated: "In all other ways it is like wild and domestic animals.[168]"

168 According to R. Ḥaggai, the list of ways in which a *koy* is equal to both wild and domestic animals is intended to be exhaustive. R. Yose notes that the cases enumerated are only given as examples; almost no lists in the Mishnah are exhaustive.

כיצד מפרישין פרק שלישי

(fol. 65b) **משנה א**: כֵּיצַד מַפְרִישִׁין אֶת הַבִּיכּוּרִין. יוֹרֵד אָדָם לְתוֹךְ שָׂדֵהוּ וְרוֹאֶה תְאֵינָה שֶׁבִּיכֵּירָה אֶשְׁכּוֹל שֶׁבִּיכֵּר רִימּוֹן שֶׁבִּיכֵּר קוֹשְׁרָן בְּגֶמִי וְאוֹמֵר הֲרֵי אֵלּוּ בִּיכּוּרִים. רִבִּי שִׁמְעוֹן אוֹמֵר אַף עַל פִּי שֶׁזֶּה כֵן חוֹזֵר וְקוֹרֵא אוֹתָם בִּיכּוּרִין מֵאַחַר שֶׁיִּתָּלְשׁוּ מִן הַקַּרְקַע.

Mishnah 1: How does one designate First Fruits? A person comes into his field and there sees an early ripening fig, an early ripening bunch of grapes, an early ripening pomegranate; he binds them with bast and says, "these are First Fruits." Rebbi Simeon says, nevertheless he repeats and calls them First Fruits after they have been separated from the ground.

(fol. 65c) **הלכה א**: כֵּיצַד מַפְרִישִׁין אֶת הַבִּיכּוּרִין כול׳. עַל דַּעְתֵּיהּ דְּרִבִּי שִׁמְעוֹן לֹא קָרָא שֵׁם בְּתָלוּשׁ לֹא קִידְּשׁוּ אֵינָן מְדַמְּעִין אֵין חַייָב עֲלֵיהֶן חוֹמֶשׁ וְאֵין לוֹקִין עֲלֵיהֶן חוּץ לַחוֹמָה. מַה טַעֲמָא דְרַבָּנִין. וְעַתָּה הִנֵּה הֵבֵאתִי אֶת רֵאשִׁית פְּרִי הָאֲדָמָה. בִּשְׁעַת הֲבָאָה פֶּרִי אַף בִּשְׁעַת הַפְרָשָׁה. אֲפִילוּ בוֹסֶר אֲפִילוּ פַגִּים. עַל דַּעְתֵּיהּ דְּרִבִּי שִׁמְעוֹן מַה בִּשְׁעַת הֲבָאָה פֶּרִי אַף בִּשְׁעַת הַפְרָשָׁה פֶּרִי.

Halakhah 1: "How does one designate First Fruits? Etc." In the opinion of Rebbi Simeon, if he did not call them when they were picked they are not sanctified, they do not create *dema'*[1], one is not required to add a fifth[2], and one is not whipped for them outside the wall[3]. What is the reason of the rabbis? (*Deut*. 26:10) "Now, behold, I brought the first of the fruits of the earth." At the moment of presentation it must be a fruit, but also at the moment of dedication? Even unripe grapes, even unripe figs! In the opinion of Rebbi Simeon, since at the moment of presentation it must be a fruit, so also at the moment of dedication it must be a fruit.

1 If they are mixed with profane fruits and are unrecognizable, the mixture is permitted to laymen.

2 If misappropriated, the amount of restitution has to be 100%, not 125%.

3 If eaten outside the city walls of Jerusalem.

רִבִּי זְעִירָא בָּעֵי. בִּיכּוּרֵי יִיחוּר מַהוּ שֶׁיַּתִּירוּ חֲנָטוֹ.

Rebbi Zeïra asked: Do First Fruits of a grafted branch permit what is budding[4]?

4 If a grafted branch produces already recognizable fruits while the tree stump only has buds, does designating a fruit from the graft prevent you from designating later a fruit of the original tree? The question is not answered since it is not relevant in real-life agriculture.

תַּנֵּי הַבִּיכּוּרִים אֶחָד מִשִּׁשִּׁים. רֵאשִׁית הַגֵּז אֶחָד מִשִּׁשִּׁים. תְּרוּמָה טְמֵיאָה אֶחָד מִשִּׁשִּׁים. תַּנֵּי רִבִּי יִשְׁמָעֵאל הַבִּיכּוּרִים אֶחָד מִשִּׁשִּׁים. פֵּיאָה אֶחָד מִשִּׁשִּׁים. רֵאשִׁית הַגֵּז אֶחָד מִשִּׁשִּׁים. תְּרוּמָה טְמֵיאָה אֶחָד מִשִּׁשִּׁים. תְּרוּמָה שֶׁאֵין הַכֹּהֲנִים מַקְפִּידִין עָלֶיהָ אֶחָד מִשִּׁשִּׁים. מַה אִית לָךְ. כְּגוֹן תְּרוּמַת הַכְּלֵיסִין וְהֶחָרוּבִין וּשְׂעוֹרִין שֶׁבְּאֱדוֹם.

It was stated: First Fruits one in sixty[5]. The first of shearings, one in sixty[6]. Impure heave, one in sixty[7]. Rebbi Ismael[8] stated: First Fruits one in sixty. *Peah* one in sixty[9]. The first of shearings, one in sixty. Impure heave, one in sixty. Heave for which the Cohanim do not care[10], one in sixty. What do you have? E. g., the heave of *kelesin*[11], carob, and red barley.

5 This statement, that First Fruits have to be $1\frac{2}{3}\%$ of the entire harvest, is accepted by Maimonides (*Bikkurim* 2:17) as rabbinic rule, even though it contradicts the statement of Talmud *Peah* that First Fruits have no rabbinic measure. It is probable that this includes not only First Fruits but also their "decorations" (Mishnah 9).

6 In the Babli, *Ḥulin* 137b, this is the opinion of Samuel only.

7 Tosephta *Terumot* 5:6.

8 In the Tosephta (Note 7): R. Ismael from Shezur and R. Simeon.

9 Mishnah *Peah* 1:2.

10 *'Orlah* 2, Note 64.

11 Cf. *Terumot* 11, Note 60; *Ma'serot* 2, Note 134.

(fol. 65b) **משנה ב**: כֵּיצַד מַעֲלִין אֶת הַבִּיכּוּרִים. כָּל־הֶעָיָרוֹת שֶׁבַּמַּעֲמָד מִתְכַּנְּסוֹת לְעִירוֹ שֶׁלַּמַּעֲמָד וְלָנִין בִּרְחוֹבָהּ שֶׁלָּעִיר וְלֹא הָיוּ נִכְנָסִין לַבָּתִּים וְלַמַּשְׁכִּים הָיָה הַמְּמוּנֶּה אוֹמֵר לָהֶם קוּמוּ וְנַעֲלֶה צִיּוֹן אֶל בֵּית יי אֱלֹהֵינוּ.

Mishnah 2: How does one bring First Fruits? All villages in the *ma'amad*[12] district come to its central city. They stay overnight in the city square and do not enter houses[13]. In the morning, the organizer says to them (*Jer*. 31:5): "Get up and let us ascend to Zion, to the Eternal's, our God's, House.[14]"

12 The district which sent Temple personnel and accompanying laymen to Jerusalem for a week; cf. *Berakhot* Chapter 1, Note 231.

13 So as not to become impure by the impurity of the dead which persists for seven days. The impurity of the dead is transmitted by the "tent" (the house) over the corpse (*Num*. 19). Any other impurity is immediately removed by immersion in a *miqweh* outside the Temple mount and does not prevent the farmer from presenting his First Fruits.

14 In the verse: אל יי אלהינו.

(fol. 65c) **הלכה ב**: כְּגוֹן יְהוֹיָרִיב וּמַכִּירָיו.

Halakhah 2: For example, Jehoyarib and its acquaintances[15].

15 The 24 *ma'amad* districts were given the names of the 24 priestly courses.

וְיָלִינוּ בְּבֵית הַכְּנֶסֶת. תַּנָּא רִבִּי חֲלַפְתָּא בֶּן שָׁאוּל מִפְּנֵי אוֹהֶל הַטּוּמְאָה.

Could they not stay in the synagogue overnight? Rebbi Ḥalaphta ben Shaul stated: Because of the tent of impurity[13].

בַּדֶּרֶךְ הָיוּ אוֹמְרִים שָׂמַחְתִּי בְּאוֹמְרִים לִי בֵּית יי נֵלֵךְ. בִּרוּשָׁלֵם הָיוּ אוֹמְרִים עוֹמְדוֹת הָיוּ רַגְלֵינוּ בִּשְׁעָרַיִיךְ יְרוּשָׁלֵם. בְּהַר הַבַּיִת הָיוּ אוֹמְרִים הַלְלוּ יָ֗הּ הַלְלוּ אֵל בְּקָדְשׁוֹ כול׳. בָּעֲזָרָה הָיוּ אוֹמְרִים כָּל הַנְּשָׁמָה תְּהַלֵּל יָ֗הּ הַלְלוּ יָ֗הּ.

On the way they were saying (*Ps*. 122:2): "I rejoiced when I was told, we shall go to the Eternal's House." In Jerusalem, they said (*Ps*. 122:3): "Our feet were standing in Jerusalem." On the Temple Mount they said (*Ps*. 150:1) "Hallelujah, praise God in His Sanctuary, etc." In the Temple courtyard they said (*Ps*. 150:6): "Praise the Eternal every soul, praise the Eternal"[17].

17 They timed the recitation of *Ps*. 150 to last from the gate of the Temple Mount to the gate of the Temple enclosure.

(fol. 65b) **משנה ג**: הַקְּרוֹבִים מְבִיאִין תְּאֵינִים וַעֲנָבִים וְהָרְחוֹקִים מְבִיאִין גְּרוֹגְרוֹת וְצִימּוּקִים. וְהַשּׁוֹר הוֹלֵךְ לִפְנֵיהֶן וְקַרְנָיו מְצוּפּוֹת זָהָב וַעֲטָרָה שֶׁלְּזַיִת בְּרֹאשׁוֹ. הֶחָלִיל מַכֶּה לִפְנֵיהֶן עַד שֶׁהֵן מַגִּיעִין קָרוֹב לִירוּשָׁלֵם. הִגִּיעוּ קָרוֹב לִירוּשָׁלֵם שָׁלְחוּ לִפְנֵיהֶן וְעִיטְּרוּ אֶת בִּיכּוּרֵיהֶן. הַפַּחוֹת הַסְּגָנִים וְהַגִּזְבָּרִים יוֹצְאִין לִקְרָאתָן. לְפִי כְבוֹד הַנִּכְנָסִין הָיוּ יוֹצְאִין. כָּל־בַּעֲלֵי אוּמָּנִיּוֹת שֶׁבִּירוּשָׁלֵם עוֹמְדִים בִּפְנֵיהֶן וְשׁוֹאֲלִין בִּשְׁלוֹמָם אַחֵינוּ אַנְשֵׁי מָקוֹם פְּלוֹנִי בָּאתֶם בְּשָׁלוֹם.

Mishnah 3: Those who live close by bring figs and grapes but those from far away bring dried figs and raisins. The bull walks before them[18], his horns covered with gold and he wears an olive crown on his head. The fife beats[19] before them until they are arriving close to Jerusalem. When they arrived close to Jerusalem, they sent ahead of them[20] and they adorned their First Fruits[21]. Civil[22] and Temple administrators and the treasurers came out to meet them; they were leaving according to the standing of the comers. All artisans in Jerusalem were getting up for them[23] to greet them: "Our brothers, people from place **X**, be welcomed."

18 The required sacrifice (Mishnah 2:4) was a communal sacrifice, not a personal one of each farmer.

19 The marching time.

20 To the Temple.

21 Cf. Mishnah 9.

22 This has to be taken with a grain of salt; the expression פחות וסגנים is from *Ez.* 23:6.

23 When the procession passed by.

(fol. 65c) **הלכה ג**: עַד הֵכָן. עַד כְּדֵי שֶׁהוּא יָכוֹל לִתְרוֹם מִן הַמּוּבְחָר. בִּיקֵּשׁ לְהָבִיא דְבֵילָה. נֹאמַר אִם הָיְתָה קְעִילִית מֵבִיא. אִם הָיְתָה בוֹצְרִית אֵינוֹ מֵבִיא.

Halakhah 3: How far? That he could give heave from the best[24]. If he wants to bring a fig cake, we shall say that if it was from Qe'ila[25] he may bring it, from Bostra he cannot bring it.

24 This refers to Mishnah *Terumot* 2:4 where it is stated that if there is no Cohen available, the farmer should not give heave from the best but from what keeps best. The meaning of the sentence here seems to be that if the time needed to bring the First Fruits to Jerusalem is enough that in the case of heave the farmer should prefer the preservable to the good-looking, the people are classified as "far away".

25 In the Babli, *Nazir* 4a, these fig cakes are classified as intoxicating. Those from Bostra, on the dry Golan heights, were dry.

פְּשִׁיטָא שֶׁהוּא מַקְרִיב שְׁלָמִים. רִבִּי אִימִּי אָמַר מַקְרִיב שְׁלָמִים. רַב אָמַר מְקֵיצִין בָּהֶן אֶת הַמִּזְבֵּחַ. רִבִּי זְעִירָא בָּעֵי. יָחִיד שֶׁנִּתְעַצֵּל וְלֹא בָא מֵבִיא גְּדִי וְקַרְנָיו מְצוּפּוֹת כֶּסֶף.

Is it obvious that it[26] will be sacrificed as a well-being offering? Rebbi Ammi said, it will be sacrificed as a well-being offering. Rav said, one uses it to occupy the altar[27]. Rebbi Zeïra asked: Does a private person who was lazy and did not come [with the group] bring a goat with its horns covered in silver[28]?

26 The bull walking in front of the procession.

27 קיץ המזבח is used for elevation offerings which are brought any time the altar would otherwise be empty. It is difficult to find the meaning in the root קיץ "summer"; it might be from a verb parallel Arabic قصّ, أقصّ, "to appear pregnant".

28 This is the interpretation of Maimonides who does not quote the statement in his Code. According to Rashba (*Responsa* 1, #291) it is a prescriptive sentence: "A private person who was lazy and did not come brings a goat with its horns covered in silver." This agrees with Z. Frankel's opinion that in the Yerushalmi, בעי does not necessarily imply a question.

וַעֲטָרָה שֶׁלְּזַיִת בְּרֹאשׁוֹ. שֶׁהוּא מִמִּין שִׁבְעָה.

"And an olive crown on his head." Since this is one of the "Seven Kinds".

תַּנֵּי מִי שֶׁהָיוּ בִּיכּוּרָיו גְּרוֹגְרוֹת הָיָה מְעַטְּרָן תְּאֵינִים. וְצִימּוּקִים הָיָה מְעַטְּרָן עֲנָבִים.

It was stated: He whose First Fruits were dried figs adorned them with fresh figs; raisins one adorned with fresh grapes.

וְכִי יֵשׁ קָטוֹן וְגָדוֹל בִּירוּשָׁלֵם. אֶלָּא כֵינִי מַתְנִיתָא בְּאוֹכְלוֹסִין. לְפִי רוֹב נִכְנָסִין הָיוּ יוֹצְאִין.

Is there small and great in Jerusalem[29]? But so is the Mishnah: By multitudes[30]. According to the number of comers they were leaving.

29 When the Mishnah states that the receiving committe of the Temple was formed according to the standing of the comers, it seems inconceivable that the social standing of the arrivals should be given any consideration.

30 A Greek word with Semitic endings; cf. *Berakhot* 9, Note 47.

וְלֹא כֵן תַּנֵּי תָקוּם וְהָדַרְתָּ. מַה קִימָה שֶׁאֵין בָּהּ חִסָּרוֹן כִּיס אַף הִידּוּר שֶׁאֵין בָּהּ חִסָּרוֹן כִּיס. שַׁנְייָא הִיא הָכָא שֶׁהוּא אַחַת לְקִיצִּים. רִבִּי יוֹסֵי בֵּירִבִּי בּוּן בְּשֵׁם רִבִּי חוּנָא בַּר חִייָא. בּוֹא וּרְאֵה כַּמָּה גָדוֹל כּוֹחָן שֶׁלְּעוֹשֵׂי מִצְוֹת. שֶׁמִּפְּנֵי זָקֵן אֵין עוֹמְדִין וּמִפְּנֵי עוֹשֵׂי מִצְוֹת עוֹמְדִין. אָמַר רִבִּי יוֹסֵי בֵּירִבִּי בּוּן אִילֵּין דְּקַייְמִין מִן קוֹמֵי מֵיתָא לָא מִן קוֹמֵי מֵיתָא אִינּוּן קַייָמִין לוֹן אֶלָּא מִן קוֹמֵי אִילֵּין דִּגְמָלִים לֵיהּ חֶסֶד.

Did we not state: (*Lev.* 19:32) "You shall rise and give respect[31]." Just as rising does not cost anything, so giving respect should not cost anything[32]? There is a difference here since it is only once in a long time. Rebbi Yose ben Rebbi Abun in the name of Rebbi Ḥuna bar Ḥiyya: Come and see how strong is the case of those who come to fulfill a commandment! For before an elder one does not have to stand[33] but before those who come to fulfill a commandment one stands! Rebbi Yose ben Rebbi Abun said, those that stand up before a dead person do not stand up before the dead but before those who serve him in charity[34].

31 "Before a white head (an old person) *you shall rise and give respect* to an Elder (a rabbinic authority)."

32 *Sifra Qedošim Pereq* 7(13). But the Mishnah requires the artisans, who are paid for their products, not for their time, to get up when the procession passes by and lose time (which is money) from their work.

33 If it costs money. The saying is

quoted in Babli *Qiddušin* 33a.

34 This sentence is added because it is a homily by R. Yose ben R. Abun and is somehow connected with the topic discussed.

עַד כַּמָּה אָדָם צָרִיךְ לַעֲמוֹד מִפְּנֵי זָקֵן. שִׁמְעוֹן בַּר בָּא בְשֵׁם רִבִּי יוֹחָנָן. פַּעֲמַיִים בַּיּוֹם. רִבִּי לָעְזָר אָמַר פַּעַם אַחַת בַּיּוֹם. לֹא כֵן תַּנֵּי רִבִּי שִׁמְעוֹן בֶּן אֶלְעָזָר אוֹמֵר. מְנַיִין לַזָּקֵן שֶׁלֹּא יַטְרִיחַ. תַּלְמוּד לוֹמַר זָקֵן וְיָרֵאתָ מֵאֱלֹהֶיךָ אֲנִי יי. עַל דַּעְתֵּיהּ דְּרִבִּי יוֹחָנָן נִיחָא. עַל דַּעְתֵּיהּ דְּרִבִּי לָעְזָר לֹא יָקוּם כָּל־עִיקָּר. רִבִּי יַעֲקֹב בַּר אָחָא בְשֵׁם רִבִּי לָעְזָר. דְּלָא יֵיחְמֵי סִייַעְתָּא דְסַבִּין וְעָבַר קוֹמֵיהוֹן בְּגִין דִּיקוּמוֹן לוֹן מִן קוֹמוֹי. כְּשֵׁם שֶׁהֵן חֲלוּקִין כָּאן כָּךְ הֵן חֲלוּקִין בִּשְׁאִילַת שָׁלוֹם.

How often does a person have to rise before an Elder? Simeon bar Abba in the name of Rebbi Joḥanan: twice a day[35]. Rebbi Eleazar said, once a day. Was it not stated thus: Rebbi Simeon ben Eleazar says, from where that an Elder should not importune? The verse says (*Lev.* 19:32): "Elder, but you should fear your God, I am the Eternal[36]." According to Rebbi Joḥanan, this is understandable[37]. According to Rebbi Eleazar one should not get up at all[36]! Rebbi Jacob bar Aḥa in the name of Rebbi Eleazar: That he should not see a group of old men[38] and pass in front of them so they should rise before him. Just as they[39] disagree here, so they disagree about greeting.

35 In the Babli, *Qiddušin* 33b, it is formulated in the name of R. Yannai: That the reverence shown to a Sage should not be greater than that given to God, before Whom one appears twice daily, for morning and afternoon/evening prayers.

36 *Sifra Qedošim Pereq* 7(15). The ending of the verse is addressed not to the person who has to show reverence to the rabbi but to the rabbi.

37 He holds that the reverence shown to a rabbi must definitely be less than that given God.

38 Or any people.

39 R. Johanan and R. Eleazar; how many times a student has to greet his teacher every day.

רִבִּי חִזְקִיָּה רִבִּי חֲנִינָה בְּרֵיהּ דְּרִבִּי אַבָּהוּ בְּשֵׁם רִבִּי אֶבְדּוּמָא דְמִן חֵיפָה. לְזָקֵן אַרְבַּע אַמּוֹת עָבַר יֵשֵׁב לוֹ. כֹּהֵן גָּדוֹל מִשֶּׁהוּא רוֹאֵהוּ וְעַד שֶׁהוּא נִכְסֶה מִמֶּנּוּ. מַה טַעֲמָא וְהָיָה כְּצֵאת מֹשֶׁה הָאֹהֱלָה יָקוּמוּ כָּל־הָעָם וגו׳. תְּרֵין אֲמוֹרִין. חַד אָמַר לִשְׁבָח וְחַד אָמַר לִגְנַאי. מָאן דְּאָמַר לִשְׁבָח. מֵיחְמֵי צַדִּיקָא וּמִזַּכֵּי. וּמָאן דְּאָמַר לִגְנַאי. חֲזִי שָׁקֵי חֲזִי כְּרָעִין אֲכִיל מִן יְהוּדָאֵי שָׁתֵי מִן יְהוּדָאֵי. כָּל־מִדְּלֵיהּ מִן יְהוּדָאֵי.

Rebbi Ḥizqia, Rebbi Ḥanina the son of Rebbi Abbahu, in the name of Rebbi Eudaimon from Haifa: For an Elder four cubits; once he passed one sits down. The High Priest, from the moment one sees him until he disappears from view.[40] What is the reason? (*Ex.* 33:8) "It was, when Moses went to the tent, the entire people rose, etc." Two Amoraïm[41], one as praise and one as shame. The one who says, as praise: To see the just person and acquire merit. The one who says, as shame: Look at his thighs, look at his feet, he eats from the Jews, he drinks from the Jews, all he has is from the Jews.

40 The statement is quoted in the Babli, *Qiddušin* 33b, with the head of the rabbinic court instead of the High Priest.

41 In the Babli, *Qiddušin* 33b, they are identified as R. Ammi and R. Isaac Nappaḥa.

אָרוֹן פָּנָיו כְּלַפֵּי הָעָם וְהַכֹּהֲנִים כְּלַפֵּי הָעָם. וְיִשְׂרָאֵל פְּנֵיהֶן כְּלַפֵּי הַקּוֹדֶשׁ.

The ark is facing the people, the Cohanim are facing the people, and the people face the holy[42].

42 In the synagogue, the people stand with their faces towards the ark (and Jerusalem); the face of the holy ark and the Cohanim while they bless the people face the people, not the ark.

אָמַר רִבִּי לָעְזָר. אֵין הַתּוֹרָה עוֹמֶדֶת מִפְּנֵי בְנָהּ. שְׁמוּאֵל אָמַר אֵין עוֹמְדִין מִפְּנֵי חָבֵר. רִבִּי הִילָא רִבִּי יַעֲקֹב בַּר אִידִי הֲווֹן יְתִיבִין. עָבַר שְׁמוּאֵל בַּר בָּא וְקָמוּ לוֹן מִן קוֹמוֹי. אָמַר לוֹן. תַּרְתֵּיי גַּבְּכוֹן. חָדָא שֶׁאֵינִי זָקֵן. וְחָדָא שֶׁאֵין הַתּוֹרָה עוֹמֶדֶת מִפְּנֵי בְנָהּ.

Rebbi Eleazar said, the Torah does not get up because of her son. Samuel said, one does not get up because of a fellow[43]. Rebbi Hila and Rebbi Jacob bar Idi were sitting[44]. Samuel bar Abba[45] passed by them and they stood up. He said to them: Two things are [wrong] with you. The first, that I am not an Elder[46]. The other, that the Torah does not get up because of her son[47].

43 But only before a genuinely ordained rabbi.

44 Studying Torah.

45 A student of R. Johanan who enjoyed great authority but never was formally ordained, cf. Note 66.

46 He never acquired a rabbinic title.

47 Study is the Torah, the Sage is only the son of the Torah.

אָמַר רִבִּי זְעִירָא. רִבִּי אָחָא מַפְסִיק וְקָאִים דּוּ חָשַׁשׁ כְּהָדֵין תַּנָּיָא. דְּתַנֵּי כּוֹתְבֵי סְפָרִים תְּפִילִין וּמְזוּזוֹת מַפְסִיקִין לִקְרִיַּת שְׁמַע וְאֵין מַפְסִיקִין לִתְפִילָּה. רִבִּי חֲנַנְיָה בֶּן עֲקַבְיָה אוֹמֵר כְּשֵׁם שֶׁמַּפְסִיקִין לִקְרִיַּת שְׁמַע כָּךְ מַפְסִיקִין לִתְפִילָּה וְלִתְפִילִין וְלִשְׁאָר מִצְוֹתֶיהָ שֶׁלְתּוֹרָה.

Rebbi Zeïra said that Rebbi Aḥa interrupted [his studies] and got up since he considered the following statement:[48] "The writers of Torah scrolls, *tefillin* and *mezuzot* do interrupt for the reading of the *Šema'* but they do not interrupt for prayer. Rebbi Ḥanania ben Aqabia says, just as they interrupt for the reading of the *Šema'* so they do interrupt for prayer, *tefillin*, and all other commandments of the Torah."

48 Tosephta *Berakhot* 2:6, quoted *Šabbat* 1:1 (fol. 3b) In the Tosephta, there is an additional statement of Rebbi to the effect that one does not interrupt the performance of one commandment for any other commandment, a statement attributed to R. Ḥanania ben Aqabia in Babli *Sukkah* 26a.

While here it is assumed that R. Aḥa follows R. Ḥanania ben Aqabia, an argument in R. Aḥa's name to support the anonymous statement is in *Berakhot* 1:5 (Note 164), *Šabbat* 1:2.

חִזְקִיָּה בְּרִיבִּי מִן דַּהֲוָה לָעֵי בְּאוֹרַיְתָא כָּל־צוֹרְכֵיהּ הֲוָה אֲזִיל וִיתִיב לֵיהּ קוֹמֵי בֵּית וַעֲדָא בְּגִין מֵיחְמֵי סַבִּין וּמֵיקָם לֵיהּ מִן קוֹמֵיהוֹן. יְהוּדָה בַּר חִייָה הֲוָה יְלִיף סְלִיק וּשְׁאִיל בִּשְׁלָמֵיהּ דְּרִבִּי יַנַּאי חָמוּהּ מֵעֶרֶב שַׁבָּת לְעֶרֶב שַׁבָּת. וַהֲוָה יְתִיב לֵיהּ עַל אֲתַר תְּלִי בְּגִין מֵיחְמִינֵיהּ וּמֵקִים לֵיהּ מִן קוֹמוֹי. אָמְרִין לֵיהּ תַּלְמִידוֹי. לֹא כֵן אַלְפָּן רִבִּי. לְזָקֵן אַרְבַּע אַמּוֹת. אָמַר לוֹן אֵין יְשִׁיבָה לִפְנֵי סִינַי. חַד זְמָן עֲנִי מַסִּיק. אָמַר לֵית אֶיפְשַׁר דִּיהוּדָה בְּרִי מְשַׁנֶּה מִנְהָגֵיהּ. אָמַר לֵית אֶיפְשַׁר דְּלָא יְגִיעוֹן יִיסוּרִין בְּהַהוּא גוּפָא צַדִּיקָא. מִסְתַּבְּרָא שֶׁאֵין לָנוּ יְהוּדָה בְּרִיבִּי.

The great Ḥizqiah[49], when he had studied Torah as much as he could, used to go and sit before the assembly hall in order to see old men and get up before them. Jehudah bar Ḥiyya used to go and greet his father-in-law Rebbi Yannai every Sabbath eve. He used to sit on a hilly place in order to see him and get up before him. His students said to him, did the teacher not instruct us, "for an Elder four cubits"? He said to them, one does not sit before Sinai. Once he did not come. He said it is impossible that my son Jehudah should change his habits, it is impossible that sufferings should come over this holy body[50]. It is reasonable that we lost the great Jehudah.

49 Ḥizqiah ben R. Ḥiyya the elder, twin brother of Jehudah ben Ḥiyya. The story must refer to the very young Ḥizqiah, before he opened his own

academy.

50 R. Yannay must disagree with the characterization that sudden death is a sign of Divine wrath (Chapter 2, Note 47), at least as far as totally just people are concerned. Proof for this position is given by the deaths of Aaron and Moses.

רִבִּי מֵאִיר חֲמֵי אֲפִילוּ סָב עַם הָאָרֶץ וּמְקִים לֵיהּ מִן קוֹמוֹי וְאָמַר לֹא מַגָּן מַאֲרִיךְ יָמִים. רִבִּי חֲנִינָא מָחֵי מָאן דְּלָא קָאִים מִקּוֹמוֹי וַהֲוָה אֲמַר לֵיהּ כִּי בְעִיתָה מְבַטְּלָה דְאוֹרָיְתָא. אָמַר רִבִּי סִימוֹן אָמַר הַקָּדוֹשׁ בָּרוּךְ הוּא מִפְּנֵי שֵׂיבָה תָּקוּם וְהָדַרְתָּ פְּנֵי זָקֵן וְיָרֵאתָ מֵאֱלֹהֶיךָ אֲנִי יי. אֲנִי הוּא שֶׁקִּייַמְתִּי עֲמִידַת זָקֵן תְּחִילָּה.

Rebbi Meïr, when he saw even a vulgar old man, rose before him. He said, not for nothing did he live so long. Rebbi Ḥanina slapped a person who did not rise before him and said, do you want to do away with the Torah? Rebbi Simon said, The Holy One, praise to Him, said (*Lev.* 19:32): "Before a white head you shall rise, give respect to an Elder, and fear your God, I am the Eternal." I am the one who first observed standing before an Elder[51].

51 *Gen.* 18:2.

כְּשֶׁהַנָּשִׂיא נִכְנָס כָּל־הָעָם עוֹמְדִים מִפָּנָיו וְאֵין רְשׁוּת לְאֶחָד מֵהֶן לֵישֵׁב עַד שֶׁיֹּאמַר לָהֶם שְׁבוּ. אַב בֵּית דִּין שֶׁנִּכְנָס עוֹשִׂין לוֹ שׁוּרוֹת. רָצָה נִכְנָס בְּזוֹ רָצָה נִכְנָס בְּזוֹ. חָכָם שֶׁנִּכְנָס אֶחָד עוֹמֵד וְאֶחָד יוֹשֵׁב אֶחָד עוֹמֵד וְאֶחָד יוֹשֵׁב עַד שֶׁמַּגִּיעַ וְיוֹשֵׁב לוֹ בִמְקוֹמוֹ. רִבִּי מֵאִיר הֲוָה יְלִיף סְלַק לְבֵית וַעֲדָא וַהֲווֹן כָּל־עַמָּא חָמְיִין לֵיהּ וְקַיְימוֹן לֵיהּ מִן קוֹמוֹי. כַּד שָׁמְעוּן הָהֵן תַּנָּיָיא תָּנֵי בָּעוֹן לְמֵיעֲבַד לֵיהּ כֵּן. כָּעַס וּנְפַק לֵיהּ. אָמַר לוֹן שָׁמַעְתִּי שֶׁמַּעֲלִין בַּקּוֹדֶשׁ וְלֹא מוֹרִידִין.

"[52]When the patriarch[53] enters, everybody stands and they may not sit down until he tells them: sit! For the chief judge[54] one forms rows; he may choose through which one to enter. For the *ḥakham*[55], one person after another stands up and then sits down until he arrives at his place." Rebbi Meïr was used to it that when he went to the assembly hall, the people saw him and stood up before him. When they heard a *Tanna* reciting this statement, they wanted to follow its rules[56]. He got angry and left. He said to them, I heard than one promotes in dignity but does not demote[57].

52 Tosephta *Sanhedrin* 7:8; the Tosephta text is identical with the Babli text, *Horaiot* 13b.

53 The president of the Synhedrion.

54 The number two man in the hierarchy of the Synhedrion. In the Babli version, one forms two passage ways on both sides of which the people stand and he may choose one of these.

55 The number three man in the hierarchy of the Synhedrion.

56 That only the persons closest to where he was at the moment would stand up and sit down immediately after he passed.

57 A principle also accepted in the Babli (*Yoma* 20b). For example, if the High Priest becomes temporarily disabled on the Day of Atonement, his substitute after that day cannot serve as High Priest, because there is one, or as simple priest, since one promotes in dignity but does not demote. R. Meïr extends the principle and rules that forms of showing respect cannot be reduced once they became accepted.

רִבִּי זְעִירָא הֲוון בָּעְייָן מַמְנִיתֵיהּ וְלָא בָּעֵי מְקַבֵּל עֲלוֹי. כַּד שְׁמַע הָהֵן תַּנָּייָא תַנֵּי חָכָם חָתָן נָשִׂיא גְּדוּלָּה מְכַפֶּרֶת. קְבִיל עֲלוֹי מַמְנִיתֵיהּ. חָכָם. מִפְּנֵי שֵׂיבָה תָּקוּם וְהָדַרְתָּ פְּנֵי זָקֵן. מַה כְתִיב בַּתְרֵיהּ וְכִי יָגוּר אִתְּכֶם גֵּר בְּאַרְצְכֶם לֹא תוֹנוּ אוֹתוֹ. מַה הַגֵּר מוֹחֲלִין לוֹ עַל כָּל־עֲווֹנוֹתָיו אַף חָכָם שֶׁנִּתְמַנֶּה מוֹחֲלִין לוֹ עַל כָּל־עֲווֹנוֹתָיו. חָתָן. וַיֵּלֶךְ עֵשָׂיו אֶל יִשְׁמָעֵאל וַיִּקַּח אֶת מָחֲלַת בַּת יִשְׁמָעֵאל. וְכִי

מָחֲלַת שְׁמָהּ. (fol. 65d) וַהֲלֹא בָּשְׂמַת שְׁמָהּ. אֶלָּא שֶׁנִּמְחֲלוּ לוֹ כָּל־עֲוֹנוֹתָיו. נָשִׂיא. בֶּן שָׁנָה שָׁאוּל בְּמָלְכוֹ. וְכִי בֶּן שָׁנָה הָיָה. אֶלָּא שֶׁנִּמְחֲלוּ לוֹ כָּל־עֲוֹנוֹתָיו כְּתִינּוֹק בֶּן שָׁנָה.

They wanted to ordain Rebbi Zeïra but he did not want to take it upon himself. When he heard a *Tanna* stating: "For an ordained person, a bridegroom, a patriarch, the dignity deletes [his sins]," he accepted being ordained. An ordained person: (*Lev.* 19:32): "Before a white head you shall rise, give respect to an Elder, and fear your God, I am the Eternal." What is written after that (*v.* 33): "If a proselyte lives in your land, you shall not trick him." Just as all his sins are forgiven to the proselyte, so all sins are forgiven to one being ordained. The bridegroom: (*Gen.* 28:9) "Esaw went to Ismael and married Maḥalat[58] bat Ismael." But was her name Maḥalat, was it not Basemat[59]? But all his sins were forgiven him. The president: (*1S.* 13:1) "Saul was one year old when he became king." Was he one year old when he became king? But all his sins were forgiven him as to a baby of one year.

58 "The one being forgiven."

59 "The perfumed." The verse would prove only that prior sins of the bride are forgiven.

רִבִּי מָנָא מֵיקִיל לָאִילֵּין דְּמִיתְמַנֵּיי בְּכְסַף. רִבִּי אִימִּי קָרָא עֲלֵיהוֹן אֱלֹהֵי כֶסֶף וֵאלֹהֵי זָהָב לֹא תַעֲשׂוּ לָכֶם. אָמַר רִבִּי יֹאשִׁיָּא וְטַלִּית שֶׁעָלָיו כְּמַרְדַּעַת שֶׁלְחֲמוֹר. אָמַר רִבִּי שַׁיָּין. זֶה שֶׁהוּא מִתְמַנֶּה בְּכֶסֶף אֵין עוֹמְדִין מִפָּנָיו וְאֵין קוֹרִין אוֹתוֹ רִבִּי. וְהַטַּלִּית שֶׁעָלָיו כְּמַרְדַּעַת שֶׁלַּחֲמוֹר. רִבִּי זְעִירָא וְחַד מִן רַבָּנָן הֲווֹן יְתִיבִין. עֲבַר חַד מִן אִילֵּין דְּמִיתְמַנֵּי בְּכְסַף. אֲמַר יָתֵיהּ דְּמִן רַבָּנִין לְרִבִּי זְעִירָא. נַעֲבִיד נַפְשָׁן תַּנָּיֵי וְלָא נֵיקוּם לוֹן מִקּוֹמוֹי.

Rebbi Mana made light of those ordained for money. Rebbi Ammi[60] read for them (*Ex.* 20:19): "Do not make for yourselves gods of silver or gods of gold." Rebbi Yoshia said, their prayer shawl is like a donkey's saddle cover. Rebbi Ashian said, if somebody is ordained for money, one does not get up before him and one does not address him as Rebbi; his prayer shawl is like a donkey's saddle cover. Rebbi Zeïra and one of the rabbis were sitting together when a person ordained for money was passing by. One of the rabbis said to Rebbi Zeïra, let us behave like *Tannaïm*[61] and not get up before him.

60 In the Babli, *Sanhedrin* 7b, this is ascribed to Rav Ashi and directed against those who ordain for money. The ordination discussed here is original ordination in the succession of Moses and the Prophets, in Mishnaic times expressed by the title of "Rebbi", in contrast to the informal (Babylonian and modern) ordination known by the title of "Rav.".

61 People of prior generations, before the patriarchate, the only authority empowered to ordain in their time, had discovered ordination as a source of income. Not to honor an ordained person was really an insult to the patriarchate.

תִּירְגֵּם יַעֲקֹב אִישׁ כְּפַר נָבוּרַיָּא. הוֹי אוֹמֵר לָעֵץ הָקִיצָה עוּרִי לְאֶבֶן דּוּמֵם הוּא יוֹרֶה. יוֹדֵעַ הוּא יוֹרֶה. הִנֵּה הוּא תָּפוּשׂ זָהָב וָכֶסֶף. לֹא בְּכַסְפִּייָא אִיתְמַנֵּי. וְכָל־רוּחַ אֵין בְּקִרְבּוֹ. לֹא חֲכִים כְּלוּם. הוֹי אוֹמֵר בְּעִיתוֹן מַמְנִייָה. וַיי בְּהֵיכַל קָדְשׁוֹ. הָא רִבִּי יִצְחָק בַּר לָעְזָר בִּכְנִישְׁתָּא מְדַרְתָּא דְקַיְסָרִין.

Jacob from Kefar Naburaia translated (*Ḥab.* 2:19-20): "Woe, to him who says to wood wake up, arise to the silent stone, should he instruct?" He who knows should instruct. "Behold, he is grabbed by gold and silver," is he not ordained by the money chest? "No spirit is in him," he does not know anything. Woe to him who says, I want to be ordained! "But the

Eternal is in His holy hall," e. g., Rebbi Isaac ben Eleazar in the fortified synagogue[62] of Caesarea.

62 Cf. *Berakhot* 3, Note 90.

רִבִּי אִמִּי שָׁאַל לְרִבִּי סִימוֹן. שָׁמַעְתָּ שֶׁמְּמַנִּין זְקֵינִים בְּחוּצָה לָאָרֶץ. אָמַר לֵיהּ. שָׁמַעְתִּי שֶׁאֵין מְמַנִּין זְקֵינִים בְּחוּצָה לָאָרֶץ. אָמַר רִבִּי לֵוִי וְלֹא מִקְרָא מָלֵא הוּא. בֶּן אָדָם בֵּית יִשְׂרָאֵל יוֹשְׁבִים עַל אַדְמָתָם. הָא כָּל־יְשִׁיבָה שֶׁלָּךְ לֹא יְהֵא אֶלָּא עַל אַדְמָתָךְ. רַבָּנִין דְּקַיְסָרִין אָמְרִין מְמַנִּין זְקֵינִים בְּחוּצָה לָאָרֶץ עַל מְנָת לַחֲזוֹר. רִבִּי יִצְחָק בַּר נַחְמָן הֲוָה בְּעַזָּה וּמְנוּנֵיהּ עַל מְנָת לַחֲזוֹר. רִבִּי זְמִינָא הֲוָה בְּצוֹר וּמְנוּנֵיהּ עַל מְנָת לַחֲזוֹר. אוֹף רִבִּי יוֹנָה הֲוָה בְּפִיתְקָא וְלָא קְבִיל עֲלוֹי מִתְמַנְּיָה. אָמַר עַד זְמָן דְּמִיתְמַנֵּי רִבִּי וּמִינָּה רִבִּי. אָמַר רִבִּי חָמָא. יְהוּדָה בֶּן טִיטֶס הֲוָה בְּרוֹמֵי וּמְנוּנֵיהּ עַל מְנָת דְּיַחֲזוֹר.

Rebbi Ammi asked Rebbi Simeon: Did you hear that one ordains Elders outside the Land? He answered, I heard that one does not ordain Elders outside the Land. Rebbi Levi said, is that not an explicit verse (*Ez.* 36:17): "Son of man, the House of Israel are dwelling on their Land;" that all your academies[63] shall only be on your Land. The rabbis of Caesarea say, one may ordain Elders outside the Land on condition they return. Rebbi Isaac bar Naḥman was in Gaza and they ordained him on condition he return[64]. Rebbi Zemina was in Tyre and they ordained him on condition he return. Also Rebbi Jonah was on the list but he refused to be ordained as long as his teacher was not ordained. They ordained his teacher. Rebbi Ḥama said, Jehudah ben Titus[65] was in Rome and they ordained him on condition he return.

63 Taking the word ישב "to sit" in the meaning: "To study in a talmudic academy."

64 The Southern border of the

Amoraic Land of Israel was Ascalon (cf. *Ševi'it* p. 496.)

65 A fourth-generation Amora.

שִׁמְעוֹן בַּר וָוא הֲוָה בְּדַמַּסְקוֹס וְאִיתְמַנּוּן דְּקִיקִין מִינֵּיהּ וְהוּא לֹא אִיתְמַנֵּי. שִׁמְעוֹן בַּר וָוא הֲוָה בָּקִי בְּמַרְגָּלִיתָא בְּכָל־מִילָּה וְלָא הֲוָה לֵיהּ עִיגּוּל מֵיכְלֵיהּ. וַהֲוָה רִבִּי יוֹחָנָן קָרֵי עֲלוֹי וְגַם לֹא לַחֲכָמִים לֶחֶם. אָמַר כָּל־מִי שֶׁאֵינוֹ מַכִּיר מַעֲשָׂיו שֶׁלְאַבְרָהָם יַכִּיר מַעֲשֶׂה אֲבוֹתָיו שֶׁלְזֶה. שִׁמְעוֹן בַּר וָוא הֲוָה בְּדַמַּסְקוֹס וְשָׁלַח לֵיהּ רִבִּי אַבָּהוּ חָדָא אִיגְּרָא וִיהַב מִן סִיבְתֵּיהּ בְּגַוָּהּ. בְּגִין אִילֵּין סִבְתָּא קוּם אֶתְהַלֵּךְ לְאַרְעָא דְיִשְׂרָאֵל. מִי יְגַלֶּה עָפָר מֵעֵינֶיךָ רִבִּי יוֹחָנָן. אַבָּהוּ רִיגְלוּתָיָה אִיתְמַנֵּי. שִׁמְעֹן דְּמַעֲפָרְיָא לָא אִתְמַנֵּי.

Simeon bar Abba[66] was in Damascus and smaller people than he were ordained but he was not ordained. Simeon bar Abba was an expert in everything concerning pearls but he did not have a loaf to eat. Rebbi Johanan quoted about him (*Eccl.* 9:11): "Also bread is not for Sages." He said, anybody who does not know the good works of Abraharn may know them through the good works of this man's ancestors. Simeon bar Abba was in Damascus when Rebbi Abbahu sent him a letter and enclosed some of his grey hair: "For these gray hairs' sake, get up and go to the Land of Israel. Who would remove the earth from your eyes, Rebbi Johanan: Abbahu the shoe-clad was ordained, Simeon the toga-clad was not ordained!"

66 Since elsewhere in the Yerushalmi (e. g., *Berakhot* 1:7, Note 137) he is given the title of Rebbi and in the Babli he appears as Rav Shimen bar Abba, he had the title of Rav before he came from Babylonia to Galilee and in the end was fully ordained in the Land of Israel.

משנה ד: הֶחָלִיל מַכֶּה לִפְנֵיהֶם עַד שֶׁמַּגִּיעִין לְהַר הַבַּיִת. הִגִּיעוּ לְהַר(fol. 65b) הַבַּיִת אֲפִילוּ אַגְרִיפַּס הַמֶּלֶךְ נוֹטֵל הַסַּל עַל כְּתֵיפוֹ וְנִכְנָס עַד שֶׁהוּא מַגִּיעַ לָעֲזָרָה. הִגִּיעַ לָעֲזָרָה וְדִבְּרוּ הַלְוִיִּם בַּשִּׁיר אֲרוֹמִמְךָ יי כִּי דִילִּיתָנִי וְלֹא שִׂמַּחְתָּ אוֹיְבַי לִי. הַגּוֹזָלוֹת שֶׁעַל הַסַּלִּים הָיוּ עוֹלוֹת וּמַה שֶּׁבְּיָדָם נוֹתְנִין לַכֹּהֲנִים.

Mishnah 4: The fife beats before them until they arrive at the Temple Mount. Arrived at the Temple Mount, even king Agrippas takes the basket on his own shoulder and enters until he arrives at the Temple courtyard. When they arrived at the Temple courtyard, the Levites sang (*Ps.* 30:2): "I shall elevate You, Eternal, for You drew me up and You did not make my enemies happy because of me." The pigeons on the baskets were elevation sacrifices and what was in their hands[67] they gave to the Cohanim.

משנה ה: עוֹדֵינוּ הַסַּל עַל כְּתֵיפוֹ קוֹרֵא מֵהִגַּדְתִּי הַיּוֹם לַיי אֱלֹהֶיךָ עַד שֶׁהוּא גוֹמֵר כָּל־הַפָּרָשָׁה. רִבִּי יוּדָה אוֹמֵר עַד אֲרַמִּי אוֹבֵד אָבִי. הִגִּיעַ לַאֲרַמִּי אוֹבֵד אָבִי מוֹרִיד הַסַּל מִן כְּתֵיפוֹ וְאוֹחֲזוֹ בִּשְׂפָתָיו וְכֹהֵן מֵנִיחַ יָדוֹ תַּחְתָּיו וּמְנִיפוֹ. וְקוֹרֵא מֵאֲרַמִּי אוֹבֵד אָבִי עַד שֶׁהוּא גוֹמֵר כָּל־הַפָּרָשָׁה. וּמַנִּיחוֹ בְּצַד הַמִּזְבֵּחַ וְהִשְׁתַּחֲוָה וְיָצָא.

Mishnah 5: As long as the basket is still on his shoulder he reads from (*Deut.* 26:3) "I am declaring today before the Eternal, your God" until he finishes the entire paragraph. Rebbi Jehudah says, until (*v.* 5): "My father was a wandering Aramean." When he comes to "my father was a wandering Aramean", he takes the basket down from his shoulder, holds it by its rim, and the Cohen puts his hand under it and weaves[68] it. Then he reads from "my father was a wandering Aramean" until he finishes the entire paragraph, he puts it down next to the altar, prostrates himself, and leaves.

67 According to Maimonides, pigeons that were not tied to the baskets. According to R. Abraham ben David and R. Simson, the baskets of First Fruits; according to the Mayence commentary ("Rabbenu Gershom") and Rashi (in *Menaḥot* 58a), the baskets themselves. The last explanation is the only one compatible with the Halakhah (Note 70).

68 Cf. Chapter 2, Note 122.

(fol. 65d) **הלכה ד**: רַב הוּנָא אָמַר כֵּינִי מַתְנִיתָא וְלָקַח הַכֹּהֵן הַטֶּנֶא מִיָּדֶיךָ.

Halakhah 4: Rav Huna said[69]: So is the Mishnah (*Deut.* 26:4): "The Cohen shall take the basket from your hand."

69 According to R. Isaac Simponti and R. Simson of Sens, this refers to Mishnah 4: The Cohen has to take the basket before the Levites start to sing. In this version, the Levites wait until the procession reaches the inner courtyard where the ceremony is held. According to others, Rav Huna gives the reason why even the king has to take the basket himself, that the Cohen has to receive it from the owner's hand. The correct interpretation seems to be that "the Cohen shall take the basket from your hand" should replace the first reference to "my father was a wandering Aramean" in the text of R. Jehudah since *v*.4 separates between two declarations.

אִית תַּנָּיֵי תַנֵּי מַחֲלִף. כְּדֵי לִסְמוֹךְ מַתָּנָה לְמַתָּנָה.

Some *Tannaïm* switch statements[70] to combine gift with gift.

70 Switch the order of Mishnaiot to have Mishnah 7 follow immediately after Mishnah 4, to explain what really was given to the Cohanim.

תַּנֵּי רִבִּי יוֹסֵי. לֹא הָיוּ נוֹתְנִין אֶת הַגּוֹזָלוֹת עַל גַּבֵּי הַסַּלִּין שֶׁלֹּא יְנַבְּלוּ הַבִּיכּוּרִין אֶלָּא תוֹלֶה אוֹתָן חוּץ לַסַּלִּים.

Rebbi Yose stated: They did not put the pigeons on top of the baskets in order not to dirty them but one hangs them on the sides of the baskets.

תַּנֵּי חַד סָב קוֹמֵי רִבִּי זְעִירָא. חוֹזֵר לְהִגַּדְתִּי הַיּוֹם. וְכִי יֵשׁ אָדָם מַגִּיד וְחוֹזֵר וּמַגִּיד. קִייַּמוּנָהּ כְּבָר הִגַּדְתִּי.

An old man stated before Rebbi Zeïra: He returns to[71] "I am declaring today." But can a person declare and repeat it[72]? We support it: I already declared[73].

71 In this version, R. Jehudah requires the farmer first to declare v. 3, then to perform the procedure of weaving, and then to read again vv. 3,5-10.

72 Usually, this is taken to mean that a witness may not change his story even if he gives a reason (Babli *Sanhedrin* 44b).

73 The repetition of v. 3 is not a declaration but a statement that this already had been declared.

הוּנָא בָּעֵי. הֲנָחָה מַהוּ שֶׁתַּתִּיר לִמְחוּסְרֵי זְמָן. אָמַר רַב מַתַּנְיָיה הָדָא דְתֵימַר בְּשֶׁחָזַר וּנְטָלָן. אֲבָל אִם הָיוּ בִמְקוֹמָן כְּהִנִּיחָן הֵן. רִבִּי יוֹנָה בָּעֵי. הִנִּיחָן בַּלַּיְלָה.

Huna asked: Does depositing it permit to those lacking time[74]? Rav Mattania said, that means[75], if he took them up again. But if they stayed in their place they are deposited[76]. Rebbi Jonah asked, if he deposited them in the night[77]?

74 Somebody brought First Fruits to the Temple before Pentecost. They should not have been accepted but if they were duly dedicated and deposited near the altar, will they automatically become regular First Fruits on Pentecost and then may be eaten by Cohanim under the rules of heave?

75 That you have a problem (which is not answered.)

76 While the owner cannot make the declaration, the Temple acquires all it is given and gives it to the Cohanim.

77 No Temple service is performed during the night except what is connected to the activities of the preceding day. Therefore, the obvious answer to R. Jonah's question is negative; First Fruits illegally deposited in the night never become permitted.

מַנִּיחָן בְּקֶרֶן דְּרוֹמִית מַעֲרָבִית. לִפְנֵי יי. יָכוֹל בְּמַעֲרָב. תַּלְמוּד לוֹמַר אֶל פְּנֵי הַמִּזְבֵּחַ. אִי לִפְנֵי הַמִּזְבֵּחַ יָכוֹל בְּדָרוֹם. תַּלְמוּד לוֹמַר לִפְנֵי יי. הָא כֵּיצַד. מַגִּישָׁן עַל קֶרֶן דְּרוֹמִית מַעֲרָבִית וּמַנִּיחָהּ בִּדְרוֹמָהּ שֶׁלְּקֶרֶן.

"[78]One puts them[79] near the South-West corner. (*Deut*. 26:10) 'Before the Eternal', that should mean the West. The verse says (*Deut*. 26:4) 'at the face of the altar.' If it is at the face of the altar that should mean the South[80]. The verse says 'before the Eternal'! How is that? He presents them at the South-Western corner and puts them down South of the corner."

78 This is a Babylonian *baraita*, quoted in Babli *Soṭa* 14b, *Zebaḥim* 66a, *Menaḥot* 19b. The Babylonian character is shown by the use of **אי** as "if".

79 The First Fruits to be deposited near the altar. The problem treated is an apparent contradiction between the prescriptions contained in verses 4 and 10 of Chap. 26.

80 The entrance to the Temple precinct was to the East. Going from East to West one has the outer and inner courtyards, then the Cohanim's court containing the altar, and to the West the Temple building containing the holiest of holies, counted as the Presence of the Eternal. The access to the altar was via the ramp built at its South side. Therefore, "before the Eternal" means before the Temple building, to the West of the altar. "At the face of the altar" means at the South side.

(fol. 65b) **משנה ו**: בָּרִאשׁוֹנָה כָּל־מִי שֶׁהוּא יוֹדֵעַ לִקְרוֹת קוֹרֵא וְכָל־מִי שֶׁאֵינוֹ יוֹדֵעַ לִקְרוֹת מַקְרִין לְפָנָיו. נִמְנְעוּ מִלְּהָבִיא הִתְקִינוּ שֶׁיְּהוּ מַקְרִין אֶת מִי שֶׁהוּא יוֹדֵעַ וְאֶת מִי שֶׁאֵינוֹ יוֹדֵעַ.

Mishnah 6: In earlier times, everybody who knew how to read, read, and everybody who did not know how to read, had someone read before him[81]. When they refrained from bringing they instituted that one read before him who knew and him who did not know.

משנה ז: הָעֲשִׁירִים מְבִיאִין אֶת בִּיכּוּרֵיהֶן בְּקָלָתוֹת שֶׁלְּכֶסֶף וְשֶׁלְּזָהָב וְהָעֲנִיִּים מְבִיאִין אוֹתָן בְּסַלֵּי נְצָרִים שֶׁלְּעֲרָבָה קְלוּפָה וְהַסַּלִּים וְהַבִּיכּוּרִים נוֹתְנִים לַכֹּהֲנִים.

Mishnah 7: Rich people bring their First Fruits in bowls[82] of silver and gold but poor people bring them in baskets of stripped willow twigs. Baskets and First Fruits are given to the Cohanim.

81 The Cohen recites the declaration word by word and the farmer repeats each word after the Cohen.

82 Greek κάλαθος, Latin *calathus* "basket; pail; bowl".

(fol. 65d) **הלכה ה**: תַּנֵּי. אֵין עֲנִייָה אֶלָּא מִפִּי אֶחָד. וְלֹא עוֹד אֶלָּא שֶׁסָּמְכוּ לְמִקְרָא וְעָנִיתָ וְאָמַרְתָּ.

Halakhah 5: It was stated: "Answering is only by a single person. Not only that but they found support in the verse (*Deut.* 26:5): 'You shall answer and say'.[83]"

83 In *Deut.* 26:5, reciting the declaration is formulated as "answering and saying." From this one deduces that even though First Fruits are brought to the Temple in a large procession, the presentation is a private ceremony for each farmer separately. They also found a biblical hint that the declaration should be repeated after the Cohen, to convince literate people to conform to the usage of the illiterate.

The corresponding statement in *Sifry Deut* (#301) reads: "'You shall answer and say'. It is said here 'answer' and it is said there (*Deut.* 27:14) 'answer'. Since the answering there is in the holy language (Hebrew), so the answering here is in the holy language. From here, they said that in earlier times, everybody who knew how to read, read, and everybody who did not know how to read, had someone read before him. When they refrained from bringing they instituted that one read before him who knew and him who did not know; they found support in the verse: 'You shall answer', answering is only to what others said." This text would read in the Halakhah: אֵין עֲנִייָה אֶלָּא מִפִּי אַחֵר

רִבִּי יוֹנָה בָּעֵי מַהוּ לַהֲבִיאָן בְּתַמְחוּיִין שֶׁלְּכֶסֶף.

Rebbi Jonah asked: May one bring in large silver bowls[84]?

84 The (probably Egyptian) word טנא which appears only in *Deut.* (Chapters 26,28) traditionally means a small (wooden or metal) bowl. Is this prescriptive? No answer is given. In the Babli (*Baba Qama* 92a), Mishnah 7 is interpreted to mean that the poor give baskets and fruits to the Cohanim but the rich come to get their silver bowl back after the Cohanim have eaten their fruits. There is no hint of this interpretation in the Yerushalmi and, since the presentation of First Fruits was always done simultaneously by a mass of people, the position of the Babli is not practical. Probably the question of R. Jonah is not answered because nobody would give a large precious bowl.

רִבִּי יוֹנָה וְרִבִּי יִרְמְיָה. חַד אָמַר מְחַזֵּר מָנָא. וְחָרְנָא אָמַר מְחַזֵּר פַּטִּירִין עִם יַרְקוֹנִין. דְּאַתְּ אָמַר פַּטִּירִין עִם מְרוֹרִין.[85] וְלָא יָדְעִינָן מָאן אָמַר דָּא וּמָאן אָמַר דָּא. מִן מַה דְּאָמַר רִבִּי יוֹנָה מַהוּ לַהֲבִיאָן בְּתַמְחוּיִין שֶׁלְּכֶסֶף. הֲוֵי הוּא דְּאָמַר דִּמְחַזֵּר מָנָא. דִּי אָמַר סַלָּה.[86] (ד)רִבִּי פִינְחָס אָמַר. מְחַזֵּר פַּטִּימִין בְּנֵי תוֹרִין. דִּי אָמַר תּוֹרִין וּבְנֵי תוֹרִין.

[87]Rebbi Jonah and Rebbi Jeremiah. One says, one repeats "vessel". The other one says, one repeats "unleavened with vegetables" because you have to say "unleavened with bitter herbs." We do not know who said what. Since Rebbi Jonah said, may one bring in large silver baskets, that

shows that he must have said that one repeats "vessel". One must say: "basket." Rebbi Phineas said, one must repeat (*Lev.* 1:14): "Fattened and young pigeons" because one must say "pigeons and young pigeons."

85 Reading of the parallel *Megillah* 4:1 (fol. 74d). Here: מרזרין.

86 Reading of the parallel *Megillah* 4:1. Here: בלה.

87 The main place of this paragraph is in *Megilla* 4:1, which deals with the rules of the Aramaic translation of the Torah in public worship. While in principle the translator may choose his own words, in a few instances rabbinic authorities insisted that certain expressions are too imprecise. The first one is the translation of טנא by "vessel" instead of "basket", the second one that of מצות ומרורים (*Num.* 9:11) by "unleavened bread and vegetables." The paragraph is included here since from the preceding paragraph it is inferred that R. Jonah is the stickler for the correct translation of טנא. The addition of the unconnected statement of R. Phineas shows that the paragraph is copied from *Megillah* and not vice-versa.

The Targumim follow R. Jonah and R. Jeremiah but not R. Phineas.

(fol. 65b) **משנה ח**: רִבִּי שִׁמְעוֹן בֶּן נָנָס אוֹמֵר מְעַטְּרִין אֶת הַבִּיכּוּרִין חוּץ מִשִּׁבְעַת הַמִּינִים. רִבִּי עֲקִיבָה אוֹמֵר אֵין מְעַטְּרִין אֶת הַבִּיכּוּרִין אֶלָּא מִשִּׁבְעַת הַמִּינִין.

Mishnah 8: Rebbi Simeon ben Nanas[88] says, one adorns First Fruits [with anything] except from the Seven Kinds[89]. Rebbi Aqiba says, one adorns First Fruits only with the Seven Kinds.

משנה ט: רִבִּי שִׁמְעוֹן אוֹמֵר שָׁלֹשׁ מִדּוֹת בַּבִּיכּוּרִים. הַבִּיכּוּרִים וְתוֹסֶפֶת הַבִּיכּוּרִים וְעִיטּוּר בִּיכּוּרִים. תּוֹסֶפֶת הַבִּיכּוּרִים מִין בְּמִינוֹ וְעִיטּוּר בִּיכּוּרִים מִין בְּשֶׁאֵינוֹ מִינוֹ. תּוֹסֶפֶת הַבִּיכּוּרִים נֶאֱכֶלֶת בְּטַהֲרָה וּפְטוּרָה מִן הַדְּמַאי וְעִיטּוּר הַבִּיכּוּרִים חַיָּיב בַּדְּמַאי.

Mishnah 9: Rebbi Simeon says, there are three components of First Fruits[90]. First Fruits, additions to First Fruits, and adornments of First Fruits. Additions to First Fruits are of the same kind, adornments of First Fruits are not of the same kind. Additions to First Fruits are eaten in purity and exempt from the rules of *demay*[91], adornments of First Fruits are subject to the rules of *demay*.

משנה י: אֵימָתַי אָמְרוּ תּוֹסֶפֶת הַבִּיכּוּרִים כַּבִּיכּוּרִים. בִּזְמַן שֶׁהִיא בָאָה מִן הָאָרֶץ. וְאִם אֵינָהּ בָּאָה מִן הָאָרֶץ אֵינָהּ כַּבִּיכּוּרִים.

Mishnah 10: When did they say that additions to First Fruits follow the rules of First Fruits? If they come from the Land. But if they do not come from the Land, they do not follow the rules of First Fruits.

88 A third generation Tanna, usually disagreeing with either R. Aqiba or R. Ismael.

89 Cf. Mishnah 1:3.

90 Since First Fruits are few, one fills the baskets with additional fruits. For R. Aqiba and R. Simeon, the additions may be of the same or of different kinds, following different rules. The "additions to First Fruits" of R. Simeon and R. Aqiba are the "adornments of First Fruits" of R. Simeon ben Nanas. The latter forbids R. Aqiba's "adornments of First Fruits".

91 They follow all rules of heave like First Fruits proper. Practically, additions to First Fruits are indistinguishable from First Fruits.

(fol. 65d) **הלכה ו:** אָמַר רִבִּי יוֹסֵי. כָּל־עַמָּא מוֹדוּ שֶׁמְּעַטְּרִין אֶת הַבִּיכּוּרִין לָאָרֶץ. שֶׁאֵין בְּנֵי אָדָם טוֹעִין שֶׁמְּבִיאִין בִּיכּוּרִין לְחוּץ. לְאֵלֶּא מַפְלִיגִין בְּעַמּוֹן וּמוֹאָב. מָאן דְּאָמַר מְעַטְּרִין אֶת הַבִּיכּוּרִין חוּץ מִשִּׁבְעַת הַמִּינִים. מְעַטְּרִין אֶת הַבִּיכּוּרִים מֵעַמּוֹן וּמוֹאָב. מָאן דְּאָמַר אֵין מְעַטְּרִין אֶלָּא מִשִּׁבְעַת הַמִּינִין. אֵין מְעַטְּרִין אֶת הַבִּיכּוּרִין מֵעַמּוֹן וּמוֹאָב. אָמַר רִבִּי מָנָא כָּל־עַמָּא מוֹדוּ שֶׁאֵין מְעַטְּרִין אֶת הַבִּיכּוּרִין מֵעַמּוֹן וּמוֹאָב. שֶׁבְּנֵי אָדָם טוֹעִין לוֹמַר שֶׁמְּבִיאִין בִּיכּוּרִין מֵעַמּוֹן וּמוֹאָב. מַה פְלִיגִין. בְּחוּצָה לָאָרֶץ. מָאן דְּאָמַר מְעַטְּרִין אֶת

הַבִּיכּוּרִין חוּץ מִשִּׁבְעַת הַמִּינִים. מְעַטְּרִין אֶת הַבִּיכּוּרִים מֵחוּץ לָאָרֶץ. מָאן דְּאָמַר אֵין מְעַטְּרִין אֶת הַבִּיכּוּרִים אֶלָּא מִשִּׁבְעַת הַמִּינִין. אֵין מְעַטְּרִין אֶת הַבִּיכּוּרִים חוּץ לָאָרֶץ.

Halakhah 6: Rebbi Yose said: Everybody agrees that one adorns First Fruits with produce of the Land since nobody errs to think that one may bring First Fruits from outside the Land. They differ about this, about Ammon and Moab[92]. For him who says, one adorns First Fruits [with anything] except from the Seven Kinds, one may adorn First Fruits with produce from Ammon and Moab[93]. For him who says, one adorns First Fruits only with the Seven Kinds, one may not adorn First Fruits with produce from Ammon and Moab.

Rebbi Mana said: Everybody agrees that one may not adorn First Fruits with produce of Ammon and Moab since people err to think that one may bring First Fruits from Ammon and Moab. About what do they differ? About outside the Land. For him who says, one adorns First Fruits [with anything] except from the Seven Kinds, one may adorn First Fruits with produce from outside the Land[93]. For him who says, one adorns First Fruits only with the Seven Kinds, one may not adorn First Fruits with produce from outside the Land..

92 In talmudic sources, "Ammon and Moab" stands for all of Transjordan, including the earlier territories of the tribes Reuben and Gad but excluding the Golan heights which were settled in the times of the return from Babylon.

93 These can never be taken as First Fruits.

משנה י: וּלְמָה אָֽמְרוּ הַבִּיכּוּרִים כְּנִכְסֵי כֹהֵן. שֶׁהוּא קוֹנֶה מֵהֶם עֲבָדִים(fol. 65b) וְקַרְקָעוֹת וּבְהֵמָה טְמֵיאָה וּבַעַל חוֹב נוֹטְלָן בְּחוֹבוֹ וְהָאִשָּׁה בִּכְתוּבָּתָהּ כְּסֵפֶר תּוֹרָה. וְרִבִּי יְהוּדָה אוֹמֵר אֵין נוֹתְנִין אוֹתָן אֶלָּא לֶחָבֵר בְּטוֹבָה וַחֲכָמִים אוֹמְרִים נוֹתְנִין אוֹתָם לְאַנְשֵׁי מִשְׁמָר וְהֵם מְחַלְּקִין בֵּינֵיהֶן כְּקָדְשֵׁי הַמִּקְדָּשׁ.

Mishnah 10: Why did they say, First Fruits are the Cohen's property[94]? He may use them to buy slaves, real estate, and impure animals. A creditor can take them for his claim and a woman for her *ketuba*[95], like a Torah scroll. And Rebbi Jehudah says, one gives them only to a fellow[96] for goodwill, but the Sages say one gives them to the people of the watch[97] and they distribute them among themselves like Temple-hallowed food.

94 Cf. Mishnah 2:1.

95 The capital payment due a wife at the dissolution of her marriage by divorce or the husband's death.

96 A Cohen who is a fellow as defined in the Introduction to *Demay*.

97 The group of Cohanim serving in the Temple during the week the First Fruits were presented. They might be from the same district as the farmers coming in procession, cf. Note 13.

(fol. 65d) **הלכה ז**: רִבִּי יַנַּאי בְּשֵׁם רִבִּי חִיָּיה בַּר וָוא. שָׁאֲלוּ אֶת רַבָּן שִׁמְעוֹן בֶּן גַּמְלִיאֵל. מָהוּ שֶׁיִּמְכּוֹר אָדָם סֵפֶר תּוֹרָה לִישָּׂא אִשָּׁה. אָמַר לוֹן אִין. לִלְמוֹד תּוֹרָה. אָמַר לוֹן אִין. מִפְּנֵי חַיָּיו. וְלֹא אֲגִיבוֹן. רִבִּי יוֹנָה בְּשֵׁם רִבִּי חִיָּיה בַּר וָוא. שָׁאֲלוּ אֶת רַבָּן שִׁמְעוֹן בֶּן גַּמְלִיאֵל. מָהוּ שֶׁיִּמְכּוֹר אָדָם סֵפֶר תּוֹרָה לִישָּׂא אִשָּׁה. אָמַר לוֹן אִין. לִלְמוֹד תּוֹרָה. אָמַר לוֹן אִין. מִפְּנֵי חַיָּיו לֹא שְׁאָלוּן וְלֹא אֲגִיבוֹן. עַל דַּעְתֵּיהּ דְּרִבִּי יוֹנָה נִיחָא. לֹא שְׁאָלוּן וְלֹא אֲגִיבוֹן. עַל דַּעְתֵּיהּ דְּרִבִּי יוֹסֵי. אִן שְׁאָלוּן לֵיהּ לָמָּה לֹא אֲגִיבוֹן. כִּי אָתָא רִבִּי חֲנַנְיָה רִבִּי פִּינְחָס רִבִּי יוֹחָנָן בְּשֵׁם רַבָּן שִׁמְעוֹן בֶּן גַּמְלִיאֵל. מוֹכֵר הוּא אָדָם לִישָּׂא אִשָּׁה וְלִלְמוֹד תּוֹרָה וְכָל־שֶׁכֵּן מִפְּנֵי חַיָּיו.

Halakhah 7: Rebbi (Yannai)[98] in the name of Rebbi Ḥiyya bar Abba: They asked Rabban Simeon ben Gamliel, may a person sell a Torah scroll in order to marry a wife? He said to them, yes. To study Torah? Yes. For his livelihood? He did not respond. Rebbi Jonah in the name of Rebbi Ḥiyya bar Abba: They asked Rabban Simeon ben Gamliel, may a person sell a Torah scroll in order to marry a wife? He said to them, yes. To study Torah? Yes. For his livelihood they did not ask and he did not respond. According to Rebbi Jonah it is understandable: They did not ask, therefore he did not respond. According to Rebbi Yose, if they asked him, why did he not respond? When Rebbi Ḥanania came, Rebbi Phineas, Rebbi Joḥanan in the name of Rabban Simeon ben Gamliel: A person may sell to marry a wife and to study Torah[99], and *a fortiori* for his livelihood.

98 As R. M. Margalit already noted, he must be R. Yose, the colleague of R. Jonah, who is quoted later. R. Yannai was R. Ḥiyya bar Abba's teacher's teacher.

Since the Mishnah ties selling First Fruits to selling a Torah scroll, the rules discussed here also apply to the sale of First Fruits by a Cohen.

99 In the Babli (*Megillah* 27a): "A person may sell a Torah scroll *only* to marry or to study Torah." There, Rabban Simeon ben Gamliel emphatically forbids selling a Torah scroll for one's livelihood; cf. Note 103.

תַּנֵּי. הַמַּדִּיר אֶת בְּנוֹ לְתַלְמוּד תּוֹרָה מוּתָּר לְמַלּוֹת לוֹ חָבִית שֶׁלְמַיִם וּלְהַדְלִיק לוֹ אֶת הַנֵּר. רִבִּי יַעֲקֹב בַּר אִידִי בְּשֵׁם רִבִּי יוֹחָנָן. אַף לוֹקֵחַ לוֹ חֲפָצָיו מִן הַשּׁוּק. וּפְלִיגִין. כָּאן בְּאִישׁ כָּאן בְּאִשָּׁה. אִם הָיָה אָדָם מְסוּיָּים עָשׂוּ אוֹתוֹ כְאִשָּׁה. מַעֲשֶׂה בְאָדָם אֶחָד שֶׁהִדִּיר אֶת בְּנוֹ לְתַלְמוּד תּוֹרָה. וּבָא מַעֲשֶׂה לִפְנֵי רִבִּי יוֹסֵי בֶּן חֲלוֹפְתָּא וְתִּיר לוֹ לְמַלְאוֹת חָבִית שֶׁלְמַיִם וּלְהַדְלִיק לוֹ אֶת הַנֵּר.

It was stated: If somebody vows[100] regarding his son to study Torah, he is permitted to fill for him an amphora of water and to light for him. Rebbi Jacob bar Idi in the name of Rebbi Joḥanan: He also can buy things for him on the market. Do they differ? Here for a man, there for a woman[101]. If he was a known personality they treated him as a woman. "[102]It happened that somebody vowed regarding his son to study Torah. The case came before Rebbi Yose ben Ḥalaphta and he permitted him to fill an amphora of water and to light for him."

100 מדיר here means מדיר הנאה, A made a vow either that A forbids to himself any benefit from B or he forbids B to enjoy any benefit from himself. {The technical term was that "A's property should be like a sacrifice (of which any profane use is criminal) to B", cf. Mishnah *Nedarim* 1:2, Matthew 15:5.} The parallel to this paragraph is in Babli *Nedarim* 38b. In the formulation there it is unclear whether the father forbids his own property to his son until the son has successfully completed his studies or whether he forbids himself to enjoy any benefit from his son (depriving his son from the rewards for honoring father and mother) for that time; cf. *Meïri Nedarim* (ed. A. Liss) p. 151b. In the formulation of the Yerushalmi, it is clear that the parent forbids himself to enjoy any benefit from his son. It is then asserted that the vow excludes small personal services.

101 It was thought demeaning for a woman of substance (as well as for a man of high station) to be seen in public buying on the market.

102 Tosephta *Bekhorot* 6:11. There, the formulation is: "He made a vow that the son should be forbidden to work for him." Nevertheless, R. Yose permitted small personal services.

תַּנֵּי. הַמּוֹכֵר סֵפֶר תּוֹרָה שֶׁלְּאָבִיו אֵינוֹ רוֹאֶה סִימַן בְּרָכָה לְעוֹלָם. וְכָל־הַמְקַיֵּים סֵפֶר תּוֹרָה בְּתוֹךְ בֵּיתוֹ עָלָיו הַכָּתוּב אוֹמֵר הוֹן וָעוֹשֶׁר בְּבֵיתוֹ וְצִדְקָתוֹ עוֹמֶדֶת לָעַד.

It was stated[103]: "He who sells his father's Torah scroll will never do well. But about everybody who keeps a Torah scroll in his house, the verse says (*Ps.* 112:3): "Property and riches in his house, his merit will stand forever."

103 In Babli *Mo'ed Qaṭan* 27a in the name of Rabban Simeon ben Gamliel: "He who sells either his father's Torah scroll or his daughter (to be married) will never do well."

Epilogue

On the Tosephta

Zacharias Frankel in his מבוא הירושלמי[1] already noted that the Tosephta sometimes agrees with the Yerushalmi, sometimes with the Babli, sometimes with both Talmudim, sometimes with neither of them. He assumed that the different Tosephtot were essentially Galilean compilations, an opinion shared by S. Lieberman regarding the Tosephta text in our hands[2].

Even when the Tosephta materially agrees with one of the Talmudim, the exact wording never is the same as in the Talmud texts. On the other hand, we know from Gaonic sources that the Tosephta, together with the halakhic Midrashim, was regularly studied in the Babylonian academies. E. Y. Kutscher, who in his time was the greatest authority on dialects of Mishnaic Hebrew, did not consider the current Tosephta a Yerushalmi text (oral communication, in a discussion of a paper on the Talmudic vocabulary[3].) While *Zeraïm* is not an ideal text to compare Babli and Yerushalmi, since there exists a Babylonian parallel only for Tractate *Berakhot*, a detailed analysis of the Tosephta texts quoted shows a definite slant towards Babylonian traditions. In the table, the following abbreviations are used:

B Agrees in meaning with Babli.

Y Agrees in meaning with Yerushalmi.

¬ Negation, does not agree.

& And.

Number of Tosephta Texts

	Quoted also in Babli				Not quoted in Babli	
	B	Y	B&Y	¬B&¬Y	Y	¬Y
Berakhot	16	6	17	3	10	0
Peah	3	1	12	0	27	1
Demay	0	0	11	1	52	9
Kilaim	4	1	2	1	26	2
Ševi'it	0	0	6	2	43	7
Terumot	9	0	9	0	51	8
Ma'serot	0	0	6	0	3	4
Ma'aser Šeni	1	2	4	2	17	6
Ḥallah	1	0	5	0	10	5
'Orlah	0	1	4	0	11	3
Bikkurim	2	0	5	0	6	2

The first two columns show that where the traditions disagree, the Tosephta reproduces the Babylonian opinion more than three times as often as the Yerushalmi one.

To the arguments given in the Introduction to these volumes (*Berakhot* SJ 18, pp. 16-27) of the influence of the Yerushalmi on the editing of the Babli one can add the dependence of Babylonian terminology on the Galilean (cf. גזירה , *Demay* SJ 19, p. 369). The Yerushalmi is based on two collections of Tannaïtic statements, the Mishnah, quoted by תנינן and a *baraita* collection containing, among others, statements parallel to those appearing in Tosephta, *Mekhiltot, Sifra, Sifry* and early Midrashim, introduced by תני. The Babli is based on three collections, Mishnah (תנן), תנו רבנן referring often to parallels to Tosephta and halakhic Midrashim, and a general *baraita* collection introduced by תניא. Since the Mishnah in the Babli has undergone some rewriting[4] and the halakhic Midrashim also show signs of Babylonian editing, something similar might have happened to the Tosephta. The material of the Yerushalmi depends in great part on the teachings of R. Joḥanan. Is it noteworthy that the most important scholars of the succession of R. Joḥanan's academy for three generations all were Babylonians [Rabbis Immi and Yasa (Ammi and Assi), Ḥiyya bar Abba, Zeïra (Zēra), Jeremiah]. There remains the possibility that the collection known as the Tosephta was originally edited by a Babylonian in Galilee or a Galilean in Babylonia [such as R. Eudaimon (Dimi) and R. Abin (Ravin).]

On the Editors of the Yerushalmi

The technical language and the structure of the Yerushalmi are so uniform in all tractates that it is clear that the Yerushalmi has undergone a thorough process of editing. The teachers of the last generation of Galilean Sages, mainly R. Berekhiah and R. Tanḥuma, express their own opinion only on homiletic subjects, not on halakhic discussions. An old tradition holds that the Yerusalem Talmud was "made" by R. Joḥanan. In this form the statement is untenable but it is undeniable that the Jerusalem Talmud is the product of R. Joḥanan's academy in Tiberias. While the detailed editorial work was probably done by R. Berekhiah, R. Tanḥuma, and their schools, they are editors but cannot be considered as collectors of the material. That role must have been played by the schools of the preceding generation, one headed by R. Yose (probably, ben Zabida) and the other, contemporary, by R. Jonah and his son R. Mana II. Of the generations between R. Joḥanan and R. Yose, only R. Zeïra (student of a student of R. Joḥanan and teacher of the teachers of RR. Yose and Jonah) appears with a frequency approximating those of the other rabbis mentioned. There are interesting differences in the numbers of times each author is quoted in each tractate. These differences may show that one or the other academy acted as main collector of the material of the tractate. Since the tractates vary in length from less than two to 13 folio pages, in order to make the figures comparable, the frequency of formal statements of R. Joḥanan in each tractate has been put equal to one. It will be seen that Tractate *Terumot* comes closest to be a product of the school of R. Joḥanan; it also contains the most formal statements of R. Simeon ben Laqish, the #2 member of R. Joḥanan's academy. It seems therefore that the uniformity of style of the different tractates goes back to a written style already developed by the second generation of Galilean Amoraïm or, less likely, imposed on the traditional material by the anonymous scholars of the last generation.

The frequency of formal statements of RR. Zeïra, Yose, Jonah, and Mana, compared to those of R. Joḥanan is given in the following table, in which the numbers which indicate a dominant role of one of the scholars are given in boldface. A detailed study of the peculiarities of the different tractates is desirable but cannot be undertaken here.

	Zeïra	Yose	Jonah	Mana	# of statements of R. Johanan
Berakhot	**0.94**	0.48	0.29	0.19	97
Peah	0.48	0.47	0.38	0.23	64
Demay	0.71	0.42	0.61	0.20	59
Kilaim	**0.82**	**0.82**	0.59	0.22	49
Ševi'it	0.61	0.78	0.37	0.39	54
Terumot	0.28	0.39	0.16	0.14	**132**
Ma'serot	0.75	0.55	0.68	0.35	40
Ma'aser Šeni	**0.90**	**0.85**	**0.85**	0.40	40
Ḥallah	0.52	**0.93**	0.75	0.18	40
'Orlah	0.37	0.40	0.45	0.12	60
Bikkurim	0.77	0.62	0.58	0.15	26

1 Breslau 1870; Reprint Jerusalem 1967.

2 For example, Introduction to *Tosefta ki-fshutah* , p. כב.

3 E. and H. Guggenheimer, *Notes on the Talmudic Vocabulary: gndryps-qntrwpis*, לשוננו 35(1971) pp. 201-207.

4 Cf. M. Schachter, The Babylonian and Jerusalem Mishnah, textually compared, Jerusalem 1959.

Indices

Index of Biographical Notes

Abba Ḥilfai bar Qirya 121

Ben Bag-Bag 29
Bar Lolita 307

Dositheos from Kefar Etma 472

Eleazar ben Mathia 77
Eleazar ben Paḥora 223

Ḥanina ben Hak̲iniah 77

Jehufah ben Paṭora 223
Joḥanan High Priest 218
Joseph the Cohen 389

Mar Zuṭra 216

Samuel, brother of Rav Berekhia 454

Rebbi Aḥa ben Pappos 211
Rebbi Curius 470
Rebbi Ḥama bar Yose 485
Rebbi Ḥanina bar 'Agil 271
Rebbi Ḥiyya bar Julianus 454
Rebbi Huna bar Aḥa 213
Rebbi Inaya ben Sinai 144
Rebbi Isaac the elder 169
Rebbi Jacob, son the the daughter of Jacob 172
Rebbi Joshua (Amora) 205
Rebbi Joshua from Ono 419
Rebbi Samuel bar Ḥiyya bar Jehudah 89
Rebbi Sidor 293
Rebbi Simeon ben Jehudah 93
Rebbi Simeon ben Barsana, Karsana 369
Rebbi Simeon ben Nanas 654
Rebbi Yudan ben Gadya 128
Rebbi Yudan bar Ḥanin 431

Yoëzer from Bira 488

Index of Biblical Quotations

Gen. 15:18 286
17:5 563
21:31 426
32:33 507

Ex. 3:8 585
3:17 585
12:3 292
13:3 513
18:8 600
Ex. 20:19 645
21:18 510
22:6 138,139
22:30 506,512
23:19 616

Ex. 33:8 639

Lev. 2:14 251
6:23 511
7:23 507,511
7:24 507,511
11:9 598
11:28 542
11:35 542
11:37 257
11:42 508
12:16 511
13:45 172
13:47,48 285
14:21 416
14:35 416
16:4 286
17:12 45
19:19 6,29,32,255
266,284,295,539
19:23 397,399,405
19:24 183,184,405
19:25 399
19:32 637,642,644
19:33 644
21:13 567
21:14 567
22:3 596
22:7 460,461
22:15 50
23:10 251
23:14 231,261,508,
537
23:40 405
25:5 421
27:21 383
27:27 89,113
27:28 15,383
27:30 335
27:31 137,184
27:33 15
27:34 281

Num. 4:18 591
Num. 4:20 591
6:3 486.487
6:4 443,487
8:25 591,592
10:29 560
15:17 285,286
15:18 285,287,415
15:19 255,335
15:20 228,260,319
15:21 211,228
18:13 616
18:17 15
18:18 19
18:21 196
18:26 198,257
18:29 257,457
18:31 199,200
33:3 289

Deut. 1:35 593
11:24 291
12:6 590,605
12:16 507
12:17 50,611
12:22 598
14:3 463
14:21 506,512
14:22 261,427
14:24 106
14:25 21,25,42,72,73
14:26 38,46,106
14:27 256
14:28 192
14:29 401
16:3 513
16:7 617
18:1 384
18:3 383
22:9 509
26:2 549
26:3 559,648
26:4 583,590,616
26:5 606,648,652
26:10 586,631
26:11 571,584
26:12 193
26:13 208,605,606
26:14 48,209
26:15 213
26:16 212
32:14 181

Jos. 1:4 291
511 289

1Sam. 1:22 592
13:1 644
25:38 595

2K. 14:25 293

Is. 28:28 233
28:29 233,234
46:12 215

Jer. 31:5 633

Ez. 33:32 616
39:15 172
44:15 195
44:22 565
44:30 616

Hab. 2:19-20 645

Ps. 10:3 281
30:2 648
78:65 222
112:3 660
121:4 222
122:2-3 634
150:1-6 634

Prov. 14:23 592

Job 5:26 593
17:2 222
24:16 174

Cant. 4:8	376	Neh. 10:39	196	2Chr. 31:4	197
Eccl. 9:11	647				

Index of Greek and Latin Words

ἄσημος	14		
ἄσπρον	76	bucella	271
δυσγνωσία	23	cancelli	449
		castra	25
ἐπίτροπος	564	caulis	530
		clibanicius	269
ἴτριον	270	cucuma	280
κερκίς	521	patella	30
κραμβαλέος	271		
κράμβιτας	271	sicarii	550
		splenium	509
λεκάνη, λεκός	123	subsellium	566
ὀποβάλσαμον	175	tiro	214
		tractum	265
ῥητίνα	46	tremes	22
		tritor	180
σπόγγος	263	triturator	180
συμβολή	157		
		vicia	387
ὑδρία	519		

Index of Hebrew and Arabic Words

אפר	595	ישב	646	إسفنج	263
גבל	317	כלח	593	حلّ	283
גזר	213	ספק	427		
				خلط	265
חכר	198	ענקוקלות	446	صبارة	76

				قسب	559
طرطور	180	فجل	278	قصّ	636
عطن	205	فُرص	321	كعك	279

General Index

Abraham ben David 74,333
Agency, for divorce 149
Albeck, H. 59
Ammon and Moab 656
Animals, tithe 13
  dedication 114
Apicius 265
Arukh 437,521
Asher ben Ieḥiel 329
Asparn 76
Atonement, Day of 51

Bachofen, J. J. 449
Borrower, liability 141
Brooks, R. 2
Buxtorf, J. 191,423

Caro, J. 145,333
Cirillo, S. 95,104,329,401,605
Citron 429,619

Dema' 323
Demay 224
Domains, for *ḥallahi* *374*
Dreams, linterpretation 159–167

Ekhah rabbati 12,179,180,181
Epstein, J.N. 22,61,73,104,271,422, 438,530
Eruv, dead-end street 140
  courtyard 278
Ettlinger, J. J. 217

Firstling 12
Fleischer, H.L. 23,198,387
Forbidden food, permitted later 608
  use of 506 ff.
Four kinds 405
Fourteen years 415
Frankel, Z. 636,661
Friedmann, M. 530
Fulda, E. 225,346,352,403,612

Genesis rabba 380
Goldschmidt, L. 558

Ḥallah of *demay* 366
Holidays, food for 158
Human blood 622
Hung sacrifice 628
Husband, inheritor 572

Impurity, preparation 297
  of houses 556

Jastrow, M. 65,123,191
Jerusalem, houses in 95
  measure 306

Kanievski, H. 1,40,226,341
Katz, E. 218
Kohout, A. 65
Koy 624
Kramer, E. (Gaon of Wilna) 1,226,495,604
Krauss, S. 23,65,279,446,555
Kutaḥ 272
Kutscher, E. Y. 661

Legal tender 14

Levy, J. 23,65,198,387
Lewis & Short 269
Liddell & Scott 76,270,519
Lieberman, S. 2,24,65,179,226,352,444, 495,555,661
Lifting 437,441
Löw, I. 65,230,444,530,555

Ma'amad 633
Maimonides 1,10,33,59,62,66,76,94, 103,109,115,117,120,145,152,155,202, 225,300,306309,311,315,323,333,340, 355,367,373,399,401,406,414,437,442, 444,452,494,502,630,633,649
Mamzer 218
Mathematics, Euclidean 505
Margalit, M. 1,99,191,226,355,658
Meïri, M. 225,530
Meḵilta (dR. Ismael) 139,229,513
Meḵilta dR. Simeon bar Iohai 612
Mending, invisible 420
Midraš haggadol 204,205
Midraš Šemuel 596,617
Midraš Tanḥuma 386
Milham, M.E. 265
Minors, legal status 139
MMT 36

Neusner, J. 226
Nearness, measure of 362
Nissim Gerondi 329

'Omer 227
'Orlah 397
Or zarua' 414,441,446
Ownership,transferral of 143
Oẓar Hageonim 230

Peruṭah 126
Pesaḥ *289*
leftover 87,90
Pesiqta rabbati 530
Phylacteries 211
Piggul 84,238

Plinius 230
Proselyte, child of 562
Publioc domain, uS 549

Qab, local 306
Qafeḥ, Y. 2,226
Qalir, E. 522
Qohelet rabbati 77,160,163,164,165,166, 167

Rashi 73,129,202,217,304,460,482,630
Real estate, claims 417
Levitic 217
Restitution, hope for 551

Sacrifices, substitute 91
Samuel, age of prophet 590
Schachter, M. 665
Second Tithe 3
Seder 'Olam 99,415
Sepphoris measure 306
Sheftel, H. J., 123
Seven kinds 585
Sifra 15,38,39,235,243,247,251,292,382 414,444,446,460,461,508,512,624
Sifry 16,21,29,31,39,193,194,195,229, 292,309,415,458,502,508,605,613, 617,652
Simponti, I. 152,312,502,617,649
Simson, of Sens 1,94,97,145,152,225,287, 312,329,366,414,494,502,617,649
Siṭ 522
Slave, Hebrew 136
Sofer, A. 225
Solomon ben Adrat 287
Sperber, D. 14,23,123
Standing, legal 208
Syria 293,369,536

Tašbeẓ 273
Temple, debts to 89,114
holiness of site 99
Tenant, hereditary 370
Ṭevel 325
Ṭevul-yom 85,346

Tort law 18
Tosephot 58

Vow of renunciation of benefit 659

Watch 383
Whore's wages 578
Wine, Gentile 521

Yalquṭ Šim'oni 596,617

Zuckermann, M. 23,123

www.ingramcontent.com/pod-product-compliance
Lightning Source LLC
Chambersburg PA
CBHW031841220426
43663CB00006B/462